Seeing Both Sides

CLASSIC CONTROVERSIES IN ABNORMAL PSYCHOLOGY

Scott O. Lilienfeld received his B.A. from Cornell University in 1982 and his Ph.D. in clinical psychology from the University of Minnesota in 1990. He completed his clinical internship at Western Psychiatric Institute and Clinic in Pittsburgh from 1986 to 1987. He was a faculty member in the Department of Psychology at the State University of New York, University at Albany, from 1990 to 1994 and is currently an assistant professor in the Department of Psychology at Emory University in Atlanta, Georgia.

Dr. Lilienfeld has authored or co-authored approximately 30 journal articles and book chapters on such issues as personality disorders, psychiatric classification and diagnosis, and anxiety disorders. His principal research interests concern the assessment and causation of psychopathic personality and risk factors for antisocial behavior in childhood and adulthood. He currently lives in Atlanta with his wife.

Seeing Both Sides

CLASSIC CONTROVERSIES IN ABNORMAL PSYCHOLOGY

SCOTT O. LILIENFELD

Emory University

Brooks/Cole Publishing Company
I(T)P™ An International Thomson Publishing Company

Pacific Grove • Albany • Bonn • Boston • Cincinnati • Detroit • London • Madrid • Melbourne
Mexico City • New York • Paris • San Francisco • Singapore • Tokyo • Toronto • Washington

Sponsoring Editor: *Marianne Taflinger*
Marketing Representative: *James Grott*
Advertising: *Jean Thompson*
Production Coordinator: *Fiorella Ljunggren*
Production: *Scratchgravel Publishing Services*
Manuscript Editor: *Rebecca Smith*
Permissions Editor: *May Clark*
Interior Design: *Anne Draus, Scratchgravel Publishing Services*
Cover Design: *Vernon T. Boes*
Cover Art: *René Magritte; not to be reproduced, 1937; Museum Boymans-van Beuningen, Rotterdam*
Typesetting: *Scratchgravel Publishing Services*
Cover Printing: *Color Dot Graphics*
Printing and Binding: *Courier Kendallville, Inc.*

For more information, contact:

BROOKS/COLE PUBLISHING COMPANY
511 Forest Lodge Road
Pacific Grove, CA 93950
USA

International Thomson Publishing Europe
Berkshire House 168–173
High Holborn
London WC1V 7AA
England

Thomas Nelson Australia
102 Dodds Street
South Melbourne, 3205
Victoria, Australia

Nelson Canada
1120 Birchmount Road
Scarborough, Ontario
Canada M1K 5G4

International Thomson Editores
Campos Eliseos 385, Piso 7
Col. Polanco
11560 México D. F. México

International Thomson Publishing GmbH
Königswinterer Strasse 418
53227 Bonn
Germany

International Thomson Publishing Asia
221 Henderson Road
#05–10 Henderson Building
Singapore 0315

International Thomson Publishing Japan
Hirakawacho Kyowa Building, 3F
2-2-1 Hirakawacho
Chiyoda-ku, Tokyo 102
Japan

Printed in the United States of America

10 9 8 7 6 5 4 3 2 1

Library of Congress Cataloging-in-Publication Data

Lilienfeld, Scott O., [date]
Seeing both sides : classic controversies in abnormal psychology / Scott O. Lilienfeld.
p. cm.
Includes bibliographical references and index.
ISBN 0-534-25134-X
1. Psychiatry. 2. Psychiatry—Philosophy. 3. Clinical psychology. 4. Clinical psychology—Philosophy. 5. Psychology, Pathological. I. Title.
RC454.4.L55 1994
616.89—dc20 94-18083
CIP

for Lori

CONTENTS

PREFACE

When a thing ceases to be a subject of controversy, it ceases to be a subject of interest.

—William Hazlett

There are two sides to every question.

—Protagoras

It is better to debate a question without settling it, than to settle it without debate.

—Joubert, *Pensées*, No. 115

Agreement exists in disagreement.

—Lucan, *Pharsalia* (1830)

Abnormal psychology is an enormously exciting, and yet at times greatly frustrating, discipline. What often makes the study of abnormal psychology frustrating to students is the multiplicity of opposing viewpoints on so many of the issues that occupy this field's center stage. Indeed, in few, if any, areas of psychology—or, for that matter, all of social science—is there such an absence of consensus regarding so many pivotal questions. As students open their abnormal psychology textbooks to the beginning chapter, for example, many are puzzled or even dismayed to discover that there is precious little agreement among psychologists concerning so fundamental an issue as the definition of "abnormality." These students are understandably apprehensive about undertaking the study of a discipline that has yet to settle on the proper domain of its subject matter.

Perplexed by contradictory views, students often leave abnormal psychology classes despairing of finding definitive answers to many of the issues they are asked to come to grips with. They in turn frequently ask their instructors, "But which is *the* correct view (theory, interpretation of the data, and so on)?" The response that most instructors give—"Well, there is no single correct view (theory, interpretation of the data, etc.)"—tends, understandably, to be less than satisfying. Unfortunately, many books of readings in abnormal psychology are composed of articles representing a myriad of diverse theoretical and research perspectives and often have the unintended effect of further heightening students' confusion and frustration.

Major Goals and Rationale

Seeing Both Sides is an effort to assist you in the difficult task of navigating your way through the diverse and often opposing viewpoints so frequently encountered in abnormal psychology courses. At the same time, this book seeks to capture the sense of excitement, even wonder, that many students experience when first reading about the attempts of theoreticians and researchers in the field of abnormal psychology to grapple with the immensely challenging questions confronting them. In this book, you will encounter nineteen issues that have been persistent lightning rods for controversy in abnormal psychology. Each of these issues is represented by two readings that adopt conflicting, and in some cases diametrically opposite, perspectives. By exposing you to a broad sampling of the major controversies in abnormal psychology, I hope both to enhance your appreciation for, and understanding of, many of the central questions facing workers in this field and to provide you with the skills required to critically evaluate divergent positions on these and related questions.

The latter point merits some elaboration. As citizens in modern Western society, we are almost incessantly bombarded with information—much of it false, oversimplified, or misleading—concerning the characteristics, causes, and treatments of abnormal behavior. One has only to open the pages of a newspaper or popular magazine or tune the television to Phil Donahue or Oprah Winfrey to encounter a discussion of questions such as "Is premenstrual syndrome a mental illness?" "Is alcoholism genetic?" "Should hyperactive kids be placed on drugs?" or "Does shock therapy cause brain damage?" Important as these questions are, they are rarely discussed at a level that permits, let alone encourages, a thoughtful or critical analysis of the issues. Thus, one of the principal goals of this book is to prepare you to become better-informed and more critical *consumers* of the vast lay and scientific literature on abnormal behavior. Moreover, I believe that you will gain skills that should allow you to better evaluate conflicting claims in other areas of psychology, as well as in social science in general.

An additional goal of this book is to increase your capacity and willingness to tolerate ambiguity. Given the plethora of competing views in abnormal psychology, some students may be tempted to dogmatically adopt a single perspective on a theoretical or empirical question while ignoring or belittling others. But as John Stuart Mill pointed out, "He who knows only of his side of the case, knows little of that."* Thus, I intend to open your mind to alternative ways of conceptualizing and evaluating psychological issues.

Readings

A few words about the selection of readings are warranted. Many of the choices I was forced to make were quite difficult, and a large number of superb and interesting readings had to be omitted. Three major principles guided my selection of readings. First, I included readings only if they adopted opposite or at least substantially different perspectives on a topic of considerable importance to the field of abnormal psychology. Consequently, readings that expressed a clear viewpoint on each topic were generally accorded first priority.

Second, the readings had to address issues that have been enduring, long-standing points of debate in abnormal psychology. It was not essential that all the readings be recent, as I want to expose you to some of the classic debates that have helped shape current thinking in abnormal psychology. Moreover, psychologists as hardened and cynical as I am know that the age of an article or book is rarely a reliable barometer of the wisdom contained within it. Wherever possible, however, I have included readings that are less than fifteen years old, as each topic I have selected continues to be an active focus of theorizing, research, or both.

Third and finally, I have striven to include selections that are interesting and accessible to undergraduates but that do not oversimplify or "water down" complex issues. You need to be able to digest material from primary sources, and one of the most valuable services that a book of this type can perform is to introduce you to original readings in a nonthreatening fashion. Thus, in virtually all cases, I have selected either articles from peer-reviewed journals in psychology and psychiatry or chapters from edited volumes.

Nevertheless, I am well aware that some students and instructors may find that certain readings or issues not included here are more to their liking. To satisfy these individuals, as well as to whet the appetites of readers who are hungry for additional knowledge, I have included an appendix that contains a list of other controversial issues in abnormal psychology, along with suggested readings representing opposing sides of each topic.

Of course, in compiling readings for a book of this sort, there is invariably a danger of creating the impression of a more polarized debate than actually exists; by selecting readings that adopt extreme viewpoints on an issue, one may in effect foment a "straw-person" controversy. I was quite cognizant of this potential problem when choosing readings. Although some of the readings I have selected represent quite controversial or contentious points of view, all of them adopt a perspective that is, in either its original or its slightly modified form, shared by a large number of thinkers in abnormal psychology. At the same time, I aimed to include readings that clearly and starkly delineate the opposing positions in each debate. Presenting these positions in bold relief highlights the differences between them and allows you to readily perceive the fundamental disagreements underlying each controversy.

Format

The book is divided into four parts: I. *Classification and Diagnosis*, II. *Psychopathology: Its Characteristics and Causes*, III. *Psychological and Somatic Treatments*, and IV. *Legal and Ethical Is-*

*J. S. Mill, "On Liberty." In M. Warnock (Ed.), *John Stuart Mill: Utilitarianism, On Liberty, Essay on Bentham, Together with Selected Writings of Jeremy Bentham and John Austin* (Cleveland, Ohio: World Publishing, 1859/1962), p. 163.

sues. Each part begins with an introduction and overview of the issues to be covered in the following chapters. Each chapter presents an issue portrayed by two readings that represent opposing positions. Each pair of readings is preceded by an introduction that provides background for the major arguments discussed in both readings, underscores the central points made by each author, introduces several key concepts and terms contained in these readings, and presents a set of preview questions designed to alert readers to the principal issues raised in both selections. Each pair of readings is followed by a discussion, which presents a critical analysis of the arguments made by the authors and, wherever possible, emphasizes the conceptual skills necessary to evaluate these and similar arguments. In several cases—particularly those in which the readings are more than a decade old—these discussion sections contain an update on recent research or theoretical developments that have a bearing on the issues covered in the readings. Finally, each chapter concludes with a set of questions designed to stimulate further discussion and an annotated bibliography of suggestions for additional reading.

Who This Book Is For

This book is suitable as a supplement for introductory courses in abnormal psychology or as a primary text for advanced courses in abnormal psychology. Because a large number of the issues included in the book (for example, the disease model of alcoholism and the safety and efficacy of electroconvulsive therapy) correspond to chapters in abnormal psychology textbooks (substance abuse disorders, somatic treatments), instructors who use an abnormal psychology textbook may wish to assign the topics in this book in conjunction with textbook chapters. In addition, instructors with small class sections may want to use the book as a didactic tool to facilitate group discussion.

Acknowledgments

This book would not have been possible without the efforts of a number of exceptionally talented, dedicated, and helpful individuals. First and foremost, I would like to extend my gratitude to my editor at Brooks/Cole, Marianne Taflinger, without whose enthusiasm, diligence, and encouragement this project would never have been initiated, let alone completed. I owe her my warmest thanks. Second, thanks go to Fiorella Ljunggren of Brooks/Cole and Anne and Greg Draus of Scratchgravel, who brought this book to life; May Clark of Brooks/Cole, who coordinated the permissions requests; and Rebecca Smith, who helped me to communicate more clearly and succinctly. Third, I extend my thanks to my secretary Jacqueline Rice, whose assistance through all phases of the project made my life immeasurably easier. Fourth, of course, I thank the authors of the readings in this book, whose intelligence, creativity, and scholarship made this book possible. In many cases, these authors were asked to give permission to reproduce their writings; I consider myself remarkably fortunate that all graciously consented. In addition, a number of reviewers provided extremely helpful suggestions concerning the choice of format, topics, and readings. They are Hal Arkowitz of the University of Arizona, Ira H. Bernstein of the University of Texas at Arlington, Mike Condra of Queen's University at Kingston, Reid Jones of Delta State University, David Lester of Stockton State College, Kurt N. Olsen of Lycoming College, Demetrios Papageorgis of the University of British Columbia, Bernard Schiff of the University of Toronto, Annette L. Stanton of the University of Kansas, Joan Stewart of York University, Geoffrey Thorpe of the University of Maine, Stephen Tiffany of Purdue University, and Michael Vasey of Ohio State University.

Last but by no means least, I wish to express heartfelt thanks to my wife, Lori Marino, who heroically (and perhaps masochistically) read every sentence of my commentaries and offered numerous valuable comments and suggestions along the way. Her tireless support and encouragement throughout this project made more of a difference to me than she probably realizes.

A Closing Note

Finally, I want to encourage readers and instructors who have used this book of readings to share their reactions with me. Such comments are the most valuable feedback an author can receive and will be given careful consideration in future revisions. I am eager to hear from you.

Scott O. Lilienfeld

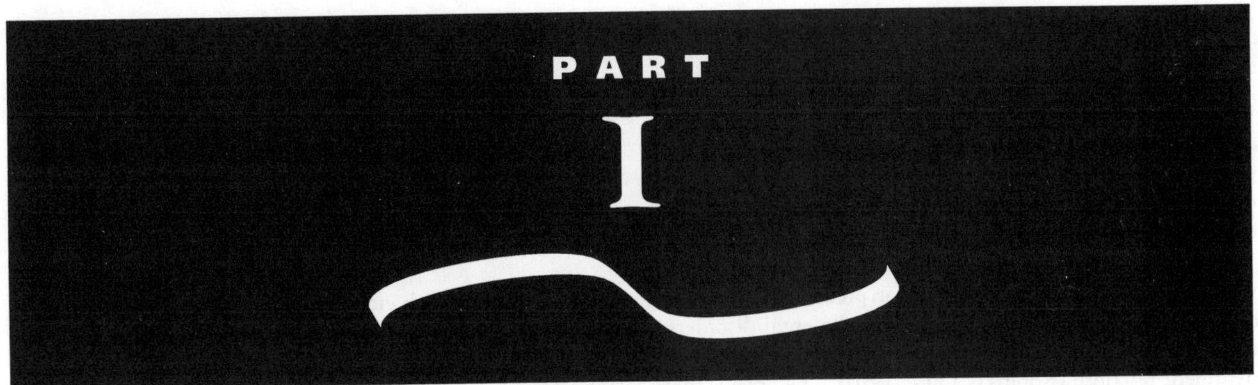

Classification and Diagnosis

The beginning of health is to know the disease.
—Cervantes, *Don Quixote* (Pt. ii, Ch. 60)

INTRODUCTION

In this first part of the book we will explore some central controversies surrounding the classification and diagnosis of psychopathology. **Classification** can be defined as the systematic delineation of the major categories of psychopathological conditions, as well as the boundaries between and relations among these categories. **Diagnosis**, in contrast, can be defined as the process of assigning individuals to the categories generated by a classification system. Thus, a psychiatric classification system is a prerequisite for psychiatric diagnosis. One must first have a system for placing individuals into categories—classification—before the process of placing individuals into these categories—diagnosis—can be performed.

No set of issues is as essential to the field of abnormal psychology as that pertaining to classification and diagnosis. If the diagnoses that psychologists and psychiatrists use to label different varieties of abnormality are fundamentally flawed, research and treatments based on these diagnoses will in all likelihood also be flawed.

As the readings in this first part of the book demonstrate, a number of prominent thinkers in abnormal psychology have called our present systems of classification and diagnosis into serious question. In general, two broad types of criticisms have been raised:

- Some authors have argued that the very premises underlying psychiatric classification and diagnosis are in error and that any attempt to categorize individuals exhibiting abnormal behavior into homogeneous classes of "psychiatric disorders" is doomed to failure.
- Other authors have not questioned the fundamental assumptions underlying the enterprise of psychiatric classification and diagnosis itself but have criticized specific features of our current classification system.

To take an analogy, some political scientists contend that our current democratic system is irrevocably flawed and must be replaced by an alternative system; other political scientists do not question our democratic system itself but instead believe that certain elements of this system (for example, campaign financing, congressional term limits) require reform or at least some extensive fine-tuning. In part I, you will encounter the views of both types of critics—those who argue for a disbanding of traditional psychiatric classification systems and those who argue for a revision of these systems—as well as the responses of staunch defenders of the present system of psychiatric classification.

Whenever we classify individuals—be it for medical, psychological, or other purposes—we strive to create groupings that are more homogeneous than the broader population from which the groupings originated. In other words, we aim to form categories of individuals who share at least some important characteristics with one another. Researchers who develop a classification system assume that the characteristics of individuals within each category are more predictable than they had been previously, thereby allowing us to learn important information about such individuals. In medicine, for example, diabetes mellitus is a useful medical diagnosis because it improves our ability to predict individuals' response to certain treatments (for example, insulin), risk for certain illnesses (for example, blindness), and other characteristics.

Similarly, in the case of a psychiatric classification system, we assume that its categories will help us predict such variables as the course and outcome of individuals' mental disorders, their family history, performance on laboratory measures, and treatment response (Robins & Guze, 1970). The hope is that such a system eventually will also provide important clues to the causes of the psychopathological disorders it encompasses. The key point, which is often missed by critics of psychiatric classification, is that valid diagnoses provide us with more than labels for abnormal behavior; they provide us with important information that we did not have before.

Probably the first major system of psychiatric classification was put forth by the Greek physician Hippocrates (c. 460–377 B.C.), who grouped all mental anomalies into three categories: mania (excessive excitement), melancholia (excessive depression), and phrenitis (brain fever). Hippocrates (and later his Roman disciple Galen) further argued that all disturbances in personality were attributable to imbalances among four fluids, or "humors": Sanguine (moody) individuals had an excess of blood, phlegmatic (apathetic) individuals an excess of phlegm, melancoholic (depressed) individuals an excess of black bile, and choleric (hot-tempered) individuals an excess of yellow bile. Compare Hippocrates' reassuringly parsimonious scheme with the current classification system in American psychiatry, the *Diagnostic and Statistical Manual of Mental Disorders*, fourth edition (DSM-IV), which contains approximately 350 conditions, most of which can only be diagnosed if certain highly complex and detailed rules are met. Despite their enormous superficial differences, Hippocrates' and DSM-IV's classifications of mental disorders share a crucial goal—to allow improved prediction, and ultimately understanding, of disordered behavior.

OVERVIEW OF PART I

This part of the book embraces four controversial issues concerning psychiatric classification and diagnosis. Chapter 1 discusses whether it is meaningful to conceptualize aberrant or socially maladaptive behavior as the product of mental illness. Chapter 2 deals with the question of whether mental health professionals can truly distinguish the abnormal from the normal. Chapter 3 examines the debate regarding the merits and liabilities of probably the most significant and controversial development in psychiatric classification in this century, the third edition of the American Psychiatric Association's *Diagnostic and Statistical Manual of Mental Disorders* (DSM-III). Finally, Chapter 4 explores the question of whether DSM-III and similar classification systems are gender biased.

You can think of the first two issues as logically prior to the last two. If the concept of mental illness is not meaningful or if psychologists and psychiatrists cannot reliably differentiate mental illness from normality, then it makes little sense to proceed with a system for classifying mental illnesses. For that matter, it would make little sense to read a book on the characteristics, etiology, or treatment of mental illnesses. Nevertheless, as you will soon see, you cannot avoid these issues quite so easily.

REFERENCES

Robins, E., & Guze, S. B. (1970). Establishment of diagnostic validity in psychiatric illness: Its application to schizophrenia. *American Journal of Psychiatry, 126*, 983–987.

CHAPTER 1

Is mental illness a myth?

PRO	Szasz, T. S. (1960). The myth of mental illness. *American Psychologist, 15*, 113–118.
CON	Ausubel, D. P. (1961). Personality disorder *is* disease. *American Psychologist, 16*, 69–74.

OVERVIEW OF THE CONTROVERSY: Thomas S. Szasz argues that "mental illness" is a mythical entity, a flawed attempt to explain interpersonal behavior that society finds unpleasant. David P. Ausubel counters that mental illness is genuine and that the notion of illness is not inconsistent with problematic interpersonal behavior.

CONTEXT OF THE PROBLEM

What is mental illness? This question, so often overlooked or given short shrift in abnormal psychology courses, poses a fundamental challenge to psychologists engaged in the study of abnormal behavior. If researchers who study mental illness cannot agree on its definition, justifiable questions can be raised concerning the scientific status of the discipline of abnormal psychology. How can scientists aspire to comprehend a phenomenon without first knowing where this phenomenon begins and ends—or, for that matter, whether it even exists?

Some rebellious authors have had the bad manners to suggest that the concept of mental illness has outlived its utility and should be discarded. Many of these authors, among them an upstart psychiatrist named Thomas Szasz, argue that "mental illness" is little more than a descriptive label for behavior that most of us find unusual, unpleasant, or annoying. Just as demonic possession was frequently invoked as a cause of abnormal behavior during much of the Middle Ages, these writers claim, an imaginary entity called "mental illness" is invoked as a "scientific" cause of abnormal behavior in our time. Moreover, the concept of "mental illness," they insist, is objectionable ethically as well as scientifically, because it encourages diagnosed individuals to shirk responsibility for their behavior.

Although the articles in this chapter are dated (published in 1960 and 1961), the issues they raise are not. Serious questions concerning the definition and even the existence of mental illness have nagged professionals in the field of abnormal psychology for decades. These questions are like the evil protagonist in the film *Cape Fear:* Time and time again, they apparently disappear once and for all, only to reappear unexpectedly in a new and often more sinister guise.

Indeed, our views on the boundaries of mental illness have been subject to marked and frequent historical changes. In recent centuries, for example, children who masturbated were given diagnoses of childhood masturbation disorder (Wakefield, 1992a). Slaves who repeatedly escaped from their masters were said to suffer from drapetomania (Wakefield, 1992a), and slaves who were disobedient to their masters were sometimes given diagnoses of dysathesia aethiopica (Tavris, 1992). Homosexuality was formally considered a psychiatric disorder in the United States as recently as 1973, when the membership of the American Psychiatric Association voted to remove it from the diagnostic nomenclature (Spitzer, 1981). An even more recent case in point: In the late 1970s the

American Psychiatric Association considered including a formal statement in DSM-III to the effect that mental disorders are a subset of medical diseases (Kirk & Kutchins, 1992). This proposal, which was never officially adopted, touched off a firestorm of protests from psychologists, as well as spirited rebuttals to these protests by several members of the psychiatric community. The intense controversy over this proposal underscores the persisting disagreement among mental health professionals regarding the nature of mental illness. In this case, the unresolved question was "How, if at all, does mental illness differ from medical illness?" Indeed, this is one of the principal issues addressed by the two readings in this chapter.

Questions over the boundaries of mental illness resurfaced in the mid-1980s and early 1990s over the issue of whether to include such syndromes as premenstrual dysphoric disorder (premenstrual syndrome), self-defeating personality disorder, and sadistic personality disorder in the official diagnostic nomenclature. Once again, these questions proved highly resistant to a simple solution, largely because of the lack of consensus regarding the definition of mental illness. Many psychologists surely experienced a sense of déjà vu as they were again asked to face the question "What is mental illness?" Some psychologists were forced to reconfront a more embarrassing question: "Is mental illness a myth?"

THE CONTROVERSY
Szasz vs. Ausubel

Szasz

Thomas Szasz, who for decades has been one of the most outspoken and controversial opponents of traditional models of psychiatric classification and diagnosis, argues that "mental illness" is an illusory entity, not unlike the unicorn of ancient mythology. Szasz does not maintain that the problematic behaviors that mental health professionals label as indicative of "mental illness" are mythical; there is no denying that the behavior of certain individuals is consistently strange, irritating, or deviant. For Szasz, however, these behaviors are not a product of an underlying disease of the brain but are better thought of as "problems in living." He likens the concept of "mental illness" to the concept of demonic possession that dominated the popular psychology of the Middle Ages. Like demonic possession, "mental illness" is a circular explanation for behavior that we otherwise find inexplicable. A diagnosis of "mental illness" essentially explains nothing, according to Szasz, and amounts only to a tautological description of the behaviors that it refers to. Moreover, Szasz argues that the "mental illness" concept is predicated on a misleading analogy between medical and mental disorders. Whereas the features of medical disorders tend to be objective and empirically verifiable, the features of mental disorders tend to be subjective and inferential. Finally, Szasz contends that labeling people as "mentally ill" diminishes their responsibility and accountability for their freely chosen actions.

Ausubel

In his response to Szasz, David Ausubel counters that mental illnesses are genuine. He takes issue with Szasz's claim that mental illness must be a product of brain illness and instead argues that illness is simply a substantial departure from socially desirable standards of behavior. Some but not all mental illnesses, according to Ausubel, can be traced to structural damage to the brain. Ausubel also maintains that Szasz has created an artificial dichotomy between mental and medical disorders. For example, the symptoms of many medical disorders (such as chronic pain) are just as subjective and inferential as are those of many mental disorders. In addition, Ausubel disagrees with Szasz that the concepts of "problems in living" and "mental illness" are fundamentally incompatible. Some individuals may experience interpersonal difficulties as a consequence of an underlying illness.

Finally, Ausubel criticizes the position on mental illness adopted by O. Hobart Mowrer in an earlier article (Mowrer, 1960). Mowrer argued that "mental illness," particularly neurosis, is best conceived of as a sin or moral failing. According to Mowrer, neurotics are individuals who have not fully acknowledged the guilt that they should feel regarding their immoral impulses, beliefs, and behaviors. Ausubel disagrees with Mowrer that mental illness and immorality are largely synonymous and further asserts that the concepts of mental illness and immorality are not mutually exclusive. Individuals may feel, think, and act unethically because of an underlying disease.

One minor point before beginning: Ausubel uses the term *personality disorder* in a rather different sense than it is typically used today (see Chapter 9). The contemporary term refers to a condition characterized by extreme levels of certain personality traits (such as impulsivity or perfectionism) that result in inflexible or maladaptive behavior; however, Ausubel uses the term as a catchall for mental illness in general. Thus, as you read his article, bear in mind that Ausubel is referring not only to the ten major conditions listed in DSM-IV as personality disorders but to all the conditions listed in DSM-IV as mental disorders.

KEY CONCEPTS AND TERMS*

problems in living Szasz's term for the interpersonal behaviors that mental health professionals label as signs of mental illness. According to Szasz, "mentally ill" individuals are not suffering from a disease but are instead experiencing difficulty in adjusting their behavior to the demands of society.

sign Feature of a psychopathological condition that is observable directly by others. For example, a sad facial expression

*The terms listed in this section clarify some of the ideas in the articles that follow. Other important terms that are presented in the discussion in boldface type do not appear in this list.

is a sign of depression, because another individual can observe it directly.

symptom Feature of a psychopathological condition that is not observable directly by others and thus must be reported by the patient. For example, intense feelings of sadness and worthlessness are symptoms of depression, because they cannot be directly observed by another individual and can only be reported by the patient.

PREVIEW QUESTIONS

1. According to Szasz, how do medical illnesses differ from what are typically called mental illnesses?
2. According to Szasz, what are problems in living and how do they relate to the concept of mental illness?
3. What does Szasz view as the major ethical problems associated with viewing problems in living as mental illnesses?
4. On what grounds does Ausubel dispute Szasz's distinction between medical and mental illnesses?
5. Does Ausubel disagree with Szasz that mental illnesses can be conceptualized as problems in living?
6. What are Ausubel's major criticisms of Mowrer's "mental illness as sin" position?

THOMAS S. SZASZ

The myth of mental illness

My aim in this essay is to raise the question "Is there such a thing as mental illness?" and to argue that there is not. Since the notion of mental illness is extremely widely used nowadays, inquiry into the ways in which this term is employed would seem to be especially indicated. Mental illness, of course, is not literally a "thing"—or physical object—and hence it can "exist" only in the same sort of way in which other theoretical concepts exist. Yet, familiar theories are in the habit of posing, sooner or later—at least to those who come to believe in them—as "objective truths" (or "facts"). During certain historical periods, explanatory conceptions such as deities, witches, and microorganisms appeared not only as theories but as self-evident *causes* of a vast number of events. I submit that today mental illness is widely regarded in a somewhat similar fashion, that is, as the cause of innumerable diverse happenings. As an antidote to the complacent use of the notion of mental illness—whether as a self-evident phenomenon, theory, or cause—let us ask this question: What is meant when it is asserted that someone is mentally ill?

In what follows I shall describe briefly the main uses to which the concept of mental illness has been put. I shall argue that this notion has outlived whatever usefulness it might have had and that it now functions merely as a convenient myth.

MENTAL ILLNESS AS A SIGN OF BRAIN DISEASE

The notion of mental illness derives its main support from such phenomena as syphilis of the brain or delirious conditions—intoxications, for instance—in which persons are known to manifest various peculiarities or disorders of thinking and behavior. Correctly speaking, however, these are diseases of the brain, not of the mind. According to one school of thought, *all* so-called mental illness is of this type. The assumption is made that some neurological defect, perhaps a very subtle one, will ultimately be found for all the disorders of thinking and behavior. Many contemporary psychiatrists, physicians, and other scientists hold this view. This position implies that people *cannot* have troubles—expressed in what are *now called* "mental illnesses"—because of differences in personal needs, opinions, social aspirations, values, and so on. *All problems in living* are attributed to physicochemical processes which in due time will be discovered by medical research.

"Mental illnesses" are thus regarded as basically no different than all other diseases (that is, of the body). The only difference, in this view, between mental and bodily diseases is that the former, affecting the brain, manifest themselves by means of mental symptoms; whereas the latter, affecting other organ systems (for example, the skin, liver, etc.), manifest themselves by means of symptoms referable to those parts of the

SOURCE: *American Psychologist, 15*, pp. 113–118, February 1960.

body. This view rests on and expresses what are, in my opinion, two fundamental errors.

In the first place, what central nervous system symptoms would correspond to a skin eruption or a fracture? It would *not* be some emotion or complex bit of behavior. Rather, it would be blindness or a paralysis of some part of the body. The crux of the matter is that a disease of the brain, analogous to a disease of the skin or bone, is a neurological defect, and not a problem in living. For example, a *defect* in a person's visual field may be satisfactorily explained by correlating it with certain definite lesions in the nervous system. On the other hand, a person's *belief*—whether this be a belief in Christianity, in Communism, or in the idea that his internal organs are "rotting" and that his body is, in fact, already "dead"—cannot be explained by a defect or disease of the nervous system. Explanations of this sort of occurrence—assuming that one is interested in the belief itself and does not regard it simply as a "symptom" or expression of something else that is *more interesting*—must be sought along different lines.

The second error in regarding complex psychosocial behavior, consisting of communications about ourselves and the world about us, as mere symptoms of neurological functioning is *epistemological*. In other words, it is an error pertaining not to any mistakes in observation or reasoning, as such, but rather to the way in which we organize and express our knowledge. In the present case, the error lies in making a symmetrical dualism between mental and physical (or bodily) symptoms, a dualism which is merely a habit of speech and to which no known observations can be found to correspond. Let us see if this is so. In medical practice, when we speak of physical disturbances, we mean either signs (for example, a fever) or symptoms (for example, pain). We speak of mental symptoms, on the other hand, when we refer to a patient's *communications about himself, others, and the world about him*. He might state that he is Napoleon or that he is being persecuted by the Communists. These would be considered mental symptoms *only* if the observer believed that the patient was *not* Napoleon or that he was *not* being persecuted by the Communists. This makes it apparent that the statement that "X is a mental symptom" involves rendering a judgment. The judgment entails, moreover, a covert comparison or matching of the patient's ideas, concepts, or beliefs with those of the observer and the society in which they live. The notion of mental symptom is therefore inextricably tied to the *social* (including *ethical*) *context* in which it is made in much the same way as the notion of bodily symptom is tied to an *anatomical* and *genetic context* (Szasz, 1957a, 1957b).

To sum up what has been said thus far: I have tried to show that for those who regard mental symptoms as signs of brain disease, the concept of mental illness is unnecessary and misleading. For what they mean is that people so labeled suffer from diseases of the brain; and, if that is what they mean, it would seem better for the sake of clarity to say that and not something else.

MENTAL ILLNESS AS A NAME FOR PROBLEMS IN LIVING

The term "mental illness" is widely used to describe something which is very different than a disease of the brain. Many people today take it for granted that living is an arduous process. Its hardship for modern man, moreover, derives not so much from a struggle for biological survival as from the stresses and strains inherent in the social intercourse of complex human personalities. In this context, the notion of mental illness is used to identify or describe some feature of an individual's so-called personality. Mental illness—as a deformity of the personality, so to speak—is then regarded as the *cause* of the human disharmony. It is implicit in this view that social intercourse between people is regarded as something *inherently harmonious*, its disturbance being due solely to the presence of "mental illness" in many people. This is obviously fallacious reasoning, for it makes the abstraction "mental illness" into a *cause*, even though this abstraction was created in the first place to serve only as a shorthand expression for certain types of human behavior. It now becomes necessary to ask: "What kinds of behavior are regarded as indicative of mental illness, and by whom?"

The concept of illness, whether bodily or mental, implies *deviation from some clearly defined norm*. In the case of physical illness, the norm is the structural and functional integrity of the human body. Thus, although the desirability of physical health, as such, is an ethical value, what health *is* can be stated in anatomical and physiological terms. What is the norm deviation from which is regarded as mental illness? This question cannot be easily answered. But whatever this norm might be, we can be certain of only one thing: namely, that it is a norm that must be stated in terms of *psychosocial, ethical*, and *legal* concepts. For example, notions such as "excessive repression" or "acting out an unconscious impulse" illustrate the use of psychological concepts for judging (so-called) mental health and illness. The idea that chronic hostility, vengefulness, or divorce are indicative of mental illness would be illustrations of the use of ethical norms (that is, the desirability of love, kindness, and a stable marriage relationship). Finally, the widespread psychiatric opinion that only a mentally ill person would commit homicide illustrates the use of a legal concept as a norm of mental health. The norm from which deviation is measured whenever one speaks of a mental illness is a *psychosocial and ethical one*. Yet, the remedy is sought in terms of *medical* measures which—it is hoped and assumed—are free from wide differences of ethical value. The definition of the disorder and the terms in which its remedy are sought are therefore at serious odds with one another. The practical significance of this covert conflict between the alleged nature of the defect and the remedy can hardly be exaggerated.

Having identified the norms used to measure deviations in cases of mental illness, we will now turn to the question: "Who defines the norms and hence the deviation?" Two basic answers may be offered: (*a*) It may be the person himself (that is, the patient) who decides that he deviates from a norm. For example, an artist may believe that he suffers from a work inhibition; and he may implement this conclusion by seeking help *for* himself from a psychotherapist. (*b*) It may be someone other than the patient who decides that the latter is deviant (for example, relatives, physicians, legal authorities, society generally, etc.). In such a case a psychiatrist may be hired by others to do something *to* the patient in order to correct the deviation.

These considerations underscore the importance of asking the question "Whose agent is the psychiatrist?" and of giving a candid answer to it (Szasz, 1956, 1958). The psychiatrist (psychologist or nonmedical psychotherapist), it now develops, may be the agent of the patient, of the relatives, of the school, of the military services, of a business organization, of a court of law, and so forth. In speaking of the psychiatrist as the agent of these persons or organizations, it is not implied that his values concerning norms, or his ideas and aims concerning the proper nature of remedial action, need to coincide exactly with those of his employer. For example, a patient in individual psychotherapy may believe that his salvation lies in a new marriage; his psychotherapist need not share this hypothesis. As the patient's agent, however, he must abstain from bringing social or legal force to bear on the patient which would prevent him from putting his beliefs into action. If his *contract* is with the patient, the psychiatrist (psychotherapist) may disagree with him or stop his treatment; but he cannot engage others to obstruct the patient's aspirations. Similarly, if a psychiatrist is engaged by a court to determine the sanity of a criminal, he need not fully share the legal authorities' values and intentions in regard to the criminal and the means available for dealing with him. But the psychiatrist is expressly barred from stating, for example, that it is not the criminal who is "insane" but the men who wrote the law on the basis of which the very actions that are being judged are regarded as "criminal." Such an opinion could be voiced, of course, but not in a courtroom, and not by a psychiatrist who makes it his practice to assist the court in performing its daily work.

To recapitulate: In actual contemporary social usage, the finding of a mental illness is made by establishing a deviance in behavior from certain psychosocial, ethical, or legal norms. The judgment may be made, as in medicine, by the patient, the physician (psychiatrist), or others. Remedial action, finally, tends to be sought in a therapeutic—or covertly medical—framework, thus creating a situation in which *psychosocial, ethical, and/or legal deviations* are claimed to be correctible by (so-called) *medical action*. Since medical action is designed to correct only medical deviations, it seems logically absurd to expect that it will help solve problems whose very existence had been defined and established on nonmedical grounds. I think that these considerations may be fruitfully applied to the present use of tranquilizers and, more generally, to what might be expected of drugs of whatever type in regard to the amelioration or solution of problems in human living.

THE ROLE OF ETHICS IN PSYCHIATRY

Anything that people *do*—in contrast to things that *happen* to them (Peters, 1958)—takes place in a context of value. In this broad sense, no human activity is devoid of ethical implications. When the values underlying certain activities are widely shared, those who participate in their pursuit may lose sight of them altogether. The discipline of medicine, both as a pure science (for example, research) and as a technology (for example, therapy), contains many ethical considerations and judgments. Unfortunately, these are often denied, minimized, or merely kept out of focus; for the ideal of the medical profession as well as of the people whom it serves seems to be having a system of medicine (allegedly) free of ethical value. This sentimental notion is expressed by such things as the doctor's willingness to treat and help patients irrespective of their religious or political beliefs, whether they are rich or poor, etc. While there may be some grounds for this belief—albeit it is a view that is not impressively true even in these regards—the fact remains that ethical considerations encompass a vast range of human affairs. Making the practice of medicine neutral in regard to some specific issues of value need not, and cannot, mean that it can be kept free from all such values. The practice of medicine is intimately tied to ethics; and the first thing that we must do, it seems to me, is to try to make this clear and explicit. I shall let this matter rest here, for it does not concern us specifically in this essay. Lest there be any vagueness, however, about how or where ethics and medicine meet, let me remind the reader of such issues as birth control, abortion, suicide, and euthanasia as only a few of the major areas of current ethicomedical controversy.

Psychiatry, I submit, is very much more intimately tied to problems of ethics than is medicine. I use the word "psychiatry" here to refer to that contemporary discipline which is concerned with *problems in living* (and not with diseases of the brain, which are problems for neurology). Problems in human relations can be analyzed, interpreted, and given meaning only within given social and ethical contexts. Accordingly, it *does* make a difference—arguments to the contrary notwithstanding—what the psychiatrist's socioethical orientations happen to be; for these will influence his ideas on what is wrong with the patient, what deserves comment or interpretation, in what possible directions change might be desirable, and so forth. Even in medicine proper, these factors play a role, as for instance, in the divergent orientations which physicians, depending on their religious affiliations, have toward such things as birth control and therapeutic abortion. Can anyone really believe that a psychotherapist's ideas concerning religious belief, slavery, or other similar issues play no role in his practical work? If they do make a difference, what are we to infer from it? Does it not seem reasonable that we ought to have different psychiatric therapies—each expressly recognized for the ethical positions which they embody—for, say, Catholics and Jews, religious persons and agnostics, democrats and communists, white supremacists and Blacks, and so on? Indeed, if we look at how psychiatry is actually practiced today (especially in the United States), we find that people do seek psychiatric help in accordance with their social status and ethical beliefs (Hollingshead & Redlich, 1958). This should really not surprise us more than being told that practicing Catholics rarely frequent birth control clinics.

The foregoing position, which holds that contemporary psychotherapists deal with problems in living, rather than with mental illnesses and their cures, stands in opposition to a currently prevalent claim, according to which mental illness is just as "real" and "objective" as bodily illness. This is a confusing claim since it is never known exactly what is meant by such words as "real" and "objective." I suspect, however, that what is intended by the proponents of this view is to create the idea in the popular mind that mental illness is some sort of disease entity, like an infection or a malignancy. If this were true, one could *catch* or *get* a "mental illness," one might *have* or *harbor* it, one might *transmit* it to others, and finally one could get *rid* of it. In my opinion, there is not a shred of evidence to support this idea. To the contrary, all the evidence is the other way and supports the view that what people now call mental illnesses are for the most part *communications* expressing unacceptable ideas, often framed, moreover, in an unusual idiom. The scope of this essay allows me to do no more than mention this alternative theoretical approach to this problem (Szasz, 1957c).

This is not the place to consider in detail the similarities and differences between bodily and mental illnesses. It shall suffice for us here to emphasize only one important difference between them: namely, that whereas bodily disease refers to public, physicochemical occurrences, the notion of mental illness is used to codify relatively more private, sociopsychological happenings of which the observer (diagnostician) forms a part. In other words, the psychiatrist does not stand *apart* from what he observes, but is, in Harry Stack Sullivan's apt words, a "participant observer." This means that he is *committed* to some picture of what he considers reality—and to what he thinks society considers reality—and he observes and judges the patient's behavior in the light of these considerations. This touches on our earlier observation that the notion of mental symptom itself implies a comparison between observer and observed, psychiatrist and patient. This is so obvious that I may be charged with belaboring trivialities. Let me therefore say once more that my aim in presenting this argument was expressly to criticize and counter a prevailing contemporary tendency to deny the moral aspects of psychiatry (and psychotherapy) and to substitute for them allegedly value-free medical considerations. Psychotherapy, for example, is being widely practiced as though it entailed nothing other than restoring the patient from a state of mental sickness to one of mental health. While it is generally accepted that mental illness has something to do with man's social (or interpersonal) relations, it is paradoxically maintained that problems of values (that is, of ethics) do not arise in this process.[1] Yet, in one sense, much of psychotherapy may revolve around nothing other than the elucidation and weighing of goals and values—many of which may be mutually contradictory—and the means whereby they might best be harmonized, realized, or relinquished.

The diversity of human values and the methods by means of which they may be realized is so vast, and many of them remain so unacknowledged, that they cannot fail but lead to conflicts in human relations. Indeed, to say that human relations at all levels—from mother to child, through husband and wife, to nation and nation—are fraught with stress, strain, and disharmony is, once again, making the obvious explicit. Yet, what may be obvious may be also poorly understood. This I think is the case here. For it seems to me that—at least in our scientific theories of behavior—we have failed to *accept* the simple fact that human relations are inherently fraught with difficulties and that to make them even relatively harmonious requires much patience and hard work. I submit that the idea of mental illness is now being put to work to obscure certain difficulties which at present may be inherent—not that they need be unmodifiable—in the social intercourse of persons. If this is true, the concept functions as a disguise; for instead of calling attention to conflicting human needs, aspirations, and values, the notion of mental illness provides an amoral and impersonal "thing" (an "illness") as an explanation for *problems in living* (Szasz, 1959). We may recall in this connection that not so long ago it was devils and witches who were held responsible for men's problems in social living. The belief in mental illness, as something other than man's trouble in getting along with his fellow man, is the proper heir to the belief in demonology and witchcraft. Mental illness exists or is "real" in exactly the same sense in which witches existed or were "real."

CHOICE, RESPONSIBILITY, AND PSYCHIATRY

While I have argued that mental illnesses do not exist, I obviously did not imply that the social and psychological occurrences to which this label is currently being attached also do not exist. Like the personal and social troubles which people had in the Middle Ages, they are real enough. It is the labels we give them that concerns us and, having labeled them, what we do about them. While I cannot go into the ramified implications of this problem here, it is worth noting that a demonologic conception of problems in living gave rise to therapy along theological lines. Today, a belief in mental illness implies—nay, requires—therapy along medical or psychotherapeutic lines.

What is implied in the line of thought set forth here is something quite different. I do not intend to offer a new conception of "psychiatric illness" nor a new form of "therapy." My aim is more modest and yet also more ambitious. It is to suggest that the phenomena now called mental illnesses be looked at afresh and more simply, that they be removed from the category of illnesses, and that they be regarded as the expressions of man's struggle with the problem of *how* he should live. The last mentioned problem is obviously a vast one, its enormity reflecting not only man's inability to cope with his environment, but even more his increasing self-reflectiveness.

By problems in living, then, I refer to that truly explosive chain reaction which began with man's fall from divine grace by partaking of the fruit of the tree of knowledge. Man's awareness of himself and of the world about him seems to be a steadily expanding one, bringing in its wake an ever larger *burden of understanding* (an expression borrowed from Susanne Langer, 1953). *This burden*, then, *is to be expected and must not be misinterpreted.* Our only *rational* means for lightening it is *more understanding*, and appropriate *action* based on such understanding. The main alternative lies in acting as though the burden were not what in fact we perceive it to be and taking refuge in an outmoded theological view of man. In the latter view, man does not fashion his life and much of his world about him, but merely lives out his fate in a world created by superior beings. This may logically lead to pleading nonresponsibility in the face of seemingly unfathomable problems and difficulties. Yet, if man fails to take increasing responsibility for his actions, individually as well as collectively, it seems unlikely that some higher power or being would assume this task and carry this burden for him. Moreover, this seems hardly the proper time in human history for obscuring the issue of man's responsibility for his actions by hiding it behind the skirt of an all-explaining conception of mental illness.

CONCLUSIONS

I have tried to show that the notion of mental illness has outlived whatever usefulness it might have had and that it now functions merely as a convenient myth. As such, it is a true heir to religious myths in general, and to the belief in witchcraft in particular; the role of all these belief-systems was to act as *social tranquilizers*, thus encouraging the hope that mastery of certain specific problems may be achieved by means of substitutive (symbolic-magical) operations. The notion of mental illness thus serves mainly to obscure the everyday fact that life for most people is a continuous struggle, not for biological survival, but for a "place in the sun," "peace of mind," or some other human value. For man aware of himself and of the world about him, once the needs for preserving the body (and perhaps the race) are more or less satisfied, the problem arises as to what he should do with himself. Sustained adherence to the myth of mental illness allows people to avoid facing this problem, believing that mental health, conceived as the absence of mental illness, automatically insures the making of right and safe choices in one's conduct of life. But the facts are all the other way. It is the making of good choices in life that others regard, retrospectively, as good mental health!

The myth of mental illness encourages us, moreover, to believe in its logical corollary: that social intercourse would be harmonious, satisfying, and the secure basis of a "good life" were it not for the disrupting influences of mental illness or "psychopathology." The potentiality for universal human happiness, in this form at least, seems to me but another example of the I-wish-it-were-true type of fantasy. I do not believe that human happiness or well-being on a hitherto unimaginably large scale, and not just for a select few, is impossible. This goal could be achieved, however, only at the cost of many men, and not just a few being willing and able to tackle their personal, social, and ethical conflicts. This means having the courage and integrity to forgo waging battles on false fronts, finding solutions for substitute problems—for instance, fighting the battle of stomach acid and chronic fatigue instead of facing up to a marital conflict.

Our adversaries are not demons, witches, fate, or mental illness. We have no enemy whom we can fight, exorcise, or dispel by "cure." What we do have are *problems in living*—whether these be biologic, economic, political, or sociopsychological. In this essay I was concerned only with problems belonging in the last mentioned category, and within this group mainly with those pertaining to moral values. The field to which modern psychiatry addresses itself is vast, and I made no effort to encompass it all. My argument was limited to the proposition that mental illness is a myth, whose function it is to disguise and thus render more palatable the bitter pill of moral conflicts in human relations.

NOTE

1. Freud went so far as to say that: "I consider ethics to be taken for granted. Actually I have never done a mean thing" (Jones, 1957, p. 247). This surely is a strange thing to say for someone who has studied man as a social being as closely as did Freud. I mention it here to show how the notion of "illness" (in the case of psychoanalysis, "psychopathology," or "mental illness") was used by Freud—and by most of his followers—as a means for classifying certain forms of human behavior as falling within the scope of medicine, and hence (by *fiat*) outside that of ethics!

REFERENCES

Hollingshead, A. B., & Redlich, F. C. *Social class and mental illness*. New York: Wiley, 1958.

Jones, E. *The life and work of Sigmund Freud*. Vol. III. New York: Basic Books, 1957.

Langer, S. K. *Philosophy in a new key*. New York: Mentor Books, 1953.

Peters, R. S. *The concept of motivation*. London: Routledge & Kegan Paul, 1958.

Szasz, T. S. Malingering: "Diagnosis" or social condemnation? AMA *Arch Neurol. Psychiat.*, 1956, *76*, 432–443.

Szasz, T. S. *Pain and pleasure: A study of bodily feelings*. New York: Basic Books, 1957. (a)

Szasz, T. S. The problem of psychiatric nosology: A contribution to a situational analysis of psychiatric operations. *Amer. J. Psychiat.*, 1957, *114*, 405–413. (b)

Szasz, T. S. On the theory of psychoanalytic treatment. *Int. J. Psycho-Anal.*, 1957, *38*, 166–182. (c)

Szasz, T. S. Psychiatry, ethics and the criminal law. *Columbia Law Rev.*, 1958, *58*, 183–198.

Szasz, T. S. Moral conflict and psychiatry. *Yale Rev.*, 1960, *49*, 555–566.

DAVID P. AUSUBEL

Personality disorder is disease

In two recent articles in the *American Psychologist*, Szasz (1960) and Mowrer (1960) have argued the case for discarding the concept of mental illness. The essence of Mowrer's position is that since medical science lacks "demonstrated competence . . . in psychiatry," psychology would be wise to "get out" from "under the penumbra of medicine," and to regard the behavior disorders as manifestations of sin rather than of disease (p. 302). Szasz' position, as we shall see shortly, is somewhat more complex than Mowrer's, but agrees with the latter in emphasizing the moral as opposed to the psychopathological basis of abnormal behavior.

For a long time now, clinical psychology has both repudiated the relevance of moral judgment and accountability for assessing behavioral acts and choices, and has chafed under medical (psychiatric) control and authority in diagnosing and treating the personality disorders. One can readily appreciate, therefore, Mowrer's eagerness to sever the historical and professional ties that bind clinical psychology to medicine, even if this means denying that psychological disturbances constitute a form of illness, and even if psychology's close working relationship with psychiatry must be replaced by a new rapprochement with sin and theology, as "the lesser of two evils" (pp. 302–303). One can also sympathize with Mowrer's and Szasz' dissatisfaction with prevailing amoral and nonjudgmental trends in clinical psychology and with their entirely commendable efforts to restore moral judgment and accountability to a respectable place among the criteria used in evaluating human behavior, both normal and abnormal.

Opposition to these two trends in the handling of the behavior disorders (i.e., to medical control and to nonjudgmental therapeutic attitudes), however, does not necessarily imply abandonment of the concept of mental illness. There is no inconsistency whatsoever in maintaining, on the one hand, that most purposeful human activity has a moral aspect the reality of which psychologists cannot afford to ignore (Ausubel, 1952, p. 462), that man is morally accountable for the majority of his misdeeds (Ausubel, 1952, p. 469), and that psychological rather than medical training and sophistication are basic to competence in the personality disorders (Ausubel, 1956, p. 101), and affirming, on the other hand, that the latter disorders are genuine manifestations of illness. In recent years psychology has been steadily moving away from the formerly fashionable stance of ethical neutrality in the behavioral sciences; and in spite of strident medical claims regarding superior professional qualifications and preclusive legal responsibility for treating psychiatric patients, and notwithstanding the nominally restrictive provisions of medical practice acts, clinical psychologists have been assuming an increasingly more important, independent, and responsible role in treating the mentally ill population of the United States.

It would be instructive at this point to examine the tactics of certain other medically allied professions in freeing themselves from medical control and in acquiring independent, legally recognized professional status. In no instance have they resorted to the devious stratagem of denying that they were treating diseases, in the hope of mollifying medical opposition and legitimizing their own professional activities. They took the position instead that simply because a given condition is defined as a disease, its treatment need not necessarily be turned over to doctors of medicine if other equally competent professional specialists were available. That this position is legally and politically tenable is demonstrated by the fact that an impressively large number of recognized diseases are legally treated today by both medical *and* nonmedical specialists (e.g., diseases of the mouth, face, jaws, teeth, eyes, and feet). And there are few convincing reasons for believing that psychiatrists wield that much more political power than physicians, maxillofacial surgeons, ophthalmologists, and orthopedic surgeons, that they could be successful where these latter specialists have failed, in legally restricting practice in their particular area of competence to holders of the medical degree. Hence, even if psychologists were not currently managing to hold their own vis-à-vis psychiatrists, it would be far less dangerous and much more forthright to press for the necessary ameliorative legislation than to seek cover behind an outmoded and thoroughly discredited conception of the behavior disorders.

THE SZASZ-MOWRER POSITION

Szasz' (1960) contention that the concept of mental illness "now functions merely as a convenient myth" (p. 118) is grounded on four unsubstantiated and logically untenable propositions, which can be fairly summarized as follows:

1. Only symptoms resulting from demonstrable physical lesions qualify as legitimate manifestations of disease. Brain pathology is a type of physical lesion, but its symptoms, properly speaking, are neurological rather than psychological in nature. Under no circumstances, therefore, can mental symptoms be considered a form of illness.
2. A basic dichotomy exists between *mental symptoms,* on the one hand, which are subjective in nature, dependent on subjective judgment and personal involvement of the observer, and referable to cultural-ethical norms, and *physical symptoms*, on the other hand, which are allegedly objective in nature, ascertainable without personal involvement of the observer, and independent of cultural norms and ethical standards. Only symptoms possessing the latter set of characteristics are genuinely reflective of illness and amenable to medical treatment.
3. Mental symptoms are merely expressions of problems of living and, hence, cannot be regarded as manifestations of a pathological condition. The concept of mental illness is misleading and demonological because it seeks to explain psychological disturbance in particular and human disharmony in general in terms of a metaphorical but nonexistent disease entity, instead of attributing them to inherent difficulties in coming to grips with elusive problems of choice and responsibility.
4. Personality disorders, therefore, can be most fruitfully conceptualized as products of moral conflict, confusion, and aberration. Mowrer (1960) extends this latter proposition to include the dictum that psychiatric symptoms are primarily reflective of unacknowledged sin, and that individuals manifesting these symptoms are responsible for and deserve their suffering, both because of their original transgressions and because they refuse to avow and expiate their guilt (pp. 301, 304).

Widespread adoption of the Szasz-Mowrer view of the personality disorders would, in my opinion, turn back the psychiatric clock twenty-five hundred years. The most significant and perhaps the only real advance registered by mankind in evolving a rational and humane method of handling behavioral aberrations has been in substituting a concept of disease for the demonological and retributional doctrines regarding their nature and etiology that flourished until comparatively recent times. Conceptualized as illness, the symptoms of personality disorders can be interpreted in the light of underlying stresses and resistances, both genic and environmental, and can be evaluated in relation to *specifiable* quantitative and qualitative norms of appropriately adaptive behavior, both cross-culturally and within a particular cultural context. It would behoove us, therefore, before we abandon the concept of mental illness and return to the medieval doctrine of unexpiated sin or adopt Szasz' ambiguous criterion of difficulty in ethical choice and responsibility, to subject the foregoing propositions to careful and detailed study.

Mental Symptoms and Brain Pathology

Although I agree with Szasz in rejecting the doctrine that ultimately some neuroanatomic or neurophysiologic defect will be discovered in *all* cases of personality disorder, I disagree with his reasons for not accepting this proposition. Notwithstanding Szasz' straw man presentation of their position, the proponents of the extreme somatic view do not really assert that the *particular nature* of a patient's disordered beliefs can be correlated with "certain definite lesions in the nervous system" (Szasz, 1960, p. 113). They hold rather that normal cognitive and behavioral functioning depends on the anatomic and physiologic integrity of certain key areas of the brain, and that impairment of this substrate integrity, therefore, provides a physical basis for disturbed ideation and behavior, but does not explain, except in a very gross way, the particular kinds of symptoms involved. In fact, they are generally inclined to attribute the *specific* character of the patient's symptoms to the nature of his preillness personality structure, the substrate integrity of which is impaired by the lesion or metabolic defect in question.

Nevertheless, even though this type of reasoning plausibly accounts for the psychological symptoms found in general paresis, various toxic deliria, and other comparable conditions, it is an extremely improbable explanation of *all* instances of personality disorder. Unlike the tissues of any other organ, brain tissue possesses the unique property of making possible awareness of and adjustment to the world of sensory, social, and symbolic stimulation. Hence by virtue of this unique relationship of the nervous system to the environment, diseases of behavior and personality may reflect abnormalities in personal and social adjustment, quite apart from any structural or metabolic disturbance in the underlying neural substrate. I would conclude, therefore, that although brain pathology is probably not the most important cause of behavior disorder, it is undoubtedly responsible for the incidence of *some* psychological abnormalities *as well as* for various neurological signs and symptoms.

But even if we completely accepted Szasz' view that brain pathology does not account for any symptoms of personality disorder, it would still be unnecessary to accept his assertion that to qualify as a genuine manifestation of disease a given symptom must be caused by a physical lesion. Adoption of such a criterion would be arbitrary and inconsistent both with medical and lay connotations of the term "disease," which in current usage is generally regarded as including any marked deviation, physical, mental, or behavioral, from normally desirable standards of structural and functional integrity.

Mental versus Physical Symptoms

Szasz contends that since the analogy between physical and mental symptoms is patently fallacious, the postulated parallelism between physical and mental disease is logically untenable. This line of reasoning is based on the assumption that the two categories of symptoms can be sharply dichotomized with respect to such basic dimensions as objectivity-subjectivity, the relevance of cultural norms, and the need for personal involvement of the observer. In my opinion, the existence of such a dichotomy cannot be empirically demonstrated in convincing fashion.

Practically all symptoms of bodily disease involve some elements of subjective judgment—both on the part of the patient and of the physician. Pain is perhaps the most important and commonly used criterion of physical illness. Yet, any evaluation of its reported locus, intensity, character, and duration is dependent upon the patient's subjective appraisal of his own sensations and on the physician's assessment of the latter's pain threshold, intelligence, and personality structure. It is also a medical commonplace that the severity of pain in most instances of bodily illness may be mitigated by the administration of a placebo. Furthermore, in taking a meaningful history the physician must not only serve as a participant observer but also as a skilled interpreter of human behavior. It is the rare patient who does not react psychologically to the signs of physical illness; and hence physicians are constantly called upon to decide, for example, to what extent precordial pain and reported tightness in the chest are manifestations of coronary insufficiency, of fear of cardiac disease and impending death, or of combinations of both conditions. Even such allegedly objective signs as pulse rate, BMR [basal metabolic rate], blood pressure, and blood cholesterol have their subjective and relativistic aspects. Pulse rate and blood pressure are notoriously susceptible to emotional influences, and BMR and blood cholesterol fluctuate widely from one cultural environment to another (Dreyfuss & Czaczkes, 1959). And anyone who believes that ethical norms have no relevance for physical illness has obviously failed to consider the problems confronting Catholic patients and/or physicians when issues of contraception, abortion, and preferential saving of the mother's as against the fetus' life must be faced in the context of various obstetrical emergencies and medical contraindications to pregnancy.

It should now be clear, therefore, that symptoms not only do not need a physical basis to qualify as manifestations of illness, but also that the evaluation of *all* symptoms, physical as well as mental, is dependent in large measure on subjective judgment, emotional factors, cultural-ethical norms, and personal involvement on the part of the observer. These considerations alone render no longer tenable Szasz' contention (1960, p. 114) that there is an inherent contradiction between using cultural and ethical norms as criteria of mental disease, on the one hand, and of employing medical measures of treatment on the other. But even if the postulated dichotomy between mental and physical symptoms were valid, the use of physical measures in treating subjective and relativistic psychological symptoms would still be warranted. Once we accept the proposition that impairment of the neural substrate of personality can result in behavior disorder, it is logically consistent to accept the corollary proposition that other kinds of manipulation of the same neural substrate can conceivably have therapeutic effects, irrespective of whether the underlying cause of the mental symptoms is physical or psychological.

Mental Illness and Problems of Living

"The phenomena now called mental illness," argues Szasz (1960), can be regarded more forthrightly and simply as "expressions of man's struggle with the problem of how he should live" (p. 117). This statement undoubtedly oversimplifies the nature of personality disorders; but even if it were adequately inclusive it would not be inconsistent with the position that these disorders are a manifestation of illness. There is no valid reason why a particular symptom cannot both reflect a problem in living *and* constitute a manifestation of disease. The notion of mental illness, conceived in this way, would not "obscure the everyday fact that life for most people is a continuous struggle . . . for a 'place in the sun,' 'peace of mind,' or some other human value" (p. 118). It is quite true, as Szasz points out, that "human relations are inherently fraught with difficulties" (p. 117), and that most people manage to cope with such difficulties without becoming mentally ill. But conceding this fact hardly precludes the possibility that some individuals, either because of the magnitude of the stress involved, or because of genically or environmentally induced susceptibility to ordinary degrees of stress, respond to the problems of living with behavior that is either seriously distorted or sufficiently unadaptive to prevent normal interpersonal relations and vocational functioning. The latter outcome—gross deviation from a designated range of desirable behavioral variability—conforms to the generally understood meaning of mental illness.

The plausibility of subsuming abnormal behavioral reactions to stress under the general rubric of disease is further enhanced by the fact that these reactions include the same three principal categories of symptoms found in physical illness. Depression and catastrophic impairment of self-esteem, for example, are manifestations of personality disorder which are symptomologically comparable to edema in cardiac failure or to heart murmurs in valvular disease. They are indicative of underlying pathology but are neither adaptive nor adjustive. Symptoms such as hypomanic overactivity and compulsive striving toward unrealistically high achievement goals, on the other hand, are both adaptive and adjustive, and constitute a type of compensatory response to basic feelings of inadequacy, which is not unlike cardiac hypertrophy in hypertensive heart disease or elevated white blood cell count in acute infections. And finally, distortive psychological defenses that have some adjustive value but are generally maladaptive (e.g., phobias, delusions, autistic fantasies) are analogous to the pathological situation found in conditions like pneumonia, in which the excessive outpouring of serum and phagocytes in defensive response to pathogenic bacteria literally causes the patient to drown in his own fluids.

Within the context of this same general proposition, Szasz repudiates the concept of mental illness as demonological in nature, i.e., as the "true heir to religious myths in general and to the belief in witchcraft in particular" (p. 118) because it allegedly employs a reified abstraction ("a deformity of personality") to account in causal terms both for "human disharmony" and for symptoms of behavior disorder (p. 114). But again he appears to be demolishing a straw man. Modern students of personality disorder do not regard mental illness as a cause of human disharmony, but as a comanifestation with it of inherent difficulties in personal adjustment and interpersonal relations; and in so far as I can accurately interpret the literature, psychopathologists do not conceive of mental illness as a cause of particular behavioral symptoms but as a generic term under which these symptoms can be subsumed.

Mental Illness and Moral Responsibility

Szasz' final reason for regarding mental illness as a myth is really a corollary of his previously considered more general proposition that mental symptoms are essentially reflective of problems of living and hence do not legitimately qualify as manifestations of disease. It focuses on difficulties of ethical choice and responsibility as the particular life problems most likely to be productive of personality disorder. Mowrer (1960) further extends this corollary by asserting that neurotic and psychotic individuals are responsible for their suffering (p. 301), and that unacknowledged and unexpiated sin, in turn, is the basic cause of this suffering (p. 304). As previously suggested, however, one can plausibly accept the proposition that psychiatrists and clinical psychologists have erred in trying to divorce behavioral evaluation from ethical considerations, in conducting psychotherapy in an amoral setting, and in confusing the psychological explanation of unethical behavior with absolution from accountability for same, *without* necessarily endorsing the view that personality disorders are basically a reflection of sin, and that victims of these disorders are less ill than responsible for their symptoms (Ausubel, 1952, pp. 392–397, 465–471).

In the first place, it is possible in most instances (although admittedly difficult in some) to distinguish quite unambiguously between mental illness and ordinary cases of immorality. The vast majority of persons who are guilty of moral lapses knowingly violate their own ethical precepts for expediential reasons—despite being volitionally capable at the time, both of choosing the more moral alternative and of exercising the necessary inhibitory control (Ausubel, 1952, pp. 465–471). Such persons, also, usually do not exhibit any signs of behavior disorder. At crucial choice points in facing the problems of living they simply choose the opportunistic instead of the moral alternative. They are not mentally ill, but they are clearly accountable for their misconduct. Hence, since personality disorder and immorality are neither coextensive nor mutually exclusive conditions, the concept of mental illness need not necessarily obscure the issue of moral accountability.

Second, guilt may be a contributory factor in behavior disorder, but is by no means the only or principal cause thereof. Feelings of guilt may give rise to anxiety and depression; but in the absence of catastrophic impairment of self-esteem induced by *other* factors, these symptoms tend to be transitory and peripheral in nature (Ausubel, 1952, pp. 362–363). Repression of guilt is more a consequence than a cause of anxiety. Guilt is repressed in order to avoid the anxiety producing trauma to self-esteem that would otherwise result if it were acknowledged. Repression per se enters the causal picture in anxiety only secondarily—by obviating "the possibility of punishment, confession, expiation, and other guilt reduction mechanisms" (Ausubel, 1952, p. 456). Furthermore, in most types of personality disorder other than anxiety, depression, and various complications of anxiety such as phobias, obsessions, and compulsion, guilt feelings are either not particularly prominent (schizophrenic reactions), or are conspicuously absent (e.g., classical cases of inadequate or aggressive, antisocial psychopathy).

Third, it is just as unreasonable to hold an individual responsible for symptoms of behavior disorder as to deem him accountable for symptoms of physical illness. He is no more culpable for his inability to cope with sociopsychological stress than he would be for his inability to resist the spread of infectious organisms. In those instances where warranted guilt feelings *do* contribute to personality disorder, the patient is accountable for the misdeeds underlying his guilt, but is hardly responsible for the symptoms brought on by the guilt feelings or for unlawful acts committed during his illness. Acknowledgment of guilt may be therapeutically beneficial under these circumstances, but punishment for the original misconduct should obviously be deferred until after recovery.

Lastly, even if it were true that all personality disorder is a reflection of sin and that people are accountable for their behavioral symptoms, it would still be unnecessary to deny that these symptoms are manifestations of disease. Illness is no less real because the victim happens to be culpable for his illness. A glutton with hypertensive heart disease undoubtedly aggravates his condition by overeating, and is culpable in part for the often fatal symptoms of his disease, but what reasonable person would claim that for this reason he is not really ill?

CONCLUSIONS

Four propositions in support of the argument for discarding the concept of mental illness were carefully examined, and the following conclusions were reached:

First, although brain pathology is probably not the major cause of personality disorder, it does account for *some* psychological symptoms by impairing the neural substrate of personality. In any case, however, a symptom need not reflect a physical lesion in order to qualify as a genuine manifestation of disease.

Second, Szasz' postulated dichotomy between mental and physical symptoms is untenable because the assessment of *all* symptoms is dependent to some extent on subjective judgment, emotional factors, cultural-ethical norms, and personal involvement of the observer. Furthermore, the use of medical measures in treating behavior disorders—irrespective of whether the underlying causes are neural or psychological—is defensible on the grounds that if inadvertent impairment of the neural substrate of personality can have distortive effects on behavior, directed manipulation of the same substrate may have therapeutic effects.

Third, there is no inherent contradiction in regarding mental symptoms both as expressions of problems in living *and* as manifestations of illness. The latter situation results when individuals are for various reasons unable to cope with such problems, and react with seriously distorted or maladaptive behavior. The three principal categories of behavioral symptoms—manifestations of impaired functioning, adaptive compensation, and defensive overreaction—are also found in bodily disease. The concept of mental illness has never been advanced as a demonological cause of human disharmony, but only as a co-manifestation with it of certain inescapable difficulties and hazards in personal and social adjustment. The same concept is also generally accepted as a generic term for all behavioral symptoms rather than as a reified cause of these symptoms.

Fourth, the view that personality disorder is less a manifestation of illness than of sin, i.e., of culpable inadequacy in meeting problems of ethical choice and responsibility, and that victims of behavior disorder are therefore morally accountable for their symptoms, is neither logically nor empirically tenable. In most instances immoral behavior and mental illness are clearly distinguishable conditions. Guilt is only a secondary etiological factor in anxiety and depression, and in other personality disorders is either not prominent or conspicuously absent. The issue of culpability for symptoms is largely irrelevant in handling the behavior disorders and in any case does not detract from the reality of the illness.

In general, it is both unnecessary and potentially dangerous to discard the concept of mental illness on the grounds that only in this way can clinical psychology escape from the professional domination of medicine. Dentists, podiatrists, optometrists, and osteopaths have managed to acquire an independent professional status without rejecting the concept of disease. It is equally unnecessary and dangerous to substitute the doctrine of sin for illness in order to counteract prevailing amoral and nonjudgmental trends in psychotherapy. The hypothesis of repressed guilt does not adequately explain most kinds and instances of personality disorder, and the concept of mental illness does not preclude judgments of moral accountability where warranted. Definition of behavior disorder in terms of sin or of difficulties associated with ethical choice and responsibility would substitute theological disputation and philosophical wrangling about values for specifiable quantitative and qualitative criteria of disease.

REFERENCES

Ausubel, D. P. Ego *development and the personality disorders*. New York: Grune & Stratton, 1952.

Ausubel, D. P. Relationships between psychology and psychiatry: The hidden issues. *Amer. Psychologist*, 1956, *11*, 99–105.

Dreyfuss, F., & Czaczkes, J. W. Blood cholesterol and uric acid of healthy medical students under the stress of an examination. AMA *Arch. intern. Med.*, 1959, *103*, 708.

Mowrer, O. H. "Sin," the lesser of two evils. *Amer. Psychologist*, 1960, *15*, 301–304.

Szasz, T. S. The myth of mental illness. *Amer. Psychologist*, 1960, *15*, 113–118.

DISCUSSION

The question "What is mental illness?" has been vexing to abnormal psychology theorists, researchers, and practitioners for decades. The authors of the two articles in this chapter present us with quite different answers. Szasz maintains that "mental illness" is a convenient label for behavior that either society or the individual in question finds unwanted or unpleasant. "Mentally ill" persons, he contends, do not suffer from diseases but rather from problems in living: They march to the beat of a decidedly different drummer, and thus their behavior does not conform to the norms of society. One potential weakness in Szasz's reasoning, however, is the fact that many highly undesirable behaviors are not typically considered diagnostic, let alone indicative, of mental illness. Laziness, obnoxiousness, and messiness—although not generally regarded as ideals to aspire to—are not in and of themselves viewed as pathological (Wakefield, 1992a).

Ausubel, in contrast, argues that mental illness is a tangible entity. He conceptualizes mental illness as "a gross deviation from a designated range of desirable behavioral variability" (p. 72). As Gorenstein (1984) has pointed out, however, Ausubel's definition of mental illness seems to beg the question to some extent. Namely, how are we to define *desirable?* Or turning the question around, how are we to define *undesirable?* Should the undesirability of a condition (which is utterly central to Ausubel's conception of mental illness) be defined purely on the basis of societal values, such as judgments concerning whether a condition is unwanted or unpleasant? Ausubel appears to give a negative response to this question, although he acknowledges that such judgments inevitably play some role in the definition of mental illness. Or should the undesirability of a condition be defined purely on the basis of scientific criteria, such as reduced biological fitness (defined by evolutionary theorists as the extent to which one's genes are represented in subsequent generations) or life span (see, for example, Kendell, 1975)? Like defining illness in terms of purely value-laden criteria, defining illness in terms of purely scientific criteria runs afoul of obvious counterexamples. Many characteristics that drastically reduce average fitness (for example, being a priest) or average life span (for example, being a soldier in a devastating war) would not qualify as illnesses in anyone's book. Thus, the definition of an "undesirable" characteristic, which plays an essential role in Ausubel's conception of illness, proves to be surprisingly elusive.

Wakefield (1992a, 1992b) has recently attempted to remedy the shortcomings in the positions of Szasz, Ausubel, and others by positing a novel conception of illness, including mental illness. Whereas most previous conceptions are premised on either purely value-laden criteria or purely scientific criteria, Wakefield argues that the correct definition of illness incorporates both value-laden and scientific criteria. Specifically, Wakefield proposes that illness is best conceptualized as a "harmful dysfunction," whereby *harm* is a social value judgment concerning the undesirability or unpleasantness of a condition and *dysfunction* is the failure of a physical or mental system to perform its evolutionarily designed function. Thus, according to Wakefield, paranoia (or, as it is called in DSM-IV, delusional disorder) is an illness because (1) it is generally viewed as unwanted by society (after all, interacting with people who are convinced we are out to get them is seldom enjoyable) and (2) humans are not designed by evolution to fear or mistrust actual people (such as the president) or imagined individuals (such as Martians) who pose no physical threat.

Nevertheless, Wakefield's analysis too appears to have its potential hitches. For one thing, he seems to presume that evolution has designed a single response for all physical and mental systems. But this assumption is doubtful. Evolution may well have designed an anxiety response to dangerous stimuli, for example, but it has probably not designed a universal value for this response across all individuals. In other words, it seems in principle impossible to determine what constitutes an evolutionarily designed level of anxiety following a frightening situation (such as being involved in a car accident). The most adaptive response to a car accident for one person may be to talk to friends about the accident and repeatedly relive it in vivid detail; for another, it may be to forget the accident and find helpful distractions. For the evolution of physical and mental systems across organisms, variability in responses, not uniformity, is the rule.

A second possible problem with Wakefield's analysis is that many widely accepted mental disorders probably represent extreme variations of evolutionarily adaptive functions rather than failures of evolutionarily designed functions. Consider panic disorder, a condition in which people tend to experience recurrent surges of intense anxiety and anxiety-related symptoms, often with no apparent cause. Is panic disorder truly a failure of the anxiety system to perform its designed function, as Wakefield would contend? Or is it instead a reflection of the anxiety system performing its proper function (that is, alerting the organism to potential danger) but in an inappropriate situation? The latter interpretation appears more consistent with the available evidence (Barlow, 1991).

Where does this discussion leave us? How should mental illness be defined? My own position (which, I should warn you, is almost undoubtedly a minority opinion) is that all attempts to provide an explicit definition of illness, including mental illness, are doomed to failure. My view is that illness is a nonscientific concept that exists exclusively in our minds rather than in nature. Like many mental concepts, such as chair (also see Discussion in Chapter 3), the concept of illness has inherently fuzzy and unclear boundaries and thus can never be fully or explicitly defined. These wavering boundaries help to explain persistent disagreement regarding whether behavioral patterns such as homosexuality, premenstrual syndrome, alcoholism, and attention-deficit/hyperactivity disorder constitute mental disorders.

Whether you agree with my argument or not, you must nevertheless accept the fact that our present concepts of mental illness are characterized by a certain unavoidable degree of fuzziness. Nevertheless—and this is a crucial point—even if I am correct that the concept of mental illness is intrinsically nebulous around the edges, this would *not* imply that entities such as schizophrenia, depression, alcoholism, and panic disorder are not genuine and not worthy of scientific study. To take a corresponding example, the concept of drug possesses fuzzy boundaries: informed people do not agree on whether substances like caffeine and nicotine should be classified as drugs (Gorenstein, 1992). Nevertheless, such disagreement does not imply that caffeine and nicotine do not exist or do not merit scientific inquiry. Similarly, mental illness is a fuzzy concept, at least as we currently conceive of it, but the principal entities we subsume under that concept are far from mythical.

QUESTIONS TO STIMULATE DISCUSSION

1. Do you concur with Szasz that mental illnesses are no more than problems in living? If so, why? If not, can you generate examples of mental illnesses that do not seem to fit his conceptualization?
2. Szasz argues that the label *mental illness* often encourages people to shirk responsibility for their problematic behaviors. Do you agree? To what extent is Szasz's contention a moral, as opposed to a scientific, issue?
3. Prior to 1973, homosexuality was officially defined as a mental disorder in the United States psychiatric classification system, but it was dropped from the classification system that year following a vote by members of the American Psychiatric Association. What factors do you suspect were responsible for this decision? What are the implications of this decision for our conceptualizations of mental disorder?
4. Most individuals who have attempted to define disorder have used the same criteria to define both psychological and physical disorder. For example, Wakefield intended his "harmful dysfunction" analysis to apply to all illnesses, both mental and medical. Should the same criteria be used to define both psychological and physical disorder? Or is a different set of criteria needed for each?
5. Do attempts to define *mental illness*, such as those of Ausubel and Wakefield, help to inform us primarily about the true nature of mental illness? Or do they instead help to inform us primarily about how we think about mental illness? Explain.

SUGGESTIONS FOR FURTHER READING

Ellis, A. (1967). Should some people be labeled mentally ill? *Journal of Consulting Psychology, 31*, 435–446.
Ellis argues that labeling certain individuals mentally ill is not intrinsically wrong but that such labeling frequently carries an evaluative component that is gratuitous. He contends that if we define *mental illness* operationally and strip away its pejorative connotations, most of the problems associated with diagnostic labeling will disappear.

Gorenstein, E. E. (1984). Debating mental illness: Implications for science, medicine, and social policy. *American Psychologist*, 39, 50–56. (Reprinted in Hooley, J. M., Neale, J. M., & Davison, G. C. [1989]. *Readings in abnormal psychology*. New York: Wiley).
This is a highly readable and informative account of the debate regarding the existence of mental illness. Gorenstein contends that although the definition of *disease* is value-laden and devoid of scientific content, the entities that are currently

known as mental illnesses, such as schizophrenia and depression, are nevertheless real.

Gorenstein, E. E. (1992). *The science of mental illness*. San Diego: Academic Press.
This book provides a first-rate summary of the conceptual underpinnings of psychopathology. The first chapter overlaps extensively with Gorenstein's *American Psychologist* article (1984). Chapter 5, particularly the section titled "Three Errors of Common Biological Approaches to Deviant Behavior," is a must for all serious students of biological psychopathology.

Kendell, R. E. (1975). The concept of disease and its implications for psychiatry. *British Journal of Psychiatry, 127*, 305–315.
Kendell provides an excellent overview of changing concepts of disease in medicine, including psychiatry, and criticizes a number of previous attempts to define disease (for example, the disease-as-lesion view, the statistical view). He concludes that disease must ultimately be defined in terms of a biological disadvantage that is intrinsic to the organism.

Kety, S. S. (1974). From rationalization to reason. *American Journal of Psychiatry, 131*, 957–963.
Kety launches a spirited defense of the medical model of psychiatric disorder. He argues that schizophrenia is substantially influenced by genetic factors and concludes with some irony that "if schizophrenia is a myth, it is a myth with a strong genetic component" (p. 961). See the readings by Gorenstein (1984, 1992), however, for a trenchant critique of Kety's logic.

Murphy, J. M. (1976). Psychiatric labeling in cross-cultural perspective. *Science, 191*, 1019–1028 (Reprinted in Hooley, J. M., Neale, J. M., & Davison, G. C. [1989]. *Readings in abnormal psychology*. New York: Wiley).
Murphy describes the results of her classic investigations of psychopathology and psychiatric labeling among the Eskimos in the Bering Strait and the Yorubas in Nigeria. She reports that these cultures appear to possess labels for conditions very similar to what would be called schizophrenia and psychopathy in Western culture and that these cultures' attitudes toward the mentally ill are strikingly reminiscent of ours. Murphy concludes that psychopathology and psychiatric labeling are far less culturally relative than has been suggested by most proponents of labeling theory.

Sarbin, T. (1967). On the futility of the proposition that some people be labeled "mentally ill." *Journal of Consulting Psychology, 31*, 447–453.
In his response to Ellis (1967), Sarbin agrees with Szasz that mental illness is a mythical entity attached to individuals who engage in certain violations of social norms. He contends that the key decision confronting society is how to deal with such individuals.

Szasz, T. S. (1974). *The myth of mental illness: Foundations of a theory of personal conduct* (rev. ed.). New York: Harper & Row.
In this classic and controversial book, first published in 1961, Szasz elaborates on his thesis that mental illness is a mythical entity. Using hysteria as an example, he traces our changing historical conceptions of mental illness through the ages. Szasz also puts forth his hypothesis that the signs of mental illness are typically veiled communications of socially unacceptable ideas.

Wakefield, J. C. (1992a). The concept of mental disorder: On the boundary between biological facts and social values. *American Psychologist, 47*, 373–388.
Wakefield analyzes a number of different definitions of mental disorder, including mental disorder as myth, mental disorder as pure value concept, mental disorder as statistical deviation, and mental disorder as biological disadvantage. He finds all of them wanting. He suggests that disorder, including mental disorder, is best conceived of as a "harmful dysfunction," whereby the term *harmful* involves a value judgment on the part of society and *dysfunction* involves the failure of a system to adequately perform a task that it is has been designed by evolution to perform.

Wakefield, J. C. (1992b). Disorder as harmful dysfunction: A conceptual critique of DSM-III-R's definition of mental disorder. *Psychological Review, 99*, 232–247.
Wakefield extends his "harmful dysfunction" analysis of mental illness to the mental disorders contained in DSM-III-R (a revision of DSM-III). He argues that DSM-III-R fails to adequately operationalize the concept of dysfunction, and thus errs frequently in its attempt to distinguish disorders from nondisorders. This article is appropriate for more advanced readers.

REFERENCES

Barlow, D. H. (1991). Disorders of emotion. *Psychological Inquiry, 2*, 58–71.

Gorenstein, E. E. (1984). Debating mental illness: Implications for science, medicine, and social policy. *American Psychologist, 39*, 50–56.

Gorenstein, E. E. (1992). *The science of mental illness*. San Diego: Academic Press.

Kendell, R. E. (1975). The concept of disease and its implications for psychiatry. *British Journal of Psychiatry, 127*, 305–315.

Kirk, S. A., & Kutchins, H. (1992). *The selling of DSM-III: The rhetoric of science in psychiatry*. New York: Aldine de Gruyter.

Mowrer, O. H. (1960). "Sin," the lesser of two evils. *American Psychologist, 15*, 301–304.

Spitzer, R. L. (1981). The diagnostic status of homosexuality in DSM-III: A reformulation of the issues. *American Journal of Psychiatry, 138*, 210–215.

Tavris, C. (1992). *The mismeasure of woman*. New York: Simon & Schuster.

Wakefield, J. C. (1992a). The concept of mental disorder: On the boundary between biological facts and social values. *American Psychologist, 47*, 373–388.

Wakefield, J. C. (1992b). Disorder as harmful dysfunction: A conceptual critique of DSM-III-R's definition of mental disorder. *Psychological Review, 99*, 232–247.

CHAPTER

2

Are mental health professionals incapable of distinguishing abnormality from normality?

PRO Rosenhan, D. L. (1973). On being sane in insane places. *Science*, *179*, 250–258.

CON Spitzer, R. L. (1975). On pseudoscience in science, logic in remission, and psychiatric diagnosis: A critique of Rosenhan's "On being sane in insane places." *Journal of Abnormal Psychology*, *84*, 442–452.

OVERVIEW OF THE CONTROVERSY: David L. Rosenhan reports the results of a study that he claims demonstrates that mental health professionals are unable to distinguish sane from insane individuals. Robert L. Spitzer finds Rosenhan's design and conclusions to be catastrophically flawed and contends that careful scrutiny of Rosenhan's findings actually indicates that mental health professionals are capable of distinguishing sane from insane individuals with uncanny accuracy.

CONTEXT OF THE PROBLEM

Reliability of diagnosis is a fundamental prerequisite for a valid classification system. **Reliability** traditionally refers to consistency or replicability of measurement. Thus, a reliable measure of a psychopathological syndrome assesses that syndrome consistently—that is, with a minimal degree of error. Although a variety of types of reliability are applicable to abnormal psychology, the type of reliability most relevant to psychiatric diagnosis is **interrater reliability**, or the extent to which different raters (for example, two psychologists or two psychiatrists) agree on the diagnosis of a set of individuals. Psychologists and psychiatrists also sometimes refer to **test-retest reliability**, or the extent to which the diagnoses of a set of individuals remain consistent over relatively brief (such as one-month) intervals. In the domain of psychiatric diagnosis, however, test-retest reliability is typically emphasized considerably less than is interrater reliability, because a number of psychopathological conditions (such as depression) appear and disappear rather frequently and thus would not be expected to be highly consistent over time.

Without adequate reliability, the **validity** of a psychiatric diagnosis, which can essentially be thought of as the extent to which this diagnosis identifies what it is intended to identify, becomes moot. Reliability is a necessary (but not sufficient) condition for validity. Imagine yourself attempting to construct a new room in your house using a rubber ruler, a ruler whose units change radically in length from one moment to the next. Your task would be all but impossible, because your measurements of the floor, walls, and ceiling would be wildly inconsistent over time. Such an endeavor would be tantamount to attempting to construct a psychiatric classification system without reliable diagnostic categories. One cannot measure something validly without first possessing a dependable measuring stick.

In general, when psychologists discuss the reliability of psychiatric diagnosis, they are referring to the ability of raters to distinguish among different varieties of mental illness. For example, psychologists are often interested in the ability of trained interviewers to distinguish between patients with schizophrenia and those with mood disorders (such as depression or mania). The article by David Rosenhan in this chapter, however, is concerned with an even more basic issue. Rosenhan is simply interested in the extent to which mental health professionals can distinguish between individuals with mental illness versus those without it. Although Rosenhan's article is not technically a study of interrater reliability (his subjects were not assessed by more than one rater), his findings have significant implications for the reliability of psychiatric diagnosis. If mental health professionals cannot differentiate between the mentally ill and the mentally healthy, the question of whether they can distinguish among different varieties of mental illness seems premature and perhaps even pointless.

A separate but related issue concerns the effect of diagnostic labeling on individuals. A number of prominent authors, such as sociologist Thomas Scheff (1984), have hypothesized that psychiatric labels tend to become self-fulfilling prophecies. These writers, who are sometimes referred to as **labeling theorists**, contend that once a person is labeled mentally ill, others will interpret that person's behavior in light of the label. Thus, innocuous habits that many of us exhibit from time to time—twirling our hair under stress, muttering to ourselves while reading—are construed by others as indications of psychological abnormality. The implications of this thesis for Rosenhan's study seem clear: A mentally healthy person who is labeled mentally ill may appear mentally ill to observers, because that person's actions will tend to be interpreted as signs of mental illness. Do Rosenhan's findings provide support for this bold prediction?

THE CONTROVERSY: Rosenhan vs. Spitzer

Rosenhan

Since its publication in the prestigious journal *Science* in 1973, David Rosenhan's article has become arguably the best-known and most controversial paper in all of abnormal psychology. Rosenhan's methodology and logic are brutally simple. Eight pseudopatients (normal individuals who feign mental illness), including himself, obtained admission to twelve psychiatric hospitals by simulating symptoms of mental illness. Specifically, these pseudopatients informed the admitting officers that they were hearing a voice saying "empty," "hollow," and "thud." All were promptly admitted, and in all but one case, they were discharged with diagnoses of "schizophrenia in remission" (one was discharged with a diagnosis of "manic depression in remission"). Remarkably, many of the pseudopatients were hospitalized for several weeks prior to their discharge. No less remarkably, many of the hospitalized psychiatric patients apparently recognized the pseudopatients as normal, whereas staff members did not.

Rosenhan contends that the psychiatric labels became self-fulfilling prophecies, as evidenced by the fact that commonplace behaviors exhibited by the pseudopatients (such as note taking and pacing) were interpreted as signs of mental illness. Rosenhan concludes emphatically that psychiatrists and other mental health professionals cannot reliably distinguish sane from insane individuals and that psychiatric labeling has pernicious effects. He recommends replacing global psychiatric diagnosis with a descriptive system focusing upon specific behaviors. Needless to say, Rosenhan's conclusions, if correct, have dire implications for both the reliability and utility of psychiatric diagnosis.

Spitzer

Robert Spitzer, who subsequently became the principal architect of DSM-III and DSM-III-R (a revision), takes aim at both Rosenhan's methods and conclusions, caustically referring to the latter as a case of "logic in remission." Spitzer points out that all the pseudopatients were discharged as "in remission," demonstrating that the mental health professionals who treated them were well aware that they were no longer exhibiting indications of mental illness. Spitzer bolsters his claim by showing that the diagnosis of schizophrenia in remission is extremely rare, suggesting that the psychiatric staff who made these diagnoses in Rosenhan's study recognized that the pseudopatients were substantially different from virtually all individuals who initially present with symptoms typical of schizophrenia. Spitzer further maintains that Rosenhan failed to provide convincing evidence that the psychiatric staff considered the pseudopatients' behavior to be abnormal. Finally, Spitzer vigorously disputes Rosenhan's claim that psychiatric diagnosis is not useful, as well as Rosenhan's suggestion that it be abandoned in favor of describing specific behaviors.

KEY CONCEPTS AND TERMS

hallucination Perception of a stimulus that is not physically present. The hallucinations of individuals with schizophrenia are usually auditory and typically consist of voices.

in remission No longer exhibiting indications of an illness.

malingering Deliberate feigning of the signs or symptoms of an illness (including a psychopathological condition) in order to achieve a tangible goal (for example, to obtain disability payments).

psychosis Mental disorder characterized by cognitive and emotional impairments so profound that they result in a substantial loss of contact with "reality."

schizophrenia Mental disorder characterized by severe disturbances in thought, emotion, and behavior. Thinking abnormalities, disturbances in emotional expression, withdrawal from others, and ambivalence in relationships are particularly frequent characteristics of schizophrenia.

PREVIEW QUESTIONS

1. What is Rosenhan's central hypothesis, and how does he proceed to test it?
2. What evidence does Rosenhan provide to buttress his claim that diagnostic labels are "sticky"?
3. What does Rosenhan suggest as an alternative to traditional methods of psychiatric diagnosis?
4. Why is Spitzer not impressed with Rosenhan's finding that 11 of the 12 diagnoses on discharge were "schizophrenia in remission?"
5. Does Spitzer believe the admitting psychiatrists were mistaken to give the pseudopatients an initial diagnosis of schizophrenia?
6. According to Spitzer, what would be the result if Rosenhan's proposal to abandon psychiatric labeling were adopted?

DAVID L. ROSENHAN

On being sane in insane places

If sanity and insanity exist, how shall we know them?

The question is neither capricious nor itself insane. However much we may be personally convinced that we can tell the normal from the abnormal, the evidence is simply not compelling. It is commonplace, for example, to read about murder trials wherein eminent psychiatrists for the defense are contradicted by equally eminent psychiatrists for the prosecution on the matter of the defendant's sanity. More generally, there are a great deal of conflicting data on the reliability, utility, and meaning of such terms as "sanity," "insanity," "mental illness," and "schizophrenia"(*1*). Finally, as early as 1934, Benedict suggested that normality and abnormality are not universal(*2*). What is viewed as normal in one culture may be seen as quite aberrant in another. Thus, notions of normality and abnormality may not be quite as accurate as people believe they are.

To raise questions regarding normality and abnormality is in no way to question the fact that some behaviors are deviant or odd. Murder is deviant. So, too, are hallucinations. Nor does raising such questions deny the existence of the personal anguish that is often associated with "mental illness." Anxiety and depression exist. Psychological suffering exists. But normality and abnormality, sanity and insanity, and the diagnoses that flow from them may be less substantive than many believe them to be.

At its heart, the question of whether the sane can be distinguished from the insane (and whether degrees of insanity can be distinguished from each other) is a simple matter: do the salient characteristics that lead to diagnoses reside in the patients themselves or in the environments and contexts in which observers find them? From Bleuler, through Kretchmer, through the formulators of the recently revised *Diagnostic and Statistical Manual* of the American Psychiatric Association, the belief has been strong that patients present symptoms, that those symptoms can be categorized, and, implicitly, that the sane are distinguishable from the insane. More recently, however, this belief has been questioned. Based in part on theoretical and anthropological considerations, but also on philosophical, legal, and therapeutic ones, the view has grown that psychological categorization of mental illness is useless at best and downright harmful, misleading, and pejorative at worst. Psychiatric diagnoses, in this view, are in the minds of the observers and are not valid summaries of characteristics displayed by the observed (*3–5*).

Gains can be made in deciding which of these is more nearly accurate by getting normal people (that is, people who do not have, and have never suffered, symptoms of serious psychiatric disorders) admitted to psychiatric hospitals and then determining whether they were discovered to be sane and, if so, how. If the sanity of such pseudopatients were always detected, there would be prima facie evidence that a sane individual can be distinguished from the insane context in which he is found. Normality (and presumably abnormality) is distinct enough that it can be recognized wherever it occurs, for it is carried within the person. If, on the other hand, the sanity of the pseudopatients were never discovered, serious difficulties would arise for those who support traditional

SOURCE: *Science*, *179*, pp. 250–258, 1973.

modes of psychiatric diagnosis. Given that the hospital staff was not incompetent, that the pseudopatient had been behaving as sanely as he had been outside of the hospital, and that it had never been previously suggested that he belonged in a psychiatric hospital, such an unlikely outcome would support the view that psychiatric diagnosis betrays little about the patient but much about the environment in which an observer finds him.

This article describes such an experiment. Eight sane people gained secret admission to 12 different hospitals (6). Their diagnostic experiences constitute the data of the first part of this article: the remainder is devoted to a description of their experiences in psychiatric institutions. Too few psychiatrists and psychologists, even those who have worked in such hospitals, know what the experience is like. They rarely talk about it with former patients, perhaps because they distrust information coming from the previously insane. Those who have worked in psychiatric hospitals are likely to have adapted so thoroughly to the settings that they are insensitive to the impact of that experience. And while there have been occasional reports of researchers who submitted themselves to psychiatric hospitalization (7), these researchers have commonly remained in the hospitals for short periods of time, often with the knowledge of the hospital staff. It is difficult to know the extent to which they were treated like patients or like research colleagues. Nevertheless, their reports about the inside of the psychiatric hospital have been valuable. This article extends those efforts.

PSEUDOPATIENTS AND THEIR SETTINGS

The eight pseudopatients were a varied group. One was a psychology graduate student in his 20's. The remaining seven were older and "established." Among them were three psychologists, a pediatrician, a psychiatrist, a painter, and a housewife. Three pseudopatients were women, five were men. All of them employed pseudonyms, lest their alleged diagnoses embarrass them later. Those who were in mental health professions alleged another occupation in order to avoid the special attentions that might be accorded by the staff, as a matter of courtesy or caution, to ailing colleagues (8). With the exception of myself (I was the first pseudopatient and my presence was known to the hospital administrator and chief psychologist and, so far as I can tell, to them alone), the presence of pseudopatients and the nature of the research program was not known to the hospital staffs (9).

The settings were similarly varied. In order to generalize the findings, admission into a variety of hospitals was sought. The 12 hospitals in the sample were located in five different states on the East and West coasts. Some were old and shabby, some were quite new. Some were research-oriented, others not. Some had good staff-patient ratios, others were quite understaffed. Only one was a strictly private hospital. All of the others were supported by state or federal funds or, in one instance, by university funds.

After calling the hospital for an appointment, the pseudopatient arrived at the admissions office complaining that he had been hearing voices. Asked what the voices said, he replied that they were often unclear, but as far as he could tell they said "empty," "hollow," and "thud." The voices were unfamiliar and were of the same sex as the pseudopatient. The choice of these symptoms was occasioned by their apparent similarity to existential symptoms. Such symptoms are alleged to arise from painful concerns about the perceived meaninglessness of one's life. It is as if the hallucinating person were saying, "My life is empty and hollow." The choice of these symptoms was also determined by the *absence* of a single report of existential psychoses in the literature.

Beyond alleging the symptoms and falsifying name, vocation, and employment, no further alterations of person, history, or circumstances were made. The significant events of the pseudopatient's life history were presented as they had actually occurred. Relationships with parents and siblings, with spouse and children, with people at work and in school, consistent with the aforementioned exceptions, were described as they were or had been. Frustrations and upsets were described along with joys and satisfactions. These facts are important to remember. If anything, they strongly biased the subsequent results in favor of detecting sanity, since none of their histories or current behaviors were seriously pathological in any way.

Immediately upon admission to the psychiatric ward, the pseudopatient ceased simulating *any* symptoms of abnormality. In some cases, there was a brief period of mild nervousness and anxiety, since none of the pseudopatients really believed that they would be admitted so easily. Indeed, their shared fear was that they would be immediately exposed as frauds and greatly embarrassed. Moreover, many of them had never visited a psychiatric ward; even those who had, nevertheless had some genuine fears about what might happen to them. Their nervousness, then, was quite appropriate to the novelty of the hospital setting, and it abated rapidly.

Apart from the short-lived nervousness, the pseudopatient behaved on the ward as he "normally" behaved. The pseudopatient spoke to patients and staff as he might ordinarily. Because there is uncommonly little to do on a psychiatric ward, he attempted to engage others in conversation. When asked by staff how he was feeling, he indicated that he was fine, that he no longer experienced symptoms. He responded to instructions from attendants, to calls for medication (which was not swallowed), and to dining-hall instructions. Beyond such activities as were available to him on the admissions ward, he spent his time writing down his observations about the ward, its patients, and the staff. Initially these notes were written "secretly," but as it soon became clear that no one much cared, they were subsequently written on standard tablets of paper in such public places as the dayroom. No secret was made of these activities.

The pseudopatient, very much as a true psychiatric patient, entered a hospital with no foreknowledge of when he would be discharged. Each was told that he would have to get out by his own devices, essentially by convincing the staff that he was sane. The psychological stresses associated with hospitalization were considerable, and all but one of the pseudopatients desired to be discharged almost immediately after being admitted. They were, therefore, motivated not only to behave sanely, but to be paragons of cooperation. That their behavior was in no way disruptive is confirmed by nursing reports, which have been obtained on most of the patients. These reports uniformly indicate that the patients were "friendly," "cooperative," and "exhibited no abnormal indications."

THE NORMAL ARE NOT DETECTABLY SANE

Despite their public "show" of sanity, the pseudopatients were never detected. Admitted, except in one case, with a diagnosis of schizophrenia (*10*), each was discharged with a diagnosis of schizophrenia "in remission." The label "in remission" should in no way be dismissed as a formality, for at no time during any hospitalization had any question been raised about any pseudopatient's simulation. Nor are there any indications in the hospital records that the pseudopatient's status was suspect. Rather, the evidence is strong that, once labeled schizophrenic, the pseudopatient was stuck with that label. If the pseudopatient was to be discharged, he must naturally be "in remission"; but he was not sane, nor, in the institution's view, had he ever been sane.

The uniform failure to recognize sanity cannot be attributed to the quality of the hospitals, for, although there were considerable variations among them, several are considered excellent. Nor can it be alleged that there was simply not enough time to observe the pseudopatients. Length of hospitalization ranged from 7 to 52 days, with an average of 19 days. The pseudopatients were not, in fact, carefully observed, but this failure clearly speaks more to traditions within psychiatric hospitals than to lack of opportunity.

Finally, it cannot be said that the failure to recognize the pseudopatients' sanity was due to the fact that they were not behaving sanely. While there was clearly some tension present in all of them, their daily visitors could detect no serious behavioral consequences—nor, indeed, could other patients. It was quite common for the patients to "detect" the pseudopatients' sanity. During the first three hospitalizations, when accurate counts were kept, 35 of a total of 118 patients on the admissions ward voiced their suspicions, some vigorously, "You're not crazy. You're a journalist or a professor [referring to the continual note-taking]. You're checking up on the hospital." While most of the patients were reassured by the pseudopatient's insistence that he had been sick before he came in but was fine now, some continued to believe that the pseudopatient was sane throughout his hospitalization (*11*). The fact that the patients often recognized normality when staff did not raises important questions.

Failure to detect sanity during the course of hospitalization may be due to the fact that physicians operate with a strong bias toward what statisticians call the type 2 error (*5*). This is to say that physicians are more inclined to call a healthy person sick (a false positive, type 2) than a sick person healthy (a false negative, type 1). The reasons for this are not hard to find: it is clearly more dangerous to misdiagnose illness than health. Better to err on the side of caution, to suspect illness even among the healthy.

But what holds for medicine does not hold equally well for psychiatry. Medical illnesses, while unfortunate, are not commonly pejorative. Psychiatric diagnoses, on the contrary, carry with them personal, legal, and social stigmas (*12*). It was therefore important to see whether the tendency toward diagnosing the sane insane could be reversed. The following experiment was arranged at a research and teaching hospital whose staff had heard these findings but doubted that such an error could occur in their hospital. The staff was informed that at some time during the following 3 months, one or more pseudopatients would attempt to be admitted into the psychiatric hospital. Each staff member was asked to rate each patient who presented himself at admissions or on the ward according to the likelihood that the patient was a pseudopatient. A 10-point scale was used, with a 1 and 2 reflecting high confidence that the patient was a pseudopatient.

Judgments were obtained on 193 patients who were admitted for psychiatric treatment. All staff who had had sustained contact with or primary responsibility for the patient—attendants, nurses, psychiatrists, physicians, and psychologists—were asked to make judgments. Forty-one patients were alleged, with high confidence, to be pseudopatients by at least one member of the staff. Twenty-three were considered suspect by at least one psychiatrist. Nineteen were suspected by one psychiatrist *and* one other staff member. Actually, no genuine pseudopatient (at least from my group) presented himself during this period.

The experiment is instructive. It indicates that the tendency to designate sane people as insane can be reversed when the stakes (in this case, prestige and diagnostic acumen) are high. But what can be said of the 19 people who were suspected of being "sane" by one psychiatrist and another staff member? Were these people truly "sane," or was it rather the case that in the course of avoiding the type 2 error the staff tended to make more errors of the first sort—calling the crazy "sane"? There is no way of knowing. But one thing is certain: any diagnostic process that lends itself so readily to massive errors of this sort cannot be a very reliable one.

THE STICKINESS OF PSYCHODIAGNOSTIC LABELS

Beyond the tendency to call the healthy sick—a tendency that accounts better for diagnostic behavior on admission than it does for such behavior after a lengthy period of exposure—the data speak to the massive role of labeling in psychiatric assessment. Having once been labeled schizophrenic, there is nothing the pseudopatient can do to overcome the tag. The tag profoundly colors others' perceptions of him and his behavior.

From one viewpoint, these data are hardly surprising, for it has long been known that elements are given meaning by the context in which they occur. Gestalt psychology made this point vigorously, and Asch (*13*) demonstrated that there are "central" personality traits (such as "warm" versus "cold") which are so powerful that they markedly color the meaning of other information in forming an impression of a given personality (*14*). "Insane," "schizophrenic," "manic-depressive," and "crazy" are probably among the most powerful of such central traits. Once a person is designated abnormal, all of his other behaviors and characteristics are colored by that label. Indeed, that label is so powerful that many of the pseudopatients' normal behaviors were overlooked entirely or profoundly misinterpreted. Some examples may clarify this issue.

Earlier I indicated that there were no changes in the pseudopatient's personal history and current status beyond those of name, employment, and, where necessary, vocation. Otherwise, a veridical description of personal history and circumstances was offered. Those circumstances were not psychotic. How were they made consonant with the diagnosis of psychosis? Or were those diagnoses modified in such a way as to bring them into accord with the circumstances of the pseudopatient's life, as described by him?

As far as I can determine, diagnoses were in no way affected by the relative health of the circumstances of pseudopatient's life. Rather, the reverse occurred: the perception of his circumstances was shaped entirely by the diagnosis. A clear example of such translation is found in the case of a pseudopatient who had had a close relationship with his mother but was rather remote from his father during his early childhood. During adolescence and beyond, however, his father became a close friend, while his relationship with his mother cooled. His present relationship with his wife was characteristically close and warm. Apart from occasional angry exchanges, friction was minimal. The children had rarely been spanked. Surely there is nothing especially pathological about such a history. Indeed, many readers may see a similar pattern in their own experiences, with no markedly deleterious consequences. Observe, however, how such a history was translated in the psychopathological context, this from the case summary prepared after the patient was discharged.

> This white 39-year-old male . . . manifests a long history of considerable ambivalence in close relationships, which begins in early childhood. A warm relationship with his mother cools during his adolescence. A distant relationship to his father is described as becoming very intense. Affective stability is absent. His attempts to control emotionality with his wife and children are punctuated by angry outbursts and, in the case of the children, spankings. And while he says that he has several good friends, one senses considerable ambivalence embedded in those relationships also. . . .

The facts of the case were unintentionally distorted by the staff to achieve consistency with a popular theory of the dynamics of a schizophrenic reaction (*15*). Nothing of an ambivalent nature had been described in relations with parents, spouse, or friends. To the extent that ambivalence could be inferred, it was probably not greater than is found in all human relationships. It is true the pseudopatient's relationships with his parents changed over time, but in the ordinary context that would hardly be remarkable—indeed, it might very well be expected. Clearly, the meaning ascribed to his verbalizations (that is, ambivalence, affective instability) was determined by the diagnosis: schizophrenia. An entirely different meaning would have been ascribed if it were known that the man was "normal."

All pseudopatients took extensive notes publicly. Under ordinary circumstances, such behavior would have raised questions in the minds of observers, as, in fact, it did among patients. Indeed, it seemed so certain that the notes would elicit suspicion that elaborate precautions were taken to remove them from the ward each day. But the precautions proved needless. The closest any staff member came to questioning these notes occurred when one pseudopatient asked his physician what kind of medication he was receiving and began to write down the response. "You needn't write it," he was told gently. "If you have trouble remembering, just ask me again."

If no questions were asked of the pseudopatients, how was their writing interpreted? Nursing records for three patients indicate that the writing was seen as an aspect of their pathological behavior. "Patient engages in writing behavior" was the daily nursing comment on one of the pseudopatients who was never questioned about his writing. Given that the patient is in the hospital, he must be psychologically disturbed. And given that he is disturbed, continuous writing must be a behavioral manifestation of that disturbance, perhaps a subset of the compulsive behaviors that are sometimes correlated with schizophrenia.

One tacit characteristic of psychiatric diagnosis is that it locates the sources of aberration within the individual and only rarely within the complex of stimuli that surrounds him. Consequently, behaviors that are stimulated by the environment are commonly misattributed to the patient's disorder. For example, one kindly nurse found a pseudopatient pacing the long hospital corridors. "Nervous, Mr. X?" she asked. "No, bored," he said.

The notes kept by pseudopatients are full of patient behaviors that were misinterpreted by well-intentioned staff. Often enough, a patient would go "berserk" because he had, wittingly or unwittingly, been mistreated by, say, an attendant. A nurse coming upon the scene would rarely inquire even cursorily into the environmental stimuli of the patient's behavior. Rather, she assumed that his upset derived from his pathology, not from his present interactions with other staff members. Occasionally, the staff might assume that the patient's family (especially when they had recently visited) or other patients had stimulated the outburst. But never were the staff found to assume that one of themselves or the structure of the hospital had anything to do with a patient's behavior. One psychiatrist pointed to a group of patients who were sitting outside the cafeteria entrance half an hour before lunchtime. To a group of young residents he indicated that such behavior was characteristic of the oral-acquisitive nature of the syndrome. It seemed not to occur to him that there were very few things to anticipate in a psychiatric hospital besides eating.

A psychiatric label has a life and an influence of its own. Once the impression has been formed that the patient is schizophrenic, the expectation is that he will continue to be schizophrenic. When a sufficient amount of time has passed, during which the patient has done nothing bizarre, he is considered to be in remission and available for discharge. But the label endures beyond discharge, with the unconfirmed expectation that he will behave as a schizophrenic again. Such labels, conferred by mental health professionals, are as influential on the patient as they are on his relatives and friends, and it should not surprise anyone that the diagnosis acts on all of them as a self-fulfilling prophecy. Eventually, the patient himself accepts the diagnosis, with all of its surplus meanings and expectations, and behaves accordingly (*5*).

The inferences to be made from these matters are quite simple. Much as Zigler and Phillips have demonstrated that there is enormous overlap in the symptoms presented by patients who have been variously diagnosed (*16*), so there is enormous overlap in the behaviors of the sane and the insane. The sane are not "sane" all of the time. We lose our tempers, "for no good reason." We are occasionally depressed or anxious, again for no good reason. And we may find it difficult to get along with one or another person—again for no reason that we can specify. Similarly, the insane are not always insane. Indeed, it was the impression of the pseudopatients while living with them that they were sane for long periods of time—that the bizarre behaviors upon which their diagnoses were allegedly predicated constituted only a small fraction of their total behavior. If it makes no sense to label ourselves permanently depressed on the basis of an occasional depression, then it takes better evidence than is presently available to label all patients insane or schizophrenic on the basis of bizarre behaviors or cognitions. It seems more useful, as Mischel (*17*) has pointed out, to limit our discussions to *behaviors*, the stimuli that provoke them, and their correlates.

It is not known why powerful impressions of personality traits, such as "crazy" or "insane," arise. Conceivably, when the origins of and stimuli that give rise to a behavior are remote or unknown, or when the behavior strikes us as immutable, trait labels regarding the *behaver* arise. When, on the other hand, the origins and stimuli are known and available, discourse is limited to the behavior itself. Thus, I may hallucinate because I am sleeping, or I may hallucinate because I have ingested a peculiar drug. These are termed sleep-induced hallucinations, or dreams, and drug-induced hallucinations, respectively. But when the stimuli to my hallucinations are unknown, that is called craziness, or schizophrenia—as if that inference were somehow as illuminating as the others.

THE EXPERIENCE OF PSYCHIATRIC HOSPITALIZATION

The term "mental illness" is of recent origin. It was coined by people who were humane in their inclinations and who wanted very much to raise the station of (and the public's sympathies toward) the psychologically disturbed from that of witches and "crazies" to one that was akin to the physically ill. And they were at least partially successful, for the treatment of the mentally ill *has* improved considerably over the years. But while treatment has improved, it is doubtful that people really regard the mentally ill in the same way that they view the physically ill. A broken leg is something one recovers from, but mental illness allegedly endures forever (*18*). A broken leg does not threaten the observer, but a crazy schizophrenic? There is by now a host of evidence that attitudes toward the mentally ill are characterized by fear, hostility, aloofness, suspicion, and dread (*19*). The mentally ill are society's lepers.

That such attitudes infect the general population is perhaps not surprising, only upsetting. But that they affect the professionals—attendants, nurses, physicians, psychologists, and social workers—who treat and deal with the mentally ill is more disconcerting, both because such attitudes are self-evidently pernicious and because they are unwitting. Most mental health professionals would insist that they are sympathetic toward the mentally ill, that they are neither avoidant nor hostile. But it is more likely that an exquisite ambivalence characterizes their relations with psychiatric patients, such that their avowed impulses are only part of their entire attitude. Negative attitudes are there too and can easily be detected. Such attitudes should not surprise us. They are the natural offspring of the labels patients wear and the places in which they are found.

Consider the structure of the typical psychiatric hospital. Staff and patients are strictly segregated. Staff have their own living space, including their dining facilities, bathrooms, and assembly places. The glassed quarters that contain the professional staff, which the pseudopatients came to call "the cage," sit out on every dayroom. The staff emerge primarily for caretaking purposes—to give medication, to conduct a therapy or group meeting, to instruct or reprimand a patient. Otherwise, staff keep to themselves, almost as if the disorder that afflicts their charges is somehow catching.

So much is patient-staff segregation the rule that, for four public hospitals in which an attempt was made to measure the degree to which staff and patients mingle, it was necessary to use "time out of the staff cage" as the operational measure. While it was not the case that all time spent out of the cage was spent mingling with patients (attendants, for example, would occasionally emerge to watch television in the dayroom), it was the only way in which one could gather reliable data on time for measuring.

The average amount of time spent by attendants outside of the cage was 11.3 percent (range, 3 to 52 percent). This figure does not represent only time spent mingling with patients, but also includes time spent on such chores as folding laundry, supervising patients while they shave, directing ward cleanup, and sending patients to off-ward activities. It was the relatively rare attendant who spent time talking with patients or playing games with them. It proved impossible to obtain a "percent mingling time" for nurses, since the amount of time they spent out of the cage was too brief. Rather, we counted instances of emergence from the cage. On the average, daytime nurses emerged from the cage 11.5 times per shift, including instances when they left the ward entirely (range, 4 to 39 times). Late afternoon and night nurses were even less available, emerging on the average 9.4 time per shift (range, 4 to 41 times). Data on early morning nurses, who arrived usually after midnight and departed at 8 a.m., are not available because patients were asleep during most of this period.

Physicians, especially psychiatrists, were even less available. They were rarely seen on the wards. Quite commonly, they would be seen only when they arrived and departed, with the remaining time being spent in their offices or in the cage. On the average, physicians emerged on the ward 6.7 times per day (range, 1 to 17 times). It proved difficult to make an accurate estimate in this regard, since physicians often maintained hours that allowed them to come and go at different times.

The hierarchical organization of the psychiatric hospital has been commented on before (20), but the latent meaning of that kind of organization is worth noting again. Those with the most power have least to do with patients, and those with the least power are most involved with them. Recall, however, that the acquisition of role-appropriate behaviors occurs mainly through the observation of others, with the most powerful having the most influence. Consequently, it is understandable that attendants not only spend more time with patients than do any other members of the staff—that is required by their station in the hierarchy—but also, insofar as they learn from their superiors' behavior, spend as little time with patients as they can. Attendants are seen mainly in the cage, which is where the models, the action, and the power are.

I turn now to a different set of studies, these dealing with staff response to patient-initiated contact. It has long been known that the amount of time a person spends with you can be an index of your significance to him. If he initiates and maintains eye contact, there is reason to believe that he is considering your requests and needs. If he pauses to chat or actually stops and talks, there is added reason to infer that he is individuating you. In four hospitals, the pseudopatient approached the staff member with a request which took the following form: "Pardon me, Mr. [or Dr. or Mrs.] X, could you tell me when I will be eligible for grounds privileges?" (or ". . . when I will be presented at the staff meeting?" or ". . . when I am likely to be discharged?"). While the content of the question varied according to the appropriateness of the target and the pseudopatient's (apparent) current needs the form was always a courteous and relevant request for information. Care was taken never to approach a particular member of the staff more than once a day, lest the staff member become suspicious or irritated. In examining these data, remember that the behavior of the pseudopatients was neither bizarre nor disruptive. One could indeed engage in good conversation with them.

The data for these experiments are shown in Table 1, separately for physicians (column 1) and for nurses and attendants (column 2). Minor differences among these four institutions were overwhelmed by the degree to which staff avoided continuing contacts that patients had initiated. By far, their most common response consisted of either a brief response to the question, offered while they were "on the move" and with head averted, or no response at all.

The encounter frequently took the following bizarre form: (pseudopatient) "Pardon me, Dr. X. Could you tell me when I am eligible for grounds privileges?" (physician) "Good morning, Dave. How are you today?" (Moves off without waiting for a response.)

It is instructive to compare these data with data recently obtained at Stanford University. It has been alleged that large and eminent universities are characterized by faculty who are so busy that they have no time for students. For

TABLE 1 Self-Initiated Contact by Pseudopatients with Psychiatrists and Nurses and Attendants, Compared to Contact with Other Groups

	Psychiatric Hospitals		*University Campus (Nonmedical)*	*University Medical Center*		
				Physicians		
Contact	*(1) Psychiatrists*	*(2) Nurses and Attendants*	*(3) Faculty*	*(4) "Looking for a Psychiatrist"*	*(5) "Looking for an Internist"*	*(6) No Additional Comment*
Responses						
Moves on, head averted (%)	71	88	0	0	0	0
Makes eye contact (%)	23	10	0	11	0	0
Pauses and chats (%)	2	2	0	11	0	10
Stops and talks (%)	4	0.5	100	78	100	90
Mean number of questions answered (out of 6)	*	*	6	3.8	4.8	4.5
Respondents (no.)	13	47	14	18	15	10
Attempts (no.)	185	1283	14	18	15	10

*Not applicable

this comparison, a young lady approached individual faculty members who seemed to be walking purposefully to some meeting or teaching engagement and asked them the following six questions.

1. "Pardon me, could you direct me to Encina Hall?" (at the medical school: ". . . to the Clinical Research Center?").
2. "Do you know where Fish Annex is?" (There is no Fish Annex at Stanford.)
3. "Do you teach here?"
4. "How does one apply for admission to the college?" (at the medical school: "... to the medical school?").
5. "Is it difficult to get in?"
6. "Is there financial aid?"

Without exception, as can be seen in Table 1 (column 3), all of the questions were answered. No matter how rushed they were, all respondents not only maintained eye contact, but stopped to talk. Indeed, many of the respondents went out of their way to direct or take the questioner to the office she was seeking, to try to locate "Fish Annex," or to discuss with her the possibilities of being admitted to the university.

Similar data, also shown in Table 1 (columns 4, 5, and 6), were obtained in the hospital. Here too, the young lady came prepared with six questions. After the first question, however, she remarked to 18 of her respondents (column 4), "I'm looking for a psychiatrist," and to 15 others (column 5), "I'm looking for an internist." Ten other respondents received no inserted comment (column 6). The general degree of cooperative responses is considerably higher for these university groups than it was for pseudopatients in psychiatric hospitals. Even so, differences are apparent within the medical school setting. Once having indicated that she was looking for a psychiatrist, the degree of cooperation elicited was less than when she sought an internist.

POWERLESSNESS AND DEPERSONALIZATION

Eye contact and verbal contact reflect concern and individuation: their absence, avoidance and depersonalization. The data I have presented do not do justice to the rich daily encounters that grew up around matters of depersonalization and avoidance. I have records of patients who were beaten by staff for the sin of having initiated verbal contact. During my own experience, for example, one patient was beaten in the presence of other patients for having approached an attendant and told him, "I like you." Occasionally, punishment meted out to patients for misdemeanors seemed so excessive that it could not be justified by the most radical interpretations of psychiatric canon. Nevertheless, they appeared to go unquestioned. Tempers were often short. A patient who had not heard a call for medication would be roundly excoriated, and the morning attendants would often wake patients with, "Come on, you m——f——s, out of bed!"

Neither anecdotal nor "hard" data can convey the overwhelming sense of powerlessness which invades the individual as he is continually exposed to the depersonalization of the psychiatric hospital. It hardly matters *which* psychiatric hospital—the excellent public ones and the very plush private hospital were better than the rural and shabby ones in this regard, but, again, the features that psychiatric hospitals had in common overwhelmed by far their apparent differences.

Powerlessness was evident everywhere. The patient is deprived of many of his legal rights by dint of his psychiatric commitment (*21*). He is shorn of credibility by virtue of his psychiatric label. His freedom of movement is restricted. He cannot initiate contact with the staff, but may only respond to such overtures as they make. Personal privacy is minimal. Patient quarters and possessions can be entered and examined by any staff member, for whatever reason. His personal history and anguish is available to any staff member (often including the "grey lady" and the "candy striper" volunteer) who chooses to read his folder, regardless of their therapeutic relationship to him. His personal hygiene and waste evacuation are often monitored. The water closets may have no doors.

At times, depersonalization reached such proportions that pseudopatients had the sense that they were invisible or at least unworthy of account. Upon being admitted, I and other pseudopatients took the initial physical examinations in a semipublic room, where staff members went about their own business as if we were not there.

On the ward, attendants delivered verbal and occasionally serious physical abuse to patients in the presence of other observing patients, some of whom (the pseudopatients) were writing it all down. Abusive behavior, on the other hand, terminated quite abruptly when other staff members were known to be coming. Staff are credible witnesses. Patients are not.

A nurse unbuttoned her uniform to adjust her brassiere in the presence of an entire ward of viewing men. One did not have the sense that she was being seductive. Rather, she didn't notice us. A group of staff persons might point to a patient in the dayroom and discuss him animatedly, as if he were not there.

One illuminating instance of depersonalization and invisibility occurred with regard to medications. All told, the pseudopatients were administered nearly 2100 pills, including Elavil, Stelazine, Compazine, and Thorazine, to name but a few. (That such a variety of medications should have been administered to patients presenting identical symptoms is itself worthy of note.) Only two were swallowed. The rest were either pocketed or deposited in the toilet. The pseudopatients were not alone in this. Although I have no precise records on how many patients rejected their medications, the pseudopatients frequently found the medications of other patients in the toilet before they deposited their own. As long as they were cooperative, their behavior and the pseudopatients' own in this matter, as in other important matters, went unnoticed throughout.

Reactions to such depersonalization among pseudopatients were intense. Although they had come to the hospital as participant observers and were fully aware that they did not "belong," they nevertheless found themselves caught up in and fighting the process of depersonalization. Some examples: a graduate student in psychology asked his wife to bring his textbooks to the hospital so he could "catch up on his homework"—this despite the elaborate precautions taken to conceal his professional association. The same student, who had trained for quite some time to get into the hospital, and who had looked forward to the experience, "remembered" some drag races that he had wanted to see on the weekend and insisted that he be discharged by that time. Another pseudopatient attempted a romance with a nurse. Subsequently, he informed the staff that he was applying for admission to graduate school in psychology and was very likely to be admitted, since a graduate professor was one of his regular hospital visitors. The same person began to engage in psychotherapy with other patients—all of this as a way of becoming a person in an impersonal environment.

THE SOURCES OF DEPERSONALIZATION

What are the origins of depersonalization? I have already mentioned two. First are attitudes held by all of us toward the mentally ill—including those who treat them—attitudes characterized by fear, distrust, and horrible expectations on the one hand, and benevolent intentions on the other. Our ambivalence leads, in this instance as in others, to avoidance.

Second, and not entirely separate, the hierarchical structure of the psychiatric hospital facilitates depersonalization. Those who are at the top have least to do with patients, and their behavior inspires the rest of the staff. Average daily contact with psychiatrists, psychologists, residents, and physicians combined ranged from 3.9 to 25.1 minutes, with an overall mean of 6.8 (six pseudopatients over a total of 129 days of hospitalization). Included in this average are time spent in the admissions interview, ward meetings in the presence of a senior staff member, group and individual psychotherapy contacts, case presentation conferences, and discharge meetings. Clearly, patients do not spend much time in interpersonal contact with doctoral staff. And doctoral staff serve as models for nurses and attendants.

There are probably other sources. Psychiatric installations are presently in serious financial straits. Staff shortages are pervasive, staff time at a premium. Something has to give, and that something is patient contact. Yet, while financial stresses are realities, too much can be made of them. I have the impression that the psychological forces that result in depersonalization are much stronger than the fiscal ones and that the addition of more staff would not correspondingly improve patient care in this regard. The incidence of staff meetings and the enormous amount of record-keeping on patients, for example, have not been as substantially reduced as has patient contact. Priorities exist, even during hard times. Patient contact is not a significant priority in the traditional psychiatric hospital, and fiscal pressures do not account for this. Avoidance and depersonalization may.

Heavy reliance upon psychotropic medication tacitly contributes to depersonalization by convincing staff that treatment is indeed being conducted and that further patient contact may not be necessary. Even here, however, caution needs to be exercised in understanding the role of psychotropic drugs. If patients were powerful rather than powerless, if they were viewed as interesting individuals rather than diagnostic entities, if they were socially significant rather than social lepers, if their anguish truly and wholly compelled our sympathies and concerns, would we not seek contact with them, despite the availability of medications? Perhaps for the pleasure of it all?

THE CONSEQUENCES OF LABELING AND DEPERSONALIZATION

Whenever the ratio of what is known to what needs to be known approaches zero, we tend to invent "knowledge" and assume that we understand more than we actually do. We seem unable to acknowledge that we simply don't know. The needs for diagnosis and remediation of behavioral and emotional problems are enormous. But rather than acknowledge that we are just embarking on understanding, we continue to label patients "schizophrenic," "manic-depressive," and "insane," as if in those words we had captured the essence of understanding. The facts of the matter are that we have known for a long time that diagnoses are often not useful or reliable, but we have nevertheless continued to use them. We now know that we cannot distinguish insanity from sanity. It is depressing to consider how that information will be used.

Not merely depressing, but frightening. How many people, one wonders, are sane but not recognized as such in our psychiatric institutions? How many have been needlessly stripped of their privileges of citizenship, from the right to vote and drive to that of handling their own accounts? How many have feigned insanity in order to avoid the criminal consequences of their behavior, and, conversely, how many would rather stand trial than live interminably in a psychiatric hospital—but are wrongly thought to be mentally ill? How many have been stigmatized by well-intentioned, but nevertheless erroneous, diagnoses? On the last point, recall again the a "type 2 error" in psychiatric diagnosis does not have the same consequences it does in medical diagnosis. A diagnosis of cancer that has been found to be in error is cause for celebration. But psychiatric diagnoses are rarely found to be in error. The label sticks, a mark of inadequacy forever.

Finally, how many patients might be "sane" outside the psychiatric hospital but seem insane in it—not because craziness resides in them, as it were, but because they are responding to a bizarre setting, one that may be unique to institutions which harbor nether people? Goffman (4) calls the process of socialization to such institutions "mortification"—an apt metaphor that includes the processes of depersonalization that have been described here. And while it is impossible to know whether the pseudopatients' responses to these processes are characteristic of all inmates—they were, after all, not real patients—it is difficult to believe that these processes of socialization to a psychiatric hospital provide useful attitudes or habits of response for living in the "real world."

SUMMARY AND CONCLUSIONS

It is clear that we cannot distinguish the sane from the insane in psychiatric hospitals. The hospital itself imposes a special environment in which the meanings of behavior can easily be misunderstood. The consequences to patients hospitalized in such an environment—the powerlessness, depersonalization, segregation, mortification, and self-labeling—seem undoubtedly counter-therapeutic.

I do not, even now, understand this problem well enough to perceive solutions. But two matters seem to have some promise. The first concerns the proliferation of community mental health facilities, of crisis intervention centers, of the human potential movement, and of behavior therapies that, for all of their own problems, tend to avoid psychiatric labels, to focus on specific problems and behaviors, and to retain the individual in a relatively nonpejorative environment. Clearly, to the extent that we refrain from sending the distressed to insane places, our impressions of them are less likely to be distorted. (The risk of distorted perceptions, it seems to me, is always present, since we are much more sensitive to an individual's behaviors and verbalizations than we are to the subtle contextual stimuli that often promote them. At issue here is a matter of magnitude. And, as I have shown, the magnitude of distortion is exceedingly high in the extreme context that is a psychiatric hospital.)

The second matter that might prove promising speaks to the need to increase the sensitivity of mental health workers and researchers to the *Catch 22* position of psychiatric patients. Simply reading materials in this area will be of help to some such workers and researchers. For others, directly experiencing the impact of psychiatric hospitalization will be of enormous use. Clearly, further research into the social psychology of such total institutions will both facilitate treatment and deepen understanding.

I and the other pseudopatients in the psychiatric setting had distinctly negative reactions. We do not pretend to describe the subjective experiences of true patients. Theirs may be different from ours, particularly with the passage of time and the necessary process of adaptation to one's environment. But we can and do speak to the relatively more objective indices of treatment within the hospital. It could be a mistake, and a very unfortunate one, to consider that what happened to us derived from malice or stupidity on the part of the staff. Quite the contrary, our overwhelming impression of them was of people who really cared, who were committed, and who were uncommonly intelligent. Where they failed, as they sometimes did painfully, it would be more accurate to attribute those failures to the environment in which they, too, found themselves than to personal callousness. Their perceptions and behavior were controlled by the situation, rather than being motivated by a malicious disposition. In a more benign environment, one that was less attached to global diagnosis, their behaviors and judgments might have been more benign and effective (*22*).

REFERENCES AND NOTES

1. P. Ash, *J. Abnorm. Soc. Psychol.* 44, 272 (1949); A. T. Beck, *Amer. J. Psychiat.* 119, 210 (1962); A. T. Boisen, *Psychiatry* 2, 233 (1938); N. Kreitman, *J. Ment. Sci.* 107, 876 (1961); N. Kreitman, P. Sainsbury, J. Morrisey, J. Towers, J. Scrivener, *ibid.*, p. 887; H. O. Schmitt and C. P. Fonda *J. Abnorm. Soc. Psychol.* 52, 262 (1956); W. Seeman, *J. Nerv. Ment. Dis.* 118, 541 (1953). For an analysis of these artifacts and summaries of the disputes, see J. Zubin, *Annu. Rev. Psychol.* 18, 373 (1967); L. Phillips and J. G. Draguns, *ibid.* 22, 447 (1971).
2. R. Benedict, *J. Gen. Psychol.* 10, 59 (1934).
3. See in this regard H. Becker, *Outsiders: Studies in the Sociology of Deviance* (Free Press, New York, 1963); B. M. Braginsky, D. D. Braginsky, K. Ring, *Methods of Madness: The Mental Hospital as a Last Resort* (Holt, Rinehart & Winston, New York, 1969); G. M. Crocetti and P. V. Lemkau, *Amer. Sociol. Rev.* 30, 577 (1965); E. Goffman, *Behavior in Public Places* (Free Press, New York, 1964); R. D. Laing, *The Divided Self: A Study of Sanity and Madness* (Quadrangle, Chicago, 1960); D. L. Phillips, *Amer. Sociol. Rev.* 28, 963 (1963); T. R. Sarbin, *Psychol. Today* 6, 18 (1972); E. Schur, *Amer. J. Sociol.* 75, 309 (1969); T. Szasz, *Law, Liberty and Psychiatry* (Macmillan, New York, 1963); *The Myth of Mental Illness: Foundations of a Theory of Mental Illness* (Hoeber-Harper, New York, 1963). For a critique of some of these views, see W. R. Gove, *Amer. Sociol. Rev.* 35, 873 (1970).
4. E. Goffman, *Asylums* (Doubleday, Garden City, N.Y., 1961).
5. T. J. Scheff, *Being Mentally Ill: A Sociological Theory* (Aldine, Chicago, 1966).
6. Data from a ninth pseudopatient are not incorporated in this report because, although his sanity went undetected, he falsified aspects of his personal history, including his marital status and parental relationships. His experimental behaviors therefore were not identical to those of the other pseudopatients.
7. A. Barry, *Bellevue Is a State of Mind* (Harcourt Brace Jovanovich, New York, 1971); I. Belknap, *Human Problems of a State Mental Hospital* (McGraw-Hill, New York, 1956); W. Caudill, F. C. Redlich, H. R. Gilmore, E. B. Brody, *Amer. J. Orthopsychiat.* 22, 314 (1952); A. R. Goldman, R. H. Bohr, T. A. Steinberg, *Prof. Psychol.* 1, 427 (1970); unauthored, *Roche Report* 1 (No. 13), 8 (1971).
8. Beyond the personal difficulties that the pseudopatient is likely to experience in the hospital, there are legal and social ones that, combined, require considerable attention before entry. For example, once admitted to a psychiatric institution, it is difficult, if not impossible, to be discharged on short notice, state law to the contrary notwithstanding. I was not sensitive to these difficulties at the outset of the project, nor to the personal and situational emergencies that can arise, but later a writ of habeas corpus was prepared for each of the entering pseudopatients and an attorney was kept "on call" during every hospitalization. I am grateful to John Kaplan and Robert Bartels for legal advice and assistance in these matters.
9. However distasteful such concealment is, it was a necessary first step to examining these questions. Without concealment, there would have been no way to know how valid these experiences were; nor was there any way of knowing whether whatever detections occurred were a tribute to the diagnostic acumen of the staff or to the hopsital's rumor network. Obviously, since my concerns are general ones that cut across individual hopsitals and staffs, I have respected their anonymity and have eliminated clues that might lead to their identification.
10. Interestingly, of the 12 admissions, 11 were diagnosed as schizophrenic and one, with the identical symptomatology, as manic-depressive psychosis. This diagnosis has a more favorable prognosis, and it was given by the only private hospital in our sample. On the relations between social class and psychiatric diagnosis, see A. deB. Hollingshead and F. C. Redlich, *Social Class and Mental Illness: A Community Study* (Wiley, New York, 1958).
11. It is possible, of course, that patients have quite broad latitudes in diagnosis and therefore are inclined to call many people sane, even those whose behavior is patently aberrant. However, although we have no hard data on this matter, it was our distinct impression that this was not the case. In many instances, patients not only singled us out for attention, but came to imitate our behaviors and styles.
12. J. Cumming and E. Cumming, *Community Ment. Health* 1, 135 (1965); A. Farina and K. Ring, *J. Abnorm. Psychol.* 70, 47 (1965); H. E. Freeman and O. G. Simmons, *The Mental Patient Comes Home* (Wiley, New York, 1963); W. J. Johannsen, *Ment. Hygiene* 53, 218 (1969); A. S. Linsky, *Soc. Psychiat.* 5, 166 (1970).
13. S. E. Asch, *J. Abnorm. Soc. Psychol.* 41, 258 (1946); *Social Psychology* (Prentice-Hall, New York, 1952).
14. See also I. N. Mensh and J. Wishner, *J. Personality* 16, 188 (1947); J. Wishner, *Psychol. Rev.* 67, 96 (1960); J. S. Bruner and R. Tagiuri, in *Handbook of Social Psychology*, G. Lindzey, Ed. (Addison-Wesley, Cambridge, Mass., 1954), vol. 2, pp. 634–654; J. S. Bruner, D. Shapiro, R. Tagiuri, in

Person Perception and Interpersonal Behavior, R. Tagiuri and L. Petrullo, Eds. (Stanford Univ. Press, Stanford, Calif., 1958), pp. 277–288.
15. For an example of a similar self fulfilling prophecy, in this instance dealing with the "central" trait of intelligence, see R. Rosenthal and L. Jacobson, *Pygmalion in the Classroom* (Holt, Rinehart & Winston, new York, 1968).
16. E. Zigler and L. Phillips, *J. Abnorm. Soc. Psychol.* 63, 69 (1961). See also R. K. Freudenberg and J. P. Robertson, A.M.A. *Arch. Neurol. Psychiatr.* 76, 14 (1956).
17. W. Mischel, *Personality and Assessment* (Wiley, New York, 1968).
18. The most recent and unfortunate instance of this tenet is that of Senator Thomas Eagleton.
19. T. R. Sarbin and J. C. Mancuso, *J. Clin. Consult. Psychol.* 35, 159 (1970); T. R. Sarbin, *ibid.* 31, 447 (1967); J. C. Nunnally, Jr., *Popular Conceptions of Mental Health* (Holt, Rinehart & Winston, New York, 1961).
20. A. H. Stanton and M. S. Schwartz, *The Mental Hospital: A Study of Institutional Participation in Psychiatric Illness and Treatment* (Basic, New York, 1954).
21. D. B. Wexler and S. E. Scoville, *Ariz. Law Rev.* 13, 1 (1971).
22. I thank W. Mischel, E. Orne, and M. S. Rosenhan for comments on an earlier draft of this manuscript.

ROBERT L. SPITZER

On pseudoscience in science, logic in remission, and psychiatric diagnosis: A critique of Rosenhan's "On being sane in insane places"

Some foods taste delicious but leave a bad aftertaste. So it is with Rosenhan's study, "On Being Sane in Insane Places" (Rosenhan, 1973a), which, by virtue of the prestige and wide distribution of *Science*, the journal in which it appeared, provoked a furor in the scientific community. That the *Journal of Abnormal Psychology*, at this late date, chooses to explore the study's strengths and weaknesses is a testament not only to the importance of the issues that the study purports to deal with but to the impact that the study has had in the mental health community.

Rosenhan apparently believes that psychiatric diagnosis is of no value. There is nothing wrong with his designing a study the results of which might dramatically support this view. However, "On Being Sane in Insane Places" is pseudoscience presented as science. Just as his pseudopatients were diagnosed at discharge as "schizophrenia, in remission," so a careful examination of this study's methods, results, and conclusions leads me to a diagnosis of "logic, in remission."

Let us summarize the study's central question, the methods used, the results reported, and Rosenhan's conclusions. Rosenhan (1973a) states the basic issue simply: "Do the salient characteristics that lead to diagnoses reside in the patients themselves or in the environments and contexts in which observers find them?" Rosenhan proposed that by getting normal people who had never had symptoms of serious psychiatric disorders admitted to psychiatric hospitals "and then determining whether they were discovered to be sane" was an adequate method of studying this question. Therefore, eight "sane" people, pseudopatients, gained secret admission to 12 different hospitals with a single complaint of hearing voices. Upon admission to the psychiatric ward, the pseudopatients ceased simulating any symptoms of abnormality.

The diagnostic results were that 11 of the 12 diagnoses on admission were schizophrenia and 1 was manic-depressive psychosis. At discharge, all of the patients were given the same diagnosis, but were qualified as "in remission."[1] Despite their "show of sanity" the pseudopatients were never detected by any of the professional staff, nor were

I wish to acknowledge the many valuable suggestions made by Jean Endicott, Joseph Fleiss, and Joseph Zubin.

SOURCE: *Journal of Abnormal Psychology*, 84(5), pp. 442–452, 1975.

any questions raised about their authenticity during the entire hospitalization.

Rosenhan (1973a) concluded: "It is clear that we cannot distinguish the sane from the insane in psychiatric hospitals" (p. 257). According to him, what is needed is the avoidance of "global diagnosis," as exemplified by such diagnoses as schizophrenia or manic-depressive psychosis, and attention should be directed instead to "behaviors, the stimuli that provoke them, and their correlates."

THE CENTRAL QUESTION

One hardly knows where to begin. Let us first acknowledge the potential importance of the study's central research question. Surely, if psychiatric diagnoses are, to quote Rosenhan, "only in the minds of the observers," and do not reflect any characteristics inherent in the patient, then they obviously can be of no use in helping patients. However, the study immediately becomes confused when Rosenhan suggests that this research question can be answered by studying whether or not the "sanity" of pseudopatients in a mental hospital can be discovered. Rosenhan, a professor of law and psychology, knows that the terms "sane" and "insane" are legal, not psychiatric, concepts. He knows that no psychiatrist makes a diagnosis of "sanity" or "insanity" and that the true meaning of these terms, which varies from state to state, involves the inability to appreciate right from wrong—an issue that is totally irrelevant to this study.

DETECTING THE SANITY OF A PSEUDOPATIENT

However, if we are forced to use the terms "insane" (to mean roughly showing signs of serious mental disturbance) and "sane" (the absence of such signs), then clearly there are three possible meanings to the concept of "detecting the sanity" of a pseudopatient who feigns mental illness on entry to a hospital, but then acts "normal" throughout his hospital stay. The first is the recognition, when he is first seen, that the pseudopatient is feigning insanity as he attempts to gain admission to the hospital. This would be detecting sanity in a sane person simulating insanity. The second would be the recognition, after having observed him acting normally during his hospitalization, that the pseudopatient was initially feigning insanity. This would be detecting that the currently sane never was insane. Finally, the third possible meaning would be the recognition, during hospitalization, that the pseudopatient, though initially appearing to be "insane," was no longer showing signs of psychiatric disturbance.

These elementary distinctions of "detecting sanity in the insane" are crucial to properly interpreting the results of the study. The reader is misled by Rosenhan's implication that the first two meanings of detecting the sanity of the pseudopatients, which involve determining the pseudopatient to be a fraud, are at all relevant to the central research question. Furthermore, he obscures the true results of his study—because they fail to support his conclusion—when the third meaning of detecting sanity is considered, that is, a recognition that after their admission as "insane," the pseudopatients were not psychiatrically disturbed while in the hospital.

Let us examine these three possible meanings of detecting the sanity of the pseudopatient, their logical relation to the central question of the study, and the actual results obtained and the validity of Rosenhan's conclusions.

THE PATIENT IS NO LONGER "INSANE"

We begin with the third meaning of detecting sanity. It is obvious that if the psychiatrists judged the pseudopatients as seriously disturbed while they acted "normal" in the hospital, this would be strong evidence that their assessments were being influenced by the context in which they were making their examination rather than the actual behavior of the patient, which is the central research question. (I suspect that many readers will agree with Hunter who, in a letter to *Science* [Hunter, 1973], pointed out that, "The pseudopatients did *not* behave normally in the hospital. Had their behavior been normal, they would have walked to the nurses' station and said, 'Look, I am a normal person who tried to see if I could get into the hospital by behaving in a crazy way or saying crazy things. It worked and I was admitted to the hospital, but now I would like to be discharged from the hospital' " [p. 361].)

What were the results? According to Rosenhan, all the patients were diagnosed at discharge as "in remission."[2] The meaning of "in remission" is clear: It means without signs of illness. Thus, all of the psychiatrists apparently recognized that all of pseudopatients were, to use Rosenhan's term, "sane." However, lest the reader appreciate the significance of these findings, Rosenhan (1973a) quickly gives a completely incorrect interpretation: "If the pseudopatient was to be discharged, he must naturally be 'in remission'; but he was not sane, nor, in the institution's view, had he ever been sane" (p. 252). Rosenhan's implication is clear: The patient was diagnosed "in remission" not because the psychiatrist correctly assessed the patient's hospital behavior but only because the patient had to be discharged. Is this interpretation warranted?

I am sure that most readers who are not familiar with the details of psychiatric diagnostic practice assume, from Rosenhan's account, that it is common for schizophrenic patients to be diagnosed "in remission" when discharged from a hospital. As a matter of fact, it is extremely unusual. The reason is that a schizophrenic is rarely completely asymptomatic at discharge. Rosenhan does not report any data concerning the discharge diagnoses of the real schizophrenic patients in the 12 hospitals used in his study. However, I can report on the frequency of a discharge diagnosis of schizophrenia "in remission" at my hospital, the New York State Psychiatric Institute, a research, teaching, and community hospital where diagnoses are made in a routine fashion, undoubtedly no different from the 12 hospitals of Rosenhan's study. I examined the official book that the record room uses to record the discharge diagnoses and their statistical codes for all patients. Of the over 300 patients discharged in the last year with a diagnosis of schizophrenia, not one was diagnosed "in remission." It is only possible to code a diagnosis of "in remission" by adding a fifth digit (5) to the 4-digit code number for the subtype of schizophrenia (e.g., paranoid schizophrenia is coded as 295.3, but paranoid schizophrenia "in remission" is coded as 295.35). I therefore realized that a psychiatrist might intend to make a discharge diagnosis of "in remission" but fail to use the fifth digit, so that the official recording of the diagnosis would not reflect his full assessment. I therefore had research assistants read the discharge summaries of the last 100 patients whose discharge diagnosis was schizophrenia to see how often the term "in remission," "recovered," "no longer ill," or "asymptomatic" was used, even if not recorded by use of the fifth digit in the code number. The result was that only one patient, who was diagnosed paranoid schizophrenia, was described in the summary as being "in remission" at discharge. The fifth digit code was not used.

To substantiate my view that the practice at my hospital of rarely giving a discharge diagnosis of schizophrenia "in remission" is not unique, I had a research assistant call the record room librarians of 12 psychiatric hospitals, chosen catch as catch can.[3] They were told that we were interested in knowing their estimate of how often, at their hospital, schizophrenics were discharged "in remission" (or "no longer ill" or "asymptomatic"). The calls revealed that 11 of the 12 hospitals indicated that the term was either never used or, at most, used for only a handful of patients in a year. The remaining hospital, a private hospital, estimated that the term was used in roughly 7% of the discharge diagnoses.

This leaves us with the conclusion that, because 11 of the 12 pseudopatients were discharged as "schizophrenia in remission," a discharge diagnosis that is rarely given to real schizophrenics, the diagnoses given to the pseudopatients were a function of the patients' behaviors and not of the setting (psychiatric hospital) in which the diagnoses were made. In fact, we must marvel that 11 psychiatrists all acted so rationally as to use at discharge the category of "in remission" or its equivalent, a category that is rarely used with real schizophrenic patients.

It is not only in his discharge diagnosis that the psychiatrist had an opportunity to assess the patient's true condition incorrectly. In the admission mental status examination, during a progress note, or in his discharge note the psychiatrist could have described any of the pseudopatients as "still psychotic," "probably still hallucinating but denies it now," "loose associations," or "inappropriate affect." Because Rosehan had access to all of this material, his failure to report such judgments of continuing serious psychopathology strongly suggests that they were never made.

All pseudopatients took extensive notes publicly to obtain data on staff and patient behavior. Rosenhan claims that the nursing records indicate that "the writing was seen as a aspect of their pathological behavior." The only datum presented to support this claim is that the daily nursing comment on one of the pseudopatients was, "Patient engages in writing behavior." Because nursing notes frequently and intentionally comment on nonpathological activities that patients engage in so that other staff members have some knowledge of how the patient spends his time, this particular nursing note in no way supports Rosenhan's thesis. Once again, the failure of Rosenhan to provide data regarding instances where normal hospital behavior was categorized as pathological is remarkable. The closest that Rosenhan comes to providing such data is his report of an instance where a kindly nurse asked if a pseudopatient, who was pacing the long hospital corridors because of boredom, was "nervous." It was, after all, a question and not a final judgment.

Let us now examine the relation between the other two meanings of detecting sanity in the pseudopatients: the recognition that the pseudopatient was a fraud, either when he sought admission to the hospital or during this hospital stay, and the central research question.

DETECTING "SANITY" BEFORE ADMISSION

Whether or not psychiatrists are able to detect individuals who feign psychiatric symptoms is an interesting question but clearly of no relevance to the issue of whether or not the salient characteristics that lead to diagnoses reside in the patient's behavior or in the minds of the observers. After all, a psychiatrist who believes a pseudopatient who feigns a symptom *is* responding to the pseudopatient's behavior. And Rosenhan does not blame the psychiatrist for believing the pseudopatient's fake symptom of hallucinations. He blames him for the diagnosis of schizophrenia. Rosenhan (1973b) states:

> The issue is not that the psychiatrist believed him. Neither is it whether the pseudopatient should have been admitted to the psychiatric hospital in the first place. . . . The issue is the diagnostic leap that was made between the single presenting symptom, hallucinations, and the diagnosis schizophrenia (or in one case, manic-depressive psychosis). Had the pseudopatients been diagnosed "hallucinating," there would have been no further need to examine the diagnosis issue. The diagnosis of hallucinations implies only that: no more. The presence of hallucinations does not itself define the presence of "schizophre-

nia." And schizophrenia may or may not include hallucinations. (p. 366)

Unfortunately, as judged by many of the letters to *Science* commenting on the study (Letters to the editor, 1973), many readers, including psychiatrists, accepted Rosenhan's thesis that it was irrational for the psychiatrists to have made an initial diagnosis of schizophrenia as *the most likely condition* on the basis of a single symptom. In my judgment, these readers were wrong. Their acceptance of Rosenhan's thesis was aided by the content of the pseudopatients' auditory hallucinations, which were voices that said "empty," "hollow," and "thud." According to Rosenhan (1973a), these symptoms were chosen because of "their apparent similarity to existential symptoms [and] the *absence* of a single report of existential psychoses in the literature" (p. 251). The implication is that if the content of specific symptoms has never been reported in the literature, then a psychiatrist should somehow know that the symptom is fake. Why then, according to Rosenhan, should the psychiatrist have made a diagnosis of hallucinating? This is absurd. Recently I saw a patient who kept hearing a voice that said, "It's O.K. It's O.K.," I know of no such report in the literature. So what? I agree with Rosenhan that there has never been a report of an "existential psychosis." However, the diagnoses made were schizophrenia and manic-depressive psychosis, not existential psychosis.

DIFFERENTIAL DIAGNOSIS OF AUDITORY HALLUCINATIONS

Rosenhan is entitled to believe that psychiatric diagnoses are of no use and therefore should not have been given to the pseudopatients. However, it makes no sense for him to claim that within a diagnostic framework it was irrational to consider schizophrenia seriously as the most likely condition without his presenting a consideration of the differential diagnosis. Let me briefly give what I think is a reasonable differential diagnosis, based on the presenting picture of the pseudopatient when he applied for admission to the hospital.

Rosenhan says that "beyond alleging the symptoms and falsifying name, vocation, and employment, no further alterations of person, history, or circumstances were made" (p. 251). However, clearly the clinical picture includes not only the symptom (auditory hallucinations) but also the desire to enter a psychiatric hospital, from which it is reasonable to conclude that the symptom is a source of significant distress. (How often did the admitting psychiatrist suggest what would seem to be reasonable care: outpatient treatment? Did the pseudopatient have to add other complaints to justify inpatient treatment?) This, plus the knowledge that the auditory hallucinations are of 3 weeks' duration,[4] establishes the hallucinations as significant symptoms of psychopathology as distinguished from so-called "pseudohallucinations" (hallucinations while falling asleep or awakening from sleep, or intense imagination with the voice heard from inside of the head).

Auditory hallucinations can occur in several kinds of mental disorders. The absence of a history of alcohol, drug abuse, or some other toxin, the absence of any signs of physical illness (such as high fever), and the absence of evidence of distractibility, impairment in concentration, memory or orientation, and a negative neurological examination all make an organic psychosis extremely unlikely. The absence of a recent precipitating stress rules out a transient situational disturbance of psychotic intensity or (to use a nonofficial category) hysterical psychosis. The absence of a profound disturbance in mood rules out an affective psychosis (we are not given the mental status findings for the patient who was diagnosed manic-depressive psychosis).

What about simulating mental illness? Psychiatrists know that occasionally an individual who has something to gain from being admitted into a psychiatric hospital will exaggerate or even feign psychiatric symptoms. This is a genuine diagnostic problem that psychiatrists and other physicians occasionally confront and is called "malingering." However, with the pseudopatients there was no reason to believe that any of them had anything to gain from being admitted into a psychiatric hospital except relief from their alleged complaint, and therefore no reason to suspect that the illness was feigned. Dear reader: There is only one remaining diagnosis for the presenting symptom of hallucinations under these conditions in the classification of mental disorders used in this country, and that is schizophrenia.

Admittedly, there is a hitch to a definitive diagnosis of schizophrenia: Almost invariably there are other signs of the disorder present, such as poor premorbid adjustment, affective blunting, delusions, or signs of thought disorder. I would hope that if I had been one of the 12 psychiatrists presented with such a patient, I would have been struck by the lack of other signs of the disorder, but I am rather sure that having no reason to doubt the authenticity of the patients' claim of auditory hallucinations, I also would have been fooled into noting schizophrenia as the most likely diagnosis.

What does Rosenhan really mean when he objects to the diagnosis of schizophrenia because it was based on a "single symptom"? Does he believe that there are real patients with the single symptom of auditory hallucinations who are misdiagnosed as schizophrenic when they actually have some other condition? If so, what is the nature of that condition? Is Rosenhan's point that the psychiatrist should have used "diagnosis deferred," a category that is available but rarely used? I would have no argument with this conclusion. Furthermore, if he had presented data from real patients indicating how often patients are erroneously diagnosed on the basis of inadequate information and what the consequences were, it would have been a real contribution.

Until now, I have assumed that the pseudopatients presented only one symptom of psychiatric disorder. Actually, we know very little about how the pseudopatients presented themselves. What did the pseudopatients say in the study reported in *Science*, when asked, as they must have been, what effect the hallucinations were having on their lives and why they were seeking admission into a hospital? The reader would be much more confident that a single presenting symptom was involved if Rosenhan had made available for each pseudopatient the actual admission work-up from the hospital record.

DETECTING SANITY AFTER ADMISSION

Let us now examine the last meaning of detecting sanity in the pseudopatients, namely, the psychiatrist's recognition, *after* observing him act normally during his hospitalization, that the pseudopatient was initially feigning insanity and its relation to the central research question. If a diagnostic condition, by definition, is always chronic and never remits, it would be irrational not to question the original diagnosis if a patient were later found to be asymptomatic. As applied to this study, if the concept of schizophrenia did not admit the possibility of recovery, then failure to question the original diagnosis when the pseudopatients were no longer overtly ill would be relevant to the central research question. It would be an example of the psychiatrist allowing the context of the hospital environment to influence his diagnostic behavior. But neither any psychiatric textbook nor the American Psychiatric Association's *Diagnostic and Statistical Manual of Mental Disorders* (American Psychiatric Association, 1968) suggests that mental illnesses endure forever. Oddly enough, it is Rosenhan (1973a) who, without any reference to the psychiatric literature, says: "A broken leg is something one recovers from, but mental illness allegedly endures forever" (p. 254). Who, other than Rosenhan, alleges it?

As Rosenhan should know, although some American psychiatrists restrict the label of schizophrenia to mean chronic or process schizophrenia, most American psychiatrists include an acute subtype from which there often is a remission. Thus, the *Diagnostic and Statistical Manual*, in describing the subtype, acute schizophrenic episode, states that "in many cases the patient recovers within weeks."

A similar straw man is created when Rosenhan (1973a) says,

> The insane are not always insane . . . the bizarre behaviors upon which their [the pseudopatients] behaviors were allegedly predicated constituted only a small fraction of their total behavior. If it makes no sense to label ourselves permanently depressed on the basis of an occasional depression, then it takes better evidence than is presently available to label all patients insane or schizophrenic on the basis of behaviors or cognitions. (p. 254)

Who ever said that the behaviors that indicate schizophrenia or any other diagnostic category comprise the total of a patient's behavior? A diagnosis of schizophrenia does not mean that all of the patient's behavior is schizophrenic any more than a diagnosis of carcinoma of the liver means that all of the patient's body is diseased.

Does Rosenhan at least score a point by demonstrating that, although the professional staff never considered the possibility that the pseudopatient was a fraud, this possibility was often considered by other patients? Perhaps, but I am not so sure. Let us not forget that all of the pseudopatients "took extensive notes publicly." Obviously this was highly unusual patient behavior and Rosenhan's quote from a suspicious patient suggests the importance it had in focusing the other patients' attention on the pseudopatients: "You're not crazy. You're a journalist or a professor [referring to the continual note-taking]. You're checking up on the hospital." (Rosenhan, 1973a, p. 252).

Rosenhan presents ample evidence, which I find no reason to dispute, that the professional staff spent little time actually with the pseudopatients. The note-taking may easily have been overlooked, and therefore they developed no suspicion that the pseudopatients had simulated illness to gain entry into the hospital. Because there were no pseudopatients who did not engage in such unusual behaviors, the reader cannot assess the significance of the patients' suspicions of fraud when the professional staff did not. I would predict, however, that a pseudopatient in a ward of patients with mixed diagnostic conditions would have no difficulty in masquerading convincingly as a true patient to both staff and patients if he did nothing unusual to draw attention to himself.

Rosenhan presents one way in which the diagnosis affected the psychiatrist's perception of the patient's circumstances: Historical facts of the case were often distorted by the staff to achieve consistency with psychodynamic theories. Here, for the first time, I believe Rosenhan has hit the mark. What he described happens all the time and often makes attendance at clinical case conferences extremely painful, especially for those with a logical mind and a research orientation. Although his observation is correct, it would seem to be more a consequence of individuals attempting to rearrange facts to comply with an unproven etiological theory than a consequence of diagnostic labeling. One could as easily imagine a similar process occurring when a weak-minded, behaviorally-oriented clinician attempts to rewrite the patient's history to account for "hallucinations reinforced by attention paid to patient by family members when patient complains of hearing voices." Such is the human condition.

One final finding requires comment. In order to determine whether "the tendency toward diagnosing the sane insane could be reversed," the staff of a research and teaching hospital was informed that at some time during the following three months, one or more pseudopatients would attempt to be admitted. No such attempt was actually made. Yet approximately 10% of 193 real patients were suspected by two or more staff members (we are not told how many made judgments) to be pseudopatients. Rosenhan (1973a) concluded: "Any diagnostic process that lends itself so readily to massive errors of this sort, cannot be a very reliable one" (p. 179). My conclusion is that his experimental design practically assures only one outcome.

ELEMENTARY PRINCIPLES OF RELIABILITY OF CLASSIFICATION

Some very important principles that are relevant to the design of Rosenhan's study are taught in elementary psychology courses and should not be forgotten. One of them is that a measurement or classification procedure is not reliable or unreliable in itself but only in its application to a specific population. There are serious problems in the reliability of psychiatric diagnosis as it is applied to the population to which psychiatric diagnoses are ordinarily given. However, I fail to see, and Rosenhan does not even attempt to show, how the reliability of psychiatric diagnoses applied to a population of individuals seeking help is at all relevant to the reliability of psychiatric diagnoses applied to a population of pseudopatients (or one including the threat of pseudopatients). The two populations are just not the same. Kety (1974) has expressed it dramatically:

> If I were to drink a quart of blood and, concealing what I had done, come to the emergency room of any hospital vomiting blood, the behavior of the staff would be quite predictable. If they labeled and treated me as having a bleeding peptic ulcer, I doubt that I could argue convincingly that medical science does not know how to diagnose that condition. (p. 959)

(I have no doubt that if the condition known as pseudopatient ever assumed epidemic proportions among admittants to psychiatric hospital, psychiatrists would in time become adept at identifying them, though at what risk to real patients, I do not know.)

ATTITUDES TOWARD THE INSANE

I shall not dwell on the latter part of Rosenhan's study, which deals with the experience of psychiatric hospitalization. Because some of the hospitals participated in residency training programs and were research oriented, I find it hard to believe that conditions were quite as bad as depicted, but they may well be. I have always believed that psychiatrists should spend more time on psychiatric wards to appreciate how mind dulling the experience must be for patients. However, Rosenhan does not stop at documenting the horrors of life on a psychiatric ward. He asserts, without a shred of evidence from his study, that "negative attitudes [toward psychiatric patients] are the natural offspring of the labels patients wear and the places in which they are found." This is nonsense. In recent years large numbers of chronic psychiatric patients, many of them chronic schizophrenics and geriatric patients with organic brain syndromes, have been discharged from state hospitals and placed in communities that have no facilities to deal with them. The affected communities are up in arms not primarily because they are mental patients labeled with psychiatric diagnoses (because the majority are not recognized as expatients) but because the behavior of some of them is sometimes incomprehensible, deviant, strange, and annoying.

There are at least two psychiatric diagnoses that are defined by the presence of single behaviors, much as Rosenhan would prefer a diagnosis of hallucinations to a diagnosis of schizophrenia. They are alcoholism and drug abuse. Does society have negative attitudes toward these individuals because of the diagnostic label attached to them by psychiatrists or because of their behavior?

THE USES OF DIAGNOSIS

Rosenhan believes that the pseudopatients should have been diagnosed as having hallucinations of unknown origin. It is not clear what he thinks the diagnosis should have been if the pseudopatients had been sufficiently trained to talk, at times, incoherently and had complained of difficulty in thinking clearly, lack of emotion, and that their thoughts were being broadcast so that strangers knew what they were thinking. Is Rosenhan perhaps suggesting multiple diagnoses of (a) hallucinations, (b) difficulty thinking clearly, (c) lack of emotion, and (d) incoherent speech . . . all of unknown origin?

It is no secret that we lack a full understanding of such conditions as schizophrenia and manic-depressive illness, but are we quite as ignorant as Rosenhan would have us believe? Do we not know, for example, that hallucinations, in the context just described, are symptomatic of a different condition than are hallucinations of voices accusing the patient of sin when associated with depressed affect, diurnal mood variation, loss of appetite, and insomnia? What about hallucinations of God's voice issuing commandments, associated with euphoric affect, psychomotor excitement, and accelerated and disconnected speech? Is this not also an entirely different condition?

There is a purpose to psychiatric diagnosis (Spitzer & Wilson, 1975). It is to enable mental health professionals to (a) communicate with each other about the subject matter of their concern, (b) comprehend the pathological processes involved in psychiatric illness, and (c) control psychiatric disorders. Control consists of the ability to predict outcome, prevent the disorder from developing, and treat it once it has developed. Any serious discussion of the validity of psychiatric diagnosis, or suggestions for alternative systems of classifying psychological disturbance, must address itself to these purposes of psychiatric diagnosis.

In terms of its ability to accomplish these purposes, I would say that psychiatric diagnosis is moderately effective as a shorthand way of communicating the presence of constellations of signs and symptoms that tend to cluster together, is woefully inadequate in helping us understand the pathological processes of psychiatric disorders, but does offer considerable help in the control of many mental disorders. Control is possible because psychiatric diagnosis often yields information of value in predicting the likely course of illness (e.g., an early recovery, chronicity, or recurrent episodes) and because for many mental disorders it is useful in suggesting the best available treatment.

Let us return to the three different clinical conditions that I described, each of which had auditory hallucinations as one of its manifestations. The reader will have no difficulty in identifying the three hypothetical conditions as schizophrenia, psychotic depression, and mania. Anyone familiar with the literature on psychiatric treatment will know that there are numerous well-controlled studies (Klein & Davis, 1969) indicating the superiority of the major tranquilizers for the treatment of schizophrenia, of electroconvulsive therapy for the treatment of psychotic depression, and, more recently, of lithium carbonate for the treatment of mania. Furthermore, there is convincing evidence that these three conditions, each of which is often accompanied by hallucinations, are influenced by separate genetic factors. As Kety (1974) said, "If schizophrenia is a myth, it is a myth with a strong genetic component."

Should psychiatric diagnosis be abandoned for a purely descriptive system that focuses on simple phenotypic behaviors before it has been demonstrated that such an approach is more useful as a guide to successful treatment or for understanding the role of genetic factors? I think not. (I have a vision. Traditional psychiatric diagnosis has long been forgotten. At a conference on behavioral classification, a keen research investigator proposes that the category "hallucinations of unknown etiology" be subdivided into three different groups based on associated symptomatology. The first group is characterized by depressed affect, diurnal mood variation, and so on, the second group by euphoric mood, psychomotor excitement. . . .)

If psychiatric diagnosis is not quite as bad as Rosenhan would have us believe, that does not mean that it is all that good. What is the reliability of psychiatric diagnosis? A review of the major studies of the reliability of psychiatric diagnosis prior to 1972 (Spitzer & Fleiss, 1974) revealed that "reliability is only satisfactory for three categories: mental deficiencies, organic brain syndrome, and alcoholism. The level of reliability is no better than fair for psychosis and schizophrenia, and is poor for the remaining categories." So be it. But where did Rosenhan get the idea the psychiatry is the only medical specialty that is plagued by inaccurate diagnosis? Studies have shown serious unreliability in the diagnosis of pulmonary disorders (Fletcher, 1952), in the interpretation of electrocardiograms (Davies, 1958), in the interpretation of X-rays, (Cochrane & Garland, 1952; Yerushalmy, 1947), and in the certification of causes of death (Markush, Schaaf, & Siegel, 1967). A review of diagnostic unreliability in other branches of physical medicine is given by Garland (1960) and the problem of the vagueness of medical criteria for diagnosis is thoroughly discussed by Feinstein (1967). The poor reliability of medical diagnosis, even when assisted by objective laboratory tests, does not mean that medical diagnosis is of no value. So it is with psychiatric diagnosis.

Recognition of the serious problems of the reliability of psychiatric diagnosis has resulted in a new approach to psychiatric diagnosis—the use of specific inclusion and exclusion criteria, as contrasted with the usually vague and ill-defined general descriptions found in the psychiatric literature and in the standard psychiatric glossary of the American Psychiatric Association. This approach was started by the St. Louis group associated with the Department of Psychiatry of Washington University (Feighner, Robins, Guze, Woodruff, Winokur, & Munoz, 1972) and has been further developed by Spitzer, Endicott, and Robins (1974) as a set of criteria for a selected group of functional psychiatric disorders, called the Research Diagnostic Criteria (RDC). The Display shows the specific criteria for a diagnosis of schizophrenia from the latest version of the RDC.[5]

Diagnostic Criteria for Schizophrenia from the Research Diagnostic Criteria

1. At least two of the following are required for definite diagnosis and one for probable diagnosis:
   a. Thought broadcasting, insertion, or withdrawal (as defined in the RDC).
   b. Delusions of control, other bizarre delusions, or multiple delusions (as defined in the RDC), of any duration as long as definitely present.
   c. Delusions other than persecutory or jealousy, lasting at least 1 week.
   d. Delusions of any type if accompanied by hallucinations of any type for at least 1 week.
   e. Auditory hallucinations in which either a voice keeps up a running commentary on the patient's behaviors or thoughts as they occur, or two or more voices converse with each other (of any duration as long as definitely present).
   f. Nonaffective verbal hallucina-

tions spoken to the subject (as defined in this manual).

g. Hallucinations of any type throughout the day for several days or intermittently for at least 1 month.

h. Definite instances of formal thought disorder (as defined in the RDC).

i. Obvious catatonic motor behavior (as defined in the RDC).

2. A period of illness lasting at least 2 weeks.
3. At no time during the active period of illness being considered did the patient meet the criteria for either probable or definite manic or depressive syndrome (Criteria 1 and 2 under Major Depressive or Manic Disorders) to such a degree that it was a prominent part of the illness.

Reliability studies utilizing the RDC with case record material (from which all cues as to diagnosis and treatment were removed), as well as with live patients, indicate high reliability for all of the major categories and reliability coefficients generally higher than have ever been reported (Spitzer, Endicott, Robins, Kuriansky, & Gurland, 1975). It is therefore clear that the reliability of psychiatric diagnosis can be greatly increased by the use of specific criteria. (The interjudge reliability [chance corrected agreement, K] for the diagnosis of schizophrenia using an earlier version of RDC criteria with 68 newly admitted psychiatric inpatients at the New York State Psychiatric Institute was .88, which is a thoroughly respectable level of reliability.) It is very likely that the next edition of the American Psychiatric Association's *Diagnostic and Statistical Manual* will contain similar specific criteria.

There are other problems with current psychiatric diagnosis. The recent controversy over whether or not homosexuality per se should be considered a mental disorder highlighted the lack of agreement within the psychiatric profession as to the definition of a mental disorder. A definition has been proposed by Spitzer (Spitzer & Wilson, 1975), but it is not at all clear whether a consensus will develop supporting it.

There are serious problems of validity. Many of the traditional diagnostic categories, such as some of the subtypes of schizophrenia and of major affective illness, and several of the personality disorders, have not been demonstrated to be distinct entities or to be useful for prognosis or treatment assignment. In addition, despite considerable evidence supporting the distinctness of such conditions as schizophrenia and manic-depressive illness, the boundaries separating these conditions from other conditions are certainly not clear. Finally, the categories of the traditional psychiatric nomenclature are of least value when applied to the large numbers of outpatients who are not seriously ill. It is for these patients that a more behaviorally or problem-oriented approach might be particularly useful.

I have not dealt at all with the myriad ways in which psychiatric diagnostic labels can be, and are, misused to hurt patients rather than to help them. This is a problem requiring serious research which, unfortunately, Rosenhan's study does not help illuminate. However, whatever the solutions to that problem, the misuse of psychiatric diagnostic labels is not a sufficient reason to abandon their use because they have been shown to be of value when properly used.

In conclusion, there are serious problems with psychiatric diagnosis, as there are with other medical diagnoses. Recent developments indicate that the reliability of psychiatric diagnosis can be considerably improved. However, even with the poor reliability of current psychiatric diagnosis, it is not so poor that it cannot be an aid in the treatment of the seriously disturbed psychiatric patient. Rosenhan's study, "On Being Sane in Insane Places," proves that pseudopatients are not detected by psychiatrists as having simulated signs of mental illness. This rather unremarkable finding is not relevant to the real problems of the reliability and validity of psychiatric diagnosis and only serves to obscure them. A correct interpretation of his own data contradicts his conclusions. In the setting of a psychiatric hospital, psychiatrists are remarkably able to distinguish the "sane" from the "insane."

NOTES

1. The original article only mentions that the 11 schizophrenics were diagnosed "in remission." Personal communication from D. L. Rosenhan indicates that this also applied to the single pseudopatient diagnosed as manic-depressive psychosis.
2. In personal communication D. L. Rosenhan said that "in remission" referred to a use of that term or one its equivalents, such as recovered or no longer ill.
3. Rosenhan has not identified the hospitals used in this study because of his concern with issues of confidentiality and the potential for ad hominem attack. However, this does make it impossible for anyone at those hospitals to corroborate or challenge his account of how the pseudopatients acted and how they were perceived. The 12 hospitals used in my mini-study were Long Island Jewish–Hillside Medical Center, New York; Massachusetts General Hospital, Massachusetts; St. Elizabeth's Hospital, Washington, D.C.; McLean Hospital, Massachusetts; UCLA, Neuropsychiatric Institute, California; Meyer-Manhattan Hospital (Manhattan State), New York; Vermont State Hospital, Vermont; Medical College of Virginia, Virginia; Emory University Hospital, Georgia; High Point Hospital, New York; Hudson River State Hospital, New York and New York Hospital–Cornell Medical Center, Westchester Division, New York.
4. This was not in the article but was mentioned to me in personal communication by D. L. Rosenhan.
5. For what it is worth, the pseudopatient would have been diagnosed as

"probable" schizophrenia using these criteria because of 1(f). In personal communication, Rosenhan said that when the pseudopatients were asked how frequently the hallucinations occurred, they said, "I don't know." Therefore, Criterion 1(g) is not met.

REFERENCES

American Psychiatric Association. *Diagnostic and statistical manual of mental disorders* (2nd ed.). Washington, D.C.: American Psychiatric Association, 1968.

Cochrane, A. L., & Garland, L. H. Observer error in interpretation of chest films: International investigation. *Lancet*, 1952, *2*, 505–509.

Davies, L. G. Observer variation in reports on electrocardiograms. *British Heart Journal*, 1958, *20*, 153–161.

Feighner, J. P., Robins, E., Guze, S. B., Woodruff, R. A., Winokur, G., & Munoz, R. Diagnostic criteria for use in psychiatric research. *Archives of General Psychiatry*, 1972, *26*, 57–63.

Feinstein, A. *Clinical judgment*. Baltimore, Md.: Williams & Wilkins, 1967.

Fletcher, C. M. Clinical diagnosis of pulmonary emphysema—an experimental study. *Proceedings of the Royal Society of Medicine*, 1952, *45*, 577–584.

Garland, L. H. The problem of observer error. *Bulletin of the New York Academy of Medicine*, 1960, *36*, 570–584.

Hunter, F. M. Letters to the editor. *Science*, 1973, *180*, 361.

Kety, S. S. From rationalization to reason. *American Journal of Psychiatry*, 1974, *131*, 957–963.

Klein, D., & Davis, J. *Diagnosis and drug treatment of psychiatric disorders*. Baltimore, Md.: Williams & Wilkins, 1969.

Letters to the editor. *Science*, 1973, *180*, 356–365.

Markush, R. E., Schaaf, W. E., & Siegel, D. G. The influence of the death certifier on the results of epidemiologic studies. *Journal of the National Medical Association*, 1967, *59*, 105–113.

Rosenhan, D. L. On being sane in insane places. *Science*, 1973, *179*, 250–258. (a)

Rosenhan, D. L. Reply to letters to the editor. *Science*, 1973, *180*, 365–369. (b)

Spitzer, R. L., Endicott, J., & Robins, E. *Research diagnostic criteria*. New York: Biometrics Research, New York State Department of Mental Hygiene, 1974.

Spitzer, R. L., Endicott, J., Robins, E., Kuriansky, J., & Gurland, B. Preliminary report of the reliability of research diagnostic criteria applied to psychiatric case records. In A. Sudilofsky, B. Beer, & S. Gershon (Eds.), *Predictability in psychopharmacology*. New York: Raven Press, 1975.

Spitzer, R. L., & Fleiss, J. L. A reanalysis of the reliability of psychiatric diagnosis. *British Journal of Psychiatry*, 1974, *125*, 341–347.

Spitzer, R. L., & Wilson, P. T. Nosology and the official psychiatric nomenclature. In A. Freedman & H. Kaplan (Eds.), *Comprehensive textbook of psychiatry*. New York: Williams & Wilkins, 1975.

Yerushalmy, J. Statistical problems in assessing methods of medical diagnosis, with special reference to X-ray techniques. *Public Health Reports*, 1947, *62*, 1432–1449.

DISCUSSION

This chapter provides one of the very few cases in this book in which the question that serves as the chapter's title can be answered in a reasonably straightforward fashion: no. Robert Spitzer's rebuttal clearly points out that mental health professionals can, in at least some cases, differentiate the mentally ill from the non–mentally ill. (As Spitzer points out, however, the terms *sane* and *insane* used by Rosenhan refer technically to legal, rather than psychiatric, concepts.) The fact that in all but one case David Rosenhan's pseudopatients were discharged with diagnoses of schizophrenia in remission strongly suggests that the mental health professionals who had been observing the pseudopatients' behavior following admission were aware that they had not been behaving in a grossly pathological fashion. Regrettably, this fact is often neglected in discussions of Rosenhan's findings.

Spitzer's arguments are compelling in another respect. Because the diagnosis of schizophrenia in remission is apparently very uncommon, Rosenhan's results paradoxically imply that the psychiatrists who made this diagnosis had performed a difficult task with nearly perfect "reliability." (I place quotation marks around this term because the pseudopatients were not diagnosed by multiple raters.) Simply put, these psychiatrists successfully recognized that the individuals who exhibited symptoms of a disorder that rarely disappears completely had in fact experienced "remission." Thus, far from indicting diagnostic reliability, Rosenhan's study suggests that mental health professionals can actually distinguish psychotic from nonpsychotic individuals with surprisingly high levels of accuracy.

Another thoughtful critique of Rosenhan's article, by Theodore Millon (1975), makes a further telling point concerning Rosenhan's conclusions. As Millon notes, the admitting officer in a psychiatric institution can make one of two errors: type 1 or type 2. A type 1 error involves calling an ill person healthy; a type 2 error involves calling a healthy person ill. The admitting clinicians in Rosenhan's study uniformly committed type 2 errors. Although Rosenhan admits that type 2 errors are often justifiable in medical diagnosis, he appears to deny that they are justifiable in psychiatric diagnosis. But what Rosenhan's analysis overlooks, according to Millon, is that there are good medical, legal, and social reasons for mental health professionals to err on the side of type 2 errors, particularly in the case of a disorder as serious as schizophrenia. Schizophrenia is associated with a markedly increased risk of suicide, depression, substance abuse (Goodwin & Guze, 1989), and perhaps violence. Thus, a failure to make this diagnosis when appropriate could result in substantial harm to both the patient and others. In assigning initial diagnoses of schizophrenia, argues Millon, the psychiatrists in Rosenhan's study were thus exercising good scientific and professional judgment.

Do these criticisms imply that Rosenhan's paper was not worth publishing? No, they do not, for at least two reasons. First, Rosenhan's observations dramatically underscore a potential hazard of diagnostic labels: their capacity to become self-fulfilling. As Spitzer observes, the example in which the details of a pseudopatient's discharge summary were gerrymandered to fit his ostensible psychiatric status provide a good illustration of this danger. This case provides a sorely needed reminder of the human mind's propensity to rearrange or reframe facts to achieve consistency with preexisting beliefs. Such a tendency is probably no less rampant among mental health experts than among nonexperts, and it helps to explain why the editors of psychological and psychiatric journals have increasingly come to insist that researchers remain "blind" to (unaware of) the diagnostic status of their subjects.

All that said, however, it would be a mistake to interpret Rosenhan's results as a resounding affirmation of labeling theory. For one thing, if the effects of psychiatric labels (like *schizophrenic*) and global psychological judgments (like *mentally ill*) are so powerful, why were the genuine psychiatric patients apparently not swayed by them? It seems likely that the pseudopatients' actual behaviors overpowered whatever adverse effects the labels assigned to them may have exerted on the perceptions of observers. Observers may in some cases be influenced by labels, but the capacity of these labels to affect the interpretation of behavior probably has its limits.

A second intriguing point raised by Rosenhan's findings concerns what Ulric Neisser (1973) has referred to as the "irreversibility" of diagnostic labels. In his comment on Rosenhan's study, Neisser reminds us that all the pseudopatients were ultimately diagnosed as in remission; a discharge diagnosis of normal or of "normal; initial diagnosis in error" was not made in any case. It is almost as though the diagnostician can never be wrong, according to Neisser. If the initial diagnosis is schizophrenia and subsequent behavior confirms that diagnosis, the patient is discharged with "schizophrenia"; but if the initial diagnosis is schizophrenia and subsequent behavior contradicts that diagnosis, the patient is discharged with "schizophrenia in remission." Such "heads I win, tails you lose" reasoning is potentially dangerous, asserts Neisser, because it effectively immunizes diagnostic practices from disproof. This point has probably not received sufficient attention in discussions of Rosenhan's findings.

But even here the picture may be more complex than first meets the eye. The fact is that the diagnosis of schizophrenia in remission does communicate useful information, because schizophrenia tends to be a chronic disorder that often reappears following periods of remission. Thus, such a diagnosis is usually more informative than a simple diagnosis of normal, because only the former diagnosis indicates that the patient is at increased risk for subsequent schizophrenic episodes. Similarly, a diagnosis of cancer in remission is usually more informative than a diagnosis of normal, because only the former diagnosis alerts physicians to the heightened probability of a reoccurrence. Psychiatrists' unwillingness to reverse a diagnosis, although perhaps sometimes a self-serving refusal to admit error, can also be viewed as a prudent and calculated diagnostic decision to err on the side of patient safety.

QUESTIONS TO STIMULATE DISCUSSION

1. From the standpoint of research design, are there features of Rosenhan's study that seem wanting? Can you propose a design that would provide a better test of his central hypotheses?
2. Rosenhan suggests that the pseudopatients should have been given initial diagnoses of "hallucinating" rather than "schizophrenia." Do you agree? What do you view as the advantages and disadvantages of this suggestion?
3. What do you suspect would happen if Rosenhan's study were "replicated" in a series of medical hospitals, with 12 pseudopatients all falsely complaining of severe chest pain? What findings would you predict, and what would be the implications of these findings for the practice of medical diagnosis?
4. Rosenhan states, "The fact that the patients often recognized normality when staff did not raises important questions" (p. 252). What conclusions, if any, can you draw from this observation? What questions raised by this observation remain unanswered?

SUGGESTIONS FOR FURTHER READING

Braginsky, B. M., Braginsky, D. D., & Ring, K. (1969). *Methods of madness: The mental hospital as a last resort.* New York: Holt, Rinehart & Winston.

This is a classic work on the social psychology of hospitalized psychiatric patients. The authors argue that psychiatric patients are no different from "normals" in their pursuit of pleasure and comfort or in the methods they use to obtain these goals. Note the double meaning of *resort* in the book's title.

Matarazzo, J. D. (1983). The reliability of psychiatric and psychological diagnosis. *Clinical Psychology Review, 3,* 103–145. (Reprinted in abridged form in Hooley, J. M., Neale, J. M., & Davison, G. C. [1989]. *Readings in abnormal psychology.* New York: Wiley).

Matarazzo provides a comprehensive review of the history of diagnostic judgments and of recent studies of diagnostic reliability. He concludes that the reliabilities of most psychopathological conditions are now quite high and that the use of explicit diagnostic criteria has contributed substantially to this improved state of affairs.

Millon, T. (1975). Reflections on Rosenhan's "On being sane in insane places." *Journal of Abnormal Psychology, 84,* 456–461. (See also critiques of Rosenhan's article by B. Weiner and S. Crown in the same issue, as well as the letters in the issue of *Science* immediately following Rosenhan's article.)
Millon criticizes the methodology of Rosenhan's study and argues that it provides a grossly inadequate test of Rosenhan's central hypothesis. He also takes issue with Rosenhan's proposal to substitute labeling of specific behaviors for psychiatric diagnosis, arguing that Rosenhan failed to differentiate labeling (which simply describes the patient's behavior) from diagnosis (which helps to explain the patient's behavior).

Rosenhan, D. L. (1975). The contextual nature of psychiatric diagnosis. *Journal of Abnormal Psychology, 84,* 462–474.
Rosenhan responds to his critics, arguing that situational context plays a potent role in psychiatric diagnosis. In addition, he disputes many of Spitzer's claims (including the claim that *in remission* is essentially equivalent to *sane*) and reemphasizes the "stickiness" of diagnostic labels.

Scheff, T. J. (1984). *Being mentally ill: A sociological theory.* Chicago: Aldine.
Scheff presents his sociological model of labeling. He contends that the label of mental illness is applied to individuals who exhibit chronic and severe violations of implicit or unwritten societal norms ("primary or residual deviance"). Once labeled, such individuals internalize these labels and begin to adopt the role of the mentally ill individual ("secondary deviance").

Spitzer, R. L., & Fleiss, J. L. (1974). A re-analysis of the reliability of psychiatric diagnosis. *British Journal of Psychiatry, 125,* 341–347.
The authors reanalyze the major pre–DSM-III reliability studies using indices of chance-corrected diagnostic agreement. They conclude that the reliabilities for most diagnostic categories are satisfactory but in need of improvement. They suggest that the use of explicit diagnostic criteria, in conjunction with structured psychiatric interviews, is necessary to improve reliability.

REFERENCES

Goodwin, D. W., & Guze, S. B. (1989). *Psychiatric diagnosis* (4th ed.). Oxford: Oxford University Press.

Millon, T. (1975). Reflections on Rosenhan's "On being sane in insane places." *Journal of Abnormal Psychology, 84,* 456–461.

Neisser, U. (1973). Reversibility of psychiatric diagnoses. *Science, 180,* 1116.

Scheff, T. J. (1984). *Being mentally ill: A sociological theory.* Chicago: Aldine.

CHAPTER

3

Was DSM-III an important advance?

PRO	Spitzer, R. L., Williams, J. B. W., & Skodol, A. E. (1980). DSM-III: The major achievements and an overview. *American Journal of Psychiatry, 137*, 151–164.
CON	Vaillant, G. E. (1984). The disadvantages of *DSM-III* outweigh its advantages. *American Journal of Psychiatry, 141*, 542–545.

OVERVIEW OF THE CONTROVERSY: Robert L. Spitzer, Janet B. W. Williams, and Andrew E. Skodol review the major achievements of DSM-III, including its definition of mental disorder, use of explicit diagnostic criteria, emphasis on reliability, and provision of multiple axes. They conclude that DSM-III represents a substantial improvement over previous systems of psychiatric classification. George E. Vaillant argues that DSM-III largely ignores cross-cultural considerations, is oversimplified, mixes classifications based on states and on traits, fails to appreciate the distinction between disease and symptom, and emphasizes reliability at the expense of validity.

CONTEXT OF THE PROBLEM

During the 1960s and 1970s, the American system of psychiatric classification and diagnosis was under siege from numerous directions. Although the second edition of the American Psychiatric Association's Diagnostic and Statistical Manual of Mental Disorders (DSM-II), which appeared in 1968, was almost surely a marked improvement over its rather vague and sketchy predecessor (DSM-I), significant problems with most psychiatric categories remained. Psychiatric diagnosis tended to be plagued by mediocre and in some cases downright abysmal levels of interrater reliability (Spitzer & Fleiss, 1974); even highly trained clinicians frequently failed to reach adequate agreement on the diagnoses of a set of patients. As a consequence, many outsiders questioned the scientific pretensions of psychiatry and began to raise serious concerns regarding the enterprise of psychiatric diagnosis.

In part, these disappointing levels of reliability were probably due to the fact that DSM-II and similar systems provided diagnosticians with quite global, impressionistic, and often imprecise descriptions of each syndrome. For example, for the diagnosis of asthenic personality (which has since been retired from the diagnostic nomenclature, with few apparent mourners), DSM-II stated only that "this behavior pattern is characterized by easy fatigability, low energy level, lack of enthusiasm, marked incapacity for enjoyment, and oversensitivity to physical and emotional stress" (p. 43). One can easily imagine why even trained diagnosticians might disagree regarding the presence or absence of such a diagnosis. For example, what constitutes a lack of enthusiasm? (Indeed, you might be nervously wondering whether you would be judged to be lacking in enthusiasm.) How does one infer whether an individual is unenthusiastic? Where does one draw the line between garden-variety apathy and a clinically significant absence of enthusiasm? Moreover, must patients be unenthusiastic to be given a diagnosis of asthenic personality? What if they possess all the other features of this diagnosis but are highly enthusiastic? The criteria for many of the other disorders in DSM-II suffered from similar ambiguity.

To make matters worse, DSM-II implicitly embraced a particular theoretical stance—Freudian psychoanalysis—in its descriptions of many diagnoses. Although psychoanalysis certainly has fervent adherents, DSM-II's adoption of this paradigm effectively excluded many clinicians who do not believe it to be a useful model of the **etiology** (causes and origins) of mental disorders. For example, in its description of paranoid schizophrenia, DSM-II stated that the patient with this condition "uses the [defense] mechanism of projection, which ascribes to others characteristics he cannot accept in himself" (p. 34). Perhaps so, but how is the clinician who does not believe in defense mechanisms (and many do not) to make use of this information?

In response to these and other problems, the American Psychiatric Association appointed a task force, headed by Robert Spitzer, to revise the DSM. DSM-III, which was finally published in 1980 after a lengthy process of review and revision, instituted a number of daring changes in the diagnostic system. To address the problem of reliability, DSM-III specified explicit criteria, as well as detailed and precise algorithms (decision rules), for virtually all diagnostic categories. Thus, DSM-III gave clinicians more guidance, and less leeway, in diagnostic decision making. DSM-III also mandated that patients be described along a series of **axes**, or dimensions of functioning, that included not only their psychiatric disorder (Axes I and II), but also their medical status (Axis III), recent history of psychosocial stressors (Axis IV), and level of functioning (Axis V). In addition, DSM-III eschewed any particular theoretical stance in favor of a purely descriptive system. The goal was to give clinicians of greatly varying theoretical persuasions a manual they could use with equal ease and comfort.

Several years before its publication, DSM-III set off a firestorm of controversy that has yet to subside fully. Did the innovations introduced in DSM-III truly mark an improvement in psychiatric diagnosis? Or in their fervent quest to make psychiatric diagnosis more rigorous and "scientific" did the developers of DSM-III deprive the diagnostic system of much of its richness, theoretical depth, and thus validity?

You may wonder why, given the fact that DSM-III-R appeared in 1987 and DSM-IV in 1994, I have elected to focus on the controversies surrounding DSM-III. I have two reasons: (1) DSM-III was probably the most significant development in psychiatric classification and diagnosis in this century, and (2) because both DSM-III-R and DSM-IV share all of the principal features of DSM-III (such as its atheoretical stance, provision of explicit diagnostic criteria, and multiaxial system), virtually all the defenses and criticisms of DSM-III discussed in the readings in this chapter apply to its two revisions.

THE CONTROVERSY
Spitzer, Williams, and Skodol vs. Vaillant

Spitzer, Williams, and Skodol

Robert Spitzer, Janet Williams, and Andrew Skodol begin by summarizing the major achievements of DSM-III. They argue that the participation of a large number of organizations and researchers in the development of DSM-III made the decision-making process more objective, open to criticism, and less politicized than was the case with earlier editions of the manual. They contend that DSM-III's reasonably explicit definition of mental disorder—a syndrome associated with either significant distress or disability—helps to resolve a number of knotty and controversial issues, such as the question of whether to include homosexuality in the diagnostic nomenclature. Spitzer and his colleagues also describe some of the other new features of DSM-III—such as its use of operational diagnostic criteria, its emphasis on reliability, and its multiple axes—and assert that these features represent a major advance in psychiatric classification. Finally, they review in detail the principal diagnostic categories in DSM-III and discuss the rationale for the revisions in each of these categories.

Vaillant

George Vaillant contends that DSM-III, although fulfilling an understandable desire for increased diagnostic rigor, is a fatally flawed document. He cites five major shortcomings of DSM-III. First, DSM-III is "parochial" in that it largely neglects differing cross-cultural manifestations of psychopathological syndromes. Second, DSM-III is concrete and overly simplistic in its conceptualization of psychopathology. Third, DSM-III fails to account adequately for developmental changes in the expression of psychopathological syndromes. Fourth, DSM-III, by ignoring etiology, confuses underlying diseases with reactions to those diseases. Finally, DSM-III has paradoxically increased reliability and decreased validity.

KEY CONCEPTS AND TERMS

ego-dystonic homosexuality Category included for the first time in DSM-III but deleted from DSM-III-R that allowed homosexual individuals to be diagnosed as mentally ill if they were disturbed by their sexual preference.

homeostatic mechanism Psychological or physiological mechanism within the organism that tends to maintain constancy and equilibrium. Psychodynamic theorists contend that, just as many physical signs and symptoms are a product of homeostatic mechanisms (for example, fever), many psychopathological symptoms are a product of such mechanisms.

multiaxial system Diagnostic system requiring clinicians to describe each patient along several axes, or dimensions of functioning. DSM-III and its two successors contain five axes.

state versus trait Distinction between relatively transient and short-lived emotional experiences (states) and relatively stable and enduring predispositions (traits). State fluctuations can greatly complicate the assessment and diagnosis of traits.

PREVIEW QUESTIONS

1. What do Spitzer, Williams, and Skodol view as the major advantages of DSM-III over DSM-II and previous psychiatric classification systems?
2. How does DSM-III define *mental disorder*? According to Spitzer, Williams, and Skodol, how does this definition help to resolve the controversies regarding the classification of conditions as mental disorders?
3. What are the five axes of DSM-III? According to Spitzer, Williams, and Skodol, what are the advantages of a multiaxial system for psychiatric diagnosis?
4. What does Vaillant mean when he says that DSM-III is parochial?
5. In what ways, according to Vaillant, is DSM-III adynamic?
6. How can DSM-III have simultaneously increased reliability and decreased validity?

ROBERT L. SPITZER, JANET B. W. WILLIAMS, & ANDREW E. SKODOL

DSM-III: The major achievements and an overview

Then the diagnostic team come in an' diagnozzles the whole she-bang!

Di-agnostic? . . . Lessee . . . agnostic means "one what don't know" . . . an' di is a Greek prefix denotin' twofold—so the di-agnostic team don't know twice as much as an ordinary agnostic . . . right?

—POGO, *NEW YORK POST*, AUGUST 1, 1966

The reader of this article could not have escaped, during the last five years, reading or otherwise hearing about the development of *DSM-III*, the third edition of the American Psychiatric Association's *Diagnostic and Statistical Manual of Mental Disorders* (published in 1980). Surely, no classification of mental disorders has received such attention and has stirred such controversy before its official adoption. In the first part of this article the authors, battle-weary at the time of this writing and in the final throes of reviewing galleys and page proofs, describe the major achievements of *DSM-III* (the content and the process of its development), and in the second part we will present an overview of *DSM-III*—with its departures from *DSM-II* and the reasons for these changes.

This article will not attempt to present much of the material that is covered in the introduction to *DSM-III*, such as the goals of the Task Force on Nomenclature and Statistics, and some of the basic concepts, for example, the generally atheoretical (descriptive) approach taken toward defining and classifying the disorders. Whereas this article was written by the authors alone, without the help of colleagues, the introduction to *DSM-III* was written by the senior author (with the help of the second author) but was extensively reviewed and edited by well over 50 colleagues from the task force, the Assembly Liaison Committee on *DSM-III*, the Council on Research and Development, the Reference Committee, and the Board of Trustees. Because of this help we believe that what is said in the introduction to *DSM-III* cannot be said any better, and we urge all readers of this article to read it.

THE MAJOR ACHIEVEMENTS

DSM-III, both in its process of development and its content, differs in numerous ways from its predecessor, *DSM-II*, and from other official classifications of mental disorders, such as the ninth revision of the *International Classification of Diseases* (*ICD-9*), and its Clinical Modification (*ICD-9-CM*) for use in this country. What follows is

---

SOURCE: *American Journal of Psychiatry, 137*, pp. 151–164, 1980.

a discussion of what we regard as some of the major achievements of *DSM-III*.

The Process

DSM-III was five years in development, two years more than had initially been anticipated. This extension—granted because of the heated controversy that surrounded the project—was necessary to work out solutions to many of the problematic aspects of drafts of the document. Drafts of *DSM-III* were prepared by members of the advisory committees and reviewed by members of the Task Force on Nomenclature and Statistics, whose job it was to guide the development of *DSM-III*. This process involved over 100 individuals with expertise in either specific areas of the classification (e.g., the Advisory Committee on Psychosexual Disorders) or in psychiatric nosology in general (the Task Force on Nomenclature and Statistics).

Throughout the development of *DSM-III* the evolving document was reviewed by components of the American Psychiatric Association [(APA)], such as a liaison committee appointed by the Assembly, and committees appointed by various national organizations, such as the American Psychological Association and the American Psychoanalytic Association. At some time each of these groups raised serious objections (to put it mildly) to the task force's approach.

The task force made every effort to be responsive to these groups and in many instances eventually reversed its position on a particular issue. For example, in 1976 the task force planned to include in *DSM-III* an explicit statement that the mental disorders in *DSM-III* are "medical" disorders. This led to a bitter exchange of letters with the American Psychological Association, which challenged the basis for designating the *DSM-III* disorders as "medical." The American Psychiatric Association responded by noting that it had never attempted to tell the American Psychological Association what constituted a "psychological" disorder, and therefore. . . . After much soul searching, the task force concluded that the purpose of *DSM-III* was to classify and describe mental disorders and not to clarify the relationship between psychiatry and medicine, the reason why the task force initially wished to include such a statement. With the removal of this statement (although there are, of course, references to the fact that the *DSM-III* classification is a subset of the *ICD-9-CM* classification), the American Psychological Association liaison committee on *DSM-III* was able to evaluate *DSM-III* as a scientific document and concluded that *DSM-III* represents "substantive advances in the 'state of the art' of psychopathologic diagnosis" (1).

In addition, drafts of *DSM-III* were scrutinized and reviewed by individual members of the mental health professions, many of whom made valuable suggestions for changes. Within the limitation of an imperfect filing system, every critique of *DSM-III* (which numbered in the hundreds) was considered and personally responded to with a letter from either the senior or second author.

A major achievement in the process of the development of *DSM-III* was the involvement of over 800 clinicians in a series of field trials. These began in December 1976, using those portions of the draft that were then available. The final field trial was a two-year National Institute of Mental Health–sponsored project that used several versions of the completed draft and involved over 400 clinicians in more than 120 facilities across the country and approximately 80 clinicians in private practice. As a result of these field trials, continual revisions were made in the classification and text of *DSM-III*. This is the first time that a classification of mental disorders has been attempted and modified in a systematic and comprehensive manner before its formal adoption and use.

We regard the involvement of such a large number of professional organizations and colleagues in the development of *DSM-III* as a major achievement that contrasts sharply with the process of development of *DSM-II* (published in 1968). It is significant that, even in those controversies that became highly politicized, such as the classification of "neurotic" disorders, the final decisions, after considerable debate and attempts at compromise, were always made by the experts who had been given the task of developing the document. In other words, this process was successful in avoiding the appointment of a committee, separate from the task force and its advisory committees, to rewrite parts of the manual to ensure its acceptability to the membership of APA. Of even greater significance, a referendum of the membership to change some aspect of *DSM-III* was avoided, although only narrowly so on the issue of the classification of neurotic disorders. No one wanted to repeat the scene of the general membership voting on a presumably "scientific" issue, as was done in 1973 on the issue of the elimination of homosexuality from the *DSM-II* classification.

Consensus on Controversial Diagnostic Categories

The process described above made it possible for consensus to be reached on many controversial diagnostic categories. A few are mentioned below.

A confrontation between the task force and various APA components over the issue of the classification of neurotic disorders was avoided by the task force's proposal that the term "neurotic disorders" be used in a strictly descriptive sense and distinguished from the term "neurotic process," and by the task force's acceptance of a suggestion made by an ad hoc committee of the Board of Trustees to include the names of the *DSM-II* neuroses in parentheses after the corresponding *DSM-III* terms.

Although the category of Borderline Personality or Borderline State is of great importance to many clinicians, it has had confusing multiple meanings, and before work on *DSM-III*, it was never included in an official classification of mental disorders. Despite the task force's initial reluctance to include this category because of the difficulty in defining the boundaries of the concept and the admittedly ambiguous name of the category, the results of a study (discussed later in this article) that involved over 800 members of APA were used to describe the category and to distinguish it from what later was called Schizotypal Personality Disorder. That an impressive degree of consensus was reached in our field on this difficult category is attested to by the fact that such major investigators in this area as Drs. John Gunderson and Otto Kernberg are relatively satisfied with the way in which *DSM-III* defines Borderline Personality Disorder.

The classification of so-called "psychophysiological" or "psychosomatic" disorders has not been satisfactory for many reasons (discussed below). With the help of an advisory committee of psychiatrists with a special interest in liaison psychiatry, and with help from members of the American Psychosomatic Society, it was possible to reach a consensus as to how the classification of mental disorders could enable a clinician to indicate the role of psychological factors in the initiation or exacerbation of a physical condition: the *DSM-III* category of Psychological Factors Affecting Physical Condition.

It should not surprise the reader to be told that consensus was not *always* reached, and in a few instances a formal vote had to be taken with the majority opinion determining the outcome. Several noteworthy examples come to mind. The task force believed that it was important to be able to identify, within major depressive episodes, those with what has been referred to as "endogenous" features. However, the term endogenous was judged unsuitable because of its historical etiological meanings, which imply the absence of a reactive component. In a search for an alternative term, the task force and a group of "affective mavens" resurrected and chose "melancholia" as the most suitable term from a larger number of choices. A significant minority could not be swayed from their view that this term was inappropriate.

Another example where consensus could not be reached involved the notorious *DSM-II* category of Sexual Orientation Disorder, which replaced Homosexuality when it was removed from the classification in 1973. Many of those who championed the 1973 change were strongly opposed to the inclusion in *DSM-III* of any category that specifically was limited to homosexuals. This controversy, which resulted in over 180 pages of correspondence, could not be resolved within the Advisory Committee on Psychosexual Disorders and eventually had to be resolved by the task force. Again, a significant minority within the advisory committee and the task force believe that the final solution, the inclusion of the *DSM-III* category of Ego-dystonic Homosexuality, was a serious mistake. (The final definition of the category, however, answered many of the major objections that had been raised to initial drafts of the category.)

The *DSM-III* approach to defining Schizoaffective Disorder is unique in that eventually a consensus could only be reached on the inability to reach a consensus on a specific definition. Thus Schizoaffective Disorder is the only specific category in *DSM-III* without diagnostic criteria. The task force accepted the recommendation of a special committee that it appointed to review the category that there was no definition of the condition that seemed acceptable to most clinicians at the present time.

DSM-III Definition of Mental Disorder

Since a frequent charge made by critics of nosology is the absence of a definition of mental disorder, the task force was initially eager to include within *DSM-III* such a definition. However, despite several attempts early in the development of *DSM-III* to develop such a definition, none that was proposed was acceptable (2, 3). However, in the final months of *DSM-III's* development it was possible to draft a definition that was acceptable not only to the task force but to the various APA components that oversaw the development of *DSM-III*. Every word and comma was carefully examined, resulting in the final definition that was included in both the introduction and the glossary of technical terms:

> In *DSM-III*, a mental disorder is conceptualized as a clinically significant behavioral or psychologic syndrome or pattern that occurs in an individual and that is typically associated with either a painful symptom (distress) or impairment in one or more important areas of functioning (disability). In addition, there is an inference that there is a behavioral, psychologic or biologic dysfunction and that the disturbance is not only in the relationship between the individual and society. When the disturbance is limited to a conflict between an individual and society, this may represent social deviance, which may or may not be commendable, but is not by itself a mental disorder.

This definition provides basic concepts that were useful in the many decisions that the task force had to make regarding what conditions to include in the classification and how to define the boundaries of the various disorders. It does not pretend to offer precise boundaries between "disorder" and "normality."

The concepts contained in this definition were helpful in deciding that it was not necessary to require distress before a psychosexual dysfunction, such as Inhibited Sexual Excitement (frigidity, impotence), would be diagnosed. Similarly, it was helpful in deciding that the diagnosis of such Paraphilias (Sexual Deviations in *DSM-II*) as Fetishism and Exhibitionism also need not require distress. The task force concluded that inability to experience the normative sexual response cycle (as in frigidity or impotence) represented a *disability* in the *important area* of sexual functioning, whether or not the individual was distressed by the symptom. The same logic applied to the requirement or preference for inanimate objects (as in Fetishism) or bizarre acts (as in Exhibitionism) for sexual arousal. (Many expected that the logic of the 1973 decision to delete homosexuality from the classification of mental disorders would lead the task force on *DSM-III* to define Necrophilia as a disorder only if the individual complained of the symptom!)

Does this definition help to clarify the issues in the controversy as to whether or not all or some cases of homosexuality should be regarded as a mental disorder? With this definition it becomes clear (at least to us) that the issue is not one of *factual* matters about homosexuality, such as whether or not certain familial patterns predispose to the development of the condition, but rather a *value* judgment about the importance of heterosexual functionings. On the one hand, the gay activists and their supporters argue that homosexuality represents no impairment in an "important area of functioning" since *sexual* functioning is unimpaired. They refuse to accept *hetero*sexual functioning as the norm. On the other hand, those who argue that exclusive homosexuality always should be conceptualized as a mental disorder believe that *hetero*sexual functioning represents an "important" area of functioning in its own right.

The *DSM-III* position (and the 1973 decision) can be viewed as acknowledging that at the present time mental health professionals are unable to agree on whether it is *hetero*sexual or *sexual* functioning that should be regarded as an "important area of functioning," so that inability to function in that area justifies the designation of mental disorder. Therefore, in *DSM-III* only those homosexuals distressed by their inability to function heterosexually are classified as having a mental disorder (Ego-dystonic Homosexuality). In other words, in this controversial condition it is the *patient* who judges whether or not the absence of his or her heterosexual functioning represents impairment in an important area of functioning.

Diagnostic Criteria

Diagnostic criteria appear at the end of the text describing each specific *DSM-III* diagnosis. These criteria are offered as useful guides for making the diagnosis, since it has been demonstrated that the use of such criteria enhances diagnostic agreement among clinicians. In *DSM-I* and *DSM-II*, as well as in *ICD-9*, the clinician is to a large degree on his or her own in defining the content and boundaries of the diagnostic categories, since explicit detailed definitions are not provided.

We are not alone in believing that the incorporation into *DSM-III* of diagnostic criteria is a significant achievement. Alvan Feinstein, an authority on medical nosology, made the following remarks while discussing the inclusion of diagnostic criteria in *DSM-III* (4):

> The production of operational identifications has been a pioneering, unique advance in nosology. . . . In the field of diagnostic nosology, the establishment of operational criteria represents a breakthrough that is as obvious, necessary, fundamental, and important as the corresponding breakthrough in obstetrics and surgery when Semmelweiss, Oliver Wendell Holmes, and, later on, Lord Lister, demanded that obstetricians and surgeons wash their hands before operating on the human body. . . . The absence of such criteria is what has made the rest of the ICD (International Classification of Diseases) such a shambles because of the inconsistent variations with which the nomenclature is applied. (pp. 194–195)

More recently Robin M. Murray, in an article in *Lancet* titled "A Reappraisal of American Psychiatry" (5), noted,

> The incorporation of operational definitions into the DSM-III diagnostic manual gives the U.S.A. an everyday classificatory system potentially superior to those in use elsewhere in the world. (p. 256)

Diagnostic Reliability

The need for reliability, that is, agreement among clinicians on assigning diagnoses to patients, is universally acknowledged. Studies of the reliability of psychiatric diagnosis using *DSM-I* and *DSM-II* indicated generally poor or only fair reliability for most of the major diagnostic categories (6). In the *DSM-III* field trials over 450 clinicians participated in the largest reliability study ever done, involving independent evaluations of nearly 800 patients—adults, adolescents, and children. For most of the diagnostic classes the reliability was quite good, and in general it was much higher than that previously achieved with *DSM-I* and *DSM-II* (7).

Multiaxial System

A multiaxial system for psychiatric evaluation provides for the systematic evaluation of an individual's condition in terms of several variables, or axes, that are conceptualized and rated as quasi-independent of each other. The potential advantages of such a system include comprehensiveness and the recording of nondiagnostic data that are valuable in understanding possible etiological factors and in treatment planning and prognosis. Although many multiaxial systems have been proposed (8), none has come into widespread clinical use.

There are five axes in the *DSM-III* multiaxial classification; each individual should be evaluated on each axis. The first three axes constitute the official diagnostic assessment:

Axis I: Clinical Syndromes
Conditions Not Attributable to a Mental Disorder That Are a Focus of Attention or Treatment (V Codes)
Additional Codes

Axis II: Personality Disorders
Specific Developmental Disorders

Axis III: Physical Disorders and Conditions

Axes IV and V are available for use in special clinical and research settings and provide information supplementing the official *DSM-III* diagnoses (Axes I, II, and III).

Axis IV: Severity of Psychosocial Stressors
Axis V: Highest Level of Adaptive Functioning Past Year

The experience of clinicians using this multiaxial system in the *DSM-III* field trials demonstrated that it was possible to achieve at least fair reliability for Axis IV and quite good reliability for Axis V (9). Furthermore, despite the greater demand placed on the clinician by the multiaxial system, the vast majority of field trial participants indicated their belief that the *DSM-III* multiaxial system is a useful addition to the traditional diagnostic evaluation.

DSM-III: AN OVERVIEW[1]

Each of the 17 major diagnostic classes in *DSM-III* follows, with a discussion of the corresponding *DSM-II* categories and the reasons for the changes.

Disorders Usually First Evident in Infancy, Childhood, or Adolescence

The *DSM-III* classification begins with disorders that are usually first evident in infancy, childhood, or adolescence. Adults will occasionally be given diagnoses from this class, and children and adolescents will sometimes be given diagnoses from outside of this class. In *DSM-II* these disorders were limited to children. There are more than four times as many categories in this section as there were in the childhood section of *DSM-II*, reflecting a great increase in knowledge in this area. The diagnoses in this *DSM-III* class can be divided into five major groups based on the predominant area of disturbance: *intellectual, behavioral, emotional, physical,* and *developmental.*

There is only one category in the *intellectual* group: Mental Retardation. This diagnosis is made if an individual before the age of 18 shows significantly subaverage general intellectual functioning with concurrent deficits in adaptive behavior. This category no longer includes individuals with IQs above 70 who previously were given the label of Borderline Mental Retardation, since the large majority of these persons do not have marked impairment in adaptive behavior (10). *DSM-III* includes Borderline Intellectual Functioning as a V code for Conditions Not Attributable to a Mental Disorder because such a condition may be a focus of attention or treatment (11). Etiological physical conditions that in *DSM-II* were designated in the fourth digit are listed in *DSM-III* on Axis III. The fifth digit in the *DSM-III* diagnostic code for Mental Retardation permits the clinician to indicate the presence or absence of behavioral symptoms associated with the retardation that, while not due to another mental disorder, may be the primary focus of attention or treatment. Examples of such symptoms include aggressive or suicidal behavior.

The *behavioral* group has two categories: Attention Deficit Disorder and Conduct Disorder. In the past Attention Deficit Disorder was often called Minimal Brain Dysfunction, and in *DSM-II* it was called Hyperkinetic Reaction of Childhood. The term minimal brain dysfunction is based on unsubstantiated assumptions of altered brain function (12). The *DSM-III* term, Attention Deficit Disorder with Hyperactivity, is used because attentional difficulties are prominent and virtually always present in hyperkinetic children. The essential features of Attention Deficit Disorder are signs of developmentally inappropriate inattention and impulsivity. When hyperactivity is absent, this is indicated in the fifth digit. In addition, some adults who as children had Attention Deficit Disorder with Hyperactivity continue to have attentional difficulties (but no hyperactivity) as adults (13, 14). These are classified as a residual type.

Conduct Disorder is characterized by a repetitive and persistent pattern of aggressive or nonaggressive conduct in which either the basic rights of others or major age-appropriate societal norms or rules are violated. *DSM-III* divides Conduct Disorder into four types. There is an aggressive-nonaggressive distinction, based on the obvious difference in clinical picture, which has implications for management and may be predictive of adult antisocial behavior (15). The socialized-undersocialized dichotomy also is relevant to treatment planning and may also have prognostic significance, although this remains controversial (16). The *DSM-II* categories of Runaway Reaction of Childhood, Unsocialized Aggressive Reaction of Childhood, and Group Delinquent Reaction of Childhood are all subsumed within the *DSM-III* category of Conduct Disorder.

The *emotional* group of childhood disorders includes a large number of diagnoses under the subclasses of Anxiety Disorders of Childhood or Adolescence and Other Disorders of Infancy, Childhood, or Adolescence. There were relatively few *DSM-II* diagnoses that covered these kinds of difficulties in children. Withdrawing Reaction of Childhood is now divided into Avoidant Disorder of Childhood or Adolescence and Schizoid Disorder of Childhood or Adolescence based on whether or not there is a defect in the motivation and capacity for emotional involvement (Schizoid) or a fear of, but desire for, contact with strangers (Avoidant). Overanxious Reaction of Childhood continues as Overanxious Disorder. By including Separation Anxiety Disorder (17, 18), Elective Mutism (19), and Identity Disorder (20), well-recognized clinical syndromes have been added to the classification. Reactive Attachment Disorder of Infancy has been described in the literature under a variety of names including "failure to thrive" (21). Oppositional Disorder was a diagnosis first included in the classification of childhood disorders prepared by the Group for the Advancement of Psychiatry (22).

The *physical* disorders include Eating Disorders, Stereotyped Movement Disorders, and Other Disorders with Physical Manifestations such as Stuttering,

Functional Enuresis, and sleep disturbances. The Eating Disorders (Anorexia Nervosa, Bulimia, Pica, and Rumination Disorder of Infancy) correspond to the *DSM-II* diagnosis of Special Symptoms, Feeding Disturbance, and are described separately because of different clinical features, course, and treatment implications (23). The *DSM-II* diagnosis of Tic is also elaborated in the *DSM-III* category Stereotyped Movement Disorders as three distinguishable disorders, Transient Tic Disorder, Chronic Motor Tic Disorder, and Tourette's Disorder, also because the symptom pictures, usual course, and treatment approaches vary (24). A number of other *DSM-II* Special Symptom categories, Speech Disturbance, Disorders of Sleep, Enuresis, and Encopresis, have been grouped together in *DSM-III* because their manifestations are primarily physical. The only speech disturbance likely to come to the attention of a mental health professional is Stuttering. The two disorders of sleep included in *DSM-III* are Sleepwalking Disorder and Sleep Terror Disorder. Both have marked behavioral manifestations and are often treated by mental health professionals because they are traditionally thought of as mental disorders (25, 26). *DSM-III* prefixes the term Functional to the diagnosis of Enuresis and Encopresis to emphasize that these diagnoses are made after the exclusion of physical etiologies.

The fifth group of Disorders Usually First Evident in Infancy, Childhood, or Adolescence consists of the *developmental* disorders—Pervasive Developmental Disorders and Specific Developmental Disorders. Pervasive Developmental Disorders correspond to Schizophrenia, Childhood Type, in *DSM-II*. When there is the onset of grossly impaired emotional relationships or unresponsiveness to others, bizarre behavior, and gross impairment in language development before the age of 30 months, this is classified as Infantile Autism. There is evidence that this syndrome bears little relationship to the psychotic disorders of adult life, particularly adult onset Schizophrenia (27). When the profound disturbance in social relations and multiple oddities of behavior develop between the ages of 30 months and 12 years, this is termed, in *DSM-III*, Childhood Onset Pervasive Developmental Disorder. It is likely that some children with this disorder will develop Schizophrenia as adults, but currently there is no way to predict this outcome (28).

Specific Developmental Disorders in *DSM-III* are characterized by specific delays in development and are divided according to the predominant area of functioning that is impaired (29–32). These were grouped together in *DSM-II* as Specific Learning Disturbance, but each warrants a different treatment focus. In *DSM-III* they are coded on Axis II to ensure that they are not overlooked when the individual has a more florid Axis I disorder. Examples of Specific Developmental Disorders are Developmental Reading, Arithmetic, Language, and Articulation Disorders.

Organic Mental Disorders

The Organic Brain Syndromes of the *DSM-II* implied the notion of a single syndrome due to global impairment of brain tissue functioning and with a limited number of manifestations. *DSM-II* also divided the organic brain syndromes into psychotic and nonpsychotic types according to the "severity of functional impairment" and "the capacity to meet the ordinary demands of life"—a distinction that was not only difficult to make, but that did not correspond to the usual meaning of "psychotic," which implies impaired reality testing. *DSM-II* also preserved the *DSM-I* distinction of acute versus chronic brain syndrome, based on the potential reversibility of the syndrome, rather than its course. This approach had many limitations; in particular, it discouraged recognition of potentially reversible but chronic brain syndromes such as Dementia due to hypothyroidism (33–35).

In contrast, *DSM-III* describes nine different organic brain syndromes—Delirium, Dementia, Amnestic Syndrome, Organic Delusional Syndrome, Hallucinosis, Organic Affective Syndrome, Organic Personality Syndrome, Intoxication, and Withdrawal—each with characteristic clinical features, course, and complications. When a Dementia is due to certain neurological diseases characteristically appearing in the senium (Primary Degenerative Dementia, Multi-infarct Dementia) or is an organic brain syndrome caused by the direct effects of a substance on the nervous system, these diagnoses are made on Axis I from Section I of the Organic Mental Disorders. When there is another organic etiology, such as infection, tumor, or metabolic disturbance, or the etiology or pathophysiological process is unknown, an Organic Brain Syndrome from Section 2 of the Organic Mental Disorders is noted on Axis I and the specific physical disorder, if known, is listed on Axis III.

Organic Mental Disorders appearing in later life include the single category of Primary Degenerative Dementia, subdivided into Senile and Presenile Onset. Formerly this disorder was either Senile and/or Presenile Dementia. In the *DSM-III* diagnoses the fifth digit is used to code features often associated with these dementias, such as delirium, delusions, or depression, which may require additional treatment. Another *DSM-II* diagnosis that falls in this group is Psychosis with Cerebral Arteriosclerosis, now called Multi-Infarct Dementia, since the dementia is evidently related to the presence of multiple infarcts rather than the degree of cerebral arteriosclerosis (36).

The *DSM-II* category Drug Intoxication (other than alcohol) has been greatly expanded in the *DSM-III* section on Substance-induced Organic Mental Disorders to allow for the identification of both the class of substance involved and the specific type of organic brain syndrome caused. Thus, depending on the substance, one or more of the nine organic brain syndromes is associated with alcohol, barbiturates or similarly acting sedatives or hypnotics, opioids, cocaine, amphetamines or similarly acting sympathomimetics, phencyclidine (PCP) or similarly acting arylcyclohexylamines, hallucinogens, cannabis, tobacco, caffeine, or other substances.

Within the category of alcohol-related disorders, *DSM-III* makes several changes. Delirium Tremens is now more descriptively termed Alcohol Withdrawal Delirium; Korsakoff's Psychosis is Alcohol Amnestic Disorder; Other Alcoholic Hallucinosis is Alcohol Hallucinosis; and, since there is no compelling evidence that a paranoid state due to alcohol use is a distinct entity, *DSM-III* eliminates the diagnosis of Alcohol Paranoid State. If an individual dependent on alcohol became paranoid, this could be diagnosed as Alcohol Dependence and a Paranoid Disorder. In addition, since alcohol has not been shown to be the causative factor in the Dementia found in some individuals with chronic Alcohol Dependence (37), this condition is called Dementia Associated with Alcoholism, rather than Alcoholic Deterioration (*DSM-II*) or Alcoholic Dementia (*ICD-9*). Finally, Alcohol Idiosyncratic Intoxication replaces Pathological Intoxication, since the former is a more accurate descriptive term.

Substance Use Disorders

This section of *DSM-III* includes disorders in which there are behavioral changes associated with more or less regular use of substances that affect the central nervous system and that in almost all subcultures would be viewed as undesirable. This category combines the *DSM-II* categories of Drug Dependence and Alcoholism to emphasize that the effects of the maladaptive uses of all substances of potential abuse and dependence are similar.

The Substance Use Disorders are divided into two major types: Abuse and Dependence. In general, Substance Abuse is defined by a pattern of pathological use for at least one month that causes impairment in social or occupational functioning. Examples of pathological use include inability to reduce or discontinue use or remaining intoxicated throughout the day. Substance Dependence is defined by the presence of either tolerance or withdrawal. For Alcohol and Cannabis Dependence, impairment in social or occupational functioning is also required. In the case of tobacco, the presence of a serious physical disorder that the individual knows is exacerbated by tobacco use is also considered evidence of Dependence. *DSM-III's* restricted definition of dependence generally departs from *DSM-II* usage in referring to physiological dependence only, not psychological dependence.

Many substances are associated with both abuse and dependence, including alcohol, barbiturates or similarly acting sedatives or hypnotics, opioids, amphetamines or similarly acting sympathomimetics, and cannabis. However, the *DSM-III* text acknowledges that the existence and significance of Cannabis Dependence is controversial (38, 39). Substances for which abuse but not dependence has been demonstrated include cocaine, phencyclidine (PCP) or similarly acting arylcyclohexylamines, and hallucinogens. (Phencyclidine is distinguished from hallucinogens despite some similarities in their effects [see reference 40].) There is also a category of Tobacco Dependence, justifiably included in this section by the potentially serious medical complications of long-term use (41–43) and its inclusion in *ICD-9*. Although the absence of an intoxication state and the severe social complications associated with other substances of dependence argues for classifying Tobacco Dependence as a physical disorder, the difficulty in controlling use and the significant withdrawal syndrome bring it conceptually close to the other Substance Use Disorders. Poly-substance Use may be classified as such when it is not possible to identify each of the substances involved.

For each Substance Use Disorder in *DSM-III*, the pattern of use or course of the disorder is coded in the fifth digit as continuous, episodic, or in remission.

Schizophrenic Disorders

The *DSM-III* concept of Schizophrenia is more narrowly defined than the *DSM-II* concept. Specifically, the diagnosis of Schizophrenia requires (1) a period of active psychotic symptomatology such as delusions, hallucinations, or certain characteristic disturbances in the form of thought, and (2) a duration of disturbance or impairment, including prodromal and residual phases, of at least six months. The rationale for restricting the diagnosis in this way was to identify a more homogeneous population with regard to a tendency toward onset in early adult life, recurrent episodes, an increased prevalence among family members, severe functional impairment, and differential response to somatic therapies (44, 45). The *DSM-II* diagnoses of Simple Type (46) and Latent Type, in which psychotic symptoms are absent, are not included and would correspond in *DSM-III* to a severe personality disorder, such as Schizotypal or Borderline Personality Disorder. Acute Schizophrenic Episode is also excluded from this class and in *DSM-III* is included as Schizophreniform Disorder, in the class Psychotic Disorders Not Elsewhere Classified, with the expectation that in most cases the long-term prognosis is more favorable than for Schizophrenia.

Because of the recognition in recent years that Affective Disorder may be accompanied by psychotic symptoms that used to be thought of as pathognomonic for Schizophrenia, such as auditory hallucinations and bizarre delusions, some individuals who may have been diagnosed as having Paranoid or Catatonic Schizophrenia in *DSM-II* will in *DSM-III* be diagnosed as having an Affective Disorder (47).

In *DSM-II* two subtypes (Acute and Chronic Undifferentiated) were defined by course, and the remaining subtypes by symptom picture. In *DSM-III* the fourth digit is used to designate the phenomenologic subtype: Disorganized, Paranoid, Catatonic, Undifferentiated, and Residual; and the fifth digit is used to indicate the course of the illness as either Subchronic, Chronic, Subchronic with Acute Exacerbation, Chronic with Acute Exacerbation, or In Remission. Among the subtypes, the term "hebephrenic" was changed to "disorganized" to emphasize that aspect of the individual's behavior rather than restricting the concept to the regressed and silly patient uncommonly seen today (48).

Finally, Schizophrenia, Schizoaffective type, is not included among the Schizophrenic Disorders in *DSM-III*. Such cases might be classified under the new system as Schizophrenia with a superimposed Affective Disorder, Major Affective Disorder with Psychotic Features, or as Schizoaffective Disorder or one of several other Psychotic Disorders Not Elsewhere Classified—reflecting the heterogeneous nature of this category (49, 50).

Paranoid Disorders

A Paranoid Disorder in *DSM-III* is characterized by a clinical picture in which the predominant symptoms are persistent persecutory delusions or delusional jealousy, not accounted for by another psychotic disorder. There are three specific Paranoid Disorders in *DSM-III*: Paranoia, Shared Paranoid Disorder, and Acute Paranoid Disorder. Involutional Paranoid State has not been included because there is no compelling evidence that a paranoid disorder occurring in the involutional period is distinct from one occurring at other phases of the life cycle (51).

Paranoia is a disorder in which a persecutory delusional system develops insidiously and becomes chronic and stable. By definition it requires a duration of at least six months. Shared Paranoid Disorder is traditionally known as Folie à Deux. Although rare, it is included in the classification because of its distinctive clinical picture and special treatment implications (52). Acute Paranoid Disorder is the most common Paranoid Disorder; it is characterized by persistent persecutory delusions or delusional jealousy of acute onset and brief duration.

Psychotic Disorders Not Elsewhere Classified

This is an important group of psychotic disorders that do not meet the diagnostic criteria for Organic, Schizophrenic, Paranoid, or Affective Disorders. These diagnoses will be commonly made, in part because of the more narrow concept of Schizophrenia in *DSM-III* and the uncertainty that exists about the boundaries between Affective and Schizophrenic Disorders. The three specific disorders included here are Schizophreniform Disorder, Brief Reactive Psychosis, and Schizoaffective Disorder. There is also a residual category, Atypical Psychosis.

Schizophreniform Disorder will, under many circumstances, replace the *DSM-II* diagnosis of Acute Schizophrenic Episode. The essential clinical features of this disorder are identical with those of Schizophrenia, with the exception that the duration is less than six months but more than two weeks. There is also evidence suggesting that Schizophreniform Disorder is accompanied by a greater likelihood of emotional turmoil and confusion, a tendency toward acute onset and resolution, a better prognosis as measured by return to the premorbid level of functioning, and no increase in the prevalence of Schizophrenia among family members (53, 54).

Brief Reactive Psychosis always follows a psychosocial stressor and has a duration of less than two weeks. If a Brief Reactive Psychosis persists beyond two weeks, a diagnosis of Schizophreniform Disorder must be considered. Many of these cases were formerly diagnosed Acute Schizophrenic Episode or Schizoaffective Schizophrenia in *DSM-II*.

In *DSM-III*, Schizoaffective Disorder is reserved for conditions for which the clinician is unable to make a differential diagnosis between Schizophrenia (or Schizophreniform Disorder) and Affective Disorder (55). Examples would include episodes of affective illness in which a mood-incongruent delusion or hallucination dominates the clinical picture after the affective symptoms have resolved or episodes of mixed psychotic and affective disturbance in which the history of the onset of the psychotic features in relation to the affective symptoms is not clear. Schizoaffective Disorder has the distinction of being the only specific diagnosis in *DSM-III* that does not have diagnostic criteria because of the inability, at this time, to reach a consensus on the defining characteristics.

Affective Disorders

In contrast to *DSM-II*, which divided Affective Disorders based on the presence of psychosis and classified all Major Affective Disorders as psychoses except for those precipitated by stressful life experiences, *DSM-III* groups Affective Disorders together (other than those due to a known organic factor). There are three subclasses: Major Affective Disorder, Other Specific Affective Disorders, and Atypical Affective Disorders.

Major Affective Disorder includes Bipolar Disorder and Major Depression. Bipolar Disorder is used for all individuals who have had a manic episode, since research shows that virtually all such cases eventually develop major depressive episodes (56). The current episode may be classified in the fourth digit as manic, depressed, or mixed, and in the fifth digit the presence and type of psychotic features are noted. The *DSM-III* diagnosis of Bipolar Disorder corresponds to the *DSM-II* diagnosis of Manic-Depressive Illness, Manic or Circular type.

Whereas the *DSM-II* classification implied the unity of manic-depressive illness, *DSM-III* accepts the evidence that distinguishes between unipolar and bipolar forms of Affective Disorder (57, 58). Therefore, Manic-Depressive Illness, Depressed, is now classified as Major Depression with the notation of recurrent episodes in the fourth digit. The *DSM-II* concept of Involutional Melancholia is also included in Major Depression in *DSM-III* because of the absence of compelling evidence that depression occurring during the involutional period is different from that occurring at other stages of life (59).

DSM-III recognizes the heterogeneous nature of Major Depressive Episodes (60) and uses the term Melancholia (fifth digit) to designate a subtype (often referred to as "endogenous") that tends to be more severe, is associated with classic vegetative signs, and is particularly responsive to somatic therapy (61). The presence of psychotic features, whether mood-congruent or mood-incongruent, may also be noted in the fifth digit.

Other Specific Affective Disorders are characterized by a relatively sustained mood disturbance of at least two years' duration. A full affective syndrome, defined by mood and associated symptoms, is not present, and there are no psychotic features. There are two disorders in this subclass: Cyclothymic Disorder (Cyclothymic Personality in *DSM-II*) and Dysthymic Disorder (roughly equivalent to the concept of Depressive Personality and Depressive Neurosis) (62).

Anxiety Disorders

DSM-III groups the disorders in which anxiety is experienced directly in the class of Anxiety Disorders. This is in contrast to *DSM-II*, in which all disorders in which anxiety was "felt and expressed directly" or "controlled unconsciously" by conversion, displacement, and various other psychological defense mechanisms were classified together as Neuroses. In *DSM-III* other neurotic disorders are distributed among other classes based on shared symptoms or other descriptive features.

The *DSM-II* category Anxiety Neurosis is divided into Panic Disorder and Generalized Anxiety Disorder based on whether there are sudden attacks of fear, apprehension, or terror and associated physical symptoms (Panic Disorder) or generalized persistent motor tension, autonomic hyperactivity, apprehension, and vigilance in the absence of recurrent panic attacks. There is evidence that Panic Disorder, as a distinct entity, has a differential treatment response as compared with other disorders in which anxiety is prominent (63, 64).

In *DSM-III* there are three distinct forms of Phobic Disorders: Agoraphobia (with or without a history of panic attacks), Simple Phobia, and Social Phobia. These three differ not only in clinical picture and characteristic age at onset but also in differential treatment approach and response (65).

Another important *DSM-III* Anxiety Disorder is Post-traumatic Stress Disorder. In this disorder, sometimes referred to as Traumatic Neurosis, symptoms of reexperiencing stressful events, numbness toward and reduced involvement with the external world, and other affective, physiological, and cognitive symptoms develop after a psychologically traumatic event that is outside the range of usual human experience. The disorder is divided into acute and chronic or delayed forms because longitudinal studies have shown differential outcomes for each (66).

Obsessive-Compulsive Neurosis appears in *DSM-III* as Obsessive-Compulsive Disorder and is included in the Anxiety Disorders because anxiety is experienced if the individual resists the obsessions or compulsions.

Somatoform Disorders

In this group of disorders there are physical symptoms suggesting physical disorders for which there are no demonstrable organic findings or known physiological mechanisms to account for the disturbance. There usually is strong presumptive evidence that the symptoms are linked to psychological factors or conflicts.

The *DSM-II* category of Hysterical Neurosis has been split in *DSM-III* into several different classes (67). Hysterical Neurosis, Conversion Type, is now either Conversion Disorder, in which there is a loss or alteration in physical functioning, or Psychogenic Pain Disorder, in which the predominant features are a complaint of pain and positive evidence of the etiological role of psychological factors (68).

Another form of "Hysteria," also known as Briquet's Disorder, is Somatization Disorder (69). In this disorder there are recurrent and multiple somatic complaints of several years' duration for which medical attention is sought but which are not apparently due to any physical disorders. This is distinguished from Hypochondriasis by the former's having an earlier age at onset and by a preoccupation with symptoms rather than fear of having specific diseases.

Dissociative Disorders

The Dissociative type of Hysterical Neurosis in *DSM-II* is now divided into three adult forms and one for childhood. The unifying features are the sudden, temporary alteration and loss in functioning of consciousness, identity, or motor behavior. Psychogenic Amnesia, Psychogenic Fugue, and Multiple Personality are distinguished by differing clinical pictures, predisposing factors, and courses (70, 71). Sleepwalking Disorder, although involving dissociation, is classified in the *DSM-III* class of Disorders Usually First Evident in Infancy, Childhood, or Adolescence.

Depersonalization Disorder (Depersonalization Neurosis in *DSM-II*) is included in the class of Dissociative Disorders because the feeling of one's own reality, a component of identity, is lost, although some question this inclusion because a memory disturbance is absent (72).

Psychosexual Disorders

Psychological factors are assumed to be of major etiological significance in the development of these disorders. There are four subclasses: Gender Identity Disorders, Paraphilias, Sexual Dysfunctions, and Other Psychosexual Disorders.

The Gender Identity Disorders are characterized by the individual's feelings of discomfort and inappropriateness about his or her anatomic sex and by persistent behavior patterns usually associated with the other sex. There was no adequate *DSM-II* diagnosis corresponding to this disorder. Transsexualism (73) and Gender Identity Disorder of Childhood (74) are the two specific diagnoses in this class.

DSM-II Sexual Deviations are now termed Paraphilias, emphasizing that the deviation (para) is in that to which the individual is attracted (philia). Paraphilias are defined as conditions that are associated with either (1) preference for the use of a nonhuman object for sexual arousal, (2) repetitive sexual activity with humans involving real or simulated suffering or humiliation, or (3) repetitive sexual activity with nonconsenting or inappropriate partners. Examples of *DSM-III* Paraphilias include Fetishism, Transvestism, Zoophilia, Pedophilia, Exhibitionism, Voyeurism, Sexual Masochism, and Sexual Sadism.

The *DSM-II* category of Psychophysiologic Genitourinary Disorder, which included Dyspareunia and Impotence, has been greatly expanded into the *DSM-III* subclass of Psychosexual Dysfunctions, due to the substantial increase in interest in this area and the development of diverse treatment techniques (75, 76). The essential feature of the Psychosexual Dysfunctions is inhibition in the appetite or psychophysiological changes that characterize the complete sexual response cycle. Diagnoses for inhibitions in sexual desire, sexual excitement, and female or male orgasm, as well as premature ejaculation, functional dyspareunia, and functional vaginismus are included in this group. These diagnoses are not made if the sexual dysfunction is entirely due to organic factors (physical illness, medication) or another Axis I mental disorder.

Whether or not to classify homosexuality as a mental disorder has stirred considerable controversy (77). The seventh and subsequent printings of the *DSM-II* substituted the category of Sexual Orientation Disturbance for Homosexuality, following a decision by the APA Board of Trustees to eliminate homosexuality per se as a diagnosis. The new category was to be used for homosexuals who were "either disturbed by, in conflict with, or wish to change their sexual orientation." This category in *DSM-III* is given a more accurate name, Ego-dystonic Homosexuality, and the definition slightly changed to emphasize impaired heterosexual arousal and explicit dissatisfaction and distress from a homosexual pattern of sexual arousal (78). Ego-dystonic Homosexuality is included in a residual category of Other Psychosexual Disorders. (Sexual Orientation Disturbance in *DSM-II* was included in the Sexual Deviations.)

Factitious Disorders

Individuals who simulate physical or psychological symptoms in such a way that they are not discovered, and therefore appear to voluntarily produce illness, have disorders that are classified in *DSM-III* as Factitious Disorders. The actions of these individuals are compulsive and voluntary in the sense that they are deliberate and purposeful, but not in the sense that they can be controlled. The prototype of Factitious Disorders, Munchausen Syndrome (79), is called Chronic Factitious Disorder with Physical Symptoms in *DSM-III*. There is also a category for individuals who simulate psychological symptoms (Ganser Syndrome): Factitious Disorder with Psychological Symptoms. Factitious Disorders are distinguished from Malingering, where, although the individual is also in voluntary control of the symptoms, the goal is obviously recognizable with a knowledge of the environmental circumstances rather than by an understanding of the individual's psychological makeup.

Disorders of Impulse Control Not Elsewhere Classified

This residual class is for disorders of impulse control that are not classified as Substance Use Disorders or Paraphilias. The hallmarks of these disorders are (1) the failure to resist an impulse to perform an act harmful to the individual or others, (2) increasing tension before committing the act, and (3) an experience of pleasure, gratification, or release at the time of committing the act. These acts may be ego-syntonic at the moment of discharge but may also be accompanied by regret or guilt afterwards. Included in this class are Pathological Gambling (80), Kleptomania (81), Pyromania (82), and Isolated Explosive Disorder (83) (roughly equivalent to Explosive Personality in *DSM-II*). These disorders may have important forensic implications, and have differing treatment implications as well as obviously distinct clinical features.

Adjustment Disorder

Adjustment Disorder replaces the *DSM-II* category of Transient Situational Disturbances. Adjustment Disorder is characterized by a maladaptive reaction to an identifiable psychosocial stressor occurring within three months of the onset of the stress. The category is not used if the disturbance meets the criteria for another specific mental disorder. It is assumed that the disturbance will eventually remit after the stressor ceases, or when a new level of adaptation is reached.

Significant changes in the *DSM-III* concept from *DSM-II* are as follows:

1. Adjustment Disorder excludes reactions of psychotic proportions that can be classified adequately elsewhere, while Transient Situational Disturbances included disorders of any severity.
2. Adjustment Disorder may be given to individuals with other underlying mental disorders, such as Personality Disorders, who, in fact, may be especially vulnerable to stress (84).
3. Adjustment Disorder is subtyped by predominant symptomatology to aid in treatment planning, while Transient Situational Disturbances were classified by stage in life.

DSM-III Adjustment Disorder is subclassified as with depressed mood, anxious mood, mixed emotional features, disturbance of conduct, mixed disturbance of emotions and conduct, work or academic inhibition, or withdrawal.

Psychological Factors Affecting Physical Condition

The *DSM-II* approach to the classification of psychophysiologic or "psychosomatic" disorders had several practical and theoretical limitations (85). As defined in *DSM-II*, the various categories of psychophysiologic disorders were rarely diagnosed and the differentiation of these disorders from physical illnesses tended to be made idiosyncratically by clinicians. The *DSM-II* definition perpetuated simplistic, unicausational concepts of disease etiology and did not encourage collaboration between mental health practitioners and medical specialists.

The *DSM-III* category of Psychological Factors Affecting Physical Condition enables a clinician to note that psychological factors contribute to the initiation or exacerbation of a physical condition. Using the multiaxial approach, the clinician records the physical condition or disorder on Axis III. The judgment that psychological factors are involved requires evidence of a temporal relationship between the occurrence of environmental stimuli with symbolic meaning and the onset or exacerbation of the physical symptoms. Physical conditions for which this category may be appropriate include (but are not limited to) obesity, tension headache, migraine headache, angina pectoris, painful menstruation, sacroiliac pain, neurodermatitis, acne, rheumatoid arthritis, asthma, pylorospasm, nausea and vomiting, regional enteritis, ulcerative colitis, frequency of micturition, and hyperthyroidism.

Personality Disorders

Personality Disorders are characterized by enduring patterns of relating to, perceiving, and thinking about the environment and oneself that become inflexible and maladaptive, causing significant impairment in social or occupational functioning, or subjective distress. Personality Disorders are distinguished from personality traits that are not necessarily pathological. Personality Disorders in *DSM-III* are coded on Axis II to ensure that they will not be overlooked in the presence of a more florid Axis I disorder.

Several of the *DSM-II* Personality Disorders persist relatively unchanged in *DSM-III*, several have had slight modification or have been expanded, two have been deleted, and several new diagnoses—commonly used in clinical practice—have been added. Paranoid Personality, Obsessive-Compulsive Personality (without the term "Obsessive"), Antisocial Personality, and Passive-Aggressive Personality all remain in the *DSM-III* classification, but are described with much greater detail. The *DSM-II* diagnosis of Passive-Aggressive Personality Disorder, Dependent Type, is equivalent to the *DSM-III* diagnosis of Dependent Personality Disorder. Cyclothymic Personality has been included as Cyclothymic Disorder within the Affective Disorders section of *DSM-III* because of evidence suggesting a relationship to Bipolar Disorder (86). Explosive Personality has also been removed from the Personality Disorders section because, by definition, the explosive behavior is in contrast to the individual's usual behavior and therefore is inconsistent with the *DSM-III* definition of Personality Disorder.

Asthenic Personality has not been retained since it is not clinically distinguishable from mild chronic depression (Dysthymic Disorder in *DSM-III*). Inadequate Personality was not retained because it was defined not by a distinctive behavior pattern, but merely by nonspecific functional impairment. Hysterical Personality was changed to Histrionic Personality Disorder, to avoid confusion caused by the historical relationship of the term "hysteria" to female anatomy and conversion symptoms (87), and to focus appropriately on the histrionic pattern of behavior.

The *DSM-II* category of Schizoid Personality has been divided into three separate Personality Disorders: Schizotypal, Schizoid, and Avoidant. The eccentric features of the *DSM-II* diagnosis are best described by the *DSM-III* Schizotypal Personality Disorder. The criteria for Schizotypal Personality Disorder were developed to identify individuals often described as having Borderline Schizophrenia. These individuals have been noted to have an increased prevalence of chronic Schizophrenia among family members (88, 89). The distinction between Schizoid and Avoidant Personalities is based on whether there is a defect in the motivation and capacity for emotional involvement (Schizoid) or avoidance of desired close relationships because of fear of rejection (Avoidant). This descriptive distinction appears to have therapeutic and prognostic significance.

Borderline Personality Disorder is a new *DSM-III* category, although it has been a widely used diagnosis both in clinical practice and in the literature (90). The enduring personality features, characterized by instability—in sense of identity, interpersonal relationships, impulse control, and mood and affect regulation—are supported by the results of a factor analytic study of the symptoms of a group of over 800 patients clinically diagnosed as "borderline" (89). These patients were most often classified as having Schizophrenia, Latent Type, in *DSM-II*. The refined *DSM-III* definition will have important treatment and outcome implications. Narcissistic Personality has received considerable attention in the psychoanalytic literature (91). It is included as a Personality Disorder, characterized by a grandiose sense of self, fantasies of unlimited success, exhibitionistic need for attention and admiration, and other characteristic disturbances, such as feelings of entitlement, interpersonal exploitiveness, relationships that alternate between extremes of overidealization and devaluation, and lack of empathy.

V Codes

Conditions without Manifest Psychiatric Disorder (*DSM-II*) are now referred to as V Codes for Conditions Not Attributable to a Mental Disorder That Are a Focus of Attention or Treatment. The *DSM-II* category was limited to "individuals who are psychiatrically normal but who nevertheless have severe enough problems to warrant examination by a psychiatrist." No definition of normality was provided. In *DSM-III* these codes can be applied to an individual who has a mental disorder, if the condition that is a "focus of attention or treatment" itself is not attributable to a mental disorder. Several of the *DSM-II* social maladjustments have been preserved as V Codes: Marital Problem, Phase of Life Problem or Other Life Circumstance Problem, Occupational Problem. Dyssocial Behavior has been divided into Adult and Childhood or Adolescent Antisocial Behavior. New Problems useful to distinguish from mental disorders have been added: Malingering (92), Parent-Child Problem, Other Interpersonal Problem, Academic Problem, Uncomplicated Bereavement (93), Non-compliance with Medical Treatment, and Other Specified Family Circumstances.

Circumstances in which one of these conditions will be noted include the following: (1) after a thorough evaluation no mental disorder is found, (2) the evaluation is as yet incomplete to determine the presence or absence of a mental disorder but the reason for contact is needed, or (3) an individual has a mental disorder but the focus of attention or treatment is on a condition or problem not due to the disorder. An example of this would be an individual with Bipolar Disorder who had marital problems that antedated the development of the Affective Disorder and therefore were apparently unrelated to the Affective Disorder but were the focus of marital therapy.

Nonspecific conditions are now spelled out in *DSM-III* with greater precision. There is an opportunity to diagnose an Unspecified Mental Disorder that is nonpsychotic, or, if psychotic, the diagnosis may be Atypical Psychosis from the Psychotic Disorders Not Elsewhere Classified section. No Mental Disorder can be more specifically noted as referring to No Diagnosis or Condition on Axis I or No Diagnosis on Axis II.

THE FUTURE

When the Task Forces on Nomenclature and Statistics each began their work on *DSM-II* and *DSM-III*, there was no systematically collected information on the experience of clinicians using the previous manual to guide them in their work. *DSM-III* represents a major investment by our profession. The real payoff, in terms of advancing the field and better understanding and care of our patients, will come from careful study in the next few years of the strengths and weaknesses of this system. This will be of great help to those brave souls given the responsibility for developing *DSM-IV*. Pogo notwithstanding, the word "diagnosis" comes from the Greek root "gnosis," which means knowledge.

NOTE

1. This section is an elaboration of material presented in tabular form in Appendix C of *DSM-III*, "Annotated Comparative Listing of *DSM-II* and *DSM-III*," prepared by Robert L. Spitzer, M.D., Steven E. Hyler, M.D., and Janet B. W. Williams, M.S.W. The references were provided by members of the various advisory committees.

REFERENCES

1. Report of the American Psychological Association's Liaison Committee on DSM-III, Fall 1979
2. Spitzer RL, Endicott J: Medicine and mental disorder: proposed definition and criteria, in Critical Issues in Psychiatric Diagnosis. Edited by Spitzer RL, Klein DF. New York, Raven Press, 1978
3. Klein DF: A proposed definition of mental illness. Ibid
4. Feinstein AR: A critical overview of diagnosis in psychiatry, in Psychiatric Diagnosis. Edited by Rakoff VM, Stancer HC, Kedward HB. New York, Brunner/Mazel, 1977
5. Murray RM: A reappraisal of American psychiatry. Lancet 1:255–258, 1979
6. Spitzer RL, Fleiss JL: A re-analysis of the reliability of psychiatric diagnosis. Br J Psychiatry 125:341–347, 1974
7. Spitzer RL, Forman JBW, Nee J: DSM-III field trials: I. Initial interrater diagnostic reliability. Am J Psychiatry 136:815–817, 1979
8. Mezzich JE: Patterns and issues in multiaxial psychiatric diagnosis. Psychol Med 9:125–137, 1979
9. Spitzer RL, Forman JBW: DSM-III field trials: II. Initial experience with the multiaxial system. Am J Psychiatry 136:818–820, 1979
10. Gross HJ: Manual on Terminology and Classification in Mental Retardation. Baltimore, Garamond/Pridemark Press, 1977, p 19
11. Gift JE, Strauss JS, Ritzler BA: Failure to detect low IQ in psychiatric assessment. Am J Psychiatry 135:345–349, 1978
12. Cantwell D: The Hyperactive Child: Diagnosis, Management, Current Research. New York, Spectrum Publications, 1975
13. Weiss G, Minde K, Werry JS, et al: Studies on the hyperactive child: VIII. Five year follow-up. Arch Gen Psychiatry 24:409–414, 1971
14. Wood DR, Reimherr FW, Wender PH, et al: Diagnosis and treatment of minimal brain dysfunction in adults. Arch Gen Psychiatry 33:1453—1460, 1976
15. Robins L: Sturdy childhood predictors of adult outcomes: replications from longitudinal studies. Psychol Med 8:611–622, 1978
16. Jenkins RL: Behavior Disorders of Childhood and Adolescence. Springfield, Ill, Charles C Thomas, 1973

17. Bowlby J: Separation anxiety: a critical review of the literature. J Child Psychol Psychiatry 1:251–259, 1960
18. Gittelman-Klein R, Klein DF: School phobia diagnostic considerations in the light of imipramine effects. J Nerv Ment Dis 156:199–215, 1973
19. Elson A, Pearson C, Jones CD, et al: Follow up study of childhood elective mutism. Arch Gen Psychiatry 13: 182–187, 1965
20. Erikson E: Identity: Youth and Crisis. New York, WW Norton, 1968
21. Fischhoff J: Failure to thrive, in Basic Handbook of Child Psychiatry. Edited by Noshpitz J. New York, Basic Books, 1979
22. Group for the Advancement of Psychiatry: Psychopathological Disorders in Childhood: Theoretical Considerations and a Proposed Classification. Report 62. New York, GAP, 1966
23. Halmi KA: Anorexia nervosa, in Comprehensive Textbook of Psychiatry, 3rd ed. Edited by Kaplan H, Freedman A, Sadock B. Baltimore, Williams & Wilkins Co, 1980
24. Shapiro AK, Shapiro ES, Bruun KD, et al: Gilles de la Tourette Syndrome. New York, Raven Press, 1978
25. Jacobson A, Kales A, Lehmann D, et al: Somnambulism: all-night electroencephalographic studies. Science 148:975–977, 1965
26. Fisher C, Kahn E, Edwards A, et al: A psychophysiological study of nightmares and night terrors: III. Mental content and recall of stage 4 night terrors. J Nerv Ment Dis 158:174–188, 1974
27. Rutter M, Schopler E: Autism: A Reappraisal of Concepts and Treatments. New York, Plenum Press, 1978
28. Kolvin I, Ounsted C, Humphrey M, et al: Studies in the childhood psychoses: I–VI. Br J Psychiatry 118: 381–419, 1971
29. Baker L, Cantwell DP: Developmental language disorder, in Comprehensive Textbook of Psychiatry, 3rd ed. Edited by Kaplan H, Freedman A, Sadock B. Baltimore, Williams & Wilkins Co 1980
30. Baker L, Cantwell DP: Developmental articulation disorder. Ibid
31. Cantwell DP, Baker L: Specific arithmetic disorders. Ibid
32. Rutter M, Yule W: The concept of specific reading retardation. J Child Psychol Psychiatry 16:181–197, 1975
33. Lipowski ZB: Organic brain syndromes: a reformulation. Compr Psychiatry 19: 309–322, 1978
34. Seltzer B, Sherwin I: "Organic brain syndromes": an empirical study and critical review. Am J Psychiatry 135:13–21, 1978
35. Wells CE: Chronic brain disease: an overview. Am J Psychiatry 135:22–28, 1978
36. Hachinski VC, Lassen NA, Marshall J: Multi-infarct dementia: a cause of mental deterioration in the elderly. Lancet 2:207–210, 1974
37. Goodwin DW, Hill SY: Chronic effects of alcohol and other psychoactive drugs on intellect, learning and memory, in Alcohol, Drugs and Brain Damage. Edited by Rankin JG. Toronto, Addiction Research Foundation, 1975
38. Jones RT, Benowitz N, Bachman J: Clinical studies of cannabis tolerance and dependence. Ann NY Acad Sci 282:221–239, 1976
39. Petersen RC: Marihuana Research Findings. NIDA Research Monograph 14. Rockville, Md, US Department of Health, Education, and Welfare, 1977
40. Petersen RC, Stillman RC: Phencyclidine (PCP) Abuse: An Appraisal. NIDA Research Monograph 21. Rockville, Md, US Department of Health, Education, and Welfare, 1978
41. Report on Smoking and Health. Rockville, Md, US Department of Health, Education, and Welfare, Office of the Surgeon General, 1979
42. Jaffe JH, Jarvik ME: Tobacco use and tobacco use disorder, in Psychopharmacology: A Generation of Progress. Edited by Lipton MA, DiMascio A, Killam KF. New York, Raven Press, 1978
43. Larson PS, Silvetle H: Tobacco: Experimental and Clinical Studies. Baltimore, Williams & Wilkins Co, 1975
44. Spitzer RL, Andreasen N, Endicott J: Schizophrenia and other psychotic disorders in DSM-III. Schizophr Bull 4:489–509, 1978
45. Kendell RE, Brockington IF, Leff JP: Prognostic implications of six alternative definitions of schizophrenia. Arch Gen Psychiatry 36:25–34, 1979
46. Stone AA, Hopkins R, Mahnke MW, et al: Simple schizophrenia: syndrome or shibboleth. Am J Psychiatry 125:305–312, 1968
47. Abrams R, Taylor MA: Catatonia: prediction of response to somatic treatments. Am J Psychiatry 134:78–80, 1977
48. Tsuang M, Winokur G: Criteria for subtyping schizophrenia: clinical differentiation of hebephrenic and paranoid schizophrenia. Arch Gen Psychiatry 31:43–47, 1974
49. Procci WR: Schizo-affective psychosis: fact or fiction? A survey of the literature. Arch Gen Psychiatry 33: 1167–1178, 1976
50. Brockington IF, Leff JP: Schizo-affective psychosis: definitions and incidence. Psychol Med 9:91–99, 1979
51. Retterstol N: Paranoid and Paranoiac Psychosis. Springfield, Ill, Charles C Thomas, 1966
52. McNeil JN, Verwoerdt A, Peak D: Folie à deux in the aged: review and case report of role reversal. J Am Geriatr Soc 20:316–323, 1972
53. Sartorius N, Jablensky A, Shapiro R: Cross-cultural differences in the short term prognosis of schizophrenic psychoses. Schizophr Bull 4:102–113, 1978
54. Tsuang M, Dempsey M, Rauscher F: A study of atypical schizophrenia: comparison with schizophrenia and affective disorder by sex, age of admission, precipitant, outcome and family history. Arch Gen Psychiatry 33:1157–1160, 1976
55. Pope HG Jr, Lipinski J: Diagnosis in schizophrenia and manic-depressive illness: a reassessment of the specificity of "schizophrenic" symptoms in the light of current research. Arch Gen Psychiatry 35:811–828, 1978
56. Nurnberger J, Roose S, Dunner D, et al: Unipolar mania: a distinct clinical entity? Am J Psychiatry 136:1420–1423, 1979

57. Winokur G, Clayton P, Reich T: Manic Depressive Illness. St Louis, CV Mosby Co, 1969
58. Perris C: A study of bipolar (manic depressive) and unipolar recurrent depressive psychosis. Acta Psychiatr Scand, Supplement 194, 1966, pp 9–188
59. Weissman M: The myth of involutional melancholia. JAMA 242:742–744, 1979
60. Nelson JC, Charney DS: Primary affective disorder criteria and the endogenous-reactive distinction. Arch Gen Psychiatry 37:787–793, 1980
61. Bielski RJ, Friedel RO: Prediction of tricyclic antidepressant response: a critical review. Arch Gen Psychiatry 33:1479–1489, 1976
62. Klerman GL, Endicott J, Spitzer RL, et al: Neurotic depressions: a systematic analysis of multiple criteria and multiple meanings. Am J Psychiatry 136:57–62, 1979
63. Klein DF, Zitrin CM, Woerner MG: Antidepressants, anxiety, panic and phobia, in Psychopharmacology: A Generation of Progress. Edited by Lipton MA, DiMascio A, Killam KF. New York, Raven Press, 1978
64. Zitrin CM, Klein DF, Woerner MG: Behavior therapy, supportive psychotherapy, imipramine and phobias. Arch Gen Psychiatry 35:307–316, 1978
65. Marks I: Fears and Phobias. New York, Academic Press, 1969, p 109
66. Keiser L: The Traumatic Neurosis. Philadelphia, JB Lippincott Co, 1968
67. Hyler SE, Spitzer RL: Hysteria split asunder. Am J Psychiatry 135:1500–1504, 1978
68. Sternbach RA: Pain: A Psychophysiological Analysis. New York, Academic Press, 1968
69. Guze S: The validity and significance of the clinical diagnosis of hysteria (Briquet's syndrome). Am J Psychiatry 132:138–140, 1975
70. Nemiah J: Hysterical neurosis, dissociative type, in Comprehensive Textbook of Psychiatry, 2nd ed, vol 1. Edited by Freedman A, Kaplan H, Sadock B. Baltimore, Williams & Wilkins Co, 1975
71. Ludwig AM, Brandsma JM, Wilbur CB, et al: The objective study of multiple personality. Arch Gen Psychiatry 26:298–310, 1972
72. Lehmann L: Depersonalization. Am J Psychiatry 131:1221–1224, 1974
73. Green R, Money J: Transsexualism and Sex Reassignment. Baltimore, Johns Hopkins Press, 1969
74. Green R: Sexual Identity Conflict in Children and Adults. New York, Penguin, 1975
75. Masters WH, Johnson VE: Human Sexual Inadequacy. Boston, Little, Brown and Co, 1970
76. Kaplan HS: The New Sex Therapy. New York, Brunner/Mazel, 1974
77. Spitzer RL: A proposal about homosexuality and the APA nomenclature: homosexuality as an irregular form of sexual behavior and sexual orientation disturbance as a psychiatric disorder. A symposium: should homosexuality be in the APA nomenclature? Am J Psychiatry 130:1207–1216, 1973
78. Spitzer RL: Homosexuality and mental disorder: a reformulation of the issues, in Proceedings of the Closure of Scientific Disputes Symposium of the Institute of Society, Ethics and the Life Sciences, The Hastings Center, October 5–6, 1979 (in press)
79. Sussman N, Hyler S: Factitious disorders, in Comprehensive Textbook of Psychiatry, 3rd ed. Edited by Kaplan H, Freedman A, Sadock B. Baltimore, Williams & Wilkins Co, 1980
80. Lesieur HR: The compulsive gambler's spiral of options and involvement. Psychiatry 42:79–87, 1979
81. Wihels F: Kleptomania and other psychopathic crimes. J Criminal Psychopathol 4:205–216, 1942
82. Lewis NDC, Yarnell H: Pathological firesetting. Res Publ Assoc Res Nerv Ment Dis 82, 1951
83. Bach-y-Rita G, Lion JR, Climent CS, et al: Episodic dyscontrol: a study of 130 violent patients. Am J Psychiatry 127:49–54, 1971
84. Looney JG, Gunderson EKE: Transient situational disturbances: course and outcome. Am J Psychiatry 135:660–663, 1978
85. Looney JG, Lipp MR, Spitzer RL: A new method of classification for psychophysiologic disorders. Am J Psychiatry 135:304–308, 1978
86. Akiskal HS, Djenderedjian AH, Rosenthal RH, et al: Cyclothymic disorder: validating criteria for inclusion in the bipolar affective group. Am J Psychiatry 134:1227–1233, 1977
87. Chodoff P: The diagnosis of hysteria: an overview. Am J Psychiatry 131:1073–1078, 1974
88. Rosenthal D, Kety SS: The Transmission of Schizophrenia. London, Pergamon Press, 1968
89. Spitzer RL, Endicott J, Gibbon M: Crossing the border into borderline personality and borderline schizophrenia: the development of criteria. Arch Gen Psychiatry 36:17–24, 1979
90. Gunderson JG, Singer MT: Defining borderline patients: an overview. Am J Psychiatry 132:1–9, 1975
91. Kernberg O: Borderline Conditions and Pathological Narcissism. New York, Jason Aronson, 1975
92. David D, Weiss JMA: Malingering and associated syndromes, in Adult Clinical Psychiatry: American Handbook of Psychiatry, 2nd ed, vol III. Edited by Arieti S, Brody E; Arieti S, editor-in-chief. New York, Basic Books, 1974
93. Clayton PJ, Halikas JA, Maurice WL: The bereavement of the widowed. Dis Nerv Syst 32:597–604, 1971

GEORGE E. VAILLANT

The disadvantages of DSM-III *outweigh its advantages*

. . . Having long suffered under *DSM-II*, clinicians and researchers alike thirsted for greater diagnostic precision. *DSM-III* attempted to quench this thirst, and for these good intentions we are grateful and filled with admiration. Certainly, *DSM-III* deserves praise as a vessel that held water when our lips were dry, but *DSM-III* must also be recognized for what it is: a glass less full than empty. Its disadvantages outweigh its advantages, and we can all learn from its limitations. We have faith that *DSM-IV* will offer a more generous draught for our thirst for diagnostic precision and clinical sensitivity.

We all know the story of the committee that tried to design a racehorse. Instead, by combining the ideas of everyone, the committee invented the brontosaurus—a truly remarkable beast. *DSM-III*, too, is a most remarkable creation, but, like the dinosaur, its disadvantages clearly outweigh its advantages and it must be allowed to become extinct.

This essay will focus attention on five major disadvantages of *DSM-III*. These disadvantages may have arisen because the authors listened too much to committees and too little to the views of great individual psychiatrists who, in the past, have made seminal contributions to diagnostic clarity. First, *DSM-III* is parochial; second, it is reductionistic; third, it ignores the distinction between trait and state; fourth, it is adynamic—it ignores conflict, adaptation, longitudinal course, and development; and finally, it has consistently sacrificed diagnostic validity on the altar of diagnostic reliability.

DSM-III IS PAROCHIAL

DSM-III ignores other cultures and other historical epochs and ignores any aspect of learning that does not come under the heading of American practical technology. Sinclair Lewis' Babbitt would have no trouble appreciating *DSM-III*.

Recently, Samuel Guze and I were privileged to be part of an international committee sponsored by the Alcohol, Drug Abuse, and Mental Health Administration, a committee inspired and created by the imaginative foresight of Gerald Klerman. The charge of our multinational group was to begin coordinating the evolving [International Classification of Diseases *(ICD-10)*] nomenclature on neuroses and personality disorders with that of *DSM-III*. To a room filled with European psychiatrists, we earnestly described how antisocial personality—by far the best researched of all axis II disorders—could be reliably, even validly, defined by the Chinese menu strategy of *DSM-III*. Unfortunately, we had stepped right out of the pages of Henry James. We were archetypes of Americans in Europe. Our defense of *DSM-III* was practical, concrete, naive, and above all parochial. A wise Pole, fluent in five languages and educated in five countries, looked hard at these two earnest and enthusiastic Americans, who were enormously pleased with their brand-new technology. Our markers of antisocial personality did not ring true for him or for the five cultures that he knew. "You know," he said sadly, "I begin to understand why in your country psychiatry has become so unpopular!" Without adequate sensitivity to value judgment and to cross-cultural and cross-generational mores and without putting the accent on the overall forest rather than the trees, *DSM-III* had defined antisocial personality with a language and with a certainty that seemed utterly preposterous to this experienced European.

How much more vulnerable than antisocial personality are the axis II classifications of borderline and narcissistic personality disorders! Only 10–20 years old, these disorders are still usually observed only in American cities that have opera houses and psychoanalytic institutes. Borderline and narcissistic personalities are rarely seen in Iowa City or in Mobile; certainly, they are not recognized in Tangiers or Bucharest. One wonders if these disorders were included in *DSM-III* as a committee-like compromise for also including somatization disorder (or Briquet's disease)—a disorder quite as regional as kuru. For unknown reasons Briquet's disease is rarely encountered outside of Missouri, Kansas, and Iowa. Perhaps, like hysteria in *DSM-III*, the diagnosis of borderline disorder or Briquet's disease lies in the eyes of the beholder.

Had they wished international consensus, *DSM-III* committees might have followed the path set by Kurt Schneider (1). They might have tried to focus on

SOURCE: *American Journal of Psychiatry, 141*(4), pp. 542–545, April 1984.

those personality types that over generations and across national boundaries have acquired some sort of cross-cultural validity. Schneider's typology resembles personality types, not fashions. The authors of *DSM-IV* will do well to listen less to committees and more to individuals, like Kurt Schneider, with a synthetic view.

DSM-III IS REDUCTIONISTIC

DSM-III ignores the fact that most of the diagnoses with which we deal in psychiatry reflect dimensions and continua. Pregnancy is a black-and-white diagnosis; schizophrenia (2) and dysthymic disorder are not. There are necessary and sufficient criteria for the diagnosis of pregnancy, but not for schizophrenia. It almost seems that committee writing leads to group regression in Piagetian cognitive development. In *DSM-III* there is little evidence of Piaget's formal operations. Concrete, reductionistic thinking served Linnaeus well, but unlike Linnaeus, *DSM-III* rarely sees to the heart of the matter. Karl Menninger (3) suggested that a few years' additional experience allowed Phillipe Pinel to prune his list of diagnoses from 2,400 to four. *DSM-IV* would do well to do likewise. If *ICD-9* can encompass the world's mental ills in 36 pages, does *DSM-III* need 300?

In its reductionism and its laundry lists, *DSM-III* becomes needlessly complex and trendy. Its categories are too numerous and its avoidance of old-fashioned general terms such as "neurosis" and "psychosis" only makes things worse. Instead, the committee's pet neologisms are included, while neurosis, a term with a 200-year history, is dropped. Why? Because the authors of *DSM-III* feared that neurosis was associated with a century-old theory. We hope that the authors of *DSM-IV* will pay more attention than their predecessors did to history, and that they will also pay attention to the genius of Adolf Meyer—a man who saw beyond black-and-white reductionism and taught us to see schizophrenia not as a disease entity but as a reaction pattern.

DSM-III CONFUSES STATE AND TRAIT

DSM-III pays too much attention to transient surface phenomena and too little attention to clinical course and human development. Emil Kraepelin made his great contribution to psychiatry in part because he distinguished manic-depressive patients from schizophrenic patients by their clinical course as much as by their presenting symptoms.

Diagnosis depends as much upon appreciation of clinical trajectory as it does upon cross-sectional detail. Even the best defined disease can have very different symptoms in the same patient at different ages. As reflected by the 1966 report of the Group for the Advancement of Psychiatry (GAP) (4), child psychiatry fully appreciated that sensitivity to development was essential to diagnosis. By ignoring development and longitudinal course, *DSM-III* is unlikely to serve child psychiatry as well as the GAP volume written 15 years earlier.

For years psychiatric diagnosis had been retarded by its insistence that paranoid, catatonic, and hebephrenic schizophrenic patients reflected different clinical traits rather than that they were the same individuals viewed at different stages in their lives. Fortunately, *DSM-III* does not repeat this particular mistake, but it makes others. *DSM-III* tries to split schizoid, schizotypal, schizophrenic, and schizophreniform psychoses into four discrete disorders; it fails to appreciate that when viewed cross-sectionally at different points in time, many individuals will pass from one category to another. For example, in the *DSM-III* nomenclature a person hitherto diagnosed as having a schizotypal personality disorder after a parent's death will be diagnosed as having a reactive psychosis, which 2 weeks later will be relabeled schizophreniform disorder, and 6 months later, without any real change in clinical manifestations, will be rediagnosed as undifferentiated schizophrenia. Kraepelin might have been confused.

Even neurology takes pains to point out that Parkinson's disease looks different at different ages. Akathisia and dystonia in youth reflect the same disorder that festination and pill-rolling tremor reflect in the elderly. Psychiatry can be no less aware of life trajectory than neurology is. Thus, the authors of *DSM-IV* will do well to listen to Samuel Guze's injunction that to be meaningful, diagnosis must imply not only "uniform clinical picture" and "predictable response to treatment" but also, within reason, "a uniform course" (5).

DSM-III IS ADYNAMIC

Not only does *DSM-III* pay too little attention to longitudinal course but it also pays too little attention to pathogenesis. Yet to ignore pathogenesis is to risk confusing symptom with disease.

In psychiatry, as in medicine, rational therapeutics depend on understanding pathophysiology. Yet nowhere does *DSM-III* pay adequate attention to the difference between disease process, on the one hand, and homeostatic mechanisms, on the other. Cough is sometimes a sign of illness but more often a healthy nonspecific adaptive pattern. Too often *DSM-III* gives us only criteria for classifying the extent of our patients' inflammation and ignores what lies beneath. It is as if fracture were not distinguished from callus formation and cough not distinguished from pneumonia. There is no place in *DSM-III* for encouraging physicians to concern themselves with pathogenesis, and ego defense mechanisms are deliberately ignored.

Apparently the *DSM-III* creators believed that since etiology in psychiatry is uncertain, it would be an advantage to ignore etiology altogether. But modern psychiatrists must be expert at both descriptive and dynamic diagnoses. The effort to make *DSM-III* a descriptive nosology that is atheoretical with regard to etiology creates a polarity between classification and explanatory formulation that is artificial. It may be the task of an adequate diagnostic system to appreciate the fact that most psychiatric disorders, like arteriosclerotic vascular disease, are the sum of multiple interacting causes, but that does not mean that diagnosis can ever ignore cause.

The historian of philosophy Walter Kaufmann suggested that Freud created a "poetic science" (6). Poets and novelists have always been able to take etiology into account, even when they were not sure. How? They paid attention to dynamics. Perhaps in parasitology, in orthopedics, and in computer technology one can escape from humanism, but not in psychiatry. Like it or not, psychiatry *is* dynamic. It has more in common with the inevitable ambiguity of great drama than with *DSM-III's* quest for algorithms compatible with the cold binary logic of computer science.

Axis VI was going to encompass Freud's defense mechanisms, but because defense mechanisms implied unconscious etiology, axis VI was abandoned by the [American Psychiatric Association] task force on *DSM-III*. For *DSM-III* to ignore defense mechanisms as obvious as displacement, projection, and reaction formation and yet to include disorders as vague and as poorly defined as dependent, avoidant, and narcissistic personality disorders is indefensible.

Ultimately, a diagnostic axis that includes defenses may prove to be the most valuable dimension in *DSM-IV*. For example, patients who have compulsive personality disorders typically display isolation of affect. In the interview situation, as in the rest of life, they are unable to experience simultaneously powerful affects and the ideas connected with them. This observation, although it originates in the psychodynamic concept of defense, can be made reliably and provides useful nosological data about compulsive personalities. Again, it is not at all uncommon for patients simultaneously to display symptoms of both panic and somatization, yet in *DSM-III* these two symptoms have become separate disorders, and the accompanying text provides contradictory instructions about their possible coexistence (7).

The authors of *DSM-III* imply that because emotional conflict is difficult to verify, it should not be taken into account. They forget that long before medicine had ever identified viruses, physicians were willing to postulate their existence. Before Koch, physicians learned to view cough and "laudable" pus not as disease entities but as evidence of adaptive response to unseen pathogens. But *DSM-III* chooses to ignore defense mechanisms because they cannot be identified with certainty and to reify the manifestations of conflict like simple phobia and the dissociative and dysthymic disorders. Yet too often such disorders are symptoms, and as such they are merely the visible flame of unseen combustion. They no more reflect diagnostic entities than do dropsy or cough. For example, hypochondriasis and somatization are treated as discrete disorders. *DSM-III* suggests that the hypochondriac complains of an imaginary disease and that the individual afflicted with somatization disorder complains of imaginary symptoms—as if that were an important distinction to anybody but a Thomist. In fact, both are defense mechanisms more often than diagnoses; hypochondriasis often conveys unconscious reproach, whereas somatization can reflect a wish for secondary gain or merely a desire to communicate an unconscious or unverbalized affective state.

A more flagrant example of the adynamic nature of *DSM-III* is that of dysthymic disorder, by which term *DSM-III* means garden-variety depression. As such, dysthymic disorder is a symptom par excellence. Depression can be due to anger turned against the self—for example, the retroflected rage of a woman toward an alcoholic husband; depression can also be due to the sequential loss of a woman's family through a series of catastrophes. Grief and rage are hardly identical clinical states. But as long as insomnia, tearfulness, and recurrent thoughts of suicide are intermittently present for 2 years, *DSM-III* cares not about etiology. It is almost as if *DSM-III* were hysterically blind to perceiving psychodynamics.

We must remember, too, that depression, like a child's tears, is often designed to get someone in the dysthymic person's environment to *do* something, rather than reflecting a discrete defect of twisted genes or of disordered amine metabolism. In other words, much that *DSM-III* suggests as signs of illness reflects efforts at communication. But systems theory, like conflict theory, is dynamic, and as such it is difficult to fit into a computer or into a static conception of the universe. Thus, systems theory and defense mechanisms have no place in *DSM-III*.

Clearly, psychiatry must concern itself with the uncertain, affective interplay between the hypothalamus, the limbic system, and the motor cortex—an interplay distorted by both the dimension of time and the alchemy of memory. Somehow, appreciation of this complexity got lost in the *DSM-III* committee work.

The authors of *DSM-IV* will do well to listen to Sigmund Freud's poetic science. For, like Kurt Schneider, Adolf Meyer, and Samuel Guze, Freud was a smart man. With his elucidation of defense mechanisms (8), Freud revolutionized our classification of neuroses. *DSM-III* is a step backward.

DSM-III SACRIFICES VALIDITY FOR RELIABILITY

At the Rochester Schizophrenia Conference, I asked Robert Spitzer why in the differential diagnosis of schizophrenia he ignored the importance of Bleuler's concept of autism. Did he not agree that autism (i.e., substituting fantasized human relationships for real ones) was a far more specific and valid hallmark of schizophrenia than were the criteria of Feighner or the Research Diagnostic Criteria (RDC)? Perhaps, he replied, but it was hard to get rater agreement on autism.

Yet to diagnose schizophrenia, as does *DSM-III*, by noting "auditory hallucinations on several occasions with a content of more than one or two words" is like trying to make the criterion for drafting professional basketball players that they be at least 7 feet tall. Obviously, measuring the height of a basketball player is a far more reliable procedure than judging his ball handling. But preoccupation with height rather than with ball handling is unlikely to lead to a championship team. The authors of *DSM-IV* will do well to listen not to Feighner but to Eugen Bleuler. By his focus on the still-difficult-to-grasp concept of autism, Bleuler was striving for truth, not rater reliability.

CONCLUSIONS

DSM-III represents a bold series of choices based on guess, taste, prejudice, and hope. Some of these choices are undoubtedly right, but few are based on fact or truth. In 1976, even while still on the drawing board, *DSM-III* represented a real evolutionary step forward. For that, Robert Spitzer and all who came to his aid deserve psychiatry's ungrudging gratitude and admiration. But today our task is to recognize *DSM-III* for what it is—a first draft.

In the future, we will want to pay attention to brilliant individuals who, like Linnaeus and Darwin, were able to see to the heart of the matter. We will want to find clinicians on the right evolutionary track who are capable of succinct thinking, capable of Piagetian formal operations, and capable of seeing the forest through the trees. For heuristic purposes my nominees are Kurt Schneider, Adolf Meyer, Samuel Guze, Sigmund Freud, and Eugen Bleuler, but I am sure that the reader can nominate others.

Certainly I hope that the authors of *DSM-IV* will rectify the mistakes of *DSM-III*. We want a psychiatric nomenclature that, like medical nomenclature, is international and not parochial. We want nomenclature that is not reductionistic but sees broad, unifying patterns. We want a nomenclature that embraces clinical course and is based on etiology and dynamism, not on static symptoms. Finally, we want a diagnostic system that is valid as well as reliable—on to *DSM IV*!

REFERENCES

1. Schneider K: Clinical Psychopathology. Translated by Hamilton MW. New York, Grune & Stratton, 1959
2. Zubin J, Spring B: Vulnerability: a new view of schizophrenia. J Abnorm Psychol 86:103–126, 1977
3. Menninger K: The Vital Balance. New York, John Wiley & Sons, 1963
4. Group for the Advancement of Psychiatry: Psychopathological Disorders in Childhood: Report Number 62. New York, GAP, 1966
5. Guze SB: The role of follow-up studies: their contribution to diagnostic classification as applied to hysteria. Seminars in Psychiatry 2:292–402, 1970
6. Kaufmann W: Discovering the Mind, vol 3. New York McGraw-Hill, 1980
7. Frances A, Cooper AM: Descriptive and dynamic psychiatry: a perspective on *DSM-III*. Am J Psychiatry 138: 1198–1202, 1981
8. Freud S: The neuro-psychoses of Defence (1894), in Complete Psychological Works, standard ed, vol 3. London, Hogarth Press, 1962

DISCUSSION

Philosophers of science distinguish between two types of concepts that can be used to describe entities in the real world: closed and open (Pap, 1953). A **closed concept**, such as a triangle, has clear-cut "boundaries." (Warning: Do not take the word *boundaries* too literally.) A shape is either a triangle or it is not. In addition, each of the features of a closed concept is perfectly correlated with the concept itself—that is, a closed concept possesses *perfectly defining* features. All triangles possess exactly three sides, and all shapes that possess exactly three sides are triangles.

In contrast, an **open concept**, such as a chair, has fuzzy boundaries (see Neisser, 1979). Many objects are not clearly either chairs or nonchairs. Is a beanbag a chair? How about a bar stool, a park bench, or a crate? If you are unsure of the answers to these questions, you are in good company. In addition, each of the features of an open concept is only imperfectly correlated with the concept itself—that is, an open concept does not possess perfectly defining features. Try naming a characteristic that all chairs possess and that no objects that are not chairs do not possess. For example, the characteristic "something that one can sit on" is not perfectly defining of a chair, because one can sit on many things—including a couch, a boulder, and a person's lap—that are not chairs.

How are triangles and chairs relevant to DSM-III? Virtually all psychopathological conditions—such as schizophrenia, bipolar disorder, and obsessive-compulsive disorder—are best thought of as open concepts (Cantor, Smith, French, & Mezzich, 1980; Meehl, 1986). That is, essentially all the conditions that fall under the umbrella of abnormal psychology are characterized by fuzzy boundaries and an absence of perfectly defining features. This openness is responsible for many of the dilemmas plaguing psychiatric diagnosis. Because most psychopathological syndromes have unclear and vaguely defined boundaries, interrater reliability will often tend to be less than optimal. Moreover, because most of these syndromes cannot be diagnosed with absolute certainty based on the presence or absence of one (or even several) features, disagreement almost inevitably arises concerning which features should be used as diagnostic criteria.

Crudely speaking, there are two ways in which one can deal with the extreme openness of most psychopathological categories. First, one can simply accept this openness as a fact of life and allow the descriptions of psychiatric diagnoses to reflect this openness. This is essentially the approach adopted by the developers of DSM-I and DSM-II, who permitted the descriptions of most categories to remain somewhat vague and fuzzy (see, for example, DSM-II's description of asthenic personality in the introduction to this chapter). The potential advantage of this approach is that it allows diagnosticians considerable flexibility, because they are free to consider a wide variety of information in arriving at a diagnostic decision. This flexibility, however, may be purchased at a substantial price: low interrater reliability.

Second, one can attempt to reduce the openness of psychiatric diagnoses by closing them up—that is, by making them more similar to closed concepts. This is essentially the approach adopted by the developers of DSM-III. By providing explicit criteria and decision rules for each category, and thereby limiting diagnostician flexibility, DSM-III has embraced a more closed approach to psychiatric diagnosis. The potential advantage of this approach is its increased interrater reliability. Nevertheless, increased reliability may also be purchased at a substantial price: decreased validity. Specifically, because a closed approach prevents diagnosticians from considering potentially relevant information, a closed approach may result in categories that are highly reliable but overly narrow.

Here is an example of the dangers of using a closed approach: DSM-III delineated two ways of meeting the criterion of recklessness in the diagnosis of antisocial personality disorder: "driving while intoxicated" and "recurrent speeding" (American Psychiatric Association, 1980, p. 321). The assessment of recklessness using DSM-III will probably be highly reliable, because diagnosticians will presumably experience relatively little difficulty agreeing on the presence or absence of either of these behaviors. But DSM-III's assessment of recklessness may result in less than ideal validity, because the clinician is prevented from considering other forms of recklessness, such as driving a motorcycle without adequate training or hunting while intoxicated. Thus, a relatively closed approach, like a relatively open approach, involves a trade-off. A closed approach aims to emphasize reliability but does so at the potential expense of validity. In contrast, an open approach aims to emphasize validity but does so at the potential expense of reliability.

Herein lies the crux of the dispute between the proponents and opponents of DSM-III: Do the benefits of shifting from a relatively open approach toward a closed approach outweigh its costs? Many of the criticisms leveled by Vaillant at DSM-III, such as its "black-and-white reductionism" (p. 543) and overemphasis on interrater reliability, reflect his conviction that the adoption of a more closed approach stripped the diagnostic system of much of its richness and complexity. In an important paper published several years after Vaillant's, David Faust and Richard A. Miner (1986) similarly contend that Spitzer and his colleagues' single-minded pursuit of rigor resulted in a more objective and reliable, but greatly oversimplified, system of classification. "In the long run," Faust and Miner assert, "there is little to be gained by attempting to measure poorly understood things precisely" (p. 966).

Nevertheless, the accomplishments of the developers of DSM-III should not be underestimated. DSM-III and its successors have rendered the process of arriving at psychiatric diagnoses considerably more explicit and thus more open to informed criticism and feedback. Moreover, by providing standard criteria and algorithms that most or virtually all diagnosticians use, these manuals have increased the likelihood that investigators who conduct research on a disorder, such as schizophrenia, are studying the same or at least reasonably similar groups of individuals. The importance of this achievement cannot be overlooked, because readers of the abnormal psychology literature can now more easily draw appropriate generalizations across studies. Similarly, this achievement has facilitated communication among clinicians, because what two different clinicians mean by *schizophrenia*, for example, has been brought into closer alignment.* Whatever DSM-III's shortcomings, there seems little doubt that its increased explicitness and standardization have exerted a long-term beneficial impact on both the science and the practice of psychiatric diagnosis.

QUESTIONS TO STIMULATE DISCUSSION

1. If you were placed in charge of the committee to develop DSM-V, what alterations would you make in the general format and design of the manual? (Note: This question does not concern alterations in the criteria for specific disorders.)
2. Do you agree with Vaillant that DSM-III is parochial? If so, how would you go about making the diagnostic manual less time- and culture-bound?
3. Vaillant and others have harshly criticized DSM-III's adoption of an atheoretical stance. What problems might ensue if the DSM were to incorporate a specific theoretical orientation—say, behaviorism or psychoanalysis—into its criteria for psychiatric disorders? Would these problems be offset by the potential benefits of a more theory based system?

*This conclusion should be tempered by the finding that many clinicians apparently ignore the DSM when assigning diagnoses (Kirk & Kutchins, 1992).

4. As you learned in Chapter 2, reliability is a prerequisite for validity. But might there be cases in which reducing the reliability of a diagnostic category might actually increase its validity? If so, how could this occur? Finally, if you have a copy of DSM-III, DSM-III-R, or DSM-IV handy, can you locate any examples in which lowering the reliability of a diagnostic category might increase its validity?

SUGGESTIONS FOR FURTHER READING

Faust, D., & Miner, R. A. (1986). The empiricist and his new clothes: DSM-III in perspective. *American Journal of Psychiatry, 143*, 962–967.
Faust and Miner provide a thoughtful and penetrating critique of the implicit philosophical bases underlying DSM-III. They argue that DSM-III represents an attempt to return to an outmoded and naive scientific methodology: strict empiricism. This article is appropriate for more advanced readers.

Himmelhoch, J., Mezzich, J., & Ganguli, M. (1991). Controversies in psychiatry: The usefulness of DSM-III. *Psychiatric Annals, 21*, 621–631.
This article is an edited transcript of a debate between the first two authors on the utility of DSM-III. Among the primary issues discussed are the advantages and disadvantages of the multiaxial system, the atheoretical stance adopted by the authors of DSM-III, and the extent to which DSM-III has prematurely closed off research on alternative classification systems.

Kendell, R. E. (1983). DSM-III: A major advance in psychiatric nosology. In R. L. Spitzer, J. B. W. Williams, & A. E. Skodol (Eds.), *International perspectives on DSM-III* (pp. 55–68). Washington, DC: American Psychiatric Press.
Don't be fooled by the title of this chapter: The great British psychiatrist spills most of his ink over the potential weaknesses of DSM-III, including its selection of axes, proliferation of unvalidated disorders, and unnecessarily restrictive diagnostic criteria. Kendell nevertheless concludes that the principal structural innovations of DSM-III, such as its use of operational definitions, render it a decided improvement over previous classification systems.

Kirk, S. A., & Kutchins, H. (1992). *The selling of DSM-III: The rhetoric of science in psychiatry*. New York: Aldine de Gruyter.
This is an entertaining and critical account of the political machinations involved in the development and marketing of DSM-III. Kirk and Kutchins' discussion of the DSM-III field trials, particularly the interpretation of the reliability data resulting from these trials, is especially enlightening. But beware: Certain sections of the book (for example, the discussion of the kappa coefficient as an index of interrater reliability) are marred by Kirk and Kutchins' polemical tone and less than impartial coverage of the critical issues.

Klerman, G. L. (1984). The advantages of DSM-III. *American Journal of Psychiatry, 141*, 539–542.
Klerman contends that the major new features of DSM-III—particularly its avoidance of theory in favor of description, use of operational criteria, emphasis on reliability, and multiaxial format—make it an enormously significant contribution to American psychiatry. His conclusion: "The judgment is in: DSM-III has already been declared a victory" (p. 542).

Millon, T. (1983). The DSM-III: An insider's account. *American Psychologist, 38*, 804–815.
This article provides the reader with an overview of DSM-III from one of the few major psychologists intimately involved in its construction. Millon discusses what he views as the major conceptual strengths and shortcomings of DSM-III and concludes with a list of suggestions for its revision, including the adoption of a consistent theoretical framework, development of a formal scheme for assessing psychosocial stressors, and increased emphasis on interpersonal approaches to diagnosis.

Millon, T., & Klerman, G. L. (Eds.). (1986). *Contemporary directions in psychopathology: Toward the DSM-IV*. New York: Guilford Press.
This is a superb and diverse collection of chapters dealing with conceptual and methodological problems in psychiatric classification and with proposals for improving DSM-III. The chapter by P. E. Meehl is a must for all who wish to think clearly about classification and diagnosis.

REFERENCES

American Psychiatric Association. (1980). *Diagnostic and statistical manual of mental disorders* (3rd ed.). Washington, DC: Author.

Cantor, N., Smith, E. E., French, D. R., & Mezzich, J. (1980). Psychiatric diagnosis as prototype categorization. *Journal of Abnormal Psychology, 89*, 181–193.

Faust, D. & Miner, R. A. (1986). The empiricist and his new clothes: DSM-III in perspective. *American Journal of Psychiatry, 143*, 962–967.

Kirk, S. A., & Kutchins, H. (1992). *The selling of DSM-III: The rhetoric of science in psychiatry*. New York: Aldine de Gruyter.

Meehl, P. E. (1986). Diagnostic taxa as open concepts: Metatheoretical and statistical questions about reliability and construct validity in the grand strategy of nosological revision. In T. Millon & G. L. Klerman (Eds.), *Contemporary directions in psychopathology: Toward the DSM-IV* (pp. 215–231). New York: Guilford Press.

Neisser, U. (1979). The concept of intelligence. *Intelligence, 3*, 217–227.

Pap, A. (1953). Reduction sentences and open concepts. *Methodos, 5*, 3–30.

Spitzer, R. L., & Fleiss, J. L. (1974). A re-analysis of the reliability of psychiatric diagnosis. *British Journal of Psychiatry, 125*, 341–347.

CHAPTER

Is the diagnostic system biased against women?

PRO	Kaplan, M. (1983). A woman's view of DSM-III. *American Psychologist*, 38, 786–792.
CON	Williams, J. B. W., & Spitzer, R. L. (1983). The issue of sex bias in DSM-III: A critique of "A woman's view of DSM-III" by Marcie Kaplan. *American Psychologist*, 38, 793–798.

OVERVIEW OF THE CONTROVERSY: Marcie Kaplan argues that the observed sex differences in the prevalence of many psychopathological conditions—particularly females' higher rates of depression and certain personality disorders—are due to implicit gender biases in diagnostic criteria. Janet B. W. Williams and Robert L. Spitzer respond by pointing out that sex differences in diagnostic rates may reflect genuine differences in the nature of societal pressures on males and females and that Kaplan's assertions regarding the existence of masculine biases in diagnostic criteria are unsubstantiated.

CONTEXT OF THE PROBLEM

Men and women differ in their measured levels of psychological characteristics. Few would dispute this statement, although many would argue about the number or magnitude of these differences. In the domain of personality, several sex differences are reasonably well documented. Males tend to score higher than females on indices of aggressiveness (Maccoby & Jacklin, 1974), whereas females tend to score higher than males on indices of dependency (Lazarus & Monat, 1979). But how are we to explain these differences? It is here that the principal controversy begins.

To oversimplify matters slightly, there are three major explanations for sex differences in measured personality traits. First, some authors argue that many or most of these differences stem primarily from biological factors. Such authors might attribute sex differences in measured aggressiveness, for example, largely to males' higher levels of testosterone (see, for example, Edwards, 1970). Second, some authors argue that sex differences in psychological traits stem primarily from societal and cultural factors. These authors might seek to explain sex differences in measured aggressiveness in terms of society's stronger prohibitions on females' overt expression of aggression (see, for example, Feshbach, 1969). Incidentally, these first two explanations are not incompatible; sex differences may arise from a combination or from the interaction of a biological predisposition with sociocultural factors.

The third explanation for sex differences in measured personality characteristics is rather different from the first two. Whereas the first two explanations accept the reality of such differences, the third explanation calls this reality into question. Proponents of this view contend that the measures psychologists use to assess many personality traits, including aggressiveness and dependency, are gender biased and that the reported sex differences in these traits are largely or entirely illusory. When psychologists refer to a measure as **biased**, they mean that this measure assesses a characteristic more validly in one group (such as males) than in another (such as females). In psychological lingo, a biased test contains **systematic error:** It preferentially misclassifies the members of one group. When some psychologists argue that intelligence tests are biased against certain ethnic groups, such as African-Americans, they are in effect asserting that such tests systematically misclassify the members of these ethnic groups as less intelligent than the members of other ethnic groups. The same argument can be extended to sex differences: Certain psychological measures may systematically misclassify the members of one gender, producing the appearance of sex differences that do not in fact exist.

Note that, according to this definition of bias, differences between groups are not necessarily biases. No one would seriously contend that bathroom scales are biased against males (although many males probably wish this were the case) simply because they tend to yield higher weights for males than for females. Such scales are not gender biased, because they assess the variable of weight with equal validity in both males and females: Males, after all, are heavier on average than females. A measuring instrument is biased only if it assesses a characteristic with lower validity in one group than in another.

The existence of substantial sex differences in the rates of a number of psychiatric diagnoses is well known. Major depression, anorexia nervosa, and somatization disorder, for example, are much more commonly diagnosed in females than in males. Antisocial personality disorder, alcohol dependence (alcoholism), and fetishism, in contrast, are much more commonly diagnosed in males than in females. But might these sex differences be a product of implicit gender biases in the diagnostic criteria for these conditions, or what Widiger and Spitzer (1991) have referred to as **diagnostic criterion sex bias**? More specifically, might these criteria reflect gender-specific ways of expressing certain psychological difficulties? These are the central questions addressed by the readings in this chapter.

THE CONTROVERSY: Kaplan vs. Williams and Spitzer

Kaplan

Marcie Kaplan begins by noting that women's rates of psychological treatment tend to be higher than men's. She reviews three major explanations for this sex difference: (1) Women are more willing than men to express psychological problems, (2) societal pressures place women at elevated risk for psychological problems, and (3) women are penalized (in other words, diagnosed) for both overconforming and underconforming to traditional female roles. Although Kaplan finds merit in some of these explanations, she proposes a different hypothesis: that the diagnostic criteria in DSM-III and similar systems frequently embody masculine-biased assumptions regarding what behaviors are indicative of mental normality and abnormality. For example, she asserts that the diagnosis of dependent personality disorder in DSM-III includes stereotypically feminine ways of expressing dependency (for example, leaving major career decisions up to one's spouse) but not stereotypically masculine ways of expressing dependency (for example, allowing one's spouse to cook, clean, and take care of all major household duties). To bolster her argument, Kaplan creates two fictitious personality disorders—"independent" and "restricted" personality disorders—that appear to be exaggerations of traditionally masculine characteristics. Why, she asks rhetorically, are these conditions not included in the diagnostic nomenclature? Finally, Kaplan maintains that many of the female sexual disorders in DSM-III suffer from similar male-biased assumptions.

Williams and Spitzer

Janet Williams and Robert Spitzer take issue with Kaplan's logic on several grounds. They maintain that Kaplan confuses the etiology of a psychiatric problem with the question of whether this problem should be considered a mental disorder. Specifically, Williams and Spitzer contend that recognizing sociocultural pressures as relevant to the etiology of a problem (such as depression) does not imply that this problem should be excluded from the diagnostic nomenclature. Williams and Spitzer also find Kaplan's charge that DSM-III omits male examples of psychopathology and exaggerations of male stereotypes to be unwarranted. In addition, they dispute her claim that several of DSM-III's categories for psychosexual dysfunction are gender biased. Finally, Williams and Spitzer present data from the DSM-III field trials demonstrating that a number of mental disorders are more common in males than in females, suggesting that DSM-III does not contain a pervasive masculine bias.

KEY CONCEPTS AND TERMS

dependent personality disorder Personality disorder characterized by excessive passivity and reliance on others.

histrionic personality disorder Personality disorder characterized by excessively dramatic and emotional behavior.

learned helplessness Hypothesis advanced by Martin Seligman and his colleagues to explain the origins of depression. According to this hypothesis, depression is a consequence of chronic exposure to uncontrollable events.

personality disorder Condition in which personality traits have reached extreme levels, resulting in inflexible and maladaptive behavior.

PREVIEW QUESTIONS

1. What are some of the explanations Kaplan cites (other than her own) to explain the overall sex difference in treatment rates for mental illness?

2. What is Kaplan's major criticism of DSM-III's definition of mental disorder?
3. Why does Kaplan believe that the diagnostic criteria for a number of DSM-III personality disorders (for example, dependent personality disorder) are biased against females?
4. How do Williams and Spitzer attempt to refute Kaplan's claim that DSM-III's definition of mental disorder is inherently biased against females?
5. Why do Williams and Spitzer disagree with Kaplan that the criteria for several personality disorders are gender biased?
6. Williams and Spitzer report a number of findings (from the DSM-III field trials) on sex ratios for various mental disorders. What are these findings, and why do Williams and Spitzer believe them to be damaging to Kaplan's central thesis?

MARCIE KAPLAN

A woman's view of DSM-III

More adult women than adult men are treated for mental illness (e.g., Gove & Tudor, 1973; Rohrbaugh, 1979). There are a variety of theories, most of which concern sex roles, that account for this sex difference. There is good reason for the sex role related explanation. According to Bem (1974) and Berzins, Welling, and Wetter (1978), most females are feminine typed and most males are masculine typed. Kelly (1983) concludes that sex differences in behavioral disorders may be associated not with sex but with sex role typing.

In this article I will review several of the popular sex role related theories on sex differences in mental illness treatment rates and then posit an additional one: A contributor to the sex differences in treatment rates is clinicians' diagnostic criteria—that is, in DSM-II (American Psychiatric Association, 1968) and now DSM-III (American Psychiatric Association, 1980). In other words, masculine-biased assumptions about what behaviors are healthy and what behaviors are crazy are codified in diagnostic criteria; these criteria then influence diagnosis and treatment rates and patterns. In my discussion of the influence of diagnostic criteria on sex differences in treatment patterns, I will look at some criteria for specific diagnoses.

THEORIES ABOUT SEX DIFFERENCES IN TREATMENT RATES

One theory (which has not adequately been supported by data) that accounts for the sex difference in treatment rates is that women are not sicker, they are just more willing to express symptomatology (Phillips & Segal, 1969). Another (more data-supported) theory is that women actually are sicker; their disadvantaged status in society makes them more at risk for mental illness. For instance, the Subpanel on the Mental Health of Women of the President's Commission on Mental Health (1978) documented ways in which inequality creates dilemmas for women in certain contexts (e.g., marriage, child rearing, aging, work). Carmen, Russo, and Miller (1981) add that this same inequality facilitates the occurrence of events (e.g., incest, rape, and marital violence) that heighten women's vulnerability to mental illness. They also point out the link between alienation, powerlessness, and poverty—many women's lot—and impaired mental health.

The theories that women are more willing to express symptomatology and that women's disadvantaged status makes them more vulnerable to mental illness are broad ones. Gove (1979) and Gove and Tudor (1973) formulated several more specific sex role related explanations for gender differences in disordered behavior. First they refined the finding that adult women have higher rates of mental illness and reported that women's higher rate is primarily due to the higher rate of mental illness among married women than among married men. (Widowed, divorced, and never-married men have higher rates of mental illness, respectively, than widowed, divorced, and never-married women [Gove, 1972].) Gove and Tudor offer several sex role related explanations for married women's greater vulnerability to mental illness. These are (a) Whereas men have two sources of gratification (family and work), traditional married women have only one source of gratification (family); (b) even when a married woman works, she is discriminated

SOURCE: *American Psychologist, 38*, pp. 786–792, July 1983.

against in the workplace and expected to work and be a homemaker, whereas the man is only expected to work; (c) homemaking is a frustrating, low-prestige job, unconsonant with the education and intellectual attainment of a large number of women; (d) the role of housewife is unstructured and invisible, allowing the individual time to brood alone; (e) expectations confronting women are unclear; for instance, women are supposed to adjust to and prepare for contingencies (Gove, 1979). (Data supporting these explanations are not supplied.)

Another sex role related theory accounting specifically for married women's higher treatment rates is based on Gilligan's (1979) work. Gilligan claims that whereas for men identity precedes intimacy (Erikson, 1950), sex roles dictate that for women identity and intimacy tasks are simultaneous. In other words, women claim an identity through intimate relationships. Bernard (1975) and Mischel (1966) suggest that women are thus more dependent on others than are men. Nadelson and Notman (1981) mention some resulting difficulties for women (and for men who marry early). For instance, those who marry before establishing identities may find their marital choices inappropriate later, and those who are "burdened by excessive dependency needs, unrealistic expectations of their partners, or unresolved psychological issues" (p. 1355) may find their intimate relationships difficult and stressful and their mental health at risk.

SEX RATIOS OF SPECIFIC DISORDERS

I turn now from the subject of women's higher treatment rates for disordered behavior in general to the subject of specific behavioral disorders. Table 1 divides those adult disorders for which (according to DSM-III) there are data on sex ratio into two categories: those more commonly diagnosed in adult women and those more commonly diagnosed in adult men. (Disorders whose onset is in adolescence are not included in the table; thus, Anorexia and Bulimia, primarily diagnosed in females, are not listed.) Inspecting Table 1 might lead one to the conclusion that women internalize conflict and that men act it out or, to use Allport's (1958) terms, that women are intropunitive and men, extropunitive.

TABLE 1 Disorders for Which There Are Data on Sex Ratio

More Commonly Diagnosed in Women	*More Commonly Diagnosed in Men*
Primary degenerative dementia	Multi-infarct dementia
Depression	Alcohol hallucinosis
Cyclothymic disorder	Substance use disorders
Dysthymic disorder	Transsexualism
Agoraphobia	Paraphilias
Simple phobia	Factitious disorder
Panic disorder	Impulse control disorder
Somatization disorder	Paranoid personality disorder
Psychogenic pain disorder	Antisocial personality disorder
Multiple personality	Compulsive personality disorder
Inhibited orgasm	
Inhibited sexual desire	
Histrionic personality disorder	
Borderline personality disorder	
Dependent personality disorder	

Note: Information adapted from DSM-III

What are some of the more specific sex role related explanations for so-called female disorders? There are two popular sex role related theories that account for depression (Weissman, 1980). One is the social status hypothesis: Sex discrimination results in "legal and economic helplessness, dependency on others, chronically low self-esteem, low aspirations, and, ultimately, clinical depression" (Weissman & Klerman, 1977, p. 106). The second sex role related popular theory that accounts for depression is the learned helplessness hypothesis (Seligman, 1973, 1975). Another theory less frequently cited than the above two is drawn from Lewinsohn (1974): Women have sex role related deficits in their capacity to obtain reinforcement from the environment. Thus, according to Kelly (1983), feminine-typed responses such as kindness, emotionality, self-subordination, and gentleness may not obtain reinforcement as effectively as masculine-typed responses such as assertiveness and forcefulness. Thus, those limited to feminine-typed responses might reach fewer goals than others might reach and thus would be more vulnerable to depression.

That Dependent and Histrionic Personality Disorders, Agoraphobia, and Anorexia are more commonly diagnosed in females has been explained as follows: These disorders represent caricatures of the traditional female role. In other words, as Chesler (1972) claimed, women's high treatment rates for mental illness reflect partially a labeling of women who overconform to sex role stereotypes as pathological. Thus, the individual with Dependent Personality Disorder is passive and subordinate; the individual with Histrionic Personality Disorder is vain, dependent, and given to exaggerated expression of emotions; the agoraphobic may fear entering and coping with a man's world (Chambless & Goldstein, 1980); and the anorexic may have faithfully followed her model—the fashion model—to a society-condoned anorexic weight level.

Many of the sex role related theories accounting for female disorders have some basis in data, but that data may be tangentially related. For instance, Hare-Mustin (1983) connected Linehan's (Note 1) study on the prevalence of behavior modification that teaches women to be thin with the prevalence of Anorexia in women. Another example of an indirect relationship between clinical and research data is the application of Seligman's (1974) learned helplessness studies to depressed women (an example of analogue studies). Most sex role related theories about women's higher treatment rates await empirical validation. Kelly (1983) suggests that a goal for the 1980s is to "integrate more directly sex role 'personality' research with research on clinical disorders" (p. 24).

OVERCONFORMING AND UNDERCONFORMING: A THEORY SUPPORTED BY DATA

One might say that of all the sex role explanations for women's higher treatment rates, one explanation is more directly supported by data than the others: Chesler's (1972) assertion that women are diagnosed for both overconforming and underconforming to sex role stereotypes. Data supporting this assertion are supplied by Broverman, Broverman, Clarkson, Rosenkrantz, and Vogel's (1970) study and similar subsequent studies. Broverman et al. found that therapists' criteria for healthiness in men and healthiness in adults were the same, but their criteria for healthiness in women were different:

> healthy women differ from healthy men [and thus healthy adults] by being more submissive, less independent, less adventurous, more easily influenced, less aggressive, less competitive, more excitable in minor crises, having their feelings more easily hurt, being more emotional, more conceited about their appearance, less objective, and disliking math and science. (p. 4)

Sherman (1980) reviewed 10 studies of therapists' and counselors' attitudes toward women that have been conducted since the Broverman study and found that despite the publicity of the Broverman findings and supposed changes in society's attitude toward women, stereotyping, albeit less severe than 10 years ago, still exists. Many studies showed that men stereotyped more than women; and some studies showed that older people and those with Freudian orientations stereotyped more than others.

The implications of the stereotyping described by Broverman et al. (1970) and the other researchers are that to be considered an unhealthy adult, women must act as women are supposed to act (conform too much to the female sex role stereotype); to be considered an unhealthy woman, women must act as men are supposed to act (not conform enough to the female sex role stereotype). Not only does this Catch-22 predict that women are bound to be labeled unhealthy one way or another, but also the double bind itself could drive a woman crazy.

DSM-III

Bearing in mind this discussion of sex role explanations for women's higher treatment rates, I turn to my own argument, which I advance not as an alternative to the above explanations but as an additional explanation. As previously mentioned, my thesis is that masculine-biased assumptions about what behaviors are healthy and what behaviors are crazy were codified in DSM-II and are now codified in DSM-III, and thus influenced and will continue to influence diagnosis and treatment rates. These masculine-biased assumptions are codified most explicitly in diagnostic criteria for Personality Disorders, which will be discussed in detail below. However, for the record, the assumptions are also codified in criteria for disorders other than Personality Disorders. For instance, classical Freudians would find Gender Identity Disorder of Childhood in every little girl and Atypical Gender Identity Disorder in many women, according to the Freudians' and DSM-III's (p. 263) respective assumptions about penis envy.

Definitions

DSM-III's definition of Mental Disorder and criteria for Personality Disorders is as follows:

> a clinically significant behavioral or psychological syndrome or pattern that occurs in an individual and that is typically associated with either a painful symptom (distress) or impairment in one or more important areas of functioning (disability). In addition, there is an inference that there is a behavioral, psychological, or biological dysfunction, and that the disturbance is not only in the relationship between the individual and society. (When the disturbance is *limited* to a conflict between an individual and society, this may represent social deviance, which may or may not be commendable, but is not by itself a Mental Disorder.) (p. 6)

According to DSM-III, all Personality Disorders entail "either significant impairment in social or occupational functioning or subjective distress" (p. 305), which spells out one of the criteria for Mental Disorder: "impairment in one or more important areas of functioning (disability)" (p. 6).

Problems

What does impairment in social or occupational functioning mean? I believe these criteria contain assumptions and then generate diagnoses accordingly. For instance, is a woman unemployed outside the home impaired in occupational functioning? Is a man who is employed outside the home and thus never there when his children come home from school impaired in social functioning? Evidently users of DSM-III assume not, or many "healthy" individuals who assume traditional sex roles would have diagnoses; yet a woman who neglects her children and a man who can't hold down a job—perhaps healthy individuals who assume nontraditional roles—may be labeled *impaired* by a diagnostician.

The above examples of potential diagnoses concern individuals who may experience no primary subjective distress, that is, no distress related directly to these behaviors mentioned (although they may experience distress related to society's and thus to their own reactions to these behaviors). These nondistressed, perhaps healthy, people are labeled *unhealthy*. What about individuals who perhaps are healthy and are subjectively distressed? Through arbitrary assumptions implicit in diagnostic criteria, do they too win diagnoses? For instance, consider the woman who experiences subjective distress because of the double bind inherent in wanting to be a healthy adult—self sufficient—and also in wanting to be a healthy woman—dependent on a man. She may have very real symptoms of unhappiness; according to DSM-III she may have Major Depression. But in her unhappiness, she may be reacting to an impossible situation the way any normal, healthy person would. Her unhappiness and her label of *depressed* may be manifestations that she is a scapegoat for society's illness, its unjust sex role imperatives. In other words, in terms of DSM-III's definitions of Mental Disorder and social deviance, it is difficult, if not impossible, to say when a disturbance is only brought about by a conflict between an individual and society. It is difficult to say when society should be labeled as *unjust* and when an individual should be labeled as *crazy*. This difficulty makes one wonder what assumptions clinicians make—and which diagnostic criteria encourage and support those assumptions—when they designate the individual, as opposed to society, as the problem.

Histrionic Personality Disorder ("Hysterical Personality" in DSM-II)

To make more specific this discussion of assumptions about what is healthy and what is crazy, I will turn to a specific DSM-III diagnosis—Histrionic Personality Disorder. Compare the criteria for that diagnosis with the findings of the Broverman et al. (1970) study concerning clinicians' criteria for healthiness in women. To earn the label of Histrionic Personality Disorder, which according to DSM-III is "diagnosed far more frequently in females than in males" (p. 314), an individual must satisfy three out of five criteria in Category A and two out of five criteria in Category B (p. 315). Three Category A criteria are "self-dramatization, e.g., exaggerated expression of emotions" (cf. Broverman et al.'s [p. 3] "being more emotional"), "overreaction to minor events" (cf. Broverman et al.'s "more excitable in minor crises"), and "irrational, angry outbursts or tantrums" (cf. Broverman et al.'s "more excitable," "more emotional," "less objective," i.e., less rational). Two Category B criteria are "vain and demanding" (cf. Broverman et al.'s "more conceited about their appearance") and "dependent, helpless, constantly seeking reassurance" (cf. Broverman et al.'s "more submissive, less independent, less adventurous, more easily influenced"). It appears then that via assumptions about sex roles made by clinicians, a healthy woman automatically earns the diagnosis of Histrionic Personality Disorder or, to help female clients, clinicians encourage them to get sick.

Dependent Personality Disorder ("Passive-Dependent Personality" in DSM-II)

Look at another set of assumptions codified in DSM-III about what is healthy and what is crazy. These assumptions result in the selective application of the label *dependency*. Why is dependency considered so subjectively distressing or impairment causing that it earns in its extreme expression the diagnosis of a Personality Disorder? The diagnosed individual

> passively allows others to assume responsibility for major areas of life because of inability to function independently, . . . subordinates own needs to those of persons on whom he or she depends in order to avoid any possibility of having to rely on self . . . [and] lacks self-confidence. (pp. 325, 326)

Again, these criteria echo the clinicians' idea of healthy women as described in the Broverman et al. (1970) study; they also echo Miller's (1976) description of subordinate-group members (women) in situations of inequality (society). Thus as in the Histrionic Personality Disorder, clinicians help individuals to attain a diagnosis, or clinicians label the individual *ill* in lieu of labeling society *unjust*.

As regards dependency, there is another means, besides the assumption that women should act more dependently than men, by which DSM-III guides clinicians to label women. That is, DSM-III singles out for scrutiny and therefore diagnosis the ways in which women express dependency but not the ways in which men express dependency. For instance, DSM-III does not mention the dependency of individuals—usually men—who rely on others to maintain their houses and take care of their children. (These are the others *from whom the individuals are independent.*) DSM-III does not mention the dependency of individuals—usually men—who, when widowed, seek a new spouse to take care of them (widowed women seek a new spouse to take care of [Troll, 1979]). DSM-III does not mention the dependency of individuals—usually men—whose mental illness rates are higher when they are alone than when they are married (women's rates are higher when they are married than when they are alone [Gove, 1972]). In short, men's dependency, like women's dependency, exists and is supported and sanctioned by society; but men's dependency is not labeled as such, and men's dependency is not considered sick, whereas women's dependency is.

To summarize, DSM-III makes three major assumptions about dependency. One is that there is something unhealthy about it. Another is that dependency's extreme expression in women is reflective not simply of women's relationship to (e.g., subordinate position in) society but also of women's behavioral, psychological, or biological dysfunction. A third assumption is that whereas women's expression of dependency merits clinicians' labeling and concern, men's expression of dependency does not.

DSM-III makes similar assumptions regarding histrionicness (as did DSM-II regarding hysteria). For instance, DSM-III assumes that the constellation of histrionic personality traits is not mostly reflective of women's subordinate position in society; however, contrast Miller's (1976) discussion of subordinate-group members carrying unsolved aspects of human experience such as childishness. Another DSM-III and DSM-II assumption is that histrionicness (hysteria) is unhealthy, but its opposite (see Restricted Personality below) is not.

Independent Personality Disorder and Restricted Personality Disorder

To underscore the above points regarding DSM-III's assumptions about dependency and histrionics, consider the following two fictitious diagnostic categories (presented in the DSM-III's format) and compare the first to the diagnosis of Dependent Personality Disorder and the second to the diagnosis of Histrionic Personality Disorder.

Diagnostic Criteria for Independent Personality Disorder

The following are characteristic of the individual's current and long-term functioning, are not limited to episodes of illness, and cause either significant impairment in social functioning or subjective distress.

A. Puts work (career) above relationships with loved ones (e.g., travels a lot on business, works late at night and on weekends)
B. Is reluctant to take into account the others' needs when making decisions, especially concerning the individual's career or use of leisure time, e.g., expects spouse and children to relocate to another city because of individual's career plans
C. Passively allows others to assume responsibility for major areas of social life because of inability to express necessary emotion (e.g., lets spouse assume most child-care responsibilities)

Differential diagnosis In Compulsive Personality Disorder, there is a perfectionism and an indecisiveness that are lacking in the Independent Personality Disorder. In Avoidant Personality Disorder there is more social withdrawal; the individual with Independent Personality Disorder has relationships with people but behaves as if she or he were independent of those people. However, all three of these disorders may coexist. Restricted Personality Disorder might coexist with Independent Personality Disorder.

Diagnostic Criteria for Restricted Personality Disorder

The following are characteristic of the individual's current and long-term functioning, are not limited to episodes of illness, and cause either significant impairment in social or occupational functioning (though usually not the latter) or subjective distress.

A. Behavior that is overly restrained, unresponsive, and barely expressed, as indicated by at least three of the following:
   1. Limited expression of emotions, e.g., absence of crying at sad moments
   2. Repeated denial of emotional needs, e.g., of feeling hurt
   3. Constant appearance of self-assurance
   4. Apparent underreaction to major events, e.g., is often described as stoic
   5. Repeatedly choosing physical or intellectual activities over emotional experiences
B. Characteristic disturbances in interpersonal relationships as indicated by at least two of the following:
   1. Perceived by others as distant; e.g., in individual's presence others feel uncomfortable disclosing their feelings
   2. Engages others (especially spouse) to perform emotional behaviors such as writing the individual's thank-you notes or telephoning to express the individual's concern
   3. Engages in subject-changing, silence, annoyance, physical behavior, or leave taking when others introduce feeling-related conversation topics
   4. Indirectly expresses resistance to answering others' expressed needs (e.g., by forgetting, falling asleep, claiming need to tend to alternate responsibilities)

The above two diagnoses share criteria with DSM-III's Compulsive Personality Disorder. For instance, three criteria for Compulsive Personality Disorder are "restricted ability to express warm and tender emotions," . . . "insistence that others submit to his or her way of doing things, . . . [and] excessive devotion to work and productivity to the exclusion of pleasure and the value of interpersonal relationships" (pp. 327–328). But satisfying those criteria alone will not win a DSM-III diagnosis. An individual must also be a perfectionist (e.g., preoccupied with details, lists, etc.) or be indecisive. In other words, whereas behaving in a feminine stereotyped manner alone will earn a

DSM-III diagnosis (e.g., Dependent or Histrionic Personality Disorder), behaving in a masculine stereotyped manner alone will not. A masculine stereotyped individual, to be diagnosed, cannot just be remarkably masculine. Masculinity alone is not clinically suspect; femininity alone is.

WOMEN'S SEXUALITY

As a final illustration of my argument that masculine-biased assumptions shape diagnosis and treatment patterns, I turn to the past literature on and conceptions of women's sexuality. Freud's classic theory that vaginal orgasms are different from and more mature than clitoral orgasms caused clinicians, their clients, and the public to believe that women who experienced clitoral orgasms were arrested in their psychological development. It was not until Masters and Johnson published *Human Sexual Response* in 1966 and claimed that there is only one female orgasm, and it is clitoral, that women who experienced clitoral orgasms were considered cured. In other words, women who before 1966 were immature or even dysfunctional were suddenly, in 1966, mature and functional. The women's sexual behavior did not change, but diagnostic criteria did. The DSM-III is compiled mostly by men, and the Psychosexual Disorder Advisory Committee is made up of approximately two-thirds men. That the DSM-III currently identifies Inhibited Orgasm and Inhibited Sexual Desire as (a) disorders, and (b) disorders more commonly found in females, in the light of psychiatry's past mistake regarding women's sexuality, should encourage some thought when one is considering women's sexual pathology. (The diagnostic criteria of Inhibited Female Orgasm acknowledge that diagnosis requires a "difficult judgment" [p. 279].)

CONCLUSION

Evidence discussed in this article should give one pause when one is considering women's pathology in general, sexual or otherwise. Our diagnostic system, like the society it serves, is male centered. In a female-centered system and society, the public mental health profile might be different. All young macho males seeking psychotherapy might tempt clinicians to award a diagnosis of restricted Personality Disorder (cf. clinicians' current generosity with the labels *histrionic* or *hysterical*). A Broverman study might discover the belief that healthy adult traits were dependence and emotionality; men might be caught in the double bind of choosing between male and adult healthiness; men's treatment rates might be higher than women's.

What is the significance of women's higher rates? As discussed earlier, Chesler (1972) asserts (and the Broverman et al. [1970] study supports the assertion) that one reason healthy women are labeled disordered is that they refuse to play the traditional female role. But Franks and Rothblum (1983) claim that women are disordered; that is, they are depressed, agoraphobic, and experience sexual dysfunction. If Franks and Rothblum are correct, then the demands of traditional sex roles may be more maladaptive for women than they are for men. Another explanation and the one explored in this article is that adaptiveness and maladaptiveness are arbitrarily defined. In other words, not only are women being punished (by being diagnosed) for acting out of line (not acting like women) and not only are traditional roles driving women crazy, but also male-centered assumptions—the sunglasses through which we view each other—are causing clinicians to see normal females as abnormal.

REFERENCE NOTE

1. Linehan, M. Behavior therapy for women: When equal treatment is unequal. In S. B. Sobel (Chair), *Clinical psychology of women: Old concerns and new approaches*. Symposium presented at the meeting of the American Psychological Association, Montreal, September 1980.

REFERENCES

Allport, G. W. *The nature of prejudice*. Garden City, N.Y.: Doubleday, 1958.

American Psychiatric Association. *Diagnostic and statistical manual of mental disorders* (2nd ed.). Washington, D.C.: Author, 1968.

American Psychiatric Association. *Diagnostic and statistical manual of mental disorders* (3rd ed.). Washington, D.C.: Author, 1980.

Bem, S. L. The measurement of psychological androgyny. *Journal of Consulting and Clinical Psychology*, 1974, *42*, 155–162.

Bernard, J. *Women, wives and mothers: Values and options*. Chicago: Aldine, 1975.

Berzins, J. I., Welling, M. A., & Wetter, R. E. A new measure of psychological androgyny based on the Personality Research Form. *Journal of Consulting and Clinical Psychology*, 1978, *46*, 126–138.

Broverman, I. D., Broverman, D. M., Clarkson, F. E., Rosenkrantz, P. S., & Vogel, S. R. Sex-role stereotypes and clinical judgments of mental health. *Journal of Consulting and Clinical Psychology*, 1970, *34*, 1–7.

Carmen, E. H., Russo, N. F., & Miller, J. B. Inequality and women's mental health: An overview. *American Journal of Psychiatry*, 1981, *138*(10), 1319–1330.

Chambless, D. L., & Goldstein, A. J. Anxieties: Agoraphobia and hysteria. In A. M. Brodsky & R. I Hare-Mustin (Eds.), *Women and psychotherapy: An assessment of research and practice*. New York: Guilford, 1980.

Chesler. P. *Women and madness*. New York: Avon Books, 1972.

Erikson, E. *Childhood and society*. New York: W. W. Norton, 1950.

Franks, V., & Rothblum, E. D. Concluding comments, criticism and caution: Consistent conservatism or constructive change? In V. Franks & E. D. Rothblum (Eds.), *The stereotyping of women: Its effects on mental health*. New York: Springer, 1983.

Gilligan, C. Woman's place in a man's life cycle. *Harvard Educational Review*, 1979, *49*, 431–446.

Gove, W. R. The relationship between sex roles, mental illness and marital status. *Social Forces*, 1972, *51*, 34–44.

Gove, W. R. Sex differences in the epidemiology of mental disorder: Evidence and explanations. In E. S. Gomberg & V. Franks (Eds.), *Gender and disordered behavior: Sex differences in psychopathology*. New York: Brunner/Mazel, 1979.

Gove, W. R., & Tudor, J. Adult sex roles and mental illness. *American Journal of Sociology*, 1973, *73*, 812–835.

Hare-Mustin, R. T. An appraisal of the relationship between women and psychotherapy: 80 years after the case of Dora. *American Psychologist*, 1983, 38, 593–601.

Kelly, J. A. Sex role stereotypes and mental health: Conceptual models in the 1970's and issues for the 1980's. In V. Franks & E. D. Rothblum (Eds.), *The stereotyping of women: Its effects on mental health*. New York: Springer, 1983.

Lewinsohn, P. H. A behavioral approach to depression. In R. J. Friedman & M. M. Katz (Eds.), *The psychology of depression: Contemporary theory and research*. Washington, D.C.: Winston-Wiley, 1974.

Masters, W. H., & Johnson, V. E. *Human sexual response*. Boston: Little, Brown, 1966.

Miller, J. B. *Toward a new psychology of women*. Boston: Beacon Press, 1976.

Mischel, W. A social learning view of sex differences and behavior. In E. Maccoby (Ed.), *The development of sex differences*. Stanford, Calif.: Stanford University Press, 1966.

Nadelson, C. C., & Notman, M. T. To marry or not to marry: A choice. *American Journal of Psychiatry*, 1981, *138*(10),1352–1356.

Phillips, D., & Segal, B. E. Sexual status and psychiatric symptoms. *American Sociological Review*, 1969, *34*(1), 58–72.

President's Commission on Mental Health: Subpanel on the Mental Health of Women. In *Report to the President* (Vol. 3). Washington, D.C.: U.S. Government Printing Office, 1978.

Rohrbaugh, J. B. *Women: Psychology's puzzle*. New York: Basic Books, 1979.

Seligman, M. E. P. Depression: Fall into helplessness. *Psychology Today*, June 1973, pp. 43–46, 48.

Seligman, M. E. P. Depression and learned helplessness. In R. J. Friedman & M. M. Katz (Eds.), *The psychology of depression: Contemporary theory and research*. Washington, D.C.: Winston-Wiley, 1974.

Seligman, M. E. P. *Helplessness: On depression, development and death*. San Francisco: Freeman, 1975.

Sherman, J. A. Therapist attitudes and sex-role stereotyping. In A. M. Brodsky & R. T. Hare-Mustin (Eds.), *Women and psychotherapy: An assessment of research and practice*. New York: Guilford, 1980.

Troll, L. Sex differences in aging. In E. S. Gomberg & V. Franks (Eds.), *Gender and disordered behavior: Sex differences in psychopathology*. New York: Brunner/Mazel, 1979.

Weissman, M. M. Depression. In A. M. Brodsky & R. T. Hare-Mustin (Eds.), *Women and psychotherapy: An assessment of research and practice*. New York: Guilford, 1980.

Weissman, M. M., & Klerman, G. L. Sex differences and the epidemiology of depression. *Archives of General Psychiatry*, 1977, *34*, 98–111.

JANET B. W. WILLIAMS & ROBERT L. SPITZER

The issue of sex bias in DSM-III: A critique of "A woman's view of DSM-III" by Marcie Kaplan

It is well-known that certain mental disorders are more frequently diagnosed in women than in men (Dohrenwend & Dohrenwend, 1976). The best example of this is the diagnosis of depression, which in nearly all studies in Europe and in the United States is found to be approximately twice as common in females as in males (Weissman & Klerman, 1977). Various theories have been proposed to account for this unequal sex ratio. These include theories about how certain biological and/or cultural factors affect the true prevalence or expression of a disorder in the two sexes, how certain psychological factors differentially affect the likelihood of whether an individual will seek treatment or in some other way come into the mental health system and therefore be diagnosed, and how bias on the part of clinicians affects the relative frequency with which a diagnosis is applied to females rather than males.

SOURCE: *American Psychologist*, 38, pp. 793–798, July 1983.

In . . . her article, "A Woman's View of DSM-III," Marcie Kaplan (Kaplan, 1983) asserts yet another explanation to account for the greater frequency with which women are diagnosed as having certain mental disorders:

A contributor to the sex differences in treatment rates [of mental disorders] is clinicians' diagnostic criteria—that is, in DSM-II (American Psychiatric Association, 1968) and now DSM-III (American Psychiatric Association, 1980). In other words, masculine-biased assumptions about what behaviors are healthy and what behaviors are crazy are codified in diagnostic criteria; these criteria then influence diagnosis and treatment rates and patterns" (p. 786).

Kaplan's charge of sex bias in DSM-III is a serious one which, if true, would constitute a major flaw in the scientific and clinical value of DSM-III. This article examines the logic of Kaplan's arguments and the accuracy of her statements about DSM-III. Although Kaplan's article raises important issues, she unfortunately presents no data to support her hypothesis, nor does she predict what data would either support or negate her view. We therefore present data from the field trials of DSM-III that describe the sex ratios of the major Axis I clinical syndromes, in order to determine the extent to which they are consistent with Kaplan's hypothesis. . . .

The authors of this article were both heavily involved in the development of DSM-III. The senior author, a woman deeply concerned about women's issues, was the text editor of DSM-III. The coauthor was the chair of the American Psychiatric Association's Task Force on Nomenclature and Statistics that guided the development of DSM-III. Together we attempted to insure that DSM-III avoid any manifestations of sex bias. Thus the text was carefully scrutinized to insure that whenever possible, clinical examples were not limited to either sex. In addition, we invited the American Psychiatric Association's Committee on Women to review drafts of DSM-III and made several changes in response to their suggestions (one being to change Hysterical Personality Disorder to Histrionic Personality Disorder to avoid the historical connotation of a wandering uterus as the cause of the disorder). This article can thus be considered "Another Woman's (and Man's) View of DSM-III."

KAPLAN'S VIEW OF DSM-III AS SEX-BIASED

Kaplan asserts that DSM-III is sex-biased in five ways: (1) in its definitions of mental disorder and of personality disorder; (2) in sex-biased assumptions in the criteria for some disorders; (3) in omitting male examples of pathology; (4) in its omission of diagnostic categories that correspond to masculine stereotypes; and (5) in the categories of psychosexual dysfunctions. Each of these are discussed below.

The DSM-III Definitions of Mental Disorder and Personality Disorder

Kaplan quotes the paragraph in DSM-III in which the concept of mental disorder is presented. This paragraph ends with the disclaimer that "when the disturbance is *limited* to a conflict between an individual and society, this may represent social deviance, which may or may not be commendable, but is not by itself a mental disorder" (p. 6). (This disclaimer was added to indicate that the diagnosing of political dissidents as mentally ill, as is done in some countries, is a misuse of psychiatric diagnosis.) She then gives an example of a woman experiencing "very real symptoms of unhappiness" (p. 789) because she is caught in the double bind of wanting to be self-sufficient but also wanting to be dependent on a man; Kaplan says that "according to DSM-III she may have major depression" (p. 789). Although Kaplan's point in giving this example is not absolutely clear to us, she apparently thinks that this woman's depression is only the result of a conflict with society and that the woman nevertheless, according to the DSM-III definition, will be diagnosed as having a mental disorder in spite of her "normal," "healthy" reaction to society's "unjust sex role imperatives" (p. 789). Kaplan concludes that in terms of DSM-III's definition of mental disorder and social deviance, "it is difficult to say when society should be labeled as *unjust* and when an individual should be labeled as *crazy*," (*p*. 789) and that clinicians probably frequently make the wrong assumptions about the attribution of symptoms of distress "when they [diagnose] the individual as opposed to society" (p. 789).

Kaplan seems to be confusing the etiology of a mental disorder with whether or not it should be diagnosed as such. We certainly agree, as would most clinicians who use DSM-III, that in many cases societal pressures are an important contributing factor to the development of mental disorders such as depression in women (as well as in men!). However, if the woman in Kaplan's example truly developed a full depressive syndrome, and not just "unhappiness," then we believe the diagnosis of a depressive disorder is appropriate. Presumably, psychotherapy would, at least in part, focus on helping her deal more effectively with whatever societal pressures contributed to the development of her depression.

The consequences of Kaplan's dichotomy that the problem lies *either* with society *or* the individual are staggering. Would Kaplan really argue that if unemployment and poverty contributed to someone's becoming physiologically dependent on alcohol, it would be wrong for a clinician to diagnose him or her as having Alcoholism?

Kaplan also seems to be confusing the misuse of the DSM-III definition of mental disorder with the definition itself. Consider her examples: She speculates that a healthy woman who rejects the traditional family role might be accused of neglecting her children (p. 789) and that a healthy man who chooses to reject the traditional male work role would be judged as not being able to "hold down a job" (p. 789). Clearly, there is nothing in the DSM-III definition itself, and Kaplan cites no specific phrases in the definition that would direct a clinician to make such sex-biased judgments.

Kaplan quotes the DSM-III definition of Personality Disorder that requires "either significant impairment in social or occupational functioning or subjective distress" (p. 305). She then says "I believe these criteria contain assumptions and then generate diagnoses accordingly" (p. 788). Significantly, Kaplan never states what these underlying sex-biased assumptions are and instead poses a series of questions that she apparently believes reveals them to the reader: "For instance, is a woman unemployed outside the home impaired in occupational functioning? Is a man who is employed outside the home and thus never there when his children come home from school impaired in social functioning?" (p. 788–789). Presumably, the answer she would assume DSM-III to have to her first question is Yes, and to the second, No, although the basis for this assumption of *hers* is never stated. We think her point is that the concepts of "occupational" and "social functioning" contained in the DSM-III definition of mental disorder are sex-biased by assuming that homemaking for a female is not an "occupation," and that family relationships for a male are not considered part of "social functioning."

It is hard for us to understand how Kaplan concludes that the DSM-III concepts of social and occupational functioning contain sex-biased assumptions. Although these concepts are not specifically defined in DSM-III, there are examples and criteria throughout the text that make it clear that "occupational functioning" includes homemaking and that "social relationships" include family relations for both sexes. One example is contained in the Axis V scale for Highest Level of Adaptive Functioning Past Year. The adult example for "superior functioning" (in which there must be "unusually effective functioning in social relations, occupational functioning, and use of leisure time" [p. 29]) is "single parent living in deteriorating neighborhood takes excellent care of children and home, has warm relations with friends, and finds time for pursuit of hobby" (p. 29). The reader will note that no sex is given for the example, implying that taking "excellent care of children and home" constitutes superior occupational functioning for a man or a woman.

Sex-Biased Assumptions in the Diagnostic Criteria

Kaplan charges that

> masculine-biased assumptions . . . are codified in criteria for other disorders besides Personality Disorders. For instance, classical Freudians would find Gender Identity Disorder of Childhood in every little girl, and Atypical Gender Identity Disorder in many women, according to the Freudians' and DSM-III's (p. 263) respective assumptions about penis envy. (p. 788)

First, let us examine the DSM-III diagnostic criteria for Gender Identity Disorder of Childhood, which unfortunately Kaplan did not quote in her article. The following criteria are for females (there is a corresponding category for males):

A. Strongly and persistently stated desire to be a boy, or insistence that she is a boy (not merely a desire for any perceived cultural advantages from being a boy).
B. Persistent repudiation of female anatomic structures as manifested by at least one of the following repeated assertions:
   (1) that she will grow up to become a man (not merely in role)
   (2) that she is biologically unable to become pregnant
   (3) that she will not develop breasts
   (4) that she has no vagina
   (5) that she has, or will grow, a penis. (pp. 265–266)

Under "differential diagnosis" for this category, DSM-III states that "children whose behavior merely does not fit the cultural stereotype . . . of femininity should not be given this diagnosis unless the full syndrome is present" (p. 265).

These criteria were developed with the help of the American Psychiatric Association's Committee on Women. They reviewed all of DSM-III prior to its final submission and made specific suggestions about this particular category; these suggestions were incorporated into the final version of DSM-III. The reader examining these diagnostic criteria and the statement regarding differential diagnosis may have difficulty, as we do, seeing how any reasonable clinician using DSM-III could diagnose Gender Identity Disorder of Childhood "in every little girl."

Now let us examine Kaplan's reference to "DSM-III's . . . assumptions about penis envy" (p. 788) that according to her appear on page 263. The reader who expects to find a reference to penis envy on page 263 of DSM-III will look in vain. This page contains a discussion of Transsexualism, a disorder in which there is a persistent sense of discomfort and inappropriateness about one's anatomic sex and a persistent wish to be rid of one's genitals and to live as a member of the other sex. Kaplan evidently was referring to the following sentences under the heading of "differential diagnosis":

> Other individuals with a disturbed gender identity may, in isolated periods of stress, wish to belong to the other sex and to be rid of their own genitals. In such cases, the diagnosis Atypical Gender Identity Disorder should be considered, since the diagnosis of Transsexualism is made only when the disturbance has been continuous for at least two years. (p. 263)

This is merely a caution about diagnosing Transsexualism in individuals with a transient stress-related desire to be of the opposite sex and be rid of their own genitals.

DSM-III does assume that a wish to belong to the other sex and to be rid of one's own genitals constitutes psychopathology, but this widely held clinical assumption is hardly the same as the Freudian theory of penis envy, which postulates that all girls go through an inevitable developmental phase in which they yearn to have a penis.

Omitting Male Examples of Pathology

In her critique of the DSM-III category of Dependent Personality Disorder, Kaplan states that DSM-III makes

> the assumption that women *should act* more dependently than men—by which DSM-III guides clinicians to label women. That is, DSM-III singles out for scrutiny and therefore diagnosis the ways in which women express dependency, but not the ways in which men express dependency. For instance, DSM-III does not mention the dependency of individuals—usually men—who rely on others to maintain their houses and take care of their children. (p. 789)

The reader of Kaplan's discussion of the DSM-III category of dependent personality disorder can only assume that in the text and criteria of DSM-III for this category, there are numerous examples of female dependency and none of male. In the criteria themselves there are three examples of dependent features: "lets spouse decide what kind of job he or she should have," "tolerates abusive spouse," and "sees self as helpless, stupid" (p. 326). Clearly these three examples are applicable for men as well as for women. In the text one specific example is given that hardly indicates DSM-III's insensitivity to women's issues: "For example, a wife with this disorder may tolerate a physically abusive husband for fear that he will leave her" (p. 325). The text provides many other examples of dependent features, but all of them use the phrase "he or she." It is true that the reference to tolerating a physically abusive spouse could have been written so that it applied equally to a male or a female, but it is hardly sexist to recognize that physically abusive spouses are usually husbands rather than wives.

Omission of Diagnostic Categories That Correspond to Male Stereotypes

Kaplan discusses the DSM-III category of Histrionic Personality Disorder and notes, as have many others, that it corresponds to a stereotype of femininity. She then invents two fictitious disorders, Independent and Restricted Personality Disorders, to show that whereas "behaving in a feminine stereotyped manner alone will earn a DSM-III diagnosis (e.g., Dependent or Histrionic Personality Disorder), behaving in a masculine stereotyped manner alone will not" (p. 791).

It never occurs to Kaplan that there are other DSM-III personality disorders that correspond to masculine stereotypes and therefore are more commonly diagnosed in men. Many would consider the features of Antisocial and Schizoid Personality Disorders to be caricatures of masculinity. According to DSM-III, Antisocial Personality Disorder is characterized by "lying, stealing, fighting, truancy, . . . resisting authority, . . . unusually early or aggressive sexual behavior, excessive drinking, . . . use of illicit drugs, . . . impaired capacity to sustain lasting, close, warm, and responsible relationships" (p. 318). Schizoid Personality Disorder is characterized by "emotional coldness and aloofness . . . absence of warm, tender feelings for others . . . indifference to the feelings of others" (p. 311).

The DSM-III Categories of Psychosexual Dysfunctions

Kaplan reviews past conceptions of female sexuality to show how male-biased judgments about woman's sexuality influenced judgments about female psychosexual dysfunctions. Without actually critiquing the DSM-III categories of psychosexual dysfunctions, she concludes that "in the light of psychiatry's past mistake regarding women's sexuality" (p. 791) one should question the accuracy of the DSM-III assumption that Inhibited Female Orgasm and Inhibited Sexual Desire are disorders. She also notes that the Psychosexual Disorders Advisory Committee was composed of two-thirds men.

We certainly agree with Kaplan that in the past, conceptions about female sexuality were male biased. The psychosexual dysfunctions classification of DSM-III was largely based on the work of Dr. Helen Singer Kaplan (Kaplan, 1974), a woman to be sure, and perhaps the most influential member of the Psychosexual Disorders Advisory Committee. Female members of the committee (with no opposition from male members) helped ensure that male-biased conceptions were avoided. For example, in the criteria for Inhibited Female Orgasm, there is a discussion of the difficulty of distinguishing a pathological inhibition of female orgasm from a normal variation of the female sexual response, thus avoiding the frequent male assumption that female inability to have orgasm always indicates pathology. If Marcie Kaplan detects male-biased assumptions in the DSM-III section on psychosexual dysfunctions, the burden is on her to point to them rather than to merely imply that they exist.

SEX RATIOS OF DSM-III AXIS I CLINICAL SYNDROMES

If Kaplan is correct in asserting that the DSM-III definition of mental disorder is generally biased toward diagnosing healthy women as disordered, then one would expect there to be a tendency for more females than males to be diagnosed in all diagnostic categories. Table 1 presents the sex ratios of Axis I clinical syndromes for 2,712 adults (1,297 males, 1,415 females) evaluated during the second phase of the DSM-III field trials. (These evaluations were done by several hundred clinicians at a large number of mental health facilities that included many different kinds of clini-

TABLE 1 Sex Ratios of Axis I Diagnoses in DSM-III Phase 2 Field Trials for Adults

Diagnosis	*Males*	*Females*	*Sex Ratio (M/F)*	*Chi square*[a]
Eating disorders	5	17	.29	4.58*
Affective disorders	272	457	.60	31.7**
Bipolar	84	72	1.17	2.05
Major depression	100	232	.43	40.88**
Cyclothymic	7	13	.54	.85
Dysthymic	67	129	.52	101.47
Adjustment disorder	174	261	.67	10.06**
Senile and presenile dementias	26	33	.79	.196
Anxiety disorders	99	123	.80	.76
Somatoform disorders	38	47	.81	.24
Somatization	1	13	.08	7.72**
Conversion	7	10	.70	.09
Psychogenic pain	9	18	.50	1.72
Hypochondriasis	21	8	2.62	6.09*
Mental retardation	14	14	1.00	.06
Psychosexual dysfunction	17	13	1.31	.39
Schizophrenia	258	170	1.52	26.04**
Substance-induced organic mental disorders	49	31	1.58	5.52*
Substance use disorders	297	131	2.27	78.4*
Paraphilias	15	0	∞	∞**

Note: $N = 2{,}712$; 1,297 males and 1,415 females ages 18 or over
[a]Observed sex ratio versus expected sex ratio based on overall sex ratio (.92)
$^{*}p < .05$ $^{**}p < .01$

cal services, for example, inpatient clinics, outpatient clinics, specialized clinics, private practice.) Approximately two thirds of the patients were outpatients, the remainder inpatients. The details of the method of the field trials is described elsewhere (Williams & Spitzer, 1980). Only those diagnostic categories with at least 10 males or females are presented. Subgroups of the major diagnostic classes are shown when they differ from the overall sex ratio of the major class. Sex ratios are calculated by dividing the number of males with the disorder by the number of females with the disorder. Therefore, sex ratios of less than one indicate that the disorder is more commonly diagnosed in females.

As can be seen, there is no overall tendency for the sex ratios to be less than 1.00 even though the overall sex ratio for the entire sample is .92. There are several categories more commonly diagnosed in females, but there are also several categories more commonly diagnosed in males, a finding that is consistent with the Dohrenwends' 1976 survey of over 80 studies designed to count both untreated and treated cases of psychiatric disorder conducted in different parts of the world since the turn of the century (Dohrenwend & Dohrenwend, 1976).

As expected, Major Depression is more commonly diagnosed in females, but Bipolar Disorder is approximately equally common in the two sexes. A recent community survey of the prevalence of affective disorders among the Amish in Pennsylvania reveals an equal proportion of males and females with both Major Depression and Bipolar Disorder (Egeland & Hostetter, 1983). This finding in the total absence of all forms of alcoholism in the Amish suggests that in the larger culture, alcoholism in males may represent a masked form of affective disorder and certainly offers no support to Kaplan's assertion that the criteria for depression contain sex-biased assumptions.

The sex ratios for two specific Somatoform Disorders are intriguing. Somatization Disorder (a chronic illness involving multiple unexplained physical symptoms) is far more common in women, whereas Hypochondriasis (morbid fear of or preoccupation with the belief of having a serious physical disease) is more common in men. Examination of the diagnostic criteria for these two disorders does not reveal any sex bias in the way in which the criteria are written. For whatever reason, men and women apparently express emotionally based physical symptoms in different ways.

Table 1 indicates that the nine Paraphilias (formerly called Sexual Perversions) were diagnosed only in men, although the criteria, with only one exception (Transvestism—never observed in females), are written so that they could apply to either males or females. Schizophrenia and Substance Use Disorders are more common in men.

SUMMARY AND CONCLUSIONS

During the development of DSM-III, strenuous efforts were made to avoid the introduction of male-biased assumptions. A careful analysis of Kaplan's critique of DSM-III fails to support her contention that "masculine-biased assumptions about what behaviors are healthy and what behaviors are crazy are codified in diagnostic criteria; these criteria then influence diagnosis and treatment rates and patterns" (p. 786). Kaplan's argument is based on the faulty assumption that recognizing a societal problem (e.g., sexism) excludes the utility of clinical diagnosis of the individual. Many of the hypothetical clinical examples that she uses to illustrate her point have no relationship to the actual content of DSM-III and only show one of the many ways in which DSM-III conceivably could be misused. No specific examples of sex-biased assumptions are provided, and frequently she implies the existence of a sex-biased statement in DSM-III that cannot be found. If Kaplan's thesis is correct that there is a general bias toward diagnosing females as having a mental disorder, then one would expect a general tendency for all major categories to be given more frequently to women. Examination of the sex ratios for the DSM-III Axis I clinical syndromes reveals many categories that are more commonly diagnosed in men, providing no support to her thesis.

REFERENCES

American Psychiatric Association. *Diagnostic and statistical manual of mental disorders* (2nd ed.). Washington, D.C.: Author, 1968.

American Psychiatric Association, *Diagnostic and statistical manual of mental disorders* (3rd ed.). Washington, D.C.: Author, 1980.

Dohrenwend, B. P., & Dohrenwend, B. S. Sex differences and psychiatric disorders. *The American Journal of Sociology*, 1976, *81*, 1447–1454.

Egeland, J. A., & Hostetter, A. M. Amish study, 1: Affective disorders among the Amish, 1976–1980. *American Journal of Psychiatry*, 1983, *140*, 56–61.

Kaplan, H. S. *The new sex therapy: Active treatment of sexual dysfunctions*. New York: Brunner/Mazel, 1974.

Kaplan, M. A woman's view of DSM-III. *American Psychologist*, 1983, *38*, 786–792.

Kass, F., Sptizer, R. L., & Williams, J. B. W. An empirical study of the issue of sex bias in the diagnostic criteria of DSM-III Axis II personality disorders. *American Psychologist*, 1983, *38*, 799–801.

Weissman, M. M., & Klerman, G. L. Sex differences and the epidemiology of depression. *Archives of General Psychiatry*, 1977, *34*, 98–111.

Williams, J. B. W., & Spitzer, R. L. DSM-III field trials: Interrater reliability. In *Diagnostic and statistical manual of DSM-III* (3rd ed.). Washington, D.C.: American Psychiatric Association, 1980.

DISCUSSION

Since the publication of the two articles in this chapter over a decade ago, the controversy regarding gender bias in psychiatric diagnosis has grown increasingly intense and acrimonious. Prior to the publication of DSM-III-R in 1987, heated disputes erupted in several quarters concerning the possible inclusion of four additional disorders in the diagnostic nomenclature:

- Premenstrual syndrome (officially called at that time, perhaps euphemistically, late luteal phase dysphoric disorder), a condition characterized by marked emotional, behavioral, and physical changes occurring around the menstrual period
- Self-defeating personality disorder (initially called, less euphemistically, masochistic personality disorder), a syndrome characterized by a chronic history of self-destructive and masochistic actions
- Sadistic personality disorder, a syndrome marked by a repeated pattern of cruelty, humiliation, and violence toward others
- Paraphilic coercive disorder, a condition intended primarily to identify rapists who are sexually aroused by the coercive quality of the act (Holden, 1986)

The first two conditions are much more common among females (the first is, of course, exclusive to females), whereas the last two conditions are much more common among males. Proponents of these diagnoses argued that these conditions were seen in a relatively large number of individuals, that they often produced significant impairment, and that there was sufficient evidence for their validity to merit at least their provisional inclusion in the DSM.

Nevertheless, numerous feminist mental health professionals, as well as researchers concerned with the issue of gender bias, raised serious questions regarding both the validity and ethical implications of all four conditions. Many writers contended that the diagnosis of premenstrual syndrome would stigmatize females for normal biological events (hormonal changes beginning prior to menstruation) and would be difficult to assess reliably and validly (Gallant & Hamilton, 1988; Hamilton & Gallant, 1990). Moreover, self-defeating personality disorder, critics argued, is often or usually a consequence of physically, sexually, or emotionally abusive relationships. Because the diagnosis of a personality disorder implies a longstanding and pervasive pattern of behavior that does not arise solely in response to an environmental stressor, many critics insisted that self-defeating personality disorder was better thought of as an understandable reaction to prolonged maltreatment than as a personality disorder.

The criticisms concerning the two predominantly male disorders were different. The inclusion of these conditions in the diagnostic manual, opponents charged, would legitimize or excuse physically and sexually abusive behaviors by males. For example, males who repeatedly battered their spouses or lovers could defend themselves—ethically, legally, or both—by explaining that their behavior was due to sadistic personality disorder. Similarly, males who raped because they enjoyed humiliating or dominating females could potentially be exculpated by invoking their paraphilic coercive disorder.

Because of the controversies surrounding all four conditions, Robert Spitzer and the other developers of DSM-III-R settled for a compromise, which left neither the proponents nor the opponents of their inclusion entirely satisfied: The first three syndromes were included in the appendix of DSM-III-R as "categories needing further study" (American Psychiatric Association, 1987, p. 367), whereas paraphilic coercive disorder was dropped entirely. Moreover, a clause was added to DSM-III-R stating that the diagnosis of self-defeating personality disorder should not be made if the behaviors occurred "exclusively in response to, or in anticipation of, being physically, sexually, or psychologically abused" (APA, 1987, p. 374). Nevertheless, this clause failed to placate many of the critics of this diagnosis, who claimed that more subtle and insidious forms of abuse and mistreatment were being disregarded.

The controversies surrounding most of these syndromes resurfaced in the early 1990s as DSM-IV approached publication. Once again, the developers of DSM-IV opted for a compromise. Both self-defeating and sadistic personality disorders were omitted entirely, whereas premenstrual syndrome (now called premenstrual dysphoric disorder) was listed in the text under a "wastebasket" category titled "Depressive Disorders Not Otherwise Specified"; its diagnostic criteria were placed in the appendix.

In evaluating the recent controversies concerning these diagnoses, a point made by Williams and Spitzer in their article is worth reiterating. As they note, it is essential to divorce the question of what causes a condition from the question of whether that condition constitutes a valid diagnosis. Several years ago, I had a discussion with a colleague regarding the well-documented sex difference in the rates of major depression (virtually all investigators have reported that major depression is approximately twice as frequent among females as among males). "I don't believe that there is a true sex difference in depression rates," he said. When I confronted him with the overwhelming research evidence to the contrary, he responded, "Yes, but women so have many more stressors to deal with than men; so of course they will have higher rates of depression." My good colleague had fallen into the same trap that Williams and Spitzer caution us against. Simply because one can identify a plausible cause for a disorder does not render that disorder any less real or any less worthy of study or treatment. If, for example, a greater number of life stressors were found to be the principal cause of the elevated rate of essential hypertension (high blood pressure of unknown origin) among African-Americans, would we stop considering their essential hypertension a disorder and thus disregard it? A physician who elected to do so could justifiably be accused of malpractice, because essential hypertension is no less a risk factor for heart attacks among blacks than among whites.

The more important question to be answered in evaluating these controversial diagnoses, as well as those discussed by Kaplan (for example, histrionic and dependent personality disorders), is whether they are biased against females. As you will recall from the introduction to this chapter, the issue of bias concerns whether a diagnosis assesses certain characteristics more validly in one group (in this case, on the basis of gender) than in another. In other words, a biased diagnosis is one that has a different meaning in one group than in another. Critics who maintain that the diagnosis of self-defeating personality disorder, for example, is biased against females are asserting that this diagnosis tends to reflect one set of characteristics (such as masochism) in males and a different set of characteristics (such as mistreatment by a spouse or lover) in females.

The opposition toward including sadistic personality disorder in the nomenclature, however, seems premised less on its potential bias than on its potential misuse (for example, excusing males for their abusive behavior). This argument raises an intriguing question: Should the potential abuse of a psychiatric diagnosis constitute a reason for its exclusion from the diagnostic manual? Some would contend that the decision of whether to include a condition in the diagnostic nomenclature should be based on purely scientific considerations; any diagnosis can be misused by those sufficiently determined to do so. For example, the diagnosis of paranoid schizophrenia was used frequently in the former Soviet Union to stigmatize political dissidents, but few would maintain that this misuse justifies the omission of paranoid schizophrenia from the psychiatric classification system.

Finally, the analysis of bias presented here raises yet another puzzling question, this time in the case of premenstrual syndrome. Can one determine whether a diagnosis is gender biased if, by definition, it is present only in one gender? Indeed, the gender-specific nature of premenstrual syndrome has been one of the major reasons why many researchers have never felt entirely comfortable about its inclusion in the DSM (Gallant & Hamilton, 1988). Along these lines, Carol Tavris (1992) has asked, only half facetiously, why a corresponding diagnosis such as "excessive testosterone syndrome" is not made among males. Extremely high testosterone levels are, after all, associated with increased rates of antisocial and criminal behaviors. Although Tavris's analogy is imperfect (women can possess elevated levels of testosterone, whereas men cannot suffer from premenstrual symptoms), it raises an intriguing question. Does the diagnosis of premenstrual syndrome, and perhaps other conditions, reflect the implicit use of males as a benchmark for mental health?

QUESTIONS TO STIMULATE DISCUSSION

1. Do you believe that ethical issues (for example., the extent to which a diagnosis may unfairly stigmatize or legitimize the behaviors of one gender) should be considered before deciding whether to include a diagnosis (such as self-

defeating personality disorder or sadistic personality disorder) in the DSM? Or should this decision be based solely on scientific considerations?

2. Kaplan and others contend that histrionic personality disorder—which is characterized by traits such as vanity, emotionality, seductiveness, and craving for attention—is in essence a caricature of "traditional" femininity. Should there then be a predominantly male diagnostic category of macho personality disorder, characterized by such traits as aggressiveness, tendency to degrade and dominate women, unwillingness to express tender emotions, and male chauvinist attitudes? What arguments could you make both for and against the inclusion of this category?
3. If you were appointed a consultant to DSM-V, what recommendations would you make concerning the inclusion of premenstrual syndrome (premenstrual dysphoric disorder)?
4. Given that all individuals (including those who sit on DSM committees) probably hold implicit gender biases, is at least some degree of gender bias inevitable in any diagnostic manual? Or are there ways of ensuring that gender bias is minimized or even eliminated from the DSM?
5. At the conclusion of their article, Williams and Spitzer present data showing that many Axis I conditions are more prevalent among males than females. Do their findings compellingly refute Kaplan's claims? Defend your answer.
6. Must a diagnosis exhibit a sex difference in order to be gender biased? Explain.

SUGGESTIONS FOR FURTHER READING

Chodoff, P. (1982). Hysteria and women. *American Journal of Psychiatry, 139*, 545–551.

Chodoff reviews the history of the concept of hysteria and concludes that hysteria is a caricature of traditional femininity. He argues that sex differences in stereotypically "feminine" characteristics stem primarily from biological factors. Finally, Chodoff conjectures that the sociopath, or perhaps the "macho" personality, is a caricature of traditional masculinity, and raises the question of why "macho personality disorder" is not recognized by the diagnostic system as a male analogue of histrionic personality disorder.

Earls, F. (1987). Sex differences in psychiatric disorders: Origins and developmental influences. *Psychiatric Developments, 1*, 1–23.

Earls reviews the literature on sex differences in major adult psychiatric disorders, including alcoholism, depression, antisocial personality, and eating disorders. He argues that these sex differences stem from temperamental differences in childhood, and he discusses both biological (for example, sex hormones) and social (for example, parenting styles) influences on these temperaments.

Gomberg, E. S., & Franks, V. (Eds.). (1979). *Gender and disordered behavior: Sex differences in psychopathology*. New York: Brunner/Mazel.

This is a useful compilation of readings touching on such topics as sex differences in depression, suicidal behavior, criminality, and alcoholism. The chapter by Gove provides a good overview of the literature on the epidemiology of mental illnesses in males and females, as well as a discussion of explanations for sex differences in the prevalence of various mental illnesses.

Kaplan, M. (1983). The issue of sex bias in DSM-III: Comments on the articles by Spitzer, Williams, and Kass (1983). *American Psychologist, 38*, 802–803.

Kaplan responds to Williams and Spitzer's critique and to the critique written by Kass, Spitzer, and Williams (see following listing). She contends that her arguments do not necessarily predict higher psychopathology rates among females across all diagnostic categories. In addition, she proposes that different diagnoses in some cases reflect sex-typed manifestations of the same underlying problem (for example, depression in females and alcoholism in males).

Kass, F., Spitzer, R. L., & Williams, J. B. W. (1983). An empirical study of the issue of sex bias in the diagnostic criteria of DSM-III Axis II personality disorders. *American Psychologist, 38*, 799–801.

In a further reply to Kaplan's original article, Kass, Spitzer, and Williams report data from the DSM-III field trials on the prevalences and sex ratios of personality disorders. They found no difference in the overall rate of personality disorders between males and females and significantly higher rates of several personality disorders, including antisocial and paranoid personality disorders, among males than among females.

Lilienfeld, S. O. (1992). The association between antisocial personality and somatization disorders: A review and integration of theoretical models. *Clinical Psychology Review, 12*, 641–662.

Lilienfeld reviews the evidence suggesting that antisocial personality disorder and somatization disorder reflect sex-differentiated expressions of the same underlying predisposition and evaluates the evidence for four models explaining their association. He concludes that social and cultural factors shape the expression of a genetically influenced predisposition toward these two syndromes.

Tavris, C. (1992). *The mismeasure of woman*. New York: Simon & Schuster.

Adapting her title from Steven Jay Gould's book "*The Mismeasure of Man*," Tavris takes aim at most psychologists' implicit assumption that males should be used as the standard with which to gauge psychological normality. Chapter 5 ("Misdiagnosing the Mind") provides an entertaining critique of sex bias in psychiatric diagnosis but is marred by several errors and misstatements.

Warner, R. (1978). The diagnosis of antisocial and hysterical personality disorders: An example of sex bias. *Journal of Nervous and Mental Disease, 166*, 839–845.

Warner reports the results of a study purporting to show sex bias in the diagnosis of antisocial personality disorder and hysteria. He provided a group of clinicians with a hypothetical case history of a patient who is immature, self-centered, guiltless, and flirtatious but told half these clinicians that the patient is female and the other half that the patient is male. Warner found that clinicians are much more likely to make a diagnosis of hysterical personality disorder when the patient is female but are about equally likely to diagnose antisocial personality disorder when the patient is male. Warner's somewhat premature conclusion: "We should modify our present diagnostic schema, which is confusingly tied to behavior patterns and sexual stereotypes, to achieve a more functional system" (p. 844).

Widiger, T. A., & Spitzer, R. L. (1991). Sex bias in the diagnosis of personality disorders: Conceptual and methodological issues. *Clinical Psychology Review, 11*, 1–22.

The authors provide a helpful overview of the literature on sex bias in the diagnosis of DSM-III and DSM-III-R personality disorders and discuss problems that have led to misinterpretations of research findings. They argue that investigators must be careful to distinguish sex bias from sex differences stemming from genuine biological or sociocultural influences.

REFERENCES

American Psychiatric Association. (1987). *Diagnostic and statistical manual of mental disorders* (3rd ed., rev.). Washington, DC: Author.

Edwards, D. A. (1970). Post-neonatal androgenization and adult aggressive behavior in female mice. *Physiology and Behavior, 5*, 465–467.

Feshbach, N. D. (1969). Sex differences in children's modes of aggressive responses toward outsiders. *Merrill-Palmer Quarterly, 15*, 249–258.

Gallant, S. J., & Hamilton, J. A. (1988). On a premenstrual syndrome diagnosis: What's in a name? *Professional Psychology: Research and Practice, 19*, 271–278.

Hamilton, J. A., & Gallant, S. J. (1990). Problematic aspects of diagnosing premenstrual phase dysphoria: Recommendations for psychological research and practice. *Professional Psychology: Research and Practice, 21*, 60–68.

Holden, C. (1986). Proposed new psychiatric diagnoses raise charges of gender bias. *Science, 231*, 327–328.

Lazarus, R. S., & Monat, A. (1979). *Personality*. Englewood Cliffs, NJ: Prentice-Hall.

Maccoby, E. E., & Jacklin, C. N. (1974). *The psychology of sex differences*. Stanford, CA: Stanford University Press.

Tavris, C. (1992). *The mismeasure of woman*. New York: Simon & Schuster.

Widiger, T. A., & Spitzer, R. L. (1991). Sex bias in the diagnosis of personality disorders: Conceptual and methodological issues. *Clinical Psychology Review, 11*, 1–22.

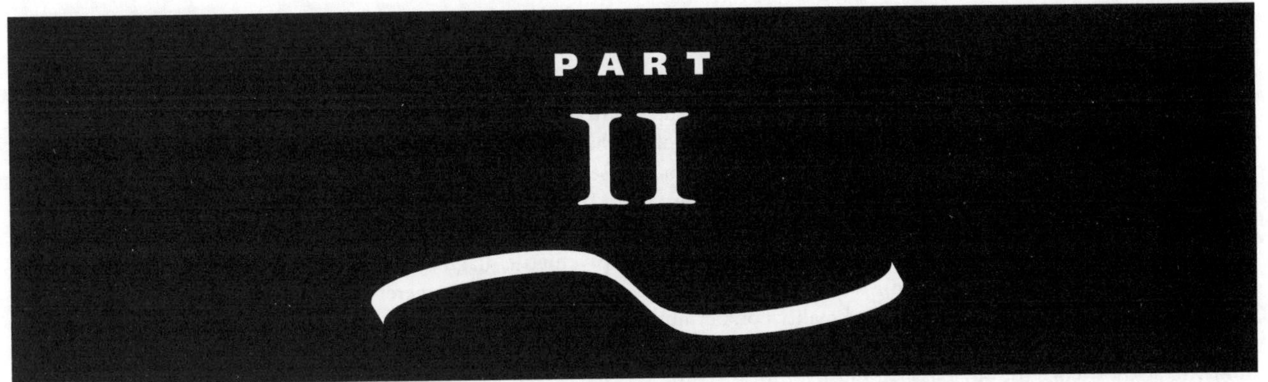

Psychopathology: Its Characteristics and Causes

Though this be madness, yet there is method in 't.

—Shakespeare, *Hamlet* (Act II, Sc. II)

INTRODUCTION

Dating back at least to Hippocrates, scientists have been in the business of attempting to subdivide the enormously heterogeneous domain of abnormal behavior into more meaningful and homogeneous categories. Although there have been a variety of schemes for subdividing mental disorders, the distinction that held sway for much of the 20th century was that between neuroses and psychoses. Indeed, this distinction has managed to find its way into our popular language and continues to exert influence on our modern classification systems. Despite the shortcomings associated with this distinction (which, as you will see shortly, led to its deletion from the official diagnostic nomenclature), it does provide a useful starting point with which to conceptualize the similarities and differences among mental disorders.

The term *neurosis* was apparently coined by William Cullen of the University of Edinbourg in 1769 (Postel & Quetel, 1983). Cullen's choice of this term was predicated on his conviction that neuroses were of physiological origin (*neurosis* literally means "disease of the nerves"). *Neurosis* later came to refer to a diverse group of conditions characterized by such symptoms as anxiety, depression, and somatic complaints lacking a clearly demonstrated physical basis. In addition, most neurotic individuals were viewed as possessing a common set of characteristics: intact contact with "reality" (note that I am cleverly sidestepping the philosophical debate regarding the existence of an objective "reality"), adequate orientation (that is, awareness of who one is, of where one is, and of time), awareness of their illness (commonly referred to as insight), and relatively mild social and occupational impairment. Most neurotic individuals were treated on an outpatient basis, often by means of psychotherapy alone.

Psychoses, in contrast, referred to a group of conditions characterized by such symptoms as **delusions** (fixed false beliefs not shared by members of one's culture or subculture) and hallucinations (perceptions of stimuli that are not physically present). (Incidentally, most beginning abnormal psychology students seem to confuse delusions with hallucinations; I passionately implore you not to become a member of this unsavory majority.) In contrast to neurotic individuals, most psychotic individuals were believed to be characterized by substantially impaired contact with "reality," grossly impaired orientation, little or no awareness of their illness, and severe social and occupational impairment. Many or most psychotic individuals required inpatient hospitalization, often involving a mix of psychotherapy and somatic treatments (for example, medications or electroconvulsive therapy).

As handy as the distinction between neuroses and psychoses was, it became increasingly evident that it was problematic in a number of respects. First, many individuals (such as depressed patients) exhibited relatively mild symptoms, adequate contact with reality, and additional characteristics of neurosis at certain times but seemed to develop severely incapacitating symptoms, markedly impaired contact with reality, and additional characteristics of psychosis at other times. Second, some conditions did not seem to fit neatly into either category. Many individuals with alcoholism, for example, were found to exhibit adequate orientation and reality contact but marked social and occupational impairment and a striking inability to acknowledge the obvious facts of their illness. Third, a number of psychopathologists had serious reservations concerning the excess theoretical baggage associated with the term *neurosis*. To many, this term had come to be inextricably embedded in concepts derived from psychoanalytic theory, such as unconscious conflict, repression, and neurotic anxiety. As a result, many theorists and researchers who were not psychoanalytically oriented felt understandably uncomfortable about the term's use.

In response to these and other difficulties, the *Diagnostic and Statistical Manual*, Third Edition (DSM-III) omitted the term *neurosis* from the formal diagnostic system and, with it, the classic distinction between neuroses and psychoses. The fourth edition, DSM-IV, now has 17 classes of mental disorders, many of which cut across the traditional boundaries of neurosis and psychosis. In this second part of the book, I will touch on conditions from seven of the major diagnostic classes listed in DSM-IV: schizophrenia, anxiety disorders, mood disorders, dissociative disorders, personality disorders, psychoactive substance use disorders, and childhood disorders. Because of space limitations, I have elected not to discuss controversial issues relevant to conditions in a number of other important diagnostic classes, such as somatoform disorders, sleep disorders, impulse control disorders, organic mental disorders, and psychological factors affecting physical condition (previously referred to as "psychosomatic" or "psychophysiological" disorders by some writers). If you are interested, you can explore some of the unresolved issues concerning these conditions by consulting the works listed in the appendix.

At this point, you may justifiably wonder whether the choice of a classification scheme isn't arbitrary. Isn't the decision of how to subdivide the domain of mental disorders simply a matter of personal taste and preference? Although there may be at least a grain of truth in such accusations—psychologists and psychiatrists can be just as irrational as the rest of humanity—the true picture is considerably more complex. Recall from the introduction to Part I that valid psychiatric diagnoses share an extremely important characteristic: They provide us with novel information. In this respect, a valid *diagnosis* differs from a *label*, which simply provides a summary term for a set of behaviors. In an article that should be required reading for all serious students of abnormal psychology, Robins and Guze (1970) delineate several criteria for establishing the validity of psychiatric diagnoses (also see Chapter 9 in this book). Valid psychiatric diagnoses, according to Robins and Guze, inform us about such characteristics as diagnosed individuals' family history, course and outcome, and performance on laboratory and personality tests. Thus, the choice of a classification system is far from arbitrary. Psychopathologists, whatever their disagreements, share a commitment to developing a classification system that will yield the most valid (that is, most informative) diagnoses. I urge you to bear this point in mind while reading the selections in this section of the book.

OVERVIEW OF PART II

In this second part of the book, we examine a broad spectrum of issues relevant to the diagnosis, clinical features, and etiology of various mental disorders. Although the articles in this part span a remarkably diverse set of issues, the common thread running through them is their focus on controversial issues relevant to specific forms of psychopathology.

In Chapter 5, we revisit the age-old "nature versus nurture" issue in the context of the debate over the genetic basis of schizophrenia. In Chapter 6, we explore the question of whether anxiety and depression can be meaningfully distinguished. In Chapter 7, we explore the utility of the "disease model" of alcoholism and encounter important questions regarding the conceptualization of socially problematic behaviors as "addictions." In Chapter 8, we explore the complex issues regarding the validity of one of the most controversial of all psychopathological syndromes—multiple personality disorder. In Chapter 9, we examine the controversy surrounding the diagnosis of borderline personality disorder and, in the process, confront some of the difficulties that have bedeviled the classification of personality disorders in general. Chapter 10 concerns the question of whether sex-reassignment surgery improves the long-term adjustment of transsexuals. Finally, in Chapter 11 we examine the longstanding controversy regarding the existence of clinical depression in children.

REFERENCES

Postel, J., & Quetel, C. (Eds.). (1983). *Nouvelle histoire de la psychiatrie*. Toulouse, France: Privat.

Robins, E., & Guze, S. B. (1970). Establishment of diagnostic validity in psychiatric illness: Its application to schizophrenia. *American Journal of Psychiatry, 126*, 983–987.

CHAPTER

5

Does schizophrenia have a substantial genetic component?

PRO Straube, E. R., & Oades, R. D. (1992). Genetic studies. In E. R. Straube & R. D. Oades (Eds.), *Schizophrenia: Empirical research and findings* (pp. 361–384). San Diego: Academic Press.

CON Lewontin, R. C., Rose, S., & Kamin, L. J. (1984). Schizophrenia: The clash of determinisms. In R. C. Lewontin et al. (Eds.), *Not in our genes* (pp. 197–231). New York: Pantheon Books.

OVERVIEW OF THE CONTROVERSY: Eckart R. Straube and Robert D. Oades review the evidence from twin and adoption studies of schizophrenia and conclude that schizophrenia is substantially influenced by genetic factors. Richard C. Lewontin, Steven Rose, and Leon J. Kamin find the evidence for the heritability of schizophrenia to be unconvincing and argue that greater attention should be focused on social and cultural factors in the genesis of schizophrenia.

CONTEXT OF THE PROBLEM

The so-called "nature versus nurture" issue has been one of the most persistent and longstanding debates in psychology, including abnormal psychology. This issue, which I will argue in the Discussion of this chapter is essentially a pseudoissue, concerns whether differences among individuals are attributable to differences in their genetic endowment (nature) or to differences in their experience (nurture). The term **heritability**, which is often misused and misunderstood (not least of all by psychologists), refers to the extent to which differences among individuals in a characteristic (for example, their levels of intelligence or extroversion) are due to differences in their genetic makeup. Please note: Heritability does not refer to the importance of genes in the origin of a characteristic. For example, although genes are responsible for producing the proteins that lead to the development of our arms (and are thus extremely important in the development of our arms), the heritability of having both arms is close to zero. Why? Because the *differences* among individuals in whether or not they possess both arms are due largely or entirely to environmental factors (such as accidents), not genetic factors. Keep this point in mind, because a great deal of unnecessary confusion has resulted from the failure to understand what heritability means.

In the arena of psychopathology, the heritability of schizophrenia, which is a severe disorder of thought and emotion frequently associated with delusions and hallucinations, has for decades served as a focal point for the nature versus nurture debate. More recently, that debate in abnormal psychology has to some extent shifted to behavior problems, such as alcoholism (See Chapter 7) and violent criminality. Nevertheless, the same methodological issues that have been bones of contention in the debate concerning the genetics of schizophrenia are also relevant to the investigation of the heritability of these conditions.

Three major **behavior-genetic designs** (that is, research designs that provide information regarding genetic influences on behavior) help to elucidate the heritability of a condition: family studies, twin studies, and adoption studies. Family studies typically involve a comparison of the prevalence of a condition among the relatives of affected individuals (in other words, those with the condition) with the prevalence of this condition among the relatives of unaffected individuals. Although family studies are quite useful for certain purposes, such as estimating relatives' risk of developing a condition, they are severely limited in one respect. Specifically, because genetic and environmental influences are confounded (inextricably entangled) in intact families, family studies are indeterminate regarding genetic versus environmental causation. In other words, because individuals in intact families share both genes and environment, family studies cannot provide conclusive information regarding the extent to which a condition is influenced by genetic or environmental factors. Family studies do provide useful information about heritability in one respect, however: If a condition does not run in families, it is highly unlikely that it is influenced by genetic factors. (For discussion of an important but presumably rare possible exception, see Lykken, McGue, Tellegen, & Bouchard, 1992). Because of the limitations of family studies, behavior-geneticists have generally turned to more definitive methodologies, particularly twin and adoption studies, to clarify the role of genetic factors in the etiology of mental illnesses.

In the traditional twin study, the investigator compares the concordance (the occurrence in both members of a pair) rate of a condition in monozygotic (MZ) or identical twins, who share 100% of their genes, with the concordance rate of that condition in same-sex dizygotic (DZ) or fraternal twins, who share 50% of their genes on average. (An aside: The word *genes* in the preceding sentence technically refers only to those genes that differ from one human to another, which actually constitute only about one-fifth of one percent of the human genetic material.) DZ twins are thus no more genetically similar or dissimilar than ordinary same-sex siblings. If the concordance of a condition among MZ twins exceeds that among same-sex DZ twins, we can conclude with reasonable certainty that this condition is at least partly heritable. The twin design is, however, premised on an important assumption—the **equal environments assumption**. This assumption, which is more complex than it might appear at first blush, essentially posits that (1) MZ twins are not treated more similarly than are same-sex DZ twins or (2) if MZ twins are in fact treated more similarly than same-sex DZ twins, this greater similarity in treatment does not increase MZ twins' similarity for the characteristic in question relative to that of same-sex DZ twins. If you are confused at this point, do not despair: The equal environments assumption is discussed in greater detail in the reading by Lewontin, Rose, and Kamin and in the Discussion section.

Finally, in the typical adoption study, the investigator compares the prevalence of a condition among the adopted-away biological relatives of affected individuals with its prevalence among the adopted-away biological relatives of unaffected individuals. If a condition is influenced by genetic factors, the prevalence of this condition in the former group should be higher than that in the latter group. In many ways, the adoption design provides the most unequivocal test of genetic influence on a characteristic, because it allows the cleanest separation of genetic and environmental factors. Unlike the family study, in which genetic and environmental influences are hopelessly and inextricably confounded, the adoption study permits investigators to examine the independent effects of genes and environment. Like the twin study, however, the adoption study is premised on a key assumption—**random placement**, which is also discussed in the reading by Lewontin, Rose, and Kamin. Essentially, the assumption of random placement (the opposite of selective placement) posits that adoptees are placed with parents who are no more similar to these adoptees' biological parents than would be expected by chance.

As you will see, many of the differences in the way that Straube and Oades, on the one hand, and Lewontin, Rose, and Kamin, on the other, interpret the data on the heritability of schizophrenia stem from differences in their evaluation of the two principal assumptions of the twin and adoption designs—equal environments (twin studies) and random placement (adoption studies). Whereas Straube and Oades view these assumptions as largely or entirely warranted, Lewontin, Rose, and Kamin do not. For Lewontin, Rose, and Kamin, these assumptions represent serious, if not fatal, stumbling blocks in the effort to detect genetic influences on schizophrenia.

THE CONTROVERSY
Straube and Oades vs. Lewontin, Rose, and Kamin

Straube and Oades

Eckart Straube and Robert Oades first point out that schizophrenia has a pronounced tendency to aggregate in families, although they acknowledge that this finding does not provide definitive evidence for genetic transmission. They then review evidence from several studies demonstrating that the concordance rate for schizophrenia among MZ twins considerably exceeds that among same-sex DZ twins and conclude that these data argue strongly for a genetic component to schizophrenia. Straube and Oades also review the major findings from adoption studies of schizophrenia, which consistently show that the adopted-away biological relatives of schizophrenics exhibit a higher rate of schizophrenia than do the adopted-away biological relatives of nonschizophrenics, or normals, and again conclude that these data indicate a substantial genetic influence on schizophrenia. Straube and Oades next discuss evidence that the offspring of the unaffected MZ co-twins of schizophrenics are at elevated risk for schizophrenia, suggesting that these offspring have inherited a predisposition toward schizophrenia from their parents. In addition, they review findings suggesting that schizophrenia spectrum conditions—conditions that appear to represent mild or attenuated forms of schizophrenia—are partially under genetic control and are genetically associated with schizophrenia. Straube and Oades discuss several models for the transmission of schizophrenia and conclude that models involving the action of multiple genes, in conjunction with environmental factors, appear to be the most plausible in light of existing evidence. Finally, Straube and Oades review the findings of molecular genetic (linkage) studies of schizophrenia, which involve examining the extent to which known genetic material segregates with schizophrenia within families. They conclude that the results of these studies are inconclusive although promising.

Lewontin, Rose, and Kamin

In this reading, which has been abridged for the purposes of this book, Richard Lewontin, Steven Rose, and Leon Kamin begin by noting the "clash of determinisms"—biological versus cultural—that has bedeviled the study of schizophrenia for decades. They trace the history of the search for the genetic basis of schizophrenia to the eugenics movement of the early part of the 20th century, which aimed to "improve" the gene pool by eliminating genes ostensibly predisposing toward schizophrenia, criminality, alcoholism, and other socially undesirable conditions. Lewontin, Rose and Kamin review Kallman's classic twin studies of schizophrenia and find his results to be highly questionable. They also review the findings from other major twin studies of schizophrenia, including Gottesman and Shield's 1972 study, and again find these results to be unconvincing. Not only are these studies plagued by methodological problems, the reading's authors claim, but the greater concordance among MZ twins than among DZ twins reported by most investigators can be plausibly attributed to greater environmental similarity among MZ twins than DZ twins. Lewontin, Rose, and Kamin then discuss the results of the Danish adoption studies, which are frequently cited as the most persuasive evidence for the heritability of schizophrenia. They argue that close inspection of these studies reveals little or no evidence of a genetic basis for schizophrenia *per se*, as well as serious methodological problems such as selective placement by adoption agencies. Lewontin, Rose, and Kamin conclude that the evidence for the heritability of schizophrenia is extremely weak and that investigators interested in the etiology of schizophrenia must begin to attend seriously to broad social and cultural influences.

KEY CONCEPTS AND TERMS

concordance Occurrence of a given condition in both individuals of a pair (typically a twin pair). Concordance is the opposite of discordance.

cross-fostering design Adoption design in which individuals are raised by adoptive parents who have a particular psychiatric condition. This design allows investigators to determine whether the presence of this condition in the adoptive parents increases the children's risk of developing this condition.

discordance Occurrence of a given condition in only one member of a pair (typically a twin pair). Discordance is the opposite of concordance.

eugenics Policy of attempting to "improve" the gene pool of a population by practices such as mandatory sterilization and limits on immigration.

genotype Organism's genetic endowment. Genotype must be distinguished from phenotype.

Mendelian inheritance Pattern of inheritance characterized by the action of single genes. Mendelian inheritance differs from polygenic inheritance.

penetrance Extent to which a characteristic (for example, schizophrenia) is manifested in individuals with a given genotype. In a genetic condition with a high penetrance, such as Huntington's chorea, many or all individuals with the genotype will develop the condition.

phenotype Observable characteristic of the organism. Phenotypes result from a combination of or interaction between the genotype and environmental influences.

polygenic inheritance Pattern of inheritance characterized by the action of multiple genes. Polygenic inheritance differs from Mendelian inheritance.

schizophrenia spectrum Broad class of conditions including both schizophrenia and milder syndromes thought to be genetically related to schizophrenia. Although investigators disagree somewhat on the boundaries of this spectrum, it typically includes such conditions as schizotypal, paranoid, and sometimes schizoid personality disorders.

schizotypal personality disorder Personality disorder characterized by oddities in thinking, behavior, and appearance and by abnormalities in social relationships.

selective placement Tendency for adoptees to be placed in homes on a nonrandom basis. Typically, selective placement involves the placement of adoptees with adoptive parents who are more similar on relevant characteristics (such as psychopathology, personality traits, and intelligence) to the adoptees' biological parents than would be expected by chance.

zygosity Classification of twins as monozygotic ("identical," originating from the same zygote, or fertilized egg) or dizygotic ("fraternal," originating from two different zygotes or fertilized eggs).

PREVIEW QUESTIONS

1. What are the three major research designs that behavior-geneticists use for examining the influence of genetic factors on a condition, and what is the logic behind each?

What are the potential weaknesses and limitations of each design?
2. What are the major findings from twin studies of schizophrenia? How do Straube and Oades, on the one hand, and Lewontin, Rose, and Kamin, on the other, differ in their interpretations of these findings?
3. What are the major findings from adoption studies of schizophrenia? Once again, how do these two sets of authors differ in their interpretations of these findings?
4. What is the schizophrenia spectrum, and why is it potentially relevant to the genetics of schizophrenia?
5. According to Straube and Oades, what are the most plausible models for the mode of inheritance of schizophrenia? What makes these models more likely than alternative models?

ECKART R. STRAUBE & ROBERT D. OADES

Genetic studies

I. IS SCHIZOPHRENIA INHERITED?

A. Familial Aggregation of Schizophrenia

A schizophrenic is more likely than a nonschizophrenic to have a blood relation who is also schizophrenic. All research reports agree on this point (e.g., Gottesman and Shields, 1982; Frangos *et al.*, 1985; Kendler *et al.*, 1985; Winokur *et al.*, 1985; McGue *et al.*, 1986). The risk of a first-degree relative developing schizophrenia is about 10 times higher than that of a relative of a nonschizophrenic subject (see Table 1). (The risk for someone without close relatives with schizophrenia is approximately 0.85%). . . .

It should be emphasized that about 90% of schizophrenics have no schizophrenic parents, brothers, or sisters (Gottesman and Shields, 1982; McGue and Gottesman, 1989). However, the probability that the monozygotic (MZ) twin of a schizophrenic also suffers in some degree from schizophrenia is higher than that of the twin that comes from another egg and does not share 100% of the genetic material [i.e., dizygotic (DZ); Table 1].

It appears that schizophrenia has a genetic component, but that inheritance may not follow classical Mendelian rules, with dominant and recessive genes for the major features, as for example, Huntington's chorea does. However, other illnesses pose problems similar to those encountered in the study of schizophrenia. There are many illnesses with a psychiatric and/or somatic character in which the hereditary mechanism is poorly understood. For example, the incidence of diabetes mellitus is also higher in the families of those who have the illness but, like schizophrenia, it seems to have a relatively low penetrance. The expression of the phenotype is apparently affected by other factors, since not all of the carriers of the relevant genes succumb to the illness.

Not just the incidence of schizophrenia, but also the incidence for subgroups and for specific symptoms, has been investigated. In earlier reports there seemed to be an increased incidence (concordance) for the symptoms of traditional subgroups in the kindred or twins studied (Fischer *et al.*, 1969; Pollin *et al.*, 1969; Diebold *et al.*, 1977; Kallman, cited in Gottesman and Shields, 1982). However, more recent studies (e.g., Kendler *et al.*, 1988) and a critical review (McGuffin *et al.*, 1987) have questioned these reports.

Even if the question of whether prominent symptom patterns have a genetic basis is disregarded, the reader should be cautioned against assuming that there is enough evidence from family studies alone to understand the genetic influence in schizophrenia, since the putative genetic and the putative environmental influences cannot be separated. If, for example, a child is raised by a mentally disturbed parent, then the poor milieu and a negative influence on the development of the child may theoretically also cause a mental handicap.

It may also be noted that, in most cases, the psychiatrists who were retrospectively attempting to establish diagnoses were often not blind to the type of family to which the subjects be-

---

SOURCE: *Schizophrenia: Empirical Research and Findings*, by E. R. Straube and R. D. Oades (Eds.), pp. 361–384.

TABLE 1 Rates of Definite Schizophrenia among Relatives of Schizophrenics[a]

Familial Relationship	*n*	*% Affected*
Offspring of two schizophrenics	134	37
Offspring of one schizophrenic	1678	9
Siblings	7523	7
Grandchildren	739	3
Monozygotic twins	106	41
First cousins	1600	2
Dizygotic twins	149	12
Spouses	399	1

[a]Adapted from McGue and Gottesman, 1989

longed. Bias favoring achievement of a positive result for the investigation(s) may be involved. . . .

B. Twin Studies

When searching for semiquantitative information on the degree of influence exerted by hereditary and environmental factors in the etiology of schizophrenia, the measures of concordance from twin studies are the appropriate gauge. If genetic inheritance has a decisive influence, then MZ twins who share the same genetic material should show a far greater incidence of schizophrenia when one of them is schizophrenic than DZ twins. (If dominant genes were involved, the incidence in the MZ twin should approach 100% whereas that in the DZ twin would be about 50%.)

As can be seen in Table 1, the incidence rates of concordance are considerably lower than would be expected from a straightforward Mendelian inheritance. Because of the relatively numerous twin studies carried out, we must select and summarize the information. (For more complete discussions of both results and criticism of methods, see Jackson, 1960; Zerbin-Rüdin, 1972; Neale and Oltmanns, 1980; Gottesman and Shields, 1982; McGuffin *et al.*, 1984; Gottesman *et al.*, 1987; Kringlen, 1987; McGue and Gottesman, 1989.) The more recent studies attempt to consider the criticism of Jackson (1960), among others, of the methods formerly used.

The study of Gottesman and Shields (1982) at the Maudsley Hospital in London shall serve as an example for genetic research with twins. In this study, the selection and diagnosis of the subjects was carefully carried out: six evaluators blind to the zygosity of the subjects were employed. (The authors exerted much effort establishing the zygosity of their subjects. This was not as easy as it might appear and was treated relatively generously in earlier studies.) The degree of concordance depends on the diagnosis, but no matter what diagnostic scheme was used, or how narrowly or generously the criteria were applied, the concordance for schizophrenia was higher with the MZ than with the DZ twins in all cases. On the basis of the judgment of the six evaluators, the concordance was 50% for MZ and 9% for DZ twins (see Table 2; Gottesman and Shields, 1982).

The data are in good agreement with concordance rates derived from other more recent studies. However, older studies reported higher concordances. If justifiable criticisms of the methods are disregarded, one of the reasons for this higher concordance is most likely to be the inclusion of subjects with widely varying degrees of illness (i.e., the severity of the illness of the index twin also plays a role in the concordance rates). Relevant here is the reanalysis of an earlier study reported by Gottesman and Shields (1982) in their review. When this group of twins was divided into severely and mildly ill groups, the concordance rates for MZ twins were 75% and 17%, respectively. (The total concordance, without taking the severity of symptoms into account, was 46% for MZ and 14% for DZ twins.)

It is interesting to compare these results with those of Kendler and Robinette (1983) based on the twin register of the American Academy of Sciences. . . . From a base of 16,000 twins, 590 pairs had two or at least one schizophrenic twin. The concordance rate for schizophrenia was 31% for MZ and 6.5% for DZ twins. This concordance can be compared with that for diabetes mellitus, 19% versus 8%, and that for high blood pressure, 26% versus 11%. These concordance values are lower than those found in the Maudsley study, but do confirm the more general experience that concordance rates tend to be higher when the subjects are taken from a purely clinical background, than from the population at large. Once again, selection factors can be seen to play a role. It is also relevant that after Kendler and Robinette divided their population according to the severity of the illnesses, higher

TABLE 2 Effects of Diagnostic Criteria on Twin Concordance for Schizophrenia[a]

	Monozygotic	*Dizygotic*	*MZ:DZ*
Chart diagnoses	10/24 (42)[b]	3/33 (9)	4.6
Consensus of six judges	11/22 (50)	3/33 (9)	5.5
Broad criteria (Meehl)	14/24 (58)	8/33 (24)	2.4
Narrow criteria (Birley)	3/15 (20)	3/22 (14)	1.5

[a]From Gottesman and Shields, 1982
[b]Numbers in parentheses indicate percentages.

concordance rates were found in the more severely ill, which confirms the findings of Gottesman and Shields (1982).

Of course radical proponents of the influence of environmental factors still object to interpretations of these findings in terms of a genetic component in the transmission of schizophrenia. Some suggest that monozygocity and the necessary similarity of looks and behavior incur problems in the development of the "ego" and of the individual's identity, which are precisely the problems that these psychoanalysts suggest are uppermost in the anomalous development leading to schizophrenia (cf. Arieti, 1955). However, contrary to this argument, it should be noted that the incidence of schizophrenia in samples of MZ-twin probands or DZ-twin probands is no higher than in nontwin samples (Gottesman and Shields, 1982).

In order to counter the criticism of the "environmentalists," the development of MZ twins who were separated immediately after birth and grew up apart must be followed. This is a very rare circumstance. The numbers of cases available do not allow a statistically significant conclusion to be drawn. Evidence from 7 MZ twins (all separated in early childhood) speaks against interpretations that consider an identity problem the cause of the higher concordance rates in MZ twins: 5 of these twins were concordant for schizophrenia (see review and personal observations of Kringlen, 1987).

C. *Adoption Studies*

Adoption studies provide a useful complementary paradigm for investigating the contribution of hereditary and environmental factors in the development of schizophrenia. If there is a hereditary component, there is an increased likelihood of a child of a schizophrenic patient to develop schizophrenia after adoption into a healthy family. The comparison is drawn with children of healthy parents adopted into healthy families. The control and index groups discussed here were carefully matched according to the relevant demographic features.

Several adoption studies have been carried out in Denmark, where there is a particularly comprehensive register of psychiatric illnesses. These studies have mostly been instigated by workers at the National Institutes of Mental Health (NIMH)(e.g., Rosenthal *et al.*, 1968, 1971, who searched the register for schizophrenic patients who had given their children up for adoption, and Kety *et al.*, 1975, 1978, who started with registered adopted probands who had developed schizophrenia). An earlier comprehensive study was carried out by Heston (1966) in the United States with a procedure similar to that adopted by Rosenthal.

The principal finding of the studies of Heston, Rosenthal, and colleagues was that a higher proportion of the children of schizophrenic biological parents than of the children of parents with no recorded illness who were adopted into healthy families eventually developed a schizophrenia-like illness. Some of the individuals concerned were adopted at an early age (i.e., <1 yr). For example, in the study of Heston (1966), 5 (11%) of the 47 adopted offspring of schizophrenic mothers became schizophrenic. None of the children in the control group became schizophrenic. Interestingly, Heston reported that not only schizophrenia, but also "sociopathy, neurosis, and mental deficiency," even greater artistic gifts were more frequent in the index group than in the control group.

The Danish–American study (Rosenthal *et al.*, 1968) and, more recently, a Finnish adoption study (Tienari *et al.*, 1985) reported lower frequencies than Heston (1966). However, cases with schizophrenia were still higher in the index group than in the control group. For example, Rosenthal *et al.* recorded a definitive schizophrenia in 6% of the adopted offspring deriving from a parent with schizophrenia (n = 52). This point is emphasized by the re-analysis of their results by Lowing *et al.*(1983). Using more modern diagnostic criteria, only 3% could be diagnosed as schizophrenic (DSM-III). However, as in the Heston study, the authors noted a higher incidence of milder psychiatric problems, especially schizotypal personality disorder, in the index offspring than in the control group. (This finding will be discussed in more detail in a subsequent section.)

It could therefore be claimed that modern diagnostic criteria uncover a lower incidence of fully developed schizophrenia in offspring of schizophrenic patients adopted into healthy families than the earlier studies (see also Tienari *et al.*, 1985, and subsequent text). The reported incidences are slightly lower than those expected from reports in which the offspring was reared by a schizophrenic biological parent and not by a healthy nonbiological parent. In the former case, 10% of the offspring were expected to be affected. This discrepancy permits consideration of the possible role of differences in the familial milieu (i.e., high risk offspring reared by a disturbed or by a healthy person).

This was the starting point for an additional project in Denmark by the NIMH team. Wender *et al.* (1974) wanted to know what the influence of the adoptive father or mother on the adopted child might be. They searched in the Danish registers for those cases in which the adopting parent eventually became schizophrenic after adopting a child from healthy biological parents. (Compared with the previous design, this is the reverse procedure. Adopting schizophrenic *parents*, not the offspring of schizophrenic biological parents, formed the index group. This procedure is called a *cross-fostering* design.)

The result was that no more deviance was observed in the children of healthy biological parents (raised by a schizophrenic parent; n = 28) than in those children raised by healthy parents (n = 79). [For more details of the design and the results in this and the other two Danish–American adoption studies, the reader is referred to Gottesman and Shields (1982), who gave an extensive review of the field.] The unavoidable weakness of the study by Wender *et al.* (1974) is that there is no information about the nature of the interaction between the adopting parents and the child, since it is based on retrospective, if blind, analysis of case register data.

Indeed, these results did arouse controversy. Prominent in the debate over the validity of the conclusions have been Lidz and Blatt (1983) at Yale University, who maintained that environmental factors had played a much larger role than had been admitted. They argued that factors such as the age at adoption, the size of the family, and the age of illness onset were not considered. They further criticized that the inclusion of schizophrenia-like illnesses, such as borderline and spectrum diagnoses, may make the picture less rather than more clear. (Other problems include the small number of children appropriate for study and the even smaller number that might be expected to develop schizophrenia.) Thus, in their opinion, evidence from which to attempt to distinguish between genetic and environmental contributions to the development of schizophrenia is limited.

The Finnish team of Tienari and colleagues (1985) also criticized the results of the Danish–American adoption studies, which they felt had not considered sufficiently the different familial environments encountered by the adopted children. This factor can be seen in their own exhaustive study of the fate of 91 children adopted from schizophrenic mothers and 91 control children adopted from healthy mothers. Nevertheless, as in the Danish–American study, they found that more children of schizophrenic mothers developed schizophrenia or schizophrenia-like illnesses. Tienari *et al.* (1985) reported six (7%) schizophrenic cases in the index group and one (1%) psychotic proband in the control group. From 128 (133) matched pairs examined in a later re-analysis (Tienari *et al.*, 1989, 1991), there was no further incidence of illness in the control group, but three cases of paranoia and one of manic-depression had developed in the index group.

However, additional findings from Tienari *et al.* (1991) concerning the role of the family environment are of considerable relevance for a theory of gene-environment interactions in schizophrenia. In contrast to the Danish–American adoption studies, they examined the family members themselves and recorded their patterns of interactions. They found more disturbed offspring in the more disturbed family environments (independent of the index status of the offspring). However, they also found that the likelihood of a severe disturbance (including schizophrenia) was greater if the offspring of a schizophrenic mother was brought up in an adoptive family with a disturbed family atmosphere (compared with the offspring of the control group, who did not have the same risk status). From the index group, 20% of the offspring brought up in a disturbed adoptive family developed a severe character disorder or worse, whereas only 7% of the control group received the same rating (Table 3). These results appear to show the joint effects of genetic vulnerability and family environment (Tienari *et al.*, 1991).

Naturally, Tienari and colleagues (1985, 1989, 1991) asked whether the disturbed family situation could have arisen through the adoption of the potentially psychotic child. However, since similar disturbances of the interactions between members of the family also occurred with the adoption of children from healthy parents, the authors doubt if this was the primary cause. Furthermore, they compared the incidence of clear clinical cases of schizophrenia in children who came directly from the biological parents or came indirectly by way of an institution. The incidence was higher in the latter case. Thus, Tienari *et al.* (1985, 1991) concluded that although a genetic predisposition played a role, unfavorable environmental conditions were important for the development of a complete schizophrenic illness. From this evidence, one might also argue that a "good" family environment can exert a protective effect (Tienari *et al.*, 1985, 1991; Gottesman *et al.*, 1987). However, all these comments must be regarded as tentative; the conclusions may yet be strengthened or weakened. Not all subjects in these studies had reached the critical age for the development of schizophrenia.

TABLE 3 Demonstration of the Putative Gene-Environment Interaction in Adopted Offspring of Schizophrenic or Healthy Biological Mothers as a Function of the Family Atmosphere in the Adoptive Family[a]

	Family Atmosphere		
Offspring	*Healthy*	*Disturbed*	*Severely Disturbed*
Schizophrenic biological mother (n = 133)			
Healthy	33	10	4
Neurotic	7	8	9
Psychotic/personality disorder/borderline	3	8	20
Nonschizophrenic biological mother (n = 131)			
Healthy	31	15	5
Neurotic	12	13	11
Psychotic/personality disorder/borderline	2	5	7

[a]Percentage of offspring with or without a disturbance in the different family groups. Adapted from Tienari *et al.*, 1991.

II. PATTERNS OF DISTURBANCE IN FIRST-DEGREE RELATIVES OF SCHIZOPHRENICS

A. *Offspring of Monozygotic Twins Discordant for Schizophrenia*

Even if the results described so far are accepted as indicative of a heritable component in schizophrenia, it may explain only a part of the variance. At least 50% of the MZ twins with a schizophrenic parent are discordant for the illness. However, it is possible that those who do not develop schizophrenia are carriers. Factors may be present that suppress the release of the symptoms, as suggested earlier (i.e., the threshold for expression of the illness is not exceeded). This interpretation is supported by the conclusions of an elegant study by Fischer (1971, 1973) in Denmark.

Fischer studied the children of the nonschizophrenic twin partners of MZ twin pairs in which the other twin was schizophrenic (n = 25). In this group, she found a 13% incidence of schizophrenia. A recent re-analysis of the same material by Gottesman . . . and Bertelsen . . . (1989) confirms these findings (17% with a schizophrenic or schizophrenic-like psychosis; ICD diagnosis). This percentage is astonishingly close to that expected from a genetic model if one parent was schizophrenic (Figure 1; i.e., healthy twins with the same genetic complement as the schizophrenic partners seem to be carriers). In the offspring of the schizophrenic MZ twin, schizophrenia occurred with about the same incidence (16%) as in the offspring of the schizophrenic DZ twins (18%). The offspring of nonschizophrenic DZ twins had a much lower incidence of schizophrenia (3%; Figure 1).

Kringlen (1987) reported similar findings with 155 offspring of discordant MZ and DZ twins. There were 13% schizophrenic offspring in the former group and 3% in the latter. From such results it seems that, although schizophrenia cannot be attributed to genetic factors alone, an increased risk of developing schizophrenia must be genetically transmitted, even if one of the twins does not show a schizophrenia phenotype.

B. *Disturbances in Nonschizophrenic Relatives of Schizophrenics*

It is rather important to provide a little more background at this time. The present concern is the mental health of the nonschizophrenic subjects. As mentioned briefly earlier, it is known from more detailed analyses that many of the discordant nonschizophrenic members of MZ twins are not necessarily completely mentally normal. (All too often the data presented in tables are crude and oversimplified. Subjects who do not develop schizophrenia may be classed along with healthy subjects when, in fact, a category of nonschizophrenic would be more appropriate.) Using data from several reports, Table 4 shows that schizoid disturbances (as far as they were recorded as such) and other psychiatric disturbances are relatively frequent among discordant twins. This does not mean that the evaluators did not find completely normal subjects among the partners of MZ twins that are schizophrenic. However, from the results described earlier, it would be expected that, if disturbed, the nonschizophrenic partners would show a less severe form of a (perhaps) schizophrenia-like personality disturbance.

Let us now return to the adoption studies. One of the earlier investigations (Rosenthal *et al.*, 1968, 1971) reported that many of the offspring adopted from their biological parents could be given a spectrum diagnosis,

FIGURE 1 Schematic Illustration of the Number of Offspring of Members of Dizygotic (DZ) and Monozygotic (MZ) Twin Pairs Who Developed Schizophrenia as a Function of Whether Their Parent Was the Healthy or Ill Member of the Twin Pair (after Propping, 1989)

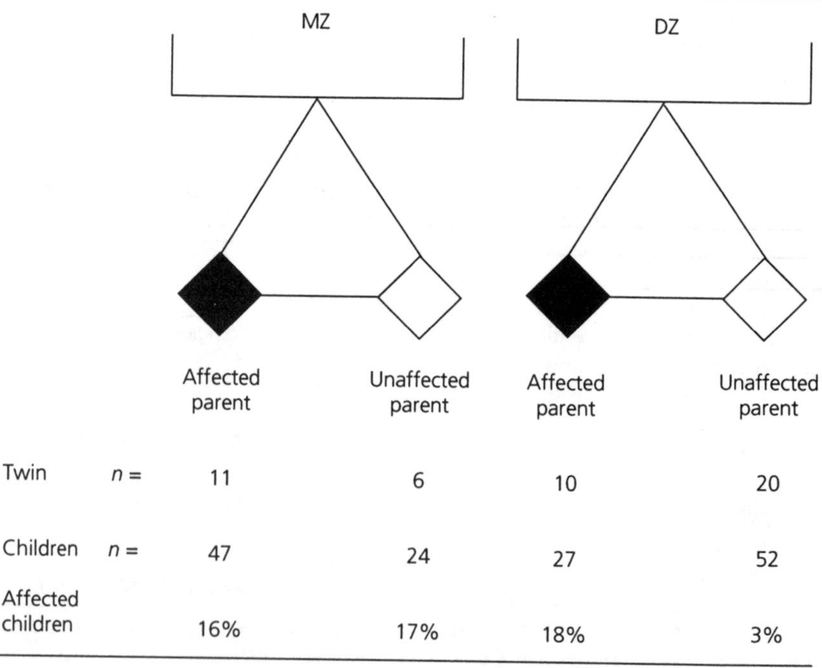

	MZ Affected parent	MZ Unaffected parent	DZ Affected parent	DZ Unaffected parent
Twin n =	11	6	10	20
Children n =	47	24	27	52
Affected children	16%	17%	18%	3%

TABLE 4 Pairwise Monozygotic Rates for Schizophrenia/Questionable Schizophrenia, Schizoid, Other Psychiatric Conditions, and Normality in Some Schizophrenic Twin Studies[a,b]

	n	S (%)	Si (%)	P (%)	N (%)
Luxenburger	14	72	14	—	14
Rosanoff *et al.*	41	61	—	7	32
Kallmann	174	69	21	5	5
Slater	37	64	—	14	22
Kringlen	45	38	—	29	33
Fischer	21	48	5	5	43
Gottesman & Shields	22	50	9	18	23

[a]From Gottesman and Shields, 1982
[b]S, schizophrenia/questionable schizophrenia; Si, schizoid; P, other psychiatric conditions; N, normal

that is, mental disturbances were recorded that could be ascribed to schizophrenia and the periphery of a conventional diagnosis of schizophrenia (e.g., personality disorders with mild schizophrenia-like features). From the index group, 32% of adopted offspring without schizophrenic parents were given a spectrum diagnosis; from the control group, the figure was 16%. Since these diagnoses were somewhat vague, the outcome of this study was criticized (e.g., Lidz *et al.*, 1981). Lowing *et al.* (1983) from the NIMH re-analyzed the material, as already reported. Both analyses were carried out blind to the status of the offspring of the probands. Lowing *et al.* (1983) then used DSM-III criteria. There was some change in the diagnosis of the parents, but the higher incidence of spectrum subjects was confirmed. They diagnosed only one case of schizophrenia (2.5%), but 38% of the index group and 13% of the control group were considered spectrum cases. Within the spectrum diagnosis, schizotypal and schizoid personality disorders had the highest frequency (Table 5). This was also true if only the adopted offspring of chronic schizophrenics were considered.

The incidence of borderline cases and borderline personality disturbances (DSM-III) did not distinguish the two groups re-analyzed by Lowing and colleagues. Kendler and Gruenberg (1984) also found, in their re-analysis of another Danish–American adoption study, an increased incidence of DSM-III-defined spectrum personality disturbances (rated blind) among the biological parents of the adopted children that eventually developed schizophrenia. Prominent were schizotypal and paranoid personality disorders, but not borderline cases.

TABLE 5 Re-analysis of the Rosenthal *et al.* (1968, 1971) Adoption Study by Lowing *et al.* (1983)

	Adopted Offspring	
DSM-III Diagnosis	Schizophrenic Biological Parent (n = 39)	Nonschizophrenic Biological Parent (n = 39)
Schizophrenia	1	0
Spectrum personality disorder[a]	14	5
No spectrum disorder	24	34

[a]Schizotypal personality disorder, schizoid personality disorder, borderline personality disorder, and "mixed spectrum"

Kendler and Gruenberg used the material of Kety *et al.* (1975), who were interested in adopted offspring with schizophrenia (from the Danish register) and in the rate of schizophrenia in the biological *parents* of these children. [The so-called "Kety strategy" represented the third Danish adoption study of the NIMH, along with the "conventional strategy" of the study of Rosenthal *et al.* (1968, 1971) and the "cross-fostering strategy" of Wender *et al.*, 1974.]

This argument will now be extended to a large-scale study of the incidence of spectrum personality disturbances in first-degree relatives of unequivocally diagnosed chronic schizophrenics (Baron *et al.*, 1983; Baron, 1987). This study was run by the New York Psychiatric Institute at two major hospitals. It found a significantly higher incidence of spectrum personality disturbances in 376 first-degree relatives of 90 schizophrenics (RDC; DSM-III) than in a control group of 346 first-degree relatives of 90 nonschizophrenics.

In detail, Baron found a schizotypal personality disturbance in 15% of the first-degree relatives of the schizophrenics but in only 2% of the control relatives. Paranoid personality disturbances and chronic schizophrenia were less frequent than schizotypal traits among the relatives of the schizophrenics, but were still significantly more frequent than in the controls, with incidences of 7% and 6%, respectively. Kendler and colleagues (1984) from another clinic in New York presented similar results in a study of first-degree relatives. Coryell and Zimmerman (1989) found no differences, but the diagnoses of the relatives were mostly attained through telephone interviews, which may be a disadvantage. Schulz *et al.* (1986) in Pittsburgh wanted to know whether the incidence of schizophrenia or schizotypal disturbances was higher among the first-degree relatives of patients with a schizotypal personality disturbance. They obtained negative results. Unfortunately there were several weaknesses in the study. In particular, the experimental group used was too small ($n = 22$), and only 44 relatives were investigated. If the incidence is considered, it may be expected from the previous studies that the use of small groups extremely reduces the chance of finding subjects with schizotypal or schizophrenic symptoms. Therefore, little weight can be placed on these negative results.

The reasons for classifying the spectrum diagnosis under the DSM largely arose from the adoption studies (particularly those of Rosenthal and colleagues). Unfortunately, it provides no clear, broadly accepted definition. However, most of the authors cited included schizotypal, paranoid, or schizoid personality disorders. Borderline personality disorder seemed to be less frequent in the first-degree relatives of schizophrenics, but no definitive answer can yet be given. Some of the personality disorders defined in the DSM-III-R do overlap. (See Gottesman, McGuffin, and Farmer, 1987, for an extensive discussion.)

Relevant to whether a narrow or broad definition of the illness relates to the putative common genetic element is a study by Gottesman. . . . This American–English study (Farmer *et al.*, 1987) revealed that the inclusion of schizotypal personality disturbances, atypical psychoses, and mood-incongruent delusions along with definitive cases of schizophrenia markedly increased concordance values for MZ over DZ twins. They calculated the concordance rates for a number of diagnostic constellations, but this particular constellation of diagnoses showed the largest difference between MZ and DZ twins. The other extreme shows that if a very narrow definition of schizophrenia is used (e.g., Abrams and Taylor, 1983, Chicago), extremely few schizophrenic patients are reported from the families of these schizophrenics.

In summary, it can be said that there is an increased incidence of schizophrenic spectrum personality disturbances that are genetically in some way related to schizophrenia among the first-degree relatives of schizophrenics (e.g., schizotypal, schizoid, paranoid, and probably other psychotic disturbances such as atypical psychosis, mood-incongruent delusions, and schizo-affective disorder). Remarkable, though, is the absence in all studies of reports of (DSM-III-R) borderline personality disturbances among the relatives of schizophrenic patients. This is in contrast to prior expectations (see review by Schied, 1990).

These findings could form part of a working hypothesis for current research, to facilitate the assembly of new symptom constellations from an empirical base for studies of the nature of genetic transmission in schizophrenia (cf. Morey, 1988).

III. GENETIC MODELS AND GENETIC ANALYSIS

A. *Single Major Locus Models*

From the data discussed earlier, it seems evident that the classic Mendelian single major locus models cannot adequately explain the observations (i.e., one dominant or recessive gene). In other words, it is unlikely that a direct pathway from the genotype to the phenotype exists. For example, not all the twin partners of affected MZ twins are schizophrenic themselves. They must, however, transmit "something" in their genetic material, since more offspring of the unaffected become ill than would be expected if no transmission had occurred.

Several authors have therefore proposed that a dominant or recessive single gene with reduced penetrance may explain the data. Debray and colleagues (1979) from France ran likelihood estimates for 12 different potential genetic models of transmission, including single major locus models with low penetrance. Their data were based on 1333 individuals from 25 families with a schizophrenic member, covering 4 generations. The authors were not able to decide among several models, since they obtained similar likelihood estimates, but they were able to conclude that modified (low penetrance) single major locus models were untenable (later confirmed by Tsuang *et al.* 1982, and others; see reviews by Faraone *et al.*, 1988; McGue and Gottesman, 1989; see Crow, 1990, for a continuation of the argument for a single locus in a modified form).

B. *Polygenic Models*

Polygenic models propose that several genes found at several loci may explain the pattern of transmission in schizophrenia. There are three main reasons to propose this alternative: (1) different degrees of severity of schizophrenia may be better explained by differences in the number of loci responsible (additive effects) than by single major locus models; (2) the puzzling heterogeneity may be better explained by different genes (i.e., by different combinations of genes in different schizophrenic patients); or (3) schizophrenia may be the result of the interaction of several genes. Also, (4) the fact that the rate of schizophrenia in the population is constant despite the reduced rate of reproduction of schizophrenic patients cannot be explained by single major locus models.

There have been several studies performed so far, but no clear support has become evident for the one or the other variant two-locus model, several-locus model, and so on. (See reviews by Gottesman and Shields, 1982; Faraone *et al.*, 1988.)

C. *Multifactorial Models*

A multifactorial model assumes that the phenotype is the result of a combination of genetic transmissions *and* environmental influences. A multifactorial model was first proposed by Gottesman and Shields (1967) for the mode of transmission in schizophrenia, but such models have been applied earlier to account for other nonstraightforward familial distributions of (psycho)somatic illnesses, such as high

FIGURE 2 Schematic Illustration of the Multifactorial Model. Several genes (most likely a dominant gene and its genetic background) as well as environmental factors contribute to the "multifactorial" illness (after Propping, 1989).

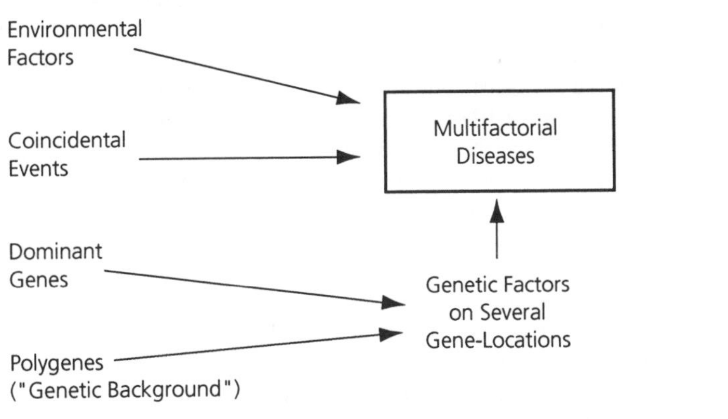

blood pressure, allergies, and diabetes mellitus. In the case of schizophrenia, it is suggested that all individuals have some unobservable liability or predisposition to develop the illness. The model assumes that the mode of transmission is polygenic; therefore the arguments given previously also apply here. The main advantage is that the model also considers environmental factors (Figure 2). Another special feature is that a normal distribution of the predisposition in the general population is assumed. The appearance of the illness is seen as the crossing of a threshold. The model also accounts for spectrum personality disorders (second threshold)(see . . . Figure 3).

There are several old "goodness-of-fit" calculations that have yielded mixed results (cf. Matthysse and Kidd, 1976; review by Gottesman and Shields, 1982). More recent analyses incorporate the two-threshold assumption (i.e., different degrees of the expression of the phenotype from schizoid personality disorder to schizophrenia) and use path analysis in order to disentangle the effects of genetic and environmental factors. Several studies were again initiated by Gottesman and co-workers (see Rao *et al.*, 1981; McGue *et al.*, 1983, 1987) using all information available from several Western European family and twin databases. The results of the "goodness-of-fit" calculations for these data were all similar, favoring the assumption of a multifactorial model and rejecting single major locus models. The authors also concluded that genetic factors accounted for most of the variance (about 60%) but that environmental factors were also important, just to a lesser degree (see review by Faraone *et al.*, 1988, for more details).

FIGURE 3 Gaussian Distribution of the Disposition to Illness in the Population (i.e., the Subclinical Spectrum or Threshold Region). The illness is overt in the area to the right (after Propping, 1989).

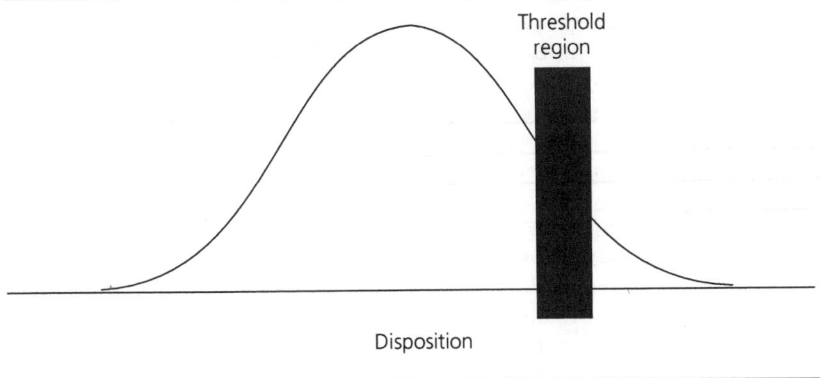

D. Mixed Models

A variant of the multifactorial model is the mixed model. The mixed model assumes that a major locus gene exists with a polygenic background and environmental factors (see Figure 2). The model therefore takes into account the heterogeneity and the similarity of the phenotype. Carter and Chung (1980) were not able to find support for a mixed model, but they only used hospital diagnoses to calculate the "goodness-of-fit" with the data from 507 siblings. Baron (1987) also included spectrum disorders in his analysis, using diagnoses based on a standardized interview (79 chronic schizophrenics and their first-degree relatives). The result of this study was discussed already. Baron (1987) found that a single recessive major locus makes the largest contribution to the transmission of the liability (63%). In the model, there was also a statistical likelihood for a polygenic influence, but it was considerably lower (20%). The contribution of environmental effects (random and common sibling environment) to the variance in liability was estimated to be 17%.

In summary, both mixed and polyfactorial models can be supported to some extent. Thus, as yet, no clear decision can be made about which mode of transmission is the most likely, although single major locus models can probably be rejected (see also McGue and Gottesman, 1989). A problem for these mathematical models and the "goodness-of-fit" estimations is that they depend on the reliability of the diagnosis and, more critically, on the concept of schizophrenia. Therefore, no definitive answers can be expected from this type of calculation. If a researcher decides to include only hospitalized schizophrenic patients, or even only DSM-III-R defined chronic schizophrenic patients, he or she gets a different picture of the mode of transmission than the researcher who believes that spectrum disorders, including schizoid or paranoid personality traits, belong to the genetic concept of schizophrenia. Another problem is, then, to define the borders of the spectrum (see the comprehensive discussion of this problem by Gottesman *et al.*, 1987). Since it is not clear what the appropriate phenotype for analysis should be in schizophrenia research, we must await more precisely defined biological or genetic markers. (These markers will be discussed in the next section.)

E. Molecular Genetic Approaches

Three recent studies conducted by teams from London (Sherrington *et al.*, 1988). Edinburgh (St. Clair *et al.*, 1989), and Yale (Kennedy *et al.*, 1988) have not waited for improved diagnosis and recognition of schizophrenia, but plunged into the material from well-known pedigrees with the newer techniques of molecular biology. Sherrington and colleagues claimed to have demonstrated that the inheritance of a disposition to psychiatric disorders belonging to the schizophrenia spectrum can be associated with genetic material on chromosome 5. The latter two studies, with negative results, have shown that not all cases of schizophrenia can be so explained. How did this all come about?

Three conditions were necessary: the availability of pedigrees providing psychiatric information and genetic material, the methods for locating the genetic fragments responsible, and a sign of where to look among the vast library of genes available.

The analysis of large family clans will be considered first. Sherrington *et al.* (1988) studied two British and five Icelandic pedigrees covering three generations. The Icelandic families were those described by Karlsson (1982, 1988). This database of 104 persons included 39 cases of schizophrenia, 5 with schizoid disturbances, and a further 10 cases of disorders including phobias, anxiety, and depression. Kennedy *et al.* (1988) searched northern Swedish pedigrees. This material covers 157 persons in seven branches. They were able to diagnose 31 cases of schizophrenia and found 50 unaffected subjects. St. Clair *et al.* (1989) used the same phenotypic descriptions as the London group, with 15 families in Scotland. Of 166 members whose DNA was examined, 75 had some mental disturbance; for 44 this was schizophrenia, and, for a further 5 cases, a psychosis or spectrum personality was determined.

We will now discuss the methods. Basically, these tools involve the use of restriction enzymes to identify places at which the different genomes vary. When following the inheritance of parts of a chromosome through a family, one can use the variations of the sequences of DNA as genetic markers. These variations become visible when they disrupt the recognition site for a restriction enzyme. The sequences of DNA marked by these sites are called restriction fragment length polymorphisms (RFLPs). Among the thousands of such sequences already known in humans, it has been possible to track RFLPs that pass from generation to generation with a disease (e.g., Huntington's chorea, manic depression; Egeland *et al.*, 1987). It can be concluded that the genes contributing to the disease lie in a chromosomal region near the RFLP.

Why did these groups look at chromosome 5? The sign was provided by a case reported by Bassett *et al.* (1988). The case concerned an uncle and nephew who were both schizophrenic and had certain unusual facial features in common. They both carried an extra copy of the region known as 5q11–13 translocated to chromosome 1. (Additionally, at the time it was thought that the glucocorticoid receptor was encoded near the 5q region. Disturbance of glucocorticoid metabolism can give rise to psychoses. This locus has since been shown not to be as close as originally thought.)

Sherrington *et al.* (1988) reported finding strong concordance with a putative dominant character predisposing to schizophrenia. The concordance has been improved by including the other psychiatric illnesses, but in view of the relatively inadequate information provided by the individuals concerned, this finding must be treated with reserve. The transmission of schizophrenia and of the genetic markers was $10^{6.49}$-fold more likely if they were genetically linked than unlinked (i.e., the relatively high lod score of 6.49 speaks in favor of a single gene locus[1]). Two features, one in the design and the other in the methods, must qualify this result. There was a deliberately biased sampling of families for signs of genes with a high penetrance. This was deemed a necessary design feature to increase the likelihood of finding what their methods could detect, namely, a single gene locus. However, it is difficult to believe that the lod score increased when they broadened the diagnostic criteria to include various depressive illnesses. Family, twin, and adoption studies have not provided evidence for a genetic link between these two types of psychiatric disturbance (e.g., Loranger, 1981).

However, reasonable criticism can also be made of the reports of negative results (Byerley *et al.*, 1989). The pedigree studied by Kennedy *et al.* (1988) may prove to be an exceptional case. There is reason to suppose that it is also demonstrating segregation for mental retardation. This adds considerable complexity to the analysis. Although the report of St. Clair *et al.* (1989) is laudable for its attempt to test several hypotheses for the linkage of different syndromes, their basic assumption of an autosomal dominant mode for inheritance is unlikely. Byerley is not alone in suggesting that a recessive mode is more likely (see previous section).

What might the combined results mean? It seems that schizophrenia may rarely be linked to defects in an unknown gene on chromosome 5. It may be a dominant gene, the inheritance of which leads to the inheritance of a susceptibility to schizophrenia. However, carriers do not necessarily develop schizophrenia. It has not been shown that a chromosome 5 defect is sufficient for the development of schizophrenia nor that all schizophrenia develops from this or any other gene. Using five RFLPs, Kennedy *et al.* (1988) found no evidence of a link between chromosome 5 and schizophrenia, but noted that a demonstration of the heterogeneity of schizophrenia would require finding another genetic locus (Lander, 1988).[2] Striking in the results of Sherrington *et al.*(1988) is that apparently several subtypes of schizophrenia may have a common genetic source. Again, the suggestion is that the etiology does not match the results of current diagnostic practices. Future studies should aim to attain more psychiatric and genetic information from more members. This information should be combined with recently developed genetic maps to demonstrate linkage. Such techniques could already be applied to other behavioral and physiological markers correlating with schizophrenia (e.g., pursuit eye movements, sensitivity to amphetamine; Lander, 1988). . . .

[Section IV has been omitted here.]

V. SUMMARY STATEMENTS AND INTERPRETATIONS

A. *Monozygotic (MZ) and Dizygotic (DZ) Twin Studies*

The rate of schizophrenia is higher in MZ than in DZ twins. The concordance is generally less than 50%, but is higher if one of the twins is severely ill.

The numbers speak for a genetic contribution, but are far lower than those expected for a straightforward dominant-recessive model of inheritance.

B. *Adoption Studies*

The adopted (index) offspring of schizophrenic parents are at higher risk for developing schizophrenia than control children. However, the incidence of schizophrenia is lower than in children living with the affected parent. In some adoption studies, schizophrenia is rare, but spectrum personality disorder (e.g., schizotypal personality disorder) is more frequent.

These results demonstrate that both the genetic disposition and the environment play a role in the development of schizophrenia.

C. *First-Degree Relatives of Schizophrenics*

About 15% of the relatives of schizophrenics have personality disorders which have some similarity with schizophrenia (i.e., schizotypal personality disorder and other spectrum features).

A common heritable factor seems to be the basis of both the fully developed illness and the spectrum personality disorder. There may be at least two influences that determine the severity of the expression as spectrum or fully developed schizophrenia: environmental stress and the degree of genetic load (reflected, for example, by the number of afflicted relatives; Odegaard, 1972, in Propping, 1989). The phenotype is the product of a genetic/environment interaction but the genetic predisposition seems to be the necessary condition. Birth complications and slight cortical atrophy seem to play the same unfavorable role as aversive environmental influences. . . . Another possibility is that of a phenocopy, if the same putative pathognomonic area is afflicted by atrophic processes.

D. *Mechanisms of Inheritance*

The exact mode of inheritance is not clear, although most researchers exclude at least the possibility of a single major locus gene. Psychiatric genetics today favor polyfactorial or mixed models (i.e., this is the result of most mathematical likelihood estimations when comparing the model with the appearance of schizophrenia or spectrum disorders in pedigrees).

The polyfactorial model assumes that several genes are responsible for schizophrenia and the additional influence of the environment results in the crossing of a second threshold. The appearance of spectrum disorders is being considered as the crossing of an initial threshold. In general, it is suggested that the liability or the disposition to develop the illness is distributed continuously in the population (Gaussian distribution). The mixed model assumes that, in addition to the factors involved in the polyfactorial mode of transmission, a single major gene locus is responsible.

The mixed and polyfactorial models seem to be plausible with respect to the fact that the phenotype is heterogeneous, the illness can appear without family history of schizophrenia, and schizophrenia does not die out despite the fact that schizophrenic patients have fewer offspring than healthy persons. However, the exact proof for one or the other model is difficult to present because of the variable nature of and the difficulty defining the borders of the various expressions of the phenotype in the general population, from mild spectrum features to severe breakdown.

E. *Molecular Genetics*

A recent claim that the genetic locus is on chromosome 5 is not supported by several other studies.

It is theoretically possible, as discussed earlier, that more than one locus is required to bring about a sufficient liability for developing schizophrenia. If so, a search for a single locus would only make sense if the existence and contribution of a major gene could be assumed. Information pertinent to a decision between the alternatives is not available.

NOTES

1. The "lod" score or "log of the odds" refers to the usual parametric statistic for assessing the strength of a linkage. The conventional threshold for acceptance of linkage is 3.0, whereas that for rejection of a linkage between a polymorphic test marker and a particular disease locus is –2.0. For example, in 1990 the status of combined studies on a marker for Huntington's disease on the short arm of chromosome 4 was 87.7 at a recombination frequency of 0.04; in contrast, for the 11p marker for bipolar affective disorder, the lod score has decreased from 4.08 in the original study to –9.3 after subsequent additional investigations.
2. There are at least two other reports of features with an increased incidence in small groups of schizophrenics, the origin of which has been traced to a locus on chromosome 19 (19p13) (see discussion in Byerley *et al.*, 1989). It should not be overlooked that there may be a number of genetic defects necessary for the expression of the phenotype. It may be a combination of all or only some of these that is sufficient for the illness to appear.

REFERENCES

Abrams, R., and Taylor, M. A. (1983). The genetics of schizophrenia: A reassessment using modern criteria. *American Journal of Psychiatry, 140*, 1971–175.

Andrew, B., Watt, D. C., Gillespie, C., and Chapel, H. (1987). A study of genetic linkage in schizophrenia. *Psychological Medicine, 17*, 363–370.

Arieti, S. (1955). *Interpretation of schizophrenia*. New York: Brunner.

Baron, M. (1982). Genetic models of schizophrenia. *Acta Psychiatrica Scandinavica, 65*, 263.

Baron, M. (1986a). Genetics of schizophrenia: I. Familial patterns and mode of inheritance. *Society of Biological Psychiatry, 21*, 1051–1066.

Baron, M. (1986b). Genetics of schizophrenia: II. Vulnerability traits and gene markers. *Society of Biological Psychiatry, 21*, 1189–1211.

Baron, M. (1987). Genetic models and the transmission of schizophrenia. In H. Häfner, W. F. Gattaz and W. Janzarik (Eds.), *Search for the causes of schizophrenia*. Berlin: Springer.

Baron, M., Gruen, R., Asnis, L., and Kane, J. (1983). Familial relatedness of schizophrenia and schizotypal states. *American Journal of Psychiatry, 140*, 1437–1442.

Baron, M., Gruen, R., Rainer, J. D., Kane, J., Asnis, L., and Lord, S. (1985). A family study of schizophrenic and normal control probands: Implications for the spectrum concept of schizophrenia. *American Journal of Psychiatry, 142*, 447–454.

Basset, A. S., Jones, B. D., McGillivray, B. C., and Pantzar, J. T. (1988). Partial trisomy chromosome 5 cosegregating with schizophrenia. *Lancet, I*, 799–800.

Byerley, W., Mellon, C., O'Connell, P., Lalouel, J. M., Nakamura, Y., Leppert, M. and White, R. (1989). Mapping genes for manic-depression and schizophrenia with DNA markers. *Trends in Neurosciences, 12*, 46–48.

Carter, C. L., and Chung, C. S. (1980). Segregating analysis of schizophrenia under a mixed genetic model. *Human Heredity, 30*, 350.

Coryell, W. H., and Zimmerman, M. (1989). Personality disorder in the families of depressed, schizophrenic, and never-ill probands. *American Journal of Psychiatry, 146*, 496–502.

Crow, T. J. (1990). Nature of the genetic contribution to psychotic illness—a continuum viewpoint. *Acta Psychiatrica Scandinavica, 81*, 401–408.

Debray, Q., Coillard, V., and Stewart, J. (1979). Schizophrenia: A study of genetic models. *Human Heredity, 29*, 27–36.

Diebold, K., Arnold, E., and Pfaff, W. (1977). Statistische Untersuchungen zur Symptomatik und Syndromatik von 120 endogen psychotischen Elter- Kind- und Geschwisterpaaren. *Fortschr. d. Neurologie. Psychiat. u. ihrer Grenzgeb, 45*, 349–364.

Egeland, J. A., Gerhard, D. S., Pauls, D. L., Sussex, J. N., Kidd, K. K., Allen, C. R., Hostetter, A. M., and Housman, D. E. (1987). Bipolar affective disorders linked to DNA markers on chromosome 11. *Nature, 325*, 783–787.

Faraone, S. V., Lyons, M. J., and Tsuang, M. T. (1988). Mathematical models of genetic transmission. In M. T. Tsuang and J. C. Simpson (Eds.), *Handbook of schizophrenia, Vol. 3: Nosology, epidemiology and genetics*. (pp. 501–530). Amsterdam: Elsevier.

Farmer, A. E., McGuffin, P., and Gottesman, I. I. (1987). Twin concordance for DSM-III schizophrenia. *Archives of General Psychiatry, 44*, 634–644.

Fischer, M. (1971). Psychoses in the offspring of schizophrenic monozygotic twins and their normal co-twins. *British Journal of Psychiatry, 118*, 43–52.

Fischer, M. (1973). Genetic and environmental factors in schizophrenia. *Acta Psychiatrica Scandinavica*, Suppl. 238.

Fischer, M., Harvald, B., and Hauge, M. (1969). A Danish twin-study of schizophrenia. *British Journal of Psychiatry, 115*, 981–990.

Frangos, E., Athanassenas, G., Tsitourides, S., Katsanou, N., and Alexandrakou, P. (1985). Prevalence of DSM-III schizophrenia among the first-degree relatives of schizophrenic probands. *Acta Psychiatrica Scandinavica, 72*, 382–386.

Gershon, E. S., Merril, C. R., Golding, L. R., DeLisi, L. E., Berrettini, W. H., and Nurnberger, J. I., Jr. (1987). The role of molecular genetics in psychiatry. *Biological Psychiatry, 22*, 1388–1405.

Gottesman, I. I., and Bertelsen, A. (1989). Confirming unexpressed genotypes for schizophrenia. *Archives of General Psychiatry, 46*, 867–872.

Gottesman, I. I., McGuffin, P., and Farmer, A. E. (1987). Clinical genetics as clues to the "real" genetics of schizophrenia. *Schizophrenia Bulletin, 13*, 23–47.

Gottesman, I. I., and Shields, J. A. (1967). A polygenic theory of schizophrenia. *Proceedings in North Atlantic Academic Sciences, 58*, 199–205.

Gottesman, I. I., and Shields, J. (1982). *Schizophrenia: The epigenetic puzzle*. Cambridge: Cambridge University Press.

Helmchen, H., and Henn, A. (Eds.) (1987). *Biological perspectives of schizo-*

phrenia. Dahlem workshop reports. New York: Wiley.

Heston, L. L. (1966). Psychiatric disorders in foster home reared children of schizophrenic mothers. *British Journal of Psychiatry, 112*, 819–825.

Holzman, P. S., Kringlen, E., Mattysse, S., Flanagan, S. D., Lipton, R. B., Cramer, G., Levin, S., Lange, K., and Levy, D. L. (1988). A single dominant gene can account for eye tracking dysfunction and schizophrenia in offspring of discordant twins. *Archives of General Psychiatry, 45*, 641–647.

Jackson, D. D. (1960). A critique of the literature on the genetics of schizophrenia. In D. D. Jackson (Ed.), *The study of schizophrenia*. New York: Basic Books.

Karlsson, J. L. (1982). Family transmission of schizophrenia: A review and synthesis. *British Journal of Psychiatry, 140*, 600–606.

Karlsson, J. L. (1988). Partly dominant transmission of schizophrenia in Iceland. *British Journal of Psychiatry, 152*, 324–329.

Kelsoe, J. R., Ginns, E. I., Egeland, J. A., Gerhard, D. S., Goldstein, A M., Bale, S. J., Pauls, D. L., Long, R. T., Kidd, K. K., Conte, G., and Housman, D. E. (1989). Reevaluation of the linkage relationship between chromosome lip loci and the gene for bipolar affective disorder in the old order Amish. *Nature, 342*, 238–243.

Kendler, K. S., and Gruenberg, A. M. (1984). An independent analysis of the Danish adoption study of schizophrenia. *Archives of General Psychiatry, 41*, 555–564.

Kendler, K. S., Gruenberg, A. M., and Tsuang, M. T. (1985). Psychiatric illness in first-degree relatives of schizophrenic and surgical control patients. *Archives of General Psychiatry, 42*, 770–779.

Kendler, K. S., Gruenberg, A. M., and Tsuang, M. T. (1988). A family study of the subtypes of schizophrenia. *American Journal of Psychiatry, 145*, 57–62.

Kendler, K. S., Masterson, C. C., Ungaro, R., and Davis, K. L. (1984). A family history study of schizophrenia-related personality disorders. *American Journal of Psychiatry, 141*, 424–427.

Kendler, K. S., and Robinette, C. D. (1983). Schizophrenia in the National Academy of Sciences–National Research Council Twin Registry: A 16-year update. *American Journal of Psychiatry, 140*, 1551–1563.

Kennedy, J. L., Guiffra, L. A., Moises, H. W., Cavalli-Sforzas, L. L., Pakstis, A. J., Kidd, J. R., Castiglione, C. M., Sjogren, B., Wetterberg, L., and Kidd, K. K. (1988). Evidence against linkage of schizophrenia to markers on chromosome 5 in a north Swedish pedigree. *Nature, 336*, 167–170.

Kety, S. S., Rosenthal, D., Wender, P. H., Schulsinger, F., and Jacobsen, B. (1975). Mental illness in the biological and adoptive families of adopted individuals who have become schizophrenic: A preliminary report based on psychiatric interviews. In R. R. Fieve, D. Rosenthal, H. Brill (Eds.), *Genetic research in psychiatry*. Baltimore: Johns Hopkins University Press.

Kety, S. S. Rosenthal, D., Wender, P. H., Schulsinger, F., and Jacobsen, B. (1978). The biological and adoptive families of adopted individuals who become schizophrenic: Prevalence of mental illness and other characteristics. In L. C. Wynne, R. L. Cromwell, S. Matthysse (Eds.), *The nature of schizophrenia*. New York: Wiley.

Kringlen, E. (1987). Contributions of genetic studies on schizophrenia. In H. Häfner, W. F. Gattaz, and W. Janzarik (Eds.), *Search for the causes of schizophrenia*. Berlin: Springer.

Lander, E. S. (1988). Splitting schizophrenia. *Nature, 336*, 105–106.

Lidz, T. and Blatt, S. (1983). Critique of the Danish-American studies of the biological and adoptive relatives of adoptees who became schizophrenic. *American Journal of Psychiatry, 140*, 426–434.

Lidz, T., Blatt, S., and Cook, B. (1981). Critique of the Danish-American studies of the adopted-away offspring of schizophrenic parents. *American Journal of Psychiatry, 138*, 1063–1068.

Loranger, A. W. (1981). Genetic independence of manic-depression and schizophrenia. *Acta Psychiatrica Scandinavica, 63*, 444–452.

Lowing, P. A., Mirsky, A. R., and Pereira, R. (1983). The inheritance of schizophrenia spectrum disorders: A reanalysis of the Danish adoptee study data. *American Journal of Psychiatry, 140*, 1167–1171.

Matthysse, S. W., and Kidd, K. K. (1976). Estimating the genetic contribution to schizophrenia. *American Journal of Psychiatry, 133*, 185–191.

McGue M., and Gottesman, I. I. (1989). Genetic linkage in schizophrenia: Perspectives from genetic epidemiology. *Schizophrenia Bulletin, 15*, 453–464.

McGue M., Gottesman, I., and Rao, D. C. (1983). The transmission of schizophrenia under a multifactorial threshold model. *American Journal of Human Genetics, 35*, 1161.

McGue, M., Gottesman, I. I., and Rao, D. C. (1986). The analysis of schizophrenia family data. *Behavior Genetics, 16*, 75–87.

McGue, M., Gottesman, I. I., and Rao, D. C. (1987). Resolving genetic models for the transmission of schizophrenia. *Genetics and Epidemiology, 2*, 99.

McGuffin, P., Farmer, A., and Gottesman, I. I. (1987). Is there really a split in schizophrenia? *British Journal of Psychiatry, 150*, 581–592.

McGuffin, P., Farmer, A. E., and Gottesman, I. I., Murray, R. M., and Reveley, A. M. (1984). Twin concordance for operationally defined schizophrenia. *Archives of General Psychiatry, 41*, 541–545.

McGuffin, P., and Sturt, E. (1986). Genetic markers in schizophrenia. *Human Heredity, 36*, 65–88.

Morey, L. C. (1988). The categorical representation of personality disorder: A cluster analysis of DSM-III-R personality features. *Journal of Abnormal Psychology, 97*, 314–321.

Neale, J. M., and Oltmanns, T. F. (1980). *Schizophrenia*. New York: John Wiley & Sons.

Odegaard, O. (1972). The multifactorial theory of inheritance in predisposition of schizophrenia. In A. K. Kaplan (Ed.), *Genetic factors in schizophrenia* (pp. 256–275). Springfield, Illinois: Charles C Thomas.

Pollin, W., Allen, M. G., Hoffer, A., Stabenau, J. R., and Huber, Z. (1969).

Psychopathology in 15,909 pairs of veteran twins. *American Journal of Psychiatry, 7,* 597–609.

Propping, P. (1989) *Psychiatrische Genetik. Befunde und Konzepte*. Berlin: Springer.

Rao, D. C., Marton, N. E., Gottesman, I. I., and Lew, R. (1981). Path analysis of qualitative data on pairs of relatives: Application to schizophrenia. *Human Heredity, 31,* 325–333.

Rosenthal, D., Wender, P. H., Kety, S. S., Schulsinger, F., Welner, J., and Oatergaard, L. (1968). Schizophrenics' offspring reared in adoptive homes. In D. Rosenthal and S. S. Kety (Eds.), *The transmission of schizophrenia*. New York: Pergamon Press.

Rosenthal, D., Wender, P. H., Kety, S. S., Welner, J., and Schulsinger, F. (1971). The adopted away offspring of schizophrenics. *American Journal of Psychiatry, 128,* 307–311.

Schied, H. W. (1990). Psychiatric concepts and therapy. In E. R. Straube and K. Hahlweg (Eds.), *Schizophrenia: Concepts, vulnerability, and intervention*. Berlin: Springer.

Schulz, P. M., Schulz, S. C., Goldberg, S. C., Ettigi, P., Resnick, R. J., and Friedel, R. O. (1986). Diagnoses of the relatives of schizotypal outpatients. *Journal of Nervous and Mental Disease, 174,* 457–463.

Sherrington, R., Brynjolfsson, J., Petursson, H., Potter, M., Dudleston, K., Barraclough, B., Wasmuth, J., Dobbs, M., and Gurling, H. (1988). Localization of a susceptibility locus for schizophrenia on chromosome 5. *Nature, 336,* 164–167.

St. Clair, D., Blackwood, D., Muir, W., Baillie, D., Hubbard, A., Wright, A., and Evans, H. J. (1989). No linkage of chromosome 5q11–q13 markers to schizophrenia in Scottish families. *Nature, 339,* 305–309.

Tienari, P., Kaleva, M., Lahti, I., Laksy, K., Moring, J., Naarala, M., Sorri, A., Wahlberg, K. E., and Wynne, L. (1991). Adoption studies on schizophrenia. In C. Eggers (Ed.), *Schizophrenia and youth*. Berlin: Springer Verlag.

Tienari, P., Lahti, I., Sorri, A., Naarala, M., Moring J., and Wahlberg, K.-E., (1989). The Finnish adoptive family study of schizophrenia: Possible joint effects of genetic vulnerability and family environment. *British Journal of Psychiatry, 155,* Suppl. 5, 29–32.

Tienari, P., Sorri, A., Lahti, I., Naarala, M., Wahlberg, K.-E., Rönkkö, T., Pohjola, J., and Moring, J. (1985). The Finnish adoptive family study of schizophrenia. *The Yale Journal of Biology and Medicine, 58,* 227–237.

Tsuang, M. T., Bucher, K. D., and Fleming, J. A. (1982). Testing the monogenetic theory of schizophrenia: An application of segregation analysis to blind family study data. *British Journal of Psychiatry, 140,* 595.

Wender, P. H., Rosenthal, D., Kety, S. S., Schulsinger, F., and Welner, J. (1974). Crossfostering: A research strategy for clarifying the role of genetic and experiential factors in the etiology of schizophrenia. *Archives of General Psychiatry, 30,* 212–128.

Winokur, G., Scharfetter, C., and Angst, J. (1985). A family study of psychotic symptomatology in schizophrenia, schizoaffective disorder, unipolar depression, and bipolar disorder. *European Archives of Psychiatry and Neurological Sciences, 234,* 295–298.

Zerbin-Rüdin, E. (1972). Genetic research and the theory of schizophrenia. *International Journal of Mental Health, 1,* 42–63.P

RICHARD C. LEWONTIN, STEVEN ROSE, & LEON J. KAMIN

Schizophrenia: The clash of determinisms

THE CASE OF SCHIZOPHRENIA

The diagnosis and treatment of schizophrenia are paradigms of the determinist mode of thinking, for this is the mental disorder on which more biochemical and genetic research has been lavished than any other, the one in which claims to have discovered *the* cause in a particular molecule or gene have been made most extensively. It is now so widely believed that psychiatry has proved the disorder to be biological that if the case fails here, where it is strongest, it must be even weaker elsewhere. But schizophrenia is interesting from another point of view as well, for in opposition to the biologizing tendencies of medical psychiatry there has grown up a strong countermovement in recent years. Antipsychiatry, in the hands of practitioners like R. D. Laing and theorists like Michel Foucault, has gone far in the opposite direction, almost to the point of denying the existence of a disorder or group of disorders diagnosable as schizophrenia at all. Thus in the case of schizophrenia we find precisely that clash of determin-

---

isms, on the one hand biological and on the other cultural, . . . which it is one of the purposes of our book to transcend.

What Is Schizophrenia?

Schizophrenia literally means "split mind." The classic picture of a schizophrenic is of a person who feels in some fundamental way cut off from the rest of humanity. Unable to express emotion or interact normally or express themselves verbally in a way that is rational to most others, schizophrenics appear blank, apathetic, dull. They may complain that their thoughts are not their own or that they are being controlled by some outside force. According to the textbooks, dramatically ill schizophrenics appear not to be able to or wish to do anything for themselves—they take little interest in food, sexual activity, or exercise; they experience auditory hallucinations; and their speech seems rambling, incoherent, and disconnected to the casual listener. Some psychiatrists doubt whether schizophrenia is a single entity at all, or speak of core schizophrenia and a wider range of schizophrenia-like symptoms.

The idea of a single disease of schizophrenia may be a hangover from the nineteenth-century definition of madness—so-called dementia praecox—which preceded it. The diagnosis of schizophrenia in a patient with a given set of symptoms can vary between doctor and doctor and culture and culture. It is true that when matched and carefully controlled transnational surveys are done there is some concordance of diagnosis; however, in real life the diagnostic and prescribing practices of doctors and psychiatrists differ sharply from the more controlled procedures of clinical trials. Comparisons of figures in different countries have shown that the most frequent use of the diagnosis of schizophrenia occurs in the United States and the Soviet Union. Nonetheless, even in Britain, where it is defined in a somewhat narrower sense, up to 1 percent of the population is said to suffer from schizophrenia,[1] and 28,000—or 16 percent—of the admissions to hospitals for mental illness in 1978 were for a diagnosis of schizophrenia or its related disorders.

Faced with the complex phenomena that result in a diagnosis of schizophrenia, the biological determinist has a simple question: What is it about the biology of the individual schizophrenic that predisposes him or her toward the disorder? If no obvious gross brain difference can be found, predisposition must lie in some subtle biochemical abnormality—perhaps affecting the connections between individual nerve cells. And the thrust of the determinist argument is that the causes for these abnormalities, although they might have been environmental, are most likely to lie in the genes. . . .

THE GENETICS OF SCHIZOPHRENIA

The statement that the brain of a person manifesting schizophrenia shows biochemical changes compared with that of a normal person may be no more than a reaffirmation of a proper materialism that insists on the unity of mind and brain. But the ideology of biological determinism goes much deeper that this. It is, as we have reiterated, linked to an insistence that biological events are ontologically prior to and cause the behavioral or existential events, and hence to a claim that if brain biochemistry is altered in schizophrenia, then underlying this altered biochemistry must be some type of genetic predisposition to the disorder. By 1981 psychologists were claiming to be able to detect potential schizophrenics when they are only three years old—up to fifty years before the disease manifests itself. The claim, made by Venables to a meeting of the British Association for the Advancement of Science, is based on a survey of three-year-olds in Mauritius; "potentially abnormal" children were said to show "abnormal autonomic responses.[2]

Push the diagnosis back beyond the three-year-old and we are soon with embryo or gene. But the hunt for a genetic basis for schizophrenia goes far beyond an interest in therapy, as there is no way in which the mere demonstration of a genetic basis for the disorder would aid in its treatment.* As we have seen, the lineage of the effort to find genetic predispositions runs back through the eugenic thinking of the 1930s and 1920s, with its belief in genes for criminal degeneracy, sexual profligacy, alcoholism, and every other type of activity disapproved of by bourgeois society. It is deeply embedded in today's determinist ideology. Only thus can we account for the extraordinary repetitive perseverance and uncritical nature of research into the genetics of schizophrenia. Whatever such research may say about the disorder it proposes to explain, an examination of the claims of its protagonists says a very great deal about the intellectual history of our contemporary determinist society, and hence is worth analyzing in some detail.

The belief that schizophrenia has a clear and important genetic basis is now very widely held. The father of psychiatric genetics, Ernst Rüdin, was so convinced of this that, arguing on the basis of statistics collected by his co-workers,

*These words were true when we wrote them. However, reductionist science moves faster than the Gutenberg technology of book production. For if it were the case that there were schizophrenia-producing genes, then techniques that excised those abnormal genes from the genome of affected individuals and replaced them with their normal alleles would presumably prevent the expression of the disorder. If schizophrenia were a single or even a two- or three-gene defect, such techniques are not wholly beyond the reach of contemporary molecular genetics—what is sometimes called genetic engineering. There are serious research programs now under way in several laboratories to make gene libraries from schizophrenics and isolate and clone the "schizophrenic genes" with a view to studying their possible replacement. Granted the reductionist premise, the therapeutic logic would be impeccable. And if one can have schizophrenic urine, why not, indeed, schizophrenic genes?

he advocated the eugenic sterilization of schizophrenics. When Hitler came to power in 1933, Rüdin's advocacy was no longer merely academic. Professor Rüdin served on a panel, with Heinrich Himmler as head, of the Task Force of Heredity Experts who drew up the German sterilization laws of 1933.

Perhaps the most influential psychiatric geneticist in the English-speaking world was a student of Rüdin's, the late Franz Kallmann. The blizzard of statistics published by Kallmann seemed to indicate conclusively that schizophrenia was a genetic phenomenon. From his study of a thousand pairs of affected twins, Kallmann concluded that if one member of a pair of identical twins was schizophrenic there was an 86.2 percent chance that the other would be also. Further, if two schizophrenic parents produced a child, there was a 68.1 percent chance that the child would be schizophrenic. These figures led Kallmann to argue that schizophrenia could be attributed to a single recessive gene.

The particular genetic theory espoused by Kallmann has made it possible for latter-day psychiatric geneticists to attempt a spectacular rewriting of their history. Thus, in a recent textbook the following note appears: "Kallmann's [theory] was apparently not based solely on his data. His widow has indicated that Kallmann advocated a recessive model because he could then argue convincingly against the use of sterilization to eliminate the gene. As a Jewish refugee, Kallmann was very sensitive to this issue and afraid of the possible social consequences of his own research."[3] The point here is that if a disease such as schizophrenia is caused by a recessive gene, many carriers of the gene will not themselves display symptoms. Thus, sterilization merely of those who do show symptoms would be inefficient and would fail to eliminate the disease.

The picture of Kallmann as a bleeding-heart protector of schizophrenics, adjusting his scientific theories to mirror his compassion, is grotesquely false. The first Kallmann publication on schizophrenia is in a German volume edited by Harmsen and Lohse that contains the proceedings of the frankly Nazi International Congress for Population Science.[4] There, in Berlin, Kallmann argued vigorously for the sterilization of the apparently healthy relatives of schizophrenics, as well as of schizophrenics themselves. This was necessary, according to Kallmann, precisely because his data indicated that schizophrenia was a genetically recessive disease. Two Nazi geneticists, Lenz and Reichel, rose to argue that there were simply too many apparently healthy relatives of schizophrenics to make their sterilization feasible.

The eugenicist views of Kallmann were not confined to obscure Nazi publications but also made widely available in English after his arrival in the United States in 1936. In 1938 he wrote of schizophrenics as a "source of maladjusted crooks, asocial eccentrics, and the lowest type of criminal offenders. Even the faithful believer in . . . liberty would be much happier without those. . . . I am reluctant to admit the necessity of different eugenic programs for democratic and fascistic communities . . . there are neither biological nor sociological differences between a democratic and a totalitarian schizophrenic."[5]

The extremity of Kallmann's totalitarian passion for eugenic sterilization was clearly indicated in his major 1938 text. Precisely because of the recessivity of the illness, it was above all necessary to prevent the reproduction of the apparently healthy children and siblings of schizophrenics. Further, the apparently healthy marriage partner of a schizophrenic "should be prevented from remarrying" if any child of the earlier marriage is even a suspected schizophrenic, and even if the second marriage is with a normal individual.[6]

These views of the future president of the American Society for Human Genetics are so bloodcurdling that one can sympathize with the efforts of present-day geneticists to misrepresent or to suppress them. They have not, however, suppressed the mountains of published statistics with which Kallmann attempted to prove that schizophrenia (like tuberculosis and homosexuality) was a hereditary form of degeneracy. Those figures are presented to students in today's textbooks as the fruits of impartial science. We begin our review of the data concerning the genetics of schizophrenia with a detailed examination of Kallmann's work, which should make clear that Kallmann's figures cannot be regarded seriously.

KALLMANN'S DATA

The Kallmann data were collected under two very different sets of circumstances. The earlier data, published in 1938, were based upon the records of a large Berlin mental hospital. Working with records from the period 1893–1902, Kallmann made an "unambiguous diagnosis" of schizophrenia in 1,087 index cases. To make these diagnoses it was necessary to ignore "earlier diagnoses or the contemporary notes on hereditary taint conditions in the family of the patient." Then Kallmann attempted to locate, or to acquire information about, relatives of the index cases—many of whom were long since dead. That task often involved

> formidable difficulties . . . we were dealing with inferior people. . . . They sometimes escaped our search for years. . . . Quite a few were bad-humored . . . we had to overcome the suspicion with which certain classes regarded any kind of official activity. . . . Whenever we encountered serious opposition we found ourselves to be dealing with either officials and members of the academic world, or people with exaggerated suspicions, schizoid types, and possible schizophrenics . . . our private sources of information were amplified from the records of police bureaus. . . . In making inquiries about people already dead or living too far away, we employed . . . local bureaus and trusted agents.[7]

With information gathered in this way, Kallmann felt able to diagnose the relatives of the index cases, and thus to report the probability of schizophrenia for each type of relative. The rates reported by Kallmann in this German

TABLE 1 Age-Corrected Morbidity Rates for Schizophrenia, as Reported by Kallmann

Relationship to Index Case	*Berlin, 1938*	*New York, 1946*	*New York, 1953*
MZ twin	—	85.8	86.2
DZ twin	—	14.7	14.5
Parents	10.4	9.2	9.3
Children	16.4	—	—
Full siblings	11.5	14.3	14.2
Half-siblings	7.6	7.0	7.1
Grandchildren	4.3	—	—
Nephews, nieces	3.9	—	—
Step-siblings	—	1.8	1.8
Spouse	—	2.1	—

sample are reproduced in the left-hand column of Table 1. The reported rates, it should be noted, were "age-corrected." That was necessary because some of the relatives were quite young and might develop schizophrenia as they grew older. The arbitrary correction employed by Kallmann can sometimes produce rates in excess of 100 percent.

The second set of data collected by Kallmann came from a very different sample, studied in New York State. The index cases were now individuals who were schizophrenic twins who had been admitted to public mental hospitals. When Kallmann reported in 1946, there were 794 such index cases.[8] By 1953, the number had increased to 953. There were, of course, some identical (MZ) twins, and some fraternal (DZ) twins. Thus, by obtaining information about the co-twins of index cases, Kallmann could report the probability that both members of a pair were schizophrenic. That probability is called the "pairwise concordance rate." The age-corrected concordances were reported for different types of twins, along with the corrected morbidity rates for various types of relatives. These had been determined by collecting information about the relatives of the twin index cases. There was virtually no information given about the procedures employed in this massive study, but Kallmann wrote that "classification of both schizophrenia and zygosity were made on the basis of personal investigation and extended observation." This obviously allowed for "contaminated diagnosis." That is, the decision as to whether or not a co-twin was said to be schizophrenic could be influenced by the decision as to whether the twin pair was MZ or DZ and vice versa. The Kallmann 1946 data, and the even more sketchily reported data of 1953,[9] are also presented in Table 1.

These data are obviously consistent with an overwhelming genetic determination of schizophrenia—particularly the remarkable rate of 86 percent among MZ twins. Where direct comparisons can be made, the change of countries and of eras—as well as the switch to relatives of twin index cases—has had little effect on the reported figures.

The correspondence between Kallmann's theoretical expectations and the results he discovered is sometimes quite remarkable. Thus, in 1938 Kallmann indicated that the work of earlier twin researchers suggested that schizophrenia manifested itself, even among those with the full genetic predisposition, only about 70 percent of the time.[10] That meant, according to Kallmann's single recessive gene theory, that 70 percent of the children of two schizophrenic parents should themselves be schizophrenic. The Kallmann data indicated that the expectation of schizophrenia in the offspring of two schizophrenics was precisely 68.1 percent. That result, of course, nicely validated Kallmann's theory. Four other studies of the children of two schizophrenic parents suggest a risk of only between 34 and 44 percent.[11]

Kallmann stressed repeatedly that, in his data, the " morbidity figure for the siblings . . . corresponds perfectly with the concordance rate for two-egg twin pairs, whose chance of inheriting a similar genotypical combination is exactly the same as that for any ordinary pair of brothers and sisters."[12] The same close correspondence was described as a notable finding in 1953. We shall soon see, however, that—as an embarrassment to a simple genetic theory—other investigators have not found the close correspondences of data with theory routinely detected by Kallmann. . . .

The research conducted by others who followed Kallmann has in any event made it clear that his extraordinarily high figures cannot be repeated. The Kallmann data are still presented, unblushingly, in purportedly serious reviews of research, but they are now counterbalanced by more recent and more modest results. Perhaps the chief harm brought about by Kallmann's deluge of incredible and poorly documented data was to create a climate in which the findings of subsequent workers seemed so reasonable and moderate that they escaped serious critical scrutiny. Thus, Kallmann's data have faded from the body of acceptable evidence, but the belief for which he was largely responsible—that a genetic basis for schizophrenia has been clearly established—still remains powerful in and out of science.

Family Studies

There are basically three kinds of inquiries that attempt to demonstrate a genetic basis for schizophrenia: family studies, twin studies, and adoption studies. There is no need to spend much time on the first. The simple idea behind them is that if schizophrenia is inherited, the relatives of schizophrenics are likely to display the disease as well.

Further, the more closely related a person is to a schizophrenic, the more likely it should be that the person will be affected. The problem is, of course, that these predictions would also follow from a theory that maintained that schizophrenia was environmentally produced. There is an obvious tendency for close relatives to share similar environments.

For what such data are worth, the major compilation of family studies seems to have been made by Zerbin-Rüdin.[13] The compilation was presented to English-readers in "simplified form" by Slater and Cowie.[14] Their table indicates, e.g., that fourteen separate studies yield a 4.38 percent expectation of schizophrenia among the parents of schizophrenic index cases. The expectation among sibs, in ten studies, was 8.24 percent; and among children 12.31 percent in five studies. For uncles and aunts, grandchildren, and cousins the figures were all under 3 percent, but still higher than the expected 1 percent.

The exactness of these figures, however, is more apparent that real. The same basic set of studies was also summarized by Rosenthal in 1970.[15] The relatives diagnosed in these studies, Rosenthal noted, had often been dead for many years. The studies are quite old, and methods of diagnoses and of sampling are not always spelled out. The combined figures are dominated by Kallmann's massive samples and by data gathered by other members of Rüdin's "Munich school." The Rosenthal tables make clear a fact that is obscured by the Slater and Cowie summary. There are vast differences in the rates of schizophrenia reported in different studies. For parents of index cases, reported risks range from 0.2 percent (lower than in the population at large) to 12.0 percent. For sibs, the range is between 3.3 and 14.3 percent. The risk for sibs is in one study twenty-nine times larger than that for parents; but in another the risk for parents is 1½ times larger than that for sibs. These studies at best demonstrate what nobody would have contested. There is at least a rough tendency for diagnosed schizophrenia to "run in families."*

Twin Studies

[T]he basic logic of twin studies depends upon the fact that while MZ twins are genetically identical, DZ twins on average share (like ordinary siblings) only half their genes. Thus, if a trait is genetically determined, one would obviously expect MZs to be concordant for that trait more often than DZs. The major logical problem with twin studies is that MZ twins, who typically resemble one another strikingly in appearance, are treated much more similarly than are DZs by parents and peers. There is abundant evidence . . . that the environments of MZs are very much more similar than those of DZs. (Twin studies typically compare concordance rates among MZs, who are always of the same sex, with concordance rates among same-sexed DZs.) The demonstration that concordance is higher among MZs does not necessarily establish a genetic basis for the trait in question. Perhaps the difference is due to the greater environmental similarity of MZs. We shall soon discuss evidence which indicates that this possibility is not at all farfetched.

Well-designed twin studies should take as their index cases all schizophrenic twins admitted to a particular hospital during a particular time period. The alternative—feasible in small Scandinavian countries, which maintain population registers—is to start with the entire population of twins and to locate index schizophrenic cases. With either technique, a number of procedural problems are inevitable. The co-twins of index cases are often dead or unavailable for personal examination. Thus, informed guesses often must be made both about whether a given pair is MZ or DZ, and whether or not the co-twin is schizophrenic. The guesses are typically made by the same person, opening the way for contaminated diagnoses. There is sometimes an effort to have blind diagnoses made of individual cases by independent judges, working from written case histories.[17]

The case histories, however, contain selective material gathered and prepared by investigators who were not themselves "blind." Further, the case records of those twins who have in fact been hospitalized—and their diagnoses—had been written up by doctors who questioned the ill twins in detail about possible taint in their family lines. The diagnosis of schizophrenia, as should by now be clear, is by no means a cut-and-dried affair. The fact that a person's relative may have suffered from schizophrenia is often used to help doctors make a diagnosis.

The biases that contaminate twin studies stand out clearly from an attentive reading of the published case history materials. The very first case described by Slater in 1953 is the story of Eileen, a hospitalized schizophrenic, and of her identical twin, Fanny. Eileen had been hospitalized in 1899, "suffering from acute mania," and died in the hospital in 1946. With Eileen as the index case, Slater's task was to investigate the mental status of Fanny, who died, aged seventy-one in 1938. We are told by Slater:

> While still in the twenties she had a mental illness, of which no details are available. . . . Fanny in [1936] proved very difficult to examine . . . so that only the barest details were obtainable. She suppressed all mention of her own mental illness in early years, which fact was obtained from the history of her twin sister given at the time of her admission to hospital. Though there was no sign of any present schizophrenic symptoms, this suspicion and reserve are such as are commonly found as sequelae of a schizophrenic psychosis. Unfortunately, no facts are obtainable about the nature of her past mental illness,

*Even this modest conclusion is not unchallenged in the literature. Two studies in the United States found rates of schizophrenia among the first-degree relatives of schizophrenics which were scarcely above the rate in the general population.[16]

but the probabilities are very greatly in favour of it having been a schizophrenic one . . . she made a fairly complete and permanent recovery . . . though psychologically her reserve and lack of frankness suggest that the schizophrenia was not entirely without permanent after-effect. . . . According to her daughter-in-law, who had not heard of her mental illness, she led a hard life. Neither her family nor the neighbours noticed anything odd about her.[18]

These MZ twins, according to Slater, were concordant for schizophrenia. The only evidence that Fanny had once suffered from schizophrenia was her twin's assertion—while "suffering from acute mania" in 1899—that Fanny had had some kind of mental illness. Fanny herself, in 1936, was difficult and suppressed all mention of her illness. That lack of frankness, Slater noted, was typical of recovered schizophrenics, who otherwise appear normal. Fanny's dead identical twin had clearly been schizophrenic. For Slater this made it obvious that Fanny's supposed mental illness fifty years earlier had been schizophrenia. Fanny's neighbors and family, unlike Slater and other students of the Munich school, had not the wit to detect Fanny's schizophrenia.

Consider now the first pair of discordant DZ twins described by Gottesman and Shields in their 1972 study. Twin A was a hospitalized schizophrenic. What about Twin B? "No psychiatric history. Family unwilling for him to be contacted for Twin Investigation. . . . The pair differs from most in that neither twin was seen by us." The investigators concluded that Twin B was normal: and six blind judges, pondering a case study summary prepared by the investigators, unanimously agreed that Twin B was free of psychopathology. With DZ Pair 16 of the same study, all judges again agreed that the co-twin was normal, making the pair discordant. The diagnosis of the co-twin had not been made under ideal conditions: "He refused to be seen for the Twin Investigation, remaining upstairs out of sight, but his wife was seen at the door. . . . He was regarded as a healthy, levelheaded, solid happy person." That might in fact be the case—but few will agree that diagnoses of co-twins made in this way are solid or levelheaded.

Problems of this sort affect all twin studies, and that should be borne in mind as we review the results reported by various investigators. To obtain reasonable estimates of concordance rates, it seems sensible to require that a study contain at least twenty pairs of MZ and twenty pairs of same-sexed DZ twins. There have been seven such studies, and their results are summarized in Table 2.

TABLE 2 Reported Concordance Rates

	"Narrow" Concordance		*"Broad" Concordance*	
Study	*% MZs*	*% DZs*	*% MZs*	*% DZs*
Rosanoff et al., 1934[19] (41 MZs, 53 DZs)	44	9	61	13
Kallmann, 1946[8] (174 MZs, 296 DZs)	59	11	69	11–14
Slater, 1953[18] (37 MZs, 58 DZs)*	65	14	65	14
Gottesman and Shields, 1966[20] (24 MZs, 33 DZs)	42	15	54	18
Kringlen, 1968[21] (55 MZs, 90 DZs)	25	7	38	10
Allen et al., 1972[22] (95 MZs, 125 DZs)	14	4	27	5
Fischer, 1973[23] (21 MZs, 41 DZs)	24	10	48	20

*There is no simple way to derive separate narrow and broad concordance rates for Slater.

The table presents raw, pairwise concordance rates, without any age correction. Two sets of rates are given for each study, one narrow and one broad. The narrow rates are based on the investigator's attempt to apply a relatively strict set of criteria when diagnosing schizophrenia. The broad rates include as concordant cases in which one twin is described as "borderline schizophrenic" or as "schizo-affective psychosis" or a "paranoid with schizophrenic-like features." The tabled concordance rates, it should be noted, depend upon the different investigators' varying sets of diagnostic criteria. They have not been concocted ad hoc by us.

The table makes clear that in all studies concordance is higher for MZ than DZ twins. But it is also clear that the concordance reported for MZs is much higher in the three older studies than in the four more recent ones. There is in fact no overlap between the two sets of studies. For narrow concordance, the average has plunged from 56 to 26 percent for MZs; for DZs, the corresponding averages are 11 and 9 percent. For broad concordance, MZ rates have dropped from 65 to 42 percent, while the DZ rate remained at a constant 13 percent. These average values, which weight all studies equally, should not be taken too literally. The data do make clear, however, that even in genetically identical MZs environmental factors must be of enormous importance. The concordance for MZs reported by modern researchers, even under the broadest criteria, does not remotely approach the preposterous 86 percent figure claimed by Kallmann.

Those who perform such studies still claim, however, that the higher concordance observed among MZs—a unanimous finding—demonstrates at least some genetic basis for schizophrenia. We

TABLE 3 Reported Risks for DZ Twins and Sibs

	% DZs	*% Sibs*
Luxenburger, 1935[24]	14.0	12.0
Kallmann, 1946[8]	14.7	14.3
Slater, 1953[18]*	14.4	5.4
Gottesman and Shields, 1972[17]	9.1	4.7
Fischer, 1973[23]*	26.7	10.1
Kringlen, 1976[21]	8.5	3.0

*Probability that the differences between DZs and sibs are due only to sampling error is less than 0.01%.

have already noted that MZs not only are genetically more similar than DZs but also experience much more similar environments than do DZs. The environmental similarity, no less that the genetic similarity, might plausibly account for the higher concordance of MZs.

There are in fact some simple and critical tests that can be made of this environmental hypothesis. There is no doubt that DZ twins experience more similar environments than do ordinary siblings. The DZ twins, however, are genetically no more alike than are ordinary siblings—they are only siblings who happen to have been born at the same time. Thus, from an environmental viewpoint—and only from such a viewpoint—we would expect concordance among DZs to be higher than among ordinary sibs. There have been a number of studies that reported rates of schizophrenia concordance among DZ twins, as well as rates among siblings of the twins. The results of all such studies are summarized in Table 3.

Though the reported differences are very small in the early studies, all studies agree in showing a higher concordance rate among DZs than among sibs. Within more modern studies, the difference is often statistically significant, with the risk for DZs reported as two or three times that for sibs. When we note that similarity of environment can double or triple the concordance of DZs above that of sibs, it seems entirely plausible to attribute the still higher concordance of MZs to their still greater environmental similarity.

The same kind of point can be demonstrated by comparing the concordance rates of same-sexed and of opposite-sexed DZs. Though both types of DZ twins are equally similar genetically, it is obvious that same-sexed pairs experience more similar environments than do opposite-sexed pairs. The available data, summarized in Table 4, again support the environmentalist expectation. There have been statistically significant differences reported by several investigators, always indicating a higher concordance among same-sexed twins. The results of the one study that appears to reverse the otherwise universal trend were not statistically significant.

TABLE 4 Concordance in Same- and Opposite-Sexed DZ Twins

	% Same-Sexed	*% Opposite-Sexed*
Rosanoff et al., 1934 (53 SS, 48 OS)[19]*	9.4	0.0
Luxenburger, 1953[24]	19.6	7.6†
Kallmann, 1946 (296 SS, 221 OS)[8]*	11.5	5.9
Slater, 1953 (61 SS, 54 OS)[18]*	18.0	3.7
Inouye, 1961 (11 SS, 6 OS)[25]	18.1	0.0
Harvald and Hauge, 1965 (31 SS, 28 OS)[26]	6.5	3.6
Kringlen, 1968 (90 SS, 82 OS)[21]	6.7	9.8

*Probability that differences between same- and opposite-sexed twins are due only to sampling error is less than 0.05%.
†Estimated

Consider, finally, some implications of a finding casually reported by Hoffer and Pollin.[27] Those authors studied the hospital records of the American war veteran twins later reported on by Allen et al. Several hundred diagnosed schizophrenic twins were located by searching through records, but the twins were not personally examined by the investigators. Thus, to determine whether a twin pair was MZ or DZ, questionnaires were mailed to all twins, asking whether they looked as much alike as two peas in a pod, whether they were confused for each other, etc. There were many occasions when only one twin of a discordant pair returned the questionnaire. When the twin returning the questionnaire had been diagnosed as schizophrenic, 31.3 percent gave answers indicating that they were MZ. When the answering twin was not the diagnosed schizophrenic, only 17.2 percent indicated that they were MZ. The difference is statistically significant, and it was produced by an unrealistically small proportion of MZs among the nonschizophrenic twins.

That is easily understandable. When you are normal and your twin is schizophrenic, you are well advised to tell twin investigators and other authorities that you are not a carbon copy of your twin—even if you really are MZs. To admit that you are the MZ twin of a schizophrenic is clearly to invite a similar diagnosis—even, perhaps, sterilization—for yourself. We recall that in all the twin studies some decisions about zygosity are made on the basis of questions put to nonaffected twins and to their relatives. With a little sensitivity to the real lives of people, we must recognize an all-too-human tendency to deny that the nonaffected MZ twins of schizophrenics really are identical. This must be still another source of error, tending to remove some discordant pairs from the MZ and into the DZ category. That, of course, artificially inflates the difference in concordance rates between MZs and DZs. There is little wonder in the fact that even psychiatric geneticists have not found twin studies to be wholly convincing, and have turned to studies of adoption. The adoption studies, in theory at least, might be able to disentangle genetic from environmental effects in a way that twin studies cannot.

Adoption Studies

The basic procedure of adoption studies is to begin with a set of schizophrenic index cases, and then to study the biological relatives from whom they have been separated by the process of adoption. Thus—at least in theory—the index case and his or her biological relatives have only genes, and not environment, in common. The question of interest is whether the biological relatives of the index cases, despite the lack of shared environments, display an increased incidence of schizophrenia. To answer that question it is necessary to compare the rate of schizophrenia among the biological relatives with the rate observed in some appropriate control group.

The adoption studies carried out in Denmark in recent years by a collaborative team of American and Danish investigators have had enormous impact. To some critics who could detect the methodological weaknesses of twin studies, the Danish adoption studies appeared to establish the genetic basis of schizophrenia beyond any doubt. The eminent neuroscientist Solomon Snyder referred to these studies as a landmark "in the history of biological psychiatry. It's the best work that's been done. They take out all the artifacts in the nature vs. nurture argument."[28] Paul Wender, one of the authors of the studies, was able to announce: "We failed to discover any environmental component. . . . That's a very strong statement."[29] Though Wender's total excision of environmental factors is extreme, the Danish studies have been universally accepted as an unequivocal demonstration of an important genetic basis for schizophrenia. Clearly these studies require detailed critical examination.

Though they have been described in many separate publications, there are basically two major Danish adoption studies. The first, with Kety as senior investigator, starts with adoptees as the schizophrenic index cases and examines their relatives. The second, with Rosenthal as senior investigator, starts with schizophrenic parents as index cases and examines the children whom they gave up for adoption.

The study that began with adoptees as index cases was first reported by Kety in 1968.[30] Based on Copenhagen records, the investigators located thirty-four adoptees who had been admitted to psychiatric hospitals as adults and who could be diagnosed from the records as schizophrenics. For each schizophrenic adoptee a control adoptee who had never received psychiatric care was selected. The control was matched to the index case for sex, age, age at transfer to the adoptive parents, and socioeconomic status (SES) of the adoptive family.

The next step was to search the records of psychiatric treatment for all Denmark, looking for relatives of both the index and control cases. Those who searched the records did not know which were the relatives of index cases and which were the relatives of controls. Whenever a psychiatric record was found, it was summarized and then diagnosed blindly by a team of researchers who came to a consensus. The relatives were not at this stage personally examined.

The researchers traced 150 biological relatives (parents, sibs, or half-sibs) of the index cases, and 156 biological relatives of the controls. The first point to note is one not stressed by the authors: There were virtually no clear cases of schizophrenia among the relatives either of the index or of the control cases. To be precise, there was one chronic schizophrenic among the index relatives and one among the controls. To obtain apparently significant results the authors had to pool together a "schizophrenic spectrum of disorders." The spectrum concept lumps into a single category such diagnoses as chronic schizophrenia, "borderline state," "inadequate personality," "uncertain schizophrenia," and "uncertain borderline state." With such a broad concept, 8.7 percent of the biological relatives of index cases and 1.9 percent of the biological relatives of controls were diagnosed as displaying spectrum disorders. There were nine biological families of index cases in which at least one spectrum diagnosis had been made, compared to only two such families among the controls. That difference is the supposed evidence for the genetic basis of schizophrenia. Without the inclusion of such vague diagnoses as "inadequate personality" and "uncertain borderline schizophrenia" there would be no significant results in the Kety study.

From the Kety data of 1968 it is possible to demonstrate that such vague diagnoses—falling within the "soft spectrum"—are not in fact associated with schizophrenia. Among the sixty-six biological families reported on in 1968 there were a total of six in which at least one "soft" diagnosis had been made.* There was *no* tendency for such diagnoses to occur any more frequently in families in which definite schizophrenia had been diagnosed than in other families. However, the "soft spectrum" diagnoses very definitely tended to occur in the same families in which "outside the spectrum" psychiatric diagnoses had been made—that is, such clearly nonschizophrenic diagnoses as alcoholism, psychopathy, syphilitic psychosis, etc. There were "outside the spectrum" diagnoses in 83 percent of the families containing "soft spectrum"

---

*We here include as "soft" diagnoses the two least certain diagnoses employed by Kety et al.—their D-3 diagnosis ("uncertain borderline") and their C diagnosis ("inadequate personality").

diagnoses, and in only 30 percent of the remaining families—a statistically significant difference. Thus it appears that the Kety et al. results depend upon their labeling as schizophrenia vaguely defined behaviors that tend to run in the same families as do alcoholism and criminality—but which do not tend to run in the same families as does genuine schizophrenia. However, it remains the case that these frowned-upon behaviors did occur more frequently among the biological relatives of adopted schizophrenics than among the biological relatives of adopted controls. What might account for such a finding?

The most obvious possibility is that of selective placement, a universal phenomenon in the real world in which adoptions in fact occur, and a phenomenon that undermines the theoretical separation of genetic and environmental variables claimed for adoption studies. The children placed into homes by adoption agencies are never placed randomly. For example, it is well known that biological children of college-educated mothers, when put up for adoption, are placed selectively into the homes of adoptive parents with higher socioeconomic and educational status. The biological children of mothers who are grade-school dropouts are usually placed into much lower status adoptive homes. Thus it seems reasonable to ask: Into what kinds of adoptive homes are infants born into families shattered by alcoholism, criminality, and syphilitic psychosis likely to be placed? Further, might not the adoptive environment into which such children are placed cause them to develop schizophrenia?

From raw data kindly made available to one of us by Dr. Kety, we have been able to demonstrate a clear selective placement effect. Whenever a record of psychiatric treatment of a relative was located by Kety's team, notation was made about whether the relative had been in a mental hospital, in the psychiatric department of a general hospital, or in some other facility. When we check the adoptive families of the schizophrenic adoptees, we discover that in eight of the families (24 percent) an adoptive parent had been in a mental hospital. That was not true of a single adoptive parent of a control adoptee. That, of course, is a statistically significant difference—and it suggests as a credible interpretation of the Kety et al. results that the schizophrenic adoptees, who indeed had been born into shattered and disreputable families, acquired their schizophrenia as a result of the poor adoptive environments into which they were placed. The fact that one's adoptive parent goes into a mental hospital clearly does not bode well for the psychological health of the environment in which one is reared. There is, by the way, no indication that the biological parents of the schizophrenic adoptees have been in mental hospitals at an excessive rate. That occurred in only two families (6 percent), a rate in fact lower than that observed in the biological families of the control adoptees.

The same set of subjects had also been reported on in a later paper by Kety et al.[31] For this later work as many as possible of the relatives of index and control adoptees had been traced down personally and interviewed by a psychiatrist. The interviews were edited, and consensus diagnoses were then made blindly by the investigators. The basic picture did not change much. There were more spectrum diagnoses among relatives of index cases than among relatives of controls, although the interview procedure greatly increased the overall frequency of such diagnoses. This time, however, diagnoses of inadequate personality had to be excluded from the spectrum, since they occurred with equal frequency in both sets of relatives. The significance of the 1968 results, based on records rather than interviews, had depended upon including inadequate personality in the elastic spectrum.

Personal correspondence with the psychiatrist who conducted the interviews with relatives has revealed a few interesting details. The 1975 paper speaks only of "interviews," but it turns out that in several cases, when relatives were dead or unavailable, the psychiatrist "prepared a so-called pseudo interview from the existing hospital records." That is, the psychiatrist filled out the interview form in the way in which he guessed the relative would have answered. These pseudo interviews were sometimes diagnosed with remarkable sensitivity by the team of American investigators. The case of the biological mother of S-II, a schizophrenic adoptee, is one particularly instructive example.

The woman's mental hospital records had been edited and then diagnosed blindly by the investigators in 1968. The diagnosis was inadequate personality—at that time, inside the spectrum. The 1975 paper—by which time inadequate personality is outside the spectrum—indicates that, upon personal interview, the woman had been diagnosed as a case of uncertain borderline schizophrenia—again inside the spectrum. But personal correspondence had revealed that the woman was never in fact interviewed; she had committed suicide long before the psychiatrist attempted to locate her, and so—from the original hospital records—she was "pseudo interviewed." Perhaps the most remarkable aspect of the story, also revealed by personal correspondence, is that the woman had been hospitalized twice—and each time had been diagnosed as manic-depressive by the psychiatrists who actually saw and treated her. That is, she had been diagnosed as suffering from a mental illness unrelated to schizophrenia, and very clearly outside the schizophrenia spectrum. We can only marvel at the fact that the American diagnosticians, analyzing abstracts of these same records, were twice able to detect—without ever seeing her—that she really belonged within the shifting boundaries of the spectrum.

The Kety study has more recently been expanded to include all of Denmark (rather than merely Copenhagen). The hospital records of relatives have been searched and the results briefly referred to in a couple of publications. The relatives are also being interviewed. There have been no detailed data published or made available for the larger sample, so critical analysis is not yet possible. Though Kety asserts that results from the expanded sample confirm those earlier reported in detail, there is no reason to suppose that the more recent work is free of the invalidating flaws we have outlined above.

These results must be evaluated together with the results of a companion study reported by Rosenthal et al. using the same Danish files.[32] This study first identified a number of schizophrenic parents who had given up children for adoption. The question is whether those children, not reared by their schizophrenic biological parents, will tend to develop schizophrenia. The control group for the index children was made up of adoptees whose biological parents had no record of psychiatric treatment. The index adoptees and the controls, when grown up, were interviewed—blindly—by a Danish psychiatrist. Based upon those interviews, decisions were made as to whether particular individuals were in or out of the spectrum of schizophrenic disorders. Countless textbooks now indicate that a higher frequency of spectrum disorders were diagnosed in the adopted children of schizophrenics than in children of normal controls. That claim is based on preliminary (and inadequately reported) accounts of the study.

The preliminary reports did claim to observe a barely significant tendency for spectrum disorders to be more frequent among the index cases. (There was only one adoptee who had ever in fact been hospitalized for schizophrenia, and the authors frankly admitted that if they had looked only for hospitalized cases of schizophrenia, "we would have concluded that heredity did not contribute significantly to schizophrenia.")[33] The early papers, however, are entirely vague as to when and how or by whom decisions were made about whether individual cases were in or out of the spectrum. The papers indicate merely that the interviewing Danish psychiatrist made a "thumbnail diagnostic formulation" for each interview, and that these were somehow related to whether or not the interviewee was placed into the spectrum. Personal correspondence with several of the collaborators had made it clear that the "thumbnail diagnostic formulation" of the interviewer did not specify whether the individual was in or out of the spectrum. For the early papers, that decision was made in a manner and by parties unknown.

When consensus diagnoses like those in the Kety study were reported on for the first time in 1978, it developed that there was no significant tendency for spectrum cases to occur more frequently among index subjects.[34] Thus, despite the widely cited misleading early reports of the Rosenthal et al. study, its outcome was in fact negative.

Wender et al. added a new refinement to the Rosenthal study by reporting on a new group of twenty-eight "cross-fostered" subjects.[35] These were adoptees whose biological parents had been normal but whose adoptive parents had become schizophrenic. The new group was added to observe whether the experience of being reared by a schizophrenic adoptive parent would produce pathology in a child. The cross-fostered children, according to Wender et al., did not show more pathology than did the control adoptees. But it is important to note that in this paper the concept of diagnosing a schizophrenia spectrum had been abandoned; instead, the Danish interviews were now being rated for "global psychopathology." Consensus diagnoses—or any other diagnoses—of whether or not the cross-fostered children were in the schizophrenia spectrum have not appeared in any of the many papers concerned with the genetics of schizophrenia.

There is, however, an obscure paper from the Kety and Rosenthal group concerned with the characteristics of people who refuse to take part in psychological studies that contains some important and relevant information.[36] The paper includes as an aside an incidental table (Table 14) showing the percentage of spectrum diagnoses made in each group by a Danish Psychiatrist, Schulsinger. We learn from that table that fully 26 percent of the cross-fostered adoptees were diagnosed as being in the schizophrenia spectrum—a rate not significantly different from that of the index adoptees themselves. Further, that obscure table is the only place where data on an immensely relevant control group have been reported. The Danish investigators, it turns out, also interviewed (and diagnosed) a number of nonadopted children of schizophrenics, who had been reared by their mentally ill biological parents. The rate of spectrum disorder among this group did not differ from that observed among cross-fostered children. Thus, had they taken the design of their own study seriously, the investigators might have concluded that they had shown schizophrenia to be entirely of environmental origin. The cross-fostered biological children of normal parents, when merely reared by schizophrenic adoptive parents, show just as great a frequency of spectrum disorders as do the nonadopted biological children of schizophrenics. The reader may not be surprised to learn that consensus diagnoses of the nonadopted group, like consensus diagnoses of the cross-fostered group, have never been reported.

The weaknesses of the Danish adoption studies are so obvious upon critical review that it may be difficult to understand how distinguished scientists could have regarded them as eliminating all the artifacts that beset family and twin studies of nature and nurture. In fact, a team of investigators from the French National Institute of Medical Research have published, quite independently, an analysis of the Danish adoption studies that reaches the conclusion that they are gravely deficient.[37] Perhaps one factor encouraging the usually uncritical acceptance of the investigators' claims has been indicated by Wender and Klein in an article written for the popular magazine *Psychology Today*.[38] They cite the Danish adoption study—based upon a broad concept of schizophrenia spectrum—as indicating that "for each schizophrenic there may be 10 times as many people who have a milder form of the disorder that is genetically . . . related to the most severe form . . . 8 percent of Americans have a lifelong form of personality disorder that is genetically produced. This finding is extremely important." The importance of the finding is spelled out by Wender and Klein in the following language: "The public is largely unaware that different sorts of emotional illnesses are now responsive to specific medications and, unfortunately, many doctors are similarly unaware." The logic, erroneous at every step, is as follows: The Danish adoption studies have shown that schizophrenia, and a number of behavioral eccentricities, are genetically produced. Since the genes influence biological mechanisms, it must follow that the most effective treatment for schizophrenia, and for behavioral eccentricity, is drug treatment. Focusing on social or environmental conditions as a cause of disordered behavior would be fruitless.

Yet any materialist understanding of the relationship of brain to behavior must recognize that even if schizophrenia were largely genetic in origin, it would in no way follow that drugs—or any biological, as opposed to social, treatment—would necessarily be the most effective therapy. Just as drugs change behavior, so will altered behavior imposed by talking therapies change brains (as indeed the latent theory behind behavior modification would itself agree). The logic of this does not depend on a belief in any more explicit integration of the biological and the social.

SCHIZOPHRENIA AS SOCIALLY DETERMINED

To reveal, as we have tried, the theoretical and empirical impoverishment of the conventional wisdom of biological determinism in relationship to schizophrenia does not then argue that there is nothing relevant to be said about the biology of the disorder, and still less does it deny that schizophrenia exists. The problem of understanding the etiology of schizophrenia and a rational investigation of its treatment and prevention is made vastly more difficult, perhaps even hopelessly tangled, by the extraordinary latitude and naiveté of diagnostic criteria. Certainly one may wonder about the relevance of biology to the diagnosis of schizophrenia either by the forensic psychiatrists of the Soviet Union or by the British psychiatrist who diagnoses a young black as schizophrenic on the basis of his use of the religious language of Rastafarianism.[39]

Misgivings are not eased when one recalls a well-known study by Rosenhan and his colleagues in California in 1973.[40] Rosenhan's group of experimenters presented themselves individually at mental hospitals complaining of hearing voices. Many were hospitalized. Once inside the hospital, according to the strategy of the experiment, they declared that their symptoms had ceased. However, it did not prove so easy to achieve release. The experimenters' claims to normality were disregarded, and most found themselves treated as mere objects by nurses and doctors and released only after considerable periods of time. A pseudo-patient who took notes in one of the hospitals, for instance, was described by nurses as showing "compulsive writing behavior."

Even more revealing, perhaps, was the drop in hospital admissions for schizophrenia in the area after Rosenhan circulated the results of the first experiment among doctors and indicated that they might be visited by further pseudo-patients in the future, although none were actually sent.

It is this sort of experience that lies behind the argument, developed in its most extreme form by Michel Foucault and his school over the last two decades, that the entire category of psychological disorders is to be seen as a historical invention, an expression of power relationships within society manifested within particular families. To simplify Foucault's intricate argument, he claims that all societies require a category of individuals who can be dominated or scapegoated, and over the centuries since the rise of science—and particularly since the industrial revolution of the nineteenth century—the mad have come to fill this category. In medieval times, he says, houses of confinement were built for lepers, and madness was often explained in terms of possession by demons or spirits.[41] According to Foucault the idea of institutionalizing the mad developed during the eighteenth and nineteenth centuries after the clearing of the leper houses left a gap for new scapegoats to replace the old ones.

In this view madness is a matter of labeling; it is not a property of the individual but merely a social definition wished by society on a proportion of its population. To look for correlates of madness in the brain or the genes is therefore a meaningless task, for it is not located in the brain or the individual at all. To dismiss the suffering and the deranged behavior of the schizophrenic merely as a problem of social labeling by those who have power over those who have not seems a quite inadequate response to a complex social and medical problem. Despite Foucault's historiography and the enthusiasm of its reception in Britain and France at the crest of the wave of antipsychiatry of the 1960s and 1970s, the actual historical account he gives of when and how asylums for the insane arose has been called into question.[42] And by cutting the phenomenon of schizophrenia completely away from biology and locating it entirely in the social world of labeling, Foucault and his followers arrive, from a very different starting point, back in the dualist Cartesian camp, which . . . preceded the full-blown materialism of the nineteenth century. So much has Foucault retreated that at certain points in his argument he even seems to be ambiguous as to whether "physical" quite apart from "mental" illness exists except in the social context that proclaims it.

More modest than Foucault's grand theorizing but nonetheless culturally determinist are the social and familial theories of schizophrenia developed by R. D. Laing.[43] For Laing—at least the Laing of the sixties and early seventies—schizophrenia is essentially a family disorder, not a product of a sick individual but of the interactions of the members of a sick family. Within this family, locked together by the nuclear style of living of contemporary society, one particular child comes to be picked upon, always at fault, never able to live up to parental demands or expectations. Thus the child is in what Laing calls (in a term derived from Gregory Bateson) a double bind; whatever he or she does is wrong. Under such circumstances the retreat into a world of private fantasy becomes the only logical response to the intolerable pressures of existence. Schizophrenia is thus a rational, adaptive response of individuals to the constraints of their life. Treatment of the schizophrenic by hospitalization or by drugs is therefore not seen as liberation from the disease but as part of that person's oppression.

Family context may be crucial in the development of mental illnesses such as schizophrenia, but it is clear that a larger social context is also involved. The diagnosis is made most often of working-class, inner-city dwellers, least often of middle- and upper-class suburban dwellers.[44] To a social theorist, the argument about the social context that determines the diagnosis is clear. An example of the class nature of the diagnosis of mental illness comes from the studies of depression by Brown and Harris in 1978 in Camberwell, an inner-city, largely working-class area of London, with some pockets of middle-class infiltration.[45] They showed that about a quarter of working-class women with children living in Camberwell were suffering from what they defined as a definite neurosis, mainly severe depression, whereas the incidence among comparable middle-class women was only some 6 percent. A large proportion of these depressed individuals, who if they had attended psychiatric clinics would wave been diagnosed as ill and medicalized or hospitalized, had suffered severe threatening events in their lives within the past year, such as loss of husband or economic insecurity. The use of drugs—mainly tranquilizers—among such groups of women is clearly very high.

Biological determinism faces such social evidence with arguments that, for example, people with genotypes predisposing toward schizophrenia may drift downward in occupation and living accommodation until they find a niche most suited to their genotype. But it would by a brave biological determinist who would want to argue that in the case of the depressed housewives of Camberwell it was their genes that were at fault.

An adequate theory of schizophrenia must understand what it is about the social and cultural environment that pushes some categories of people toward manifesting schizophrenic symptoms; it must understand that such cultural and social environments themselves profoundly affect the biology of the individuals concerned and that some of these biological changes, if we could measure them, might be the reflections or correspondents of that schizophrenia with the brain. It may well be that, in our present society, people with certain genotypes are more likely than others to suffer from schizophrenia—although the evidence is at present entirely inadequate to allow one to come to that conclusion. This says nothing about the future of "schizophrenia" in a different type of society, nor does it help us build a theory of schizophrenia in the present. Neither biological nor cultural determinism, nor some sort of dualistic agnosticism, is adequate to the task of developing such a theory. For that, we must look to a more dialectical understanding of the relationship between the biological and the social.

NOTES

1. *Schizophrenia: Report of an International Pilot Study* (Geneva: WHO, 1973).
2. P. H. Venables, "Longitudinal Study of Schizophrenia," Paper 146 of Annual Meeting, British Association of Advanced Science (September 1981).
3. J. M. Neal and T. F. Oltmanns, *Schizophrenia* (New York: John Wiley, 1980), p. 202.
4. H. Harmsen and F. Lohse, *Bevölkerungsfragen* (Munich: J. F. Lehmanns, 1936).
5. Informal discussion in F. R. Moulton and P. O. Komoro, eds., *Mental Health*, Publication no. 9 (1939) American Association for the Advancement of Science, p. 145.
6. F. J. Kallmann, *The Genetics of Schizophrenia* (Locust Valley, N.Y.: J. J. Augustin, 1938), pp. 99, 131, and pp. 267–268.
7. F. J. Kallmann, "Heredity, Reproduction and Eugenic Procedure in the Field of Schizophrenia," *Eugenical News* 23 (1938): pp. 105–13.
8. F. J. Kallmann, "The Genetic Theory of Schizophrenia: An Analysis of 691 Schizophrenic Twin Index Families," *American Journal of Psychiatry* 103 (1946): 309–22.
9. F. J. Kallmann, *Heredity in Health and Mental Disorder* (New York: Norton, 1953).
10. F. J. Kallmann, "Eugenic Birth Control in Schizophrenic Families," *Journal of Contraception* 3 (1938): 195–99.
11. D. Rosenthal, "The Offspring of Schizophrenic Couples." *Journal of Psychiatric Research* 4 (1966): 167–88.
12. F. J. Kallmann, "The Heredo-constitutional Mechanisms of Predisposition and Resistance to Schizophrenia." *American Journal of Psychiatry* 98 (1942): 544–51.
13. E. Zerbin-Rüdin, "Schizophrenien," in *Humangenetik*, vol. 2, ed. P. E. Becker (Stuttgart: Thieme, 1967).
14. E. Slater and V. Cowie, *The Genetics of Mental Disorders* (London: Oxford Univ. Press, 1971).
15. D. Rosenthal, *Genetic Theory and Abnormal Behavior* (New York: McGraw-Hill, 1970).

16. I. I. Gottesman and J. Shields, *Schizophrenia and Genetics: A Twin Study Vantage Point* (New York: Academic Press, 1972).
17. H. M. Pollock and B. Malzberg, "Hereditary and Environmental Factors in the Causation of Manic-depressive Psychoses and Dementia Praecox," *American Journal of Psychiatry* 96 (1940): 1227–47. Also see G. Winokur, J. Morrison, J. Clancy, and R. Crowe, "The Iowa 500: II. A Blind Family History Comparison of Mania, Depression and Schizophrenia," *Archives of General Psychiatry* 27 (1972): 462–64.
18. E. Slater, *Psychotic and Neurotic Illnesses in Twins*, Medical Research Council Special Report Series no. 278 (London: Her Majesty's Stationery Office, 1953).
19. A. J. Rosanoff, L. M. Handy, I. R. Plesset, and S. Brush, "The Etiology of So-called Schizophrenic Psychoses with Special Reference to Their Occurrence in Twins," *American Journal of Psychiatry* 91 (1934):247–86.
20. I. I. Gottesman and J. Shields, "Schizophrenia in Twins: 16 years' Consecutive Admissions to a Psychiatric Clinic," *British Journal of Psychiatry* 112 (1966): 809–18.
21. E. Kringlen, "An Epidemiological-clinical Twin Study on Schizophrenia," in *The Transmission of Schizophrenia*, eds. D. Rosenthal and S. S. Kety (Oxford: Pergamon, 1968).
22. M. G. Allen, S. Cohen, and W. Pollin, "Schizophrenia in Veteran Twins. A Diagnostic Review," *Archives of General Psychiatry* 128 (1972): 939–45.
23. M. Fischer, "Genetic and Environmental Factors in Schizophrenia: A Study of Schizophrenic Twins and Their Families," *Acta Psychiatrica Scandinavica*, Suppl. 238 (1973).
24. H. Luxenburger, "Untersuchungen an schizophrenen Zwillingen und ihren Geschwistern Zur Prüfung der Realität von Manifestationsschwankungen," Zeitschrift für die Gesamte *Neurologie und Psychiatrie* 154 (1935): 351–94.
25. E. Inouye, "Similarity and Dissimilarity of Schizophrenia in Twins," *Proceedings of the Third World Congress of Psychiatry, Montreal* (Toronto: Univ. of Toronto Press, 1961): I: 524–30.
26. B. Harvald and M. Hauge, "Hereditary Factors Elucidated by Twin Studies," in *Genetics and the Epidemiology of Chronic Disease*, ed. J. V. Neel, M. W. Shaw, and W. J. Schull (Washington D.C.: Department of Health, Education, and Welfare, 1965).
27. A. Hoffer and W. Pollin, "Schizophrenia in the NAS-NRC Panel of 15,909 Veteran Twin Pairs," *Archives of General Psychiatry* 23 (1970): 469–77.
28. S. Snyder, *Medical World News*, 17 May 1976, p. 24.
29. P. Wender, *Medical World News*, 17 May 1976, p. 23.
30. S. S. Kety, D. Rosenthal, P. H. Wender, and F. Schulsinger, "The Types and Prevalence of Mental Illness in the Biological and Adoptive Families of Adopted Schizophrenics," in *The Transmission of Schizophrenia*, ed. D. Rosenthal and S. S. Kety (Oxford: Pergamon, 1968).
31. S. S. Kety, D. Rosenthal, P. H. Wender, F. Schulsinger, and B. Jacobsen, "Mental Illness in the Biological and Adoptive Families of Adopted Individuals Who Have Become Schizophrenic," in *Genetic Research in Psychiatry*, ed. R. R. Fieve, D. Rosenthal, and H. Brill (Baltimore: Johns Hopkins Univ. Press, 1975).
32. D. Rosenthal, P. H. Wender, S. S. Kety, F. Schulsinger, J. Welner, and L. Ostergaard, "Schizophrenics' Offspring Reared in Adoptive Homes," in *The Transmission of Schizophrenia*, ed. D. Rosenthal and S. S. Kety (Oxford: Pergamon, 1968), p. 388.
33. E. Rosenthal, P. H. Wender, S. S. Kety, J. Welner, and F. Schulsinger, "The Adopted-away Offspring of Schizophrenics," *American Journal of Psychiatry* 128 (1971): 307–11.
34. R. J. Haier, D. Rosenthal, and P. Wender, "MMPI Assessment of Psychopathology in the Adopted-away Offspring of Schizophrenics," *Archives of General Psychiatry* 35 (1978): 171–75.
35. P. H. Wender, D. Rosenthal. S. S. Kety, F. Schulsinger, and J. Welner, "Cross-fostering: A Research Strategy for Clarifying the Role of Genetic and Experiential Factors in the Etiology of Schizophrenia," *Archives of General Psychiatry* 30 (1974): 121–28.
36. H. Paikin, B. Jacobsen, F. Schulsinger, K. Gottfredsen, D. Rosenthal, P. Wender, and S. S. Kety, "Characteristics of People Who Refused to Participate in a Social and Psychopathological Study," in *Genetics, Environment and Psychopathology*, ed. S. Mednick., F. Schulsinger, J. Higgins, and B. Bell (Amsterdam: North-Holland, 1974).
37. B. Cassou, M. Schiff, and J. Stewart, "Génétique et schizophrénie: réévaluation d'un consensus," *Psychiatrie de l'Enfant* 23 (1980): 87–201. See also T. Lidz and S. Blatt, "Critique of the Danish-American Studies of the Biological and Adoptive Relatives of Adoptees Who Became Schizophrenic," *American Journal of Psychiatry* 140 (1983): 426–31.
38. P. M. Wender and D. R. Klein, "The Promise of Biological Psychiatry," *Psychology Today*, February 1981, pp. 25–41.
39. "Rampton Prisoner Victim of Bungle," *The Guardian* (London), 23 March 1981. Also see R. Littlewood and M. Lipsedge, *Aliens and Alienists: Ethnic Minorities and Psychiatry* (Harmondsworth, Middlesex, England: Penguin, 1982).
40. D. L. Rosenhan, "On Being Same in Insane Places," *Science* 179 (1973): 250–58.
41. Foucault, *Madness and Civilization*.
42. P. Sedgwick, *Psychopolitics* (London: Pluto, 1982).
43. R. K. Laing, *The Divided Self* (London: Tavistock, 1960) Also see R. D. Laing, *The Politics of Experience and the Bird of Paradise* (Harmondsworth, Middlesex, England: Penguin, 1969); R. D. Laing and A. Esterson, *Sanity, Madness and the Family* (Harmondsworth, Middlesex, England: Penguin, 1970); D. Cooper, *The Death of the Family* (Harmondsworth, Middlesex, England: Penguin, 1972); R. Boyers and R. Orrill (eds.), *R. D. Laing and*

Anti-Psychiatry (Harmondsworth, Middlesex, England: Penguin, 1972).
44. A. B. Hollingshead and F. C. Redlich, *Social Class and Mental Illness* (New York: John Wiley, 1958). Also see J. K. Wing, *Reasoning About Madness* (New York: Oxford Univ. Press, 1978).
45. G. W. Brown and T. Harris, *Social Origins of Depression: Study of Psychiatric Disorder in Women* (London: Tavistock, 1978).

DISCUSSION

A discussion of the issues contained in this and similar chapters almost invariably begins with this question: Nature or nurture? In this chapter, the question can be rephrased in the following way: Is schizophrenia caused by genetic factors or by environmental factors? But as you will see throughout this book, the human mind's tendency to oversimplify complicated issues by dichotomizing them into mutually exclusive alternatives often leads us badly astray. The "nature versus nurture" debate is no exception.

Indeed, one could make a reasonable argument that, for all or virtually all forms of psychopathology, the "nature versus nurture" debate is actually a pseudocontroversy. Ponder this simple fact: There are approximately 100,000 genes in the human genome, affecting virtually every aspect of the structure and functioning of the brain and remainder of the nervous system. Is it really plausible to think that not even one of these genes influences, even to the most trivial extent, an individual's risk for developing a condition as enormously complex and multifaceted as schizophrenia? It seems exceedingly unlikely that the heritability of schizophrenia would be precisely zero, because this would imply that individual differences in the propensity to develop schizophrenia are entirely independent of every one of these 100,000 genes. Moreover, an accumulating body of evidence suggests that most or all personality traits—including extroversion-introversion, impulse control, interpersonal alienation, stress reactivity, and fearfulness—are influenced substantially by genetic factors (Tellegen et al., 1988). Again, it seems rather implausible that none of these personality traits would affect, even to a minor degree, an individual's susceptibility to schizophrenia.

But what does the evidence concerning the heritability of schizophrenia indicate? In particular, how are we to reconcile the conclusions of Straube and Oades with those of Lewontin, Rose, and Kamin? As noted in the introduction to this chapter, many of the differences between these two sets of authors can be traced to their differing evaluations of the principal assumptions underlying behavior-genetic designs: Straube and Oades consider these assumptions to rest on reasonably firm ground, whereas Lewontin, Rose, and Kamin do not. In particular, Lewontin, Rose, and Kamin voice serious concerns regarding the equal environments assumption, which, as noted in the introduction, is a crucial presupposition underlying the twin research methodology. Because MZ twins tend to be treated more similarly than DZ twins are (a fact that few researchers would dispute), the higher concordance for schizophrenia among MZ twins is potentially attributable to their greater environmental similarity rather than to their greater genetic similarity. But do the data bear out Lewontin, Rose, and Kamin's criticism of the equal environments assumption?

In fact, the equal environments assumption has stood up surprisingly well to careful empirical scrutiny (Kendler, 1983). This assumption has been tested in several ways. First, researchers have identified MZ and DZ twins whose zygosity has been misclassified—that is, MZ twins who were mistakenly believed by themselves and others to be DZ twins and DZ twins who were mistakenly believed by themselves and others to be MZ twins. If similarity in rearing is the key factor underlying the greater similarity of MZ twins than DZ twins, then perceived zygosity, rather than actual zygosity, should be the best predictor of twin similarity in psychological characteristics. In fact, twin resemblance in personality and cognitive ability is related much more closely to actual, rather than to perceived, zygosity (Scarr & Carter-Saltzman, 1979). Second, investigators have found that similarity in parental rearing among MZ twins is essentially uncorrelated with their actual similarity in either personality or intelligence (Loehlin & Nichols, 1976). Third and perhaps most important, the greater similarity in parental rearing for MZ twins than for DZ twins appears to be due largely or entirely to the fact that MZ twins evoke more similar reactions from their parents than do DZ twins (Lytton, 1977). Thus, the greater similarity of MZ twins than DZ twins seems to be a cause, rather than a consequence, of more similar parental treatment of MZ twins. This conclusion reminds us of an important point: Children's behavior influences their parents' behavior, as well as the converse (Bell, 1968).

Lewontin, Rose, and Kamin have no doubt performed an important service by pointing out methodological shortcomings in many of the twin and adoption studies of schizophrenia. They are surely correct that much of the evidence concerning the heritability of schizophrenia is far from perfect and in some cases has been overstated by overly enthusiastic proponents of genetic explanations of psychopathology. They are also correct that more recent estimates of the heritability of schizophrenia tend to be lower than earlier estimates (Kringlen, 1987), although even these newer estimates suggest that the heritability of schizophrenia is sizable.

Perhaps the weakest link in Lewontin, Rose, and Kamin's reasoning is their failure to explain the consistency of results in studies by different investigators, in different countries, and with different methodologies. Why do virtually all studies in this literature, even with their shortcomings, show a strong genetic influence on schizophrenia? Lewontin, Rose, and Kamin would presumably have to argue that the methodological weaknesses associated with these studies are all systematically biased in the direction of detecting substantial heritability. Although such a uniform bias is possible, it seems rather implausible. Perhaps the most reasonable conclusion one can draw is that, although the evidence concerning the heritability of schizophrenia is far from flawless, converging evidence from multiple sources—studies of MZ twins and DZ twins reared together, studies of offspring of MZ twins discordant for schizophrenia, and adoption studies—implicates genetic factors in the etiology of schizophrenia. It is this consistency of findings across numerous studies (each in isolation admittedly imperfect) that leads most impartial readers to conclude that schizophrenia is strongly influenced by genetic factors. Moreover, the heritability of schizophrenia appears to be comparable to that of many medical conditions in which genetic factors are known to play a major role, such as diabetes, hypertension, coronary artery disease, and breast cancer (Kendler, 1983).

As Straube and Oades note, however, considerable controversy remains concerning the mode of genetic transmission in schizophrenia. To oversimplify matters somewhat, there are two principal camps of researchers. One camp, which currently represents a clear majority, believes that schizophrenia is a polygenic disorder, a disorder produced by multiple genes acting in concert with environmental influences. According to these researchers, schizophrenia is like height and weight in that it is produced by environmental factors and by the combined effects of a large number of genes, each of which makes only a relatively minor contribution to the phenotype of interest. The second camp, which represents a small but active minority of researchers, believes that schizophrenia is a monogenic, single-gene disorder. These researchers maintain that one gene, again in combination or in interaction with environmental factors, is necessary but not sufficient to produce schizophrenia. This gene is necessary in that one cannot develop schizophrenia without it; but it is not sufficient in that environmental factors are required to trigger schizophrenia in genetically predisposed individuals. According to Meehl (1962), Heston (1970), and most proponents of this position (but see Iacono & Grove, 1993, for a dissenting view), this gene is **dominant** in that only one "copy" of it is necessary to produce the vulnerability to schizophrenia.

Some advocates of this second view have conducted **linkage studies**, which, as noted in the reading by Straube and Oades, allow investigators to ascertain whether a psychopathological condition, in this case schizophrenia, is associated with known genetic material within families. Although several investigative teams have reported linkage between areas of certain chromosomes (for example, chromosome 5) and schizophrenia, the search for genetic linkage has been plagued by failures to replicate previous results. Such replication failures may indicate one of three things (Iacono & Grove, 1993):

- Researchers have not yet been fortunate enough to locate the gene predisposing to schizophrenia.
- Schizophrenia is not in fact a monogenic disorder.
- What we currently call schizophrenia is actually a heterogeneous category comprising two or more etiologically different conditions.

With respect to the last point, it is worth pointing out that Eugen Bleuler, the individual who coined the term *schizophrenia*, referred to "the group of schizophrenias" in the title of his classic 1911 book. Bleuler, who was firmly committed to the view that schizophrenia was not one condition but many, would not have been terribly surprised by the inability of modern-day researchers to locate "the gene" underlying schizophrenia. One should not expect to find a unitary etiology for a heterogeneous disorder.

The conclusion that schizophrenia is substantially influenced by genetic factors should not, however, be taken to imply that Lewontin, Rose, and Kamin's critique is devoid of value. Far from it. Indeed, their call for increased attention to the role of environmental influences in the development of schizophrenia is well taken. One fact is not in dispute: Environmental factors play a key role in the etiology of schizophrenia. We can be certain of this conclusion because, in all twin studies, the MZ concordance rate for schizophrenia is well below 100%, with the average figure lying between 40% and 50%. Consequently, an increasing number of researchers have argued that a **diathesis-stress model** provides the most reasonable framework for the etiology of schizophrenia. According to this model, individuals who possess a genetic predisposition to schizophrenia (*diathesis*, by the way, means "predisposition") will develop schizophrenia if, and only if, they are exposed to sufficient environmental stress. If the diathesis-stress model is correct, both genetic factors and environmental factors are necessary but not sufficient to produce schizophrenia. Each set of factors is needed, but neither alone will do the trick. Although the diathesis-stress model has considerable intuitive appeal, it has yet to be tested adequately.

The less than perfect concordance between MZ twins for schizophrenia indicates that nonshared (also known as within-family) environmental factors—factors responsible for making individuals within the same family different from one another—must make a significant contribution to the development of schizophrenia.* A behavior-genetic design that is

---

*A number of investigators have also examined the potential role of shared (also known as between-family) environmental influences in the etiology of schizophrenia. In contrast to nonshared environmental influences, shared environmental influences make individuals within the same family similar to one another. See Straube and Oades'

ideal for exploring the role of nonshared environmental factors in the etiology of schizophrenia is the study of MZ twins who are discordant for schizophrenia. Because MZ twins are genetically identical, the factors accounting for their discordance are, by definition, environmental. Thus, investigators can use this design to attempt to identify the nonshared environmental variables that are responsible for this discordance.

The literature on MZ twins discordant for schizophrenia has been reviewed by Wahl (1976). Although Wahl's review is somewhat dated, the overall picture he paints has not changed greatly. Wahl concludes that researchers who have sought to pinpoint nonshared environmental influences on schizophrenia have generally come away empty-handed. Factors such as differential patterns of parental treatment in childhood and birth order seem not to have panned out as variables distinguishing the schizophrenic twin from the nonschizophrenic twin. Moreover, even when differences between discordant twins have been reported, they have often been difficult to interpret. For example, several investigators have found that the schizophrenic twin was more submissive, dependent, and fearful in childhood compared with the nonschizophrenic twin. But such personality differences are not necessarily a consequence of environmental influences; they may instead reflect an early manifestation of schizophrenic symptomatology in the preschizophrenic twin. Consequently, schizophrenia researchers find themselves in a peculiar and mildly embarrassing quandary. They know that nonshared environmental factors are relevant to the etiology of schizophrenia, because of the high rate of MZ twin discordance for this condition. Nevertheless, they have had considerable difficulty identifying any of these factors.

There appear to be two major explanations for the failure to detect specific nonshared environmental influences on schizophrenia. These explanations are not mutually exclusive, and there may be some truth to both. The first explanation, which is the most commonly invoked, is simply that investigators have not been clever enough (or fortunate enough) to detect the specific nonshared environmental influences relevant to schizophrenia. The second explanation is quite different from the first and tends to make some readers—not to mention schizophrenia researchers—a bit uncomfortable. According to this explanation, the principal environmental variables that are causally related to schizophrenia are random rather than systematic (Meehl, 1978). Unlike systematic environmental influences, which are experienced by a large number of individuals, random environmental influences are highly unique and idiosyncratic to each individual. Thus, random occurrences—such as losing a close friend at age 6, getting injured in a car accident at age 13, being rejected for a date at age 15, or witnessing a shooting at age 17—might actually be the nonshared environmental factors most critical to the development of schizophrenia. A progressive accumulation of such random events could help to explain why one MZ twin develops schizophrenia while his or her co-twin does not—and, by extension, why one person genetically predisposed to schizophrenia develops this condition while the other remains healthy. From this perspective, chance and luck, especially bad luck, may be among the most crucial etiological factors in schizophrenia (Meehl, 1978).

If this explanation has at least a kernel of truth to it, investigators interested in the environmental causes of schizophrenia may be forced to abandon a purely nomothetic approach to environmental factors in favor of a more idiographic approach, the approach championed by the American personality psychologist Gordon Allport (1937). Psychologists using a **nomothetic** approach attempt to draw generalizations across a large number of individuals. In contrast, psychologists using an **idiographic** approach attempt to understand the unique configuration of personal characteristics and life history factors within a single individual. An idiographic approach may be a bitter pill for some schizophrenia researchers to swallow, because it implies that any attempt to explain the environmental etiology of schizophrenia in terms of a universal set of life experiences is bound to be incomplete or inadequate. At the same time, however, an idiographic approach captures much of the richness and complexity that is often missed by a nomothetic approach, which ignores or deemphasizes experiences that are unique to each person. No less than a full appreciation of such richness and complexity may be necessary for an adequate understanding of the factors that lead a given individual to schizophrenia.

review, in their reading in this chapter, of the adoption studies of Wender, Rosenthal, Kety, Schulsinger, and Welner (1974) and of Tienari et al. (1989) for a discussion of the relationship between shared environmental factors and schizophrenia. Suffice it to say that the evidence that such factors are causally associated with schizophrenia is promising but highly preliminary. The primary difficulty with interpreting these findings is that many of the apparent "environmental" factors (such as disturbed parental communication and parental hostility and criticality) may be a consequence, rather than a cause, of the child's psychopathology.

QUESTIONS TO STIMULATE DISCUSSION

1. Lewontin, Rose, and Kamin attempt to refute the equal environments assumption underlying the twin research design with two different sources of data: comparisons of DZ twins with ordinary siblings and comparisons of same-sex and opposite-sex DZ twins. Do you find this evidence compelling? Why or why not?
2. Lewontin, Rose, and Kamin contend that one of the principal underlying agendas of behavior-genetic researchers in the schizophrenia literature is the prescription of antipsychotic medication. Do you agree with them? Is the heritability of schizophrenia relevant to whether it should be

treated by means of medication (as opposed to psychotherapy or other interventions)?

3. Is it plausible to think that the predisposition to a disorder as complicated as schizophrenia could be produced largely or entirely by a single gene? Explain your reasoning.
4. If schizophrenia is a heterogeneous disorder etiologically, as many researchers have suggested, how should research on the causes of schizophrenia be conducted? What types of research strategies might help to identify meaningful subtypes of schizophrenia?
5. As noted in the Discussion section, the diathesis-stress hypothesis has been an extremely influential model among schizophrenia researchers. How might one attempt to test this model?
6. Judging from what you have read, do you believe any important environmental factors have been ignored or neglected in the search for the causes of schizophrenia? What might they be?
7. If chance and luck were found to play an important role in the etiology of schizophrenia, what would be the implications of this finding, if any, for the treatment of schizophrenia? What might be the implications of this finding for the prevention of schizophrenia?

SUGGESTIONS FOR FURTHER READING

Gottesman, I. I. (1991). *Schizophrenia genesis: The origins of madness.* New York: W. H. Freeman.

This is an interesting and highly readable introduction to research on the characteristics and etiology of schizophrenia. Gottesman intersperses reviews of such topics as the diagnosis, genetics, epidemiology, and neurobiology of schizophrenia with first-person accounts of schizophrenics and family members of schizophrenics. This book is highly recommended for beginning readers who wish to gain an overview of the major research findings and trends in the schizophrenia literature.

Gottesman, I. I., & Shields, J. (1972). *Schizophrenia and genetics: A twin study vantage point.* New York: Academic Press.

Gottesman and Shields review the early behavior-genetic studies of schizophrenia and present the methods and results of their landmark twin study of schizophrenia at Maudsley Hospital. Paul E. Meehl provides an afterword.

Gottesman, I. I., & Shields, J. (1982). *Schizophrenia: The epigenetic puzzle.* Cambridge, England: Cambridge University Press.

This is a superb and comprehensive review of the evidence regarding the roles of genetic and environmental influences in the etiology of schizophrenia. In Sherlockian fashion, Gottesman and Shields lead the reader through the findings from family, twin, and adoption studies, as well as from studies of childhood schizophrenia and autism, environmental influences, and epidemiology and social biology. They conclude with a discussion of models of genetic and environmental transmission. This book is appropriate for advanced readers.

Kendler, K. S. (1983). Overview: A current perspective on twin studies of schizophrenia. *American Journal of Psychiatry, 140,* 1413–1425.

Kendler provides a first-rate review of the major twin studies of schizophrenia. The discussion of the validity of the twin methodology is particularly clear and thorough, and it helps to dispel a number of frequent misconceptions regarding twin studies.

Kringlen, E. (1987). Contributions of genetic studies of schizophrenia. In H. Hafner, W. F. Gattaz, & W. Janzarik (Eds.), *Search for the causes of schizophrenia* (pp. 123–142). Berlin: Springer-Verlag.

This is a clear and readable overview of the major evidence regarding the role of genetic factors in schizophrenia. Kringlen clearly delineates the logic underlying each of the major behavior-genetic designs and reviews the principal findings derived from each. He concludes that, although genetic influences upon schizophrenia are undeniable, many of the earlier studies probably overestimated their contribution.

Meehl, P. E. (1962). Schizotaxia, schizotypy, schizophrenia. *American Psychologist, 17,* 827–838.

In this seminal article, Meehl introduces his model of the etiology of schizophrenia. According to Meehl, certain individuals inherit a dominant gene (perhaps producing a neuronal abnormality he terms "synaptic slippage") that leads to an "integrative neural defect" called "schizotaxia." Given existing social learning factors, all schizotaxics develop a personality constellation known as "schizotypy"; in turn, however, only a subset of schizotypes develop full-blown schizophrenia. Thus, for Meehl, a dominant gene defect is a necessary but not sufficient condition for schizophrenia. Although this article is not easy to read, it is well worth the effort. Ambitious readers whose appetite is whetted by this paper may want to move on to Meehl, P. E. (1989). Schizotaxia revisited. *Archives of General Psychiatry, 46,* 935–944; and Meehl, P. E. (1990). Toward an integrated theory of schizotaxia, schizotypy, and schizophrenia. *Journal of Personality Disorders, 4,* 1–99.

Plomin, R., DeFries, J. C., & McClearn, G. E. (1990). *Behavior genetics: A primer* (2nd ed.). New York: W. H. Freeman.

This is an excellent and relatively nontechnical introduction to behavior-genetic methods and findings. Plomin et al. begin with an overview of basic genetic concepts and methods (such as gene mechanisms, population genetics, and quantitative genetics) and then discuss the application of family, twin, and adoption designs to the study of psychopathology, personality, intelligence, and other psychological characteristics. The book is appropriate for readers with little or no background in genetics.

Sarbin, T. R., & Mancuso, J. C. (1980). *Schizophrenia: Medical diagnosis or moral verdict?* New York: Pergamon Press.

Sarbin and Mancuso put forth their thesis that schizophrenia is more fruitfully conceptualized as a set of behaviors that is condemned in certain societies than as the product of a biological "disease." Chapter 7 contains a critique of the evidence for the genetic basis of schizophrenia.

Torrey, E. F., Bowler, A. E., Taylor, E. H., & Gottesman, I. I. (1994). *Schizophrenia and manic-depressive disorder: The biological roots of mental illness as revealed by the landmark study of identical twins*. New York: Basic Books.
The authors explore the environmental and genetic antecedents of schizophrenia and bipolar disorder in a study of 66 identical twin pairs, many of whom were discordant for these conditions. They conclude that schizophrenia, although influenced substantially by genetic factors, is probably triggered in many cases by a virus or other biological agent in utero or shortly after birth. In addition, they document alterations in brain structure and function among identical twins with schizophrenia.

Wahl, O. (1976). Monozygotic twins discordant for schizophrenia: A review. *Psychological Bulletin, 83*, 91–106.
Wahl provides a comprehensive review of studies of identical twins discordant for schizophrenia. This paradigm offers investigators a unique opportunity to examine the role of nonshared (within-family) environmental influences in the etiology of schizophrenia. As Wahl's review shows, however, this design has generally failed to yield striking differences between schizophrenic and nonschizophrenic co-twins; the major reported differences have been in early personality characteristics and birth weight, and even these findings have not always been consistent across studies.

REFERENCES

Allport, G. W. (1937). *Personality: A psychological interpretation*. New York: Holt.

Bell, R. Q. (1968). A reinterpretation of the direction of effects in studies of socialization. *Psychological Bulletin, 75*, 81–95.

Bleuler, E. (1950). *Dementia praecox or the group of schizophrenias*. New York: International Universities Press (originally published in 1911).

Heston, L. L. (1970). The genetics of schizophrenia and schizoid disease. *Science, 167*, 249–256.

Iacono, W. G., & Grove, W. M. (1993). Schizophrenia revisited: Toward an integrative genetic model. *Psychological Science, 4*, 273–276.

Kendler, K. S. (1983). Overview: A current perspective on twin studies of schizophrenia. *American Journal of Psychiatry, 140*, 1413–1425.

Kringlen, E. (1987). Contributions of genetic studies of schizophrenia. In H. Hafner, W. F. Gattaz, & W. Janzarik (Eds.), *Search for the causes of schizophrenia* (pp. 123–142). Berlin: Springer-Verlag.

Loehlin, J. C., & Nichols, R. C. (1976). *Heredity, environment, and personality*. Austin: University of Texas Press.

Lykken, D. T., McGue, M., Tellegen, A., & Bouchard, T. J. (1992). Emergenesis: Genetic traits that may not run in families. *American Psychologist, 47*, 1565–1577.

Lytton, H. (1977). Do parents create, or respond to, differences in twins? *Developmental Psychology, 13*, 456–459.

Meehl, P. E. (1962). Schizotaxia, schizotypy, schizophrenia. *American Psychologist, 17*, 827–838.

Meehl, P. E. (1978). Theoretical risks and tabular asterisks: Sir Karl, Sir Ronald, and the slow progress of soft psychology. *Journal of Consulting and Clinical Psychology, 46*, 806–834.

Scarr, S., & Carter-Saltzman, L. (1979). Twin method: Defense of a critical assumption. *Behavior Genetics, 9*, 527–542.

Tellegen, A., Lykken, D. T., Bouchard, T. J., Wilcox, K. J., Segal, N. L., & Rich, S. (1988). Personality similarity in twins reared apart and together. *Journal of Personality and Social Psychology, 54*, 1031–1039.

Tienari, P., Lahti, I., Sorri, A., Naarala, M., Moring, J., & Wahlberg, K. E. (1989). The Finnish adoptive family study of schizophrenia: Possible joint effects of genetic vulnerability and family environment. *British Journal of Psychiatry, 155*, Supplement 5, 29–32.

Wahl, O. (1976). Monozygotic twins discordant for schizophrenia: A review. *Psychological Bulletin, 83*, 91–106.

Wender, P. H., Rosenthal, D., Kety, S. S., Schulsinger, F., & Welner, J. (1974). Cross-fostering: A research strategy for clarifying the role of genetic and experiental factors in the etiology of schizophrenia. *Archives of General Psychiatry, 30*, 121–128.

CHAPTER

6

Can anxiety and depression be meaningfully differentiated?

PRO Hamilton, M. (1988). Distinguishing between anxiety and depressive disorders. In C. G. Last & M. Hersen (Eds.), *Handbook of anxiety disorders* (pp. 143–155). Needham Heights, MA: Allyn & Bacon.

CON Dobson, K. S. (1985). The relationship between anxiety and depression. *Clinical Psychology Review*, *5*, 307–324.

OVERVIEW OF THE CONTROVERSY: Max Hamilton reviews evidence from several sources—including studies of genetics, personality factors, natural history, treatment response, and clinical features—and concludes that anxiety and depression are separable entities. Keith S. Dobson argues that anxiety and depression share fundamental emotional features and overlap so substantially that they are difficult to distinguish at the level of either personality traits or psychiatric diagnoses.

CONTEXT OF THE PROBLEM

Crudely speaking, the two different approaches to psychiatric classification are "splitting" and "lumping." "Splitters" tend to emphasize the differences among psychopathological syndromes and to favor cleaving broad groupings of signs and symptoms into narrower and more homogeneous categories. "Lumpers" tend to emphasize the commonalities among psychopathological syndromes and to favor aggregating narrowly defined groupings of signs and symptoms into broader and more heterogeneous categories. Splitters strive for precision and accuracy, lumpers for parsimony and economy. The distinction between splitters and lumpers, like most black-and-white classifications, is something of an oversimplification. Nonetheless, the history of psychiatric classification has been marked by an incessant and sometimes bitter struggle between proponents of these two approaches. If the popularity of DSM-III and its progeny in most Western countries is any indication, the splitters appear to have triumphed, at least temporarily, in the world of contemporary psychiatric classification. DSM-IV, for example, contains roughly 350 psychiatric categories, many of them subsuming highly circumscribed patterns of behavior; in contrast, DSM-I, published in 1952, contained a mere 60 categories. Diagnoses such as adjustment disorder with depressed mood, mathematics disorder, trichotillomania (failure to resist impulses to pull out one's hair), telephone scatologia (repetitive making of obscene telephone calls, listed in the draft version of DSM-IV) attest to the DSM's penchant for subdividing the enormous pie of abnormality into rather thin slices.

Perhaps nowhere in the domain of psychiatric classification are the battle lines between splitters and lumpers so clearly demarcated as in the debate over the distinction between anxiety and depression. Over the past several decades, two competing views of the relation between these two entities have emerged (Klerman, 1988). Advocates of the "dualistic" view contend that anxiety and depression, although similar in certain ways, represent fundamentally different emotions. Moreover, these theorists assert, extreme variations of these emotions are manifested in two distinct classes of psychopathological syndromes—anxiety disorders and mood disorders. Advocates of the "unitary" view, in contrast, contend that anxiety and depression, although superficially different in certain ways, represent expressions of the same underlying emotional processes. Moreover, these individuals contend, the overlap between "anxiety" and "mood" disorders is so great as to render distinctions between them essentially meaningless.

Which view best fits the existing evidence? As proponents of the dualistic view are quick to point out, anxiety and depression seem to differ subjectively. Certainly, we all recognize anxiety and depression as different, if not qualitatively distinct, mood states. All of us can differentiate between feeling jittery and on edge as opposed to feeling sad and **anhedonic** (unable to experience pleasure). In addition, DSM-IV contains separate sections for anxiety disorders (comprising such conditions as panic disorder, simple phobia, obsessive-compulsive disorder, and generalized anxiety disorder) and mood disorders (comprising such conditions as major depression, bipolar disorder, and dysthymia). This taxonomic scheme appears to acknowledge that extreme levels of anxiety and depression are expressed as substantially different classes of disorders. Indeed, the classic Newcastle studies of Sir Martin Roth and his colleagues (for example, Roth, Gurney, Garside, and Kerr, 1972) seemed to indicate that patients with anxiety could be differentiated from those with depression on the basis of certain clinical features (see the article by Dobson in this chapter).

But proponents of the unitary view remain undaunted. They note that measures of anxiety and depression tend to be highly correlated and that anxiety and mood disorders frequently co-occur within both individuals and families (Maser & Cloninger, 1990). Indeed, DSM-IV has added the diagnosis of mixed anxiety-depression to its appendix (as a disorder warranting further study) in recognition of the extensive overlap of anxiety and depression within individuals. Moreover, there is considerable overlap among the biological treatments that anxious and depressed individuals respond to. For example, tricyclics, a class of medications initially marketed as antidepressants, alleviate the symptoms of a number of anxiety disorders, including generalized anxiety disorder and obsessive-compulsive disorder (Frances et al., 1992).

Thus, there appears to be some empirical support for both the dualistic and unitary positions. The nagging question remains: Should we split or should we lump?

THE CONTROVERSY: Hamilton vs. Dobson

Hamilton

Max Hamilton argues that an increasing body of evidence points to the existence of important distinctions among the "affective disorders" (which, unlike most writers, he defines as comprising both the anxiety disorders and the mood disorders of depression and mania). He reviews the evidence from several sources indicating that anxiety and depression are fundamentally different entities:

- Anxiety and depressive disorders appear to be influenced by different genetic factors.
- Whereas individuals with anxiety disorders tend to have histories of nervousness, low self-confidence, oversensitivity, and shyness prior to their illness, individuals with endogenous depression (depression originating in the absence of a marked psychosocial stressor) tend to have histories of stable interpersonal relationships and high achievement.
- The course of anxiety disorders tends to be chronic with few periods of complete recovery, whereas the course of depressive disorders tends to be episodic with frequent periods of complete or almost complete recovery.
- Anxiety and depression tend to respond to different treatments; for example, individuals with depression tend to improve following the administration of tricyclic antidepressants and electroconvulsive ("shock") therapy (see Chapter 16), whereas individuals with anxiety and anxious depressions tend to improve following the administration of monoamine oxidase inhibitors and benzodiazepines.
- Finally, a number of investigators have succeeded in differentiating anxiety and depression in terms of clinical features and physiological variables.

Dobson

Keith Dobson points out that anxiety and depression have been hypothesized by a number of theorists to be separable constructs. Cognitive models, for example, posit that, whereas anxiety is an emotional reaction to potential threat, depression is an emotional reaction to harm that is imminent or that has already occurred. Similarly, a number of models of emotion postulate other fundamental differences between anxiety and depression. Nevertheless, as Dobson points out, anxiety and depression share important emotional features: Fear is often an integral component of depression, and sadness is often an integral component of anxiety. Dobson next reviews studies examining the association between trait measures of anxiety and depression. He notes that the correlations between indices of anxiety and depression tend to be moderate to very high, nearly as high as the correlations between anxiety indices alone and depression indices alone. Dobson then discusses the efforts of investigators who have attempted to differentiate anxiety and depression as clinical syndromes. According to Dobson, these investigators have generally found substantial overlap between anxiety and depressive disorders. Dobson concludes that the existing evidence does not convincingly demonstrate that anxiety and depression can be differentiated and offers a longitudinal model to account for their association.

KEY CONCEPTS AND TERMS

benzodiazepines Class of medications typically used to treat relatively mild forms of anxiety. Benzodiazepines include diazepam (Valium) and chlordiazepoxide (Librium).

discriminant function analysis Statistical procedure that allows investigators to determine which variables best distinguish two or more groups of individuals. One might perform a discriminant function analysis, to ascertain, for example, which variables (such as personality traits, family history, and response to medications) best differentiate a group of anxious individuals from a group of depressed individuals.

discriminant validity Extent to which a measure does not correlate with other measures that it is theoretically not expected to correlate with. Discriminant validity is sometimes referred to as divergent validity.

endogenous depression Depression originating in the absence of a marked psychosocial stressor. Compare endogenous depression with reactive depression.

factor analysis Statistical procedure for uncovering the major underlying dimensions shared by a set of items on a test. One might perform a factor analysis to determine, for example, whether the relationships among the items on a 100-item measure of mood states can be accounted for by two underlying dimensions, as well as to determine what entities (for example, anxiety and depression) these two dimensions appear to represent.

monoamine oxidase inhibitors Class of medications typically used to treat depression, particularly "atypical" forms of depression characterized by excessive appetite, weight gain, difficulty falling asleep, agitation, and anxiety. Monoamine oxidase inhibitors (often referred to as MAOI's) include phenelzine.

neurotic depression Form of depression characterized by marked signs and symptoms of anxiety.

reactive depression Depression that appears following a marked psychosocial stressor. Compare reactive depression with endogenous depression.

response style Tendency to respond to the items on a test in a fashion that is largely or entirely independent of the test's content. Response styles commonly discussed in the psychological literature include acquiescence (responding "yes" to many or most of the items, irrespective of their content) and social desirability (responding to items in such a way as to give "healthy" or "socially appropriate" answers).

tricyclic antidepressants Class of medications typically used to treat depression. Tricyclic antidepressants include imipramine and amitriptyline.

PREVIEW QUESTIONS

1. On what bases does Hamilton find the distinction between neuroses and psychoses to be inadequate?
2. According to Hamilton, how do anxious and depressed individuals differ in terms of their familial/genetic pattern, premorbid personality, natural history, and treatment response?
3. According to Dobson, what do cognitive models of psychopathology posit to be the major difference between anxiety and depression?
4. What do the psychometric data on the relationship between measures of anxiety and depression indicate?
5. According to Dobson, what major conclusions can be drawn from studies that attempt to differentiate anxiety and depression as diagnostic syndromes?
6. What is Dobson's developmental model of the relationship between anxiety and depression, and what does it predict about the chronological sequence of these two emotions?

MAX HAMILTON

Distinguishing between anxiety and depressive disorders

There is a long tradition in psychiatry, now waning in importance, of believing that all mental disorders are of the same essence and that the notion of separate mental "diseases" has no real meaning. In its modern form, this idea dates from the 19th century theory of the "unitary psychosis." In the United States, this tradition was continued and developed by Adolf Meyer, who regarded all mental disturbance as a reaction to the environment, with the form based on the circumstances, constitution, and personality of the individual. When psychoanalysis began to dominate clinical psychiatry, this theory fit well with psychoanalytic ideas, which minimized the difference between diagnostic categories and instead emphasized the importance of mental mechanisms. The difference between different "disorders" was then regarded as essentially one of individual balance between the mental mechanisms. Most clinical psychologists adhere to variations of this theme, even when unconscious mechanisms are replaced by conditioning and learning theories.

Although sociologists recognize, to some extent, the differences between different disorders, because they are concerned solely with the social factors relating to incidence and prevalence, they too have an essentially unitary approach.

In particular, concerning anxiety and depressive states, the fundamental unity of these two syndromes is implied in both Seligman's theory of "learned helplessness" (Abramson, Seligman, & Teasdale, 1978) and Bowlby's concept of "separation anxiety" (Bowlby, 1969).

There is, of course, considerable justification for this way of looking at the affective disorders, comprising the three groups of manias, depressions (melancholias), and anxiety states. Affective disorders involve a change in mood, are more common in women than in men, and have overlapping symptoms. These characteristics apply when we consider anxiety states and "neurotic" depression, but apply also to mania and depression, much more than one would gather from traditional clinical descriptions. It is not only that patients may swing from one mood disorder to another (most easily recognized in manic-depressive disorder), but that in any one phase there is overlap of symptoms.

Nevertheless, on the basis of accumulating evidence, opinion is swinging over to emphasizing the differences and distinctions between the affective disorders. This chapter concentrates on depressive and anxiety disorders. . . .

Depressive disorders are now classified as either bipolar or unipolar, but the relationship of the latter to those depressive conditions variously described as "reactive" or "neurotic" is still under debate. This is partly a legacy of the distinction, once regarded as central in psychiatry, between the psychoses and the neuroses. Clearly, the recurrent depressions, both bipolar and unipolar, could be classified as psychotic disorders, but the reactive depressions fit very badly into this category, as is shown by the alternative name of "neurotic depression."

It has been increasingly recognized that the dichotomy between psychosis and neurosis, however useful it may have been once, has become increasingly a handicap rather than an aid to classification in psychiatry. An example of this is the abandonment in DSM-III of the term *neurotic*. Before going further, it would be useful to review briefly this old distinction, to make clear why it has been abandoned. It could be said that it was made on five criteria.

1. *Etiology*—Psychoses were said not to be psychogenic, in contrast to the neuroses. This distinction has become very thin, now that the role of environmental experiences in the precipitation of acute phases of mania and schizophrenia have become increasingly recognized. On the other hand, the role of infantile experiences in the causation of neuroses has received much adverse criticism.
2. *Response to treatment*—It was said that neuroses responded to psychotherapy and psychoses did not. The value of social therapy and rehabilitation is quite clear even for chronic schizophrenics, and many respond to behavioral therapy. The continual proliferation of

SOURCE: *Handbook of Anxiety Disorders*, by Cynthia G. Last and Michel Hersen, pp. 143–155. Copyright © 1988 by Allyn and Bacon. Adapted by permission.

psychotherapies for the neuroses suggests that these treatments are not as effective as has been suggested in the past.

3. *Insight*—Psychotics were said to have no insight into their condition, but in the early stages of the disorder, schizophrenics are often only too well aware of what is happening to them, and there are few patients who show less insight than the classical hysterics.
4. *The personality is wholly involved in psychosis, but not in neurosis*—It is difficult to make out what this means, but in manic-depressive disorder and some types of schizophrenia, the patient may show complete restoration between acute phases, indicating that however severe may have been the patient's disorganization and maladjustment, the personality survived intact.
5. *Social adaptation*—This is largely a question of the severity of the disorder, not of type.

Once it is accepted that the distinction between psychotic and neurotic can be ignored, the depressions can be left as depressions, with differences in the clinical manifestations (anxious vs. retarded) and in precipitating stresses (endogenous vs. reactive) recognized to be varying in quantity rather than quality. However, another distinction remains important, that between a normal reaction to environmental stresses and an abnormal or pathological condition. This applies equally to both depressive and anxiety states. A terrifying experience (fright) may produce appropriate reactions which may take considerable time to fade away. Even though the person's condition is recognized as not being pathological (diseased state), it is accepted that, in addition to sympathy and understanding, it is appropriate that such help as can be provided by modern medicine should be available. In some cases, it is nevertheless recognized that the response to the precipitating stress has produced a state that continues independently of its origin (i.e., the stress has introduced a pathological condition).

The same applies to those persons who have undergone a severe loss. Even when taking into account the significance of the loss to the individual and the reactivity of the personality (the variations here are greater than most psychiatrists recognize), it may become evident that the original stress has precipitated a pathological process which then continues independently of its origin. There are some features that help to distinguish between normal and abnormal reactions, but however carefully examined, there remains a residuum of cases where the nature of the condition remains in doubt. This does not invalidate the general usefulness of the distinction. The same considerations apply to those patients suffering from a severely debilitating or mortal illness.

The problems relating to the differences between the various forms of depressive states are not irrelevant to the distinction between depressions and anxiety states. If all the forms of depressive disturbances are included, then the distinction between them and the anxiety states is easy, but if the reactive (anxious, neurotic) depressions only are considered, then the distinction becomes difficult.

The best way of approaching the subject is to separate the two aspects: The first is to consider the theoretical problem of whether the two groups of disorders are truly separate, though overlapping in their manifestations; and the second is to make a practical decision (e.g., as a basis for treatment).

GENETIC AND FAMILY STUDIES

Both family and twin studies have given clear evidence that there is a hereditary component to depressive disorders. Thus, the incidence of such disorders in parents of children of patients is about 10%; in monozygotic twins the concordance rate is 68%; and in same-sexed dizygotic twins it is only 23%. Much of the work on the genetics of the depressions has been on manic-depressive disorder, obviously because it is the most clinically identifiable. The evidence indicates that there are different genes producing the same clinical effect. Many reports have shown that there is a sex-linked dominant gene (e.g., Dunner & Fieve, 1975; Winokur 1970), though Loranger (1975) and Fieve, Mendlewicz, Rainer et al. (1975) have warned that this applies only to some families. Where there is no evidence of the presence of the disorder in the family, it has been suggested (Mendlewicz, Fieve, Rainer et al. 1973) that the inheritance is polygenic.

Unipolar depressions appear to have a distinct mode of inheritance. The pattern of risks in children and parents is incompatible with an X-linked dominant gene, despite the marked preponderance of depressions among the female relatives of female probands. Cadoret, Winokur, and Clayton (1970) have suggested that there are at least two genetic varieties of depressive disorder: one in which the sex is limited to women, and the other in which the two sexes have equal morbidity rates. Although most series of depressives include twice as many women as men, it is not yet certain that this represents the true prevalence in the general population.

Other evidence for the genetic heterogeneity of the depressions is derived from the response to treatment. This response is much the same among first-degree relatives given a particular antidepressant drug, but not for different antidepressants. This suggests that there is more than one biochemical abnormality underlying the depressions and that these are genetically specific (Pare & Mack, 1971).

In contrast to unipolar and bipolar depressive illnesses, neurotic depressions (which must in practice overlap the latter to some extent) show little evidence of genetic factors. Torgersen (1980) found that the proband concordance rate was 21% for monozygotic twins and 28% for same-sexed dizygotic twins. This conforms to the general opinion that those with neurotic depressions are a very mixed group. In my opinion, it also accords well with the supposition that the group of people with neurotic depressions often includes those who are not ill (i.e., not in a pathological state, but "overreacting" to the stresses of life). In other words, they are constitutionally different from most persons.

Much of the genetic work on the anxiety states was made before the current subdivisions came into use and therefore need be considered only briefly. Suffice it to say that there is good evidence for genetic factors, though further work that distinguishes between the varieties of anxiety states will have to be done in due course. The prevalence of anxiety states in the population is estimated to be 3.4% among women and 1.5% among men (Cloninger, Martin, Clayton, & Guze, 1981). Corresponding to this, there is a higher prevalence among the female relatives of anxiety patients (19%) than among the male relatives (8%), that is, a ratio of about two to one. The pooled risk for second-degree relatives (6%) is slightly less than half that for first-degree relatives (16%). Roth, Gurney, Garside, and Kerr (1972) found that 20% of the parents and 17% of the siblings of anxiety state patients suffered from neurotic disorder. The corresponding figures for depressives were 5% and 9%. Personality disorder was found in the parents of anxiety state patients in 68% of all cases and in the siblings 32% of the time. The corresponding figures for the depression were 28% and 14%.

Torgersen (1980) found that the proband concordance rate for anxiety states was 39% for monozygotic twins and 12% for dizygotic same-sexed pairs. These figures are close to those reported by Slater and Shields (1969), which were 41% and 4%, respectively. Even more to the point, all investigators agree that the genetic factors for depressions are distinct from those for anxiety states.

PREMORBID PERSONALITY

Persons with anxiety disorders, on the whole, tend to have poorly adjusted personalities. They have what is commonly described as an anxious disposition. In other words, they have a low threshold for the appearance of anxiety, including minor nondisabling phobias. Their most important traits are immaturity, lack of confidence, dependence on relatives, hypersensitivity, a shy and anxious disposition, and hysterical features. All these go a long way back in the life of the individual and are evident in a poor record during school life. On the Maudsley Personality Inventory, those with anxiety disorder show higher Neuroticism and more Introversion than depressives (Kerr, Roth, Schapira, & Gurney, 1972). Among women, 39% show premorbid frigidity; whereas among the depressives, this is found in only 8% (Roth et al., 1972).

Neurotic depressives tend to have the same personality characteristics as those suffering from anxiety states (Zerssen, 1980). In contrast, endogenous depressives tend to have rigid personality structures, and to be orderly and traditionally minded, with a tendency to close personal relationships with family members. They are solid characters, oriented toward achievement, reliable in social relations, and conforming to social roles (Tellenbach, 1980). None of these characteristics are necessarily beyond the normal range; this type of personality is very common. Bech, Shapiro, Sihm, Nielsen, Sørensen, and Rafaelsen (1980) tested 13 unipolar and 23 bipolar depressives on the Marke-Numan Temperament (Bech, Allerup, & Rosenberg, 1978), the Zerssen Personality and the Cesarec-Marke Personality Scales, and the Eysenck Personality Inventory, and found that the score patterns of their subjects lay within the normal range. The bipolar cases scored significantly lower on Neuroticism than did neurotics. It must be said that there is little evidence for a "depression-prone" personality.

PRECIPITATING EVENTS

We are all afraid when we are in a potentially harmful situation and we become depressed when we experience a major loss or feel that our circumstances are hopeless. These are normal reactions, but the important question is whether this is true of the precipitation of pathological states. Finlay-Jones and Brown (1981) have no doubt. They found that the frequency of such appropriate precipitating stresses in the year previous to the onset of illness in 164 young women attending a general practitioner was significantly greater than in a control series. They even found that cases of mixed anxiety and depression had experienced both a severe loss and a severe danger before the onset of their illness.

This would be conclusive evidence if it could be certain that the young women investigated by Finlay-Jones and Brown were suffering from true pathological disorders, and there is still controversy on this. Another investigation adds to this doubt. Popkin, Callies, and MacKenzie (1985) examined the data pertaining to 50 medical inpatients suffering from various illnesses such as malignant neoplasm, insulin-dependent diabetes, and epilepsy, and who had been diagnosed by a psychiatric consultant as suffering also from a major depressive syndrome. Earlier investigators had concluded that over two thirds of such disorders were reactive responses to physical illness. The patients were treated with antidepressant drugs and only 40% responded, a result that is very inferior to that usually experienced. Incidentally, 16 of the patients had to terminate their antidepressant treatment because of unacceptable side effects (half of which were delirium). As this inquiry was retrospective and uncontrolled, its relevance is by no means great, but it would have been very important had the results of treatment been a good response in 70% to 80%. In contrast to this report, Clayton and Lewis (1981) found that depressive disorders arising secondarily to other nonaffective psychiatric illness responded to drugs in the same manner as primary depressive disorders.

However, there is no doubt that both anxiety states and depressive illness are quite frequently precipitated by external events. Roth et al. (1972) found that physical and psychological stresses were more severe and more numerous in anxiety cases. Is there any fundamental difference between primary depressive disorder with or without a precipitating stressful life event? Garvey, Schaffer, and Tuason (1984) found no difference, after 4 and 6 weeks, in the response to treatment.

COURSE

During the course of the illness, the anxiety states are, in general, much more responsive to the situation of the patient than the depressive illnesses. Thus the placebo response is much greater in the former than in the latter. Recovery from an acute phase is often incomplete and is followed by a subsequent recrudescence. Noyes, Clancy, Holuk, and Slymen (1980) followed up 112 anxiety neurotics for 6 years and compared them with 110 surgical subjects. Recovery or mild impairment was found in 68% of the patients, with the majority showing persisting symptoms and some social impairment. Patients who originally had an illness of less than 5 years duration showed a more favorable outcome than those who had been ill for 6 years or more. Thus, the course of the illness is irregularly recurrent with periods of remission, which are not always complete. This might account for the usual descriptions of the personalities of these patients.

In contrast, the course of the depressions shows a regular cycle of acute phases with (usually) clear intervening periods. The frequency distribution of the length of acute phases and of cycles is lognormal, and there is a tendency for the cycles to become shorter in the course of time (Angst, Grof, Hippius, Poldinger, Varga, Weis, & Wyss, 1969). On the whole, although about 40% of depressives do recover spontaneously (i.e., they have no further attacks), the prognosis of these patients is not good in the long run (Angst, 1980) in the sense that, however well they may be between acute phases, recurrence is to be expected.

According to Keller, Klerman, Lavori, Coryell, Endicott, and Taylor (1984), in the shorter run, after 2 years, only about 20% of depressives will still not have recovered and 65% will have made a complete recovery. These authors give the ultimate complete recovery rate as approaching 80%.

Although anxiety states are usually not as disabling during the acute phase as are the depressions, in between acute periods those suffering from anxiety disorders are more likely to experience symptoms and to have recurrences. It is of particular interest that these patients almost invariably remain in the same diagnostic category (Shapira, Roth, Kerr, & Gurney, 1972).

RESPONSE TO TREATMENT

The treatment for anxiety states has always been essentially some form of psychotherapy. This was true also for the depressions, until the discovery of the first of the modern antidepressants, Imipramine pamoate, except that more severe cases were treated with convulsive therapy. As antidepressant drugs came increasingly into use, the range of severity of depressions treated with convulsive therapy was considerably reduced. At the same time, introduction of the benzodiazepine drugs also diminished the emphasis on psychotherapy for anxiety states. In recent years there has been a recrudescence of interest in the psychotherapy for the depressions, so that in one sense, the differences in the approach to treatment for these disorders has become much less.

As stated earlier, one way of examining the relationship between the two types of disorder is to examine their response to treatment. When the nature of the treatment is clearly understood, together with its mode of action, this can be very illuminating, but otherwise it can be very misleading. In the first place, most treatments are not completely effective, as there are always some patients who do not respond. Only rarely do we know why this should be so. In the long-term treatment of endogenous depressions with nortriptyline hydrochloride, Kragh-Sørenson, Hansen, Larsen, Naestoft, and Hvidberg (1974) found that in the few cases where relapse occurred, the plasma levels of the drug were too low. Paykel (1972) found that there was no significant difference between psychotic and neurotic depressives in the results of treatment with amitriptyline. However, when he classified his patents into the four groups he had described (using a clustering method), he found that the psychotics had the best outcome, the anxious depressives the worst, and the other two groups came in between. Subsequently, Paykel, Klerman, and Prusoff (1974) found that the outcome of treatment with amitriptyline was better among endogenous than reactive depressions. In these cases, the different outcomes between different groups adds plausibility to the distinction made between them.

It would be very unwise to be more certain about this conclusion. For example, aspirin is used for the long-term treatment of both rheumatoid arthritis and coronary thrombosis. We understand why this does not imply that they are the same or even related disorders, because the treatment effects depend on two different actions of the drug. In the treatment of bacterial infections, the same antibiotic will be used for different infections, and different antibiotics will affect the same infection. Were the nature of the diseases and the mode of action of the treatments unknown, it would be impossible to draw conclusions about the classification of either.

Accepting these reservations, it is still worthwhile considering what light is shed on the distinction between the depressions and anxiety states by their response to different treatments. Even within the depressive disorders, it was quickly realized that the disorder that responded best to convulsive therapy was the endogenous or psychotic syndrome. For example, Carney, Roth, and Garside (1965) found that the similarity between the features that distinguished depressions from anxiety states were very similar to those that indicated the response to convulsive therapy. In their diagnostic index and Electro-Convulsive Therapy (ECT) predictive index (Carney, Roth, & Garside, 1965) it was loss of weight, early wakening, and a previous episode that favored the diagnosis of depressive disorder and good response to the treatment. On the opposite side were anxiety, worsening of symptoms late in the day, together with hysterical and hypochondriacal features in the illness.

Mendels (1965) similarly found that those features characteristic of anxiety states and neurotic depressions were inimical to a good outcome with convulsive therapy. These included, among others, inadequate personality and neurotic traits in childhood and adult life.

The response to antidepressant drugs was similar. Clinical experience soon showed that the tricyclic antidepressants were more effective for the retarded depressions than for the anxious type, and this was fully confirmed in a double-blind controlled trial by Hollister et al. (1967), whose report went as far as to recommend the phenothiazines for the latter syndrome. Raskin, Schulterbrandt, Reatig, Crook, and Odle (1974) found in their double-blind controlled trial that whereas phenelzine sulfate was effective for most depressions, for the anxiety-depressives, diazepam was a better treatment as shown by the subsidence of symptoms when it was taken and their worsening when it was discontinued. Rickels, Hesbacher, and Downing (1970) evaluated drug treatments for neurotic depressives and found that tricyclics were better for high depression and low anxiety, but chlordiazepoxide was better for the reverse pattern. In a controlled trial of amitriptyline hydrochloride, phenelzine, and placebo, Rowan, Paykel and Parker (1982) found that both drugs were effective antidepressants, but differed in detail in their effects. Examination of the changes in individual symptoms showed that phenelzine produced greater improvement on ratings of anxiety, and amitriptyline on anergia and loss of interest.

With the exception of convulsive therapy, drug treatment of the depressions seems to show a gradation in the response to treatment corresponding to the changeover from typical retarded depressions to anxious depressions.

Comparisons between the outcome of treatment in depressions and anxiety states yield much the same results. Once again, convulsive therapy is obviously better for the depressions (Gurney, Roth, Kerr, & Schapira, 1970). Drug therapy does not show such clear results. In a controlled trial comparing diazepam with phenelzine or with placebo on groups with anxiety, depressive and phobic neuroses, Mountjoy, Roth, Garside, and Leitch (1977) found that phenelzine did better than placebo in the depressive neuroses but, if anything, it fared worse than placebo in the anxiety groups. This is an unusual finding, as most controlled trials of phenelzine have shown it to be an effective treatment in anxiety states, though often in an unpredictable fashion. For example, Tyrer, Candy, and Kelly (1973) found it to be an effective treatment for chronic agoraphobic and social phobic patients when compared with placebo, though the difference between the results of the two treatments had diminished at follow-up a year later (Tyrer & Steinberg, 1975).

The first report on the effect of imipramine on agoraphobia and panic attacks was by Klein (1964). This has since been confirmed many times, for example, by Zitrin, Klein, and Woerner (1980), who showed in a controlled trial that the drug was more effective than placebo for primary phobias and spontaneous panic attacks. It is of interest that in this trial the more depressed patients fared worse than those who were less depressed.

Other antidepressant drugs have also been found effective in the treatment of agoraphobia and panic attacks and particular interest has been directed toward the monoamine oxidase inhibitors (e.g., phenelzine). The effectiveness of phenelzine was confirmed by Nies, Howard, and Robinson (1982) (who emphasized the importance of adequate dosage), especially on the phobic, somatic, and psychic components of anxiety. In a controlled trial comparing the effect of imipramine, phenelzine, and placebo, combined with supportive group therapy, on chronic anxiety states (mean length of illness 13 years), Sheehan, Ballenger, and Jacobsen (1980) found that although all patients showed improvement, those receiving the active drugs did significantly better. Phenelzine was better than imipramine for phobic avoidance, and work and social disability.

Concerning the relationship between depressive and anxiety disorders, it would appear that the response to treatment is equivocal. On the one hand, convulsive therapy and the tricyclics show obviously better results with the retarded type of depressions than with the anxious depressions and anxious states, though they are not ineffective in the last two. On the other hand, the monoaminase oxidase inhibitors, although sometimes effective for retarded depressions, produce a response that is much the same in the anxious depressions and anxiety states, and that appears to ignore the difference between them.

Psychotherapy is too big a subject to be dealt with adequately in this chapter, but it cannot be ignored. Psychotherapy has always been regarded as the basic and essential treatment for the anxiety states, aside from symptomatic treatment with sedatives (anxiolytics). However, since the last century, new approaches and techniques have been continually proposed, which suggests that none of them was all that satisfactory. The last two decades have witnessed the increasing development and use of behavioral techniques, and controlled trials have demonstrated their value. For the depressions, clinicians have tended to use psychotherapy only when other treatments were unavailable or had failed.

A new technique, cognitive psychotherapy, has been introduced in the last decade and has aroused not only considerable interest, but even attempts at evaluation with controlled trials. Two examples will suffice: Blackburn and Bishop (1983) tested cognitive and drug therapy and their combination and found that in hospital outpatients the combination was significantly superior to cognitive therapy and about equal in general practice. Drugs alone came out most poorly. It is particularly meaningful clinically that the improvement was not only on cognitive variables, but also on measures of mood and overall severity. "Treatment as usual," with or without cognitive therapy, was evaluated by Teasdale, Fennell, Hibbert, and Amies (1984), who found that the combined treatment was significantly better. At 3 months follow-up, there was no difference between the two groups.

Even when the ultimate outcome of different treatments is the same, this does not imply that these treatments are of equal value. Any treatment that shortens the duration of suffering and of deprivation of normal life for the patients is of value. Perhaps in the milder cases the cost in time, effort, and money, and so on may have to be weighed in relation to the benefit from a shorter duration of illness; but this is very much an individual matter.

COMPARISON OF FEATURES

The clear difference in the dominant mood of the two disorders is obviously the basis on which they were first distinguished. But mood is not an abstract entity, it is a form of (internal and external) behavior of human beings, and the difference between the two moods is easy to demonstrate on most physiological variables. For example, differences between the two were found by Shagass (1955) in the photically activated electroencephalogram; by Kelly and Walter (1969) in forearm blood flow and heart rate, both under resting conditions and experimentally induced anxiety; and also by Noble and Lader (1972) together with differences in the electromyogram, skin conductance and its fluctuations, and rate of salivation.

Depression and anxiety can be subdivided into many symptoms, many of which are quite different, but some of which are similar. It is an obvious step, once the data have been gathered systematically, to apply factor analysis and discriminant function analysis to them to see what light these mathematical techniques cast on the distinction under consideration. Of course, such mathematical analyses must be confirmed in the end by independent information, (e.g., genetic studies, course and prognosis, and response to treatment).

Roth et al. (1972) factor analyzed their data by the method of principal components. The first component clearly distinguished between anxiety and depressive states. The distribution of scores on this component was unimodal, but the patients diagnosed as depressive or anxious occupied different ends of the distribution, with considerable overlap. However, discriminant function analysis of the same data (Gurney, Roth, Garside, Kerr, & Schapira, 1972) produced a bimodal distribution of the discriminant function scores. The conclusion was that the two diagnostic categories formed two distinct groups with overlapping manifestations. Subsequent follow-up studies (Shapira et al., 1972) confirmed the distinction. The items that contributed most to the discriminant function (in descending order of importance) were panic attacks, neuroticism, suicidal tendencies, retardation, and agoraphobia.

Most of the patients in these studies had been admitted into the hospital. Prusoff and Klerman (1974) studied outpatients and did not obtain such clear-cut results. Using self-assessment questionnaire items, they found that a discriminant function led to a 35% incorrect assignment of the patients' diagnoses.

At the time the mathematical analyses are made, they are validated against clinical diagnosis. Despite constant efforts to refine diagnostic criteria and procedures, these are still by no means satisfactory. In a follow-up study by Nelson, Charney, and Vingiano (1978), among the 40 patients who had been diagnosed as reactive depression and who had responded to treatment with psychosocial therapy without antidepressant drugs, 18 *clearly* met the research diagnostic criteria for primary affective disorder and 11 *probably* did so. Feinberg, Carroll, Steiner, and Commorato (1979) confirmed that the research diagnostic criteria mixed together endogenous and neurotic depressions, and were convinced that no mere checklist of clinical features could be expected to select a completely homogeneous group of patients.

CLINICAL PRACTICE

It must not be forgotten that whereas an organic condition can present as a psychiatric disorder (e.g., thyrotoxicosis may look like an anxiety state and dementia may resemble a depressive illness), the reverse is also true. This will be particularly important when patients are reluctant to mention their psychological symptoms, for fear of being labeled "neurotic," or sometimes when they think that doctors are concerned only with somatic symptoms. Either way, the patients do not mention their psychological symptoms or minimize them or explain them away. For this reason, even when the diagnosis seems obvious, it is wise to consider the possibility of organic disease. A simple clinical examination should rule out the possibility of the commonest organic conditions. After that, it is not worth carrying out investigations for uncommon diseases. Because they are uncommon, most of the time nothing will be found and a fruitless search for the uncommon is obviously wasteful when one considers that anxiety and depressive states are common. The same applies to uncommon psychiatric conditions. Careful routine history taking will soon reveal the hallucinations of the paraphrenic who presents as a depressive, or the compulsive rituals of the obsessional who mentions only the symptoms of anxiety.

In the majority of cases, there is no difficulty in recognizing the anxiety or depressive disorders. In the case of the depressions, the chief difficulty is when the various symptoms associated with anxiety are prominent and "mask" the underlying disorder. In ordinary clinical practice, symptoms of anxiety are extremely common in depressive illness, as has been pointed out above. Thus, anxiety is present in 96% and somatic symptoms of anxiety in 86%, difficulty in falling asleep in 86% of men and 79% of women, and agitation in 61% of men and 72% of women (Hamilton, 1980). Even attacks of panic occur in a minority of patients (Klein, 1964).

The diagnosis of depressive disorder is therefore made on positive grounds. Apart from the depressed mood which, however mild it may be, is always more persistent than in the anxiety states and is usually worse in the mornings, the most important symptom to look for is a loss of interest in life, work, hobbies, and normal activities. After that the clinician places great weight on the somatic symptoms of loss of appetite, energy, libido, and weight. Feelings of self-reproach, guilt, and thoughts of suicide will often be present, but usually will be elicited only on questioning. Delayed insomnia is relatively specific for depressive illness, but is very much related to the severity of illness. A particularly useful sign when it is detected is psychomotor retardation. Finally, if there is still doubt about the diagnosis, it is well to take into account the background of the current illness: a first attack in the 30s, a history of previous attacks of depression, and/or family history of depression or suicide. The patients may have well-adjusted personalities when they are well.

In anxiety states, although the patient may suffer from depressed mood, depression tends to be episodic and fluctuating, responsive to external circumstances, similar to but not as marked as anxious mood. Patients often say that they can more or less easily "shake themselves out of it." Agoraphobic patients may not mention their disability, even when they are almost completely housebound, and they have been known to deny its existence even when questioned. In case of doubt, the patients' statements should be checked with the relatives. Somatic symptoms are frequent and may dominate the clinical picture. They are of the type associated with over-activity of the adrenergic autonomic nervous system. Sexual function is disturbed. In men, it takes the form usually of premature ejaculation or inability to maintain an erection; in women, it appears as dyspareunia or anorgasmia. Inquiry into the background will sometimes reveal a history of symptoms in childhood and a family history of neurosis, personality disorder, or alcoholism. The onset of anxiety states tends to be more abrupt than the depressions and the first breakdown occurs earlier, in the 20s or teens.

CONCLUDING REMARKS

The importance of distinguishing between anxiety and depressive illnesses lies in the approach to treatment which, in the current state of the art, differs considerably between them. For the depressions, the basic treatment is antidepressant drug therapy supplemented, if appropriate, by psychotherapy. For the more severe cases, convulsive therapy should be considered, especially if there is any possibility of suicide. Long-term treatment would also possibly involve administration of lithium. For the anxiety states, psychotherapy is the basic treatment, supplemented by anxiolytic drugs for short-term use. For the phobic anxieties, behavior therapy may be the most appropriate form of treatment.

REFERENCES

Abramson, L. Y., Seligman, M. E. P., & Teasdale, J. (1978). Learned helplessness in humans: Critique and reformulation. *Journal of Abnormal Psychology*, 87, 49–74.

Angst, J., Grof, P., Hippius, H., Poldinger, W., Varga, E., Weis, P., & Wyss, F. (1969). Verlaufsgesetzlichkeiten depressiver Syndrom, in H. Hippius and H. Selbach (Eds.) *Das depressiver Syndrom*. Munich: Urban & Schwarzenberg.

Angst, J. (1980). Verlauf unipolar depressiver, bipolar manisch-depressiver und schizoaffectiver Erkrankungen und Psychosen. Ergebnisse einer prospectiveren Studie. *Fortschrift Neurologia und Psychiatria*, 48, 3–30.

Bech, P., Allerup, P., & Rosenberg, R. (1978). The Marke-Nyman Temperament Scale. *Acta Psychiatrica Scandinavica*, 57, 49–58.

Bech, P., Shapiro, R. W., Sihm, F., Nielsen, B. F., Sørensen, B., and Rafaelsen, O. J. (1980). Personality in unipolar and bipolar manic-melancholic patients. *Acta Psychiatrica Scandinavia*, 62, 245–247.

Blackburn, I. M., & Bishop, S. (1983). Changes in cognition with pharmacotherapy and cognitive therapy. *British Journal of Psychiatry, 143*, 609–717.

Bowlby, J. (1969). *Attachment and Loss.* London: Hogarth Press.

Cadoret, R. J., Winokur, G., & Clayton, P. J. (1970). Family history studies: VI. Manic-depressive disease versus depressive disease. *British Journal of Psychiatry, 116*, 625–635.

Carney, M. W. P., Roth, M., & Garside, R. F. (1965). The diagnosis of depressive syndromes and the prediction of ECT response. *British Journal of Psychiatry, 111*, 659–674.

Cesarec, L., & Marke, S. (1968). *Mätning av psypkogena behavmed frageformulärsteknik.* Stockholm, Skand: Testförlaget.

Clayton, P. J., & Lewis, C. E. (1981). The significance of secondary depression. *Journal of Affective Disorders, 3*, 25–35.

Cloninger, C. R., Martin, R. L., Clayton, P., & Guze, S. B. (1981). A blind follow-up and family study of anxiety neurosis: Preliminary analysis of the St. Louis 500, in D. F. Klein and J. G. Rabkin (Eds.) *Anxiety: New Research and Changing Concepts*, pp. 137–148.

Dunner, D. L., & Fieve, R. R. (1975). Psychiatric illness in fathers of men with bipolar primary affective disorder. *Archives of General Psychiatry, 32*, 1134–1137.

Eysenck, H. J., & Eysenck, S. B. G. (1964). *Manual of the Eysenck Personality Inventory.* London: University of London Press.

Feinberg, M., Carroll, B. J., Steiner, M., & Commorato, A. J. (1979). Misdiagnosis of endogenous depression with research diagnostic criteria. *Lancet, 1*, 267, Feb. 3rd.

Fieve, R. R., Mendlewicz, J., Rainier, J. D., et al. (1975). A dominant-linked factor in manic-depressive illness: Studies with color blindness. *Proceedings of the American Psychopathological Association, 63*, 241–255.

Finlay-Jones, R., & Brown, G. W. (1981). Types of stressful life events and the onset of anxiety and depressive disorders. *Psychological Medicine, 11*, 803–815.

Garvey, M. J., Schaffer, C. B., & Tuason, V. B. (1984). Comparison of pharmacological treatment response between situational and non-situational depressions. *British Journal of Psychiatry, 145*, 363–365.

Gurney, C., Roth, M., Kerr, T. A., & Schapira, K. (1970). The bearing of treatment on the classification of the affective disorders. *British Journal of Psychiatry, 117*, 251–255.

Gurney, C., Roth, M., Garside, R. F., Kerr, T. A., & Schapira, K. (1972). Studies in the classification of affective disorders. The relation between anxiety states and depressive illnesses II. *British Journal of Psychiatry, 121*, 162–166.

Hamilton, M. (1980). Psychopathology of depressions: Quantitative aspects, in K. Achte, V. Aalberg, and J. Lonnqvist (Eds.) "Psychopathology of Depression." *Psychiatria Fennica Supplementum*, pp. 201–205.

Hollister, L. E., Shelton, J., Overall, J. E., Pennington, V., Kimbell, I., & Johnson, M. (1967). Selective choice for drugs for depression. *Archives of General Psychiatry, 17*, 486–493.

Keller, M. B., Klerman, G. L., Lavori, P. W., Coryell, W., Endicott, J., & Taylor, J. (1984). Long-term outcome of episodes of depression. *Journal of the American Medical Association, 252*, 788–792.

Kelly, D., & Walter, C. J. S. (1969). A clinical and physiological relationship between anxiety and depression. *British Journal of Psychiatry, 115*, 401–406.

Kerr, T. A., Roth, M., Schapira, K. & Gurney, C. (1972). The assessment and prediction of outcome in affective disorders. *British Journal of Psychiatry, 121*, 167–174.

Klein, D. F. (1964). Delineation of two drug-responsive anxiety syndromes. *Psychopharmacologia, 5*, 397–408.

Kragh-Sørenson, P., Hansen, C. E., Larsen, N. E., Naestoft, J., & Hvidberg, E. F. (1974). Long-term treatment of endogenous depression with nortriptyline with control of plasma levels. *Psychological Medicine, 4*, 174–180.

Loranger, A. W. (1975). X-linkage and manic-depressive illness. *British Journal of Psychiatry, 127*, 482–488.

Mendels, J. (1965). Electroconvulsive therapy and depression I. The prognostic significance of clinical factors. *British Journal of Psychiatry, 111*, 675–681.

Mendlewicz, J., Fieve, R. R., Rainier, J. D. et al. (1973). Affective disorder on paternal and maternal sides. Observations in bipolar (manic-depressive) patients with and without a family history. *British Journal of Psychiatry, 122*, 31–34.

Meyer, A. (1951). *The Collected Papers Vol. II. Psychiatry*, Ed. by Eunice Winters. Baltimore: Johns Hopkins Press.

Mountjoy, C. Q., Roth, M., Garside, R. F., & Leitch, I. M. (1977). A clinical trial of phenelzine in anxiety, depressive and phobic neuroses. *British Journal of Psychiatry, 131*, 486–492.

Nelson, J. C., Charney, D. S., & Vingiano, A. W. (1978). False positive diagnosis with primary affective disorder criteria. *Lancet, 2*, 1252–1253, Dec. 9th.

Nies, A., Howard, D., & Robinson, D. S. (1982). Anti-anxiety effects of MAO inhibitors. In *The Biology of Anxiety*, R. J. Matthew (Ed.) pp. 123–133. New York: Brunner/Mazel.

Noble, P., & Lader, H. (1972). A physiological comparison of 'endogenous' and 'reactive' depression. *British Journal of Psychiatry, 120*, 541–542.

Noyes, R., Clancy, J., Holuk, P. R., & Slymen, D. J. (1980). The prognosis of anxiety neurosis. *Archives of General Psychiatry, 37*, 173–178.

Pare, C. M., & Mack, J. W. (1971). Differentiation of two genetically specific types of depression by the response to antidepressant drugs. *Journal of Medical Genetics, 8*, 306–309.

Paykel, E. S. (1972). Depressive typologies and response to amitriptyline. *British Journal of Psychiatry, 120*, 147–156.

Paykel, E. S., Klerman, G. L., & Prusoff, B. A. (1974). Prognosis of depression and the endogenous-neurotic distinction. *Psychological Medicine, 4*, 57–64.

Popkin, M. K., Callies, A. L., & Mackenzie, B. (1985). The outcome of antidepressant use in the medically ill. *Archives of General Psychiatry, 42*, 1160–1163.

Prusoff, G., & Klerman, G. L. (1974). Differentiating depressed from neurotic outpatients. Use of discriminant function analysis for separation of neurotic affective states. *Archives of General Psychiatry, 30,* 301–309.

Raskin, A., Schulterbrandt, J. G., Reatig, N., Crook, T. H., & Odle, D. (1974). Depression subtypes and response to phenelzine, diazepam, and a placebo. *Archives of General Psychiatry, 30,* 66–75.

Ravaris, C. L., Nies, A., Robinson, D. S., Ives, J. O., Bartlett, D. (1976). A multiple dose controlled study of phenelzine in depressive-anxiety states. *Archives of General Psychiatry, 33,* 347–350.

Rickels, K., Hesbacher, P., & Downing, R. W. (1970). Differential drug effects in neurotic depression. *Diseases of the Nervous System, 31,* 468–475.

Roth, M., Gurney, C., Garside, R. F., & Kerr, T. A. (1972). Studies in the classification of affective disorders. The relationship between anxiety states and depressive illness I. *British Journal of Psychiatry, 121,* 147–161.

Rowan, P. R., Paykel, E. S., & Parker, R. R. (1982). Phenelzine and amitriptyline: Effects on symptoms of neurotic depression. *British Journal of Psychiatry, 140,* 475–483.

Schapira, K., Roth, M., Kerr, T. A., & Gurney, C. (1972). The prognosis of affective disorders: The differentiation of anxiety states from depressive illnesses. *British Journal of Psychiatry, 121,* 175–181.

Shagass, C. (1955). Differentiation between anxiety and depression by the photically activated EEG. *American Journal of Psychiatry, 112,* 41–46.

Sheehan, D. V., Ballenger, J., & Jacobsen, G. (1980). Treatment of endogenous anxiety with phobic, hysterical and hypochondriacal components. *Archives of General Psychiatry, 37,* 51–59.

Slater, E., & Shields, J. (1969). Genetical aspects of anxiety, in M. H. Lader (Ed.) *Studies of Anxiety,* pp. 62–71. British Journal of Psychiatry Special Publications No. 3, Ashford, Kent, England.

Teasdale, J. D., Fennell, M. J. V., Hibbert, G. I., & Amies, P. L. (1984). Cognitive therapy for major depressive therapy in primary care. *British Journal of Psychiatry, 144,* 400–406.

Tellenbach (1976). *Melancholie.* Berlin: Springer.

Tellenbach (1980). Zur Phänomenologie des Gesundseins and deren Konsequenzen für den Arzt. Z. Klin. *Psychol. Psychother., 28,* 57–67.

Torgersen, S. (1980). Hereditary and environmental differentiation and general neurotic, obsessive, and impulsive hysterical personality traits. *Acta Genetica Medical Genrellol, 29,* 193–207.

Torgerson, S. (1983). Genetic factors in anxiety disorders. *Archives of General Psychiatry, 40,* 1085–1089.

Tyrer, P., Candy, J., & Kelly, D. (1973). A study of the clinical effects of phenelzine and placebo in the treatment of phobic anxiety. *Psychopharmacologia, 432,* 237–254.

Tyrer, P., & Steinberg, D. (1975). Symptomatic treatment of agoraphobia and social phobias: A follow-up study. *British Journal of Psychiatry, 127,* 163–168.

Winokur, G. (1970). Genetic findings and methodological considerations in manic-depressive disease. *British Journal of Psychiatry, 117,* 267–274.

Zerssen, D. v. (1977). Premorbid personality and affective disorders, in G. D. Burrows (Ed.) "*Handbook of Studies on Depression,*" pp. 79–103. Amsterdam: Excerpta Medica.

Zerssen, D. v. (1980). Personlichkeitsforschung bei Depressionen, in H. Heimann and H. Gideke (Eds.) "*Neue Perspektiven in der Depressionsforschung,*" pp. 155–178. Bern: Huber.

Zitrin, C. M., Klein, D. F., & Woerner, M. G. (1980). Treatment of agoraphobia with group exposure in vivo and imipramine, *Archives of General Psychiatry, 37,* 63–71.

KEITH S. DOBSON

The relationship between anxiety and depression

While there has been a longstanding distinction drawn between the concepts of anxiety and depression, it is the intent of this paper to explore whether these two constructs can be meaningfully separated. Both conceptual and empirical arguments will be advanced. Conceptual distinctions that have been drawn between the constructs of anxiety and depression will also be reviewed, although it will be shown that these conceptual distinctions are not reflected in current assessment technology. Rather, assessment tools for anxiety and depression demonstrate considerable overlap and lack divergent validity.

It should be noted that in any comparison between constructs the analysis may be aimed at a number of levels. For the constructs of anxiety and depression it is possible to analyze differences at the item, state, trait, and syndromal (or clinical state) levels. Of most importance for this discussion are the trait and syndromal comparisons, since the comparisons involve multiple components of each construct and are aimed at relatively broad levels of analysis. Further, to the extent that anxiety and depression differ at the trait and syndromal levels, the corresponding states and items on tests will reflect those larger differences. Thus, this review will focus upon the relationship of anxiety and depression at the syndromal and trait levels of analysis, although discussion of the mood states of anxiety and depression will also be presented.

I wish to thank Debbie Dobson and Brian F. Shaw in the development of the ideas, and Kathy Stanfield and Elizabeth McCririck in the production of the manuscript. Work on this manuscript was aided by a British Columbia Mental Health Foundation Research Grant.

THE CONSTRUCT OF ANXIETY

Anxiety has been variously defined, but in general it seems to be considered an affective, physiological, cognitive, and behavioral state (Spielberger, 1975a; Beck, Laude, & Bohnert, 1974). Epstein (1976) has noted that anxiety may eventuate from the perception of threat: "threats to future happiness, threats to self-esteem, and threats to the individual's ability to make sense of the data of his experience" (pp. 188–189). Beck and Emery (1979) have distinguished between fear and anxiety, defining "fear as awareness and appraisal of danger, and anxiety as the unpleasant feeling state and physiological reaction that occurs when fear is provoked" (p. 2). Typically, the state of anxiety is considered to be one of unfocused arousal, discomforting to the person involved, and a state to be avoided. The literature on anxiety has made a notable distinction between the trait of anxiety (i.e. the tendency to become anxious, although not be necessarily anxious at the moment), and state anxiety (i.e. to be experiencing anxiety) (Glanzmann & Laux, 1978; Spielberger, 1972, 1975b; Endler & Magnusson, 1976). Evidence for the empirical integrity of the state-trait model of anxiety is widely available (see Spielberger, 1975b, for a review), and there have been a number of attempts to define more situationally-specific predispositions for anxiety. This latter person-situation interaction model for anxiety (Magnusson & Endler, 1977) has led to the development of situationally-related measures of trait anxiety and an increase in the ability to make differential predictions of anxiety in different situations (Dobson, 1983; Endler, 1975; Magnusson & Endler, 1977).

Beyond the trait-state model of anxiety, there has been considerable effort at defining a syndromal anxiety pattern. Thus, while anxiety has been implicated in almost all neurotic patterns, the current Diagnostic and Statistical Manual (DSM-III: American Psychiatric Association, 1980) distinguishes phobic disorders and anxiety states or neuroses. Of the anxiety-states the Generalized Anxiety Disorder is the closest to a "pure" anxiety reaction. Epidemiological evidence suggest wide cross-cultural variability in the prevalence of anxiety neuroses. Carey, Gottesman, and Robins (1980) provided estimated prevalence rates that ranged from 0.6 per 1000 (Bille & Juel-Nielson, 1968) to 39.2 per 1000 (Brunetti, 1976). Based upon the work of Carey et al. (1980), there appears to be a consistent sex difference in the prevalence of anxiety neuroses, with the average prevalence rate for women being 2.17 times that for men.

SOURCE: *Clinical Psychology Review*, 5, pp. 307–324, 1985.

THE CONSTRUCT OF DEPRESSION

In contrast to anxiety, unipolar depression has been defined as a multifaceted state (Craighead, 1980) that eventuates from a perception of an important loss or threat of such a loss (Beck, 1976; Costello, 1976, 1980; Lloyd, 1980). For example, depression can be triggered from the loss of a spouse through divorce, or the perception that such a loss is imminent. The state itself has emotional, cognitive, behavioral, and physiological components as in anxiety, but the general nature of the components of depression is one of avoidance, withdrawal, and diminished activity. With regard to the distinction between trait and state depression, some conceptual and empirical work has been accomplished (Zuckerman & Lubin, 1965; Costello & Comrey, 1967), but the thrust of research has been on the nature and effect of the experience of the state of depression. This work has been spurred by the question of the distinction between "normal" state depression (in which the individual shows elevated signs of a depressive type) and "clinical" state depression, which consists of a diagnosable syndrome of symptoms (Craighead, 1980). The limited work to date in the area of trait depression has been on the prediction of sub-clinical phenomena, such as increases in depressed mood or changes in depressive behavior.

Clinical depression has been widely researched, and a comprehensive review of the psychological literature is neither intended nor possible here (see Doerfler, 1981). It is important, though, to note that there are a number of categories of affective disorders according to the DSM-III (American Psychiatric Association, 1980). Included in DSM-III's diagnostic scheme are major affective disorders (manic episode and major depressive episode), bipolar disorder, major depression, specific affective disorders (cyclothymic disorder, depressive neuroses), and atypical disorders. Generally, research in clinical unipolar depression is aimed at the major depressive episode (also the major depressive disorder) group. Estimates of the prevalence of depression (Carey et al., 1980) range from 0.43 per 1000 (Lemkau, Tietze, & Cooper, 1942) to 117.6 per 1000 (Brown, Davidson, Harris, MacLean, Pollock, and Prudo, 1977). The average female:male prevalence rate is 2.28:1 based on the data of Carey et al. (1980).

Only recently have some trait predictors of clinical depression begun to be developed (e.g. Dobson & Breiter, 1983; Dobson & Shaw, 1986; Weissman & Beck, 1978), and some of the most promising appear to be physiological in nature (Carroll et al., 1981).

ANXIETY AND DEPRESSION

Conceptually, there are both similarities and differences between the constructs of anxiety and depression (Costello, 1976). In this section, the evidence from cognitive and emotional models of affect, psychometric evidence related to the separation of anxiety and depression, and the data on clinical diagnosis of anxiety and depressive states will be reviewed. These reviews represent increasingly broad definitions of anxiety and depression, from emotions to traits to clinical syndromes.

Cognitive Models of Anxiety and Depression

Cognitive models of anxiety and depression converge upon the idea that there is a perception of threat for both anxiety and depression. In the case of anxiety, it appears that the threat is potential, in that a threat to self-esteem, happiness, or ability to deal with the world may occur (Beck, 1976; Beck, Laude, & Bohnert, 1974; Epstein, 1976; Lazarus & Averill, 1972). In the case of depressive reactions, however, the threat to self-esteem, happiness, or ability to cope is perceived as either *imminent* and certain, or having already occurred (Beck, 1976). Thus, a major difference between anxiety and depression is that the one emotional pattern, anxiety, is future oriented and predictive of threat, whereas depressive responses are either tied to imminent or past events which have a direct bearing on self-esteem and so on.

Theories of Emotion

Theories of emotion vary in their description of anxiety and depression, but generally suggest that anxiety and depression are general emotions comprised of combinations of more fundamental emotions (Izard, 1971, 1977; Klerman, 1977; Plutchik, 1980a, 1980b). In the discussion of differential emotions theory (Izard, 1977), for example, it is stated that:

> In the analysis of anxiety in terms of Differential Emotions Theory, fear was found to be the key emotion of anxiety with which other important fundamental emotions interrelate and interact. . . . Similarly, Differential Emotions Theory posits distress—anguish, the emotion which predominates in grief, as the key emotion in depression and the one with which other fundamental emotions interact. (p. 94)

Elsewhere in his book, Izard (1977) suggests that fear is predominantly a future-oriented emotion and that grief is past-oriented, in keeping with the cognitive perspective on threat (Beck, 1976; Lazarus & Averill, 1972). Izard, however, goes on to document what other emotional patterns also emerge in anxiety and depression. Thus, Izard states that anxiety includes interest (or curiosity, alertness) and distress (largely defined as sadness). Also, depression is more than distress and anguish, involving elements of fear (anxiety) and hostility. In related work, Ekman and Friesen (1975) found that for a sample of 40 patients the rank order of important emotions in depression were: (a) distress (sadness, anguish), (b) fear (anxiety), and (c) inner-directed hostility.

In contrast to Izard's perspective that emotions can be uniquely defined and then examined for their relationships, other theorists and researchers have attempted to determine high-order emotional dimensions that might order or pattern more basic affective experiences. For example, Russell (1980) presented evidence that 28 emotion adjectives could be ordered in a circular array that was defined by the two dimensions of pleasure-displeasure and degree-of-arousal (arousal vs. sleep). Within his circumplex model of affect, the adjectives "depressed," "sad," "tense," "distressed," and "afraid" were located on the extreme displeasure side of the pleasure-displeasure dimension (Russell, 1980, p. 1168). The adjectives "depressed" and "sad" were different from the other adjectives, however, in that they were placed towards the "sleepy" end of the degree-of-arousal dimension, while the anxiety-related adjectives were placed towards the "aroused" end of the degree-of-arousal dimension. Russell's work, therefore, suggests that while the emotions of anxiety and depression are comparable in terms of their degree of unpleasantness, anxiety states reflect a more aroused condition than depression.

Tellegen (1985; Zevon & Tellegen, 1982) has presented a circumplex model of affect which is remarkable in its similarity to Russell. Tellegen's model employs the two primary dimensions of positive affect (high scores reflecting "pleasurable engagement"; low scores reflecting "the absence of pleasurable engagement") and negative affect (high scores reflecting "unpleasurable engagement"; low scores reflecting "nonpleasurable disengagement"). Parenthetically, Tellegen uses the word "engagement" in a manner that is roughly synonymous with Russell's use of "arousal." Anxiety and depression, using Tellegen's (1985) model, fall close in the circumplex space. "Jittery," "nervous," and "fearful" are defined primarily as high negative affect terms, whereas "blue," "sad," and "unhappy" are both negative and low positive affect (low arousal) terms. Both Russell (1980) and Tellegen (1985), then, are arguing that the emotions of anxiety and depression are comparable in their being "unpleasant" or "high negative" emotions. Both provide data, as well, that depression involves less arousal (Russell, 1980) or lower positive affect (Tellegen, 1985) than depression. This convergence of findings is important both theoretically and procedurally, in that Russell's studies involved the general rating of adjectives by subjects, and Tellegen's research involved self-ratings by subjects.

Based upon theories of emotion, it appears that there is a fair degree of similarity between the emotions involved in anxiety and depression. Thus, while the emotional patterns are not identical, there are fear elements in depression and sadness elements in fear (anxiety), although this "sharing" of elements may be more true in depression, where there is a larger fear element than visa versa (Izard, 1971, 1977). The emotional models of anxiety and depression complement the cognitive models, although relatively little literature exists which attempts to directly relate the two areas of theory. One reason why such relations have not been examined is that the nature of threat that eventuates in anxiety or depression has never been fully explained. For example, it is not clear that one type of situational threat is more associated with anxiety or depression. Thus, although it seems clear that loss events, or threats where loss is certain, have a high probability of engendering a depressive affect (Costello, 1980; Lloyd, 1980; Paykel, Myers, Dienelt, Klerman, Lindenthal, & Pepper, 1969), we do not know much about the anxiety potential of possible loss events. Theoretically, such possible threats should engender significant elements of anxiety (Beck, Laude, & Bohnert, 1974; Lazarus & Averill, 1972), but this area has not been well explored.

Psychometric Evidence

In addition to cognitive and emotional models of anxiety and depression, there also exists a psychometrically-based literature that addresses the empirical relationship between trait anxiety and depression. A review of this literature would provide important information about the relationship between these two important constructs, and it is the intent of this section to provide this review. It should be mentioned that there is an inherent difficulty in this review process, due to the fact that most of the self-report measures in the area of depression are intended to be measures of the degree of current depression (i.e., are state measures), while there have been a number of trait measures of anxiety developed. As such, this state-trait distinction will be considered in the interpretation of any relationships between anxiety and depression inventories where the instrument is a trait measure in one instance while a state measure in the other.

Before proceeding to provide a summary of this information, it is important to note that a similar exercise was conducted by Mendels, Weinstein, and Cochrane (1972). They provided information on the Costello-Comrey (1967) anxiety and depression scales, the Zung Depression Inventory (Zung, 1965), and the Multiple Affect Adjective Check List (MAACL; Zuckerman & Lubin, 1965). By way of summary, they found that the relationship among all of these scales was positive and significant, and that the relationship between the constructs of anxiety and depression, at least as measured by these instruments, was strong. The current review draws upon that earlier work, and also provides a summary of several other anxiety and depression scales not employed by Mendels et al. (1972).

The instruments actually chosen for use in this review consist of those listed in Table 1. These eight scales include three state depression scales, two trait depression scales, and three trait anxiety scales (for a review of psychometric data, see Derogatis, 1982). The literature was surveyed for studies that reported correlations between any combination of two or more of these scales, and the results are reported here. Of im-

TABLE 1 List of Anxiety and Depression Scales Reviewed

Title	*Reference*	*Type*	*Acronym*
Institute for Personality and Ability Testing—Anxiety Form	Cattell & Scheier, 1961	Trait anxiety	IPAT
State-Trait Anxiety Inventory	Spielberger, Gorsuch, & Lushene, 1970	Trait anxiety	STAI
Multiple Affect Adjective Check List	Zuckerman & Lubin, 1965	Trait anxiety Trait depression	MAACL-A MAACL-D
Costello-Comrey scale	Costello & Comrey, 1967	Trait anxiety Trait depression	CC-A CC-D
Self-rating Depression scale	Zung, 1965	State depression	SDS
Beck Depression Inventory	Beck, Ward, Mendelson, Mock, & Erbaugh, 1961	State depression	BDI
Minnesota Multiphasic Personality Inventory—D scale	Hathaway & McKinley, 1942	State depression	MMPI-D

portance is the fact that the studies reviewed varied in their use of subject populations, and of their numbers of subjects, thus making the comparability between some of the correlations tenuous. A list of the subject types and numbers of subjects, broken down by sex, appears in Table 2. In all, data from 16 studies are summarized.

The actual correlations from the studies reviewed have been recorded in Table 3 (these are the correlations with the matching letter, which corresponds to the letter assigned to the studies from Table 2). Simple visual inspection of Table 3 reveals that every correlation is positive and statistically significant at the .05 level of significance or better. The absolute range of values is .24 to .94. At first glance, it appears that the relationship among the scales is such that the distinction between anxiety and depression is more fictitious than substantive. As a further test of this hypothesis, average correlations between anxiety-anxiety, depression-depression, and anxiety-depression scales were computed, through the process of r-to-z transformations, averaging, and z-to-r transformations. The results of this computation showed that the average correlation was .66 (n = 8, range = .24–.90) among anxiety scales, .69 (n = 30, range = .29–.83) among depression scales, and .61 (n = 34, range = .27–.94) between anxiety and depression scales. In all three cases, the average correlation is positive and highly statistically significant. Also, the amount of shared variance, r^2, for each average correlation is high, ranging from 37.2% to 47.6%.

On the basis of the results shown . . . in Table 3, and the average intercorrelations between anxiety and depression scales, a tempting conclusion is that the two concepts cannot be meaningfully differentiated, at least as practiced by the self-report inventories used in this review. In fact, it appears that the two constructs of anxiety and depression demonstrate relatively poor divergent validity (Campbell & Fiske, 1959). Other evidence supporting this conclusion lies in the fact that there are a number of studies where an attempt was made to define two orthogonal dimensions of trait anxiety and depression for the completion of a two-by-two (low vs. high) factorial design (Gotlib & Asarnow, 1979; Kennedy & Craighead, 1979; Miller, Seligman, & Kurlander, 1975). In each of these studies, the investigators used predetermined cut-off scores, but were unable to identify a sufficiently large number of high depressed, low anxious subjects to complete the factorial design. Yet again, this suggests that trait anxiety and depression cannot be meaningfully separated, and that in the case of high trait depression scores, the trait anxiety scores will also be elevated.

Diagnostic Symptoms

Clinical research on the relationship between anxiety and depressive syndromes has long been controversial (see Gersh & Fowles, 1979, for a review), with research perspectives varying from those aimed at documenting separate anxiety and depression syndromes (Downing & Rickels, 1974; Prusoff & Klerman, 1974), a unitary model of anxiety and depression (Crinker & Nunally, 1968), secondary depression in anxiety disorders (Clancy, Noyes, Hoenk, & Slymen, 1978; Cloninger, Martin, Clayton, & Guze, 1981; Dealy, Ishiki, Avery, Wilson, & Dunner, 1981), and anxiety disorders secondary to depressive disorders (Leckman, Merikangas, Pauls, Prusoff, & Weissman, 1983; Leckman, Weissman, Merikangas, Pauls, & Prusoff, 1983). While there has been relatively little research documenting secondary anxiety or depression, there is an extensive literature

TABLE 2 References for Table 3

Reference	Table 3 Index Letter	Subject Description: Number & Sex	Subject Description: Description
Bloom & Brady, 1968	a	82 F; 18 M	Psychiatric inpatients
Costello, Christensen, & Rogers, 1974	b	63 F; 27 M	Psychiatric inpatients
Costello & Comrey, 1967	c	91 F; 24 M	Psychiatric inpatients
DeMonbreun & Craighead, 1977	d	48 M	Psychiatric patients and normals
Dobson, 1980	e-1	157 F	College students
	3-2	119 M	College students
Hatzenbeuhler, Parpal, & Mathews, 1983	f	65 mixed	College students
Hesselbrock, Hesselbrock, Tennen, Meyer, & Workman, 1983	g	250 mixed	Alcoholic patients
Mendels, Weinstein, & Cochrane, 1972	h	100 F	Psychiatric inpatients
Miller, Seligman, & Kurlander, 1975	i	68 mixed	College students
Nussbaum, Wittig, Hanlon, & Kurland, 1963	j	30 F	Depressed psychiatric patients
Seitz, 1970	k	30 M	Depressed psychiatric patients
Shipley & Fazio, 1973	l	22 mixed	"Depressed" college students
Spielberger, Gorsuch, & Lushene, 1970	m-1	80 M	College students
	m-2	126 F	College students
	m-3	129 M	Psychiatric inpatients
	m-4	79 M	Psychiatric inpatients
Zuckerman & Lubin, 1965	n-1	21 M	Normal adults
	n-2	246 mixed	College students
	n-3	19 mixed	Psychiatric patients
	n-4	32 mixed	Not reported
	n-5	40 mixed	Patients and normals
	n-6	46 mixed	College students
	n-7	26 M	Psychiatric patients
	n-8	47 F	Psychiatric patients
Zung, 1969	o	182 mixed	Depressed psychiatric patients
Zung, Richards, & Short, 1965	p	152	Psychiatric patients
Total		3419	

in the symptom patterns in anxiety and depressive disorders.

In one of the earliest studies on anxiety and depression symptom patterns, Derogatis, Lipman, Covi, and Rickels (1972) administered the Symptom Distress Checklist (SCL; Parloff, Kellman, & Frank, 1954) to 641 male and female anxious neurotic outpatients and 251 female neurotic depressed outpatients, and factor analyzed the resultant symptom patterns separately for each group. The results showed five statistically significant and interpretable dimensions each for anxi-

TABLE 3 Correlations among Selected Anxiety and Depression Scales[a]

Scales[b]	*STAI*	*MAACL-A*	*MAACL-D*	*CC-A*	*CC-D*	*SDS*	*BDI*	*MMPI-D*
IPAT	.76 (m-1) .75 (m-2)	—	.51 (m-1) .57 (m-2) .63 (n-1) .56 (n-2) .38 (n-3)	—	—	—	.41 (i)	—
STAI	—	.63 (e-1) .24 (e-2) .58 (m-1) .52 (m-2)	.62 (e-1) .51 (e-2)	—	—	—	.64 (e-1) .65 (e-2)	.57 (m-3) .61 (m-4)
MAACL-A		—	.69 (e-1) .61 (e-2) .87 (h) .94 (n-5) .75 (n-6) .86 (n-7) .85 (n-8)	.90 (d) .54 (h)	.58 (h)	.51 (h)	.50 (h) .51 (e-1) .27 (e-2)	.59 (h) .61 (n-4) .68 (n-5)
MAACL-D			—	.42 (h)	.67 (b) .65 (h)	.57 (h) .29 (o)	.66 (a) .70 (d) .40 (e-1) .61 (e-2) .59 (h)	.59 (h) .73 (n-5)
CC-A				—	.40 (c) .59 (h)	.53 (h)	.44 (h)	.30 (c) .35 (h)
CC-D					—	.74 (d) .65 (h)	.76 (b) .70 (f)	.70 (h)
SDS						—	.78 (f) .79 (h) .83 (k) .76 (o)	.76 (h) .58 (k) .83 (l) .70 (p)
BDI							—	.59 (g) .70 (h) .75 (j) .41 (k)

[a]All correlations have $p < .001$. The references to the correlations are found in Table 2.
[b]The references to the scales (listed by acronym) are found in Table 1.

ety and depression: somatization, obsessive-compulsiveness, interpersonal sensitivity, and depression were found for both groups, and anxiety for the anxiety neurotics and hostility for the depressives alone. It should be noted, though, that the somatization dimension incorporated several items that also appeared in the anxiety dimension, and so the depressives, while not having a unique anxiety dimension, did evidence several anxiety symptoms. It is also noteworthy that the depressive dimension seen among the anxiety neurotics was unusual in the types of symptoms identified, leading the authors to conclude "the construct of depression is defined somewhat differently among the anxious patients than it is among the depressed neurotics . . ." (p. 663). Finally, Derogatis, Lipman, et al. (1972) noted that the anxiety dimension was not satisfactory in its presentation, and noted that a revision of the SCL included more anxiety items.

In 1974, Prusoff and Klerman reported a study in which 364 depressed women were contrasted with 364 matched anxious women again using the SCL. Through configural analyses of the symptom endorsement, they found that depressed patients had higher scores on the depression dimension, while anxious patients had higher scores on the anxiety dimension. In terms of items, though, 34 of the 58 SCL items were significantly different between the two groups, with the depressed group scoring higher. The total SCL scores were also significantly higher for the depressed group. Based upon various classification methods,

Prusoff and Klerman also reported misclassification rates of 31.9% to 39.6%. Thus, while there was obviously high overlap in symptom patterns between the two groups, the authors concluded that "the pluralistic view is closest to the data and theoretically and empirically the most compelling" (p. 307).

Downing and Rickels (1974) also reported a study in which an anxious (n = 122) and depressed (n = 149) sample of patients were contrasted. In their study they used a 35-item SCL and showed that while both patient groups evidenced both anxiety and depressive symptoms, that the relative severity of the symptoms was highest for the within-group designation. Using a physician assignment to treatment (anxiolytics or antidepressant medication) as the reference, Downing and Rickels found that they could correctly differentiate 85.2% of the sample. They concluded that a unitary syndrome point of view was not consistent with their data, and that by careful consideration of symptom patterns, more specific diagnoses could be made, and in fact should be made for the assignment of medication to patients.

The Newcastle group in Britain has also reported data relevant to the question of the relationship between the syndromes of anxiety and depression (Gurney, Roth, Garside, Kerr, & Schapira, 1972; Roth, Gurney, Garside, & Kerr, 1972; Schapira, Roth, Kerry, & Gurney, 1972). One of the major points that they made (Roth et al., 1972) was that the anxious patients had such pervasive amounts of depression that they would also meet the inclusion criteria for depression in most studies of depressive disorders. Nonetheless, they argued that two separable groups existed, based upon the severity of subtypes of symptoms. They reported that the major difference was the presence of more symptoms in the depressed group, largely of an "endogenous" nature (e.g., older age of onset, early morning awakening, absence of obvious environmental precipitants, etc.). Examination of persistent versus episodic anxiety and depression showed that episodic anxiety and depression were present for both groups, but that persistent anxiety was more common in the anxiety group (31% versus 16%) and persistent depression was more common in the depressed group (65% versus 21%).

Other evidence bearing on the anxiety-depression relationship is offered by Cooke (1980). In that study a community sample of 408 subjects completed a symptom inventory, and the results were subjected to a principal component analysis. Within this nonclinical sample three main components were identified. The largest was one which was entitled "anxiety-depression," including such symptoms as agitation, irritability, guilt, nervousness, being scared, being restless, having repetitive thoughts, panic attacks, and tension. The second component was a cognitive depressive component, incorporating self-devaluation and indecision, while the third component was largely comprised of somatic features of depression (crying, loss of libido, sleep and eating difficulties, etc.).

Finally, Leckman, Weissman et al. (1983) present data on a large number of carefully diagnosed depressed patients. Utilizing the DSM-III method of diagnosis, it was determined that 77 of the 133 depressed patients also met the diagnostic features for a diagnosis of agoraphobia, panic disorder, or generalized anxiety disorder. Further, there was evidence that some of the shared variance for these disorders may derive from familial patterns, and that further examination of family data may provide data about the extent of the relationship and risk factors for depression. One of their conclusions was that "panic disorder and major depression may partially have a common underlying diathesis" (p. 1060).

In summary, the clinical literature on anxiety and depression consistently documents a relationship between anxious and depressive neuroses, although the patterning and severity of the symptoms is at times such that statistical separation of diagnostic groups is possible. While estimates of the overlap between anxiety and depressive disorder vary, the commonly cited 25%–40% overlap (Klerman, 1977) is sufficient to necessitate careful consideration of the psychological mechanisms by which patients develop concommitant anxiety and depressive symptomatology (Derogatis, Klerman, & Lipman, 1972). Also, it has been pointed out that the failure to perfectly separate anxiety and depressive disorders has very serious implications for the consideration and application of therapies (and particularly psychoactive medications) for anxiety and depressive disorders (Downing & Rickels, 1974; Fann & Wheless, 1977; Hamilton, 1973).

DIFFERENTIATING ANXIETY AND DEPRESSION

While it will be argued that a true distinction exists between anxiety and depression, the above review leads to the conclusion that our current self-report and syndromal assessment of these two constructs does not adequately reflect this distinction.

If the conclusion that the two constructs cannot be meaningfully separated is borne out by future research, a number of consequences may follow. For one, it may be necessary for future investigators who are interested in one or the other construct to assess and statistically control for the other, as through analysis of covariance. Second, the theoretical nature of the constructs of anxiety and depression, and in particular their reference to each other, may require further consideration and possible change. A third consequence may be the need for the development of standardized instruments that maximize the discriminant validity between anxiety and depression (cf. Dobson, 1980; Tellegen, 1985). Tellegen (1985), for example, has argued that one method for constructing less correlated scales is to "turn the Anxiety scale into more nearly a measure of Negative Affect and the Depression scale in to more nearly a measure of (reversed) Positive Affect," thus altering the items of the scales to conform to more nearly orthogonal dimensions. One problem with this method, of course, is that reversed Positive Affect in Tellegen's model of affect does not define depression, but identifies adjectives such as "drowsy," "dull," "sleepy," and "sluggish." Thus, a depression scale with more reversed positive affect items may not adequately represent the construct of depression. A contrasted approach is that of Dobson (1985), who used rationally defined anxiety and depression items and then created anxiety and depression scales whose items were chosen by the criterion of correlating more closely with their own scale than that of the other construct (cf. Jackson, 1970). This method of scale construction ensures high within-scale item-total scale correlations, but lower cross-construct correlations. Dobson (1985) reports that correlations between anxiety and depression scales was .59 for males and .44 for females, notably lower than the average anxiety-depression correlations reported in Table 3.

Several extant issues bear exploration with respect to self-report of anxiety and depression. Because of insufficient data in the publication of research and relatively small numbers of studies reviewed in Tables 1 to 3, more detailed analyses than those conducted here are not feasible. However, examination of such factors as the sex of subjects, their psychiatric status, and type of assessment instrument (trait versus state; self-report versus interview) will aid in circumscribing the generality of the conclusion that anxiety and depression are indiscriminable. For example, this review only examined self-report instruments. Contrasts between self-report and interview measures may yield more divergent results, as self-report measures rely on self-perceptions of functioning and internally-normed criteria for judgments, whereas clinical interviews incorporate externally-normed judgments (e.g., how anxious is this person compared to others in general?). Yet another class of variables that require assessment are those that might be construed as personality or response styles that would affect the report of anxiety and depression. In particular, acquiescent response styles and those affected by social desirability require elucidation (Linden, Paulhus, & Dobson, 1986; Linehan & Nielsen, 1983). Further research exploring these possible mitigating factors is clearly warranted, as for example in a multitrait (in this case, construct)—multimethod matrix (Campbell & Fiske, 1959).

Examination of situational variables may also assist in the separation of anxiety and depression. The work of Endler (1975; Endler & Magnusson, 1977; Endler & Shedletsky, 1973) has generally indicated that trait anxiety may not be a unitary construct, but may be related to situationally-relevant dimensions. Endler has developed the S-R Inventory of General Trait Anxiousness (Endler & Okada, 1975) on this basis, and this tool has been used to demonstrate that the type of situation a person is engaged in will to some extent dictate the relative predictive usefulness of trait anxiety scores (Dobson, 1983; Dobson & Neufeld, 1979). In the case of depression, there is also reason to believe that only some types of situations will engender a depressive response (most notably, situations involving loss; Costello, 1980; Lloyd, 1980; Paykel et al., 1969), and attempts to devise situation-specific trait measures for depression may improve the discriminability of situation-dependent anxiety and depression scores.

With a view to examining the dimensionality of situations, Dobson (1980) studied 69 situations that had been identified in the literature as related to anxiety or depression. Using a sample of 78 female and 122 male university students, ratings of "How anxiety-inducing is the situation?" were performed, and the results were factor analyzed. The VARIMAX solutions indicated that for ratings of anxiety, potential situations such as going into an interview for an important job, going to meet a new date, entering a final examination, and so on, were the most important. These "anticipatory situations" accounted for 68.1% and 41.7% of the variance for males and females, respectively. Interestingly, for the ratings of depression, potential situations such as having someone close die, being left by one's friend, being excluded or left out, and so on—"social loss situations"—accounted for 57.5% of the situational variance for the women, while for males anticipatory situations again emerged as the primary factor, accounting for 60.3% of the variance. For males, social loss situations only emerged as a third factor, following "situations requiring assertiveness and persistence," and accounted for only 5.8% of the depressiveness variance. These data suggest not only that the types of situational threats may vary in terms of their potential to engender anxiety or depression, but that there may also be a sex difference in the sensitivity to social losses. If women are in fact found to be more loss sensitive this may help to account for the observation of sex differences in the prevalence rates of depression.

Finally, it may be that the constructs of anxiety and depression are highly correlated because they are truly coexistent aspects of human functioning. In such an event, and given the evidence that high-depressed but low-anxious people are rare, it may be that the two constructs are hierarchically arranged, in that depression is a superordinate response. If this supposed hierarchical arrangement is valid, then a given individual when faced with a relevant situation has three trait possibilities: no trait anxiety or depression, with little or no attendant reaction to the situation; trait anxiety, with an anxious response to the situation; or trait anxiety and depression, with an anxious and depressive response to the situation.

Yet another possibility is that there is a developmental sequence in the development of anxious and depressive responses, as a function of an individual's trait predispositions. For example, the possibility of being fired from a place of employment may be experienced as a threat of loss of self-esteem. If the threat is far in the future, or is of only moderate probability, a person with the relevant "matched" trait for anxiety is most likely to suffer anxiety. As the potential firing approaches in time, and as the likelihood of the event becomes more certain, the person's degree of certainty of the threatening event will increase. Finally, as the event becomes imminent and predictable, anxiety will become a strong response, and given a relevant "matched" trait for depression, the person will react to the imminent event and then manifest loss of employment with a further depression response. In the absence of the relevant trait for depression, an attenuated depressive response would be seen, while little anticipatory anxiety would be shown without the trait for unemployment anxiety. Figure 1 shows these possible configurations. In keeping with the results from Table 3, of course, it is hypothesized that both anxiety and depressive traits will tend to co-occur for specific situations. The hypothesis argues that patterns a and d in Figure 1 should predominate in the reaction to life events. In order to assess this developmental possibility, cross-sectional and longitudinal data are required. Such a longitudinal study may have the form of first determining subjects' sensitivities through a multidimensional trait scale for anxiety and depression, and second, of examining the development of anxiety and depression as life events which impinge on the subjects' traits. Examination of event types and sex differences in sensitivity to events would provide evidence about mechanisms of anxiety and depression, and potentially begin to address the question of sex differences in prevalence of anxiety and depression.

Experimental and naturalistic data relevant to the above hierarchical and developmental hypotheses would do much to determine if a depressive response is in fact beyond, or in addition

FIGURE 1 Possible Trait Configurations and Responses to the Threat of Unemployment

a) No trait anxiety or depression for unemployment.

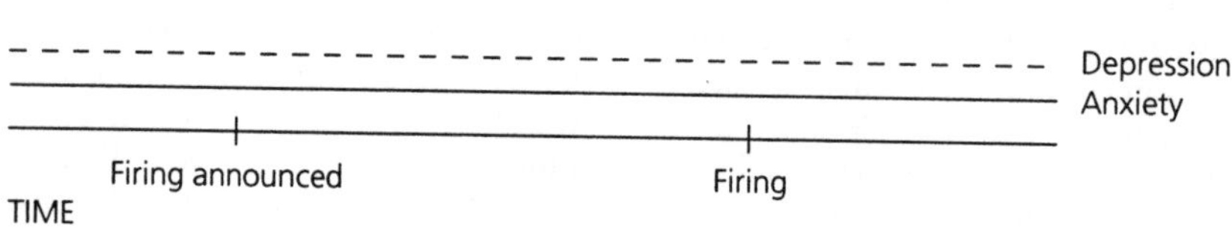

b) Trait anxiety, but no trait depression for unemployment.

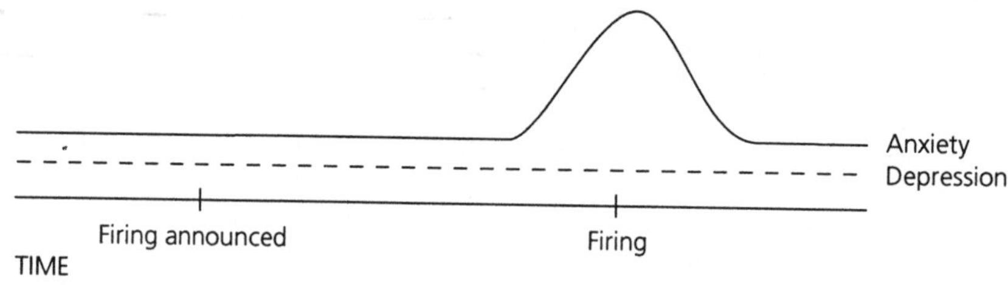

c) No trait anxiety, but trait depression for unemployment.

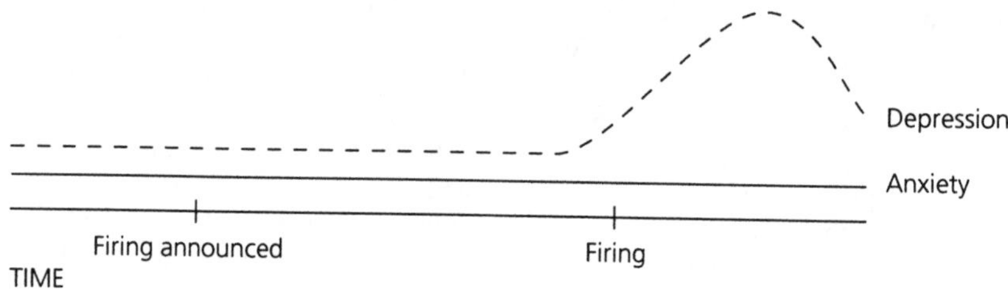

d) Trait anxiety and trait depression for unemployment.

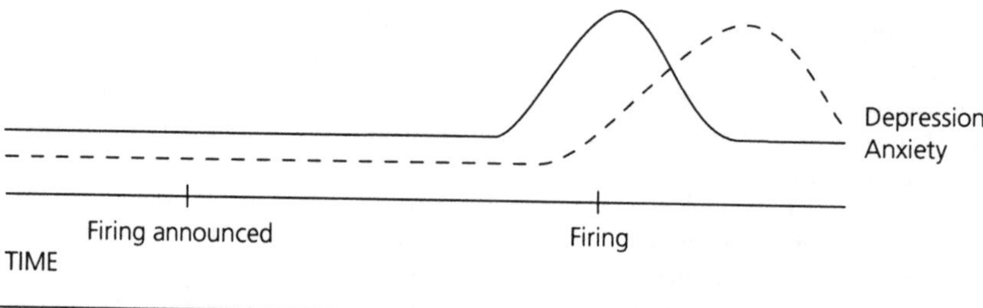

to, anxiety. Clearly, as the data stand it must be questioned whether trait anxiety and trait depression constitute two separate constructs, and yet there it is equally clear that two separable groups of clinically anxious and clinically depressed clients exist (Derogatis, Klerman, & Lipman, 1972; Derogatis, Lipman, Covi, & Rickels, 1972; Prusoff & Klerman, 1974). Investigation of the cognitive, emotional, and behavioral distinctions between trait anxiety and trait depression would be the next logical point of inquiry.

REFERENCES

American Psychiatric Association. (1980). *Diagnostic and statistical manual—III*. Washington, DC: Author.

Beck, A. T. (1976). *Cognitive therapy and the emotional disorders*. New York: International Universities Press.

Beck, A. T. & Beamesderfer, A. (1974). Assessment of depression: The depression inventory. *Psychological Measurements in Psychopharmacology and Modern Problems in Pharmacopsychiatry*, **7**, 151–189.

Beck, A. T. & Emery, G. (1979). *Cognitive therapy and anxiety and phobic disorders*. Philadelphia: Center for Cognitive Therapy.

Beck, A. T., Laude, R., & Bohnert, M. (1974). Ideational components of anxiety neurosis. *Archives of General Psychiatry*, **31**, 319–325.

Beck, A T., Ward, C. M., Mendelson, M., Mock, J., & Erbaugh, J. (1961). An inventory for measuring depression. *Archives of General Psychiatry*, **4**, 561–571.

Bille, M., & Juel-Nielsen, N. (1968). Incidence of neurosis in psychiatric and other medical services in a Danish county. *Danish Medical Bulletin*, **10**, 172–176.

Bloom, P. M., & Brady, J. P. (1968). An ipsative validation of the multiple affect adjective check list. *Journal of Clinical Psychology*, **24**, 45–46.

Brown, G. W., Davidson, S., Harris, T., MacLean, U., Pollock, S., & Prudo, R. (1977). Psychiatric disorder in London and North Ulster. *Social Science and Medicine*, **11**, 367–377.

Brunetti, P. M. (1976). Rural Vaucluse: Two surveys on the prevalence of mental disorders. In T. Andersen, C. Astrup, & Forsdahl (Eds.) *Social, somatic and psychiatric studies of geographically defined populations* (pp. 12–15). *Acta Psychiatrica Scandinavica Supplemental*, 263.

Campbell, D. T., & Fiske, D. W. (1959). Convergent and discriminant validation by the multitrait-multimethod matrix. *Psychological Bulletin*, **56**, 81–105.

Carey, G., Gottesman, I. I., & Robins, C. (1980). Prevalence rates for the neuroses: Pitfalls in the evaluation of familiarity. *Psychological Medicine*, **10**, 437–443.

Carroll, B. J., Feinberg, M., Greden, J. F., Tarika, J., Albala, A. A., Haskett, R. F., James, N., Kronfol, Z., Lohr, N., Steiner, M., de Vigne, J. P., & Young, E. (1981). A specific laboratory test for the diagnosis of melancholia: Standardization, validation and clinical utility. *Archives of General Psychiatry*, **38**, 15–22.

Cattell, R. B., & Scheier, I. L. (1961). *The meaning and measurement of neuroticism and anxiety*. New York: Ronald Press.

Clancy, J., Noyes, R., Hoenk, P., & Slymen, M. S. (1978). Secondary depression in anxiety neurosis. *Journal of Nervous and Mental Disease*, **166**, 846–850.

Cloninger, C. R., Martin, R. L., Clayton, P., & Guze, S. B. (1981). A blind follow-up and family study of anxiety neurosis: Preliminary analysis of the St. Louis 500. In D. F. Klein & J. Rabkin (Eds.), *Anxiety: New research and changing concepts*. New York: Raven Press.

Cooke, D. J. (1980). Conceptual and methodological considerations of the problem inherent in the specification of the simple event-syndrome link. In I. G. Sarason & C. D. Spielberger (Eds.), *Stress and anxiety: Volume 7*. Washington: Hemisphere.

Costello, C. G. (1976). *Anxiety and depression: The adaptive emotions*: Montreal: McGill–Queen's University Press.

Costello, C. G. (1980). Loss as a source of stress in psychopathology. In R. W. J. Neufeld (Ed.), *Psychological stress and psychopathology*. New York: McGraw Hill.

Costello, C. G., Christensen, S. J., & Rogers, T. B. (1974). The relationship between measures of general depression and the endogenous versus reactive classification. *Canadian Psychiatric Association Journal*, **19**, 259–265.

Costello, C. G., & Comrey, A. L. (1967). Scales for measuring depression and anxiety. *Journal of Psychology*, **66**, 303–313.

Craighead, W. E. (1980). Away from a unitary model of depression. *Behavior Therapy*, **11**, 122–128.

Crinker, R. R., & Nunally, J. C. (1968). In M. M. Katz, J. O. Cole, & W. F. Borton (Eds.), *The role and methodology of classification in psychiatry and psychopathology*. Chevy Chase, MD: Public Health Service.

Dealy, R. S., Ishiki, D. M., Avery, D. H., Wilson, L. G., & Dunner, D. L. (1981). Secondary depression in anxiety disorders. *Comprehensive Psychiatry*, **22**, 612–618.

DeMonbreun, B. G., & Craighead, W. E. (1977). Distortion of perception and recall of positive and neutral feedback in depression. *Cognitive Therapy and Research*, **1**, 311–329.

Derogatis, L. R. (1982). Self-report measures of stress. In L. Goldberger & S. Breznitz (Eds.), *Handbook of stress: Theoretical and clinical aspects*. New York: The Free Press.

Derogatis, L. R., Klerman, G. L., & Lipman, R. S. (1972). Anxiety states and depressive neuroses. *Journal of Nervous and Mental Disease*, **155**, 392–403.

Derogatis, L. R., Lipman, R. S., Covi, L., & Rickels, K. (1972). Factorial invariance of symptom diversions in anxious and depressive neuroses. *Archives of General Psychiatry*, **27**, 659–685.

Dobson, K. S. (1980). *Assessing anxiety and depression: Development and application of the differential anxiety and depression inventory*. Unpublished doctoral dissertation, University of Western Ontario, London, Canada.

Dobson, K. S. (1983). A regression analysis of the interactional approach to anxiety. *Canadian Journal of Behavioural Science*, **15**, 163–173.

Dobson, K. S. (1985). Defining an interactional approach to anxiety and depression. *The Psychological Record*, **35,** 471–489.

Dobson, K. S. & Breiter, H. J. (1983). Cognitive assessment of depression: Reliability and validity of three measures. *Journal of Abnormal Psychology*, **92,** 107–109.

Dobson, K. S., & Neufeld, R. W. J. (1979). Stress-related appraisals: A regression analysis. *Canadian Journal of Behavioural Science*, **11**(4), 274–285.

Dobson, K. S., & Shaw, B. F. (1986). Cognitive assessment with major depressive disorders. *Cognitive Therapy and Research*, **10,** 13–29.

Doerfler, L. A. (1981). Psychological research in depression: A methodological review. *Clinical Psychology Review*, **1,** 119–137.

Downing, R. W., & Rickels, K. (1974). Mixed anxiety depression: Fact or myth? *Archives of General Psychiatry*, **30,** 312–317.

Ekman, P., & Friesen, W. V. (1975). *Unmasking the face*. Englewood Cliffs, NJ: Prentice-Hall.

Endler, N. S. (1975). The case for person-situation interactions. *Canadian Psychological Review*, **16,** 12–21.

Endler, N. S., & Magnusson, D. (1976). Toward an interactional psychology of personality. *Psychological Bulletin*, **83,** 956–974.

Endler, N. S., & Magnusson, D. (1977). The interactional model of anxiety: An empirical test in an examination situation. *Canadian Journal of Behavioural Science*, **9,** 101–107.

Endler, N. S., & Okada, M. (1975). A multidimensional measure of trait anxiety: The S-R inventory of general trait anxiousness. *Journal of Consulting and Clinical Psychology*, **43,** 319–329.

Endler, N. S., & Shedletsky, R. (1973). Trait versus state anxiety, authoritarianism and ego threat versus physical threat. *Canadian Journal of Behavioural Science*, **5**(4), 347–361.

Epstein, S. (1976). Anxiety, arousal, and the self-concept. In I. G. Sarason & C. D. Spielberger (Eds.), *Stress and anxiety: Volume 3*. Washington, DC: Hemisphere.

Fann, W. E., & Wheless, J. C. (1977). Pharmacological treatment of the moderately anxious and depressed patient. In W. E. Fann, I. Karacan, A. D. Pokorny, & R. L. Williams (Eds.), *Phenomenology and treatment of depression*. New York: Spectrum Pub.

Gersh, F. S., & Fowles, D. C. (1979). Neurotic depression: The concept of anxious depression. In R. A. Depue (Ed.), *The psychobiology of the depressive disorders*. New York: Academy Press.

Glanzmann, P., & Laux, L. (1978). The effects of trait anxiety and two kinds of stressors on state anxiety and performance. In C. D. Spielberger & I. G. Sarason (Eds.), *Stress and anxiety: Volume 5*. New York: Wiley.

Gotlib, I. H., & Asarnow, R. T. (1979). Interpersonal and impersonal problem-solving skills in mildly and clinically depressed university students. *Journal of Consulting and Clinical Psychology*, **47**(1), 86–95.

Gurney, C., Roth, M., Garside, R. F., Kerr, T. A., & Schapira, K. (1972). Studies in the classification of affective disorders: The relationship between anxiety states and depressive illness: II. *British Journal of Psychiatry*, **11,** 162–166.

Hamilton, M. (1973). Combined anxiety-depressive states. In W. L. Rees (Eds.), *Anxiety factors in comprehensive patient care*. New York: American Elsevier Co.

Hathaway, S. R., & McKinley, J. C. (1942). A multiphasic personality schedule (Minnesota): III. The measurement of symptomatic depression. *Journal of Psychology*, **14,** 73–84.

Hatzenbuehler, L. C., Parpal, M., & Matthews, L. (1983). Classifying college students as depressed or nondepressed using the Beck Depression Inventory: An empirical analysis. *Journal of Consulting and Clinical Psychology*, **51,** 360–366.

Hesselbrock, M. M., Hesselbrock, V. M., Tennen, H., Meyer, R. E., & Workman, K. L. (1983). Methodological consideration in the assessment of depression in alcoholics. *Journal of Consulting and Clinical Psychology*, **51,** 399–405.

Izard, C. E. (1971). *The face of emotion*. New York: Appleton-Century-Crofts.

Izard, C. E. (1977). *Human emotions*. New York: Plenum Press.

Jackson, D. N. (1970). A sequential system for personality scale development. In C. D. Spielberger (Ed.), *Current topics in clinical and community psychology: Vol. 2*. New York: Plenum Press.

Kennedy, R. E., & Craighead, W. E. (1979). *Differential effects of various types of reinforcement and punishment on learning, expectations and recall in depression and anxiety*. Paper presented at the annual meeting of the Association for the Advancement of Behavior Therapy, Chicago, Illinois.

Klerman, G. L. (1977). Anxiety and depression. In G. D. Burrows (Ed.), *Handbook of studies on depression*. New York: Excerpta Medica.

Lazarus, R. S., & Averill, J. (1972). Emotion and cognition: With special reference to anxiety. In C. D. Spielberger (Ed.), *Anxiety: Current trends in theory and research: Vol. II*. New York: Academic.

Leckman, J. F., Merikangas, K. R., Pauls, D. L., Prusoff, B., & Weissman, M. M. (1983). Anxiety disorders and depression: Contradictions between family study data and DSM-III conventions. *American Journal of Psychiatry*, **140,** 880–882.

Leckman, J. F., Weissman, M. M., Merikangas, K. R., Pauls, D. L., Prusoff, B. (1983). Panic disorder and depression: Increased risk of depression, alcoholism, panic, and phobic disorders in families of depressed probands with panic disorder. *Archives of General Psychiatry*, **40,** 1055–1060.

Lemkau, P., Tietze, C., & Cooper, M. (1942). Mental hygiene problems in an urban district. *Mental Hygiene*, **26,** 100–119.

Linden, W., Paulhus, D. L., & Dobson, K. S. (1986). The effects of response styles on the report of psychological and somatic distress. *Journal of Consulting and Clinical Psychology*, **54,** 309–313.

Linehan, M. M., & Nielsen, S. L. (1983). Social desirability: Its relevance to the measurement of hopelessness and suicidal behavior. *Journal of Consulting and Clinical Psychology*, **51,** 141–143.

Lloyd, C. (1980). Life events and depressive disorder revisited: II. Events as precipitating factors. *Archives of General Psychiatry*, **37,** 541–548.

Magnusson, D., & Endler, N. S. (Eds.). (1977). *International psychology and personality*. New York: Wiley.

Mendels, J., Weinstein, N., & Cochrane, C. (1972). The relationship between depression and anxiety. *Archives of General Psychiatry*, **27**, 649–653.

Miller, W. R., Seligman, M. E. P., Kurlander, H. M. (1975). Learned helplessness, depression and anxiety. *Journal of Nervous and Mental Disease*, **161** (5), 317–357.

Nussbaum, K., Wittig, B. A., Hanlon, T. E., & Kurland, A. A. (1963). Intravenous nialamide in the treatment of depressed female patients. *Comprehensive Psychiatry*, **4**, 105–116.

Parloff, M., Kellman, H., & Frank, J. (1954). Comfort, effectiveness and self-awareness criteria of improvement. *American Journal of Psychiatry*, **111**, 343–351.

Paykel, E. S., Myers, J. K., Dienelt, M. N., Klerman, G. L., Lindenthal, J. J., & Pepper, M. P. (1969). Life events and depression—A controlled study. *Archives of General Psychiatry*, **21**, 753–760.

Plutchik, R. (1980a). *Emotions in humans and animals: A psychoevolutionary synthesis*. New York: Harper & Row.

Plutchik, R. (1980b). Measurement implications of a psychoevolutionary theory of emotions. In K. R. Blankstein, P. Pliner, & J. Polivy (Eds.), *Assessment and modification of emotional behavior*. New York: Plenum Press.

Prusoff, B., & Klerman, G. L. (1974). Differentiating depressed from anxious neurotic outpatients. *Archives of General Psychiatry*, **30**, 302–309.

Roth, M., Gurney, C., Garside, R. F., & Kerr, T. A. (1972). Studies in the classification of affective disorders: The relationship between anxiety states and depressive illness—I. *British Journal of Psychiatry*, **121**, 147–161.

Russell, J. A. (1980). A circumplex model of affect. *Journal of Personality and Social Psychology*, **39**, 1161–1178.

Schapira, K., Roth, M., Kerry, T. A., & Gurney, C. (1972). The prognosis of affective disorders: The differentiation of anxiety states from depressive illness. *British Journal of Psychiatry*, **121**, 175–181.

Seitz, R. (1970). Five psychological measures of neurotic depression: A correlational study. *Journal of Clinical Psychology*, **26**, 504–505.

Shipley, C. R., & Fazio, A. F. (1973). Pilot study of a treatment for psychological depression. *Journal of Abnormal Psychology*, **83**, 372–378.

Spielberger, C. D. (1972). Anxiety as an emotional state. In C. D. Spielberger (Ed.), *Anxiety: Current trends in theory and research: Vol. 1*. New York: Academic.

Spielberger, C. D. (1975a). The measurement of state and trait anxiety: Conceptual and methodological issues. In L. Levi (Ed.), *Emotions—Their parameters and measurement*. New York: Raven Press.

Spielberger, C. D. (1975b). Anxiety: State-trait process. In C. D. Spielberger & I. G. Sarason (Eds.), *Stress and anxiety: Vol 1*. New York: Wiley.

Spielberger, C. D., Gorsuch, R. L., & Lushene, R. E. (1970). *STAI—Manual for the State-Trait Anxiety Inventory*. Palo Alto, CA: Consulting Psychologists Press.

Tellegen, A. (1985). Structures of mood and personality and their relevance to assessing anxiety, with an emphasis on self-report. In A. H. Tuma & J. D. Maswer (Eds.), *Anxiety and the anxiety disorders*. Hillsdale, NJ: Lawrence Erlbaum Associates.

Weissman, A. N., & Beck, A. T. (1978). *Development and validation of the dysfunctional Attitude Scale: A preliminary investigation*. Paper presented at the annual meeting of the American Education Research Association, Toronto, Ontario.

Zevon, M. A., & Tellegen, A. (1982). The structure of mood changes: An idiographic/nomothetic analysis. *Journal of Personality and Social Psychology*, **43**, 111–122.

Zuckerman, M. A., & Lubin, B. (1965). *The multiple affect adjective check list*. San Diego, CA: Educational and Industrial Testing Service.

Zung, W. W. (1965). A self-rating depression scale. *Archives of General Psychiatry*, **12**, 63–70.

Zung, W. W. (1969). A cross-cultural survey of symptoms in depression. *American Journal of Psychiatry*, **126**, 116–121.

Zung, W. W., Richards, C. B., & Short, M. J. (1965). Self-rating depression scale in an outpatient clinic. *Archives of General Psychiatry*, **13**, 508–516.

DISCUSSION

Much to the dismay and occasional annoyance of beginning students in abnormal psychology courses, many important questions concerning mental illness turn out to have more than one correct answer. So it is with the query constituting the title of this chapter: Anxiety and depression both can and cannot be differentiated. What do I mean by this statement, and how can it be interpreted as anything other than sheer nonsense?

In the sciences (and let us not forget that psychology is a branch of science), we can often explain phenomena on multiple levels. Consider the human brain, that 3-pound blob of jellylike material occupying the space between your ears. At one level, your brain is an enormous, sprawling organ consisting of approximately 100 billion neurons and intracellular material. At a more specific level, however, your brain is an agglomeration of countless molecules of enormous variety. At an even more specific level, your brain consists of an even more unfathomable number of atoms—and so on. The point is that we can quite appropriately describe your brain at a number of different levels of generality or specificity. None of these levels is the only correct level of analysis; each provides us with different, but perfectly valid, information.

Similarly, one can often study psychopathological entities on multiple levels. The relationship between anxiety and depression is such a case. If we examine propensities to experience mood states, we find that individuals differ from one another on two extremely broad and general personality dimensions: **positive affectivity** (PA) and **negative affectivity** (NA) (Tellegen, 1985; Watson & Clark, 1984). PA represents an enduring disposition to experience positive moods of many kinds, including cheerfulness, enthusiasm, interest, and pride. NA, in contrast, represents an enduring disposition to experience negative moods of many kinds, including anxiety, depression, guilt, and anger. Interestingly, PA and NA are almost entirely uncorrelated. An individual who is high in PA is not necessarily low in NA, or vice versa. A person who is capable of experiencing the heights of joy and happiness is just as capable as everyone else of experiencing the depths of despair and anguish.

Auke Tellegen (1985) and Leanna Clark and David Watson (1991) have used the distinction between PA and NA to explain both the overlapping and the unique features of anxiety and depression. According to these authors, anxiety and depression are alike in that they are both characterized by elevated levels of NA. The presence of high NA in both anxiety and depression helps to explain why authors such as Dobson have maintained that anxiety and depression are often extremely difficult to distinguish. In contrast, anxiety and depression are different in that they are each uniquely characterized by the presence of specific factors that are unrelated to the more general dimension of NA. Anxiety is marked by the presence of elevated levels of physiological arousal, whereas depression is marked by the presence of low levels of PA, or what might be termed anhedonia (loss of pleasure). These differences help to explain why authors like Hamilton have contended that anxiety and depression can be meaningfully distinguished on the basis of natural history, treatment response, physiological factors, and other variables.

Thus, at a very general level of explanation, anxiety and depression are indeed difficult or impossible to differentiate, because both share elevated levels of NA. But at a more specific level of explanation, anxiety and depression can be differentiated, because each entity is characterized by a distinctive element not shared by the other. If this analysis is on the mark, both Hamilton and Dobson would be correct to some extent; they appear to disagree only because each has elected to focus on a different level of explanation.

One implication of this analysis is that anxiety and depression should frequently coexist within individuals, because anxiety and depression share elevated levels of NA and because the specific factors associated with anxiety and depression (physiological overarousal and low levels of PA, respectively) are not mutually exclusive. Moreover, some individuals may exhibit a fairly equal mixture of both anxiety and depression, with no marked predominance of either emotional state. As noted in the introduction to this chapter, DSM-IV has provisionally introduced the diagnostic category of mixed anxiety-depression to accommodate such individuals, who previously were either undiagnosed or relegated somewhat arbitrarily to one or the other broad diagnostic class. Careful research on these individuals should help to clarify the association between anxiety and depression and to elucidate the underlying factors that are both common and unique to these two entities.

QUESTIONS TO STIMULATE DISCUSSION

1. Do the two readings in this chapter provide stronger support for the dualistic view or for the unitary view? Or is there no clear "winner"? Explain your reasoning.
2. Because of the extremely high correlation between anxiety and depression, it is typically quite difficult to assess one construct without assessing the other. Some researchers have attempted to deal with this problem by developing relatively "pure" measures of anxiety or depression (that is, measures that primarily assess the features specific to each condition). What are the potential advantages and disadvantages of this strategy?
3. We sometimes become anxious in response to stressful life events; at other times, we become depressed. What situational factors might account for this difference?
4. Similarly, some individuals habitually tend to become anxious following stressors, whereas others habitually tend to become depressed. What predisposing influences (for example, personality variables) might be responsible for this difference?

SUGGESTIONS FOR FURTHER READING

Barlow, D. H. (1988). *Anxiety and its disorders: The nature and treatment of anxiety and panic*. New York: Guilford Press.

Barlow provides a superb, interesting, and extremely comprehensive treatment of the major theoretical and methodological issues in the study of anxiety and anxiety disorders. The first two chapters, with discussions of the subjective experience of anxiety and the relationship between anxiety and other emotions, contain valuable introductory information that is presented in few other textbooks on anxiety or anxiety disorders.

Clark, L. A., & Watson, D. (1991). Tripartite model of anxiety and depression: Psychometric evidence and taxonomic implications. *Journal of Abnormal Psychology, 100*, 316–336.

The authors review evidence that anxiety and depression can be distinguished by their levels of positive affectivity (PA) (with depression characterized by low PA levels and anxiety by relatively normal PA levels) but that they share high levels of negative affectivity (NA). They conclude that anxiety and depression possess significant common and unique factors and that a tripartite model incorporating two lower-order factors (specific anxiety and specific depression) and one higher-order NA factor best accounts for the existing data.

Coryell, W. (1990). Anxiety secondary to depression. *Psychiatric Clinics of North America, 13*, 685–698.
Coryell reviews the literature on the occurrence of anxiety following depression. He concludes that data from studies of behavior-genetics, epidemiological patterns, treatment response, and course all point to the existence of fundamental differences between anxiety and depressive disorders.

Frances, A., Manning, D., Marin, D., Kocsis, J., McKinney, K., Hall, W., & Kline, M. (1992). Relationship of anxiety and depression. *Psychopharmacology, 106*, S82–S86.
The authors review the evidence for four different models of the association between anxiety and depression: a unitary model, a pluralistic model positing multiple discrete syndromes, a predispositional model in which anxiety increases the risk for subsequent depression, and a measurement model in which anxiety and depression co-occur largely because of artifactual overlap between anxiety and depression measures. They find some merit in each of these hypotheses and discuss proposals for handling the problem of diagnostic overlap between anxiety and depression.

Kendall, P. C., & Watson, D. (1989). *Anxiety and depression: Distinctive and overlapping features*. San Diego: Academic Press.
This edited volume contains a variety of chapters dealing with the similarities and differences between anxiety and depression. The issues covered include the relationship of anxiety and depression to positive and negative affect, the differential diagnosis of anxiety and depressive disorders, self-report assessment of anxiety and depression, the role of life events in the etiology of anxiety and depression, and behavioral and cognitive treatments of anxiety disorders.

Klerman, G. L. (1980). Anxiety and depression. In G. D. Burrows and B. Davies (Eds.), *Handbook of studies on anxiety* (pp. 145–164). Amsterdam: Elsevier/North Holland Biomedical Press.
Klerman reviews the evidence for the distinction between anxiety and depression from studies of autonomic activity, skeletal and facial muscle activity, mood, and psychopharmacological response. He concludes that the evidence strongly favors the pluralistic position over the unitary position. Readers may also want to see an updated discussion of Klerman's views on the anxiety-depression relationship: Klerman, G. L. (1988). Relationship between anxiety and depression. In M. Roth, R. Noyes, & G. D. Burrows (Eds.), *Handbook of anxiety, Vol. 1: Biological, clinical, and cultural perspectives* (pp. 59–82). Amsterdam: Elsevier.

Maser, J., & Cloninger, C. (1990). *Comorbidity of mood and anxiety disorders*. Washington, DC: American Psychiatric Press.
This important edited volume contains 40 chapters dealing with various aspects of the "comorbidity" (co-occurrence within individuals) between anxiety and depressive disorders. Some of the issues covered include the effect of classification schemes upon "comorbidity," epidemiological evidence for the overlap between anxiety and depression, biological and psychosocial models of this overlap, and research and assessment strategies for the study of anxiety and depression. Readers should beware of using the term *comorbidity*, however: It originated in medical epidemiology and has rather different connotations in psychiatry than in organic medicine (see Chapter 9).

Racagni, G., & Smeraldi, E. (Eds.) (1987). *Anxious depression: Assessment and treatment*. New York: Raven Press.
This edited volume contains a number of chapters dealing with the within-individual overlap of anxiety and depression. The topics covered include the assessment of anxiety and depression, the descriptive psychopathology of anxious depression, the familial/genetic association between anxiety disorders and mood disorders, biological models of anxiety and depression, and considerations in the pharmacological treatment of anxious depression.

Tyrer, P. (1985). Neurosis divisible? *Lancet, i*, 685–688.
Tyrer presents his concept of the "general neurotic syndrome" and argues that individuals with anxiety and those with depression frequently exhibit slightly different manifestations of a shared pathological process. He concludes that "the 'lumpers' deserve another try" (p. 688).

REFERENCES

Clark, L. A., & Watson, D. (1991). Tripartite model of anxiety and depression: Psychometric evidence and taxonomic implications. *Journal of Abnormal Psychology, 100*, 316–336.

Frances, A., Manning, D., Marin, D., Kocsis, J., McKinney, K., Hall, W., & Kline, M. (1992). Relationship of anxiety and depression. *Psychopharmacology, 106*, S82–S86.

Klerman, G. L. (1988). Relationship between anxiety and depression. In M. Roth, R. Noyes, & G. D. Burrows (Eds.), *Handbook of anxiety: Vol. 1. Biological, clinical, and cultural perspectives* (pp. 59–82). Amsterdam: Elsevier.

Maser, J., & Cloninger, C. (1990).*Comorbidity of mood and anxiety disorders*. Washington, DC: American Psychiatric Press.

Roth, M., Gurney, C., Garside, R. F., & Kerr, T. A. (1972). Studies in the classification of affective disorders: The relationship between anxiety states and depressive illness—I. *British Journal of Psychiatry, 121*, 147–161.

Tellegen, A. (1985). Structures of mood and personality and their relevance to assessing anxiety, with an emphasis on self-report. In A. H. Tuma & J. Maser (Eds.), *Anxiety and the anxiety disorders* (pp. 681–706). Hillsdale, NJ: Erlbaum.

Watson, D., & Clark, L. A. (1984). Negative affectivity: The disposition to experience aversive emotional states. *Psychological Bulletin*, 96, 465–490.

CHAPTER 7

Does evidence support the "disease model" of alcoholism?

PRO Milam, J. R., & Ketcham, K. (1981). *Under the influence: A guide to the myths and realities of alcoholism* (pp. 31–46, 136–142). New York: Bantam Books.

CON Peele, S. (1989). *The diseasing of America: Addiction treatment out of control* (pp. 55–83). Lexington, MA: Lexington Books.

OVERVIEW OF THE CONTROVERSY: James R. Milam and Katherine Ketcham contend that alcoholism is a physiological disease resulting from the combined action of genetic, metabolic, hormonal, and perhaps other biological factors. Stanton Peele argues that the principal assumptions of the "disease model" of alcoholism—such as the loss-of-control phenomenon, the genetic basis of alcoholism, and the necessity for Alcoholics Anonymous treatment—are either false or severely overstated.

CONTEXT OF THE PROBLEM

No one knows for sure when the human race first discovered alcohol. One thing is for certain, however: The use of alcohol for recreational purposes is not a recent development in our history. Humans were apparently familiar with beer, wine, and mead dating back at least to Paleolithic times. Remnants of early civilizations suggest that alcohol was used for religious ceremonies and medicinal purposes (Mello & Mendelson, 1974). References to the recreational use of alcohol appear in the Old Testament, Mesopotomanian sayings, and Egyptian hieroglyphics (Goodwin & Guze, 1989). The technique of distilling alcohol from sugar was invented in Arabia in about A.D. 800. By the 1600s, distilled liquor had become a drug of abuse throughout much of the Western world. It was not until 1849, however, that a Swedish health official, Magnus Huss, coined the term *alcoholism* (Goodwin & Guze, 1989).

DSM-IV distinguishes between two conditions characterized by excessive drinking: **alcohol dependence** (which is essentially equivalent to alcoholism) and **alcohol abuse** (which is milder than alcohol dependence and involves a maladaptive pattern of drinking, resulting in repeated negative consequences, such as legal problems, drunk driving, absences from work, and physical fights). Alcohol dependence is characterized by a constellation of problematic signs and symptoms. For example, alcohol-dependent individuals often consume alcohol in greater amounts or over longer durations than initially intended, spend a great deal of time ingesting or obtaining alcohol or recovering from its effects, and sacrifice important activities (such as time with family members) because of drinking. In addition, they frequently continue to drink despite a serious problem that is caused or exacerbated by drinking and make repeated unsuccessful attempts to reduce or stop drinking. Finally, these individuals commonly experience marked **tolerance**—the need to use greater amounts of alcohol to experience the same effect or a decreased effect with the same amount of alcohol—and **withdrawal** symptoms while not drinking. The major withdrawal symptoms of alcoholism include "the shakes," seizures ("rum fits"), and **delirium tremens** (the "DTs"), which are characterized by fever, rapid heart beat, excessive sweating, confusion, and extremely vivid hallucinations (which are often visual).

Benjamin Rush, considered by many to be the father of American psychiatry, is typically credited with being the first major figure to conceptualize alcoholism as a "disease" (in the early 1800's). At about the same time, a British physician, Thomas Trotter, likened alcoholism to a medical disorder (see the reading by Milam and Ketcham in this chapter). Both Rush and Trotter believed alcoholism to be the product of a discrete biological defect or dysfunction, much as diabetes, cancer, and tuberculosis are. Specialized medical institutes for the treatment of alcoholism appeared in various regions of the United States during the middle and late 1800s (the first in Boston in 1841), reinforcing the belief that the treatment of alcoholism was properly within the province of the medical profession.

It was not long, however, before societal attitudes toward alcohol changed. Following the passage of the 18th amendment to the U.S. Constitution in 1920, which prohibited the use of alcoholic beverages, alcoholism came to be viewed more as a behavioral and moral problem than as a disease or physiological defect (Goodwin & Guze, 1989; Miller & Chappel, 1991). After the repeal of the 18th amendment in 1933, marking the legal end of Prohibition, the concept of alcoholism as a disease experienced a renaissance. In 1935, two former alcoholics, one a physician (Robert Smith) and the other a stockbroker (William Wilson), founded Alcoholics Anonymous (AA). AA is premised on the assumption that certain individuals possess a physiological susceptibility to alcohol analogous to an allergy. For such individuals, a single drink is believed to set off a unquenchable desire for still more alcohol, leading inevitably to a loss of control over drinking (Fingarette, 1988).

Perhaps the individual most responsible for promulgating the disease model of alcoholism was a physiological researcher at Yale University, Elvin Morton Jellinek. Drawing on questionnaire research with AA members, Jellinek (1946, 1952) concluded that alcoholism was a biological illness with a highly characteristic and predictable progression. He described four major phases of alcoholism: prealcoholic, prodromal, crucial, and chronic. In the prealcoholic phase, individuals discover that alcohol provides a means of reducing tension and increasing self-confidence. In the prodromal phase, they begin to drink secretly and heavily and to experience **blackouts** (periods of memory loss for events that occurred while drinking, not to be confused with passing out). In the crucial phase, drinkers begin to lose control over drinking, engage in "benders" (prolonged bouts of drinking lasting days or even weeks), and experience severe withdrawal symptoms while not drinking. Finally, in the chronic phase, they drink almost constantly and neglect virtually all social and occupational responsibilities. Jellinek (1960) also distinguished among five "species" of alcoholics: alpha (who drink to minimize tension), beta (who experience physical damage from drinking, such as cirrhosis of the liver, but are not dependent on alcohol), delta (who are unable to abstain from drinking), epsilon (who lose control of their drinking and go on periodic benders), and gamma (who lose control of their drinking, experience withdrawal symptoms, and are physically dependent on alcohol) (Vaillant, 1988).

Jellinek's description of the natural history of alcoholism and his typology of alcoholics have not gone unchallenged, however. For example, the course of alcoholism appears to be far more variable than implied by Jellinek. Moreover, although Jellinek's "species" clearly exist, a number of alcoholics do not fit neatly into any of his five categories (Goodwin & Guze, 1989). Despite its shortcomings (also see Fingarette, 1988, for a discussion of methodological problems with Jellinek's work), Jellinek's research was instrumental in persuading a number of scientists that alcoholism is best conceived of as a physiological illness with a distinctive natural history.

Nevertheless, the "disease model" of alcoholism—the notion that alcoholism is a consequence of a specifiable physiological defect or dysfunction—continues to be a source of substantial controversy among alcoholism researchers and practitioners. Moreover, this model has been extended to a wide variety of other problematic behaviors, including illegal drug use, gambling, overeating, sexual promiscuity, and even excessive shopping (Peele, 1989). Many critics contend, however, that such extrapolation is premature. Should not the proponents of the disease model, these skeptics ask, first demonstrate that it applies to the condition that it was initially invoked to explain—alcoholism?

THE CONTROVERSY: Milam and Ketcham vs. Peele

Milam and Ketcham

James Milam and Katherine Ketcham first discuss the history of the disease concept of alcoholism in the United States. They note that public and scientific conceptions of alcoholism have alternated between two opposing perspectives: Alcoholism is a moral weakness for which the affected individual bears responsibility, and alcoholism is a physiological disease for which the victim bears little or no responsibility. Milam and Ketcham argue that Alcoholics Anonymous (AA), although correctly adopting the disease model, mistakenly blames the alcoholic for deep-seated personality flaws. Nevertheless, they contend, the AA approach has helped thousands of alcoholics to achieve abstinence. Milam and Ketcham then review the evidence for the role of five factors (some of which overlap) in the etiology of alcoholism: abnormal metabolism of alcohol, innate preferences for alcohol, genetic influences, prenatal influences, and biologically related ethnic differences in alcohol susceptibility. They conclude that, although nonalcoholics and alcoholics begin drinking for the same reasons, physiological factors are entirely responsible for determining which drinkers progress to alcoholism.

Peele

Stanton Peele begins by listing six major assumptions of the disease model promulgated by the contemporary alcoholism movement and contends that none of these six assumptions has been upheld by scientific research. For example, there is no compelling evidence, says Peele, that AA or related approaches are effective treatments for alcoholism. Peele then discusses the empirical support for a number of widely held beliefs consistent with the disease model of alcoholism. For example, he questions the reality of the loss-of-control phenomenon in alcoholism and argues that alcoholics are entirely capable of moderating their drinking when it is in their best interests. Moreover, Peele asserts, the evidence for the role of genetic and biological factors in the etiology of alcoholism has been considerably overstated by proponents of the disease model. He then takes issue with several other assumptions of the disease model: the notion of alcoholism as a "primary" disease that is not symptomatic of other problems, the assertion that alcoholism is largely independent of sociocultural factors, the belief in the efficacy of AA and similar treatments, and the claim that enormous numbers of drinkers "deny" their alcoholism. Peele concludes that most of the currently favored treatments for alcoholism are demonstrably ineffective, whereas a number of demonstrably effective treatments have been largely or entirely ignored.

KEY CONCEPTS AND TERMS

acetaldehyde Metabolic (that is, breakdown) product of alcohol. Acetaldehyde is highly toxic, and it produces nausea, low blood pressure, and other negative effects when present at high levels.

alcohol dehydrogenase Liver enzyme responsible for metabolizing alcohol.

dopamine Neurotransmitter (chemical messenger in the nervous system) implicated in reward-seeking behaviors, including drinking.

fetal alcohol syndrome Syndrome occurring in children of mothers who drink excessively during pregnancy. Fetal alcohol syndrome is characterized by abnormalities in four major areas: central nervous system dysfunction (often including mental retardation), low birth weight, facial abnormalities (for example, flattened nose and narrow eyes), and a variety of nonspecific body malformations.

proband In a behavior-genetic study, the family member who exhibits the disorder of interest.

serotonin Neurotransmitter (chemical messenger in the nervous system) implicated in drinking, eating, and sex, among other drive-related behaviors.

PREVIEW QUESTIONS

1. According to Milam and Ketcham, what are the practical and moral implications of viewing alcoholism as a disease?
2. According to Milam and Ketcham, what are the major strengths and weaknesses of the AA approach?
3. According to Milam and Ketcham, what are the five major physiological factors that can increase an individual's propensity for alcoholism? What is the research evidence for each of these five factors?
4. According to Peele, what are the six major assumptions of the disease model of alcoholism?
5. What are Peele's major criticisms of the so-called loss-of-control phenomenon among alcoholics?
6. What are Peele's major criticisms of the genetic data relevant to alcoholism?
7. According to Peele, what does the research evidence on the effectiveness of AA and similar treatments indicate?

JAMES R. MILAM & KATHERINE KETCHAM

Under the influence: A guide to the myths and realities of alcoholism

It's a long road to a good sobriety. But I can wait. I can put one foot in front of the other: Life has meaning if not perfection. I'll be with my family tonight and find joy in being with them. I'll get up tomorrow and go to work—without cold sweat, headache, and misery in just the thought of another day of exertion with another hangover: I don't have life all worked out—I never will, or there would be no challenge to it. But working on the mystery of it has its own rare rewards. There's a chance for happiness now. I didn't have that before.

A RECOVERED ALCOHOLIC

HISTORICAL PERSPECTIVE

In 1804 Thomas Trotter, an Edinburgh physician, wrote a paper stating his belief that habitual drunkenness was a disease:

In medical language, I consider drunkenness, strictly speaking, to be a disease, produced by a remote cause, and giving birth to actions and movements in the living body that disorder the functions of health.[1]

Trotter's essay provoked an explosive controversy that continues to this day. In one sentence, he challenged the moral code of a society, threatened a basic tenet of the Christian church, and questioned the medical profession's traditional lack of involvement with the drunkard. Ever since Trotter, society has been deeply divided over the question: Is alcoholism primarily a physiological disease, or is it, after all, a symptom of character inadequacy and emotional weakness? This is still the root source of conflict and confusion in the alcoholism field today.

The church's vehement opposition to Trotter's essay was based on several points. By elevating "depravity" to the status of "disease" and insisting that the victim was not responsible for his actions, Trotter threatened society's moral code, over which the church stood guardian. Throughout history, the habitual drunkard was considered a sinful and pitiful creature who, preferring vice to virtue, was responsible for his many troubles. This was part of the moral code which proclaimed: Drunkenness is bad; moderation is good. Drunkards are to be pitied and despised; abstainers are virtuous and admirable.

If excessive drinking is a disease, as Trotter proclaimed, the drinker cannot be held responsible for his own actions and is thus protected from moral condemnation and judgment. By shifting the blame from the alcoholic's character to a "remote cause" outside the alcoholic's control, Trotter's new theory confused the lines between "good" (that is, will power, self-control, and moderation) and "evil" (that is, weakness of character, gluttony, and intemperance).

The medical profession was equally upset by Trotter's essay, which suggested that the treatment of this "disease" was mainly their responsibility. The physician's involvement with the drunkard had been limited to treating the physical complications accompanying excessive drinking, performing autopsies, and signing death certificates. The average physician viewed alcoholics with the same mixture of fear and disgust expressed by the rest of society, and most had no desire to spend their time ministering to men and women who presumably lacked motivation and ambition, consorted with unsavory characters, and carelessly threw their lives away in pursuit of debauchery.

Without the moral approval of the church or the professional cooperation of the physician, the fledgling "disease concept" did not catch on. In fact, the first attempts to treat alcoholism as something other than a mental or social aberration encountered fierce and effective opposition. Almost a quarter century after Trotter s essay appeared, Eli Todd, medical superintendent of the Hartford Retreat for the Insane, suggested that it might be better to give "inebriates" a separate retreat rather than lump them with the insane and mentally incompetent. His indignant colleagues forced him to abandon the idea. A similar suggestion by the Connecticut State Medical Society two years later was also hastily scrapped for lack of support.

Not until 1841, when the Washington Home first opened in Boston, was an "institution for inebriates" able to

SOURCE: *Under the Influence: A Guide to the Myths and Realities of Alcoholism*, by James R. Milam, pp. 31–46, 136–142, 1981.

withstand public disapproval and keep its doors open. The next sixty years witnessed an age of enlightenment in the study and treatment of inebriates; by 1900 over fifty public and private facilities had opened for the sole purpose of treating inebriates. In 1870, the American Association for the Cure of Inebriates (soon renamed the Association for the Study of Inebriety) was founded by a group of physicians and superintendents of inebriate asylums. In 1876 the Association launched the Quarterly Journal of Inebriety, which, until it ceased publication in 1914, stimulated research and discussion by publishing hundreds of articles on alcohol-related issues.

Yet despite these significant advances, most people continued to view drunkards as moral degenerates rather than the innocent and unwilling victims of a disease. The church insisted that the chronic inebriate was responsible for his unhappy state and needed the church's moral guidance to be reformed. The belief that alcoholism was a disease failed to ignite the interest of most physicians, and their acceptance of this revolutionary concept was halfhearted, at best.

Almost one hundred years after Trotter's essay first generated heated controversy, the moral and religious attitudes toward drunkards and drunkenness were, if anything, even more intense and intolerant. By the end of the nineteenth century, the burgeoning Temperance movement had organized a crusade against alcohol at the national level, launching attacks from the pulpit with Bibles in hand and hymns of salvation firing passions. The Volstead Act, establishing national Prohibition in 1919, effectively eclipsed further study of alcoholism as a disease. Although Prohibition did reduce total alcohol consumption in the country, it had no apparent effect on alcoholism and thus missed its mark. As typically happens with misguided attempts to legislate morality, Prohibition not only failed to curb the original problem; it added a host of others. Bootlegging, hijacking, and syndicated crime became so widespread that the whole experiment had to be abandoned.

Shortly after the repeal of Prohibition in 1933, an event occurred which reinstated alcoholism as a subject worthy of scientific interest and, at the same time, ushered in the present age of compromise and confusion. In 1935 the fellowship of Alcoholics Anonymous (A.A.) was begun by two men who had been given up as "hopeless" drunkards by their physicians. Both men were able to stay sober, and they went on to help thousands of other alcoholics recover in a program that relied on simple spiritual principles and the compassion and understanding of fellow sufferers to achieve total abstinence from alcohol. A.A. demonstrated for the first time that alcoholics in significant numbers could recover and return to productive, useful lives. Most importantly, it proved that alcoholics, when they stayed sober, were decent, normal human beings and not hopeless degenerates.

The significance of these insights was undermined, however, for A.A. had also embraced the moral attitudes of the day: while asserting that alcoholism is a disease, the program fixed the blame for contracting the disease squarely on the victim. In *Alcoholics Anonymous*, the A.A. "Bible," and in *Twelve Steps and Twelve Traditions*, A.A.'s cofounder Bill Wilson refers repeatedly to "glaring personality defects" and "character flaws" that caused excessive drinking and thus alcoholism:

> We reluctantly come to grips with those serious character flaws that made problem drinkers of us in the first place, flaws which must be dealt with to prevent a retreat into alcoholism once again.[2]

Thus, from its inception, A. A., like the rest of society, has mistaken the psychological consequences of alcoholism for its causes, and the moral approach of the program followed logically. The Christian formula of sin, repentance, and redemption can be clearly seen in A.A.'s Twelve Steps, especially Steps 4 through 7:

> Step 4: Made a searching and fearless moral inventory of ourselves.
> Step 5: Admitted to God, to ourselves, and to another human being, the exact nature of our wrongs.
> Step 6. Were entirely ready to have God remove all these defects of character.
> Step 7: Humbly asked Him to remove our shortcomings.[3]

Despite its moralistic foundation, however, A.A. worked as no other approach to alcoholism had before, and as a long-term sobriety maintenance program, there still is not even a distant rival. Thus A.A. stands as a colossal paradox. The fellowship has undoubtedly been the most powerful force in getting society to accept alcoholism as a treatable disease. Yet at the same time, it has become a powerful obstacle to accepting the otherwise overwhelming evidence that biological factors, not psychological or emotional factors, usher in the disease.

Nevertheless, A.A. has helped tens of thousands of alcoholics to get and stay sober. Inspired by A.A.'s early success, several major developments followed; like A.A., they moved the disease concept forward but also retained the belief that the onset of the disease is caused by defects of character. In 1940, the Quarterly Journal of Studies on Alcohol was established within the Laboratory of Applied Physiology at Yale University. Now titled the Journal of Studies on Alcohol and published by the Rutgers Center of Alcohol Studies at Rutgers University, this publication renewed scientific interest in the physiological and biological aspects of alcoholism, and reestablished alcoholism as a "field" worthy of scientific research. Once again, however, this influential effort was undermined by the age-old assumption that the cause of the disease was to be found in some mysterious character flaw or personality defect.

Having encouraged the development of the Quarterly Journal at Yale, Marty Mann, one of the first women members of A.A., also founded the voluntary lay organization which was later to become the National Council on Alcoholism (NCA). Along with A.A., NCA has helped to spread the idea that alcoholism is a treatable disease, while also maintaining the belief that psychological problems are the primary predisposing factors.

The impact of these developments was enormous, and the church and medical profession were finally forced to modify their positions. One hundred forty-two years after Trotter's essay, the Presbyterian Church became the first religious organization to acknowledge formally alcoholism's status as a disease. Note, however the allowance for moral censure in the qualifying phrase of the proposition accepted at the Church's 158th Assembly in 1946:

> *Once drinking has passed a certain point,* alcoholism is a disease; that is, the drinking cannot be stopped by a mere resolution on the part of the drinker. [Italics added]

The medical profession shuffled its feet for another ten years until the American Medical Association (AMA) finally "voted" alcoholism a disease in 1956. Yet even here the disease concept was seriously compromised, for the main body of the medical profession continued to view alcoholism as a self-inflicted symptom of an underlying psychological inadequacy and relegated treatment of the disease to its psychiatric branch, where it still languishes. . . .

WHY PEOPLE DRINK ALCOHOL

The alcoholic starts drinking the same ways and for the same reasons the nonalcoholic starts drinking. He drinks to gain the effects of alcohol—to feel euphoric, stimulated, relaxed, or intoxicated. Sometimes he drinks to ease his frustrations; other times he drinks to put himself in a good mood. If he is tense, he may drink more than usual in an effort to unwind and get his mind off his troubles; if shy, he may drink to gain confidence; if extroverted, he may drink because he likes the company of other drinkers.

The alcoholic, like the nonalcoholic, is influenced in the way he drinks, where he drinks, how much, and how often he drinks by numerous psychological, social, or cultural factors. He may start drinking to impress his girl friend, to prove he is not afraid of his parent's disapproval, or because he is taunted into it by his friends. He may drink regularly because alcohol makes him laugh and forget his troubles or because he feels self-assured after a few drinks. If his wife has a cocktail every night, he may drink to keep her company. If his coworkers are heavy drinkers, he may learn to drink heavily.

Again like the nonalcoholic, the alcoholic learns to drink a variety of alcoholic beverages, and he develops preferences among beers, wines, and liquors. He learns how much and how fast people ordinarily drink on various occasions, and he learns how well he can "hold his liquor," how much it takes for him to feel good, to get high, or to get drunk.

Alcoholics as well as nonalcoholics may change their drinking habits because of life changes: death of a loved one, divorce, loss of a job. Loneliness, depression, fears, and insecurities may also affect the way a person drinks. *The point is that none of these psychological or social factors are unique to either the alcoholic or nonalcoholic. Members of both groups drink together for the same reasons and with the same reinforcement by alcohol's stimulating and energizing effects.* The same variety of personality traits is found in both groups. Earlier advocates of an "alcoholic personality" have abandoned this hypothesis, and the theory of an "addictive personality" has also been discredited by lack of supportive evidence.

At some point, however, the drinking patterns of both groups begin to diverge. The alcoholic starts to drink more and more often. He does not want to stop drinking once he has started. In the later stages of his drinking, he may keep a six pack of beer in his desk drawer or a pint of whiskey in the glove compartment. He may stop regularly at the corner tavern for a few quick ones after work. He may gulp his first drink or switch to martinis or straight whiskey.

Particular personality traits may become intensified or may undergo bizarre transformations. The sensitive may become insensitive, the extrovert introverted, the gentle violent, the tactful belligerent, and the compassionate uncaring. An early alcoholic is often irritable, moody, and depressed when he is not drinking. He angrily denies that he is drinking too much, blames his drinking on his nagging wife or his slave-driving boss, and stubbornly refuses to stop drinking. His promises to cut down are broken within days or weeks. His marriage slowly and painfully deteriorates, friendships dissolve, and interest in his work wanes.

The alcoholic appears to be using alcohol to solve his problems. His drinking appears to be an effort to drown his depression, forget work or marriage difficulties, obliterate loneliness and insecurities, and ease mounting tensions. *The reality, however, is very different from the appearance. In reality, an abnormal physiological reaction is causing the alcoholic's increasing psychological and emotional problems. Something has gone wrong inside.*

WHY SOME PEOPLE ARE ALCOHOLIC

Researchers have worked relentlessly, detectives on a tough case, to discover exactly what goes wrong. Their accumulated evidence shows that no one mysterious X factor causes alcoholism; no silver bullet exists which can be carefully extracted to make the alcoholic well again. Instead, their studies have uncovered a number of physiological differences between alcoholics and nonalcoholics. When taken together, these "predisposing factors" explain the alcoholic's vulnerability to alcohol and the onset of alcoholism.

The susceptible person must drink, of course, if he is to become addicted to alcohol. If he stops drinking for any reason—religious, cultural, social, or psychological—the disease is arrested. Furthermore, although psychological factors do not cause alcoholism, they can influence the alcoholic's attempts to control his drinking and his reaction to the addiction. A professional athlete trained to believe in the importance of health and fitness may go on the wagon repeatedly in an effort to halt his growing addiction to alcohol. When he starts drinking again, he may suffer crippling feelings of guilt and shame. A lonely and bored widow, on the other hand, may slide helplessly and resignedly into the disease, having few psychological or social incentives to help her fight the addiction.

In other words, while psychological, cultural, and social factors definitely influence the alcoholic's drinking patterns and behavior, they have no effect on whether or not he becomes alcoholic in the first place. *Physiology, not psychology, determines whether one drinker will become addicted to alcohol and another will not.* The alcoholic's enzymes, hormones, genes, and brain chemistry work together to create his abnormal and unfortunate reaction to alcohol. Discussions of the basic predisposing factors to alcoholism—abnormal metabolism, preference, heredity, prenatal influences, and ethnic susceptibilities—follow.

Abnormal Metabolism

Acetaldehyde, the intermediate byproduct of alcohol metabolism, appears to be one of the major villains in the onset of alcoholic drinking. The trouble probably begins in the liver. Charles Lieber, chief of the research program on liver disease and nutrition at the Bronx Veterans Administration Hospital, found that the same amount of alcohol produced very different blood acetaldehyde levels in alcoholics and nonalcoholics. Much higher levels were reached in alcoholics. Lieber theorized that this unusual buildup of acetaldehyde was caused in part by a malfunctioning of the liver's enzymes.[4]

Marc Schuckit, a psychiatrist and researcher at the University of California in San Diego, took this acetaldehyde difference in alcoholics one step further. His studies confirmed that, in alcoholics, the breakdown of acetaldehyde into acetate—the second step in alcohol metabolism—is performed at about half the rate of "normal," i.e., nonalcoholic, metabolism. It is this slowdown in metabolism which apparently causes acetaldehyde to accumulate.[5]

Both Lieber and Schuckit wanted to find out whether this enzyme malfunctioning was caused by heavy drinking or preceded heavy drinking. In other words, they hoped to answer the question: Does the alcoholic drink too much because his body is somehow abnormal or does his body become abnormal because he drinks too much? Lieber discovered that the liver mitochondria in alcoholics are abnormal and unable to change acetaldehyde into acetate at as great a rate as in nonalcoholics. Significantly, this low capacity was evident even in the early stages of heavy alcohol consumption, indicating that the alcoholic's cells are altered before he starts drinking heavily and continually.[6] Schuckit's studies with the offspring of alcoholics also indicate that the metabolic abnormality exists prior to heavy drinking. Like their alcoholic parents, the children of alcoholics (who before this experiment had never drunk alcohol) were unable to convert acetaldehyde to acetate at normal speed.[7] Heredity is clearly implicated in these studies.

Alcoholics, then, appear to have a liver cell malfunction which causes acetaldehyde to accumulate when they drink. Unfortunately for the alcoholic, acetaldehyde is a dangerous substance to have around in any quantity. Directly irritating to the cells and capable of hampering cellular activities, acetaldehyde can also react explosively when combined with other chemical substances. In the liver, Lieber suggests that the rising levels of acetaldehyde disturb many of the intricate activities of the cells, making it even more difficult for them to get rid of acetaldehyde, which, in turn, results in further damage to the cells. The cells may be permanently damaged if acetaldehyde is present in large quantities for long periods of time.

Moreover, acetaldehyde's harmful effects are not confined to the liver. High acetaldehyde levels can inhibit the synthesis of proteins in heart muscle, leading to impaired cardiac function. In the brain, a piling up of acetaldehyde can lead to bizarre and complicated chemical reactions. When acetaldehyde flows through the brain, it competes with other chemical substances known as brain amines (or neurotransmitters) for the attention of certain enzymes. Acetaldehyde wins this competition and, as a result, blocks the enzymes from accomplishing their primary duty of inhibiting the amines' activity.[8]

If acetaldehyde stopped interfering with the brain's chemical activities at this point, addiction to alcohol might never occur. Acetaldehyde, however, is a volatile substance which reacts with just about any other chemical which happens to be in the vicinity. The brain amines, which have been piling up while the acetaldehyde preoccupies their enzyme, interact with acetaldehyde to form compounds called "isoquinolines." These chemical agents are responsible for a number of fascinating and far-reaching events.

Like acetaldehyde, the isoquinolines suppress the enzyme which is responsible for deactivating many of the brain amines. The isoquinolines also release stored brain amines. In mice, they can aggravate alcohol withdrawal symptoms. For alcoholics, the isoquinolines have one characteristic which makes their other properties pale in significance. They are astonishingly like the opiates, and researchers suggest that they may act on the opiate receptors in the brain, thus contributing to the addiction of alcohol.[9]

In summary, addiction to alcohol may, in part, be traced back to a liver enzyme malfunction which results in a buildup of acetaldehyde throughout the body. In the brain, these large amounts of acetaldehyde interact with the brain amines to create the isoquinolines. These mischievous substances may trigger the alcoholic's need to drink more and more alcohol to counter the painful effects of the progressive buildup of acetaldehyde.

Preference for Alcohol

Everyone has a different reaction to the taste and effect of alcohol. Some people appear driven by the desire to drink; some enjoy the taste and effect and so drink whenever they have the chance; others like a drink every once in a while but prefer nonalcoholic beverages most of the time; still others feel sick to their stomachs, dizzy, flushed, or drunk after just one or two drinks. The last group will generally avoid drinking alcohol.

The same range of likes and dislikes for alcohol is found in rats and mice bred to be genetically alike. The DBA strain of mice, for example, are teetotallers. These animals probably find alcohol's taste or effect unpleasant. The C57BL strains, on the other hand, are heavy drinkers and will consistently choose an alcohol solution over a water or sugar and water solution. Other animals are more mixed in their likes and dislikes and can be compared to the typical social drinker who will slowly sip one or two drinks over the course of an evening.

Preference for alcohol is undoubtedly regulated by complicated chemical activities in the brain. In a 1968 experiment, rats dramatically reduced or completely stopped drinking alcohol when given a chemical substance which depleted the brain's supply of serotonin.[10] Serotonin, a brain amine responsible for relaying messages from one brain cell to another, appears to increase the animal's preference for alcohol. The brains of alcohol-seeking mice and rats, for example, contain higher levels of serotonin than the brains of alcohol-avoiding animals. Further, drinking alcohol increases serotonin concentrations in the brains of the animals that show a preference for alcohol but not in those which avoid it.[11]

Serotonin is only one of many chemical substances which regulate how much an animal will drink. Tetrahydropapaveroline (THP), the product of the interaction of acetaldehyde and dopamine, a brain amine similar to serotonin, is another. When THP was injected into rats' brains, it caused rats that normally rejected alcohol to drink excessive amounts.[12] In what the experimenters called an "addictive-like intake," rats injected with THP drank to the point of intoxication and suffered withdrawal symptoms when they stopped drinking. They continued to drink as though to avoid the disagreeable and painful withdrawal symptoms. The animals' behavior, in short, mimicked the alcoholic's drinking behavior.

An animal's initial liking or dislike for alcohol is clearly only one factor involved in a biological predisposition to alcoholism. The THP study shows that preference is not even a necessary factor, since rats which at first refused to drink could be made to drink addictively when THP was injected into their brains. A number of chemical activities in the brain, therefore, appear to be at the roots of addictive drinking. Future research should further clarify the mechanisms of acetaldehyde, the brain amines, and the products of their interaction.

Heredity

Accumulated evidence clearly indicates that alcoholism is hereditary. Professionals and researchers, however, are often reluctant to accept heredity as a major cause of alcoholism, in part because they are committed to the common misconception that alcoholism is caused by social, cultural, and psychological factors. Genes may influence the alcoholic's reaction to alcohol, these professionals admit, but can genes explain every nuance of the alcoholic's behavior? What about his personal problems, including his troubled marriage, financial difficulties, emotional insecurities, and his belligerent refusal to stop drinking? People do not inherit functional, or nonorganic, psychological problems; therefore, if these problems are the causes of alcoholism, as many insist, then obviously alcoholism cannot be hereditary.

Once again, the consequences of alcoholism are confused with the causes. The weight of evidence clearly links alcoholism to heredity. In a recent study, psychiatrist and researcher Donald Goodwin provides clear and strong corroboration that alcoholism is, indeed, passed from parent to child through genes.[13] Goodwin was able to separate hereditary influences from environmental influences by studying the children of alcoholics who were taken from their parents at birth and adopted by nonrelatives. He postulated that if alcoholism were indeed, inherited, these children would have a high rate of alcoholism even though they were not living with their biological alcoholic parent. If environmental influences were more important, the adopted child would be no more likely to become alcoholic than the children of nonalcoholic parents.

Goodwin found that the children of alcoholics do have a much higher risk of becoming alcoholics themselves—four times that of nonalcoholics—despite having no exposure to their alcoholic parent after the first weeks of life. They were also likely to develop the disease earlier in life, usually in their twenties. The children of nonalcoholic parents, on the other hand, showed relatively low rates of alcoholism even if reared by alcoholic foster parents.

In an effort to discover the relationship, if any, between alcoholic drinking and psychiatric problems, Goodwin compared the children of alcoholics with the children of nonalcoholics. The two groups were "virtually indistinguishable" with regard to depression, anxiety neurosis, personality disturbance, psychopathology, criminality, and drug abuse. As already indicated, psychiatric problems are clearly not relevant to the onset of alcoholism.

In a second adoption study, Goodwin compared the sons of alcoholics who were adopted and raised by an unrelated family with their brothers who had been raised by the alcoholic parent. He found that the children raised by the biological alcoholic parent were no more likely to become alcoholic than their brothers who were raised by nonrelatives.

These astonishing findings shatter those theories which insist that the children of alcoholics become alcoholics themselves because they learn bad habits from their parents or model their behavior on that of their alcoholic parent. They also destroy one other misconception—the belief that problem drinking and alcoholism are directly related. The terms "alcohol abuse and alcoholism" are commonly used to imply that the former causes the latter. Most people believe problem drinkers, or those people who use alcohol to solve personal problems, become alcoholics. Problem drinkers, the theory goes, abuse alcohol because they are unhappy, lonely, depressed, angry, hostile, unemployed, divorced, poor, or generally dissatisfied with life. As they drink more and more often for relief, they become addicted to alcohol.

Goodwin not only failed to find this connection between alcoholism and problem drinking; he found an inverse relationship: the children of nonalcoholic parents had a much lower rate of alcoholism but were more likely to be heavy or problem drinkers. As Goodwin summarized the results, "Our findings tend to contradict the oft-repeated assertion that alcoholism results from the interaction of multiple causes—social, psychological, biological. . . . The 'father's sins' may be visited on the sons even in the father's absence."[14] Problem drinking, then, appears to be caused by psychological, emotional, or social problems, while alcoholic drinking is caused by hereditary factors.

Goodwin's studies provide compelling evidence that alcoholics do not drink addictively because they are depressed, lonely, immature, or dissatisfied. They drink addictively because they have inherited a physical susceptibility to alcohol which results in addiction if they drink. Furthermore, this evidence has profound implications for treatment. While it may be possible to teach the problem drinker how to drink in a more responsible way, the alcoholic's drinking is controlled by physiological factors which cannot be altered through psychological methods such as counseling, threats, punishment or reward. In other words, the alcoholic is powerless to control his reaction to alcohol.

Prenatal Influences

When a pregnant woman drinks, the fetus drinks with her. If the mother drinks too much, so does the fetus. The fetus, of course, has no defenses against these large doses of alcohol. The fetal alcohol syndrome (FAS), in which the children of alcoholic mothers suffer from mental retardation, stunted growth, and facial disfigurations such as flattened noses and narrowed eyes, is a well-known and documented reaction of the vulnerable fetus to large and continuous doses of alcohol.

Since alcoholism is hereditary, the fetus that is subjected to large amounts of alcohol may also become addicted while still in the womb. When the baby is born and the umbilical cord supplying alcohol is severed, the newborn child may experience withdrawal symptoms. As one researcher describes it:

> The alcoholic mother who has been drinking heavily through pregnancy and particularly that mother who has actually had acute alcoholic withdrawal during pregnancy may have ingested sufficient alcohol to have developed incipient signs and symptoms of tolerance and physical dependence in the newborn child. . . . Such a child, in addition to having the hypothesized genetic propensity toward alcoholism, has probably been exposed to high levels of alcohol during his intrauterine development. Such a child may actually have developed some level of tolerance and physical dependence during pregnancy and may be born—in a manner similar to that of children of heroin addicts—in an acute alcoholic withdrawal state.[15]

The newborn is, in fact, an alcoholic. Years later when he takes his "first" drink, he may experience an instant reactivation of this addiction. Many alcoholics do appear to be instantly addicted to alcohol from their very first drink, experiencing immediate tolerance changes, craving for alcohol, and withdrawal symptoms when they stop drinking. This "instant alcoholic" may actually have triggered an addiction that began before he was born.

Ethnic Susceptibilities to Alcohol

Extreme differences in alcoholism rates have been found among various ethnic groups. For example, Jews and Italians have low alcoholism rates, about 1 percent, while at the other extreme, Native Americans have extraordinarily high rates, somewhere around 80–90 percent. Once again, physical factors—not psychological, social, or cultural factors—explain these different ethnic susceptibilities to alcohol.

Dr. Bert Vallee and his colleagues at Harvard Medical School have been studying biochemical and genetic aspects of alcoholism. They have isolated fifteen different forms of the alcohol dehydrogenase (ADH) liver enzyme and discovered that the number and variety of these enzymes vary widely from person to person. The complex patterns appear to be genetically controlled, and different racial groups have a typical variation of the number and type of these "isoenzymes." Vallee suspects that each combination of isoenzymes reacts with alcohol differently and determines the person's specific physiological response. Flushing, nausea, violent behavior, sleepiness, and hyperactivity, for example, are probably brought about by the drinker's specific grouping of isoenzymes.[16]

Vallee's findings help to explain the abundance of research showing different physiological reactions to alcohol among various ethnic groups. Fenna, for example, discovered that a group of Native Americans were unable to oxidize and eliminate alcohol as quickly as Caucasians; and Wolff found that Japanese, Koreans, and Taiwanese had aversive reactions including flushing and mild to moderate intoxication with alcohol doses causing no obvious reaction in the majority of Caucasians. He ruled out the possibility that this reaction was acquired or learned by testing Oriental and Caucasian newborn infants and finding similar responses.[17] Researchers have also found higher levels of acetaldehyde, alcohol's highly toxic breakdown product, in Orientals than in Caucasians after drinking alcohol.[18] These high acetaldehyde levels are probably the result of enzyme deficiencies; the flushing and nausea that result could explain why Orientals tend to drink sparingly or not at all.

Another interesting finding of recent research is the discovery that a direct relationship exists between the length of time an ethnic group has been exposed to alcohol and the rate of alcoholism within that group [see Table 1]. Jews and Italians, for example, have had access to large amounts of alcohol for more than 7,000 years, and their alcoholism rate is very low. Alcohol was first introduced in quantity to the northern European countries, including France, Ireland, and the Scandinavian countries, some 1,500 years ago, and the rates of alcoholism are relatively higher there. Native Americans, who suffer from extremely high alcoholism rates, did not have large supplies of alcohol until approximately 300 years ago.[19]

These differences in susceptibility are exactly what we should expect given the fact that alcoholism is a hereditary disease. The implication is that the longer an ethnic group is exposed to alcohol, the lower its members' susceptibility to alcoholism. This relationship is consistent with the principle of natural selection whereby those people with a high genetic susceptibility are eliminated over many generations, resulting in a lower susceptibility rate for the entire group. People with low susceptibility to alcoholism survive and pass on their low susceptibility. Thus, the rate of alcoholism among high susceptibility groups such as Native Americans should lower significantly over time if they continue to drink.

Interbreeding among ethnic groups will also have a dramatic effect on alcoholism rates. If ethnic groups with high susceptibility rates interbreed with ethnic groups with a lower susceptibility, the alcoholism rates for both groups will change. In fact, it has been observed that alcoholism rates among both Jews and Italians are rising steadily as they increasingly interbreed with peoples who have a higher susceptibility to alcoholism.

The scientific evidence clearly indicates an interplay of various hereditary, physiological factors—metabolic, hormonal, and neurological—which work together and in tandem to determine the individual's susceptibility to alcoholism. It would be a mistake to simplify the interactions in the body, making it appear that one specific gene, one enzyme, or one hormone is solely responsible for a chain of events leading in a straight line to physical dependence and addiction. Even a slight difference in the number or type of liver enzymes, for example, could alter a person's drinking patterns, preference, and problems. Yet, while additional predisposing factors to alcoholism will undoubtedly be discovered, abundant knowledge already exists to confirm that alcoholism is a hereditary, physiological disease and to account fully for its onset and progression. . . .

[TABLE 1 Ethnicity and Alcoholism]

Ethnic Group	*Time Exposure*	*Susceptibility to Alcoholism*	*Alcoholism Rate*
Jews, Italians	7,000+ years	Low	Low
Scandinavians, Irish, French	l,500 years	Medium	Medium
North American Indians, Eskimos	300 years	High	High

From James R. Milam, *The Emergent Comprehensive Concept of Alcoholism* (ACA Press, PO. Box 286, Kirkland, WA 98033).

NOTES AND REFERENCES

1. Thomas Trotter, "An Essay, Medical, Philosophical, and Chemical, on Drunkenness and Its Effects on the Human Body."
2. *Twelve Steps and Twelve Traditions*, p. 74. Both *Alcoholics Anonymous* (3rd ed., 1976) and *Twelve Steps and Twelve Traditions (1952)* are published by A.A. World Services, New York, NY 10017.
3. From *Twelve Steps and Twelve Traditions*.
4. Lieber summarized his research in an article titled, "The Metabolism of Alcohol," in the March 1976 issue of *Scientific American*, pp. 25–33. In this article, Lieber suggests that increased microsomal ethanol oxidizing activity (MEOS) in alcoholics is a possible factor in high acetaldehyde levels. Intensified MEOS activity would result in faster metabolism of alcohol to acetaldehyde. For a detailed review of Lieber's research on acetaldehyde levels in alcoholics, and nonalcoholics, see C. S. Lieber, Y. Hasumara, R. Teschke, S. Matsuzaki, and M. Korsten "The Effect of Chronic Etha-

nol Consumption on Acetaldehyde Metabolism," in *The Role of Acetaldehyde in the Actions of Ethanol*, ed. K. O. Lindros and C. J. P Ericksson (Helsinki: Finnish Foundation for Alcohol Studies, vol. 23, 1975), pp. 83–104.

5. Marc A. Schuckit and V. Rayses, "Ethanol Ingestion: Differences in Blood Acetaldehyde Concentrations in Relatives of Alcoholics and Controls," *Science*, vol. 203 (1979), p. 54.
6. Lieber speculated in the *Scientific American* (see n. 4 above) that the high acetaldehyde level may be responsible for altering the mitochondria. He summarized: "The alcoholic may therefore be the victim of a vicious circle: a high acetaldehyde level impairs mitochondrial function in the liver, acetaldehyde metabolism is decreased, more acetaldehyde accumulates and causes further liver damage" (p. 32).
7. Marc Schuckit, "Alcoholism and Genetics: Possible Biological Mediators," in *Biological Psychiatry*, vol. 15 (1980), no. 3, pp. 437–47.
8. Brain amines (or neurotransmitters) are responsible for relaying information from one neuron to another. Each of the 30 different substances known or suspected to be transmitters in the brain (including serotonin, norepinephrine, and dopamine) has a characteristic excitatory or inhibitory effect on neurons. See *Scientific American*, September 1979, pp. 134–49, for more information on the actions of these complex chemical substances.
9. The theory that acetaldehyde, rather than or in addition to alcohol itself, may be responsible for addiction is gaining popularity among researchers. Acetaldehyde's specific actions in the brain have not yet been pinpointed, but several researchers have made intriguing proposals. See V. E. Davis and M. J. Walsh, "Alcohol, Amines, Alkaloids: A Possible Biochemical Basis for Alcohol Addiction," *Science*, vol. 167 (1970), pp. 1005–7; and G. Cohen and M. A. Collins, "Alkaloids from Catecholamines in Adrenal Tissue: Possible Role in Alcoholism," *Science*, vol. 167 (1970), pp. 1749–51.
10. R. D. Myers and W. L. Veale, "Alcohol Preference in the Rat: Reduction Following Depletion of Brain Serotonin," *Science*, vol. 160 (1968), pp. 1469–71.
11. L. Ahtee and K. Eriksson, "5-Hydroxytryptamine and 5-Hydroxyindoleacetic Acid Content in Brain of Rat Strains Selected for Their Alcohol Intake," *Physiology and Behavior*; vol. 8 (1972), pp. 123–26; and J. L. Perhach, Jr., R. H. Cox, Jr., and H. C. Ferguson, "Possible Role of Serotonin in the Voluntary Selection of Ethanol by Mice," *Proceedings of the Federation of American Societies for Experimental Biology*, vol. 32 (1973), p. 697.
12. R. D. Myers and C. L. Melchior, "Alcohol Drinking: Abnormal Intake Caused by Tetrahydropapaveroline in Brain," *Science*, vol. 196 (1977), pp 554–56.
13. Donald Goodwin, Is *Alcoholism Hereditary?* (New York: Oxford University Press, 1976).
14. *Ibid.*, p. 77.
15. B. Kissin and H. Begleiter, eds., *The Biology of Alcoholism* (New York: Plenum Press, 1974), vol. 3, p. 10.
16. In June 1980, Harvard Medical School received a $5.8 million gift from Joseph E. Seagram and Sons, Inc., U.S. subsidiary of the world's largest distiller and winemaker. The gift is to be used for research on the fundamental biological, chemical, and genetic aspects of alcohol metabolism and alcoholism. Dr. Bert Vallee is directing the research supported by the grant. From the *Harvard Gazette*, June 27, 1980.
17. D. Fenna, L. Mix, O. Schaefer, and J. A. L. Gilbert, "Ethanol Metabolism in Various Racial Groups," *Canadian Medical Association Journal*, vol. 105 (1971), pp. 472–75; and P. H. Wolff, "Ethnic Differences in Alcohol Sensitivity," *Science*, vol. 175 (1972), pp. 449–50.
18. Several sources report higher acetaldehyde levels in Orientals than in Caucasians. See M. A. Korsten, S. Matsuzaki, L. Feinman, and C. S. Lieber, "High Blood Acetaldehyde Levels after Ethanol Administration: Differences between Alcoholic and Nonalcoholic Subjects," *New England Journal of Medicine*, vol. 292 (1975), pp. 386–89; J. A. Ewing, B. A. Rouse, and E. D. Pellezzari. "Alcohol Sensitivity and Ethnic Background," *American Journal of Psychiatry*, vol. 131 (1974), pp. 206–10; and T. E. Reed, H. Kalant, R. J. Gibbins, B. M. Kapur, and J. G. Rankin, "Alcohol and Acetaldehyde Metabolism in Caucasians, Chinese and Amerinds," *Canadian Medical Association Journal*, vol. 115 (1976), pp. 851–55.
19. James R. Milam, *The Emergent Comprehensive Concept of Alcoholism* (ACA Press, PO. Box 286, Kirkland, WA 98033).

STANTON PEELE

The diseasing of America: Addiction treatment out of control

AA, treatment centers and alcohol counseling are the only known successful methods of arresting the compulsion to drink or take drugs. Alcoholism was totally untreatable and fatal until 1935, when AA was founded.

—RUTH HARRIS, WOMENSPACE SHELTER PROJECT, CLEVELAND

What we "know" about alcoholism, like the points in Ruth Harris's quote above, has been determined by an active group of proselytizers for AA and the alcoholism movement, most of whom are alcoholics. These advocates have had very specific experiences with drinking. At the same time, many of their experiences and views were distinctive even *before* they became alcoholics and were in fact quite different from those of people *less* likely to become alcoholics. Nonetheless, public opinion surveys show that Americans at large have accepted all or most of the contentions of the modern alcoholism movement. Still, not everyone agrees.

The core beliefs that the alcoholism movement has successfully promulgated are:

1. Alcoholics don't drink too much because they intend to, but only because they can't control their drinking.
2. Alcoholics inherit their alcoholism and thus are born as alcoholics.
3. Alcoholism always grows worse without treatment, so that alcoholics can never cut back or quit drinking on their own.
4. Alcoholism as a disease can strike any individual—it is an "equal-opportunity destroyer"—and respects no social, religious, ethnic, or sexual bounds.
5. Treatment based on AA principles is the *only* effective treatment for alcoholism—in the words of one proponent, a modern medical "miracle"—without which no one can hope to arrest a drinking problem.
6. Those who reject the AA approach for their drinking problems, or observers who contradict any of the contentions about alcoholism listed here, are practicing a special *denial* that means death for alcoholics.

These keynotes to the AA and National Council on Alcoholism perspective existed before any research had been conducted to verify them—they represent folk wisdom. This folk wisdom has come to be accepted by most Americans. For example, according to a 1987 Gallup poll, 87 percent of Americans endorse the idea that alcoholism is a disease (although only 68 percent express *strong* agreement with this idea). This figure has increased steadily, jumping from 79 percent who agreed in 1982, as Americans are told they must accept the "truths" of alcoholism, which are said to represent modern scientific breakthroughs in our understanding of drinking problems. For example, Gallup presented Americans' growing acceptance of the disease viewpoint under the heading "Misconceptions About Alcoholism Succumb to Educational Efforts."[1]

The actual scientific evidence, however, strongly *contradicts* the contentions of the alcoholism movement. For example, the standard wisdom is that AA is unmatched in effectiveness for dealing with alcoholism and that alcoholism would be licked if only everyone joined AA. Certainly, many people who belong to AA tell us that AA stopped them from drinking. However, this no more demonstrates the general effectiveness of AA than testimony that some people decide not to kill themselves after they discover Christ is evidence that Christianity is the cure for suicide. In fact, research has not found AA to be an effective treatment for general populations of alcoholics. Consider the following summary by researchers at the Downstate (New York) Medical Center Department of Psychiatry:

> The general applicability of AA as a treatment method is much more limited than has been supposed in the past. Available data do not support AA's claims of much higher success rates than clinic treatment. Indeed, when population differences are taken into account, the reverse seems to be true.[2]

Not one study has ever found AA or its derivatives to be superior to any other approach, or even to be better than not receiving any help at all for eliminating alcoholism when alcoholics are assigned to different kinds of treatment. At the same time, other methods that have regularly been found superior to AA and other standard therapies for alcoholism have been completely rejected by American treatment programs. To preview the startling proposition that therapies that are universally advocated have already been shown to be ineffective and that more effective approaches are available, consider the prevailing approach to drunk-driving convictions in America—remanding drinking drivers for treatment. Advocates of a humane, informed approach to the problem continually plead for more such referrals and bemoan primitive programs that simply arrest, imprison, or place on probation those caught driving while intoxicated (DWI). Meanwhile, *every comparative study of standard treatment programs versus legal proceedings for drunk drivers finds that those who received ordinary judicial sanctions had fewer subsequent accidents and were rearrested less.*[3]

While standard disease treatments and education programs for drunk drivers have conclusively been shown to fail at their mission, nondisease rehabilitation programs—such as those teaching DWIs social skills (like those needed to reject additional drinks), enhanced personal responsibility in decision making, and methods for drinking moderately—*have* shown beneficial results.[4] Yet almost no such nondisease programs for drunk drivers remain in the United States, and these few are under strong attack. In 1985, the attorney general of New York and the State Division of Alcoholism and Alcohol Abuse attempted to close such a program in Rochester, although the program had operated successfully for years under the auspices of the county DA's office. (Eventually, the New York State Supreme Court ruled in favor of the program, Creative Interventions, mainly on technical grounds.[5])

AA's undeserved status as a universal cure for alcoholism and the beleaguered state of skill-training approaches for drunk drivers are some of the many indicators that alcoholism practices are based on the prejudices of a few rather than on scientific data. That this situation prevails in the United States is clear in a remarkable quote from the current director of the National Institute on Alcohol Abuse and Alcoholism, Enoch Gordis:

> In the case of alcoholism, our whole treatment system, with its innumerable therapies, armies of therapists, large and expensive programs, endless conferences . . . and public relations activities is founded on hunch, not evidence, and not on science. . . . Yet the history of medicine demonstrates repeatedly that unevaluated treatment, no matter how compassionately administered, is frequently useless and wasteful and sometimes dangerous or harmful. The lesson we have learned is that *what is plausible may be false, and what is done sincerely may be useless or worse.* (emphasis in original)[6]

While alcoholism movement experts strive to declare that the dominant American approaches to alcoholism represent the end point of a long process of scientific discovery, other countries have repudiated the disease approach entirely. Consider this quote from British psychiatrist Robin Murray:

> There can be no doubt that current British and American perspectives on alcoholism differ widely. . . . Even R. E. Kendell, one of the British psychiatrists most interested in categorical diagnostic systems, states that for alcoholism it is "increasingly clear that most of the assumptions of the 'disease model' are unjustified and act as a barrier to a more intelligent and effective approach to the problem."[7]

The following is a list of some of the widely promulgated and generally accepted ideas about the disease of alcoholism, along with the research that contradicts them.

LOSS OF CONTROL

The core idea of the AA version of the disease of alcoholism is that alcoholics cannot cease drinking once they start. The first step of AA, admitting that the alcoholic is "powerless over alcohol," means that alcoholics simply cannot regulate their drinking in any way. According to AA, even a single taste of alcohol (such as that in an alcoholic dessert) sets off uncontrollable binge drinking. Alcoholism professionals have attempted to translate AA's view into scientific-sounding terms. For example, in a popular book on alcoholism, *Under the Influence*, James Milam claims: "The alcoholic's drinking is controlled by physiological factors which cannot be altered through psychological methods such as counseling, threats, punishment, or reward. In other words, the alcoholic is powerless to control his or her drinking."[8]

In fact, this statement has been demonstrated to be false by every experiment designed to test it. For example, alcoholics who are not aware that they are drinking alcohol do not develop an uncontrollable urge to drink more.[9] Psychologist Alan Marlatt and his colleagues found that alcoholics drinking heavily flavored alcoholic beverages did not drink excessive amounts—as long as they thought the drinks did not contain alcohol. The alcoholics in this experiment who drank the most were those who believed they were imbibing alcohol—*even when their beverage contained none.*[10] From this study, we see that what alcoholics believe is more important to their drinking than the "facts" that they are alcoholics and that they are drinking alcohol.

Rather than losing control of their drinking, experiments show, alcoholics aim for a desired state of consciousness when they drink.[11] They drink to transform their emotions and their self-image—drinking is a route to achieve feelings of power, sexual attractiveness, or control over unpleasant emotions.[12] Alcoholics strive to attain a particular level of intoxication, one that they can describe before taking a drink. Nancy Mello and Jack Mendelson of Harvard Medical School and McLean Hospital—the former a psychologist and the latter a physician—found that alcoholics would continue working to gain credits with which to buy alcohol until they could stockpile the amount they needed to get as drunk as they wanted. They continued to work for credits as they were undergoing withdrawal from previous binges, even though they could stop and turn in their credits for drink at any time.[13]

Alcoholics are influenced by their environments and by those around them, even when they are drinking and intoxicated. For example, researchers at Baltimore City Hospital offered alcoholics the opportunity to drink whenever they wanted in a small, drab isolation booth. These street inebriates curtailed their drinking significantly in order to spend more time in a comfortable and interesting room among their companions. In these and other studies, alcoholics' drinking behavior was molded simply by the way the alcohol was administered or by the rewards alcoholics received or were denied based on their drinking styles.[14]

What does this research prove? *Alcoholism* is the term we use to describe people who get drunk more than other people and who often suffer problems due to their drinking. Alcoholism exists—overdrinking, compulsive drinking, drinking beyond a point where the person knows he or she will regret it—all these occur. (In fact, these things happen to quite a high percentage of all drinkers during their lives.) But this drinking is *not* due to some special, uncontrollable biological drive. Alcoholics are no different from other human beings in exercising choices, in seeking the feelings that they believe alcohol provides, and in evaluating the mood changes they experience in terms of their alternatives. No evidence disputes the view that alcoholics continue to respond to their environments and to express personal values even while they are drinking.

THE GENETICS OF ALCOHOLISM

AA originally claimed that alcoholics inherit an "allergy" to alcohol that underlies their loss of control when they drink. Today this particular idea has been discarded. Nonetheless, a tremendous investment has been made in the search for biological inheritances that may cause alcoholism, while many grandiose claims have been made about the fruits of this search. In 1987, almost two-thirds of Americans (63 percent) agreed that "alcoholism can be hereditary"; only five years earlier, in 1982, more people had disagreed (50 percent) than agreed (40 percent) with this statement. Furthermore, it is the better educated who agree most with this statement.[15] Yet widely promulgated and broadly accepted claims about the inheritance of alcoholism are inaccurate, and important data from genetic research call into doubt the significance of genetic influences on alcoholism and problem drinking. Moreover, prominent genetic researchers themselves indicate that cultural and environmental influences are the major determinants of most drinking problems, even for the minority of alcoholics who they believe have a genetic component to their drinking.

Popular works now regularly put forward the theory—presented as fact—that the inherited cause of alcoholism has been discovered. In the words of Durk Pearson and Sandra Shaw, the authors of *Life Extension*, "Alcohol addiction is not due to weak will or moral depravity; it is a genetic metabolic defect . . . [just like the] genetic metabolic defect resulting in gout." One version of this argument appeared in the newsletter of the Alcoholism Council of Greater New York:

> Someone like the derelict . . . , intent only on getting sufficient booze from the bottle poised upside-down on his lips . . . [is] the victim of metabolism, a metabolism the derelict is born with, a metabolic disorder that causes excessive drinking.[16]

Is it really possible that street inebriates are destined from the womb to become alcoholics? Don't they really have a choice in the matter, or any alternatives? Don't their upbringings, or their personal and social values, have any impact on this behavior?

Several well-publicized studies have found that close biological relatives of alcoholics are more likely to be alcoholics themselves. The best-known research of this kind, examining Danish adoptees, was published in the early 1970s by psychiatrist Donald Goodwin and his colleagues. The researchers found that male adoptees with alcoholic biological parents became alcoholics three to four times more often than adoptees without alcoholic relatives. This research has several surprising elements to it, however. In the first place, only 18 percent of the males with alcoholic biological parents became alcoholics themselves (compared with 5 percent of those without alcoholic parentage). Note that, accepting this study at face value, the vast majority of men whose fathers are alcoholics do not become alcoholic solely because of biological inheritance.[17]

Some might argue that Goodwin's definition of alcoholism is too narrow and that the figures in his research severely understate the incidence of alcoholism. Indeed, there was an additional group of problem drinkers whom Goodwin and his colleagues identified, and many people might find it hard to distinguish when a drinker fell in this rather than in the alcoholic group. However, more of the people in the problem drinking group did not have alcoholic parents than did! If alcoholic and heavy problem drinkers are combined, as a group they are not more likely to be offspring of alcoholic than of nonalcoholic parents, and the finding of inherited differences in alcoholism rates disappears from this seminal study. One last noteworthy result of the Goodwin team's research: in a separate study using the same methodology as the male offspring study, the investigators did not find that daughters of alcoholic parents more often became alcoholic themselves (in fact, there were more alcoholic women in the group *without* alcoholic parents).[18]

Other studies also discourage global conclusions about inheritance of alcoholism. One is by a highly respected research group in Britain under Robin Murray, dean of the Institute of Psychiatry at Maudsley Hospital. Murray and his colleagues compared the correlation between alcoholism in identical twins with that between fraternal twins. Since the identical pair are more similar genetically, they should more often be alcoholic or nonalcoholic together than twins whose relationships are genetically equivalent to ordinary siblings. No such difference appeared. Murray and his colleagues and others have surveyed the research on inheritance of alcoholism.[19] According to a longtime biological researcher in alcoholism, David Lester, these reviews "suggest that genetic involvement in the etiology of alcoholism . . . is weak at best." His own review of the literature, Lester wrote, "extends and . . . strengthens these previous judgments." Why, then, are genetic viewpoints so popular? For Lester, the credibility given genetic views is "disproportionate with their theoretical and empirical warrant," and the "attraction and persistence of such views lies in their conformity with ideological norms."

Several studies of male children of alcoholics (including two ongoing Danish investigations) have not found that these children drink differently as young adults or adolescents from their cohorts without alcoholic relatives.[20] These children of alcoholics are not generally separated from their parents, and we know that for whatever reason, male children brought up by their alcoholic parents more often will be alcoholic themselves. What this tells us is that these children aren't born as alcoholics but develop their alcoholism over the years. In the words of George Vaillant, who followed the drinking careers of a large group of men over forty years:

> The present prospective study offers no credence to the common belief that some individuals become alcoholics after the first drink. The progression from alcohol use to abuse takes years.[21]

What, then, do people inherit that keeps them drinking until they become alcoholics? Milam asserts in *Under the Influence* that the source of alcoholism is acetaldehyde, a chemical produced when the body breaks down alcohol. Some research has found higher levels of this chemical in children of alcoholics when they drink[22]; other research (like the two Danish prospective studies) has not. Such discrepancies in research results also hold for abnormalities in brain waves that various teams of researchers have identified in children of alcoholics—some find one EEG pattern, while other researchers discover a distinct but different pattern.[23] Psychiatrist Marc Schuckit, of the University of California at San Diego Medical School, found no such differences between young men from alcoholic families and a matched comparison group, leading him to "call into question . . . the replicability and generalizability" of cognitive impairments and neuropsychologic deficits "as part of a predisposition toward alcoholism."[24]

Washington University psychiatrist Robert Cloninger (along with several other researchers) claims that an inherited antisocial or crime-prone personality often leads to both criminality and alcoholism in men.[25] On the other hand, antisocial acting out when drinking, as well as criminality, are endemic to certain social and racial groups—particularly young working-class and ghetto males.[26] The Cloninger view gets into the slippery realm of explaining that the underprivileged and ghettoized are born the way they are. In addition, Schuckit has failed to find any differences in antisocial temperament or impulsiveness to differentiate those who come from alcoholic families and those without alcoholic siblings or parents.[27] Instead, Schuckit believes, one—perhaps *the*—major mechanism that characterizes children of alcoholics is that these children are born with a diminished sensitivity to the effects of alcohol[28] (although—once again—other researchers do not find this to be the case[29]).

In Schuckit's view, children of alcoholics have a built-in tolerance for alcohol—they experience *less* intoxication than other people when drinking the same amounts. (Note that this is the opposite of the original AA view that alcoholics inherit an allergy to alcohol.) In the Schuckit model, alcoholics might unwittingly drink more over long periods and thus build up a dependence on alcohol. But as a theory of alcoholism, where does this leave us? *Why* do these young men continue drinking for the years and decades Vaillant tells us it takes them to become alcoholics? And even if they *can* drink more without experiencing physical effects, why do they tolerate the various drinking problems, health difficulties, family complaints, and so on that occur on the road to alcoholism? Why don't they simply recognize the negative impact alcohol is having on their lives and resolve to drink less? Certainly, some people do exactly this, saying things like "I limit myself to one or two drinks because I don't like the way I act after I drink more."

One insight into how those with similar physiological responses to alcohol may have wholly different predispositions to alcoholism is provided by those who manifest "Oriental flush"—a heightened response to alcohol marked by a visible reddening after drinking that frequently characterizes Asians and Native Americans. Oriental flush has a biochemical basis in that Asian groups display higher acetaldehyde levels when they drink: here, many believe, is a key to alcoholism. But individuals from Asian backgrounds who flush do not necessarily . . . differ in their susceptibility to drinking problems from those who don't flush.[30] Moreover, groups that show flushing have both the *highest* alcoholism rates (Native Americans and Eskimos) and the *lowest* rates (Chinese and Japanese) among ethnic groups in the United States. What distinguishes between how people in these two groups react to the same biological phenomenon? It would certainly seem that Eskimos' and Indians' abnegated state in America and their isolation from the American economic and achievement-oriented system inflate their alcoholism rates, while the low alcoholism rates of the Chinese and Japanese must be related to their achievement orientation and economic success in our society.

Not even genetically oriented researchers (as opposed to popularizers) deny that cultural and social factors are crucial in the development of alcoholism and that, in this sense, alcoholism is driven by values and life choices. Consider three quotes from prominent medical researchers. Marc Schuckit: "It is unlikely that there is a single cause for alcoholism. . . . At best, biologic factors explain only a part of" the alcoholism problem;[31] George Vaillant: "'I think it [finding a biological marker for alcoholism] would be as unlikely as finding one for basketball playing.' . . . The high number of children of alcoholics who become addicted, Vaillant believes, is due less to biological factors than to poor role models";[32] Robert Cloninger: "The demonstration of the critical importance of sociocultural influences in most alcoholics suggests that major changes in social attitudes about drinking styles can change dramatically the prevalence of alcohol abuse regardless of genetic predisposition."[33] In short, the idea that alcoholism is an inherited biological disease has been badly overstated, and according to some well-informed observers, is completely unfounded. . . .

ALCOHOLISM ISN'T DUE TO ANYTHING BUT ALCOHOLISM— ALCOHOLISM AS A "PRIMARY DISEASE"

Members of AA and representatives of the alcoholism movement argue that alcoholism is not the result of other problems that the alcoholic drinks to forget or disguise. Rather, they claim, alcoholism is a self-contained disease that exists independent of other aspects of the alcoholic's life and personal functioning. In this view, alcoholics have no special difficulties other than those produced by their drinking, and improving their lives in any other way aside from getting them to stop drinking will not affect their disease.

At this point, I introduce the personage of George Vaillant, the psychiatrist and author of *The Natural History of Alcoholism*, to whom I have already referred. Vaillant is a remarkable figure in the modern history of alcoholism research. He is actually one of the first epidemiologists to investigate the sources of alcoholism from a disease perspective, as opposed to the social perspective used by the Berkeley Alcohol Research Group. Vaillant emphatically endorses the disease model of alcoholism and of medical treatment for it. He sees alcoholism as a primary disease that has "a life of its own and is not a moral or psychological problem." However, Vaillant's claims are frequently contradicted by his own data.

For example, while Vaillant repeatedly stresses that alcoholism is an independent disease and not a response to some other set of problems, he reports the following research results from his own and other studies:

> The most important single prognostic variable associated with remission among alcoholics who attend alcohol clinics is having something to lose if they continue to abuse alcohol. . . . Patients cited changed life circumstances rather than clinic intervention as most important to their abstinence. . . . Improved working and housing conditions made a difference in 40 percent of good outcomes, intrapsychic change in 32 percent, improved marriage in 32 percent, and a single 3-hour session of advice and education about drinking . . . in 35 percent.[34]

In other words, people get over alcoholism because of changes in other parts of their lives that make it worthwhile to quit, that counterbalance their urge to drink, or that remove the stresses (such as marital problems) that led them to drink alcoholically. Vaillant urges those who want to help alcoholics to "learn to facilitate natural healing processes" since these processes are the key to alcoholic recovery. Yet Vaillant seeks mainly to warn these helpers "*not to interfere* with the recovery process," because his research shows that "it may be easier for improper treatment to retard recovery than for proper treatment to hasten it." More than anything, Vaillant's actual findings are that the course of alcoholism depends mainly on how well people can resolve their life problems. . . .

ALCOHOLISM, THE "EQUAL-OPPORTUNITY" DISEASE

One of the most popular items produced by the alcoholism movement is a poster entitled "The Typical Alcoholic American." It depicts a range of people from different ethnic, racial, and social groups, of different ages, and of both sexes. The point of the poster is that anyone from any background may be alcoholic—a point often driven home in educational programs about alcoholism. Strictly speaking, this idea can be true (although there are virtually no cases of adolescents who demonstrate a physical dependence on alcohol). But there are demographic categories that enhance the possibility of becoming alcoholic so significantly that it is hard to imagine that someone experienced with alcoholism would fail to notice these. Indeed, were it possible to isolate a measurable biological factor that distinguished those at risk for alcoholism as well as the drinker's sex, social class, ethnic background, and disadvantaged minority status, the discoverer of such a mechanism would win the Nobel Prize.

Epidemiologists such as Cahalan and Room have been able to predict extremely well which American men will develop drinking problems based purely on demographic categories: those who live in disadvantaged social settings, blacks and Hispanics, specific religious and ethnic groups, and certain social groups like young working-class men are highly predisposed to problem drinking. Sociologist Andrew Greeley led an investigation at the National Opinion Research Center into "ethnic drinking subcultures" around the country. He found that "there is overwhelming evidence of differences among American ethnic groups and drinking patterns, particularly among Italians, Jews, and Irish."[35] George Vaillant found that the Irish subjects in his study were *seven times* as likely to become alcoholic as their Italian neighbors. Moreover, Italians were more likely than others to moderate their drinking—rather than to abstain—after they *developed* a drinking problem. Vaillant described this Italian-Irish difference as follows: "It is consistent with Irish culture to see the use of alcohol in terms of black or white, good or evil, drunkenness or complete abstinence, while in Italian culture it is the distinction between moderate drinking and drunkenness that is most important."

Others, like James Milam in *Under the Influence*, have proposed farfetched racial theories to account for why the Irish, Indians, and other high-alcoholism groups more often become drunkards. Here, of course, the disease theory—developed to remove the stigma from alcoholism—starts sounding a lot more invidious. Are blacks and Hispanics and Indians and Eskimos in the United States really alcoholics more often because of inherited racial differences? Are lower-class or ghettoized or non-college-bound people really in these positions because of genetic differences that make them prone to drunkenness or criminality? Although proponents do not intend harm, such racial interpretations of human differences can be and have been used in prejudicial and very damaging ways.

Along with social and ethnic differences, gender differences in the incidence of alcoholism are monumental. In every type of measure, from drunk driving to treatment referrals to consumption levels, women display from one-third to one-tenth or less the drinking problems of men. No epidemiological research has ever disputed this fact. Yet contemporary alcoholism specialists frequently bemoan the large number of "hidden" women alcoholics who refuse to seek treatment because of the greater stigma attached to female drunkenness. In this view, *apparent* gender differences in alcoholism rates are the result of women and other groups with a reputation for fewer drinking problems underreporting their drinking problems because they are too ashamed to acknowledge their alcoholism.

Research has established that women with drinking problems are actually *more* likely to seek treatment than men, just as they seek more psychotherapy of every kind. In addition to the lower alcoholism rates for women in general, research finds that alcoholism occurs for middle-class women even less frequently. Once again, any summary of actual findings of research in an area of alcoholism reveals conclusions exactly the opposite of those presented to the public and maintained as gospel by the alcoholism movement. According to Barbara Lex, of the Harvard Medical School, in her exhaustive survey of alcoholism in special populations:

> The stereotype of the typical "hidden" female alcoholic as a middle-aged suburban housewife does not bear scrutiny. The highest rates of problem drinking are found among younger, lower-class women . . . who are single, divorced, or separated.[36]

Without an awareness of such fundamental ethnic, social, and gender differences, it is hard to imagine how a researcher or clinician can make sense out of the most elementary aspects of alcoholism.

Jews have been the object of a similar campaign to uncover hidden alcoholics, marked by the special shame they carry because they belong to a group that is not *supposed* to be alcoholic. Programs like the Chemical Dependency division of Jewish Family Services of Cleveland have energetically mounted campaigns "to deal with whole community denial and to emphasize that the disease can strike any member of the community."[37] In 1980, two sociologists—convinced that the number of Jewish alcoholics was increasing—conducted a survey of Jewish drinking in an upstate New York city. They found no sign that any of their eighty-eight respondents had ever abused alcohol. Following up leads from doctors, alcoholism counselors, and rabbis about Jewish alcoholics, the sociologists never actually located one. Nearly all these informants claimed to know of at most one or two Jewish alcoholics, and one—who reported, "There is an alarming problem with alcoholism in the Jewish community"—claimed that there were five in this city with about ten thousand Jews. In other words, the most dire, unsubstantiated claim was that the Jews in the city had an alcoholism rate of one-twentieth of one percent, or perhaps 0.1 percent of adults.[38]

Interviews by these researchers reveal that Jews have an extreme aversion to problem drinking and problem drinkers. They avoid people who drink too much and/or become obstreperous when they drink, and they make jokes about non-Jews' excessive drinking, embodied in the phrase "*shikker* [drunk] as a goy." What is more, non-Orthodox Jews in this study did not accept the disease theory of alcoholism (It was actually Orthodox Jews, generally lower in socioeconomic status, who were more willing to believe in this disease.) In the words of the authors, "Reform and nonpracticing Jews define alcoholism in terms of psychological dependence and view suspected alcoholics with condemnation and blame."[39] If they suddenly were to accept the idea that problem drinking is the result of an unavoidable, inbred biological mechanism, one wonders if they would then begin to show the rates of alcoholism common to other ethnic groups in the United States!

The modern alcoholism movement insists that all people recognize that alcoholism is a disease, and it emphasizes the need for a value-free view of alcoholism. Jews and other groups with extremely low alcoholism rates (like the Chinese) avoid alcohol problems within a very different social context. These cultures divest alcohol of its magical powers and instead incorporate drinking in a low-key way in a family context where the young drink mild alcoholic beverages in the company of parents and older relatives. They disapprove strongly of overdrinking, especially when it leads to inappropriate behavior. There is a strong moralism here, but the moralism is not toward alcohol as evil incarnate; it is toward larger values of community, proper deportment, and self-control. Sociologist Milton Barnett describes the drinking in New York City's Chinatown:

They drink and become intoxicated, yet for the most part drinking to intoxication is not habitual, dependence on alcohol is uncommon and alcoholism is a rarity. . . . The children drank, and they soon learned a set of attitudes that attended the practice. While drinking was socially sanctioned, becoming drunk was not. The individual who lost control of himself under the influence of liquor was ridiculed and, if he persisted in his defection, ostracized.

Barnett examined the police blotters in the Chinatown police district between the years 1933 and 1949; among 15,515 arrests, he found not one record of public drunkenness.[40]

It's hard to understand what people mean when they discount cultural differences in alcoholism and insist that those groups with apparently low alcoholism rates are merely disguising their drinking problems out of shame. Sometimes they argue that they know an Italian alcoholic, or that there are French alcoholics in the Paris subways and Jewish alcoholics in Tel Aviv, or that some Jews have joined AA. *Yet there is no aspect of drinking and alcoholism more self-evident than that it varies tremendously across groups, particularly ethnic groups.* Indeed, Jellinek himself, in *The Disease Concept of Alcoholism*, was convinced that cultural differences are fundamental, major, and crucial to the nature of alcoholism.

When one sees a film like *Moonstruck*, the benign and universal nature of drinking in New York Italian culture is palpable on the screen. If one can't detect the difference between drinking in this setting, or at Jewish or Chinese weddings, or in Greek taverns, and that in Irish working-class bars, or in Portuguese bars in the worn-out industrial towns of New England, or in run-down shacks where Indians and Eskimos gather to get drunk, or in Southern bars where men down shots and beers—and furthermore, if one can't connect these different drinking settings, styles, and cultures with the repeatedly measured differences in alcoholism rates among these same groups, then I can only think one is blind to the realities of alcoholism.

THE INFALLIBILITY OF AA AND MEDICAL TREATMENT FOR ALCOHOLISM

Although alcoholism is billed as an *incurable* disease, we are told that there *is* effective medical treatment for it. Private treatment centers claim remarkable remission rates of 70, 80, and 90 percent. Meanwhile, Father Martin, the lecturing alcoholic priest, calls AA a "modern medical miracle," and one often hears claims that *everyone* who *seriously* embarks on an AA program will become sober. Along with television specials about the treatability of alcoholism, we now have a popular feature-length film, *Clean and Sober*, that trumpets the success and importance—the essentialness—of getting treated for alcohol and drug abuse.

Yet the research on treatment paints a very different picture. It has been remarkably hard to find systematic proof that treatment for alcoholism and other addictions accomplishes *anything at all*. The discrepancy between grandiose claims by treatment centers and the research results occurs because treatment centers cannot be counted on to do assessments of their programs that truly take into account the number of people who drop out of their programs; whether patients remain sober after leaving the treatment center; how different their patients are from average alcoholics (since well-off, employed, and middle-class patients have a superior prognosis under any circumstances); and how often people cut back or stop drinking on their own even if they don't enter treatment.

When researchers trace every case that enters treatment (including those who drop out) and compare treated populations with comparable groups of untreated alcoholics, the results often surprise even the treatment advocate. Consider George Vaillant's reactions to his research results for the patients he treated in Cambridge Hospital with an AA-based program:

It seemed perfectly clear that by meeting the immediate individual needs of the alcoholic . . . , by disregarding "motivation," by turning to recovering alcoholics rather than to Ph.D.'s for lessons in breaking self-detrimental and more or less involuntary habits, and by inexorably moving patients from dependence upon the general hospital into the treatment system of AA, I was working for the most exciting alcohol program in the world.

But then came the rub. Fueled by our enthusiasm, I . . . tried to prove our efficacy. Our clinic followed up our first 100 detoxification patients . . . every year for the next 8 years. . . . After initial discharge, only 5 patients in the Clinic sample *never* relapsed to alcoholic drinking, and there is *compelling evidence that the results of our treatment were no better than the natural history of the disease*. (emphasis added)[41]

What Vaillant did was to compare his treatment results over eight years with remission rates in "natural history" studies of alcoholics, in which drinking alcoholics were simply followed in their natural settings for a number of years. Certainly, a percentage of Vaillant's treated patients were not actively alcoholic when followed up eight years later. Only this percentage was not significantly different from that for untreated alcoholics. Remarkably, in this book that is cited as a beacon of defense for the often-assailed efficacy of medical treatment for alcoholism, the author—a research psychiatrist—reveals that alcoholics who are left to their own devices do about as well as did those in his expensive treatment program! Why, we may wonder, did Vaillant begin his book by indicating that "in order to *treat* alcoholics effectively we need to invoke the model of the medical practitioner"? (We may also wonder if Vaillant is any more skeptical about "turning to recovering alcoholics for lessons in breaking self-detrimental and more or less involuntary habits.")

Why does everyone believe AA and related treatments for alcoholism are so tremendously successful? The universal praise for AA focuses on its successes and disregards its failures, while we hear little about the successful recovery of those who don't attend AA. People who overcome drinking problems on their own, despite their numbers, are not an organized and visible group on the American alcoholism landscape. For example, George Vaillant found that many of his alcohol abusers cut back their drinking—nearly all without treatment. But even a solid majority of those among Vaillant's subjects who quit drinking altogether did not join AA. Yet not one of the successful cases of remission Vaillant highlights in his book involves a person who quit a drinking problem without AA or treatment—Vaillant simply ignores the bulk of his data when it comes to his case studies.

In order to evaluate a treatment's *general* effectiveness, research must assign patients randomly to different treatments and/or to a group that receives no treatment (called a control group). Two psychologists, William Miller and Reid Hester, reported every controlled study of alcoholism treatment—that is, studies that employed various treatment and no-treatment comparison groups.[42] These researchers discovered only two controlled studies of AA's effectiveness. Keith Ditman, a physician and head of the Alcoholism Research Clinic at UCLA in the 1960s, studied outcomes for three groups of alcoholics—those assigned by a court either to AA, to an alcoholism clinic, or to an untreated control group.[43] Forty-four percent of the control group were not rearrested in the follow-up period, compared with only 31 percent of AA clients and 32 percent of clinic clients. In the other controlled study of AA, Jeffrey Brandsma and his colleagues reported in 1980 that those randomly assigned to AA engaged in binge drinking significantly more frequently at three months than those assigned either to the nontreatment control group or to other therapies. (At twelve months they did as well, but no better, than the other groups.)[44]

Nor does comparative research find that group counseling sessions, such as those portrayed in the film *Clean and Sober*, are better for recovery than doing nothing. Three researchers have evaluated the most popular group technique in alcoholism and addiction treatment, confrontation therapy, in comparison with other group therapies, from transactional analysis to T-groups. Confrontation therapy is based on the Synanon "game," in which one member of the group at a time is put on the hot seat and has all his or her defenses shot down by other group members. While all the other group therapy techniques in this study came out even in the evaluations, confrontation therapy was found to produce the most significant negative outcomes, requiring psychiatric treatment for some group members.[45]

In addition to AA, group, and confrontation therapy, Miller and Hester found that alcoholism education, drug therapy, and individual alcoholism counseling have not shown positive results in controlled studies. However, the standard treatments for alcoholism in the United States consist entirely of these therapies for which Miller and Hester found no evidence of effectiveness! In the researchers' words, "American treatment of alcoholism follows a standard formula that appears impervious to emerging research evidence, and has not changed significantly for at least two decades." Miller and Hester's survey also showed that hospital (or inpatient) treatment is no better than far less expensive outpatient treatment.[46] As a 1987 *Science* article also indicated, a large body of research has established that intensity of treatment has no bearing on results. Instead, the *Science* article summarizes, the best predictors of patient outcome are the characteristics of the patient who enters the treatment.[47]

Miller and Hester did find a number of therapies that have shown better results than chance or natural recovery: therapy that conditions aversive reactions to drinking, behavioral self-control training, marital and family therapy, social skills training, and stress management. A therapy that showed particular effectiveness with a group of hospitalized alcoholics was the community reinforcement approach, which offered training in problem solving and job skills, behavioral family therapy, and social skills training. The community reinforcement approach would seem to address the natural processes that Vaillant found were the keys to remission in alcoholism. Yet the therapies that have been shown to be effective, like the community reinforcement approach, exist only in research studies and are not used as standard treatments practically anywhere in the United States.

In addition to the most effective types of treatment, another question is how we should measure the results of treatment. And the most controversial question of all in the alcoholism field is whether alcoholics can or should drink again, perhaps with the goal of moderating their drinking. In the United States (unlike most other countries), virtually no treatment centers allow nonabstinence alternatives. Nonetheless, all systematic treatment assessments (like Vaillant's) have found that nearly all alcoholics drink again following treatment and that some can sustain moderate drinking for long periods when they do drink again. At the same time, most alcoholics who drink again return to their previous levels of alcoholism. Is there some way to build upon the group who manages to continue drinking at less severe levels to get more of the alcoholics who perpetually relapse to moderate their drinking?

Dr. Edward Gottheil (who holds both an M.D. and a Ph.D. in psychology) of Jefferson Medical College reported that 33 to 59 percent of patients engaged in some moderate drinking during a two-year follow-up of alcoholism treatment at a VA hospital. Moreover, only 8 percent of this hospitalized group actually abstained throughout the two years. Gottheil commented:

> If the definition of successful remission is restricted to abstinence, these treatment centers cannot be considered especially effective and would be difficult to justify from cost-benefit analyses. If the remission criteria are relaxed to include . . . moderate levels of drinking, success rates increase to a more respectable range. . . . [Moreover] when the moderate drinking groups were included in the remission category, remitters did significantly and consistently better than nonremitters at subsequent follow-up assessments.[48]

Although Gottheil's findings about abstinence following treatment are typical, his conclusions are anything but acceptable in American alcoholism treatment. That is, studies that find hardly any remission due to strict abstinence criteria still refuse to consider the possibility that patients might improve while continuing to drink. One remarkable illustration of this is a highly publicized study by John Helzer, of the Washington University Department of Psychiatry, and his colleagues.[49] The most notorious result of this study, published in the prestigious *New England Journal of Medicine* and widely quoted in newspapers around the country, is that a minuscule *1.6 percent* of the alcoholics treated at a hospital subsequently became moderate drinkers.

In addition to the 1.6 percent of alcoholics who drank moderately and regularly throughout the three years of this study, an additional 4.6 percent of treated alcoholics drank moderately for up to thirty of those thirty-six months and abstained the rest of the time. In other words, these treated alcoholics drank moderately but not in *every* month of the three years; Helzer et al. therefore did not categorize them as moderate drinkers. Furthermore, the researchers discovered that 12 percent of treated alcoholics reported that they had had more than six drinks three times in one month in the previous three years but had had no drinking problems. The investigators were very careful to scrutinize any claims by patients that they had drunk without problems—the researchers questioned those who knew such patients and checked hospital and police records. Nonetheless, despite the absence of information to contradict these former patients' claims, the investigators decided that they were denying their continued alcoholic drinking.

Consider the overall results of the Helzer et al. study: 6 percent of treated alcoholics never got drunk but drank lightly over the previous three years; another 12 percent sometimes drank heavily but reported no dependence symptoms and were not discovered to have alcohol problems. Yet the researchers indicated that moderate drinking by former alcoholics was next to impossible to attain. Clearly, one might give these data a different cast. One could say that 18 percent of these hospitalized alcoholism patients drank sometimes but were no longer drinking alcoholically (compared with the 15 percent who abstained). When the notorious Rand Report presented almost exactly the same results in two studies in 1976 and 1980,[50] the National Council on Alcoholism attempted to suppress the report before publication and viciously attacked it in the press after it appeared.[51]

Of course, we need to know what is best for the alcoholic patient in assessing these data. That is, how well did these alcoholic patients do, once these investigators discarded the possibility of moderate-drinking outcomes? The overall prognosis for alcoholics treated in the hospitals Helzer et al. studied was shockingly bad following treatment. Before reciting these statistics, we must keep in mind that not all alcoholic patients in Helzer et al.'s study actually received alcoholism treatment; in fact, only one of four groups did. This group had the lowest remission rate of the four! Twice as many alcoholic patients treated in a medical-surgical ward were in remission from alcoholism when assessed after treatment as those who actually received alcoholism treatment: only 7 percent of those in the alcoholism treatment unit survived and were judged to be in remission from five to eight years after treatment.

Thus, in a study widely taken to legitimize standard alcoholism treatment in America, *less than 10 percent of those treated specifically for alcoholism survived and were not drinking alcoholically five to eight years after receiving treatment*. The percentage of alcoholics aided in recovery by the hospital treatment in this study is actually far smaller than those Vaillant found when he examined natural-history studies of alcoholism. In this sense, the parading of minimal moderate-drinking outcomes in a setting where people were discouraged from believing they could moderate their drinking seems almost bizarre, as though the researchers and hospital staff were proud of eliminating one category of remission while finding they could not encourage any other. This is not the stuff of which announcements of great medical breakthroughs of the past were made.

THE CATCH-22 OF DENIAL

What if you are told you are an alcoholic and that you must abstain for life, and you don't agree? Then you are, according to treatment wisdom, practicing denial. Many, many people have been told they drink too much or that they are alcoholic. Scott Peck, a psychiatrist and author of the book *The Road Not Taken*, once remarked in an interview in *People* magazine that he regularly drank at home in the evening and that as a result he had had to deal with accusations that he was an alcoholic. After careful consideration, Peck rejected this idea. Many people without Peck's confidence, however, may eventually accept others' characterizations of their drinking or drug use. If, on the other hand, they continue to disagree with such diagnoses, this denial can then be used as *evidence* that they are really alcoholic or addicted. Modern treatment philosophy insists that denial is a keystone of alcoholism and must be attacked before recovery can occur.

Yet we have seen that people from different cultural backgrounds and with varied personal experiences may view drinking and alcoholism very differently. The picture of different views of alcoholism does not indicate that those who don't accept that they have a "disease" should be attacked and converted to a particular treatment's point of view. Nonetheless, the standard approach in the alcoholism movement is to bombard problem drinkers with the disease message until their previous beliefs are exorcised and, thus purified, they can join the movement. Often this approach backfires, since people tend to reject communications that attack their existing self-conceptions. But if people should refuse or drop out of or fail at treatment, then the supposedly benign model that alcoholism is a disease blames the drinkers for their failures—after all, they were told not to drink.

A group of studies have questioned people about their beliefs about drinking problems for which they are seeking treatment and their goals for treatment. In direct opposition to the denial hypothesis, three research teams in Britain have all found that problem drinkers' beliefs that they are capable of moderating their drinking and their lack of involvement in previous abstinence training are crucial factors in managing to control their drinking.[52] Those more oriented toward abstinence succeed better at totally abstaining. These British findings held for drinkers *no matter how dependent on alcohol they were*. In other words, people respond best to treatment that builds on their existing perceptions and experiences. This model applies as well, of course, to the people who are comfortable in AA.

Whether people seek help at all for a drinking problem is another decision steeped in people's views of themselves and the world. Barry Tuchfeld interviewed former alcoholics who had quit or reduced their drinking on their own.[53] Most had simply refused to seek help from some outside agency like AA or a therapist:

> I'd never consider going to a doctor or minister for help. Good Lord, no! That would make me drink twice as much.
>
> The one thing I could never do is go into formal rehab. For me to have to ask somebody else to help with a self-made problem, I'd rather drink myself to death.
>
> I would sit there and listen to their stories . . . and I couldn't fit myself into their patterns.

Certainly there are people who say they are going to improve on their own and don't do so. But in the cases Tuchfeld investigated, people found their own routes to recovery and made them work. On the other hand, there are also those in treatment who claim they are trying to abstain or that they are abstaining but who are not. One cannot compare the imperfections of those rejecting treatment or trying to cut back their drinking with some rose-colored idea that all those who *go* to treatment are successfully abstaining. As Griffith Edwards, Britain's leading addiction researcher, asserts: "the number of times members have 'slipped' since joining AA [the majority of his AA subjects had done so] serves to emphasize that AA is as much a society of alcoholics who are having difficulty in remaining sober as it is one in which they are staying off drink."[54]

AND RESEARCHERS WHO DENY THE "TRUTHS" OF ALCOHOLISM MUST BE CRAZY TOO

While problem drinkers may be assailed for denying the "truths" about alcoholism—particularly that they need treatment—researchers in the field who deny these truths can encounter even more trouble. (I think I can speak from personal experience about this.) Psychologists and psychiatrists who have practiced controlled-drinking therapy and sociologists who report moderate drinking by hospital patients who have been *told* to abstain have had their funding suspended, have been castigated and vilified in the press, and have been accused by treatment spokespeople of causing the deaths of many alcoholics.[55] When a study was published by the Rand Corporation reporting that a strong minority of treated alcoholics return to drinking but reduce or eliminate their drinking problems, one critic reported that he had "learned that some alcoholics have resumed drinking as a result of . . . the Rand study" and that "this could mean death or brain damage for these individuals."[56] The implication was that perhaps such researchers should be jailed.

Consider, on the other hand, the following description of the Rand results in the 1985 book *Alcohol Use and Abuse in America* by Jack Mendelson and Nancy Mello:

> There have been an increasing number of clinical reports that some former alcoholics can drink socially and function well for periods of two and one-half to eleven years. Many clinicians have reported that alcoholics who drink moderately are better adjusted and have better social functioning than ex-alcoholic abstainers. Despite this gradually accumulating data base, the 1976 publication of . . . the Rand Report was responded to with outrage by many self-appointed spokesmen for the alcoholism treatment community. . . . When this national sample was followed again after four years, there were no significant differences in relapse rates between alcohol abstainers and nonproblem drinkers. . . .
>
> It is of some interest to compare the presumed data base for Jellinek's original formulation of the notion of "craving" and "loss of control" [with that of the Rand study]. . . . Jellinek was an American pioneer in alcoholism studies. In 1946, Jellinek analyzed responses to a questionnaire circulated by Alcoholics Anonymous and concluded from the 98 responses received that "loss of control means that as soon as a small quantity of alcohol enters the organism . . . the drinker has lost the ability to control the quantity [he will drink]." . . . [In comparison, re-

searchers] at the Rand Corporation chose a representative random sample of 14,000 clients . . . of geographically and demographically diverse patients.[57]

Yet the Rand data are disregarded and Jellinek's work is gospel in the alcoholism field. Mendelson and Mello are preeminent alcoholism researchers and editors of the most important journal in the alcoholism field (the *Journal of Studies on Alcohol*). However, few lay people or treatment professionals know of their views. For reasons that may by now be clear, those sympathetic to nondisease viewpoints in the United States present their ideas gingerly. As a result, the dogma that alcoholism is a disease goes unquestioned. George Vaillant, despite his own contrary data, simply quotes received opinion:

> The American Medical Association, American Psychiatric Association, American Public Health Association, American Hospital Association, American Psychological Association, National Association of Social Workers, World Health Organization, and the American College of Physicians have now each and all officially pronounced alcoholism as a disease. The rest of us can do no less.[58]*

Where has all this unanimity about alcoholism led us? We certainly don't seem to be eliminating alcoholism, despite multiplying again and again the money, effort, and people we invest in treatment and education. For one thing, many people refuse or drop out of treatment or relapse (like Joan Kennedy, who is far more typical of outcomes from treatment than Betty Ford). We rarely hear from the many people who fail at conventional treatments. Nor do we hear from those who refuse to enter treatment—except as dreaded examples of the phenomenon of "denial." We also don't hear much on public service announcements from those who moderate their drinking or, heaven forbid, their drug use. When Kareem Abdul Jabbar mentioned in his 1983 autobiography, *Giant Steps*, that he used drugs in college, reviewers were highly critical. But if he had lost control, become addicted, and been suspended from basketball while he entered treatment, he could have become a role model for our children.

*This statement is wrong in at least one particular: although the National Council on Alcoholism regularly reports that the American Psychological Association (APA) has taken the position that alcoholism is a disease, the APA has in fact never done so.

NOTES

1. These data are from 1982 and 1987 Gallup polls. The Gallup organization summarized these findings in "Misconceptions about alcoholism succumb to educational efforts," *The Gallup Report No. 265*, October 1987, 24–31.
2. F. Baekeland, L. Lundwall, and B. Kissin, "Methods for the treatment of chronic alcoholism: A critical appraisal," in *Research Advances in Alcohol and Drug Problems, vol.* 2, eds. R. J. Gibbons et al. (Wiley, 1975), 306.
3. R. E. Hagen, R. L. Williams, and E. J. McConnell, "The traffic safety impact of alcohol abuse treatment as an alternative to mandating license controls," *Accident Analysis and Prevention* 11(1979):275–91; D. F. Preusser, R. G. Ulmer, and J. R. Adams, "Driver record evaluation of a drinking driver rehabilitation program," *Journal of Safety Research* 8(1976):98–105; P. M. Salzberg and C. L. Klingberg, "The effectiveness of deferred prosecution for driving while intoxicated," *Journal of Studies on Alcohol* 44(1983):299–306.
4. R. A. Brown, "Conventional education and controlled drinking education courses with convicted drunken drivers," *Behavior Therapy* 11(1980): 632–42; S. H. Lovibund, "Use of behavior modification in the reduction of alcohol-related road accidents," in *Applications of Behavior Modification*, eds. T. Thompson and W. S. Dockens III (Academic Press, 1975).
5. "In the matter of Creative Interventions," State of New York Supreme Court County of Monroe, Decision Index #8700/85.
6. E. Gordis, "Accessible and affordable health care for alcoholism and related problems: Strategy for cost containment," *Journal of Studies on Alcohol* 48(1987):579–85.
7. R. M. Murray et al., "Economics, occupation and genes: A British perspective" (Paper presented at the American Psychopathological Association, New York, March 1986), 1–2.
8. J. R. Milam and K. Ketcham, *Under the Influence: A Guide to the Myths and Realities of Alcoholism* (Bantam Books, 1983), 42.
9. J. Merry, "The 'loss of control' myth," *Lancet* 1(1966):1257–58; J. Langenbucher and P. E. Nathan, "The 'wet' alcoholic: One drink . . . then what?" in *Identifying and Measuring Alcoholic Personality Characteristics*, ed. W. M. Cox (Jossey-Bass, 1983).
10. G. A. Marlatt, B. Demming, and J. B. Reid, "Loss of control drinking in alcoholics: An experimental analogue," *Journal of Abnormal Psychology* 81(1973):223–41 .
11. N. K. Mello and J. H. Mendelson, "A quantitative analysis of drinking patterns in alcoholics," *Archives of General Psychiatry* 25(1971):527–39.
12. G. A. Marlatt, "Alcohol, the magic elixir," in *Stress and Addiction, eds.* E. Gottheil et al. (Brunner/Mazel, 1987).
13. N. K. Mello and J. H. Mendelson, "Drinking patterns during work-contingent and non-contingent alcohol acquisition," *Psychosomatic Medicine* 34(1972): 1116–21.
14. G. Bigelow, I. A. Liebson, and R. Griffiths, "Alcoholic drinking: Suppression by a brief time-out procedure," *Behavior Research and Therapy* 12(1974):107–15; M. Cohen, I. A. Liebson, L. A. Faillace, and R. P. Allen, "Moderate drinking by chronic alcoholics: A schedule-dependent phenomenon," *Journal of Nervous and Mental Disorders* 153 (1971):434–44.
15. Gallup poll, "Misconceptions."
16. J. Mason, "The body: Alcoholism defined," *Update* (Alcoholism Council of Greater New York), January 1985, 4–5.
17. D. W. Goodwin, F. Schulsinger, I,. Hermansen et al. "Alcohol problems

in adoptees raised apart from alcoholic biological parents," *Archives of General Psychiatry* 28(1973):238–43.

18. D. W. Goodwin, F. Schulsinger, J. Knop et al. "Alcoholism and depression in adopted-out daughters of alcoholics," *Archives of General Psychiatry* 34(1977):751–55.
19. D. Lester, "Genetic theory: An assessment of the heritability of alcoholism," in *Theories of Alcoholism*, eds. C. D. Chaudron and D. A. Wilkinson (Addiction Research Foundation, 1988); R. M. Murray, C. A. Clifford, and H. M. D. Gurling, "Twin and adoption studies: How good is the evidence for a genetic role?" in *Recent Developments in Alcoholism*, vol. 1, ed. M. Galanter (Plenum, 1983); J. S. Searles, "The role of genetics in the pathogenesis of alcoholism," *Journal of Abnormal Psychology* 97(1988): 153–67.
20. A. I. Alterman, J. S. Searles, and J. G. Hall, "Failure to find differences in drinking behavior as a function of familial risk for alcoholism," *Journal of Abnormal Psychology* 98(1989):50–53; J. Knop, D. W. Goodwin, T. W. Teasdale et al., "A Danish prospective study of young males at high risk for alcoholism," and V. E. Pollock, J. Volavka, S. A. Mednick et al., "A prospective study of alcoholism," both in *Longitudinal Research in Alcoholism*, eds. D. W. Goodwin et al. (Kluwer-Nijhoff, 1984).
21. G. E. Vaillant, *The Natural History of Alcoholism* (Harvard University Press, 1983), 106.
22. M. A. Schuckit and V. Rayses, "Ethanol ingestion: Differences in blood acetaldehyde concentrations in relatives of alcoholics and controls," *Science* 213(1979):54–55.
23. S. Peele, "The implications and limitations of genetic models of alcoholism and other addictions," *Journal of Studies on Alcohol* 47(1986):63–73.
24. M. A. Schuckit et al., "Neuropsychological deficits and the risk for alcoholism," *Neuropsychopharmacology* 1(1987):45–53.
25. C. R. Cloninger, M. Bohman, S. Sigvardsson et al. "Psychopathology in adopted-out children of alcoholics," in *Recent Developments in Alcoholism*, vol. 3, ed. M. Galanter (Plenum, 1985).
26. D. Cahalan and R. Room, *Problem Drinking Among American Men* (Rutgers Center of Alcohol Studies, 1974).
27. M. A. Schuckit, "A comparison of anxiety and assertiveness in sons of alcoholics and controls," *Journal of Clinical Psychiatry* 43(1982):238–39; "Extroversion and neuroticism in young men at higher and lower risk for the future development of alcoholism," *American Journal of Psychiatry* 140(1983):1223–24.
28. M. A. Schuckit, "Ethanol-induced changes in body sway in men at high alcoholism risk," *Archives of General Psychiatry* 42(1985):375–79; B. W. Lex, S. E. Lukas, N. E. Greenwald, and J. Mendelson, "Alcohol-induced changes in body sway in women at risk for alcoholism," *Journal of Studies on Alcohol* 49 (1988):346–56.
29. C. T. Nagoshi and J. R. Wilson, "Influence of family alcoholism history on alcohol metabolism, sensitivity, and tolerance," *Alcoholism: Clinical and Experimental Research* 11(1987): 392–98.
30. R. C. Johnson et al., "Cultural factors as explanations for ethnic group differences in alcohol use in Hawaii," *Journal of Psychoactive Drugs* 19 (1987):67–75.
31. M. A. Schuckit, "Subjective responses to alcohol in sons of alcoholics and control subjects," *Archives of General Psychiatry* 41(1984):833.
32. "New insights into alcoholism," *Time*, 25 April 1983, 64, 69.
33. C. R. Cloninger et al., "Inheritance of alcohol abuse," *Archives of General Psychiatry* 38(1981):867.
34. Vaillant, *Natural History*, 188–192.
35. A. M. Greeley, W. C. McCready, and G. Theisen, *Ethnic Drinking Subcultures* (Praeger, 1980).
36. B. W. Lex, "Alcohol problems in special populations," in *The Diagnosis and Treatment of Alcoholism*, 2nd ed., eds. J. H. Mendelson and N. K. Mello (McGraw-Hill, 1985), 96–97.
37. S. Abrams, "Denial comes first: Discussing Jewish reaction to chemical dependency," *Cleveland Jewish News*, 27 December 1985, 16; D. Bean, "Jewish addicts admit it: Not-to-worry myth busted," *Cleveland Plain Dealer*, 1 June 1986, 32A.
38. B. Glassner and B. Berg, "How Jews avoid alcohol problems," *American Sociological Review* 45(1980):647–64.
39. B. Glassner and B. Berg, "Social locations and interpretations: How Jews define alcoholism," *Journal of Studies on Alcohol* 45(1984):16–25.
40. M. L. Barnett, "Alcoholism in the Cantonese of New York City," in *Etiology of Chronic Alcoholism*, ed. O. Diethelm (Charles C Thomas, 1955).
41. Vaillant, *Natural History*, 283–84.
42. W. R. Miller and R. K. Hester, "The effectiveness of alcoholism treatment: What research reveals," in *Treating Addictive Behaviors: Processes of Change*, eds. W. R. Miller and N. K. Heather (Plenum, 1986).
43. K. S. Ditman, G. G. Crawford, E. W. Forgy et al., "A controlled experiment on the use of court probation in the management of the alcohol addict," *American Journal of Psychiatry* 124(1967):160–63.
44. J. M. Brandsma, M. C. Maultsby, and R. J. Walsh, *The Outpatient Treatment of Alcoholism: A Review and Comparative Study* (University Park Press, 1980).
45. M. A. Lieberman, I. D. Yalom, and M. B. Miles, *Encounter Groups* (Basic Books, 1973).
46. W. R. Miller and R. K. Hester, "Inpatient alcoholism treatment: Who benefits?" *American Psychologist* 41 (1986):794–805.
47. C. Holden, "Is alcoholism treatment effective?" *Science* 236(1987):20–22.
48. E. Gottheil et al., "Follow-up of abstinent and nonabstinent alcoholics," *American Journal of Psychiatry* 139 (1982):564.
49. J. E. Helzer, L. N. Robins, J. R. Taylor et al. "The extent of long-term moderate drinking among alcoholics discharged from medical and psychiatric treatment facilities," *New England Journal of Medicine* 312(1985):1678–82.
50. J. M. Polich, D. J. Armor, and H. B. Braiker, *The Course of Alcoholism:*

Four Years After Treatment (Wiley, 1981).

51. S. Peele, "The cultural context of psychological approaches to alcoholism," *American Psychologist* 39(1984): 1337–51.
52. Elal-Lawrence, P. D. Slade, and M. E. Dewey, "Predictors of outcome type in treated problem drinkers," *Journal of Studies on Alcohol* 47(1986):41–47; N. Heather, S. Rollnick, and M. Winton, "A comparison of objective and subjective measures of alcohol dependence as predictors of relapse following treatment," *British Journal of Clinical Psychology* 22(1983):11–17; J. Orford and A. Keddie, "Abstinence or controlled drinking in clinical practice," *British Journal of Addiction* 81(1986):495–504.
53. B. S. Tuchfeld, "Spontaneous remission in alcoholics," *Journal of Studies on Alcohol* 42(1981):626–41.
54. G. Edwards et al., "Who goes to Alcoholics Anonymous?" *Lancet* 1 (1966):382–84.
55. Peele, "The cultural context."
56. D. J. Armor, J. M. Polich, and H. B. Stambul, *Alcoholism and Treatment* (Wiley, 1978), 232.
57. J. H. Mendelson and N. K. Mello, *Alcohol Use and Abuse in America* (Little, Brown, 1985), 346–47.
58. Vaillant, *Natural History*, 3. Vaillant's source for this quote is S. E. Gitlow, "Alcoholism: A disease," in *Alcoholism: Progress in Research and Treatment*, eds. P. B. Bourne and R. Fox (Academic Press, 1973), 8. The statement is inaccurate, however, in at least one and perhaps more instances. G. R. Vandenbos, acting chief executive officer of the American Psychological Association (APA), wrote me (29 March 1989) that the APA has never taken the position that alcoholism is a disease and that, in fact, it had explicitly rejected adopting this position. Nonetheless, the National Council on Alcoholism has stated in public documents for a number of years that the APA supports the view that alcoholism is a disease.

DISCUSSION

Milam and Ketcham, one the one hand, and Peele, on the other, appear to share a key assumption that is pivotal to both of their arguments—namely, that the concept of disease corresponds to a well-understood and clearly defined entity in nature. In other words, both sets of authors seem to agree that the statement "Alcoholism is a disease" can be confirmed or disconfirmed by data. Milam and Ketcham, for example, conclude that "alcoholism is a hereditary, physiological disease." Peele, who adopts the opposing position concerning the disease model, contends that "the dogma that alcoholism is a disease goes unquestioned."

As you learned in Chapter 1, however, there is surprisingly little consensus in either medicine or psychology concerning the criteria for identifying a condition as a disease. Although a variety of definitions for disease have been proposed—including social undesirability, reduced biological fitness, deviation from a statistical norm (see Chapter 11), and harmful dysfunction (Wakefield, 1992a, 1992b)—none has achieved universal (or even close to universal) acceptance. In addition, as discussed in Chapter 1, most or all of these definitions are subject to obvious counterexamples and are thus unable to accommodate all conditions that are widely agreed to be diseases. Thus, when authors such as Milam and Ketcham and Peele refer to the disease model of alcoholism, it is not entirely clear which of the above definitions, if any, they are referring to. Moreover, as I will discuss shortly, some of the presuppositions of the disease model (such as the heritability of alcoholism) are, when examined closely, far less central to this model than is commonly believed. Consequently, the disease model of alcoholism might better be thought of as a metaphor than as a strictly scientific set of hypotheses regarding the etiology of alcoholism.

What, then, are the principal assumptions underlying this metaphor? As you have seen, one the most crucial presuppositions underlying the disease model is traditionally believed to be the loss-of-control phenomenon. According to advocates of the disease model, alcoholics possess a biochemical anomaly (akin to an allergy) that renders them incapable of curtailing their drinking after even a single drink of alcohol. As noted briefly by Peele, however, at least one line of research raises serious questions concerning the reality of the loss-of-control phenomenon.

Alan Marlatt and his colleagues have conducted a number of studies to examine the factors influencing alcoholics' drinking in a laboratory setting (see Marlatt & Rohsenow, 1980, for a review). In one of the first applications of this design, Marlatt, Demming, and Reid (1973) randomly assigned two groups of subjects—male alcoholics and male nonalcoholic social drinkers—to one of four conditions. All subjects were falsely told that the purpose of the study was to examine how individuals rate the flavors of various beverages. In condition 1, subjects were asked to drink alcohol (a vodka and tonic mixture) and were correctly informed that they were drinking alcohol. In condition 2, subjects were asked to drink a nonalcohol beverage (tonic alone) but were falsely informed that they were drinking alcohol. In condition 3, subjects were asked to drink the nonalcohol beverage and were correctly informed that they were drinking nonalcohol. Finally, in condition 4, subjects were asked to drink alcohol (a vodka and tonic mixture) but were falsely informed that they were drinking nonalcohol. This four-condition methodology is referred to as a **balanced placebo design** because half of the subjects who believe they are drinking alcohol are in fact drinking a placebo; conversely, half of the subjects who believe they are drinking a placebo are in fact drinking alcohol. The researchers' principal dependent measure in each of the four conditions was the total amount of alcohol consumed.

Marlatt et al. (1973) found that the primary determinant of drinking behavior—for both alcoholic subjects and nonalcoholic subjects—was what subjects believed about the beverage content rather than its actual content. Specifically, subjects who thought they were drinking nonalcoholic beverages consumed less alcohol than did subjects who thought they were drinking alcohol, regardless of the beverage content. These results pose a major problem for the loss-of-control assumption, because subjects (including alcoholic subjects) did not lose control (drink heavily) after drinking alcohol if they did not believe that they were drinking alcohol.

These provocative findings, which have been replicated numerous times (Marlatt & Rohsenow, 1980), indicate that alcoholics' **expectancies** concerning the effects of alcohol may be an important determinant of their drinking habits. Moreover, although the findings of Marlatt and his colleagues are in no way incompatible with the role of genetic and physiological factors in the etiology of alcoholism, they strongly suggest that the loss-of-control assumption, at least in its pure form, is mistaken. Unlike an allergy, which is automatically (or almost automatically) triggered by exposure to the substance in question, the loss-of-control phenomenon seems to be determined largely or entirely by subjects' beliefs about the substance in question.*

Another set of data frequently invoked in support of the disease model, and reviewed both by Milam and Ketcham and by Peele, is the evidence concerning the heritability of alcoholism. Recall from Chapter 5 that heritability is a statistic describing the extent to which individual differences in a characteristic (in this case, alcoholism) are attributable to genetic influences. Although Milam and Ketcham, on the one hand, and Peele, on the other, arrive at quite different conclusions regarding the genetic data on alcoholism, the truth concerning the heritability of alcoholism appears to lie between the two extremes that they present. It is now generally agreed that the heritability of alcoholism, although probably overestimated by some authors (Searles, 1988), is modest but not insubstantial; that heritability tends to be higher in more severe cases of alcoholism (Kaij, 1960); and that it tends to be somewhat higher for male alcoholism than for female alcoholism (McGue, Pickens, & Svikis, 1992), although the reasons for this difference remain unclear. In addition, behavior-genetic studies conclusively demonstrate that environmental factors play a critical role in the etiology of alcoholism, because the concordance rate of alcoholism among monozygotic twins is considerably below 100 percent in all studies (Searles, 1988).

But is the heritability of a condition relevant to its classification as a disease, as the authors of both readings in this chapter imply? A moment's reflection indicates that the answer to this question is an unequivocal no. Many characteristics—such as height, weight, eye and hair color, extroversion (Scarr, Webber, Weinberg, & Wittig, 1981), and intelligence (Bouchard, Lykken, McGue, Segal, & Tellegen, 1990)—are substantially influenced by genetic factors but are of course not diseases according to any criteria. Conversely, some conditions, such as the common cold and AIDS, are largely or entirely environmental (that is, nongenetic) in origin but are widely considered to be diseases. Thus, the literature on the heritability of alcoholism, although potentially informative regarding the etiology of this condition, does not bear directly on the validity of the disease model.

Moreover, it is important to note that heritability (which, after all, is simply a statistic) tells us nothing about what characteristics are inherited. This point has been widely misunderstood, even by social scientists. Evidence for the heritability of a condition does not imply, for example, that the genetic influences in question are necessarily specific to this condition. The primary genetic factors predisposing a person to alcoholism might well be personality traits that influence an enormous range of behavioral characteristics in addition to drinking. Indeed, such personality traits might increase individuals' propensity for a broad spectrum of socially problematic behaviors, such as abuse of drugs other than alcohol, gambling, aggressiveness, and sexual promiscuity.*

C. Robert Cloninger (1987), for example, has proposed that three major genetically influenced dimensions—novelty seeking (a tendency to experience excitement in response to new stimuli or in anticipation of rewarding stimuli), harm avoidance (a tendency to experience fear in anticipation of

*It is also worth pointing out that the "involuntary" nature of a condition is not traditionally considered relevant to whether that condition is a disease, even though many authors have invoked the supposedly involuntary nature of alcoholics' drinking in support of the disease model of alcoholism. Individuals with high blood pressure who refuse to alter their lifestyle (for example, who continue to smoke cigarettes, eat eggs and bacon every morning, and work 80 hours a week) would still be considered to have a disease, even though the behaviors contributing to this disease are voluntary.

*This reasoning does not imply, however, that the genetic influences relevant to alcoholism cannot be specific to alcoholism. Indeed, in an important program of research, Mark Schuckit (1987) has shown that the sons of alcoholics, compared with the sons of nonalcoholics, tend to exhibit diminished subjective reactions (for example, less intense feelings of intoxication) and objective reactions (for example, less body sway) following drinking. Although Schuckit's findings are not conclusive regarding the genetic versus environmental origin of these differences (the fathers and sons in his sample were raised in the same family), they are consistent with the possibility that at least some of the genetic influences relevant to alcoholism are relatively specific to this condition.

punishing stimuli), and reward dependence (a tendency to persist in responding to rewarding stimuli, such as social approval)—underlie both normal and abnormal personality functioning. According to Cloninger, individuals' standing on these three dimensions influences their risk for alcoholism and certain other forms of substance abuse. For Cloninger, the major variables mediating the heritability of alcoholism are personality dimensions rather than factors specific to alcoholism.

Interestingly, according to Cloninger, two precisely opposite groups of individuals are at elevated risk for problem drinking: individuals low in novelty seeking, high in harm avoidance, and high in reward dependence and individuals high in novelty seeking, low in harm avoidance, and low in reward dependence. Cloninger hypothesizes, moreover, that these two groups of individuals tend to drink for very different reasons. Individuals in the first group (who are at risk for "Type 1" alcoholism) presumably drink primarily to reduce tension and anxiety. These individuals, according to Cloninger, are predominantly female, are prone to anxiety and depression, and tend to have a relatively late onset of problem drinking. In contrast, individuals in the second group (who are at risk for "Type 2" alcoholism) presumably drink primarily to relieve boredom and to give free rein to their proclivities toward risk taking and sensation seeking. These individuals, according to Cloninger, are predominantly male, are prone to antisocial and criminal behavior, and tend to have a relatively early onset of problem drinking.

Although the empirical support for Cloninger's model is so far somewhat preliminary (it derives largely from indirect evidence from adoption studies of alcoholism), his research and theorizing raise an important challenge not only for the disease model but also for any attempt to explain the causes of alcoholism. Many models of the etiology of alcoholism implicitly or explicitly assume that all individuals drink heavily for the same or at least very similar reasons. That is, alcoholism is often viewed, both by many proponents of the disease model and by others, as a homogeneous entity resulting from a single set of causal influences. But if Cloninger is correct, alcoholism may represent the culmination of two very different (and in fact essentially opposite) pathways. Thus it seems possible, if not likely, that any comprehensive model of the etiology of alcoholism will ultimately have to come to grips with the knotty problem of its heterogeneity.

QUESTIONS TO STIMULATE DISCUSSION

1. Milam and Ketcham maintain that alcoholics begin to drink for exactly the same reasons as do nonalcoholics. Do you agree? How might one proceed to test their claim?
2. Is the assertion that a condition is a disease incompatible with findings that it is strongly influenced by sociocultural or other environmental factors? Defend your reasoning, and provide examples of well-accepted diseases to buttress your argument.
3. What are the practical (for example, social policy) implications, if any, of research on the heritability of alcoholism? Does this research have implications for the treatment or prevention of alcoholism?
4. Imagine that you have been awarded a $20 million grant from the federal government to investigate the effectiveness of Alcoholics Anonymous (AA) treatment. Design a study that you believe would help to settle the question of whether AA is a beneficial treatment for alcoholism. What types of methodological difficulties are you likely to encounter in completing your study?
5. How might a proponent of the disease model attempt to account for Cloninger's findings regarding the existence of two very different pathways to alcoholism? If these findings can be corroborated by future researchers, would they pose explanatory difficulties for the disease model? Explain your reasoning.

SUGGESTIONS FOR FURTHER READING

Fingarette, H. (1988). *Heavy drinking: The myth of alcoholism as a disease*. Berkeley: University of California Press.
In this provocative book, Fingarette delineates his scientific, logical, and ethical objections to the disease model of alcoholism. He traces the history of the alcoholism-as-disease concept and critically examines the controlled-drinking controversy, the genetic and biological evidence, the effectiveness of AA and standard medical treatments, and other key issues in the debate concerning the "disease model" of alcoholism.

Goodwin, D. W. (1976). *Is alcoholism hereditary?* New York: Oxford University Press.
Goodwin provides a useful, albeit somewhat dated, overview of the literature on genetic and environmental influences on alcoholism, including the Danish adoption study of alcoholism. His book is appropriate for readers with no prior background in the study of either alcoholism or behavior genetics. (Incidentally, his answer to the question constituting the title of his book is yes.)

Jellinek, E. M. (1960). *The disease concept of alcoholism*. New Haven, CT: Hillhouse Press.
In this dated but classic work, Jellinek reviews early conceptions of alcoholism and presents his case for conceptualizing alcoholism as an illness. The third section of the book contains a discussion of Jellinek's fivefold typology of alcoholics. In addition, Jellinek discusses in detail both psychosocial and physiological models of the etiology of alcoholism.

Madsen, W. (1989). Thin thinking about heavy drinking. *The Public Interest*, 95, 112–118. (Reprinted in Slife, B., & Rubinstein, J. [1992]. *Taking sides: Clashing views on controversial psychological issues* [7th Ed.]. Guilford, CT: Dushkin Publishing Group.)

In his reply to an article by Fingarette (a partial summary of Fingarette's *Heavy drinking: The myth of alcoholism as a disease*), Madsen takes Fingarette to task for improper interpretations of the scientific literature on alcoholism, including the genetic data, research on the efficacy of AA, and the controlled-drinking studies. Madsen's article is marred, however, by overstatements and ad hominem comments.

Miller, N. S., & Chappel, J. N. (1991). History of the disease concept. *Psychiatric Annals, 21*, 196–205.

Miller and Chappel trace the roots of the disease concept of alcoholism, including its origins in the temperance movement and Alcoholics Anonymous. Nevertheless, many of their attacks on alternative views of alcoholism, such as learning models, do not withstand close scrutiny.

Peele, S. (1985). *The meaning of addiction: Compulsive experience and its interpretation*. Lexington, MA: Heath.

Peele criticizes traditional scientific models of addiction and argues that "our conventional view of addiction . . . is one more element in a pervasive loss of control that is the major contributor to drug and alcohol abuse" (p. xii). In Chapters 2 and 3, Peele skeptically examines the disease model of alcoholism and genetic and biological theories of addiction.

Schuckit, M. A. (1987). Biological vulnerability to alcoholism. *Journal of Consulting and Clinical Psychology, 55*, 301–309 (Reprinted in Hooley, J. M., Neale, J. M., & Davison, G. C. [1989]. *Readings in abnormal psychology*. New York: Wiley.)

Schuckit reviews the evidence relevant to biological factors in the etiology of alcoholism, with particular emphasis on studies of the male offspring of alcoholics. He concludes that promising biological markers for alcoholism include a diminished reaction to alcohol, a smaller P300 event-related brain potential, and lower alpha wave levels in the resting electroencephalogram (EEG).

Searles, J. S. (1988). The role of genetics in the pathogenesis of alcoholism. *Journal of Abnormal Psychology, 97*, 153–167.

Searles critiques the major behavior-genetic studies of alcoholism, particularly the Danish and U.S. adoption studies. He concludes that these studies are riddled with serious methodological flaws and that the influence of environmental factors in the etiology of alcoholism has probably been substantially underestimated.

Tarter, R. E., Alterman, A. I., & Edwards, K. I. (1985). Vulnerability to alcoholism in men: A behavior-genetic perspective. *Journal of Studies on Alcohol, 46*, 329–356.

Tarter and his colleagues comprehensively review the literature on the role of genetically influenced temperaments in the etiology of alcoholism. They focus on the potential impact of six dimensions on alcoholism risk—activity level, attention span, soothability, emotionality, reaction to food, and sociability—and discuss the evidence linking biological factors to these six dimensions.

Vaillant, G. E. (1983). *The natural history of alcoholism*. Cambridge, MA: Harvard University Press.

In this classic book, Vaillant reviews the literature on the etiology and course of alcoholism and describes the results of a large-scale prospective study of two samples (one a group of college students, the other a group of adolescent boys from inner-city Boston schools). He concludes that alcoholism is a "disorder with a life of its own" (p. 309) rather than simply a symptom of underlying pathology and that alcoholism tends to be a chronic condition characterized by three stages of increasingly heavy drinking. In addition, he tentatively concludes that existing treatments for alcoholism are no more effective than "the natural healing processes" (p. 316) of the disorder.

Vaillant, G. E. (1990). We should retain the disease concept of alcoholism. *Harvard Medical School Mental Health Letter*, 6(9), 4–6.

Using hypertension and coronary heart disease as exemplars, Vaillant argues that alcoholism fulfills the same criteria as do many established medical diseases. Moreover, he attempts to refute the implicit claims of Fingarette and others that diseases necessarily have a single etiology, differ qualitatively from normality, and are unaffected by situational factors. (Also see Fingarette, H. (1990). We should reject the disease concept of alcoholism. *Harvard Medical School Mental Health Letter*, 6(8), 4–6.)

REFERENCES

Bouchard, T. J., Lykken, D. T., McGue, M., Segal, N. L., & Tellegen, A. (1990). Sources of human psychological differences: The Minnesota study of twins reared apart. *Science, 250*, 223–228.

Cloninger, C. R. (1987). Neurogenetic adaptive mechanisms in alcoholism. *Science, 236*, 410–416.

Fingarette, H. (1988). *Heavy drinking: The myth of alcoholism as a disease*. Berkeley: University of California Press.

Goodwin, D. W., & Guze, S. B. (1989). *Psychiatric diagnosis* (4th ed.). New York: Oxford University Press.

Jellinek, E. M. (1946). Phases in the drinking history of alcoholics. *Quarterly Journal of Studies on Alcohol, 7*, 1–88.

Jellinek, E. M. (1952). The phases of alcohol addiction. *Quarterly Journal of Studies on Alcohol, 13*, 673–684.

Jellinek, E. M. (1960). *The disease concept of alcoholism*. New Haven, CT: Hillhouse Press.

Kaij, L. (1960). *Studies on the etiology and sequels of abuse of alcohol*. Lund, Sweden: University of Lund.

Marlatt, G. A., Demming, B., & Reid, J. B. (1973). Loss of control drinking in alcoholics: An experimental analogue. *Journal of Abnormal Psychology, 81*, 233–241.

Marlatt, G. A., & Rohsenow, D. J. (1980). Cognitive processes in alcohol use: Expectancy and the balanced placebo design. In N. K. Mello (Ed.), *Advances in substance abuse: Behavioral and biological research* (Vol. 1, pp. 159–199). Greenwich, CT: JAI Press.

McGue, M., Pickens, R. W., & Svikis, D. S. (1992). Sex and age effects on the inheritance of alcohol problems: A twin study. *Journal of Abnormal Psychology, 101*, 3–17.

Mello, N. K., & Mendelson, J. K. (1974). Alcoholism: A biobehavioral disorder. In S. Arieti (Ed.), *American handbook of psychiatry* (2nd ed., pp. 371–403). New York: Basic Books.

Miller, N. S., & Chappel, J. N. (1991). History of the disease concept. *Psychiatric Annals, 21*, 196–205.

Peele, S. (1989). *The diseasing of America: Addiction treatment out of control*. Lexington, MA: Lexington Books.

Scarr, S., Webber, P. L., Weinberg, R. A., & Wittig, M. A. (1981). Personality resemblance among adolescents and their parents in biologically related and adoptive families. *Journal of Personality and Social Psychology, 40*, 885–898.

Schuckit, M. A. (1987). Biological vulnerability to alcoholism. *Journal of Consulting and Clinical Psychology, 55*, 301–309

Searles, J. S. (1988). The role of genetics in the pathogenesis of alcoholism. *Journal of Abnormal Psychology, 97*, 153–167.

Vaillant, G. E. (1988). The alcohol-dependent and drug-dependent person. In A. M. Nicholi, Jr. (Ed.), *The new Harvard guide to psychiatry* (pp. 700–713). Cambridge, MA: Belknap Press.

Wakefield, J. C. (1992a). The concept of mental disorder: On the boundary between biological facts and social values. *American Psychologist, 47*, 373–388.

Wakefield, J. C. (1992b). Disorder as harmful dysfunction: A conceptual critique of DSM-III-R's definition of mental disorder. *Psychological Review, 99*, 232–247.

CHAPTER

8

Is multiple personality disorder a distinct syndrome?

PRO Kluft, R. P. (1987). An update on multiple personality disorder. *Hospital and Community Psychiatry, 38*, 363–373.

CON Fahy, T. A. (1988). The diagnosis of multiple personality disorder: A critical review. *British Journal of Psychiatry, 153*, 597–606.

OVERVIEW OF THE CONTROVERSY: Richard P. Kluft discusses the history of the concept of multiple personality disorder, as well as recent research on its diagnosis, etiology, and treatment, and concludes that multiple personality disorder is a distinct syndrome that has, until recently, been unjustly neglected in American psychiatry. Thomas A. Fahy reviews the evidence for the validity of the diagnosis of multiple personality disorder and concludes that it is a nonspecific symptom of a variety of psychopathological conditions rather than a distinct syndrome.

CONTEXT OF THE PROBLEM

Multiple personality disorder (MPD), officially known as dissociative identity disorder in DSM-IV, is perhaps the most puzzling and unusual of all psychopathological syndromes. Along with psychogenic amnesia, psychogenic fugue, and depersonalization disorder, MPD is categorized as a dissociative disorder by DSM-IV, meaning that it is characterized by disturbances in identity, memory, perception, or awareness.

Before discussing what MPD is, let us first be clear about what it is not: Contrary to popular misconception, MPD is not equivalent to schizophrenia. Schizophrenia, unlike MPD, involves the splitting of normally integrated functions, such as feeling and thinking, within a single personality. You should therefore look askance at statements like "I have a rather schizophrenic attitude toward the field of abnormal psychology" or "My feelings about my mother are schizophrenic," which have become part of our popular lingo. Such statements almost always refer to the existence of two or more states of mind regarding an issue and are thus an allusion to MPD, not schizophrenia.

Now let us examine what MPD is. According to DSM-IV, MPD involves the simultaneous existence of two of more distinct personalities or personality states within the same individual. Each of these personalities or personality states is characterized by its own relatively stable pattern of relating to and interpreting the world. In addition, at least two of the personalities or personality states seize control of the individual's behavior on a repeated basis. It is this coexistence of multiple distinct personalities or personality states that most clearly demarcates MPD from schizophrenia and other conditions.

MPD has a number of other characteristic features. In most cases, the "original" personality possesses little or no direct awareness of the alternate personalities, although it is frequently aware of substantial periods of lost time. The alternates, in contrast, typically have at least some awareness of the original personality or of each other. The transitions from one personality to another typically occur quite rapidly—in seconds to minutes—but occasionally occur more slowly. In the literature, the number of reported personalities existing in a single individual ranges from 2 to over 100; approximately half of the cases have 10 or more personalities (American Psychiatric Association, 1987).

The reported differences among the personalities range from the bizarre to the spectacular. Not uncommonly, personalities differ in stated gender, age, family of origin, and even race. Even more remarkably, personalities have been reported to differ in their eyeglass prescriptions, handedness, allergies, susceptibilities to alcohol, presence versus absence of headaches, and IQ (American Psychiatric Association, 1987; Putnam, Guroff, Silberman, Barban, & Post, 1986). Quite often, the personalities are polar opposites; the celebrated case described in *The Three Faces of Eve* (Thigpen & Cleckley, 1954) is such an example. Eve White (Eve's original personality) was the incarnation of utter purity and conventionality, and Eve Black (one of Eve's two alternates) was the incarnation of utter seductiveness and licentiousness. Eve, whose actual name is Chris Sizemore, later claimed to possess 21 personalities (Sizemore & Pittillo, 1977).

The MPD diagnosis has had its vocal critics. A number of authors have called attention to the "epidemic" in the diagnosis of MPD in the United States over the last several decades (Boor, 1982). Between 1934 and 1971, only 12 cases of MPD were reported in the American literature (Rosenbaum, 1980), but a number of investigators have recently reported that they have each seen over 50 patients with MPD (Spanos, Weekes, & Bertrand, 1985), and a prominent MPD researcher recently published a report of 100 cases (Putnam et al., 1986). It is perhaps not entirely coincidental that this epidemic has followed the immense publicity surrounding such cases as Sybil (Schreiber, 1973) and Billy Milligan (Keyes, 1981). Is it not plausible, these critics ask rhetorically, that the precipitous rise in the number of reported MPD cases reflects an increase in the public's awareness of, and thus ability to mimic, its symptomatology? Moreover, skeptics point to the frequent emergence of what appear to be additional personalities in MPD patients during hypnosis. Are these personalities discovered by hypnosis, as most proponents of the MPD diagnosis contend, or are they created?

Some critics have gone even further to conceptualize MPD as a social-psychological phenomenon akin to role playing. According to these authors, patients with MPD are enacting "parts" synthesized from a number of information sources, including media reports and unintentional cues from their therapists (Spanos et al., 1985). Some individuals (such as criminals) may adopt MPD in order to shirk responsibility for their shortcomings and misbehaviors.

In evaluating claims for the validity of the MPD diagnosis, it is perhaps worth bearing in mind the classic scientific dictum (introduced by the British philosopher David Hume) that extraordinary claims require extraordinary evidence. Certainly, many of the assertions made about MPD are extraordinary. Is the evidence for these assertions equally extraordinary?

THE CONTROVERSY: Kluft vs. Fahy

Kluft

Richard P. Kluft begins by noting that MPD was, until fairly recently, largely neglected by American psychiatrists. He contends that the burgeoning interest in this condition has been spurred by a number of factors, including the use of standardized diagnostic criteria, increased awareness of the prevalence and adverse consequences of child abuse, and appreciation of the similarities of MPD to posttraumatic stress disorder, an anxiety disorder resulting from exposure to an extremely anxiety-provoking event. Kluft examines claims that MPD is a consequence of hypnosis and other interventions and finds them to be unsubstantiated. He proposes a four-factor model of the etiology of MPD, which involves complex interactions between the individual's capacity for dissociation and severe environmental stressors. Kluft goes on to discuss considerations in the diagnosis, clinical presentation, and differential diagnosis of MPD and argues that MPD is a condition distinct from schizophrenia, partial-complex seizure disorder (a form of epilepsy), and malingering. Finally, he discusses recent findings in the MPD literature—such as the detection of MPD in children and the discovery that MPD aggregates in certain families—and concludes with a review of the psychotherapeutic treatment of MPD. MPD, Kluft argues, can be effectively treated by long-term therapy aimed at integration of the alternate personalities.

Fahy

Thomas Fahy first summarizes the literature on the diagnosis, phenomenology, and differential diagnosis of MPD. He notes that MPD is often difficult to distinguish from other phenomena, such as other dissociative disorders, malingering, borderline personality disorder (see Chapter 9), and somatization disorder. Fahy discusses the results of physiological investigations of MPD and argues that there is no compelling evidence of specific changes during the transitions among personalities. What changes are observed, Fahy contends, appear attributable to generalized differences in arousal across personalities. Fahy next addresses the possibility that MPD is an iatrogenic (doctor-produced) condition and discusses suggestions that alternate personalities are often induced by hypnosis. He then examines four different models of MPD: MPD as the consequence of childhood trauma, MPD as self-hypnosis, MPD as a disorder of state-dependent learning, and MPD as a personality disorder. Fahy concludes that MPD is a nonspecific symptom of a variety of psychopathological syndromes rather than a distinct condition and that recent societal changes, such as increased media publicity, are probably responsible for the dramatic rise in its prevalence.

KEY CONCEPTS AND TERMS

alter One of the alternate personalities in a patient with MPD. Alters are distinguished from the "original" personality.

amytal interview Interview that involves the administration of the barbiturate sodium amobarbital (amytal), or "truth serum." The function of the amytal interview is to lessen inhibitions so that deeply buried memories can be retrieved. Note: The term "truth serum" is a misnomer, because amytal probably lowers the threshold for recalling all "memories," both accurate and inaccurate.

borderline personality disorder Personality disorder characterized by pervasive instability in identity, mood, and interpersonal relationships (see Chapter 9).

Briquet's syndrome Older term for somatization disorder, a condition characterized by an early and chronic history of multiple bodily symptoms lacking any demonstrated physical basis.

dissociative disorders Class of disorders characterized by disturbances in identity, memory, perception, or awareness.

evoked potential Physiological measure obtained by averaging the brain's electrical responses to a large number of identical stimuli. Evoked potentials are also referred to as event-related potentials (ERPs).

first-rank symptoms Symptoms of schizophrenia first identified by the German psychiatrist Kurt Schnieder. First-rank symptoms include audible thoughts, voices arguing with one another, thought withdrawal (the delusion that one's thoughts are being withdrawn from one's head by some external force), and delusions of control (the delusion that one's actions are under the control of an external force).

iatrogenic Produced by a physician or other medical professional.

partial-complex seizure disorder Form of epilepsy, involving the brain's temporal lobe and closely associated structures, frequently associated with hallucinations, "automatic" behaviors (such as "automatic" writing, in which the person writes passages that he or she is subsequently unable to recognize as his or her own), and other emotional and behavioral disturbances.

posttraumatic stress disorder Syndrome resulting from exposure to an extremely traumatic event, such as military combat, rape, or severe physical or sexual abuse. Its symptoms include repeated and extremely disturbing recollections of the event, recurrent nightmares of the event, avoidance of stimuli that remind the individual of the event, feelings of detachment from others, and intense autonomic arousal.

state-dependent learning Learning that occurs more accurately or efficiently when the organism is in the same state (for example, in a particular mood or under the influence of a particular drug) as when the material being learned was originally encountered.

PREVIEW QUESTIONS

1. According to Kluft, what factors have sparked the recent increase in interest in MPD?
2. What does Kluft make of skeptics' assertions that MPD is iatrogenic?
3. What is Kluft's four-factor model of the etiology of MPD?
4. According to Kluft, what are the primary principles involved in the psychotherapeutic treatment of MPD?
5. According to Fahy, what are the principal conditions that tend to be confused with MPD?
6. What does Fahy conclude from studies of physiological changes occurring during the transitions from one personality to another?
7. According to Fahy, is MPD a distinct condition? If not, what is it?

RICHARD P. KLUFT

An update on multiple personality disorder

Multiple personality disorder is a complex, chronic dissociative psychopathology characterized by disturbances of identity and memory (1). What distinguishes it from all other psychiatric syndromes is the ongoing coexistence of relatively consistent but alternating separate identities plus recurrent episodes of memory distortion, frank amnesia, or both (2,3).

Until quite recently multiple personality disorder was relegated to a marginal position in American psychiatry by the prevailing general consensus that the condition is quite rare (reflected in *DSM-III* [4]), its relative absence from the scientific literature, and the propensity of both the professional and the lay communities to react to its often-dramatic phenomenology with either fascination or skepticism. However, within a relatively brief span of time, multiple personality disorder has become the focus of considerable interest. It is diagnosed, treated, and studied with increasing frequency.

Since 1974 at least 11 investigators or groups have reported clinical or research experience with ten or more multiple personality disorder patients (5–15); several additional large series were reported at the First, Second, and Third International Conferences on Multiple Personality/Dissociative States held in 1984 through 1986. Among the papers is Putnam and associates' description (14) of 100 multiple personality disorder patients diagnosed by 92 clinicians; the presentations included Schultz and associates' study (16) of 355 such patients contributed by 355 therapists. Between 1983 and 1985 five journals devoted special issues to the disorder (17–21). The field is growing with such rapidity that a comprehensive bibliography published in 1983 (22) required revision within two years (23).

This rise in reportage has rekindled long-standing controversies. Several writers have suggested that the increase is largely spurious, reflecting misdiagnosis and iatrogenesis (24–26). Others have wondered whether the disorder's prevalence has increased, whether diagnostic criteria have changed, whether the diagnosis is now made more astutely, or whether a small number of clinicians are contributing a disproportionate amount of current cases (27). There is general curiosity and considerable consternation about why a condition thought to be rare, if not extinct, is entering the psychiatric mainstream at this point in history. This paper will attempt to put the current status of multiple personality disorder in historical perspective, to explore the implications of the polarized conflicts that surround the disorder, and to demonstrate that current findings may allow a degree of resolution of many venerable controversies.

THE GROWTH OF INTEREST IN THE DISORDER

Since 1984 much of the increased case-finding has been related to the more widely available information on multiple personality disorder in the general psychiatric literature. However, the confluence of several forces was already at work. *DSM-III*, in grouping multiple personality disorder with the dissociative disorders and severing its longstanding association with hysteria, called attention to the condition. Also, by tightening the definitions of schizophrenia and the affective disorders, *DSM-III* diminished (but did not eliminate) the danger that multiple personality disorder patients, who often have symptoms such as hallucinations (14,28–30) and first-rank symptoms of schizophrenia (30), and almost invariably have affective stigmata (7,14,29,30), would be misdiagnosed perfunctorily.

Further, advances in psychopharmacology have encouraged greater diagnostic precision and closer scrutiny of treatment failures. A characteristic presentation of multiple personality disorder is failure to respond to appropriate treatment for some other condition that the patient is believed to have (2,3).

In addition, the helping professions are increasingly aware of the hitherto-unacknowledged high prevalence of child abuse and incest, and their sequelae in adult psychopathology. Workers in these areas are discovering multiple personality disorder among the adult survivors of such experiences. Increasingly clinicians are listening to adult patients' retrospective accounts of abuse without discounting them in advance as fantasies. As these accounts are explored in the process of therapy, multiple personality disorder may emerge spontaneously (31). More than

SOURCE: *Hospital and Community Psychiatry*, 38(4), pp. 363–373, April 1987.

a dozen therapists have told me that this is a common event in groups of incest victims. The impact of feminism and the increasing numbers of women in the mental health professions have encouraged serious attention to multiple personality disorder; the condition has a reported 9:1 predominance of females among its victims (10,14), who report a 75 to 88 percent prevalence of sexual abuse during childhood (14, 16,29).

Lay interest in celebrated cases of multiple personality disorder and the exploitation of its dramatic potential in innumerable television productions have gradually brought the disorder to the attention of the professional community. The impact of Schreiber's description of Wilbur's treatment of "Sybil" (32) was profound, and it reached a professional as well as a general public audience.

It is a historical fact that interest in multiple personality disorder increases when interest in hypnosis is high; a renaissance of interest in hypnosis has been under way for more than a decade. The tragic struggles of our Vietnam veterans have also alerted psychiatrists to posttraumatic stress disorder. Many clinicians working with both multiple personality disorder and posttraumatic stress disorder have remarked on the similarity of the two conditions (3,33–36). Some consequences of this have been a new credibility for multiple personality disorder, an enhanced appreciation of the dissociative aspects of posttraumatic stress disorder, and an application of the treatment approaches useful for posttraumatic stress disorder patients to multiple personality disorder populations (36).

The psychophysiological aspects of multiple personality disorder have spurred considerable excitement. Several investigators have attempted to study possible interfaces between this condition and partial complex seizure disorders (37–39). It has long been appreciated that personalities may differ in characteristics that indicate psychophysiological differences, including handedness. However, scientific studies exploring psychophysiological differences are in their infancy; in most cases the personalities of only one or two patients have been studied (39–42). Thus, given the clinical heterogeneity of multiple personality disorder (30), any generalizations must be tentative.

In one larger investigation Putnam (43) studied 11 patients across at least three personalities, along with matched normal controls who simulated multiple personalities. For the patients he found that certain parameters of the average evoked potentials of the different personalities were stably different, and that controls feigning alternate personalities could not duplicate the parameters. He also found differences among the patients' personalities in topographic power spectral electroencephalographic studies. Putnam cautions that although his findings may reflect neurophysiological differences in perception across alternate personalities, they instead may result from a systematic artifact, as yet uncharacterized, that is generated by the alternate personalities.

Braun (44), collaborating with Putnam, obtained baseline evoked potentials on the separate personalities of some of his patients. After he achieved integration of the personalities, he found that the patients' evoked potentials were stably different from those of the previously separate personalities. The study of multiple personality disorder may well offer unique opportunities to explore the interaction of mind and body. Braun (45) has offered a speculative synthesis of several neuropsychophysiologic models.

A final contributor to the rising interest in multiple personality disorder has been the teaching efforts of several pioneers in the field. For example, several hundred psychiatrists have attended courses on multiple personality disorder offered at the annual meetings of the American Psychiatric Association.

THE CONTROVERSIES REVISITED

Although the prevalence and phenomenology of multiple personality disorder will be controversial issues for the foreseeable future, it is useful to review the polarized positions outlined in a recent exchange of letters (26,35,46–48). One view is that the condition is rare or nonexistent, and that the apparent exponential increase in its reportage reflects iatrogenesis, cultural factors, loose diagnostic criteria, the personal agendas of a few individuals, and the efforts of misguided patients who search out clinicians who will sanction the diagnosis.

The evidence adduced for this view is largely based on the opinions of respected authorities, buttressed by perpetuation of the assumption that hypnosis or encouragement to enact multiple personality behaviors creates the disorder (49); indeed, it is clearly established that many phenomena of the disorder can be induced with hypnosis or other interventions (49–53).

Those inclined to be skeptical feel that many traumata patients complain of reflect fantasy, confabulation, or pseudomemory. From this stance, it follows that although the patient should be treated with respect, the condition is primarily a social-psychological event rather than an intrinsic disorder, and that the essence of treatment is the nonreinforcement of multiple personality phenomena. The phenomena should neither be encouraged to emerge nor explored. In the absence of secondary gain, the disorder should subside.

The opposing view espoused in the discussion is that the phenomenology of multiple personality disorder reflects the maladaptive persistence of an overwhelmed child's desperate efforts to flee inward when flight from traumatic external circumstances is impossible (3,7,33,35), and that the prevalence of the disorder is much higher than formerly believed (5–16). Those who take this view believe that the present increase in diagnosis redresses longstanding patterns of misdiagnosis and underdiagnosis, and they consider a false-positive diagnosis the more conservative diagnostic error (10).

Some feel that the current diagnostic criteria for multiple personality disorder are unduly restrictive (7,28) and that the recognition of less-than-classic cases is long overdue (30,54,55). From this stance, it follows that the structures and the memories of the personalities, and the conflicts among them, are the embodiment of the patient's past and present difficulties as well as the key to accessing and working through them. Bringing the personalities into communication with one another and the therapist becomes essential to an uncovering, change-oriented psychotherapy. The personalities' emergence and interaction with the therapist is seen as analogous to the gradual uncovering of hidden mental contents in any other psychodynamic treatment.

In approaching resolution of these two views, it is well to bear in mind that no new area is immune from instances of overenthusiasm and misapplication of recent advances. It would be naive to assume that as awareness of multiple personality disorder increases, and before the full dimensions of this syndrome are explored and understood, there will be no occasions of "trendy" overdiagnosis (30).

On the whole, the skeptical literature consists of opinions that, however eloquent, do not constitute scientific data. A review of the large series of cases clearly demonstrates that, excepting Bliss' aggressive casefinding studies (28,56–58), which often endorsed criteria less stringent than *DSM-III*, most workers are adhering to *DSM-III* criteria or using even more demanding measures (9,59). Most workers are reporting large series of patients referred to them with the diagnosis of multiple personality disorder already made or strongly suspected. Patients in my series of more than 250 subjects were initially diagnosed by more than 150 colleagues (35). Hence, in the main, a few authors are reporting the diagnostic experience of many clinicians.

Although some phenomena of multiple personality disorder are readily induced, and the worsening of multiple personality disorder by iatrogenic error has been reported (60), there is no evidence that clinical multiple personality disorder can be produced *de novo* by iatrogenic manipulations (60,61). As I observed elsewhere: "Phenomena analogous to and bearing dramatic but superficial resemblance to clinical multiple personality can be elicited experimentally or in a clinical situation if one tries to do so or makes technical errors. Furthermore, the phenomena described in Hilgard's hidden observer work [62] and the Watkins' ego state articles [63] can be elicited by hypnosis and overinterpreted as multiple personality" (60). Gruenewald (64) states: "Although injudicious use of hypnosis may have a variety of untoward effects, causation *de novo* of multiple personality does not seem to be one of them." When I repeated efforts of other investigators to induce iatrogenic multiple personality disorder, I found the resultant phenomena were unlike clinical multiple personality disorder (65). The outcome of treatment according to the postulates of skeptics about the syndrome is discussed below.

Information bearing on the broader view is accumulating. As noted, many large series have been reported by workers who draw cases from many sources. Virtually all modern series confirm the high incidence of child abuse in multiple personality disorder patients; in two large cohorts the rate is 97 percent (14,16). These reports are not easily discounted. In another series Coons and Milstein (29) documented allegations of mistreatment of 85 percent of their patients. I have reported on abused children who, when they were serendipitously assessed before being abused, were without signs of multiple personality disorder, but who developed the disorder after being abused (66,67).

Putnam and associates (14) have found that for patients with multiple personality disorder, an average of 6.8 years elapses between the time they are first assessed for symptoms referable to the disorder and the time they receive an accurate diagnosis; during that period they receive an average of 3.6 erroneous diagnoses. Longitudinal study of multiple personality disorder patients lends support to a broad rather than a narrow construction of the disorder (30). Approximately 94 percent of the patients try to hide, deny, or dissimulate their condition rather than dramatize or exploit it. Approximately 80 percent experience substantial periods of time in which the various personalities do not emerge overtly but instead are in relative harmony or influence one another without assuming complete executive control. Some cases of multiple personality disorder never fulfill *DSM-III* criteria because the personalities pass as one another or influence one another without completely emerging (30,54, 55). Some patients have so many personalities that no single alternate personality fulfills *DSM-III* criteria for the syndrome (30).

Although the discussion above argues for a revision of many long-held notions about multiple personality disorder, one can ask whether this polarized debate, however venerable, has clinical relevance. Does it matter whether we diagnose and treat according to one view or the other? P. D. Scott wrote, "The follow-up is the great exposer of truth, the rock on which many fine theories are wrecked and upon which better ones can be built. It is to the psychiatrist what the post-mortem is to the physician" (quoted in 68). Recent studies indicate that patients whose multiple personality disorder remains untreated do not experience remission (30,69), that those who prematurely leave treatment relapse into rather than cease multiple personality disorder behaviors (13,30,70), and that those whose treatment does not deal directly with the disorder may cease to show multiple personalities to their therapist but continue to experience them.

In contrast, patients who enter treatment with a therapist experienced with the condition usually have a stormy treatment but achieve remission of symptoms. In one ongoing study, at follow-up at 27 or more months after their personalities were integrated, 94 percent of the patients were without behavioral evidence of the disorder (13, 70). When treatment is offered by less experienced therapists at a less-than-optimal intensity, less optimistic results can be expected (69).

Taken as a whole, the above findings are most consistent with the stance that the current rise in reportage of multiple personality disorder is one of several indicators of substantial advances in psychiatry's understanding of this venerable but long-misunderstood condition.

THE ETIOLOGY OF THE DISORDER

According to the four-factor theory, multiple personality disorder occurs when a child with the capacity to dissociate (factor 1) is exposed to overwhelming stimuli (factor 2) that cannot be managed with less drastic defenses (13). Hence the capacity to dissociate is enlisted in the service of defense. Dissociated contents become linked with one of many possible substrates and shaping influences for personality organization (factor 3). If there are inadequate stimulus barriers and restorative experiences, or an excess of double-binding messages that inhibits the child's capacity to process his experience (factor 4), multiple personality disorder can result.

For example, if a dissociation-prone child with an imaginary companion is harshly molested by an adult, and either the abuser is a parent or the caregiver fails to detect and respond to the child's hurt, the child might develop a personality, based on the imaginary companion, to encapsulate the abuse experience, and he might develop an intropunitive personality, based on the abuser, using the mechanism of identification with the aggressor. The child might also develop a protector or helper personality in the face of the caregiver's empathic failures or abusive behaviors. Over a period of time, anger over the abuse and any sexual stimulation experienced along with it might become organized into personalities as well.

Once established, this defensive pattern, which disposes of upsetting material and pressures rapidly and efficiently, may be repeated to cope both with further overwhelming experiences and with more mundane developmental issues. With the onset of adolescence, it is common for personalities to be formed to handle school and work and to encapsulate sexual pressures and behaviors. By this time the multiple personality disorder that developed to cope with intolerable childhood circumstances has achieved some secondary autonomy and is increasingly maladaptive. As the adolescent achieves increasing autonomy, the independent actions of the personalities are subject to fewer external restraints, and the condition may become more overt. This is a major reason why multiple personality disorder, although it originates in childhood, is rarely diagnosed before late adolescence (27).

This theory is buttressed by findings that patients with multiple personality disorder are highly hypnotizable (57, 71). Whether this is because severely disciplined (72) and abused (73) individuals are more hypnotizable, whether the diminution of hypnotizability that normally occurs with age is precluded by its being enlisted as a defense (11), or whether only individuals with a biologically based high degree of hypnotizability develop multiple personality disorder remains uncertain. As noted above, some series report child abuse in 97 percent of patients (14,16). Nonabuse etiologies are also known (13), among which are exposure to the death of a loved one, accidents, and the carnage of war, as well as severe pain, illness, near-death experience, cultural dislocation, and family chaos.

One young girl was sitting on her grandfather's lap, chatting in the language of his native land when he suddenly died of a heart attack and fell over on her. She split off a personality that spoke in the grandfather's native language and grieved for him. As an adult, the patient presented with a depression refractory to medication, psychotherapy, and ECT. When her multiple personality disorder was discovered and the grieving personality treated, she made a full and lasting recovery.

The diversity of the substrates and shaping confluences of factor 3 explains why multiple personality disorder is so heterogeneous and why theories about the syndrome drawn from single case studies or small samples often contradict one another. There is no common psychodynamic pattern across all cases. Multiple personality disorder is most parsimoniously understood as a posttraumatic pathology, the form of which will be determined by factors unique to each case. For example, it stands to reason that a girl whose life was uneventful before being molested by her uncle at age eight has had a different developmental experience from a young woman abused from infancy on by her father and exploited in child prostitution and "kiddy-porn." To infer a pregenital origin of the multiple personality disorder in both cases because analogies are drawn between the presence of separate personalities and the psychodynamic concept of splitting unduly strains the meanings and boundaries of these ideas.

DIAGNOSTIC CRITERIA

DSM-III offers three diagnostic criteria for multiple personality disorder: "A. The existence within the individual of two or more distinct personalities, each of which is dominant at a particular time. B. The personality that is dominant at any particular time determines the individual's behavior. C. Each individual personality is complex and integrated with its own unique behavior patterns and social relationships." Inclusion of criteria for the disorder in the diagnostic manual was a major step forward, but since the manual's publication in 1980, findings from the longitudinal study of multiple personality disorder patients (30) suggest the need for further revision.

Criterion B is misleading, because it has been discovered that even in unquestioned classic cases, personalities may influence behavior without emerging, personalities may share control, or personalities may contend for control for protracted periods. At such times both the experience of being passively influenced and the special hallucinations, considered first-rank symptoms of schizophrenia (74), can be documented in multiple personality disorder (30). Such normative phenomena of multiple personality disorder often lead to misdiagnosis of the condition as schizophrenia.

It has also been learned that personalities often try to pass as one another, and that, according to two series, the average contemporary patient has 13.3 to 13.9 personalities (14,13). These entities have a wide range of distinctness and complexity; their importance, dominance, and elaborateness may vary over time (30). In view of these findings, criterion C is misleading as well, inadvertently encouraging false-negative diagnoses.

In retrospect, *DSM-III* criteria reflect an older view of multiple personality disorder, drawn from a small number of patients with very overt disorders, many of whom were highly intelligent and creative women, and most of whom had very few personalities. Recognizing the findings in larger series, the forthcoming revised manual, *DSM-III-R*, proposes to eliminate criterion C and use more flexible and less reified criteria: "A. The existence within the individual of two or more distinct personalities or personality states (each with its own relatively enduring pattern of perceiving, relating to, and thinking about the environment and self). B. Each of these personality states recurrently takes full control of the individual's behavior" (75).

In *DSM-III-R* less well-developed cases would be acknowledged as forms of multiple personality disorder but classified as a form of dissociative disorder not otherwise specified: "variants of Multiple Personality Disorder, such as cases in which there is more than one entity capable of assuming executive control of the individual, but not more than one entity is sufficiently complex and integrated to meet the full criteria for Multiple Personality Disorder, or cases in which a second personality never assumes complete executive control" (75). Most cases of multiple personality disorder can be easily subsumed under these rubrics.

THE PRESENTATION OF THE DISORDER

As noted above, study of the natural history of this disorder (30) illustrates that relatively few patients with genuine multiple personality disorder demonstrate the classic phenomena in an overt and ongoing manner. Most who do are skilled at dissimulation. Excepting the small minority of patients who flaunt their condition, most patients, with their secretiveness, suppression, denial, and periods of relatively little conflict among the personalities, have only certain temporal "windows of diagnosability" (3) during which the classic signs are easily discerned.

"The patient is often polysymptomatic but shows little of the overt symptoms of MPD. If the alters are narcissistically invested in separateness, and have specialized roles, but contention is low, a smooth but overt system of alters may be evident. Such patients often value their MPD. If the same conditions prevail, but with contention, the patient may show the classic picture of major shifts of personality dominance in response to psychosocial stressors and inner battles, and emphatic differences among the alters will become manifest" (3). This view is no more than a restatement for multiple personality disorder of the psychoanalytic concept that the structures of the mind do not become manifest except under conditions of conflict (76).

Multiple personality disorder rarely presents as a freestanding condition. Almost invariably its manifestations are embedded within a polysymptomatic presentation suggestive of one or more commonplace conditions. Therefore it usually is a superordinate diagnosis (2) that may encompass a plethora of manifestations consistent with other conditions. Symptoms of anxiety and somatoform disorders are common, as are phobic and borderline manifestations. Depressive symptoms are nearly universal, and hallucinations and passive-influence experiences are very common (7,12,14,16,28–30).

In sum, unless the clinician's index of suspicion for multiple personality disorder is high, almost inevitably his attention will be held by phenomena that suggest other disorders, and multiple personality disorder will not be considered. A patient I recently diagnosed had 22 years of prior therapy, without relief, and carried the diagnoses (and was on medication for) schizophrenia, major depression, and partial complex seizure disorder.

Review of the initial presentations of patients in a large contemporary series (30) indicates that virtually all patients with multiple personality disorder complain of depression. A small number of patients claim from the outset that they have multiple personality disorder, and almost all are initially disbelieved. Some 15 percent show classic signs from the first, or early on; either they are diagnosed promptly, or the diagnosis is missed because the diagnostician's index of suspicion is low. However, the classic presentation of a depressed, neurasthenic, compulsive individual complaining of severe headaches and reluctantly acknowledging amnesia is increasingly recognized.

The most common presentation is seen in the patient who has failed to improve in a straightforward way when given competent and adequate treatment for what appear to be medical or mental health complaints or both. Another common presentation occurs when multiple personality disorder mimics somatoform or psychosomatic disorder. Many times the patient reexperiences the physical sensations of some mistreatment without awareness of their origin. One woman referred by a surgeon complained of tearing rectal pain and the sensation of a foreign body in her rectum. They proved related to an anal penetration experienced during her exploitation in child pornography. The patient's hypnotically retrieved memories were confirmed by a sister who was also present at the time and was similarly abused but had not repressed the experience.

Many patients with multiple personality disorder present with signs suggestive of psychosis. They report the hearing of voices of alternate personalities and the revivification of past experiences as hallucinations, experiences of feeling controlled or influenced, interference with their thoughts, and similar phenomena. If they see visual evidences of other personalities attempting to seize control, they may report that their bodies are being transformed.

It is crucial to avoid inferring the presence of schizophrenia from such manifestations. The chaotic lives of many patients with multiple personality disorder suggest borderline states. Indeed, the presence of concomitant *DSM-III* borderline features has ranged from 15 percent in a series of successfully treated patients (13) to 70 percent in a series of patients studied in depth (12). The presence of concomitant borderline features is correlated with lower levels of psychosocial function (12).

Many patients present in connection with antisocial behaviors. Often they maintain they do not remember such behaviors, but this excuse is so common among offenders that it is usually discounted. Also, many patients abuse substances in order to control or cover their dissociative experiences. The experience of "blackouts" by a recovering alcoholic, for example, may suggest unsuspected multiple personality disorder.

Patients with multiple personality disorder may be quite difficult to diagnose. They frequently withhold or are amnestic for crucial information. It is not uncommon for the patient to hear an inner voice warning against giving complete answers. The clinician routinely expects deception and dissimulation in a forensic context, but may not be alert to it under more routine conditions. False-negative diagnoses are quite common, even among clinicians experienced with multiple personality disorder (30).

Nonetheless, clinicians can inquire about certain signs commonly associated with multiple personality disorder and can pursue afffirmative answers as opportunity permits. The existence of any of the following signs should be scrutinized carefully:

- A history of prior treatment failure
- Three or more prior diagnoses
- Concurrent psychiatric and somatic symptoms
- Fluctuating symptoms and an inconsistent level of functioning
- Severe headaches, often refractory to narcotics
- A history of time distortion or time lapses
- The patient's having been told by others of behaviors he has forgotten
- The patient's having been told by others of observable changes in his facies, voice, and behavioral style
- The patient's discovery in his domicile, vehicle, or place of work of productions, possessions, or strange handwriting that he can neither account for nor recognize
- Auditory hallucinations, which should be assessed with special care
- The use of "we" in a collective sense
- The eliciting of what appear to be separate personalities with hypnosis or amytal. This phenomenon suggests but does not confirm the disorder because phenomena resembling multiple personality disorder can be elicited by these means. Indeed, that is the basis for the Watkins' ego-state therapy (63).
- A history of child abuse

DIFFERENTIAL DIAGNOSIS

Many axis I and axis II entities coexist with multiple personality disorder, and most differential diagnostic issues are less problematic than generally perceived. Bearing in mind the concept of superordinate diagnosis (2), if a "patient manifests alternating separate identities and episodes of amnesia or time distortion, notwithstanding problems with the second criterion . . . MPD is the only clinical entity in which both coexist and are recurrent" (3).

If these criteria are present, so is some form of multiple personality disorder. Then, instead of "Is this multiple personality disorder or something else?" the issue becomes "Does this condition fulfill current criteria for multiple personality disorder or should it be considered an atypical dissociative disorder with the features of multiple personality?" and "Which concomitant diagnoses ought to be rendered?" Many cases probably will best be classified as atypical dissociative disorders until they are fully explored.

More than 90 percent of multiple personality disorder patients have symptoms of depression or anxiety disorders. Most have received prior diagnoses of depression; half or more have had prior diagnoses of schizophrenia (14). Many of these symptoms reflect the interactions of the personalities. A certain number of patients have concomitant drug-responsive depressive disorders (77). If exploration of the personalities does not fully explain affective symptoms or if all personalities have affective symptoms, a trial of antidepressants is warranted.

It is crucial to realize that with *DSM-III* and proposed *DSM-III-R* criteria, multiple personality disorder and schizophrenia may still be confused. Also, some patients with multiple personality disorder have brief psychotic episodes, and some schizophrenics have dissociative features (3,78).

In considering the possible presence of schizophrenia, it is useful to avoid reliance on first-rank symptoms of schizophrenia, which are common in multiple personality disorder (30), and to search for Bleuler's primary symptoms (3,78). The four As of flat or inappropriate affect, loose or illogical associations, ambivalence, and autism are not characteristic of multiple personality disorder. Affects are usually appropriate, given the personalities' assumptive worlds, and patients with multiple personality disorder usually handle ambivalence by different personalities' espousing different points of view. Most schizophrenic patients experience auditory hallucinations as being outside their head, while most multiple personality disorder patients experience them as within their head (3,30). Once anxiety is allayed, most multiple personality disorder patients preserve reality testing and establish a good rapport with others.

Several features of temporal lobe or partial complex seizures overlap with multiple personality disorder; two reports have postulated that these disorders are etiologies of multiple personality disorder (37,38). However, discussion of this point is impeded because many patients described in these articles did not fulfill recognized diagnostic criteria for multiple personality disorder, and many patients' descriptions of their personalities were not documented by clinicians' observations. Also, the patients' responses to anticonvulsants were often unconvincing (37,38; noted in 3,77,78).

The presence or absence of electroencephalographic findings is helpful but may be inconclusive. Patients with such seizures may not regularly show EEG findings, and patients with multiple personality disorder may have intercurrent and unrelated EEG abnormalities. Since multiple personality disorder patients often have placebo responses (77), a trial of anticonvulsants, unless accompanied by vigorous observation and a prolonged follow-up, may be inconclusive. Often hypnosis, amytal interview, or observation by skilled nursing personnel can contribute to resolving the dilemma of this differential diagnosis.

Malingering often enters the differential diagnosis, especially when a patient's circumstances would make the enacting of multiple personality disorder behaviors useful in the pursuit of an obviously understandable goal. Many patients with multiple personality disorder run afoul of the law; antisocial behaviors by personalities are not uncommon. One may encounter a patient with legitimate multiple personality disorder who augments his disorder or partially malingers to try to escape the consequences of antisocial actions.

The problem of malingering in multiple personality disorder has been addressed in several articles in a recent journal (20) and in a recent study (79). Malingering may be maintained even under hypnosis and in amytal interviews. In practice, most malingering by individuals trying to simulate multiple personality disorder is crude. It reveals itself by inconsistency and by the patient's preoccupation with the stressful circumstances that he is feigning the disorder to avoid. Genuine multiple personality disorder patients usually remain entrapped by their inner conflicts even when under stress and thus have trouble relating to their pressing problems; their dissociative defenses come into play to evade the current stressors.

In my experience, persons who are completely malingering base their presentations on lay sources of information; theirs is a blatant picture of multiple personality disorder rather than the polysymptomatic presentations usually encountered. They overstate their case and do not maintain consistent alternate personalities in areas unrelated to the motivations for their malingering (3,79). While differential diagnosis remains problematic, the evaluator with state-of-the-art knowledge usually unmasks the malingerer. In a recent case, a woman's classic presentation of multiple personality disorder lacked any of the features commonly associated with the condition. When confronted, she admitted she was basing her ersatz disorder on a representation in a popular soap opera.

ADDITIONAL RECENT FINDINGS

One of the most exciting advances in the understanding of multiple personality disorder is its discovery and successful treatment in children (66,67,80–82). In children the syndrome is often less florid than in adults, perhaps because the child's personalities are less invested in maintaining autonomy.

Children can often be successfully treated in much less time than adults. If the patient can be protected from retraumatization, the prognosis is excellent. Two of my index patients remain healthy and integrated after five and seven years of follow-up. In the face of retraumatization, however, the dissociative defenses are so efficient that the relapse rate verges on 100 percent.

It has recently been found that multiple personality disorder has a familial pattern. Anecdotal reports of the disorder in three generations of a single family (66) were followed by an in-depth study of 18 families in which dissociative disorders proved quite common (59). In an anterospective study of parents with multiple personality disorder, instances of multiple personality disorder and dissociative disorders were discovered among the children (9).

Tragically it is not uncommon for a parent with multiple personality disorder to abuse a child and create the syndrome in that child. Nor is it uncommon for a parent with the disorder to block out evidence that suggests the child may be exposed to danger and thereby facilitate others' abuse of the child. The impact on a child of being raised by, and identifying with, a parent with the disorder remains to be studied. Identifying with a parent with multiple personality disorder may prove to be an alternative pathway to the development of the condition. All children of multiple personality disorder patients should receive a comprehensive psychiatric evaluation at regular intervals (9,81).

Traditionally multiple personality disorder has been considered most common in women. Workers in the field have long suspected that males with multiple personality disorder were underrepresented in clinical populations because they ran afoul of the law and entered the criminal justice system. Anecdotal observations to this effect have been made (30). Bliss and Larson (83) interviewed 33 convicted male sexual offenders and found that seven of their subjects had multiple personality disorder by *DSM-III* criteria, and another six had suggestive but not definitive signs. Assessment of a substantial number of males with multiple personality disorder may lead to considerable revisions of our understanding of this condition.

It also has been found that a fraction of multiple personality disorder patients function at a very high level and evade detection for long periods. Instances of multiple personality disorder in physicians have been described (84).

TREATMENT OF MULTIPLE PERSONALITY DISORDER

Braun's *Treatment of Multiple Personality Disorder* (85) and a recent review (86) have attempted to summarize what is currently known about the treatment of the syndrome, covering both general principles and the application of various modalities. Multiple personality disorder is found in a diverse group of individuals with a wide range of concomitant axis I and axis II diagnoses and many different constellations of ego strengths and dynamics (77,86,87). Therefore treatments must be highly individualized. For example, if a patient's personalities are readily available and accessible, there may be little reason to introduce hypnosis or amytal interviews. However, the majority of successful treatments have been accomplished in intense but supportive psychodynamic psychotherapies facilitated with hypnotherapeutic interventions.

The tasks of therapy are the same as those in any intense, change-oriented approach but are pursued with a patient whose personality is not unified. Therefore one cannot assume the presence of an ongoing and available observing ego, and the therapist may encounter profound disruptions of usually autonomous ego functions, such as memory. Personalities may have different perceptions, recollections, priorities, goals, and degrees of commitment to the therapy, the therapist, and one another (77,86). For therapy to succeed, it becomes essential for the personalities to gradually arrive at a unity of purpose and a common motivation. Efforts to achieve such cooperation and facilitate the personalities' integration distinguishes the therapy of multiple personality disorder (13,70,77).

While integration is desirable, pragmatism must prevail. Caul (88) argues, "It seems to me that after treatment you want a functional unit, be it a corporation, a partnership, or a one-owner business." O'Brien (55) tersely notes, "A negotiated 'detente' may be the best result achievable at the time."

In discussions of treatment objectives, usually fusion, integration, and unification are used as synonyms; they "connote the spontaneous or facilitated coming together after adequate therapy has helped the patient to see, abreact, and work through the reasons for being of each separate alter. Consequently, the therapy serves to erode the barriers between the alters, and allow mutual acceptance, empathy, and identification. It does not indicate the dominance of one alter, the creation of a new 'healthy' alter, or a premature compression or suppression of alters into the appearance of a resolution" (86).

More recently integration has been used to describe an ongoing intrapsychic process of undoing all aspects of dissociative dividedness that begins long before there is any reduction in the number or distinctness of the personalities, that persists throughout the treatment of the divided individual, and that continues at a deeper level even when the separate personalities have blended into one. Fusion has come to mean "three stable months of 1) continuity of contemporary memory, 2) absence of overt behavioral signs of multiplicity, 3) subjective sense of unity, 4) absence of alter personalities on hypnotic re-exploration (hypnotherapy cases only), 5) modification of transference phenomena consistent with the bringing together of personalities, and 6) clinical evidence that the unified patient's self-representation included acknowledgment of attitudes and awarenesses which were previously segregated in separate personalities" (60). Such a stable period usually occurs after the collapse of several apparent fusions that occurred prematurely, before all necessary therapeutic work had been achieved.

Virtually every aspect of treatment depends on the strength of the therapeutic alliance, which must be cultivated globally and with each personality. The personalities are treated equally, with respect and empathic concern. As they increasingly accept themselves as dissociated aspects of a total person, their inner battles and claims on autonomy gradually diminish. This is often a painful, prolonged, and arduous process (77,86). Attempts to take sides in the personalities' inner wars or to suppress personalities generally prolong treatment.

These cautions do not mean the therapist should not be a firm advocate of reality. He should attempt to explore and, when necessary, discourage irresponsible or self-destructive behaviors.

Braun (89) has outlined treatment issues and described an approach that is universal enough to apply to most modalities and formats. Most of the steps he recommends are overlapping and ongoing rather than sequential. Treatment begins with the creation of an atmosphere of safety or trust (step 1). Operationally this means enough trust to carry on the work of a difficult therapy. The diagnosis must be made and shared with the accessible personalities (step 2), soon after the patient is comfortable with the therapist and enough data are available to place the issue before the patient in a tactful and circumspect way. Only when the patient appreciates his situation can the true treatment of multiple personality disorder begin.

Next one must establish communication with the accessible personalities (step 3). In patients whose personalities rarely emerge spontaneously and cannot switch voluntarily, the use of hypnosis may be helpful. Thereafter, it is important to assess the personalities' pressures toward harming self, others, or the body they share and to contract against such activities (step 4). Failing such an agreement, aspects of the treatment may require a hospital setting. Then the therapist must learn the origin, functions, and problems of each alter and the manner in which they relate to one another (step 5).

Subsequently work is done to address the personalities' issues and problems (step 6). Difficult times are likely, because most personalities were developed in connection with traumatic events and distressing relationships. In connection with this step, it becomes possible to comprehend the structure of the system of personalities (step 7), a process that often involves special procedures such as art therapy, movement therapy, or hypnosis. Building on the above foundation, therapy increasingly focuses on enhancing communications among the personalities (step 8), either directly via inner dialogues or through the therapist. Hypnosis has proven extremely valuable in such interventions. On occasion the personalities are helped to interact in an "inner group therapy" (90).

With communications established, therapy works toward achieving a resolution of the personalities' conflicts and their integration (step 9). Hypnosis is often a useful facilitator of these processes. Once integrated, the patient must develop new defenses and coping skills (step 10) to obviate the pressure to reconstitute dissociative mechanisms. He must learn more appropriate interpersonal behaviors, including how to optimize available social supports (step 11). Thereafter, a considerable amount of working-through and ongoing support is necessary to solidify gains (step 12), and long-term follow-up is essential (step 13).

Multiple personality disorder responds well to intense psychotherapies that gain access to its inner structure and then use that access to bring treatment to bear on the traumatic experiences, maladaptive patterns, and intrapsychic conflicts manifested in the structure and interaction of the several personalities. These objectives may be achieved in an individual psychotherapy alone, or in a series of coordinated therapies provided by several therapists. There are no reports of achieving a complete resolution of multiple personality disorder with group or family therapy alone, although these approaches have a valuable, if circumscribed, role to play (90–93).

Financial problems may provide an obstacle to the provision of an optimal treatment. Ideally the patients should be seen twice a week or more, and hospitalization should be considered during crises and for safety during work on particularly distressing issues. Often the resources to support such a treatment are not available.

The core symptoms of multiple personality disorder are not responsive to pharmacotherapy, although concomitant anxiety, somatoform, and depressive symptoms may be. Consequently anxiolytics, sedatives, antidepressants, and mood stabilizers may play a valuable ancillary role. There is no firm role for antipsychotics in the management of this disorder; the role of anticonvulsants remains equivocal (77,94). It is crucial to be aware that medications may have different effects on different personalities.

Follow-up studies of patients treated in intense individual psychotherapy in accord with the principles described above indicate that the vast majority of patients, if treated at a suitable degree of intensity by a therapist experienced with multiple personality disorder, do well. In one study 52 patients were reassessed after appearing to fulfill criteria for fusion for a minimum of 27 months (70). They were interviewed at length, and rather aggressive hypnotic and nonhypnotic efforts were made to elicit signs of residual separateness. For 94.2 percent of the patients there was clear evidence of improved function and progress in life. The same proportion, 94.2 percent, had not relapsed into behaviorally manifest multiple personality disorder, and 78.8 percent had not suffered residual or recurrent dissociative difficulties of any form. These findings suggest that when motivated patients are offered appropriate treatment and energetic follow-up, they can achieve a stable remission of the symptoms that characterize the condition and can have stable and productive lives as unified individuals.

CONCLUSIONS

Multiple personality disorder is in the process of reentering the mainstream of psychiatry after a long and unfortunate absence. Newer findings have made it necessary to reconsider, and in most cases revise, longstanding beliefs about its phenomenology, etiology, and clinical management (95). Notwithstanding the fact that work with patients with multiple personality disorder is demanding and arduous, evidence is accumulating to suggest that the treatment of this syndrome is one of the more optimistic areas of contemporary psychiatric practice.

REFERENCES

1. Nemiah JC: Dissociative disorders, in Comprehensive Textbook of Psychiatry, 3rd ed. Edited by Kaplan H, Freedman A, Sadock B. Baltimore, Williams & Wilkins, 1981
2. Putnam RW, Loewenstein RJ, Silberman EK, et al: Multiple personality disorder in a hospital setting. Journal of Clinical Psychiatry 45:172–175, 1984
3. Kluft RP: Making the diagnosis of multiple personality disorder (MPD), in Directions in Psychiatry, Vol 5,

Lesson 23. Edited by Flach FF. New York, Hatherleigh, 1985

4. Diagnostic and Statistical Manual of Mental Disorders, 3rd ed. Washington, DC, American Psychiatric Association, 1980
5. Allison RB: A new treatment approach for multiple personalities. American Journal of Clinical Hypnosis 17:15–32, 1974
6. Beahrs JO: Unity and Multiplicity. New York, Brunner/Mazel, 1982
7. Bliss EL: Multiple personalities. Archives of General Psychiatry 37: 1388–1397, 1980
8. Clary WF, Burstin KJ, Carpenter JS: Multiple personality and borderline personality disorder. Psychiatric Clinics of North America 7:89–100, 1984
9. Coons PM: Children of parents with multiple personality disorder, in Childhood Antecedents of Multiple Personality. Edited by Kluft RP. Washington, DC, American Psychiatric Press, 1985
10. Greaves GB: Multiple personality: 165 years after Mary Reynolds. Journal of Nervous and Mental Disease 168:577–596, 1980
11. Hicks RE: Discussion: a clinician's perspective, in Childhood Antecedents of Multiple Personality. Edited by Kluft RP. Washington, DC, American Psychiatric Press, 1985
12. Horevitz RP, Braun BG: Are multiple personalities borderline? Psychiatric Clinics of North America 7:69–88, 1984
13. Kluft RP: Treatment of multiple personality disorder: a study of 33 cases. Psychiatric Clinics of North America 7:9–29, 1984
14. Putnam FW, Guroff JJ, Silberman EK, et al: The clinical phenomenology of multiple personality disorder: review of 100 recent cases. Journal of Clinical Psychiatry 47:285–293, 1986
15. Solomon RS, Solomon V: Differential diagnosis of multiple personality. Psychological Reports 51:1187–1194, 1982
16. Shule R, Braun BG, Kluft RP: Creativity and the imaginary companion phenomenon: prevalence and phenomenology in MPD. Presented at the Second International Conference on Multiple Personality/Dissociative States, Chicago, Oct 1985
17. Braun BG (ed): American Journal of Clinical Hypnosis 26:(2), 1983
18. Kluft RP (ed): Psychiatric Annals 14:(1), 1984
19. Braun BG (ed): Psychiatric Clinics of North America 7:(1), 1984
20. Orne MT (ed.): International Journal of Clinical and Experimental Hypnosis 32:(2), 1984
21. O'Regan B (ed): Investigations 1:(3/4), 1985
22. Boor M, Coons PM: A comprehensive bibliography of literature pertaining to multiple personality. Psychological Reports 53:295–310, 1983
23. Damgaard J, Van Benschoten S, Fagen J: An updated bibliography of literature pertaining to multiple personality. Psychological Reports 57: 131–137, 1985
24. Kline MV: Multiple personality: facts and artifacts in relation to hypnotherapy. International Journal of Clinical and Experimental Hypnosis 32:198–209, 1984
25. Thigpen CH, Cleckley HM: On the incidence of multiple personality disorder. International Journal of Clinical and Experimental Hypnosis 32: 63–66, 1984
26. Chodoff P: More on multiple personality disorder (ltr). American Journal of Psychiatry 144:124, 1987
27. Orne MT, Dinges DF, Orne EC: On the differential diagnosis of multiple personality in the forensic context. International Journal of Clinical and Experimental Hypnosis 32:118–169, 1984
28. Bliss EL, Larson EM, Nakashima SR: Auditory hallucinations and schizophrenia. Journal of Nervous and Mental Disease 171:30–33, 1983
29. Coons PM, Milstein V: Psychosexual disturbances in multiple personality: characteristics, etiology, and treatment. Journal of Clinical Psychiatry 47:106–110, 1986
30. Kluft RP: The natural history of multiple personality disorder, in Childhood Antecedents of Multiple Personality. Edited by Kluft RP. Washington, DC, American Psychiatric Press, 1985
31. Ross CA: Diagnosis of multiple personality during hypnosis: a case report. International Journal of Clinical and Experimental Hypnosis 32: 222–235, 1984
32. Schreiber FR: Sybil. New York, Henry Regnery, 1973
33. Spiegel D: Multiple personality as a post-traumatic stress disorder. Psychiatric Clinics of North America 7: 101–110, 1984
34. Putnam FW: Dissociation as a response to extreme trauma, in Childhood Antecedents of Multiple Personality. Edited by Kluft RP. Washington, DC, American Psychiatric Press, 1985
35. Kluft RP: More on multiple personality disorder: reply (ltr). American Journal of Psychiatry 144:124–125, 1987
36. Spiegel D: Dissociation, double binds, and posttraumatic stress in multiple personality disorder, in Treatment of Multiple Personality Disorder. Edited by Braun BG. Washington, DC, American Psychiatric Press, 1986
37. Mesulam M: Dissociative states with abnormal temporal lobe EEG. Archives of Neurology 38:176–181, 1981
38. Schenk L, Bear D: Multiple personality and related dissociative phenomena in patients with temporal lobe epilepsy. American Journal of Psychiatry 138:1311–1316, 1981
39. Cocores JA, Bender AL, McBride E: Multiple personality, seizure disorder, and the electroencephalogram. Journal of Nervous and Mental Disease 172:436–438, 1984
40. Coons PM, Milstein V, Marley C: EEG studies of two multiple personalities and a control. Archives of General Psychiatry 39:823–825, 1982
41. Brende JO: The psychophysiologic manifestations of dissociation: electrodermal responses in a multiple personality patient. Psychiatric Clinics of North America 7:41–50, 1984
42. Mathews RJ, Jack RA, West WS: Regional blood flow in a patient with multiple personality. American Journal of Psychiatry 142:504–505, 1985

43. Putnam FW: The psychophysiologic investigation of multiple personality disorder: a review. Psychiatric Clinics of North America 7:31–39, 1984
44. Braun BG: Neurophysiologic changes in multiple personality due to integration: a preliminary report. American Journal of Clinical Hypnosis 26: 84–92, 1983
45. Braun BG: Towards a theory of multiple personality and other dissociative phenomena. Psychiatric Clinics of North America 7:171–193, 1984
46. Bliss EL: How prevalent is multiple personality disorder? Reply (ltr). American Journal of Psychiatry 142: 1527, 1985
47. Ludolph PS: How prevalent is multiple personality? (ltr). American Journal of Psychiatry 142:1526–1527, 1985
48. Kluft RP: The prevalence of multiple personality (ltr). American Journal of Psychiatry 143:802–803, 1986
49. Spanos NP, Weekes JR, Bertrand LD: Multiple personality: a social psychological perspective. Journal of Abnormal Psychology 94:362–376, 1985
50. Harriman P: The experimental production of some phenomena of multiple personality. Journal of Abnormal and Social Psychology 37: 244–255, 1942
51. Harriman P: A new approach to multiple personality. American Journal of Orthopsychiatry 13:638–643, 1943
52. Leavitt H: A case of hypnotically produced secondary and tertiary personalities. Psychoanalytic Review 34:274–295, 1947
53. Kampman R: Hypnotically induced multiple personality. International Journal of Clinical and Experimental Hypnosis 24:215–227, 1976
54. Ross CA: DSM-III: problems in diagnosing partial forms of multiple personality disorder: discussion paper. Journal of the Royal Society of Medicine 78:933–936, 1985
55. O'Brien P: The diagnosis of multiple personality syndromes: overt, covert, and latent. Comprehensive Therapy 11:59–66, 1985
56. Bliss EL: Multiple personalities, related disorders, and hypnosis. American Journal of Clinical Hypnosis 26:114–123, 1983
57. Bliss EL: Spontaneous self-hypnosis in multiple personality disorder. Psychiatric Clinics of North America 7:135–148, 1984
58. Bliss EL, Jeppsen EA: Prevalence of multiple personality among inpatients and outpatients. American Journal of Psychiatry 142:250–251, 1985
59. Braun BG: The transgenerational incidence of dissociation and multiple personality disorder: a preliminary report, in Childhood Antecedents of Multiple Personality. Edited by Kluft RP. Washington, DC, American Psychiatric Press, 1985
60. Kluft RP: Varieties of hypnotic interventions in the treatment of multiple personality. American Journal of Clinical Hypnosis 24:230–240, 1982
61. Braun BG: Hypnosis creates multiple personality: myth or reality? International Journal of Clinical and Experimental Hypnosis 32:191–197, 1984
62. Hilgard E: Multiple Controls in Human Thought and Action. New York, Wiley, 1977
63. Watkins JG, Watkins HH: Ego-state therapy, in Handbook of Innovative Therapies. Edited by Corsini R. New York, Wiley, 1981
64. Gruenewald D: On the nature of multiple personality: comparisons with hypnosis. International Journal of Clinical and Experimental Hypnosis 32:170–190, 1984
65. Kluft RP: Using hypnotic inquiry protocols to monitor treatment progress and stability in multiple personality disorder. American Journal of Clinical Hypnosis 28:63–75, 1985
66. Kluft RP: Multiple personality in childhood. Psychiatric Clinics of North America 7:121–134, 1984
67. Kluft RP: Childhood multiple personality disorder: predictors, clinical findings, and treatment results, in Childhood Antecedents of Multiple Personality. Edited by Kluft RP. Washington, DC, American Psychiatric Press, 1985
68. Woodruff RA, Goodwin DW, Guze SB: Psychiatric Diagnosis. New York, Oxford University Press, 1974
69. Coons PM: Treatment progress in 20 patients with multiple personality disorder. Journal of Nervous and Mental Disease 174:715–721, 1986
70. Kluft RP: Personality unification in multiple personality disorder: a follow-up study, in Treatment of Multiple Personality Disorder. Edited by Braun BG. Washington, DC, American Psychiatric Press, 1986
71. Lipman LS: Hypnotizability and multiple personality. Presented at the annual meeting of the American Psychiatric Association, Dallas, May 18–24, 1985
72. Hilgard J: Personality and Hypnosis. Chicago, University of Chicago Press, 1970
73. Nash MR, Lynn SJ, Givens DL: Adult hypnotic susceptibility, childhood punishment, and child abuse: a brief communication. International Journal of Clinical and Experimental Hypnosis 32:6–11, 1984
74. Schneider K: Clinical Psychopathology, 5th ed. New York, Grune & Stratton, 1959
75. Work Group to Revise DSM-III: Draft: DSM-III-R in Development 10/5/85. Washington, DC, American Psychiatric Association, 1985
76. Arlow JA, Brenner C: Psychoanalytic Concepts and the Structural Theory. New York, International Universities Press, 1964
77. Kluft RP: Aspects of the treatment of multiple personality disorder. Psychiatric Annals 14:51–55, 1984
78. Coons PM: The differential diagnosis of multiple personality. Psychiatric Clinics of North America 7:51–68, 1984
79. Kluft RP: The simulation and dissimulation of multiple personality disorder. American Journal of Clinical Hypnosis 30:104–118, 1987
80. Fagan J, McMahon PP: Incipient multiple personality in children: four cases. Journal of Nervous and Mental Disease 172:26–36, 1984
81. Kluft RP: Treating children who have multiple personality disorder, in Treatment of Multiple Personality Disorder. Edited by Braun BG. Washington, DC, American Psychiatric Press, 1986

82. Weiss M, Sutton PJ, Utecht AJ: Multiple personality in a 10-year-old girl. Journal of the American Academy of Child Psychiatry 24:495–501, 1985
83. Bliss EL, Larson EM: Sexual criminality and hypnotizability. Journal of Nervous and Mental Disease 173: 522–526, 1985
84. Kluft RP: High-functioning multiple personality patients. Journal of Nervous and Mental Disease 174:722–726, 1986
85. Braun BG (ed): Treatment of Multiple Personality Disorder. Washington, DC, American Psychiatric Press, 1986
86. Kluft RP: The treatment of multiple personality disorder (MPD): current concepts, in Directions in Psychiatry, Vol 5, Lesson 24. Edited by Flach FF. New York, Hatherleigh, 1985
87. Kernberg OF: Some clinical observations on the multiple personality, in Multiple Personality and Dissociation. Edited by Braun BG, Kluft RP. New York, Brunner/Mazel (in press)
88. Hale E: Inside the divided mind. New York Times Magazine, Apr 17, 1983, pp 100–106
89. Braun BG: Issues in the psychotherapy of multiple personality disorder, in Treatment of Multiple Personality Disorder. Edited by Braun DG. Washington, DC, American Psychiatric Press, 1986
90. Caul D: Group and videotape techniques for multiple personality disorder. Psychiatric Annals 14:43–55, 1984
91. Kluft RP, Braun BG, Sachs RG: Multiple personality, intrafamilial abuse, and family psychiatry. International Journal of Family Psychiatry 5:283–301, 1984
92. Caul D, Sachs RG, Braun BG: Group therapy in the treatment of multiple personality disorder, in Treatment of Multiple Personality Disorder. Edited by Braun BG. Washington, DC, American Psychiatric Press, 1986
93. Coons PM, Bradley K: Group psychotherapy with multiple personality patients. Journal of Nervous and Mental Disease 173:515-521, 1985
94. Barkin R, Braun BG, Kluft RP: The dilemma of drug therapy for multiple personality disorder, in Treatment of Multiple Personality Disorder. Edited by Braun BG. Washington, DC, American Psychiatric Press, 1986
95. Kluft RP: Dissociative disorders, in An Annotated Bibliography of DSM-III. Edited by Skodol AE, Spitzer RL. Washington, DC, American Psychiatric Press (in press)

THOMAS A. FAHY

The diagnosis of multiple personality disorder: A critical review

> Eve seemed momentarily dazed. Suddenly her posture began to change. Her body slowly stiffened until she sat rigidly erect. An alien, inexplicable expression then came over her face. This was suddenly erased into utter blankness. . . . She relaxed easily into an attitude of comfort the physician had never before seen in this patient. A pair of blue eyes popped open. There was a quick reckless smile. In a bright unfamiliar voice that sparkled the woman said, "Hi, there, Doc!"
>
> —*THE THREE FACES OF EVE* (THIGPEN & CLECKLEY, 1957), P. 26

Acknowledgments: I am grateful to Drs. A. David, S. Wessely, and J. Cutting.

S. L. Mitchill is usually credited with the first description of a case of multiple personality disorder following his publication in 1816 of a case of double consciousness (Mitchill, 1816). The patient was a young English woman, Mary Reynolds, who had emigrated with her family to a rural area of Pennsylvania. She was a bright and healthy child, but during her teenage years developed fits and episodes of blindness which were thought to be symptoms of psychological disturbance. In her early 20s:

> Unexpectedly, and without any kind of forewarning, she fell into a profound sleep, which continued several hours beyond the ordinary term. On waking she was discovered to have lost every trait of acquired knowledge. Her memory was *tabula rasa*; all vestiges both of words and of things, were obliterated and gone. It was found necessary for her to learn everything again . . . after a few months another fit of somnolency invaded her. On rousing from it, she found herself restored to the state she was before the paroxysm; but she was wholly ignorant of every event and occurrence that had befallen her afterwards . . . she is as unconscious of her *double* character as two distinct persons are of their respective natures . . . During four years and upwards, she has undergone periodical transitions

SOURCE: *British Journal of Psychiatry, 153*, pp. 597–606, 1988. Reprinted by permission of The Royal College of Psychiatrists, Publications Office, London, England.

from one of these states to the other. (Mitchill, 1816)

The old and new personalities continued to alternate until her death (Mitchell, 1888). This patient, like many others, attracted a great deal of interest from the medical profession and lay public alike, and she became known as *la dame de MacNish* after an account written by MacNish which achieved some popularity in France (MacNish, 1830; Ellenberger, 1970). The small number of references to the condition in the first half of the 19th century included two British reports of dual consciousness (Mayo, 1845; Skae, 1845). No cases of the disorder were published between 1846 and 1873.

After the turn of the century, Morton Prince reviewed a collection of 20 patients (Prince, 1905) and later published a celebrated account of one patient, Christine Beauchamp (Prince, 1920). From this time, most cases were reported as having more than two personalities, and the condition became known as multiple personality disorder (MPD). Prince's use of hypnosis to investigate the alternate personalities, and his speculations on their function, had a profound influence on later observers. In an attempt to explain his patients' bizarre symptoms, he postulated the existence of a physiological cerebral mechanism that allowed disintegration of the personality. He believed that anatomical changes occurred, which were an extreme variation of normal function and were similar to those occurring in sleep (Prince, 1901). Taylor & Martin, in their classic review (1944), identified 28 cases in the literature between 1874 and 1900. They described three types of organization, based on the amount of "leakage" of information between alternates; these were the mutually amnesic, one-way amnesic, and co-conscious types. They were adamant that hypnosis did not account for the unusual symptoms.

The diagnosis was made infrequently in the first half of the 20th century. This decline has been ascribed by Rosenbaum (1980) to the introduction of the term schizophrenia by Bleuler in 1911, but there is little evidence, except for the coincidence of dates, to support this assertion. The diagnosis was heavily criticized from the first case descriptions. It was commonly held that these patients were clever and suggestible "mythomaniacs," who were capable of impressing less-clever and gullible clinicians (Ellenberger, 1970). Cutler & Reed (1975) have suggested that many of the early cases were brain damaged, but supporters of the diagnosis may have interpreted the possibility of an organic hypothesis as contributing to the authenticity of the diagnosis.

The recent history of the condition has been punctuated by the appearance of several widely publicized biographical accounts of MPD patients (multiples) (Thigpen & Cleckley, 1957; Schreiber, 1973; Hanksworth & Schwarz, 1977; Keyes, 1981) and alleged multiples (Schwartz, 1981; Levin & Fox, 1985). The number of reports in the literature has also increased dramatically since 1970. Bliss (1986) estimates that 300 cases have been reported in the world literature, at least 79 occurring between 1970 and 1981 (Greaves, 1980; Boor, 1982), but only eight cases were identifiable in the 25-year period prior to this. This "epidemic" (Boor, 1982) is indicative of the renewed interest in the disorder, particularly in North America, a trend also reflected in the need for a detailed bibliography published in 1983 to require major revision only 2 years later (Boor & Coons, 1983; Damgaard *et al*, 1985).

The nosological status of MPD was altered when it was listed as a diagnosis among the dissociative states in DSM-III (American Psychiatric Association, 1980), having been included as a symptom in the hysteria section in DSM-II (American Psychiatric Association, 1968). MPD will also be accorded special recognition in ICD-10 [*International Classification of Diseases*, 10th edition], where it will become a separate diagnosis classified under the dissociative disorders of memory, awareness, and identity (World Health Organization, 1987).

Supporters of the diagnosis of MPD attribute the increase in case reporting to greater accuracy in diagnosis following clarification of the definition of schizophrenia by DSM-III (Kluft, 1987), and greater awareness of the condition among professionals, which may be due in part to wider availability of "educational" material, including annual workshops on the topic held by the American Psychiatric Association. Public awareness of the condition has also been raised following the release of dramatized written and cinematic biographies of sufferers, and this may have led to an increased number of patients presenting themselves to experts (Thigpen & Cleckley, 1984). An upsurge of interest in child abuse, hypnosis, and post-traumatic stress disorder may also have attracted researchers to the diagnosis. Some critics have suggested that the increase in case reporting reflects iatrogenic and cultural influences on suggestible patients (Chodoff, 1987). It is also significant, as Orne *et al* (1984) have pointed out, that a small number of clinicians are responsible for the increased number of reports, suggesting that estimates of prevalence require cautious interpretation, because of possible selection bias. Until basic epidemiological studies are performed, all estimates of prevalence are no more than speculative.

DIAGNOSTIC CRITERIA

According to DSM-III, multiple personality disorder can be diagnosed by the presence of the following criteria:

a. The existence within the person of two or more distinct personalities, each of which is dominant at a particular time.
b. The personality that is dominant at any particular time determines the individual's behavior.
c. Each individual is complex and integrated with its own unique behavior patterns and social relationships.

These criteria have been justifiably criticized by Ludolph (1985) as excessively vague and open to a wide variety of interpretations. The failure to provide a satisfactory description of "personality" in the context of the diagnostic criteria is a significant weakness of DSM-III. In addition, the criteria do not specify if the diagnosis can be established when the patient demonstrates symptoms only after hypnosis. Most significantly, inter-rater reliability for detection of these criteria has not been assessed in any major studies. No attempts have been made to eliminate problems of possible selection bias and poor case definition by using standardized interviews as opposed to "standardized criteria."

Surprisingly, the DSM-III criteria have been criticized from some quarters for being over-strict, excluding patients with incomplete forms of the disorder and those with so many alternates that it is impossible for any single personality to meet DSM-III criteria (Bliss, 1983; Kluft, 1985*a*). DSM-III-R takes these incomplete forms of the disorder into account by classifying them as dissociative reactions not otherwise specified (Work group to revise DSM-III, 1985).

PHENOMENOLOGY

Putnam *et al* (1986) have made the most detailed assessment of the clinical phenomenology of MPD. They circulated a 386-item questionnaire, employing symptom checklists, multiple-choice questions, and rating scales, to 400 clinicians with a known interest in MPD, seeking information on cases of MPD meeting DSM-III criteria. One hundred cases were selected, including 92 females, based on the number of questions completed by clinicians. Unfortunately, no demographic data were given on the excluded cases. The average age at diagnosis was 31.3 years. The patients were well educated, and many had achieved a high occupational status. Ninety-five per cent had received one or more psychiatric or neurological diagnoses prior to the diagnosis of MPD; the interval between first presentation and diagnosis of MPD was on average 7 years. The patients presented with an impressive array of symptoms, most prominently depression, anxiety, eating disorders and auditory and visual hallucinations. Many presented with "hysterical" or "dissociative" symptoms, including psychogenic amnesia (55%), conversion symptoms (50%), and fugue episodes (50%). The number of personalities ranged from 1 to 60, the average being 13.3. In 85 cases, one of the alternates was reported to be a child. In 61%, suicidal behavior was associated with the alternate personality, and 34% had indulged in self-mutilation. Violent behavior toward others was commonly attributed to alternates. Homicidal behavior was alleged in 6%, and sexual assault in 20%. Somatic symptoms and drug abuse were common, and in 50%, one of the alternates was sexually promiscuous. Amnesia was a symptom in 95% of patients. These findings resemble the symptom profiles reported by other authors (Boor, 1982; Bliss, 1984*a*). Bliss has stressed the importance of amnesia and lost time as symptoms that should raise the clinical suspicion of MPD (Bliss, 1980).

DIFFERENTIAL DIAGNOSIS

MPD can present with a diversity of symptoms, including those commonly associated with affective disturbance and schizophrenia. Most patients have received one of these diagnoses before the diagnosis of MPD is made. Unlike schizophrenia, reality testing is said to be well preserved, and affect is likely to be appropriate, although compartmentalized. Up to 50% of patients experience auditory hallucinations (Bliss, 1980; Bliss *et al*, 1983). The EEG is of little help in distinguishing MPD from temporal-lobe epilepsy, since a high rate of non-specific abnormalities has been detected in MPD patients, most commonly, bilateral temporal-lobe slowing (Putnam, 1986).

Malingering is said to be an important differential diagnosis where an obvious gain may result from psychiatric intervention, for example in subjects on remand for serious offenses. The presentation in cases of conscious simulation may be crude, inconsistent, and overstated (Orne *et al*, 1984; Kluft, 1987). A recent notorious case was that of Kenneth Bianchi, better known as the "Hillside Strangler." Bianchi was found guilty of the sadistic murder of ten young women in Los Angeles between 1977 and 1978. A diagnosis of MPD was proposed by expert witnesses for the defense, but their case was rejected by the court when it was revealed that Bianchi had previously impersonated a psychologist and that he had free access to his psychiatric files during the course of the examinations. He also managed to produce a third personality when it was suggested to him that true cases of MPD rarely had only two personalities.

Borderline personality disorder has been diagnosed in 70% of a sample of 33 patients (Horevitz & Braun, 1983) and 23% of 70 patients (Kluft, 1982). In Bliss' series of 21 DSM-III multiples, 76% qualified for designation as Briquet's syndrome (Bliss, 1986) and eight out of ten of a series of Coons' patients satisfied RDC [Research Diagnostic Criteria] criteria for Briquet's syndrome (Coons, 1984). Putnam acknowledges that a large number of his cases bear a resemblance to Briquet's syndrome or somatization disorder, but like other investigators, he proposes that once the diagnostic criteria for MPD are satisfied, MPD should be considered the superordinate diagnosis, since working with the alternates can provide a therapeutic device that cannot be utilized in the "unified" individual (Putnam, 1987).

MPD may prove difficult to distinguish from other dissociative amnesic disorders. In these states, behavior may be complex, but recovery is often complete, recurrences are less common, and the onset of the amnesic spell may be intimately related to a stressful event. Prince mistakenly diagnosed Ansel Bourne as suffering from MPD. The turn-of-the century itinerant preacher disappeared after a disagreement with his wife and reassumed awareness of his former life after 8 weeks as a shopkeeper in a distant town under the name A. J. Brown. His condition did not recur after this episode and was more typical of a fugue state than MPD (Hogson, 1891).

PSYCHOLOGICAL AND PHYSIOLOGICAL INVESTIGATIONS

The complex nature of MPD has been demonstrated in results from serial psychological assessments of individual cases. Loewenstein has used an experiential sampling method to investigate a single MPD patient. In this type of study, information on the patient's mood, self-perception, and clinical state is collected on a random basis, comparing self-reporting of symptoms with results obtained on standardized rating scales, in a naturalistic setting (Loewenstein *et al*, 1987). It is claimed that these investigations show alternates to display characteristics that are as different as those that occur between separate individuals, for example, on rating scales measuring quantitative differences in mood and motivation. In other studies, differences across alternates were noted on the MMPI, Adjective Check Lists, and McDougal's Scale of Emotions (Ludwig *et al*, 1972; Larmore *et al*, 1977). Ludwig *et al* (1972), in a study of a patient with four personalities, found that emotionally neutral material could become general to other personalities by a practice effect, but emotionally laden words generalized less well, implying that the different personalities were relatively independent in emotionally relevant areas. Silberman *et al* (1985) administered two distinct lists of non-emotive words to MPD patients and simulating control subjects (pretending to be multiple-personality disordered). They hypothesized that if MPD patients were truly dissociated, they would show a special ability to discriminate the two sets of stimuli. The study failed to demonstrate such an ability, but it was found that dissociation enhanced the underlying compartmentalization capabilities of the patients, while in control subjects, attempts to mimic dissociation disrupted this ability.

Others have searched for physiological measures on which alternates can be compared with normal separate individuals. The purpose of this type of research is unclear. These authors clearly do not think that patients have more than one brain, but there is implicit in their work the equally unlikely assumption that MPD and allied hysterical or dissociative disorders may be the result of a specific neurophysiological or anatomical anomaly. Prince & Peterson (1908) investigated skin-resistance response to emotionally laden words, and found variations in reactions between alternates. Latterly, studies have concentrated on EEGs. Thigpen & Cleckley (1954), investigating their patient, Eve, found dissimilarities between alternates on EEGs, with differing muscle tension and alpha background frequency. Condon *et al* (1969), investigating the same patient, discovered differences in three types of divergent eye movement across the alternates. Coons *et al* (1982) compared a simulating control subject with two MPD patients and found that all differed in EEG recordings across alternates, which they attributed to changes in the levels of arousal and mood among the subjects, a conclusion supported by the work of Cocores *et al* (1984). Putnam studied the P100, N120, and P200 components of the visual evoked response in a group of MPD patients and simulating control subjects. He also found differences in both groups, the MPD patients being less similar across alternates (Putnam, 1986). In a single case, Bahnson & Smith (1975) found the transitions between alternates were accompanied by bradycardia, a reduction in skin potential, and dramatic respiratory pauses of up to 2 min duration. Paroxysmal abnormalities in the EEG have been reported in one case of MPD, a 16-year-old girl who presented with four distinct personalities and amnesic somnambulism, whose EEG showed paroxysmal discharges and abortive spikes (Horton & Miller, 1972). Clinical descriptions analyzed by Sutcliffe & Jones (1962) suggest that many additional cases in the literature may have been epileptic. Mesulam (1981) reports seven MPD-like patients with abnormal EEGs, most commonly temporal-lobe abnormalities. Cerebral blood flow patterns in a single-case study (Mathews *et al*, 1985) showed right temporal hyperperfusion following transition between alternates.

The significance of these results is unknown but there is no evidence to support a specific physiological change occurring with transition, and the results of physiological and psychological investigations are consistent with a generalized alteration in the level of arousal in the subject.

AN IATROGENIC DISORDER?

Since the earliest case descriptions of dual consciousness, critics have suggested that the presentation could be strongly influenced by the clinician through selective reinforcement of certain symptoms (Ellenberger, 1970; Greaves, 1980). The skepticism of critics and the frustration of supporters of MPD were recorded by Taylor & Martin (1944) and seems as apposite today as then:

> Apparently most ready to accept multiple personality as real are (1) persons who are very naive and (2) persons who have worked with actual cases or near cases.

The issue of iatrogenicity remains unresolved (Chodoff, 1987; Margetts, 1987). Although supporters of the diagnosis can point to the wide distribution of cases in time and place (Kluft, 1987), this distribution no longer extends outside the USA. Just one British case has appeared in the literature over the past 15 years (Cutler & Reed, 1975).

Spanos acknowledges the iatrogenic dimension within his social psychological conceptualization of the disorder

(Spanos *et al*, 1985). This model considers the patient to be actively involved in using the information available to him to create a social impression that is compatible with his objectives. An individual may learn to enact the MPD role collecting impressions from popular books and films, where these patients are often portrayed sympathetically. The powerful attraction of this high-status diagnosis was illustrated by the reaction to Thigpen & Cleckley's publication of *The Three Faces of Eve* (1957). The authors were overwhelmed by the number of people who contacted them, having diagnosed themselves as multiples (Thigpen & Cleckley, 1984). They were also referred "thousands" of patients for assessment, but considered only one of these to be a genuine case.

The psychotherapist could be an unwitting accomplice in molding the presentation, both by providing the patient with information and by selective reinforcement of symptoms. The practice of interviewing the alternates at length and giving them names may add to the complexity of the alternate. Each personality may thus acquire a history, a function, and elaborate patterns of behavior. Reactivity within an interview setting has been demonstrated in a case with three personalities. Selective reinforcement of one alternate produced an increase in the frequency of occurrence of this personality (Kohlenberg, 1973). Although this and similar experiments highlight the extent to which symptoms can be shaped iatrogenically, they do not prove that the disorder has its etiology within the clinical setting.

During the late 19th century, it was discovered that the symptoms of most hysterical disorders could be induced in good hypnotic subjects under the influence of hypnosis (Bramwell, 1906). These observations have led investigators to examine the relevance of hypnosis to hysterical disorders, including MPD. Putnam *et al* (1986) found that hypnosis was used to facilitate first revelation of the alternates in a minority of cases (23%). Since hypnosis has been used to diagnose and treat MPD, it has been important to clarify the extent to which it is responsible for the disorder. Under hypnosis, alternate personalities may reveal themselves when required by the therapist. That there is a relationship between hypnosis and MPD is suggested by the high hypnotizability scores of most MPD patients (Bliss, 1983; Putnam *et al*, 1986).

In an attempt to assess the influence of the clinician, some researchers have tried to induce symptoms of MPD in volunteers. Harriman studied "automatic writing" under the influence of hypnotic suggestion (Harriman, 1942). He concluded that normal subjects had many features in common with MPD patients, namely the production of alternates with different behavior patterns and mutual amnesia. These ill-defined "personalities" included one responsible for the cryptic automatic writing, another in a post-hypnotic somnambulistic state who knew nothing about the meaning of the writing, and finally, the normal integrated personality. However, Harriman was unable to produce more-complex personalities, similar to those found in the clinical setting, under hypnotic suggestion (Harriman, 1943).

Kampman (1976) has also studied the induction of alternates in hypnotized normal subjects. She found that 7% of normal individuals were able to respond to suggestions to create a secondary personality using an age regression test, i.e. the ability to comply with a request to regress to an earlier age. In 43 out of 78 good hypnotic subjects, she was able to create an age-regressed alternate. However, the age-regression model, like the automatic writing model, does not provide an entirely satisfactory comparison with MPD, lacking the complexity and chronicity of the clinical syndrome. There is scanty evidence that short-term exposure to hypnosis can induce well-developed alternates through the use of hypnosis alone. The experimentally induced personalities tend to be transitory, and their presence does not extend beyond the hypnotic experience (Erickson, 1980; Stern, 1984). The effects of long-term exposure to hypnosis within a clinical setting remain unknown, but there is little evidence that the therapeutic use of hypnosis is directly responsible for the disorder (Kluft, 1982). Nevertheless, Gruenewald (1971) urges caution in the use of hypnosis as an investigative tool, believing that it may sanction and reinforce the dissociative trend.

EXPLANATORY MODELS

Many authors have been ready to offer explanations for the development of MPD; indeed, there is a confusion of theories proposing psychological, sociological, and physiological causes. A small number of explanations are firmly grounded in research findings, including the following.

Traumatic Childhood Experiences

Traumatic childhood experiences, especially of physical abuse and neglect, are said to be common in MPD (Wilbur, 1984). Several studies have reported high rates of abuse but none have included control groups and most have relied on self-reports. Saltman & Solomon (1982) reported six cases of MPD occurring in incest victims. Bliss (1984*b*), in a series of 70 patients, estimated that 60% had been victims of sexual abuse and 40% were victims of other types of physical abuse during childhood. Coons & Milstein (1986) found similar rates of 75% and 55%, respectively. The highest figures have been reported by Putnam *et al* (1986), where 97% were reported by their clinicians to have a history of abuse in childhood. Sexual abuse, usually incest, was reported in 83%. Other types of physical abuse were reported in 75%, and a combination of physical and sexual abuse in 68%. In this study, the average age of onset of MPD was estimated at approximately 6 years. There was a negative relationship between the number of different types of trauma and the age at which an alternate was reported to have first appeared, but there was a negative correlation with the number of alternates.

How these traumatic experiences might lead to a presentation of MPD in later life is unclear. The effects of exposure to situations of extreme ambivalence and abuse in early childhood may be coped with, in a psychodynamic formulation, by an elaborate form of denial, so that the child believes the event to be happening to someone else (Lovinger, 1983). This process may be facilitated in childhood, a time when there is a rich fantasy life, often including imaginary companions. This elaborate and exotic form of defense may be a function of a higher level of ego organization than occurs in borderline or narcissistic personalities, where splitting into "all good and all bad" alternatives, denial or projective identification, are employed (Greaves, 1980).

It is also possible that traumatic experiences in childhood may enhance the individual's ability to dissociate. A positive correlation has been found between reporting of strict discipline and punishment in childhood and hypnotizability in adults (Cooper & London, 1976; Hilgard, 1970; Nash *et al*, 1984; Nowlis, 1969). Usually, hypnotizability diminishes with age, but in these individuals, traumatic experiences may preserve their high childhood scores.

Spontaneous Self-Hypnosis

The term self-hypnosis or autohypnosis usually refers to a consciously self-induced trance, brought on by a subject who has been taught the method by a skilled hypnotist. Bliss (1986) proposes that the MPD patient spontaneously undergoes a rapid, unpremeditated withdrawal into a hypnotic trance when faced with an anxiety-provoking situation. There is, as I have already outlined, a considerable amount of evidence linking hypnotic susceptibility with MPD. Bliss found that many of his patients entered trances rapidly, even though most had not been hypnotized previously (Bliss, 1984*b*). He believes that the patients were probably expert at slipping into self-induced trances, but had failed to recognize that this was a hypnotic process. Bliss also observed that multiples frequently enter trances during painful moments in therapy (Bliss, 1984*c*) and he suggests that patients embark on similar withdrawals when confronted with repugnant memories and stresses outside the clinical setting. That the MPD patient should manifest such symptoms may also be a function of the colorful fantasy life of the excellent hypnotic subject (Wilson & Barber, 1982). The world of deep hypnosis is seen as a bizarre and frightening domain, a place of hallucinations, conversion symptoms, terrors, and amnesia. British workers are relatively inexperienced in this area, and their objections to this theory of MPD may justifiably be criticized as lacking this perspective.

Despite his claim to be able to induce further alternates (including one named "Dr. Bliss") in patients, Bliss (1984*c*), like many others with a large collection of cases, is content to minimize the influence of the therapist on the symptom profile of his highly hypnotizable patients. That patients are excellent hypnotic subjects and prone to self-hypnosis does not prove that the relationship between hypnosis and MPD is causal. If the relationship was uncomplicated, it could be supposed that the condition is also treatable by hypnosis. This is also a controversial issue, but the compilers of the best established treatment guidelines consider hypnotherapy to be of limited value (Kluft, 1985*b*; Braun, 1986). An aptitude for self-hypnosis will not, in the absence of adversity, explain the bizarre presentation of MPD.

State-Dependent Learning

A state-dependent learning model of MPD attempts to explain the phenomenon of directional awareness between personalities, which occurs with mutual or one-way amnesia. It is postulated that memories specific to one state may only be accessed if the physiological cues of that alternate are present (Putnam, 1986). Likewise, memories acquired in one state of physiological arousal may be less easily retrieved in another state. As outlined above, physiological investigations of multiples suggest that alternates may be distinguished by measurement of correlates of arousal, including muscle tension. Although Silberman *et al* (1985) found that two lists of words were recalled separately better across mutually amnesic than mutually cognizant personalities, there has been little evidence to show that the ability to segregate memories is correlated with any measures of physiological arousal. The relationship of changes in the level of arousal to the amount of leakage between personalities needs to be clarified by proponents of this model. Although state-dependent learning could explain the common symptom of amnesia, it fails to provide a clue to the true origins of the disturbance.

MPD as a Personality Disorder

In view of implications for treatment, it is important to consider the extent to which MPD may be part of a specific personality disorder. Central to theories explaining MPD as a disorder of personality is the view that adverse experiences in early childhood can have a profound effect on the course of personality development. Kernberg (1975) characterizes the borderline personality-disordered patient as an individual with primitive defense mechanisms involving splitting, projective identification, idealization, omnipotence, devaluation, and denial. He has proposed that borderline narcissistic and hysterical disorders form a continuum according to the degree to which repression or splitting predominate. Borderline and MPD patients have many similarities, including their presentation with polyneurotic, conversion, and dissociative symptoms. Several authors view the multiple as a special instance of the borderline, where the underlying process is splitting of the internalized self and object concepts into "all-good" and "all-bad" parts which cannot coexist in consciousness and may abruptly displace each other, allowing the individual to function without contradiction (Lasky, 1978; Marmer, 1980; Buck, 1983; Clary *et al*, 1984). Using this model, the alternates show several borderline features, including primitive idealization, identity disturbance, and dramatic splitting. Greaves (1980) acknowledges that MPD patients may be personality disordered, possibly through exposure to an atmosphere of extreme ambivalence in the narcissistic period of ego development. He contrasts the borderline, with poverty of object relations and a highly fragmented ego lacking in a central core, with the multiple who has a more sophisticated personality organization where alter egos may represent a higher and more stable form of ego organization. Gruenewald (1977) also maintains that MPD is a form of narcissistic personality disorder, rooted in Oedipal conflicts and triggered by childhood trauma and deprivation. Most of these authors are analysts, and their views are largely based on consideration of underlying psychodynamic processes they have detected in their patients. In general, their explorations fail to take into account the influences of the therapy itself and the broader social influences that may have a special relevance to the personality-disordered individual.

DISCUSSION

In ICD-10, the dissociative states will be classified according to the prominence of selected symptoms, although the diagnostic guidelines advise that evidence of psychogenic causation, in the form of a clear association in time with stressful events or disturbed relationships, should be elicited. The failings of such a system of classification, where symptoms are held to be superordinate, and to an extent, separate from the underlying disturbance, is highlighted in the precipitous elevation of MPD to the status of a diagnostic entity. There is little evidence to suggest that MPD is a distinct diagnosis rather than an intriguing symptom of a wide range of psychological disturbances. Patients undoubtedly present with dual behavior occurring before contact with a therapist and without experience of hypnosis. This behavior, which includes mood swings, psychogenic amnesia, and alterations in behavior, attitudes, and taste, cannot easily be dismissed as a consequence of diagnostic fashion or the influence of the therapist if it is present prior to the patient's contact with the clinician. Patients may describe an inner world where splitting of a most sophisticated nature occurs, but splitting is found as a symptom in many psychiatric disorders (Benner & Joscelyne, 1984). In a series of cases by Putnam *et al* (1986), a similar heterogeneity of diagnosis was found before MPD was eventually diagnosed, with over 70% having received a diagnosis of depression, 60% a neurotic disorder, and 50% a personality disorder. When MPD was finally diagnosed, it arbitrarily became the primary diagnosis, although other dissociative or hysterical symptoms that were equally common in these patients, e.g. conversion symptoms and fugue states, failed to be accorded an equivalent diagnostic primacy.

In a similar manner, MPD appears to acquire priority as a diagnostic entity in cases where the diagnosis coexists with Briquet's syndrome or borderline personality disorder. In these cases of overlapping diagnoses, it is inappropriate that the diagnosis of MPD should receive priority, as the restricted criteria of MPD ignore the polyneurotic disturbance central to the later diagnostic categories, and afford the most parsimonious explanation for the patients' behavior.

The failure to elicit a clear pattern of psychiatric diagnosis among first-degree relatives of patients also supports the view that MPD is a non-specific symptom of a variety of psychiatric disorders. Instead, an above-average level of psychiatric morbidity of all types has been reported (Putnam *et al*, 1986). Physiological investigations have likewise failed to prove the existence of MPD as a specific entity, most investigations pointing instead to a difference in the level of arousal between personalities that may also occur in other types of dissociative reactions.

In considering these criticisms, there is no reason to doubt the existence of symptoms suggestive of MPD that are recorded as increasingly common in numerous published case reports. However, no conclusive evidence has been presented over the past 25 years to challenge Sutcliffe & Jones' (1962) contention that the disorder is most commonly reported during periods when the diagnosis is fashionable, in conditions of acceptance on the part of the therapist, by workers who have a strong interest in hypnosis, and where patients have been treated, often over a lengthy period, in psychotherapy.

Kluft (1984, 1987) has proposed a "four factor theory" to explain the genesis of MPD. He views the condition as a chronic, dissociative, post-traumatic stress disorder originating in childhood. With some modifications, his theory can be applied to view MPD as the convergence point of a wide variety of psychological disturbances. The individual may have an innate potential to dissociate (Kluft's factor 1) which is reflected in hypnotizability ratings. Traumatic experiences in early childhood may disturb personality development (factor 2), leading to a greater potential for "psychodynamic dividedness." Experience of trauma may also enhance the individual's dissociative capacity, possibly leading to an autodissociative phenomenon allied to autohypnotic potential. The individual may be denied the chance to recover spontaneously through continued deprivation (factor 4), but the final presentation is shaped by psychodynamic and extrinsic factors including psychosocial influences (factor 3). Kluft suggests that errors in interview technique and influences from the media and literature are of limited importance, but this does not explain the culture-bound nature of the diagnosis. The effects of developmental experiences, psychodynamic factors, and hypnotic susceptibility are unlikely to vary greatly between cultures. The principal variables that may contribute to differences in rates of diagnosis include the extent to which the condition is promoted as a high-status disorder, with consequent sick-role privileges, by the media, and through subtle inadvertent reinforcement within the patient-doctor relationship, reflecting acceptance of the nosological validity of the disorder. The role of the media in shaping the presentation of psychiatric illness is poorly understood. The most detailed research in this area has investigated imitative behavior following reports of suicide, attempted suicide, or violence in the media (Philips, 1986) and has found a stronger imitative effect for non-fictional reports. However, little research has been done on imitative responses among the mentally ill following fictional or non-fictional depictions of psychiatric illness in the media.

The attempt to create a separate syndrome of MPD follows the precedent of hysteria in the 19th century when the diagnosis was conferred with a "halo of glory" (Major, 1974). Slater's (1965) caution that the diagnosis of hysteria may not only be a delusion but also a snare is especially appropriate to MPD, where the hysterical symptom has been precipitously and uncritically inflated to a final diagnosis.

REFERENCES

American Psychiatric Association (1968) *Diagnostic and Statistical Manual of Mental Disorders* (2nd edn). Washington, DC: APA.

——— (1980) *Diagnostic and Statistical Manual of Mental Disorders* (3rd edn). Washington, DC: APA.

Bahnson, C. B. & Smith, K. (1975) Autonomic changes in a multiple personality. *Psychosomatic Medicine*, **37**, 85–86.

Benner, D. G. & Joscelyne, B. (1984) Multiple personality as a borderline disorder. *Journal of Nervous and Mental Disease*, **172**, 98–104.

Bliss, E. L. (1980) Multiple personalities: A report of 14 cases with implications for schizophrenia and hysteria. *Archives of General Psychiatry*, **37**, 1388–1397.

——— (1983) Multiple personalities, related disorders and hypnosis. *American Journal of Clinical Hypnosis*, **26**, 114–123.

——— (1984*a*) A symptom profile of patients with multiple personalities, including MMPI results. *Journal of Nervous and Mental Disease*, **172**, 197–202.

——— (1984*b*) Hysteria and hypnosis. *Journal of Nervous and Mental Disease*, **172**, 203–206.

——— (1984*c*) Spontaneous self-hypnosis in multiple personality disorder. *Psychiatric Clinics of North America*, **7**, 135–148.

——— (1986) *Multiple Personality, Allied Disorders, and Hypnosis*. Oxford: Oxford University Press.

——— Larson, E. M. & Nakashima, S. R. (1983) Auditory hallucinations and schizophrenia. *Journal of Nervous and Mental Disease*, **171**, 30–33.

Boor, M. (1982) The multiple personality epidemic. *Journal of Nervous and Mental Disease*, **170**, 302–304.

——— & Coons, P. M. (1983) A comprehensive bibliography of literature pertaining to multiple personality. *Psychological Reports*, **53**, 295–310.

Bramwell, J. M. (1906) *Hypnosis: Its History, Practice and Theory*. London: Delamore Press.

Braun, B. G. (1986) *Treatment of Multiple Personality Disorder*. Washington, DC: American Psychiatric Press.

Buck, O. D. (1983) Multiple personality as a borderline state. *Journal of Nervous and Mental Disease*, **171**, 62–65.

Chodoff, P. (1987) More on multiple personality disorder. *American Journal of Psychiatry*, **144**, 124.

Clary, W. F., Burstin, K. J. & Carpenter, J. S. (1984) Multiple personality and borderline personality disorder. *Psychiatric Clinics of North America*, **7**, 89–99.

Cocores, J. A., Bender, A. L. & McBride, E. (1984) Multiple personality, seizure disorder and the electroencephalogram. *Journal of Nervous and Mental Disease*, **172**, 436–438.

Condon, W. S., Ogston, W. D. & Pacoe, L. V. (1969) Three faces of Eve revisited: A study of transient microstrabismus. *Journal of Abnormal Psychology*, **74**, 618–620.

Coons, P. M. (1984) The differential diagnosis of multiple personality disorder. *Psychiatric Clinics of North America*, **7**, 51–67.

——— & Milstein, V. (1986) Psychosexual disturbances in multiple personality: Characteristics, etiology, and treatment. *Journal of Clinical Psychiatry*, **47**, 106–110.

———, ——— & Marley, C. (1982) EEG studies of two multiple personalities and a control. *Archives of General Psychiatry*, **39**, 823–825.

Cooper, L. M. & London, P. (1976) Children's hypnotic susceptibility. *International Journal of Clinical and Experimental Hypnosis*, **24**, 140–148.

Cutler, B. & Reed, J. (1975) Multiple personality: A single case study with a 15 year follow-up. *Psychological Medicine*, **5**, 18–26.

Damgaard, J., Van Benschoten, S. & Fagen, J. (1985) An updated bibliography of literature pertaining to multiple personality. *Psychological Reports*, **57**, 131–137.

Ellenberger, H. F. (1970) *The Discovery of the Unconscious*. New York: Basic Books.

Erickson, M. H. (1980) *The Collected Papers of Milton H. Erickson on Hypnosis*, vol. 3, p. 264. New York: Irvington.

Greaves, G. B. (1980) Multiple personality: 165 years after Mary Reynolds. *Journal of Nervous and Mental Disease*, **168**, 577–596.

Gruenewald, D. (1971) Hypnotic technique without hypnosis in the treatment of dual personality. *Journal of Nervous and Mental Disease*, **153**, 41–46.

——— (1977) Multiple personality and splitting phenomena: A reconceptualization. *Journal of Nervous and Mental Disease*, **164**, 385–393.

Hanksworth, H. & Schwarz, T. (1977) *The Five of Me*. New York: Pocket Books.

Harriman, P. L. (1942) The experimental induction of multiple personality. *Psychiatry*, **5**, 179–186.

——— (1943) A new approach to multiple personality. *American Journal of Orthopsychiatry*, **13**, 638–643.

Hilgard, E. R. (1970) *Personality and Hypnosis: A Study of Imaginative Involvement*. Chicago: University of Chicago Press.

Hogson, R. (1891) A case of double consciousness. *Proceedings of the Society for Psychical Research*, **7**, 221–257.

Horevitz, R. P. & Braun, B. G. (1983) Are multiple personality disorder patients borderline? An analysis of 33 patients. *Psychiatric Clinics of North America*, **7**, 69–87.

Horton, P. & Miller, D. (1972) The etiology of multiple personality. *Comprehensive Psychiatry*, **13**, 151–159.

Kampman, R. (1976) Hypnotically induced multiple personality: An experimental study. *International Journal of Clinical and Experimental Hypnosis*, **3**, 215–227.

Kernberg, O. F. (1975) *Borderline Conditions and Pathological Narcissism*. New York: Jason Aronson.

Keyes, D. (1981) *The Minds of Billy Milligan*. New York: Bantam.

Kluft, R. P. (1982) Varieties of hypnotic interventions in the treatment of multiple personality. *American Journal of Clinical Hypnosis*, **24**, 230–240.

——— (1984) Treatment of multiple personality disorder. *Psychiatric Clinics of North America*, **7**, 9–29.

——— (1985*a*) The natural history of multiple personality disorder. In *Childhood Antecedents of Multiple Personality*. Washington, DC: American Psychiatric Press.

——— (1985*b*) The treatment of multiple personality disorder (MPD): Current concepts. In *Directions in Psychiatry* (ed. F. F. Flach). New York: Hatherleigh.

——— (1987) An update on multiple personality disorder. *Hospital and Community Psychiatry*, **38**, 363–373.

Kohlenberg, R. J. (1973) Behavioristic approach to multiple personality: A case study. *Behavior Therapy*, **4**, 137–140.

Larmore, R. J., Ludwig, A. M. & Cain, R. L. (1977) Multiple personality; An objective case study. *British Journal of Psychiatry*, **131**, 35–40.

Lasky, R. (1978) The psychoanalytic treatment of a case of multiple personality disorder. *Psychoanalytic Review*, **65**, 353–380.

Levin, J. & Fox, J. A. (1985) *Mass Murder*. New York: Plenum Press.

Loewenstein, R. J., Hamilton, J., Algona, S., Reid, N. & deVries, M. (1987) Experiential sampling in the study of multiple personality disorder. *American Journal of Psychiatry*, **144**, 19–24.

Lovinger, S. L. (1983) Multiple personality: A theoretical view. *Psychotherapy: Research and Practice*, **20**, 425–434.

Ludolph, P. S. (1985) How prevalent is multiple personality? *American Journal of Psychiatry*, **142**, 1526–1527.

Ludwig, A. M., Bradsma, J. & Wilbur, C. (1972) The objective study of a multiple personality. *Archives of General Psychiatry*, **26**, 298–310.

MacNish, R. (1830) *The Philosophy of Sleep*. Glasgow: W. R. McPhun.

Major, R. (1974) The revolution of hysteria. *International Journal of Psycho-Analysis*, **55**, 385–392.

Margetts, E. L. (1987) Culture bound disorders. *Bulletin of the Royal College of Psychiatrists*, **11**, 275–276.

Marmer, S. S. (1980) Psychoanalysis of multiple personality disorder. *International Journal of Psychoanalysis*, **61**, 439–459.

Mathews, R. J., Jack, R. A. & West, W. S. (1985) Regional blood flow in a patient with multiple personality. *American Journal of Psychiatry*, **142**, 504–505.

Mayo, T. (1845) Case of double consciousness. *Medical Gazette* (new series), **1**, 1202–1203.

Mesulam, M. M. (1981) Dissociative states with abnormal temporal lobe EEG. *Archives of Neurology*, **38**, 176–181.

Mitchell, S. W. (1888) Mary Reynolds: A case of double consciousness. *Transactions of the College of Physicians of Philadelphia* (3rd series), **10**, 366–389.

Mitchill, S. L. (1816) A double consciousness, or duality of person in the same individual. *Medical Repository*, **3**, 185–186.

Nash, M. R., Lynn, S. J. & Givens, D. L. (1984) Adult hypnotic susceptibility, childhood punishment, and child abuse: A brief communication. *International Journal of Clinical and Experimental Hypnosis*, **32**, 6–11.

Nowlis, D. P. (1969) The child-rearing antecedents of hypnotic susceptibility and of naturally occurring hypnotic-like experience. *International Journal of Clinical and Experimental Hypnosis* **17**, 109–120.

Orne, M. T., Dinges, D. F. & Orne, E. C. (1984) The differential diagnosis of multiple personality disorder in the forensic context. *International Journal of Clinical and Experimental Hypnosis*, **32**, 118–167.

Philips, D. P. (1986) Natural experiments on the effects of mass media violence on fatal aggression: Strengths and weaknesses of a new approach. *Advances in Experimental Social Psychology*, **19**, 207–250.

Prince, M. (1901) The development and genealogy of the Misses Beauchamp. *Proceedings of the Society for Psychical Research*, **15**, 466–483.

——— (1905) *The Dissociation of a Personality*. New York: Longmans.

——— (1920) Miss Beauchamp: The psychogenesis of multiple personality. *Journal of Abnormal Psychology*, **16**, 67–137.

——— & Peterson, F. (1908) Experiments in psychogalvanic reactions from co-conscious ideas in a case of multiple personality. *Journal of Abnormal Psychology*, **3**, 114–131.

Putnam, F. W. (1986) The scientific investigation of multiple personality disorder. In *Split Minds, Split Brains: Historical and Current Perspectives*. New York: New York University Press.

——— (1987) Multiple personality disorder? *Journal of Clinical Psychiatry*, **48**, 174.

——— Guroff, J. J., Silberman, E. K., Barban, L. & Post, R. M. (1986) The clinical phenomenology of multiple personality disorder: Review of 100 recent cases. *Journal of Clinical Psychiatry*, **47**, 285–293.

Rosenbaum, M. (1980) The role of the term schizophrenia in the decline of diagnoses of multiple personality.

Archives of General Psychiatry, **37,** 1383–1385.

Saltman, V. & Solomon, R. S. (1982) Incest and the multiple personality. *Psychological Reports*, **50,** 1127–1141.

Schreiber, F. R. (1973) *Sybil*. Chicago: Regnery.

Schwartz, J. R. (1981) *The Hillside Strangler: A Murderer's Mind*. New York: New American Library.

Silberman, E. K., Brandsma, J. M., Wilbur, C. B., Bendfeldt, F. & Post, R. M. (1985) Dissociative states in multiple personality disorder: A quantitative study. *Psychiatric Research*, **15,** 253–260.

Skae, D. (1845) Case of intermittent mental disorder of the tertiary type, with double consciousness. *Northern Journal of Medicine*, **4,** 10–13.

Slater, E. (1965) Diagnosis of hysteria. *British Medical Journal*, ***i,*** 1395–1399.

Spanos, N. P., Weekes, J. R. & Bertland, L. D. (1985) Multiple personality: A social psychological perspective. *Journal of Abnormal Psychology*, **94,** 362–376.

Stern, C. R. (1984) The etiology of multiple personalities. *Psychiatric Clinics of North America*, **7,** 150–159.

Sutcliffe, J. P. & Jones, J. (1962) Personal identity, multiple personality and hypnosis. *International Journal of Clinical and Experimental Hypnosis*, **10,** 231–269.

Taylor, W. S. & Martin, M. F. (1944) Multiple personality. *Journal of Abnormal and Social Psychology*, **39,** 281–300.

Thigpen, C. H. & Cleckley, H. (1954) A case of multiple personality. *Journal of Abnormal and Social Psychology*, **49,** 135–151.

——— & ——— (1957) *The Three Faces of Eve*. London: Secker and Warburg.

——— & ——— (1984) On the incidence of multiple personality disorder. *International Journal of Clinical and Experimental Hypnosis*, **32,** 63–66.

Wilbur, C. B. (1984) Multiple personality and child abuse. *Psychiatric Clinics of North America*, **7,** 3–7.

Wilson, S. C. & Barber, T. X. (1982) The fantasy prone personality: Implications for understanding imagery, hypnosis and parapsychological phenomena. In *Imagery: Current Theory, Research and Application* (ed. A. A. Sheikh). New York: Wiley.

Work Group to Revise DSM-III (1985) *Draft: DSM-III-R in Development 10/5/85*. Washington, DC: American Psychiatric Association.

World Health Organization (1987) ICD-10: *1986 Draft of Chapter V*. Geneva: World Health Organization.

DISCUSSION

As the articles in this chapter illustrate, the controversies concerning MPD are exceedingly complex and resistant to a straightforward solution. Of all the perplexing findings in the MPD literature, however, perhaps the fact most in need of explanation is the apparent dramatic increase in the prevalence of this diagnosis over the past several decades. How can this massive increase be explained? Is it attributable to an actual increase in the incidence of the disorder, perhaps resulting from such iatrogenic influences as hypnosis? Is it attributable to an incorrect lowering of the diagnostic threshold for MPD, resulting in an excessive number of individuals being mistakenly diagnosed as having the disorder? Or is it attributable to a correct lowering of the diagnostic threshold for MPD, resulting in the successful detection of many individuals with the disorder who previously went undiagnosed? The existing data do not seem to permit a clear choice among these three alternatives.

Moreover, many findings in the MPD literature appear either to have been misinterpreted or at least interpreted in a questionable fashion. Specifically, data that do not clearly support the validity of MPD have sometimes been interpreted as providing persuasive evidence for its validity, whereas data that do not clearly undermine the validity of MPD have sometimes been interpreted as providing persuasive evidence against its validity.

Let me explain what I mean. As both Kluft and Fahy point out, a number of investigators have reported that the alternate personalities of MPD patients often exhibit interesting psychological and physiological differences. For example, alternates have frequently been found to obtain different scores on personality measures and to display different event-related brain potentials in response to repeated stimuli. But do these findings, intriguing as they are, truly support the validity of MPD? As Fahy notes, it is not clear that they do, because differences among alternate personalities may be attributable to nonspecific differences in arousal level. Or perhaps even more to the point, differences among alternates may be due to differences in current mood. An individual who is extremely happy at one moment and extremely sad at another, for example, might exhibit striking differences on personality and physiological indices. It is known, for example, that individuals' current moods often dramatically influence how they describe their long-standing personality traits. This phenomenon is often referred to as the state-trait problem in personality assessment (Loranger et al., 1991). Clearly, to provide compelling evidence for the validity of MPD, the differences among alternates should be shown to be due to something more than short-lived mood changes.*

*It is true that, according to DSM-IV, MPD can be characterized by the presence of coexisting personality states. Nevertheless, DSM-IV asserts that each of these personality states must be associated with its own relatively enduring and distinctive pattern of relating to and interpreting the world.

Some investigators (for example, Putnam, 1984) have attempted to rule out this competing explanation by including in their studies a comparison group of normal individuals who are asked to simulate MPD. The inclusion of such a comparison group may not entirely solve the problem, however: The mood changes of individuals asked to feign MPD seem unlikely to approach the depth or intensity of mood changes experienced by individuals with MPD.

On the flip side of the coin, at least one team of investigators has reported that many of the features of MPD are potentially attributable to role playing. In an ingenious study, Nicholas Spanos and his colleagues (1985) demonstrated that college students could be induced to generate some of the characteristics of MPD when provided with the proper instructions and cues from experimenters. The researchers derived their instructions to their subjects almost verbatim from hypnosis sessions involving Kenneth Bianchi, the so-called Hillside Strangler, who was arrested in 1979 for the rape and murder of several women in Los Angeles. Bianchi initially denied the murders but later pleaded not guilty by reason of insanity (see Chapter 17) on the grounds that he suffered from MPD. Nevertheless, a number of experts (for example, Orne, Dinges, & Orne, 1984) now believe that Bianchi faked MPD.

Although Spanos et al.'s design was somewhat complex, their key comparison for our purposes involved two conditions: the "Bianchi" treatment and the control treatment. Subjects in the Bianchi condition went through a hypnotic induction procedure and were asked to play the part of a fictional murderer, Harry (or, for female subjects, Betty) Hodgins. They were then given instructions, virtually identical to those given to Bianchi during a hypnotic interview, designed to elicit an alternate personality. For example, at one point subjects were told, "I've talked a bit to Harry (Betty), but I think perhaps there might be another part of Harry (Betty) that I haven't talked to. . . . Would you talk to me, Part, by saying 'I'm here'?" (Spanos et al., 1985, p. 367). In contrast, subjects in the control treatment were administered neither the hypnotic induction procedure nor the Bianchi instructions.

Subjects in both conditions returned for a second session, during which they completed a series of tasks. Prior to these tasks, subjects in the Bianchi condition were again hypnotized and asked to play the role of the murderer. Interestingly, Spanos et al. found that subjects in the Bianchi treatment successfully reproduced a number of characteristics of MPD. For example, these subjects exhibited markedly different scores on personality tests when asked to assume the role of each personality, frequently adopted a second name, and demonstrated spontaneous "amnesia" when asked to recall details from the first session. In contrast, subjects in the control treatment exhibited few or no characteristics of MPD.

Do Spanos et al.'s findings truly raise questions concerning the validity of MPD, as some have claimed? Not necessarily. As Spanos and his colleagues themselves point out, individuals predisposed to MPD may possess a propensity toward suggestibility and fantasy, leading them to be especially susceptible to cues from others, including psychotherapists. This same propensity may also confer a talent for adopting and enacting imaginary roles. From this perspective, the role-taking explanation favored by Spanos et al. does not necessarily demonstrate that MPD does not exist. Instead, patients with MPD can perhaps be conceptualized as uniquely capable of creating and entering a fantasy world inhabited by their own imaginary identities.

QUESTIONS TO STIMULATE DISCUSSION

1. Virtually all of us experience brief episodes during which "we are not ourselves" or during which we surprise ourselves or others by behaving dramatically out of character. Do these episodes differ in kind from those of patients with MPD or only in degree?
2. The alternate personalities of MPD have been reported to differ in terms of such characteristics as their allergies and susceptibility to alcohol. Do you find these differences credible? Can they be explained in terms of what we know about the physiology of the human nervous system?
3. Patients with MPD often enter psychotherapy with two or three known personalities, only to discover shortly thereafter that they actually have 10, 20, or even more personalities. Are these personalities in fact discovered during the course of psychotherapy? Or are they instead created, intentionally or unintentionally, by cues emitted by their therapists?
4. As both Kluft and Fahy observe, a very high proportion of patients with MPD report histories of severe physical or sexual abuse in childhood. Presuming that these reports are accurate, how might such abuse predispose a person to MPD?
5. What problems are associated with the retrospective reporting of child abuse among patients with MPD and similar disorders? How might these problems be overcome?

SUGGESTIONS FOR FURTHER READING

Aldridge-Morris, R. (1989). *Multiple personality: An exercise in deception*. Hove and London: Lawrence Erlbaum Associates.
Aldridge-Morris provides a comprehensive overview of MPD from experimental, developmental, social, and cultural perspectives. Chapter 3 ("The Voice of the Skeptics") summarizes the debate regarding the validity of the MPD diagnosis. Aldridge-Morris concludes that most cases of MPD can be explained from a role-playing perspective and that iatrogenic factors often play a major part in the etiology of this syndrome.

Bloch, J. P. (1991). *Assessment and treatment of multiple personality and dissociative disorders.* Sarasota, FL: Professional Resource Press.

This is a relatively concise and accessible introduction to the literature on the etiology, clinical presentation, assessment and diagnosis, and treatment of MPD and related dissociative disorders. When evaluating Bloch's recommendations for the treatment of MPD, bear in mind that he has a very strong psychodynamic orientation.

Putnam, F. W. (1991). Recent research on multiple personality disorder. *Psychiatric Clinics of North America, 14,* 489–502.

Putnam provides a good update of new developments in research on MPD, including studies of psychophysiological variables, state-dependent learning and retrieval, and personality characteristics.

Putnam, F. W., Guroff, J. J., Silberman, E. K., Barban, L., & Post, R. M. (1986). The clinical phenomenology of multiple personality disorder: Review of 100 recent cases. *Journal of Clinical Psychiatry, 47,* 285–293.

This is probably the most detailed and comprehensive report on the characteristics of MPD patients in the psychological and psychiatric literature. The authors' findings on psychological differences among the alternate personalities are themselves worth reading. Nevertheless, Putnam et al.'s exclusive reliance on clinicians' reports renders many of their conclusions tentative.

Rosenbaum, M. (1980). The role of the term schizophrenia in the decline of diagnoses of multiple personality. *Archives of General Psychiatry, 37,* 1383–1385.

Rosenbaum examines changes in the prevalence of the MPD diagnosis over time and argues that it declined dramatically following the introduction of the term *schizophrenia*, particularly in the United States. He contends that a number of individuals diagnosed as schizophrenics in the United States during the early and middle part of this century actually had MPD.

Ross, C. A. (1989). *Multiple personality disorder: Diagnosis, clinical features, and treatment.* New York: Wiley.

Ross provides a broad overview of the theoretical and research literature on MPD and discusses MPD's assessment and relationship to other psychiatric disorders. The appendices include interview and checklist measures for MPD and other dissociative conditions.

Schreiber, F. R. (1973). *Sybil.* Chicago: Regnery.

This is a remarkable popularized account of psychiatrist Cornelia Wilbur's treatment of "Sybil," a woman with a severe history of physical and sexual abuse who reportedly developed 16 personalities. Readers interested in other popularized accounts of MPD should also see Thigpen, C. H., & Cleckley, H. (1954). *The three faces of Eve.* London: Secker and Warburg; and Keyes, D. (1981). *The minds of Billy Milligan.* New York: Bantam.

Spanos, N. P., Weekes, J. R., & Bertrand, L. D. (1985). Multiple personality: A social psychological perspective. *Journal of Abnormal Psychology, 94,* 362–376. (Reprinted in Hooley, J., Neale, J. M., & Davison, G. C. [1989]. *Readings in abnormal psychology.* New York: Wiley.)

Spanos and his colleagues present their role-taking model of MPD in this article. Using the text of a monologue with serial killer Kenneth Bianchi (the Hillside Strangler), who is believed by a number of experts to have feigned the symptoms of MPD, they conduct a study to illustrate how experimenter cuing can lead normal subjects to successfully enact the part of an MPD patient.

Spiegel, D., & Cardena, E. (1991). Disintegrated experience: The dissociative disorders revisited. *Journal of Abnormal Psychology, 100,* 366–378.

The authors outline the principal revisions in the dissociative disorders section of DSM-IV and review empirical evidence regarding the association between psychological trauma and dissociation. They also discuss diagnostic issues relevant to MPD and proposed changes in the MPD criteria.

REFERENCES

American Psychiatric Association (1987). *Diagnostic and statistical manual of mental disorders* (3rd ed., rev.). Washington, DC: Author.

Boor, M. (1982). The multiple personality epidemic. *Journal of Nervous and Mental Disease, 170,* 302–304.

Keyes, D. (1981). *The minds of Billy Milligan.* New York: Bantam.

Loranger, A. W., Lenzenweger, M. F., Gartner, A. F., Susman, V. L., Herzig, J., Zammit, G. K., Gartner, J. D., Abrams, R. C., & Young, R. C. (1991). Trait-state artifacts and the diagnosis of personality disorders. *Archives of General Psychiatry, 48,* 720–728.

Orne, M. T., Dinges, D. F., & Orne, E. C. (1984). On the differential diagnosis of multiple personality in the forensic context. *International Journal of Clinical and Experimental Hypnosis, 32,* 118–169.

Putnam, F. W. (1984). The psychophysiological investigation of multiple personality disorder: A review. *Psychiatric Clinics of North America, 7,* 31–39.

Putnam, F. W., Guroff, J. J., Silberman, E. K., Barban, L., & Post, R. M. (1986). The clinical phenomenology of multiple personality disorder: Review of 100 recent cases. *Journal of Clinical Psychiatry, 47,* 285–293.

Rosenbaum, M. (1980). The role of the term schizophrenia in the decline of diagnoses of multiple personality disorder. *Archives of General Psychiatry, 37,* 1383–1385.

Schreiber, F. R. (1973). *Sybil.* Chicago: Regnery.

Sizemore, C. C., & Pittillo, E. S. (1977). *I'm Eve.* Garden City, NY: Doubleday.

Spanos, N. P., Weekes, J. R., & Bertrand, L. D. (1985). Multiple personality: A social psychological perspective. *Journal of Abnormal Psychology, 94,* 362–376.

Thigpen, C. H., & Cleckley, H. (1954). *The three faces of Eve.* London: Secker and Warburg.

CHAPTER

9

Is borderline personality disorder a diagnosis of questionable validity?

PRO Akiskal, H. S., Chen, S. E., Davis, G. C., Puzantian, V. R., Kashgarian, M., & Bolinger, J. M. (1985). Borderline: An adjective in search of a noun. *Journal of Clinical Psychiatry, 46*, 41–48.

CON Berelowitz, M., & Tarnopolsky, A. (1993). The validity of borderline personality disorder: An updated review of recent research. In P. Tyrer & G. Stein (Eds.), *Personality disorder reviewed* (pp. 90–112). London: Royal College of Psychiatrists Press.

OVERVIEW OF THE CONTROVERSY: Hagop S. Akiskal and his colleagues report the results of a study that they claim demonstrates that the diagnosis of borderline personality disorder is hopelessly heterogeneous. Mark Berelowitz and Alex Tarnopolsky review the recent research literature on borderline personality disorder and conclude that this diagnosis has a promising degree of validity.

CONTEXT OF THE PROBLEM

Although a large number of psychiatric diagnoses remain highly controversial, no group of conditions in the DSM have been so persistently plagued by criticism as have the personality disorders. Personality disorders, which you have previously encountered in Chapter 1 and in Chapter 4, were largely ignored or were accorded scant attention by researchers throughout much of the 20th century. Personality disorders were catapulted into the forefront of controversy in 1980, when DSM-III devoted its Axis II to chronic, long-standing conditions that have generally persisted since childhood or adolescence. Since its inception, Axis II has generated an unprecedented flurry of research on personality disorders. Much of this research, however, has been bedeviled by serious conceptual and methodological problems. Three of these problems have been especially vexing:

- The levels of interrater reliability for personality disorders have consistently been among the lowest for all disorders in the DSM. In part, low interrater reliability is surely due to the considerable inference and judgment required to apply many of the diagnostic criteria for the personality disorders. Consider, for example, the difficulty of deciding whether a patient "is often envious of others" (one of the DSM-IV criteria for narcissistic personality disorder). It is easy to imagine why clinicians might disagree regarding such a judgment; pathological envy in one clinician's eyes might simply be healthy competitiveness in another's.
- Many of these disorders possess questionable or dubious levels of validity, which should not be surprising given that reliability imposes a ceiling on validity (see Chapter 2). As discussed in the introductions to Part I and Part II, one useful way of conceptualizing validity is the extent to which a diagnosis provides information over and above the behaviors described by the label itself. In other words, a valid diagnosis informs us about characteristics—such as diagnosed individuals' family history, performance on labora-

tory and personality tests, course and outcome, and response to treatment—none of which we knew prior to making the diagnosis (Robins & Guze, 1970). By this standard, the validities for many or most of the DSM-IV personality disorders can most charitably be described as less than impressive.

- There is enormous within-individual overlap among different personality disorders, a phenomenon often referred to, perhaps misleadingly, as **comorbidity**. I say misleadingly, because comorbidity is technically the co-occurrence of two or more diseases within the same individual (Feinstein, 1970); whether the DSM-IV personality disorders truly represent distinct disease entities, however, remains an open question (see Lilienfeld, Waldman, & Israel, in press). Semantic considerations aside, it is clear that the "comorbidity" among personality disorders is extensive. Approximately 50% of patients with a personality disorder satisfy diagnostic criteria for at least one other personality disorder (Grove & Tellegen, 1991), and it is not uncommon to find patients who simultaneously meet criteria for three, four, or five different personality disorder diagnoses. These high levels of "comorbidity" raise troublesome questions regarding the current classification of personality disorders. Does this overlap reflect the simultaneous existence of multiple conditions within individuals, or does it instead reflect DSM-IV's failure to "carve nature at its joints"—that is, to develop a classification scheme that identifies the true entities in nature?

Of the 10 major personality disorders in DSM-IV, perhaps none has been the subject of more intense debate than borderline personality disorder (BPD). The term *borderline* originated from the belief, no longer widely held, that patients with this personality constellation were on the border between neurosis and psychosis. Although BPD is a rather difficult condition to define, the feature that perhaps best characterizes BPD patients is their "stable instability" (Grinker, 1979); about the only thing one can safely predict about these individuals is that they will be unpredictable. Patients with BPD, who are predominantly female, tend to possess an unstable sense of identity and to be uncertain of such issues as their self-image, values, long-term goals, and sexual orientation. In addition, they are typically emotionally unstable and subject to sudden and unexpected mood swings, temper outbursts, suicidal and self-mutilatory behaviors, and such impulsive actions as promiscuous sex and binge eating. Finally, patients with BPD are characterized by unstable interpersonal relationships; their friendships and romantic partnerships often alternate between the extremes of overidealization ("You are wonderful"; "I never knew someone like you existed") and devaluation ("You are the worst person in the world"; "I wish I had never met you"). Many readers will recognize the character played by Glenn Close in the film *Fatal Attraction* as possessing many of the features of BPD.

Some theorists, particularly those of a psychoanalytic bent, argue that BPD represents a single personality organization that is distinct from other personality disturbances. Many of these theorists, such as Otto Kernberg (1984), believe that BPD stems from a failure to develop an integrated sense of identity in early childhood. In contrast, other authors contend that the BPD category is etiologically heterogeneous and that it overlaps extensively with many other psychopathological syndromes. George Vaillant (1992) has wryly commented that the diagnosis of BPD tends to be applied whenever a patient elicits hostile and resentful reactions from therapists. For Vaillant and other critics, the BPD diagnosis encompasses a mélange of conditions with diverse etiologies, including some forms of mood disorder, certain personality disorders (such as antisocial and histrionic personality disorders), and perhaps "schizophrenic spectrum" disorders (see Chapter 5), which share little but for their noxious impact on others. If these claims are warranted, they would imply that the BPD diagnosis is of questionable validity.

THE CONTROVERSY: Akiskal et al. vs. Berelowitz and Tarnopolsky

Akiskal et al.

Hagop Akiskal and his colleagues point out that BPD overlaps extensively with a number of other conditions, particularly mood disorders and antisocial and histrionic personality disorders. They hypothesize that BPD is etiologically heterogeneous but that in most cases it represents an atypical manifestation of mood disorder. Akiskal et al. report the results of a study in which they examined 100 patients with BPD and followed them for intervals ranging from 6 months to 3 years. This group of patients was compared with four other groups—57 patients with schizophrenia, 50 patients with other personality disorders, 50 patients with bipolar disorder, and 40 patients with unipolar disorder. Akiskal et al. found that, at intake, patients with BPD presented with an enormous variety of other diagnoses, including major depression, dysthymia, cyclothymia, schizotypal personality disorder, antisocial personality disorder (which they refer to as sociopathy), somatization disorder, panic disorder with agoraphobia, obsessive-compulsive disorder, and epilepsy. The biological family members of BPD patients also exhibited high rates of mood disorders, particularly bipolar disorder. At follow-up, BPD patients were found to have an elevated rate of depressive, but not schizophrenic, episodes compared with patients in the other groups. Akiskal et al. conclude that the BPD diagnosis is highly heterogeneous and that it overlaps with mood disorders, anxiety disorders, personality disorders, schizophrenia, and perhaps certain organic mental disorders. For Akiskal et al., *borderline* is "an adjective in search of a noun," meaning that the BPD diagnosis borders on so many conditions as to render it virtually meaningless.

Berelowitz and Tarnopolsky

Mark Berelowitz and Alex Tarnopolsky note that there are two major systems for assessing BPD: the Diagnostic Interview for Borderlines (DIB) and the DSM-III/DSM-III-R criteria. Both of these assessment procedures, according to Berelowitz and Tarnopolsky, possess adequate levels of reliability. Berelowitz and Tarnopolsky then examine the evidence for the validity of the BPD diagnosis using a minor modification of Robins and Guze's (1970) criteria. As noted earlier, Robins and Guze contend that a valid diagnosis should provide clinicians and researchers with a variety of sources of information besides the behaviors described by the diagnostic label itself. Accordingly, Berelowitz and Tarnopolsky review the evidence for the validity of the BPD diagnosis from six sources: identification of a homogeneous group of patients, differentiation from other disorders, natural history, family history, laboratory and personality tests, and response to treatment. In each case, they argue that the BPD diagnosis, although still requiring further research, demonstrates a promising degree of validity. BPD, they contend, appears to be distinguishable from schizophrenia, mood disorders, and perhaps other personality disorders. Berelowitz and Tarnopolsky conclude by reviewing the evidence concerning the childhood antecedents of BPD and argue that a history of childhood abuse and neglect appears to be a common feature among individuals with this syndrome.

KEY CONCEPTS AND TERMS

antisocial personality disorder Personality disorder characterized by a chronic history of antisocial, criminal, and irresponsible behaviors beginning prior to age 15. Antisocial personality disorder is sometimes referred to as sociopathy.

assortative mating Tendency for individuals with similar or identical characteristics (including similar or identical psychopathological conditions) to mate (or marry) one another. Assortative parental psychopathology (discussed in the Akiskal et al. article) is thus the presence of the same or similar psychopathological conditions in both parents of an individual.

bipolar disorder Condition characterized by the presence of both manic and depressive episodes or, more rarely, manic episodes alone. Compare with unipolar depression.

cluster analysis Statistical procedure for detecting relatively homogeneous subgroups of individuals within a larger group of individuals. One might use cluster analysis, for example, to determine whether a diagnosis such as BPD comprises several more homogeneous conditions.

cyclothymia Condition characterized by frequent up-and-down mood swings that do not reach the intensity of full-blown depressive or manic episodes. Cyclothymia is hypothesized by many researchers to be a mild form of bipolar disorder.

depersonalization Feeling that one is somehow disconnected or estranged from oneself or one's body. Individuals experiencing an episode of depersonalization may feel as though their body parts have changed in size or feel as though they are observing themselves from a distance.

derealization Feeling that one is somehow disconnected or estranged from one's surroundings.

dexamethasone suppression test Promising "biological marker" for at least some forms of depression. In the dexamethasone suppression test (DST), the patient is administered dexamethasone, a synthetic form of cortisol. About 90% of normal individuals will show suppression of cortisol in response to dexamethasone, but approximately 50% of depressed individuals will not.

dysthymia Mild but chronic form of depression. According to DSM-IV, dysthymia (officially known in DSM-IV as dysthymic disorder) is characterized by the presence of a persistent depressed mood for at least 2 years, accompanied by symptoms such as low self-esteem, pessimism, and chronic fatigue.

episodic dyscontrol Sudden outburst of uncontrolled anger and physical aggressiveness that is apparently triggered by seizures in the brain's temporal lobe and closely associated structures.

formes frustes Unusual or atypical manifestation of an illness. Some investigators propose that BPD is a formes frustes of other conditions, such as bipolar disorder or schizophrenia.

hypomania Mild form of mania.

micropsychotic episode Extremely brief period of psychosis, which is apparently sometimes experienced by individuals with BPD, schizotypal personality disorder, and perhaps related conditions in response to severe stressors.

pharmacological hypomania Period of hypomania accidentally triggered by the administration of antidepressant medication. A moderately high percentage of depressed individuals experience hypomanic episodes (and in some cases, manic episodes) after taking antidepressants.

pseudoneurotic schizophrenia Controversial diagnostic entity, not officially listed in DSM-IV, which is characterized by multiple neurotic symptoms (for example, excessive social anxiety, panic attacks, obsessions, and compulsions) that are believed by some theorists to represent manifestations of underlying schizophrenia.

unipolar depression Condition characterized by the presence of depressive episodes alone. Compare with bipolar disorder.

PREVIEW QUESTIONS

1. According to Akiskal et al., into what two categories has DSM-III partitioned the borderline concept? What are the principal features of these categories?
2. What are Akiskal et al.'s major findings, and what are the implications of these findings for the validity of BPD?
3. Why do Akiskal et al. conclude that *borderline* is "an adjective in search of a noun"?
4. According to Berelowitz and Tarnopolsky, what is the evidence concerning the reliability of the BPD diagnosis?
5. What are the Robins and Guze (1970) criteria for validating psychiatric disorders?
6. According to Berolowitz and Tarnopolsky, how well does the BPD diagnosis satisfy the Robins and Guze criteria? Using each Robins and Guze criterion, briefly describe the evidence for the validity of BPD.
7. What do Berelowitz and Tarnopolsky conclude from the literature on the childhood antecedents of BPD?

HAGOP S. AKISKAL, SHEN E. CHEN, GLENN C. DAVIS, VAHE R. PUZANTIAN, MARK KASHGARIAN, & JOHN M. BOLINGER

Borderline: An adjective in search of a noun

The diagnosis of borderline conditions enjoys great clinical popularity in North American psychiatry. The most prevalent opinion is that these are primitive disorders of developmental origin, characterized by an unstable sense of self and low-level defensive operations.[1] It is also thought that borderline patients have an unusually high liability for transient breaks with reality.[2] Despite criticism by phenomenologically oriented clinical investigators,[3–5] the borderline concept has been introduced into DSM-III. DSM-II had recognized such conditions only as "dilute or "latent" forms of schizophrenia. In restricting the operational territory of schizophrenia to "process" . . . schizophrenia, DSM-III has now pushed the borderline concept into the domain of personality disorders, where it is listed under two overlapping rubrics: 1) *borderline personality disorder*, manifested by such unstable characterologic attributes as impulsivity, drug-seeking, polymorphous sexuality, extreme affective lability, boredom, anhedonia, and bizarre attempts at self-harm, and 2) *schizotypal personality disorder*, the hallmarks of which are oddities of communication or perception and other soft signs of "micropsychosis," typically, although not exclusively, associated with a schizoid existence.

Despite efforts to identify a distinct schizotypal disorder,[6–9] considerable overlap exists between schizotypal, schizoid, and avoidant types. Likewise, borderline patients are not easily discriminable from antisocial and histrionic personality disorders. One is reminded of Mack's suggestion that "borderline" refers to a personality disorder without a characterologic specialty.[10] Implicit in the DSM-III position is that schizotypal disorders, believed to be on the border of schizophrenia, should be separated from the more nebulous mélange of unstable characterologic attributes constituting borderline conditions. In line with these developments, recent research, exemplified by Stone's work,[11] has suggested a shift of the borderline concept from a subschizophrenic to a subaffective disorder. Gunderson, however, who was among the first to attempt to bring operational clarity to this murky psychopathologic area, in recent collaborative work with Pope et al.,[12] seems to espouse the view that the characterologic pathology of borderline patients is distinct from any concurrent affective episodes. Monroe,[13] who subscribes to the existence of a third (neither schizophrenic nor affective) psychosis related to epilepsy, has postulated that "episodic dyscontrol" manifested by unmodulated affects is at the core of borderline psychopathology. Kernberg's concept,[1] probably the broadest of all, embraces a wide spectrum of subpsychotic temperamental

SOURCE: *Journal of Clinical Psychiatry*, 46(2), pp. 41–48, 1985. Reprinted by permission of the Physicians Postgraduate Press, Inc.

and polysymptomatic neurotic disorders tied together by identity diffusion and common, primitive defensive operations like splitting and projective identification, in the presence of grossly intact reality testing.

Despite a considerable amount of empirical work in the past few years, several controversies regarding the nosologic status of borderline conditions remain unresolved:

1. Is borderline a personality disorder?
2. Does it refer *to formes frustes* or interepisodic manifestations of affective, schizophrenic, or epileptic psychoses?
3. Is it an intermediate mode of functioning between neurosis and psychosis?

Several interview schedules for a descriptive identification of borderline and schizotypal personality disorders have been developed. Khouri et al.,[7] in their attempt to focus on subschizophrenic disorders, have excluded affective symptoms from their inventory. By contrast, the Gunderson et al.[14] diagnostic interview for borderlines (DIB) casts a wider net which includes circumscribed psychotic, affective, acting out, interpersonal, and social areas. Pope et al.[12] attempted to validate DIB borderlines by using the Washington University approach to validating psychiatric entities. Soloff and Millward[15] and Loranger et al.,[16] who used the same instrument, focused on the familial aspects of the disorder. Perry and Klerman,[17] using a related instrument, examined the phenomenologic features of the disorder. The data from these studies indicate 1) lack of relationship of the disorder to schizophrenia, 2) failure to discriminate from antisocial and histrionic character disorders, and 3) at least some degree of overlap with primary affective disorder.

Considering the general confusion in this area, the substantive findings of these studies are quite impressive. Nevertheless, one must bear in mind the following limitations: First, they were not generally conducted in outpatient settings, where the largest number of borderlines are encountered clinically. Second, proband Axis I diagnosis and family history were often based on chart review. Third, a control group of bipolar affective disorder was not specifically provided. Fourth, repeated evaluations at follow-up were not instituted, minimizing the chances of detecting hypomanic episodes. Finally, the degree of overlap of borderlines with antisocial and histrionic personality disorders could not be estimated in the absence of a control group consisting of such personalities.

We have elsewhere reported preliminary family history and follow-up data suggesting substantial overlap of borderline personality disorders with dysthymic and cyclothymic temperaments and atypical bipolar II disorder.[18] Our findings were tentative because data collection on control groups had not been completed when our report was published. In the present article, we attempt to address the methodologic issues raised above and provide comparisons with schizophrenic, bipolar, unipolar, and personality disorder controls. Furthermore, we explore the possibility that childhood object loss and unstable home environment due to assortative parental psychopathology may form the developmental background of borderline conditions. The overall aim of this exercise is to prospectively delineate the range of psychopathologic conditions for which the adjective "borderline" is currently applicable.

Our main hypothesis is that borderlines are heterogeneous groups of patients who meet specific criteria for more explicit Axis I psychiatric diagnoses. Based on prior work, we also hypothesized that borderlines would show high rates of familial affective (but not of schizophrenic) disorders, and would develop full-blown affective (rather than schizophrenic) breakdowns during prospective follow-up similar to affective but unlike nonaffective controls. Because borderline patients are often considered to have complicated biographies, we wished to test the possibility that increased rates of early separations and broken homes—associated with assortative parental psychopathology—might underlie their character pathology.

METHOD

Selection of Subjects

We selected 100 borderline patients from a large pool of general psychiatric outpatients by examining *consecutive* admissions in two urban mental health centers. These subjects met at least five of the six Gunderson-Singer criteria.[2] (This study was conducted prior to the availability of the DIB.[14]) Most probands had extensive psychiatric histories dating back to adolescence or early adulthood, and had been considered complex diagnostic problems by referring clinicians. They had often been presented at diagnostic staff conferences and had received such diagnoses as borderline and mixed personality disorder, as well as "latent" and "pseudoneurotic" schizophrenia. Although 40% had had one or more psychiatric hospitalizations prior to the index outpatient interview, none had received the diagnosis of a definite affective or schizophrenic disorder.

Four control groups were selected from consecutive admissions in the same outpatient settings: 57 schizophrenic subjects, 50 nonaffective personality disorders (definite or probable somatization and antisocial), 50 classical (bipolar I) manic-depressives, and 40 episodic major (unipolar) depressives.

Diagnostic Procedures

All probands and control subjects were evaluated in semistructured diagnostic interviews based on the Washington University criteria.[19] Since DSM-III is more widely known to practicing psychiatrists, we have translated diagnoses to the corresponding DSM-III terms.

All Gunderson-Singer borderline probands also met the DSM-III criteria for borderline personality, but only 16 fully met those for schizotypal personality. Borderline, schizotypal, and antisocial personalities were the only Axis II diagnoses used in this study; all other diagnoses were based on Axis I. Since DSM-III does not specifically distinguish hypomania from mania, we found it useful to set the following threshold for hypomania: 1) symptomatic criteria for mania of at least 2 days; 2) absence of querulous belligerence; 3) no psychotic symptoms; and 4) no hospitalization.

Each proband received principal and, when applicable, concurrent diagnoses. "Principal diagnosis" refers to the chronologically primary or most incapacitating disorder which usually brought the patient to clinical attention. "Concurrent diagnoses" include all additional diagnoses, which often followed the principal disorder chronologically.

Substance (including ethanol) use disorders were so prevalent in our borderline probands (unsurprisingly, because these are among the Gunderson-Singer and DSM-III defining criteria) that it was more meaningful to consider them independently from descriptive diagnoses. They were classified as sedative-hypnotic abuse or dependence, alcohol abuse or dependence, or psychedelic (hallucinogen-cannabis-psychostimulant) abuse or dependence.

Patients were seen at 1–8 week intervals (as warranted clinically), and followed over a 6–36 month prospective observation period. Mean duration of follow-up was comparable for study and control groups. Pharmacologic, psychotherapeutic, and sociotherapeutic interventions were provided as deemed clinically appropriate. Schizophreniform, hypomanic, manic, and major depressive episodes, as well as mixed states, were carefully noted during follow-up. Hypomanic responses to antidepressants were considered pharmacologically occasioned if they occurred within 6 weeks after administration of tricyclic antidepressants or monoamine oxidase inhibitors.

Criteria for Familial and Developmental Factors

One-third of affected family members were patients in our mental health clinics, one-third were directly interviewed to ascertain their diagnoses, and, in the remaining third, diagnostic information was obtained from other family members, using the Research Diagnostic Criteria–Family History version.[20] Except for familial schizophrenia (which included both first- and second-degree relatives), all other family history items refer to *first*-degree biologic relatives. Assortative mating, i.e., where both parents suffered from psychiatric disorders, was noted in particular. Of the 100 probands, 3 were adopted and were unable to provide family histories.

Developmental object loss was assessed by the following criteria, modified from Amark:[21] 1) proband born out of wedlock and parents not subsequently married or living together; 2) one or both parents lost by death before proband reached age 15; 3) parents separated or divorced before proband reached age of 15; 4) proband adopted or lived in foster homes or orphanages.

Statistical Techniques

Except for age distribution, which was analyzed by ANOVA, comparisons between groups were made by chi-square analysis, with Yates' correction when appropriate.

RESULTS

Demographic and Family History Characteristics

Borderline and control probands were preponderantly from Hollingshead-Redlich classes III and IV. The mean age at index evaluation was 29 years for borderline probands, 34 for schizophrenics, 30 for nonaffective personalities, 38 for the bipolar controls, and 47 for recurrent major depressive controls; these differences in age were not statistically significant. About two-thirds of the subjects in each group were women.

Borderline probands, when compared with schizophrenic controls, had a significantly higher rate of familial affective disorders (35% vs. 9%, $\chi^2 = 11.76$, $p < .001$) and a significantly lower rate of schizophrenia (3% vs. 21%, $\chi^2 = 11.21$, $p < .001$).

Borderlines and control groups did not differ in family history for major depression (see Table 1). However, with respect to familial bipolar disorder, borderlines were similar to bipolar controls but significantly different from personality disorder and unipolar controls.

Diagnoses at Index Evaluation

Table 2 provides diagnostic information on the 100 borderline probands at index evaluation. These probands can be categorized into five groups based on principal diagnosis. The largest group

TABLE 1 Family History for Major Depression and Bipolar Disorder in Borderline and Control Groups

	Borderline Group (N = 97)		Personality Controls (N = 50)		Bipolar Controls (N = 50)		Unipolar Controls (N = 40)	
Family History	N	%	N	%	N	%	N	%
Major depression	17	17.5	5	10	11	22	8	20
Bipolar disorder	17	17.5[a]	1	2	13	26	1	3

[a]Significantly different from personality controls, $\chi^2 = 6.03$, $p < .02$; and from unipolar controls, $\chi^2 = 4.36$, $p < .05$

TABLE 2 Axis I Diagnoses in 100 Borderline Patients at Index Evaluation*

Principal Diagnosis	*Concurrent Diagnosis*	*Substance Use Disorders*
Affective group (N = 45)		
Recurrent major depression (6)		Sedative-hypnotics (2)
Dysthymic disorder (14)	Schizotypal disorder (3)	Sedative-hypnotics (2) Alcohol (1) Psychedelics (1)
Cyclothymic disorder (7)	Somatization disorder (1)	Sedative-hypnotics (4) Psychedelics (2) Alcohol (1)
(Atypical) bipolar II disorder (17)	Sociopathy (1) Somatization disorder (1) Residual (adult) attention deficit disorder (1)	Sedative-hypnotics (4) Alcohol (1) Psychedelics (2)
Personality (N = 21)		
Sociopathy (9)	Residual (adult) attention deficit disorder (1) Schizotypal disorder (1) Temporal lobe epilepsy (1) Dysthymia (3)	Sedative-hypnotics (8) Psychedelics (6) Alcohol (5)
Somatization disorder (12)	Panic disorder (2) Sociopathy (2) Temporal lobe epilepsy (1) Schizotypal disorder (1) Dysthymia (7)	Sedative-hypnotics (12) Alcohol (2) Psychedelics (2)
Polysymptomatic neurosis group (N = 18)		
Panic and agoraphobic disorders (10)	Dysthymia (6) Sociopathy (1) Somatization disorder (1) Schizotypal disorder (1)	Sedative-hypnotics (8) Alcohol (2) Psychedelics (1)
Obsessive-compulsive disorder (8)	Dysthymia (5) Schizotypal disorder (1)	Sedative-hypnotics (1)
Schizotypal group (N = 9)		
Schizotypal disorder (9)		Sedative-hypnotics (2) Alcohol (1) Psychedelics (2)
Organic group (N = 3)		
Grand mal epilepsy (1)		Alcohol (1)
Temporal lobe epilepsy (1)		Sedative-hypnotics (1)
Residual (adult) attention deficit disorder (1)		Psychedelics (1) Alcohol (1)
Undiagnosed group (N = 4)		
"Chronic identity disorder" (4)		Alcohol (3) Psychedelics (2) Sedative-hypnotics (2)

*Numbers in parentheses refer to the numbers of patients with given disorder or condition.

(N = 45) consisted of affective disorders, primarily cyclothymic or dysthymic and atypical (bipolar II) rather than "classic" forms. The next largest group, personality disorders (N = 21), consisted of probable or definite somatization disorder and antisocial personalities. An almost equal category was the polysymptomatic neurosis group (N = 18), consisting of panic, agoraphobic, and obsessive-compulsive disorders. There were 9 patients with schizotypal personality and no concurrent disorders. The organic group is represented by 2 epileptic patients and 1 with adult (residual) attention deficit disorder.

The remaining 4 probands were considered undiagnosed at index evaluation; they had some affinity to adolescent identity disorder as defined in DSM-III, except that their condition had persisted beyond adolescence, was chronic, and had its basis in physical defects or abnormalities that could be expected to produce an irreconcilable identity conflict. For example, one subject was an albino girl born to black parents, and another was a very intelligent college educated woman with multiple congenital abnormalities and short stature. The profound identity disturbance in these patients was based on realistic anatomic factors.

Also displayed in Table 2 are the concurrent diagnoses given to 37 cases. Of these, secondary or superimposed dysthymia with chronic fluctuating course was the most common (N = 21). Of the remaining patients with multiple diagnoses, 7 met the criteria for schizotypal personality disorder, 2 for epilepsy, 2 for adult (residual) attention deficit disorder, and 5 for somatization, sociopathic, and panic disorders. Patients with multiple concurrent diagnoses were not uncommon (e.g., an agoraphobic woman who suffered from preexisting somatization disorder and superimposed or secondary dysthymic disorder).

Substance abuse/dependence occurred in 55% of the probands and was equally distributed across all diagnostic groups (Table 2). Sedative-hypnotics were the most frequent drugs of abuse (46%), followed by alcohol (21%) and psychedelics (19%); many patients abused multiple drugs.

Follow-Up Course

As shown in Table 3, major depressive episodes with melancholic features developed in 29 borderline probands; 11 others had brief hypomanic excursions (6 on tricyclic challenge), 4 had manic episodes (1 of which was on tricyclic administration), and 8 evolved into mixed affective states (coexisting manic and depressive features). Four probands were known to have committed suicide after dropping out of treatment; their diagnoses ranged from obsessive-compulsive to somatization, schizotypal, and epileptic disorders.

Schizophreniform episodes (nonaffective psychotic symptoms that cleared within weeks) occurred in 4 borderlines and 1 personality disorder control. One borderline proband developed full-fledged paranoid schizophrenia, and 2 others (who at follow-up satisfied the Hoch and Polatin[22] description of pseudoneurotic schizophrenia) were classified as chronic undifferentiated type. Thus, 8 % of the borderline group developed "schizophrenia-related" disorders (assuming schizopreniform illness is related to schizophrenia), compared with 2% of personality disorder controls (χ^2 = 1.19, .05 < p < .1). This nonsignificant trend for borderlines to develop schizophrenia-related outcomes should be contrasted with their highly significant liability for affective breakdowns (χ^2 = 19.1, p < .001).

The link of borderline personality to affective disorder was further strengthened when we examined rates for pharmacologically-occasioned hypomanic switches: 20% of the 45 affective borderlines and 35% of bipolar controls

TABLE 3 Prospective Follow-Up Outcome in Borderlines and Nonaffective Personality Disorder Controls

	Borderline Group (N = 100)		*Personality Controls (N = 50)*			
Outcome	*N*	*%*	*N*	*%*	*χ^2(df = 1)*	*p*
Affective episodes						
Major depression	29	29	2	4	11.22	< .001
Hypomania or mania[a]	15	15	0	0	6.75	< .01
Mixed states[a]	8	8	0	0	2.79	NS
Suicide	4	4	0	0	0.80	NS
Schizophrenia-related outcome						
Schizophreniform psychosis	5	5	1	2	0.20	NS
Pseudoneurotic schizophrenia	2	2	0	0	0.06	NS
Paranoid schizophrenia	1	1	0	0	0.13	NS

[a]Includes full episodes during antidepressant drug administration which did not remit upon reduction of drug dosage and required lithium administration

had such switches as compared with no personality controls and 2.5% of unipolar controls ($\chi^2 = 29.02$, $p < .001$).

As expected, most of the affective episodes occurred in those given primary affective diagnoses at index evaluation (26 of 45). It is also noteworthy that 20% of those without primary affective diagnoses, including the 4 completed suicides, developed major affective episodes. Schizophreniform episodes were equally distributed in the nonaffective groups, but a chronic schizophrenic denouement was strictly limited to the pure schizotypal group (3 out of 9).

Developmental Object Loss and Parental Assortative Mating

With respect to childhood object loss, borderlines were intermediate between affective and personality controls (Table 4). Borderlines were not different from personality controls on parental assortative mating, but differed significantly from affective controls. Parental units with alcoholism and affective disorder were the most common, followed by alcoholism and sociopathy. These data suggest that many borderlines had troubled home environments due to psychiatric disorder in both parents (roughly two-thirds of patients with early breaks in attachment bonds had assortative parental psychopathology) that led to frequent separations, foster care, or adoption experience.

DISCUSSION

The major finding of the present study is that the borderline rubric encompasses a heterogeneous group of psychopathologic conditions lying predominantly on the border of affective, anxiety, and somatization-antisocial disorders, and, to a minimal extent, that of schizophrenic and organic disorders.

The Border Condition

The affective border Our data favor the notion that borderline disorders are located predominantly on the border of affective rather than schizophrenic psychoses. At index evaluation, nearly half the sample met criteria for subaffective disorders, and two-thirds had a strong affective component, if concurrent or follow-up episodes are taken into account. The relationship to affective disorder is also supported by high rates of pharmacologic hypomania and of familial affective disorder, especially bipolar illness. This finding is in line with earlier reports by our group regarding a lowered threshold for pharmacologic hypomania in cyclothymic[23] and dysthymic disorders,[24] and suggests a common neuropharmacologic substrate for subaffective and borderline disorders. The relatively young age of the borderline group is also in keeping with the insidious onset of bipolar disorders in adolescence or early adulthood. Many seem to suffer from life-long cyclothymia and dysthymia, and make transient shifts into melancholic, hypomanic, manic, and mixed affective episodes, with rapid return to their habitual temperaments. Hence, their diagnosis is best described as borderline manic-depressive psychosis. The 20% rate of depressive episodes with melancholic depth—including 4 suicides on follow-up in the 55 borderline probands who were placed into nonaffective subgroups at index evaluation—suggests that the entire cohort of borderlines suffers from intense affective arousal. This is not surprising, since six of the eight DSM-III criteria for borderline personality are affectively loaded. In brief, the clinical data on the close link between borderline and affective conditions reported here support other findings that have emerged from the application of neuroendocrine[25–27] and sleep electroencephalographic[18,28,29] techniques to borderlines.

The border with anxiety disorders These disorders conform to what the British literature describes as atypical depression[30] or phobic-anxiety-depersonalization syndrome.[31] Intermittent depression occurs in the context of a chronically anxious multiphobic, usu-

TABLE 4 Developmental Factors in Borderline and Control Groups*

	Borderlines		Controls				Comparisons			
			Primary Affective		Personality Disorder		Three-Way		Pairwise[a]	
History	*N*	*%*	*N*	*%*	*N*	*%*	χ^2	*p*	*Groups*	*p*
Parental assortative mating	40	41	5	13	14	47	12.29	< .005	BL vs PA	< .01
									PD vs PA	< .01
									BL vs P	NS
Developmental object loss	36	37	7	18	18	60	13.46	< .005	BL vs PA	< .05
									PD vs PA	< .01
									BL vs PA	< .05

*N = 97 for borderlines (three cases of early adoption excluded); N = 30 for personality controls because of unavailability of reliable data in 20 subjects.
[a]BL = borderline; PA = primary affective; PD = personality disorder.

ally agoraphobic, illness with spontaneous panic attacks characterized by fears of cardiac catastrophe or total mental collapse and associated helplessness and dependency. The highly idiosyncratic manner in which depersonalization and derealization (as part of a panic attack) are experienced, coupled with strong histrionic or obsessional elements, may simulate bizarre but short-lived reactive or schizophreniform psychotic episodes. Work by Klein et al.[32] suggests that some of these patients may represent affective variants with history of childhood school phobia, dependent and histrionic features in adulthood, and positive response to imipramine or monoamine oxidase inhibitors.

The schizophrenia border Nine percent of our sample appears to lie on a schizophrenia spectrum identified in the Danish adoption studies.[7,8] This modest affinity to schizophrenia is evidenced by clinical schizotypal features with familial background for schizophrenia, and progression to soft" schizophrenic illnesses (schizophreniform and pseudoneurotic) and, in 3 instances, to process schizophrenia. All 3 patients with chronic schizophrenic denouement on follow-up belonged to this schizotypal group. Seven other patients, who had other principal diagnoses, also met the criteria for schizotypal disorder. None of these patients had family history for schizophrenia, suggesting that many of the schizotypal features defined in DSM-III may be nonspecific accompaniments of chronic psychiatric or affective disorders, and that they have diagnostic value in suggesting a subschizophrenic disorder only when they occur in the absence of validated psychiatric disorder.

The personality border This subgroup consists of a spectrum of histrionic and sociopathic individuals[4] who have parents with similar or related disorders, who have suffered the developmental vicissitudes of unstable parental marriages, and who complain of lifelong intermittent dysphoria. Brief dysphoric psychotic episodes are often precipitated by substance abuse, but may also result from other organic factors (described next).

The organic border This very small subgroup in our study is similar to patients described by Androlunis et al.[33] in their larger inpatient sample of borderline men. These authors suggest that subtle temporal lobe pathology underlies the impulsivity, affective lability, and anger outbursts of some of these patients. Until the nature of this pathology is defined in a more rigorous fashion, it may be preferable to limit the concept of episodic dyscontrol to those who evidence electroencephalographic findings of a seizure disorder or who show unequivocal response to anticonvulsant medication such as carbamazepine.

The Nature of Micropsychotic Episodes

Our data suggest that schizophreniform episodes are the exception in borderline patients. Grandiose or irritable forms of hypomania, which are sometimes mobilized by antidepressant treatment, as well as depressive delusions, are more common. Drug-induced psychoses (i.e., secondary to ethanol, sedative-hypnotic, psychedelic, and stimulant abuse, or withdrawal states) represent another plausible explanation for micropsychotic episodes. Finally, depersonalization, derealization, and brief reactive psychoses, which are not uncommon in panic, sociopathic, and somatization disorders, could easily simulate schizophreniform symptomatology.

The Origin of Character Pathology

Borderline patients appear to suffer from early breaks in attachment bonds, largely because of assortative parental psychopathology. In this respect they seem intermediate between nonaffective personality disorder and unipolar affective controls. There is some evidence that among the affective disorders, history of assortative parental psychopathology is most common in bipolar II disorders.[34] Such findings strengthen the link between borderline and atypical bipolar disorders. More importantly, our findings suggest that borderline probands are at a double disadvantage: they may inherit the illnesses of one or both parents, and may develop exquisite vulnerability to adult object loss as a result of the troubled early home environment. As stated in Bowlby's latest formulations,[35] childhood object loss may not predispose to affective disorder *per se*, but to character-based affective expressions. Since loss of parents is not an uncommon experience in the early life history of affective probands,[36] their adult affective illnesses can be complicated by separation-related characterologic disturbances, similar to the hysteroid dysphoric women described by Liebowitz and Klein.[37] It is also likely that when one parent has affective disorder and the other a sociopathic or somatization disorder, their children may inherit both illnesses and thereby exhibit manifestations of both disorders. Another possible source of characterologic pathology in borderline disorders, such as cyclothymia or bipolar II, is in the hindrance to optimal ego maturation due to the high-frequency episodes beginning in early adolescence.[18] Indeed, in an adolescent sample studied at Cornell,[38] borderline personality disturbances generally *followed* affective episodes. Thymoleptic therapy or long-term lithium stabilization can bring many such patients to a level of ego stability that had not been achieved in years of psychotherapy and nonspecific pharmacotherapy.[39] However, this outcome is not universal, suggesting that maladaptive personality patterns may become irreversible after many years of inadequately treated affective disorders. The reversibility of "conduct disorders" in depressed children treated with thymoleptics illustrates the importance of early energetic and specific pharmacologic therapies in preventing post-depressive personality disturbances.[40] In brief, the characterologic disturbances of borderline patients sometimes represent primary character pathology but more often are secondary to or concurrent with an affective disorder (i.e., to be coded on an axis orthogonal to the phenomenologic diagnosis).

Lack of Predictive Utility

Borderline conditions emerge as an enormously heterogeneous group of disorders that embrace the gamut of psychopathology. Proportions of specific subtypes in different studies are probably a function of the different populations sampled. Borderline conditions do not seem to represent a definable personality type and, therefore, do not belong on Axis II in DSM-III. We suggest that the potential utility of the concept might be explored on a distinct psychodynamic axis. Despite an unwieldy degree of diagnostic heterogeneity, the concept may still prove useful in setting the stage for a psychotherapeutic intervention geared to the common developmental vicissitudes and ego functioning of patients with certain low level defenses as described in Kernberg's work.[1]

It would seem however, that the very heterogeneity of disorders within the borderline realm argues against a unitary therapeutic modality. For instance, if the clinician were to consider pharmacologic approaches, one could make the case for tricyclics, MAO inhibitors, lithium carbonate, neuroleptics, stimulants, and anticonvulsants—as well as for avoidance of pharmacotherapy—for the various subtypes.

In summary, the current nosologic use of the concept of borderline seems to map a large universe of chronically and seriously ill "difficult" patients outside the area of the classical psychoses and neuroses.[41] It is necessary to look beyond the characterologic "masks" in order to appreciate the phenomenologic diversity of these conditions. A specific personality type or psychopathologic entity as the proper noun for the borderline adjective has not been found yet. Nor is it likely to be found, because, similar to the imprecise adjectival use of terms like "neurotic" and "psychotic," it has no place in modern descriptive psychopathology; there are simply too many neurotic and psychotic conditions which render futile all descriptive efforts to identify a specific "border."[5,41] In a very literal sense, borderline personality can be considered to be a borderline diagnosis.

REFERENCES

1. Kernberg OF: Structural interviewing. Psychiatr Clin North Am 4:169–195, 1981
2. Gunderson JG, Singer MT: Defining borderline patients: An overview. Am J Psychiatry 132:1–10, 1975
3. Klein D: Psychopharmacology and the borderline patient. In Mack JE (ed): Borderline States in Psychiatry. New York, Grune & Stratton, 1975
4. Guze SB: Differential diagnosis of the borderline patient. In Mack JE (ed): Borderline States in Psychiatry. New York, Grune & Stratton, 1975
5. Rich CL: Borderline diagnoses. Am J Psychiatry 135:1399–1401, 1978
6. Spitzer R, Endicott J, Gibbon M: Crossing the border into borderline personality and borderline schizophrenia: The development of criteria. Arch Gen Psychiatry 36:17–24, 1979
7. Khouri PJ, Haier RJ, Rieder RO, et al: A symptom schedule for the diagnosis of borderline schizophrenia: A first report. Br J Psychiatry 137:140–147, 1980
8. Kendler KS, Gruenberg AM, Strauss JS: An independent analysis of the Copenhagen sample of the Danish adoption study of schizophrenia: II. The relationship between schizotypal personality disorder and schizophrenia. Arch Gen Psychiatry 38:928–987, 1981
9. Siever LJ, Gunderson JG: The search for a schizotypal personality: Historical origins and current status. Compr Psychiatry 24:199–212, 1983
10. Mack JE: Borderline states: An historical perspective. In Mack JE (ed): Borderline States in Psychiatry. New York, Grune & Stratton, 1975
11. Stone MH: The Borderline Syndrome: Constitution, Personality, and Adaptation. New York, McGraw-Hill, 1980
12. Pope HG, Jones JM, Hudson JI, et al: The validity of DSM-III borderline personality disorder. Arch Gen Psychiatry 40:23–30, 1983
13. Monroe RR: Episodic Behavioral Disorders. Cambridge, Harvard University Press, 1970
14. Gunderson JG, Kolb JE, Austin V: The diagnostic interview for borderline patients. Am J Psychiatry 138: 896–903, 1981
15. Soloft PH, Millward JW: Psychiatric disorders in the families of borderline patients. Arch Gen Psychiatry 40: 37–44, 1983
16. Loranger AW, Oldham JM, Tulis EH: Familial transmission of DSM-III borderline personality disorder. Arch Gen Psychiatry 39:795–799, 1982
17. Perry JC, Klerman GL: Clinical features of the borderline personality disorder. Am J Psychiatry 137:167–173, 1980
18. Akiskal HS: Subaffective disorders: Dysthymic, cylothymic, and bipolar II disorders in the "borderline" realm. Psychiatr Clin North Am 4:25–46, 1981
19. Feighner JP, Robins E, Guze SB, et al: Diagnostic criteria for use in psychiatric research. Arch Gen Psychiatry 26:57–63, 1972
20. Andreasen NC, Endicott J, Spitzer RL, et al: The family history method using diagnostic criteria—Reliability and validity. Arch Gen Psychiatry 34:1229–1235, 1977
21. Amark C: A study in alcoholism Acta Psychiatr Neurol Scand 70 (Suppl), 1951
22. Hoch P, Polatin P: Pseudoneurotic forms of schizophrenia. Psychiatr Q 23:248–276, 1949
23. Akiskal HS, Djenderedjian AH, Rosenthal RH, et al: Cyclothymic disorder: Validating criteria for inclusion in the bipolar affective group. Am J Psychiatry 134:1227–1233, 1977

24. Akiskal HS: Dysthymic disorder: Psychopathology of proposed chronic depressive subtypes. Am J Psychiatry 140:11–20, 1983
25. Carroll BJ, Greden JF, Feinberg M, et al: Neuroendocrine evaluation of depression in borderline patients. Psychiatr Clin North Am 4:89–99, 1981
26. Garbutt JC, Loosen PT, Tipermas A, et al: The TRH test in patients with borderline personality disorders. Psychiatry Res 9:107–113, 1983
27. Baxter L, Edell W, Gerner R, et al: Dexamethasone suppression test and axis I diagnoses of inpatients with DSM-III borderline personality disorder. J Clin Psychiatry 45:150–153, 1984
28. Bell J, Lycaki H, Jones D, et al: Effect of preexisting borderline personality disorder on clinical and EEG sleep correlates of depression. Psychiatry Res 9:115–123, 1983
29. McNamara ME, Reynolds CF, Soloff FH, et al: EEG sleep evaluation of depression in borderline patients. Am J Psychiatry 141:182–186, 1984
30. West ED, Dally PJ: Effect of iproniazid in depressive syndromes. Br Med J 1:2491–2494, 1959
31. Roth M: The phobic-anxiety-depersonalization syndrome. Proc Roy Soc Med 52:587–595, 1959
32. Klein DF, Gittleman R, Quitkin F, et al: Diagnosis and Drug Treatment of Psychiatric Disorder: Adult and Children, 2nd ed. Baltimore, Williams & Wilkins, 1980
33. Andrulonis PA, Glueck BC, Stroebel CF, et al: Borderline personality subcategories. J Nerv Ment Dis 170:670–679, 1982
34. Dunner DL, Fleiss JL, Addonizio G, et al: Assortative mating in primary affective disorder. Biol Psychiatry 11: 43–51, 1976
35. Bowlby J: The making and breaking of affectional bonds: I. Aetiology and psychopathology in the light of attachment theory. Br J Psychiatry 130: 201–210, 1977
36. Akiskal HS, Tashjian R: Affective disorders: Part 11. Recent advances in laboratory and pathogenetic approaches. Hosp Community Psychiatry 34:822–830, 1983
37. Liebowitz MR, Klein DF: Hysteroid dysphoria. Psychiatr Clin North Am 2:555–575, 1979
38. Friedman RC, Clarkin JF, Corn R, et al: DSM-III and affective pathology in hospitalized adolescents. J Nerv Ment Dis 170:511-521, 1982
39. Akiskal HS, Khani MK, Scott-Strauss A: Cyclothymic temperamental disorders. Psychiatr Clin North Am 2:527–554, 1979
40. Kroll J, Sines L, Martin K, et al: Borderline personality disorder. Construct validity of the concept. Arch Gen Psychiatry 38:1021–1026, 1981
41. Dickes R: The concept of borderline states: An alternative proposal. Int J Psychoanal Psychother 3:1–27, 1974

MARK BERELOWITZ & ALEX TARNOPOLSKY

The validity of borderline personality disorder: An updated review of recent research

In 1987 we reviewed the data on the validity of the diagnosis of borderline personality (Tarnopolsky & Berelowitz, 1987), using the research that had become available since the statement by Liebowitz (1979) that:

> When the St Louis approach to diagnostic validity is used as a guideline, the conclusion reached is that available data do not weight for or against borderline's status as an independent entity.

We concluded in our review that the scale had tipped in favor of the validity of the diagnosis, but that much research was still needed.

The key developments between 1979 and 1987 that made this change possible were the introduction of reliable clinical diagnostic criteria in the DSM-III (American Psychiatric Association, 1980), and reliable research instruments such as the Diagnostic Interview for Borderlines (DIB; Gunderson *et al*, 1981). It became possible, using these instruments, to test the validity of the diagnosis against the criteria of Robins & Guze (1970):

a. Identification of a characteristic phenomenology
b. Phenomenological independence from other psychiatric disorders
c. Follow-up data

SOURCE: *Personality Disorder Reviewed*, by P. Tyrer and G. Stein (Eds.), pp. 90–112, 1993. Reprinted by permission of The Royal College of Psychiatrists, Publications Office, London, England.

d. Family studies
e. Laboratory investigations and psychological tests
f. Treatment response

We also concluded in 1987 that data were lacking in several areas. It seems appropriate therefore to reassess the situation in the light of recent developments. These include:

a. General developments in the field of personality disorders
b. New empirical studies using diagnostic instruments that examine a wider range of DSM-III Axis II diagnoses
c. New data and new concepts on etiology and long-term outcome
d. Treatment studies
e. Childhood antecedents

For the convenience of the reader we will follow the basic structure of our 1987 review, updating each section systematically, and adding new sections as appropriate.

As in 1987, the literature remains predominantly from the US, although there is a burgeoning Canadian literature on the subject, as well as a few papers from the UK.

CONCEPTUAL MODELS AND DIAGNOSTIC SYSTEMS

The term "borderline" has been used in a number of specific ways in psychiatry and psychoanalysis (Jackson & Tarnopolsky, 1990). Firstly, there is a long history of the notion of a condition which was borderline to schizophrenia, in terms of symptoms, course, and prognosis. Many of these patients would fit into the category of schizotypal personality disorder in DSM-III-R (American Psychiatric Association, 1987).

Secondly, following Stern (1938), psychoanalysts use the word "borderline" to describe a group of patients, apparently with neurotic disorders, who are prone to brief psychotic episodes under stress, including the stress of psychoanalysis. These patients were not defined precisely in phenomenological terms, and possibly covered a wide group of diagnostic labels. The clearest contemporary account of such patients has been given by Kernberg (1967), including a diagnostic system (Kernberg, 1981) and a modification of the psychotherapeutic method (Kernberg *et al*, 1989).

Thirdly, a number of psychotherapeutically sophisticated American psychiatrists (Grinker *et al*, 1968; Gunderson & Kolb, 1978; Spitzer *et al*, 1979) combined the psychoanalytic ideas, empirical research, and their own clinical experience to construct phenomenological profiles for borderline personality disorder (BPD). The specific consequences of their work include a semistructured research instrument, the Diagnostic Interview for Borderlines (DIB) (Gunderson *et al*, 1981; Zanarini *et al*, 1989*b*), and the DSM-III diagnostic set for Borderline Personality Disorder (Spitzer *et al*, 1979). These instruments identify a group of patients with a specific personality disorder characterized by a particular instability in areas of behavior, relationships, identity, and emotional experience, as well as a vulnerability to psychotic-like episodes. Although a term like unstable or labile personality disorder may well have been more appropriate for this group, the word "borderline" has persisted, for better or for worse. It is the validity of borderline personality as defined by Spitzer and Gunderson that will be the focus of this paper.

We will begin by reviewing the reliability of the diagnostic instruments; we will then assess the validity of the diagnosis, using the criteria of Robins & Guze (1970); lastly we will examine some of the data on childhood antecedents.

RELIABILITY

Reliability refers to the agreement between different assessors about the presence of a disorder, and to the consistency of the assessment over time. Reliable diagnostic instruments are a precondition for empirical research. The coefficient kappa (κ) is a good measure of reliability with $\kappa = 0$ indicating chance agreement and $\kappa = 1$ showing full agreement. In general, κ values above 0.7 are considered acceptable.

Two instruments will be considered here.

a. Diagnostic Interview for Borderlines (DIB; DIB-R) (Gunderson *et al*, 1981; Zanarini *et al*, 1989*b*). This is a semi-structured interview which identifies characteristic affects, impulse-action patterns, interpersonal relationships, and cognitions, including psychotic-like phenomena. The new version (DIB-R) contains 186 questions, divided into several sections, which are weighted to provide a numerical score.

Acceptable agreement, with κ values in some cases above 0.8, has been demonstrated for live interviews (Kroll *et al*, 1981*a*; Frances *et al*, 1984; Hurt *et al*, 1984) and case notes (McGlashan, 1983*a*; Armelius *et al*, 1985), and for two interviews of the same patient by different clinicians at least one week apart (Cornell *et al*, 1983). Inter-rater reliability for the subscales of the DIB was also high, with the exception of the section on affects (Frances *et al*, 1984).

b. DSM-III Borderline Personality Disorder. Spitzer *et al* (1979) partitioned a muddled field into two distinct personality disorders: schizotypal personality, related to schizophrenia, and borderline personality, discussed here. This work formed part of the development of the DSM-III, and the form and content of the diagnostic method are very much within the spirit of the DSM-III—there is an eight-item checklist, five of which must be present for the diagnosis. The checklist identifies chronically unstable, vulnerable individuals, with difficult relationships, poor self-control, and identity problems. The definitions of three items were improved for DSM-III-R. The DSM-III criteria have latterly been incorporated into research instruments (e.g. Spitzer *et al*, 1987). Good reliability with κ values above 0.7 was obtained with clinical interviews

(Frances *et al*, 1984), case notes (McGlashan, 1983*a*), and with new research interviews (κ = 0.85, Stangl *et al*, 1985; κ between 0.52 and 1.0, Zanarini *et al*, 1987; see also Kavoussi *et al*, 1990).

VALIDITY: AN APPLICATION OF THE CRITERIA OF ROBINS AND GUZE

The paucity of objective indicators of psychiatric disorder means that validity is best assessed by marshaling data from a number of different areas. The criteria of Robins & Guze (1970) remain useful for this purpose, despite criticism (Livesley, 1991).

A Unitary Clinical Description

"In general, the first step is to describe the clinical picture of the disorder" (Robins & Guze, 1970). Does the research identify a homogeneous group of patients?

During the 1980s many studies have applied both the DIB and the DSM-III criteria to case notes (McGlashan, 1983*a*; Pope *et al*, 1983) and interviews (Frances *et al*, 1984; Akiskal *et al*, 1985*a*). Kroll's group (Kroll *et al*, 1981*b*, 1982; Barrash *et al*, 1983) thoroughly examined a series of 252 admissions in the US and the UK, applying both sets of criteria in interviews. The DIB identified a larger number of patients than the DSM-III. There were some false positives and false negatives, mostly cases which met the DIB criteria and not the DSM-III. The commonest diagnosis for these discordant cases was "non-borderline" personality disorder. Cluster analysis further improved the agreement and yielded a high sensitivity (0.83) and specificity (0.89) for the DIB against the DSM-III. However, there is a problem in assessing these data: the DIB is a research tool, whereas the DSM-III criteria are in the form of an unstructured clinical interview.

Zanarini *et al* (1991) tested the DSM-III and the DSM-III-R criteria against so-called LEAD diagnoses (i.e. clinical diagnoses made by experienced clinicians—Longitudinal Expert All Data, see also Spitzer, 1983). There were a number of misclassified cases, indicating that the DSM criteria did not accurately reflect what senior clinicians had in mind when diagnosing BPD. Overall the DSM criteria identified a wider range of personality pathology than did the clinical diagnoses.

By means of this and other research (Gunderson, 1977; Sheehy *et al*, 1980; Soloff & Ulrich, 1981) a characteristic phenomenological set of core features has been identified: unstable interpersonal relationships, idealization and denigration of others, intense unpredictable feelings, and impulsive and self-destructive behavior. Similarly, Maudsley [a mental hospital in Great Britain] psychiatrists thought that the most frequent items among the borderline patients were a pattern of unstable, intense interpersonal relationships, and impulsiveness and unpredictability in potentially self-damaging areas (both DSM-III items); the most discriminating item, however, was brief, stress-related, psychotic episodes or regressions (a Gunderson item) (Tarnopolsky & Berelowitz, 1984). With regard to psychotic features, Links *et al* (1989) found that loosely defined "psychotic" symptoms such as depersonalization/derealization and drug-free paranoid experiences predict a diagnosis of BPD, while borderline patients with highly specific symptoms like delusions and hallucinations often merited additional diagnoses of major affective disorder or drug/alcohol abuse.

Bateman (1989) reported the only diagnostic study of UK patients undertaken by a local author. He compared in-patient DIB-diagnosed borderline patients with PSE-diagnosed neurotic and psychotic controls. A particularly high level of anxiety and irritability, externalized as violent destructive behavior, anger, and hostility at interview, distinguished borderline patients from neurotic patients. In addition, they presented with depressive and non-specific psychotic features.

Kroll *et al* (1982) highlighted certain differences between British and American patients: "The British borderlines (DIB and DSM-III criteria) reported minimal drug abuse and no drug-related psychosis . . . [they] evidenced no interest in caretaker roles; and although the majority reported derealization and depersonalization, so did the majority of British non-borderline patients."

Although there is some persistent discordance between the diagnostic instruments, they do nevertheless appear to be tapping the same core of pathology. The agreement between the DIB and the DSM-III is relatively high, particularly considering the uncertainty about psychiatric diagnosis generally.

Phenomenological Discrimination from Other Disorders

The question here is whether patients with an operationally diagnosed borderline personality can be distinguished from patients with other psychiatric conditions, especially schizophrenia, affective disorders, and other personality disorders.

Schizophrenia

Several studies in different centers and using different methods have now placed the phenomenological distinction between borderline personalities and schizophrenic in-patients beyond reasonable doubt (Gunderson *et al*, 1975; Kolb & Gunderson, 1980; Soloff & Ulrich, 1981; Kroll *et al*, 1981*b*, 1982; Pope *et al*, 1983). For example, Gunderson *et al* (1975), using patients drawn from the International Pilot Study of Schizophrenia (Carpenter *et al*, 1973), found that the borderline in-patients had significantly fewer psychotic symptoms than the schizophrenic group, with no evidence of thought disorder. The borderline group was characterized by derealization, a frenetic and stormy life-style, unusual and occult experiences, marked interpersonal difficulties, and suicide threats.

Other writers confirmed that the psychotic symptoms of borderline patients are not typically schizophrenic (Pope *et al*, 1983; Chopra & Beatson, 1986; Links *et al*, 1989). Kroll *et al* (1981*b*) found only one DSM-III schizophrenic among 21 DIB positive in-patients, and Pope *et al* (1983) found no DSM-III schizophrenics among 33 in-patients diagnosed as borderline according to Gunderson criteria.

However, the distinction between out-patients from these two groups is less clear and less well studied. Sheehy *et al* (1980), comparing borderlines (diagnosed according to their own criteria) and schizophrenics diagnosed by Carpenter criteria (Carpenter *et al*, 1973), found that deficient management of impulses, intolerably unpleasant feelings, and idealization/denigration of others were significantly more prevalent among the borderline patients. Pronounced failure of reality testing was more prevalent among the schizophrenic patients, and was the best predictor of group differences. But Koenigsberg *et al* (1983) found that borderline out-patients had only non-significantly higher DIB scores than schizophrenic out-patients. These results are conflicting and throw doubt on the accuracy of the distinction between the disorders.

Affective Disorders

The coincidence of affective illness with borderline personality is greater than might be expected statistically (Gunderson & Elliot, 1985; Perry, 1985). The relationship between borderline personality and affective illness is potentially more complicated than the postulated link with schizophrenia. The issue remains complex, and the debates are often heated.

Gunderson & Elliot (1985) listed four possible explanations for the high coincidence. The first two possibilities were that one disorder is a consequence of the other: (a) drug-taking or promiscuity are used to relieve feelings of dysphoria or depression, or (b) depression may be secondary to poor impulse control and unsatisfactory relationships. The third (c) is that both disorders coexist independently in the same subjects; and the fourth (d) postulates that affective symptoms or character traits arise from an interaction of symptoms peculiar to each individual. Research data partially support each hypothesis, although Gunderson & Elliot's analyses at the time led them to accept the fourth.

Turning now to the empirical evidence, Gunderson & Kolb (1978) were able to discriminate borderline personality from neurotically depressed in-patients by the presence of drug-related psychotic experiences, anhedonia and dysphoria, interpersonal difficulties, and paranoid experiences. Sheehy *et al* (1980), with less formal methods, obtained similar results in a series of out-patients. Barrash *et al* (1983), summarizing the findings of Kroll's group of 252 in-patients, found 48 with DIB positive borderline personality and 77 patients with affective disorders (unspecified); only three patients with affective disorders were DIB positive. Soloff & Ulrich (1981) found that total scores, scaled section scores, and 19 individual DIB items all effectively differentiated borderline personality from Research Diagnostic Criteria (RDC; Spitzer *et al*, 1975) (major) unipolar depressives. It was also repeatedly noted that the items characteristic of each disorder are different (e.g. impulsivity v. affective state), and that the attendant emotions are different, the depression of the borderline patient having the more schizoid qualities of boredom and emptiness. Borderline personalities also feel easily disappointed and let down, want to hurt themselves, and may be well aware of their rage. These symptomatic differences were confirmed by McGlashan (1978*b*), who also found that borderline patients broke down at an earlier age, and had fewer premorbid instrumental skills than unipolars.

By contrast, other studies of in-patients (Pope *et al*, 1983) and out-patients (Akiskal *et al*, 1985*a*) have found proportions as high as 50% of major and minor affective illnesses among DIB-positive patients. Akiskal argued that the symptom set for BPD could easily be rearranged to look like an affective disorder. It is of local interest that the British sample ($n = 47$) studied by Kroll *et al* (1982) showed seven DIB-positive cases, three with a secondary diagnosis of depressive neurosis and one with a primary diagnosis of major affective illness (DSM-III). Also, Bateman's (1989) study in London found that among 11 borderline in-patients (DIB), ten met the PSE criteria for minor, and one for major, depressive disorders, although they differed in other ways (see above). James & Berelowitz (in preparation) found similar results in adolescents.

Soloff *et al* (1987) studied patients who were both borderline and depressed to see if a particular depressive syndrome emerged (i.e. one that could replace BPD as a diagnostic category)—it did not.

Fyer *et al* (1988) used an epidemiological approach to examine comorbidity, and found no increase of affective disorder in BPD patients compared with other patients. Certainly depression was common in other personality disorders as well. Other studies have shown that many affectively disordered patients have abnormal personalities (Friedman *et al*, 1983; Shea *et al*, 1987), but these are not exclusively or even predominantly borderline (Shea *et al*, 1987; Pilkonis & Frank, 1988).

Gunderson has recently updated his review (Gunderson & Phillips, 1991), and now concludes that their third hypothesis is the most tenable, namely that BPD and affective illnesses commonly occur together, but are unrelated. Overall the findings are conflicting, and the field remains unclear. Certainly, affective symptoms and borderline traits are both common, and often occur together, but depression occurs in other personality disorders as well. It is likely that more conceptual as well as empirical work will be needed to clarify these matters.

Personality Disorders

In our first review we reported several studies that failed to distinguish between in-patients with borderline (DIB) and non-borderline personality disorders (Kolb & Gunderson, 1980; Kroll *et al*, 1981*b*, 1982). Pope *et al* (1983) found that borderline personality overlapped with histrionic personality disorder in women, and antisocial personality disorder in men (all diagnoses according to DSM-III criteria). However, borderline cases could be clearly distinguished in at least three out-patient samples (Sheehy *et al*, 1980; Perry & Klerman, 1980; Koenigsberg *et al*, 1983). As mentioned above for the comparison with schizophrenia, it is possible that the symptoms which determine admission may be of particular importance. In one refinement of the in-patient studies quoted above, Barrash *et al* (1983) applied cluster analytic methods to the DIB items in Kroll's series, and were then able to distinguish between borderline and other personality disorders.

Several points should be noted. Firstly, in the early 1980s the diagnosis of non-borderline personalities was not standardized. Secondly, the studies quoted made little allowance for dimensional aspects of personality. Thirdly, the use of the DSM-III has become more refined.

Several newer studies have dealt with these points in different ways. Stangl *et al* (1985), studying out-patients, found good overall agreement ($\kappa > 0.7$) for the presence of any personality disorder, and for three particular DSM-III types, borderline, histrionic, and dependent. The most frequent combination was borderline and histrionic. Zanarini *et al* (1990) applied the DIB as well as their own interview for the assessment of other personality disorders to a large sample of in- and out-patients. They were able to distinguish between frequent, discriminating, and specific borderline traits. The latter included seven features evident in both sexes and both settings: quasi-psychotic thought; self-mutilation; manipulative suicide efforts; concerns about abandonment, engulfment, and annihilation; demandingness and entitlement; treatment regressions; and countertransference difficulties. But when the DSM-III and DSM-III-R were compared with so-called LEAD criteria ("expert criteria") on the same sample, the DSM criteria were found to be "overinclusive," and the LEAD criteria restrictive. The authors suggest that the DSM criteria may identify a relatively non-specific type of severe character pathology. Nurnberg *et al* (1991), using DSM-III-R, reached a similar conclusion.

Borderline personalities can be distinguished at a descriptive level from schizophrenic and affective patients. However, there continue to be problems in distinguishing them from other personality disorders. It may be that the term is being used in two ways, as a relatively precise and distinctive cluster of symptoms which identify a specific personality disorder (DIB), and as a more general measure of severe character pathology (DSM-III, DSM-III-R). The latter notion would also fit with psychoanalytic views such as those of Kernberg (1967). This problem may reflect a fundamental weakness in the concept of borderline personality; alternatively it may merely reflect the conceptual and theoretical difficulties which bedevil the whole field of personality disorders. In summary, the data suggest that borderline personality disorders, as currently described, may be distinct and also coexist, at different levels of severity. This is illustrated by the overlap and distinctiveness of borderline and schizotypal personalities (Spitzer *et al*, 1979; Barrash *et al*, 1983; Frances *et al*, 1984; McGlashan, 1987*a*). Other writers have identified large sets of traits shared by what had been assumed to be separate personality disorders. For example, Nurnberg *et al* (1991) found two broad groups which straddle the boundaries of the DSM-III clusters. Borderline personality is in one group, schizotypal in the other.

Follow-Up

Follow-up studies help to establish whether or not, over time, patients who are thought to have one particular condition can be shown to have some other disorder which can better explain their original symptoms (Robins & Guze, 1970). Early studies of borderline personality were not specifically designed for follow-up, and had small sample sizes and short observation periods (Pope *et al*, 1983; Barasch *et al*, 1985; Akiskal *et al*, 1985*a*; Mitton & Links, 1988). Some studies have extended over longer periods (as much as 15 years), but most have problems relating to diagnostic reliability, selectivity of the samples, and treatment effects (McGlashan, 1986; Stone *et al*, 1987; Paris *et al*, 1988; Cardish & Silver, 1991). . . .

A central question initially was whether borderline personalities were manifesting an early form of schizophrenia. In a five-year follow-up of borderline and schizophrenic patients, before the DIB and DSM-III were introduced (Carpenter & Gunderson, 1977), all the schizophrenic patients retained their original diagnoses, but there was persistent diagnostic uncertainty about the borderline group. Despite this uncertainty, however, only one of the 24 borderlines was subsequently rediagnosed as schizophrenic. No schizophrenics were found among DIB or DSM-III borderline samples after 4–7 years (Pope *et al*, 1983, $n = 27$) and after three years (Barasch *et al*, 1985, $n = 30$). McGlashan (1983*b*) found that after 15 years 24% of borderline personalities and 55% of schizotypals developed schizophrenia. No specific borderline trait was predictive of schizophrenia (Fenton & McGlashan, 1989).

The second question concerned the relationship between borderline personality and affective illness. Pope *et al* (1983) found that of the mixed cases (borderline personality plus affective illness), 74% had possible/probable affective illness at follow-up, while the corresponding figure for the "pure" borderline group was only 23%. Akiskal *et al* (1985*a*) found a similar figure of 20% for melancholic episodes among "pure" borderlines. Moreover, some workers have found major depression to be equally prevalent among borderline and other personality disorders at three years, which argues against a specific link between borderline and affective disorders (Barasch *et al*, 1985). The vast majority of borderline patients do not become depressives: only 11% changed from borderline personality to affective disorder over time (McGlashan 1983*b*, 1987*b*). McGlashan (1987*b*) also found that one-third of unipolar depressives developed BPD.

The third question concerns the stability of borderline personality over time. The majority retained their original diagnosis (65%: Pope *et al*, 1983; 60–90%: Barasch *et al*, 1985; 44–70%: McGlashan, 1983*b*, 1987*b*), but some, in addition, received other personality disorder diagnoses as well, mainly in the DSM-III dramatic or flamboyant group (Pope *et al*, 1983). In only one or two cases was the diagnosis of schizotypal personality considered possible or definite.

The last question concerns social functioning. The presence of similar social outcome is a weaker argument for validity than the persistence of the diagnosis, since there is no one-to-one relationship between psychopathology and social functioning. Nevertheless, when followed up over several years, borderline patients show better social functioning than schizophrenics. This was evident at five years (Carpenter & Gunderson, 1977), although at two years there had been no discernible difference (Gunderson *et al*, 1975). In later studies, "pure" borderline personalities presented outcomes intermediate between those for schizophrenic illness (worst) and affective illness (best) at around five years (Pope *et al*, 1983; McGlashan, 1983*b*, 1986), and similar to affective illness at 15 years (McGlashan, 1983*b*). Unlike schizophrenics, they tend to improve over time, and are at their best 10–20 years after discharge (McGlashan, 1986; Cardish & Silver, 1991). By comparison with schizophrenics they were more likely to be autonomous, in employment, to be married and have children, despite needing repeated brief hospital admissions (McGlashan, 1986). There was also less completed suicide (Stone *et al*, 1987). The diagnostic distinction between borderline and schizophrenia was found to be a powerful predictor of the type of discharge, circumstances of discharge, and course following discharge (McGlashan & Heinssen, 1988).

In summary, borderline personalities usually retain their diagnoses over time, but in addition they may present with other personality disorders, frequently within the DSM-III "dramatic" group. Several studies show that only a minority develop schizophrenia, in contrast with schizotypals. Most borderline personalities do not develop affective illness; a variable number display affective symptoms at follow-up, but possibly no more than for other personality disorders. One-third of unipolars appear to develop BPD. Comorbidity with affective disorders (McGlashan, 1978*b*; Shea *et al*, 1987) and alcoholism (Dulit *et al*, 1990) affects the presentation, interpretation, and course of the disorder.

At follow-up, patients with BPD either retain their diagnoses or acquire another Axis II diagnosis. It appears that a distinctive course is becoming clearer, with long-term social functioning similar to that of unipolar depressives, and improvement early in the fifth decade.

Family Studies

Robins & Guze (1970) argue that finding an increased prevalence of the disorder in the relatives and in the index patients supports the validity of the diagnosis. In particular, twin studies help to disentangle the relative etiological importance of environment and heredity.

Because of their respective historical roots, in this section we will consider both borderline (DSM-III and DIB criteria) and schizotypal personalities, and their relationship to schizophrenia. In the Danish Adoption Study, Kety *et al* (1968) found evidence supporting a genetic link between "B-3 borderline schizophrenics" and the chronic schizophrenic index cases. A sample of B-3 cases was then used by Spitzer to define the criteria for DSM-III Schizotypal Personality Disorder (Spitzer *et al*, 1979). Kendler *et al* (1981) applied Spitzer's criteria blindly to the Danish records and confirmed that schizotypal personality was more common among the biological relatives of chronic schizophrenic patients than among either relatives of controls or relatives of B-3 index cases. Gunderson *et al* (1983) further showed that among the B-3 relatives of chronic schizophrenics, the most common diagnosis was schizotypal personality, not borderline; the commonest diagnosis in the B-3 *index* cases was borderline personality (9 cases out of 10), and their B-3 relatives had borderline rather than schizotypal features. These two studies therefore allow for two genetic propositions: (a) the mentally ill biological relatives of schizophrenics are schizotypal and not borderline, and (b) the mentally ill relatives of borderline personalities are, in the main, themselves borderline. These findings are supported by other studies (Loranger *et al*, 1982; Baron *et al*, 1985). The latter group found that borderline personality was ten times more common among the treated relatives of borderline patients than in the relatives of schizophrenic patients. Links *et al* (1988*a*) found no schizophrenic patients among the relatives of borderlines. A substantive twin study by Torgersen (1984) showed that monozygotic twins of schizotypal patients have schizotypal (33%) and not borderline (0%) disorders.

With regard to the genetic link with affective disorders, Soloff & Millward (1983) are often quoted as they found that more borderline than depressed probands had relatives with mood swings. This result, however, refers to a mixed group of 19 borderline patients, 9 schizotypal patients, and 20 patients who met both criteria; further analysis revealed that depression was actually more prevalent among the relatives of the schizotypal than the borderline patients! Links *et al* (1988*a*) examined the relatives of a sample of borderline patients. The vast majority of patients also had a depressive condition; among the relatives the most frequent diagnoses were alcoholism and recurrent unipolar depressions.

Pope *et al* (1983) and Andrulonis & Vogel (1984) simply separated pure borderline patients from those who also had an effective illness, and found that the prevalence of affective illness was raised only in the relatives of the latter group. Torgersen (1984) found the same: "all the co-twins with an affective disorder were co-twins of schizotypal and borderline patients with a concurrent affective disorder as well." Zanarini *et al* (1988) supported these conclusions. They examined a sample of patients with borderline, antisocial, and other personality disorders. The latter also had dysthymic disorder. The borderline patients were separated into "pure" and "depressed" subgroups. In summary, they found that relatives of borderlines were more frequently borderline and relatives of "antisocials" were more frequently antisocial and relatives of depressed borderlines more frequently had major depressions. Relatives of dysthymic patients with "other" personality disorders had an even higher rate of major depressions.

Although a number of objections can be raised against these studies (see Tarnopolsky & Berelowitz, 1987, p. 730) we are nevertheless left with consistent evidence, albeit of variable quality, confirming the separateness of borderline and schizotypal personalities, and of borderline personality and major depressive illness. In 1987 we suggested that diagnostically rigorous multicenter research was needed to further clarify these issues—such a study is currently being carried out (Loranger *et al*, 1991).

Laboratory Investigations and Psychological Tests

Biological data are as sparse and inconclusive in the area of borderline personalities as they were for the whole of psychiatry 20 years ago (Robins & Guze, 1970).

Much of the work with biological markers to assess the relationships with affective disorders is questionable, either because the patient had both syndromes concurrently (Carroll *et al*, 1981), or because good controls were not available. Only Kontaxakis *et al* (1987) found similar proportions of dexamethasone non-suppressors (about 50%) among borderline patients and depressive controls. Korzekwa *et al* (1991) found an abnormal DST [dexamethasone suppression test] in only a quarter of borderline personalities comorbid with depression, and paradoxically, in only 17% of those with endogenous features. Several reviews (Steiner *et al*, 1988; Tarnopolsky, 1991; Korzekwa, 1991) all agree that the DST findings are inconsistent in studies of BPD.

Other indicators have been studied. The findings by Korzekwa (1991) for thyrotropin-releasing hormone were inconclusive. Akiskal *et al* (1985*b*) described a REM sleep pattern in borderline patients similar to that found in depressive patients; there were differences, however, between those borderline patients who had an affective illness at any time in the past and those who had not. Silk *et al* (1988) argued that the sleep EEG may be a more useful predictor of endogenous depression among borderline patients than the DST. Coid *et al* (1984) found a raised level of plasma metenkephalin (a neuropeptide that blocks pain perception) among self-mutilators who met DSM-III borderline criteria. Coccaro *et al* (1989) found that low CSF [cerebrospinal fluid] 5-HIAA correlates more with traits of aggression and impulsivity than with BPD per se. Only Kutcher *et al* (1987, 1989) are able to argue for a common biological element to BPD and schizophrenia. Using the EEG under experimental conditions, they obtained auditory evoked responses (P300) that distinguished BPD from other personality disorders and from affective disorder, but were shared by schizotypal and schizophrenic patients.

Some of these findings are intriguing, but we have to conclude that there is as yet no diagnostic biological marker of BPD, and no biological proof of its affiliation with another psychiatric disorder.

Singer (1977) has reviewed the literature on psychological tests. In brief, borderline personalities show ordinary reasoning on highly structured tests, but on projective ones they "demonstrate flamboyantly deviant reasoning and thought processes." Test results distinguish between borderline and schizophrenic in-patients, but for out-patients the distinction is less clear. Borderline patients' responses to the Wechsler (1958) Adult Intelligence Scale, Rorshach (1942) and other tests have been reported (Kernberg *et al*, 1981; Soloff & Ulrich, 1981). Borderline personalities in both the USA and the UK showed a characteristic Minnesota Multidimensional Personality Inventory (MMPI; Hathaway & McKinley, 1967) profile, namely 8,4,2 (8 = schizophrenia, 4 = psychopathic deviate, and 2 = depression) (Kroll *et al*, 1981*b*, 1982). MMPI scores also differentiate borderline from schizotypal personality (Goldberg, 1985; Stangl *et al*, 1985).

Western *et al* (1990) compared borderline adolescent girls with other psychiatric cases and with normal controls, using the Thematic Apperception Test (TAT). Borderline patients demonstrated more malevolent representations, lower-level capacity for emotional investment in people, relationships, and moral values, and attributions of causality which were less accurate, complex, or logical. However, some of their representations of people were overly complex. These interesting findings need replication.

Treatment Response

Although not specifically mentioned by Robins & Guze (1970), treatment response contributes to the delineation of a disorder: therapeutic success may suggest the existence of a specific etiological or pathological factor (e.g. Teitelman *et al*, 1979).

Few controlled studies of treatment of borderline patients exist; this is probably because of the lack, until recently, of reliable diagnostic criteria; because psychoanalytic psychotherapy is often described only in case reports; and because of the lack of optimism among many psychiatrists about the treatment of patients with personality disorders.

Pharmacotherapy

Both antidepressants (Klein, 1977) and low-dose neuroleptics have been used (Brinkley *et al*, 1979; Serban & Siegel, 1984). Recently, two double-blind, placebo-controlled trials reported the efficacy of moderate doses of neuroleptics on chronic severe populations. In one sample of out-patients, thiothixene had an effect on psychotic-like symptoms (Goldberg *et al*, 1986); in an in-patient sample haloperidol had an effect on both psychotic-like and affective symptoms (Soloff *et al*, 1986), but patients on amitryptiline got worse.

Other studies of antidepressants (Cowdry & Gardner, 1988; Cole *et al*, 1984) have not shown substantial benefits for antidepressants; in fact they may be positively harmful in some cases (Soloff *et al*, 1986).

Recently there has been an interest in the possible efficacy of serotonin reuptake inhibitors. A trial by Cornelius *et al* (1990) showed that fluoxetine may be effective in treating the depressive and impulsive symptoms of borderline patients, but not the other symptoms.

In a helpful review article Kutcher & Blackwood (1989) provide guidelines for the rational use of medication with borderline patients. . . .

Individual Psychoanalytic Psychotherapy

The classic Meninger Clinic project (Kernberg *et al*, 1972) remains the most comprehensive study in this area. The investigators compared supportive psychotherapy, classical psychoanalysis, and "expressive psychotherapy" conducted in an in-patient setting; borderline patients responded best to the latter. The sophistication of this study makes replication daunting (the researchers raised one million dollars in 1955!), but it is nevertheless surprising that smaller replications have not been attempted.

Recently there has been a shift towards combining pharmacotherapy and psychotherapy, a protocol that has some face validity. This has been described by Waldinger & Frank (1989), Stone (1990), and Brockman (1990), among others, but we are unaware of clinical trials of this treatment combination.

Family Therapy

We are unaware of controlled studies of the efficacy of this treatment. However, given our increasing breadth of knowledge about the family histories of borderline patients, such a treatment makes intuitive sense, especially for adolescent patients. This has been reviewed by Clarkin *et al* (1991).

Conclusion

With regard to treatment, our 1987 conclusions remain unchanged. Good studies of treatment are only just becoming available, and have not yet contributed substantially to the issue of validity. Further work needs to be done on medication, on the relative merits of in-patient and out-patient treatment, on different models of psychotherapy, and on combined treatments. The effects of treatment will have to be analyzed carefully, both with regard to target symptoms, and also to non-specific measures such as social and psychological morbidity.

CHILDHOOD ANTECEDENTS

In our previous paper we did not deal with etiology except with regard to genetics, mainly because of a lack of suitable empirical data. However, over the last five years a number of relevant papers have appeared which test certain etiological theories.

The theory which went unchallenged for many years, especially in the United States, was that of Mahler's group (Mahler *et al*, 1975). They observed a group of mothers and toddlers in a seminaturalistic setting, and observed a particular type of mother-child interaction, during a specific development phase, which they felt was the foundation of future personality disorder. They noticed that toddlers aged 18–24 months repeatedly explore away from mother, and then return to her for comfort and reassurance—this phenomenon is called the rapprochement phase of separation—individuation. They argued that through repetitions of this cycle the infant learns both object constancy and the capacity for ambivalence. It was noted that some mothers responded to their returning infants with either aggression or withdrawal, and the infants then alternated between clinginess and withdrawal. The behavior of the infant was thought to be similar to that of borderline adults.

This research was welcomed uncritically by those seeking a psychological cause for borderline personality disorder. Mahler's ideas fit with Bowlby's empirical work (Bowlby, 1982), and one can see similarities to the way in which the so-called group C infants responded to maternal separation in the strange situation (Bretherton, 1985).

However, there are a number of problems with Mahler's work. Firstly, we are unaware of any follow-up data on the original children which would confirm or deny the hypothesis. Secondly, there is the important caution expressed by Balint (1968) and Stern (1985) about the links that can be drawn between certain types of apparently similar adult and child behavior. Thirdly, Mahler's sample was unusual in being a volunteer sample of middle-class intellectual academics or spouses of academics, and we are unaware of similar work on more representative samples.

Perhaps in keeping with the spirit of the times, the focus of the more recent empirical research has been on overt physical and sexual abuse, separation and neglect, in the childhood histories of borderline adults, and there has recently been a flurry of papers dealing with this issue.

Links *et al* (1988*b*) compared in-patients with confirmed BPD and those with borderline traits. The BPD cases experienced more separations, family breakdown, foster placement, and physical and sexual abuse. The reason for the separation also differed—in the former group it was usually due to marital breakdown, in the latter group to bereavement.

Herman *et al* (1988) studied patients with BPD and those with other personality disorders, looking specifically for experiences of childhood trauma. Histories of physical and sexual abuse and the witnessing of serious domestic violence characterized the borderline patients.

Ogata and colleagues compared borderline and depressed patients. Borderline patients had a much higher rate of sexual abuse. Mental illness, personality disorder, drug abuse, and marital discord were more common in their parents (Ogata *et al*, 1990).

Nigg *et al* (1991) used projective measures to study the quality of childhood experiences in sexually abused borderline adults. They found that the early memories of the subjects were particularly malevolent and unpleasant.

Also using projective tests, Paris & Frank (1989) found that borderline patients perceived themselves as having received less care as children than did non-borderline controls.

Brown & Anderson (1991) studied the childhood abuse (physical and sexual) histories of nearly 1000 patients admitted to a military center. An increase in the proportion of patients with borderline personality disorder was noted with increasing levels of reported abuse; 3% of non-abused patients, 13% with either type of abuse, and 29% of those who had suffered both types of abuse had BPD. Borderline personality disorder accounted for nearly 50% of the personality disorder diagnoses in the abused group.

Byrne *et al* (1990) compared early life histories of a sample of 29 borderline and schizophrenic patients. Both physical and sexual abuse were much more common in the borderline group. The pattern of sexual abuse suggested neglectful and disordered family relationships.

Zanarini *et al* (1989*a*) have made a detailed study of this area, with the aim of investigating whether abuse, neglect, disturbed parenting, or separation are etiologically important. They compared the childhood histories of 50 out-patients with borderline personality disorder, 29 with antisocial personality disorder, and 26 who were dysthymic as well as having a non-borderline Axis II diagnosis. The borderline patients reported significantly more abuse, with 48% reporting physical abuse, 26% reporting sexual abuse, and 80% reporting verbal abuse. There was also a substantial degree of neglect. Abuse was found to be both common and highly discriminating, and neglect and separation were common but less discriminating. Many patients experienced a combination of all three.

All these papers have the problem that they are based on retrospective recall of childhood events. We are unaware of any prospective studies of sexually and physically abused children which demonstrate the later development of BPD. However, the retrospective nature of the above work does not invalidate it. All of the papers were investigating persistent patterns of maltreatment and neglect, rather than one-off incidents. They therefore lend substantial support to the idea that the breeding ground for borderline personality disorder is a childhood environment which combines neglect and instability, marital discord, physical and sexual abuse, and the absence of a good relationship which will buffer the effects of the adverse environment.

There is less support now for the etiological significance of multiple separations from the mother, as suggested by earlier writers. It seems that those authors overestimated the effects of the separations alone, and did not pay sufficient attention to the family context which led to the separation—namely discord, neglect, and abuse.

These papers also contribute to the discussion (see below) about whether BPD is really best thought of as synonymous with "severely disabling personality disorder."

CONCLUSIONS

The validity of borderline personality disorder has been scrutinized more intensely than any other personality disorder category. The diagnosis has a complex history, which has led to understandable confusion. However, the rigorous examination of the concept has been greatly assisted by several developments in the last 15 years. Firstly, Spitzer's group partitioned a muddled field into two discrete disorders, namely borderline and schizotypal personalities, and from there developed the DSM-III clinical diagnostic criteria. Secondly, Gunderson's group has developed and refined the DIB, still the best research interview for diagnosing BPD. Thirdly, diagnostic instruments of acceptable quality have been devised for the diagnosis of non-borderline personality disorders. In 1987 we concluded that there was support for the validity of the diagnosis. The evidence since 1987 has not led to any major new breakthroughs, but serves to add some modest additional validation. We are unaware of any substantial work that calls the diagnosis into question more strongly than before.

The DSM and the DIB continue to be useful instruments, and identify a characteristic phenomenological core. The patients thus identified can be readily distinguished from schizophrenic in-patients, and, with less success, from schizophrenic out-patients. The accumulated evidence suggests that BPD cannot be subsumed under the category of affective illness. There continue to be problems in distinguishing BPD from certain other personality disorders. Follow-up studies show that patients retain their diagnoses over time, or acquire other Axis II diagnoses. They do not appear to develop affective illness or schizophrenia. The condition becomes less disabling in the fifth decade. The family studies thus far indicate that the disorder is genetically distinct, and not linked to schizophrenia or affective illness. The biological research remains speculative. The data on treatment suggest that there is no specific treatment, either psychological or pharmacological. A combination of treatments may be most sensible.

With regard to etiology, the period since 1987 saw a substantial interest in the quality of care which borderline adults received in childhood. The evidence for a history of abuse and neglect is strong.

Borderline personality disorder is common, disabling, and difficult to treat. It probably has a multifactorial etiology, and requires a flexible treatment approach. This raises the question of whether it would be easier to see it as a measure of severe personality dysfunction, rather than as a discrete diagnostic entity. However, this issue is complicated by the fact that most personality disorder diagnoses depend partly on the identification of specific symptoms, and partly on measures of social and interpersonal functioning. Nevertheless it may be that "severe" cases of antisocial personality, borderline personality, and histrionic personality have more in common with one another than with "mild" cases within the same specific diagnostic category. Further conceptual work is required to clarify these issues.

REFERENCES

Akiskal, H. S., Chen, E. S., Davis, G. C., *et al* (1985*a*) Borderline: an adjective in search of a noun. *Journal of Clinical Psychiatry*, **46,** 41–48.

———, Yeravanian, B. I., Davis, G. C., *et al* (1985*b*) The nosological status of borderline personality: clinical and polysomnographic study. *American Journal of Psychiatry*, **142,** 192–198.

American Psychiatric Association (1980) *Diagnostic and Statistical Manual of Mental Disorders* (3rd edn) (DSM-III). Washington, DC: APA.

——— (1987) Diagnostic and Statistical Manual of Mental Disorders (3rd edn, revised) (DSM-III-R). Washington, DC: APA.

Andrulonis, P. A. & Vogel, N. G. (1984) Comparison of borderline sub-categories to schizophrenic and affective disorders. *British Journal of Psychiatry*, **144,** 358–363.

Armelius, B., Kulgreu, G. & Renberg, E. (1985) Borderline diagnosis from hospital records. *Journal of Nervous and Mental Disease*, **173,** 32–34.

Balint, M. (1968) The Basic Fault. London: Tavistock Publications.

Barasch, A., Frances, A., Hurt, S., *et al* (1985) Stability and distinctness of borderline personality disorder. *American Journal of Psychiatry*, **142,** 1484–1486.

Baron, M., Gruen, R., Asnis, L., *et al* (1985) Familial transmission of schizotypal and borderline disorders. *American Journal of Psychiatry*, **142,** 927–934.

Barrash, J., Kroll, J., Carey, K., *et al* (1983) Discriminating borderline personality disorder from other personality disorders: cluster analysis of the Diagnostic Interview for Borderlines. *Archives of General Psychiatry*, **40,** 1297–1302.

Bateman, A. W. (1989) Borderline personality in Britain: a preliminary study. *Comprehensive Psychiatry*, **30,** 385–390.

Bowlby, J. (1982) *Attachment and Loss. Vol 1. Attachment* (2nd edn). New York: Basic Books.

Bretherton, I. (1985) Attachment theory: retrospect and prospect. In *Growing Points of Attachment Theory and Research* (eds I. Bretherton & E. Waters). *Monographs of the Society for Research in Child Development*, **50,** 3–35.

Brinkley, J. R., Beiteman, B. D., & Freidel, R. O. (1979) Low-dose neuroleptic regimens in the treatment of borderline patients. *Archives of General Psychiatry*, **36,** 319–326.

Brockman, R. (1990) Medication and transference in psychoanalytically oriented psychotherapy of the borderline patient. *Psychiatric Clinics of North America*, **13,** 287–296.

Brown, G. R. & Anderson, B. (1991) Psychiatric morbidity in adult inpatients with childhood histories of sexual and physical abuse. *American Journal of Psychiatry*, **148,** 55–61.

Byrne, C. P., Velamoor, V. R., Cernovsky, Z. Z., *et al* (1990) A comparison of borderline and schizophrenic patients for childhood life events and parent-child relationships. *Canadian Journal of Psychiatry*, **35,** 590–595.

Cardish, R. J., & Silver, D. (1991) The long term outcome of borderline personality disorder. *Proceedings of the Conference on Borderline Personality Disorder, Hamilton, Ontario, January, 1991*.

Carpenter, W., Strauss, J. & Bartko, J. (1973) Flexible system for the diagnosis of schizophrenia. *Science*, **182,** 1275–1278.

——— & Gunderson, J. G. (1977) Five year follow-up comparison of borderline and schizophrenic patients. *Comprehensive Psychiatry*, **18,** 567–571.

Carroll, B. J., Greden, J. T., Feinberg, M., *et al* (1981) Neuroendocrine evaluation of depression in borderline patients. *Psychiatric Clinics of North America*, **4,** 89–99.

Chopra, H. D. & Beatson, J. A. (1986) Psychotic symptoms in borderline personality disorder. *American Journal of Psychiatry*, **143,** 1605–1607.

Clarkin, J. F., Marziali, E. & Munroe-Blum, H. (1991) Group and family treatments for borderline personality disorder. *Hospital and Community Psychiatry*, **42**, 1038–1043.

Coccaro, E. F., Siever, L. J., Klar, H. M., *et al* (1989) Serotonergic studies in patients with affective and personality disorders. *Archives of General Psychiatry*, **46**, 587–599.

Coid, J. C., Allalio, B. & Rees, L. H. (1984) Raised plasma metenkephalin in patients who habitually harm themselves. *Lancet*, ***ii***, 545–546.

Cole, J. O., Salomon, M., Gunderson, J., *et al* (1984) Drug therapy in borderline patients. *Comprehensive Psychiatry*, **25**, 249–254.

Cornelius, J. R., Soloff, P. H., Perel, J. M., *et al* (1990) Fluoxetine trial in borderline personality disorder. *Psychopharmacology Bulletin*, **26**, 151–154.

Cornell, D. G., Silk, K. R., Ludolph, P. S., *et al* (1983) Test-retest reliability of the Diagnostic Interview for Borderlines. *Archives of General Psychiatry*, **40**, 130–131.

Cowdry, R. & Gardner, D. (1988) Pharmacotherapy of borderline personality disorder. *Archives of General Psychiatry*, **45**, 111–119.

Dulit, R .A., Fyer, M. R., Haas, G. L., *et al* (1990) Substance use in borderline personality disorder. *American Journal of Psychiatry*, **147**, 1002–1007.

Fenton, W. S. & McGlashan, T. H. (1989) Borderline personality disorder and unipolar affective disorder: long-term effects of comorbidity. *Journal of Nervous and Mental Disease*, **167**, 467–473.

Frances, A., Clarkin, J. F., Gilmore, M., *et al* (1984) Reliability of criteria for borderline personality disorder—a comparison of DSM-III and the Diagnostic Interview for Borderline Patients. *American Journal of Psychiatry*, **141**, 1080–1084.

Friedman, R. C., Arnold, M. S., Clarkin, J. E., *et al* (1983) History of suicidal behavior in depressed borderline patients. *American Journal of Psychiatry*, **140**, 1023–1026.

Fyer, M. R., Frances, A., Sullivan, T., *et al* (1988) Comorbidity of borderline personality disorder. *Archives of General Psychiatry*, **45**, 348-352.

Goldberg, S. (1985) The MMPI as a predictor of borderline and schizotypal personality disorders. *Abstracts, Annual Meeting of the Royal College of Psychiatrists*. London: Royal College of Psychiatrists.

———, Schulz, S. C., Schulz, P. M., *et al* (1986) Borderline and schizotypal personality disorders treated with low-dose thiothixene versus placebo. *Archives of General Psychiatry*, **43**, 698–700.

Grinker, R. R., Werble, B. & Drye, R. C. (1968) *The Borderline Syndrome*. New York: Basic Books.

Gunderson, J. G. (1977) Characteristics of borderlines. In *Borderline Personality Disorders* (ed. P. Hartocollis), pp. 173–192. New York: International Universities Press.

———, Carpenter, W. T. & Strauss, J. S. (1975) Borderline and schizophrenic patients: a comparative study. *American Journal of Psychiatry*, **132**, 1257–1264.

——— & Kolb, J. E. (1978) Discriminating features of borderline patients. *American Journal of Psychiatry*, **135**, 792–796.

———, ——— & Austin, V. (1981) The diagnostic interview for borderline patients. *American Journal of Psychiatry*, **138**, 896–903.

———, Siever, L. J. & Spaulding, E. (1983) The search for a schizotype: crossing the border again. *Archives of General Psychiatry*, **40**, 15–22.

——— & Eliot, G. R. (1985) The interface between borderline personality disorder and affective disorder. *American Journal of Psychiatry*, **142**, 277–288.

——— & Phillips, K. A. (1991) A current view of the interface between borderline personality disorder and depression. *American Journal of Psychiatry*, **148**, 967–975.

Hathaway, S. R. & McKinley, J. C. (1967) *Minnesota Multiphasic Personality Inventory: Manual for Administration and Scoring*. New York: Psychological Corporation.

Herman, J. L., Perry, J. C. & van der Kolk, B. A. (1988) Childhood trauma in borderline personality disorder. *American Journal of Psychiatry*, **146**, 490–495.

Hurt, S. W., Hyler, S. E., Frances, A., *et al* (1984) Assessing borderline personality with self-report, clinical interview, or semi-structured interview. *American Journal of Psychiatry*, **141**, 1228–1231.

Jackson, M. & Tarnopolsky, A. (1990) Borderline personality. In *Principles and Practice of Forensic Psychiatry* (eds R. Bluglass & P. Bowden). Edinburgh: Churchill Livingstone.

Kavoussi, R. J., Cocarro, E. F., Klar, H. M., *et al* (1990) Structured interviews for borderline personality disorder. *American Journal of Psychiatry*, **147**, 1522–1525.

Kendler, K. S., Gruenberg, A.M. & Strauss, J. S. (1981) An independent analysis of the Copenhagen sample of the Danish adoption study of schizophrenia: II. The relationship between schizotypal personality disorder and schizophrenia. *Archives of General Psychiatry*, **38**, 982–984.

Kernberg, O. F. (1967) Borderline personality organisation. *Journal of the American Psychoanalytic Association*, **15**, 641–685.

——— (1981) Structural interviewing. *Psychiatric Clinics of North America*, **4**, 169–195.

———, Burstein, E. D., Coyne, L., *et al* (1972) Psychotherapy and psychoanalysis: final report of the Menninger Foundation's Psychotherapy Research Project. *Bulletin of the Menninger Clinic*, **36**, 1–277.

———, Goldstein, E. G., Carr, A. C., *et al* (1981) Diagnosing borderline personality: a pilot study using multiple diagnostic methods. *Journal of Nervous and Mental Disease*, **169**, 225–231.

———, Selzer, M. A., Koenigsberg, H. W., *et al* (1989) *Psychodynamic Psychotherapy of Borderline Patients*. New York: Basic Books.

Kety, S. S., Rosenthal, D., Wender, P. H., *et al* (1968) The types and prevalence of mental illness in the biological and adopted families of adopted schizophrenics. In *The Transmission of Schizophrenia* (eds D. Rosenthal & S. S. Kety), pp. 345–362. New York: Pergamon Press.

Klein, D. F. (1977) Pharmacological treatment and delineation of borderline disorders. In *Borderline Personality Disorders* (ed. P. Hartocollis). New York: International Universities Press.

Koenigsberg, H., Kernberg, O. F. & Schomer, J. (1983) Diagnosing borderline patients in an outpatient setting. *Archives of General Psychiatry*, **40,** 60–63.

Kolb, J. E. & Gunderson, J. G. (1980) Diagnosing borderline patients with a semi-structured interview. *Archives of General Psychiatry*, **37,** 37–41.

Kontaxakis, V., Markionis, M., Vaslamtsis, J., *et al* (1987) Multiple neuroendocrinological responses in borderline personality disorder patients. *Acta Psychiatrica Scandinavica*, **76,** 593–597.

Korzekwa, M. I. (1991) Biological markers in borderline personality disorders. *Proceedings of the Conference on Borderline Personality Disorders, Hamilton, Ontario, January, 1991.*

———, Steiner, M., Links, P, *et al* (1991) The dexamethasone suppression test in borderline personality disorders: Is it useful? *Canadian Journal of Psychiatry*, **36,** 26–28.

Kroll, J., Pyle, R., Zander, J., *et al* (1981*a*) Borderline personality disorder: interrater reliability of the Gunderson Diagnostic Interview for Borderlines (DIB). *Schizophrenia Bulletin*, **7,** 269–272.

———, Sines, L., Martin, K., *et al* (1981*b*) Borderline personality disorder: construct validity of the concept. *Archives of General Psychiatry*, **38,** 1021–1026.

———, Carey, K., Sines, L., *et al* (1982) Are there borderlines in Britain? *Archives of General Psychiatry*, **39,** 60–63.

Kutcher, S. P., Blackwood, D. H. R., St. Clair, D. M., *et al* (1987) Auditory P300 in borderline personality disorder and in schizophrenia. *Archives of General Psychiatry*, **44,** 645–650.

——— & ——— (1989) Pharmacotherapy of the borderline patient: a critical review and clinical guidelines. *Canadian Journal of Psychiatry*, **34,** 347–353.

———, ———, St. Clair, D. M., *et al* (1989) Auditory P300 does not differentiate borderline personality disorder from schizotypal personality disorder. *Biological Psychiatry*, **26,** 645–650.

Liebowitz, M. R. (1979) Is borderline a distinct entity? *Schizophrenia Bulletin*, **5,** 23–37.

Links, P. S., Steiner, M. & Huxley, G. (1988*a*) The occurrence of borderline personality disorder in the families of borderline patients. *Journal of Personality Disorders*, **2,** 14–20.

———, ———, Offord, D. R., *et al* (1988*b*) Characteristics of borderline personality disorder: a Canadian study. *Canadian Journal of Psychiatry*, **33,** 336–340.

———, ——— & Mitton, J. (1989) Characteristics of psychosis in borderline personality disorder. *Psychopathology*, **22,** 188–193.

Livesley, W. J. (1991) Borderline personality disorder: aspects of validity. *Proceedings of the Conference on Borderline Personality Disorder, Hamilton, Ontario, January 1991.*

Loranger, A. W., Oldham, J. M. & Tulis, E. H. (1982) Familial transmission of DSM-III borderline personality disorder. *Archives of General Psychiatry*, **39,** 795–799.

———, Hirshfield, R. M. A., Sartorius, N., *et al* (1991) The WHO/ADAMHA International Pilot Study of Personality Disorders: background and purpose. *Journal of Personality Disorders*, **5,** 296–306.

Mahler, M. S., Pine, F., & Bergmann, A. (1975) *The Psychological Birth of the Human Infant*. London: Hutchinson.

McGlashan, T. H. (1983*a*) The borderline syndrome: I. Testing three diagnostic systems. *Archives of General Psychiatry*, **40,** 1311–1318.

——— (1983*b*) The borderline syndrome: II. Is it a variant of schizophrenia or affective disorder? *Archives of General Psychiatry*, **40,** 1319–1323.

——— (1986) Long-term outcome of borderline patients. *Archives of General Psychiatry*, **40,** 20–30.

——— (1987*a*) Testing DSM-III symptoms criteria for schizotypal and borderline personality disorders. *Archives of General Psychiatry*, **44,** 143–148.

——— (1987*b*) Borderline personality disorder and unipolar affective disorder: long term effects of comorbidity. *Journal of Nervous and Mental Disease*, **167,** 467–473.

——— & Heinssen, R. K. (1988) Hospital discharge status and long term outcome for patients with schizophrenia, schizoaffective disorder, borderline personality disorder and unipolar affective disorder. *Archives of General Psychiatry*, **45,** 363–368.

Mitton, J. E. & Links, P. S. (1988) Two year prospective follow up of borderlines. *Proceedings and Summary, 141st Annual Meeting, American Psychiatric Association*, p. 225. Washington, DC: APA.

Nigg, J. T., Silk, K. R., Westen, D., *et al* (1991) Object representations in the early memories of sexually abused borderline patients. *American Journal of Psychiatry*, **148,** 864–869.

Nurnberg, H. G., Raskin, M., Levine, P. E., *et al* (1991) The comorbidity of borderline personality disorder and other DSM-III-R Axis II personality disorders. *American Journal of Psychiatry*, **148,** 1371–1377.

Ogata, S. N., Silk, K. R. & Goodrich, S. (1990) The childhood experience of the borderline patient. In *Family Environment and Borderline Personality Disorder* (ed. P. Links). Washington, DC: American Psychiatric Press.

Paris, J., Knowles, D. & Brown, R. (1988) Developmental factors in the outcome of BPD. *Proceedings and Summary, 141st Annual Meeting, American Psychiatry Association*, p. 157. Washington, DC: APA.

——— & Frank, H. (1989) Perceptions of parental bonding in borderline patients. *American Journal of Psychiatry*, **146,** 1498–1499.

Perry, J. C. (1985) Depression in borderline personality disorder: lifetime prevalence at interview and longitudinal course of symptoms. *American Journal of Psychiatry*, **142,** 15–21.

——— & Klerman, G. L. (1980) Clinical features of the borderline personality disorder. *Archives of General Psychiatry*, **137,** 165–173.

Pilkonis, P. A. & Frank, E. (1988) Personality pathology in recurrent depression: nature, prevalence and relationship to treatment response. *American Journal of Psychiatry*, **145,** 435–441.

Pope, H. G., Jonas, J. M., Hudson, J. I., *et al* (1983) The validity of DSM-III borderline personality disorder. *Archives of General Psychiatry*, **40**, 23–30.

Robins, E. & Guze, S. G. (1970) Establishment of diagnostic validity in psychiatric illness: its application to schizophrenia. *American Journal of Psychiatry*, **126**, 983–987.

Rorschach, H. (1942) Psychodiagnostics (5th edn). Berne: Hans Huber.

Serban, G. & Siegel, S. (1984) Response of borderline and schizotypal patients to small doses of thiothixene and haloperidol. *American Journal of Psychiatry*, **141**, 1455–1458.

Shea, M. T., Glass, D. R., Pilkonis, P. A., *et al* (1987) Frequency and implications of personality disorders in a sample of depressed outpatients. *Journal of Personality Disorders*, **1**, 27–42.

Sheehy, M., Goldsmith, L. & Charles, E. (1980) A comparative study of borderline patients in a psychiatric outpatient clinic. *American Journal of Psychiatry*, **137**, 1374–1379.

Silk, K. R., Lohr, E., Shipley, E., *et al* (1988) Sleep EEG and DST in borderlines with depression. *Proceedings and Summary, 141st Annual Meeting, American Psychiatric Association*, p. 206. Washington, DC: APA.

Singer, M. (1977) The borderline diagnosis and psychological tests: review and research. In *Borderline Personality Disorders* (ed. P. Hartocollis). New York: International Universities Press.

Soloff, P. H. & Ulrich, R. F. (1981) The Diagnostic Interview for Borderlines: a replication study. *Archives of General Psychiatry*, **38**, 686–692.

——— & Millward, J. W. (1983) Psychiatric disorders in the families of borderline patients. *Archives of General Psychiatry*, **40**, 37–44.

———, George, A., Nathan, S., *et al* (1986) Progress in pharmacotherapy of borderline disorders. *Archives of General Psychiatry*, **38**, 686–692.

———, ———, ———, *et al* (1987) Characterising depression in borderline patients. *Journal of Clinical Psychiatry*, **48**, 155–157.

Spitzer, R. L. (1983) Psychiatric diagnosis: are clinicians still necessary? *Comprehensive Psychiatry*, **24**, 399–411.

———, Endicott, J. & Robins, E. (1975) Research Diagnostic Criteria (RDC). *Psychopharmacology Bulletin*, **11**, 22–24.

———, ——— & Gibbon, M. (1979) Crossing the border into borderline personality and borderline schizophrenia. *Archives of General Psychiatry*, **36**, 17–24.

———, Williams, J. B. W. & Gibbon, M. (1987) *Structured Clinical Interview for DSM-III-R Axis II Disorders (SCID-II)*. New York: New York State Psychiatric Institute, Biometrics Research.

Stangl, D., Peohl, B., Zimmerman, M., *et al* (1985) A structured interview for the DSM-III personality disorders. *Archives of General Psychiatry*, **42**, 591–596.

Steiner, M., Links, P. & Korzekwa, M. I. (1988) Biological markers in borderline personality disorders: an overview. *Canadian Journal of Psychiatry*, **33**, 350–354.

Stern, A. (1938) Psychoanalytic investigation of and therapy in the borderline group of neuroses. *Psychoanalytic Quarterly*, **7**, 467–489.

Stern, D. N. (1985) *The Interpersonal World of the Infant*. New York: Basic Books.

Stone, M. H. (1990) Treatment of borderline patients: a pragmatic approach. *Psychiatric Clinics of North America*, **13**, 265–286.

———, Stone, D. K. & Hurt, S. (1987) The natural history of borderline patients treated by intensive hospitalization. *Psychiatric Clinics of North America*, **10**, 185–206.

Tarnopolsky, A. (1991) The validity of the borderline personality disorder. In *Handbook of Borderline Personality Disorder* (eds D. Silver & M. Rosenbluth). New York: IUP.

——— & Berelowitz, M. (1984) "Borderline personality": diagnostic attitudes at the Maudsley Hospital. *British Journal of Psychiatry*, **144**, 364–369.

——— & ——— (1987) Borderline personality: a review of recent research. *British Journal of Psychiatry*, **151**, 724–734.

Teitelman, E., Glass, J. B., Blyn, C., *et al* (1979) The treatment of female borderlines. *Schizophrenia Bulletin*, **5**, 111–117.

Torgersen, S. (1984) Genetic and nosological aspects of schizotypal and borderline personality disorders. *Archives of General Psychiatry*, **41**, 546–554.

Waldinger, R. J. & Frank, A. F. (1989) Clinicians' experiences in combining medication and pharmacotherapy in the treatment of borderline patients. *Hospital and Community Psychiatry*, **40**, 712–718.

Wechsler, D. (1958) *The Measurement and Appraisal of Adult Intelligence* (4th edn). Baltimore: Williams & Wilkins.

Westen, D., Ludolph, P., Lerner, H., *et al* (1990) Object relations in borderline adolescents. *Journal of the American Academy of Child and Adolescent Psychiatry*, **29**, 338–348.

Zanarini, M., Gunderson, J. G. & Frankenburg, F. R. (1987) The diagnostic interview for personality disorders: test-retest and interrater reliability. *Comprehensive Psychiatry*, **28**, 467–480.

———, ———, Marino, M. F., *et al* (1988) DSM-III disorders in the families of borderline outpatients. *Journal of Personality Disorders*, **2**, 292–302.

———, ———, ———, *et al* (1989*a*) Childhood experiences of borderline patients. *Comprehensive Psychiatry*, **30**, 18–25.

———, ———, ———, *et al* (1989*b*) The revised diagnostic interview for borderlines. *Journal of Personality Disorders*, **3**, 10–18.

———, ———, ———, *et al* (1990) Discriminating borderline personality disorder from other Axis II disorders. *American Journal of Psychiatry*, **147**, 161–167.

———, ———, ———, *et al* (1991) The face validity of the DSM-III and DSM-III-R criteria sets for borderline personality disorder. *American Journal of Psychiatry*, **148**, 870–874.

DISCUSSION

The readings in this chapter highlight a knotty and complicated problem that has long plagued the study of personality disorders: the phenomenon of "comorbidity" (but remember not to take this term too literally)—that is, diagnostic overlap within individuals. Most or all of the personality disorders in DSM-IV, including BPD, co-occur frequently with both Axis I and Axis II conditions (see the article in Chapter 3 by Spitzer, Williams, and Skodol for a discussion of these two axes). As a result, individuals with a personality disorder tend to satisfy criteria for additional disorders (including other personality disorders).

The phenomenon of comorbidity raises potentially serious questions regarding the validity of many of the DSM-IV personality disorders, because it appears to challenge the implicit assumption that these disorders are separable syndromes. If a diagnosis overlaps so extensively with other conditions that it rarely occurs in isolation, one can justifiably ask whether it represents an independent entity. Both Akiskal and his colleagues and Berelowitz and Tarnopolsky acknowledge that BPD exhibits high rates of comorbidity with mood disorders, other personality disorders (such as histrionic and antisocial personality disorders), and perhaps schizophrenia, although Berelowitz and Tarnopolsky seem less convinced that this diagnostic overlap is damaging to the validity of BPD. Akiskal et al., in contrast, conclude that BPD is an extremely vague and etiologically heterogeneous category "that embrace[s] the gamut of psychopathology" (p. 47).

The weak link in Akiskal et al.'s argument seems to be their reliance on questionable diagnostic measures. Akiskal et al. state that "subjects were evaluated in semistructured diagnostic interviews based on the Washington University criteria" (p. 42). In the following sentence, however, they note that "since DSM-III is more widely known to practicing psychiatrists, we have translated diagnoses to the corresponding DSM-III terms" (p. 42). There is a potential problem here. The Washington University criteria, which appeared in the early 1970s, are quite discrepant in many cases from the DSM-III criteria, which appeared in 1980. Thus, Akiskal et al. were presumably forced to extrapolate from one criteria set to a rather different criteria set. Moreover, several of the diagnoses Akiskal et al. examined, including BPD, are not even included in the Washington University criteria. Because we are provided with no information about how these diagnoses were made, many of Akiskal et al.'s findings are difficult to evaluate.

Why do I make so much of Akiskal et al.'s diagnostic methods? A few moments' reflection leads one to the conclusion that perhaps the easiest way to obtain high rates of comorbidity with many other disorders is to use unreliable diagnostic measures. The use of such measures tends to result in heterogeneous categories and thus high rates of diagnostic overlap with numerous other conditions. For example, if Akiskal et al.'s diagnoses of BPD were highly unreliable, many patients who satisfied criteria for BPD in their sample may actually have had disorders other than BPD, such as depression or schizophrenia. As a consequence, Akiskal et al.'s BPD group would be expected to be highly heterogeneous and to exhibit "comorbidity" with a number of other conditions.

Up to this point, I have assumed that extremely high rates of comorbidity raise grave questions concerning a disorder's validity. Playing devil's advocate, however, one could contend that extensive comorbidity sometimes indicates that a disorder is extremely disabling or widespread in its effects. Otto Kernberg (1984), for example, maintains that BPD (which he prefers to call borderline personality organization) is not a specific disorder but rather a pervasive personality structure that stems from early difficulties in parental relationships. According to Kernberg, this personality structure predisposes individuals to a broad spectrum of psychological disturbances, including depression, anxiety, and various DSM-IV personality disorders. Thus, for Kernberg, high rates of diagnostic overlap between BPD and other conditions are not only to be expected but are entirely consistent with BPD's validity. If Kernberg is correct, substantial comorbidity may sometimes be a reflection of a condition's severity or pervasiveness.

Medical science offers some precedent for this argument. Acquired immune deficiency syndrome (AIDS), for example, exhibits high rates of comorbidity with a wide variety of medical conditions, such as tuberculosis, Kaposi's sarcoma, and pneumonia. But of course such comorbidity does not call the validity of AIDS into question, because we know that a severely compromised immune system leaves individuals vulnerable to a wide variety of opportunistic infections.

This example underscores a fundamental distinction between most medical conditions, including AIDS, and most psychopathological conditions, including BPD. In the case of AIDS, we possess reasonably good knowledge of how the disorder gives rise to the medical conditions that accompany it. Specifically, we understand quite a bit about how certain underlying causal processes (such as immune system deficits) produce the co-occurrence of AIDS with other disorders. In contrast, in the case of BPD, we understand virtually nothing about the underlying causal processes that produce its co-occurrence with other conditions. Although certain theorists, such as Kernberg, have postulated specific etiological processes (such as a borderline personality organization) to explain the association between BPD and other conditions, these theories have yet to be tested adequately—largely because they deal with unobservable constructs and are thus quite difficult to test.

The key point is that the concept of comorbidity tends to have a markedly different meaning in medicine than in abnormal psychology, because our understanding of the etiological processes underlying most psychopathological syndromes, including personality disorders, is poor or nonexistent. Inevitably some individuals, such as Kernberg, will maintain that the substantial comorbidity among personality disorders is consistent with certain theoretical predictions. At the same time, however, some will inevitably maintain that this "comorbidity" indicates that something is profoundly wrong with our current classification of personality disorders.

QUESTIONS TO STIMULATE DISCUSSION

1. Berelowitz and Tarnopolsky conclude that reasonably strong support exists for the validity of BPD. Do you agree with their conclusion? Or do you find their conclusion to be overly optimistic given the literature that both they and Akiskal et al. review?
2. Berelowitz and Tarnopolsky clearly believe that further work is necessary to clarify the validity of BPD. What types of investigations do you believe would shed the most light on BPD's validity?
3. If you were asked to revise the diagnostic criteria for BPD, would you attempt to alter these criteria to decrease BPD's comorbidity with other conditions, such as major depression and other personality disorders? What might be the potential advantages and disadvantages of doing so?
4. A number of authors, such as George Vaillant, argue that BPD is often little more than a pejorative label clinicians attach to patients whom they find annoying or difficult to treat. If Vaillant and others are correct, what could be done to minimize such misuse? What features of the BPD diagnosis render it especially susceptible to this misuse?

SUGGESTIONS FOR FURTHER READING

Akiskal, H. S., Yerevanian, B. I., Davis, G. C., King, D., & Lemmi, H. (1985). The nosological status of borderline personality: Clinical and polysomnographic study. *American Journal of Psychiatry, 142*, 192–198.

In the companion paper to the one reprinted in this chapter, Akiskal and his colleagues report that BPD patients who were not concurrently depressed tended to exhibit shortened rapid eye movement (REM) latency, an abnormality found in a large subset of depressed individuals. Moreover, the REM latencies of BPD patients were comparable to those of depressed patients and shorter than those of patients with other personality disorders. Finally, Akiskal et al. find that BPD overlaps considerably with a variety of other syndromes, including mood disorders, anxiety disorders, and somatization disorder. They conclude that "the contemporary operational criteria for borderline disorder identify a wide net of temperamental disorders with strong affective coloring rather than a unitary nosological entity" (p. 192).

Goldstein, E. G. (1990). *Borderline disorders: Clinical models and techniques*. New York: Guilford Press.

This books provides a good introduction to the complex and often confusing psychoanalytic models of the etiology of BPD, including those of Mahler, Masterson and Rinsley, Kernberg, and Kohut. The second half of the book provides an overview of treatment models for BPD.

Grove, W. M., & Tellegen, A. (1991). Problems in the classification of personality disorders. *Journal of Personality Disorders, 5*, 31–41.

Grove and Tellegen provide an excellent discussion of conceptual and methodological difficulties in the classification of personality disorders. Among the problems they identify are prematurely focusing on applied questions, ignoring findings from research on "normal" personality traits, and using research designs that are inappropriate for the study of personality disorders. This article should be required reading for all those interested in interpreting or conducting research on personality disorders.

Gunderson, J. G., & Sabo, A. N. (1993). The phenomenological and conceptual interface between borderline personality disorder and PTSD. *American Journal of Psychiatry, 150*, 19–27.

The authors review evidence suggesting that BPD and related conditions stem in part from early psychological trauma. They conclude that BPD is closely related to posttraumatic stress disorder (PTSD), a condition resulting from acute exposure to severe stressors (see Chapter 8).

Millon, T. (1987). On the genesis and prevalence of the borderline personality disorder: A social learning thesis. *Journal of Personality Disorders, 2*, 354–372.

Millon contends that the BPD diagnosis has increased dramatically in prevalence over the past several decades. He attributes this trend to large-scale social changes, such as the loss of meaningful goals and aspirations, the decline in positive role models, and the erosion of unifying cultural traditions.

Perry, J. C., & Klerman, G. L. (1978). The borderline patient: A comparative analysis of four sets of diagnostic criteria. *Archives of General Psychiatry, 35*, 141–150.

The authors review four influential criteria sets for BPD: those of Knight, Kernberg, Grinker and his colleagues, and Gunderson and Singer. They find that these four sets exhibit minimal overlap and tentatively conclude that different theorists have emphasized different subtypes within a broad and heterogeneous group of "borderline" syndromes.

Pope, H. G., Jonas, J. M., Hudson, J. I., Cohen, B. M., & Gunderson, J. G. (1983). The validity of DSM-III borderline personality disorder: A phenomenologic, family history, treatment response, and long-term family study. *Archives of General Psychiatry, 40*, 23–30.

Pope and his colleagues report the results of a 4- to 7-year follow-up study of 33 patients with BPD. They conclude that, although BPD can be distinguished from schizophrenia on a variety of indices, BPD is difficult to distinguish from histrionic, antisocial, and perhaps narcissistic personality disorders on the basis of criteria such as outcome, family history, and treatment response. They conclude that these findings raise questions regarding the discriminant validity of the BPD diagnosis.

Stone, M. H. (1986). Borderline personality disorder. In A. M. Cooper, A. J. Frances, & M. H. Sacks (Eds.), *The personality disorders and neuroses* (pp. 203–217). New York: Basic Books.
This chapter provides a good, although now slightly dated, overview of the different conceptions of BPD, as well as of the research literature on the assessment, differential diagnosis, natural history, biology, and treatment of BPD. The discussion of the history of the "borderline" concept is especially useful.

Taylor, S. (1993). DSM-IV criteria for borderline personality disorder: A critical evaluation. *Journal of Psychopathology and Behavioral Assessment*, *15*, 97–112.
Taylor reviews the proposed criteria for BPD in DSM-IV and argues that the revisions to these criteria are likely to increase the overlap (comorbidity) of BPD with other diagnoses, including schizotypal personality disorder, and thus further reduce BPD's discriminant validity. He suggests that BPD is better conceptualized within a dimensional than within a categorical perspective and that it probably represents an essentially arbitrary cutoff corresponding to elevated levels of neuroticism.

REFERENCES

Feinstein, A. R. (1970). The pre-therapeutic classification of comorbidity in chronic disease. *Journal of Chronic Diseases*, *23*, 455–468.

Grinker, R. R. (1979). Diagnosis of borderlines: A discussion. *Schizophrenia Bulletin*, *5*, 47–52.

Grove, W. M., & Tellegen, A. (1991). Problems in the classification of personality disorders. *Journal of Personality Disorders*, *5*, 31–42.

Kernberg, O. F. (1984). *Severe personality disorders*. New Haven, CT: Yale University Press.

Lilienfeld, S. O., Waldman, I. D., & Israel, A. C. (in press). A critical examination of the use of the term and concept of comorbidity in psychopathology research. *Clinical Psychology: Science and Practice*.

Robins, E., & Guze, S. G. (1970). Establishment of diagnostic validity in psychiatric illness: Its application to schizophrenia. *American Journal of Psychiatry*, *126*, 983–987.

Vaillant, G. E. (1992). The beginning of wisdom is never calling a patient borderline. *Journal of Psychotherapy Research and Practice*, *1*, 117–134.

CHAPTER

10

Is sex reassignment surgery ineffective in improving the adjustment of transsexuals?

PRO Meyer, J. K., & Reter, D. J. (1979). Sex reassignment: Follow-up. *Archives of General Psychiatry, 36,* 1010–1015.

CON Abramowitz, S. I. (1986). Psychosocial outcomes of sex reassignment surgery. *Journal of Consulting and Clinical Psychology, 54,* 183–189.

OVERVIEW OF THE CONTROVERSY: Jon K. Meyer and Donna J. Reter report the findings of a study that they interpret as indicating that sex reassignment has few, if any, positive effects on psychosocial adjustment. Stephen I. Abramowitz criticizes Meyer and Reter's methodology and interpretations and concludes that approximately two-thirds of the individuals who undergo sex reassignment surgery exhibit positive outcomes at follow-up.

CONTEXT OF THE PROBLEM

Transsexualism (known officially as gender identity disorder in DSM-IV) is undoubtedly one of the most enigmatic of all psychopathological conditions. Little or nothing is known about its causes, and consistently effective treatments for it have remained elusive. As DSM-IV notes, the core feature of transsexualism is a profound and enduring discomfort with one's biological sex. Almost invariably, transsexuals report that they feel trapped in the wrong body and are preoccupied with the thought of ridding themselves of their primary and secondary sex characteristics. Transsexualism is extremely rare; its prevalence has been estimated to be approximately 1 among each 30,000 males and 1 among each 100,000 females (American Psychiatric Association [APA], 1987). The reasons for this sex difference are unknown.

Transsexualism is associated with a number of other characteristics. Most transsexuals, although technically "homosexual" in their sexual orientation, view their sexual orientation as heterosexual because they subjectively perceive themselves to be members of the opposite sex. (Note, however, that transsexuals are not delusional in the sense of literally believing themselves to be members of the opposite sex.) Dressing in the clothes of the opposite sex is also common. The reader should be careful, however, not to confuse transsexualism with **transvestism** (known in DSM-IV as transvestic fetishism), which is also associated with cross-dressing. Transvestites, who are essentially always heterosexual males, typically obtain sexual gratification from cross-dressing. For transsexuals, however, cross-dressing is not a source of sexual arousal but is simply a reflection of greater subjective comfort in the clothing of the opposite sex. Not surprisingly, many transsexuals experience frequent periods of profound depression, anxiety, and despair. Suicide attempts are not uncommon. More rarely, transsexual males have been reported to mutilate or even attempt to remove their genitals (APA, 1987).

To alleviate their intense feelings of distress, a number of transsexuals seek and eventually undergo sex reassignment surgery. Although the first sex-change operation was performed in Europe in 1930 (Abraham, 1931), the first such operation to receive widespread international attention was conducted in Copenhagen in 1952 on a former soldier, George (subsequently Christine) Jorgensen. A number of other well-known cases helped to bring the results of sex reassignment surgery into the public eye. Jan (previously James) Morris, a prominent British journalist who covered Sir Edmund Hillary's ascent of Mount Everest, authored the book *Conundrum* (1974), a poignant account of her painful dilemma as a male transsexual and subsequent successful adjustment as a woman. The transformation of a professional tennis player, Dr. Richard Raskin, into Renee Richards attracted considerable publicity in the United States.

How are these operations performed? In male-to-female sex reassignment surgery, the male's genitals are almost entirely removed, and some of the remaining tissue is used to create an artificial vagina. Electrolysis is often necessary to remove facial and body hair, as is training to alter voice pitch. In some cases, plastic surgery is performed on facial features and on the Adam's apple. Approximately 1 to 2 years prior to the operation, female hormones are prescribed to soften the skin and to develop the breasts and other secondary sex characteristics. In female-to-male sex reassignment surgery (which is considerably more complicated than the reverse operation), the breasts, ovaries, and uterus are surgically removed, and the vagina is closed. A penis is constructed from rib cartilage, from tissue taken from other parts of the body, or from plastic. This penis does not function entirely normally, and the individual is unable to engage in sexual intercourse without a prosthesis. Male hormones are administered prior to the operation to facilitate hair growth, alter the distribution of fat throughout the body, deepen the voice, and halt menstruation. Following neither operation is the individual capable of having children, because gonads (sex glands)—the ovary in the case of the woman and the testicles in the case of the man—cannot be surgically constructed given the limits of current medical technology.

In the case of both male-to-female and female-to-male operations, transsexuals typically undergo a 1- to 2-year trial period (the "real-life" test) in which they gradually adopt the lifestyle of the opposite sex. The advantages and disadvantages of this trial period, however, are a point of some contention (Oppenheim, 1986).

By the mid 1970s, approximately 2500 individuals had undergone sex reassignment surgery in the United States (Gagnon, 1977). The popularity of this procedure was bolstered by preliminary reports suggesting that the postsurgical functioning of most transsexuals was quite positive (Pauly, 1968). The enthusiasm for sex reassignment surgery changed dramatically in 1979, however, when the article by Meyer and Reter reprinted in this chapter first appeared in a prominent medical journal. In this article, Meyer and Reter conclude that the adjustment of a group of transsexuals who had received operations at the Johns Hopkins University's Gender Identity Clinic, then one of the country's leading centers for sex reassignment surgery, was no more favorable than that of an unoperated comparison group. Following the publication of this article, the Johns Hopkins clinic was closed, and an increasing number of investigators raised serious questions about the efficacy of sex reassignment surgery. The results of Meyer and Reter's study were widely publicized: *Time* magazine cited it as demonstrating "no differences in long-term adjustment between transsexuals who go under the scalpel and those who do not," and Meyer was quoted in Associated Press reports as stating that "surgical intervention has done nothing objective beyond time and psychotherapy" (quoted in Fleming, Steinman, & Bocknek, 1980).

Although Meyer and Reter's study has been harshly criticized by a number of authors (for example, Fleming et al., 1980; see also the article by Abramowitz in this chapter), the controversy over the effectiveness of sex reassignment surgery has not fully subsided. While the debate rages, sex reassignment operations continue—at a rate of approximately 1000 annually in the United States alone (Bootzin, Acocella, & Alloy, 1993).

THE CONTROVERSY: Meyer and Reter vs. Abramowitz

Meyer and Reter

Jon Meyer and Donna Reter first review the literature on the psychosocial outcomes of transsexuals who have undergone sex reassignment surgery. They conclude that, although serious postoperative casualties are relatively rare, the adjustment of transsexuals following surgery appears to be less favorable than was initially reported. Meyer and Reter go on to report the findings of a follow-up study of 29 transsexuals who had received sex reassignment surgery at the Johns Hopkins Gender Identity Clinic. Fifteen of these patients had received surgery prior to 1971, and 14 had received surgery by 1974, when the study was completed. These 29 patients were compared with a group of 21 transsexuals who were not operated on. The major measure administered to all subjects was a 2- to 4-hour interview assessing several aspects of psychosocial adjustment, including social stability, psychiatric contacts, requests for reversal of surgery, and further pursuit of sex reassignment. Meyer and Reter found that the 15 patients who had received surgery prior to 1971 and the 21 unoperated transsexuals exhibited moderate and roughly equal rates of improvement and that the 14 patients who later received surgery exhibited minimal improvement. Meyer and Reter conclude that "sex reassigment surgery confers no objective advantage in terms of social rehabilitation" (p. 1015).

Abramowitz

Stephen Abramowitz begins by reviewing the data from the early, "prequantitative" studies of the outcome of sex reassignment surgery, in which outcome was measured simply in terms of degree of adjustment. He finds that improvement rates in these studies ranged from approximately 60% to 85%, although serious psychiatric casualties were reported in all studies. Abramowitz then reviews the findings from the later, "quantitative" studies of the outcome of sex reassignment surgery, in which outcome was assessed using multiple criteria and standardized instruments. Improvement and casualty rates in these studies are generally similar to those in the prequantitative studies, although several factors—including gender, preoperative personality, and the extent to which the operated transsexual adopts the characteristics of his or her new gender—appear to influence outcome. Abramowitz criticizes the Meyer and Reter study on a number of grounds, including the use of arbitrary coding procedures and an unequal length of follow-up for the experimental and comparison groups. Abramowitz concludes that approximately two-thirds of individuals appear to exhibit positive outcomes following sex reassignment surgery, that the psychological casualty rate of such surgery is approximately 7%, and that the outcome tends to be more favorable among female-to-male than among male-to-female transsexuals. He also observes that the lack of adequate control groups makes it difficult to unequivocably attribute either success or failure of the outcome to the surgery itself. Note: I have therefore oversimplified matters somewhat by suggesting that Abramowitz is on the con side of the question constituting the title of this chapter. Abramowitz is not absolutely convinced that sex reassignment surgery improves the adjustment of transsexuals, although he does believe that the overall improvement rate is fairly high. In addition, he clearly believes that it would be premature to terminate sex reassignment surgery on the basis of Meyer and Reter's findings.

KEY CONCEPTS AND TERMS

gender reorientation Extent to which the individual who has received sex reassignment surgery has successfully adopted the physical appearance and mannerisms of his or her newly assigned sex. A number of investigators have suggested that gender reorientation is a predictor of postsurgical outcome among transsexuals.

internal validity Confidence with which one can determine whether an independent variable (the variable being manipulated) has a causal effect on the dependent variable (the variable being measured). In an internally valid study, the observed effect can confidently be attributed to the treatment. Internal validity differs from external validity, which is the extent to which the results of a study can be generalized.

moderator Third variable that affects the strength of the relationship (in statistical terms, the magnitude of the correlation) between two other variables. Thus, if age at operation were found to influence the strength of the relationship between sex reassigment surgery and postsurgical psychological adjustment, age at operation would be a moderator variable.

PREVIEW QUESTIONS

1. What is the design of Meyer and Reter's study? What are their experimental and comparison groups? What are the major measures administered to each group?
2. What is Meyer and Reter's principal conclusion, and what evidence do they provide for it?
3. What are Abramowitz's major criticisms of Meyer and Reter's design and conclusions?
4. What conclusions does Abramowitz draw concerning the overall improvement rate following sex reassignment surgery and the influence of patient variables (such as gender and presurgical psychological adjustment) on improvement rate? What do the outcome studies suggest regarding the rate of psychological casualties following sex reassignment surgery?
5. What are Abramowitz's major recommendations for improving the methodology of sex reassignment outcome studies?

JON K. MEYER & DONNA J. RETER

Sex reassignment: Follow-up

Historical, mythological, and cross-cultural aspects of "transsexualism" have been reviewed by Green.[1,2] Desires to identify with and assume the role of the opposite sex have been recognized since antiquity. Cauldwell[3] introduced the term transsexualism to signify individuals wishing to be the opposite sex, distinguishing them from transvestites. Common usage of the term came about, however, as a consequence of the publication of *The Transsexual Phenomenon* by Benjamin.[4]

Abraham[5] is credited with the first surgical procedure on a transsexual patient. Occasional operative reports followed this initial venture, but the procedure did not become well-known until 1953, when Hamburger et al[6] reported the case of Christine Jorgensen. The treatment of Ms Jorgensen differed from preceding reports in that surgery was performed after a period of hormonal castration and psychiatric observation. In 1960, a bilateral reduction mammoplasty in a female wishing to be male constituted the first procedure at The Johns Hopkins Hospital.

The establishment of The Johns Hopkins Gender Identity Clinic and Committee in 1965 is detailed by Money and Schwartz.[7] The public controversy surrounding the beginnings of the program died away in a surprisingly short time. Initial objections to sex reassignment[8] yielded to an almost routine acceptance, leading Stoller[9] to comment on the neglect of assessment, diagnosis, and treatment selection. Previous reports from the Hopkins series have emphasized the clinical characteristics of applicants for sex reassignment[10,11] and have remarked on their close relationship to the perversions[12] and their inclusion within the borderline personality syndromes.[13]

The presentation of a biologically normal male or female requesting ablation of sexual and reproductive organs and construction of opposite sex facsimiles still presents a clinical and scientific problem of no small degree. Familiarity has sometimes obscured the essential problematic character of this request. The attempt in this article is to step back from "normalization" of sex reassignment procedures in order to look objectively at the long-range effects of surgery.

SEX REASSIGNMENT FOLLOW-UP: THE LITERATURE

Benjamin,[4] reporting on 51 reassigned biological males, estimated "good" results in 33% (integration into the world of women, acceptance by the family, and reasonable sexual adjustment); "satisfactory" in 53% (less successful adjustment, although meeting most of the patient's wishes); and "doubtful" in 10% (appearance and sexual function unsatisfactory, despite some relief from unhappiness). One patient was deemed to have an unsatisfactory result and one was lost to follow-up. Results were based on personal contact in 46 cases.

Benjamin[4] also reported anecdotal experience with 20 female patients:

> The results of either androgen therapy or operations or both have generally been decidedly satisfactory. With one doubtful exception . . . all patients under my observation . . . were benefitted.

Randall[14] reported on 29 biological males and six females assessed from three months to several years postoperatively. Five men had shown "psychopathic and antisocial propensities" and nine, "depressive illnesses of varying degrees" prior to operation. Three had depressive relapses postsurgically and two committed suicide. Comparing preoperative and postoperative adjustment of male patients by means of social and subjective criteria, Randall reported a shift from 86% fair or poor adjustment preoperatively to 72% excellent or good postoperatively. Twenty-two males were satisfied with surgery, six were dissatisfied, and one wished the reassignment undone. The six females received androgens and underwent various surgical procedures (although none underwent hysterectomy and oophorectomy). Results were judged to be excellent in three, good in two, and fair in one.

This study was supported by Foundations' Fund for Research in Psychiatry grant 71-518.

The authors gratefully acknowledge the support, stimulation, and counsel of their colleagues: John E. Hoopes, MD, Milton T. Edgerton, MD, John Money, PhD, Howard Jones, MD, Lonnie Burnett, MD, Claude Migeon, MD, Natalia Chapanis, PhD, Dietrich Blumer, MD, and Horst Schirmer, MD, all of whom were members of The Johns Hopkins Gender Identity Committee at the time follow-up began. Leonard R. Derogatis, PhD, associate professor of medical psychology and director of research, The Sexual Behaviors Consultation Unit, assisted in data analysis.

SOURCE: *Archives of General Psychiatry*, 36, pp. 1010–1015, August 1979.

Money[15] published "prefatory remarks" on outcome in 17 males and seven females. All but one expressed an unequivocal feeling of having done the right thing by undergoing reassignment. Nine males improved in employment status and eight maintained the status quo; among females, the figures were three and four, respectively. No females had police records. Six males had been arrested prior to reassignment; the two with more serious charges were arrested again postoperatively. None became psychotic. Seven males and three females married for the first time after reassignment.

Edgerton and Meyer[16] reported early psychosocial follow-up in 13 biological males surveyed by questionnaire. All reported "no regrets" and claimed relief from anxiety associated with "illegal" presurgical cross-dressing. One patient attempted suicide, but none of the others experienced a gross emotional disorder. Sexual adjustment was mixed, 60% reporting feelings identified as orgiastic.

Hastings[17] presented data from halfway in a planned ten-year follow-up of 25 reassigned males. No patients with a known history of overt mental illness were accepted into the program, but two psychotic episodes were seen postoperatively, four patients made serious suicidal attempts, and one was shot and seriously wounded. Adjustment in this series was rated on a 4-point scale (from poor to excellent) in each of four major categories: economic, social, sexual, and emotional. Criteria for ratings of poor, fair, good, or excellent were defined in terms of observable or readily inferrable variables. Hastings' data indicate postoperative adjustments that averaged between good and fair.

Hore et al[18] reported brief follow-up experience with 16 reassigned males. Eleven were reported to have "definitely benefitted from the operation . . . feeling more female and having increased confidence in their new role." Five were dissatisfied, three citing surgical complications and two not feeling "fully female."

Follow-up makes it clear that obvious psychiatric disturbance, serious postsurgical ambivalence, and gross dyssocial behavior are infrequent complications of surgical intervention. The careful study by Hastings, however, is somewhat more even-handed about postoperative adjustment than the more dramatic improvement indicated in earlier reports.

THE HOPKINS STUDY

In 1971, a follow-up was inaugurated of 100 Gender Identity Clinic (GIC) patients, 34 operated and 66 unoperated. All had applied to the GIC for sex reassignment and had been evaluated prior to the study. The 34 operated patients constituted the total group of patients well known to the Hopkins Clinic who had been operated on at the time follow-up began. Twenty-four were operated on at The Johns Hopkins Hospital, ten at other institutions. The 66 unoperated patients (all of whom had been seen by the first author) comprised the total active unoperated file at the time of follow-up inauguration.

The pivotal point separating baseline from follow-up differed in the operated and unoperated groups. In the operated group, it was the point of sex reassignment surgery, and in the unoperated, it was the initial GIC interview, in which the patient was accepted as an applicant and the criteria to qualify for formal consideration of sex reassignment were explained (living and working in the desired role with concurrent hormones for at least one year). At the point of initial GIC interview (ie, the time follow-up began), the unoperated patients had not met the criterion of a trial period and could not be considered for surgery. The situation among the operated subjects was more complex. At the beginning of the Hopkins program, a formal, documented, and GIC-supervised trial period was not insisted on. Therefore, the surgical qualifying requirements for the earlier operated patients were not as structured as in subsequent years. Among the 34 operated patients, 21 (62%) had documented trial periods that would satisfy current standards. The remaining 13 had all been well established in the cross-gender role at surgery, but might not have worked in that role or taken hormones with regularity.

Sustained efforts were made to bring the patients to Baltimore for follow-up. Some distant patients were reluctant to return, so the first author traveled to a more centrally located city for some interviews. All patients included in the follow-up were personally interviewed. Interviews were conducted and utilized only with the informed consent of the patient. When the follow-up effort was completed in late 1974, 52 patients had been interviewed; 50 gave consent for publication of their data. In all instances, patient permission was sought to contact other physicians for confirmation of surgical procedures, medical treatment, and hormone administration.

Follow-up interviews were organized into three components: the first covering the more observable criteria of adaptation (eg, residence, education, and job); the second, family relationships and adaptational patterns at major life intervals (eg, grade school, high school); and the third, fantasy, dreams, and sexual activity. Interviews ranged from two to four hours in length. Sessions were recorded and transcribed, providing, along with notes, the corpus of research data. Material for this article, intended to report the observable and objective factors in adjustment, was taken almost exclusively from the first interview component.

The inclusion of unoperated subjects is an important departure from the usual procedure of reporting only postsurgical patients. These unoperated individuals were considered a comparison group for the operated subjects. While not a rigorous control group, they provided the only available approximation to it. From the medical point of view, because of the serious and irreversible nature of the surgery, random assignment to the operative group was not possible. From the patient's perspective, the passionate demands for reassignment did not allow random assignment to the nonoperative group. To reiterate, the inclusion of the unoperated subjects in follow-up was considered essential, not only as an approximation of a control group, but also, as a group of unoperated subjects who might contribute to an understanding of the natural course of the wish for sex reassignment.

RESULTS

Follow-Up and Attrition

Follow-up was achieved and data could be published for 50% of the sample. Hoped-for follow-up percentages in the 70% to 80% range were mitigated against by the realities of a national sample and the difficulty in reestablishing contact with some patients.

Considering the low follow-up percentage, subject representability must be assessed. Table 1 compares sex, race, Hollingshead socioeconomic level, age at initial interview, and surgical and consultation variables for subjects and those patients lost to follow-up, who appeared comparable along these indices.

Exceptions to this comparability include the racial distribution and trial period completion in the operated group. The four blacks in the operated group lived in close proximity to the interview sites, accounting in part for their complete inclusion. Of the operated subjects, 73% (11 of 15) had by current standards completed a formal trial period prior to surgery. Two of the remaining four had long established themselves in the cross-gender role, but had not taken hormones regularly; one patient had taken hormones regularly, but had not established a full-time cross-sexual identity. The remaining subject had a still more qualified trial period. Among operated patients lost to follow-up, 59% (ten of 17) had completed a "formal" trial period prior to surgery. In both operated and unoperated groups, subjects in comparison with those lost to follow-up tended more to live in Maryland, the District of Columbia, and surrounding states.

Average follow-up for operated subjects was 62 months (range, 19 to 142) and for unoperated subjects, 25 months (range, 15 to 48). The difference in length of follow-up is a product of having very complete records on the operated cases from the earlier years, but having comprehensive records on the unoperated cases dating only from mid-1969.

Social Change

Frequency of change of residence was selected as one index of social stability. In looking at this variable, the average number of months per given address was compared for equal time periods prior to and during follow-up. Applicants for sex reassignment have been noted to be unsettled, moving frequently and often leaving no forwarding address, behavior attributed to the insecurity of "masquerading" prior to genital surgery. For both operated and unoperated subjects, however, there was slightly more residential instability following surgery or interview. The average number of months between moves for operated subjects was 20 (presurgery) and 18 (follow-up); for unoperated subjects, 12 (precontact) and 10 (follow-up).

Job and educational levels (Hollingshead) were selected as the two other indices of social adjustment. Job levels indicated a slight upward trend for both groups, somewhat more for operated subjects (5.2 to 4.9) than for unoperated subjects (5.2 to 5.1), but occurring over a longer average follow-up period. Educational levels initially and at follow-up showed essentially no change: operated subjects, 5.1 and 5.1, respectively (no change), and unoperated subjects, 4.0 to 3.9, respectively. In general, the operated subjects were less well educated than the unoperated subjects. Socioeconomic levels of individual patients were usually the same as those of the family of origin.

Since job level is an important index, subjects were used as their own controls in a frequency distribution of job level change during follow-up. There was little observable difference between operated and unoperated subjects. Forty-seven percent of operated subjects and 43% of unoperated subjects showed no change, and 74% of operated and 71% of unoperated subjects were bracketed between a decrease or increase of one job level in comparison with baseline.

Psychiatric Contact

Psychiatric contacts were compared for unoperated and operated subjects. Seventy-two percent of unoperated subjects had psychiatric contact prior to the initial interview; in the follow-up, only 28% had further contacts. This contrasts with 33% and 8% for operated subjects at comparable times. The bulk of the psychiatric contacts represented forays in search of "understanding" or certification for sex reassignment.

Two unoperated patients were psychiatric inpatients prior to being interviewed, and one was followed up continuously in posthospital care. One unoperated subject was hospitalized during follow-up after undergoing sex reassignment elsewhere. One operated subject had been psychiatrically hospitalized prior to surgery and one was hospitalized after surgery.

Reversal of Surgery

One of the serious potential complications of sex reassignment surgery is the possibility that the patient will consider that a mistake has been made. Reports of such cases have been both anecdotal and documented.[14,19] In the Hopkins' series, a biological female who had undergone mastectomy, removal of internal reproductive organs, and phallus construction eventually requested removal of the phallus, but not negation of the entire reassignment procedure. This request came after many surgical complications. She was later hospitalized briefly for pentazocine dependency and suicidal ideation. None of the other patients were known to have requested an "undoing" of the surgical procedure.

TABLE 1 Comparison of Subjects and Patients Lost to Follow-Up

							Residence at Initial Interview, %					*Where Operated, %*		*Surgical Complications*	
		Sex, %		*Race, %*											
Group	*No. of Patients*	*M*	*F*	*W*	*B*	*Other*	*Maryland or District of Columbia*	*Sur-rounding States*	*Other*	*Average Age, yr*	*Socio-economic Level*	*Johns Hopkins*	*Other*	*%*	*Per Patient*
Operated															
Followed	15*	73	27	66	27	7	27	40	33	30.1	3.9	67	33	53	1.8
Lost to follow-up	17	76	24	100	0	0	6	41	53	30.5	3.8	70	30	52	1.7
Unoperated															
Followed	35	80	20	94	6	0	34	43	23	28.4	3.9	(43)†	(57)‡	N/A	N/A
Lost to follow-up	31	77	23	90	10	0	29	32	39	29.5	3.7	(39)†	(61)‡	N/A	N/A

*Two patients refused permission for publication of their data. Their inclusion would bring the number to 17.
†First consultation at Johns Hopkins
‡First consultation elsewhere

TABLE 2 Comparison of Original Operated, Operated during Follow-Up, and Unoperated Patients

		Sex, %		Race, %					Average No. of Gender Identity Clinic Consultations		Where Operated, %		Surgical Complications	
Status	*No. of Patients*	*M*	*F*	*W*	*B*	*Other*	*Average Age, yr*	*Socio-economic Level*	*Before Follow-Up*	*During Follow-Up*	*Johns Hopkins*	*Other*	*%*	*Per Patient*
Operated*	15	73	27	66	27	7	30.1	3.9	5.8	1.2	67	33	53	1.8
Unoperated, subsequently operated*	14	93	7	100	0	0	30.9	4.2	2.4	2.9	36	64	29	1.3
Unoperated, not subsequently operated	21	76	24	90	10	0	26.7	3.5	2.0	1.2		—	—	—

*Patients with full genital reassignment or surgical removal of reproductive organs

Continued Pursuit of Sex Reassignment

Of the 35 unoperated patients, 14 (40%) pursued surgical reassignment essentially to completion during follow-up. Five underwent their surgery at Hopkins, and nine elsewhere. Another was approved for surgery at Hopkins, but did not follow through. At other institutions, one patient underwent augmentation and castration, but not genital reassignment, and another underwent rhinoplasty and thyroid cartilage shave.

In other words, of the 35 unoperated subjects, five (14%) completed a trial period satisfactorily, were offered sex reassignment at Hopkins, and underwent surgery. (One patient completed a trial period and was offered surgery, but declined. He is included with the residual unoperated subjects.) Nine (26%) of the 35 sought surgery elsewhere without satisfactorily completing the trial period.

Five male unoperated subjects (14%) had given up anything approaching pursuit of sex reassignment during the follow-up, although they did at times nourish fantasies of being female. The remaining 21 (60% of the original 35) still stated an active interest in sex reassignment without either completing the trial period or pushing on to surgery.

Overall Assessment of Outcome

The observation that some unoperated patients did subsequently undergo reassignment establishes three groups of interest: the original operated group; an originally unoperated but subsequently operated group; and an unoperated and not subsequently operated group, constituting the residual unoperated subjects.

Table 2 outlines demographic and surgical data for the three groups. Originally unoperated but subsequently operated patients, like operated subjects, are, on the average, slightly older and of lower socioeconomic level than unoperated and not subsequently operated subjects. There was no difference in psychiatric contacts between the residual unoperated subjects and those who were unoperated originally but subsequently operated on. The residual unoperated group was followed up for an average of 27 months (range, 17 to 48), whereas the subsequently operated group was followed up for an average of 21 months (range, 15 to 34).

In order to compare outcome for the three subject categories, initial and follow-up adjustment scores were calculated by summing scores based on concrete behaviors in four categories: legal, economic, marriage or cohabitation, and psychiatric. An effort was made to weight the scores so that no one category was overrepresented as a determiner of outcome. Table 3 indicates the scoring system. Most of the scoring is self-evident. However, if the patient is male requesting reassignment as female, a gender-appropriate cohabitation or marriage means that he lives with, or marries, a man as a female; a non-gender appropriate situation would be one in which the patient, while requesting sex reassignment, nonetheless cohabitated or married as a man.

Table 4 lists the means and standard deviations in each group initially and at follow-up, as well as change scores. The lowest initial mean score was in operated subjects. However, there is no significant difference among the initial adjustment levels for the three subject categories.

Adjustment scores at follow-up reflect a positive shift in means, a narrowing of the ranges, and a tightening of the standard deviations. The operated and unoperated (not subsequently operated) subjects show nearly equal means, both more highly positive than the group operated on during follow-up. There is again, however, no significant difference in follow-up scores.

On the other hand, change scores for operated patients approach significance ($P < .10$) and for unoperated patients (not subsequently operated) are clearly significant ($P < .001$). Change scores for unoperated subjects subsequently operated on, as a whole, are not significant. The poorest follow-up scores (mean, −0.4) were seen among that subgroup of subsequently operated patients who precipitously pursued surgery elsewhere. Those unoperated, subsequently operated patients who underwent surgery at Hopkins have a mean adjustment score of +1.0.

In the original operated group, a comparison of initial and follow-up adjustment scores, as well as change scores, was made for those subjects who had completed a formal trial period (N = 11) and those whose presurgical trial was less exacting (N = 4). No statistically significant difference was found. Interpretation is difficult because of the small number of patients, but there was a tendency for those subjects without formal trial periods to have lower initial and follow-up adjustment scores than those subjects with more rigorous trial periods.

At the most simple level, these data suggest that significant change in adjustment scores may be achieved either through surgery or through the passage

TABLE 3 Adjustment Scoring System

Category	Score
Legal	
Arrested only	−1
Arrested and jailed	−2
Economic: Hollingshead job level	
1 or 2	+3
3 or 4	+2
5 or 6	+1
7 or 8	0
Cohabitation	
Cohabit	
Gender-appropriate	+1
Nongender-appropriate	−1
Marriage	
Gender-appropriate	+2
Nongender-appropriate	−2
Psychiatric	
Contact	−1
Outpatient treatment	−2
Hospitalization	−3

TABLE 4 Adjustment Scores Initially and at Follow-Up, with Change Scores

Group	*Initial*			*Follow-Up*			*Change*		
	Mean	*Range*	*SD*	*Mean*	*Range*	*SD*	*Mean*	*Range*	*SD*
Operated	−2.07	−18 − +4	6.68	+1.07	−1 − +4	1.53	+3.13*	−2 − +19	6.33
Operated during follow-up	−1.14	−9 − +2	2.91	+0.21	−4 − +2	1.89	+1.36	−3 − +10	3.03
Unoperated	−1.33	−7 − +2	2.61	+1.10	−4 − +4	1.97	+2.43†	−2 − +8	2.73

*Borders on significance: $P < .10$ (two-tail); $P < .05$ (one-tail)
†Significant: $P < .001$ (two-tail)

of time in association with some contact and acceptance into an organized evaluation program. Operated patients who could not withstand the rigors of a trial period of living and working in the desired gender role clearly did less well than the unoperated subjects or their fellow operated subjects.

COMMENT

Although only 52% of the sample was interviewed, subjects' initial values seemed comparable to those of patients lost to follow-up along important demographic indices. None of the operated patients voiced regrets at reassignment, the operative loss of reproductive organs, or substitution of opposite sex facsimiles (except one, previously noted). Socioeconomically, operated and unoperated patients changed little, if at all, with operated patients demonstrating no superiority in job or education. The operated group showed greater residential stability. Unoperated subjects made more use of psychiatric contacts both before and after the initial interview, which relates to their somewhat higher educational level and the recent greater emphasis on psychiatric screening. Additionally, these patients, being unoperated, continued to seek various psychiatric endorsements for their quest. Forty percent of the original unoperated group pursued surgery to the point of genital ablation during follow-up; 14% gave up all active pursuit.

It is important to recall, in interpreting the data, that while both operated and unoperated subjects were followed up for substantial periods, the original operated group was followed up for an average of 62 months, whereas the original unoperated group was followed up for an average of 25 months. This difference may influence data interpretation in a variety of ways. For example, it is important to realize that the group of unoperated subjects may continue to characterize itself more definitively as time goes on. It seems likely that the percentages of subjects who are eventually operated on or who drop all pursuit of sex reassignment will change from what is reported here. On the other hand, five-year follow-up is certainly ample to demonstrate socioeconomic improvement and stability. The failure of the operated group to demonstrate clear objective superiority over the unoperated is all the more striking.

Initial adjustment scores indicate that the original operated group was slightly more distressed than the unoperated. Over follow-up, the original operated group and the residual unoperated group (not subsequently operated on) reached comparable adjustment levels, with the degree of positive change approaching significance for operated subjects and being clearly significant for the unoperated. Those patients who pursued surgery, particularly those who pursued it precipitously, showed levels of distress closer to initial levels. It seems clearly beneficial for patients to be considered for surgery within the environs of an organized program. Abandonment of a program and precipitous requests for surgery are contraindications for it.

In the Hopkins' program, no attempt was made to habilitate unoperated patients in the cross-gender role. The patients were seen infrequently (Table 2), were not given hormones, and were not urged or instructed in either direction. The program is interested, concerned, but noninterventive, recognizing the strength of the wish for sex reassignment, but adopting a position of watchful waiting with regard to it.[20] For those patients who elected to pursue surgery, however, there came to be an insistence on full completion of a trial period of living and working in the desired gender role for at least a year, with concurrent hormones, prior to formal consideration of surgery. Selection for sex reassignment was essentially self-determined by the patient, dependent on his motivation, capacity to organize, and degree of ambivalence. It was not thought, because of the serious, irreversible nature of the surgery, that patients could be randomly assigned to operative or nonoperative categories.

Although other constructions are possible, the most conservative interpretation of the data is that among the applicants for sex reassignment, there are operationally two groups who, in the face of a trial period, will self-select for or against surgery and that in either instance, improvement will be demonstrated over time, as judged by observable behavioral variables. Sex reassignment surgery confers no objective advantage in terms of social rehabilitation, although it remains subjectively satisfying to those who have rigorously pursued a trial period and who have undergone it.

REFERENCES

1. Green RL: Transsexualism: Mythological, historical, and cross-cultural aspects, in Benjamin H (ed): *The Transsexual Phenomenon*. New York Julian Press, 1966, pp 173–186.
2. Green RL: Mythological, historical, and cross-cultural aspects of transsexualism, in Green R, Money J (eds): *Transsexualism and Sex Reassignment*. Baltimore, Johns Hopkins Press, 1969, pp 235–242.
3. Cauldwell DO: Psychopathia transsexualis. *Sexology* 16:274–280, 1949.
4. Benjamin H: *The Transsexual Phenomenon*. New York, Julian Press, 1966.
5. Abraham F: Genitalumwandlung an zwei maennlichen transvestiten. *Z Sexualwissenschafft* 18:223–226, 1931.
6. Hamburger C, Sturup GK, Dahl-Iverson E: Transvestism: Hormonal, psychiatric and surgical treatment. *JAMA* 152:391–396, 1953.
7. Money J, Schwartz F: Public opinion and social issues in transsexualism: A case study in medical sociology, in Green R, Money J (eds): *Transsexualism and Sex Reassignment*. Baltimore, Johns Hopkins Press, 1969, pp 253–269.
8. Green RL: Attitudes toward transsexualism and sex reassignment procedures, in Green R, Money J (eds): *Transsexualism and Sex Reassignment*. Baltimore, Johns Hopkins Press, 1969, pp 235–242,
9. Stoller R: Male transsexualism: Uneasiness. *Dan Med Bull* 19:301–316, 1972.
10. Meyer JK: Some thoughts on nosology and motivation among "transsexuals," in Laub D, Gandy P (eds): *Proceedings of the Second Interdisciplinary Symposium on the Gender Dysphoria Syndrome*. Stanford, Calif, Division of Reconstructive and Rehabilitation Surgery, Stanford University Medical Center, 1974, pp 31–33.
11. Meyer JK: Clinical variants among applicants for sex reassignment. *Arch Sex Behav* 3:527–558, 1974.
12. Meyer JK: Individual psychotherapy of sexual disorders, in Freedman A, Kaplan H, Sadock B (eds): *Comprehensive Textbook of Psychiatry*, ed 2. Baltimore, Williams & Wilkins Co, 1975, pp 1544–1555.
13. Meyer JK: Training and accreditation for the treatment of sexual disorders. *Am J Psychiatry* 133:389–394,1976.
14. Randall J: Preoperative and postoperative status of male and female transsexuals, in Green R, Money J (eds): *Transsexualism and Sex Reassignment*. Baltimore, Johns Hopkins Press, 1969, pp 355–382.
15. Money J: Prefatory remarks on outcome of sex reassignment in 24 cases of transsexualism. *Arch Sex Behav* 1:163–165, 1971.
16. Edgerton MT Jr, Meyer JK: Surgical and psychiatric aspects of transsexualism, in Horton C (ed): *Surgery of the External Genitalia*. Boston, Little Brown & Co, 1973, pp 117–161.
17. Hastings D: Postsurgical adjustment of male transsexual patients, in Meyer JK (ed): Sex Assignment and Sex Reassignment: Intersex and Gender Identity Disorders. *Clin Plast Surg* 1:335–344, 1974.
18. Hore B, Nicolle F, Calnan J: Male transsexualism in England: 16 cases with surgical intervention. *Arch Sex Behav* 4:81–88, 1975.
19. Money J, Wolff G: Sex reassignment: Male to female to male. *Arch Sex Behav* 2:245–250,1973.
20. Meyer JK, Hoopes JE: The gender dysphoria syndromes: A position statement on so-called "transsexualism." *Plast Reconstr Surg* 54:444–451, 1974.

STEPHEN I. ABRAMOWITZ

Psychosocial outcomes of sex reassignment surgery

Transsexualism is a psychiatric disorder characterized by the conviction that gender identity has not conformed to one's biological sex. Although many transsexuals derive some gratification from assuming roles appropriate to their desired gender, a substantial number are convinced that only a sexual transformation can effect meaningful relief from anguish and despair. The lives of these individuals often become a quest to find a sympathetic physician. The treatment of choice—indeed, often the only treatment acceptable to the transsexual—is sex-reassignment surgery. The ethical and conceptual dilemmas posed by this request have evoked

Thanks are due Larry E. Beutler and anonymous reviewers for careful readings of earlier drafts of this article.

SOURCE: *Journal of Consulting and Clinical Psychology*, 54(2), pp. 183–189, 1986.

heated controversy and debate. From the perspective of many psychiatrists and psychologists, the surgeon who performs a sex-change operation is at best naively colluding in a psychotic odyssey and at worse surrendering to mercenary instincts. To physicians skeptical of psychosocial models of mental illness and face-to-face with the agony of a pleading transsexual, however, surgical treatment holds out the promise of a lasting cure. Although generally not regarded as curative in and of itself, the sex change is thought to offer reassurance for a weak gender identity under constant cultural siege (Sorensen, 1981a).

Transsexual patients are in fact notoriously resistant to psychotherapy aimed at reconstructive rehabilitation rather than presurgical counseling. Although some success in modifying certain transsexual symptoms via behavioral techniques has been reported (Barlow, Abel, & Blanchard, 1979) and the potential of conventional psychotherapy is undergoing reevaluation (Lothstein & Levine, 1981), comparative outcome studies involving interpersonal or uncovering psychotherapy are virtually nonexistent.

BACKGROUND AND OBJECTIVES

The modern era of sex reassignment was ushered in by the celebrated Christine Jorgensen case (Hamburger, Stürup, & Dahl-Iversen, 1953), but comprehensive reviews of the research did not appear for over a decade. Although acknowledging the anecdotal nature and lack of rigor of much of the early follow-up reports, Pauly (1968) concluded that the data compel tentative acceptance of reassignment as the treatment of choice pending further research. This positive conclusion was tempered only slightly in an update that incorporated the findings of the comparatively rigorous studies of the 1970s (Pauly, 1981), including the influential Hopkins report (Meyer & Reter, 1979). In the context of a thoughtful historical overview, Lothstein (1982) emphasized increasing awareness of the selective nature of the successful outcomes and the need to restrict the surgical procedure to the most qualified candidates.

The objectives of the present review are to (a) reassess the past two decades of empirical research on sex-change surgery from a methodological perspective; (b) reexamine the controversial Hopkins research published in 1979; and (c) bring to bear the increasingly more rigorous research that has appeared since that time. Incidental reports and case histories were not reviewed. The former provide insufficient information with which to evaluate the credibility of the inferences made about outcome, whereas the latter impose severe constraints on internal and external validity.

Methodological Overview

Before turning to the review proper, it will prove helpful to acclimate the reader to the still primitive methodological state of this literature. Departures from usual scientific and report-writing procedures are more the rule than the exception. Control groups have only been introduced over the last 5 years. In defense of the investigators, the unique clinical dilemmas raised by the transsexual's insistence on sex transformation virtually preclude random assignment, waiting-list or attention-placebo controls, and psychotherapy comparison cases. Nonetheless, the paucity of control groups makes attribution of either improvement or deterioration to the surgical intervention scientifically untenable.

Recruitment procedures and selection criteria are inadequately described more often than not, and data on attrition are generally not provided. We are typically left in the dark about such obviously critical subject variables as psychiatric status and diagnosis, extent of gender reorientation, and previous early-stage sex-change procedures. Subjects included in subsequent reports by the same investigators sometimes appear to overlap with samples from earlier series. Incredibly, subjects who committed suicide are occasionally not included in computation of the improvement rate because they were not available for follow-up. The extent of hormonal and surgical modification is often not given, and the experience of the treatment team is left unspecified. Although adjunctive counseling or psychotherapy is sometimes made available, we are typically left to wonder about its type, extent, and use.

The research is rife with violations of generally acceptable assessment practices. Subject and investigator biases are rarely taken into account, and the criteria of standardization, specific as well as global judgments, quantification, and multiple data sources have until recently gone unheeded. Data have typically been collected at only one point in time (follow-up) rather than over the reasonable expectation of three (pre and post in addition to follow-up). The application of conventional statistical procedures is a recent innovation.

Organization of Review

Consistent with the emphasis of the review, the main sections are organized by methodological approach to the question of outcome: prequantitative and quantitative. These discussions are followed by a closer look at the disputatious Hopkins findings. An evaluative overview in the context of the inferences drawn by previous reviewers concludes the article.

PREQUANTITATIVE STUDIES

Ten investigations on the results of sex-change surgery were classified as prequantitative (Benjamin, 1966; Edgerton & Meyer, 1973; Hastings & Markland, 1978; Hoenig, Kenna, & Youd, 1971; Hore, Nicolle, & Calnan, 1975; Money, 1971; Money & Brennan, 1968; Money & Primrose, 1968; Randell, 1969, 1971). Randell's (1969, 1971) samples appear to be partly overlapping.

In this group of studies, outcome is rated in terms of degree of improvement or satisfaction, and the distribution of patients is reported by category or converted to percentages. These investigations are characterized by some differentiation of outcome domains and specification of patient parameters. The former development reflects recognition that the consequences of surgical intervention reverberate beyond cosmetic satisfaction and sexual functioning to psychiatric status and psychosocial adjustment. The latter refinement reflects clinical concern for poor risks and encourages investigation of moderators of treatment success beyond patient sex. Hence, despite the absence of controls and of standardized psychometric assessment devices, these studies represent a modest methodological advance from the incidental reports and case histories.

Duration of follow-up in these studies has been intermediate (3 months to 5.5 years). Only Benjamin (1966) was not a member of the original surgical team and did not have a preponderantly Anglo-American sample. Surprisingly, all of the prequantitative articles appeared before 1980.

Main Results

The overall tenor of the evidence from the prequantitative research is positive but qualified. The thrust of each of the reports is favorable, with about 60% to 85% of patients rated as satisfied or improved. However, at least one serious postoperative incident—generally defined as a reversal request, psychotic episode, hospitalization, or suicide—is reported in six of the articles, and 14 complications (6.4%) are documented in all. Furthermore, character pathology was implicated as a risk factor by no less than four investigative teams (Edgerton & Meyer, 1973; Hastings & Markland, 1978; Hoenig et al., 1971; Randell, 1969).

Results were best along the dimensions of cosmetic satisfaction, interpersonal relationships, and psychological well-being. Improvement was less pronounced in the work and economic spheres, the legal arena and, interestingly, in the realm of sexual relations.

Sex Differences

Forty-four of the 220 postoperative patients were females-to-males. No trend toward greater improvement emerged in the six studies having such a sample, including the five that permitted a direct comparison with the biological males. However, females-to-males had a slightly lower rate of serious complications (4.5%) than did their male counterparts (6.8%). This difference, though intriguing and consistent with the conventional wisdom, is not amenable to statistical test because the varying definitions of serious complications and unequal number of cases across investigations violate the assumption of event independence.

These prequantitative efforts did not incorporate psychometric instruments and were authored by persons having a stake in the surgical outcome. Such weaknesses may, however, be partly offset by the greater articulation of outcome variables and potential patient mediators. The large-series character of the populations, in contrast to the idiosyncratic nature of the case history, argues for a representativeness that lends credence to the findings—the worrisome complications as well as the encouraging overall figures. Once again, however, the lack of control subjects precludes the drawing of inferences regarding the extent to which the success and casualty rates exceed the corresponding base rates from spontaneous remission, maturation, and placebo among transsexuals motivated for but refused sex transformation.

QUANTITATIVE STUDIES

Fourteen investigations were classified as quantitative (Bentler, 1976; Blanchard & Steiner, 1983; Fleming, Cohen, Salt, Jones, & Jenkins, 1981; Fleming, Jones, & Simons, 1982; Fleming, MacGowan, Robinson, Spitz, & Salt, 1982; Hunt & Hampson, 1980; Laub & Fisk, 1974; Lothstein, 1980; Meyer & Reter, 1979; Sadoughi, Jayaram, & Bush, 1978; Sorensen, 1981a, 1981b; Walinder, Lundström, & Thuwe, 1978; Walinder & Thuwe, 1975). None of these data sets appears to be overlapping.

In addition to dimensionalizing the multiple outcome criteria and possible mediating variables other than patient sex, these studies employed psychometric inventories or standardized rating scales. Some of the results are based on the application of conventional statistical procedures. Although most of the research remains preexperimental, control groups are occasionally incorporated. The upshot is greater scientific credibility, seemingly more careful documentation of complications, and more systematic examination of outcome moderators and the processes that may underlie them. Both Scandinavian and Anglo-American populations are well represented, and the average follow-up period of about 4 years is substantial. Not surprisingly, virtually all of these more methodologically sound investigations were published within the last decade.

In examining the results, it will help to keep in mind the three kinds of studies included in this section. Nine investigations (one with controls) fit the larger scale, longitudinal paradigm; three employed smaller samples in relatively well-controlled, cross-sectional designs; and two were essentially correlational and aimed at identifying moderator variables. Investigators of the larger scale, follow-up projects appear on the whole to have had more of a hand in the decision to operate than did their counterparts in the quasi-experimental and process-oriented studies.

Improvement Rates

Taking the longitudinal follow-ups without an unoperated comparison group, we again encounter overall improvement rates that hover around two-thirds. A rate of about 50% sets the lower level of the range (Sorensen, 1981a, 1981b), and one of over 85% establishes the ceiling (Laub & Fisk, 1974). For the studies having control groups, of course, success is reflected by an increment of the operated group over the unoperated group, rather than by absolute improvement rates. In two of the three quasi-experimental investigations carried out by the Boston research group, the direction of the evidence was favorable to the matched postsurgical patients (Fleming et al., 1981; Fleming, MacGowan, et al., 1982). Results based on quantified Rorschach responses, however, were equivocal (Fleming, Jones, et al., 1982).

Particularly unsettling findings were reported by the team at Johns Hopkins, which conducted the lone pre–post follow-up that incorporated a control condition. Although originally operated patients showed slight positive change in overall adjustment, unoperated patients demonstrated a greater and statistically significant amount of such change (Meyer & Reter, 1979). If representative, this finding would flout the bulk of the longitudinal follow-ups by suggesting that the ubiquitous two-thirds improved rate largely reflects such factors as remission, maturation, and placebo. The implications of the Hopkins report and the controversies surrounding it have therefore been accorded separate treatment later.

Situation-Specific Improvement

Gains were greatest in the sexual and relationship spheres and least impressive with respect to socioeconomic considerations and cosmetic appearance. An intermediate level of change was indicated for psychiatric status and legal problems, such as frequency of arrests. The greater improvement in interpersonal life and lesser improvement in economic well-being are consistent with the configurations obtained from the dimensionalized analysis of the prequantitative findings. However, the poor results for cosmetic satisfaction are puzzling because quantitative studies are relatively recent and incorporate the many advances in surgical technique. The overall lack of correspondence across studies may reflect the absence of a standard assessment battery and the method variance introduced by the use of different rating scales that purport to tap the same construct.

Casualties

Beyond the sobering Hopkins data (Meyer & Reter, 1979), at least one casualty was reported in all but one of the larger scale follow-ups. Moreover, the more rigorous studies represented in this section yielded an overall complications rate of 9.1%. Although this figure is mitigated somewhat by the overrepresentation of casualties from two related series (Sorensen, 1981a, 1981b), it does not include the transient and spontaneously clearing psychotic episodes reported by Lothstein (1980). Walinder et al. (1978) noted that their 5 cases having regrets about undergoing sex-change procedures were culled from about 100 patient files, and Fleming, Jones, et al. (1982) reported postoperative suicide attempts to be rare. Ironically, the rates of possible casualties for the Hopkins operated and unoperated groups appear comparable.

Sex Differences

Forty-nine of the 217 subjects in the 8 longitudinal follow-ups in which sex of subject was reported were biological females, and 8 of the 13 investigations overall included women. Of the 5 that employed men as well, results were at least as good for the women in 2 and clearly superior in 2 others. Walinder and Thuwe (1975) commented directly on the demonstrably more favorable outcome for the females-to-males. Sorensen (1981a, 1981b) drew a similar conclusion in comparing data from his study of females-to-males with data from his study of males-to-females. These sentiments are also reflected in the casualty rate for the two groups: fully 9.6% for the males-to-females but only 4.1% for the females-to-males. Keep in mind that this difference is based on events whose occurrences are not statistically independent of one another and which are thus not congenial to conventional tests. It nonetheless appears that the greater serious complications rate obtained in the more rigorous studies is attributable primarily to the biological men.

Mediator Variables

Several additional outcome mediators were identified. Good premorbid (core) males-to-females and less overdriven phallic females-to-males fared relatively well in Sorensen's (1981a, 1981b) otherwise complications-plagued samples, and stable personality discriminated Walinder et al.'s (1978) satisfied from dissatisfied cases. Both findings are compatible with conclusions from the prequantitative research implicating character pathology as a negative factor in the surgical outcome equation.

Although the prevailing clinical wisdom regards heterosexuality as a contraindication for surgery, the empirical returns are inconclusive. Walinder et al. (1978) obtained evidence in support of such an expectation. However, Bentler (1976) reported lesser relationship stress and overall adjustment problems among heterosexually oriented patients. Surgical success was found to be unrelated to type of psychosexual disorder (Laub & Fisk, 1974).

Gender reorientation, the degree of approximation of the status of the opposite biological sex, may mediate outcome. Blanchard and Steiner (1983) found that greater resocialization in the adopted gender role was associated with lesser depression and greater social adjustment among a sample of female-to-male transsexuals that included some postoperative cases. The investigators raise the methodologically disturbing possibility that gender reorientation operates as a confound in the uncontrolled longitudinal follow-ups of surgical success. The heightened level of dedication and commitment to reorientation encouraged (if not required) by the treatment team, rather than the surgery itself, may explain any improvement. Such a scenario only underscores the limitations on interpretation imposed by the lack of a motivated control group.

Among other treatment-related factors that have been positively associated with postoperative satisfaction are consistency in early-stage administration of hormones (Walinder et al., 1978) and extent of surgical modification (Fleming, MacGowan, et al., 1982). However, Lothstein (1980) found greater susceptibility to depression among females-to-males receiving phalloplasty, which despite technical advances remains a procedure fraught with potential surgical complications and disappointments (Edgerton & Meyer, 1973). Superior outcome has also been reported by patients undergoing sex-change surgery for the first time relative to patients receiving follow-up surgery (Laub & Fisk, 1974). This would appear to implicate poor adaptive capacities among those requesting further surgery and underlines the need to control for such subject factors.

Sorensen found no effect of follow-up duration among males (1981a) or females (1981b). Inadequate family support has been isolated as a negative factor in the quantitative (Walinder et al., 1978) as well as the prequantitative (Hoenig et al., 1971) research. Poor results have also been reported for older patients and those with criminal records, inappropriate physique, and inadequate self-support (Walinder et al., 1978).

HOPKINS REPORT

Meyer and Reter (1979) reported outcome data for 50 patients seen at the Gender Identity Clinic of Johns Hopkins University. They found the following:

> Among the applicants for sex reassignment, there are operationally two groups who, in the face of a trial period, will self-select for or against surgery and that in either instance, improvement will be demonstrated over time, as judged by observable behavioral variables. (p. 1015)

This conclusion, which flew in the face of the previous research and prevailing clinical wisdom, was dramatically punctuated by the closing of the Hopkins Gender Identity Clinic soon thereafter. Because of the reputation of the surgical investigative team, the inclusion of a control group of unoperated transsexuals, and perhaps the shift toward conservatism and away from alternative sexual life-styles in the broader culture, the Hopkins research has had a far-ranging impact on the field. Citing a personal communication (Money, 1979, cited in Lothstein, 1980), Lothstein contended that the decision to shut down the program was not based on the empirical findings of the study but was the result of political pressure.

Main Findings

Three groups of surgery-seekers were compared. The primary operated group consisted of 15 patients who had qualified for and had undergone sex transformation prior to 1971, when the study began. The unoperated group consisted of 35 patients who had failed to so qualify and had not been reassigned by that date. This cohort was later divided into two subgroups, composed of 14 patients who were reassigned by 1974, when the study ended, and 21 others who had not been operated on by the time follow-up ended in 1974. Average length of follow-up was about 5 years for the original operated group but only about 2 years for the subsequently operated and unoperated groups, a threat to internal validity that has not been fully appreciated by observers. For most patients, the bulk of the follow-up information was gathered at one 2- to 4-hour interview. The primary measure of outcome was an overall adjustment index derived by combining scores along the dimensions of legal complications, appropriateness of living arrangement, employment status, and psychiatric record.

Patients who had been refused but later obtained the surgery manifested negligible positive change, but those originally reassigned and those still not reassigned demonstrated moderate and roughly equivalent improvement. The somewhat greater variation in outcome among the primary operated group, which suggests that the direction of surgical impact depended on patient characteristics, was ignored. These results prompted the inference that "Sex reassignment confers no advantage in terms of social rehabilitation" (Meyer & Reter, p. 1015). Probably because the earlier studies that their data contradicted had not included unoperated controls, the Hopkins team made little attempt at integration, thereby underscoring their unhedged conclusion.

Critique

Considerable criticism has already been directed at the Hopkins data. The researchers have been taken to task for overgeneralizing "without seemingly being aware of its impact on the general population" (Fleming, Steinman, & Bocknek, 1980, p. 455). Pauly (1981) believes that the significant positive change in adjustment among the unoperated group is "interesting but hardly justifies the conclusion that surgery is not indicated for any applicants" (p. 50).

Incorporation of a control group of unoperated patients is unique among the large-series follow-ups in this literature and helps, almost by itself, to explain the initial enthusiasm that greeted the appearance of the Hopkins report. Other things being equal, this feature enhances the internal validity of the Hopkins study relative to some otherwise similar or even superior efforts (e.g., Walinder & Thuwe, 1975). Those other things may not be equal, however. Among the oversights pointed out in previous critiques are the failure to note whether subjects' biological sex was male or female and to report the data accordingly, to assess the expressly surgical-cosmetic dimension as an outcome variable or possible mediator, and to present information on subjective-psychological criteria even though such data appear to have been collected.

Approximately 50% of those who initially enrolled in the study were lost to attrition. Although this clearly limits inferences to cooperative patients, it should be kept in mind that the figure is not given in most studies and is not inconsistent with the comparable figures that have been reported. Moreover, the rate of attrition was roughly comparable across the operated and unoperated groups.

Statistical procedures are applied in an arbitrary fashion. Nominal pre–post change data routinely submitted to chi-square analysis are reported in the apparent absence of any statistical conventions. When component scores are combined (in the arbitrary manner described next) into the overall adjustment scale and change scores for each group are analyzed, the statistical test used is not given. It appears that three separate correlated *t* tests were performed, when the more appropriate choice would have been a single Group × Time analysis of variance (ANOVA). Although such lack of precision detracts from the authors' claim for objectivity, it is nonetheless unlikely that the more efficient ANOVA procedure would have yielded an outcome more favorable to the surgical treatment.

The compellingness of the control group of unoperated sex-reassignment candidates has been called into serious question (Fleming et al., 1980; Levine & Lothstein, 1981). Although all of the subjects were surgery-seekers, ultimate classification was determined partly by self-selection and partly by clinical suitability, rather than by random assignment into operated and unoperated subgroups. The subgroups are thus unlikely to be equivalent with respect to motivation and qualifications, both of which represent threats to internal validity. Any such group-selection biases, however, should have operated in favor of those deemed best motivated and qualified—the original operated group. The gender reorientation variable discussed in the previous section might well have been such a confound. Thus, although the degree of control represented by the subsequently operated group is weak (Fleming et al., 1980; Levine & Lothstein, 1981), that weakness would be expected to magnify rather than nullify any tendency for the operated patients to report superior outcome. To the extent that assessment of outcome was reasonably valid, the absence of an increment in favor of those who originally underwent reassignment assumes added significance. By implication, it would also call into question the extent to which the postoperative improvement reported in the less well-controlled prior studies was actually attributable to the surgical intervention. The control group employed in the Hopkins research was far from perfect, but its imperfections do not alone provide a logical basis for casting aside the sobering findings.

Assessment Problems

Although many serious inadequacies of the overall measure of adjustment have already received some attention, this index deserves even closer scrutiny. Fleming et al. (1980) pointed out that the instrument is sufficiently lacking in scientific credibility to constitute, in and of itself, grounds for regarding the Hopkins data with skepticism. Some of the value judgments about the positive versus negative direction of outcome variance appear to have been arbitrary. Living alone, for example, was coded as less adjusted than living with a gender-appropriate person but was coded as more adjusted than living with a gender-inappropriate person. In addition, each dimension of the index had a different number of response categories and a different possible score range. Hence, again in a seemingly arbitrary manner, the various components of the index did not contribute equally to the overall score and were therefore weighted unequally in the final outcome equation.

Basing their deductions on the possible score ranges and actual means reported in the Hopkins article, Fleming et al. (1980) made a convincing case that the number of certain negative events figured cumulatively but that the duration of those events was disregarded. Thus, two arrests were treated as worse than one, but a longer incarceration was apparently no worse than a shorter one. Likewise, two brief hospitalizations were considered to have more negative implications for psychological well-being than a single extended stay.

If Fleming et al. (1980) are correct in the inference that number of negative psychosocial outcomes carried more weight in the global adjustment index than did their duration, then the confound introduced by the differential lengths of follow-up must be reckoned with. Because length of follow-up was about 5 years for the operated group and 2 years for the unoperated group, the reassigned patients had more time in which to accumulate negative events. To correct for this outcome bias against the operated group, certain raw negative-events scores of the unoperated subjects should have been multiplied by a factor of roughly 2½. Although it seems incomprehensible that such a straightforward psychometric error would have eluded investigators and critics alike, it appears that the method of calculating adjustment was biased against the primary surgical group and thus that the findings are misleading as reported. Under the circumstances, it may even be argued that the absence of an outcome difference that favors the unoperated group argues indirectly for the surgical case. Levine and Lothstein (1981) attributed uncritical acceptance of the Hopkins report to its reassurance of what we all "know in our hearts" (p. 107) to be true. An observer may well suspect that this incident warrants a chapter in the social psychology of medicine.

CONCLUSIONS

The main substantive finding of this review is the approximately two-thirds improvement rate reported in the prequantitative and quantitative studies. On the basis of previous reviews, Lothstein (1982) found an overall improvement rate of 68%–86%, and Pauly (1981) reported an overall satisfaction rate of slightly under three-quarters. The present figure seems compatible with both of its predecessors because Lothstein's calculations excluded some of the more rigorous studies included herein, and the evidence consistently indicates that satisfaction is a more lenient criterion of global outcome than improvement per se. The relatively lackluster results within the socioeconomic sphere represent another area of convergence (Lothstein, 1982).

Casualties

The rate of tragic outcomes that emerges from the current review is about 7%, or about the same as the rate of unsatisfactory outcomes detected by Pauly (1981). Because the current criteria of casualty—a reversal request, psychotic episode, hospitalization, or suicide—appear to be the more stringent, the disturbing possibility of a trend toward an increased number of serious postoperative incidents is raised. Some of the discrepancy may be explained by the inclusion in this review of the problem-riddled Sorensen (1981a, 1981b) samples, the present method of counting multiple complications per patient, and the likelihood that a portion of the 15% of cases classified by Pauly (1981) as uncertain would ultimately become unsatisfactory. Altogether, the data reinforce Lothstein's (1982) call for caution in generalizing from the results of the earlier, poorly controlled research. The scientific basis for this restraint, however, is the cumulative evidence of the quantitative research of the last decade and not the Hopkins report. In extrapolating from the foregoing success and complications rates to clinical practice, it is important to keep in mind that transsexuals who undergo sex-change surgery at multidisciplinary, university-based centers are a highly select sample representing only a small fraction of those who have submitted to the procedure on a fee-for-service basis.

Sex Differences

The best appreciated moderator of follow-up adjustment is the patient's biological sex. The sex ratio of applicants for reassignment surgery was previously reported as 3.2:1 (Lothstein, 1982) and 3.4:1 (Pauly, 1981) in favor of males-to-females. The corresponding figure from this review is roughly 3.7:1. Although the latter may be inflated by the exclusion of studies in which the apparent sex ratio of surgery-seekers might have been affected by matching procedures, it is apparent that the overrepresentation of male-to-female candidates has survived surgical refinements in reconstructing the penis (Edgerton & Meyer, 1973) and more tolerant cultural attitudes toward females who desire to become males than toward their male counterparts (Sorensen, 1981b). Some observers had expected an increase in the proportion of female-to-male applicants (Pauly, 1981; Sorensen, 1981b).

Consistent with the conclusion reached by several individual investigators and by Pauly (1981), outcome indeed looks to be superior for females-to-males than for males-to-females. Evidence from the more recent and rigorous studies brings this differential in favor of the former into particularly sharp focus. Although determination of the mechanisms underlying this phenomenon are properly the province of future research, part of the answer may lie in the aforementioned surgical advances and relatively benign resocialization norms for females-to-males.

Methodological Suggestions

From a methodological point of view, the need for greater controls remains paramount. Pauly (1981) has provided an incisive analysis of the difficulties encountered in attempting to attribute casualties such as suicide to the surgery in the absence of carefully matched controls. The quasi-experimental approach of Fleming has been productive, and the matched, posttest-only design of his Boston group offers an intriguing exit from the ethical maze created by the prospect of random assignment.

The many temporal factors that impinge on this research literature have been best appreciated by Lothstein (1982). We cannot determine the role of age and physical appearance in limiting results unless investigators provide information about these parameters. Similarly, although study of length of follow-up as a mediating variable has barely begun, continuing to view the process of resocialization as linear and static rather than multifaceted and dynamic is both clinically and methodologically insensitive. Gender reorientation, a critical selection criterion and possible moderator variable, may itself be a function of a temporal factor—time immersed in the transsexual underground or spent fulfilling a cross-gender trial for surgery. From a broader perspective, the complex interplay of advances in surgical technique, greater selectivity in terms of trial criteria and character structure, and the design of more sensitive follow-up research places yet another temporal qualification on the findings.

Assessment remains a high priority for methodological refinement. Measures should be standardized and should include dimensionalized as well as global components, should reflect the perceptions of significant others as well as patient and investigator, and should entail pre and post as well as longer term follow-up periods and target variables previously identified as potential moderators or confounds. Investigators would do well to use those standardized measures (such as the Minnesota Multiphasic Personality Inventory) that have been employed productively in earlier research. Data should be routinely submitted to statistical procedures that can accommodate the small subsamples often encountered in this field. Attention must be paid to such matters as subject recruitment, selection and attrition, extent of surgical modification, and any adjunctive psychotherapy or counseling utilized. Investigator or subject biases and demand characteristics operative at the data-gathering points should be explored. Finally, such methodological considerations should be dealt with clearly enough that informed readers can assess for themselves the credibility of the research.

Epilogue

I am left with a distinct feeling of déjà vu. The methodological shortcomings are all too reminiscent of those that characterized the preexperimental era of psychotherapy outcome research. Are there not certain lessons here, a moral or two for the next generation of researchers who alight on a controversial clinical enterprise? The present review suggests a couple.

The pitfalls of investigator biases and the need to control for them cannot be overemphasized. Clinicians in the vanguard of new practices are compelled by personal and professional pressures to double as objective scientists. If this literature is any indication—and I think that it is—then perhaps we should resist the impulse to be so noble. Our ego involvements are stronger than our superegos and obviously more persuasive than those graduate seminars on research design. At least one member of a clinical research team, preferably one of the principals, should not have a major clinical stake in the outcome. As the brouhaha over the Hopkins report underscores only too clearly, this caveat extends as well to broader professional and political stakes, to readers of the literature, and to reviewers.

Research is merely human behavior, no more and no less, and every bit as subject to personal whim and commitments. One can even look on the failure to incorporate proper controls as motivated forgetting, in the service of retaining personal control over the ultimate interpretation of the results. Perhaps the absence of control groups need not be viewed so harshly. After all, they are impractical (and sometimes unethical) in addition to being inconvenient. The failure to follow reasonable assessment practices, which are relatively simple to ascertain, seems less easily understood without invoking the notion of ego involvement.

After three decades of case historical, prequantitative, and quantitative research on the outcome of sex-reassignment surgery, we have yet to see either the replicative use of standardized assessment devices to facilitate cross-study comparison or the development of a multidimensional inventory to tap the various subdomains of postsurgical rehabilitation. In addition to cosmetic appearance and sexual functioning, these include self-esteem, body image, socioeconomic adjustment, family life, social relationships, and legal situations. In light of the tentative evidence that certain personality disorders contraindicate reassignment surgery, the failure to incorporate any of the available measures of borderline and antisocial personality is especially puzzling. This collective reluctance to bring state-of-the-art methods to bear on the difficult treatment decision becomes less perplexing, however, when we have recourse to scientist-as-person variables in our model of the development of a research literature.

REFERENCES

Barlow, D. H., Abel, G. G., & Blanchard, E. B. (1979). Gender identity change in transsexuals: Follow-up and replication. *Archives of General Psychiatry, 36,* 1001–1007.

Benjamin, H. (1966). *The transsexual phenomenon*. New York: Julian Press.

Bentler, P. N. (1976). A typology of transsexualism: Gender identity theory and data. *Archives of Sexual Behavior, 5,* 567–583.

Blanchard, R., & Steiner, B. W. (1983). Gender reorientation, psychological adjustment, and involvement with female partners in female-to-male transsexuals. *Archives of Sexual Behavior, 12,* 149–157.

Edgerton, M. T., Jr., & Meyer, J. K. (1973). Surgical and psychiatric aspects of transsexualism. In C. Horton (Ed.), *Surgery of the external genitalia* (pp. 117–161). Boston: Little, Brown.

Fleming, M., Cohen, D., Salt, P., Jones, D., & Jenkins, S.(1981). A study of pre- and post surgical transsexuals: MMPI characteristics. *Archives of Sexual Behavior, 10,* 161–170.

Fleming, M., Jones, D., & Simons, J. (1982). Preliminary results of Rorschach protocols of pre- and postoperative transsexuals. *Journal of Clinical Psychology, 38,* 408–514.

Fleming, M., MacGowan, B. R., Robinson, L., Spitz, J., & Salt, P. (1982). The body image of the postoperative female-to-male transsexual. *Journal of Consulting and Clinical Psychology, 50,* 461–462.

Fleming, M., Steinman, C., & Bocknek, G. (1980). Methodological problems in assessing sex-reassignment surgery: A reply to Meyer and Reter. *Archives of Sexual Behavior, 9,* 451–456.

Hamburger, C., Stürup, G. K., & Dahl-Iversen, E. (1953). Transvestism: Hormonal, psychiatric and surgical treatment. *Journal of the American Medical Association, 152,* 391–396.

Hastings, D., & Markland, C. (1978). Post-surgical adjustment of twenty-five transsexuals (male-to-female) in the University of Minnesota study. *Archives of Sexual Behavior, 7,* 327–336.

Hoenig, J., Kenna, J. C., & Youd, A. (1971). Surgical treatment for transsexualism. *Acta Psychiatrica Scandinavica, 47,* 106–133.

Hore, B. D., Nicolle, F. V., & Calnan, J. S. (1975). Male transsexualism in England: Sixteen cases with surgical intervention *Archives of Sexual Behavior, 4,* 81–88.

Hunt, D. D., & Hampson, J. L. (1980). Follow-up of 17 biologic male transsexuals after sex-reassignment surgery. *American Journal of Psychiatry, 137,* 432–438.

Laub, D. R., & Fisk, N. (1974). A rehabilitation program for gender dysphoria syndrome by surgical sex-change. *Plastic and Reconstructive Surgery, 53*, 388–403.

Levine, S. B., & Lothstein, L. M. (1981). Transsexualism or the gender dysphoria syndromes. *Journal of Sex and Marital Therapy, 7*, 85–113.

Lothstein, L. M. (1980). The postsurgical transsexual: Empirical and theoretical considerations. *Archives of Sexual Behavior, 9*, 547–564.

Lothstein, L. M. (1982). Sex reassignment surgery: Historical, bioethical, and theoretical issues. *American Journal of Psychiatry 139*, 417–426.

Lothstein, L. M., & Levine, S. B. (1981). Expressive psychotherapy with gender dysphoric patients. *Archives of General Psychiatry, 38*, 924–929.

Meyer, J. K., & Reter, D. J. (1979). Sex reassignment: Follow-up. *Archives of General Psychiatry, 36*, 1010–1015.

Money, J. (1971). Prefatory remarks on outcome of sex reassignment in twenty-four cases of transsexualism. *Archives of Sexual Behavior, 1*, 163–165.

Money, J., & Brennan, J. G. (1968). Sexual dimorphism in the psychology of female transsexuals. *Journal of Nervous and Mental Disease, 147*, 487–499.

Money, J., & Primrose, C. (1968). Sexual dimorphism and dissociation in the psychology of male transsexuals. *Journal of Nervous and Mental Disease, 147*, 472–486.

Pauly, I. B. (1968). The current status of the change of sex operation. *Journal of Nervous and Mental Disease, 147*, 460–471.

Pauly, I. B. (1981). Outcome of sex reassignment surgery for transsexuals. *Australian and New Zealand Journal of Psychiatry, 15*, 45–51.

Randell, J. (1969). Preoperative and postoperative status of male and female transsexuals. In R. Green & J. Money (Eds.), *Transsexualism and sex reassignment* (pp. 355–381). Baltimore, MD: Johns Hopkins University Press.

Randell, J. (1971). Indications for sex reassignment surgery. *Archives of Sexual Behavior, 1*, 153–161.

Sadoughi, W., Jayaram, B., & Bush, I. (1978). Postoperative changes in the self-concept of transsexuals as measured by the Tennessee Self-Concept Scale. *Archives of Sexual Behavior, 7*, 347–349.

Sorensen, T. (198la). A follow-up study of operative transsexual males. *Acta Psychiatrica Scandinavica, 63*, 486–503.

Sorensen, T. (1981b). A follow-up study of operative transsexual females. *Acta Psychiatrica Scandinavica, 64*, 50–64.

Walinder, J., Lundström, B., & Thuwe, I. (1978). Prognostic factors in the assessment of male transsexuals for sex reassignment. *British Journal of Psychiatry, 132*, 16–20.

Walinder, J., & Thuwe, 1. (1975). *A social-psychiatric follow-up study of 24 sex-reassigned transsexuals*. Gotheborg, Sweden: Scandinavian University Books.

DISCUSSION

What makes the effects of sex reassignment surgery so difficult to assess? Superficially, ascertaining whether such surgery improves the functioning of transsexual individuals would seem to be a reasonably straightforward task: One compares the adjustment of individuals who have undergone this procedure with the adjustment of those who have not. Alas, as you have probably already surmised, the answers to questions in abnormal psychology are rarely this simple.

In psychological research, the ideal method for determining the effects of a manipulation is the **experimental design.** An experiment is technically a study characterized by (1) random assignment of subjects to experimental and control groups and (2) manipulation of an independent variable to ascertain its effects on one or more dependent variables. If a study does not possess both of these features, it is not an experiment. (Many people carelessly use the term *experiment* to refer to any kind of study.) Moreover, unless a study is an experiment, we cannot draw definitive inferences regarding cause-and-effect relationships. That is, unless a study incorporates both random assignment of subjects and manipulation of an independent variable, we cannot know for certain whether the manipulation has exerted a causal effect on the dependent measure(s).

Herein lies perhaps the central stumbling block to determining the success of sex reassignment surgery. For ethical and practical reasons, random assignment of subjects to surgery and nonsurgery conditions is difficult, if not impossible. As Meyer and Reter note in their method section, "because of the serious and irreversible nature of the surgery, random assignment to the operative group was not possible" (p. 1011). In principle, one could randomly assign one group of subjects to receive surgery and another group to be placed on a waiting list for surgery. Because of difficulties in implementation, however, this approach has been used in only one major study (Mate-Kole, Freschi, & Robin, 1990), which found some support for the effectiveness of sex reassignment surgery.

Researchers who cannot use random assignment must be content to rely on a **quasi-experimental design** (sometimes referred to as a mixed design or an ex post facto design). In a quasi-experimental design, the differences between subjects in the two conditions are not manipulated by the researcher, as in an experimental design. Instead, the researcher uses the preexisting differences that subjects bring with them to the study. For example, imagine that one wished to examine differences in communication patterns between schizophrenics and normals. One would be forced to use a quasi-experimental design in such a case, because one cannot randomly assign individuals to become schizophrenic or normal; this "assignment" has already been performed by Mother Nature. Thus, in contrast to an experimental design, in which the investigator creates differences between groups, in a quasi-experimental design, group differences exist before the study has even begun. Because of the absence of random assignment, a quasi-experimental design cannot be used to draw conclusive inferences regarding the causal effects of a manipulation. Whatever causal inferences one hazards must remain tentative—and may be erroneous.

A number of potential pitfalls are associated with quasi-experimental designs. Cook and Campbell (1979) have delineated a number of threats to the internal validity of such designs. One that is especially relevant to research on sex reassignment surgery is **selection**. Selection occurs when differences in outcome between the experimental and comparison groups are due to preexisting differences between these groups rather than to the manipulation of interest (in this case, sex reassignment surgery). In the Meyer and Reter study, which used a quasi-experimental design, selection is a potentially serious threat to internal validity because the operated and unoperated transsexuals might have differed on a number of important variables. For example, individuals in the unoperated group may have self-selected against surgery or taken longer to decide whether to proceed with surgery (Fleming et al., 1980), perhaps because they possessed lower motivation for this surgery. In addition, individuals in this group may have been deemed by the treatment team to be less suitable candidates for surgery compared with those in the operated group.

As Abramowitz points out in his article, however, one could argue that whatever differences might have existed between the operated and unoperated groups should have worked in the direction of superior outcome for the operated group, because this group was presumably both more motivated and qualified for surgery. Playing devil's advocate, however, one could make a plausible case for precisely the opposite argument: Perhaps individuals in the operated group felt a more pressing need for surgery because they were more severely disturbed compared with individuals in the unoperated group. Indeed, Meyer and Reter point out that "initial adjustment scores indicate that the original operated group was slightly more distressed than the unoperated" (p.1014). These initial differences in functioning might have made sex reassignment surgery appear less effective than it actually was, because individuals in the operated group probably started from a lower baseline of psychological adjustment.

An additional threat to internal validity that is not unique to quasi-experimental designs is the **placebo effect**, which can be defined as improvement resulting from the mere expectation of improvement. In psychotherapy research, this effect is typically controlled for (albeit sometimes imperfectly) by administering a **placebo**, usually a sugar pill or other psychologically inactive manipulation (see Chapter 12). In the case of sex reassignment surgery, however, the placebo effect is in principle an insoluble problem, because there is no way to control for the knowledge that one has undergone such surgery. Consequently, greater improvements among operated than among unoperated subjects might always be explained by operated subjects' greater expectation of improvement. Moreover, individuals who have had sex reassignment surgery may "improve" on certain measures, such as self-report indices and interviews, because they feel a psychological need to justify this surgery to themselves.* In the social psychological literature, this phenomenon is known as **effort justification** (Cooper, 1980): Individuals who willingly undertake an especially arduous or painstaking procedure may exhibit improvements because they need to justify the time and suffering they have undergone.

Because of the formidable difficulties involved in recruiting appropriate comparison groups in sex reassignment research, some investigators have elected to forgo comparison groups entirely and instead have chosen to compare the adjustment of a single group of subjects before and after surgery. This methodology is often referred to as a **pre-post design.** For example, Hunt and Hampson (1980) reported that a group of 17 transsexuals exhibited improvements in economic functioning and social relationships following reassignment surgery. But here, too, possible threats to internal validity lurk menacingly. If one observes improvements in adjustment following the operation, can one confidently attribute such improvements to the effects of surgery? No. Such improvements could be due to a variety of factors other than the surgery, one of the most important being what Cook and Campbell (1979) refer to as **maturation**—that is, naturally occurring changes in subjects over time that are not produced by the manipulation in question. In other words, it is conceivable that Hunt and Hampson's subjects might have improved on their own, even without surgery. And the placebo effect and effort justification again are potential explanations for improvement in pre-post designs.

So what is the current consensus regarding the effects of sex reassignment surgery? Green and Fleming (1990) conclude that the effectiveness of sex reassignment surgery has yet to be convincingly demonstrated. They note several impediments to drawing inferences concerning the results of sex reassignment, including the fact that only a small fraction of individuals who have undergone such operations have been included in published follow-up studies. As Green and Fleming point out, it is difficult to gauge the representativeness of these individuals; perhaps the published cases were operated on by more experienced and more reputable treatment teams. If so, the research literature may overestimate the success of sex reassignment surgery.

In addition, Green and Fleming tentatively suggest that four factors are associated with a positive postsurgical out-

*Alternatively, "improvements" on such measures could result from impression management—specifically, the need to justify having undergone the surgery to others.

come: favorable preoperative psychological adjustment (which was noted by Abramowitz), preoperative counseling preparing the individual for the operation and its aftermath, good adaptation to the opposite gender role during the trial period prior to surgery, and adequate appreciation of the limitations of sex reassignment surgery. The last point merits additional discussion. Although little research concerning individuals' expectations of the consequences of sex reassignment surgery has been done, it seems plausible to conjecture that individuals who have a realistic understanding of what surgery can and cannot accomplish will be more likely to exhibit adequate postoperative functioning. Although the outcome literature on sex reassignment surgery is open to a plethora of interpretations, one fact that is not in dispute is that such surgery is rarely, if ever, a panacea for the problems of the transsexual. Even the most optimistic reading of this literature clearly indicates that difficulties in interpersonal, sexual, and occupational functioning persist for a large number of individuals. Paradoxically, individuals who are fully cognizant of these sobering facts prior to surgery may be the most likely to make a satisfactory adjustment to the often painful exigencies of life.

QUESTIONS TO STIMULATE DISCUSSION

1. Was the closing of the John Hopkins Gender Identity Clinic following the publication of Meyer and Reter's study premature? Or was it appropriate to close this clinic given the fact that the Meyer and Reter study raised legitimate questions regarding the efficacy of sex reassignment surgery? Explain your reasoning.
2. As Abramowitz notes, most investigators have found a better outcome for female-to-male than for male-to-female transsexuals. Why might this be? How could you investigate the causes of this difference?
3. Remarkably little is known about the etiology of transsexualism. If transsexualism turned out to be produced by a biological (such as hormonal) abnormality at an extremely early age (or even in utero), would this finding have implications for the treatment of this condition? Would it have implications for the use of sex reassignment surgery?
4. On what grounds, if any, should a transsexual individual be turned down for sex reassignment surgery? Is it ethical to refuse to perform this operation on an individual who has been thoroughly apprised of all the potential risks?

SUGGESTIONS FOR FURTHER READING

Fleming, M., Steinman, C., & Bocknek, G. (1980). Methodological problems in assessing sex-reassignment surgery: A reply to Meyer and Reter. *Archives of Sexual Behavior*, 9, 451–456.

The authors criticize the Meyer and Reter study on the grounds of arbitrary and misleading scoring procedures, inappropriate selection of comparison groups, and neglect of affective outcome variables. In addition, they castigate Meyer on ethical grounds for his injudicious statements to the popular press.

Green, R., & Fleming, D. T. (1990). Transsexual surgery follow-up: Status in the 1990's. *Annual Review of Sex Research*, *1*, 163–174.

Green and Fleming provide a relatively recent update of studies on the postoperative outcome of male-to-female and female-to-male transsexuals. They discuss frequent methodological problems in the literature as well as preoperative factors (including psychiatric history) that are potential moderators of successful outcome.

Lothstein, L. M. (1982). Sex reassignment surgery: Historical, bioethical, and theoretical issues. *American Journal of Psychiatry*, *139*, 417–426.

Lothstein provides a thoughtful review of the historical background and ethical issues associated with sex reassignment surgery and critiques the methodology of the major follow-up studies of postsurgical patients (including that of Meyer and Reter). The author concludes that a number of transsexuals can benefit from psychotherapy and that sex reassignment surgery "should only be considered as the last resort for a highly select group of diagnosed gender dysphoric patients" (p. 417).

Mate-Kole, C., Freschi, M., & Robin, A. (1990). A controlled study of psychological and social change after surgical gender reassignment in selected male transsexuals. *British Journal of Psychiatry*, *157*, 261–264.

The authors report the results of a 2-year follow-up study of 20 transsexuals who received sex reassignment surgery and of 20 unoperated transsexuals. They conclude that operated patients were significantly improved relative to comparison subjects in terms of several variables, including levels of neuroticism and social and sexual activity.

Money, J., & Ambinder, R. (1978). Two-year, real-life diagnostic test: Rehabilitation versus cure. In J. P. Brady & H. K. H. Brodie (Eds.), *Controversy in psychiatry* (pp. 833–845). Philadelphia: Saunders.

Money and Ambinder discuss research on the etiology, diagnosis, and clinical picture of transsexualism, along with the procedures involved in sex reassignment surgery. They contend that a 2-year trial period is a prerequisite for the proper evaluation of candidates for sex reassignment surgery.

Morris, J. (1974). *Conundrum*. New York: Harcourt Brace Jovanovich.

"I was three or perhaps four years old when I realized that I had been born into the wrong body" (p. 3) begins Jan Morris's sensitive and intimate account of her transsexualism and sex reassignment surgery in Casablanca. Her book is highly recommended for readers who wish to gain insight into the personal world of the transsexual.

Pauly, I. B. (1981). Outcome of sex reassignment surgery for transsexuals. *Australian and New Zealand Journal of Psychiatry*, *15*, 45–51.

Pauly reviews the major outcome studies of sex reassignment surgery, including the Meyer and Reter study. In addition, he reports on the postoperative outcome of two large groups of male-to-female and female-to-male transsexuals. He concludes that "a positive response to sex reassignment surgery is ten times more likely than an unsatisfactory outcome" (p. 49).

Stoller, R. J. (1978). The indications are unclear. In J. P. Brady & H. K. H. Brodie (Eds.), *Controversy in psychiatry* (pp. 846–855). Philadelphia: Saunders.

Stoller takes a less than optimistic perspective on the outcome of sex reassignment surgery. Although not advocating abandonment of sex reassignment surgery, he emphasizes the serious complications often arising from this procedure and the adjustment difficulties frequently experienced by postsurgical patients.

REFERENCES

Abraham, F. (1931). Genitalamwandlung an zwei maennlichen transvestiten. *Zeitschrift Sexualwissenschafft, 18*, 223–226.

American Psychiatric Association. (1987). *Diagnostic and statistical manual of mental disorders* (3rd ed., rev.). Washington, DC: Author.

Bootzin, R. R., Acocella, J. R., & Alloy, L. B. (1993). *Abnormal psychology: Current perspectives* (6th ed.). New York: McGraw-Hill.

Cook, T. D., & Campbell, D. T. (1979). *Quasi-experimentation: Design and analysis for field settings*. Chicago: Rand McNally.

Cooper, J. (1980). Reducing fears and increasing assertiveness: The role of dissonance reduction. *Journal of Experimental Social Psychology, 16*, 199–213.

Fleming, M., Steinman, C., & Bocknek, G. (1980). Methodological problems in assessing sex-reassignment surgery: A reply to Meyer and Reter. *Archives of Sexual Behavior, 9*, 451–456.

Gagnon, J. H. (1977). *Human sexualities*. Chicago: Scott, Foresman.

Green, R., and Fleming, D. T. (1990). Transsexual surgery follow-up: Status in the 1990's. *Annual Review of Sex Research, 1*, 163–174.

Hunt, D. D., & Hampson, J. L. (1980). Follow-up of 17 biologic male transsexuals after sex-reassignment surgery. *American Journal of Psychiatry, 137*, 432–438.

Mate-Kole, C., Freschi, M., & Robin, A. (1990). A controlled study of psychological and social change after surgical gender reassignment in selected male transsexuals. *British Journal of Psychiatry, 157*, 261–264.

Morris, J. (1974). *Conundrum*. New York: Harcourt Brace Jovanovich.

Oppenheim, G. (1986). The snowball effect of the "real-life" test for sex reassignment. *Journal of Sex Education and Therapy, 12*, 12–14.

Pauly, I. B. (1968). The current status of the change of sex operation. *Journal of Nervous and Mental Disease, 147*, 460–471.

CHAPTER

11

Is childhood depression an imaginary entity?

PRO Lefkowitz, M. M., & Burton, N. (1978). Childhood depression: A critique of the concept. *Psychological Bulletin, 85*, 716–726.

CON Kovacs, M. (1989). Affective disorders in children and adolescents. *American Psychologist, 44*, 209–215.

OVERVIEW OF THE CONTROVERSY: Monroe M. Lefkowitz and Nancy Burton conclude that depressive features in children are sufficiently normative and short-lived as to call into question the validity of the syndrome of childhood depression. Eleven years later, Maria Kovacs concludes that the existence of childhood depression has been convincingly demonstrated and that this syndrome is more enduring and malignant in its consequences than was previously believed.

CONTEXT OF THE PROBLEM

Until fairly recently, the notion that children could become clinically depressed was alien to most theorists and researchers in abnormal psychology. For example, no textbook of child psychiatry even mentioned the existence of childhood depression until 1977 (Puig-Antich & Gittelman, 1982). The longstanding assumption that children could not be clinically depressed can be traced largely to the pervasive and deeply entrenched influence of psychoanalytic thinking on American psychology and psychiatry. According to Freud and his close followers, depression can be conceptualized as anger turned inward—that is, as hostility originally aimed at another individual that has been redirected toward the self. Psychoanalytic theorists believed that a prerequisite for this redirection of anger was the presence of an intact superego, the psychic structure posited by these theorists to represent the internalized standards of morality and to be the source of guilt. But here is the catch: Most psychoanalysts thought that the superego did not appear until about the age of 5 or 6 (aficionados of psychoanalysis will recognize this as the time of the resolution of the Oedipus complex) and did not begin to crystallize fully until adolescence or early adulthood. Consequently, traditional psychoanalysts believed that children, especially young children, were incapable of experiencing depression.

Still other theorists, particularly during the 1960s and 1970s, attempted to rescue the concept of childhood depression by hypothesizing the existence of "masked depression" or "depressive equivalents" (Malmquist, 1971). These authors postulated that childhood disturbances as diverse as conduct problems, hyperactivity, enuresis (bed-wetting), excessive separation anxiety, eating difficulties, and psychosomatic complaints were actually manifestations of an underlying depressive illness. The principal problem with this position, appealing as it was to psychologists who yearned for parsimonious explanations of the causes of childhood psychopathology, was that its advocates never provided compelling evidence that the entities attributed to masked depression were in fact interrelated. With few exceptions, researchers failed to find that the psychological problems ostensibly representing different depressive "masks" were similar in terms of such variables as family history, biological measures, course and outcome, and response to treatment. Thus, most skeptics of the traditional view of childhood depression hardly found the newer concept of masked depression to be any more convincing. Interest in research on childhood depression waned and, with it, the psychological community's belief in its existence.

The 1980s and 1990s, however, witnessed an upsurge in research interest in childhood depression. Over the past decade or so, the pendulum has progressively swung to the view that children can indeed experience clinical depression. There is persuasive evidence, for example, that a number of children fulfill the same diagnostic criteria for depression as do many adults (Ryan et al., 1987). Moreover, the pioneering work of the late Joaquim Puig-Antich and his colleagues demonstrated that children who satisfy diagnostic criteria for depression exhibit several of the same biological abnormalities (such as excessive secretion of cortisol) as do depressed adults (Puig-Antich & Gittelman, 1982). In 1980, DSM-III explicitly acknowledged the existence of childhood depression with its statement that "major depression can begin at any age, including infancy" (American Psychiatric Association, 1980, p. 215). Although DSM-IV (like DSM-III and DSM-III-R) does not contain an explicit category for childhood depression, it permits clinicians to use the criteria for adult depression to diagnose depression in children.

Nevertheless, the diagnosis of childhood depression remains controversial among some theorists and researchers. For example, critics point out that simply because some children meet the diagnostic criteria for adult depression does not imply that these children necessarily have the same underlying illness as do adults. It is important to remember, these authors note, that the diagnostic criteria for psychopathological conditions are only imperfect indicators of these underlying conditions (also see the Discussion section of this chapter). The resemblances between childhood and adult depression may thus be more superficial than real. In addition, some cognitive theorists, who believe that specific cognitive structures (such as the negative self-schema discussed in the article by Kovacs in this chapter; see also Chapter 13) predispose individuals to depression, maintain that young children may not possess the capacities for abstract thinking and forethought that are prerequisites for the development of depression. Moreover, there are indications that children who fulfill the diagnostic criteria for depression may respond less positively to antidepressant medications, such as tricyclic antidepressants, than do depressed adults (Puig-Antich, Perel et al., 1987). Finally, whereas a large percentage of depressed adults exhibit such sleep abnormalities as a quicker onset of rapid eye movement (REM) sleep (the stage of sleep typically associated with vivid dreaming) after falling asleep, children and adolescents who meet diagnostic criteria for depression generally do not (Dahl & Puig-Antich, 1990). Thus, the question of the existence of childhood depression, although not as vigorously disputed as it was a decade or two ago, appears not to be entirely settled.

THE CONTROVERSY: Lefkowitz and Burton vs. Kovacs

Lefkowitz and Burton

Monroe Lefkowitz and Nancy Burton first review early conceptions of childhood depression, including the phenomenon of anaclitic depression and the notions of masked depression and "depressive equivalents," and conclude that the evidence for these entities is less than convincing. They present data on the prevalence of depressive symptoms in children and argue that these symptoms are found so commonly among apparently "normal" children that they cannot reasonably be regarded as psychopathological. In addition, they contend that these symptoms tend to be temporary and short-lived reactions to environmental circumstances rather than indications of an enduring predisposition to depression. Finally, they argue that efforts to develop reliable and valid assessment tools for childhood depression have not met with great success. Lefkowitz and Burton conclude that the diagnosis of childhood depression is premature and caution that it may be harmful given the potential consequences of stigmatization and inappropriate treatment.

Kovacs

Maria Kovacs argues that depression in childhood and adolescence is a relatively rare but extremely important psychological problem that can be reliably and validly identified using existing measures. She contends that depressed children and adolescents are at significantly heightened risk for subsequent depression, as well as for impairment in interpersonal and academic functioning. Moreover, Kovacs notes, depressed children exhibit many of the same abnormalities as do depressed adults. For example, they tend to have deficits in social skills and negative views of themselves, the world, and the future. There is also evidence that they may benefit from some of the same psychological interventions as do depressed adults. Finally, Kovacs reviews the findings of studies on the "developmental psychopathology" of childhood depression. She concludes that, although developmental effects on the expression of the clinical features of depression have not been convincingly demonstrated, these negative findings may be a consequence of methodological shortcomings.

KEY CONCEPTS AND TERMS

anaclitic depression Depressive syndrome, exhibited by children in the first several years of life, produced by sudden loss of, or separation from, a parenting figure.

developmental psychopathology Relatively new domain of abnormal psychology that takes as its major charge the study of the influence of developmental (age-related) changes in affect, cognition, and behavior on the etiology, expression, and treatment of psychological disturbances.

hospitalism Syndrome, first documented in detail by Rene Spitz, that is often observed in institutionalized children who have experienced little or no contact with parental care-givers. It typically consists of such characteristics as severe apathy and withdrawal, weight loss (often referred to as "failure to thrive"), and delayed linguistic, intellectual, and motor development.

masked depression Hypothetical condition—consisting of disturbances such as conduct problems, hyperactivity, and excessive separation anxiety—that has been posited by some authors to represent a manifestation of underlying depression in childhood.

negative self-schema Mental structure consisting of negative views regarding oneself, the world, and the future. Such a schema is theorized by proponents of cognitive models of psychopathology (see Chapter 13) to increase individuals' risk for depression in the presence of certain life events.

PREVIEW QUESTIONS

1. Why do Lefkowitz and Burton find the evidence for Spitz's construct of anaclitic depression to be unconvincing?
2. On what bases do Lefkowitz and Burton criticize the concepts of masked depression and depressive equivalents?
3. What do Lefkowitz and Burton conclude concerning the prevalence of depressive symptoms in children, and what do they view as the implications of these findings for the existence of childhood depression?
4. According to Lefkowitz and Burton, what occurs to childhood depressive symptoms over time?
5. According to Kovacs, what do we know about the consequences and prevalence of depression in children and adolescents?
6. According to Kovacs, what are some of the major deficits exhibited by depressed children and adolescents?
7. According to Kovacs, what are the principal findings from studies on the developmental psychopathology of childhood depression? In particular, what do these studies suggest about the effects of childhood depression upon the acquisition of cognitive abilities and about the continuity of depressive features over time?

MONROE M. LEFKOWITZ & NANCY BURTON

Childhood depression: A critique of the concept

The question of whether or not there is a condition such as childhood depression provides the background for this review. Indeed this question prompted the National Institute of Mental Health to hold its first conference on childhood depression in September 1975. Two opposing points of view emerged from this conference, for which the complete contents have been published by Schulterbrandt and Raskin (1977). At one pole was the position, encompassing the majority, that depression in childhood was a real condition experienced by many children and with some degree of representation in many childhood clinical samples. This point of view is buttressed by the body of literature, mostly clinical, describing this phenomenon in childhood (Anthony, 1970; Bowlby, 1960; Chapman, 1974; Cytryn & McKnew, 1972; Frommer, 1968; Malmquist, 1975; Pearce, 1977; Poznanski & Zrull, 1970; Rie, 1966; Spitz, 1946). There seems to be little question that depression in childhood exists as a clinical entity or syndrome. The treatment by pediatricians and child psychiatrists of depressive symptoms in children, in some cases with tricyclic antidepressants, lends to the diagnosis the aura of an accomplished fact. Although it is unknown how widespread is the treatment of depressed children with psychoactive drugs, the fact that it is being done was clearly established at this conference.

The point of view at the other pole, representing a rather small minority of the participants in this conference, was that childhood depression might not be a distinct clinical syndrome but a phenomenon or condition of childhood development, evanescent in nature and dissipating with time. Proponents of

SOURCE: *Psychological Bulletin*, 85(4), pp. 716–726, 1978.

this position argued that if childhood depression exists it should ultimately be measurable. If not measurable, then the probability seems high that the condition does not exist—at least in any manner that would lend itself to scientific study. The absence of a body of significant research literature pertaining to the objective measurement and epidemiological characteristics of this condition in normal prepuberal children suggests either a lack of interest in this aspect of the problem or skepticism about existence of the syndrome.

Currently, childhood depression is diagnosed by clinical evaluation based on appearance and behavior observed during the interview supplemented by case materials. Clinically, children are described as depressed if they manifest any of a wide variety of behaviors with some degree of frequency: withdrawal, crying, school failure, aggression, somatic complaints, avoidance of eye contact, enuresis, and so on. Indeed, almost any behavior that is disturbing enough to prod parents into referring a child for professional help may earn for a child a label of depressed.

The clinical studies on childhood depression present a rather strong case for the existence of this condition as an independent syndrome. Spitz's (1945, 1946) classic studies on hospitalism delineate a major class of symptoms manifested by the infant in response to separation from his mother. Intellectual, social, skeletal, and motoric retardation are the results that Spitz attributed to such separation. Spitz (1946) encompassed these symptoms in a syndrome he termed "anaclitic depression," a clinical picture similar to that found in depressed adults. In addition to the foregoing major symptoms, Spitz noted apprehension, weepiness, sadness, listlessness, immobility, and apathy. These reports made a significant impact on students of childhood depression because they described the appearance and defined the behaviors that constitute the basis for assessing this phenomenon. Although Spitz's contribution to the delineation of symptoms has ramified even into studies on the separation of infant monkeys from their mothers (Kaufman & Rosenblum, 1967, 1969; McKinney, 1977; Spencer-Booth & Hinde, 1971), his work has not gone unquestioned. Pinneau (1955) raised serious questions about Spitz's measure—the Hetzer-Wolf (1930) baby tests—of the most prominent feature of anaclitic depression, severe developmental retardation. These tests were standardized on children largely from the poorer population of Vienna. Thus the norms were not only not representative of that population (Herring, 1937) but the test was misapplied to American children because no restandardization was effected for them. More recently, Seligman (1974) has argued that anaclitic depression, based on a model of separation-loss, may be more parsimoniously explained by a model of learned helplessness in which the organism learns that there is a noncontingent relationship between any response it makes and mitigation of the trauma, that is, no response the child makes will bring back the child's mother. It should be emphasized that whether or not Spitz's (or Seligman's) model for the origin of anaclitic depression is correct, the question is independent of the empirical issue of the existence of the syndrome. Specifically, the model may indeed be ideal, but the existence of a good model does not prove the case for the existence of the syndrome.

A significant portion of the literature dealing with the clinical assessment of childhood depression may be categorized according to whether the condition is believed to occur rarely or frequently. Those viewing the malady as rare express concern about the questions of temporal stability and validity with respect to its measurement. Those viewing it as frequent argue that the syndrome can readily be diagnosed in infancy, that the symptoms are relatively invariant, and that the condition is generally underdiagnosed. If the notions of masked depression and depressive equivalents are considered in the diagnosis, childhood depression reaches a state of omnipresence.

Ossofsky (1974) stated that endogenous depression can be diagnosed in infancy and childhood and treated with imipramine. She presented a list of 12 symptoms that have traditionally characterized children with minimal brain dysfunction and stated that the pediatrician might suspect endogenous depression in any hyperactive infant, particularly when precipitate labor has been involved. Thus, inclusion of this group of children as depressed would encompass as much as one third of the childhood population and indeed make the condition frequent. More typically, the clinical manifestations of childhood depression are viewed as a characteristic mood of sadness and unhappiness, social withdrawal, self-deprecation, poor schoolwork, and somatic complaints such as headache and stomachache (Bakwin, 1972; Connell, 1972; Malmquist, 1975; McConnville, Boag, & Purohit, 1973; Poznanski & Zrull, 1970; Weinberg, Rutman, Sullivan, Penick, & Dietz, 1973). In the extensive reviews of the symptomatology of childhood depression by Kovacs and Beck (1977) and Malmquist (1975), the list of feelings and behaviors observed in depressed children becomes so broad as to necessarily include, at one time or another during development, almost all children. When the masked symptoms and depressive equivalents such as hyperactivity, aggressive behavior, psychosomatic disturbances, hypochondriasis, delinquency (Cytryn & McKnew, 1972, 1974), temper tantrums, disobedience, truancy, boredom, and restlessness (Toolan, 1962) are added to the list, then virtually no child can escape the classification. In this regard, Weinberg et al. (1973) stated that they were "impressed by the relative frequency of depressive symptoms in prepubertal children" (p. 1070), and accordingly, 63% of their subjects were diagnosed as depressed. Cytryn and McKnew (1972) also found sad affect and depressive symptoms to be "very common in children."

Critics of the notion of masked symptoms have suggested that not the disease but perhaps the doctor is masked (Depressive illness in children, 1971) or what never existed is, by this bit of semantics, made to exist (Winsberg, Note 1). Even when the rate of childhood depression is relatively low or nonexistent, the clinician may reinterpret those findings and arrive at an opposite conclusion. Thus, Varley (1974) reviewed the cases of 1,250 children at his hospital for a 3-year period, and although he found about seven percent diagnosed as depressed, he concluded that this figure was an underestimate. Similarly, van Krevelen (1971) noted that the diagnosis of depressions and manias in children under 10 years is rare and suggested that these conditions are overlooked in that age group. Manias tend to be viewed as obstreperous behavior, and natural vitality tends to disguise depression. Furthermore, he argued that some childhood neuroses could be more parsimoniously interpreted as inchoate manifestations of later affective psychosis. Similarly, Malmquist (1975) stated that "the child from 5 years of age to puberty may actually comprise the most hidden group in terms of incidence" (p. 88)

One study permits the inference that some of the variance associated with the relatively high rates of clinically diagnosed childhood depression in the United States may be attributed to differences in training of those responsible for assessment. Makita (1973) noted that there is confusion about the term *depression*, especially in Japan, where the study of psychiatry has been heavily influenced by classical German psychiatry. Thus, depression has come to mean a depressive disease of an endogenous nature, and within this connotation Makita found childhood depression to be exceedingly rare. Of the 3,000 children in Japan who came to his attention over a 10-year period, not one case bore the diagnosis of depression. Furthermore, from over 10,000 cases studied at two Tokyo hospitals, among those bearing the diagnosis of depression, "only a few were diagnosed as depression or depression-suspect in terms of depressive disease under the age of 15 and none below the age of 10" (Makita, 1973, p. 39) . This study, illustrating the very low frequency of childhood depression, tends to be unique in the clinical literature because of the author's conclusion that the condition is rare rather than masked. Many studies finding low frequencies have concluded just the opposite, that childhood depression is, for one reason or another, underdiagnosed.

But the view that this syndrome among children occurs with high frequency is hardly monolithic, though there is an increasing tendency to group the symptoms of minimal brain dysfunction (Cytryn & McKnew, 1974; Ossofsky, 1974), conduct disorder (Glaser, 1968; Toolan, 1962; Zrull, McDermott, & Poznanski, 1970), and vegetative dysfunctions (Frommer, 1968; Ling, Oftedol, & Weinberg, 1970; Renshaw, 1974) under this syndrome. Data from longitudinal and epidemiological studies suggest that the presence of symptoms of depression in children varies as a function of other factors, but particularly age. These studies using large samples of children were not specifically designed to measure the syndrome of childhood depression, but one or more of the symptoms have inadvertently been assessed as part of these studies. Thus some information is available on samples of subjects for whom psychopathology or clinical attendance did not determine subject selection. As is discussed in greater detail below, the results show wide variation in the prevalence of symptoms thought to be psychopathologic when viewed in the clinic. Perhaps the classic in this respect is the University of California Guidance Study by MacFarlane, Allen, and Honzik, 1954). These authors studied the physical, mental, and personality development of 252 children from birth to maturity. Their subjects constituted a representative sample of the Berkeley, California Survey, which included every third child born in Berkeley between January 1, 1928 and June 30, 1929. Forty-six behaviors were studied and data were presented, describing their incidence and fate for 14 periods between 21 months and 14 years. Perusal of these data illustrates the ephemeral quality of some of the symptoms that are associated with childhood depression. For example, 37% of the girls and 29% of the boys showed insufficient appetite at age 6 and this dropped to 9% and 6%, respectively, at age 9. For both sexes across 14 age groups, an average of about 14% manifested insufficient appetite. So at ages 6–8, insufficient appetite is hardly a deviant behavior, but if still present at age 9 and above, particularly for boys, it should, given the low incidence at this age, be viewed as abnormal. Another behavior, excessive reserve (withdrawal?) exhibited an average incidence of about 35% across the years measured. Since at no time did the incidence drop lower than 17%, this behavior would not meet the criterion of 10% or less established by some epidemiologists (Shepherd, Oppenheim, & Mitchell, 1971) for being considered statistically deviant. These data illustrate pointedly that any clinical diagnosis of childhood behavior should be founded on knowledge of the incidence of such behavior in the normal population and the variations in incidence as function of development.

In the New York Longitudinal Study (Chess & Thomas, 1972) the behavioral development of 136 normal children was studied from the earliest months of life onward. To date 42, or 31%, of the children (currently aged 9–15) were identified as having behavior disorders, but none of these were classified as affective. It is worthwhile to note that a rate of behavior disorders this high in a population not selected for psychopathology can scarcely be considered statistically deviant. But these data obtained from a normal sample of children help to place in clearer perspective the seemingly high rates of childhood depression found in some clinical studies. Almost all children at one time or another during development evince signs of disturbed behavior, but these problems usually tend to remit spontaneously as a function of time (Cummings, 1946; Shepherd et al., 1971; McCaffrey, Note 2). Clinical intervention, justified only if the symptoms persist, is frequently provided when it may be unwarranted, and some psychiatrists are much concerned about the danger of pharmacotherapy, particularly the use of imipramine, with "depressed" children (Eisenberg, 1964; Winsberg, Note 1).

Perhaps the reason the diagnosis of childhood depression tends, in clinical practice, to be relatively frequent is the belief that the condition is rare and consequently significant when manifested. Were the clinician to possess as a basis for comparison the data from epidemiological surveys on childhood depression, the diagnosis and treatment of any unselected case appearing in the clinic might be notably different. Presumably, the knowledge that these symptoms are fairly common in any population of children during the period of development would tend to mitigate the salience of these symptoms. Sampling bias occurs because the clinician sees only those children referred, but many of the behaviors he sees in the clinic are broadly distributed among the general childhood population. The same behavior that is salient enough to warrant a child's referral for some parents may not be so for other parents. Moreover, the likelihood is great that referral behavior varies with parents' education and socioeconomic status. Theoretically, one would also expect temporal variability, for any one child and for groups of children, in the manifestation of symptoms classified as depressive. It is of overriding importance, if the classification of childhood depression is to have any validity, to be able to differentiate this syndrome from transient developmental phenomena visible in normal children. In this respect, Kanner (1960) noted that the exaggerated psychopathologic significance attached to single behaviors arises from the use of statistics contributed by selected groups of children from child guidance clinics and juvenile courts. In the general population of children, the occurrence and psychiatric fate of these so-called symptoms are unknown.

Kanner's observation demonstrates the need not only for data on prevalence but also for longitudinal data. Such symptoms, as Shepherd et al. (1971) noted, "may represent no more than a temporary response to external factors, or even a phase of normal development rather than a disorder of mental health, any assessment of such conduct must take the duration into account" (p. 17). Quay (1972) stated that with respect to the definition of any disorder, the first step is to demonstrate that there is in fact a constellation of behaviors that can be reliably observed in one or more situations and defines the disorder. Once a definition such as depressive disorder is applied to a child, information about etiology and outcome is necessary in order for the classification to have any clinical value. Ideally, conditions antecedent to childhood depression, such as parental rejection, should be part of the body of information generated a posteriori by the classification. Also, information about relations with peers, school performance, the likelihood of responding to a certain kind of treatment, and future behavior should be predictable from a meaningful diagnosis. Frequently, classification schemes in psychopathology lead to unwarranted inferences about underlying disorders and to circular reasoning: The disorder is inferred from the symptom and then it is claimed that the symptom is produced by the disorder.

The construct of childhood depression has not yet been subjected to the tortuous taxonomic process that, in the arena of adult depression, has produced what Kendell (1976) termed "contemporary confusion." Kendell described simple typologies containing as many as five categories of depression, tiered typologies, and dimensional systems. Until recently most of the classification studies of adult depression were based on inpatient data and on relatively unreliable clinical ratings, two features militating against a representative picture of general depressive illness. Currently, our knowledge of childhood depression is similarly almost entirely derived from clinical studies. Consequently, before the taxonomists again construct elaborate systems based on unrepresentative samples, information about the prevalence of symptoms of childhood depression needs to be acquired from normal children. Tempering the exaggerated psychopathologic significance noted by Kanner, attached to symptoms observed in a clinical sample, such data would enable the clinician to place any clinical case in proper perspective with regard to the incidence and distribution of the putatively deviant behavior in the general child population.

Although there have been no epidemiological studies of depressive symptoms in childhood, there have been at least two good epidemiological studies of deviant behavior among children that were treated with some of the behaviors frequently classified as depressive symptoms. Lapouse (1966) studied 482 children ages 6–12, randomly selected from households that were systematically sampled in Buffalo, New York. Mothers and teachers were interviewed. The results showed that over 40% of the children were reported to have had seven or more fears or worries, 20% had been enuretic in the recent past, about 50% were overactive, and 10% showed loss of temper one or more times a day. A statistically significant excess of high scores was found among the 6–8 group when compared with the 9–12 group. The author concluded,

> The strikingly high prevalence of so-called symptomatic behaviors, their excessive presence in younger as contrasted to older chil-

dren, and the weak association between these behaviors and adjustment give rise to the question whether behavior deviations are truly indicative of psychiatric disorder or whether they occur as transient developmental phenomena in essentially normal children. (p. 599)

Increased age was found to be the most important demographic factor associated with a decreased amount of deviation in behavior. Deviant behavior was related to maladjustment, but only in the low socioeconomic group. This finding has implications for the definition of childhood depression founded on a clinic sample. If that sample is not representative of the distribution of socioeconomic status in the general child population, then the clinician may formulate a spurious picture of the incidence of the problem among children.

Another pertinent epidemiological study, reported by Werry and Quay (1971), concerned "The Prevalence of Behavior Symptoms in Younger Elementary School Children." The purpose of the study was to obtain prevalence data on 55 behavior symptoms commonly found in child guidance clinic populations as they occur in schoolchildren in kindergarten through second grade. About 96% (1,753 children) of the entire population in these three grades in the Urbana, Illinois school system received teacher ratings on the Quay-Peterson Behavior Problem Checklist. Of these 55 symptoms, at least 16 have been classified by various writers (Cytryn & McKnew, 1974; Hetherington & Martin, 1972; Malmquist, 1975; Poznanski & Zrull, 1970) as symptoms of childhood depression: for example, fixed expression, lack of emotional reactivity, feelings of inferiority, crying over minor annoyances and hurts, depression, chronic sadness. The present authors have computed for each sex in this normal population the range and average prevalence of these 16 behaviors seemingly associated with depression. For 926 boys, the range of prevalence was 7.2%–46.3%, M = 22%; for 827 girls, the range was 4.6%–41.4%, M = 18%. These data are instructive because they suggest that approximately 20% of the general child population has been reliably judged to possess the symptoms of depressive disorder observed in clinical samples. Indeed, such a rate has been reported by Pearce (1977) for a sample of 547 children attending a child psychiatric clinic in England. Of this sample, 23% displayed the symptom of depression. Pearce concluded that depressive disorder can be expected to occur in 10%–20% of children attending a psychiatric clinic. Yet this rate, viewed within epidemiological guidelines, is not statistically deviant (Shepherd et al., 1971).

When compared with other childhood disorders, the rate of depressive symptoms of 20% in the general child population is quite high. For example, the prevalence of childhood psychosis estimated in the general population is from .02% (2:10,000) to .008% (8:100,000). In clinic referrals the rate is estimated at 5%–9%. For mental retardation the estimate in the population is about 3%. A conclusion reached by Werry and Quay (1971) was that "the prevalence of many symptoms of psychopathology in the general 5–8 year old population is quite high and their individual diagnostic value is therefore very limited" (p. 142). Inasmuch as these kinds of behaviors tend to become less frequent with age, what we may be observing, if this 20% rate of depressive symptoms in the population of children is at all representative, is a transient developmental phenomenon, which if left alone will diminish with the passage of time.

Even in cases of loss or separation, reports indicate that although short-term distress may occur, separation is not associated with long-term disorder (Rutter, 1971). Depression is not so much a concomitant of separation as it is of the family disturbance accompanying separation (Caplan & Douglas, 1969). Based on a survey of the pertinent studies, Hetherington and Martin (1972) concluded that most children recover from what is thought to be a depression-withdrawal phase in several weeks and show normal interest and responsiveness to their environment. These observations on humans are paralleled by results of experiments on separation in monkeys (Kaufman & Rosenblum, 1967; McKinney, 1977). Following separation from their mothers, monkeys seem to go through a depressive-withdrawal phase in which many behaviors akin to human dejection are manifested. Subsequently, however, recovery and return to a normal level of behavior occur. On the other hand, Spencer-Booth and Hinde (1971) found that even after a brief separation from their mothers, rhesus monkeys showed effects such as decreased locomotion, 24 months later. From their report, however, it is unclear if these effects were statistically significant when compared with those from nonseparated controls. Various theories have been proposed to explain the depressed behavior exhibited by children, albeit transient, seemingly associated with parent–child separation. For Spitz (1946), separation resulted in anaclitic depression due to the loss of the object (mother) on whom the child was dependent for succor and emotional support. Lewinsohn (1974) proposed that separation eventuates in a lowered rate of response-contingent positive reinforcement. Inasmuch as the parents are the chief dispensers of such reinforcement, their absence reduces the density, which results in a low rate of activity and verbal behavior. Thus, the depressed child may be considered to be on a prolonged extinction schedule. For Seligman (1974), separation results in learned helplessness. Nothing the child can do will bring back the parents. In effect, the child learns that responding and reinforcement are independent, and a deficit in response initiation ensues. Activity is depressed because the incentive for instrumental responding is reduced. Separation from the source of reinforcement proves to be an uncontrollable aversive event (Miller & Seligman, 1975).

A third epidemiological study (Shepherd et al., 1971) furnished data on a group of behaviors that play a prominent role in the practice of child psychiatry. Among these behaviors were several that are found in the syndrome of childhood depression. This survey, employing parent and teacher questionnaires, obtained data on approximately 45 behaviors for over 6,000 boys and girls. The subjects ranged in age from 5 to 15 years and resided in the County of Buckinghamshire, England. Guided by the epidemiological method of inquiry, the authors' approach to morbidity with respect to the behaviors studied was that psychopathology should be regarded as statistical deviation from a norm rather than as an independent entity. Consequently, the investigators set 10% as a criterion, so any behavior occurring at an intensity or frequency that encompassed 10% or less of either sex at any of the age groups would be classified as deviant for that age and sex. Any behavior not conforming to this criterion was not regarded as deviant. The results showed a "surprisingly high prevalence" of many behaviors generally regarded as symptoms of psychopathology in children. In accord with the epidemiological findings of Lapouse (1966) and Werry and Quay (1971), the data strongly suggest that the incidence of many of these behaviors is a direct function of age and may be a transient manifestation of developmental reactions to stress in essentially normal children. For example, crying, putatively a symptom of childhood depression, diminishes dramatically with age: At age 6 approximately 18% were reported to cry "two or three times a week," but at puberty only about 2% were reported to do so. Disobedience, one of the supposed masked symptoms of depression (Toolan, 1962), prevailed at a rate of about 10% between the age of 5 years and puberty and was unrelated to age variation. On the other hand, withdrawal, another symptom of depression, was characteristic of less than 3% of the sample—it was thus considered statistically deviant—and was also unassociated with age or sex. Shepherd et al. (1971) concluded that a composite picture of their data "indicates that behavior suggestive of emotional ill health in children tends to recede spontaneously in response to developmental changes or life circumstances" (p. 162).

The foregoing study illustrates well the disparate positions from which clinicians and epidemiologists approach the phenomenon of childhood depression. From the perspective of the former, the condition is a disease process and an independent entity; from the perspective of the latter, the symptoms of childhood depression are psychopathologic only if they are statistically deviant from a norm and even then must be interpreted in the context of age and situational variables with which they may be associated.

Although several attempts have been made to introduce some rigor into the clinical classification of depression in childhood (see, e.g., Cytryn & McKnew, 1972; Kohn & Rosman, 1973; McConville et al., 1973; Group for the Advancement of Psychiatry, Note 3), only three studies that have attempted to assess depression in samples of normal children have come to our attention. The first and most important of the three with regard to the development of method was conducted by Wiggins and Winder (1961). Concerned with adjustment in preadolescent boys, the authors developed a sociometric measure, the Peer Nomination Inventory, to assess this condition. The subjects were 710, fourth, fifth, and sixth grade boys in a middle-class community. Social adjustment was reflected in four behavior systems: aggression, dependency, withdrawal, and depression. The method used was a modification of the "guess who" technique developed by Hartshorne, May, and Maller (1929), in which statements in the form of pictures representing character traits were presented to a child who was asked to guess who among his classmates the picture described. Wiggins and Winder assembled 3,290 behavior statements, which judges were required to sort, on the basis of unanimous agreement, into categories reflecting the four behavior systems. To aid in their sorting task, the judges were provided with working definitions. Thus the depressed child, "by implication or act, can be considered as being overly moralistic in his self-evaluation and, as a consequence, is 'unhappy.' He tends to be described by others as sad, feeling inadequate, remorseful, excessively self-critical, accepts blame, etc." (p. 650). Based on this definition, 144 items were categorized under depression, from which, following extensive item analyses, 12 were culled to measure this behavior system. Subsequent to studies of the psychometric properties of the four scales, the scales were subjected to a factor analysis in which the first two centroid factors accounted for 65% of the total variance. The depression variable was not uniquely defined. Temporal stability coefficients were determined after 1 year for 339 subjects; the Pearson r for depression was .37. On the face of it, the magnitude of this correlation coefficient is not very encouraging, yet this datum may reflect the ephemeral quality of childhood depression and its transitory nature over a 1-year period. A second factor analysis indicated that the depression items have definitive loadings on the factor of social isolation (withdrawal). The authors concluded that their exploratory efforts to construct a depression scale were largely unsuccessful. More recently, Wiggins (Note 4) stated,

> This particular scale was developed at a time when considerably less was known about depression, particularly depression in children. Consequently, the somewhat disappointing psychometric properties of the scale may reflect more on the manner in which we conceptualized the category than on the feasibility of developing such a category.

The second study (Siegelman, 1966) of normal school children in which childhood depression was measured also used the Peer Nomination Inventory.

Siegelman administered the inventory to 113 fourth, fifth, and sixth grade middle-class boys and generated a 58 × 58 correlation matrix on which a principal components factor analysis was performed. Examined were five major adjustment areas—aggression, dependency, withdrawal, depression, and likability—each containing 12 items, except likability, which contained 8 plus 2 additional items relating to socioeconomic status. Four factors, accounting for 65% of the total factor variance, emerged: aggression-dependency, withdrawal-depression, likability, and crying. Four of the original depression items constituted the last factor. Interestingly, the likability factor correlated negatively both with crying (–.25) and with withdrawal-depression (–.35). In contradistinction to Wiggins and Winder (1961), Siegelman believed that withdrawal-depression is a potentially meaningful factor.

A third and more recent attempt to measure childhood depression was conducted by Kovacs and Beck (1977) and their collaborators. The short form of the Beck Depression Inventory (BDI) (Beck & Beck, 1972) containing 13 items was administered to 63 seventh and eighth grade parochial school children in a group setting. The authors found that 33% of the sample fell into the "moderate to severe" depression classification. Teacher ratings of classroom performance related inversely to depression scores. Inasmuch as 33% of this sample was classified as depressed, the authors questioned if this could reflect "genuine" depression or, more likely, the tapping of developmental phenomena in this age group. Certainly, if the incidence criterion used by Shepherd et al. (1971) of 10% or less of the sample were applied, 33% depressed would hardly be viewed as statistically deviant. Actually these data are consonant with those generated by the larger epidemiological studies (Lapouse, 1966; Shepherd et al., 1971; Werry & Quay, 1971) and the New York Longitudinal Study (Chess & Thomas, 1972), which showed an incidence of depression symptoms in 20%–40% of their samples.

CONCLUDING COMMENTS

Clinical studies of children selected on the basis of psychopathology show that childhood depression is a phenomenon of concern, whereas studies of normal children indicate that these same symptoms of depression prevail at a rate too high to be considered statistically deviant. Evidence adduced from the research literature to support the concept of a syndrome of early childhood depression is insufficient and insubstantial. Consequently, diagnosis of this presumed condition in children would appear to be premature and treatment unwarranted. The possibility of producing iatrogenic effects on the child, the risk of masking other problems, and the unknown effects on parents underscore the need for rigorous research of this question.

Examination of the literature on childhood depression demonstrates that no reliable and valid method for assessing this putative condition has been developed. Whatever epidemiological evidence has been obtained on this topic is indirect and culled from responses to questionnaires administered to parents and/or teachers for the purpose of obtaining other information about children. The one attempt to develop a peer rating measure of childhood depression (Wiggins & Winder, 1961) produced a technique possessing low reliability and impure factor structure. However, further work with this method (Siegelman, 1966) suggested that it might be more promising than had been originally judged. Were the psychometric properties of such an instrument to be perfected, it could be used both epidemiologically and longitudinally to assess the prevalence and fate of supposed symptoms of depression in a normal population of children. Without supporting normative data, the notion of a syndrome of childhood depression rests largely on surmise.

NOTES

1. Winsberg, B. Personal communication, April 13, 1976.
2. McCaffrey, I. *Elementary school children with persistent emotional disturbances*. Albany, N.Y.: New York State Department of Mental Hygiene, December 1974.
3. Group for the Advancement of Psychiatry. *Psychopathological disorders in childhood* (Report No. 62). New York: Group for the Advancement of Psychiatry, 1966.
4. Wiggins, J. S. Personal communication, March 10, 1976.

REFERENCES

Anthony, E. J. Behavior disorders. In P. H. Mussen (Ed.), *Carmichael's manual of child psychology* (3rd ed., Vol. 2). New York: Wiley, 1970.

Bakwin, H. Depression—A mood disorder in children and adolescents. *Maryland State Medical Journal*, 1972, *21*, 55–61.

Beck, A. T., & Beck, R. W. Screening depressed patients in family practice: A rapid technique. *Postgraduate Medicine*, 1972, *52*, 81–85.

Bowlby, J. Grief and mourning in infancy and early childhood. *Psychoanalytic Study of the Child*, 1960, *15*, 9–52.

Caplan, M., & Douglas, V. Incidence of parental loss in children with depressed mood. *Journal of Child Psychology and Psychiatry*, 1969, *10*, 225–232.

Chapman, A. H. *Management of emotional problems of children and adolescents* (2nd ed.). Philadelphia, Pa.: Lippincott, 1974.

Chess, S., & Thomas, A. Differences in outcome with early intervention in children with behavior disorders. In M. Roff, L. N. Robins, & M. Pollack (Eds.), *Life history research in psychopathology*. Minneapolis: University of Minnesota Press, 1972.

Connell, H. M. Depression in childhood. *Child Psychiatry and Human Development*, 1972, *4*, 71–85

Cummings, J. D. A follow-up study of emotional symptoms in school children. *British Journal of Psychiatry*, 1946, *16*, 163.

Cytryn, L., & McKnew, D. H. Proposed classification of childhood depression. *American Journal of Psychiatry*, 1972, *129*, 149–155.

Cytryn, L., & McKnew, D. H. Factors influencing the changing clinical expression of the depressive process in children. *American Journal of Psychiatry*, 1974, *131*, 879–881.

Depressive illness in children. *British Medical Journal*, 1971, *2*, 237.

Eisenberg, L. Role of drugs in treating disturbed children. *Children*, 1964, *11*, 167–173.

Frommer, E. Depressive illness in childhood. *British Journal of Psychiatry*, 1968, Special Publication No. 2, pp. 117–123.

Glaser, K. Masked depression in children and adolescents. In S. Chess & A. Thomas (Eds.), *Annual progress in child psychiatry and child development*. New York: Brunner/Mazel, 1968.

Hartshorne, H., May, M., & Maller, J. B. *Studies in the nature of character: Vol. II. Studies in service and self-control*. New York: Macmillan, 1929.

Herring, A. An experimental study of the reliability of the Buhler Baby Tests. *Journal of Experimental Education*, 1937, 6, 147–160.

Hetherington, E. M., & Martin, B. Family interaction and psychopathology in children. In H. C. Quay & J S Werry (Eds.), *Psychopathological disorders of children*. New York: Wiley, 1972.

Hetzer, H., & Wolf, K. Baby tests. In C. Buhler & H. Hetzer (Eds.), *The first year of life*. New York: John Day, 1930.

Kanner. L. Do behavioral symptoms always indicate psychopathology? *Journal of Child Psychology and Psychiatry*, 1960, *1*, 17–25.

Kaufman, I. C., & Rosenblum, L. A. The reaction to separation in infant monkeys: Anaclitic depression and conservation-withdrawal. *Psychosomatic Medicine*, 1967, *29*, 648–675.

Kaufman, I. C., & Rosenblum, L. A. Effects of separation from mother on the emotional behavior of infant monkeys. *Annals of the New York Academy of Science*, 1969, *159*, 681–695.

Kendell, R. The classification of depressions: A review of contemporary confusion. *British Journal of Psychiatry*, 1976, *129*, 15–28.

Kohn, M., & Rosman, B. L. A two-factor model of emotional disturbance in the young child—Validity and screening efficiency. *Journal of Child Psychology and Psychiatry*, 1973, *14*, 31–56.

Kovacs, M., & Beck, A. T. An empirical clinical approach towards a definition of childhood depression. In J. G. Schulterbrandt & A. Raskin (Eds.), *Depression in children: Diagnosis, treatment, and conceptual models*. New York: Raven Press, 1977.

Lapouse, R. The epidemiology of behavior disorders in children. *American Journal of Diseases of Children*, 1966, *111*, 594–599.

Lewinsohn, P. M. A behavioral approach to depression. In R. J. Freidman & M. M. Katz (Eds.), *The psychology of depression: Contemporary theory and research*. Washington, D.C.: Winston, 1974.

Ling, W., Oftedol, G., & Weinberg, W. Depressive illness in childhood presenting as a severe headache. *American Journal of Diseases of Children*, 1970, *120*, 122–124.

MacFarlane, J. W., Allen, L., & Honzik, M. P. *A developmental study of the behavior problems of normal children between 21 months and 14 years*. Berkeley: University of California Press, 1954.

Makita, K. The rarity of "depression" in childhood. *Acta Psychiatrica*, 1973, *40*, 37–44.

Malmquist, C. P. Depression in childhood. In F. Flach & S. Draghi (Eds.), *The nature and treatment of depression*. New York: Wiley, 1975.

McConville, B. J ., Boag, L. C., & Purohit, A. P. Three types of childhood depression. *Canadian Psychiatric Association Journal*, 1973, *18*, 133–138.

McKinney, W. Animal biological/behavior models relevant to depressive and affective behaviors in humans. In J. G. Schulterbrandt & A. Raskin (Eds.), *Depression in children: Treatment and conceptual models*. New York: Raven Press, 1977.

Miller, W., & Seligman, M. E. P. Depression and learned helplessness in man. *Journal of Abnormal Psychology*, 1975, *84*, 228–238.

Ossofsky, H. Endogenous depression in infancy and childhood. *Comprehensive Psychiatry*, 1974, *15*, 19–25.

Pearce, J. Depressive disorders in childhood. *Journal of Child Psychology and Psychiatry*, 1977, *18*, 79–83.

Pinneau, S. R. Infantile disorders of hospitalism and anaclitic depression. *Psychological Bulletin*, 1955, *52*, 429–452.

Poznanski, E., & Zrull, J. P. Childhood depression: Clinical characteristics of overtly depressed children. *Archives of General Psychiatry*, 1970, *23*, 8–15.

Quay, H. C. Patterns of aggression, withdrawal and immaturity. In H. C. Quay & J. S. Werry (Eds.), *Psychopathological disorders of childhood*. New York: Wiley, 1972.

Renshaw, D. C. Suicide and depression in children. *Journal of School Health*, 1974, *44*, 487–489.

Rie, H. E. Depression in childhood. *Journal of the American Academy of Child Psychiatry*, 1966, *5*, 653–685.

Rutter, M. Parent–child separation: Psychological effects on the children. *Journal of Child Psychology and Psychiatry*, 1971, *12*, 233–260.

Schulterbrandt, J. G., & Raskin, A. (Eds.). *Depression in children: Diagnosis, treatment, and conceptual models*. New York: Raven Press, 1977.

Seligman, M. E. P. Depression and learned helplessness. In R. J. Griedman & M. M. Katz (Eds.), *The psychology of depression: Contemporary theory and research*. Washington, D.C.: Winston, 1974.

Shepherd, M.,Oppenheim, B., & Mitchell, S. *Childhood behavior and mental health*. New York: Grune & Stratton, 1971.

Siegelman, M. Psychometric properties of the Wiggins and Winder Peer Nomination Inventory. *Journal of Psychology*, 1966, *64*, 143–149.

Spencer-Booth, Y., & Hinde, R. A. Effects of brief separations from mothers during infancy on behavior of rhesus monkeys 6–24 months later. *Journal of Child Psychology and Psychiatry*, 1971, *12*, 157–172.

Spitz, R. A. Hospitalism: An inquiry into the genesis of psychiatric conditions in early childhood. In *The psychoanalytic study of the child* (Vol. 1). New York: International Universities Press, 1945.

Spitz, R. A. Anaclitic depression. In *The psychoanalytic study of the child* (Vol. 2). New York: International Universities Press, 1946.

Toolan, J. M. Depression in children and adolescents. *American Journal of Orthopsychiatry*, 1962, *32*, 404–414.

van Krevelen, D. A. Cyclothymias in childhood. *Acta Paedopsychiatrica*, 1971, 38, 202–210.

Varley, J. E. Depression in prepubertal children. *Developmental Medicine and Child Neurology*, 1974, *16*, 689–690.

Weinberg, W. A., Rutman, J., Sullivan, L., Penick, E. C., & Dietz, S. G. Depression in children referred to an educational diagnostic center: Diagnosis and treatment. *Journal of Pediatrics*, 1973, *83*, 1065–1072.

Werry, J. S., & Quay, H. C. The prevalence of behavior symptoms in younger elementary school children. *American Journal of Orthopsychiatry*, 1971, *41*, 136–143.

Wiggins. J. S., & Winder, C. L. The Peer Nomination Inventory: An empirically derived sociometric measure of adjustment on preadolescent boys. *Psychological Reports*, 1961, 9(Monograph Supplement 5V9), 643–677.

Zrull, J. P., McDermott, J. F., & Poznanski, E. Hyperkinetic syndrome: The role of depression. *Child Psychiatry and Human Development*, 1970, *1*, 33–40.

MARIA KOVACS

Affective disorders in children and adolescents

Research on the affective disorders in the preadult years, which has been proceeding at an unprecedented pace over the past 10 years, has been bolstered by several factors. First, increased precision in diagnostic criteria and improved methods of assessment have made subject selection easier and more uniform in psychiatric and psychologic studies. Second, explanations of "adult" depression, based on cognitive and behavior theories, prompted questions as to whether these theories could also explain mood disorders in the younger years. And last, "developmental psychopathology" as a new field of inquiry fast embraced the study of the affective disorders in the preadult years and focused greater attention on this area.

There is now compelling evidence from a diversity of studies that school-aged children and adolescents do experience depression, whether depression is defined as a painful emotion or negative mood (a *symptom*); an aggregate of negative mood and associated complaints such as hopelessness, worthlessness, suicidal wishes, and lethargy (a *syndrome*); or a depressive syndrome with a characteristic symptom pattern and duration that impairs the person's functioning and meets other requirements for a diagnosis as well (a psychiatric *disorder*; for reviews, see Digdon & Gotlib, 1985; Puig-Antich, 1986). Some information also exists about mania among juveniles, which consists of abnormally elated or irritable mood and pathologically excessive mental, physical, and social activity. However, the study of manic disorders has been constrained by the fact that these conditions are both rare and difficult to diagnose in this age-group (for a review, see Strober, Hanna, & McCracken, 1989).

As will be documented further on, affective disorders are neither normal developmental phenomena nor transient disturbances that children "outgrow." Moreover, these disorders appear to have a negative impact on social and educational functioning. Their etiology, mechanisms, correlates, and long-term consequences must therefore be more thoroughly understood. And there is a particularly urgent need for the development and testing of effective treatments that are suitable for children and adolescents who manifest affective disorders.

The purpose of the present article is to highlight recent developments in our knowledge about the affective disorders and related syndromes in the preadult years, using the general focus of investigations as an organizing principle. It is not meant to be a comprehensive review of the field. With the exception of treatment-outcome studies, only nonbiologic investigations will be considered. Because the bulk of extant work

Preparation of this article was supported by Grant MH-33990 from the National Institute of Mental Health, Health and Human Services Administration, and by a grant from the W. T. Grant Foundation.

I am grateful to the following individuals for their helpful comments on a previous version of this article: David Brent, Constantine Gatsonis, Judith Marsh, and James Stewart.

SOURCE: *American Psychologist*, 44(2), pp. 209–215, February 1989.

concerns the depressions, the manic disorders will only be touched on briefly. Studies with a psychiatric and diagnostic emphasis will be examined first. Such studies typically involve identification, description, and validation of psychopathologic disorders and therefore lay the ground for subsequent work. Studies that test hypotheses and causal explanations of depression will be examined next. Because these studies seek to impose a theory on clinical data, they move beyond psychiatric description. Developmental psychopathology of the affective disorders will be examined last. Developmental perspectives apply both to psychiatric description and hypothesis testing and can link these areas. For each of the three approaches, conceptual and methodologic problems will be noted, and recommendations will be made concerning future research.

PSYCHIATRIC AND DIAGNOSTIC STUDIES

The Findings

Recent data on the existence, characteristics, and validity of affective disorders in the preadult years have been generated by studies in which young patients were diagnosed by means of specific (operational) psychiatric criteria. The fact that the most widely used diagnostic systems, and particularly the *Diagnostic and Statistical Manual of Mental Disorders* (third edition; *DSM-III*, American Psychiatric Association, 1980), were designed primarily for adults has made these studies the object of considerable criticism.

Notwithstanding the shortcomings of available diagnostic criteria, investigations of outpatient and inpatient samples do converge in their findings that the depressive disorders in the preadult years can be identified reliably and are more persistent and psychologically and functionally more impairing than had been thought hitherto (for a review, see Puig-Antich,1986). School-aged children and adolescents can experience both "major" and "minor" variants of depression (that is, major depressive disorder as well as dysthymic disorder, which is a milder and presumably less impairing but chronic form of depression). An episode of major depression lasts up to 7–9 months on the average, while an episode of dysthymia may exceed 3 years. The depression can manifest with or without psychotic features, and endogenous or melancholic subtypes can also be identified (Kovacs, 1985; Puig-Antich, 1986).

Although the association between depression and suicidal behaviors in younger age groups is not as firmly established as it is among adults, there are indications that suicidal children are often depressed (Pfeffer, 1981). By adolescence, depressive disorders and suicidal behaviors generally go hand in hand, which further underscores the seriousness of juvenile-onset affective disturbances (e.g., Brent et al., 1988; Robins & Alessi, 1985). Another feature of the clinical picture of depressed youths is that many of them have multiple psychiatric diagnoses, commonly referred to as psychiatric comorbidity. The most prevalent comorbid conditions are anxiety disorders and conduct disorders. These comorbid disorders can make it more difficult to diagnose and treat the depression and could also have repercussions for long-term outcome (Kovacs, 1985; Kovacs, Paulauskas, Gatsonis, & Richards, 1988; Puig-Antich, 1982).

Youngsters with major depression or dysthymia will recover from the episode of disturbance for which they were referred for treatment. However, they may show residual impairment in social functioning and their educational progress and learning may be slowed down as well (Kovacs, Gatsonis, Marsh, & Richards, 1988; Puig-Antich et al., 1985). In addition, about two thirds of juveniles with a history of depression will probably develop a new episode of depression while they are still in their teens; about 20% of a given sample may develop bipolar disorder (some form of mania alternating or intermixed with depression) before they reach adulthood; and these youngsters are also likely to develop other psychiatric conditions as complications of the depression (Kovacs & Gatsonis, 1989; Strober & Carlson, 1982).

In spite of the obvious need, scant data exist at present to guide the choice of treatments. Controlled psychotherapy trials with well-defined patient groups have not been conducted. Although some children and adolescents with depressive disorders are treated on an inpatient basis, there is no empirically based information to indicate under what circumstances inpatient management may be more desirable or effective than outpatient care. Findings from pharmacotherapy trials are puzzling, because although a large portion of children recover from their depression when they are treated with antidepressant medication, youngsters seem to be equally responsive to pharmacologically inert placebo and tricyclic antidepressants (Puig-Antich et al., 1987).

Fortunately, clinical depression in childhood does not appear to be very frequent in the general population. Prevalence rates for major depression (and dysthymia) were estimated in recent community surveys of juveniles as between 2% and 5%, depending on age (Anderson, Williams, McGee, & Silva, 1987; Kashani et al., 1987). Among psychiatrically referred samples, the rates of depressive disorders can be quite variable and would generally be much higher.

Compared with the depressions, there is scant information on the psychosocial aspects and functional outcomes of mania (or its milder form, hypomania), and a substantial portion of the information is from case reports. This is partly a reflection of the fact that for reasons that are not fully understood, manic disorders are very rare prior to puberty and the years of adolescence (Strober et al., 1989). Moreover, it is very difficult to diagnose mania in the juvenile years, and its more severe forms are often mistaken for schizophrenia. It is nonetheless known that the disorder is episodic, that it may be managed by pharmacologic means, that early-onset depression may be a risk factor for it, and that it may pose a risk for suicide (e.g., Kovacs & Gatsonis, 1989; Strober et al., 1989; Weller, Weller, Tucker, & Fristad, 1986). Unfortunately, controlled treatment outcome studies of youngsters with bipolar disorder are lacking and the usefulness of nonpharmacologic agents has not been systematically explored. Much work remains to be done before the full range of psychosocial correlates of these conditions are elucidated and their effects on the youngsters' social functioning are thoroughly understood.

Research Problems and Possible Directions

Some of the major shortcomings in our knowledge of the psychiatry of juvenile-onset affective disorders derive from limitations of the medical model, problems of psychiatric classification (nosology), constraints in clinical data gathering, and sampling biases. To start with, the explanatory model implicit in psychiatric diagnosis, commonly referred to as the medical model, entails several assumptions about the nature of functional psychiatric disorders. It is assumed that a psychiatric disorder represents an abnormal state of functioning that has a characteristic symptom picture and a (usually predictable) clinical course, responds differentially to various treatments, has distinct biologic correlates, and has a characteristic family history (e.g., Feighner et al., 1972).

Although this model has inspired important research, its major limitation is the implicit emphasis on internal (endogenous) biologic factors or vulnerabilities that predispose to psychiatric illness and are presumed to be the primary determinants of course and outcome. Insufficient attention has been paid in the model to alternative mechanisms of recovery and to psychosocial factors that, alone or in combination with "intrinsic" aspects of the condition itself, may affect the severity and the long-term outcome of a disorder.

The medical-psychiatric model is also constrained by the fact that its primary goal is to describe and organize certain phenomena. Therefore, it is difficult to derive hypotheses from it concerning cause-and-effect associations that could then be subjected to scientific study. This problem is further compounded because the relations among the components of the medical model have not been specified. For example, what is the interface between clinical course and biologic correlates of a disorder, and why? As another example, whereas it is widely accepted that early-onset affective disorders may reflect familially transmitted (perhaps genetic) vulnerability, it is unclear what mechanisms could underlie such an association. It is also hard to believe that the posited sequence is a simple "if . . . then" process.

The medical-psychiatric model has not stimulated sufficient work on the logic of present-day nosology, including better ways to describe disorders and to organize classes or groups of disorders into a coherent classificatory system. Because it is often unclear how one class of disorders is related to another, proper case selection for studies becomes difficult. Some of these dilemmas stem from the fact that for most psychiatric diagnoses, there are no singularly necessary and jointly sufficient clinical (or other) features that define the condition. The relations among various disorders are neither mutually exclusive nor clearly hierarchical (e.g., a patient can have several disorders, and it is usually a matter of clinical judgment as to which is more important). Therefore, as a classification, psychiatric diagnosis exemplifies the concept of prototypical class. This explains why some depressed patients may be more characteristic of the prototype (e.g., the *DSM-III* criteria for depression) than others or why features of mania and schizophrenia may overlap. Further development of the logic whereby prototypical classes are organized into a system, and the extent to which diagnostic classes can overlap, could help to clarify puzzling issues, such as psychiatric comorbidity (Kovacs & Gatsonis, 1989). It should also be considered that one classification or nosologic system may not serve the diverse needs of researchers and clinicians, and complementary systems may have to be designed.

Another problem in psychiatric studies concerns the best way to gather and integrate the information necessary for diagnosis. It makes common sense to interview both the parent (and other adult informants) and the child about the child's disturbance in order to reach a valid decision. Although much has been made of the fact that the accounts of young patients often differ from the reports of their parents (and teachers), in light of the developmental and social-role differences among these informants, there should be disagreement. The challenge, therefore, is to determine the best way to combine the different accounts. This could involve developing guidelines about how to weigh data from informants about different symptoms or items. Such guidelines are particularly important because depressed children may have depressed mothers whose observations of their children's disturbance may be distorted in some areas.

The *DSM-III* (American Psychiatric Association 1980) has been severely criticized as insensitive to developmental issues, which criticism is likely to apply to the *DSM-III-R* (American Psychiatric Association, 1987) as well. Such criticisms are not entirely correct because the symptom criteria for affective disorders and their associated features do include some age-related accommodations. The assessment of symptoms is far more problematic because the direct psychiatric interview of the child is made difficult by developmental factors (as discussed further on). In short, when asked about many of the symptoms of affective disorders (e.g., worthlessness and guilt), the juvenile is called on to introspect and to demonstrate some psychological orientation. It is important to recognize that age-dependent constraints on self-understanding, language, and memory organization may limit the accuracy of assessment. Guidelines in this regard should be formally incorporated in research and clinical tools.

Finally, generalizability of findings can be a problem in the psychiatric literature. Studies have typically used university- and teaching-hospital-based clinic-referred or inpatient samples which are often not demographically representative of the general population. Moreover, it is not known to what extent the available findings apply to children who are not referred to mental health practitioners at all or to youngsters who are treated by private practitioners or in private hospitals. Only studies of non-clinic-based populations can resolve such issues.

HYPOTHESIS TESTING AND CAUSAL-EXPLANATION STUDIES

The Findings

There are convergent sources of information suggesting that existing theories of depression, which were initially developed for adults, can be extended "downward" to younger ages. Thus, various theory-specific psychologic, cognitive, performance, and interpersonal deficits have been investigated among juveniles.

Consistent with the hypothesis that depression is associated with social skills deficits, children who endorse high levels of depression and/or are seen by their peers as depressed do appear more isolated and less effective in their actual social interactions than their nonsymptomatic peers. In experimental situations, they perform less skillfully on some tasks of interpersonal problem solving and are preferred less often as play- or workmates (see Altmann & Gotlib, 1988; Blechman, McEnroe, Carella, & Audette, 1986; Sacco & Graves, 1984). Compared with nonsymptomatic peers, such children also exhibit difficulties in proper self-monitoring (self-control), expect to perform more poorly on experimental tasks, set more stringent criteria for success, evaluate their own performance in a more unfavorable light, and presumably receive less positive reinforcement from their peers (see Blechman et al., 1986; Kaslow, Rehm, & Siegel, 1984).

Formulations that implicate distorted cognitive processes as central in depression have likewise received some support from studies of children. For example, youngsters who rate themselves as depressed have a generally negative view of themselves, of the future, and of their own performance, although it is not yet clear if children can have a consistently negative "self-schema" (Hammen & Zupan, 1984; Kazdin, French, Unis, Esveldt-Dawson, & Sherick, 1983; Sacco & Graves, 1984). Symptomatic school children (compared with nonsymptomatic peers) are also likely to view the causes of bad events as internal, stable, and global, and at the same time, to attribute positive events or success experiences to external, unstable, and specific factors. And children who habitually have the foregoing explanatory style (compared with those who do not) seem to be likely to get depressed when faced with negative events (Nolen-Hoeksema, Girgus, & Seligman, 1986; Seligman et al., 1984). The concept that depression is associated with problem-solving deficits and impaired learning has also received some support. For instance, children who have depressive symptoms have difficulties in solving experimental tasks such as anagrams and perform more poorly than their peers on some intelligence and achievement tests (see Blechman et al., 1986; Nolen-Hoeksema et al., 1986; Sacco & Graves, 1984).

Hypotheses about specific cognitive, social skills, or problem solving deficits have not yet been adequately tested among juveniles who have a psychiatrically diagnosable depression. Initial findings do indicate that such children are more likely to have negative expectations and unfavorable self-evaluations than youngsters with other types of diagnoses (e.g., Asarnow, Carlson, & Guthrie, 1987). The parents' behavior and attitudes may also play a role in the formation and maintenance of depressive disorders among children. For example, mothers of depressed clinic-referred youths (compared with mothers of nondepressed clinic children or controls) were generally less likely to express positive affect toward their offspring and more likely to set high standards for them (Cole & Rehm, 1986).

Finally, the available models of depression hold the promise of treatments for depressed youths. It appears that children and adolescents who complain of depressive symptoms respond well to various interventions that use cognitive techniques to alter thinking and attitudes, as well as behavioral strategies to improve problem-solving approaches or to reduce tension. The effectiveness of such approaches to ameliorate depressive symptoms has been documented in comparison with being on a waiting list (Reynolds & Coats, 1986; Stark, Reynolds, & Kaslow, 1987).

Research Problems and Possible Directions

Investigations of juveniles that had been inspired by various theories of depression have been limited by the procedures that were used to select subjects. And most of these studies have not explained the rationale or the psychologic mechanisms that could underlie the findings.

First, with a few exceptions, hypothesis-testing studies have selected cases by administering paper-and-pencil self-rating scales or by using peer nomination techniques. It is clear that subject selection strategies based on psychometric approaches are practical, economical, and often nonintrusive. But symptom scales and peer nominations were not designed to inform about the duration of depressive symptoms, which can be a major constraint. In addition, the relation between dysphoric syndromes assessed by such means and psychiatrically diagnosable depressions has not been fully established. This makes it difficult to estimate the extent to which the findings are relevant to clinical depression.

The studies can also be critiqued on conceptual grounds. It can be argued, for example, that negative cognitions such as self-deprecation, helplessness, and hopelessness are intrinsic to clinical depression. As such, they are incorporated into existing psychiatric diagnostic criteria and most rating scales of depression. Therefore, verification that youngsters who admit to negative opinions of themselves on one assessment scale endorse similar views on another scale can be seen as a validation of a given assessment technique at best, and as a tautology at worst. A more interesting issue, for instance, is the significance of the fact that (with the exception of psychotic states) depressed-negative cognitions and attitudes are characteristically self-referential (e.g., "I am bad and cannot do anything well, but everyone else is okay").

Because social-skill problems appear to be ubiquitous across youngsters with different types of psychiatric disorders and difficulties, another interesting issue is whether social-skills deficits in depression have any unique features. Clinical observations suggest, for instance, that affectively disturbed youngsters are particularly impaired in their ability to properly reciprocate social initiatives and may also have problems in recognizing the interpersonal consequences of their deficits. Observations that interpersonal problems persist after recovery from a depression also raise intriguing theoretical questions as to whether age at onset of depression in combination with the duration of the disorder may impose limits on a patient's later psychologic and social resiliency.

Another area that should be explored is the nature of the relation between cognitive, performance, and interpersonal deficits and the course of affective disorders among juveniles. There is little doubt that such deficits do exist during the episode of psychiatric disturbance. It remains to be seen, however, whether such variables may be etiologic (causative) or contributory to development of affective disorders, as opposed to being associated features of the depressions.

Extant theories of depression generally posit some prior personal history or experience that has either "primed" the patient to develop a depression or has resulted in vulnerability in that regard (e.g., negative cognitive schemata or exposure to negative uncontrollable events). The extent to which such assumptions may limit the generalizability of these theories to children deserves discussion. There is also a need to develop more sensitive measures of the theoretical constructs. It would be helpful to specify better the posited mechanisms whereby a theory can account for some aspects of affective disorders in juveniles.

The designs of most projects (generally cross-sectional and quasi-experimental), as well as the small sample sizes at times, have precluded adequate tests of causal hypotheses. This is unfortunate because the promise of theory-based research resides in the identification of both etiologic variables that play a role in the onset of depression and contributing factors that maintain it.

Finally, many of the studies employed subsamples of school populations and primarily middle-class, White subjects. Therefore, there is a need to extend the findings to more representative community samples and to clinical populations. Because the age ranges of subjects were generally restricted to 7–13 years, the applicability of the results to adolescents also has to be confirmed.

DEVELOPMENTAL PSYCHOPATHOLOGY APPROACHES

The Findings

In the most general sense, developmental psychopathology concerns three broad issues: the extent to which characteristics of the developing organism mediate what disorders develop and the forms they may take; the manner in which psychopathology may interfere with the age-appropriate progression of abilities; and the continuity or discontinuity of disorders across the age span (Digdon & Gotlib, 1985; Rutter, 1986).

The concept of "masked depression" in childhood, which was popular in the 1960s and early 1970s, can be viewed as an example of the application of principles involved in developmental psychopathology. Intrinsic to the concept of masked depression was the notion that the manifestations of affective disorders vary as a function of a youngster's age and maturity. It has been also emphasized that (a) children's cognitive, emotional, and interpersonal competencies must be taken into account in describing and understanding these conditions and (b) depression should be evaluated in relation to what is "normal" for a particular stage of development (Digdon & Gotlib, 1985; Rutter, 1986). Although it has consequently been posited that the manifestations of depression and other types of affective disorders are not constant across the age span, coherent, age-specific syndromes have not been verified. It has been suggested, for example, that in light of the "present orientation" of children, the "depth" of their depression should not be comparable to that found in adults and that suicidal ideation may have a different significance in the school-age years.

The most persuasive although somewhat indirect evidence in support of a developmental mediation of affective disorders derives from studies indicating that from childhood on, the rates of depression and suicidal behaviors gradually rise (see Rutter, 1986). On the other hand, the overall syndrome and its cardinal features (e.g., loss of the ability to experience pleasure and neurovegetative changes) are remarkably stable across the age span. Psychiatric studies that have documented some variability in the depressive symptom picture as a function of age reported, for example, that adolescents compared with younger children are more likely to show sleep disturbance as excessive sleep rather than reduced sleep and that the psychotic and endogenous forms of depression are less frequent among them than among adults (Kovacs & Gatsonis, 1989; Puig-Antich, 1986; Ryan et al., 1987). However, age-related differences or the effects of cognitive and pubertal stage on symptom expression and on the characteristics of the depressive disorders cannot be uniformly verified (Kaslow et al., 1984; Kovacs & Paulauskas, 1984).

On the other hand, there are reasons to believe that depression and other affective disturbances disrupt the acquisition and unfolding of age-appropriate competencies. For example, major depressive disorder among school-age children and adolescents appears to slow down their cognitive development in some areas and seems to interfere with the continued age-appropriate acquisition of verbal skills (Kovacs, Gatsonis, et al., 1988). Academic deterioration has also been noted as a concomitant of the onset of bipolar disorder among clinically referred adolescents (Bashir, Russell, & Johnson, 1987).

Research Problems and Possible Directions

Much of the criticism leveled at current research on the affective disorders rests on the proposition that depression must be considered in relation to what is normal for a particular state of development. However, some of the examples in support of that argument, such as excessive crying being appropriate in a young child, ignore that a depressive disorder is a *collection* of symptoms, which is disruptive or functionally impairing (American Psychiatric Association, 1980, 1987). It would be hard to argue that excessive crying together with anergia, loss of weight, inability to play, and sleep disturbance represent a normal state in an elementary-school-aged child, for instance.

It has been difficult to demonstrate significant developmental effects on symptomatology and clinical course. But the few available studies of this issue have tended to use chronologic age as the sole developmental parameter, which is probably not a sufficiently sensitive index of pertinent developmental processes. Because available theory-based developmental measures may also not be sensitive enough to detect hypothesized effects, further psychometric work in this area should be a priority. Another fact to be considered is that developmental effects may be more readily detected in younger children than the ones studied so far.

Studies are also needed on the impact of depressive and manic disorders on the development of social competence and long-term academic achievement. It should be no surprise that mood disorders could have a detrimental effect on social abilities, particularly because they may interfere with the formation of friendships and other peer relationships. Likewise, affective disturbances could have negative educational consequences, perhaps as early as in elementary school. A particularly interesting study in this regard is the one by Masters, Barden, and Ford (1979) because it documented that, even among children as young as four years old, affect strongly influences learning.

Another developmental issue concerns the limits of assessment tools. Self-descriptions rely on language and organizational memory (among other factors), which are developmentally mediated. However, most assessment approaches do not formally consider a patient's level of competence in these areas, and for some instruments an issue as basic as "readability" has been neglected. The demands and limitations of a frequently used assessment method, the psychiatric interview, have been delineated. For example, the interview entails an implicit demand for a cooperative stance, which is critical for information gathering but is subject to the child's understanding of the purpose of the interview. Evaluation of many of the symptoms requires from the patient some understanding of psychologic constructs, introspection, and proper communication of the retrieved memory, which also depend on developmental stage. More formal specifications of these demands could lead to better assessment tools.

Finally, the need for a systematic integration of developmental theory and research in juvenile psychopathology has been repeatedly articulated. However, investigators have often viewed developmental variables as "noise" that should be statistically or experimentally controlled. The mechanisms whereby developmental processes may alter or affect the characteristics and consequences of psychopathologic states remain to be tested.

CONCLUDING REMARKS

Ten years ago, Lefkowitz and Burton (1978) concluded that there was "insufficient and unsubstantial" research evidence for the concept of depressive syndromes among juveniles. Although there has been considerable progress since then, their suggestion that depression in childhood may simply be a phase that "if left alone, will diminish with the passage of time" touches on an important issue. That is, some of the strongest validational support for the diagnosis of depressive disorders in youths are further longitudinal data showing that even if the disorder "goes away," it recurs and interferes with the ability to achieve and maintain competent functioning. Along this line, more work is required on the extent to which mood disorders affect social competence and academic achievement and performance. These areas are important not only in themselves but also because they influence youngsters' eventual interpersonal success and their opportunities for higher education and careers.

There is also a need for theories of the etiology of depression that take into account some of the characteristics and situational factors that are typical of juveniles. These factors include their more limited life experiences, fewer problem-solving alternatives, and age-related aspects of information processing that may affect cognitive and attributional styles. The need for such theories has become increasingly apparent because the complexities of data from nonexperimental (naturalistic) or quasi-experimental studies make the testing of causal hypotheses exceedingly difficult. While comprehensive theories are being developed, hypothesis testing focusing on specific psychologic and psychosocial constructs could be fruitful. A major decision in this regard concerns the constructs to be studied. If the literature on the psychosocial aspects of depression among adults is any indication, the etiologic roles of negative cognitive schemas, dysfunctional attributional styles, or personality traits ought to be difficult to verify. However, the study of interpersonal and social variables leading to and maintaining affective disorders could be more feasible (Barnett & Gotlib, 1988).

The existence of affective disorders among children and adolescents is no longer a point of contention. In light of already available evidence of their persistence and negative consequences, a clear research priority is the design and testing of treatment and remediative approaches to these conditions. Psychotherapy trials must be conducted with psychiatrically diagnosable young patients. Innovative applications of existing therapies should be considered. These should include an active role for parents as therapeutic agents in the treatment of their offspring. The possible usefulness of nonsymptomatic peers could also be considered both as social role models and as agents of change in attempts to remediate the negative effects of juvenile-onset affective disorders. Ultimately, the best way to help such youngsters will be early identification and treatment in order to prevent negative, long-term consequences of these conditions.

REFERENCES

Altmann, E. O., & Gotlib, I. H. (1988). The social behavior of depressed children: An observational study. *Journal of Abnormal Child Psychology, 16*, 29–44.

American Psychiatric Association. (1980). *Diagnostic and statistical manual of mental disorders* (3rd ed.). Washington, DC: Author.

American Psychiatric Association. (1987). *Diagnostic and statistical manual of mental disorders* (3rd ed., revised). Washington, DC: Author.

Anderson, J. C., Williams, S., McGee, R., & Silva, P. A. (1987). DSM-III disorders in preadolescent children: Prevalence in a large sample from the general population. *Archives of General Psychiatry, 44*, 69–76.

Asarnow, J. R., Carlson, G. A., & Guthrie, D. (1987). Coping strategies, self-perceptions, hopelessness, and perceived family environments in depressed and suicidal children. *Journal of Consulting and Clinical Psychology, 55*, 361–366.

Barnett, P. A., & Gotlib, I. H. (1988). Psychosocial functioning and depression: Distinguishing among antecedents, concomitants, and consequences. *Psychological Bulletin, 104*, 97–126.

Bashir, M., Russell, J., & Johnson, G. (1987). Bipolar affective disorder in adolescence: A 10-year study. *Australian and New Zealand Journal of Psychiatry*, 21, 36–43.

Blechman, E. A., McEnroe, M. J., Carella, E. T., & Audette, D. P. (1986). Childhood competence and depression. *Journal of Abnormal Psychology, 95*, 223–227.

Brent, D. A., Perper, J. A., Goldstein, C. E., Kolko, D. J., Allan, M. J. Allman, C. J., & Zelenak, J. P. (1988). Risk factors for adolescent suicide: Comparison of adolescent suicide victims with suicidal inpatients. *Archives of General Psychiatry, 45*, 581–588.

Cole, D. A., & Rehm, L. P. (1986). Family interaction patterns and childhood depression. *Journal of Abnormal Child Psychology 14*, 297–314.

Digdon, N., & Gotlib, I. H. (1985). Developmental considerations in the study of childhood depression. *Developmental Review, 5*, 162–199.

Feighner, J. P., Robins, E., Guze, S. B., Woodruff, R. A., Winokur, G., & Munoz, R. (1972). Diagnostic criteria for use in psychiatric research. *Archives of General Psychiatry*, 26, 57–63.

Hammen, C., & Zupan, B. A. (1984). Self-schemas, depression, and the processing of personal information in children. *Journal of Experimental Child Psychology 37*, 598–608.

Kashani, J. H., Carlson, G. A., Beck, N. C., Hoeper, E. W., Corcoran, C. M., McAllister, J. A., Fallahi, C., Rosenberg, T. K., & Reid, J. C. (1987). Depression, depressive symptoms, and depressed mood among a community sample of adolescents. *American Journal of Psychiatry, 144*, 931–934.

Kaslow, N. J., Rehm, L. P., & Siegel, A. W. (1984). Social-cognitive and cognitive correlates of depression in children. *Journal of Abnormal Child Psychology, 12*, 605–620.

Kazdin, A. E., French, N. H., Unis, A. S., Esveldt-Dawson, K., & Sherick, R. B. (1983). Hopelessness, depression, and suicidal intent among psychiatrically disturbed inpatient children. *Journal of Consulting and Clinical Psychology, 51*, 504–510.

Kovacs, M. (1985). The natural history and course of depressive disorders in childhood. *Psychiatric Annals, 15*, 387–389.

Kovacs, M., & Gatsonis, C. (1989). Stability and change in childhood-onset depressive disorders: Longitudinal course as a diagnostic validator. In L. N. Robins, J. L. Fleiss, & J. E. Barrett (Eds.), *The validity of psychiatric diagnosis* (pp. 57–75). New York: Raven.

Kovacs, M., Gatsonis, C., Marsh, J., & Richards, C. (1988). *Intellectual and cognitive development in childhood-onset depressive disorders: A longitudinal study*. Manuscript submitted for publication.

Kovacs, M., & Paulauskas, S. L. (1984). Developmental stage and the expression of depressive disorders in children: An empirical analysis. In D. Cicchetti & K. Schneider-Rosen (Eds.), *Childhood depression: New directions for child development* (Report No. 26, pp. 59–79). San Francisco: Jossey-Bass.

Kovacs, M., Paulauskas, S. L., Gatsonis, C., & Richards, C. (1988). Depressive disorders in childhood: III. A longitudinal study of comorbidity with and risk for conduct disorders. *Journal of Affective Disorders, 15*, 205–217.

Lefkowitz, M. M., & Burton, N. (1978). Childhood depression: A critique of the concept. *Psychological Bulletin, 85*, 716–726.

Masters, J. C., Barden, R. C., & Ford, M. E. (1979). Affective states, expressive behavior, and learning in children. *Journal of Personality and Social Psychology, 37*, 380–390.

Nolen-Hoeksema, S., Girgus, J. S., & Seligman, M. E. P. (1986). Learned helplessness in children: A longitudinal study of depression, achievement, and explanatory style. *Journal of Personality and Social Psychology, 51*, 435–442.

Pfeffer, C. R. (1981). Suicidal behavior of children: A review with implications for research and practice. *American Journal of Psychiatry, 138*, 154–159.

Puig-Antich, J. (1982). Major depression and conduct disorder in prepuberty. *Journal of The American Academy of Child Psychiatry, 21*, 118–128.

Puig-Antich, J. (1986). Psychobiological markers: Effects of age and puberty. In M. Rutter, C. E. Izard, & P. B. Read (Eds.), *Depression in young people: Developmental and clinical perspectives* (pp. 341–381). New York: Guilford.

Puig-Antich, J., Lukens, E., Davies, M., Goetz, D., Brennan-Quattrock, J., & Todak, G. (1985). Psychosocial functioning in prepubertal major depressive disorders: II. Interpersonal relationships after sustained recovery from the affective episode. *Archives of General Psychiatry, 42*, 511–517.

Puig-Antich, J., Perel, J. M., Lupatkin, W., Chambers, W. J., Tabrizi, M. A., King, J., Goetz, R., Davies, M., & Stiller, R. L. (1987). Imipramine in prepubertal major depressive disorders. *Archives of General Psychiatry, 44*, 81–89.

Reynolds, W. M., & Coats, K. I. (1986). A comparison of cognitive-behavioral therapy and relaxation training for the treatment of depression in adolescents. *Journal of Consulting and Clinical Psychology, 54*, 653–660.

Robins, D. R., & Alessi, N. E. (1985). Depressive symptoms and suicidal behavior in adolescents. *American Journal of Psychiatry, 142*, 588–592.

Rutter, M. (1986). The developmental psychopathology of depression: Issues and perspectives. In M. Rutter, C. E. Izard, & P. B. Read (Eds.), *Depression in young people: Developmental and clinical perspectives* (pp. 3–30). New York: Guilford.

Ryan, N. D., Puig-Antich, J., Ambrosini, P., Rabinovich, H., Robinson, D., Nelson, B., Iyengar, S., & Twomey, J. (1987). The clinical picture of major depression in children and adolescents. *Archives of General Psychiatry, 44*, 854–861.

Sacco, W. P., & Graves, D. J. (1984). Childhood depression, interpersonal problem-solving, and self-ratings of performance. *Journal of Clinical Child Psychology, 13*, 10–15.

Seligman, M. E. P., Peterson, C., Kaslow, N. J., Tanenbaum, R. L., Alloy, L. B., & Abramson, L. Y. (1984). Attributional style and depressive symptoms among children. *Journal of Abnormal Psychology, 93*, 235–238.

Stark, K. D., Reynolds, W. M., & Kaslow, N. J. (1987). A comparison of the relative efficacy of self-control therapy and a behavioral problem-solving therapy for depression in children. *Journal of Abnormal Child Psychology, 15*, 91–113.

Strober, M., & Carlson, G. (1982). Bipolar illness in adolescents with major depression. Clinical, genetic, and psychopharmacologic predictors in a three- to four-year prospective follow-up investigation. *Archives of General Psychiatry, 39*, 549–555.

Strober, M., Hanna, G., & McCracken, J. (1989). Bipolar illness. In C. Last & M. Hersen (Eds.), *Handbook of child psychiatric diagnosis* (pp. 299–316). New York: Wiley.

Weller, R. A., Weller, E. B., Tucker, S. G., & Fristad, M. A. (1986). Mania in prepubertal children: Has it been underdiagnosed? *Journal of Affective Disorders, 11*, 151–154.

DISCUSSION

Pivotal to Lefkowitz and Burton's arguments is what is often termed a **statistical approach** to the definition of illness, including mental illness. According to proponents of a statistical approach, both physical and mental disorders should be defined exclusively in terms of statistical rarity. Thus, a behavior or other characteristic that is uncommon in the general population is deemed to be abnormal and therefore pathological. Lefkowitz and Burton implicitly adopt a statistical approach when they contend that the extremely high prevalence of depressive symptoms among children in the general population renders childhood depression nonpathological. They conclude that "studies of normal children indicate that these same symptoms of depression prevail at a rate too high to be considered statistically deviant" (p. 724).

But there appear to be at least three logical difficulties with defining illness in a statistical fashion:

- How are we to define rarity? Should it be defined in terms of a frequency of 1% in the population? Or 3%? Or 5%? What criteria would one even employ to make this determination? A statistical model suffers from an unavoidable degree of arbitrariness, because scientific criteria cannot be used to decide the crucial cutoff point demarcating abnormality from normality. In this respect, Lefkowitz and Burton's arguments concerning the prevalence of childhood depressive symptoms are somewhat difficult to evaluate, because these authors do not indicate how rare such symptoms would need to be in order to be considered pathological.
- In addition, defining illness in terms of statistical rarity leads to obvious counterexamples. When the bubonic

plague ravaged Europe during the 14th century, it afflicted two-thirds or more of the population. This staggeringly high prevalence surely does not imply that bubonic plague was not an illness, as the millions of deaths resulting from it tragically attest. The same argument can be extended to a number of modern-day medical conditions, such as dental caries (cavities) and atherosclerosis (Wakefield, 1992), that are extremely widespread in the population. This reasoning suggests that the high prevalence of childhood depressive symptoms in the population cannot, by itself, be used to argue that childhood depression is not pathological.

- A statistical approach also does not specify which dimensions are relevant to illness. Most or all of us would certainly agree that extremely high blood pressure indicates disease. Many of us, although perhaps not all, would make the same assertion regarding extremely high levels of anxiety. But would any of us say the same about extremes (either high or low) in height, neck circumference, hair length, or belly button diameter? What about extremely high levels of intelligence, creativity, or altruism? Advocates of a purely statistical approach would, paradoxically, classify many highly socially desirable characteristics as abnormal. Such an approach ultimately fails as a comprehensive model of disease because many dimensions of mental and physical functioning appear to be largely or entirely irrelevant to illness.

In fact, the question "Does childhood depression exist?" may in some respects be the wrong question to ask. There is no dispute—even among Lefkowitz, Burton, and other skeptics of the childhood depression concept—that many children exhibit profound sadness and numerous features (such as crying, appetite loss, sleep difficulties, and fatigue) characteristic of what we typically call depression. If so, what is the controversy concerning childhood depression really about? Close examination of the arguments of Lefkowitz and Burton, on the one hand, and Kovacs, on the other, suggests that the actual question at issue is "Is childhood depression the same entity as adult depression?" or, put slightly differently, "Is there is a continuity between childhood and adult depression?"

These latter two questions underscore why the construct of childhood depression has been the subject of such intense debate. It is one thing to show that many children fulfill the same diagnostic criteria for depression as do many adults, a fact that no longer appears to be in dispute. It is a quite different thing, however, to show that the depression these children are experiencing is fundamentally similar to the depression experienced by adults. How would one demonstrate such a link? To answer this question satisfactorily, I first must explain a difficult but extremely important concept in abnormal psychology research: **construct validity** (Cronbach & Meehl, 1955). We have already encountered the concept of validity in several places (for example, Chapter 2). Validity is essentially the extent to which a psychological test (or diagnosis) measures what it is intended to measure. Construct validity is a specific type of validity that is appropriate when we are evaluating the extent to which a test assesses a **construct**—that is, a hypothesized characteristic of individuals that cannot be observed directly. Extroversion, honesty, artistic ability, and intelligence are all constructs, because they cannot be observed directly and must instead be inferred. We cannot literally see someone's extroversion, for instance, but can we safely deduce that a person is extroverted if he or she has many friends, enjoys going to parties, prefers being with others to being alone, and so on. Thus, we use observable indicators—behaviors—to infer whether an individual is extroverted.

Similarly, all or virtually all psychopathological conditions, including childhood disorders, are best viewed as constructs, because they refer to latent entities that are not directly observable. For example, the diagnosis of attention-deficit/hyperactivity disorder (ADHD) (more commonly known as childhood hyperactivity), which you will encounter in Chapter 15, refers to a latent condition that is inferred by the diagnostician. The diagnostic criteria for ADHD, such as "often fidgets with hands or feet or squirms in seat" and "is often easily distracted by extraneous stimuli," can be thought of as manifest (that is, observable) but fallible (that is, imperfect) indicators of the underlying entity of ADHD. These criteria are fallible because they are not present in all cases of ADHD and are present in conditions other than ADHD. Regrettably, the distinction between **manifest indicators** and **latent entities** is often overlooked when discussing psychological disorders.

This logic helps us to understand why we need to use a construct validational approach for most or all psychopathological conditions. Because these conditions are latent (unobservable) entities, we can never know for sure whether we are measuring the condition we are interested in. Thus, we are forced to gather a variety of indirect forms of evidence to demonstrate validity. This accumulation of indirect evidence is the essence of construct validation. Like Sherlock Holmes, Columbo, or any good detective, we must gradually piece together circumstantial evidence in support of our case.

Note, however, that this situation differs substantially from what we often find in medicine. As an example, consider **general paresis**, a disorder characterized by severe psychological symptoms such as paranoia, overactivity, inappropriate elation, and delusions of grandeur. General paresis was shown in the late 19th century and early 20th century to be the final stage of syphilis, in which the syphilis bacterium has invaded the brain. To demonstrate that general paresis and syphilis were the same disorder, investigators did not need to use a construct validational approach. Why? Because they discovered that the bacterium causing syphilis is also present in all individuals with general paresis. In effect, investigators had discovered an essentially foolproof method of diagnosing general paresis. General paresis was thus transformed from a latent entity measured by highly fallible indicators (specifically, abnormal behaviors) to an observable (under the microscope, at least) entity that could be diagnosed by means of a single and virtually infallible indicator—namely, a laboratory test for the syphilis bacterium. But the situation for mental disorders is, alas, quite different, because no one has yet developed (or seems even remotely close to developing) a definitive test—biological or otherwise—for identifying whether a patient has a particular mental disorder. Much to our frustration, mental disorders remain latent entities.

What types of evidence are relevant for the construct validation of a psychiatric diagnosis? In fact, we have already discussed the answer to this question in a slightly different context: the Robins and Guze (1970) criteria for the validation of psychiatric disorders (see Chapter 9). Robins and Guze argue that a valid psychiatric diagnosis should provide us with information concerning diagnosed individuals' performance on laboratory tests and self-report measures of personality and psychopathology, natural history (that is, the disorder's course and outcome), and family history of psychopathology, as well as with information concerning the differentiation of the diagnosis from other syndromes. In addition, although the point is not discussed explicitly by Robins and Guze, a valid diagnosis also ideally informs us about diagnosed individuals' response to treatment. Each of these five sources of information can essentially be thought of as indirect evidence for the construct validity of a psychiatric syndrome.

Now we can return to the debate regarding childhood depression. As I pointed out earlier, the central controversy seems to be whether childhood depression and adult depression are the same latent entities. Because we cannot use an essentially infallible laboratory test to identify either of these two conditions, as we can in the case of general paresis, we must rely on construct validity (as Robins and Guze do) to determine whether childhood depression is the same latent entity as is adult depression.

Although Kovacs does not explicitly cast this issue within a construct validational framework, she is in effect using this framework to argue that childhood and adult depression have much in common. According to Kovacs, childhood depression, like adult depression, tends to be associated with (1) a chronic course characterized by frequent recurrences and prolonged interpersonal and academic impairment; (2) social skills deficits, cognitive distortions, and problem-solving difficulties; and (3) a positive response to certain cognitive and behavioral interventions. Thus, childhood depression appears to fulfill at least some of the Robins and Guze criteria for the construct validity of psychiatric disorders. At the same time, however, Kovacs acknowledges that depressed children (4) tend not to respond more positively to tricyclic antidepressants than to placebos and (5) tend to exhibit somewhat different biological abnormalities (such as sleep disturbances) than do depressed adults. Although the first three findings provide support for the construct validity of childhood depression, the latter two raise questions concerning the validity of this construct. As Kovacs points out, the difficulty in interpreting these and other negative findings derives from the possibility that the expression or manifestation of depressive features changes as a function of age, an issue far too complex to even attempt to tackle here. In any case, it seems clear that, although much of the evidence concerning the construct validity of childhood depression is promising, further research will be necessary to more fully delineate how this construct is both similar to and different from adult depression.

QUESTIONS TO STIMULATE DISCUSSION

1. The difficulties with a statistical approach to defining psychopathology aside, do any of Lefkowitz and Burton's arguments have merit? In particular, does the tendency of childhood depressive symptoms to dissipate over time argue against the construct validity of childhood depression, as Lefkowitz and Burton contend?
2. In their concluding comments, Lefkowitz and Burton allude to the potentially dangerous iatrogenic (doctor-induced) consequences of diagnosing childhood depression. What iatrogenic effects might they be referring to? Do you agree that this diagnosis might be harmful in certain instances?
3. Judging from what you have read in this chapter, do you concur with Kovacs that "the existence of affective disorders among children and adolescents is no longer a point of contention" (p. 214)? Defend your answer.
4. As the introduction to this chapter mentions, psychoanalysts typically maintain that young children, who do not possess a well-developed superego, are incapable of experiencing depression. Do you agree with them? What types of research evidence, if any, might help to resolve this issue?
5. The concepts of masked depression and depressive equivalents remain controversial. If you were a researcher, what types of studies would you conduct to examine the validity of these constructs? What types of findings would provide persuasive evidence for (or against) their validity?
6. Jean Piaget and several other developmental psychologists have argued that young children have a poorly developed sense of future time. Is an understanding of one's future a prerequisite for depression? If so, how?

SUGGESTIONS FOR FURTHER READING

Cantwell, D. P., & Carlson, G. A. (Eds.) (1983). *Affective disorders in childhood and adolescence: An update*. New York: SP Medical and Scientific Books.

This comprehensive volume provides coverage of issues pertaining to the diagnosis, classification, and assessment of childhood depression, as well as to masked depression and alternative expressions of depression. Research on causal factors, course and outcome, and treatment is also discussed.

Cichetti, D., & Schneider-Rosen, K. (1984). *Childhood depression*. San Francisco: Jossey-Bass.
This concise edited volume contains four chapters dealing with theoretical models of the development of depression, the effects of developmental level on the manifestation of depression, the development of depression in female children, and psychological difficulties among the children of depressed parents.

Costello, C. G. (1980). Childhood depression: Three basic but questionable assumptions in the Lefkowitz and Burton critique. *Psychological Bulletin, 87*, 185–190.
Costello criticizes Lefkowitz and Burton's assumptions that symptoms that are prevalent are not pathological and symptoms that remit spontaneously are not pathological and should not be targeted for intervention.

Kazdin, A. E. (1987). Assessment of childhood depression: Current issues and strategies. *Behavioral Assessment, 9*, 291–319.
Kazdin reviews a variety of conceptual and methodological issues in the assessment of childhood depression, including the use of dimensional versus categorical scores; possible reasons for the discrepancies among parent, teacher, and child reports; and the low levels of agreement among measures. He also discusses the assets and limitations of alternative indices, such as behavioral observations, biological measures, and projective techniques.

Lefkowitz, M. M. (1980). Childhood depression: A reply to Costello. *Psychological Bulletin, 87*, 191–194.
Lefkowitz responds to Costello's critique by noting that statistical rarity is frequently used to operationalize psychopathology and that there are no compelling data indicating that depressive symptoms that remit in childhood are predictive of subsequent depression. In addition, he argues that the treatment of problems that remit spontaneously can lead to harmful iatrogenic effects.

Puig-Antich, J., & Gittelman, R. (1982). Depression in childhood and adolescence. In E. S. Paykel (Ed.), *Handbook of affective disorders* (pp. 379–392). New York: Guilford Press.
This chapter provides a thorough (although somewhat dated) overview of the literature on the diagnosis, assessment, biological correlates, and psychopharmacological and psychotherapeutic treatment of childhood depression. Puig-Antich and Gittelman conclude with a discussion of unresolved issues in the study of childhood depression, including drug response and overlap with separation anxiety disorder.

Rancurello, M. D. (1985). Clinical applications of antidepressant drugs in childhood behavioral and emotional disorders. *Psychiatric Annals, 15*, 88–100.
This article contains an overview of the use of antidepressant medications in a number of childhood psychological disturbances, including depression, attention-deficit/hyperactivity disorder, enuresis, and separation anxiety disorder. Clinical guidelines for the administration of tricyclic antidepressants, monoamine oxidase inhibitors, and lithium carbonate are summarized.

Rutter, M. (1986). The developmental psychopathology of depression: Issues and perspectives. In M. Rutter, C. E. Izard, & P. B. Read (Eds.), *Depression in young people* (pp. 3–30). New York: Guilford Press.
In this chapter, the world's preeminent child psychiatrist discusses the rationale underlying the developmental approach to depression and reviews findings on age-related changes in depressive symptoms. In addition, he summarizes the results of studies examining the continuity of depression from childhood to adulthood.

Weller, E. B., & Weller, R. A. (Eds.) (1984). *Major depressive disorders in children*. Washington, DC: American Psychiatric Press.
This volume contains six chapters focusing on the use and efficacy of antidepressant medication to treat depressed children and on the biological correlates and assessment of childhood depression.

REFERENCES

American Psychiatric Association. (1980). *Diagnostic and Statistical Manual of Mental Disorders* (3rd ed.). Washington, DC: Author.

Cronbach, L. J., & Meehl, P. E. (1955). Construct validity in psychological tests. *Psychological Bulletin, 52*, 281–302.

Dahl, R. E., & Puig-Antich, J. (1990). Sleep disturbances in child and adolescent psychiatric disorders. *Pediatrician, 17*, 32–37.

Malmquist, C. P. (1971). Depressions in childhood and adolescence. *New England Journal of Medicine, 284*, 887–893.

Puig-Antich, J., & Gittelman, R. (1982). Depression in childhood and adolescence. In E. S. Paykel (Ed.), *Handbook of affective disorders* (pp. 379–392). New York: Guilford Press.

Puig-Antich, J., Perel, J. M., Lupatkin, W., Chambers, W. J., Tabrizi, M. A., King, J., Goetz, R., Davies, M., & Stiller, R. L. (1987). Imipramine in prepubertal major depressive disorders. *Archives of General Psychiatry, 44*, 81–89.

Robins, E., & Guze, S. B. (1970). Establishment of diagnostic validity in psychiatric illness: Its application to schizophrenia. *American Journal of Psychiatry, 126*, 983–987.

Ryan, N. D., Puig-Antich, J., Ambrosini, P., Rabinovich, H., Robinson, D., Nelson, B., Iyengar, S., & Twoney, J. (1987). The clinical picture of major depression in children and adolescents. *Archives of General Psychiatry, 44*, 854–861.

Wakefield, J. C. (1992). The concept of mental disorder: On the boundary between biological facts and social values. *American Psychologist, 47*, 373–388.

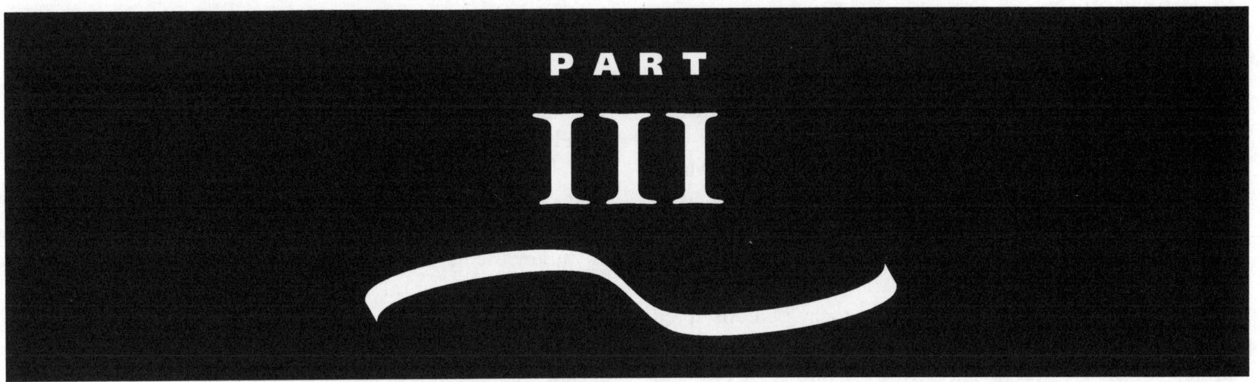

Psychological and Somatic Treatments

Canst thou not minister to a mind diseas'd;
Pluck from the memory a rooted sorrow;
Raze out the written troubles of the brain;
And with some sweet oblivious antidote
Cleanse the stuff'd bosom of that perilous stuff
Which weighs upon the heart?
—Shakespeare, *Macbeth* (Act V, Sc. III)

INTRODUCTION

Throughout history, the methods used to treat mental disorders have tended to parallel theories of their etiology. This fact should not be terribly surprising. Superficially, it would seem logical to direct the treatments for ailments at their ostensible root causes. In the case of mental disorders, treatments have traditionally been divided into two extremely broad classes—somatic and psychological—the origins of which can be traced largely to radically different assumptions concerning the etiology of mental illness.

Most early conceptions of the causation of mental disorders were largely or entirely **somatogenic**. According to somatogenic models of psychopathology, mental disorders are produced by physical disturbances, either in the brain or in other parts of the body. In turn, the treatments prescribed for these disorders were typically somatic, involving direct manipulation of body systems. For example, "hysteria" (most cases of which would today probably qualify as either conversion disorder or somatization disorder), a condition characterized by physical symptoms that lack a demonstrable organic basis—for example, anesthesias, paralyses, and seizures—was believed by the ancient Egyptians and Greeks to be caused by the aimless meandering of the uterus throughout the body. Their treatments for hysteria often involved the administration of foul-smelling substances to the nose and mouth to repel the uterus and of pleasant-smelling substances to the genital area to attract it (Loevinger, 1987). Laughable as this treatment seems today, it followed logically from the theory of etiology that spawned it. Similarly, Hippocrates, who embraced a somatogenic view of both personality and psychopathology, prescribed somatic treatments for most mental disorders. For example, he suggested that mental disorders be treated by a vegetable diet, celibacy, vigorous exercise, and bleeding.

During the Middle Ages, it became increasingly fashionable to regard mental illness as the product of demons that had infested the nervous system. In a crude sense, this etiological model can also be considered somatogenic, although in this case the presumed agents disrupting physical functioning were spiritual, rather than biological. The infamous **Malleus Maleficarum** ("The Witches' Hammer"), a manifesto issued in 1486 at the behest of Pope Innocent VIII, became a kind of popular manual for the "diagnosis" and treatment of witches. According to this manual, witches, who probably included a large number of individuals who would today be considered psychotic, were possessed by the devil. Moreover, the manual claimed, witches could be detected by a variety of physical manifestations, such as red spots and regions of insensitivity on the skin (Davison & Neale, 1994). The appropriate treatments for demonic possession involved exorcism, burning, and other brutal techniques. Once again, primitive as these interventions were, they are understandable in light of then-prevailing views of the etiology of psychopathology.

Not until the late 19th century did **psychogenic** models of the etiology of mental illness, which posit that mental illness is produced by psychological factors, begin to gain a solid foothold in both popular and scientific thinking. By "psychological" factors, I mean influences that initially impinge on the organism via sensory pathways, such as vision and hearing (Gorenstein, 1992). Much of the information reaching the sensory receptors (the eyes and ears, for example) through these pathways is cognitively processed, transformed, and interpreted and can subsequently become a source of psychological "stress." For example, if I were to inform you that you will have to take a quiz after reading this introduction (and if you were gullible enough to believe me), you would probably become anxious, angry, or both. After receiving the unwelcome news that you will be quizzed through your eyes (that is, by reading it), you would then construe this news in light of other knowledge (for example, your belief that taking a quiz is nerve-racking or unpleasant). Psychological factors thus differ from "biological" or "physical" factors, which affect bodily systems directly—that is, without the intervening activity of sensory pathways.

The clinical observations of three great neurologists—Jean Charcot, Pierre Janet, and most important, Sigmund Freud—were central in the ascendance of psychogenic explanations of mental illness. These individuals were by and large trained to regard the causes of mental illness as somatogenic, but they found themselves remarkably hard-pressed to account for certain physical symptoms of hysterics, which sometimes appeared to violate established neurological principles. For example, some hysterics presented with the spectacular symptom of **glove anesthesia**, which involves a complete loss of feeling in the hand(s) alone. With the rare exception of carpal tunnel syndrome, a condition in which the nerves of the wrist become pinched (Davison & Neale, 1994), this symptom cannot be explained in strictly physical terms, because the sensory pathways innervating the hand traverse the entire arm. Glove anesthesia and similar phenomena led Charcot, Janet, and Freud to conclude that many of the symptoms of hysteria necessitated a psychological level of explanation rather than a purely biological or physical one. In turn, this revolutionary conclusion provided the impetus for the development of the first systematic psychological treatment for mental illness—psychoanalysis.

A key theme that emerges from the study of the history of treatments for mental disorders is that these interventions have typically followed rather directly from conceptions of the etiology of psychopathology. Nevertheless, before concluding, let me disabuse you of an extremely common misconception (so common, in fact, that many psychologists seem to share it): The fact is that *the etiology of a condition bears no necessary implications for its treatment.* For example, simply because a disorder is largely or entirely biological in origin does not imply that it cannot be treated psychologically (for example, by psychotherapy). Conversely, simply because a disorder is largely or entirely psychological in origin does not imply that it cannot be treated biologically (by somatic therapy). The logic underlying these assertions can be understood if one realizes that what we call the mind is really the brain in action. That is, because the mind and brain are one, both psychological and biological interventions can influence brain function, structure, or both. What this reasoning implies is that psychological and somatic treatments differ only in terms of *how* they influence the brain. Psychological treatments affect the brain fairly indirectly, via sensory pathways, whereas somatic treatments affect the brain fairly directly. Nevertheless, both do unquestionably influence the brain.

A corollary of this conclusion is that a disorder's treatment bears no necessary implications for its etiology. For example, we cannot say that headaches are caused by a lack of aspirin; the proper treatment for headaches (aspirin) does not point directly to their causation. Similarly, you should not be misled into concluding that a disorder cannot be biological in origin if it is treatable by psychotherapy or, conversely, that a disorder cannot be psychological in origin if it is treatable by somatic therapy. Once again, the concepts of mind and brain refer to the same entities but at different levels of explanation. (See Chapter 6 for an introduction to the level of explanation problem.) You would do well to bear this point in mind when considering the implications of the readings in this section.

OVERVIEW OF PART III

In this part, you will encounter controversies regarding the effectiveness and, in some cases, safety of both psychological and somatic treatments for mental illness. In Chapter 12 I address what has consistently been one of the most nagging and persistent questions in clinical psychology: Does psychotherapy work? In Chapter 13 we explore whether cognitive-behavioral therapy, which has recently become one of the most influential schools of American psychotherapy, represents an important advance over its principal predecessor, behavior therapy. In Chapter 14 we examine the acrimonious and still largely unresolved debate regarding the efficacy and safety of controlled drinking for alcoholics. In Chapter 15, I discuss two alternative perspectives on the use of stimulants to treat children with attention-deficit/hyperactivity disorder (childhood hyperactivity). Finally, Chapter 16 deals with the ongoing scientific and societal controversy concerning the use of electroconvulsive therapy for depression and other conditions.

REFERENCES

Davison, G. C., & Neale, J. M. (1994). *Abnormal psychology* (6th ed.). New York: Wiley.

Gorenstein, E. E. (1992). *The science of mental illness*. San Diego: Academic Press.

Loevinger, J. (1987). *Paradigms of personality*. New York: W. H. Freeman.

CHAPTER

12

Is psychotherapy effective?

PRO Smith, M. L., & Glass, G. V. (1977). Meta-analysis of psychotherapy outcome studies. *American Psychologist, 32*, 752–760.

CON Prioleau, L., Murdock, M., & Brody, N. (1983). An analysis of psychotherapy versus placebo studies. *Behavioral and Brain Sciences*, 6, 275–285.

OVERVIEW OF THE CONTROVERSY: Mary Lee Smith and Gene V. Glass conduct a comprehensive meta-analysis of psychotherapy outcome studies and conclude that psychotherapy is clearly more effective than nontreatment. Leslie Prioleau, Martha Murdock, and Nathan Brody analyze a subset of the studies identified by Smith and her colleagues and conclude that psychotherapy is not demonstrably more effective than placebo treatment.

CONTEXT OF THE PROBLEM

Prior to 1952, the question constituting the title of this chapter probably would have sounded as foreign to most clinical psychologists as the question "Does fluoride help prevent tooth decay?" would have sounded to most dentists today. For many psychotherapists and researchers, the effectiveness of psychotherapy seemed so self-evident that the question hardly merited serious discussion, let alone a formal empirical demonstration. But this atmosphere of blissful complacency came to an abrupt end in 1952, when a German-born British psychologist named Hans J. Eysenck single-handedly plunged the world of clinical psychology into a state of utter disarray.

Eysenck had published an article, barely six pages long, in which he argued that the improvement rate of neurotics following psychotherapy did not exceed their natural recovery rate, which was between two-thirds and three-fourths. Psychotherapy often appears to be effective, he suggested, simply because many individuals with neurotic conditions naturally improve of their own accord. This phenomenon, gratifying to patients but annoying to psychotherapy researchers, is known as **spontaneous remission.** The efficacy of psychotherapy, Eysenck contended, was unproven at best and extremely dubious at worst. To add insult to injury, he concluded that "it seems premature to insist on the inclusion of training in . . . psychotherapy in the curriculum of the clinical psychologist" (Eysenck, 1952, p. 323).

The publication of Eysenck's article sent advocates of psychotherapy scrambling. Many simply ignored or refused to believe his findings, reassuring themselves that "I don't care what the literature says; I know it works." Of course, similar arguments had been advanced to "prove" the accuracy of astrological prediction, handwriting analysis, lie detection, and other pseudoscientific techniques. Other critics pointed to serious methodological flaws in Eysenck's analyses. For example, Eysenck's criteria for diagnosing neurosis were vague and at times seemingly inconsistent. Moreover, his criteria for improvement were in many cases based on highly subjective ratings from therapists and were in other cases highly idiosyncratic. For instance, in evaluating psychotherapy outcome, Eysenck classified all premature terminations as therapeutic failures. But some individuals may leave therapy prematurely because their symptoms have abated. Finally, Eysenck's estimates of the spontaneous remission rate of neurotics were derived from only two reports, one of which was based on the investigator's rather global and imprecise ratings of "recovery" among individuals who had filed insurance claims.

Given the plethora of problems with Eysenck's article, you might be surprised that it provoked as much furor as it did. Nevertheless, we must give Eysenck proper credit for his achievement. Whatever the merits of his arguments, he was one of the first major figures to dare to ask a fundamental question about psychotherapy: Does it work?

For the next two decades, the debate over the efficacy of psychotherapy raged with unabated intensity. Although an influential review by Luborsky, Singer, and Luborsky in 1975 provided support for the effectiveness of psychotherapy, lingering doubts remained. As Smith and Glass point out in the first article reprinted in this chapter, Luborsky et al., as well as most others who conducted reviews of psychotherapy outcome research, used what might be termed the **"voting" method** or "box score" method: The number of findings that are supportive and not supportive of the effectiveness of psychotherapy are tallied, and a total "box score" of hits and misses—not unlike that generated after a baseball game for each hitter—is tabulated.

The problem with this method is that it treats scientific research too much like a baseball game. In baseball, any contact with the ball is counted as a hit as long as the hitter successfully advances to a base without causing another player to be thrown out (with the exception of errors). Similarly, in the "voting" method of outcome research, a result is counted as a "hit" as long as it is statistically significant—that is, if it is extremely unlikely to have been produced by fluctuations in random sampling (or what some psychologists like to call "chance"). But all baseball fans know that some hits seem to be better than others; some are perfectly hit, 500-foot home runs, whereas others are poorly hit bloopers that just happen to fall between two bewildered infielders. Similarly, in research, some statistically significant results are very large in magnitude, whereas others are quite small. Moreover, some results that are quite large in magnitude are not statistically significant (especially when the number of subjects is small, because the same effect is more likely to be statistically significant with a larger sample size). The "voting" method of outcome research obscures these distinctions by lumping together all positive findings and all negative findings regardless of their magnitude. As a consequence, it provides only a crude and often misleading summary of a body of literature.

Enter an unlikely hero: a statistical technique known as **meta-analysis**. Meta-analysis, which was first formally introduced to most psychologists in the article by Smith and Glass that is reprinted in this chapter, is a procedure for aggregating and averaging the results of a large number of studies. Unlike the "voting" method, meta-analysis allows researchers to consider the magnitude of findings and yields an overall measure of **effect size**—that is, an index of the magnitude of the effects of a treatment (in the case of this chapter, psychotherapy) averaged across all studies. This measure can essentially be thought of as an indicator of the extent to which subjects who receive psychotherapy improve relative to subjects who do not receive psychotherapy. The greater the difference between these two groups of subjects, the greater the effect size. To understand the difference between statistical significance and effect size, imagine two students, Smith and Jones, who each take a 100-item true-false exam in which exactly half the items are true and half are false. For such an exam, a score of 50 represents chance performance. If Smith receives a 65 on the exam and Jones receives a 99, both students have exceeded chance performance. But Jones has clearly performed much better than Smith. The difference between these two ways of looking at Smith's and Jones's scores parallels the difference between statistical significance and effect size. A measure of statistical significance informs us whether a finding is attributable to chance, whereas a measure of effect size informs us about the magnitude of this finding.

In addition, meta-analysis permits researchers to examine whether certain variables are correlated with effect size. For example, one can examine whether studies using more experienced therapists yield larger effect sizes than those using less experienced therapists, whether studies using younger clients yield larger effect sizes than those using older clients, and so on. In this way, researchers can determine not only the overall effectiveness of psychotherapy, but what factors, if any, influence its effectiveness.

One caveat: Some of you may be put off or intimidated by some of the statistical terms and formulas presented in these two articles. For those of you who fall into this category, I offer this reassurance: The preceding paragraphs contain all the information you will need to interpret these articles. If you found these paragraphs on meta-analysis a bit confusing, you will probably want to reread them before proceeding much further.

THE CONTROVERSY: Smith and Glass vs. Prioleau, Murdock, and Brody

Smith and Glass

Mary Lee Smith and Gene Glass note that reviews conducted since Eysenck's influential articles were published contradict Eysenck's conclusion that psychotherapy is ineffective. Smith and Glass point out, however, that these reviews used the "voting" method of tabulating findings, which tends to provide an incomplete and often inaccurate picture of the overall findings. Consequently, they report the results of a meta-analysis of nearly 400 controlled investigations of psychotherapy and counseling. Sixteen variables—including the duration of therapy, therapist experience, and client IQ—were coded for each study. Smith and Glass conclude that psychotherapy is clearly more effective than nontreatment and that the average therapy client is more improved than 75 percent of untreated individuals. They also find that behavioral therapies tend to be slightly more effective than nonbehavioral therapies, although they caution that this difference may be attributable to differences in the reactivity of the outcome measures (which can be thought of as the extent to which measures are affected by subjects' knowledge that they are being measured) and perhaps other factors. Finally, Smith and Glass report that several variables were significantly correlated with the effect size of therapeutic effectiveness, including client IQ, similarity of therapist and client, and reactivity of the outcome measure. Interestingly, variables such as therapist experience and duration of psychotherapy were not significantly correlated with effect size.

Prioleau, Murdock, and Brody

Leslie Prioleau, Martha Murdock, and Nathan Brody begin by discussing the results of the meta-analysis by Smith, Glass, and Miller (1980), which was a somewhat more comprehensive version of the meta-analysis reported by Smith and Glass. Prioleau, Murdock, and Brody express reservations about some of the decisions made by Smith and her colleagues, including their choice of meta-analysis to summarize an extremely heterogeneous body of studies and their use of the outcome measure, rather than the study, as the unit of analysis. Prioleau, Murdock, and Brody focus on a set of 32 controlled studies included in Smith et al.'s (1980) meta-analysis that examined the efficacy of psychotherapy, rather than behavior therapy, and that compared psychotherapy with a placebo (psychologically inactive) treatment. Prioleau, Murdock, and Brody report a mean effect size of .42 for these 32 studies, which superficially is supportive of the effectiveness of psychotherapy. Nevertheless, they point out that their findings run counter to a number of intuitive predictions, such as that the effects of placebo treatment relative to psychotherapy should gradually diminish over time and that the effects of psychotherapy relative to placebo treatment should be greatest for less reactive outcome measures. Moreover, Prioleau, Murdock, and Brody note that the only studies demonstrating the superiority of psychotherapy over placebo treatment did not involve actual patients. The authors conclude that the effectiveness of psychotherapy for psychiatric patients has not been convincingly demonstrated.

KEY CONCEPTS AND TERMS

double-blind design Experimental design in which neither the experimenter nor the subject is aware of which condition (experimental or control) the subject is in.

ecological validity Extent to which a measure is relevant to the individual's behavior in "real life."

implosive therapy Class of treatments, typically used for anxiety disorders, that involve exposing patients to high-intensity versions of the stimuli that are the object of their fear.

multidimensional scaling Statistical procedure that allows the investigator to quantify and visualize the similarities and differences among a set of techniques, objects, or individuals on a series of dimensions. In the article by Smith and Glass, multidimensional scaling is used to quantify and visualize the similarities and differences among various psychotherapies.

reactivity Extent to which a psychological measure is potentially influenced by subjects' knowledge that their scores are being measured. Thus, a reactive measure is one that is capable of being affected by the process of measurement itself.

regression analysis Statistical procedure that allows the investigator to examine the relationship between multiple independent variables and a single dependent variable.

systematic desensitization Commonly used behavioral treatment for specific phobias and several other anxiety disorders. Systematic desensitization has two major components: deep-muscle relaxation and an anxiety hierarchy, or "ladder" of progressively anxiety-provoking experiences, constructed in conjunction with the therapist. In systematic desensitization, the client is first asked to relax and is then presented with increasingly anxiety-provoking levels of feared stimuli.

PREVIEW QUESTIONS

1. What is meta-analysis? According to Smith and Glass, how is it superior to the "voting" method?
2. What are Smith and Glass's principal findings on the overall effectiveness of psychotherapy?
3. What do Smith and Glass report concerning the relative effectiveness of different schools of therapy? What do they conclude about the magnitude of these differences?
4. What variables do Smith and Glass find to be correlated with the overall effect size of psychotherapy outcomes?
5. What are Prioleau, Murdock, and Brody's criticisms of Smith and colleagues' procedures? In what ways do their criteria for the selection of studies differ from those of Smith and Glass?
6. What criteria do Prioleau, Murdock, and Brody use to decide whether a manipulation constitutes a placebo?
7. What is Prioleau, Murdock, and Brody's principal finding on the overall effectiveness of psychotherapy relative to placebo treatment?
8. What relationships, if any, do Prioleau, Murdock, and Brody find between therapeutic effectiveness and such variables as duration of treatment, use of real patients, and type of outcome measure? What do they conclude regarding the efficacy of psychotherapy with real patients?

MARY LEE SMITH & GENE V. GLASS

Meta-analysis of psychotherapy outcome studies

Scholars and clinicians have argued bitterly for decades about the efficacy of psychotherapy and counseling. Michael Scriven proposed to the American Psychological Association's Ethics Committee that APA-member clinicians be required to present a card to prospective clients on which it would be explained that the procedure they were about to undergo had never been proven superior to a placebo ("Psychotherapy Caveat," 1974). Most academics have read little more than Eysenck's (1952, 1965) tendentious diatribes in which he claimed to prove that 75% of neurotics got better regardless of whether or not they were in therapy—a conclusion based on the interpretation of six controlled studies. The perception that research shows the inefficacy of psychotherapy has become part of conventional wisdom even within the profession. The following testimony was recently presented before the Colorado State Legislature:

> Are they [the legislators] also aware of the relatively primitive state of the art of treatment outcome evaluation which is still, after fifty years, in kind of a virginal state? About all we've been able to prove is that a third of the people get better, a third of the people stay the same, and a third of the people get worse, irregardless of the treatment to which they are subjected. (Quoted by Ellis, 1977, p. 3)

Only close followers of the issue have read Bergin's (1971) astute dismantling of the Eysenck myth in his review of the findings of 23 controlled evaluations of therapy. Bergin found evidence that therapy is effective. Emrick (1975) reviewed 72 studies of the psychological and psychopharmacological treatment of alcoholism and concluded that evidence existed for the efficacy of therapy. Luborsky, Singer, and Luborsky (1975) reviewed about 40 controlled studies and found more evidence. Although these reviews were reassuring, two sources of doubt remained. First, the number of studies in which the effects of counseling and psychotherapy have been tested is closer to 400 than to 40. How representative the 40 are of the 400 is unknown. Second, in these reviews the "voting method" was used; that is, the number of studies with statistically significant results in favor of one treatment or another was tallied. This method is too weak to answer many important questions and is biased in favor of large-sample studies.

The purpose of the present research has three parts: (1) to identify and collect all studies that tested the effects of counseling and psychotherapy; (2) to determine the magnitude of effect of the therapy in each study; and (3) to compare the effects of different types of therapy and relate the size of effect to the characteristics of the therapy (e.g., diagnosis of patient, training of therapist) and of the study. Meta-analysis, the integration of research through statistical analysis of the analyses of individual studies (Glass, 1976), was used to investigate the problem.

PROCEDURES

Standard search procedures were used to identify 1,000 documents: *Psychological Abstracts*, *Dissertation Abstracts*, and branching off of bibliographies of the documents themselves. Of those documents located, approximately 500 were selected for inclusion in the study, and 375 were fully analyzed. To be selected, a study had to have a least one therapy treatment group compared to an untreated group or to a different therapy group. The rigor of the research design was not a selection criterion but was one of several features of the individual study to be related to the effect of the treatment in that study. The definition of psychotherapy used to select the studies was presented by Meltzoff and Kornreich (1970):

> Psychotherapy is taken to mean the informed and planful application of techniques derived from established psychological principles, by persons qualified through training and experience to understand these principles and to apply these techniques with the intention of assisting individuals to modify such personal characteristics as feelings, values, attitudes, and behaviors which are judged by the therapist to be maladaptive or maladjustive. (p. 6)

Those studies in which the treatment was labeled "counseling" but whose methods fit the above definition were included. Drug therapies, hypnotherapy, bibliotherapy, occupational therapy, milieu therapy, and peer counseling were excluded. Sensitivity training, marathon encounter groups, consciousness-raising

The research reported here was supported by a grant from the Spencer Foundation, Chicago, Illinois.

SOURCE: *American Psychologist, 32*, pp. 752–760, September 1977.

groups, and psychodrama were also excluded. Those studies that Bergin and Luborsky eliminated because they used "analogue" therapy were retained for the present research. Such studies have been designated analogue studies because therapy lasted only a few hours or the therapists were relatively untrained. Rather than arbitrarily eliminating large numbers of studies and losing potentially valuable information, it was deemed preferable to retain these studies and investigate the relationship between length of therapy, training of therapists, and other characteristics of the study and their measured effects. The arbitrary elimination of such analogue studies was based on an implicit assumption that they differ not only in their methods but also in their effects and how those effects are achieved. Considering methods, analogue studies fade imperceptibly into "real" therapy, since the latter is often short term, or practiced by relative novices, etc. Furthermore, the magnitude of effects and their relationships with other variables are empirical questions, not to be assumed out of existence. Dissertations and fugitive documents were likewise retained, and the measured effects of the studies compared according to the source of the studies.

The most important feature of an outcome study was the magnitude of the effect of therapy. The definition of the magnitude of effect—or "*effect size*"—*was* the *mean difference between the treated and control subjects divided by the standard deviation of the control group*, that is, $ES = \left(\overline{X}_T - \overline{X}_C\right) / s_c$. Thus, an "effect size" of +1 indicates that a person at the mean of the control group would be expected to rise to the 84th percentile of the control group after treatment.

The effect size was calculated on any outcome variable the researcher chose to measure. In many cases, one study yielded more than one effect size, since effects might be measured at more than one time after treatment or on more than one different type of outcome variable. The effect-size measures represent different types of outcomes: self-esteem, anxiety, work/school achievement, physiological stress, etc. Mixing different outcomes together is defensible. First, it is clear that all outcome measures are more or less related to "well-being" and so at a general level are comparable. Second, it is easy to imagine a Senator conducting hearings on the NIMH [National Institute of Mental Health] appropriations or a college president deciding whether to continue funding the counseling center asking, "What kind of effect does therapy produce—on anything?" Third, each primary researcher made value judgments concerning the definition and direction of positive therapeutic effects for the particular clients he or she studied. It is reasonable to adopt these value judgments and aggregate them in the present study. Fourth, since all effect sizes are identified by type of outcome, the magnitude of effect can be compared across type of outcome to determine whether therapy has greater effect on anxiety, for example, than it does on self-esteem.

Calculating effect sizes was straightforward when means and standard deviations were reported. Although this information is thought to be fundamental in reporting research, it was often overlooked by authors and editors. When means and standard deviations were not reported, effect sizes were obtained by the solution of equations from t and F ratios or other inferential test statistics. Probit transformations were used to convert to effect sizes the percentages of patients who improved (Glass, 1977). Original data were requested from several authors when effect sizes could not be derived from any reported information. In two instances, effect sizes were impossible to reconstruct: (a) nonparametric statistics irretrievably disguise effect sizes, and (b) the reporting of no data except the alpha level at which a mean difference was significant gives no clue other than that the standardized mean difference must exceed some known value.

Eight hundred thirty-three effect sizes were computed from 375 studies, several studies yielding effects on more than one type of outcome or at more than one time after therapy. Including more than one effect size for each study perhaps introduces dependence in the errors and violates some assumptions of inferential statistics. However, the loss of information that would have resulted from averaging effects across types of outcome or at different follow-up points was too great a price to pay for statistical purity.

The effect sizes of the separate studies became the "dependent variable" in the meta-analysis. The "independent variables" were 16 features of the study described or measured in the following ways:

1. The type of therapy employed, for example, psychodynamic, client centered, rational-emotive, behavior modification, etc. There were 10 types in all; each will be mentioned in the Results section.
2. The duration of therapy in hours.
3. Whether it was group or individual therapy.
4. The number of years' experience of the therapist.
5. Whether clients were neurotics or psychotics.
6. The age of the clients.
7. The IQ of the clients.
8. The source of the subjects—whether solicited for the study, committed to an institution, or sought treatment themselves.
9. Whether the therapists were trained in education, psychology, or psychiatry.
10. The social and ethnic similarity of therapists and clients.
11. The type of outcome measure taken.
12. The number of months after therapy that the outcomes were measured.
13. The reactivity or "fakeability" of the outcome measure.
14. The date of publication of the study.
15. The form of publication.
16. The internal validity of the research design.

Definitions and conventions were developed to increase the reliability of measurement of the features of the studies and to assist the authors in estimating the data when they were not reported. The more important conventions appear in Table 1. Variables not mentioned in Table 1 were measured in fairly obvious ways. The reliability of measurement was determined by comparing the codings of 20 studies by the two authors and four assistants. Agreement exceeded 90% across all categories.*

Analysis of the data comprised four parts: (1) descriptive statistics for the body of data as a whole; (2) descriptive statistics for the comparison of therapy types and outcome types; (3) descriptive statistics for a subset of studies in which behavioral and nonbehavioral therapies were compared *in the same study*; and (4) regression analyses in which effect sizes were regressed onto variables descriptive of the study.

FINDINGS

Data from All Experiments

Figure 1 contains the findings at the highest level of aggregation. The two curves depict the average treated and untreated groups of clients across 375 studies, 833 effect-size measures, representing an evaluation of approximately 25,000 control and experimental subjects each. On the average, clients 22 years of age received 17 hours of therapy from therapists with about 3½ years of experience and were measured on the outcome variables about 3¾ months after the therapy.

For ease of representation, the figure is drawn in the form of two normal distributions. No conclusion about the distributions of the scores within studies is intended. In most studies, no information was given about the shape of an individual's scores within treated and untreated groups. We suspect that normality has as much justification as any other form.

The average study showed a .68 standard deviation superiority of the treated group over the control group. Thus, the average client receiving therapy was better off than 75% of the untreated controls. Ironically, the 75% figure that Eysenck used repeatedly to embarrass psychotherapy appears in a slightly different context as the most defensible figure on the efficacy of therapy: The therapies represented by the available outcome evaluations move the average client from the 50th to the 75th percentile.

The standard deviation of the effect sizes is .67. Their skewness is +.99. Only 12% of the 833 effect-size measures from the 375 studies were negative. If therapies of any type were ineffective and design and measurement flaws were immaterial, one would expect half the effect-size measures to be negative.

The 833 effect-size measures were classified into 10 categories descriptive of the type of outcome being assessed, for example, fear and anxiety reduction, self-esteem, adjustment (freedom from debilitating symptoms), achievement in school or on the job, social relations, emotional-somatic problems, physiological stress measures, etc. Effect-size measures for four outcome categories are presented in Table 2.

Two hundred sixty-one effect sizes from over 100 studies average about 1 standard deviation on measures of fear and anxiety reduction. Thus, the average treated client is better off than 83% of those untreated with respect to the alleviation of fear and anxiety. The improvement in self-esteem is nearly as large. The effect sizes average .9 of a standard deviation. Improvement on variables in the "adjustment" outcome class averages considerably less, roughly .6 of a standard deviation. These outcome variables are measures of personal functioning and frequently involve indices of hospitalization or incarceration for psychotic, alcoholic, or criminal episodes. The average effect size for school or work achievement—most frequently "grade point average"—is smallest of the four outcome classes.

The studies in the four outcome measure categories are not comparable in terms of type of therapy, duration, experience of therapists, number of months of posttherapy at which outcomes were measured, etc. Nonetheless, the findings in Table 2 are fairly consistent with expectations and give the credible impression that fear and self-esteem are more susceptible to change in therapy than are the relatively more serious behaviors grouped under the categories "adjustment" and "achievement."

Table 3 presents the average effect sizes for 10 types of therapy. Nearly 100 effect-size measures arising from evaluations of psychodynamic therapy, that is, Freudianlike therapy but *not* psychoanalysis, average approximately .6 of a standard deviation. Studies of Adlerian therapy show an average of .7 sigma, but only 16 effect sizes were found. Eclectic therapies, that is, verbal, cognitive, nonbehavioral therapies more similar to psychodynamic therapies than any other type, gave a mean effect size of about .5 of a standard deviation. Although the number of controlled evaluations of Berne's transactional analysis was rather small, it gave a

FIGURE 1 Effect of Therapy on Any Outcome (data based on 375 studies; 833 data points)

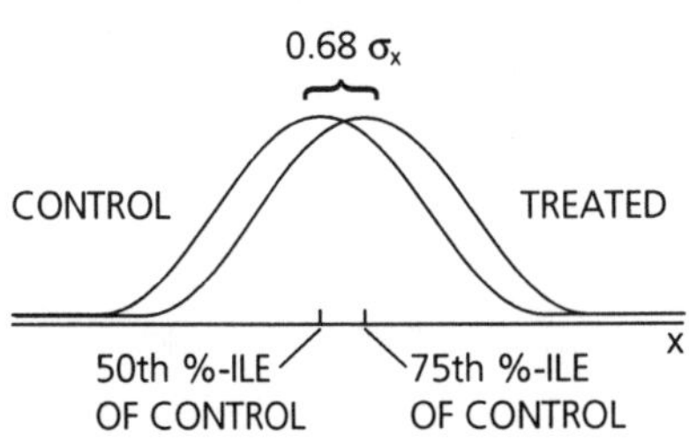

AVE. EFFECT SIZE: 0.68 σ_x
STD. DEV. OF EFFECT SIZE: 0.67 σ_x

*The values assigned to the features of the studies, the effect sizes, and all procedures are available in Smith, Glass, and Miller (Note 1).

TABLE 1 Conventions for Measurement of the Features of Studies

Study Feature	*Value*
Experience of therapist (when not given)	Lay counselor (0 years) MA candidate (1 year) MA counselor (2 years) PhD candidate or psychiatric resident (3 years) PhD therapist (4 years) Well-known PhD or psychiatrist (5 years)
Diagnosis of client (neurotic or psychotic)	Neurotic unless symptoms or labels clearly indicate otherwise
IQ of client (low, average, high)	Average unless identified as otherwise by diagnostic labels (e.g., mentally retarded) or institutional affiliation (college attendance)
Source of subjects	Clients solicited for purpose of the study Clients committed to institution, hence to therapy Clients recognized existence of problem and sought treatment
Similarity of therapist and client ("very similar" to "very dissimilar")	College students: very similar Neurotic adults: moderately similar Juveniles, minorities: moderately dissimilar Hospitalized, chronic adults, disturbed children, prisoners: very dissimilar
Type of outcome measure	Fear, anxiety: Spielberger & Cattell anxiety measures, behavioral approach tests Self-esteem: inventories, self-ideal correlations, ratings by self and others Adjustment: adjustment scales, improvement ratings, rehospitalization, time out of hospital, sobriety, symptomatic complaints, disruptive behavior Work/school achievement: grade point average, job supervisor ratings, promotions Personality traits: MMPI or other trait inventories, projective test results Social behavior: dating, classroom discipline, public speaking, information-seeking behavior, sociometrics Emotional-somatic disorder: frigidity, impotence Physiological stress: galvanic skin response, Palmer Sweat Index, blood pressure, heart rate
Reactivity of measurement	1 (low): Physiological measures; grade point average 2 Projective device (blind); discharge from hospital (blind) 3 Standardized measures of traits (MMPI, Rotter) 4 Experimenter-constructed questionnaires; client's self-report to experimenter; discharge (nonblind); behavior in presence of therapist 5 (high): Therapist rating; projective device (nonblind)
Form of publication	Journal Book Thesis Unpublished document
Internal validity (high, medium, low)	High: Randomization, low mortality Medium: More than one threat to internal validity Low: No matching of pretest information to equate groups

respectable average effect size of .6 sigma, the same as psychodynamic therapies. Albert Ellis's rational-emotive therapy, with a mean effect size of nearly .8 of a standard deviation, finished second among all 10 therapy types. The Gestalt therapies were relatively untested, but 8 studies showed 16 effect sizes averaging only .25 of a standard deviation. Rogerian client-centered therapy showed a .6 sigma effect size averaged across about 60 studies. The average of over 200 effect-size measures from approximately 100 studies of systematic desensitization therapy was .9 sigma, the largest average effect size of all therapy types. Implosive therapy showed a mean effect size of .64 of a standard deviation, about equal to that for Rogerian and psychodynamic therapies. Significantly, the average effect size for implosive therapy is markedly lower than for systematic desensitization, which was usually evaluated in studies using similar kinds of clients with similar problems—principally, simple phobias. The final therapy depicted in Table 3 is Skinnerian behavior modification, which showed a .75 sigma effect size.

Hay's ω^2, which relates the categorical variable "type of therapy" to the quantitative variable "effect size," has the value of .10 for the data in Table 3. Thus, these 10 therapy types account for 10% of the variance in the effect size that studies produce.

The types of therapy depicted in Table 3 were clearly not equated for duration, severity of problem, type of outcome, etc. Nonetheless, the differences in average effect sizes are interesting and interpretable. There is probably a tendency for researchers to evaluate the therapy they like best and to pick clients, circumstances, and outcome measures which show that therapy in the best light. Even so, major differences among the therapies appear. Implosive therapy is demonstrably inferior to systematic desensitization. Behavior modification shows the same mean effect size as rational-emotive therapy.

TABLE 2 Effects of Therapy on Four Types of Outcome Measure

Type of Outcome	*Average Effect Size*	*No. of Effect Sizes*	*Standard Error of Mean Effect Size*[a]	*Mdn Treated Person's Percentile Status in Control Group*
Fear-anxiety reduction	.97	261	.15	83
Self-esteem	.90	53	.13	82
Adjustment	.56	229	.05	71
School/work achievement	.31	145	.03	62

[a]The standard errors of the mean are calculated by dividing the standard deviation of the effect sizes (not reported) by the square root of the number of them. This method, based on the assumption of independence known to be false, gives a lower bound to the standard errors (Tukey, Note 2). Inferential techniques employing Tukey's jackknife method which take the nonindependence into account are examined in Glass (1977).

TABLE 3 Effects of Ten Types of Therapy on Any Outcome Measure

Type of Therapy	*Average Effect Size*	*No. of Effect Sizes*	*Standard Error of Mean Effect Size*	*Mdn Treated Person's Percentile Status in Control Group*
Psychodynamic	.59	96	.05	72
Adlerian	.71	16	.19	76
Eclectic	.48	70	.07	68
Transactional analysis	.58	25	.19	72
Rational-emotive	.77	35	.13	78
Gestalt	.26	8	.09	60
Client-centered	.63	94	.08	74
Systematic desensitization	.91	223	.05	82
Implosion	.64	45	.09	74
Behavior modification	.76	132	.06	78

Effects of Classes of Therapy

To compare the effect of therapy type after equating for duration of therapy, diagnosis of client, type of outcome, etc., it was necessary to move to a coarser level of analysis in which data could be grouped into more stable composites. The problem was to group the 10 types of therapy into classes, so that effect sizes could be compared among more general types of therapy. Methods of multidimensional scaling were used to derive a structure from the perceptions of similarities among the 10 therapies by a group of 25 clinicians and counselors. All of the judges in this scaling study were enrolled in a graduate-level seminar. For five weeks, the theory and techniques of the 10 therapies were studied and discussed. Then, each judge performed a multidimensional rank ordering of the therapies, judging similarity among them on whatever basis he or she chose, articulated or unarticulated, conscious or unconscious. The results of the Shepard-Kruskal multidimensional scaling analysis appear as Figure 2.

FIGURE 2 Multidimensional Scaling of 10 Therapies by 25 Clinicians and Counselors

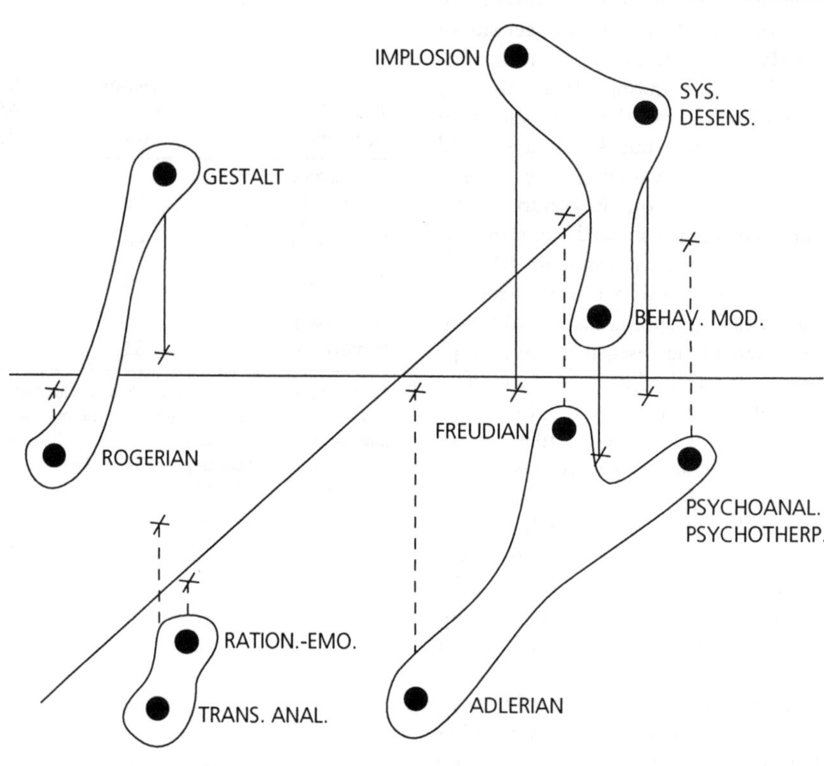

In Figure 2 one clearly sees four classes of therapies: the ego therapies (transactional analysis and rational-emotive therapy) in front; the three dynamic therapies low, in the background; the behavioral triad, upper right; and the pair of "humanistic" therapies, Gestalt and Rogerian. The average effect sizes among the four classes of therapies have been compared, but the findings are not reported here. Instead, a higher level of aggregation of the therapies, called "superclasses," was studied. The first superclass was formed from those therapies above the horizontal plane in Figure 2, with the exception of Gestalt therapy for which there was an inadequate number of studies. This superclass was then identical with the group of behavioral therapies: implosion, systematic desensitization, and behavior modification. The second superclass comprises the six therapies below the horizontal plane in Figure 2 and is termed the *nonbehavioral superclass*, a composite of psychoanalytic psychotherapy, Adlerian, Rogerian, rational-emotive, eclectic therapy, and transactional analysis.

Figure 3 represents the mean effect sizes for studies classified by the two superclasses. On the average, approximately 200 evaluations of behavioral therapies showed a mean effect of about $.8\sigma_x$, standard error of .03, over the control group. Approximately 170 evaluations of nonbehavioral studies gave a mean effect size of $.6\sigma_x$, standard error of .04. This small difference ($.2\sigma_x$) between the outcomes of behavioral and nonbehavioral therapies must be considered in light of the circumstances under which these studies were conducted. The evaluators of behavioral superclass therapies waited an average of 2 months after the therapy to measure its effects, whereas the postassessment of the nonbehavioral therapies was made in the vicinity of 5 months, on the average. Furthermore, the reactivity of susceptibility to bias of the outcome measures was higher for the behavioral superclass than for the nonbehavioral superclass; that is, the behavioral researchers showed a slightly greater tendency to rely on more subjective outcome measures. These differences lead one to suspect that the $.2\sigma_x$ difference between the behavioral and nonbehavioral superclasses is somewhat exaggerated in favor of the behavioral superclass. Exactly how much the difference ought to be reduced is a question that can be approached in at least two ways: (a) examine the behavioral versus nonbehavioral difference for only those studies in which one therapy from each superclass was represented, since for those studies the experimental circumstances will be equivalent; (2) regress "effect size" onto

FIGURE 3 Effect of Superclass #1 (Behavioral) and Superclass #2 (Nonbehavioral)

TREATMENT DESCRIPTION

	SUPERCLASS #1	SUPERCLASS #2
AVE. FOLLOW-UP	2.01 mos.	4.70 mos.
AVE. REACTIVITY	3.44	3.18

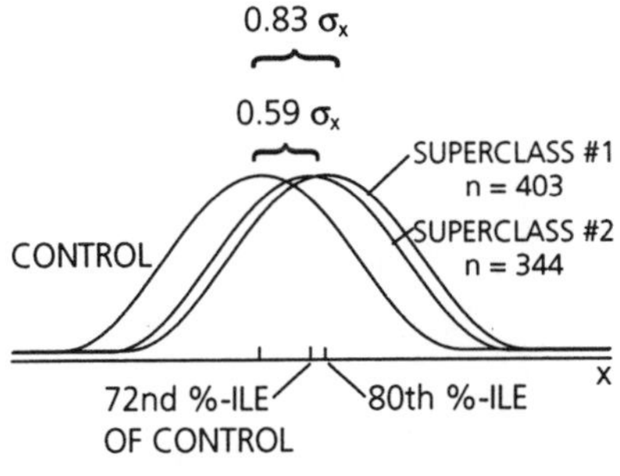

FIGURE 4 Effect of Superclass #1 (Behavioral) and Superclass #2 (Nonbehavioral) (data drawn only from experiments in which Superclass #1 and Superclass #2 were simultaneously compared with control)

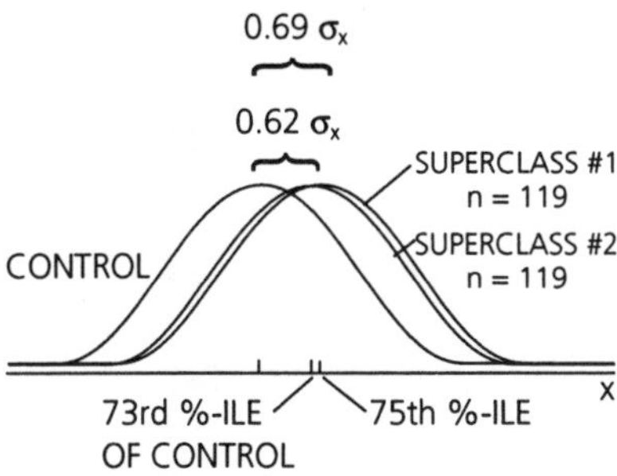

variables descriptive of the study and correct statistically for differences in circumstances between behavioral and nonbehavioral studies.

Figure 4 represents 120 effect-size measures derived from those studies, approximately 50 in number, in which a behavioral therapy and nonbehavioral therapy were compared simultaneously with an untreated control. Hence, for these studies, the collective behavioral and nonbehavioral therapies are equivalent with respect to all important features of the experimental setting, namely, experience of the therapists, nature of the clients' problems, duration of therapy, type of outcome measure, months after therapy for measuring the outcomes, etc.

The results are provocative. The $.2\sigma_x$ "uncontrolled" difference in Figure 3 has shrunk to a $.07\sigma_x$ difference in average effect size. The standard error of the mean of the 119 different scores (behavioral effect size minus nonbehavioral effect size in each study) is $.66/\sqrt{119} = .06$. The behavioral and nonbehavioral therapies show about the same average effect.

The second approach to correcting for measurable differences between behavioral and nonbehavioral therapies is statistical adjustment by regression analysis. By this method, it is possible to quantify and study the natural covariation among the principal outcome variable of studies and the many variables descriptive of the context of the studies.

Eleven features of each study were correlated with the effect size the study produced (Table 4). For example, the correlation between the duration of the therapy in hours and the effect size of the study is nearly zero, –.02. The correlations are generally low, although several are reliably nonzero. Some of the more interesting correlations show a positive relationship between an estimate of the intelligence of the group of clients and the effect of therapy, and a somewhat larger correlation indicating that therapists who resemble their clients in ethnic group, age, and social level get better results. The effect sizes diminish across time after therapy as shown by the last correlation in Table 4, a correlation of –.10 which is closer to –.20 when the curvilinearity of the relationship is taken into account. The largest correlation is with the "reactivity" or subjectivity of the outcome measure.

The multiple correlation of these variables with effect size is about .50. Thus, 25% of the variance in the results of studies can be reduced by specification of independent variable values. In several important subsets of the data not reported here, the multiple correlations are over .70, which indicates that in some instances it is possible to reduce more than half of the variability in study findings by regressing the outcome effect onto contextual variables of the study.

The results of three separate multiple regression analyses appear in Table 5. Multiple regressions were performed within each of three types of therapy: psychodynamic, systematic desensitization, and behavior modification. Relatively complex forms of the independent variables were used to account for interactions and nonlinear relationships. For example, years' experience of the therapist bore a slight curvilinear relationship with outcome, probably because more experienced therapists worked with more seriously ill clients. This situation was accommodated by entering, as an independent variable, "therapist experience" in interaction with "diagnosis of the client." Age of client and follow-up date were slightly curvilinearly related to outcome in ways most directly handled by changing exponents. These regression equations allow estimation of the effect size a study shows when undertaken with a certain type of client, with a therapist of a certain level of experience, etc. By setting the independent variables at a particular set of values, one can estimate what a study of that type would reveal under each of the three types of therapy. Thus, a statistically controlled comparison of the effects of psychodynamic, systematic desensitization, and behavior modification therapies can be obtained in this case. The three regression equations are clearly not homogeneous; hence, one therapy might be superior under one set of circumstances and a different therapy superior under others. A full description of the nature of this

TABLE 4 Correlations of Several Descriptive Variables with Effect Size

Variable	*Correlation with Effect Size*
Organization (1 = individual; 2 = group)	–.07
Duration of therapy (in hours)	–.02
Years' experience of therapists	–.01
Diagnosis of clients (1 = psychotic; 2 = neurotic)	.02
IQ of clients (1 = low; 2 = medium; 3 = high)	.15**
Age of clients	.02
Similarity of therapists and clients (1 = very similar; . . . ; 4 = very dissimilar)	–.19*
Internal validity of study (1 = high; 2 = medium; 3 = low)	–.09*
Date of publication	.09*
"Reactivity" of outcome measure (1 = low; . . . ; 5 = high)	.30**
No. of months posttherapy for follow-up	–.10*

*$p < .05$
**$p < .01$

interaction is elusive, though one can illustrate it at various particularly interesting points.

In Figure 5, estimates are made of the effect sizes that would be shown for studies in which simple phobias of high-intelligence subjects, 20 years of age, are treated by a therapist with 2 years' experience and evaluated immediately after therapy with highly subjective outcome measures. This verbal description of circumstances can be translated into quantitative values for the independent variable in Table 5 and substituted into each of the three regression equations. In this instance, the two behavioral therapies show effects superior to the psychodynamic therapy.

In Figure 6, a second prototypical psychotherapy client and situation are

TABLE 5 Regression Analyses within Therapies

	Unstandardized Regression Coefficients		
Independent Variable	*Psychodynamic (n = 94)*	*Systematic Desensitization (n = 212)*	*Behavior Modification (n = 129)*
Diagnosis (1 = psychotic; 2 = neurotic)	.174	–.193	.041
Intelligence (1 = low; . . . ; 3 = high)	–.114	.201	.201
Transformed age[a]	.002	–.002	.002
Experience of Therapist × Neurotic	–.011	–.034	–.018
Experience of Therapist × Psychotic	–.015	.004	–.033
Clients self-presented	–.111	.287	–.015
Clients solicited	.182	.088	–.163
Organization (1 = individual; 2 = group)	.108	–.086	–.276
Transformed months posttherapy[b]	–.031	–.047	.007
Transformed reactivity of measure[c]	.003	.025	.021
Additive constant	.757	.489	.453
Multiple R	.423	.512	.509
σ_e	.173	.386	.340

[a]Transformed age = $(\text{Age} - 25)(|\text{Age} - 25|)^{1/2}$
[b]Transformed months posttherapy = $(\text{No. months})^{1/2}$
[c]Transformed reactivity of measure = $(\text{Reactivity})^{2.25}$

FIGURE 5 Three Within-Therapy Regression Equations Set to Describe a Prototypic Therapy Client (Phobic) and Therapy Situation

ESTIMATED EFFECT SIZES	
PSYCHODYNAMIC	0.919
SYSTEMATIC DESENSITIZATION	1.049
BEHAVIORAL MODIFICATION	1.119

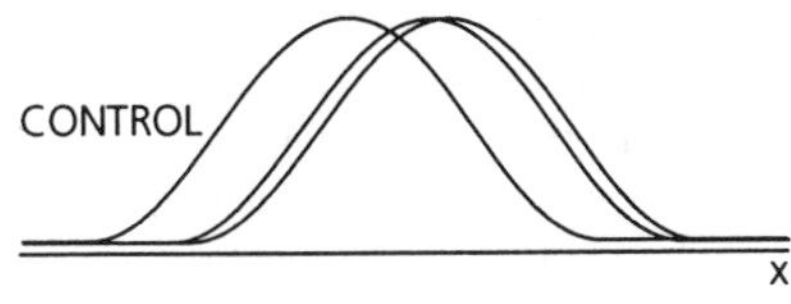

FIGURE 6 Three Within-Therapy Regression Equations Set to Describe a Prototypic Therapy Client (Neurotic) and Therapy Situation

ESTIMATED EFFECT SIZES	
PSYCHODYNAMIC	0.643
SYSTEMATIC DESENSITIZATION	0.516
BEHAVIORAL MODIFICATION	0.847

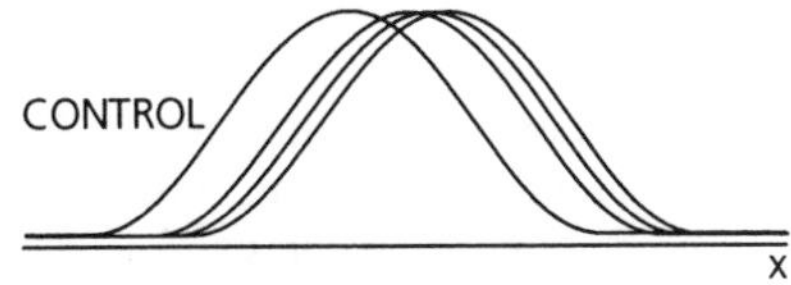

captured in the independent variable values, and the effects of the three types of therapy are estimated. For the typical 30-year-old neurotic of average IQ seen in circumstances like those that prevail in mental health clinics (individual therapy by a therapist with 5 years' experience), behavior modification is estimated to be superior to psychodynamic therapy, which is in turn superior to systematic desensitization at the 6-month follow-up point.

Besides illuminating the relationships in the data, the quantitative techniques described here can give direction to future research. By fitting regression equations to the relationship between effect size and the independent variables descriptive of the studies and then by placing confidence regions around these hyperplanes, the regions where the input-output relationships are most poorly determined can be identified. By concentrating new studies in these regions, one can avoid the accumulation of redundant studies of convenience that overelaborate small areas.

CONCLUSIONS

The results of research demonstrate the beneficial effects of counseling and psychotherapy. Despite volumes devoted to the theoretical differences among different schools of psychotherapy, the results of research demonstrate negligible differences in the effects produced by different therapy types. Unconditional judgments of superiority of one type or another of psychotherapy, and all that these claims imply about treatment and training policy, are unjustified. Scholars and clinicians are in the rather embarrassing position of knowing less than has been proven, because knowledge, atomized and sprayed across a vast landscape of journals, books, and reports, has not been accessible. Extracting knowledge from accumulated studies is a complex and important methodological problem which deserves further attention.

NOTES

1. Smith, M. L., Glass, G. V., & Miller, T. I. *The benefits of psychotherapy*. Baltimore: Johns Hopkins University Press, 1980.
2. Tukey, J. W. Personal communication, November 15, 1976.

REFERENCES

Bergin, A. E. The evaluation of therapeutic outcomes. In A. E. Bergin & S. L. Garfield (Eds.), *Handbook of psychotherapy and behavior change*. New York: Wiley, 1971.

Ellis, R. H. Letters. *Colorado Psychological Association Newsletter*, April 1977, p. 3.

Emrick, C. D. A review of psychologically oriented treatment of alcoholism. *Journal of Studies on Alcohol, 1975, 36*, 88–108.

Eysenck, H. J. The effects of psychotherapy: An evaluation. *Journal of Consulting Psychology*, 1952, *16*, 319–324.

Eysenck, H. J. The effects of psychotherapy: An evaluation. *Journal of Consulting Psychology*, 1965, *1*, 97–118.

Glass, G. V. Primary, secondary, and meta-analysis of research. *The Educational Researcher*, 1976, *10*, 3–8.

Glass, G. V. Integrating findings: The meta-analysis of research. In Lo Schulman (Ed.), *Review of research in education*. Itasca, Ill.: Peacock, 1977.

Luborsky, L., Singer, B., & Luborsky, L. Comparative studies of psychotherapies. *Archives of General Psychiatry*, 1975, *32*, 995–1008.

Meltzoff, J., & Kornreich, M. *Research in psychotherapy*. New York: Atherton, 1970.

Psychotherapy caveat. *APA Monitor*, December, 1974, p. 7.

LESLIE PRIOLEAU, MARTHA MURDOCK, & NATHAN BRODY

An analysis of psychotherapy versus placebo studies

Eysenck's well-known (1952) paper is the first of a long series of studies dealing with the question of the effectiveness of psychotherapy. Eysenck argued that many patients recover spontaneously and that the changes following psychotherapy do not exceed the spontaneous recovery rate. Eysenck has reviewed literature on psychotherapy outcome on other occasions and has continued to argue that the studies suggest that psychotherapy is an ineffective treatment (see, e.g., Eysenck 1966). Other reviewers, more favorably disposed to psychotherapy, have argued that Eysenck distorted the data and dealt with a biased sample. Meltzoff and Korneich (1970), for example, reviewed a larger body of work dealing with psychotherapy outcomes and argued that the better-designed studies tended to provide stronger evidence for the benefits of psychotherapy and that there was an ample body of convincing evidence suggesting that psychotherapy was an effective treatment.

Smith, Glass, and Miller (1980) have attempted to resolve the controversy surrounding the effectiveness of psychotherapy by using the statistical procedure of meta-analysis as a technique for reviewing systematically a substantial—and, they claim, unbiased—portion of the literature dealing with the effectiveness of psychotherapy. They analyzed all the data they could find comparing psychotherapy or behavior therapy and a control group. For each dependent variable included in each of the studies surveyed they computed a measure of effect size defined as the difference between the mean of the therapy group and the mean of the control group, divided by the standard deviation of the control group. They conclude that the mean effect size of psychological therapies is .85, indicating that when averaged over all measures in all studies, the outcome of psychological therapy is superior to that of nontreatment in control groups.

Smith et al.'s (1980) analyses appear to provide definitive evidence in favor of the effectiveness of psychological therapies. However, we felt that the research analyzed by Smith et al. should be subjected to further analyses. We had some reservations about the use of meta-analytic procedures for a body of literature as diverse as that summarized by Smith et al. (1980) (see Eysenck 1978; Strahan 1978). [See also Rosenthal and Rubin (1978).] While meta-analysis may be appropriate for summarizing the results of investigations using the same dependent variable with similar subject populations, it is questionable whether the method should be extended to the analysis of research using grossly different patient populations being subjected to grossly different methods of therapy where the outcomes are assessed using different dependent variables. Accordingly, we have tried to look in somewhat greater detail at a subset of the studies used by Smith et al. (1980) and we have tried to supplement a meta-analysis by a more traditional examination of individual studies.

The procedures used by Smith et al. (1980) in their meta-analysis may not have been ideal. In particular, these researchers performed a meta-analysis using dependent variables as their unit of measure. This procedure, in effect, weights a study by the number of dependent variables included in the analysis. Given the degree of variability across studies, we feel that it is more appropriate to use the study itself as a unit of analysis. Accordingly, we present, separately, effect size measures for each dependent variable included within a study and we obtain a mean effect size for each one (see Landman & Dawes 1982 for a comparable reanalysis of a subset of the studies used by Smith et al. 1980).

In order to permit us to examine this body of literature in greater depth we have focused on the subset of studies reported by Smith et al. (1980) using psychotherapy rather than behavior therapy. Although psychotherapy and behavior therapy may no longer be as theoretically distinct as they once were, the techniques, patients, and methods of assessment of the outcomes of therapy used in the research literature for these two broad classes of therapeutic treatments are still somewhat different. Our decision to limit the scope of our analyses to research on psychotherapy was done in part for theoretical reasons and in part in order to permit us to examine a subset of studies in somewhat greater detail.

Finally, we restricted our analysis to those studies that included a placebo

SOURCE: *Behavioral and Brain Sciences*, 6, pp. 275–285, 1983.

treatment. We believe that placebo treatments provide a more appropriate control group for assessing psychotherapeutic outcome than the more usual wait-list controls. Wait-list controls may lead to outcomes that are more negative than would have occurred merely through the passage of time. Individuals who seek therapeutic services and who are placed in a wait-list control group may be disappointed. In addition, such individuals may be experiencing an unintended reverse placebo effect. In being told they are being placed on a wait list, they are in effect told that they should not expect to improve since no therapeutic intervention will be provided for them. Since there is no appropriate control for a wait-list control group, there is no way of testing this notion. Whether wait-list controls are appropriate or not, it is relevant to inquire whether the benefits of psychotherapy exceed changes attributable to placebo expectations. Smith et al. (1980) deal with this issue only in passing. They indicate that the majority of placebo-controlled studies are in the behavior-therapy rather than the psychotherapy outcome literature. They assert that psychological treatments are approximately twice as effective as placebo treatments, and accordingly they expect that a comparison of psychotherapy against placebo would yield an effect size of approximately .42 standard deviations. We will focus on this comparison in our analysis.

We had several reasons for focusing on the comparison of psychotherapy treatments and placebo treatments. First, as a general principle, the comparison of treatment with some type of placebo control is a standard research design. The comparison is justified, since there is abundant evidence that individuals who believe they are receiving a treatment will improve as a result of the belief they are in treatment, even if there is no other theoretical reason for the treatment to be efficacious (see Shapiro & Morris 1978).

Second, we were aware of a study by Brill, Koegler, Epstein, and Forgy (1964) which provided evidence that the psychotherapy effect was equivalent to the placebo effect. Brill et al. (1964) randomly assigned psychiatric outpatients to one of several groups: a psychotherapy group that received 20 sessions of psychoanalytically oriented psychotherapy administered by psychiatric residents; a wait-list control group; a pill-placebo group that received chemically inert pills combined with occasional brief visits to psychiatrists (primarily to check on their response to medication, which was administered in a double blind design); and groups that received psychoactive drugs. Several outcome measures were used to assess therapeutic effects including the MMPI (Minnesota Multiphasic Personality Inventory), therapist and patient ratings, independent reports by a social worker, and a rating from a relative, spouse, or friend. Brill et al. (1964) report that for all measures the patients who received treatment were improved relative to the patients who were assigned to the wait-list control group. However, there were no significant differences among the various forms of treatment, including the placebo treatment. Brill et al. (1964) examine the effectiveness of psychoanalytically oriented psychotherapy of somewhat longer duration than is characteristic of many outcome studies, have a sample size exceeding that which is typical in outcome research (30 patients in each of several conditions), and use real patients. They provide evidence for the proposition that the effects of psychotherapy are equivalent to the effects of a relatively minimal placebo, which is essentially equivalent to knowledge that one is in treatment.

There are several limitations to the Brill et al. (1964) study. There was a high dropout rate; although the range of dependent variables used to assess outcomes was moderately varied, there were no behavioral measures used; and the therapy was administered by relatively inexperienced therapists. We wanted to see whether the corpus of about 500 studies included in the Smith et al. (1980) reviews would yield data that contradicted or supported the results obtained by Brill et al. (1964).

Third, an analysis of the differences between psychotherapy and placebo treatments may have implications for the provision of psychological treatment. If, for example, psychotherapy is no more effective than pill placebos, it may be cheaper and simpler to provide patients with pill placebos administered by general practitioners rather than long and relatively expensive treatment by trained psychotherapists. Our example should not be construed as advocacy of any form of treatment. Rather, we use the example as an illustration of the proposition that the results of an analysis of outcome research comparing psychotherapy to placebo treatments may have consequences for the design of treatment programs.

Fourth, there are results in the literature which are at least suggestive of the possibility that the outcomes of psychotherapy may, in part, be attributable to the influence of placebos. These include the following:

A. Duration of treatment is unrelated to the magnitude of therapeutic effect, according to Smith et al. (1980). If quite brief treatment and extended treatment produce outcomes of similar magnitude, one is led to believe that the activities engaged in by the therapist are irrelevant to the outcomes of treatment.
B. There is a body of research which suggests that experience and training in psychotherapy are unrelated to the magnitude of the psychotherapeutic effect (see Durlak 1979). Presumably, professional training would lead a therapist to engage in therapeutically relevant activities in a more accomplished manner. If the competence acquired by the therapist is unrelated to therapeutic outcome then it is possible that the activities of the therapist are not the cause of the changes in the patient.

C. Strupp (1973) and Bergin and Lambert (1978), among others, have suggested that some of the variance in outcome of psychotherapy is attributable to the characteristics of the patient. Patients who are articulate and intelligent and inclined to interpret their problems as being of psychological origin are said to have a higher probability of favorable outcome than patients without these characteristics. If there are patient characteristics that can predict the outcomes of psychotherapy, it is at least possible that these effects occur autonomously. That is, certain patients have the ability to change either as a result of their personality characteristics or the environmental circumstances in which they find themselves, or both, and a sufficient condition for the change is the knowledge that one is receiving some form of therapy. Thus it is possible that the activities of the therapist are irrelevant to the actual changes that occur.

D. Strupp (1977) and Bergin and Lambert (1978) have suggested that in a small minority of patients psychotherapy may produce adverse outcomes. While the general effect of placebo treatment is beneficial, placebo effects have also been found on occasion to produce reverse effects. Duncan and Laird (1980), for example, have suggested that individuals who are self-attentive are more likely to experience reverse placebo effects. Such individuals may become aware of the fact that a placebo has not dramatically altered their condition even though they were told it would be beneficial, and as a result they infer that their problems are more severe than they had thought. Thus placebo effects could, in principle, account for a possible deterioration effect in a minority of patients as a result of psychotherapy.

We do not mean to imply that we accept any of these conclusions about the results of outcome research on psychotherapy. We merely wish to indicate that a number of the conclusions which responsible reviewers have drawn from their examination of outcome studies are at least compatible with the assertion that part or all of the psychotherapy effect is attributable to the effects of placebos.

We have used the term "placebo" without an explicit definition. We consider a treatment a placebo treatment if the patient is led to believe that the treatment is efficacious and the treatment does not contain any other therapeutic components. Such a treatment defines an ideal case of a placebo. An operational procedure that comes close to meeting this idealized definition is the provision of a chemically inert pill to a patient combined with the assertion by a professional therapist that the pill will be an effective treatment. There are several variables than can, at least on speculative grounds, influence the effectiveness of this type of treatment. The patient must believe the assertion made by the therapist, and if the therapist harbors doubt about the effectiveness of chemically inert medications (or, in the case of a double blind study, of psychoactive drugs) for the treatment of psychological problems, the therapist may in subtle ways communicate these doubts to the patient and the effectiveness of the placebo may be mitigated. Moreover, the beliefs of the patient with respect to the potential efficacy of pill medications for the treatment of psychological problems may influence the effectiveness of such placebo treatments. Finally, in an actual experimental situation pill placebos may be accompanied by several other quasitherapeutic elements. For example, in the Brill et al. (1964) study, patients who received drug treatments including placebo were seen by resident psychiatrists for 15 minutes or less weekly, biweekly, or monthly. The sessions were brief in order to decrease the probability of psychotherapeutically relevant exchanges, and the residents were instructed to focus on the drug reactions of the patients. Despite these situations, there is no way of knowing the extent to which these conditions were adhered to in a large-scale study with several therapists. It is conceivable, as Brill and his colleagues note, that some brief psychotherapeutically relevant interchanges may have occurred on occasion.

The problem of the comparison of psychotherapy with placebo treatments is complicated by the fact that many placebo treatments include a variety of elements in addition to an attempt to manipulate the belief that one is receiving an efficacious treatment. Some studies have used placebo treatments that include discussion groups in which a therapist explicitly attempts to steer the groups' conversation toward topics that are assumed to be irrelevant to the psychological problems which led the patients to be selected for psychotherapy. Such a placebo treatment attempts to control for such features of psychotherapy as duration of treatment, meeting with fellow-patients, and having an opportunity to engage in conversation in a quasitherapeutic setting. Presumably the treatment is construed as a placebo in the belief that discussions that do not focus on specific problems are not therapeutically efficacious. But this belief may be no more than an act of faith. It may well be that the essential features of psychotherapy which account for its therapeutic effectiveness are well reproduced by this type of placebo treatment. Grünbaum (1981) has stressed the importance of theoretical assertions as a basis for ascertaining the placebogenic status of a particular form of treatment. However, since our understanding of the nature of the processes that induce change is imperfect (if not downright lacking), our attempts to distinguish between placebo treatments and treatments that reproduce several features of psychotherapy may involve imprecise theoretical and empirical distinctions. Although we prefer minimal placebo treatments we are restricted to the available research literature. We will accordingly consider as a placebo treatment any procedure so described by an investigator where we are informed or able to infer that the possibility of therapeutic benefits is conveyed to the patient. In addition, we require either implicit or explicit evidence that the authors have a theoretical rationale for the assertion that the placebo treatment omits features of psychotherapy which are essential for therapeutic effectiveness.

While the reader may feel that the variability of placebo treatments renders a comparison between placebo and psychotherapeutic treatments vexed, it should be noted that there may be considerable variability among wait-list control treatments. Duration of wait-list assignment may be a critical variable. The extent to which the assignment to a wait-list control is accompanied by preliminary assessment procedures, the kinds of information conveyed to the patient about the potential harm involved in the wait period, and the availability of psychotherapeutic services during the wait period in the event of an emergency may have a considerable influence on the changes that may occur among patients during their time on the wait list. For example, Sloane, Staples, Cristol, Yorkston, and Whipple (1975) explain their failure to find therapeutic improvement relative to their wait-list control group on follow-up as follows: The psychological assessment that preceded assignment to the wait-list group, combined with the information conveyed by the researchers that wait-listed patients could receive therapeutic treatment in an emergency, were sufficient to create therapeutic benefits in the wait-list control subjects that eventually matched the alleged benefits of psychotherapy and behavior therapy. Thus, wait-list control conditions may vary considerably, and the comparisons of such controls with psychotherapeutic treatments may involve the comparison of two forms of treatment, each variable across different investigations. Thus the comparison between psychotherapy and wait-list control treatments may raise as many theoretical problems as the comparison between psychotherapy and placebo treatments.

METHOD

We were able to locate and read in either original or abstract form 513 of the 520 studies included in the psychotherapy and drug meta-analyses included in Smith et al. (1980). Of the 513, we selected for analysis only the small subset that included both a psychotherapy treatment and a placebo treatment. The distinction between psychotherapy and behavior therapy was not problematic for the great majority of studies analyzed (for a more comprehensive treatment of this issue see Murdock 1982; Prioleau 1982). We classified as psychotherapy a number of the studies using such techniques as rational emotive therapy and even social learning therapy described in rather traditional behavioristic language, whenever we were able to infer from the description of the therapist's activities that he was required to engage in a process of exploration and clarification of the emotional experiences of the patient. In addition to classifying a study as containing a psychotherapy treatment, we looked for evidence that there was an attempt to foster and develop an emotional relationship between the therapist and the patient.

We judged that 40 of the 513 studies contained both a psychotherapy and a placebo treatment. From these 40 we discarded 8, either on the grounds that they were so seriously flawed as to render any comparison unjustified or because even with a number of ad hoc assumptions it was not possible to compute measures of effect size.

We computed a measure of effect size for each of the dependent variables included in the remaining 32 studies. Effect size was defined as the difference between the psychotherapy group mean and the placebo group mean divided by the pooled standard deviation for psychotherapy and placebo groups. If pretreatment scores existed for a measure, we obtained the difference between the pre- and posttreatment score, subtracted the comparable difference score for placebo treatment groups, and divided the difference between the change scores by the pooled standard deviation of the change scores. Where such standard deviations were not available or could not be calculated or inferred from the statistics presented, we assumed that the correlation between pre- and posttreatment scores was .5, and we adjusted the posttreatment standard deviation to obtain an estimate of the standard deviation of the change scores. If a variable was presented in terms of nominal scale measurement (e.g., percentage of improvement), we dummy coded the variables, calculated r, and converted r into a measure expressed in terms of standard deviation units. If standard deviations were not reported, we attempted to derive them from available statistics. Where the author indicated that there were no differences between therapy and placebo treatments and data were not presented, we assumed that the effect size was zero. (For a general discussion of obtaining measures of effect size, see Cohen 1969; and for a discussion of inferring effect size measures from limited data presentations, see Smith et al. 1980.) We adjusted our effect size indices such that positive scores indicated that the psychotherapy group did better on a particular measure than the placebo group. We obtained a mean effect size for each study by taking the mean of the separate effect sizes.

We have departed from the procedures used by Smith et al. (1980) in the calculation of effect sizes in three respects. First, the numerator of the fraction we use to define effect size is defined as the difference between psychotherapy and placebo treatments rather than as the difference between psychotherapy and a control group.

Second, Smith et al. (1980) use as a denominator of the fraction the standard deviation of the control group, whereas we use a pooled standard deviation. The use of the standard deviation of the control group yields the advantage of permitting one to define mean differences between two or more therapy treatments in a single study against a common base line. We chose to use a pooled standard deviation because we found that for a majority of studies included here, separate standard deviations were not available and accordingly we were forced to estimate standard deviations from such statistics as *t* and *F*. Such a procedure permits one to obtain only a pooled standard deviation rather than a separate estimate for the control and treatment group. Since we were forced to use pooled estimates for some of our calculations, it seemed to us to be more consistent to use pooled estimates for all our calculations. Smith et al. (1980) report that they found no difference in variability of control group and therapy outcomes. If a comparable result holds for the studies we examined, the decision to use pooled estimates should not appreciably influence our estimates of effect size, although it might influence an estimate in a particular set of data. Third, for the subset of studies in which data on the standard deviation of change scores were not provided, we arbitrarily assumed that the correlation between pretest and posttest scores was .5. Smith et al. (1980) used a variable value to estimate correlations depending on the nature of the outcome variables used and the duration of time intervening between pretest and posttest. We felt that for many of the measures used we were not in a position to make an informed guess about the value of the test-retest correlation. The value of .5 was at the upper end of the range of correlations used by Smith et al. (1980). It seemed to us to be somewhat less arbitrary to use a standard value rather than a variable one. In any case, this arbitrary correlation was used in fewer than one-third of our calculations and is probably not a major source of influence in the magnitude of effect sizes.

RESULTS

Table 1 presents a description of the 32 studies included in our analysis and includes the calculations of mean effect sizes for each. The mean values are corrected for the sampling bias of effect sizes (see Hedges 1981). The corrected distribution of mean effect sizes is skewed to the right. The modal category of a grouped frequency distribution with an interval of .20 occurs at an effect size value of .00. The median effect size is .15 and the mean is .42. The distribution includes one extreme value. This study, in which virtually all of the children given psychotherapy and none of the children in the placebo treatment are reported as having improved, has an effect size of 1.54 standard deviations higher than any other.

It is apparent that there is considerable diversity in magnitude of outcome in these studies. We attempted to define characteristics that might be related to the measure of effect size. We analyzed the following variables: (1) duration of treatment, (2) sample size, (3) the use of real patients as opposed to subjects solicited by the investigators, and (4) the nature of the outcome measure used.

Duration of therapy was correlated –.24 (n.s.) with effect size. Thus the nonsignificant trend is for the benefits of therapy relative to placebo to decrease as the duration of treatment increases. The correlation between sample size and effect size was –.21 (n.s.). Sample size was inversely related to therapeutic effects. The mean effect size for the eight studies using patients was .35 (median = .08) and the mean effect size for the studies using solicited subjects was .44 (median = .16). A *t* test comparing these means yields a value of .36 (n.s.).

We assigned each dependent variable to one of six categories (see Table 1). We obtained a mean effect size for the category of undisguised self-report measures and a mean effect size measure for all other measures used in each study. We compared these means in a subset of 19 studies, which permitted us to obtain within the same study a mean effect size for one or more outcomes of undisguised self-reports and one or more measures of any other type. The mean of the means for undisguised self-reports was .43 and the mean of the means for all other measures was .17. A matched group *t* test had a value of 1.58 (n.s.).

Six of the studies included in Table 1 reported follow-up data. We calculated that there were minimal changes during follow-up in mean effect sizes for three of these studies: Schwartz and Dubitzky (1967), Gillan and Rachman (1974), and DiLoreto (1971). Two showed declines of .23 and .61 in mean effect size (Paul 1964 and Hedquist & Weinhold 1970, respectively), and one (Jarmon 1972) showed a gain in effect size of .22. These data indicate that for this small subset of studies there is no tendency for the benefits of psychotherapy relative to placebo to increase during a follow-up period.

DISCUSSION

Our estimate of a mean effect size of .42 is exactly in agreement with the magnitude of the psychotherapy effect size relative to placebo treatments estimated by Smith et al. (1980). Quite apart from the central tendency of effect size in these studies, the trends in the characteristics of studies that are related to measures of effect size, albeit weakly, do not support an intuitive model, which suggests that the effects of therapy are more powerful than the effects of placebo treatments. Assume that the effects of psychotherapy are strong and that the effects of placebo are weak and emphemeral. One might argue on intuitive grounds that placebo effects would decline more than therapy through time and hence would be less likely to be equivalent to therapy where outcomes are assessed after long durations of therapy and follow-up investigation. Moreover, one might expect ephemeral and perhaps misguided beliefs in the benefits of placebo to be most strongly present for undisguised self-report measures. In addition, one would expect real patients to be more likely to benefit from the effects of a powerful treatment than solicited subjects, on the assumption that the former group are more disturbed than the latter. Our data are consistent in their bearing on this set of crude intuitions—in all respects our findings contradict these expectations. Our data suggest that as we examine these studies in a more critical manner and examine their implications for the benefits of psychotherapy, we are led to assume that the benefits of therapy relative to placebo treatments become vanishingly small.

It is possible to supplement the quantitative analysis of these studies by a somewhat more traditional analysis of their descriptive properties. And given the diversity of measures, therapies, and subjects included in these investigations, there is some question whether attempts to relate quantitative indices of effect size to other variables is entirely legitimate. After examining this set of studies we have concluded that the most informative classification is derived from an analysis of the types of patients included. It is possible to organize these studies into four subclasses as defined by the type of patient receiving therapy. The first subclass, which we consider the most crucial for an evaluation of psychotherapy outcome research, is defined as studies of outpatients, in which the patient population seeks psychological services and is not institutionalized. The three studies included in this group all deal with patients who may be described as neurotics. In addition to the Brill et al. (1964) study, which we have already described in the introduction and which we calculate to have an effect size of .07, Lorr, McNair, and Weinstein (1963) reported a similar investigation using a pill placebo treatment for psychiatric outpatients. The duration of treatment was brief (four sessions), and only two measures were used to assess outcome (global ratings by therapists and patients). However, unlike in the Brill et al. (1964) study, the therapists were described as being experienced. We calculate the effect size of Lorr et al. (1963) to be .10. The last study in this group, Gillan and Rachman (1974), provides a significant amount of therapy to a small number of patients, all multiphobic. Psychotherapy was administered by experienced therapists who are described as believing that psychotherapy is the treatment of choice for this condition. Two placebo treatments were used: relaxation training without an attempt to pair the relaxation response with the phobic stimulus and a placebo condition in which the phobic hierarchy was presented without relaxation training. Several outcome measures were used, including behavioral and psychophysiological measures. We calculate the effect size of this study to be negative, –.07.

An additional study reported by McLean and Hakstian (1979) was not included in our formal analysis since it was published too late to appear in the Smith et al. (1980) analysis. However, it is relatively well designed and does buttress the conclusions suggested by the three studies we review in the category of psychiatric outpatients. McLean and Hakstian report data for 37 randomly assigned clinically depressed outpatients who received 8–12 hours of insight-oriented psychotherapy from licensed psychologists and psychiatrists; one group of therapists had at least 2–4 years of experience and the other 5 years or more. Psychotherapy was the treatment of choice for these professionals. The experience of the therapist was unrelated to outcome and accordingly this variable was dropped from the analysis. Outcome was assessed by the use of 10 self-report measures derived from analyses of questionnaire data. A number of outcome measures were adjusted for relevant covariates. The placebo treatment was administered to 38 randomly assigned patients who received 10 hours of muscle relaxation therapy. Subjects were informed that the muscle relaxation treatment was therapeutically relevant, although McLean and Hakstian assert that they consider the variable as a placebo since there is no compelling rationale for the view that treatment of depression by muscle relaxation is therapeutically efficacious. At the end of therapy, in a comparison of the patients assigned to the psychotherapy and the placebo treatment group there was no appreciable difference on any outcome measure, although a group of subjects randomly assigned to a behavior therapy treatment condition were discernibly improved relative to the relaxation therapy patients. The relaxation therapy patients had slightly better outcomes than the psychotherapy patients. We calculate the effect size to be negative (–.11). Three months after the termination of psychotherapy there was again no discernible difference in outcome. The effect size was negative (–.08).

In a number of ways, McLean and Hakstian's is a well-designed study. It uses well-trained psychotherapists with a commitment to the virtues of psychotherapy; it includes a well-defined patient group and a follow-up. It has perhaps two limitations. There is exclusive reliance on questionnaire and self-report data (although arguably the instruments used are well standardized and have some validity for the particular target population). And it is conceivable that the placebo treatment might include a number of complex aspects (e.g., following instructions, etc.) that extend beyond the pure case of an expectancy manipulation. However, if considered in conjunction with the results of the three other studies of outpatients, this study appears to buttress the view that psychotherapy does not lead to outcomes that are more favorable than those attained by placebo treatment for outpatients.

TABLE 1 Description of Design, Placebo, Dependent Measures, and Effect Sizes of Studies in the Analysis

Author and Year	*Type of Therapy*	*Subjects*	*N*[a]	*Contact Hours*	*Therapists*	*Placebo Description*	*Dependent Measures*[b]	*Estimated Effect Sizes*[c]	*Remarks*
Winkler et al. (1965)	Rogerian	Underachieving elementary school students	60	7	M.A. level	Listened to records and stories	(2) CA [California] test of personality (6) GPA	–.55 .11 –.22	*d*
Bruyere (1975)	Group client-centered	Disruptive junior high school students	48	16	School counselors	Group problem solving	(1) Self-concept (5) Conduct GPA Behavior scale Ratings of disruptive classroom behavior	–.64 –.09 .00 + –.18	Data for effect size computation n/a for last measure
Schwartz and Dubitzky (1967)	Group therapy	Moderate smokers	72	12	Psychologists	Pill placebo	(6) Cessation of smoking	–.13	
Orlov (1972)	Group Rogerian	Maladjusted middle school students	40	15	Psychologists	Reading and discussion Books	(5) Sociometric test Rating scale Classroom behavior Improvement rating by teacher (6) GPA	.00 .00 .00 –.30 –.21 –.10	
Bruce (1971)	Group client-centered	Vocational rehabilitation clients	20	12	Psychology graduate student	Social group functions	(1) Index of adjustment (5) Job performance evaluation	.89 –1.06 – .09	
Gillan and Rachman (1974)	Group insight rational therapy	Multiphobic outpatients	24	15	Psychiatrists Psychologist	Muscle relaxation training; phobic hierarchy no relaxation training	(1) Anxiety scale (2) EPI [Eysenck Personality Inventory] (4) Therapist rating phobia and depression (5) Rating phobia and depression; external rater (6) Behavioral avoidance test Skin conductance	–.46 .00 .19 –.24 .00 .00 –.09(–.07)	*e,f*
Matthews (1972)	Group reality therapy	Maladjusted elementary school children	221	15	Elementary school teachers	Language arts classes	(2) CPI [California Psychological Inventory] (5) Problem behavior rating (6) Reading	–.11 .18 –.18 –.04	

[a]Only the number of subjects in the psychotherapy and placebo treatments are included.
[b]The number in parentheses refers to type of dependent measure according to the following code: 1 = undisguised self-report; 2 = disguised self-report; 3 = global report by therapist; 4 = rating of independent behavior by therapist; 5 = rating of independent behavior by others; 6 = independent behavior.
[c]Numbers in parentheses indicate mean effect size corrected for sampling bias.
[d]Study used two types of psychotherapy and one placebo group. Information on number of subjects and effect size is pooled across both comparisons.
[e]Study used one psychotherapy group and two types of placebo. Information on number of subjects and effect size is pooled across both comparisons.
[f]Study used real patients.

TABLE 1 *(continued)*

Author and Year	*Type of Therapy*	*Subjects*	*N*[a]	*Contact Hours*	*Therapists*	*Placebo Description*	*Dependent Measures*[b]	*Estimated Effect Sizes*[c]	*Remarks*
Jarmon (1972)	Group rational emotive therapy	Speech-anxious college students	41	3	Psychology graduate students	Group discussion of neutral topics; reading RET [rational-emotive therapy] book	(1) Fear survey schedule	–.31	e
							Confidence as a speaker	–.16	
							Social anxiety	.34	
							Fear of evaluation	.07	
							Irrational ideas	–.18	
							Fear rating	.25	
							(5) Speech anxiety rating	–.24	
							Speech disruptions	–.23	
								–.01	
Shapiro and Knapp (1971)	Group ego therapy	High-anxious college students	42	14	No information	Group discussion of general topics	(1) Personal integration	.00	
							Response bias	.00	
							Anxiety level	.00	
								.00	
Coche and Douglas (1977)	Group problem-solving training	Adult psychiatric inpatients	46	8	No information	Group play reading	(1) Adjective checklist	.26	
							(2) Minimult	.01	
							Means-ends problem solving	–.11	
								.05	
Desrats (1975)	Group Rogerian	Institutionalized adolescent orphans	39	25	Counselors with "limited counseling experience"	Viewed films and study lessons	(1) Self-esteem	.00	f
							(2) CPI	.00	
							(5) Behavior rating	.00	
							(6) GPA	.28	
							Adjustment tally	.00	
								.06	
Brill et al. (1964)	Psychoanalytic	Adult outpatients	60	20+	Psychiatric residents	Pill placebo	(1) Patient rating	.05	f
							(2) MMPI	–.12	S.D. estimate ⅓ of range
							(4) Therapist rating	.10	
							Global evaluation	.00	
							(5) Relative rating	–.12	
							Social worker rating	.38	
								.07	
Herman (1972)	Humanistic counseling (group and individual)	High-anxious junior high school students with reading problems	40	4.5	Junior high school counselors	"Bull" session	(1) MAS [Manifest Anxiety Scale]	.74	d
							(5) Anxiety rating	–.08	
							(6) Reading test	–.42	
								.08	
Lorr et al. (1963)	Individual therapy	Adult outpatients	50	4	Psychiatrists, psychologists, and social workers	Pill placebo	(1) Global improvement	.19	
							(3) Global improvement	.00	
								.10	
Rosentover (1974)	Group counseling	Underachieving high school students	63	7	Education graduate student	Heard speakers, viewed films, limited discussion	(2) Minnesota Counseling Inventory	.00	
							(6) GPA	.23	
								.12	
Warner (1969)	Group verbal and model reinforcement	Alienated junior high school students	102	4.5	Three high school counselors	Group discussion	(1) Alienation	.56	
							Anxiety	–.06	
							Self-concept	.11	
							(6) GPA	–.15	
								.12	

(continued)

TABLE 1 *(continued)*

Author and Year	*Type of Therapy*	*Subjects*	*N*[a]	*Contact Hours*	*Therapists*	*Placebo Description*	*Dependent Measures*[b]	*Estimated Effect Sizes*[c]	*Remarks*
Paul (1964)	Individual insight therapy	College students with speech performance anxiety	30	5	Psychologists	Pill placebo and boring task	(1) Anxiety	.22	
							(3) Global rating	.40	
							(5) Anxiety	.69	
							(6) Pulse rate	–.03	
							Palmar sweat	–.37	
								.18(.17)	
West (1969)	Group client-centered	Disruptive elementary school children with learning difficulty	16	10	Psychology graduate students	Read, played with puzzles, or sat quietly under supervision of counselor; no verbal interchange	(1) Self-esteem	.29	
							(2) Draw-a-Person	–.01	
							Apperception Test	–.27	
							(5) Sociometric	.69	
							(6) WISC [Wechsler Intelligence Scale for Children]	.16	
								.17(.16)	
Rehm and Marston (1968)	Nonspecific group	High-anxious college students	16	2.5	Psychology graduate students	General group discussion	(1) Fear of opposite sex	1.13	
							Situation test	.50	
							Fear survey	–.07	
							Anxiety scale	–.54	
							Adjective list	.16	
							(5) Situation anxiety	.07	
								.21(.19)	
Paykel et al. (1975)	Individual supportive	Clinically depressed inpatients	34	36	Psychiatric social workers	Pill placebo	(1) Psychic and somatic complaints	.00	*f*
							(4) Psychiatric rating	.00	
							Interview for depression	.00	
							Depression scale	.00	
							(3) Psychiatric evaluation	.79	
							(3) Relapse rate	.32	
							(5) Social adjustment	.78	
								.27(.26)	
Alper and Kranzler (1970)	Individual client-centered therapy	Disruptive elementary school children	18	10	Graduate students in counseling	Read and discuss stories	(2) Self social symbols	–.10	
							(5) "Out of seat" behavior	1.26	
							Sociometric test	–.12	
								+.34(.32)	
Trexler and Karst (1972)	Group rational emotive therapy	Speech-anxious college students	22	4	Psychology graduate student	Relaxation training	(1) Irrational beliefs test	1.37	
							Anxiety scale	–1.03	
							Confidence as a speaker	1.10	
							(5) Behavior checklist	.41	
							Overall estimate of anxiety	.25	
							(6) Finger sweat print	.26	
								.39(.36)	

[a]Only the number of subjects in the psychotherapy and placebo treatments are included.
[b]The number in parentheses refers to type of dependent measure according to the following code: 1 = undisguised self-report; 2 = disguised self-report; 3 = global report by therapist; 4 = rating of independent behavior by therapist; 5 = rating of independent behavior by others; 6 = independent behavior.
[c]Numbers in parentheses indicate mean effect size corrected for sampling bias.
[d]Study used two types of psychotherapy and one placebo group. Information on number of subjects and effect size is pooled across both comparisons.
[e]Study used one psychotherapy group and two types of placebo. Information on number of subjects and effect size is pooled across both comparisons.
[f]Study used real patients.

TABLE 1 *(continued)*

Author and Year	*Type of Therapy*	*Subjects*	N^a	*Contact Hours*	*Therapists*	*Placebo Description*	*Dependent Measures*[b]	*Estimated Effect Sizes*[c]	*Remarks*
Lester (1973)	Individual relationship counseling	High-anxious junior high school students	13	3	Graduate student in counseling	Guided discussion of current events	(1) Test anxiety Global self-report	.00 1.18 .59(.55)	
Coche and Flick (1975)	Group problem-solving training	Psychiatric inpatients	64	8	No information	Group play reading with discussion	(2) Means-ends problem-solving procedure	.69 .69	*f*
Hogan and Kirchner (1968)	Individual eclectic therapy	Snake-phobic college students	20	.75	No information	Bibliotherapy	(6) Ability to lift snake	.74 .74(.71)	
DiLoreto (1971)	Group client-centered and rational emotive therapy	High-anxious college students	60	9	Psychology graduate students	Group discussion over lunch focused on academic topics	(1) Interpersonal anxiety S-R [Stimulus-Response] inventory of anxiousness Trait anxiety Social desirability (5) Checklist of interpersonal anxiety	.37 .86 1.17 .50 1.25 .82	*d*
Grande (1975)	Group rational emotive therapy	High-anxious college students	34	4.5	Three graduate students and one undergraduate	Relaxation training via tape	(1) Interpersonal anxiety MAS Fear survey (5) Interpersonal anxiety Behavior rating	1.32 1.21 1.09 .50 .74 .97(.95)	
Meichenbaum et al. (1972)	Individual and group rational emotive therapy	High-anxious college students	24	8	Psychologists	Group discussion	(1) Checklist for anxiety Anxiety differential (5) Performance anxiety (6) Duration of silences Number of "ah" statements	1.34 .42 .57 2.00 1.02 .98(.95)	*d*
Hedquist and Weinhold (1970)	Group social learning	Anxious college students	30	6	Psychology graduate students	Group discussion	(1) Assertive behaviors	1.22 1.22(1.19)	
House (1970)	Group nondirective play therapy	Unpopular elementary school children	24	10	Education graduate student	Reading group	(1) Self-concept and motivation inventory (5) Sociometric test	2.50 .70 1.60(1.55)	
Roessler et al. (1977)	Group counseling	Physical rehabilitation clients	43	10	Rehabilitation counselor	Personal hygiene training	(1) Self-scale Facility outcome measure Goal attainment scale	.80 .84 3.40 1.68(1.65)	*f*
Platt (1970)	Group Adlerian	Disruptive elementary school children	24	5	No information	Listened to records and studied	(5) Rating by parents Rating by teachers	3.80 2.80 3.30(3.19)	Ratings were not "blind"

A second subset of studies deals with institutionalized patients. There are four in this group. Desrats (1975) deals with institutionalized adolescents given counseling by relatively untrained counselors and has an effect size of .06. Paykel, DiMascio, Haskell, and Prusoff (1975) deal with clinically depressed inpatients and use a pill placebo treatment. We calculate an effect size of .26 for this study. In this group, only Coche and Flick (1975) report a substantial positive effect size. It is a study of outcome among psychiatric inpatients who are given group problem-solving training. For a single measure of group problem solving, which may or may not be contaminated by the therapeutic procedures followed, we calculate an effect size of .69. However, in a study designed in part to be a replication of Coche and Flick's (1975) work, Coche and Douglas (1977) report a failure to replicate their earlier findings. For a somewhat more extended set of outcome measures used in this study, we calculate an effect size of .05. Thus the results of the only study using psychiatric inpatients with a substantial positive effect size are nonreplicable.

The third class of studies deals with students in school. One of these, Bruyere (1975), deals with students attending a special school for disruptive junior high school pupils. Bruyere's study has a negative effect size. School counseling did not lead to positive outcomes on a variety of measures. There are 21 additional studies in this group, all dealing with therapy provided to solicited subjects: groups of students who are nominated or selected for therapy because they have an extreme score on some measure. Clearly, such subjects are not representative of the patients who seek therapeutic services. Six of these studies have relatively positive effect sizes ranging from .74 to 3.19. This subset, with relatively large positive effect sizes, may be characterized collectively (with exceptions that can be noted by an examination of Table 1) as studies in which relatively brief therapy is provided to relatively small groups of subjects. Three of the six involve rational emotive therapy and one involves group social learning therapy. Therefore, these studies deal with quasi-behavioristic forms of treatment.

Our last group of studies is somewhat heterogeneous, consisting of those that do not fit into the preceding three groups. One study in this group, Schwartz and Dubitzky (1967), which has a negative effect size, deals with group therapy as a treatment for smokers who wish to stop smoking. Another with a negative effect size involves vocational rehabilitation clients. The final study in this group, Roessler, Cook, and Lillard (1977), is of the effectiveness of group counseling for physical rehabilitation clients. The effect size is 1.65 and it is the study we calculate to have the largest effect size among those that do not deal with solicited subjects. The outcome measures consist solely of undisguised self-reports, and the authors note that they do not know whether the optimism of their clients will be reflected in their actual behavior.

CONCLUDING SPECULATIONS

One can distinguish between two propositions: (1) In the research literature surveyed, psychotherapy has been found to produce changes in real patients that are equivalent to those produced by placebo treatments. (2) In general, psychotherapy produces changes in patients that are equivalent to those produced by placebo treatments. Proposition 1 is limited in its range of application to the studies we review and does not attempt to imply anything about what is true of psychotherapy in general. Yet, clearly, the goal of outcome research in psychotherapy is to discover what is true about psychotherapy and not to discover what is true about a particular body of research, which may be flawed. Accordingly, in what follows we shall speculate about the possible truth of proposition 2. Any psychotherapy outcome study has as its variables, therapists, patients, types of therapy, and measures of outcomes. Let us consider the potential limitations of the studies we have reviewed from the perspective of the several variables that jointly define an outcome study.

Some therapists may be able to produce beneficial effects through treatment. For a variety of reasons we are not sanguine about the possibility that variations among therapists is a major or important source of variance in outcome research. If the true size of the psychotherapy effect relative to placebo treatment is .0 then any allocation of main effect variance to individual differences among therapists would imply that some therapists consistently make their patients worse. The existence of individual differences among therapists as a major source of variance in outcome for diverse patients is of little practical relevance unless some way can be found of communicating to potential patients information about the competence of therapists. Since competence to produce changes among patients appears to be unrelated to professional training, it is hard to see how it could be practically determined. In addition, it is likely that some (and perhaps a major part) of the variance in outcome is not associated with a consistent effect of therapists but is best described as interaction variance in which certain therapists may have a higher likelihood of success with some types of patients. Finally, it should be noted that the hypothesis of individual differences in therapists' ability consistently to produce beneficial changes in their patients is testable in any study in which outcomes are obtained for several therapists each treating several patients. With such a design one could obtain a measure of the consistency of therapeutic outcome as a function of individual differences among therapists.

Certain types of therapy may have effect sizes that exceed those of placebo treatments. Clearly, the 32 studies we reviewed do not contain an exhaustive range of therapies. For example, rational emotive therapy appears to produce positive effect sizes in some of the work we review. However, none of the data we examined involved this type of therapy with true patients; nor was family therapy examined. It could be that some forms of therapy are more effective than placebo treatments and, similarly, there may exist certain types of patients who consistently benefit from psychotherapy. Obviously, we would be rash to deny such a possibility. However, it should be noted that such reviewers as Bergin and Lambert (1978) and Smith et al. (1980) have suggested that differences in outcome among types of therapy are minimal.

The weakest aspect of outcome research involves the measures used to assess change. It is possible that psychotherapy produces beneficial changes which exceed those attributable to minimal placebo treatments, but that the available outcome measures are too crude to detect such differences. Perhaps the major respect in which outcome research could be improved would be through the use of a wider range of dependent variables with more power to detect (possibly subtle) differences. None of the studies we examined used individually tailored measures of outcome in which one specifies at the start of treatment the kinds of changes that would indicate therapeutic progress for each patient. While it is certainly true that researchers could use a more extended and imaginative set of outcome measures than are characteristically used, there is no guarantee that such measures would increase the likelihood of demonstrating positive effects of psychotherapy. Recall that in the studies we examined the largest effects of psychotherapy relative to placebo were obtained for measures we would consider as biased and theoretically primitive: undisguised self-reports. One possible explanation of this result is that such measures are construed in part as a representation of the believability of the placebogenic component of therapy. If some patients prefer psychotherapy to, say, relaxation training as a method of treatment, they may come to believe psychotherapy to be the more powerful treatment; they would accordingly report greater benefits from psychotherapy than from relaxation treatment. Undisguised self-report measures suggesting that psychotherapy is more beneficial than placebo may be attributable to psychotherapy's being a more believable placebo treatment than most actual placebo treatments. It would be useful to include a measure of the expectations for therapeutic improvement at the start of therapy for subjects assigned to various placebo and therapy treatments. Such a measure might relate to outcome measures.

Apart from the occasional use of psychophysiological measures, the studies we have reviewed have rarely relied on laboratory procedures to define outcomes. Although laboratory measures might yield positive results, there could be questions as to their ecological validity and their relation to significant actions and judgments in the everyday life of the patient.

We recognize that our speculations about the potential for demonstrating significant effects of psychotherapy relative to placebos are just that—speculations. On the basis of the available data we see no reason to believe that subsequent research using better research procedures and investigating other types of therapy administered to other types of patients will yield clear-cut indications that psychotherapy is more beneficial than placebo treatment. Thirty years after Eysenck (1952) first raised the issue of the effectiveness of psychotherapy, twenty-eight years after Meehl (1955) called for the use of placebo controls in psychotherapy, eighteen years after Brill et al. (1964) demonstrated in a reasonably well-done study that the psychotherapy effect may be equivalent to the placebo effect, and after about 500 outcome studies have been reviewed—we are still not aware of a single convincing demonstration that the benefits of psychotherapy exceed those of placebos for real patients. Such a study would have to show that psychotherapy administered to real patients yields improvements relative to placebo on a variety of measures and that these improvements endure over time. We believe that securing such data should be viewed as an urgent task by those who practice or advocate the use of psychotherapy. Given the absence of convincing contradictory data, and considering the partial support (at least) that the available research literature provides, we regard it as likely that the benefits of psychotherapy do not exceed those of placebo in real patients. That is, our conclusion may not only be valid when its range of application is restricted to a limited set of studies but may also be true of psychotherapy in general.

REFERENCES

Alper, T. B. & Kranzler, G. D. (1970) A comparison of the effectiveness of behavioral and client-centered approaches for the behavior problems of elementary school children. *Elementary School Guidance and Counseling* 5: 35–43.

Bergin, A. E. & Lambert, M. J. (1978) The evaluation of therapeutic outcomes. In: *Handbook of psychotherapy and behavior change: An empirical analysis*, ed. S. L. Garfield & A. E. Bergin, pp. 139–89. Wiley.

Brill, N. Q., Koegler, R. R., Epstein, L. J. & Forgy, E. W. (1964) Controlled study of psychiatric outpatient treatment. *Archives of General Psychiatry* 10:581–95.

Bruce, J. (1971) The effects of group counseling on selected vocational rehabilitation clients. Ph.D. dissertation, Florida State University.

Bruyere, D. H. (1975) The effects of client centered and behavioral group counseling on classroom behavior and self concept of junior high school students who exhibited disruptive classroom behavior. Ph.D. dissertation, University of Oregon.

Coche, E. & Douglas, A. A. (1977) Therapeutic effects of problem-solving training and play-reading groups. *Journal of Clinical Psychology* 33:820–27.

Coche, E. & Flick, A. (1975) Problem-solving training groups for hospitalized patients. *Journal of Psychology* 91: 19–29.

Cohen, J. (1969) *Statistical power analysis for the behavioral sciences*. Academic Press.

Desrats, R. G. (1975) The effects of developmental and modeling group counseling on adolescents in childcare institutions. Ph.D. dissertation, Lehigh University.

DiLoreto, A. O. (1971) *Comparative psychology*. Aldine-Atherton.

Duncan, J. W. & Laird, J. D. (1980) Positive and reverse placebo effects as a function of differences in cues used in self-perception. *Journal of Personality and Social Psychology* 39:1024–36.

Durlak, J. A. (1979) Comparative effectiveness of paraprofessional and professional helpers. *Psychological Bulletin* 86:80–92.

Eysenck, H. J. (1952) The effects of psychotherapy: An evaluation. *Journal of Consulting Psychology* 16:319–24.

———. (1966) *The effects of psychotherapy*. International Science Press.

———. (1978) An exercise in mega-silliness. *American Psychologist* 33:517.

Gillan, P. & Rachman, S. (1974) An experimental investigation of desensitization and phobic patients. *British Journal of Psychology* 124:392–401.

Grande, L. M. (1975) A comparison of rational-emotive therapy, attention placebo and no-treatment groups in the reduction of interpersonal anxiety. Ph.D. dissertation, Arizona State University.

Grünbaum, A. (1981) The placebo concept. *Behavior Research and Therapy* 19:157–67.

Hedges, L. V. (1981) Distribution theory for Glass's estimator of effect size and related estimators. *Journal of Educational Statistics* 6:107–28.

Hedquist, F. S. & Weinhold, B. K. (1970) Behavioral group counseling with socially anxious and unassertive college students. *Journal of Counseling Psychology* 17:237–42.

Herman, B. (1972) An investigation to determine the relationship of anxiety and reading disability and to study the effects of group and individual counseling on reading improvement. Ph.D. dissertation, University of New Mexico.

Hogan, R. A. & Kirchner, J. H. (1968) Implosive, electric, verbal and bibliotherapies in the treatment of fears of snakes. *Behavior Research and Therapy* 6:167–71.

House, R. M. (1970) The effects of nondirective group play therapy upon the sociometric status and self-concept of selected second grade children. Ph.D. dissertation, Oregon State University.

Jarmon, D. D. (1972) Differential effectiveness of rational-emotive therapy, bibliotherapies and attention-placebo in the treatment of speech anxiety, Ph.D. dissertation, Southern Illinois University.

Landman, J. T. & Dawes, R. M. (1982) Psychotherapy outcome: Smith and Glass' conclusions stand up under scrutiny. *American Psychologist* 37:504–16.

Lester, B. G. (1973) A comparison of relationship counseling and relationship counseling combined with modified systematic desensitization in reducing test anxiety in middle school pupils. Ph.D. dissertation, University of Virginia.

Lorr, M., McNair, D. M. & Weinstein, G. J. (1963) Early effects of chlordiazepoxide (Librium) used with psychotherapy. *Journal of Psychiatric Research* 1:257–70.

Matthews, D. B. (1972) The effects of reality therapy on reported self-concept, social adjustment, reading achievement, and discipline of fourth and fifth grades in two elementary schools. Ph.D. dissertation, University of Southern California.

McLean, P. D. & Hakstian, A. R. (1979) Clinical depression: Comparative efficacy of outpatient treatments. *Journal of Consulting and Clinical Psychology* 47:818–36.

Meehl, P. E. (1955) Psychotherapy. *Annual Review of Psychology* 6:357–79.

Meichenbaum, D. H., Gilmore, J. B. & Fedoravicious. (1972) Group insight versus group desensitization in treating speech anxiety. In: *Psychotherapy 1971*, ed. J. D. Matarazzo, pp. 513–23. Aldine-Atherton.

Meltzoff, J. & Kornreich, M. (1970) *Research in psychotherapy*. Aldine-Atherton.

Murdock, M. N. (1982) A meta-analysis of psychotherapy outcome research: "Sentence first—verdict afterwards?" Honors thesis, Wesleyan University.

Orlov, L. (1972) An experimental study of the effects of group counseling with behavior problem children at the elementary school level. Ph.D. dissertation, The Catholic University of America.

Paul, G. L. (1964) Effects of insight, desensitization and attention-placebo treatment of anxiety: An approach to outcome research in psychotherapy. Ph.D. dissertation, University of Illinois.

Paykel, E., DiMascio, A., Haskell, D. & Prusoff, B. (1975) Effects of maintenance amitriptyline and psychotherapy on symptoms of depression. *Psychological Medicine* 5:67–77.

Platt, J. M. (1970) Efficacy of the Adlerian model in elementary school counseling, Ph.D. dissertation, University of Arizona.

Prioleau, L. A. (1982) A meta-analysis of psychotherapy outcome research: "Sentence first—verdict afterwards?" Master's thesis, Wesleyan University.

Rehm, L. P. & Marston, A. R. (1968) Reduction of social anxiety through modification of self-reinforcement: An investigation therapy technique. *Journal of Consulting and Clinical Psychology* 32:5.

Roessler, R., Cook, D. & Lillard, D. (1977) Effects of systematic and group counseling on work adjustment clients. *Journal of Consulting Psychology* 24:313–17.

Rosenthal, R. & Rubin, D. B. (1978) Interpersonal expectancy effects: the first 345 studies. *Behavioral and Brain Sciences* 3:377–415.

Rosentover, I. (1974) Group counseling of the underachieving high school student as related to self-image and academic success. Ph.D. dissertation, Rutgers University.

Schwartz, J. L. & Dubitzky, M. (1967) Clinical reduction of smoking. *Addictions* 14:35–44.

Shapiro, A. K. & Morris, L. A. (1978) Placebo effects in medical and psychological therapies. In: *Handbook of psychotherapy and behavior change: An empirical analysis*, ed. S. L. Garfield & A. E. Bergin, pp. 396–410. Wiley.

Shapiro, S. B. & Knapp, D. M. (1971) The effect of ego therapy on personality integration. *Psychotherapy: Theory, Research and Practice* 8:208–12.

Sloane, R. B., Staples, F. R., Cristol, A. H., Yorkston, N. J. & Whipple, K. (1975) *Psychotherapy versus behavior therapy*. Harvard University Press.

Smith, M. L., Glass, G. V. & Miller, T. I. (1980) *The benefits of psychotherapy*. Johns Hopkins University Press.

Strahan, R. F. (1978) Six ways of looking at an elephant. *American Psychologist* 33:693.

Strupp, H. (1973) *Psychotherapy: Clinical research and theoretical issues*. Aronson.

———. (1977) *Psychotherapy for better or worse. The problem of negative effects*. Aronson.

Trexler, L. D. & Karst, T. O. (1972) Rational-emotive therapy, placebo, and no-treatment effects on public-speaking anxiety. *Journal of Abnormal Psychology* 79:60–67.

Warner, R. (1969) An investigation of the effectiveness of verbal reinforcement and model reinforcement counseling on alienated high school students. Ph.D. dissertation, State University of New York–Buffalo.

West, W. B. (1969) An investigation of the significance of client-centered play therapy as a counseling technique. Ph.D. dissertation, North Texas State University.

Winkler, R.C., Teigland, J. J., Munger, P. F. & Kranzler, G. D. (1965) The effects of selected counseling and remedial techniques on underachieving elementary school students. *Journal of Counseling Psychology* 12:384.

DISCUSSION

After reading the two articles in this chapter, you may well be perplexed, if not utterly bewildered. Smith and Glass report a meta-analysis of psychotherapy studies and conclude that psychotherapy is clearly more effective than placebo treatment. In contrast, Prioleau, Murdock, and Brody report a meta-analysis derived from a subset of the same studies analyzed by Smith et al. (1980) (an expanded version of the Smith and Glass meta-analysis reprinted here) and arrive at not only different but diametrically opposed conclusions from those of Smith and Glass. According to Prioleau, Murdock, and Brody, there is no convincing evidence that psychotherapy is more effective than placebo treatment for actual patients. To make matters even more baffling, the effect size reported by Prioleau, Murdock, and Brody for psychotherapy (an estimate of the magnitude of the difference between treated and untreated groups) is .42— which is exactly the same effect size as that reported by Smith et al. (1980). Yet Smith and her colleagues triumphantly proclaim this effect size to be evidence for the effectiveness of psychotherapy. These two articles thus provide a dramatic illustration of how two groups of investigators can come to radically different conclusions on the basis of what appear to be very similar findings.

What these two articles demonstrate is that even a relatively "objective" statistical technique like meta-analysis, which was developed largely to circumvent the potential arbitrariness of informal literature reviews, inevitably entails a number of subjective (and therefore debatable) decisions. One such decision, of course, is the choice of which studies to include. Smith and Glass were harshly criticized by a number of authors (for example, Eysenck, 1978) for including many investigations of poor or dubious quality. Of course, the evaluation of a study's quality is itself a highly subjective judgment that rarely lends itself to consensus. Moreover, once a meta-analysis is conducted, its results may well be interpreted differently by investigators. These unpleasant facts help to explain why Prioleau, Murdock, and Brody draw conclusions so divergent from those of Smith and Glass.

In contrast to Smith and Glass, who adopted a very broad definition of psychotherapy, Prioleau, Murdock, and Brody restrict their definition of psychotherapy to treatments not explicitly incorporating behavioral components. Some might take issue with this decision: The distinction between behavior therapy and many other forms of therapy is often fuzzy, and a number of theorists posit that behavioral change (which probably occurs to some extent in all forms of psychotherapy) is the mechanism underlying all therapeutic improvement (see the article by Beidel and Turner in Chapter 13). Nevertheless, Prioleau, Murdock, and Brody might respond to this criticism by asserting that when individuals refer to psychotherapy they are typically speaking of traditional insight-oriented treatment aimed at uncovering and understanding psychological conflict. In this respect, their decision to exclude behavioral treatments from their analysis is perhaps defensible.

In addition, Prioleau, Murdock, and Brody base their conclusion that psychotherapy is ineffective on four studies involving neurotic clients. They in fact report positive effect sizes for studies using nonneurotic samples, such as college students with relatively mild psychological disturbances (such as speaking anxiety). Thus, their findings do not really call into question the effectiveness of psychotherapy in general; they call into question the effectiveness of psychotherapy for the individuals at whom such treatment is traditionally targeted—neurotic clients. Some might maintain that the distinction between neurosis and "normal" psychological distress is primarily one of degree rather than of kind and that differentiating between the effects of therapy for "neurotic" versus "nonneurotic" individuals creates an artificial and misleading dichotomy.* Again, however, Prioleau, Murdock, and Brody's reasoning is perhaps not entirely unreasonable. When we ask whether psychotherapy is effective, we are typically asking whether it is effective for the individuals who genuinely need it. If the benefits of psychotherapy extend only to what William Schofield (1964) referred to as "YAVIS" clients—those who are young, attractive, verbal, intelligent, and successful—one could justifiably argue that psychotherapy benefits those who presumably need it least.

Critics raised still other concerns regarding Prioleau, Murdock, and Brody's conclusions. In an especially thought-provoking commentary, Cordray and Bootzin (1983) argued that the comparisons examined by Prioleau, Murdock, and Brody—psychotherapy versus placebo—are better suited for understanding why psychotherapy works than for determining whether psychotherapy works. Specifically, Cordray and Bootzin contend that the "placebo" control conditions typically used in psychotherapy outcome studies actually contain ingredients that play an integral role in therapeutic effectiveness, such as the arousal of clients' expectations of improvement. From Cordray and Bootzin's perspective, the choice of the term *placebo* to refer to such conditions is unfortunate, because a placebo is traditionally defined as an inactive or inert manipulation. But if Cordray and Bootzin are correct, a placebo's capacity to inspire client expectations may be one of the principal active elements in psychotherapeutic success. Thus, psychotherapy-placebo comparisons may underestimate the actual efficacy of therapy (also see Wilkins, 1986).

In response to this criticism, Brody (1983), who coauthored the Prioleau, Murdock, and Brody paper, argued that if the effects of therapy do not exceed those of placebo treatment, "it would . . . be unnecessary to provide more than simple, inexpensive, and innocuous therapeutic interventions. . . . The rationale for the extensive training of professionals in the development of psychotherapeutic skills would evaporate" (pp. 305–306). Brody's point seems difficult to quarrel with. Why make lavish claims for the effectiveness of psychotherapy when much or all of this effectiveness could more easily and cheaply be accomplished by a sugar pill, a priest, or perhaps even a friend?

Nonetheless, Cordray and Bootzin draw attention to an intriguing and potentially important issue. Perhaps among the major ingredients involved in psychotherapeutic efficacy are the **nonspecific factors** shared by most or even all therapies. This argument has been stated most forcefully and articulately by psychiatrist Jerome Frank in his classic book, *Persuasion and Healing: A Comparative Analysis of Psychotherapy* (1973). The title of Frank's book is not without significance, because he contends that psychotherapy bears more than a passing resemblance to faith healing and similar techniques. Frank does not intend this comparison to be pejorative, however. Faith healing, after all, is astonishingly effective in many cases, as anyone who has watched certain religious evangelists in action can attest.

According to Frank, the success of psychotherapy can be traced largely or entirely to four nonspecific components:

- All psychotherapies prescribe clearly delineated roles for therapist and client, with the therapist defined as an "expert" possessing unique healing skills. This expert status lifts clients' hopes that help is forthcoming.
- All psychotherapies involve settings (for example, a large office building, a carpeted room containing scholarly journals and prominently displayed diplomas) that are designated by society as associated with the alleviation of psychological distress, a phenomenon that Torrey (1972) has humorously referred to as the "edifice complex."
- All psychotherapies provide a convincing theoretical rationale (such as a dearth of unconditional positive regard in client-centered therapy or irrational beliefs in rational-emotive therapy) for making sense of clients' difficulties, and this overarching framework instills a sense of confidence in clients and reassures them that their problems are not incomprehensible or unique.
- All psychotherapies include **therapeutic rituals** (such as systematic desensitization in behavior therapy or free association in psychoanalysis) that further augment clients' faith in the therapist and the therapeutic rationale. Such procedures, Frank maintains, are akin to the ceremonial rituals of faith healers in that they cultivate the impression that something deeply important and mysterious is taking place.

According to Frank, each of these four nonspecific factors helps to combat **demoralization**, which he views as the universal malady bringing individuals to psychotherapy. That is, essentially all individuals voluntarily seeking treatment are characterized by low self-esteem, despair, helplessness, alienation, and a profound sense of incompetence. All psychotherapies alleviate demoralization by raising hopes and expectations of improvement and by instilling feelings of confidence and self-worth.

Frank's arguments are buttressed by the results of meta-analyses such as those of Smith and Glass, which show that the differences among psychotherapies in their efficacy generally appear to be negligible. This is precisely the result one would expect if nonspecific factors were the sole or principal mediators of client improvement. Luborsky et al. (1975), who similarly reported minimal differences in success rates among psychotherapies, christened this finding the "dodo bird ver-

*Curiously, Hans Eysenck, who has devoted much of his career to arguing that neurosis is not fundamentally different from normality, did not even mention this issue in his highly laudatory comment on Prioleau, Murdock, and Brody's findings (Eysenck, 1983). Psychological researchers are no different from the rest of us: They have blind spots stemming from their preconceptions.

dict," after the bird in *Alice in Wonderland* who declared (following a race): "Everyone has won and all must have prizes."

It would be premature to accept the "dodo bird verdict" as the final word on therapeutic effectiveness. For one thing, the results of both Smith and Glass's meta-analysis and of several subsequent meta-analyses (for example, Shapiro & Shapiro, 1982) suggest that behavioral therapies are generally superior to nonbehavioral therapies, although admittedly this difference is difficult to interpret (see Smith and Glass's discussion of the differential reactivity of outcome measures) and relatively small in magnitude. Perhaps more important, many psychologists now believe that the so-called "null hypothesis"—the well-known hypothesis of "no difference" between groups that all students are introduced to in experimental psychology—is in reality always or almost always false (Lykken, 1968; Meehl, 1978). For reasons that I will not go into here, it is probably naive to suppose that a large number of psychological manipulations will all be exactly equal in their effects. It would be utterly remarkable if the 300 or so different therapies that have been identified all turn out to be precisely equivalent in their success rates. Thus, even if Frank's nonspecific factors were the only ingredients involved in therapeutic efficacy (which seems rather unlikely; for example, see the articles in Chapter 13), some psychotherapies are probably more heavily "saturated" with these nonspecific factors than are others. For example, certain therapies (such as behavior therapy) almost undoubtedly have a more plausible theoretical rationale—at least for most clients—than do others (such as nude marathon regression therapy; see Corsini, 1981).

Finally, it could be justifiably argued that the question constituting this chapter's title—"Is psychotherapy effective?"—although remarkably complex in some respects, is actually too simple in others. Maher (1983), for example, has likened posing this question to asking "Do physicians cure illness?" Admittedly, this comparison may be somewhat overstated: Many proponents of particular brands of psychotherapy do recommend that their method be used for all or essentially all psychological problems, whereas no physicians would recommend that open-heart surgery be used to treat kidney stones. Nevertheless, Maher has a point. Ultimately, the more important and interesting question, as Gordon Paul (1966) notes, may not be whether therapy is "effective" in general but rather "*what* treatment, by *whom*, is most effective for *this* individual with *that* specific problem, and under *which* set of circumstances" (pp. 111). Unfortunately, detecting these specific interactions has proved to be surprisingly difficult in psychotherapy research (Beutler, 1991), either because such interactions are exceedingly rare or because researchers have not been clever enough to look in the right places (or both). In any case, attempting to pin down specific interactions among therapy, therapist, and client variables will be one of the major challenges of the next generation of psychotherapy researchers.

POSTSCRIPT

In an article that may help to bring an end to the debate concerning the overall efficacy of psychotherapy, Lipsey and Wilson (1993) report a comprehensive summary of meta-analyses of psychotherapy and other psychological interventions. They conclude that psychotherapy tends to produce clear and consistent beneficial effects that cannot be explained entirely by either placebo effects or by methodological artifacts specific to meta-analysis. Moreover, they found that the effect sizes resulting from psychotherapy are generally comparable, and in some cases superior, to the effect sizes produced by standard medical treatments, such as heart bypass surgery, drug treatment for arthritis, and AZT for acquired immune deficiency syndrome (AIDS). Thus, the debate concerning the effectiveness of psychotherapy, although certainly not conclusively settled, appears to be moving closer to a resolution.

QUESTIONS TO STIMULATE DISCUSSION

1. Smith and Glass report finding little or no association between years of therapist experience and the effectiveness of psychotherapy. How can you explain this perplexing finding? What are its implications, if any, for the training of psychotherapists?
2. Cordray and Bootzin's (1983) analysis suggests that the "placebos" used in most psychotherapy outcome studies actually have active ingredients (for example, arousal of client expectations for improvement). If Cordray and Bootzin are correct, what would constitute a proper control group in psychotherapy outcome research? What types of manipulations would constitute better (that is, more inactive or inert) placebos than those typically used?
3. Eysenck (1978) has caustically referred to meta-analysis as "mega-silliness" because this technique, if used improperly, lends itself to the mindless lumping together of heterogeneous studies differing greatly in quality and methodology. How could this problem be avoided?
4. From what you have read, is meta-analysis superior to the traditional informal literature review, which simply summarizes the results of studies in a descriptive fashion? Or has meta-analysis led to more confusion than clarification in the psychotherapy literature? Defend your answer.
5. Jerome Frank and others have pointed to a variety of nonspecific factors that appear to be instrumental in the effectiveness of psychotherapy. But might specific factors, over and above these common elements, also contribute to therapeutic success? If so, what might they be?
6. As noted in the discussion section of this chapter, Gordon Paul (1966) suggests that psychotherapy researchers explicitly seek out specific interactions among therapy, therapist, and client variables. For example, he recommends that

researchers examine whether specific types of psychotherapy are better suited for specific types of clients. Can you think of any potential examples of this type of interaction? If so, how would you proceed to investigate them?

SUGGESTIONS FOR FURTHER READING

Brown, J. (1987). A review of meta-analyses conducted on psychotherapy outcome research. *Clinical Psychology Review, 7,* 1–23.

In an informal "meta-meta-analysis" of psychotherapy outcome studies, Brown reviews the six major meta-analyses of therapeutic efficacy, including those of Smith and Glass and of Prioleau, Murdock, and Brody. He discusses the major findings of these six studies as well as the limitations of meta-analysis as an analytic technique.

Christenson, A., & Jacobson, N. S. (1994). Who (or what) can do psychotherapy: The status and challenge of nonprofessional therapies. *Psychological Science, 5,* 8–14.

The authors review evidence indicating that paraprofessional therapists and professional therapists tend to be approximately equivalent in their success rates, as well as preliminary research suggesting that self-help materials such as books and videotapes may often be as effective as formal psychotherapy. They discuss the implications of these surprising findings and argue that investigators should focus primarily on comparing the efficacy of therapists (especially those with differing amounts of training) rather than therapies.

Eysenck, H. J. (1952). The effects of psychotherapy: An evaluation. *Journal of Consulting Psychology, 16,* 319–324.

In this seminal article, which triggered the controversy concerning the efficacy of psychotherapy, Eysenck compares the results of 24 studies of therapy outcome with the results of studies on the spontaneous remission rate of neurotics. His conclusion: "The figures fail to support the hypothesis that psychotherapy facilitates recovery from neurotic disorder" (p. 323). (See also Eysenck, H. J. [1965]. The effects of psychotherapy. *International Journal of Psychiatry, 1,* 99–142; and responses by J. D. Frank, P. E. Meehl, H. H. Strupp, J. Wolpe, J. Zubin, and others.)

Eysenck, H. J. (1978). An exercise in mega-silliness. *American Psychologist, 33,* 517.

Caustically referring to Smith and Glass's meta-analysis as "mega-silliness," Eysenck castigates them for thoughtlessly aggregating a large number of studies varying greatly in quality and design. Like much of Eysenck's writing on this topic, this comment is cleverly reasoned but marred by misstatements and polemics. (See also Glass, G. V., & Smith, M. L. [1978]. Reply to Eysenck. *American Psychologist, 33,* 517–518.)

Frank, J. (1973). *Persuasion and healing: A comparative analysis of psychotherapy* (2nd ed.). Baltimore: Johns Hopkins University Press.

Frank delineates the similarities between religious healing and contemporary psychotherapy and argues that the effectiveness of therapy derives largely from a set of "common factors" shared by virtually all therapeutic modalities. These common factors include the ability of the therapist to combat demoralization, instill confidence, and arouse the client's expectations and hopes of improvement. For Frank, the placebo effect, far from being a methodological artifact to be experimentally controlled, is perhaps the key ingredient in effective psychotherapy.

Kazdin, A. E. (1985). The role of meta-analysis in the evaluation of psychotherapy. *Clinical Psychology Review, 5,* 49–61.

Kazdin discusses the uses of meta-analysis in the evaluation of therapy outcome, as well as its potential limitations (such as the inevitably subjective nature of many of the judgments involved) and benefits. He places particular emphasis upon the advantages and disadvantages of meta-analysis compared with other data summary strategies, such as the traditional qualitative literature review.

Landman, J. T., & Dawes, R. M. (1982). Psychotherapy outcome: Smith and Glass' conclusions stand up under scrutiny. *American Psychologist, 37,* 504–516.

The authors reanalyze Smith and Glass's findings by excluding studies that lacked adequate control groups. They conclude that, contrary to the claims of critics, Smith and Glass's principal findings are not attributable to methodological artifacts.

Luborsky, L., Singer, B., & Luborsky, L. (1975). Comparative studies of psychotherapies. *Archives of General Psychiatry, 32,* 995–1008.

The authors use the "voting" or "box score" method to evaluate the efficacy of psychotherapy. They find that psychotherapy is generally more effective than "control" treatment, although the differences among therapies in their overall effectiveness are minimal. To summarize their results, the authors invoke the "dodo bird verdict" from *Alice in Wonderland:* "Everyone has won and all must have prizes."

Sloane, R. B., Staples, R. F., Cristol, A. H., Yorkston, N. J., & Whipple, K. (1975). *Psychotherapy versus behavior therapy.* Cambridge, MA: Harvard University Press.

In one of the classic studies of the efficacy of therapy, these authors report the results of a 1-year follow-up study of patients randomly assigned to either psychoanalytically oriented therapy, behavior therapy, or a waiting-list control group. They find that both treatments are clearly more effective than the waiting list and that the differences between these treatments in their effectiveness are generally minimal.

Smith, M. L., Glass, G. V., & Miller, T. I. (1980). *The benefits of psychotherapy.* Baltimore: Johns Hopkins Press.

These authors begin by examining the major reviews of psychotherapy outcome and discuss the central controversies surrounding the efficacy of psychotherapy. They then report the findings of their meta-analysis of therapeutic effectiveness, which is an expanded version of the Smith and Glass meta-analysis. Unlike Smith and Glass, they include studies of the efficacy of drug therapy with psychological disorders.

Zilbergeld, B. (1983). *The shrinking of America: Myths of psychological change.* Boston: Little, Brown.

Zilbergeld attacks America's infatuation with psychotherapy and attempts to explode a number of popular myths regarding its effectiveness. He contends that the changes produced by therapy tend to be far more modest and short-lived than is typically claimed and that proponents of therapy have greatly overestimated the malleability of the human personality.

REFERENCES

Beutler, L. E. (1991). Have all won and must all have prizes? Revisiting Luborsky et al.'s verdict. *Journal of Consulting and Clinical Psychology, 59*, 226–232.

Brody, N. (1983). Where are the emperor's clothes? *Behavioral and Brain Sciences, 6*, 303–308.

Cordray, D. S., & Bootzin, R. R. (1983). Placebo control conditions: Tests of theory or of effectiveness. *Behavioral and Brain Sciences, 6*, 286–287.

Corsini, R. J. (1981). *Handbook of innovative psychotherapies*. New York: Wiley.

Eysenck, H. J. (1952). The effects of psychotherapy: An evaluation. *Journal of Consulting Psychology, 16*, 319–324.

Eysenck, H. J. (1978). An exercise in mega-silliness. *American Psychologist, 33*, 517.

Eysenck, H. J. (1983). The effectiveness of psychotherapy: The specter at the feast. *Behavioral and Brain Sciences, 6*, 290.

Frank, J. (1973). *Persuasion and healing: A comparative analysis of psychotherapy* (2nd ed.). Baltimore: Johns Hopkins University Press.

Lipsey, M. W., & Wilson, D. B. (1993). The efficacy of psychological, educational, and behavioral treatment: Confirmation from meta-analysis. *American Psychologist, 48*, 1181–1209.

Luborsky, L., Singer, B., & Luborsky, L. (1975). Comparative studies of psychotherapies. *Archives of General Psychiatry, 32*, 995–1008.

Lykken, D. T. (1968). Statistical significance in psychological research. *Psychological Bulletin, 70*, 151–159.

Maher, B. (1983). Meta-analysis: We need better analysis. *Behavioral and Brain Sciences, 6*, 297–298.

Meehl, P. E. (1978). Theoretical risk and tabular asterisks: Sir Karl, Sir Ronald, and the slow progress of soft psychology. *Journal of Consulting and Clinical Psychology, 46*, 806–834.

Paul, G. L. (1966). *Insight vs. desensitization in psychotherapy: An experiment in anxiety reduction*. Stanford, CA: Stanford University Press.

Schofield, W. (1964). *Psychotherapy: The purchase of friendship*. Englewood Cliffs, NJ: Prentice-Hall.

Shapiro, D. A., & Shapiro, D. (1982). Meta-analysis of comparative therapy outcome studies: A replication and refinement. *Psychological Bulletin, 92*, 581–604.

Smith, M. L., Glass, G. V., & Miller, T. I. (1980). *The benefits of psychotherapy*. Baltimore: Johns Hopkins University Press.

Torrey, E. F. (1972). *The mind game*. New York: Emerson Hall.

Wilkins, W. (1986). Placebo problems in psychotherapy research: Social-psychological alternatives to chemotherapy concepts. *American Psychologist, 41*, 551–556.

CHAPTER

13

Is cognitive-behavioral therapy an important advance over behavior therapy?

PRO Beck, A. T. (1991). Cognitive therapy: A 30-year retrospective. *American Psychologist*, 46, 368–375.

CON Beidel, D. C., & Turner, S. M. (1986). A critique of the theoretical bases of cognitive-behavioral theories and therapy. *Clinical Psychology Review*, 6, 177–197.

OVERVIEW OF THE CONTROVERSY: Aaron T. Beck, the founder of cognitive therapy, argues that research evidence strongly supports the cognitive model of psychopathology and its application to the treatment of depression, anxiety disorders, and perhaps other conditions. Deborah C. Beidel and Samuel M. Turner criticize the cognitive model of psychopathology on a variety of theoretical grounds and contend that the effectiveness of "cognitive-behavioral" therapy derives from its incorporation of behavioral techniques.

CONTEXT OF THE PROBLEM

The school of behaviorism, rooted largely in the pioneering investigations of Ivan Pavlov in Russia and Edward Thorndike in the United States, arose largely in reaction to the "introspectionist" movement that was in vogue throughout much of the late 19th century and early 20th century. The introspectionists, whose ranks included such giants as E. B. Titchener and Wilhelm Wundt, strove to understand the human psyche by consciously reflecting upon its most basic elements. Their methodology was brutally simple: Subjects would sit in a room devoid of all unnecessary distractions and patiently and carefully take note of all the raw ingredients of their conscious experience. Ultimately, the introspectionists believed, the product of this painstaking endeavor would be something akin to a periodic table of elements—except that in this case the elements would be mental rather than chemical. Titchener claimed to have discovered approximately 44,000 mental elements, including 32,820 visual and 11,600 auditory sensations (Loevinger, 1987). Needless to say, the precise number and nature of these elements could not be objectively verified, because they were known only to the subject.

John B. Watson, the flamboyant and controversial figure who is generally considered the founder of behaviorism, rebelled against the highly subjective nature of introspectionism. Psychology, he argued, should aspire to the same standards of objectivity attained by such natural sciences as physics and biology. To accomplish this lofty goal, psychology should cast aside any trappings—such as introspection—that rendered it less than completely objective. Watson was thus a **methodological behaviorist**: He emphatically rejected the view that unobservable events should be a focus of psychological methodology. According to Watson, a finding that could not be objectively verified was worthless. In addition, Watson believed that, to achieve the status of a science, psychology must base itself on the laws of learning systematically demonstrated in the laboratory: classical (respondent) and operant (instrumental) conditioning. For Watson, both abnormal and normal behaviors could be explained by the same fundamental learning principles. One "learns" to become schizophrenic, according to Watson, in much the same way that one learns to hit a tennis ball, drive a car, or brush one's teeth.

B. F. Skinner, the brilliant Harvard psychologist who founded **radical behaviorism**, shared Watson's dream of a scientific psychology but did not agree that psychology should exclude internal events from its scope of inquiry. For Skinner, thoughts (as well as other internal events) are not metaphysical activities inaccessible to scientific investigation but simply behaviors that happen to be covert (that is, unobservable). As such, he maintained, thoughts are subject to the same laws of learning as overt behaviors, such as riding a bicycle or eating a sandwich. But Skinner and the radical behaviorists rejected the notion that thinking plays a causal role in overt behavior. They viewed thoughts, like all other behaviors, as a consequence of reinforcing and punishing stimuli (what Skinner termed **contingencies**). Thus, although thinking often accompanies overt behavior, including abnormal behavior, it does not cause it: both thinking and overt behavior are the product of contingencies.

How, you may be wondering, is the history of behaviorism relevant to psychotherapy? To understand the answer to this question, you must also understand that many of the early behaviorists were more than "ivory tower" academics concerned only with arcane theoretical issues. Instead, many were activists who vigorously lobbied for the application of their hard-won insights to the amelioration of real-world problems. It was not long before behaviorists began to translate the abstract principles of classical and operant conditioning into concrete treatment techniques.

The behavioral school of therapy, spearheaded by such forceful figures as Joseph Wolpe and Hans Eysenck, was premised on the assumption that abnormal behavior is maintained, and in many cases caused, by faulty learning experiences. Behavior therapists developed a variety of techniques based on both classical conditioning principles, such as systematic desensitization (see Chapter 12), and operant conditioning principles, such as the token economy. Many of these techniques met with sensational success: Systematic desensitization proved to be a remarkably effective treatment for specific phobias, and token economies proved to be quite useful for modifying the short-term behaviors of schizophrenics and other chronic psychiatric patients. The behavioral school of therapy came to exert increasing influence on American psychology in the early and middle years of the 20th century.

Nevertheless, a number of theorists grew increasingly dissatisfied with behaviorists' apparent neglect of, and even disdain for, cognitive factors. **Social learning** theorists—who included Julian Rotter, Albert Bandura, and Walter Mischel—argued that such factors as expectations, values, goals, and plans play an essential role in learning. Cognitive factors, they maintained, are actually the principal mediators of behavior. In other words, although environmental stimuli surely have an important effect on behavior, their effects are mediated by the organism's interpretation of these stimuli. Classical and operant conditioning are not automatic or "hard-wired" processes, social learning theorists argued, but rather manifestations of a flexible, thoughtful, and purposeful organism.

Social learning theory eventually gave rise to its own brand of treatment: cognitive therapy or as it is more frequently called, **cognitive-behavioral therapy**. Probably the most influential figure in the formative years of cognitive-behavioral therapy was Albert Ellis, the developer of **rational-emotive therapy**, or RET. According to Ellis, thinking is the principal determinant of emotion; moreover, irrational thinking is the principal determinant of neurosis. Most of us, Ellis contends, implicitly adopt an "A-C" model of emotion: We believe that certain actions (A), such as the breakup of a relationship, necessarily lead to certain emotional consequences (C), such as depression. But, Ellis insists, the correct account is actually an "A-B-C" model, in which certain beliefs (B)—such as "If someone breaks up with me, I must be a failure"—intervene between action and consequence. If one changes the underlying belief, argues Ellis, the emotional consequence will necessarily also change. Thus, the focus of RET is the alteration of irrational beliefs by means of persuasion, cajoling, rational argument, and empirical demonstration.

Later, Aaron Beck founded a similar school of treatment called cognitive therapy. (With few exceptions, authors in this literature use the terms *cognitive therapy and cognitive-behavioral therapy* interchangeably.) Beck's method, which is less confrontational than Ellis's, was initially developed to treat depression but was later extended by Beck and his students to the treatment of anxiety disorders, personality disorders, and other conditions.

Nevertheless, cognitive-behavioral therapy is controversial. Although controlled studies clearly demonstrate its efficacy for depression and perhaps other conditions, its efficacy relative to behavior therapy remains unclear. The founders of cognitive-behavioral therapy contend that it is a genuine alternative to behavior therapy, but its detractors contend that it is simply a variant of behavior therapy that places somewhat greater emphasis on a specific class of behaviors—thoughts.

THE CONTROVERSY: Beck vs. Beidel and Turner

Beck

Aaron Beck points out that recent therapy outcome studies and meta-analyses (see Chapter 12) lend considerable support to the efficacy of cognitive therapy in the treatment of depression, anxiety disorders, and perhaps other conditions. Beck then reflects on the initial observations that led him to posit the existence of schemas and automatic thoughts (see Key Concepts and Terms for definitions) and their role in the etiology of depression. The negative schemas of depressed and anxious individuals, he argues, are typically latent but are activated in response to specific environmental stressors. Beck discusses how the study of cognitive biases in psychopathology sheds light on "normal" cognitive and emotional functioning. He responds to criticisms of the cognitive model's assertions regarding the causal role of cognitions in psychopathology, purported neglect of interpersonal factors, and apparent inability to explain the phenomenon of depressive realism (the finding that depressed individuals view themselves and the world more realistically than do nondepressed individuals). Finally, Beck discusses the evidence for several key hypotheses derived from the cognitive model, including the negativity hypothesis and the hypothesis of cognitive primacy, and concludes that cognitive therapy is a promising alternative to behavior therapy.

Beidel and Turner

Deborah Beidel and Samuel Turner note that cognitive-behavioral therapy has been advanced as an alternative to behavior therapy by individuals dissatisfied with behaviorists' apparent neglect of cognitive factors. Beidel and Turner contend, however, that cognition has been defined inconsistently by cognitive-behaviorists: Some have defined it as a process, others as an object of that process. Moreover, Beidel and Turner argue, there is substantial evidence that cognitions follow the established laws of learning and can thus be accommodated within a behavioral framework. They review the evidence from studies of differences between mentally ill patients and normals, depressive realism, depressed individuals' predictions of their own and others' performance, and mood induction (the creation of moods by experimental manipulation) and conclude that none of these investigations provides convincing evidence that cognitive factors play a causal role in psychopathology. Finally, Beidel and Turner review research comparing the effectiveness of cognitive-behavioral and behavioral therapies. They conclude that the differences in efficacy appear to be minimal. Moreover, Beidel and Turner argue, because cognitive-behavioral therapies almost invariably incorporate behavioral techniques, their effectiveness probably derives largely or entirely from the application of basic learning principles.

KEY CONCEPTS AND TERMS

automatic thought According to cognitive-behavioral therapists, a thought that occurs "reflexively" and largely outside the boundaries of awareness, often in response to an external event. For example, after being treated rudely by a cashier on the supermarket checkout line, a depressed individual may have the automatic thought "Everyone dislikes me."

autonomy Personality style characterized by an emphasis on achievement and independence. Compare with *sociotropy*.

cognitive triad Individual's view of the self, the world, and the future. According to cognitive therapists, depressed individuals are characterized by a negative view of all three components of the cognitive triad.

content-specificity hypothesis Hypothesis that each form of psychopathology (for example, depression or anxiety) is characterized by a specific and distinctive pattern of cognitive distortions.

corrugator electromyogram (EMG) Measure of the electrical activity emanating from the frontalis muscle of the forehead. Corrugator EMG is frequently used as an index of muscle tension.

depressive realism Controversial notion that depressed individuals have a more realistic view of themselves and their worlds than do nondepressed individuals. Proponents of the concept of depressive realism typically posit that nondepressed individuals have a self-serving bias that leads them to evaluate themselves and the world positively.

internal dialogue Internalized "speech" that individuals use to monitor, control, and inhibit their behavior. Some cognitive-behavioral therapists believe that childhood disorders characterized by poor impulse control, such as attention-deficit/hyperactivity disorder (see Chapter 15), are due to deficits in internal dialogue.

negative cognitive shift According to cognitive-behavioral theorists, an alteration in cognitive organization that results in a tendency for negative information about oneself to enter awareness more easily than positive information.

schema Cognitive structure that helps individuals to organize information about themselves and their environment. Cognitive theorists hypothesize that schemas shape and direct such processes as attention, perception, information processing, and recall. (See also *negative self-schema* in Chapter 11.)

self-efficacy Concept introduced by Albert Bandura that refers to the expectation that one can successfully perform an action. Bandura has argued that increases in self-efficacy are the universal mechanism underlying all psychotherapeutic change.

self-statement modification Cognitive-behavioral technique in which individuals are taught to modify their internal dialogue or "self-talk" in order to produce more adaptive and rational ways of thinking.

sociotropy Personality style characterized by an emphasis upon intimacy and dependence upon others. Compare with *autonomy*.

PREVIEW QUESTIONS

1. What initial observations led Beck to posit his cognitive model of psychopathology?
2. According to Beck, what is a schema, and what role does it play in the genesis of depression?
3. According to Beck, what are the three major challenges to the cognitive model? What are his responses to these challenges?
4. What are the four principal hypotheses cited by Beck that were derived from the cognitive model, and what is the research evidence supporting each hypothesis?
5. According to Beidel and Turner, how do cognitive-behavioral therapies purportedly differ in emphasis from behavioral therapies?
6. According to Beidel and Turner, what are the different ways in which cognitive-behaviorists have defined cognition?
7. What research findings, according to Beidel and Turner, call into question the causal role of cognitive factors in psychopathology?
8. According to Beidel and Turner, what do research studies on the relative effectiveness of cognitive-behavioral and behavioral therapies indicate? What factors make it difficult to evaluate such comparisons?

AARON T. BECK

Cognitive therapy: A 30-year retrospective

Fifteen years have elapsed since I called for the admission of cognitive therapy into the therapeutic arena (Beck, 1976, p. 337), and 30 years have gone by since I first formulated my cognitive model of depression based on research on dreams and other ideational material (Beck, 1961). I suggested in 1976 that in order to qualify as a system of psychotherapy a particular brand of psychotherapy had to provide (a) a comprehensive theory of psychopathology that articulates with the structure of psychotherapy, (b) a body of knowledge and empirical findings that support the theory, and (c) credible findings based on outcome and other studies to demonstrate its effectiveness.

What is the status of cognitive therapy today? A steady flow of studies largely support the cognitive model of depression (Ernst, 1985). This model has facilitated the development of strategies and techniques to provide a psychotherapeutic structure. Numerous outcome studies have supported the effectiveness of the therapy in the treatment of unipolar outpatient depression, anxiety disorders, and panic disorder. A meta-analysis of 27 studies (Dobson, 1989), for example, has demonstrated the efficacy of cognitive therapy in unipolar depression and its superiority to other treatments, including antidepressant drugs. More striking has been the success of cognitive therapy in maintaining gains and preventing relapse. Five published studies have indicated that cognitive therapy has a greater prophylactic effect than do antidepressant drugs (Hollon & Najavits, 1988). A more recent study, the much-publicized National Institute of Mental Health collaborative study of the treatment of depression, has shown superiority of cognitive therapy in follow-up, in comparison with antidepressant drug and interpersonal therapy (Shea et al., 1990).

Even more impressive has been the application of cognitive therapy to panic disorder. On the basis of the cognitive model of panic (Beck, 1976, 1987a; D. M. Clark, 1986), practically complete reduction of panic attacks after 12–16 weeks of treatment has been reported (Sokol, Beck, & Clark, 1989; Sokol, Beck, Greenberg, Berchick, & Wright, 1989). Also impressive has been the successful application of cognitive therapy to generalized anxiety disorder (Butler, Fennell, Robson, & Gelder, 1991), eating disorders (Garner & Bemis, 1982), heroin addiction (Woody et al., 1984), and inpatient depression (Miller, Norman, & Keitner, 1989). Further clinical work suggests the utility of cognitive therapy in treating diverse disorders such as couples' problems (Beck, 1988) and schizophrenia (Perris, 1988). A striking feature of the diverse application has been the importance of cognitive specificity. Each

---

SOURCE: *American Psychologist*, 46(4), pp. 368–375, April 1991.

disorder has its own specific cognitive conceptualization and relevant strategies that are embraced under the general principles of cognitive therapy (Beck, 1976; Beck & Freeman, 1990; Beck, Rush, Shaw, & Emery, 1979).

Because of the breadth of cognitive therapy and its therapeutic eclecticism, and the ability of cognitive theory to explain changes in psychopathology, the question has been raised as to whether cognitive therapy might be viewed as the product of the integration of the effective psychotherapies (Alford & Norcross, 1991). The theoretical framework of cognitive therapy appears to articulate well with contemporary developments in cognitive psychology and social psychology (Hollon & Garber, 1990), as well as earlier concepts of developmental psychology (Beck, 1967). In fact, there appears to be a kind of convergent evolution of concepts from the cognitive model of psychopathology and those of cognitive psychology. Moreover, many of the recent studies of the cognitive model of depression and anxiety disorders have borrowed techniques from cognitive psychology (e.g., Mathews, 1990).

INITIAL OBSERVATIONS AND FORMULATIONS

My original observations of depressed patients were based on their verbalizations and free associations while they were undergoing psychoanalytic treatment with me. At one point I observed to my surprise that my patients experienced specific types of thoughts of which they were only dimly aware and that they did not report during their free associations. In fact, unless they were directed to focus their attention on these thoughts, they were not likely to be very aware of them. Although these thoughts seemed to be on the periphery of the patients' stream of consciousness, they appeared to play an important role in the psychic life of these patients (for a fuller description of this "discovery" see Beck, 1976, pp. 29–35). These thoughts (cognitions) tended to arise quickly and automatically, as though by reflex; they were not subject to volition or conscious control and seemed perfectly plausible to the individual. They were frequently followed by an unpleasant affect (in the case of the depressed patients) that the patients were very much aware of, even though they were unaware of, or barely aware of, the preceding automatic thoughts.

When I directed the patients to focus their attention on these "automatic thoughts," they began to report a string of them, particularly in response to a cognitive probe. "What are you thinking right now?" Connecting these thoughts brought out certain negative themes such as deprivation, disease, or defeat. Grouped together they fell into the category of a negative view of the present, past, and future experiences. Later, in working with more severely depressed patients, I noted that these types of thoughts were no longer peripheral but occupied a dominant position in consciousness and were repetitive.

It seemed to me that I had tapped another level of consciousness in the recognition of automatic thoughts, perhaps analogous to the phenomenon described by Freud as "preconscious." This level of consciousness seemed to be relevant to what people say to *themselves* and was involved in the system of self-monitoring rather than what they might say in the conversational mode, their customary way of communicating with other people. Thus, the automatic thoughts were conceived of as being part of an internal communication system, as opposed to the interpersonal communication that was more involved in the discussion with other people (Beck, 1976, pp. 24–46). Hence, the patients were less likely to report these cognitions in free association but were readily taught to focus on them when the therapist (or the patients themselves), noting a change in affect, used the cognitive probe. Following my initial observations, I discovered that Ellis (1962) reported similar observations.

The negativity permeated the "internal communications" such as self-evaluation, attributions, expectancies, inferences, and recall, and were manifested in low self-esteem, self-blame and self-criticism, negative predictions, negative interpretations of experiences, and unpleasant recollections. In ambiguous situations, the depressed patients were particularly prone to make a negative interpretation when a positive one would seem to be more appropriate; they would not only magnify their own unpleasant experiences but would either blot out or label as negative their experiences that other people would consider positive.

I also noted a variety of errors in the patients' depressive thinking, which I labeled selective abstraction, overgeneralization, dichotomous thinking, and exaggeration (of the negative aspects of their experiences). Furthermore, I noted that depressed patients tended to predict specific negative outcomes from specific tasks that they might undertake and expected long-range, bad outcomes to their life in general. A high degree of such negative expectations ("hopelessness") appeared to be predictive of suicide. These phenomena appeared to be universal across all types of subtypes of depression: reactive (nonendogenous), endogenous, bipolar, or organic. They also appeared whenever depressive symptomatology was present—irrespective of whether the primary diagnosis was depression, schizophrenia, or some other disorder.

To account for the regularities in negative thinking in depression, I postulated the presence of a *negative cognitive shift*. This thesis stipulates that there is a change in the cognitive organization so that much positive information relevant to the individual is filtered out (cognitive blockade), whereas negative self-relevant information is readily admitted.

MEANING, SYMBOLISM, AND SCHEMAS

I was struck by how ascertaining the idiosyncratic or special meanings people attached to events helped to explain what might otherwise have represented quite inexplicable affective and behavioral reactions. Highly personal meanings did not usually revolve around esoteric themes such as castration anxiety or psychosexual fixations, as might be suggested by classical psychoanalytic theory, but were related to vital social issues such as success or failure, acceptance or rejection, respect or disdain. Moreover, these meanings were accessible to introspection. At times I would pick out what seemed to be a common theme across diverse circumstances and then induce the patients to focus on their thoughts or images in these situations. The psychotherapy sessions consequently provided a rich source of data for theoretical constructions.

Many of the meanings were fairly elaborate and were packed into a rather discrete stimulus situation. A man, for example, always reacted with the thought "She does not respect me" when his wife did not respond to him. A wife not receiving a smile from her husband consistently interpreted this as "He doesn't care for me." For them, a discrete (although ambiguous) behavior had a fixed meaning. Of course, at times such meaning may be relatively accurate. But symbols are different from other complex stimuli in that the evoked meanings are not only powerful but invariant.

The internal representation of the meanings evoked by the symbols constitute a network of beliefs, assumptions, formulas, and rules and are often connected to memories relevant to the development and formation of such beliefs (Beck, 1964). The relevant beliefs interact with the symbolic situation to produce the "automatic thoughts."

Because of the continuity of content of beliefs over each recurrence of the disorder, I proposed that they existed in an inactive or latent state prior to and between depressions. These beliefs were encased in schemas that had a variety of properties in addition to content: valence, permeability, density, flexibility. However, whatever factors initiated the occurrence or recurrence of the disorder activated these schemas.

The depressed patients' interpretations of their experiences seemed to be shaped by certain absolute beliefs such as "I am worthless." "I can't do anything right," and "I am unlovable." Any situation that was remotely relevant to self-worth, ability, or social desirability was interpreted in terms of the corresponding belief. I suggested that these beliefs were formed earlier in life (Beck, 1967) and became embedded in a structure (cognitive schema). Subsequently, when specific life experiences impinged on these beliefs (schemas), they might precipitate a depression. I proposed that beliefs were generally framed in a conditional form such as "If I don't succeed, I am helpless."

A later observation suggested that two "types" of individuals—sociotropic and autonomous—were prone to become depressed after the occurrence of an adverse experience congruent with their personality. (Of course, these types simply represented extreme forms on the dimensions of sociotropy and autonomy.) Patients who were heavily invested in autonomy (independent achievement, mobility, solitary pleasures) were prone to become depressed after an "autonomous stressor" such as failure, immobilization, or enforced conformity. Patients who deeply valued closeness, dependency, and sharing were hypersensitive to and prone to become depressed after "sociotropic traumas" such as social deprivation or rejection (Beck, 1983).

It eventually became apparent that the same types of beliefs predisposed individuals to develop anxiety disorders—the difference being that in anxiety disorders the congruent stressors were the *threat* of failure or abandonment rather than the actual occurrence of the event.

EXTRAPOLATIONS TO THE NORMAL FROM THE ABNORMAL

I believe that we have learned and can still learn a great deal about normal functions from the study of psychopathology. For example, the systematic negative bias in depression and positive bias in mania (Beck, 1967) supports the presence of similar but more subtle biases in normal everyday reactions. Indeed, positive bias has been long recognized and demonstrated more recently in "illusory glow" experiments (Alloy & Abramson, 1979). Not so obvious is the clarification of everyday worries about health, and so forth, initiated by studies of cognitive aspects of hypochondriasis (Salkovskis, 1989) and panic (Beck, 1976, 1987a). The overconcern about evaluation in the social phobias and of physical danger in the impersonal phobias (e.g., heights, crowded spaces, small animals) point to similar sources of anxiety in the psychology of everyday life.

The biases also suggest how the "cognitive shift" can influence the content at each stage of cognitive processing. Starting with preferential selection (abstraction) of data, through the evaluation, interpretation, and recall from short-term recovery, the content of cognitive processing is determined by the activated schemas. Even retrieval from long-term memory is influenced by these schemas.

Continuity Hypothesis

Various psychopathological syndromes appear to represent exaggerated and persistent forms of normal emotional responses. Thus, there is a continuity between the content of "normal" responses and the excessive or inappropriate emotional experiences associated with psychopathology. In depression, the sense of defeat and the withdrawal of investment in people and customary goals becomes pervasive and unremitting and, consequently, sadness is pervasive and unremitting. In mania, the investment in expansion and goal-directed activity, and consequently, euphoria, is increased. Anxiety disorders are manifested by a generalized, intensified sense of vulnerability and a consequent motivation toward self-defense and escape.

The model of psychopathology proposes that the excessive dysfunctional behavior and distressing emotions or inappropriate affect found in various psychiatric disorders are exaggerations of normal adaptive processes (Beck, 1976).

Typology of Emotions

The study of the clinical data led to the formulation of a typology of "normal" emotions. I conceived of at least four basic emotions that were evoked by a specific cognitive profile or conceptualization. In short, the cognitive structuring of loss, gain, or threat led to a specific corresponding emotion. Sadness appeared to be invoked by the perception of loss, deprivation, or defeat. The response is withdrawal in the lost goals and emotional investment from the source of disappointment. In contrast, elation is produced by perception of a gain. Anxiety and anger, "negative" emotions, are both elicited by perceived threats, but the content of the focus differs. In anxiety, the focus is on the individuals' vulnerabilities, which they attempt to protect through avoidance, escape, or inhibition. (As a way of clarifying the confusing terminology, I have used the term *fear* to denote the cognitive, or intellectual, appraisal of a danger—for example, fear of falling—and the term *anxiety* to designate the emotional consequence of this appraisal; Beck & Emery, 1985.) In contrast, angry individuals focus more on the offensive qualities of the threat than on their own vulnerability and seek to eliminate the threat through counterattack. Limited support for the cognitive configurations have been provided by Wickless and Kirsch (1988).

EVOLUTIONARY ORIGINS OF COGNITIVE PROGRAMS

Another set of speculations attempts to tie in the structural patterns (cognitive schemas) to ethology and evolutionary mechanisms. I proposed that the analog of cognitive structures relevant to depression, anxiety disorders, and the like did not originate de novo with Homo sapiens but evolved through the millennia. Programs that could have had survival value in the wild that were not well adapted to the complexities of modern life could be involved in psychopathology (Beck & Freeman, 1990).

Although there are some risks in extrapolating from animal to human ethology, the similarities are so striking that writers have used animal observations as a way of clarifying human reactions (Darwin, 1872). I think that animal analogies provide a basis for clarifying many aspects of normal and abnormal human behavior (for anxiety and its disorders see Beck & Emery, 1985). More recently I have been impressed by the relevance of observations of primate behavior to depression in humans (Beck, 1987b).

CHALLENGES TO THE COGNITIVE MODEL

The Question of Causality

One of the propositions most frequently attributed to the cognitive model of depression is "cognitions cause depression" (e.g., see Lewinsohn, Steinmetz, Larson, & Franklin, 1981). I have argued elsewhere that it seems far-fetched to assign a casual role to cognitions because the negative automatic thoughts constitute an *integral* part of depression, just like the motivational, affective, and behavioral symptoms. To conclude that cognitions cause depression is analogous to asserting that delusions cause schizophrenia (Beck et al., 1979).

First, consider the definition of the term *cognitions*. I have used this word at times as a more technical term for automatic thoughts. As such, cognitions or automatic thoughts, according to my observations, exist as a common denominator of all kinds of depression and in fact may be essential signs of depression. Confusion may arise, however, as a result of the primacy hypothesis, which states that when the depression is established the interpretations as manifested in automatic thoughts or cognitions shape the affective, behavioral, and motivational responses. Intervention at the cognitive level may reduce the other symptoms, whereas persistence or exacerbation of the cognitive processes may maintain or increase the other symptoms.

Cognition as a singular noun refers to various processes in cognitive or information processing: perception, interpretation, recall, and, as such, comprises a component of a circular model. Each of the psychological systems (cognition, affection, motivation) is interconnected so that changes in one system may produce changes in other systems. Thus, an individual made artificially sad or anxious (e.g., as a side effect of a drug) may then "read" the sadness or anxiety as indicative of loss or danger. The motivational system relevant to relapse into passivity or flight may be activated.

A second source of confusion, related to the first, is that depression is commonly viewed as a mood state, pure and simple (Beck, 1971). This concept has perhaps been abetted by the subsuming of depression under the rubric of affective or mood disorders in the various diagnostic and statistical manuals of the American Psychiatric Association. Consequently, negative cognition has been treated as something apart from depression—as an epiphenomenon, cause, or consequence (Lewinsohn et al., 1981). A related source of confusion has arisen from experimental studies of mood induction. As Riskind (1983) has pointed out, these manipulations can as well be described as "cognitive priming" as mood induction.

A third source of confusion has been my postulation of the role of cognitive schemas in depression and anxiety. In this instance, the schemas (according to theory) become activated. The highly charged negative schemas preempt the more adaptive schemas and thus constitute the negative cognitive shift. Other writers may have assumed that I regarded the schematic change as the "cause" of depression. However, I have considered the activation of the schemas to be a mechanism by which the depression develops, not as the cause. The cause may be in any combination of biological, genetic, stress, or personality factors, which also may be offset by any combination of such factors (Beck, 1967).

Having said this, I acknowledge that my theory does include the notion that *in some cases* the congruence of personality and stressor, in the presence of other possibly unidentifiable factors, may play a causal role ("reactive depression").

A more complete elaboration of the role of cognition must address questions such as (a) What factors produce a shift in the information processing to the negative and what factors maintain the shift? We know, for example, that certain drugs (e.g., antihypertension drugs) can produce such a shift. (b) How do stress factors interacting with personality lead to such a shift? (c) What is the role of protective factors (e.g., social support, insight, coping mechanisms, etc.) in preventing such a shift? (d) Because antidepressant drugs and cognitive therapy produce the same end result (e.g., cognitive change as well as change in biological factors), do they operate through similar or different brain mechanisms? (e) Because follow-up studies consistently indicate greater stability of results and fewer relapses with cognitive therapy than with antidepressant drugs, is this an indication of its impact on additional brain mechanisms or of a more durable impact on the same brain mechanism?

Role of Interpersonal Factors

The cognitive model has been criticized for ignoring interpersonal factors in the genesis of depression (Coyne & Gotlib, 1983). In fact, I have argued elsewhere that in most cases (except possibly for continuous cycling bipolar cases) depression does not occur in a vacuum. Perhaps the most frequent environmental stressors have to do with relations with other people. The role of the interaction of the cognitions of one person with those of another has been described at some length in a recent volume (Beck, 1988). In essence, a dyadic interaction, as in a married couple, may lead to a pathological outcome when the individuals consistently misunderstand each other's behavior and misread each other's motives and act on this misconstruction. Thus, an autonomous wife may interpret her dependent husband's behavior as "He wants to control me." (He has a fear of abandonment and wants to get constant reassurance.) She interprets this as "He wants to control me." She withdraws angrily, which he interprets as "She doesn't really care about me." He demands more reassurance, resulting in further distancing himself [from her], and he slips into a depression: "Since she doesn't love me, I'm unlovable."

Obviously, the depressed individual's psychological systems continue to interact with those of other people even after depression has occurred. A depressed wife, for example, may interpret her husband's frustration at not being able to help her as a sign of rejection (husband's cognitions: "I can't do anything to help her"; wife's cognitions: "He has given up on me because he doesn't care"). The wife reacts with further withdrawal, which triggers further withdrawal of support by the husband (Beck, 1988). The fact that cognitive therapy can help to reverse depression indicates that interpersonal factors have an impact on depression.

Depressive Realism

A number of articles (e.g., Alloy & Abramson, 1979) have suggested that the problem in depression is that the patients see events too realistically (for a critique of this research, see Ackerman & DeRubeis, 1991). The clinical material, however, seems to suggest the following: First, when negative events occur that are complex or abstract, the patient attaches a broad global self-evaluative meaning or explanation. Second, the patient does not think of alternative explanations. Often in treatment therapists find that the patient, when prodded for a more logical explanation, is able to drop his or her negative interpretation. Third, the negative bias is more likely to be manifested when the data (a) are not immediately present in the here and now, (b) are not concrete, (c) are relevant to self-evaluation, and (d) are ambiguous (Riskind, 1983).

Thus, clinically, the patient is more likely to produce exaggerated negative inferences when integrating past events or projecting into the future, when making attributions for which there are no clear-cut criteria on which to base judgments, or when making vague (but crucial) inferences about his or her character.

At this stage of knowledge, it seems that the greatest explanatory power is provided by a model that stipulates that (a) the nondepressed cognitive organization has a positive bias, (b) as it shifts towards depression, the positive cognitive bias is neutralized, (c) as depression develops, a negative bias occurs, (d) in bipolar cases there is a pronounced swing into an exaggerated positive bias as the manic phase develops.

EMPIRICAL STUDIES OF DEPRESSION

Considerable research designed to test various hypotheses generated by the cognitive model of depression has been conducted. In a review of 180 articles incorporating 220 studies of this model, Ernst (1985) reported that 91% supported and 9% did not support the model. He divided his survey into three parts: cognitive triad (150 supportive, 14 nonsupportive), schemas (31 supportive, 6 nonsupportive), and cognitive processing (19 supportive, 0 nonsupportive). In general, he found that the more the studies approximated the clinical observations, the more likely they were to confirm the derived hypotheses. For example, studies of dysphoric student subjects were less likely to be supportive than studies of clinically depressed patients. A more recent critical analysis (Haaga, Dyck, & Ernst, 1991) pinpointed a number of methodological deficiencies in many of these studies.

Negativity Hypothesis

Of all the hypotheses, pervasiveness of negative thinking in all forms of depression, symptomatic or syndromatic, has been the most uniformly supported (Haaga et al., 1991). In early studies (Beck, 1967), dream themes, early memories, measures of self-concept, and responses to projective tests showed a heavy degree of the idiosyncratic content typical of depressives when compared with nondepressed psychiatric patients. Specific questionnaires designed to test components of the cognitive triad (e.g., Beck, Brown, Steer, Eidelson, & Riskind, 1987; Beckham, Leber, Watkins, Boyer, & Cook, 1986; Crandell & Chambless, 1986) have been well documented.

Eaves (1982), for example, showed that the Automatic Thought Questionnaire (Hollon & Kendall, 1980) correctly separated 97% of depressive from normal subjects and did not misidentify any of the normal subjects as depressed.

The *universality* of the cognitive phenomena has been found across all types and subtypes of depression, unipolar and bipolar, reactive and endogenous (see, e.g., Hollon, Kendall, & Lumry, 1986).

The *content-specificity* hypothesis proposes that each disorder has a specific, exclusive cognitive profile. Because most of the clinical overlap occurs between depressive and anxiety disorders, the bulk of the research has been directed toward contrasting the specific cognitive content of depression (loss, defeat, deprivation) with anxiety (danger, threat). The Cognition Checklist, for example, differentiated depressed and anxious patients on the basis of their reciprocal scores on the subscales. Depressive patients scored higher on Loss-Defeat subscales, whereas anxious patients scored higher on the Danger subscale (Beck et al., 1987). Furthermore, compared with anxiety patients, depressed patients assigned high probabilities of a negative outcome of their specific problems and a low probability of a positive outcome (Beck, Riskind, Brown, & Sherrod, 1986).

The specificity hypothesis was further supported by Greenberg and Beck (1989), who found that on self-endorsement and recall, depressives tended to endorse depressive-content (loss, etc.) cognitions, whereas anxiety patients endorsed anxiety-content (danger, etc.) cognitions.

Finally, a factor analysis of all of the cognitive scales designed to measure specifically the cognitive content of depression or anxiety produced the appropriate loadings on the depression and anxiety factors (D. A. Clark, Beck, & Brown, 1989).

Cognitive Primacy

I proposed that in depression the negative processing of information leads to the other symptoms (Beck, 1964). Although it is difficult to establish primacy of any single phenomenon, the tests of this hypothesis have been diverse and generally supportive. One approach indicated that changes in cognition preceded changes in affect (Rush, Weissenburger, & Eaves, 1986). Another line of inquiry showed that manipulations directed at increasing negative thought content in depressed patients increased self-report and corrugator electromyograph indices of depression. Conversely, Teasdale and Fennell (1982) demonstrated that active negative thought content reduction led to the greatest reduction in negative affect in depressed patients.

Finally, Beck, Kovacs, and Weissman (1975) attempted to address this issue through focusing on a specific hypothesis, namely, that hopelessness is the crucial cognitive ingredient of suicidal intent. Clinical studies indicated that hopelessness was the variable linking depression to suicidal wishes. Two prospective studies showed that patients with elevated scores on the Beck Hopelessness Scale were more likely to commit suicide over a five-year follow-up than were patients with lower scores (inpatients: Beck, Steer, Kovacs, & Garrison, 1985; outpatients: Beck, Brown, Berchick, Stewart, & Steer, 1990).

Cognitive Processing

Studies for the most part have supported the observation that in linking the cognitive chain—perception, recall, interpretation—a biased processing of negative material among depressives becomes obvious. It should be pointed out that this cognitive processing is no more conscious than the functioning of the internal organs, but its products may be conscious (Beck, 1987b).

Perception A number of studies (Dunbar & Lishman, 1984; Powell & Hemsley, 1984) have indicated a lower recognition threshold for briefly exposed negative verbal or pictorial stimuli in depressed patients than in nondepressed control subjects. A more "physiological" study showed more efficient processing of negative verbal stimuli in depressed than in nondepressed patients using the P300 waves as a marker (Blackburn, Roxborough, Muir, Glabus, & Blackwood, 1990). Gilson (1983) found that although normal subjects were more likely to perceive positive scenes, depressed subjects perceived negative scenes more frequently in a binocular rivalry experiment.

Recall Negative bias in recall of negative adjectives in depression has been reported by Bradley and Mathews (1988). Furthermore, depressed patients are more likely to underestimate recall of positive relative to negative feedback (DeMonbreun & Craighead, 1977; Gotlib, 1981).

Long-Term Memory D. M. Clark and Teasdale (1982) retrieved more negative memories at a time of day when patients were more depressed than at a time of day when they were less depressed.

Negative Inferences A number of studies administered scenarios to patients with multiple choices for conclusions or outcomes. The studies consistently showed a bias in favor of a negative personal meaning among depressed patients (e.g., Krantz & Hammen, 1979).

Congruence between Personality and Stressors

After my own clinical observations that patients who placed great stock in closeness, intimacy, and dependency and had relevant beliefs (e.g., "If I am not loved I can never be happy") were hypersensitive to any event that appeared to represent withdrawal of affection or support, I proposed that congruence between external events and specific personality types might produce depression. At the same time, Shaw (personal communication, 1980) suggested that the more autonomous patients he treated were hypersensitive to perceived failure.

In order to test this notion, my group developed a scale (the Sociotropy-Autonomy Scale) designed to locate patients on belief dimensions of autonomy and sociotropy. The "pure" groups selected for high scores on one dimension and low on the other would, for experimental purposes, be designated as sociotropic and autonomous. A number of studies then sought to show relations between the "personality type" and the corresponding stressor. A number of somewhat problematic retrospective studies of depressed patients provide mixed support for this hypothesis. In one study, however, Hammen and her group (Hammen, Ellicott, Gitlin, & Jamison, 1989) reported a congruence of life events and type of personality. A later, more refined study (Hammen, Ellicott, & Gitlin, 1989) showed that this relationship held only for patients scoring high on the autonomy scale. In contrast, Segal, Shaw, and Vella (1989) found congruence of life events only among sociotropic patients who relapsed.

Prospective studies of normal individuals exposed to naturalistic stressors provided useful information for understanding the stress-diathesis relationship. Stiles's (1990) study of depressive symptom formation in Norwegian Army recruits separated from their families and assigned to training in northern Norway indicated that those individuals who developed symptoms of depression scored higher on the Dysfunctional Attitude Scale (Weissman & Beck, 1978) at time of induction than those who did not. In future studies, cognitive vulnerability may best be studied during asymptomatic periods, using priming techniques such as those described by Miranda and Persons (1988).

Conclusion

To return to the question I posed in 1976, Can a fledgling psychotherapy challenge the giants in the field—psychoanalysis and behavior therapy?, it seems that the work of the past three decades supports the cognitive model of depression and, to an increasing degree, that of panic disorders, generalized anxiety disorder, and other disorders. Work has been done to address the concerns of Coyne and Gotlib (1983) and other critics, but more remains to be done to shore up the cognitive model.

Clinical studies indicate the utility of cognitive therapy in a wide variety of disorders, particularly depression and the anxiety disorders. Further systematic studies of the efficacy of cognitive therapy in the treatment of a broad range of psychopathology remain to be executed. The preparation and publication of treatment manuals incorporating specific cognitive conceptualizations and congruent strategies for diverse conditions such as delusional and impulsive disorders have already laid the groundwork for these studies. At this point in time, cognitive therapy is no longer fledgling and has demonstrated its capacity to fly under its own power. How far it will fly remains to be seen.

REFERENCES

Ackerman, R., & DeRubeis, R. (1991). Is depressive realism real? *Clinical Psychology Review, 11*, 565–584.

Alford, B., & Norcross, J. (1991). Cognitive therapy as integrative therapy. *Journal of Psychotherapy Integration, 1*, 175–190.

Alloy, L. B., & Abramson, L. Y. (1979). Judgment of contingency in depressed and nondepressed students: Sadder but wiser? *Journal of Experimental Psychology: General, 108*, 441–485.

Beck, A. T. (1961). A systematic investigation of depression. *Comprehensive Psychiatry, 2*, 163–170.

Beck, A. T. (1964). Thinking and depression: II. Theory and therapy. *Archives of General Psychiatry, 10*, 561–571.

Beck, A. T. (1967). *Depression: Clinical, experimental, and theoretical aspects*. New York: Harper & Row.

Beck, A. T. (1971). Cognition, affect, and psychopathology. *Archives of General Psychiatry, 24*, 495–500.

Beck, A. T. (1976). *Cognitive therapy and the emotional disorders*. New York: International Universities Press.

Beck, A. T. (1983). Cognitive therapy of depression: New perspectives. In P. J. Clayton & J. E. Barnett (Eds.), *Treatment of depression: Old controversies and new approaches* (pp. 265–284). New York: Raven Press.

Beck, A. T. (1987a). Cognitive approaches to panic disorder: Theory and therapy. In S. Rachman & J. Maser (Eds.), *Panic: Psychological perspectives* (pp. 91–109). Hillside, NJ: Erlbaum.

Beck, A. T. (1987b). Cognitive models of depression. *Journal of Cognitive Psychotherapy: An International Quarterly, 1*, 5–37.

Beck, A. T. (1988). *Love is never enough*. New York: Harper & Row.

Beck, A. T., Brown, G., Berchick, R. J., Stewart, B. L., & Steer, R. A. (1990). Relationship between hopelessness and ultimate suicide: A replication with psychiatric outpatients. *American Journal of Psychiatry, 147,* 190–195.

Beck, A. T., Brown, G., Steer, R. A., Eidelson, J. I., & Riskind, J. H. (1987). Differentiating anxiety and depression: A test of the cognitive content-specificity hypothesis. *Journal of Abnormal Psychology, 96,* 179–183.

Beck, A. T., & Emery, G., with Greenberg, R. L. (1985). *Anxiety disorders and phobias: A cognitive perspective.* New York: Basic Books.

Beck, A. T., & Freeman, A. (1990). *Cognitive therapy of personality disorders.* New York: Guilford.

Beck, A. T., Kovacs, M., & Weisman, A. (1975). Hopelessness and suicidal behavior: An overview. *Journal of the American Medical Association, 234,* 1146–1149.

Beck, A. T., Riskind, J. H., Brown, G., & Sherrod, A. (1986, June). *A comparison of likelihood estimates for imagined positive and negative outcomes in anxiety and depression.* Paper presented at the Annual Meeting of the Society for Psychotherapy Research. Wellesley, MA.

Beck, A. T., Rush, A. J., Shaw, B. F., & Emery, G. (1979). *Cognitive therapy of depression.* New York: Guilford.

Beck, A. T., Steer, R. A., Kovacs, M., & Garrison, B. (1985). Hopelessness and eventual suicide: A 10-year prospective study of patients hospitalized with suicidal ideation. *American Journal of Psychiatry, 142,* 559–563.

Beckham, E. E., Leber, W. R., Watkins, J. T., Boyer, J. L., & Cook, J. B. (1986). Development of an instrument to measure Beck's cognitive triad: The Cognitive Triad Inventory. *Journal of Consulting and Clinical Psychology, 54,* 566–567.

Blackburn, I. M., Roxborough, H. M., Muir, W. J., Glabus, M., & Blackburn, D. H. R. (1990). Perceptual and psychological dysfunction in depression. *Psychological Medicine, 20,* 95–103.

Bradley, B. P., & Mathews, A. (1988). Memory bias in recovered clinical depressives. *Cognition and Emotion, 2,* 235–245.

Butler, G., Fennell, M., Robson, P., & Gelder, M. (1991). A comparison of behavior therapy and cognitive theory in the treatment of generalized anxiety disorder. *Journal of Consulting and Clinical Psychology, 59,* 167–175.

Clark, D. A., Beck, A. T., & Brown, G. (1989). Cognitive mediation in general psychiatric outpatients: A test of the content-specificity hypothesis. *Journal of Personality and Social Psychology, 56,* 958–964.

Clark, D. M. (1986). A cognitive approach to panic. *Behaviour Research and Therapy, 24,* 461–470.

Clark, D. M., & Teasdale, J. D. (1982). Diurnal variation in clinical depression and accessibility of memories of positive and negative experiences. *Journal of Abnormal Psychology, 91,* 472–505.

Crandell, C. J., & Chambers, D. L. (1986). The validation of an inventory for measuring depressive thoughts: The Crandell Cognitions Inventory. *Behaviour Research and Therapy, 24,* 403–411.

Darwin, C. R. (1872). *The expression of the emotions in man and animals.* London: John Murray.

DeMonbreun, B. G., & Craighead, W. E. (1977). Distortion of perception and recall of positive and neutral feedback in depression. *Cognitive Therapy and Research, 1,* 311–329.

Dobson, K. S. (1989). A meta-analysis of the efficacy of cognitive therapy for depression. *Journal of Consulting and Clinical Psychology, 57,* 414–419.

Dunbar, G. C., & Lishman, W. A. (1984). Depression, recognition-memory and hedonic tone: A signal detection analysis. *British Journal of Psychiatry, 144,* 376–382.

Eaves, G. (1982). *Cognitive patterns in endogenous and nonendogenous unipolar major depressions.* Unpublished doctoral dissertation. University of Texas, Health Science Center, Dallas.

Ellis, A. (1962). *Reason and emotion in psychotherapy.* New York: Lyle Stewart.

Ernst, D. (1985). *Beck's cognitive therapy of depression: A status report.* Unpublished manuscript, University of Pennsylvania.

Garner, D. M., & Bemis, K. M. (1982). A cognitive-behavioral approach to anorexia nervosa. *Cognitive Therapy and Research, 6,* 123–150.

Gilson, M. (1983). *Depression as measured by perceptual dominance in binocular rivalry.* Unpublished doctoral dissertation, Georgia State University. (University Microfilms No. AAD83–27351)

Gotlib, I. H. (1981). Self-reinforcement and recall: Differential deficits in depressed and nondepressed psychiatric inpatients. *Journal of Abnormal Psychology, 90,* 521–530.

Greenberg, M. S., & Beck, A. T. (1989). Depression versus anxiety: A test of the content-specificity hypothesis. *Journal of Abnormal Psychology, 98,* 9–13.

Haaga, D. A. F., Dyck, M. J., & Ernst, D. (1991). Empirical status of cognitive therapy of depression. *Psychological Bulletin, 110,* 215–236.

Hammen, C., Ellicott, A., & Gitlin, M. (1989). Vulnerability to specific life events and prediction of course of disorder in unipolar depressed patients. *Canadian Journal of Behavioural Science, 21,* 377–388.

Hammen, C., Ellicott, A., Gitlin, M., & Jamison, K. R. (1989). Sociotropy/autonomy and vulnerability to specific life events in patients with unipolar depression and bipolar disorders. *Journal of Abnormal Psychology, 98,* 1147–1159.

Hollon, S. D., & Garber, J. (1990). Cognitive therapy for depression: A social cognitive perspective. *Personality and Social Psychology Bulletin, 16,* 58–73.

Hollon, S. D., & Kendall, P. C. (1980). Cognitive self-statements in depression: Development of an automatic thoughts questionnaire. *Cognitive Therapy and Research, 4,* 383–395.

Hollon, S. D., Kendall, P. C., & Lumry, A. (1986). Specificity of depressotypic cognitions in clinical depression. *Journal of Abnormal Psychology, 95,* 52–59.

Hollon, S. D., & Najavits, L. (1988). Review of empirical studies of cognitive therapy. In A. J. Frances & R. E. Hales (Eds.), *American Psychiatric Press review of psychiatry* (Vol. 7, pp. 643–666). Washington, DC: American Psychiatric Press.

Krantz, S., & Hammen, C. (1979). Assessment of cognitive bias in depression. *Journal of Abnormal Psychology, 88,* 611–619.

Lewinsohn, P. M., Steinmetz, J. L., Larson,

D. W., & Franklin, J. (1981). Depression-related cognitions: Antecedent or consequence? *Journal of Abnormal Psychology, 90*, 213–219.

Mathews, A. (1990). Why worry? The cognitive function of anxiety. *Behaviour Research and Therapy, 28*, 455–468.

Miller, I. W., Norman, W. H., & Keitner, G. I. (1989). Cognitive-behavioral treatment of depressed inpatients: Six- and twelve-month follow-up. *American Journal of Psychiatry, 146*, 1274–1279.

Miranda, J., & Persons, J. B. (1988). Dysfunctional attitudes are mood-state dependent. *Journal of Abnormal Psychology, 97*, 76–79.

Perris, C. (1988). *Cognitive therapy with schizophrenics*. New York: Guilford.

Powell, M., & Hemsley, D. R. (1984). Depression: A breakdown of perceptual defence? *British Journal of Psychiatry, 145*, 358–362.

Riskind, J. H. (1983, August). *Misconceptions of the cognitive model of depression*. Paper presented at the 91st Annual Convention of the American Psychological Association, Anaheim, CA.

Rush, A. J., Weissenburger, J., & Eaves, G. (1986). Do thinking patterns predict depressive symptoms? *Cognitive Therapy and Research, 10*, 225–236.

Salkovskis, P. M. (1989). Somatic problems. In K. Hawton, P. M. Salkovskis, J. W. Kirk, & D. M. Clark (Eds.), *Cognitive-behavioural approaches to adult psychological disorders: A practical guide* (pp. 235–277). Oxford, England: Oxford University Press.

Segal, Z. V., Shaw, B. F., & Vella, D. D. (1989). Life stress and depression: A test of the congruency hypothesis for life event content and depressive subtype. *Canadian Journal of Behavioural Science, 21*, 389–400.

Shea, M. T., Elkin, I., Imber, S. D., Sotsky, S. M., Watkins, J. T., Collins, J. F., Pilkonis, P. A., Leber, W. R., Krupnick, J., Dolan, R. T., & Parloff, M. B. (1992). Course of depressive symptoms over follow-up: Findings from the National Institute of Mental Health treatment of depression collaborative research program. *Archives of General Psychiatry, 49*, 782–787.

Sokol, L., Beck, A. T., & Clark, D. A. (1989, June). *A controlled treatment trial of cognitive therapy for panic disorder*. Paper presented at the World Congress of Cognitive Therapy, Oxford, England.

Sokol, L., Beck, A. T., Greenberg, R. L., Berchick, R. J., & Wright, E. D. (1989). Cognitive therapy of panic disorder: A non-pharmacological alternative. *Journal of Nervous and Mental Diseases, 177*, 711–716.

Stiles, T. C. (1990). *Cognitive vulnerability factors in the development and maintenance of depression*. Doctoral dissertation, University of Trondheim, Trondheim, Norway.

Teasdale, J. D., & Fennell, M. J. V. (1982). Immediate effects on depression of cognitive therapy interventions. *Cognitive Therapy and Research, 6*, 343–352.

Weissman, A., & Beck, A. T. (1978). *Development and validation of the Dysfunctional Attitude Scale*. Paper presented at the annual convention of the Association for Advancement of Behavior Therapy, Chicago.

Wickless, C., & Kirsch, I. (1988). Cognitive correlates of anger, anxiety, and sadness. *Cognitive Therapy and Research, 12*, 367–377.

Woody, G. E., McLellan, A. T., Luborsky, L., O'Brien, C. P., Blaine, J., Fox, S., Herman, I., & Beck, A. T. (1984). Severity of psychiatric symptoms as a predictor of benefits from psychotherapy: The Veterans Administration–Penn Study. *American Journal of Psychiatry, 141*, 1172–1177.

DEBORAH C. BEIDEL & SAMUEL M. TURNER

A critique of the theoretical bases of cognitive-behavioral theories and therapy

The resurgence of interest in cognitive psychology and information processing in general has been in part responsible for increased attention to the role of cognition in the etiology and treatment of emotional disorders. Cognitive-behavior therapy, suggested as the most recently discernible development within the field of behavior therapy (Wilson, 1978), has been defined as the conceptualization and treatment of maladaptive behavior which incorporates therapeutic attention to human cognition in addition to overt behavior. Although several recent reviews of the literature have noted that cognitive-behavior therapy procedures do not differ

This work was supported in part by grant No. MH 30915 from the National Institute of Mental Health.

substantially from those of the more traditional behavior therapies (cf. Latimer & Sweet, 1984; Ledwidge, 1978), proponents of a cognitive-behavioral model have emphasized that the merits of this approach should be evaluated not at the level of procedure, but on the basis of theory and conceptualization of psychopathology (Mahoney & Kazdin, 1979). Thus, this article is designed to evaluate cognitive-behavior therapy on that basis. Following a presentation of the definitions of cognitive-behavior therapy, the theoretical assumptions of the cognitive-behavioral approach to psychopathology will be critically examined. Finally, the empirical evidence put forth to justify the claim that cognitive-behavior therapy is an independent school of therapy, differing from both behavioral and cognitive therapies (Schwartz, 1982), will be evaluated.

DESCRIPTION OF COGNITIVE-BEHAVIOR THERAPY

As is true with the behavior therapies, there are different therapeutic approaches represented under the rubric of cognitive-behavior therapy. However, several descriptions which characterize the field as a whole have been provided. For example, Kendall and Hollon (1979) described the cognitive-behavioral therapies as purposeful attempts to preserve the demonstrated efficiencies of behavior modification within a less doctrinaire context and to incorporate cognitive activities in efforts to produce therapeutic change. Wilson (1978) described cognitive-behavior therapy not as a paradigm shift, but as a change in emphasis from a simplistic stimulus–response (S–R) psychology dominated by animal conditioning models to a more cognitive framework. The basic assumption of cognitive-behavioral theorists is that cognitions and information processing play an important part in the genesis and maintenance of maladaptive behavior. Moreover, the impact of external events is believed to be mediated by cognitive processes. There is an interest in the nature and modification of cognitions and some commitment to the use of behavior therapy procedures in promoting change (Meichenbaum & Cameron, 1982). A somewhat more radical view is held by cognitive theorists who assert that affective and behavioral responses are determined by the way in which the individual structures experiences (e.g., Kovacs, 1979). Finally, Mahoney and Arnkoff (1978) proposed three central themes for cognitive-behavior therapies: (a) human behavior and affective patterns (adaptive or maladaptive) develop through cognitive processes such as selective attention or symbolic coding; (b) these processes are activated by procedures similar to those in the human learning laboratory; and (c) the therapist functions as a diagnostician-educator, who after assessing maladaptive cognitive processes arranges for learning experiences which will alter cognition and, in turn, behavior-affect patterns. Thus, it would appear that cognitive-behavior therapy is offered as an alternative to behavior therapy, perhaps even as a reaction to the perceived neglect of cognitions by classical behavioral theories. In each of these explanations, cognition (in the form of perceiving, structuring, or evaluating environmental events) plays a vital role in determining overt behavior.

Brewer (1974) viewed cognitive mediation of behavior as paramount and argued that learning in humans is not an unconscious, automatic procedure as suggested by standard classical and operant theories, but rather is produced through the operation of higher mental processes. In the following sections, the validity of the cognitive-behavioral approach to the conceptualization of behavior will be evaluated by examining: (a) the nature and function of cognitions, as used by cognitive theorists and therapists; (b) the empirical evidence for the importance of cognitions in influencing emotional behavior; and (c) the relationship of cognitive-behavior theory to cognitive-behavior therapy.

CONCEPTUALIZATION OF COGNITION(S)

Upon reading the cognitive-behavior literature, it becomes apparent that cognition is defined both as a process and the object of that same process. Thus, cognition (thought) is a result of cognition (cognitive processing). In a recent review of the cognitive-behavior therapy literature, Schwartz (1982) concluded that the word cognition could be used to represent three different levels of activity. Cognition has been described as: (a) a response class composed of private events; (b) mediators of behavior, serving as an intervening link between stimuli and response; or (c) quasi-automatic, complex structures which organize and generate behavior but function independently of the laws of behavior (Beck, 1970). In this latter sense, cognition is equated to a mini-computer or an information-processing system. Mahoney's (1974) description of cognition is an example of this type of information-processing system. He proposed a number of abnormal cognitive activities which contribute to performance (behavioral) dysfunction. One example of a cognitive aberration is selective attention, examples of which include ignoring relevant stimuli, misperception, maladaptive focusing, and maladaptive self-arousal. Other abnormal cognitive activities include abnormalities in relational processes, response repertoire features, and experiential feedback. Thus, according to this definition, cognition is conceptualized as a process, not a specific thought, and according to cognitive-behavioral theorists, these processes function outside the framework of known laws of learning.

Rather than viewing cognition as alien to behavior, the more traditional behavioral view has classified cognitive activities such as perception and ideation as private, behavioral events. In addition, rather than being phenomena which function outside the laws of learning, cognition, when viewed as simply another behavior, is subject to the same laws of acquisition as other behaviors. In this case, the behavior, however, cannot be observed by another (Eysenck, 1979; Ullmann, 1970; Wolpe 1976, 1978, 1980). Thus, both classical behavioral and cognitive-behavioral theorists agree that thoughts and thought processes are private events. However, cognitive-behavioral theorists have not been entirely clear as to the etiology of these cognitive functions, although they imply that they are biologically determined and therefore immune to alteration by the application of principles of learning. In particular, psychopathology is often viewed as resulting from faulty cognitive processes (Mahoney, 1974). The unusual and/or negative thoughts reported by individuals with various emotional disturbances are offered as evidence of faulty cognitive processing. However, the fact that individuals can and do perceive different aspects of the same stimuli is not sufficient evidence to suggest that the process by which they perceive is necessarily different. Cognitive-behavioral theorists appear to be equating content of cognition with the process by which that content is acquired, assuming that unusual cognitions necessarily result from abnormal processing. An equally valid explanation of the attentional and/or perceptual distortions exhibited by emotionally disturbed individuals would invoke an individual's prior learning history. Individuals who previously have been rewarded for perceiving situations in a negative light are more likely to perceive new situations in a similar manner. In addition, there is further evidence that these processes follow the laws of behavior. Even in the case of severely disordered individuals, there is abundant evidence that covert behaviors such as attention and perception can be improved by utilization of learning theory principles (e.g., Lovaas et al., 1971). Finally, contingency management programs have been reported to be effective in decreasing the frequency of perceptual distortions such as delusions and hallucinations in schizophrenics (e.g., Alford & Turner, 1976). Coyne and Gotlieb (1983) discussed the importance of learning history for variation in cognitive content, suggesting that differences in attributional style may be a reflection of different background information. For example, depressives may not process information differently, but instead may have different previous experiences by which to process new stimuli. Each of the examples presents ample evidence that cognitive activities follow established laws of learning.

In addition to conceptualizing cognition as an information-processing system, cognition can also be defined as a thought (Schwartz, 1982). Maladaptive cognitions, as described in cognitive theory (Beck, 1970), are pervasive, negative misconstructions of objective experiences (Kendall & Hollon 1979). Similarly, the irrational beliefs of Ellis are described as related to "magical, empirically unvalidated hypotheses for which there is not, nor probably can ever be, any factual evidence" (Ellis, 1973, p. 6). According to Meichenbaum (1974), cognitive structures give rise to conscious thoughts termed internal dialogue, consisting of hunches and hypotheses which influence future attentional processes and behavior. Finally, Bandura (1977), in discussing his self-efficacy model of behavior, described cognitions as judgments concerning either the ability of the individual to perform a certain behavior or the belief that a behavior will lead to the desired outcome.

The explanations provided by these theorists are consistent in that all imply that a cognition (in the "thought" sense of the word) serves as a descriptive relationship between environmental antecedents and consequent behavior (e.g., "Every time I try to be nice to my spouse I end up feeling angry"). Thoughts are the individual's expression of the relationship between environmental events and their consequential effects. These relationships as understood by the individual may then be used to guide future behavior. Thus, as defined by the proponents of a cognitive-behavioral approach, cognition is more than a behavior or action, such as perception. It is also a principle or belief theoretically utilized by the individual in the course of behaving (Ledwidge, 1978; Rachlin, 1977; Zettle & Hayes, 1982). Rachlin (1977), in defending the more traditional behavioral approach, also defined thoughts as names for sets of relationships between environmental stimuli and behavior. He equated thought with a proposition, stating that for the behaviorist, the proposition is a verbal description of organized behavior. Similarly, Zettle and Hayes (1982) noted that Skinner's concept of rules is applicable to the proposed meaning of cognition as defined by cognitive-behaviorists.

Therefore, although traditional and cognitive-behavioral systems allow for the existence of cognition as a description of antecedent and consequent events, it is on the issue of causality that traditional behaviorists and cognitive-behavioral theorists deviate. Cognitive-behavioral theorists apparently believe cognitions are empowered to produce, shape, and change behavior. Both groups accept thought as a description of the relationship between antecedent stimuli and related affective states or motoric behavior. Nonetheless, in cognitive-behavioral theory, cognitions alone are endowed with the ability to influence future behavior or emotional distress, whereas for traditional behavioral theory they merely describe the relationship between antecedent events and their contingencies. In perhaps the most critical analysis of the inability of operant or classical conditioning to describe acquisition of behavior, Brewer (1974) argued that conditioning in humans is produced through the operation of higher mental processes. This "cognitive hypothesis" proposed that the experimental subject in a conditioning experiment develops conscious hypotheses about the relationship between the environmental events and the appropriate responses ("Every time the red light comes on, I get shocked") (Brewer, 1974, p. 2). It can be argued, however, that these conscious hypotheses are, in fact, descriptions of the contingencies which govern behavior. Brewer proceeded to present numerous experimental studies comparing classical, "unconscious" conditioning paradigms with conditions in which the subjects were informed of the contingencies. In each case, subjects informed of the contingencies responded (i.e., "learned") more quickly, thus appearing to support Brewer's contention.

A closer examination of these cognitive hypotheses reveals that these statements are identical to the "rules" described by Skinner (1976) in his explanation of rule-governed behavior. Many behaviors exhibited by humans have not been learned through classical or operant conditioning (e.g., driving an automobile at 55 mph). We have been instructed (given a rule) that the penalty for exceeding the speed limit is a traffic fine and perhaps a jail term. Thus, awareness of the contingencies can influence future behavior. The issue, however, is whether mere awareness of contingencies (the cognitive hypothesis) or the actual contingencies control behavior. An example may be helpful in illustrating this distinction. Over the past 10 years, it has become evident that wearing seat belts dramatically reduces the number of automobile accident fatalities. The evidence at this time is indisputable. As the result of a very vigorous publicity campaign, every licensed automobile driver has the knowledge (i.e., thought) that "Seat belts save lives." Yet, despite this thought, the percentage of drivers wearing seat belts (i.e., seat belt behavior) is quite low. Recently, several states have enacted mandatory seat belt laws, with the contingency that drivers not using their seat belts will be fined. As a result of this contingency, media reports of the number of drivers who "buckle up" (i.e., seat belt behavior) indicate increases of almost 100% compliance. Although a solid experimental design would require reversal of the contingency with the expectation that seat belt behavior would return to baseline, this example provides evidence that the contingency, and not just the thought, is responsible for behavior change. We believe at this time that the weight of the experimental evidence is in favor of the latter (e.g., it is the threat of the fine that keeps the driver at 55 mph). Therefore, it is incumbent upon cognitive theorists to present experimental evidence to the contrary. In our opinion, cognitive hypotheses probably serve to *speed* acquisition of behavior, but most likely are not responsible for its acquisition and, more important for psychopathology, maintenance of behavior. The ability to increase or decrease the rate of response is a function of the contingencies associated with that behavior (no matter how complex), not the verbal statement of the contingencies.

Generally, proponents of a cognitive-behavioral orientation hypothesize that these cognitions/rules arise as a result of a defect within the individual's information-processing system. It is suggested that patients consistently distort reality or reach unreasonable conclusions concerning their ability to cope (Meichenbaum, 1974). Such an explanation is not incompatible with traditional learning theory. However, according to Mahoney's (1974) account, these differences in cognitive processes are "hard-wired." The most elegant explanation was put forth by Beck (1970). Beck theorized that negative cognitions develop as a result of distorted information processing (including selective abstraction, arbitrary inference, overgeneralization, magnification, and all-or-nothing thinking). In Beck's conceptualization, cognitive organization is composed of primitive systems consisting of crude cognitive structures, similar to Freud's primary processes, and more mature systems corresponding to secondary processes. The concepts of the primitive structures are idiosyncratic and unrealistic and are usually held in check by the higher centers. As a result of depression, anxiety, or paranoid states, the primitive systems become hyperactive and overrun the realistic conceptualizations. In this view, the aberrant cognitive structures are initially dormant, and are released at the onset of psychological distress. In all cases, faulty cognitions are linked to psychopathology.

To summarize, cognition has been proposed both as a process and the object of that process. Cognitive-behavioral theorists have hypothesized that maladaptive cognitions are the result of deviant cognitive processing. The etiology of the deviant processing is not defined, although the implication is that it is one of genetic or physiological differences, and that the processes function outside the laws of learning. On the other hand, there is ample evidence that cognitive activities follow established laws of learning. Thus, it is questionable whether discussing them in the context of a "new theory" helps us to understand maladaptive behavior better.

THE ROLE OF COGNITION IN PSYCHOPATHOLOGY

Generally, the proponents of a cognitive-behavioral model implicate cognitions as the causal component of emotional distress and maladaptive behavior. In Beck's (1970) model, cognitive organization is represented overtly by behavioral and affective symptoms. The individual modifies his behavior and feelings consistent with his thoughts. Other theorists have suggested a similar causal relationship. In the A-B-C sequence of Rational Emotive Therapy (Ellis, 1973), A is an activating event, B represents the irrational beliefs, which lead in turn to maladaptive responses and anxiety at point C. Theoretically, the premises at point B literally cause the individual to feel and behave badly. Bandura (1977) referred to expectations concerning personal mastery and the effect on initiation and persistence of coping behaviors. Finally, distorted thought processes have been hypothesized to affect an individual's view of the world adversely and to lead to unpleasant emotions and behavioral difficulties (Meichenbaum, 1974). In this section, we will examine the evidence to support the contention that deviant thoughts cause maladaptive affect and/or behavior.

As evidence for deviant processing of information, several authors have offered examples that appear to support a central role for maladaptive thoughts in the genesis of emotional disorders. For example, Mahoney (1974) provided case examples of deviant thinking in schizophrenics. Meichenbaum (1974) noted differences in the use of internal dialogue in hyperactive and normal children, suggesting that impulsivity may be a result of the former group's inability to use constructive internal dialogue. Similarly, Hollon and Beck (1979) cited numerous studies indicating that depressives: (a) attribute negative outcome to internal factors such as personal incompetence (Abramson et al., 1978; Klein et al., 1976); (b) perceive less personal control over outcomes (Alloy & Abramson, 1979); and (c) underestimate the amount of reinforcement received relative to nondepressives (DeMonbreun & Craighead, 1977; Nelson & Craighead, 1977).

There are several lines of empirical work which examine the proposition that thoughts are causally related to behavior. First are the group difference studies which document differences in cognitive content between patient and normal groups (e.g., Alloy & Abramson, 1979; Klein et al., 1976; Lishman, 1972; Lloyd & Lishman, 1975). Evidence of this type requires inferring causality as a result of preestablished group differences, however, and does not rule out the possibility that these cognitions merely accompany or result from the psychopathological state. The tautology of the group difference argument is particularly evident in the case of schizophrenia. It is redundant to suggest that schizophrenics exhibit deviant information processing when this is the very criterion by which a diagnosis is assigned. The methodology necessary to test the hypothesis that deviant cognitive processing precedes pathology would require cognitive assessment of individuals who exhibit no form of psychopathology. Of this group, those reporting negative cognitions or exhibiting deviant processes would be reassessed at some future date for signs of psychopathology. Two attempts to predict future psychopathology based on an assessment of current cognitive style have not been successful (Coyne & Gotlieb, 1983). Peterson et al. (1981) assessed characterological blame in a group of women undergraduates. When assessed for depressive symptoms 6 or 12 weeks later, there was no relationship between prior characterological blame and depressive symptomatology. In a 1-year longitudinal study, Lewinsohn et al. (1981) assessed depression-related cognitions and self-esteem. Those who became depressed during the study did not differ from the controls on premorbid measures of locus of control, positive and negative outcome expectancies, irrational beliefs, perception of control, and self-esteem. The results of these studies suggest that depressive cognitions are correlates of depression and not causal factors. In reviewing these studies, Coyne and Gotlieb (1983) concluded, however, that more stringent tests are necessary before the cognitive hypothesis is abandoned, although they provided no specific suggestions for future research.

A second difficulty for cognitive-behavioral theory concerns studies that have examined the estimation accuracy when judging relationships between behavior and environmental consequences (Alloy & Abramson, 1979, 1982; Lewinsohn et al., 1980). These studies have demonstrated that depressed subjects perceived the situation *accurately*, whereas nondepressed individuals were more likely to view the events through "rose-colored lenses." Kuiper and MacDonald (1982) reported that mildly depressed individuals were able to recall positive and negative information about themselves, whereas nondepressed subjects recalled far more positive pieces of information than negative. In a slightly different approach to examining the "truth" of negative cognitions, Layne (1983) argued that cognitive theorists sometimes equate a tendency to think negatively with high scores on an irrational beliefs test. However, Layne noted that examination of the items on an irrational beliefs test (Jones, 1969) revealed that individuals scoring high on this measure may be pessimistic but not necessarily irrational (e.g., "It is impossible to overcome the influence of past history"). After evaluating the evidence regarding differences between depressives and normals on a number of variables including expectancies, perception, self-monitoring, memory, and attributions, Layne concluded that there is evidence that depressives are less optimistic, but that they do not manifest distortions in cognitive processes. Depressed subjects appear to be "sadder but wiser" (Alloy & Abramson, 1979). Finally, in an exhaustive review of the role of cognition in depression, Coyne and Gotlieb (1983) concluded that although depressed persons present themselves negatively, differences in cognition between depressed and nondepressed persons have been small but inconsistent and not specific to depression. The bulk of the research is contrary to that suggested by cognitive theory. Although the cognitions of depressives may seem more negative, there is little evidence that these cognitions are irrational or patently false, or that they precede the onset of the depressed state.

A third problem for the cognitive-behavioral model is revealed by research which demonstrated that although depressed individuals predicted negative outcomes would result from their own abilities or performance, the explanations they generated for another's performance were identical to those generated by nondepressed individuals (Garber & Hollon, 1977). This would also appear difficult to resolve in terms of cognitive-behavior theory. Why should cognitive processes be deviant with respect to only one class of behaviors, i.e., those pertaining to prediction for the individual? To make this a viable explanation, one would have to postulate two information-processing systems for each individual: one for interpretation of events directed at themselves and a second for the processing of information concerning others. In addition, there would have to be a switching mechanism by which to engage one of the two systems. Such an explanation is inherently cumbersome and has not been postulated.

Thus, it appears that based on comparative studies of patient and non-patient populations, distorted cognitive structures have not been shown to be independent of or to precede a given psychopathological state. Proponents of cognitive theory discount the importance of these studies, claiming that the research is based on a misinterpretation of Beck's (1970) theory. According to Riskind and Steer (1984), cognitive theory does not propose maladaptive *thinking* as a predisposition to depression. Rather, thinking is a result of cognitive schemata activation, which follows a stressful event. These schemata, consisting of attitudes and concepts, may not be prominent or discernible at all times. Rather, they persist only in a latent state until activated by stressful conditions. By defining the schemata as latent, they are rendered inaccessible to measurement, except during depressive episodes. Therefore, causality can never be empirically determined, but must be accepted on faith alone.

In further attempts to demonstrate empirically the validity of the cognitive-behavioral hypothesis, cognitive induction procedures have been used to induce negative mood states in non-patient groups (e.g., Coleman, 1975; Strickland et al., 1975; Teasdale & Bancroft, 1977; Velten, 1968). In the earliest study to use such a procedure, Velten (1968) had subjects read elating, depressing, or neutral statements for a period of 20 minutes. The subjects were subsequently assessed for differences in various motor behaviors such as writing speed, distance approximation, decision time, perceptual ambiguity, word association, and spontaneous verbalization. These tasks were considered motoric indicants of mood, inasmuch as depressed individuals have sometimes demonstrated abnormalities on these variables (Goodwin & Williams, 1982). There were differences between the elating and depressing statement groups on several, but not all, of the measures. Coleman (1975), using a similar procedure, reported that subjects who read depressing cognitions had poorer scores on a word association task, on the Multiple Affect Adjective Check List (MAACL), and had poorer scores on ratings of general demeanor and interaction quality after completion of the statement reading task when compared with subjects who read neutral or elating statements. Strickland et al. (1975) reported that those who read depressing statements were more depressed as measured by the MAACL, more anxious, and more hostile. They were more constricted on a graphic constriction–expansion task, and women reported a preference during the post-test period for solitary behaviors. Finally, Teasdale and Bancroft (1977) measured mood and corrugator EMG level when five individuals were thinking happy vs. unhappy thoughts. Correlation between mood and EMG level were reported as positive and significant for all subjects when happy and unhappy thought periods were collapsed. However, when measured separately, only one of the five subjects had a significant correlation between unhappy thoughts and EMG level. Two others had significant correlations only between the happy thoughts and EMG level.

More recently, the ability to induce a particular mood has been accepted, and studies have used mood-induction procedures to examine the effects of "depressed" mood on cognitive capacities, including self-reference bias in recall (Mathews & Bradley, 1983), retrieval of pleasant and unpleasant events from episodic memory (Teasdale & Fogarty, 1979), estimates of past success (Teasdale & Spencer, 1984), and removal of intrusive, unwanted cognitions (Sutherland et al., 1982). It should be noted that in these studies, dysphoric mood was determined by the subject's rating of depression on a 10-cm visual analogue scale. In each of these studies, cognitive aberrations in the form of distorted memory or recall were related to the subjects' depressed mood. In each case, however, the cognitive deficits followed the mood change rather than preceding it. Thus, these studies, although illustrating the concurrent nature of cognition and affect, cannot be used to demonstrate the causal role of cognition in creating a depressed mood.

Thus although these results are suggestive, there are several methodological problems which mediate against full acceptance of the conclusions of the mood-induction studies. The first concerns the method of inducing the depressed mood. Experimenter instructions prior to reading the depressed or elating statements emphasized that the subject "should try to feel the mood suggested by these statements, that she could do it, that there was nothing to worry about" (Velten, 1968, p. 474). Similar instructions by Coleman (1975) required the subject to talk herself into the mood suggested by the statements. Although both studies attempted to control for the instructions by including demand instruction conditions comprised of groups receiving the same instructions but not the affective statements, recent evidence suggests that the effects may have been due to the demand characteristics (Buchwald et al., 1981) or to the effect of suggesting somatic states such as "I feel tired" rather than depressive beliefs (Frost et al., 1979; Small et al., 1983).

Perhaps more damaging than the influence of demand, however, is that laboratory simulations require the subject to concentrate on acquiring a *mood* rather than merely concentrating on the cognitions. These instructions deviate radically from cognitive-behavioral theory, which proposes that these feelings occur automatically as a result of negative cognitions, rather than requiring conscious effort on the part of the patient. It is possible that given the command to concentrate on acquiring a mood, subjects may use a variety of techniques to acquire the mood, not necessarily *only* the cognitions. Second, the validity of these motoric measures as indicative of a *major depression* is suspect. There has been no demonstration that the responses produced by the depressed group are necessarily specific to depression. Other states of emotional distress, such as anxiety, may produce similar results. Coleman (1975) justified his assessment battery by noting that although a variety of measures of emotion have been used to study the elation-depression paradigm, few have demonstrated much replicability. The dependent variables in this particular study included psychomotor speech, word association, the MAACL, an anagram task, estimate of success on the anagram task, response of subjects to a cartoon, quality of interaction with a confederate, rating of general demeanor, and length of verbalization with a confederate. This variety of measures was selected "to insure a reliable and objective assessment of emotion." Perhaps the *validity* of these measures as they relate specifically to depressed affect and not necessarily to reliability or replicability is the crucial issue. Third, in reviewing the effects produced by mood induction procedures, Goodwin and Williams (1982) noted that in most of the studies induction of a depressed mood was contrasted with induction of an elated mood. Without the inclusion of a neutral condition, any significant differences reported by between-group comparisons may be attributed to changes in the scores of the subjects in the elated condition rather than to those in the depressed condition. These authors further noted that in the few studies in which comparisons included a neutral condition, the scores of depressed subjects were not different from those in the control group. Finally, with the exception of corrugator EMG, there were no physiological or biochemical indices of change in affective states as a result of these mood-induction procedures.

One final criticism has been directed at the mood-induction procedure as proposed by Velten (1968). Sutherland et al. (1982) described the effects of this procedure as "erratic" in that a number of subjects must be excluded from the study because they do not acquire the proper mood. In the Sutherland et al. (1982) sample, 32% of the subjects administered the Velten procedure were excluded for failure to reach a "depressed" criterion. In response to this, more recent studies of mood and cognition (Sutherland et al., 1982; Teasdale & Spencer, 1984) have used a music mood-induction procedure in order to induce the appropriate mood state.

In summarizing the evidence presented by these mood-induction studies, although there is some evidence that speed and type of memory recall may be a result of depressed mood, there is no evidence that these cognitive deficits precede the mood inducement. Perhaps more important, there is no evidence that clinically relevant changes in mood can be induced by the reading of depressive statements.

Evidence presented for the causal role of cognitions in RET (Zettle & Hayes, 1980) is limited in that most studies are purely correlational in nature and are based on paper and pencil measures. For example, measures of emotional distress have been reported to correlate highly with measures of irrational beliefs. However, the construct validity of the irrational belief measures has recently been called into question. For example, the irrational belief items include statements of emotional arousal and not just beliefs. Furthermore, the lack of discriminant validity data for these measures may suggest that the instruments do not assess anything other than general emotional distress (Smith, 1982).

The results of three studies that examined the relationship of irrational beliefs to physiological indicants of emotional arousal deserve special mention. Rimm and Litvak (1969) measured GSR [galvanic skin response] and repiration rates of college students presented with statement triads composed of high (affectively laden) or low (neutral) personal concern. The statements were modeled after Ellis' A-B-C paradigm. Although significant differences were noted in both physiological measures, the authors noted that any form of affectively laden statement, and not specifically an irrational one, may be physiologically arousing. Russell and Brandsma (1974), using the identical dependent variables, had subjects read aloud a sentence dyad (A–B in Ellis's scheme) consisting of affectively loaded (B) or neutral statements (A). However, the statements used in this study had a greater range of personal relevance for the speaker; this factor has been hypothesized to play a factor in arousal response. The authors reported a significant main effect for personal relevance and an interaction between relevance and scene type. Equal emotional response, as measured by respiration rate and GSR, was recorded to A and B statements when the content was highly relevant, but only to B statements when there was low relevancy. There was, however, no reported relationship between neuroticism and emotional responsivity. In a third study, Rogers and Craighead (1977) used a single subject design to measure responses to positively, negatively, and neutrally valenced evaluative conclusion statements. This study assessed physiological responsivity in terms of heart rate, GSR, and finger pulse volume. The valence of the statement had no effect upon any of the physiological measures.

In summarizing the results of these studies, Zettle and Hayes (1980) highlighted the inconsistencies in study findings and concluded that any type of affectively laden statement may function to alter physiological arousal. These studies have yet to determine that it is, in fact, the irrationality of the statement as suggested by RET theory that is causal in the manifested emotionality. Thus, it appears that evidence for an etiological role for cognitions in emotional arousal is too equivocal to allow definitive conclusions at this time.

COGNITIVE-BEHAVIORAL THEORY AND COGNITIVE-BEHAVIOR THERAPY

The nature of theory in psychopathology is to provide both a framework by which to understand human behavior and to provide direction for treatment development and implementation. Conceptualization of the etiology of psychological disorders should lead naturally to a therapeutic strategy. As noted above, cognitive-behavioral theorists propose that there is a propensity for individuals who manifest psychopathology to draw inaccurate conclusions from environmental events. In turn, these conclusions may create emotional upset and may possibly affect behavior. Changing these inaccurate conclusions should lead to a change in emotional state. Thus, cognitive-behavior therapists promote their approach to therapy as an attempt to change the inaccurate inferences of the individual.

An examination of the methodology used in such therapy studies, however, reveals that cognitions are rarely, if ever, altered directly. Instead, the focus of change is behavior and the changes in cognition seem secondary to behavioral alteration. To account for this discrepancy, several cognitive-behavioral theorists have argued that cognitive change is most efficacious when achieved through the incorporation of established behavioral procedures (Bandura, 1977; Mahoney, 1977a). Yet, the use of such procedures hopelessly confounds classical behavioral and cognitive-behavioral procedures so that no firm conclusion can be drawn. For example, Bandura's (1977) mastery experiences are based on confrontation of feared situations through exposure and modeling procedures. This can be viewed in effect as a counterconditioning procedure in which exposure to a feared situation, without the occurrence of the imagined negative consequences, is used to overcome anticipatory anxiety. Cognitive change occurs as a result of the repeated opportunity to practice new behaviors and exposure to the feared situation. As the client masters fear, belief in his own self-efficacy changes dramatically. Thus, it seems that cognitive changes occur only after behavioral change.

Mahoney (1977b) proposed his own brand of cognitive-learning therapy, "Personal Science." Similar to Bandura's position, this cognitive-learning therapy is described as recognizing "the simultaneous importance of cognitive *process* and learning *procedures*" (Mahoney, 1977b, p. 353), and highlights the teaching of coping skills that allow the client to acquire a capacity for independent functioning. Personal Science uses a problem-solving approach which includes assessment of current status, generation of alternative behaviors, and application of these new behaviors and review of the results, with further revision if necessary. The emphasis is placed on testing the contingencies of new behavioral strategies by engaging in new behaviors. The problem-solving approach is similar to operant conditioning strategies in which the appropriateness of engaging in a particular behavior is determined by the reinforcement received.

Ellis (1973) described Rational Emotive Therapy as a cognitive-emotive-behavioristic approach to psychotherapy. The cognitive component includes discrimination training by teaching the client to differentiate between rational and irrational beliefs. Clients are praised (reinforced) for the ability to identify correctly "irrational" beliefs. The client is taught to replace these irrational beliefs with more rational ones, and is then given homework assignments, another procedure commonly used by classical theorists and one of several behavioral components in the theory. These assignments function to assist the client in disputing irrational beliefs. Once again, a counterconditioning model can be used to account for changes, inasmuch as the client enters feared situations without the client's "worst fears" occurring. As in the therapeutic techniques proposed earlier, overt behavioral practices are expected to play a major role in changing cognitions.

Meichenbaum and Cameron (1982) proposed a cognitive-behavioral theory of therapeutic change that focuses on three areas of the individual: (a) behavior, (b) private speech and images, and (c) cognitive structures. The authors posit that by changing the client's behavior, environmental reactions to the client are also altered. Modifying private speech allows the client to interpret the world in a more heuristic manner. By cognitive structures, the authors are referring to the client's implicit assumptions and habitual style of thinking. The first phase of therapy involves self-observation or training the client to observe more critically his or her own behavior. This, according to Meichenbaum and Cameron, sets the stage for more concrete change. In the second stage, new behaviors are learned to deal effectively with the problem and gradually to establish new ways of thinking and behaving. Again, the emphasis is on changing behavior; later, in a gradual fashion, cognitions begin to change. The relationship between cognitive change and behavior change is described as complex and interactive, with change in one domain promoting change in the other. Behavior change, for example, may induce a number of cognitive changes, including increased feelings of competency, self-control, and self-efficacy. Meichenbaum and Cameron appear to endorse Mahoney's statement that the most effective way to modify cognitions is to modify behavior. Cognitive change for these theorists is equated with self-awareness and the ability to recognize and prevent maladaptive behaviors. In effect, clients must monitor internal dialogue, catch themselves falling into old behavior patterns, and remind themselves that they possess alternative, and more productive behaviors. In the final phase of therapy, the client focuses on recognizing and consolidating the meaningful changes that have occurred. This definition of cognition differs from that which had been proposed when discussing etiology, however. In this context, cognition refers not to a specific thought or deviant process, but to self-awareness that certain behaviors are maladaptive. If cognitive change means merely an increase in self-awareness, this change in self-awareness could affect behavior provided that alternative behaviors already exist in the individual's repertoire. If they do not, the therapist would have to assist the individual in acquiring appropriate behaviors. Nonetheless, viewing cognitive change as increased self-awareness does not seem consistent with the definitions provided by cognitive-behavioral theorists when discussing the etiology of psychopathology.

Cognitive therapy, as proposed by Beck (Hollon & Beck, 1979), also incorporates both behavioral and cognitive techniques. Behavioral procedures include self-monitoring, graded task assignments, scheduling pleasurable activities, and entering feared situations. Techniques designed to evaluate cognitions include identifying automatic thoughts, evaluating thought content, prospective hypothesis testing, and identifying underlying assumptions. These latter procedures are designed to identify and promote the systematic evaluation of the maladaptive thought. In cognitive therapy, behavioral strategies are selected and used in an effort to maximize client participation in the therapeutic process and to enhance the probability of disconfirmation of previously held beliefs. Therefore, it appears that therapist-directed behavioral activities provide a mechanism through which inappropriate cognitions can be evaluated and cognitive change can occur. In attempting to align the therapeutic procedures with Beck's primary and secondary structures cited earlier, one might hypothesize that the therapist is functioning as the individual's secondary structures and discrediting the cognitions of the hyperactive primary structures. For, as proposed above, emotional distress is what creates the cognitive shift from secondary to primary thinking structures. There is no evidence that the secondary structures have been destroyed; they have merely been overrun. Thus, the task of the therapist appears to be one of serving as the evaluator of the deviant cognitions of the primary structures until one of two events occurs—either the cognitive shift reverses, or the secondary structures are sufficiently bolstered to regain control over the hyperactive primary structures. Behavioral change is viewed as an important first step for the development of change in cognitive activities such as perception.

The activation of these primary processes, which in turn lead to maladaptive cognitions and emotional distress, is the cornerstone of cognitive theory. Cognitive therapists direct a great deal of attention during therapy sessions to the evaluation of cognitions. However, when behavioral procedures are included in the therapeutic process, particularly in the initial phases, identification of the mechanism of change becomes extremely difficult, if not impossible. Change in emotional distress may be attributed to direct interventions to increase level of activity. By confounding these procedures, the etiological model cannot be tested. Thus, cognitive therapists have not substantiated their claim that it is the cognitive procedures which effect change in psychopathological status.

All of the above cognitive-behavioral therapies are aimed at changing cognitive processing (as defined in an earlier part of this article) by encouraging clients to evaluate their thoughts in a more critical light by more careful monitoring of environmental events (contingencies). As such, this can be conceptualized as a stimulus discrimination process. Clients are required to observe more closely both the environmental cues and the behaviors, including their own, that occur within the confines of certain events. In addition, the individual is encouraged, in the spirit of collaborative empiricism (Hollon & Beck, 1979), to try new behaviors and to monitor the consequences. Cognitive change occurs as a result. Mahoney (1977a), in describing the interventions of a cognitive-behavior therapist, stated "his (the therapist's) intervention upon cognitive phenomena must always take the form of behavioral operations (lectures, assignments, modeling, etc.)" (p. 676). Although a viable therapeutic approach, these strategies run counter to the theoretical arguments of these same cognitive-behavioral theorists. For if these deviant information-processing systems are hard-wired and function outside the usual laws of learning, as several theories suggest, why should alterations in overt behavior serve to alter genetic programming or physiological brain structures? However, if cognitive-behavioral therapists are using stimulus discrimination training by encouraging patients to monitor contingencies more carefully, sharpening of perceptual skills would provide material for the construction of more valid rules by which to govern future behavior.

In proposing a resolution to the controversy, Mahoney and Kazdin (1979) argued that categorical distinctions should be based on theoretical assumptions rather than on therapeutic techniques. However, we believe that therapeutic procedures should follow from one's theoretical assumptions. Although espousing a different model of the etiology of psychopathology, the cognitive-behavioral therapists easily forsake this model in their procedural approach to treatment. Their approach is, in effect, not very different from that of their more traditionally oriented behavioral colleagues. They differ, however, in the dependent variables by which they evaluate therapeutic change. Cognitive-behavioral therapists have highlighted the importance of assessing change in attitudes and beliefs in addition to overt behaviors.

In reviewing the empirical evidence for cognitive-behavioral therapies, one would be remiss not to address the recent proliferation of reviews and meta-analytic studies purporting to compare the cognitive-behavioral therapies with more traditional behavior therapies. In the earliest comparison, Ledwidge (1978) concluded that controlled comparisons showed the two types of therapeutic procedures to be equally effective. Ledwidge's conclusions, however, have been criticized on the basis of the restrictiveness of his sampling procedures (e.g., Mahoney & Kazdin, 1979), and his use of a box-score type of evaluation. More recent and statistically superior analyses, however (Dush, et al., 1983; Miller & Berman, 1983; Zettle & Hayes, 1980), have essentially supported Ledwidge's earlier conclusion.

In evaluating outcome studies using RET, Zettle and Hayes (1980) reported that the methodological weaknesses of the studies were so great that the clinical efficacy of RET had yet to be demonstrated. More recently, a meta-analytic study of self-statement modification (SSM) by Dush et al. (1983) concluded that although SSM was more effective than no treatment, the results were less impressive when compared to placebo control groups. Studies that used SSM in combination with other procedures such as cognitive restructuring, behavior rehearsal, and modeling were more effective than was SSM alone. In comparison with "other" forms of cognitive or behavioral therapies, SSM was advantageous only when compared with a relaxation-training-only procedure. Finally, SSM appeared most effective when Meichenbaum was directly involved, suggesting that as with Ellis, the characteristics of the therapist may contribute in part to the efficacy of the procedures.

Miller and Berman (1983) reached similar conclusions in another review using meta-analysis. Although results were superior to those of no-treatment controls, there was no firm evidence that cognitive approaches were superior to other psychotherapies. This was especially evident when they were compared with established therapeutic procedures such as systematic desensitization.

Finally, Hollon and Beck (1979) reviewed studies comparing behavior therapy, cognitive-behavior therapy, and cognitive therapy. The authors divided the studies into two groups: studies utilizing volunteer subjects, and studies in which the subjects were actual patients seeking treatment. All studies were directed at treatment for depression. Of the six studies using volunteer subjects, four were reported to demonstrate some superiority for a cognitive-behavioral intervention when compared with a strictly behavioral intervention, a strictly cognitive intervention, or waiting-list control group. However, as noted by Hollon and Beck (1979), these samples were comprised of community volunteers; suicidal subjects (an indication of the severity of depression) were routinely screened out. Thus, generalizability to a clinic population cannot be assumed. At the time of Hollon and Beck's review, only three studies that used Beck's cognitive therapy with a clinical population had been conducted. Two of these studies were case studies or single-case designs; thus, treatment gains cannot be compared with those of other interventions or to a waiting-list control. The third study (Rush et al., 1977) compared the effects of cognitive therapy with a tricyclic medication. Cognitive therapy appeared equal to antidepressant medication in terms of symptom remission, although when assessed at follow-up, significantly more of the drug-treated clients had sought additional help for their depression. A more recent study was reported by Beck et al. (1985), in which cognitive therapy was compared with cognitive therapy combined with amitriptyline in the treatment of depression. At the termination of 12 weeks of treatment, there were no statistically significant differences between the groups. However, at the 6-month follow-up, and particularly at the 12-month follow-up, nonsignificant trends favoring the combined treatment were clearly evident on a number of measures. Although the differences were not statistically significant, they were fairly large and may well have been clinically significant. However, it is difficult to evaluate these data because a large number of subjects from both groups received additional treatment during the follow-up phase.

Other comparisons of these procedures have addressed not only outcome, but also the author's designation of specific procedures as either cognitive, cognitive-behavioral, or behavioral. Phillips (1981) surveyed issues of *Behavior Therapy* for the years 1977, 1978, and 1979. Seventeen outcome studies were available, but one was deleted because the population consisted of college student snake phobics. Of the 16 clinical studies, 6 reported no difference between cognitive and behavioral therapy, 5 showed positive results in favor of cognitive treatment, 2 showed mixed results, and 1 favored behavioral treatment. However, Phillips pointed out that in each case, the cognitive "therapy" was confounded by the inclusion of established behavioral techniques as part of cognitive treatment. The behavioral strategies used included modeling, behavior rehearsal, desensitization, semantic counterconditioning, relaxation, differential rates of reinforcement, and extinction procedures. Inclusion of these procedures makes it impossible to identify the exact mechanism of change.

In a second review, Latimer and Sweet (1984) surveyed the table of contents of *Behavior Research and Therapy*, the *Journal of Behavior Therapy and Experimental Psychiatry*, *Behavior Therapy*, *Cognitive Therapy and Research*, and the *Journal of Consulting and Clinical Psychology*, between the years 1970 and 1983. These authors were interested in the results of two types of comparison studies, all using clinical samples. The first type of study were those which compared a behavioral treatment of known efficacy to the same treatment plus cognitive procedures. The authors believed that studies of this type would be important in determining if cognitive procedures address issues ignored by more classic behavioral treatments. If they do, the combination of treatments should prove superior. Of the five studies which incorporated this design, none demonstrated a clinically significant effect for treatments incorporating cognitive procedures. The second study design reviewed by the authors were those in which cognitive therapy was compared with other treatments. In this review, cognitive therapies did not include established behavioral procedures. Among the 7 studies meeting this criterion, behavioral treatments were superior in 4, cognitive methods were superior in 1, and in the remaining 2, the two strategies were considered equivalent. The authors concluded that the effectiveness of cognitive therapy (when behavioral components are excluded) has not been demonstrated in clinical populations. The conclusions of Phillips (1981) and Latimer and Sweet (1984) are consistent with those of meta-analytic studies discussed earlier.

Cognitive-behavior theorists claim that cognitive-behavioral treatments provide attention to areas overlooked by traditional behavior therapy. Cognitive-behavior therapy has focused increasingly on the individual's thoughts and cognitive style. The issue that remains, however, is whether this expansion of therapeutic attention to a different behavioral domain (e.g., thoughts) constitutes a paradigm shift. The cognitive-behavioral theorists have a view of the etiology of emotional disorders that is radically different from that of their more traditional behavioral colleagues. Yet, this etiological view has not been adequately tested in treatment studies because cognitive-behavioral treatments include elements of traditional behavioral strategies known to be effective.

SUMMARY AND CONCLUSIONS

Cognitive-behavior therapy has been described as a new approach to treatment of psychological disorders. In this critique, we have evaluated the theoretical bases proposed by cognitive-behavioral theorists as the foundation for this new approach, including descriptions of cognition, the etiology of maladaptive thoughts, and the role that these cognitions play in the onset of emotional disorders. In addition, we have examined the relationship between cognitive-behavioral theory and cognitive-behavior therapy. In each case, we are forced to conclude that at this time there is no empirical support for the claims made by cognitive-behavioral theorists that their treatments are superior to traditional behavior therapy, or that their treatments address aspects of a disorder not addressed by classic behavioral techniques.

There are several reasons for reaching this conclusion. First, cognitive processes such as attention and perception can be altered by applications of learning-theory based therapy. Thus, these activities obey the established laws of learning, negating the need to postulate a separate set of laws or structural abnormalities. Some theorists have even suggested that learning of motoric behaviors is mediated by higher cognitive functions and as evidence for this hypothesis have proposed that knowledge of the contingencies increases learned responses over "usual conditioning" procedures. Proponents of this view are guilty of equating speed of acquisition with method of acquisition. Knowledge of the contingencies may hasten the process of learning, but in and of itself is probably not responsible for acquisition and/or maintenance of behavior. Thus, the power is in the application of the contingency, not in the thought itself.

Second, thoughts of depressed individuals, a group especially targeted by cognitive-behavior therapists, do not distort reality. They may be pessimistic and negative, but their thoughts are not necessarily irrational or untrue. In contrast, there is some evidence (Alloy & Abramson, 1979, 1982) that individuals without psychopathology are more guilty than their depressed counterparts of cognitive distortions. In addition, two studies have demonstrated that cognitive distortions did not precede the onset of depressive symptoms, although further investigation is warranted. Moreover, studies that have attempted to induce mood changes by having subjects read types of cognitive statements suffer from several methodological flaws so that no positive conclusions can be drawn at this time.

A third unresolved issue is the designation of a technique as a behavioral or a cognitive procedure. Traditionally, therapeutic procedures that have evolved from the principles of behavior established in experimental laboratories have been termed behavior therapy. Inasmuch as anything an individual does is considered behavior, these principles are assumed to apply to all types of behavior (overt and covert).

On the other hand, it appears that cognitive therapists and cognitive-behavioral theorists have a much narrower view of behavior, restricting its use to overt motoric acts observable by others. If one accepts this more restrictive definition of behavior, cognitions may be seen as something other than behavior and therefore may require a separate approach or special attention in treatment approaches. However, cognitive-behavior therapy bears little relationship to cognitive-behavioral theory. Claims that cognitive-behavior therapy represents a deviation from standard behavior therapy practices are not substantiated when one examines cognitive-behavior procedures. Rather, such strategies are found to include many traditional behavior therapy elements. Even the procedures used to address cognitions (e.g., recognition of a maladaptive thought and reevaluation in light of the evidence) fit neatly into a stimulus discrimination paradigm. In fact, cognitive-behavior therapists may be their own worst enemies. By relying on behavioral procedures, they demonstrate that cognitions follow the laws of learning and need not be considered as something separate from overt behavior. Mahoney's (1977a) suggestion that cognitions change by changing behavior serves to reinforce the earlier contention that cognitive-behavior therapists and theorists have not proposed a new theory by which to understand human behavior, but rather an additional set of dependent variables by which to ascertain therapeutic change. This contribution should not be discounted, however. Verbal and covert behaviors are important variables in the assessment of treatment outcome and therefore represent valid objects for scientific investigation.

Rather than cognitive-behavior therapy, perhaps cognitive behavior therapy (the same words, but minus the hyphen) is a more appropriate term to describe these new approaches to changing behavior. In contrast to defining these procedures as a combination of two different approaches (as indicated by the hyphen), cognitive behavior therapy would be conceived as therapeutic strategies based on established laws of learning but directed specifically at one subclass of behavior (i.e., cognition). Although subtle, the change and resulting refined definition more accurately describes what actually occurs in the current use of these therapeutic strategies. This conceptualization would attend to the individual's thoughts without requiring postulation of a set of rules based on an empirically unsubstantiated model. On the other hand, it is difficult to see how any beneficial results can be attained by expanding our already overtaxed verbal repertoire.

The proponents of cognitive-behavior therapy have argued that the merits of their approach should be evaluated not at the level of procedure, but on the basis of theory and conceptualization of psychopathology. It is on this very basis, however, that the evidence against their case is most damaging. At this time, we must conclude that this new approach to therapy is without a theoretical base. We hasten to point out that we do not wish to challenge the contributions of basic cognitive psychology to our knowledge of human behavior. Moreover, research from this basic area of inquiry may well prove to be useful in theories of psychopathology and in development of treatment. However, those of a cognitive-behavior persuasion have ignored this rich data base in constructing their theories (Ross, 1985). That findings from basic cognitive psychology can be important at the clinical level is demonstrated by Lang's work on the processing of imagery in the area of anxiety disorders. This work could lead to new theories of anxiety states and have a profound effect on the way in which these disorders are assessed and treated (Lang & Cuthbert, 1984). Thus, it is not the importance of cognition in psychopathological states nor the importance of findings from cognitive psychology that we criticize. Rather, we lament the failure of the cognitive-behavioral theorists to use these data and to construct theories based on empirically derived findings.

REFERENCES

Abramson, L. Y., Seligman, M. E. P., & Teasdale, J. J. (1978). Learned helplessness in humans: Critique and reformulation. *Journal of Abnormal Psychology*, **17**, 56–67.

Alford, G., & Turner, S. M. (1976). Stimulus interference and conditioned inhibition of auditory hallucinations. *Journal of Behavior Therapy and Experimental Psychiatry*, **7**, 155–160.

Alloy, L. B., & Abramson, L. Y. (1979). Judgment of contingency in depressed and nondepressed students: Sadder but wiser? *Journal of Experimental Psychology: General*, **108**, 441–485.

Alloy, L. B., & Abramson, L. Y. (1982). Learned helplessness, depression and the illusion of control. *Journal of Personality and Social Psychology*, **42**, 1114–1126.

Bandura, A. (1977). Self-efficacy: Toward a unifying theory of behavioral change. *Psychological Review*, **84**, 191–215.

Beck, A. T. (1970). Cognitive therapy: Nature and relation to behavior therapy. *Behavior Therapy*, **1**, 184–200.

Beck, A. T., Hollon, S. D., Young, J. E., Bedrosian, R. C., & Budenz, D. (1985). Treatment of depression with cognitive therapy and amtriptyline. *Archives of General Psychiatry*, **42**, 142–152.

Brewer, W. F. (1974). There is no convincing evidence for operant or classical conditioning in adult humans. In W. B. Weiner & D. S. Palermo (Eds.), *Cognition and the symbolic processes* (pp. 1–42). Hillsdale, NJ: Erlbaum.

Buchwald, A. M., Strack, S., & Coyne, J. C. (1981). Demand characteristics and the Velten mood induction procedure. *Journal of Consulting and Clinical Psychology*, **49**, 478–479.

Coleman, R. E. (1975). Manipulation of self-esteem as a determinant of mood of elated and depressed women. *Journal of Abnormal Psychology*, **84**, 693–700.

Coyne, J. C., & Gotlieb, I. H. (1983). The role of cognition in depression: A critical appraisal. *Psychological Bulletin*, **94**, 472–505.

DeMonbreun, B. G., & Craighead, W. E. (1977). Distortion of perception and recall of positive and neutral feedback in depression. *Cognitive Therapy and Research*, **1**, 311–330.

Dush, D. M., Hirt, M. L., & Schroeder, H. (1983). Self-statement modification with adults: A meta-analysis. *Psychological Bulletin*, **94**, 408–422.

Ellis, A. (1973). Rational-emotive therapy. In R. Corsini (Ed.), *Current psychotherapies* (pp. 167–207). Itasca, IL: Peacock.

Eysenck, H. J. (1979). Behavior therapy and the philosophers. *Behaviour Research and Therapy*, **17**, 511–514.

Frost, R., Graf, M., & Becker, J. (1979). Self-devaluation and depressed mood. *Journal of Consulting and Clinical Psychology*, **47**, 958–962.

Garber, J., & Hollon, S. D. (1977). Universal versus personal helplessness in depression: Belief in uncontrollability or incompetence? Unpublished manuscript, University of Pennsylvania.

Goodwin, A. M., & Williams, M. G. (1982). Mood-induction research—Its implications for clinical depression. *Behaviour Research and Therapy*, **20**, 373–382.

Hollon, S. D., & Beck, A. T. (1979). Cognitive therapy of depression. In P. C. Kendall and S. D. Hollon (Eds.), *Cognitive-behavioral interventions: Theory, research and procedures* (pp. 153–196). Orlando, FL: Academic.

Jones, R. G. (1969). A factored measure of Ellis' Irrational Belief System. *Dissertation Abstracts*, **29**,4379B–4380B.

Kendall, P. C., & Hollon, S. D. (1979). Cognitive-behavioral interventions: Overview and current status. In P. C. Kendall and S. D. Hollon (Eds.), *Cognitive-behavioral interventions: Theory, research and procedures* (pp. 1–7). Orlando, FL: Academic.

Klein, D. C., Fencil-Morse, E., & Seligman, M. E. P. (1976). Learned helplessness, depression and the attribution of failure. *Journal of Personality and Social Psychology*, **33**, 508–516.

Kovacs, M. (1979). Treating depressive disorders: The efficacy of behavior and cognitive therapies. *Behavior Modification*, **3**, 496–517.

Kuiper, N. A., & MacDonald, M. R. (1982). Self and other perceptions in mild depression. *Social Cognition*, **1**, 223–239.

Lang, P. J., & Cuthbert, B. N. (1984). Affective information processing and the assessment of anxiety. *Journal of Behavioral Assessment*, **6**, 369–395.

Latimer, P. R., & Sweet, A. A. (1984). Cognitive vs. behavioral procedures in cognitive-behavior therapy: A critical review of the evidence. *Journal of Behavior Therapy and Experimental Psychiatry*, **15**, 9–22.

Layne, C. (1983). Painful truths about depressives' cognitions. *Journal of Clinical Psychology*, **39**, 848–853.

Ledwidge, B. (1978). Cognitive behavior modification: A step in the wrong direction. *Psychological Bulletin*, **85**, 353–375.

Lewinsohn, P. M., Mischel, W., Chaplin, W., & Barton, R. (1980). Social competence and depression: The role of illusory self-perceptions. *Journal of Abnormal Psychology*, **90**, 213–219.

Lewinsohn, P. M., Steinmetz, J. L., Larson, D. W., & Franklin, J. (1981). Depression related cognitions: Antecedent or consequences? *Journal of Abnormal Psychology*, **90**, 213–219.

Lishman, W. A. (1972). Selective factors in memory: II. Affective disorders. *Psychological Medicine*, **2**, 248–253.

Lloyd, G. G., & Lishman, W. A. (1975). Effect of depression on the speed of recall of pleasant and unpleasant experiences. *Psychological Medicine*, **5**, 173–180.

Lovaas, O. I., Schreibman, L., Koegel, R., & Rehm, R. (1971). Selective responding by autistic children to multiple sensory input. *Journal of Abnormal Psychology*, **77**, 211–222.

Mahoney, M. J. (1974). *Cognition and behavior modification*. Cambridge, MA: Ballinger.

Mahoney, M. J. (1977a). On the continuing resistance to thoughtful therapy. *Behavior Therapy*, **8**, 673–677.

Mahoney, M. J. (1977b). Personal science: A cognitive learning therapy. In A. Ellis and R. Grieger (Eds.), *Handbook of rational-emotive therapy* (pp. 352–366). New York: Springer.

Mahoney, M. J., & Arnkoff, D. (1978). Cognitive and self-control therapies. In S. L. Garfield and A. E. Bergin (Eds.), *Handbook of psychotherapy and behavior change*, 2nd ed. (pp. 689–722). New York: Wiley.

Mahoney, M. J., & Kazdin, A. E. (1979). Cognitive-behavior modification: Misconception and premature evacuation. *Psychological Bulletin*, **86**, 1044–1049.

Mathews, A., & Bradley, B. (1983). Mood and the self-reference bias in recall. *Behaviour Research and Therapy*, **21**, 233–239.

Meichenbaum, D. (1974). *Cognitive behavior modification*. Morristown, NJ: General Learning.

Meichenbaum, D., & Cameron, R. (1982). Cognitive behavior therapy. In G. T. Wilson and C. M. Franks (Eds.), *Contemporary behavior therapy: Conceptual and empirical foundations* (pp. 310–338). New York: Guilford.

Miller, R. C., & Berman, J. S. (1983). The efficacy of cognitive behavior therapies: A quantitative review of the research evidence. *Psychological Bulletin*, **94**, 39–53.

Nelson, R. E., & Craighead, W. E. (1977). Selective recall of positive and negative feedback, self-control behaviors and depression. *Journal of Abnormal Psychology*, **86**, 379–388.

Peterson, C., Schwartz, S. M., & Seligman, M. E. P. (1981). Self-blame and depressive symptoms. *Journal of Personality and Social Psychology*, **41**, 253–259.

Phillips, L. W.(1981). Roots and branches of behavioral and cognitive practice. *Journal of Behavior Therapy and Experimental Psychiatry*, **12**, 5–17.

Rachlin, H. (1977). Reinforcing and punishing thoughts. *Behavior Therapy*, **8**, 659–665.

Rimm, D. C., & Litvak, S. B. (1969). Selfverbalization and emotional arousal. *Journal of Abnormal Psychology*, **74**, 181–187.

Riskind, J. H., & Steer, R. (1984). Do maladaptive attitudes "cause" depression: Misconception of cognitive theory. *Archives of General Psychiatry*, **41**, 1111.

Rogers, T., & Craighead,W. E. (1977). Physiological responses to self-statements: The effect of statement valence and discrepancy. *Cognitive Research and Therapy*, **1**, 99–119.

Ross, A. O. (1985). To form a more perfect union it is time to stop standing still. *Behavior Therapy*, **16**, 192–204.

Rush, A. J., Beck, A. T., Kovacs, M., & Hollon, S. (1977). Comparative efficacy of cognitive therapy and pharmacotherapy in the treatment of depressed outpatients. *Cognitive Therapy and Research*, **1**, 17–37.

Russell, P. L., & Brandsma, J. M. (1974). A theoretical and empirical integration of the rational-emotive and classical conditioning theories. *Journal of Consulting and Clinical Psychology*, **42**, 389–397.

Schwartz, R. M. (1982). Cognitivebehavior modification: A conceptual review. *Clinical Psychology Review*, **2**, 267–293.

Skinner, B. F. (1976). *About behaviorism*. New York: Vintage.

Small, A., Gessner, T., & Williams, K. (1983). A comparison of self-devaluation and somatic suggestion content in depressive mood manipulation. *Journal of Clinical Psychology*, **39**, 709–711.

Smith, T. W. (1982). Irrational beliefs in the cause and treatment of emotional distress: A critical review of the rational-emotive model. *Clinical Psychology Review*, **2**, 505–522.

Strickland, B. R., Hale, W. D., & Anderson, L. K. (1975). Effect of induced mood states on activity and self-reported affect. *Journal of Consulting and Clinical Psychology*, **43**, 587.

Sutherland, G., Newman, B., & Rachman, S. (1982). Experimental investigation of the relations between mood and intrusive unwanted cognitions. *British Journal of Medical Psychology*, **55**, 127–138.

Teasdale, J. D., & Bancroft, J. (1977). Manipulation of thought content as a determinant of mood and corrugator electromyographic activity in depressed patients. *Journal of Abnormal Psychology*, **86**, 235–241.

Teasdale, J. D., & Fogarty, S. J. (1979). Differential effects of induced mood on retrieval of pleasant and unpleasant events from episodic memory. *Journal of Abnormal Psychology*, **88**, 248–257.

Teasdale, J. D., & Spencer, P. (1984). Induced mood and estimates of past success. *British Journal of Clinical Psychology*, **23**, 149–150.

Ullmann, L. P. (1970). On cognitions and behavior therapy. *Behavior Therapy*, **1**, 201–204.

Velten, E. (1968). A laboratory task for the induction of mood states. *Behaviour Research and Therapy*, **6**, 473–482.

Wilson, G. T. (1978). Cognitive-behavior therapy: Paradigm shift or passing phase. In J. P. Foreyt and D. P. Rathjen (Eds.), *Cognitive behavior therapy: Research and application* (pp. 7–33). New York: Plenum.

Wolpe, J. (1976). Behavior therapy and its malcontents: II. Multimodal eclectricism, cognitive-exclusivism, and "exposure" empiricism. *Journal of Behavior Therapy and Experimental Psychiatry*, **7**, 109–116.

Wolpe, J. (1978). Cognition and causation in human behavior and its therapy. *American Psychologist*, **33**, 437–446.

Wolpe, J. (1980). Cognitive behaviour and its roles in psychotherapy: An integrative account. In M. J. Mahoney (Ed.), *Psychotherapy process: Current issues and future directions* (pp. 185–203). New York: Plenum.

Zettle, R. D., & Hayes, S. C. (1980). Conceptual and empirical status of rational-emotive therapy. In M. Hersen, R. M. Eisler, and P. M. Miller (Eds.), *Progress in behavior modification* (Vol. 9) (pp. 125–162). Orlando, FL: Academic.

Zettle, R. D., & Hayes, S. C. (1982). Rule-governed behavior: A potential theoretical framework for cognitive-behavior therapy. In P C. Kendall (Ed.), *Advances in cognitive-behavioral research and therapy* (Vol. l) (pp. 73–108). Orlando, FL: Academic.

DISCUSSION

Superficially, Beck, on the one hand, and Beidel and Turner, on the other, appear to agree on a surprisingly large number of central issues. The authors of both articles concur that distorted thinking processes are associated with many forms of psychopathology, including depression and anxiety. The authors of both articles concur that cognitive-behavioral theories and techniques have helped to rekindle interest in a largely neglected class of mental experiences that are useful for assessing therapeutic change: thoughts. Finally, the authors of both articles concur that cognitive techniques often produce therapeutic improvement. So where does the fundamental disagreement lie?

The crux of the dispute between the supporters and detractors of cognitive-behavioral theory and therapy appears to revolve around the question of the causal role of cognition—particularly cognitive structures—in the genesis of both abnormal and normal emotions and behavior. Cognitive-behaviorists contend that certain cognitive structures, particularly schemas, influence the way that individuals perceive and construe themselves and their environments. Schemas and similar structures are posited by cognitive-behaviorists to be causally primary in psychopathology in that they affect the processing and interpretation of information; Beck refers to this assertion as his "primacy hypothesis." Certain individuals are mentally ill, assert cognitive-behaviorists, because they think about the world in fundamentally maladaptive and irrational ways. Beck, for example, maintains that the negative schema (see Chapter 11)—a cognitive structure involving a propensity to interpret oneself, the world, and the future in a negative light—predisposes individuals to clinical depression in response to certain life stressors. Similarly, Beck and his followers assert that the **danger schema**, which entails a tendency to perceive harm across a wide variety of ambiguous situations, increases individuals' risk for developing anxiety disorders following certain stressful events (Beck & Emery, 1985). Although Beck denies that thoughts play a causal role in psychopathology, he does contend that certain cognitive structures, such as schemas, can give rise to psychopathology in the presence of specific environmental triggers.

In contrast, behaviorists (especially radical behaviorists, such as Skinner and his followers) deny that cognitive factors play a causal role in either normal or abnormal emotions or behavior. Indeed, Skinnerians maintain that the postulation of cognitive structures, such as schemas, is a tautological and redundant enterprise that gets us no closer to understanding the roots of psychopathology. Beidel and Turner would presumably side with Skinnerians on this issue. Cognitive structures, radical behaviorists contend, simply duplicate within the organism what is already evident in their overt behavior. In other words, such structures merely take what is "outside," namely observable behavior, and place it "inside," namely within the head of the organism (Skinner, 1974). Nothing has been accomplished in this process, say Skinnerians, except to shift the explanation of psychopathology a step farther away from its true causes: environmental contingencies (that is, reinforcing and punishing stimuli) and perhaps genetic predispositions in some cases.

As an example, take the danger schema posited by Beck and his colleagues to lie at the heart of anxiety disorders. How is the presence of this schema to be inferred in a given individual? Cognitive-behaviorists would probably argue that we can safely deduce the existence of a danger schema if a person is easily frightened by relatively innocuous stimuli, refuses to take extremely minor risks, and so on. But what evidence do we have that this individual possesses a danger schema? Presumably, our evidence is that this individual is easily frightened by relatively innocuous stimuli, refuses to take extremely minor risks, and so on. In such a case, hypothesizing the presence of a danger schema is entirely tautological: No gain in knowledge or understanding has been achieved.

But does this objection imply that cognitive structures are inherently tautological or that they are not useful for understanding or explaining psychopathology? Not necessarily. Cognitive structures are not tautological if the investigators who postulate them can generate fresh predictions that are not derived from the same data base upon which these structures were inferred. Thus, the proof of the pudding lies in the ability of researchers to produce testable predictions concerning the relationship between cognitive structures and real-world clinical phenomena such as depression and anxiety. As Beidel and Turner note, however, investigators have generally failed to provide convincing evidence that individuals who receieve elevated scores on measures of irrational thinking are at heightened risk for subsequent psychopathology. Are not these findings an enormous embarrassment for the cognitive-behavioral paradigm? Perhaps not. Beck and his colleagues argue that the schemas predisposing to psychopathology are normally latent (unobservable) but become activated (or, in Beck's terms, hypervalent) only in response to specific environmental events. Thus, such schemas normally lie dormant and inactive and are observable only when psychopathology is present.

The potential problem here, as Beidel and Turner point out, is **falsifiability**. Many philosophers of science (for example, Popper, 1959) have argued that falsifiability is the cornerstone of scientific theories. That is, a theory is scientific only if it can generate predictions that are potentially refutable. But if the schemas posited by cognitive-behavioral theorists are inaccessible to assessment prior to the appearance of psychopathology, the hypothesis that such schemas predispose individuals to later psychopathology becomes difficult, if not impossible, to falsify.

The literature comparing the effectiveness of cognitive-behavioral and behavioral therapies (which is reviewed by Beidel and Turner) is similarly fraught with interpretational ambiguities. As Albert Bandura (1977) notes, it is essential to distinguish the procedures used to alter behavior from the mechanisms by which such behavior is altered. For example, cognitive-behavioral theorists typically contend that the effectiveness of many behavioral procedures, such as systematic desensitization, derives from their capacity to effect changes in cognition. Indeed, Bandura argues that increases in self-efficacy—that is, the expectation that one will be able to perform a given act—underlie all forms of psychotherapeutic change. Clients benefit from therapy, according to Bandura, to the extent that their self-efficacy improves. Bandura further contends that behavioral techniques, including systematic desensitization and "flooding,"* are often the most effective methods for increasing self-efficacy, because they provide clients with concrete and tangible evidence that they are capable of successfully confronting their fears. If Bandura is correct, many behavioral procedures may, paradoxically, be even more potent than cognitive procedures in producing cognitive change.

On the flip side of the coin, the effectiveness of many cognitive procedures might in principle be traceable to the basic learning principles posited by behavioral theorists, such as classical conditioning. For example, in self-statement modification, the replacement of distressing self-speech ("Oh no, I'm going to screw up again") with comforting self-speech ("Relax, I know I can do it") may produce a counterconditioning process (similar to that which most behaviorists believe occurs in systematic desensitization), in which clients replace an unpleasant and anxiety-provoking unconditioned stimulus (UCS) with a pleasant and anxiety-reducing UCS. (Readers for whom the term *UCS* rings only a very distant bell, or no bell at all, will probably want to briefly refresh their memories of Pavlov and his dogs.) Once again, therapeutic procedures must be differentiated from the therapeutic mechanisms underlying their efficacy. A cognitive technique may work via behavioral (learning) principles and vice versa.

Consequently, the results of studies comparing the effectiveness of cognitive-behavioral and behavioral therapies are not terribly informative regarding the validity of either cognitive-behavioral or behavioral theories. Recall from the introduction to Part III that one must be careful to divorce treatment from etiology: The appropriate treatment for a disorder bears no necessary implications for its causation or vice versa. This reasoning leads us to a most peculiar paradox regarding studies comparing the effectiveness of cognitive-behavioral and behavioral therapies. Regardless of their outcome, the results of such studies could potentially be interpreted as supporting the validity of cognitive-behavioral theories. If cognitive-behavioral therapies were found to be more effective than behavioral therapies, cog-

*"Flooding" can be defined as prolonged exposure to a highly feared stimulus. Flooding in the case of height phobics (acrophobics), for example, would typically consist of exposing them to an extremely frightening stimulus (for example, looking down from the top floor of the World Trade Center) and preventing them from performing the response they would typically perform in that situation (for example, escaping immediately).

nitive-behaviorial theorists could understandably rejoice that the implementation of cognitive techniques adds to the well-established efficacy of behavioral techniques. But if cognitive-behavioral therapies were found to be less effective than behavioral therapies, cognitive-behavioral theorists could maintain that the addition of cognitive techniques only dilutes the efficacy of behavioral techniques, which, as Bandura points out, may frequently be the optimal means of evoking cognitive change. The implication of this paradox seems clear. Compelling evidence for the validity of the cognitive-behavioral model of psychopathology must ultimately derive from data other than therapeutic effectiveness.

QUESTIONS TO STIMULATE DISCUSSION

1. Beck conjectures that the cognitive schemas predisposing to psychopathology have their origins in basic evolutionary processes. In what ways might the schemas predisposing to depression and anxiety, for example, be evolutionarily adaptive?
2. Both Beck, on the one hand, and Beidel and Turner, on the other, agree that depression is typically accompanied by cognitive changes, such as extremely negative and pessimistic thinking. Are these cognitive changes best conceptualized as causes of depression, consequences of depression, or neither? Explain your reasoning.
3. Do you believe that systematic desensitization works by means of classical conditioning processes, as its developers claimed, or by altering cognitions, such as self-efficacy? What sort of study could one design to distinguish between these two possibilities?
4. Radical behaviorists, such as Skinner, hold that thoughts are simply behaviors that happen to be covert (unobservable) and that they are subject to the same laws of learning (that is, classical and operant conditioning) as are other behaviors. Beidel and Turner also adhere to this position. Do you agree with them? If so, why? If not, in what way(s) do you see thoughts as qualitatively different (that is, different in kind) from observable behaviors?
5. The phenomenon of depressive realism (which is discussed by both sets of authors) has been quite controversial. What factors might account for this puzzling phenomenon? What studies might be designed to provide further evidence for it?

SUGGESTIONS FOR FURTHER READING

Beck, A. T. (1976). *Cognitive therapy and the emotional disorders*. New York: International Universities Press.

In this general introduction to cognitive therapy, Beck delineates the major principles of his cognitive model of psychopathology and its implications for understanding both normal and abnormal emotions. In addition, he discusses the application of his cognitive model to the treatment of depression, anxiety disorders, and hysteria, as well as the specific procedures involved in cognitive therapy.

Beck, A. T., & Emery, G. (1985). *Anxiety disorders and phobias*. New York: Basic Books.

The first part of the book, by Aaron Beck, provides a clear and readable overview of the cognitive model of anxiety and anxiety disorders, as well as its application to specific anxiety disorders, including simple (specific) and social phobias, generalized anxiety disorder, and panic disorder. The second part of the book, by Gary Emery, contains a description and explanation of assorted cognitive techniques for the treatment of anxiety, such as cognitive restructuring and imagery methods. One warning, however: The two halves of the book read almost like two different books, so you should not expect Emery's section to incorporate much of Beck's theorizing.

Beck, A. T., Rush, A. J., Shaw, B. F., & Emery, G. (1979). *Cognitive therapy of depression*. New York: Guilford Press.

This now-classic monograph provides an overview of the role of cognitive factors in depression, along with a detailed how-to manual for the use of cognitive therapy with depressed clients. Other chapters contain information on more specialized topics, such as the application of cognitive techniques to suicidal individuals and the use of cognitive techniques in group therapy.

Coyne, J. C., & Gotlib, I. H. (1983). The role of cognition in depression: A critical appraisal. *Psychological Bulletin*, *94*, 472–505.

Coyne and Gotlib carefully examine the evidence for the cognitive model of depression from five major sources, including studies of recall of information, cognitive distortions, and attribution. They conclude that Beck's model of depression is not strongly supported by existing data and that cognitive differences between depressed and nondepressed individuals tend to be relatively small in magnitude and are potentially attributable to factors other than depression. Moreover, they conclude that the specificity of cognitive biases to depression has not been convincingly demonstrated.

Ellis, A. (1962). *Reason and emotion in psychotherapy*. New York: L. Stuart.

Ellis traces the origins and theoretical principles underlying rational-emotive therapy, and outlines common irrational beliefs that predispose individuals to psychological disturbance. He then discusses the application of RET to specific clinical problems, including marital conflict, impotence, schizophrenia, and psychopathy.

Freeman, A., Pretzer, J., Fleming, B., & Simon, K. M. (1990). *Clinical applications of cognitive therapy*. New York: Plenum Press.

The authors first review the fundamental principles of cognitive therapy and discuss common misconceptions surrounding its theory and practice. They then examine the application of cognitive therapy to specific conditions, with particular emphasis on personality disorders.

Haaga, D. A., Dyck, M. J., & Ernst, D. (1991). Empirical status of cognitive theory of depression. *Psychological Bulletin*, *110*, 215–236.

In contrast to Coyne and Gotlib (1983), Haaga et al. conclude that several components of Beck's theory of depression—including the negativity hypothesis, the hypothesis of mood-dependent retrieval, and the content specificity hypothesis—have been adequately corroborated. Nevertheless, they argue that little evidence supports the claim that depressive thinking is illogical or irrational or that dysfunctional beliefs increase susceptibility to depression.

Kendall, P. C., & Hollon, S. D. (Eds.) (1979). *Cognitive-behavioral interventions: Theory, research, and procedures*. New York: Academic Press.

This edited volume contains chapters on such topics as cognitive therapy for depression (by Hollon and Beck), cognitive treatment for anxiety disorders, development of self-control in impulsive children, and anger-control training. The opening chapter by Kendall and Hollon provides an overview of cognitive-behavioral therapy and its conceptual and historical underpinnings.

Layne, C. (1983). Painful truths about depressives' cognitions. *Journal of Clinical Psychology*, *6*, 848–853. (Reprinted in Hooley, J. M., Neale, J. M., & Davison, G. C. [1989]. *Readings in abnormal psychology*. New York: Wiley).

Layne critically reviews the evidence concerning the existence of cognitive distortions in depressed individuals. He concludes that, contrary to the assumptions of cognitive models of depression, depressed individuals appear to be more realistic than nondepressed individuals across a number of quite different tasks. He briefly discusses the puzzling therapeutic implications of this conclusion.

Ledwidge, B. (1978). Cognitive behavior modification: A step in the wrong direction? *Psychological Bulletin*, *3*, 353–375.

Ledwidge reviews the empirical literature on the relative efficacy of cognitive-behavioral and behavioral therapies. He finds that controlled studies show these two therapeutic modalities to be approximately equally effective and concludes that acceptance of the claims of cognitive-behavior therapists would be premature and potentially harmful to the reputation of behavior therapy.

Mahoney, M. J., & Kazdin, A. E. (1979). Cognitive behavior modification: Misconceptions and premature evacuation. *Psychological Bulletin*, *86*, 1044–1049.

Mahoney and Kazdin challenge Ledwidge's (1978) claims regarding the effectiveness of cognitive-behavior therapy and contend that Ledwidge's arguments are plagued by misconceptions regarding the distinction between cognitive-behavior therapy and behavior therapy. They contend that that therapies should be classified by their hypothesized theoretical mechanisms rather than by their procedures or strategies.

REFERENCES

Bandura, A. (1977). Self-efficacy: Toward a unifying theory of behavioral change. *Psychological Review*, *84*, 191–215.

Beck, A. T., & Emery, G. (1985). *Anxiety disorders and phobias: A cognitive perspective*. New York: Basic Books.

Loevinger, J. (1987). *Paradigms of personality*. New York: W. H. Freeman.

Popper, K. R. (1959). *The logic of scientific discovery*. New York: Basic Books.

Skinner, B. F. (1974). *About behaviorism*. New York: Knopf.

CHAPTER

14

Can alcoholics successfully achieve controlled drinking?

PRO Sobell, M. B., & Sobell, L. C. (1973). Individualized behavior therapy for alcoholics. *Behavior Therapy*, *4*, 49–72.

CON Pendery, M. L., Maltzman, I. M., & West, L. J. (1982). Controlled drinking by alcoholics? New findings and a reevaluation of a major affirmative study. *Science*, *217*, 169–175.

OVERVIEW OF THE CONTROVERSY: Mark B. Sobell and Linda C. Sobell report the results of a behavior therapy experiment with chronic alcoholics that they interpret as demonstrating that some alcoholics can successfully develop and maintain controlled drinking habits. Mary L. Pendery, Irving M. Maltzman, and L. Jolyon West report the results of an 11-year follow-up study of the alcoholics in the Sobells' original controlled drinking condition and strongly dispute the Sobells' conclusion that controlled drinking is an effective treatment for some alcoholics.

CONTEXT OF THE PROBLEM

On March 6, 1983, the CBS news magazine *60 Minutes* featured a sensational story about what appeared to be an emerging scientific scandal of potentially enormous proportions (Marlatt, 1983). Harry Reasoner, a CBS correspondent, stood beside the grave of an alcoholic patient who had been a subject in a behavior therapy experiment designed to teach alcoholics techniques of **controlled drinking**—that is, drinking in moderation. This experiment, initiated at Patton State Hospital in California in the early 1970s by two enterprising young students, Mark Sobell and Linda Sobell, was interpreted by its authors as indicating that controlled drinking was an effective treatment for at least some alcoholics. But in 1982 Mary Pendery, Irving Maltzman, and L. Jolyon West published a paper in the prestigious journal *Science* calling the Sobells' findings and conclusions into question. Pendery, Maltzman, and West's article led to a fierce and bitter debate that has yet to be fully resolved. The Sobells, *60 Minutes* pointed out, asserted that controlled drinking is effective for many alcoholics, yet several patients in the controlled drinking condition had died in the intervening decade from alcohol-related causes!

The controlled drinking controversy provides an excellent example of how theoretical preconceptions can shape real-world decisions and policies—in this case, the selection of treatment goals. As you learned in Chapter 7, proponents of the "disease model" of alcoholism typically maintain that alcoholics possess a physiological defect that renders them susceptible to a catastrophic loss of control over drinking. After even a single drink, these proponents contend, alcoholics are unable to curtail their urge to ingest additional alcohol, leading to an ineluctable downward spiral. The implication of this disease view is clear: The only defensible goal of alcoholism treatment is abstinence. Indeed, abstinence is the ultimate aim of virtually all traditional alcoholism treatment programs, including Alcoholics Anonymous. From the perspective of advocates of the disease model, controlled drinking is utterly doomed to failure, because the physiology of alcoholics precludes them from moderating their drinking habits.

Nevertheless, in the early 1960s a small but persistent cadre of researchers began to raise questions concerning the disease model and its implications for the treatment of alcoholism. In 1962, Davies published a paper reporting that some alcoholics can acquire and maintain drinking habits, only to be met with an onslaught of criticism (Sobell & Sobell, 1984). Similarly, the well-known Rand reports of the late 1970s and early 1980s (Armor, Polich, & Stambul, 1978; Polich, Armor, & Braiker, 1981), which appeared to indicate that controlled drinking is a viable goal for some alcoholics, drew sharp attacks from several sources (Peele, 1989). The Rand reports stirred considerable controversy about their findings that, for alcoholics who are under 40 and who exhibit relatively mild dependence on alcohol, controlled drinking is associated with lower relapse rates than is abstinence. The results of these reports ran so counter to prevailing wisdom in the alcoholism field that several attempts were apparently made to delay and perhaps even to suppress their publication (Sobell & Sobell, 1984).

But the controlled drinking controversy was not fully thrust into the public eye until Pendery, Maltzman, and West's reply to the Sobells' studies appeared in print. Pendery, Maltzman, and West not only claimed that the Sobells had greatly exaggerated the safety and efficacy of controlled drinking but also impugned the Sobells' honesty and scientific responsibility by questioning the veracity of their findings. Maltzman told the *New York Times*, "Beyond any reasonable doubt, it's fraud." In the same article, co-author West similarly asserted that the results of Pendery, Maltzman, and West's study paper cast "grave doubt on the scientific integrity of the original research" (Boffey, 1983).

These allegations, serious as they are, divert attention from the central question that is the focus of this chapter. The Sobells' specific findings aside, is their empirical generalization concerning the efficacy of controlled drinking correct? If so, what does this generalization imply about the treatment of alcoholism?

THE CONTROVERSY: Sobell and Sobell vs. Pendery, Maltzman, and West

Sobell and Sobell

The husband-and-wife team of Mark Sobell and Linda Sobell begin by outlining a rationale for a behavioral intervention program for alcoholism that emphasizes controlled drinking as a goal. They point out that several lines of evidence are consistent with the hypothesis that drinking is an operant response (a response maintained by reinforcement) which is maintained by the reduction of anxiety. In addition, the Sobells note that an increasing body of literature suggests that at least some alcoholics are capable of acquiring and maintaining controlled drinking habits. The Sobells then describe the design of their study in detail. Seventy alcoholics were first provisionally assigned to two groups—nondrinker and drinker—on the basis of their preferences and characteristics. Then subjects within each of these two groups were randomly assigned either to traditional hospital treatment involving Alcoholics Anonymous meetings and physiological interventions or to a 17-session experimental treatment. Thus, half the subjects who received the experimental treatment had abstinence as a goal and half had controlled drinking as a goal. The experimental treatment comprised a variety of behavioral techniques, including identification of the variables that help to trigger or set off excessive drinking and aversive conditioning involving electric shock. The Sobells reported that experimental subjects in the controlled drinking condition tended to exhibit superior outcome to other subjects at both 6-week and 6-month follow-up intervals. For example, compared with subjects in the other conditions, controlled drinking subjects were generally reported to have had fewer days of intoxication and were more often rated by friends and family as improved. The Sobells conclude that controlled drinking is a feasible goal for at least some alcoholics and that rigid insistence on abstinence as a treatment goal may actually be countertherapeutic.

Pendery, Maltzman, and West

Mary Pendery, Irving Maltzman, and Jolyon West first review the design of the Sobells' investigation. Although they note that the Sobells' design comprised several conditions, they elect to focus on the outcome of the controlled drinking subjects only. Pendery, Maltzman, and West cite three reasons for this decision:

- Experimental subjects who were assigned to the abstinence condition were aware that other subjects were assigned to the controlled drinking condition and may thus have been resentful.
- The experimental and control groups were not equivalent with respect to all important variables.
- In their view, the critical question is not whether controlled drinking is superior to other treatments but whether it is a viable treatment at all.

Pendery, Maltzman, and West come to dramatically different conclusions than do the Sobells regarding the outcome of the controlled drinking subjects. For example, Pendery, Maltzman, and West argue that the hospitalizations of these subjects during the first 6 months following discharge did not reflect voluntary efforts to curb drinking, as the Sobells had claimed, but rather a pattern of serious drinking-related problems. Moreover, Pendery, Maltzman, and West report that the long-term outcome of the controlled drinking group was exceedingly poor. In the decade or so after the Sobells' initial report, four of these subjects died from alcohol-related causes, a fifth was missing, and most of the surviving subjects had exhibited a chronic pattern of heavy drinking accompanied by serious complications. Pendery, Maltzman, and West conclude that the Sobells' assertions regarding the efficacy of controlled drinking do not withstand close scrutiny.

KEY CONCEPTS AND TERMS

gamma alcoholic Alcoholic who is physically dependent on alcohol and who experiences a loss of control over drinking and withdrawal symptoms (see also Chapter 7).

operant response Response that is maintained by reinforcement. Advocates of controlled drinking typically maintain that drinking is an operant response maintained by reinforcing consequences, such as stress reduction.

stimulus control variable Variable that helps to set off or trigger the behavior in question. For some alcoholics, for example, sitting alone on the couch on a Friday night might be a stimulus control variable.

stress reduction hypothesis Hypothesis that alcoholics drink to alleviate short-term anxiety.

variable ratio schedule Schedule in which a stimulus is administered a variable number of times depending on the number of responses emitted by the subject.

PREVIEW QUESTIONS

1. According to the Sobells, what are three reasons that individuals might drink to reduce anxiety?
2. What evidence and rationale do the Sobells provide for proposing controlled drinking as a treatment goal for at least some alcoholics?
3. What were the four conditions in the Sobells' experiment? What were the principal procedures they used in their two experimental conditions?
4. What were the Sobells' primary findings at the conclusion of their study? What did they report at follow-up?
5. What do the Sobells see as the major implications of their findings for the treatment of alcoholism?
6. Why do Pendery, Maltzman, and West elect to report follow-up data from the Sobells' controlled drinking condition only, rather than from all four conditions?
7. What are Pendery, Maltzman, and West's major findings, and how do those findings appear to differ from those of the Sobells?
8. What do Pendery, Maltzman, and West conclude regarding the efficacy of controlled drinking for alcoholism?

MARK B. SOBELL & LINDA C. SOBELL

Individualized behavior therapy for alcoholics

Until recently, behavioral studies of alcoholism have emphasized classical aversive conditioning and neglected the instrumental nature of drinking. Rachman and Teasdale (1969) have thoroughly reviewed the aversive-conditioning literature and pointed out that the primary purpose of such techniques is to suppress drinking responses. Seldom have attempts been made concurrently to train socially acceptable behaviors in the place of heavy drinking. Lack of generalization has been perhaps the most severe problem plaguing such studies, but it is a problem not unexpected if heavy drinking is considered to be an operant, i.e., controlled by its consequences. These consequences are usually absent in a treatment environment but are an integral part of our society.

Cohen, Liebson, and Faillace (1971) have recently provided convincing demonstrations that the drinking of alcoholic beverages by alcoholics can be regarded as an operant response and manipulated according to the various laws of operant psychology. They also demonstrated that Gamma alcoholics could maintain a pattern of moderate drinking of 95-proof ethanol for extended periods, if reinforcement contingencies were appropriately arranged. In a very real sense, their results have shown that one can buy controlled drinking behavior from an alcoholic—if the price is right!

THE RATIONALE OF THE WORK REPORTED HERE

Several studies using both animal and human subjects have investigated the hypothesis that a voluntary increase in alcohol consumption is associated with increases in stress. Clark and Polish (1960) conducted a well-controlled baseline replication design study in which rhesus monkeys could drink either water, a solution of 20% alcohol in water, or both during initial baseline (no treatment) sessions, followed by electric shock avoidance sessions, and finally, baseline sessions once again. They reported that: "Alcohol consumption increased during, and decreased after, avoidance sessions. Water intake remained the same or decreased during avoidance sessions and stayed at this level after the sessions" (p. 223). In another animal study, Cicero, Myers, and Black (1968) found that hooded rats increased their intake of ethanol in the presence of cued unavoidable electric shock. More recently, von Wright, Pekanmäki, and Malin (1971) found that . . . albino rats increase their alcohol intake significantly when subjected to an approach-avoidance conflict. They also present a critical review of additional experiments investigating the stress-reduction hypothesis.

Hershenson (1965), in a study based on self-reports by problem drinkers, concluded that their use of alcohol was stress induced. Also working with human alcoholic subjects, Schaefer, Sobell, and Mills (1971b) found substantial indirect evidence indicating that binge drinking could be stress induced. Bandura (1969) provided an excellent review of other studies supporting a stress-reduction hypothesis.

A behavioral approach to alcoholism, which has been proposed by various investigators (Masserman & Yum, 1946; Conger, 1951; Bandura, 1969; Lundin, 1969) but never developed into a full treatment design, considers heavy drinking of alcoholic beverages as an alcoholic individual's predominant learned response to a stressful, anxiety-laden situation. The response of drinking is conceived as having been acquired because the problem drinker has been rewarded, consciously or not, for such drinking. Among the possible rewarding consequences which could result from heavy drinking in a stressful situation are:

1. Alcohol is an extremely effective sedative (Carpenter, 1957; Lienert & Traxel, 1959), and thus, by

This investigation was supported (in part) by Public Health Service Grant 1 RO 1 MH 16547-02 and California Department of Mental Hygiene Grant RP-69-11-15. The opinions or conclusions stated in this paper are those of the authors and are not to be construed as official or as necessarily reflecting the policy of the Department of Mental Hygiene.

The authors are considerably indebted to Halmuth H. Schaefer for assistance throughout all phases of the study and preparation of the manuscript and to Timothy Baker, David Bangsund, William Christelman, Kenneth C. Mills, Natalie Olsen, Robert Pilkington, Dee Schucker, and Donald Stern who constituted the research staff. Joseph V. Brady helped plan the study and Francis Tierney, Sebastian Casalaina, and the alcohol program staff of Patton State Hospital were instrumental in its accomplishment.

drinking, a person experiencing an aversive situation may significantly reduce the physiological components of that state. Once a drunken stupor is reached there is little doubt that a complete, although temporary, escape from the aversive situation has been attained.

2. Alcohol consumed in large quantities is physically debilitating. During a debilitated state the drinker can avoid participating in many situations which, for whatever reasons, he finds unpleasant. Knowledge of this means of avoidance could lead a person to initiate a binge. At the very least, if the person is made to go through the aversive situation, the sedative nature of intoxication would reduce the magnitude of the accompanying anxious state.
3. Alcohol intoxication is socially accepted as an excuse for engaging in certain otherwise inappropriate behaviors, such as extremes of flirtation, or extremes of aggression, which are generally considered socially unacceptable when engaged in by a sober individual, but are tolerated from a person who is drunk. Consequently, the opportunity to engage in these behaviors with minimal chastisement can act as a reinforcer for the drinking behavior.

While it is our contention that the alcoholic's primary use of alcohol is to escape from or avoid stressful or potentially stressful situations, other contingencies might also control the excessive drinking response to some extent. Cohen *et al.* (1971) have remarked that many powerful reinforcers, such as medical and psychiatric care, attention, money, welfare, rehabilitation programs, guidance, and counseling are: "... sometimes dispensed when the alcoholic is sober, but they are often dispensed during or following excessive drinking."

It deserves mention that not all experimental studies have supported the stress-reduction hypothesis. Nathan, Titler, Lowenstein, Solomon, and Rossi (1970) reported that, although alcoholic subjects said they drank to decrease anxiety and depression, when put to the test of actual intoxication they behaved as though their anxiety and depression had increased. Likewise, McNamee, Mello, and Mendelson (1968) found that 9 of 12 alcoholic subjects who became inebriated as part of an experiment experienced an increase in anxiety and depression after the first day or two of drinking. In each of these studies, however, the subjects were volunteers from correctional institutions who probably: (1) had lower pre-experimental levels of stress and anxiety than the typical nonincarcerated alcoholic who is about to begin a drinking binge, and (2) were aware that they would eventually (at the designation of the experimenters) have to "dry out" and return to institutional life. Given these conditions, one might expect an increase in anxiety above pre-experimental levels as drinking progressed.

TREATMENT GOALS

Among professionals in the field of alcoholism there is a predominant belief that excessive drinking of alcoholic beverages signifies a progressive disease which can be arrested, but is irreversible (Williams, 1948; Jellinek, 1960; Knott & Beard, 1966). Many have considered the basis of this view as axiomatic (e.g., Lemere, 1963; Thimann, 1963), but contradictory evidence is mounting. There is an ever-increasing amount of reports demonstrating that persons who were at one time unquestionably "alcoholic" have been able to acquire, often without therapeutic intervention other than detoxification, a pattern of social, normal, or controlled drinking (Lemere, 1953; Selzer & Holloway, 1957; Pfeffer & Berger, 1957; Davies, 1962; Mukasa, Ichihara, & Eto, 1964; Kendell, 1965; Bailey & Stewart, 1967; Mukasa & Arikawa, 1968; Reinert & Bowen, 1968; Anant, 1968; Quirk, 1968; Mills, Sobell, & Schaefer, 1971). Excellent reviews of this literature have been published by Pattison (1966) and Pattison, Headley, Gleser, and Gottschalk (1968). They, as well as Gerard, Saenger, and Wile (1962), also found no necessary association between abstinence and other criteria commonly accepted as indices of emotional adjustment. In short, while there is presently no evidence that controlled drinking by former alcoholics is impossible, there is extensive evidence to the contrary. Certainly the pattern of moderate drinking acquired by a former alcoholic is a special kind of drinking. Reinert and Bowen (1968) have suggested using the term "controlled drinker" to identify such persons. By their definition, the controlled drinker, unlike the normal or social drinker, "... must be on guard ... must choose carefully and even compulsively the time, the place, and the circumstances of drinking, and he must rigidly limit the amount he drinks" (p. 286).

Persons working in the field of alcoholism, however, have been slow to accept these repeated findings of successful drinking by former alcoholics. For instance, when Davies innocently reported some positive results in a 1962 follow-up study, the report elicited a deluge of negative comments (see *Quarterly Journal of Studies on Alcohol*, 1963). The basis for much of the concern seemed to be a fear that the report might somehow mislead alcoholics the world over into beginning their own form of therapy aimed at controlled drinking. What some of the commentators (e.g. Lemere, 1963; Bell, 1963) overlooked, however, is that such a treatment goal should be the result of a treatment program and not merely acquired as a result of the patient's own initiative.

As long as the objections of traditionalists to controlled drinking had been mentioned, the other side of the issue should also be explored. The question asked is how many persons consistently deny that they have a drinking problem until they have truly become chronic alcoholics—and how much is such a denial based upon a resistance to being condemned to abstinence for life? Others have pondered this question as well (Gerard *et al.*, 1962; Brunner-Orne, 1963; Pattison, 1966; Reinert, 1968).

Any effective form of therapy must consider the kinds of behavior which our society reinforces. If the goal of therapy is to be abstinence, then the patient must be prepared to identify with certain social groups (e.g. AA, certain religious groups, etc.) which specifically reinforce nondrinking. If a patient cannot, or chooses not to identify with social groups supportive of abstinence, then the constraint of nondrinking might actually be a stressor for that patient rather than a support. The majority of our society reinforces a pattern of moderate drinking. If controlled drinking is the treatment goal which is most practical and potentially beneficial for a given individual, it should be the one pursued.

The experiment reported in the remainder of this paper was designed in accordance with the preceding rationale. Treatment sessions dealt directly with the inappropriate behavior of excessive drinking and emphasized a patient's learning alternative, more appropriate responses to stimulus conditions which had previously functioned as setting events for his heavy drinking. The treatment took into account the learning history of each individual patient and was specifically tailored to meet each patient's needs.

METHOD

Subjects

Seventy male patients who had voluntarily admitted themselves to Patton State Hospital for treatment of alcoholism and volunteered to serve in research studies were used as subjects. All subjects were screened for health problems and psychosis by a thorough medical and psychiatric examination. The staff then interviewed each subject for 45 min to determine his desire for treatment and which of the two treatment goals offered was most appropriate: nondrinking or controlled drinking. Those subjects who could socially identify with AA, requested abstinence, and/or lacked outside support for controlled drinking were always assigned to nondrinking. Subjects who requested controlled drinking, had available significant outside social support for such behavior, and/or had successfully practiced social drinking at some time in the past were considered potential candidates for the controlled drinking goal. After a majority staff decision had determined a subject's treatment goal, the subject was then randomly assigned to either a control group receiving only the conventional hospital treatment (large therapy groups, AA meetings, drug, physio-, and industrial therapy), or an experimental group receiving 17 behavioral treatment sessions in addition to the conventional hospital treatment.

Statistics describing educational, demographic, and sociological characteristics of subjects in each of the four groups appear in Table 1. All subjects had experienced some withdrawal symptoms, damaged their physical health, finances, and social standing as a result of excessive drinking. Thus, all subjects met the criteria of Jellinek's (1960) Gamma alcoholics. There were no statistically significant differences between respective experimental and control groups, with the exception that nondrinker, experimental subjects had a significantly ($p < .05$) higher level of education than nondrinker, control subjects.

Facilities

The research ward at Patton State Hospital contained the central research facilities, a simulated bar and cocktail lounge, and a simulated home environment. The bar environment, which has been fully described elsewhere (Schaefer *et al.*, 1971b), was equipped with a television camera which could be remotely controlled from an adjacent room which contained videorecording apparatus.

The simulated home environment was located immediately adjacent to the bar and separated from it by heavy, floor-length draperies. It was carpeted and included a sofa, a love seat, a soft chair, two end tables with lamps, two coffee tables, a pole lamp, a television set, and a phonograph.

Operant conditioning equipment which independently controlled two shock generators (1 BRS Foringer, 1 Grason-Stadler) was located behind the bar and could be operated by hand-held push button switches. The same shock equipment could be used in the home environment by attaching longer cables to the electrodes and switches. A large variety of confiscated alcoholic beverages were supplied by the California State Alcoholic Beverage Control Board.

Procedure

The 17 experimental treatment sessions emphasized specifically defining prior setting events for heavy drinking, and training the subject in alternative, socially acceptable responses to those situations. The treatment was designed so that each subject's sessions could be individually tailored for specific setting events and alternative responses appropriate to his case. Stimulus control variables, or setting events, for drinking were defined as those specific factors which had either immediately preceded or accompanied the onset of heavy drinking in the past. Intervening variables such as "depression" were not considered as stimulus controls for drinking unless the various defining situations could be precisely specified. A subject was always asked to generate a universe of possible alternative responses to each setting event and then evaluate each alternative for its appropriateness (effective as compared to self-destructive consequences) for the situation. To discriminate effective from ineffective responses, situations were constructed to practice various alternative responses. For each subject a cumulative treatment file of all delineated stimulus

TABLE 1 Summary of Descriptive Statistics for Subjects in Four Experimental Conditions

	Experimental Conditions[a]			
Descriptive Variable	*CD-E*	*CD-C*	*ND-E*	*ND-C*
Age (years)				
Mean	40.30	41.25	40.40	43.27
SD	9.42	10.58	9.32	10.06
Education (years)				
Mean	12.60	12.45	13.03	11.27
SD	1.54	2.35	2.29	2.09
Drinking problem (years)				
Mean	9.70	8.65	11.33	11.86
SD	6.21	4.51	6.95	8.16
Alcohol-associated arrests (no.)				
Mean	6.25	5.70	8.85	9.86
SD	6.99	5.33	10.06	13.96
Prior hospitalization for alcoholism (no.)				
Mean	2.10	1.90	3.43	4.13
SD	2.83	1.29	4.97	2.83
Marital status				
Married	6	4	3	6
Single	4	5	3	2
Divorced, Separated	10	11	9	6
Widower	0	0	0	1
Religion				
Protestant	16	13	13	13
Catholic	2	5	1	1
L.D.S.	1	1	1	1
Agnostic	1	1	0	0
Occupation				
Blue collar	17	16	11	15
White collar	1	2	3	0
Retired	1	1	1	0
Student	1	1	0	0
Withdrawal symptoms				
Tremors, sweating	9	12	5	5
Convulsions, blackouts	4	4	3	2
Hallucinations, delirium tremens	7	4	7	8
N	20	20	15	15

[a]Experimental conditions were controlled drinker, experimental (CD-E), controlled drinker, control (CD-C), nondrinker, experimental (ND-E), and nondrinker, control (ND-C).

control variables and alternative responses was maintained.

In all except probe sessions (8, 12, and 16), inappropriate drinking behaviors (respective to treatment goal) were punished by electric shocks delivered on a variable ratio 2 (VR 2) avoidance schedule. An avoidance rather than escape schedule was used to increase resistance to extinction. A larger ratio schedule (e.g., VR 3, VR 10) was not used because it was suspected that the reinforcing effects of drinking might be sufficient to completely nullify the occasional receipt of shocks. Probe sessions during which drinks were available but shock contingencies absent made it possible to assess whether the drinking patterns demonstrated in shock sessions could be expected to generalize to situations not having immediate aversive consequences for inappropriate drinking.

The types of drinks available during sessions were: (1) mixed—1 oz liquor (43% alcohol content) with 2 oz mixer, (2) beer—12 oz (3–4% alcohol con-

TABLE 2 Characteristics of Experimental Sessions[a]

Session Number	*Type of Session*	*Shock Avoidance Contingencies*	*Max. Alcohol Available (oz)*[b]
1–2	Drunk, videotaped, 3 hr[c]	No	16
3	Education, 90 min	No	N.A.
4–5	Videotape replay, 90 min[d]	Yes	6
6	Failure experience, 90 min	Yes	6
7	Stimulus control, 90 min	Yes	6
8	Stimulus control, probe, 90 min	No	6
9–11	Stimulus control, 90 min	Yes	6
12	Stimulus control, probe, 90 min	No	6
13–15	Stimulus control, 90 min	Yes	6
16	Stimulus control, probe, videotaped, 90 min	No	6
17	Summary, videotape contrast, 90 min	N.A.	N.A.

[a]A more detailed description of experimental procedures is included in the expanded version of this manuscript, available from the authors upon request.
[b]An ounce was defined as 1 oz of 86-proof liquor or its equivalent in alcohol content.
[c]During these sessions only, subjects were run in pairs and allowed to consume up to 16 drinks during each session. Sessions were conducted in the experimental bar and were separated by 1 sober day. The final 90 min of each session were videotaped.
[d]Replay was of sessions 1 and 2, respectively. These sessions, as well as session 6, allowed an evaluation of each subject's responses to a novel stressful situation.

tent), (3) wine—2½ oz (20% alcohol content) or 4 oz (12% alcohol content), and (4) straight—1 oz liquor (43% alcohol content) served in three one third-oz portions to guard against taking advantage of the variable shock schedule.

When shock contingencies were in effect, nondrinker subjects occasioned a 1-sec shock (delivered on a VR 2 schedule) by ordering any drink. The drink was then served and subjects occasioned a continuous shock from the time they touched the glass until the time they released it (the drink could be consumed). Rules for controlled drinking were derived from actual data collected from social drinkers who had participated in experimental baseline drinking studies conducted in the simulated bar (Sobell, Schaefer, & Mills, 1972; Schaefer, Sobell, & Mills, 1971a). Controlled drinker subjects occasioned a 1-sec shock (delivered on a VR 2 schedule) for the following inappropriate drinking behaviors: (1) ordering a straight drink, (2) taking a sip larger than one sixth (mixed) or one twelfth (beer) of the drink's total volume (glasses were demarcated), (3) ordering a drink within 20 min of previously ordering a drink, or (4) ordering any more than three total drinks. After consuming three drinks within a session, controlled drinker subjects were placed on the same shock contingencies as nondrinker subjects.

Table 2 presents a description of session characteristics, and the following describes the experimental procedures used in more detail:

> *Sessions 1 and 2, drunk, videotaped.* Taking advantage of the sedative effects of alcohol, staff members probed each subject for stimulus controls for the drinking response, discussed fear-laden topics, and evaluated the subject's verbal and nonverbal reactions to potentially stressful situations. These sessions further served to demonstrate to each subject that he could become quite drunk and then sober up the next day without suffering from withdrawal symptoms or severe cravings for alcohol.

The majority of sessions 3 through 17 were conducted in either the home or bar environment, whichever most closely approximated the subject's usual drinking environment. In these sessions, subjects were run individually, with one staff member (determined on a rotating basis) assigned to each session.

> *Session 3, education.* The subject, irrespective of treatment goal, was instructed about: (1) when and why various shock contingencies would apply, (2) the occurrence of probe (no shock) days, (3) the treatment rationale—emphasizing that drinking is considered to be a learned behavior which occurs in certain stimulus situations and not in others (discriminated response) and is controlled by its consequences, and (4) a response repertoire for refusing alcoholic beverages—structured situations where subjects could practice resisting social pressures to drink were used. Additionally, controlled drinker subjects were trained in a response repertoire for mixed drinks, as a previous study (Sobell, Sobell, & Schaefer, 1971) had demonstrated that many Gamma alcoholics had a gross deficiency in familiarity with types of mixed drinks.

During sessions 4 through 16, data were recorded for the following quantifiable drinking behaviors: drinks ordered, infractions of controlled or nondrinking rules (shocks occasioned), shocks actually received, sips per drink, kinds of drinks ordered, and time (sec) between successively ordered drinks.

Sessions 4 and 5, videotape replay. Videotape self-confrontation of drunken behavior was used because it had been found to be quite stress inducing for sober alcoholics and had seemed to increase a subject's spoken motivation for changing his drinking behavior (Schaefer *et al.*, 1971b). More importantly, it served to demonstrate various behavioral deficiencies (e.g. lack of overt emotional expression) as well as various setting events to a subject.

Session 6, failure experience. Twenty minutes before the session a series of plausible but impossible to complete tests were administered to the subject who was then informed of his poor test performance. The therapy session, conducted by a staff member other than the person who administered the tests, concentrated on the way the subject had responded to failure experiences, past and present. All subjects were debriefed after the session.

Sessions 7 through 16, stimulus control. An emphasis was placed on: (1) elucidating stimulus controls for heavy drinking, (2) generating a universe of possibly effective alternative responses to those situations, (3) evaluating the probable consequences of exercising each response, and (4) practicing the most beneficial alternative responses under simulated conditions. Thirty minutes of session 16 were videotaped.

When a nondrinker subject ordered no drink for two consecutive sessions during sessions 4 through 16, a priming prompt of a free drink was offered at the start of the next session. If the subject consumed the free drink, any applicable shock contingencies were then reinstated. If he chose not to consume the drink, he had to pour it down the sink and this procedure continued at 15-min intervals for the entire session.

Session 17, summary, videotape contrast. Selected replays of drunken behavior which occurred during sessions 1 and 2 were contrasted with videotape of sober behavior during session 16. The subject's progress was discussed and he was presented with a wallet-sized research program card which included a list of *Do's* and *Do Not's* specific to his treatment. He was encouraged to extend the principles of self-behavioral analysis and exercising alternative responses to all phases of his life.

In almost all cases, subjects chose to discharge from the hospital within 2 weeks after session 17. An in-depth interview was conducted with each subject before discharge, and after discharge continuous phone and personal contact was maintained with all experimental and control subjects and their respective collateral sources. Formal follow-up intervals of 6 weeks, 6 months, and 1 year were scheduled. For each subject the following information was obtained over each follow-up interval:

1. Drinking disposition (1 oz defined as 1 oz of 86-proof liquor or its equivalent in alcohol content)—(a) drunk days defined as any days during which 10 or more oz were consumed or any days more than 2 consecutive days when between 7 and 9 oz were consumed, (b) controlled drinking days defined as any days during which 6 oz or less were consumed or any isolated 1- or 2-day sequence when between 7 and 9 oz were consumed, (c) abstinent days, and (d) abstinent days resulting from hospital or jail incarceration for alcohol-related incidents (all incarcerations were verified through the holding facility and by inspecting the subject's rap sheet)
2. Vocational status as to improved, same as, or worse than prior to treatment
3. Use or nonuse of therapeutic supports outside the hospital after treatment (e.g., AA, community counseling services, etc.)
4. Evaluation by a collateral of the subject's general adjustment to interpersonal relationships and stressful situations as compared to the year preceding his hospitalization (improved, same, or worse)

In all cases, both self-reports by the subject and collateral confirmation were sought in follow-up interviews.

RESULTS

Nondrinker Experimental Subjects

Nondrinker subjects who drank during treatment sessions 4–16 could minimize the number of electric shocks they received by ordering straight drinks (minimizing drink volume) and consuming those drinks in the smallest number of sips possible. The 11 subjects who ordered drinks during these sessions ordered a total of 59 drinks, the majority (74.57%) being straight drinks. No subject ordered drinks during more than six treatment sessions. Additionally, subjects consumed all but one of the 44 straight drinks ordered in the minimum number (three) of sips possible.

As a result of the VR 2 avoidance schedule, subjects received only 61 of the 120 total shocks occasioned. A shaping effect over sessions is evident in Figure 1 which presents the total number of drinks ordered as a function of treatment sessions. Some subjects apparently formed a discrimination between shock contingency sessions and probe (no shock) sessions, but all four subjects who ordered drinks during session 12 and one of the three subjects who ordered drinks during session 16 ordered only one or two of the six total drinks available without penalty.

Drinks consumed as priming prompts (see Method) are not included in the data. Priming prompt drinks were offered to 11 subjects during a total of 17 sessions, but were consumed in only

FIGURE 1 Total Number of Drinks Ordered per Session by Nondrinker Subjects (N = 15) during Experimental Treatment Sessions 4 through 16

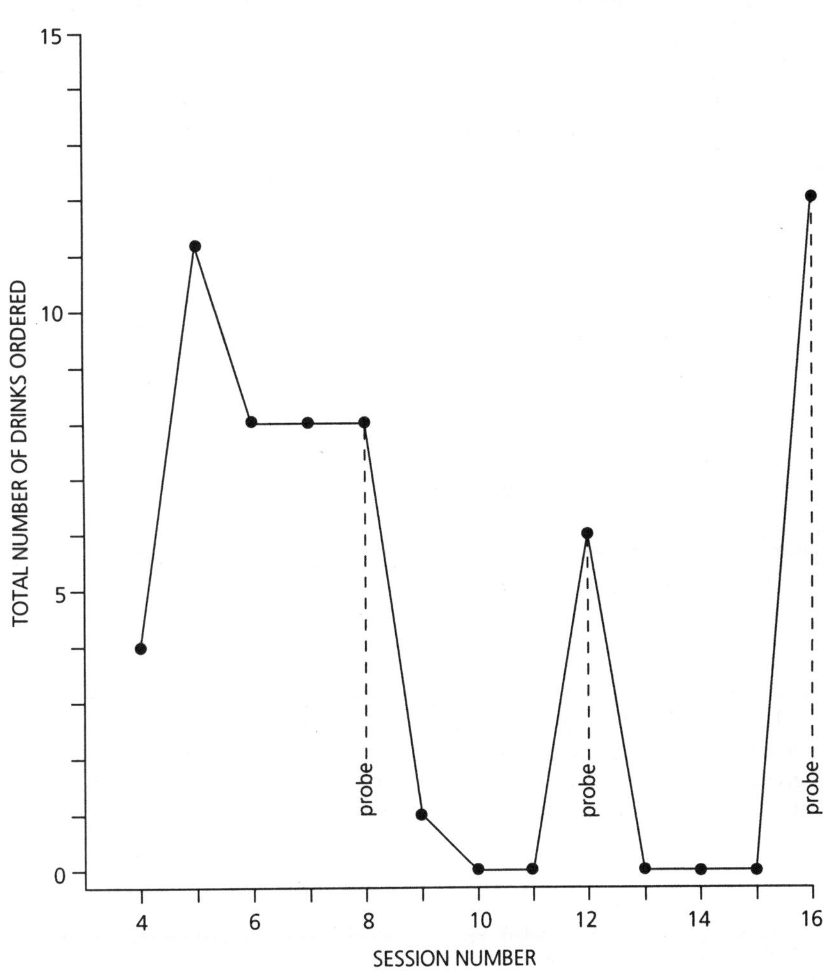

three cases. On each occasion when a priming prompt drink was consumed, the subject then proceeded to order and fully consume only one additional drink. Thus, there is no evidence that priming prompts were effective in producing increased drinking.

Controlled Drinker Experimental Subjects

All 20 controlled drinker experimental subjects ordered drinks at some time during sessions 4–16 with a mean of 27.80 drinks ordered per subject and a range from 9 to 43. Like the nondrinker subjects, controlled drinker subjects practiced drinking patterns which somewhat minimized the number of shocks they received. For instance, controlled drinker subjects never ordered straight drinks during any treatment session, and of the 556 total drinks ordered, 80.75% were mixed drinks, 13.48% were beer, and 6.57% were wine. During only 14 total sessions did any subject order more than three drinks, with 11 of these occasions occurring on probe days and the remainder during session 6. During the 248 total sessions where drinks were ordered, the mean number of drinks ordered was 2.24 (SD = 0.92).

Table 3 displays the frequency with which drinking behaviors defined as inappropriate occurred during each treatment session and the number of subjects who engaged in those behaviors. Subjects received 30 total electric shocks for the total of 63 inappropriate behaviors in which they engaged. Fourteen subjects received two or fewer total

TABLE 3 Number of Inappropriate Drinking Behaviors Emitted by Controlled Drinker Experimental Subjects during Treatment Sessions. Figures in parentheses indicate the number of subjects who emitted the inappropriate behavior at least one time during that session.

	Inappropriate Behavior[a]			
Session Number	*Ordering < 20 Min Apart*	*Ordering > Three Drinks*	*Sips > 1/6 of Drink Volume*	*Total Inappropriate Drinking Behaviors*
4	0	0	3(3)	3(3)
5	1(1)	0	0	1(1)
6	2(2)	2(1)	4(2)	8(3)
7	1(1)	0	1(1)	2(1)
8–Pr[b]	3(3)	4(3)	8(4)[c]	15(6)
9	0	0	0	0
10	1(1)	1(1)	0	2(1)
11	2(2)	1(1)	1(1)	4(3)
12–Pr[b]	8(4)	8(4)	9(4)[c]	25(7)
13	1(1)	0	0	1(1)
14	1(1)	0	0	1(1)
15	0	0	0	0
16–Pr[b]	8(6)	5(4)	3(2)[c]	16(6)

[a]Each inappropriate drinking behavior which occurred was counted separately.
[b]Pr indicates probe session, no shock contingencies in effect.
[c]Known minimum value. Total number of occasions when a drink was consumed in fewer than six sips.

shocks throughout the entire experiment, and the greatest number of shocks received by any single subject was six. Seven subjects never emitted an inappropriate drinking behavior. While receipt of electric shocks obviously was not important in controlling the subject's drinking behaviors, there was evidence that the threat of shocks effectively suppressed inappropriate drinking behaviors. The number of inappropriate drinking behaviors emitted during probe sessions ($\overline{X} = 18.67$) was considerably greater than the number of those behaviors emitted during other treatment sessions ($\overline{X} = 2.20$). This difference is statistically significant ($t(11) = 7.84, p < .01$). As in the case of the nondrinker subjects, this difference could not be attributed to any particular small group of subjects.

With the exception of subjects learning to drink with smaller sips, little or no shaping of drinking behavior was evident over sessions. This finding might be interpreted as reflecting a practice effect resulting from the instructions given subjects during session 3. The fact that no straight drink was ordered even during probe sessions also suggests that the subjects sincerely practiced controlled drinking patterns. This interpretation is additionally supported by Figure 2 which presents the mean number of ounces of 86-proof alcohol or equivalent which were actually consumed during each treatment session by those subjects who ordered drinks. With the exception of probe sessions, the initial drinking pattern was one of exaggerated sipping (more than six sips per drink) with sip size then increasing to fulfill the minimum requirements necessary to avoid shocks.

What Staff Members Learned

To the authors' knowledge, there is no reported precedent for the theoretical foundation of this experiment being as systematically applied to behavior therapy talk sessions as is here reported. This experiment, therefore, constituted a major learning experience for all the staff members involved. The staff consisted of permanent, paid employees who were either upper division students at a local university, or research assistants who had already obtained their B.A. in psychology. Staff learning is documented in Figure 3. A major stimulus control variable or alternative response was defined as meeting the criteria of specificity discussed in the Method section of this paper, as compared to vague descriptive terminology.

Follow-Up Results

All 70 of the subjects had been discharged from the hospital for at least 6 weeks prior to the preparation of this report, and 48 subjects had been discharged for longer than 6 months. Table 4 shows the number of subjects from each experimental condition who were due for follow-up, the percentage of subjects located, and the percentage of

FIGURE 2 Mean Number of Ounces of 86-Proof Alcohol (or the Equivalent in Alcohol Content) Consumed per Session by Controlled Drinker Subjects Who Ordered Drinks during Experimental Treatment Sessions 4 through 16. Numbers in parentheses indicate the number of subjects who ordered drinks during each session.

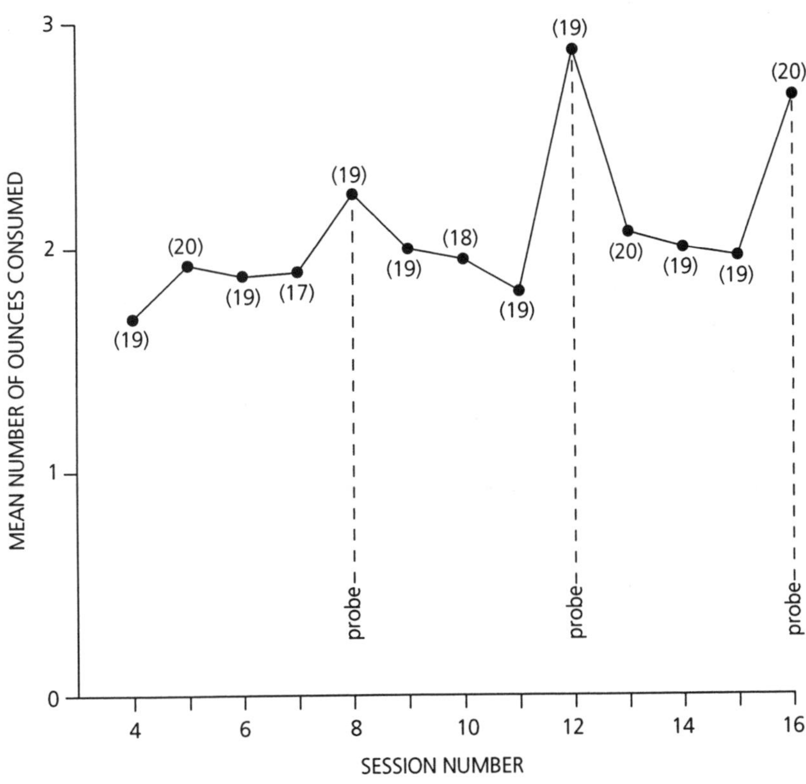

cases in which one or more collateral sources were interviewed.

The use of controlled drinking as a treatment goal made it necessary to obtain estimates of daily alcohol consumption. The criteria for different drinking dispositions have already been discussed (see Method). In most cases, there was little difficulty in obtaining reliable data, although the accuracy of reports based on memory is, of course, open to some question. However, reports by collaterals typically agreed well with reports by subjects. When there was reason to question the accuracy of a report, the data recorded were secured from the source who could best present evidence to substantiate the data. This method of follow-up data collection was selected as being more representative of behavior occurring over the entire follow-up interval than more traditional probe-day-status techniques.

Table 5 presents the drinking dispositions of subjects during a majority of the 6-week and 6-month follow-up intervals. Drinking dispositions were grouped according to whether the subject was functioning well (abstinent or controlled drinking days) or not functioning well (drunk or incarcerated, alcohol-related days). The one subject in the category of deceased, alcohol, or drug related will be discussed later in this paper.

Fisher-Yates Exact Probability Tests (McNemar, 1962) were calculated comparing respective experimental and control groups by drinking dispositions (functioning well, not functioning well) at the two follow-up intervals. Differences between the controlled drinker experimental and control subjects were found to be statistically significant ($p < .05$) for each follow-up interval. At the time of this report, only 48 of the 70 total subjects were due for 6-month follow-up. However, continuing follow-up suggests that complete 6-month data will substantiate the data in Table 5. Differences between the nondrinker experimental and control subjects at the 6-week interval are not statistically significant, although in the predicted direction. At 6 months, the difference

FIGURE 3 Mean Number of Major Stimulus Control Variables and Alternative Responses Recorded by Staff Members in Treatment Notes for Controlled Drinker Subjects ($N = 20$) and Nondrinker Subjects ($N = 15$) as a Function of Temporally Consecutive Groups of Five Subjects Each

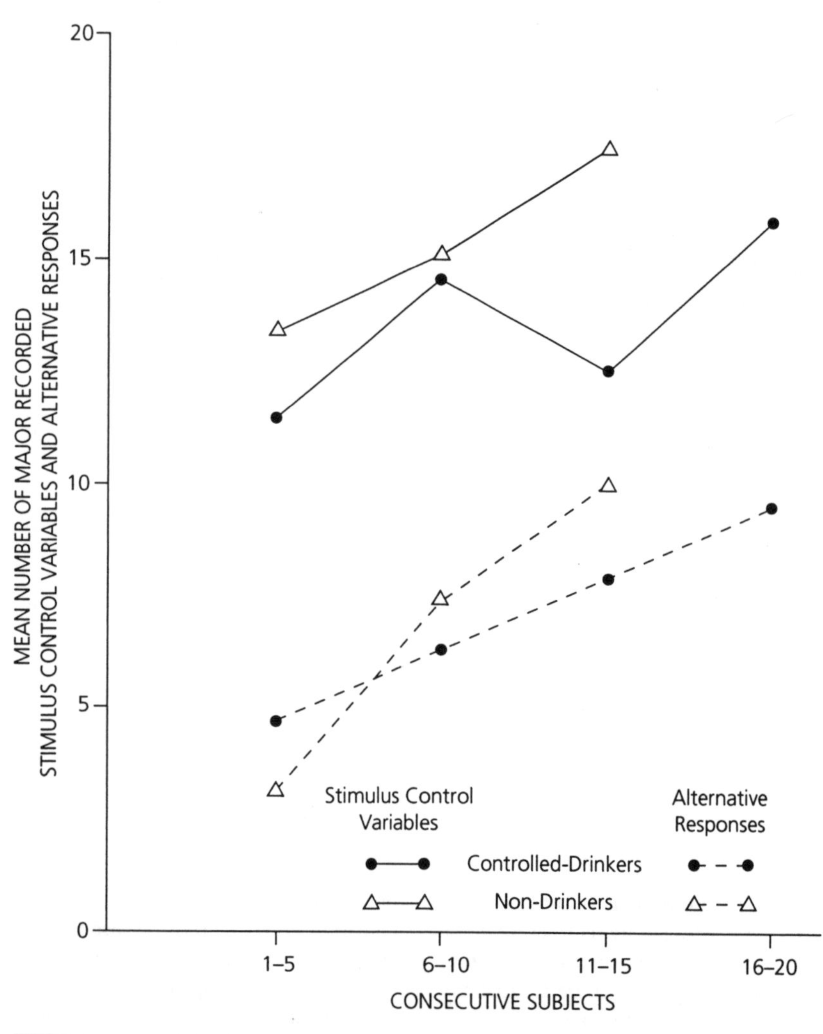

between these groups is significant ($p < .05$). For this computation, the one subject who died in an automobile accident was included as not functioning well. Although this subject had remained abstinent until the time of his death (about 2 months after discharge), an autopsy found a heavy incidence (0.4 mgm) of barbiturates in his blood. Once again, continuing follow-up suggests that the 6-month differences between groups will still be significant when data are complete.

Table 6, which presents the mean percentage of days spent in each drinking disposition by subjects from different experimental conditions for 6-week and 6-month follow-up periods, supports the data of Table 5. It is interesting that the majority of incarcerations of experimental subjects were in hospitals, while control subjects were predominantly incarcerated in jails. This difference might have been the result of voluntary hospitalizations among the experimental subjects, either to curb the start of a binge or to avoid starting

TABLE 4 Summary of the Number of Subjects Due for Follow-Up at 6-Week and 6-Month Intervals, Percentage of Subjects Found, and Percentage of Cases in Which One or More Collateral Sources Were Interviewed

Experimental Condition[a]	*N Due for Follow-Up at This Time*	*Found (%)*	*One or More Collateral Sources Interviewed (%)*
Six-week follow-up			
CD-E	20	100	90.0
CD-C	20	100	90.0
ND-E	15	100	93.4
ND-C	15	100	93.4
Total	70	100	92.9
Six-month follow-up			
CD-E	18	100	94.4
CD-C	10	100	80.0
ND-E	8	100	87.5
ND-C	12	100	100.0
Total	48	100	91.6

[a]Experimental conditions were controlled drinker, experimental (CD-E), controlled drinker, control (CD-C), nondrinker, experimental (ND-E), and nondrinker, control (ND-C).

drinking at all. This particular behavior had frequently been discussed during sessions as an alternative favorable to starting or continuing to drink.

Three other indices of behavior change were obtained for all subjects in addition to drinking status. The measures of vocational status, use of therapeutic supports, and evaluation of subjects' general functioning by collateral sources have already been described (see Method). Table 7 presents 6-week and 6-month adjunctive measure follow-up data for subjects from each treatment group. As is evident in Table 7, these data support those reported earlier for drinking disposition. Continuing follow-up indicates that the figures reported in Table 7 will not change substantially when 6-month follow-up has been completed.

DISCUSSION

The results of the present study can be succinctly summarized: Male Gamma alcoholics treated by the method of

TABLE 5 Drinking Disposition during Majority of Follow-Up Interval for Subjects from Each Experimental Condition

Drinking Disposition	*Experimental Condition*[a]			
	CD-E	*CD-C*	*ND-E*	*ND-C*
Six-week follow-up				
Controlled drinking or abstinent, not incarcerated (%)	85.5	45.0	73.4	53.3
Drunk or incarcerated, alcohol-related (%)	15.0	55.0	26.6	46.7
Six-month follow-up[b]				
Controlled drinking or abstinent, not incarcerated (%)	77.8	30.0	75.0	16.7
Drunk or incarcerated, alcohol-related (%)	22.2	70.0	25.0	75.0
Deceased, alcohol or drug related (%)	0.0	0.0	0.0	8.3

[a]Experimental conditions were controlled drinker, experimental (CD-E), controlled drinker, control (CD-C), nondrinker, experimental (ND-E), and nondrinker, control (ND-C).
[b]Not all subjects were due for 6-month follow-up. Data are presented for 18 CD-E, 10 CD-C, 8 ND-E, and 12 ND-C subjects.

TABLE 6 Mean Percentage of Days Spent in Different Drinking Dispositions by Subjects in Four Experimental Groups for 6-Week and 6-Month Follow-Up Intervals

Drinking Disposition	*Experimental Condition*[a]			
	CD-E	*CD-C*	*ND-E*	*ND-C*
Six-week follow-up				
Controlled drinking[b]	41.80	10.70	7.20	12.93
Abstinent, not incarcerated	30.95	39.32	60.33	42.13
Drunk	17.55	42.70	23.20	41.60
Incarcerated, alcohol-related				
Hospital	9.15	2.00	6.94	3.20
Jail	0.55	5.35	2.33	0.14
Total	100.00	100.00	100.00	100.00
Six-month follow-up[c]				
Controlled drinking	27.33	9.10	2.87	14.54
Abstinent, not incarcerated	37.89	29.40	62.63	16.55[d]
Drunk	20.33	50.50	19.38	40.91
Incarcerated, alcohol-related				
Hospital	12.12	4.10	12.25	8.09
Jail	2.33	6.90	2.87	19.91
Total	100.00	100.00	100.00	100.00

[a]Experimental conditions were controlled drinker, experimental (CD-E), controlled drinker, control (CD-C), nondrinker, experimental (ND-E), and nondrinker, control (ND-C).

[b]Thirteen of the CD-E subjects successfully practiced substantial controlled drinking, eight of them doing so for an average of more than 50% of all days since discharge, and the remaining five to a lesser extent (an average of about 30% of all days since discharge). One subject in each of the other three groups also successfully practiced substantial controlled drinking. The ND-E subject doing so was not yet due for 6-month follow-up. A more detailed description of the incidence of controlled drinking among subjects is included in the expanded version of this manuscript which is available from the authors upon request.

[c]Not all subjects were due for 6-month follow-up. Data are presented for 18 CD-E, 10 CD-C, 8 ND-E, and 11 ND-C subjects. The one ND-C subject who died was not included in this presentation.

[d]Abstinent, not incarcerated days reported for ND-C subjects at 6 months include 26 days when one subject was not drinking but used other drugs heavily.

individualized behavior therapy described in this paper were found to function significantly better after discharge than respective control subjects treated by conventional techniques. Differences between experimental and control subjects were found not only for drinking behaviors, but for other adjunctive measures of functioning as well. Moreover, subjects who clearly met the criteria required by most experts for classification as "alcoholics" were able to acquire and maintain patterns of controlled drinking. These findings directly contradict the concept of irreversibility of alcoholic drinking which, lacking evidence, is but a *post hoc* tautology of little descriptive or predictive value.

A treatment goal of controlled drinking is uncommon and creates certain problems of data evaluation. The criteria used to distinguish controlled drinking days from drunk days were derived from data collected on actual social drinkers who had participated in baseline drinking behavior studies and, thus, were not completely arbitrary. The baseline data, however, were obtained from single drinking sessions. If a longitudinal baseline study were conducted, normal drinking patterns would probably be found to consist of a major proportion of abstinent days, a certain proportion of controlled drinking days, and a small proportion of drunk days. Thus, any appraisal of how well the controlled drinking patterns acquired by some of the subjects in this experiment approximated normal drinking behaviors must allow for a small proportion of drunk days. Furthermore, the extent of drunkenness which is typical among normal drinkers is probably greatly dependent upon socio-economic status.

At times, many of the controlled drinker experimental subjects who were able to practice controlled drinking successfully after discharge from the hospital placed themselves on extended periods of abstinence. However, this self-imposed abstinence was not maintained by a fear of the supposedly unavoidable consequences of drinking. Instead, subjects reported they were abstinent either because drinking now served no useful purpose, or because

TABLE 7 Adjunctive Follow-Up Measures for Subjects in Four Experimental Conditions

Adjunctive Measure[a]	*Experimental Condition*[b]			
	CD-E	*CD-C*	*ND-E*	*ND-C*
Six-week follow-up				
Vocational status				
Improved (%)	20.0	20.0	33.3	33.3
Same (%)	80.0	75.0	60.0	53.3
Worse (%)	0.0	5.0	6.7	13.4
Use of therapeutic supports				
Yes (%)	35.0	20.0	60.0	33.3
No (%)	65.0	80.0	40.0	66.7
Evaluation of general adjustment by collaterals				
Improved (%)	80.0	30.0	73.3	46.7
Same (%)	20.0	55.0	20.0	53.3
Worse (%)	0.0	15.0	6.7	0.0
Six-month follow-up[c]				
Vocational status				
Improved (%)	55.6	20.0	62.5	9.1
Same (%)	44.4	70.0	37.5	72.7
Worse (%)	0.0	10.0	0.0	9.1
Use of therapeutic supports				
Yes (%)	66.7	10.0	87.5	18.2
No (%)	33.3	90.0	12.5	81.8
Evaluation of general adjustment by collaterals				
Improved (%)	88.9	30.0	75.0	18.2
Same (%)	11.0	60.0	25.0	72.7
Worse (%)	0.0	10.0	0.0	9.1

[a]See text for fuller explanation of adjunctive measures used.
[b]Experimental conditions were controlled drinker, experimental (CD-E), controlled drinker, control (CD-C), nondrinker, experimental (ND-E), and nondrinker, control (ND-C).
[c]Not all subjects were due for 6-month follow-up. Data are presented for 18 CD-E, 10 CD-C, 8 ND-E, and 11 ND-C subjects. The one ND-C subject who died was not included in this presentation.

they were dealing with stress-inducing situations and believed drinking might interfere with their effective handling of those problems. For instance, in all cases the extended periods of abstinence were occasionally interrupted by one or two days of controlled drinking. It is reasonable to suppose that the degree of self-respect associated with this sort of abstinence is much greater than that accompanying a period of abstinence which is maintained by fear, and this might help the individual to deal better with problem situations.

While reports of successful controlled drinking by a small proportion of control subjects may surprise some readers, as substantiated by numerous studies cited earlier in this paper such findings are not at all unusual. No doubt, the nature of the follow-up results one obtains are in large part a function of the measures used. Thus, if a category of controlled drinking is not included in a follow-up scale, an acquiescent subject may soon realize that this is not an expected behavior for an alcoholic and fail to report incidents which have occurred.

In many cases, an insistence upon abstinence as the only possible treatment goal for alcoholics may even be unrealistic or harmful. For instance, consider a heavy drinker who has greatly identified with social groups whose members are mostly normal drinkers. Such a person may well decide to continue drinking until he is physically debilitated, rather than risking the loss of most of his friends by being abstinent. The issue here is not the mortality of such social consequences, but their reality. If, by definition, an alcoholic may never drink in a fashion even approximating normal drinking and must always be "different" from most other individuals, then abstinence will not make an alcoholic a functioning member of society *per se*, but only a member of a special society—a subculture which specifically reinforces nondrinking. If faced with this choice, many individuals may well decide to continue drinking rather than change their social identification.

The same is true for the problem drinker, as traditional beliefs about alcoholism leave such individuals little to gain from curtailing their drinking, and, in fact, may provide an incentive for them to repeatedly attempt to prove that they are not "alcoholics." One would expect problem drinkers to find the controlled drinker treatment described in this report to be both appealing and acceptable.

The effects of certain of the various treatment procedures used in this study have already been discussed to some extent. However, stimulus control sessions constituted the bulk of the experimental treatment. It became rapidly apparent in conducting follow-up that, for some subjects, the effects of stimulus control sessions had been much more than learning how to handle specific situations. In particular, subjects who were found to be functioning well after discharge seemed to have experienced a more general form of learning sometimes called rule learning, or learning to learn. Typically, the successful subject could apply what he had learned to novel situations. For example, approximately 1 month subsequent to discharge, nondrinker experimental subject J. A. was able to analyze an experienced desire to drink as resulting form the fact that his brother was living in his house, free-loading off of him, and attempting to seduce his wife. J. A. then generated a number of possible responses to this situation, including migrating to Chicago. After analyzing the various alternatives in terms of long-range consequences, he decided to confront his brother and demand that he move out of the house. To J. A.'s amazement, his brother did move out, and J. A.'s marital relationship improved considerably thereafter.

While the contribution of each component of the treatment procedure used must be evaluated experimentally, it is our contention that stimulus control sessions not only constituted the bulk of the treatment sessions, but were primarily responsible for the behavior changes which later occurred. In a refined treatment, it would seem logical to seek as a desired outcome the kind of rule learning which has just been described. Additionally, it would be desirable to conduct at least part of the treatment on an outpatient basis where the patient could deal with situations which were real, rather than simulated, setting events for drinking. If such a treatment approach continues to be successful as applied to drinking problems, it is possible that a modified version of the same treatment could be used for various of the neuroses, especially those which could be analyzed as involving escape and avoidance responses.

The generality of these results remains to be evaluated for other subject populations such as females and subjects from other types of socioeconomic backgrounds. The subjects who served in this study—male, voluntary Gamma alcoholic patients in a state hospital—may have been more deficient in a knowledge of appropriate alternative responses to setting events for drinking than subjects with a higher education or income. It is reasonable to expect that working with middle and upper class individuals will require dealing with different and perhaps more sophisticated alternative responses.

The findings of the present study are indeed highly encouraging, but only on the basis of continued investigation and outcome studies can one expect to develop an effective and efficient short-term treatment for alcoholism. The scientific method requires that statements of opinion, such as the supposed irreversibility of alcoholism, be evaluated by experimental test if at all possible. One such evaluative experiment is reported in this paper and clearly establishes that some alcoholic individuals can acquire and maintain controlled drinking patterns. Whether those patterns will persist over longer follow-up intervals can be determined only by continued follow-up.

REFERENCES

Anant, S. S. Former alcoholics and social drinking: An unexpected finding. *The Canadian Psychologist*, 1968, **9**, 35.

Bailey, M. B., & Stewart, J. Normal drinking by persons reporting previous problem drinking. *Quarterly Journal of Studies on Alcohol*, 1967, **28**, 305–315.

Bandura, A. *Principles of behavior modification*. New York: Holt, Rinehart & Winston, 1969.

Bell, R. G. Comment on "Normal drinking in recovered alcohol addicts." *Quarterly Journal of Studies on Alcohol*, 1963, **24**, 321–322.

Brunner-Orne, M. Comment on "Normal drinking in recovered alcohol addicts." *Quarterly Journal of Studies on Alcohol*, 1963, **24**, 730–733.

Carpenter, J. A. Effects of alcoholic beverages on skin conductance: An exploratory study. *Quarterly Journal of Studies on Alcohol*, 1957, **18**, 1–18.

Cicero, T. J., Myers, R. D., & Black, W. C. Increase in volitional ethanol consumption following interference with a learned avoidance response. *Physiology and Behavior*, 1968, **3**, 657–669.

Clark, R., & Polish, E. Avoidance conditioning and alcohol consumption in rhesus monkeys. *Science*, 1960, **132**, 223–224.

Cohen, M., Liebson, I., & Faillace, L. The modification of drinking of chronic alcoholics. In N. K. Mello & J. H. Mendelson (Eds.), *Recent advances in studies on alcoholism*. Washington, D. C.: U. S. Government Printing Office, 1971, pp. 745–766.

Conger, J. J. The effects of alcohol on conflict behavior in the albino rat. *Quarterly Journal of Studies on Alcohol*, 1951, **12**, 1–29.

Davies, D. L. Normal drinking in recovered alcohol addicts. *Quarterly Journal of Studies on Alcohol*, 1962, **23**, 94–104.

Gerard, D. L., Saenger, G., & Wile, R. The abstinent alcoholic. *Archives of General Psychiatry*, 1962, **6**, 99–111.

Hershenson, D. B. Stress-induced use of alcohol by problem drinkers as a function of their sense of identity. *Quarterly Journal of Studies on Alcohol*, 1965, **26**, 213–222.

Jellinek, E. M. The disease concept of alcoholism. New Haven: Hillhouse Press, 1960.

Kendell, R. E. Normal drinking by former alcohol addicts. *Quarterly Journal of Studies on Alcohol*, 1965, **26**, 247–257.

Knott, D. H., & Beard, J. D. The disease concept of alcoholism. Paper presented at the 115th Annual Meeting of the American Medical Association, Chicago, 1966.

Lemere, F. What happens to alcoholics. *American Journal of Psychiatry*, 1953, **109**, 674–676.

Lemere, F. Comment on "Normal drinking in recovered alcohol addicts." *Quarterly Journal of Studies on Alcohol*, 1963, **24**, 727–728.

Lienert, G. A., & Traxel, W. The effects of meprobamate and alcohol on galvanic skin response. *Journal of Psychology*, 1959, **48**, 329–334.

Lundin, R. W. *Personality: A behavioral analysis*. London: MacMillan Company, 1969.

Masserman, J. H., & Yum, K. S. An analysis of the influence of alcohol on experimental neuroses in cats. *Psychosomatic Medicine*, 1946, **8**, 36–52.

McNamee, H. B., Mello, N. K., & Mendelson, J. H. Experimental analysis of drinking patterns of alcoholics: concurrent psychiatric observations. *American Journal of Psychiatry*, 1968, **124**, 81–87.

McNemar, Q. *Psychological statistics*. New York: John Wiley & Sons, Inc. 1962.

Mills, K. C., Sobell, M. B., & Schaefer, H. H. Training social drinking as an alternative to abstinence for alcoholics. *Behavior Therapy*, 1971, **2**, 18–27.

Mukasa, H., & Arikawa, K. A new double medication method for the treatment of alcoholism using the drug cyanamide. *The Kurume Medical Journal*, 1968, **15**, 137–143.

Mukasa, H., Ichihara, & Eto, A. A new treatment of alcoholism with cyanamide (H_2NCN), *The Kurume Medical Journal*, 1964, **11**, 96–101.

Nathan, P. E., Titler, N. A., Lowenstein, L. M., Solomon, P., & Rossi, A. M. Behavioral analysis of chronic alcoholism. *Archives of General Psychiatry*, 1970, **22**, 419–430.

Pattison, E. M. A critique of alcoholism treatment concepts with special reference to abstinence. *Quarterly Journal of Studies on Alcohol*, 1966, **27**, 49–71.

Pattison, E. M., Headley, E. B., Gleser, G. C., & Gottschalk, L. A. Abstinence and normal drinking: An assessment of changes in drinking patterns in alcoholics after treatment. *Quarterly Journal of Studies on Alcohol*, 1968, **29**, 610–633.

Pfeffer, A. Z., & Berger, S. A follow-up study of treated alcoholics. *Quarterly Journal of Studies on Alcohol*, 1957, **18**, 624–648.

Quirk, D. A. Former alcoholics and social drinking: an additional observation. *The Canadian Psychologist*, 1968, **9**, 498–499.

Rachman, S., & Teasdale, J. *Aversion therapy and behavior disorders: An analysis*. Florida: University of Miami Press, 1969.

Reinert, R. E. The concept of alcoholism as a disease. *Bulletin of the Menninger Clinic*, 1968, **32**, 24–25.

Schaefer, H. H., Sobell, M. B., & Mills, K. C. Baseline drinking behaviors in alcoholics and social drinkers: Kinds of drinks and sip magnitude. *Behaviour Research and Therapy*, 1971a, **9**, 23–27.

Schaefer, H. H., Sobell, M. B., & Mills, K. C. Some sobering data on the use of self-confrontation with alcoholics. *Behavior Therapy*, 1971b, **2**, 28–39.

Selzer, M. L., & Holloway, W. H. A follow-up of alcoholics committed to a state hospital. *Quarterly Journal of Studies on Alcohol*, 1957, **18**, 98–120.

Sobell, M. B., Schaefer, H. H. & Mills, K. C. Differences in baseline drinking behaviors between alcoholics and normal drinkers. *Behaviour Research and Therapy*, 1972, **10**, 257–268.

Sobell, L. C., Sobell, M. B., Schafer, H. H. Alcoholics name fewer mixed drinks than social drinkers. *Psychological Reports*, 1971, **28**, 493–494.

Thimann, J. Comment on "Normal drinking in recovered alcohol addicts." *Quarterly Journal of Studies on Alcohol*, 1963, **24**, 324–325.

von Wright, J. M., Pekanmäki, L., & Malin, S. Effects of conflict and stress on alcohol intake in rats. *Quarterly Journal of Studies on Alcohol*, 1971, **32**, 420–433.

Williams, R. J. Alcoholics and metabolism. *Scientific American*, 1948, **179**, 50–53.

MARY L. PENDERY, IRVING M. MALTZMAN, & L. JOLYON WEST

Controlled drinking by alcoholics? New findings and a reevaluation of a major affirmative study

Conventional wisdom in the health professions has long held that persons who have become physically dependent on alcohol must be advised to abstain completely. In 1962, Davies sparked debate by reporting that 7 of 93 alcoholic patients were found on long-term follow-up to be able to drink moderately (*1*). Since then, the controversy has been intensified by conclusions of other investigators that some alcoholics can safely resume social, moderate, or controlled drinking as an alternative to abstinence (*2, 3*).

In particular, success has been reported by Sobell and Sobell (3–7) with a selected group of *gamma* alcoholics who were trained to practice controlled drinking as part of an experimental treatment program conducted at Patton State Hospital, in California, in 1970 and 1971. This group was reported to have functioned significantly better throughout a 2-year follow-up period than a control group that had been treated with the traditional goal of abstinence (*7*, p. 198). An additional third year of follow-up by Caddy *et al.* (8) confirmed the Sobells' conclusions.

Gamma alcoholism, as defined by Jellinek, is characterized by physical dependence with withdrawal symptoms and loss of control (9). Of all forms of alcohol problems, it produces the greatest damage. A new and effective treatment would accordingly have great medical and social value and might also call into question basic concepts regarding the nature of alcoholism.

The Sobells' findings have been published in a series of articles and books (*3–7, 10–13*) and are widely quoted (*14–16*). The study was welcomed as a breakthrough, particularly among behavioral and social scientists (*16*), and it seemed to offer a major advance over more traditional approaches that emphasized abstinence.

We have completed an independent clinical follow-up of the Sobells' subjects with the cooperation of Patton State Hospital. Our purpose was to evaluate treatment outcomes and to assess short- and long-term risks and benefits associated with the experimental controlled drinking treatment. Our findings differ greatly from those of the Sobells and of Caddy *et al.* (*8*).

The Sobells' subjects were 40 male alcoholic inpatients at Patton State Hospital (*17*)—all characterized as *gamma* alcoholics—"who requested controlled drinking, had available significant outside support for such behavior, and/or had successfully practiced social drinking at some time in the past" (*5*, p. 54); they were selected by staff decision, on the basis of history and interview criteria (*18*), as appropriate for the controlled drinking goal. The Sobells reported that 20 of these subjects were randomly assigned to an experimental group in which they received behavioral treatment designed to enable them to practice controlled drinking after discharge [controlled drinker-experimental (CD-E) group.] (In this report we refer to these as controlled drinking subjects.) The other 20 were assigned to a control group receiving conventional treatment designed to promote total abstinence after discharge [controlled drinker-control (CD-C)]. (We refer to these as the abstinence subjects.) The Sobells' study compared treatment outcomes of these two groups after discharge.

Controlled drinking subjects received 17 individualized behavior therapy sessions in a simulated bar at the hospital. In the first two sessions, their drunken behavior was videotaped as they were consuming as much as 16 ounces of 86 proof liquor (or its equivalent). The Sobells stated that these sessions further "served to demonstrate to each subject that he could in fact, become quite drunk and then sober up on the next day without suffering from withdrawal symptoms or severe cravings for more alcohol. This information was communicated to the subject in session 3 when the 'myth of one drink' was discussed" (*3*, p. 92;19). Session 3 also included "a 'mini-drink' procedure, whereby subjects actually sampled small amounts (½ oz) of various types of mixed drinks," based on the assumption

SOURCE: *Science*, *217*, pp. 169–175, July 1982.

FIGURE 1 [Simulation] of One of the Wallet-Sized Cards (Name Deleted) Given to All Controlled Drinking Subjects When They Were Discharged from the Research Project. The back of the card (right) contains individualized drinking instructions. This card was given to subject CD-E 3.

PATTON STATE HOSPITAL **ALCOHOLISM RESEARCH PROGRAM** has completed the research program being trained as a SOCIAL DRINKER. A social drinker drinks mixed drinks, sips these drinks, paces these drinks, (about every 20 minutes) and sets himself a moderate cutoff point. Mark B. Sobell Mark B. Sobell, M.A. Alcoholism Project Director	DO NOT DRINK: By gulping; straight vodka with any kind of chaser; in morning or afternoon; when alone or bored; not working consistently; when thinking of past; DO DRINK: Vodka & 7, or Tom Collins (tall); or beer; after 6:00 p.m.; with friends; when relaxed and comfortable with self.

that alcoholics have a "gross deficiency in familiarity with mixed [as opposed to straight] drinks" (*3*, pp. 92–93). Sessions 4 through 16 included ten aversion conditioning sessions with electric shock, interspersed with three probe (no shock) sessions. Subjects were shocked for "inappropriate drinking behaviors" such as ordering a straight drink, drinking more than a prescribed amount in a single sip, or ordering drinks too frequently (*5*, p. 56). Sessions 4 and 5 also had videotape replays to confront the subjects with their own drunken behavior. Session 6 was preceded by a simulated failure experience and focused on subjects' past and present responses to such experiences. Sessions 7 through 16 also provided training in problem-solving, which emphasized "(1) elucidating stimulus controls for heavy drinking, (2) generating a universe of possibly effective alternative responses to those situations, (3) evaluating the probable consequences of exercising each response, and (4) practicing the most beneficial alternative responses under simulated conditions. Thirty minutes of session 16 were videotaped" (*5*, p. 57). In the last (17th) session, videotaped replays of drunken and nondrunken behavior were compared, progress was summarized, and each controlled drinking subject was given a wallet-sized card containing individualized drinking instructions (Figure 1).

Abstinence subjects reportedly received treatment procedures including "group therapy, chemotherapy, Alcoholics Anonymous, physiotherapy, and other traditional services" (*10*, p. 259). Both groups were followed throughout a 2-year period after discharge.

The Sobells reported both that "Basically, each subject and as many respective 'collateral information sources' as possible were contacted every 34 weeks throughout the entire follow-up interval" (*6*, p. 601) and that they relied on official records and collateral sources: "Discrepancies between reports of subjects and collaterals, between reports from different collaterals, or between subjects or collaterals and official records, were always extensively probed, with the final rating being determined by the most objective supporting information available" (*6*, p. 603). Two-year follow-up data were reported for all of the controlled drinking subjects and all but one of the abstinence subjects, constituting "the highest documented follow-up rate in the alcoholism literature" (*3*, p. 118).

The Sobells also reported that during the interviews, subjects and collaterals were asked, "How many days since our last contact have you [has ———, for collaterals] had anything to drink and how much did you [he] drink on each day?" Thus, for each day of a follow-up interval the specific "drinking reported by subjects and CISs [collateral information sources] were recorded verbatim" (*3*, p. 110). Each day was then coded into one of five daily drinking categories (*6*, p. 602): (i) drunk days, defined as "any day during which 10 or more oz of 86-proof liquor or its equivalent in alcohol content were consumed, or any sequence longer than 2 consecutive days when between 7 and 9 oz were consumed on each day" (*20*); (ii) controlled drinking days, defined as "any days during which 6 oz or less of 86-proof liquor or its equivalent in alcohol content were consumed or any isolated 1 or 2 day sequence when between 7 and 9 oz were consumed each day" (*21*); (iii) abstinent days (no alcohol was consumed); (iv) incarcerated days in jail; and (v) incarcerated days in a hospital. This coded daily drinking information constituted the basic data of the study (*22*). The primary measure of treatment outcome was "days functioning well" defined as the sum of abstinent and controlled drinking days, contrasted with days "not functioning well" defined as "the sum of drunk days and days incarcer-

FIGURE 2 Percentage of Days Functioning Well (Either Abstinent or Controlled Drinking) by Individual Controlled Drinking (CD-E) Subjects (Upper Panels) and Individual Abstinence (CD-C) Subjects (Lower Panels). Subjects' initials have been deleted from the original figures. Year 1 (left pairs): Reprinted (in slightly modified form) from *Behav. Res. Ther.*, **11**, M. B. Sobell and L. C. Sobell, "Alcoholics treated by individualized behavior therapy: one year treatment outcome," Figure 2, Copyright 1973, Pergamon Press, Ltd. Year 2 (right pairs): Reprinted (in slightly modified form) from *Behav. Res. Ther.*, **14**, M. B. Sobell and L. C. Sobell, "Second year treatment outcome of alcoholics treated by individualized behavior therapy: results," Figure 1, Copyright 1976, Pergamon Press, Ltd.

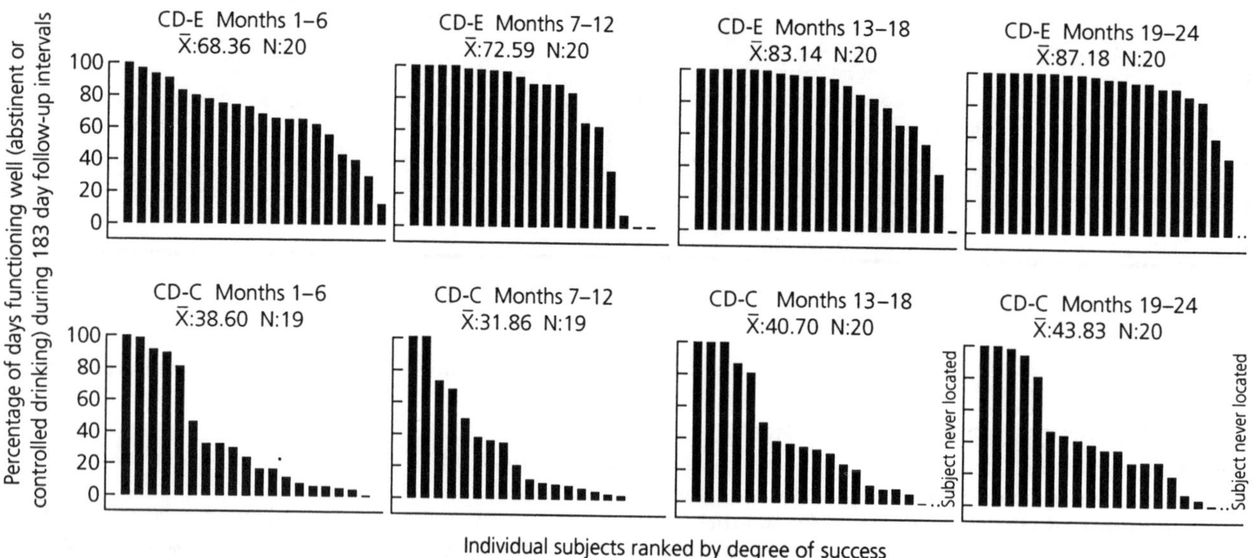

ated in a hospital or jail as a result of drinking" (7, p. 198).

The success of the controlled drinking treatment is portrayed in the graphs in Figure 2 (6, p. 606, and 7, p. 199). Results were reported as percentage of days functioning well. The apparent superiority of the controlled drinking subjects evident in the graphs was significant during each of the follow-up periods (*t*-tests: $P < .005$ for year 1 and $P < .001$ for year 2).

The Sobells referred to alcohol-related incarcerations primarily through tables showing the mean percentage of days spent in hospitals or jails for each group. For instance, during the first 6-month period, they reported that the controlled drinking subjects were incarcerated a mean of 13.09 percent of the days (11.15 percent in hospitals and 1.94 percent in jails) and the abstinence subjects 12.80 percent (3.57 percent in hospitals and 9.23 percent in jails) (6, p. 608, table 2). By the fourth 6-month period, however, they reported that the controlled drinking subjects were incarcerated only 1.09 percent of the days (0.46 percent in hospitals and 0.63 percent in jails) and the abstinence subjects 9.44 percent (2.39 percent in hospitals and 7.05 percent in jails) (7, p. 200, table 2). Thus, in contrast with the abstinence subjects, the controlled drinking subjects appeared to be improving markedly over the four follow-up periods.

The Sobells concluded: "Controlled drinking, as it was practiced by the subjects of the study, was explicitly not daily drinking; more typically it was a pattern of drinking characterized by one to four drinks on two or three occasions per week to one or two such occasions per month" (*13*, p. 160); "controlled drinking days occurred more often when subjects were at their own residences and in a social context . . ." (3, p. 139); and, "subjects who successfully engaged in controlled drinking typically did not initiate extended periods of drunk days as a result of that drinking" (3, p. 138).

Caddy *et al.* conducted an independent third-year follow-up (8), two objectives of which were "to determine how subjects functioned during their third yr of follow-up," and "to generally determine the validity of the 2-yr follow-up results already reported . . ." (7, p. 214). They also reported that the controlled drinking subjects were significantly superior to the abstinence subjects (*t*-test, $P < .03$) (8, p. 355), with half of the controlled drinking subjects included reported as "functioning well" 100 percent of the days during year 3 (8, p. 352, table 2).

In order to assess the results reported for these two shorter-term follow-up studies and to determine the long-term effects of the treatment, we located and interviewed as many as possible of the original subjects. Our initial contacts with the controlled drinking subjects and their collateral information sources were established in the period 1976 to 1979; we have had intermittent contacts with them since that time (23). One purpose of these interviews was to locate documentary data (such as records of hospitalizations for alcoholism and arrests for drunk driving) that would confirm or refute the evaluations of the original investigators. These data, supported by affidavits and records of interviews, have led us to conclusions that are very different from the conclusions of the Sobells and of Caddy *et al.*

In reporting our findings, we depart in two respects from the practice of the previous investigators. (i) In place of the subjects' initials, we have used coded numbers (CD-E's 1 to 20 and CD-C's 1 to 20) to maintain confidentiality. Our coded numbers correspond to the subjects' order of admission to the hospital within each group (as determined by their serial number of admission) (Table 1). (ii) Although we studied subjects from both the experimental and control groups, in this report, we focus on the treatment outcomes and long-term experiences of the controlled drinking–experimental group, rather than on comparisons between the groups, for three reasons. First, the Sobells acknowledged the problem of interpretation when control subjects, although directed toward abstinence, were aware that controlled drinking was considered a potentially attainable goal and that they had been selected as appropriate subjects for that goal (6, p. 616, and 3, pp. 164 and 174). Second, the available data suggest that the experimental and control groups may have differed before they were treated. For instance, most of the controlled drinking subjects were admitted to Patton State Hospital earlier than most of the abstinence subjects (Mann-Whitney $U = 82$, $P < .002$). Thus, even were group comparisons appropriate, in our view they could not be made with confidence. Third, we are addressing the question of whether controlled drinking is itself a desirable treatment goal, not the question of whether the patients directed toward that goal fared better or worse than a control group that all agree fared badly.

TABLE 1 Order of Admission to Patton State Hospital of the 20 Controlled Drinking and 20 Abstinence Subjects Studied by Sobell and Sobell (5)

Date of Admission	*Controlled Drinking Subjects*	*Abstinence Subjects*
2 April 1970		CD-C 1
28 April	CD-E 1	
1 May	CD-E 2	
2 May	CD-E 3	
4 May	CD-E 4	
5 May		CD-C 2
7 May	CD-E 5	
11 May	CD-E 6	
26 May	CD-E 7	
10 June	CD-E 8	
11 June		CD-C 3
19 June	CD-E 9	
13 July	CD-E 10	
16 July	CD-E 11	
18 July		CD-C 4
27 July	CD-E 12	
1 August	CD-E 13	
23 August	CD-E 14	
28 August*		CD-C 5
28 August*		CD-C 6
2 September	CD-E 15	
11 September*	CD-E 16	
11 September*	CD-E 17	
17 September	CD-E 18	
25 September		CD-C 7
29 September		CD-C 8
14 October		CD-C 9
15 October	CD-E 19	
16 October		CD-C 10
23 October		CD-C 11
30 October		CD-C 12
11 November		CD-C 13
30 November		CD-C 14
29 December		CD-C 15
2 February 1971		CD-C 16
3 February	CD-E 20	
10 February		CD-C 17
18 February		CD-C 18
25 February		CD-C 19
26 February		CD-C 20

*Subjects admitted on the same day are distinguished by the serial number of admission

Eighteen of the 20 subjects in the controlled drinking group were interviewed. One had died and one could not be located, but their treatment outcomes have also been documented.

The records of Patton State Hospital show that of the 20 controlled drinking subjects, the first 16 consecutive admissions were all appropriately designated *gamma* alcoholics of various levels of severity. (The last four admissions did not have all of the Sobells' specified subject characteristics and are discussed separately.)

Of the first 16, 13 were rehospitalized for alcoholism treatment within approximately 1 year of discharge (Table 2). Ten were readmitted to the alcoholism program at Patton State Hospital, where they had previously received the experimental controlled drinking treatment, and three were readmitted elsewhere (a Veterans Administration hospital in another state, Camarillo State Hospital, and Naval Hospital, Camp Pendleton). The remaining 3 of the first 16 subjects (CD = E's 3, 5, and 15) also had unfavorable outcomes throughout the first 3 years (noted below).

In our view, the references to hospital and jail incarcerations in the Sobells' tables and related discussion do not convey the reality that is evident when the actual incarceration records of each of the controlled drinking subjects are analyzed individually. For example, the Sobells noted that during the first 6 months the controlled drinking subjects were more often incarcerated in hospitals and the abstinence subjects more often in jails, and they said that this difference "might have been the result of voluntary hospitalizations among the experimental subjects, either to curb the start of a binge or to avoid starting drinking at all" (5, pp. 65–66). Records such as those reflected in Table 2, together with personal interview accounts of subjects and collaterals, seem to require a different interpretation. The rehospitalizations were not isolated setbacks in persons with otherwise benign controlled drinking outcomes. Rather, they indicated the pattern of serious problems that characterized these subjects' continued attempts to practice social drinking.

Of the 20 controlled drinking subjects, the last four admitted to the study differed somewhat from the first 16. They stated to us that, although they had had alcohol-related arrests, they had not had any prior hospitalizations [one of the characteristics specified for all subjects (3, p. 82)] or other treatment for alcohol problems. They also stated that they had not experienced physical withdrawal symptoms prior to entering Patton.

In our view, two of these four (CD-E 17, who had an unfavorable outcome, and CD-E 18, who had a favorable outcome) might have been appropriately designated *alpha* (psychologically dependent rather than physically dependent) alcoholics (9). CD-E 17 had had long-standing severe head pain, which he thought was caused by tension. He had jeopardized his job by drinking to deaden the pain. After he was discharged from the research project, his drinking worsened and he lost his job. Later his pain was attributed to compression of cervical nerves, and spinal surgery was performed in January 1973. Surgery left him disabled, but with less pain. He then began to drink moderately much of the time, but continued to become very intoxicated on weekends. Other consequences of his continued heavy drinking, such as incarcerations for multiple alcohol-related arrests, did not occur until later in our long-term follow-up.

CD-E 18, a heavy drinker for some time, had had a personal problem that led to increased drinking in the year prior to his entering Patton. After participating in the experiment and successfully resolving his problem with the help of a Patton psychiatrist, he no longer engaged in episodes of excessive drinking. His wife's statement, his Patton medical record, and his score on the Alcohol Dependence Scale (24) are consistent with his self-report that he had not experienced physical withdrawal symptoms. In our evaluation, CD-E 18 was the only one of the 20 subjects who succeeded at controlled drinking.

The remaining two controlled drinking subjects admitted, CD-E's 19 and 20, were referred by the court as a result of alcohol-related arrests. The former had been reported to be a successful controlled drinker and the latter about average for the group (6–8). Both continued to engage in intermittent excessive drinking, but neither was arrested again until the latter part of our long-term follow-up. In part because of their lower levels of alcohol dependence, documented consequences of their drinking did not occur until after the initial 3 years.

Our data relating specifically to the controlled drinking subjects' third-year treatment outcomes are very different from those of Caddy *et al.* (8). Table 3 presents our third-year findings for the six subjects ranked highest by Caddy *et al.*, all of whom they reported to be functioning well 100 percent of the days. By contrast, we found that four of the six had apparently engaged in excessive drinking that year. Of the two we evaluated as functioning well, one (CD-E 13) had done so only after three additional hospitalizations for alcoholism and incarcerations in jail and road camp for alcohol-related arrests. He then spent 5 months during his second-year follow-up in Twelve Step House, an Alcoholics Anonymous–oriented alcoholism recovery home, to which he attributed his total abstinence.

Caddy *et al.* specifically mentioned two other controlled drinking subjects in the text of their report (8, p. 351). They excluded the data of CD-E 6 from the statistical analyses because, although "abstinent," he was "incarcerated throughout the third year." They included the data of CD-E 9, who had "developed Parkinson's disease," because he reported having "used no alcohol during the third year follow-up," although "with special effort he could have obtained and consumed alcohol"; they described him as functioning well 100 percent of the time. Our documented findings regarding these two subjects reveal (i) that, during most of that year, the former was neither incarcerated nor abstinent, but free and

TABLE 2 Controlled Drinking Experimental (CD-E) Subjects Rehospitalized for Alcoholism Treatment within Approximately 1 Year of Their Participation in the Research Project. The time between discharge and first readmission is given in italics, followed by quotations from medical records of their rehospitalizations.

*CD-E I	*Readmitted to Patton 1 month, 27 days after discharge.* His record states: "Patient is threatening suicide. . . . Diagnosed as a 'paranoid' and 'social drinker' according to the patient. . . . He is brought in by police. . . . He has been drinking but is not totally inebriated."
*CD-E 2	*Readmitted* to *Patton 1 month, 15 days after discharge.* His record states: First readmission, "returned to drinking wine only was okay one week. . . . Previous stays here have not been too productive." Second readmission, "has developed a tendency to be violent when drinking, getting angry with his wife and has beat her." Third readmission, "has had problems in all aspects of adult functioning. . . . Prognosis—Extremely guarded."
*CD-E 4	*Readmitted to Patton 8 days after discharge.* His record states: "left Patton State Hospital 8 days ago, resumed drinking the next day and now earnestly requests Voluntary Alcoholic readmission. He is tremulous. . . . He is now actively hallucinating, feels he may go into DT's."
*CD-E 6	*Readmitted to Patton 7 months, 9 days after discharge.* His record states: "requests admission as a Voluntary Alcoholic. He states he hasn't had a drink for 1½ days. At present he is extremely agitated and extremely tremulous. . . . He states he sees all 'those G.D. Birds.' . . . admitted for medical care of impending DTs. . . . was averaging one fifth a day."
*CD-E 7	*Readmitted to Patton 3 months, 22 days after discharge.* "Requests admission for treatment of alcoholism—was here previously. . . . he thinks he might be close to DT's as he feels confused, sees pictures flash before his eyes and sees little moving objects on the floor. . . . he is grossly tremulous. Denies use of liquor since last night. He has consumed beer and wine over past 3 months."
*CD-E 8	*Readmitted to Patton 13 days after discharge.* His record states: "This . . . intoxicated man is taken in on a 72-hour hold partly because he is suicidal. . . . This patient was admitted . . . so intoxicated he did not even recall his own name."
*CD-E 9	*Readmitted to Patton 5 months, 11 days after discharge.* His record states: "comes in . . . as a Voluntary Alcoholic, having been here previously last year. . . . He had a quart of beer about 4:00 a.m. this morning. . . . states that he came here because he could not work, his hands were shaking so badly and he was so nervous."
*CD-E 10	*Readmitted to Patton 1 year, 19 days after discharge.* His record states: "transferred to Patton State Hospital . . . on a 14-day Certification . . . as a danger to himself and gravely disabled. . . . Patient was at Patton a year ago on the alcoholic research program. It was the program designed to convert pathological drinkers to social drinkers. Unfortunately it didn't seem to work with him and he had to go on Antabuse to put an end to his excessive drinking." Also, "abandoned the use of his Antabuse about a month ago and began drinking again."
CD-E 11	*Admitted to a Veterans Administration hospital 3 months, 4 days after discharge.* His record states: "diagnosis of Alcoholism. . . . He never drinks socially, just drinks as much as he can get. . . . He states he was drinking 24 hours a day beginning first thing in the morning. . . . He does appear to be depressed, nervous and tense."
CD-E 12	*Admitted to Camarillo State Hospital 8 months, 11 days after discharge.* His record states: "has been drinking off and on since New Year's when he lost his job. He drank heavily for 3 weeks just prior to admission. He has been through Patton's drinking training program. He has been over-dependent on tranquilizers . . . for the past 5 years."
*CD-E 13	*Readmitted to Patton 4 months, 2 days after discharge.* His record states: "Alcoholism, acute. PT been drinking heavily for past 2 weeks. Previously hospitalized for the same problem." "Had near DT's last night." Later: "Now he has lost his job and has had a 502 [charge of driving under the influence of alcohol] and is on probation. . . ." "Had 2 seizures (both in May 1971)."
*CD-E 14	*Readmitted to Patton 8 months, 8 days after discharge.* His record states: "This patient was here . . . and went through the research program that was used at that time and indications were that he might be able to resume social drinking but he realizes now this is a mistake." Patient taken to county hospital 4 months 16 days after research on a 72-hour hold. His record states: "Above patient is gravely disabled due to excessive drinking."
CD-E 16	*Admitted to Naval Hospital, Camp Pendleton 4 months, 17 days after discharge.* His record states: "Physical examination at the time of admission revealed a . . . male who was in alcoholic withdrawal. "Habits: alcohol—gallon of wine—white port" Diagnoses included: "Chronic alcoholism, toxic hepatitis."

*Readmitted to Patton State Hospital.

TABLE 3 Current Findings Regarding Third-Year Treatment Outcomes of the Six Subjects Ranked Highest by Caddy *et al.*, All of Whom They Reported as Functioning Well 100 Percent of the Days in That Year

CD-E 1	Subject and multiple collaterals state he drank heavily throughout year 3, during which he resided in three states. He used an assumed name on his driver's license because of an outstanding alcohol-related felony bench warrant issued in year 2. In February, year 3, police were called by neighbors of subject's mother, when he threatened violence and caused a disturbance while drunk, and in April, he was too drunk to attend his brother's funeral. (This trend continued and in year 4 he was arrested for drunk driving and rehospitalized.)
CD-E 5	Subject states that "the third year included some of my worst drinking experiences." In August 1972, "after drinking more than a fifth of liquor per day, I went to the San Bernardino Alcoholism Services for help. I was having shakes and other withdrawal symptoms and was very sick physically. By then, a physician had told me I had alcohol cirrhosis of the liver." A record of the subject's application for treatment there, his wife's statement, documentation of subsequent hospitalization for alcoholism treatment, and continued deterioration of his health are consistent with his self-report.
CD-E 11	Subject and collateral state that year 3 was his worst year. His records show he spent time in jail, in a state hospital, and in a Veterans Administration hospital because of actions he committed while intoxicated. Toward the end of year 3, he had additional arrests, including one for drunk driving.
CD-E 13	Subject and multiple collaterals state that he was abstinent throughout year 3. He states, however, that this was in spite of the controlled drinking treatment. He became abstinent only after additional alcohol-related incarcerations in hospitals, jail, and road camp. He then spent 5 months of year 2 at Twelve Step House, an AA-oriented alcoholism recovery home, to which he attributed his abstinence.
CD-E 15	Subject and multiple collaterals state he was drinking excessively (sometimes as much as a fifth per day and some beer) when he was not going to be at work. (His blood alcohol of 0.34 percent on a recent admission to a hospital confirms his high reported tolerance.) He had not yet experienced serious alcohol withdrawal symptoms during year 3 and did not require hospitalization. According to his family, however, his health was already beginning to deteriorate, leading to repeated alcohol-related medical problems and hospitalizations from 1976 to the present.
CD-E 18	Subject and collateral state that he successfully controlled his drinking throughout year 3, although, "it would not be entirely accurate to say I never drank excessively." We found no evidence of alcohol-related problems in any major life area. In our view this subject, who apparently had not experienced physical withdrawal symptoms, might have been appropriately designated an *alpha* (psychologically dependent) alcoholic (9).

drinking heavily, and (ii) that the latter neither had Parkinson's disease (although for a while he pretended to have it, in part to obtain Valium and other medications) nor was abstinent, but drank heavily along with taking the pills. The law enforcement records of the former (showing seven alcohol-related arrests followed by release) and the hospital record of the latter (including emergency room visits) for that year verify their self-reports.

The long-term drinking histories of the 20 controlled drinking subjects throughout the more than 10 years until the end of 1981 (the termination of our follow-up) were consistent with the data we obtained for the first 3 years. That is, the subject who had controlled his drinking after discharge was still doing so in 1981. Similarly, the subjects who had been unable to control their drinking after discharge were either still drinking heavily despite repeated damaging consequences, abstaining completely, or dead.

One controlled drinking subject (CD-E 18) continued to drink throughout the long-term follow-up period without showing symptoms of *gamma* alcoholism. He successfully maintained his pattern of controlled drinking and said his tolerance had eventually decreased to three to four drinks.

Eight controlled drinking subjects (CD-E's 2, 5, 7, 8, 9, 15, 17, and 20) continued to drink excessively—regularly or intermittently—throughout the long-term follow-up. All had one or more of the following verified alcohol-related consequences during the 1979–1981 period: job loss, arrest, marital breakup, and hospitalization for alcoholism and related serious physical illness. For example, CD-E 2 was hospitalized during December 1981 in an alcoholism treatment program, after a marital breakup and job loss as a result of his drinking; CD-E 15 was hospitalized between July 1981 and October 1981 with a brain contusion and severe retrograde amnesia from a fall (blood alcohol on admission, 0.34 percent); and CD-E 20 was arrested in 1979 after a drunk driving accident; in 1981, he consulted an alcoholism program after reaching what he called, "my own version of skid row."

Six controlled drinking subjects were abstaining completely by the end of our follow-up. The four (CD-E's 1, 4, 11, and 13) with the longest continuous abstinence (3.5 to 10 years) all stopped drinking only after multiple rehospitalizations, with their final treatment being strongly oriented toward abstinence. The fifth, CD-E 3, after years of uncontrolled drinking, decided to stop entirely in 1975 and remained abstinent through 1981 except for two or three brief (1- to 3-day) relapses when he "got drunk and went off the deep end" in reaction to serious crises. The sixth, CD-E 19, had completed more than 2 years of continuous abstinence by the end of our follow-up, ever since being hospitalized for a disabling accident sustained during a heavy drinking episode.

Four controlled drinking subjects eventually died alcohol-related deaths: CD-E 6, age 41, was found "floating face down in a lake" (blood alcohol, 0.30 percent) *(25)*. CD-E 12, age 40, died of a "massive myocardial infarction" *(26)*. The attending physician stated, "I explained the relationship of his dangerous medical condition to his drinking, and . . . [he] abstained from alcohol for approximately the last year of his life. Unfortunately, his abstinence was instituted too late to prevent his untimely death . . ." *(27)*. CD-E 14, age 41, died of "Respiratory failure, minutes, due to ethanol intoxication, days" (28). CD-E 16, age 60, died of "Suicide: Drowned when jumped from pier into bay" (blood alcohol, 0.30 percent) *(29)*.

One controlled drinking subject (CD-E 10) was still missing. His early record (Table 2) shows that he was certified about a year after discharge from the research project as gravely disabled from drinking.

We have deliberately restricted this report to issues relating to treatment outcomes rather than methodology in order not to obscure the critical question: Does the factual, objective evidence support the Sobells' statement that "many of the CD-E subjects engaged in limited, nonproblem drinking throughout the follow-up period" (3, p. 155) and their conclusion that training directed toward controlled drinking is an effective therapy for *gamma* alcoholism?

Reports of the Sobells' study have influenced some clinicians, researchers, teachers, and students to believe that controlled drinking is not only feasible for a significant proportion of *gamma* alcoholics, but also for some may even be more attainable and safer than a goal of abstinence.

The results of our independent follow-up of the same subjects, based on official records, affidavits, and interviews, stand in marked contrast to the favorable controlled drinking outcomes reported by the Sobells and Caddy *et al.* Our follow-up revealed no evidence that *gamma* alcoholics had acquired the ability to engage in controlled drinking safely after being treated in the experimental program.

REFERENCES AND NOTES

1. D. L. Davies, *Q. J. Stud. Alcohol* **23**, 94 (1962). Comments on the article and a reply by D. L. Davies ware later published [*ibid.* **24**, 109 and 321 (1963)]. More recent pertinent comments appear in "Conversation with D. L. Davies" [Br. *J. Addict.* **74**, 239 (1979)].
2. For a list of studies through 1977, see (3), pp. 16 and 218–222.
3. M. B. Sobell and L. C. Sobell. *Behavioral Treatment of Alcohol Problems* (Plenum, New York, 1978).
4. ———, *California Mental Health Research Monograph, No. 13* (California Department of Mental Hygiene, Sacramento, 1972).
5. ———, *Behav. Ther.* **4**, 49(1973).
6. ———, *Behav. Res. Ther.* **11**, 559 (1973).
7. ———, *ibid.* **14**, 195 (1976).
8. G. R. Caddy, H. J. Addington, D. Perkins, *Behav. Res. Ther.* **16**, 345 (1978).
9. E. M. Jellinek, *The Disease Concept of Alcoholism* (Hillhouse, New Brunswick, N.J., 1960).
10. E. M. Pattison, M. B. Sobell, L. C. Sobell, Eds. *Emerging Concepts of Alcohol Dependence* (Springer, New York, 1977).
11. M. B. Sobell and L. C. Sobell, in *Biological and Behavioral Approaches to Drug Dependence*, H. D. Cappell and A. E. LeBlanc, Eds. (Addiction Research Foundation, Toronto, 1975), pp. 133–167; L. C. Sobell *et al.*, Eds., *Evaluating Alcohol and Drug Abuse Treatment Effectiveness* (Pergamon, New York, 1980); L. C. Sobell and M. B. Sobell, *Int. J. Addict.* **16,** 1077 (1981); L. C. Sobell, in *(12)*, p. 166.
12. G. A. Marlatt and P. E. Nathan, Eds., *Behavioral Approaches to Alcoholism* (Rutgers Center for Alcohol Studies, New Brunswick, N.J., 1978).
13. M. B. Sobell in *(12)*, p. 149.
14. For example, E. P. Reese, J. Howard, T. W. Reese, *Human Operant Behavior* (Brown, Dubuque, 1978); P. E. Nathan and S. L. Harris, *Psychopathology and Psychology* (McGraw-Hill, New York, ed. 2, 1980).
15. J. H. Mendelson and N. K. Mello, Eds., *The Diagnosis and Treatments of Alcoholism* (McGraw-Hill, New York, 1979).
16. R. W. Lloyd and H. C. Salzberg, *Psychol. Bull.* **82,** 815 (1975); J. B. Reid, in *(12)*, p. 61; D. J. Armor, J. M. Polich, H. B. Stambal, *Alcoholism and Treatment* (Rand, Santa Monica, 1976), p. 33; *Alcoholism and Treatment* (Wiley, New York, 1978), p. 34; P. E. Nathan and T. R. Libscomb in *(15)*, pp. 336–339.
17. Thirty additional subjects, who did not meet the criteria for the controlled drinking treatment goal, were used in a parallel experiment that compared behavior therapy with conventional therapy when both had total abstinence as a goal. Since the Sobells reported no lasting differences between the two groups in the parallel experiment, we omitted it to simplify the exposition. We followed these patients also but do not report their results here.
18. "Screening factors included a reported minimal history of impulsiveness and past indications of exercise of self-control over other behaviors. . . . The staff also considered various other factors. . . . [such as] subjects having relatively few alcohol-related hospitalizations and arrests, being younger, reporting a shorter history of drinking problems, and having greater educational attainment" (3, p. 84).
19. This "myth" refers to the belief that alcoholics "will immediately or eventually proceed to drink to drunkenness

should they ingest an initial drink" (3, p. 73).

20. For the second-year follow-up, drunk days were defined as "usually consumption of greater than 6 oz of 86-proof liquor or its equivalent in alcohol" (7, p. 196).
21. For the second-year follow-up, "usually consumption of 6 oz or less. . . ." (7, p. 196).
22. The Sobells also reported additional individual drinking data including the type of beverage, the length of longest binge, and the social environment and location in which drinking typically occurred (7, p. 203, table 4).
23. We also followed the 20 abstinence subjects, but less intensively. Eleven subjects and the widows of two others were interviewed. Another had already been reported to have died (7, p. 209), and six remain unaccounted for.
24. The alcohol-dependence syndrome is described by G. Edwards and M. Gross [*Br. Med. J.* **1**, 1058 (1976)]. To assess the severity of the syndrome, we have recently begun to use a questionnaire developed by T. R. Stockwell, R. J. Hodgson, G. Edwards, C. Taylor, and H. Rankin [*Br. J. Addict.* **74**, 79 (1979)]. However, since the lowest response category on the original questionnaire is "almost never," we needed the response "never" to discriminate subjects who did not have the syndrome at all from those with low levels of severity. Therefore, for each item, if a subject responded "almost never," we asked, "Which would be the most accurate response, "never" or "almost never"? Subject CD-E 18 obtained a score of zero, having responded "never" to all relevant questions. His responses were confirmed by his wife.
25. A. D. Mahoney, Autopsy protocol, County of San Bernardino, California (1981).
26. D. R. Rodwell, Certificate of death, State of Hawaii Department of Health (1977).
27. ———, personal communication.
28. C. P. Smith, Autopsy protocol, County of San Bernardino, California (1981).
29. K. R. Bell, Coroner's report, County of San Diego, California (1979).
30. Among the many who contributed to this research, we thank especially. R. C. Miller, M. Digan, N. H. Anderson, D. Dorinson, W. McQuillan, J. Wilkins, H. D. Steward and D. Steward, the Donwood Institute of Toronto, the San Diego Trial Lawyers Association, J. Fox, and the staff of Patton State Hospital.

DISCUSSION

The two articles in this chapter provide a good illustration of how the answers to certain questions in abnormal psychology hinge as much as on definitional as on empirical considerations. In this case, underlying differences regarding the definition of an "effective" treatment appear to lie at the heart of the dispute between the Sobells and Pendery, Maltzman, and West. Is an effective treatment one that produces an outcome better than alternative conditions, even though it may not yield a high rate of success in absolute terms? Or is an effective treatment simply one that yields a high rate of success? At least in part because the answers to these questions cannot be decided on strictly scientific grounds, the efficacy of controlled drinking remains a source of active and often bitter debate in the alcoholism treatment literature.

The Sobells report that subjects in their controlled drinking condition exhibited superior outcomes relative to subjects in their other conditions. They acknowledge, however, that some subjects did not benefit from controlled drinking. Pendery, Maltzman, and West, in contrast, elect to focus exclusively on the outcomes of the subjects in the Sobells' original controlled drinking condition and do not report follow-up data for subjects in the other conditions. As Pendery, Maltzman, and West note, "we are addressing the question of whether controlled drinking is itself a desirable treatment goal, not the question of whether the patients directed toward that goal fared better or worse than a control group that all agree fared badly" (pp. 172–173).

Pendery, Maltzman, and West's decision not to report follow-up data from conditions other than the controlled drinking condition is defensible if one assumes that the principal criterion for the effectiveness of a treatment for alcoholism is that it returns many or most patients to essentially normal functioning. What these authors' data clearly indicate—and one suspects that even the Sobells would concur with this conclusion—is that controlled drinking is far from a panacea for severe alcoholism. A disquietingly large percentage of severe alcoholics treated with controlled drinking techniques exhibit markedly negative, in some cases disastrous, outcomes.

On the other hand, Pendery, Maltzman, and West's omission of follow-up data from the other groups makes the outcomes of subjects in the Sobells' controlled drinking condition difficult to interpret, because we do not have a baseline against which to gauge the efficacy of controlled drinking. Given that alcoholism, particularly when severe, is characterized by a high rate of serious psychological and medical complications—including death from such causes as cirrhosis of the liver, suicide, driving accidents, and perhaps stroke (Goodwin & Guze, 1989)—it may be unreasonable to expect any treatment for severe alcoholism to bring many or most patients to normal or even near-normal levels of adjustment. Imagine that a new treatment for cancer showed only a 25%

rate of survival after 5 years. This outcome certainly seems dismal in isolation. But if the best alternative treatment for cancer showed only a 10% rate of survival after 5 years, our evaluation of this new treatment would change dramatically (Brownell, 1984). From this perspective, Pendery, Maltzman, and West's exclusion of follow-up data from the other conditions may have unfairly given the Sobells' controlled drinking treatment a black eye.

Might the true picture concerning the efficacy of controlled drinking be somewhat more complex than I have painted it here? In discussing the literature on the effectiveness of psychotherapy, Donald Kiesler (1966) has referred to the "client uniformity myth" implicitly held by many therapists and researchers. According to Kiesler, therapists and researchers often assume that all clients will respond to a given treatment in essentially the same way, thereby neglecting the possibility of marked individual differences in therapeutic outcome. The question "Is controlled drinking an effective treatment for alcoholism?" may therefore be overly simplistic (see also Chapter 12). Instead, a more fruitful question might be "For which individuals is controlled drinking a realistic treatment goal?" Indeed, as discussed in Chapter 7, it seems plausible, if not probable, that what we currently call "alcoholism" is actually the endpoint of at least two, and perhaps many more, quite different causal pathways. Such heterogeneity might imply that different subtypes of alcoholism, or at least different client variables, could influence the effectiveness of controlled drinking.

A number of investigators have recently attempted to identify individual differences that might predict the success of controlled drinking techniques. Although the findings of these researchers must be regarded as preliminary, at least several tentative conclusions can be drawn. Alcoholics who benefit from controlled drinking appear more likely to have a milder drinking history, greater psychological and social stability, stronger social support, and a history of periods of moderate drinking. In addition, females and younger individuals may be more likely to sustain a pattern of controlled drinking (Heather & Robertson, 1983; Marlatt, Larimer, Baer, & Quigley, 1993; Rosenberg, 1993). Although the reasons for these findings are unclear, it seems plausible that the same protective factors that buffer problem drinkers from developing severe alcoholism—perhaps including greater overall coping resources—also allow them to tolerate controlled drinking. In any case, it now seems clear that at least some alcoholics can successfully achieve controlled drinking, both on their own and following treatment; the question becomes which ones (Marlatt et al., 1993; Rosenberg, 1993).

An additional set of variables that seems not to have received sufficient attention in the controlled drinking literature is clients' expectancies and beliefs concerning appropriate drinking outcomes (Marlatt et al., 1993). For example, some clients (especially those who have had previous exposure to Alcoholics Anonymous or similar groups) may believe that a single slip or lapse (for example, a drinking binge following an extremely stressful day at work) indicates a catastrophic failure that will inevitably trigger a total relapse. Clients who tend to hold an absolute, black-and-white view of abstinence may be especially susceptible to the **abstinence violation effect,** in which a single return to drinking often escalates into a full-blown return to alcoholism (Curry, Marlatt, & Gordon, 1987; Marlatt & Gordon, 1980). Individuals experiencing the abstinence violation effect may essentially say to themselves, "That's it—I blew it. I had one drink, so now I'm going to go right back to the way I was before." For such clients, the widespread belief "One drink, one drunk" can become a pernicious self-fulfilling prophecy. These clients may find it difficult or impossible to achieve controlled drinking, because they do not view occasional or moderate drinking as a feasible long-term goal. In contrast, clients who hold less dichotomous and more flexible views concerning drinking outcomes ("Every once in a while, I might slip up and drink too much, but that doesn't mean I'm going to become alcoholic again") might find it easier to achieve controlled drinking, because they believe that "One swallow doesn't make a summer" (Marlatt & Gordon, 1980), and can differentiate between a lapse and a relapse (Brownell, Marlatt, Lichtenstein, & Wilson, 1986).

There appears to be at least some preliminary empirical support for this **persuasion hypothesis** or **indoctrination hypothesis** (Orford & Keddie, 1986). Clients who believe that controlled drinking is an attainable goal or who have had little or no exposure to Alcoholics Anonymous appear more likely than other clients to successfully achieve controlled drinking (Rosenberg, 1993). Further investigation of clients' expectations and beliefs regarding controlled drinking and abstinence may thus help to pinpoint individuals for whom controlled drinking is—and is not—a realistic treatment goal.

QUESTIONS TO STIMULATE DISCUSSION

1. If you had reviewed Pendery, Maltzman, and West's manuscript for a journal, would you have accepted it in its current form? Or would you have insisted that the authors report follow-up data on the Sobells' original control groups? Explain your reasoning.
2. What are the implications of the controlled drinking debate for the "disease model" of alcoholism (see Chapter 7)? Is the possibility that some alcoholics can achieve controlled drinking incompatible with the notion that alcoholism is a disease?
3. If you were asked to design a study to assess the safety and efficacy of controlled drinking for alcoholism, what dependent variables would you select to assess outcome? How would you define a "successful" pattern of drinking? Would your selection of dependent variables be influenced by your position concerning the disease model of alcoholism,

particularly the loss-of-control assumption (see Chapter 7)? If so, how?

4. If you were placed in charge of an alcoholism treatment center, what would you select as a treatment goal for your clients: abstinence or controlled drinking? Or would your treatment goal depend on the characteristics of your clients? Explain what factors would weigh into your decision.
5. Controlled drinking, although highly controversial in the United States and Canada, is apparently widely accepted in Great Britain (see Rosenberg, 1993). What factors might account for this difference? In what ways can cross-cultural variables shape the selection of treatment goals and the long-term outcomes of individuals with alcoholism (as well as individuals with other psychological difficulties)?

SUGGESTIONS FOR FURTHER READING

Armor, D. J., Polich, J. M., & Stambul, H. B. (1976). *Alcoholism and treatment*. New York: Wiley.
The authors review existing models of the etiology and treatment of alcoholism and report preliminary findings from a large-scale follow-up study (often referred to as the Rand report) of alcoholics drawn from 45 community centers throughout the United States. They reach the controversial conclusion that "some alcoholics can return to moderate drinking with no greater chance of relapse than if they abstained" (p. vi). Interested readers should also see this 4-year follow-up of the same subjects: Polich, J. M., Armor, D. J., & Braiker, H. B. (1981). *The course of alcoholism: Four years after treatment*. New York: Wiley-Interscience.

Heather, N., & Robertson, I. (1983). *Controlled drinking* (2nd ed.). New York: Methuen.
The authors discuss the conceptual foundations of the disease model of alcoholism and comprehensively review both anecdotal and systematic empirical reports (including those of the Sobells) of controlled drinking among alcoholics. In addition, Heather and Robertson outline both behavioral and cognitive techniques to facilitate controlled drinking. They conclude with a detailed postscript concerning the Sobell affair and attempt to answer a number of unresolved questions concerning the controversies it has spawned.

Maltzman, I. (1989). A reply to Cook, "Craftsman versus professional: Analysis of the controlled drinking controversy." *Journal of Studies on Alcohol, 50*, 466–472.
Maltzman reiterates his principal charges against the Sobells and fiercely criticizes the methods and conclusions of the committees that acquitted them of scientific misconduct. In particular, he raises questions concerning the Sobells' assignment of subjects to conditions and their interview procedures.

Marlatt, G. A. (1983). The controlled-drinking controversy: A commentary. *American Psychologist, 38*, 1097–1110.
Marlatt reviews the origins of the controlled drinking debate, with particular focus on the Sobells' findings and Pendery, Maltzman, Marlatt, and West's charges. In addition, Marlatt addresses methodological difficulties in the assessment of treatment outcome among alcoholics and future directions in controlled drinking research. Marlatt concludes that, despite its problems, the work of the Sobells stands as a "landmark" in alcoholism treatment research.

Marlatt, G. A., Larimer, M. E., Baer, J. S., & Quigley, L. A. (1993). Harm reduction for alcohol problems: Moving beyond the controlled drinking controversy. *Behavior Therapy, 24*, 461–504.
The authors first provide a detailed overview of the original controlled drinking controversy, as well as a review of predictors of the efficacy of controlled drinking. They argue that "harm reduction" provides a comprehensive framework for altering drinking habits. This framework, they contend, subsumes controlled drinking and similar approaches and provides a more tolerant and realistic alternative to the traditional abstinence-oriented approaches.

Rosenberg, H. (1993). Prediction of controlled drinking by alcoholics and problem drinkers. *Psychological Bulletin, 11*, 129–139.
Rosenberg provides a comprehensive review of predictors of controlled drinking, including severity of dependence, client beliefs and expectations, treatment history, demographic factors, pretreatment drinking patterns, and family history of drinking. He concludes that, although no single variable has consistently been found to predict controlled drinking outcomes, such factors as milder severity of dependence, belief that controlled drinking is a feasible goal, stable employment history, youth, psychological and social stability, and female gender are related to successful controlled drinking.

Sobell, M. B., & Sobell, L. C. (1984). The aftermath of heresy: A response to Pendery et al.'s (1982) critique of "Individualized behavior therapy for alcoholics." *Behaviour Research and Therapy, 22*, 413–440.
In their response to Pendery, Maltzman, and West's article, the Sobells review their experimental design in detail and attempt to rebut each of the article's major accusations. The principal issues discussed by the Sobells include subject diagnoses, random assignment of subjects, interpretation of the 2-year follow-up data, and the validity of Pendery, Maltzman, and West's conclusions regarding long-term follow-up. The Sobells conclude by conceptualizing the controlled drinking controversy within the framework of Kuhn's model of scientific revolutions.

Sobell, M. B., & Sobell, L. C. (1989). Moratorium on Maltzman: An appeal to reason. *Journal of Studies on Alcohol, 50*, 473–480.
In their response to Maltzman's 1989 article, the Sobells defend their program of research against accusations of carelessness and misconduct. They contend that Maltzman has distorted their data collection procedures and findings and declare a "moratorium" on responding to his charges.

REFERENCES

Armor, D. J., Polich, J. M., & Stambul, H. B. (1978). *Alcoholism and treatment*. New York: Wiley.

Boffey, P. M. (1983, November 22). Controlled drinking gains as a treatment in Europe, *New York Times*, pp. 15, 17 (cited in Marlatt, 1983).

Brownell, K. D. (1984). The addictive disorders. In G. T. Wilson, C. M. Franks, P. C. Kendall, & K. D. Brownell (Eds.), *Annual review of behavior therapy* (Vol. 9, pp. 211–258). New York: Guilford Press.

Brownell, K. D., Marlatt, G. A., Lichtenstein, E., & Wilson, G. T. (1986). Understanding and preventing relapse. *American Psychologist, 41*, 765–782.

Curry, S., Marlatt, G. A., Gordon, J. R. (1987). Abstinence violation effect: Validation of an attributional construct with smoking cessation. *Journal of Consulting and Clinical Psychology, 55*, 145–149.

Davies, D. L. (1962). Normal drinking in recovered alcohol addicts. *Quarterly Journal on Studies of Alcohol, 23*, 94–104.

Goodwin, D. W., & Guze, S. B. (1989). *Psychiatric diagnosis* (4th ed.). New York: Oxford University Press.

Heather, N., & Robertson, I. (1983). *Controlled drinking* (2nd ed.). New York: Methuen.

Kiesler, D. J. (1966). Some myths of psychotherapy research and the search for a paradigm. *Psychological Bulletin, 65*, 110–136.

Marlatt, G. A. (1983). The controlled-drinking controversy: A commentary. *American Psychologist, 38*, 1097–1110.

Marlatt, G. A., & Gordon, J. R. (1980). Determinants of relapse: Implications for the maintenance of behavior change. In P. O. Davidson & S. M. Davidson (Eds.), *Behavioral medicine: Changing health lifestyles* (pp. 410–452). New York: Brunner/Mazel.

Marlatt, G. A., Larimer, M. E., Baer, J. S., & Quigley, L. A. (1993). Harm reduction for alcohol problems: Moving beyond the controlled drinking controversy. *Behavior Therapy, 24*, 461–504.

Orford, J., & Keddie, A. (1986). Abstinence or controlled drinking in clinical practice: A test of the dependence and persuasion hypotheses. *British Journal of Addiction, 81*, 495–504.

Peele, S. (1989). *The diseasing of America: Addiction treatment out of control*. Lexington, Massachusetts: Lexington Publishing.

Polich, M., Armor, D. J., & Braiker, H. B. (1981). *The course of alcoholism: Four years of treatment*. New York: Wiley.

Rosenberg, H. (1993). Prediction of controlled drinking by alcoholics and problem drinkers. *Psychological Bulletin, 11*, 129–139.

Sobell, M. B., & Sobell, L. C. (1984). The aftermath of heresy: A response to Pendery et al.'s (1982) critique of "Individualized behavior therapy for alcoholics." *Behaviour Research and Therapy, 22*, 413–440.

CHAPTER

15

Should attention-deficit/hyperactivity disorder be treated with stimulants?

PRO Dulcan, M. K. (1985). The psychopharmacologic treatment of children and adolescents with attention deficit disorder. *Psychiatric Annals, 15*, 69–86.

CON Jacobvitz, D., Sroufe, L. A., Stewart, M., & Leffert, N. (1990). Treatment of attentional and hyperactivity problems in children with sympathomimetic drugs: A comprehensive review. *Journal of the American Academy of Child and Adolescent Psychiatry, 29*, 677–688.

OVERVIEW OF THE CONTROVERSY: Mina K. Dulcan reviews the evidence concerning the efficacy and clinical use of stimulant medications with children diagnosed with attention-deficit/hyperactivity disorder and concludes that they are safe and effective. Deborah Jacobvitz, L. Alan Sroufe, Mark Stewart, and Nancy Leffert discuss the literature pertaining to atypical or "paradoxical" stimulant effects, the role of organic dysfunction in attention-deficit/hyperactivity disorder, the short- and long-term effects of stimulants, and stimulant side effects. They conclude that the widespread use of stimulants to treat attention-deficit/hyperactivity disorder is unwarranted.

CONTEXT OF THE PROBLEM

The diagnosis of attention-deficit/hyperactivity disorder (ADHD) has for decades been a nagging and persistent source of controversy in the field of child psychopathology. This mysterious condition been referred to over the years by a seemingly endless parade of different names: minimal brain damage, minimal brain dysfunction, behavior and learning disorder, specific learning disability, hyperkinetic-impulse disorder, hyperkinetic syndrome, hyperactive child syndrome, developmental hyperactivity, attention deficit disorder with hyperactivity, and most recently, attention-deficit/hyperactivity disorder (Lilienfeld & Waldman, 1990; Weiss & Hechtman, 1986). Almost invariably, the failure of psychopathologists to agree on a name for a condition reflects a much deeper and more fundamental confusion regarding the diagnosis and etiology of the condition itself. ADHD is no exception to this rule.

To begin with, there are enormous national differences in the diagnosis of ADHD. It is made approximately 50 (!) times more often in the United States than in Great Britain (Rutter, 1982), despite the fact that American children do not seem to possess higher rates of ADHD symptoms than English children do (Sandberg, Wieselberg, & Schaffer, 1980). Moreover, American children with ADHD exhibit an extremely diverse array of problems, such as physical aggression, temper tantrums, oppositionalism toward authority figures, enuresis (bed-wetting), motor and vocal tics, low frustration tolerance, moodiness, learning disabilities, and mild neurological abnormalities (Sandberg et al., 1980). It should thus come as no surprise that a number of authors have concluded that the American diagnosis of ADHD is almost hopelessly heterogeneous and encompasses an extremely broad spectrum of children who suffer from etiologically different conditions (Rutter & Garmezy, 1983).

Despite this chaotic state of affairs, American researchers have gradually converged on a standard set of features with which to diagnose ADHD. According to DSM-IV, ADHD children suffer from deficits in two principal areas: inattention and hyperactivity/impulsivity. The major characteristics of ADHD include being easily distracted by irrelevant stimuli, appearing not to listen to others, having difficulty maintaining prolonged concentration on a task (inattention), fidgeting frequently, having difficulty remaining seated, talking excessively (hyperactivity), frequently interrupting others' activities, answering questions before they have been completed, and engaging in dangerous activities without considering their potential consequences (impulsivity). Of course, many or most young children exhibit these behaviors at some point in their development (can any of us never recall being reprimanded for not paying attention to our parents or for talking too much in class?); but for a diagnosis of ADHD to be made, DSM-IV requires that these behaviors be considerably more frequent than among most children of the same age. As many as 3% of school-age children have been estimated to suffer from ADHD, with anywhere from four to nine times more males than females satisfying criteria for this diagnosis (American Psychiatric Association, 1994).

No less controversial than the diagnosis of ADHD is its treatment by means of stimulant medication. The use of such stimulants as methylphenidate (Ritalin), dextroamphetamine (Dexedrine), and pemoline (Cylert) in the treatment of ADHD children began in the 1930s, after researchers like Bradley (1937) discovered that they frequently exert a dramatic "calming" effect on these children. Since then, the administration of stimulants to ADHD children has skyrocketed. As Jacobvitz, Sroufe, Stewart, and Leffert point out in their article in this chapter, approximately 6% of all children in public elementary schools have been estimated to be on stimulants. Moreover, the number of children on stimulants has been doubling every 2 to 4 years since the early 1970s. One point about which there seems to be little disagreement is the remarkable short-term effect of stimulants on ADHD children. Between two-thirds and three-fourths of these children exhibit substantial decreases in inattention, overactivity, and impulsivity following the ingestion of stimulants (Satterfield, 1978).

At this point, you may be puzzled about the logic of giving children who are already hyperactive a medication that further stimulates their nervous system. For decades, so many researchers were perplexed by the "calming" effect of stimulant medications on ADHD children that they labeled it the "paradoxical effect." It was long assumed that stimulants had a unique effect on ADHD children that would ultimately be explicable in terms of their distinctive nervous system physiology.

This "paradoxical effect" turned out to be less paradoxical than was initially believed, however. Judith Rapaport and her colleagues have shown that the effects of stimulants on ADHD children are no different than their effects on normal children and on normal adults: Individuals in all three groups tend to respond with decreases in activity and improvements in attention (Rapaport et al., 1978). Although the precise mechanism of action is still a lively topic of debate, it seems likely that the decreases in activity and impulsivity that stimulants engender are actually secondary consequences of improvements in attention. Thus, the overactivity and impulsivity of ADHD children probably stem from a more fundamental inability to sustain attention. To understand this point, imagine yourself unable to maintain concentration on a task for more than a few seconds. You would probably be investigating things that arouse your immediate curiosity, perhaps by getting up out of your seat and walking (perhaps even running) around to examine whatever seems most interesting. In addition, you would probably be more likely than usual to do things on the spur of the moment, because you would not be attending to, or thinking about, the potential consequences of your actions. Thus, your attention deficit would probably cause you to be both hyperactive and impulsive.

The use of stimulants to treat ADHD has been bitterly opposed by a small but extremely vocal group of critics. Some maintain that these drugs are used indiscriminately to sedate children who are difficult for teachers, parents, and other authority figures to control. As Stephen Box argues in a 1978 article titled "Hyperactivity: The Scandalous Silence":

> Instead of recognizing the inarticulate cries of rage and despair and examining the very serious problems these hyperactive children face, there is an intense drive to individualize their problems, and blame them on organic impairments . . . Drugs are then administered to dampen and confuse the child's scarcely heard protests. In this way the minds of a generation of the ethnically and economically deprived are being hollowed out, and the revolt of a potentially delinquent population avoided. (pp. 22–24; see also O'Leary, 1980)

Still others have charged that stimulants frequently produce long-term deleterious side effects, such as growth suppression, or even that they can lead to an increased risk of violent behavior, psychosis, and addiction. For example, the defense attorney of a teenage boy who murdered a schoolmate with a baseball bat contended that his client's behavior was at least partly attributable to Ritalin (Cowart, 1988). The Church of Scientology, founded by the late L. Ron Hubbard (author of the best-selling book *Dianetics*), filed five lawsuits in Massachusetts against physicians who prescribed Ritalin, on the grounds that stimulants are addictive and can cause psychosis. Another lawsuit was filed against the American Psychiatric Association by a Georgia mother who claimed that Ritalin made her son violent and suicidal (Cowart, 1988). "I don't remember as much furor over any other issue," stated Dr. Richard Roberts, chair of the department of pediatrics at the University of Virginia (cited in Cowart, 1988, p. 2512). Are the claims of the opponents of stimulant medication warranted?

THE CONTROVERSY: Dulcan vs. Jacobvitz, Sroufe, Stewart, and Leffert

Dulcan

Mina Dulcan notes that, although little evidence exists for a "paradoxical" response of ADHD children to stimulants, there is compelling support for the effectiveness of stimulants. (Because Dulcan's article was written prior to the advent of DSM-III-R, when the term *ADHD* first appeared, she uses the DSM-III term *attention deficit disorder*, or ADD. Nevertheless, the criteria for ADD are, with relatively minor exceptions, quite similar to those for ADHD.) Approximately 75% of ADHD children, Dulcan maintains, are rated as improved following stimulant administration, as compared with 40% of ADHD children on placebo. Dulcan reviews the evidence for the efficacy of stimulants on motor behavior, cognitive functioning, and interpersonal behavior and argues that these medications have dramatic short-term effects on these variables. She acknowledges that long-term benefits of stimulants have not been found, although she contends that "it may be unreasonable to expect a drug to have long-term effects after it is terminated" (p. 74). Dulcan then reviews the evidence concerning the side effects of stimulants (such as growth suppression) and concludes that most of these effects are relatively mild and transitory. She also discusses practical concerns pertaining to the clinical administration of stimulants, as well as the use of stimulants in non-ADHD children and supplementary and alternative treatments for ADHD children. Dulcan concludes that, with appropriate precautions, stimulants are a safe and effective treatment for ADHD.

Jacobvitz, Sroufe, Stewart, and Leffert

After discussing the dramatic rise in the prescription of stimulants over the past several decades, Deborah Jacobvitz, Alan Sroufe, Mark Stewart, and Nancy Leffert acknowledge that these medications have undeniable short-term effects on attention, motor activity, and other variables relevant to ADHD. Like Dulcan, however, they find little support for a "paradoxical" effect of stimulants on ADHD. Jacobvitz, Sroufe, Stewart, and Leffert review the evidence for the existence of organic dysfunction in ADHD, which, as they note, is sometimes used to justify the use of stimulants. They conclude that the evidence for brain injury in ADHD or for psychophysiological or biochemical abnormalities specific to ADHD is inconclusive. They also review data on predictors of stimulant response and conclude that no variables have been found to consistently distinguish those who respond well to stimulants from those who respond poorly. These authors next discuss the evidence regarding the long-term effects of stimulants on three major behavioral domains: academic performance, peer relations, and antisocial behavior. They find no convincing evidence that stimulants exert beneficial effects in any of these areas. They point out that multimodal treatments combining stimulants with other techniques may ultimately prove to be effective but maintain that proper outcome studies of such treatments have yet to be conducted. Finally, these authors review the literature on the side effects of stimulants and argue that growth suppression and a chronic tic disorder known as Tourette's syndrome are potentially important long-term consequences of stimulant use. Jacobvitz, Sroufe, Stewart, and Leffert conclude that the widespread treatment of ADHD children with stimulants and the prolonged use of stimulants alone are difficult to justify given the existing data.

KEY CONCEPTS AND TERMS

anorexia Loss of appetite. Anorexia should not be confused with anorexia nervosa, a severe eating disorder characterized by extreme weight loss, profound body image distortion, and fear of becoming overweight.

catecholamine Class of neurotransmitters, or chemical messengers in the nervous system, that includes norepinephrine and dopamine.

dose response curve Curve illustrating the effects of a medication on a given behavior (for example, reading ability) at different dosages.

drug holiday Period of time during which ADHD children are temporarily taken off medication in order to minimize detrimental long-term side effects, such as growth suppression.

emanative effects Indirect and unintended psychosocial consequences of medication use, such as decreases in self-esteem.

minimal brain dysfunction Hypothesized form of mild and difficult to detect brain damage, believed by some researchers to give rise to ADHD and related syndromes. The minimal brain dysfunction concept was particularly popular in the 1960s as a model of the etiology of ADHD.

paradoxical effect Purportedly different stimulant response of ADHD children (sedation) compared with that of normal children (excitation).

Tourette's syndrome Disorder, originating in childhood or adolescence, that is characterized by frequent and persistent motor and vocal tics.

PREVIEW QUESTIONS

1. According to Dulcan, what are the principal deficits found in ADHD children?
2. According to Dulcan, what are the major short-term effects of stimulant medication, and what is the evidence for each of these effects?

3. What are the primary side effects of stimulant medication?
4. According to Dulcan, what treatments other than stimulants have been used with ADHD children? Which of these treatments appear to be effective?
5. What is Jacobvitz, Sroufe, Stewart, and Leffert's interpretation of the evidence for the atypical or "paradoxical" stimulant response among ADHD children?
6. According to Jacobvitz, Sroufe, Stewart, and Leffert, what are the major hypotheses concerning an organic etiology for ADHD, and what is the evidence for each of these hypotheses?
7. According to Jacobvitz, Sroufe, Stewart, and Leffert, what does the literature indicate regarding predictors of stimulant response among ADHD children?
8. What are the conclusions of Jacobvitz, Sroufe, Stewart, and Leffert regarding the long-term consequences of stimulant medication?

MINA K. DULCAN

The psychopharmacologic treatment of children and adolescents with attention deficit disorder

INTRODUCTION

Attention Deficit Disorder (ADD), a "new" diagnosis created for *DSM-III*,[1] includes the subtypes with hyperactivity, without hyperactivity, and residual. Douglas describes the following primary deficits in ADD: 1) lack of investment, organization, and maintenance of attention and effort in completing tasks, 2) inability to inhibit impulsive responding, 3) lack of modulation of arousal levels to meet the demands of the situation, and 4) unusually strong inclination to seek immediate reinforcement.[2] Unfortunately, the majority of studies have included a heterogeneous group of children with often unspecified degrees of learning disabilities, overactivity, aggression, brain damage, and family pathology.

Recent studies[3,4] estimate that 3% of prepubertal school children have been diagnosed by a physician as hyperactive, with an additional 3% identified as hyperactive by the school but not diagnosed by a physician. The ratio of boys to girls ranges from 4 to 1[3] to 6–8 to 1.[4]

In the 1930s clinicians began using the then available psychostimulant compounds to treat a variety of child psychiatric problems which had not responded to psychotherapy.[5,6] In the subsequent three decades, treatment with first dextroamphetamine (Dexedrine) and then in the 1950s methylphenidate (Ritalin) became an increasingly popular treatment for a disparate group of "hyperactive" children who had symptoms of anxiety, minimal brain dysfunction, aggression, psychosis, depression, hysteria, and/or school phobia. The 1970s saw a professional and lay backlash.[7–10] Teachers and physicians were accused of being in league with pharmaceutical companies to "drug" children, especially poor ones, into submission. A useful result of the outcry was a wave of more scientific studies of the characteristics of children who might benefit and the short and long term effects of stimulant medication. Currently the use of these compounds is largely limited to children with ADD. Two recent school based studies found that .6% to 1% of students are currently receiving stimulants.[3,4]

Although some have asserted that positive response to stimulants is both necessary and sufficient to make a diagnosis of ADD, this is clearly not the case. Studies of mixed diagnostic groups have not shown differential efficacy by diagnosis[6,11] and normal children respond to these medications in ways similar to hyperactive children. The evidence does not yet support either specific effects of drugs on the hyperactive syndrome or a core syndrome of hyperactivity that is uniquely responsive to drugs.[12]

PHARMACOLOGY

At present there are three psychostimulant medications in common use for treating ADD: dextroamphetamine and methylphenidate, sympathomimetic amines, and pemoline. . . .

The pharmacodynamics of the psychostimulants remain controversial.[13,14,30,31] The study of the relationship between plasma drug level and clinical effect is complicated by the finding that the dose response curves vary according to the effects measured.[20,32–34] Sprague and Sleator suggested that positive effects on behavior occurred at a higher mg/kg dose than cognitive effects and that in fact, cognitive performance was impaired at the level at which behavior improved.[35] Several studies have confirmed that drug effects on a global rating scale of behavior completed by parents and teachers (the Conners' Abbreviated Symptom Questionnaire) are maximum at a dose of 1 mg/kg.[33,36] Some studies have found improvement on tests of cognitive functioning maximal at a dose of .3 mg/kg with deteriorating of performance at 1 mg/kg.[2,35,37–40] The performance of children with ADD varies according to context and task parameters, decreasing generalizability between studies.[2] In contrast, the frequency and severity of side effects have been repeatedly shown to increase directly with increasing dose. A further complicating factor is that ADD children have been found to include negative, as well as positive placebo responders.[35]

There is a long standing myth that hyperactive children have a paradoxical response to stimulant medication. In a series of studies using dextroamphetamine, Rapoport and her colleagues amply demonstrated that this was not the case.[41–45] In response to a single dose of dextroamphetamine they found parallel responses in hyperactive boys, normal boys, and normal college men on the following measures: truncal activity during a cognitive task (decreased), reaction time (decreased), word recall (increased), vigilance (increased), non-task related speech (decreased), task related speech (increased), and insomnia (increased). The only significant difference with age was in mood. Adults reported euphoria, while children in both groups reported a wide variety of feelings with "funny" being the most common. The boys experienced a rebound period after 5 hours, characterized by increased excitability and talkativeness.[41]

THERAPEUTIC EFFECTS

On global judgments, parents, teachers, and clinicians rate 75% of hyperactive children on stimulant medication "improved" compared to 40% on placebo. Twenty-five percent are judged "no change" or "worse."[46] There is extreme inconsistency in effects within and across drug studies, with a low correlation among change scores on various measures. Conners was able to group subjects according to profiles of pretest data. Drug effects were consistent within each group with significant differences in drug response pattern and visual evoked potentials between groups.[47] Unfortunately, this preliminary finding does not seem to have been pursued or replicated.

SHORT-TERM EFFECTS

Motor Effects Stimulants have been found to decrease activity on a variety of laboratory measures.[48] In the natural environment, effects on activity depend on the context.[49,50] In an experimental classroom methylphenidate reduced hyperactive boys' gross motor movement, vocalization, noise, and disruption to a level indistinguishable from normal peers.[51] Methylphenidate also produces an improvement in handwriting.[52,53]

Cognitive Effects Stimulants improve performance on a variety of cognitive laboratory tasks measuring sustained attention, distractibility, and impulsivity, but there is no evidence of significant improvement in measures of academic achievement.[46,48,54–56] This finding is not only discouraging, but also puzzling, since there are ample case examples of children whose school grades improve on medication. It is, however, unreasonable to expect medication alone, without educational remediation, to make up for accumulated deficits. Dextroamphetamine enhances the cognitive encoding and processing operations the child typically uses.[44] Since hyperactive children use more immature strategies than their peers, with the use of drugs there may be a tendency for improvement to occur more on simple than complex tasks. Methylphenidate has not been demonstrated to increase or decrease memory 24 hours after initial learning.[38] Stimulants have been found to have no beneficial effect on primary reading retardation in the absence of hyperactivity.[57]

Interpersonal Effects The ability of stimulant medication to decrease classroom disruption[51,53,58,59] and improve behavior as rated by parents and teachers is well documented,[47,54] and the effects are interactive. In an experimental setting, when methylphenidate increases children's compliance to maternal commands and reduces off task behaviors, the mothers give fewer commands and more positive attention.[60] Teachers engage in significantly more controlling, guiding, or disciplinary actions and are more intense in all interactions with hyperactive children on placebo than with either normal children or hyperactive children on methylphenidate.[61]

LONG-TERM EFFECTS

There has not been any demonstration of long-term therapeutic effects attributable to stimulant treatment.[46,62,63] The possibility has not been conclusively disproven, however, since all of the follow-up studies have serious methodologic flaws and do not account for factors which have been shown to be associated with poor prognosis such as: low IQ, aggression, poor mother-child relationship, brain damage, low socioeconomic status, and poor family environment.[63–65] In addition, it may be unreasonable to expect a drug to have long-term effects after it is discontinued.

SIDE EFFECTS

All stimulant medications produce similar side effects. There is a group of common, short-term side effects which are usually dose related and diminish or disappear following several weeks of treatment or dose reduction. At a dose of 1 mg/kg of methylphenidate a significant proportion of children have troublesome untoward effects.[35] The most frequently reported side effects are insomnia, anorexia, weight loss, irritability, and abdominal pain.[29,46,66] It is important to compare reported side effects of medication with placebo. In one study of pemoline the only side effect for which the incidence on medication was greater than placebo was sleep problems.[28] Dextroamphetamine has actually been found to decrease the frequency of stomachaches compared to placebo.[11] It may be difficult to distinguish whether insomnia is due to drug, a preexisting sleep disorder, or a rebound effect. Sleep laboratory studies have demonstrated few clinically significant drug-induced changes in sleep parameters. Sleep disturbances reported by parents were not demonstrated, perhaps in part due to the novelty of the sleep lab setting.[67,69]

Other side effects which are occasionally reported include dizziness, nausea, euphoria, nightmares, dry mouth, constipation, lethargy, anxiety,[46] hyperacusis, and fearfulness.[67] Side effects noted only with pemoline include lip licking and biting and light picking of fingertips.

Anorexia is commonly reported, probably worsened by the tradition of giving medication one half-hour before meals, although hyperactive children are often problem eaters even prior to treatment. In a retrospective study, Loney found that 83% of the subjects treated with methylphenidate experienced no appetite suppression after one month of treatment.[71]

The most studied but still unclear side effect is growth retardation, initially reported by Safar.[72] Initial weight loss in some subjects is reported in almost all studies, probably due to anorexia. After the first few months weight loss ceases but there is a tendency for weight gain to be less than that which would be predicted. Findings regarding height are less clear, in part due to differing methodologies in measuring and predicting height and different drug doses.[73–75] To summarize, stimulant medication has a variable effect on height, which seems to be more severe with dextroamphetamine than with methylphenidate or pemoline, and increases with increasing dose. Slowing of growth may be minimized by the use of drug holidays. In a small proportion of children, growth retardation may be sufficient to reach clinical significance. Concluded from follow-up studies, adolescent height and weight were related to: severity of early weight and appetite suppression, number and length of drug holidays, duration of methylphenidate treatment, and occurrence of nausea or vomiting as an initial side effect.[71]

Endocrine studies have yet to elucidate the mechanism of growth retardation. In several studies, methylphenidate has not produced changes in human growth hormone (HGH) or prolactin.[68,76] Although dextroamphetamine does not consistently change HGH, one study found a significant decrease in the mean sleep related prolactin secretion which correlated with loss in height velocity.[67] Growth inhibition, when it occurs, may be secondary to alterations in cartilage metabolism.[68]

Some investigators have raised concerns about possible, although as yet undocumented, long-term sequelae of cardiovascular responses to stimulant medication.[77] In chronically medicated children, methylphenidate leads to significant dose-related increases in heart rate, systolic blood pressure, and mean blood pressure which are similar throughout rest, exercise, and recovery.[78] The effect on heart rate, however, varies widely, with some children even showing a reduction. Pemoline studies have shown no effect on blood pressure,[28,29,66] and an inconsistent effect on heart rate.

A rare but potentially serious side effect is the production or precipitation of a movement disorder[79,80] (Sallee R, Perel J, personal communication, March 1984) which is not related to dose or duration of drug treatment and may persist despite withdrawal of medication. Full blown Tourette's syndrome requiring treatment with haloperidol has been reported following methylphenidate,[81,82] pemoline,[82,83] and dextroamphetamine.[82] Lowe recommends that the presence of motor tics or Tourette's syndrome be an absolute contraindication to stimulant treatment, a family history of either be a relative contraindication, stimulants should be withdrawn immediately if tics appear, and haloperidol and stimulants should not be used together.[82] Comings asserts that some Tourette's syndrome children have such severe hyperactivity that methylphenidate should be added to haloperidol, and that tics are not always exacerbated by stimulants.[84]

Additional relatively rare side effects are transient if medication is withdrawn promptly. These include hypersensitivity phenomena, such as conjunctivitis, formication, skin rash, angioneurotic edema, and urticaria.[85] Psychotic episodes including hallucinations have been reported during treatment with and following withdrawal of methylphenidate and dextroamphetamine.[46,86–88] There is also a report of an acute dyskinesia.[89]

Dysphoria is a not uncommon side effect.[90,91] Cantwell reported several cases of children who developed mild to moderate depressive episodes on both methylphenidate and dextroamphetamine.[92]

Some side effects have been more controversial. Despite efforts to demonstrate, state dependent learning,[48,57,93,94] perseveration,[95] hypoactivity,[46,51,70] and decreased curiosity[96] have not been consistently found at doses less than 1 mg/kg. Although there has been one published case report of an adolescent abusing prescribed methylphenidate,[97] there is no indication that stimulant treatment increases the rate of adolescent or adult drug abuse.

There have been no reports of significant stimulant-induced changes in liver functions or blood count.[46,98] Although clinical lore cautions that stimulants may lower the seizure threshold, this has not been reported even in a large series of cases of children with known epilepsy.[99] In fact, dextroamphetamine raises the photo-Metrazol threshold of hyperkinetic children.[100] In a single case study methylphenidate decreased the frequency of temporal spike wave discharges (Strayhorn JM, personal communication, March 1984). Methylphenidate inhibits the enzymes which metabolize anticonvulsants, thus raising their blood levels.[5]

EMANATIVE EFFECTS

As described by Whalen and Henker[40,101] emanative effects are indirect and inadvertent psychosocial consequences which may be desirable or undesirable. They range from psychological changes in the treated child in self-esteem and self-efficacy, through effects on teachers and parents to influence on larger, societal attitudes and practices.

CLINICAL CONSIDERATIONS

Evaluation

Before consideration for stimulant treatment, a child or adolescent must have a thorough evaluation.[70] The interview with the child may or may not be helpful in diagnosing ADD, since these youngsters are not overactive in every setting. In addition, these children are often unaware of or deny difficulties. In a novel situation with an unfamiliar adult, children are least likely to display impulsivity, inattention, or hyperactivity. Positive findings, therefore, are much more significant than negative. If the child can be observed in an unstructured setting, for example the waiting room, this may be helpful.

Information from a child's teacher is absolutely essential for a diagnosis of ADD. In drug studies, teachers have consistently been found to be more reliable than parents in discriminating medication from placebo. It is important to remember, however, that teachers vary widely in their tolerance for activity and impulsivity, and in their ability to structure a class.

Psychological or educational testing is not necessary for a diagnosis of ADD, although it is important in assessing educational potential and achievement. The presence of inattention and impulsivity is more significant than their absence.

Any child or adolescent needing psychiatric evaluation should have a physical examination. Elaborate neurological testing or an EEG is not necessary unless there are focal symptoms. The presence or absence of soft neurological signs or minor physical anomalies is not helpful in the individual case.[102] A careful search for tics in the identified patient and family should be conducted, and baseline pulse, blood pressure, height, and weight determined.

Standard assessment measures can be extremely useful. Questionnaires tend to tap global impressions which weight heavily highly salient (novel, intense, extreme, out of context) behaviors.[103] Observational measures of attention and activity show much greater reliability and stability if behavior is sampled and averaged over more than one time period.[104]

The questionnaires most commonly used for ADD are those developed by Conners. The Parent Symptom Questionnaire (CPSQ)[105,106] has been demonstrated to differentiate between normal and clinical populations, between hyperkinetic and other clinically referred children,[107] and between stimulant and placebo treatment.[70] The most recent revision has 48 items for boys and girls ages 3 to 17.[108] The Conners Teacher Rating Scale (CTRS)[108] reliably differentiates a stimulant treated group from placebo.[46,109]

A 10-item Hyperkinesis Index contained in the CPSQ and the CTRS has been developed into an Abbreviated Symptom Questionnaire (CASQ) which has an identical format for parents and teachers.[106] It is sensitive to drug-induced changes and is useful for repeated measures. A score of 1.5 has been found to be two standard deviations greater than the mean for normals[110] and has commonly been used as a cutoff for studies of hyperactivity. Because the score on the CASQ has been found to decrease from first to second administration,[111,112] it should be given more than once to establish a baseline.

It must be remembered that these instruments measure an adult's perception of a child's behavior. There is some evidence that teacher personality characteristics are related to ratings on the CASQ.[51] A teacher's opinions regarding stimulant medication or goals for a child's class placement may affect his or her reports. The CASQ does, however, differentiate between ADD boys on medication or placebo even when raters are blind to the nature of the study.[113]

The Child Behavior Checklist[114] may be especially useful in detecting children with ADD in heterogeneous clinical populations. Parallel versions for parent and for teacher are available, with norms for boys and girls separately in age ranges 4–5, 6–11, and 12–16 years. Child Behavior Profiles can be obtained from the parent form on boys and girls in the three age ranges, and currently for 6–11 year old boys from the teacher form. . . . Each of the profiles includes factors which are relevant to ADD. The teacher profile reliably distinguishes psychiatrist diagnosed boys with ADD from other clinically referred boys, and ADD with hyperactivity from ADD without hyperactivity.[115]

Actual observation of the child in the natural environment[70] or in specially structured playroom settings,[116] while more difficult to accomplish, may be extremely useful. A school visit offers the opportunity to evaluate the child's behavior in the context of the teacher's attitudes and methods and in comparison to the rest of the class.

DECISION TO MEDICATE

Indications for stimulant medication are the presence of inattention, impulsivity, and hyperactivity which have been persistent and of sufficient severity to cause functional impairment at school, and usually also at home and with peers. There is preliminary clinical evidence that stimulants may also be indicated for children and adolescents with inattention and impulsivity but without hyperactivity. Before prescribing medication the clinician must insure that the parents are sufficiently reliable to administer the medication safely and as prescribed. It is the opinion of this author that under most circumstances interventions such as parent counseling and school consultation should be attempted first. If successful, this spares children who may not require medication. In any case, a longer period of observation is provided prior to starting medication. In addition, the clinician will have demonstrated that he or she is willing to try other approaches and does not unthinkingly medicate children. Children with severe impulsivity, which may be dangerous to themselves or others, may require more rapid institution of medication along with other interventions.

Efforts to find predictors of drug responsiveness among groups of hyperactive children have been noticeably unsuccessful. The most promising predictors are the child's behavior and laboratory measures related to attention span.[118] A better mother-child relationship and lack of parental psychopathology may predict better medication response. A high level of anxiety in the child has been found in some studies to predict poor response.[70] Taylor asserts that no current measure can predict the response of an individual child within a group of hyperactive children.[12]

The literature affords little help to the clinician in selecting one of the stimulant drugs for a specific child. Methylphenidate is the most commonly used in practice. Some clinicians advocate dextroamphetamine as the drug of first choice because it is less expensive.[89] Unfortunately, the refusal of medical assistance in some states to pay for dextroamphetamine negates this advantage for families at the lowest income levels. Experience indicates that dextroamphetamine is more likely than methylphenidate or pemoline to stimulate gratuitous comments from pharmacists to parents about "speed" or "drugs." If there is concern about possible abuse of medication, pemoline may be the safest. If short stature is a serious concern, then pemoline or methylphenidate is preferable to dextroamphetamine. Pemoline may also be indicated if administering medication during the school day is impossible or severely stigmatizing.

There have been very few studies which directly compare stimulant drugs. In large reviews combining the results of multiple separate studies one found methylphenidate slightly more efficacious than dextroamphetamine,[55] and another found no difference.[48] Two double-blind crossover studies comparing dextroamphetamine and methylphenidate found both drugs efficacious in 50% to 80% of the respondents. The remainder responded to only one of the drugs.[11,89]

In group comparison studies, methylphenidate and dextroamphetamine were found to be equal to or slightly better than pemoline.[26,27,118] Some children who improved on pemoline did not subsequently have a good response to methylphenidate.[25] Clinical experience suggests that as many as 20% of those who respond poorly to one stimulant medication have a positive response to another.[70]

INITIATING MEDICATION

Once the decision is made to prescribe stimulants, preparation of the child, the family, and the teacher is essential. Children on stimulants tend to attribute their problems to physiologic causes rather than personal or social factors and to attribute behavior change to medications or to physiologic causes such as "growing out of it."[65,101] Although not yet directly tested, it would seem clinically sound practice to emphasize that it is the child, family, and medication working together that lead to improvement. Parents should be cautioned not to look only to medication or the lack of it as a cause of the child's behavior. Whalen and Henker suggest that a "cognitive innoculation" program such as self-control training precede a medication trial to minimize possible detrimental effects on the child's sense of self-efficacy.[40]

Although most medicated hyperactive children recognize the need for stimulants and some of the beneficial effects, most dislike taking the medication.[101,119,120] Reasons given include actual or feared social stigma and humiliation by peers and teachers, a belief that taking medication means they are defective, and a belief that medication will decrease their abilities, especially at athletics. Objections often increase with age and older children are especially likely to fear drug abuse.

Myths regarding ADD and stimulants are very common among parents, and if not spontaneously brought up, they should be addressed by the clinician. Parents vary widely in their initial attitudes toward medication, ranging from highly favorable to strongly opposed, and require different emphasis in preparation.

Virtually every parent at some time changes the child's dose without consulting the physician. While this practice should be discouraged, it should not be discouraged so strongly that the practice goes underground. Parents may be given some discretion on a third daily dose. Parents should not make the child responsible for taking his own medicine. An unsupervised child is likely to forget, throw away, or worse, give away or sell the pills. Finally, there is a danger of impulsive overdose if entire bottles are left available to children. Parents should of course be instructed to inform any physician treating their child of the stimulant medication, especially if another medication is to be prescribed. Gualtieri lists known drug interactions with stimulants.[121] Although not reported in the literature, parents should be cautioned against the use of dextroamphetamine or methylphenidate with sympathomimetics, which are often included in over the counter drugs.

Teachers need just as much, if not more, education than parents, but usually receive much less.[122] Particularly to be cautioned against is the common practice of asking a loud or impulsive child in front of the class whether he has taken his pill! Teachers have been found to attribute the success of a medicated ADD child to the stimulant, not to ability or effort. This might lead a teacher to feel that a hyperactive child on medication was less worthy of credit or praise for accomplishment, leading to the child having less pride in his accomplishments and subsequently emitting less effort.[123] These effects have not been systematically studied but careful preparation of the teacher may avoid possible negative effects. Teachers surveyed reported their most common complaints regarding stimulants and hyperactivity to be: inadequate information regarding drug effects and changes in treatment regimen, side effects that may impair school performance, and disagreements with parents and physicians regarding treatment practices which were inadequately discussed.[124] Schools have a wide variety of rules and procedures regarding dispensing of medications during the school day. The parent and physician should collaborate in making an arrangement which provides the greatest supervision with the least risk of stigma.

Compliance with stimulant medication is a major problem. Kauffman suggests that poor compliance with medication regimens may be in part responsible for the variable and conflicting results from drug studies and the lack of evidence for long term efficacy of stimulants.[125] When assessed directly, compliance has been found to be no better than 60% in both short- and long-term protocols.[125,126] . . .

Since ADD is usually not a clinical emergency, the dose can be gradually increased by one pill once or twice a day each week. Since a few children can be maintained on a morning dose only, it may be useful to begin with one daily dose and add the midday dose if necessary. As noted above,[21,22] medication can be given after breakfast and lunch to minimize anorexia. The need for a third dose, usually small and given no later than 3 or 4 PM, is individually determined. Indications would be symptoms in the late afternoon or evening which interfere with homework, peer activities, or sleep, or severe behavior problems at home which cannot be managed with appropriate contingencies. Depending on the severity of symptoms and whether children are symptomatic at home as well as at school, many children can be maintained on a reduced or even no dose of medication on weekends.

MAINTENANCE

Children should have a summer "drug holiday" of at least two to four weeks to minimize possible effects on growth. If the medication seems to lose its effect, an increased dose may be required due to tolerance[89] or an increase in the child's weight, but the physician should first consider the possibility of noncompliance and/or a change in the family or school environment as a cause for clinical deterioration.

Careful monitoring of drug treatment is essential. A double-blind trial is the best way to assess effectiveness. Although this may not be possible for the individual clinician, Varley has demonstrated its practicality in a clinic.[128] In some cases it may be helpful to initially keep the teacher blind. Nearly all children should receive a trial off medication once a year. It would be ideal if the child, the parent, and the teacher were blind to this (ie, placebo substituted by clinician), but again this is not always possible. Some authors advocate a drug-free trial at the beginning of the school year but others would argue that this is the worst possible time. During the first few weeks of school, teachers form impressions of students which will be relatively unchangeable in the course of the year. If the child does still need medication, he or she is then off to a bad start. It is better to try in late winter or early spring when the child is well known to peers and teachers, and before the end of school causes whole classrooms to become inattentive and excitable. For youngsters on relatively large doses, tapering may be a better practice than abrupt discontinuation. It should be noted that medication should not be automatically discontinued at puberty, but that the duration of need for medication is a highly individual matter.

Standardized reports from teachers should be obtained on a regular basis using the CASQ. Academic testing is essential to assess the child's progress. Regular contact with the teacher is also important but unfortunately often omitted in practice. In one study, 20% of the parents surveyed stated that the physician did not even inquire whether or how the medication affected school performance![134] Parents should be seen regularly to assess both drug effects and other difficulties which might require intervention, at this time the CASQ and standardized side effect questionnaires may be used.[68,129] Height and weight should be checked at least twice a year, every three months if the child is short.[74] Blood pressure and pulse rate should be monitored at times of dose increase.

SPECIAL POPULATION

Questions often arise regarding such special populations as preschoolers, adolescents, and the mentally retarded. While ADD is often identified prior to age six, the treatment of young children is controversial. Methylphenidate is not recommended for children less than six,[24] although it is commonly used in the community. Dextroamphetamine is recommended for age 3 and over.[24] In two double-blind studies using methylphenidate vs. placebo in 3 to 6 year olds identified as hyperactive, the efficacy was found to be even more variable than in groups of older children, with a higher incidence of side effects, especially sadness, irritability, and clinginess, along with insomnia and anorexia.[130,131] Stimulants should be used in this age group only in the most severe cases where parent training and placement in a highly structured, well staffed preschool program have been unsuccessful or are not possible.

Major concerns with adolescent populations include possible growth retardation, abuse of medication, and increased sensitivity to peer opinion. Pemoline would seem to be the drug of choice for many adolescents, but a youngster who has been doing well on methylphenidate or dextroamphetamine should not automatically be switched to pemoline just because he or she reaches puberty. A double-blind crossover trial in ADD adolescents without conduct disorder previously identified as methylphenidate responders showed 70% significantly improved on methylphenidate.[132]

The evaluation and treatment of children with mental retardation is especially complex. Many studies of stimulants in mentally retarded patients have been with severely impaired institutionalized populations. Varley reports preliminary findings with a group of 10 mildly retarded children and adolescents with ADD living at home. Half of the patients improved on methylphenidate compared to placebo.[133] This is a somewhat lower rate than usually reported in children and adolescents of normal IQ.

ADDITIONAL TREATMENT

There is widespread agreement that stimulant medication should not be the only treatment for ADD for an individual's entire "career." Even children who respond positively do not show improvement in all areas where there are deficits. Unfortunately, despite long standing recommendations for multimodality treatment,[134,135] an integrated approach is not consistently carried out in practice.[3,124] The stimulant-induced decrease in intensity of problem behaviors takes the pressure off schools to evaluate and remedy academic deficiencies and off parents to learn better management techniques or to arrange for experiences which will improve a child's peer relations.

One recommendation is to make a careful evaluation and plan for treatment of specific deficits. Virtually all parents require some education regarding ADD and techniques to manage these difficult children. Although not without methodologic flaws, studies have indicated that families of hyperactive children have a higher than average incidence of marital discord, of alcoholism and sociopathy in the males, and hysteria and depression in the females.[70,136,137] Marital therapy and/or treatment of parental psychopathology may be indicated. Special classes, tutoring, and/or a change in classroom management techniques may be required. The child may benefit from individual treatment to address sequelae of ADD. Social skills training may improve peer relations.[138]

There are promising beginnings in combining pharmacologic with a variety of other treatment interventions.[135] Gittelman found ADD with hyperactivity children receiving methylphenidate and behavior modification at home and school to be equal to control children on all study measures.[139] Pelham found similar additive effects of stimulants, contingency management, and tutoring.[138] Studies with less intensive psychotherapeutic interventions have not found significant additive effects with pharmacotherapy.[140,141] Single case studies have shown additive effects of dextroamphetamine and self-control training and contingent reinforcement for correct responses on testing,[142] and activity feedback and reinforcement.[143] A great deal of work remains in the study of the interaction between stimulants and psychotherapeutic treatments.

Finally, some authors have suggested adding other medications to stimulants. Cantwell suggests that if children on stimulants develop significant depression imipramine may be added.[92] Discontinuing the stimulant with substitution of imipramine if necessary seems more parsimonious.[144] Others have suggested adding thioridiazine to stimulants to treat evening behavior problems, insomnia, and/or anorexia.[145] Given the negative effects of major tranquilizers on learning and the possibility of tardive dyskinesia, a better approach, if these side effects are severe, is to decrease the dose of stimulants, change the timing, or change to another stimulant.

ALTERNATIVE TREATMENT METHODS

Other compounds have been suggested for the treatment of hyperactivity. Imipramine is effective in some children but is not the first choice for most.[144] Thorazine[96] and haloperidol[146] are less effective than methylphenidate and have more side effects. Carbidopa/levodopa (Sinemet) is more effective than placebo but significantly less so than dextroamphetamine.[147] Caffeine has been repeatedly shown to have virtually no efficacy despite significant side effects.[11,146]

A wide variety of nonpharmacologic alternatives to stimulant treatment have been suggested. Most common is behavioral interventions via parent training, teacher training, and/or directly by the clinician.[9,148,149] Barkley describes in detail models of behavioral treatment for the home and classroom which may be useful to the clinician.[70] Behavioral treatments have been found to be effective in the short term for hyperactive children for behaviors and settings specifically targeted. Studies comparing behavioral and pharmacologic interventions have had mixed results.[141,150,151] To be effective, programs should be specifically designed for ADD.[152]

Cognitive therapy approaches for ADD children have developed from the work of Vygotsky,[153] Luria,[154] Spivack and Shure,[155] and Douglas.[156] Models use a variety of self-control and problem-solving strategies.[152,157–164] Response cost, positive reinforcers, and/or a self-reinforcement component may facilitate change.[149,152] Studies comparing methylphenidate and cognitive-behavioral treatments show each to have some benefit.[159,165]

The more controversial alternative etiologies and treatment deserve mention because they receive great attention in the media and often arise in discussions with parents and teachers. The most widely publicized has been diet.[165] Reviews of the methodologically satisfactory studies[70,166–170] indicate that 5% to 10% of hyperkinetic children may show behavioral improvement on the so called Kaiser-Permanente diet but that these changes are not as dramatic as those induced by stimulants. Preschool children are more likely to respond than older. Controversy, however, continues.[171] Although dietary treatments appeal to parents,[170] it is virtually impossible to insure compliance in a child who is of school age.

Other factors related to diet which some have implicated in the etiology of hyperactivity are food allergies, vitamin deficiencies, and sugar. Barkley[70] summarizes the lack of evidence for these theories.

Preliminary findings indicate that hyperactive children with elevated but "non-toxic" lead levels and without a "known cause" for hyperactivity (eg, birth trauma) improve after treatment with lead chelating agents.[172] Although lead toxicity is probably not causal in the majority of ADD children, it should be considered, especially if there is a history of pica or other significant environmental exposure to lead.

CONCLUSION

With appropriate evaluation and monitoring, pharmacotherapy is a safe and efficacious treatment for some symptoms in children and adolescents with ADD. The deficits which are not addressed by medication may be remediated by other interventions. Multiple measures of outcome are essential since ADD is a complex disorder and stimulants have actions which are far from simple. There are hints that combined treatments may be best, either to address multiple areas of symptoms or to increase efficacy beyond that of either intervention alone. A great deal of work remains to be done with more homogeneous and carefully described populations, standardized and controlled treatment interventions, and prospective long-term follow-up studies.

REFERENCES

1. American Psychiatric Association: *Diagnostic and Statistical Manual of Mental Disorders*, ed 3. Washington, DC, American Psychiatric Association, 1980.
2. Douglas VI: Attentional and cognitive problems, in Rutter M (ed): *Developmental Neuropsychiatry*. New York, The Guilford Press, 1983.
3. Bosco JJ, Robin SS: Hyperkinesis: Prevalence and treatment, in Whalen CK, Henker B (eds): *Hyperactive Children*. New York, Academic Press, Inc., 1980.
4. Sandoval J, Lambert NM, Sassone D: The identification and labeling of hyperactivity in children: An interactive model, in Whalen CK, Henker B (eds): *Hyperactive Children*. New York, Academic Press, Inc., 1980.
5. Wiener JM, Jaffe S: History of drug therapy in children and adolescent psychiatric disorders, in Wiener JM (ed): *Psychopharmacology in Childhood and Adolescence*. New York, Basic Books, Inc., 1977.
6 Bradley C: The behavior of children receiving benzedrine. *Am J Psychiatry* 1937; 94:517–585.
7. Fish B: The "one child one drug" myth of stimulants in hyperkinesis: Importance of diagnostic categories in evaluating treatment. *Arch Gen Psychiatry* 1971: 25:193–203.
8. Grinspoon L, Singer SB: Amphetamines in the treatment of hyperkinetic children. *Harvard Educational Review* 1973; 43:515–555.
9. O'Leary KD: Pills or skills for hyperactive children. *J Appl Behav Anal* 1980; 13:191–204.
10. Schrag P, Divoky D: *The Myth of the Hyperactive Child and Other Means of Child Control*. New York, Pantheon, 1975.
11. Arnold LE, Christopher J, Huestis R, et al: Methylphenidate vs dextroamphetamine vs caffeine in minimal brain dysfunction. *Arch Gen Psychiatry* 1978; 35:463–473.
12. Taylor E: Drug response and diagnostic validation, in Rutter M (ed): *Developmental Neuropsychiatry*. New York, The Guilford Press, 1983.
13. Brown GL, Ebert MH, Hunt RD, et al: Urinary 3- methoxy-4-hydroxyphenylglycol and homovanillic acid response to d-amphetamine in hyperactive children. *Biol Psychiatry* 1981; 16:779–787.
14. Shaywitz SE, Shaywitz BA, Cohen DJ, et al: Monoaminergic mechanisms in hyperactivity, in Rutter M (ed): *Developmental Neuropsychiatry*. New York, The Guilford Press, 1983.
15. Brown GL, Hunt RD, Ebert MH, et al: Plasma levels of d-amphetamine in hyperactive children: Serial behavior and motor responses. *Psychopharmacology* 1979; 62:133–140.
16. Brown GL, Ebert MH, Mikkelsen EJ, et al: Behavior and motor activity response in hyperactive children and plasma amphetamine levels following a sustained release preparation. *J Am Acad Child Psychiatry* 1980; 19:225–239.
17. Gualtieri CT, Kanoy R, Hauk B, et al: Growth hormone and prolactin secretion in adults and hyperactive children: Relation to methylphenidate serum levels. *Psychoneuroendocrinology* 1981; 6:331–339.
18. Greenhill LL, Puig-Antich J, Novacenko H, et al: Prolactin, growth hormone and growth responses in boys with attention deficit disorder and hyperactivity treated with methylphenidate. *J Am Acad Child Psychiatry* 1984; 23:58–67.
19. Greenhill LL, Perel J, Currans, et al: Attentional measures and plasma level correlations in methylphenidate treated males. Presented at the 1983 Meeting of the AACP, San Francisco, October 28, 1983.
20. Shaywitz SE, Hunt RD, Jatlow P, et al: Psychopharmacology of attention deficit disorder: Pharmacokinetic,

neuroendocrine, and behavioral measures following acute and chronic treatment with methylphenidate. *Pediatrics* 1982; 69:688–694.

21. Chan Y-PM, Swanson JM, Soldin SS, et al: Methylphenidate hydrochloride given with or before breakfast: II. Effects on plasma concentration of methylphenidate and ritinalic acid. *Pediatrics* 1983; 72:56–59.
22. Swanson JM, Sandman CA, Deutsch C, et al: Methylphenidate hydrochloride given with or before breakfast: I. Behavioral, cognitive, and electrophysiologic effects. *Pediatrics* 1983; 72:49–55.
23. Gilman AGG, Goodman LS, Gilman A (eds): *Goodman and Gilman's The Pharmacologic Basis of Therapeutics*, ed 6. New York, Macmillan, 1980.
24. *Physicians' Desk Reference*, Oradell, NJ, Medical Economics Co., Inc., 1984.
25. Whitehouse D, Shah U, Palmer FB: Comparison of sustained-release and standard methylphenidate in the treatment of minimal brain dysfunction. *J Clin Psychiatry* 1980; 41:282–285.
26. Dykman RA, McGrew J, Harris TS, et al: Two blinded studies of the effects of stimulant drugs on children: Pemoline, methylphenidate, and placebo, in Anderson RP (ed): *Learning Disability/MBD Syndrome*. Springfield, IL, Charles C Thomas, 1976.
27. Yaffe SJ, Danish M: The classification and pharmacology of psychoactive drugs in childhood and adolescence, in Wiener JM (ed): *Psychopharmacology in Childhood and Adolescence*. New York, Basic Books, Inc., 1977.
28. Knights RM, Viets CA: Effects of pemoline on hyperactive boys. *Pharmacol Biochem Behav* 1975; 3:1107–1114.
29. Conners CK, Taylor E: Pemoline, methylphenidate, and placebo in children with minimal brain dysfunction. *Arch Gen Psychiatry* 1980; 37:922–930.
30. Rapoport JL, Mikkelsen EJ, Ebert MH, et al: Urinary catecholamines and amphetamine excretion in hyperactive and normal boys. *J Nerv Ment Dis* 1978; 166:731–737.
31. Shekim WO, Javaid J, Dekirmenjian H, et al: Effects of d-amphetamine on urinary metabolites of dopamine and norepinephrine in hyperactive boys. *Am J Psychiatry* 1982; 139:485–488.
32. Kupietz SS, Winsberg BG, Sverd J: Learning ability and methylphenidate (Ritalin) plasma concentration in hyperactive children: A preliminary investigation. *J Am Acad Child Psychiatry* 1982; 21:27–30.
33. Winsberg BG, Kupietz SS, Sverd J, et al: Methylphenidate and dose plasma concentrations and behavioral response in children. *Psychopharmacology* 1982; 76:329–332.
34. Tomkins CP, Soldin SJ, Macleod SM, et al: Analysis of pemoline in serum by high performance liquid chromatography: Clinical application to optimize treatment of hyperactive children. *Ther Drug Monit* 1980; 2:255–260.
35. Sprague RL, Sleator EK: Methylphenidate in hyperkinetic children. Differences in dose effects on learning and social behavior. *Science* 1977; 198: 1274–1276.
36. Porges SW, Smith KM: Defining hyperactivity: Psychophysiological and behavioral strategies, in Whalen CK, Henker B (eds): *Hyperactive Children*. New York, Academic Press, 1980.
37. Brown RT, Sleator EK: Methylphenidate in hyperkinetic children: Differences in dose effects on impulsive behavior. *Pediatrics* 1979; 64: 408–411.
38. Gan J, Cantwell DP: Dosage effects of methylphenidate on paired associate learning: Positive/negative placebo responders. *J Am Acad Child Psychiatry* 1982; 21:237–242.
39. Klorman R, Salzman LF, Bauer LO, et al: Effects of two doses of methylphenidate on cross-situational and borderline hyperactive children's evoked potentials. *Electroencephalogr Clin Neurophysiol* 1983; 56:169–185.
40. Whalen CK, Henker B: Hyperactivity and the attention deficit disorders: Expanding frontiers. *Pediatr Clin North Am*, 1984; 32:397–427.
41. Rapoport JL, Buchsbaum MS, Zahn TP, et al: Dextroamphetamine: Cognitive and behavioral effects in normal prepubertal boys. *Science* 1978; 199:560 –563
42. Rapoport IL, Buchsbaum MS, Weingartner H, et al: Dextroamphetamine: Its cognitive and behavioral effects in normal and hyperactive boys and normal men. *Arch Gen Psychiatry* 1980; 37:933–943.
43. Sostek AJ, Buchsbaum MS, Rapoport JL: Effects of amphetamine on vigilance performance in normal and hyperactive children. *J Abnorm Psychol* 1980; 8:491–500.
44. Weingartner H, Ebert MH, Mikkelsen EJ, et al: Cognitive processes in normal and hyperactive children and their response to amphetamine treatment. *J Abnorm Psychol* 1980; 89:25–37.
45. Zahn TP, Rapoport JL, Thompson CL: Autonomic and behavioral effects of dextroamphetamine and placebo in normal and hyperactive prepubertal boys. *J Abnorm Child Psychol* 1980; 8:145–160.
46. Barkley RA: A review of stimulant drug research with hyperactive children. *J Child Psychol Psychiatry* 1977; 18:137–165.
47. Conners CK: Stimulant drugs and cortical evoked responses in learning and behavior disorders in children, in Smith WL (ed): *Drugs, Development and Cerebral Function*. Springfield, IL, C.C. Thomas, 1972.
48. Kavale K: The efficacy of stimulant drug treatment for hyperactivity: A meta-analysis. *Joumal of Leaning Disabilities* 1982; 15:280–289.
49. Porrino LJ, Rapoport JL, Behar D, et al: A naturalistic assessment of the motor activity of hyperactive boys. II. Stimulant drug effects. *Arch Gen Psychiatry* 1983; 40:688–693.
50. Rapoport JL, Tepsic PN, Grice J, et al: Decreased motor activity of hyperactive children on dextroamphetamine during active gym program. *Psychiatry Res* 1980; 2:225–229.
51. Whalen CK, Collins BE, Henker B, et al: Behavior observations of hyperactive children and methylphenidate (Ritalin) effects in systematically structured classroom environments:

Now you see them now you don't. *J Pediatr Psychol* 1978; 3:177–187.

52. Lerer RJ, Artner J, Lerer MP: Handwriting deficits in children with minimal brain dysfunction: Effects of methylphenidate (Ritalin) and placebo. *J Learning Disabilities* 1979; 12: 450–455.
53. Whalen CK, Henker B, Finck D: Medication effects in the classroom: Three naturalistic indicators. *J Abnorm Child Psychol* 1981; 9:419–433.
54. Keogh BK, Barkett CJ: An educational analysis of hyperactive children's achievement problems, in Whalen CK, Henker B (eds): *Hyperactive Children*. New York, Academic Press, Inc., 1980.
55. Thurber S, Walker CE: Medication and hyperactivity: A meta-analysis. *J Gen Psychol* 1983; 108:79–86.
56. Whalen CK. Henker B: Psychostimulants and children: A review and analysis. *Psychol Bull* 1976; 83:1113–1130.
57. Gittelman R, Klein DF. Feingold I: Children with reading disorders: II. Effects of methylphenidate in combination with reading remediation. *J Child Psychol Psychiatry* 1983; 24: 193–212.
58. Whalen CK, Henker BE, Finck D, et al: A social ecology of hyperactive boys: Medication effects in structured classroom environments. *J Appl Behav Anal* 1979; 12:65–81.
59. Barkley RA: Using stimulant drugs in the classroom. *School Psychology Review* 1979; 8:412–425.
60. Barkley RA: The use of psychopharmacology to study reciprocal influences in parent-child interaction. *J Abnorm Child Psychol* 1981; 9:303–310.
61. Whalen CK, Henker B, Dotemoto S: Teacher response to the methylphenidate (Ritalin) versus placebo status of hyperactive boys in the classroom. *Child Dev* 1981; 52:1005–1014.
62. Riddle KD, Rapoport JL: A 2-year follow-up of 72 hyperactive boys: Classroom behavior and peer acceptance. *J Nerv Ment Dis* 1976; 162: 126–134.
63. Weiss G: Long-term outcome: Findings, concepts, and practical implications in Rutter M (ed): *Developmental Neuropsychiatry*. New York, The Guilford Press, 1983.
64. Paternite CE, Loney J: Childhood hyperkinesis: Relationships between symptomatology and home environment, in Whalen CK, Henker B (eds): *Hyperactive Children*. New York, Academic Press, 1980.
65. Whalen CK, Henker B: The social ecology of psychostimulant treatment: A model for conceptual and empirical analysis, in Whalen CK, Henker B (eds): *Hyperactive Children: The Social Ecology of Identification and Treatment*. New York, Academic Press, 1980.
66. Page JG, Janicki RS, Bernstein JE, et al: Pemoline (Cylert) in the treatment of childhood hyperkinesis. *Journal of Learning Disabilities* 1974; 7:42–47.
67. Greenhill LL, Puig-Antich J, Chambers W, et al: Growth hormone, prolactin, and growth responses in hyperkinetic males treated with d-amphetamine. *J Am Acad Child Psychiatry* 1981; 20:84–103.
68. Greenhill L, Puig-Antich J, Goetz R, et al: Sleep architecture and REM sleep measures in prepubertal children with attention deficit disorder with hyperactivity. *Sleep* 1983; 6:91–101.
69. Chatoor I, Wells KC, Conners CK, et al: The effects of nocturnally administered stimulant medication on EEG sleep and behavior in hyperactive children. *J Am Acad Child Psychiatry* 1983; 22:337–342.
70. Barkley RA: *Hyperactive Children: A Handbook for Diagnosis and Treatment*. New York, The Guilford Press, 1981.
71. Loney J, Whaley-Klahn MA, Ponto LB, et al: Predictors of adolescent height and weight in hyperkinetic boys treated with methylphenidate. *Psychopharmacol Bull* 1981; 17:132–134.
72. Safer D. Allen R. Barr E: Depression of growth in hyperactive children on stimulant drugs. *N Engl J Med* 1972; 287:217–220.
73. Roche AF, Lipman RS, Overall JE, et al: The effects of stimulant medication on the growth of hyperactive children. *Pediatrics* 1979; 63:847–850.
74. Greenhill LL: Stimulant-related growth inhibition in children: A review, in Gittelman M (ed): *Strategic Interventions for Hyperactive Children*. New York, M.E. Sharpe, Inc., 1981.
75. Mattes JA, Gittelman R: Growth of hyperactive children on maintenance regimen of methylphenidate. *Arch Gen Psychiatry* 1983; 40:317–321.
76. Schultz FR, Hayford JT, Wolraich ML, et al: Methylphenidate treatment of hyperactive children: Effects on the hypothalamic-pituitary-somatomedin axis. *Pediatrics* 1982; 70: 987–992.
77. Aman MG, Werry JS: Methylphenidate in children: Effects on cardiorespiratory function on exertion. *International of Mental Health* 1975; 4:119–131 .
78. Ballard JE, Boileau RA, Sleator EK, et al: Cardiovascular responses of hyperactive children to methylphenidate. *JAMA* 1976; 236:2870–2874.
79. Denckla MB, Bemporad JR, MacKay MC: Tics following methylphenidate administration: A report of 20 cases. *JAMA* 1976; 235:1349–1351.
80. Margolin DI: Methylphenidate-induced tics. *JAMA* 1976; 236:917–918.
81. Bremness AB, Sverd MD: Methylphenidate-induced Tourette Syndrome. *Am J Psychiatry* 1979; 136: 1334–1335.
82. Lowe TL, Cohen DJ, Detlor J, et al: Stimulant medications precipitate Tourette's Syndrome. *JAMA* 1982; 247:1168–1169.
83. Mitchell E, Matthews KL: Gilles de la Tourette's disorder associated with pemoline. *Am J Psychiatry* 1980; 137: 1618–1619.
84. Comings DE, Comings BG: Tourette's Syndrome and attention deficit disorder with hyperactivity: Are they genetically related? *J Am Acad Child Psychiatry* 1984; 23:138–146.
85. Svard J, Hurwic MJ, David O, et al: Hypersensitivity to methylphenidate and dextroamphetamine: A report of two cases. *Pediatrics* 1977; 59:115–117.

86. Lucas AR, Weiss M: Methylphenidate hallucinosis. *JAMA* 1971; 217: 1079–1081.
87. Weiss G, Minde K, Douglas V, et al: Comparison of the effects of chlorpromazine, dextroamphetamine, and methylphenidate on the behavior and intellectual functioning of hyperactive children. *Can Med Assoc J* 1971; 104:20–25.
88. Rosenfeld M: Depression and psychotic regression following prolonged methylphenidate use and withdrawal: Case report. *Am J Psychiatry* 1979; 136:226–228.
89. Winsberg BG, Press M, Bialer I, et al: Dextroamphetamine and methylphenidate in the treatment of hyperactive/aggressive children. *Pediatrics* 1974; 53:236–24 1.
90. Gittelman R: Hyperkinetic syndrome: Treatment issues and principles, in Rutter M (ed): *Developmental Neuropsychiatry*. New York, The Guilford Press, 1983.
91. Whalen CK, Henker B, Collins BE, et al: Peer interaction in a structured communication task: Comparisons of normal and hyperactive boys and of methylphenidate (Ritalin) and placebo effects. *Child Dev* 1979; 50: 388–401.
92. Cantwell DP: Psychopharmacologic treatment of the minimal brain dysfunction syndrome, in Wiener JM (ed): *Psychopharmacology in Childhood and Adolescence*. New York, Basic Books, Inc., 1977.
93. Steinhausen HC, Kreuzer EM: Learning in hyperactive children: Are there stimulant-related and state dependent effects? *Psychopharmacology* 1981; 74: 389–390.
94. Shea VT: State-dependent learning in children receiving methylphenidate. *Psychopharmacology* 1982; 78: 266–270.
95. Dyme IZ, Sahakian BJ, Golinko BE, et al: Perseveration induced by methylphenidate in children: Preliminary findings. *Prog Neuropsychopharmacol Biol Psychiatry* 1982; 6: 269–273.
96. Fiedler NL, Ullman DG: The effects of stimulant drugs on curiosity behaviors of hyperactive boys. J *Abnorm Child Psychol* 1983: 11:193–206.
97. Goyer PF, Davis GC, Rapoport JL: Abuse of prescribed stimulant medication by a 13-year-old hyperactive boy. *J Am Acad Child Psychiatry* 1979: 18:170–175.
98. Satterfield JH, Scheid AM, Baie SD: Potential risk of prolonged administration of stimulant medication for hyperactive children. *JDBP* 1980; 1: 102–107.
99. Livingston S, Berman W, Pauli L: Amphetamines in epilepsy. *Pediatrics* 1973; 52:753–754.
100. Laufer MW, Denhoff E, Solomons G: Hyperkinetic impulse disorder in children's behavior problems. *Psychosom Med* 1957; 19:38–49.
101. Henker B, Whalen CK: The many messages of medication: Hyperactive children's perceptions and attributions, in Salzinger S, Antrobus J, Glick J (eds): *The Ecosystem of The "Sick" Child*. New York, Academic Press, 1980.
102. Ferguson HB, Rapoport JL: Nosological issues and biological validation, in Rutter M (ed): *Developmental Neuropsychiatry*. New York, The Guilford Press, 1983.
103. Collins BE, Whalen CK, Henker B: Ecological and pharmacological influences on behaviors in the classroom: The hyperkinetic behavioral syndrome, in Salzinger S, Antrobus J, Glick J (eds): *The Ecosystem of the "Sick" Child*. New York, Academic Press, 1980.
104. Rutter M: Behavioral studies: Questions and findings on the concept of a distinctive syndrome, in Rutter M (ed): *Developmental Neuropsychiatry*. New York, The Guilford Press, 1983.
105. Conners CK: Symptom patterns in hyperkinetic, neurotic, and normal children. *Child Dev* 1970; 41:667–682.
106. Conners CK: Rating scales for use in drug studies with children. *Psychopharmacol Bull* 1973; (special issue) 24–84.
107. Conners C, Rothschild G, Eisenberg L, et al: Dextroamphetamine sulfate in children with learning disorders. *Arch Gen Psychiatry* 1974; 21:182–190.
108. Goyette CH, Conners CK, Ulrich RF: Normative data on revised Conners' parent and teacher rating scales. J *Abnorm Child Psychol* 1978; 6:221–236.
109. Conners CK: A teacher rating scale for use in drug studies with children. *Am J Psychiatry* 1969; 126:884–888.
110. Werry JS, Sprague RL, Cohen MN: Conners' Teacher Rating Scale for use in drug studies with children—An empirical study. J Abnorm Child Psychol 1975; 3:217–229.
111. Werry J, Sprague R: Methylphenidate in children: Effect of dosage. *Aust NZ J Psychiatry* 1974; 8:9–19.
112. Milich R, Roberts MA, Loney J, et al: Differentiating practice effects and statistical regression on the Conners Hyperkinesis Index. *J Abnorm Child Psychol* 1980; 8:549–552.
113. Henker B, Whalen CK, Collins BE: Double-blind and triple-blind assessments of medication and placebo responses in hyperactive children. *J Abnorm Child Psychol* 1979; 7:1–13.
114. Achenbach TM, Edelbrock C: *Manual for the Child Behavior Checklist*. Queen City Printers, Inc., 1983.
115. Edelbrock C, Costello AJ, Dulcan MK: Empirical corroboration of the attention deficit disorder. *J Am Acad Child Psychiatry*, 1984; 23:285–290.
116. Routh DK: Developmental and social aspects of hyperactivity, in Whalen CK, Henker B (eds): *Hyperactive Children*. New York, Academic Press, 1980.
117. Barkley RA: Predicting the response of hyperkinetic children to stimulant drugs: A review. *J Abnorm Child Psychol* 1976; 4:327–348.
118. Conners CK, Taylor E, Meo G, et al: Magnesium pemoline and dextroamphetamine: A controlled study in children with minimal brain dysfunction. *Psychopharmacologia* 1972; 26:321–336.
119. Baxley GB, Turner PF, Greenwold WE: Hyperactive children's knowledge and attitudes concerning drug treatment. *J Pediatr Psychol* 1978; 3: 172–176.

120. Sleator EK, Ullmann RK, von Neumann A: How do hyperactive children feel about taking stimulants and will they tell the doctor? *Clin Pediatr* 1982; 21:474–479.
121. Gualtieri CT, Powell SF: Psychoactive drug interactions. *J Clin Psychiatry* 1978; 39:720–729.
122. Okolo C, Bartlett SA, Shaw SF: Communication between professionals concerning medication for the hyperactive child. *J Learning Disabilities* 1978; 11:45–58.
123. Amirkhan J: Expectancies and attributions for hyperactive and medicated hyperactive students. *J Abnorm Child Psychol* 1982; 10:265–276.
124. Gadow KD: Pharmacotherapy for behavior disorders. Typical treatment practices. *Clin Pediatr* 1983; 22:48–53.
125. Kauffman RE, Smith-Wright D, Reese CA, et al: Medication compliance in hyperactive children. *Pediatr Pharmacol* 1981; 1:231–237.
126. Firestone P: Factors associated with children's adherence to stimulant medication. *Am J Orthopsychiatry* 1982; 52:447–457.
127. Weiss G: Controversial issues of the pharmacotherapy of the hyperactive child. *Can J Psychiatry* 1981; 26:385–392.
128. Varley CK, Trupin EW: Double-blind assessment of stimulant medication for attention deficit disorder: A model for clinical application. *Am J Orthopsychiatry* 1983; 53:542–547.
129. Golinko BE: Side effects of dexedrine in hyperactive children: Operationalization and quantification in a short-term trial. *Prog Neuropsychopharmacol Biol Psychiatry* 1982; 6: 175–183.
130. Schleifer M, Weiss G, Cohen N, et al: Hyperactivity in preschoolers and the effect of methylphenidate. *Am J Orthopsychiatry* 1975; 45:38–50.
131. Conners CK: Controlled trial of methylphenidate in preschool children with minimal brain dysfunction. *I J Mental Health* 1975; 4:61–74.
132. Varley CK: Effects of methylphenidate in adolescents with attention deficit disorder. *J Am Acad Child Psychiatry* 1983; 22:351–354.
133. Varley CK, Trupin EW: Double-blind administration of methylphenidate to mentally retarded children with attention deficit disorder: A preliminary study. *Am J Ment Defic* 1982; 86:560–566.
134. Feighner AC, Feighner JP: Multimodality treatment of the hyperkinetic child. *Am J Psychiatry* 1974; 131:459–462.
135. Satterfield JH, Satterfield BT, Cantwell DP: Three-year multimodality treatment study of 100 hyperactive boys. *J Pediatr* 1981; 98: 650–655.
136. Cantwell DP: Psychiatric illness in the families of hyperactive children. *Arch Gen Psychiatry* 1972; 27:414–417.
137. Morrison JR, Stewart MA: A family study of the hyperactive child syndrome. *Bio J Psychiatry* 1971; 3:189–195.
138. Pelham WE, Schredler RW, Bologna NC, et al: Behavioral and stimulant treatment of hyperactive children: A therapy study with methylphenidate probes in a within-subject design. *J Appl Behav Anal* 1980; 13:221–236.
139. Gittelman R, Abckoff H, Pollack E, et al: A controlled trial of behavior modification and methylphenidate in hyperactive children, in Whalen CK, Henker B (eds): *Hyperactive Children*. New York, Academic Press, 1980.
140. Wolraich M, Drummond T, Salomon MK, et al: Effects of methylphenidate alone and in combination with behavior modification procedures on the behavior and academic performance of hyperactive children. *J Abnorm Child Psychol* 1978; 6:149–161.
141. Firestone P, Kelly MJ, Goodman JT, et al: Differential effects of parent training and stimulant medication with hyperactives: A progress report. *J Am Acad Child Psychiatry* 1981; 20:135–147.
142. Horn WF, Chatoor I, Conners CK: Additive effects of dexedrine and self-control training. *Behavior Modification* 1983; 7:383–402.
143. Williamson DA: Treating hyperactivity with Dexedrine and activity feedback. *Behavior Modification* 1981; 5:399–416.
144. Rancurello MD: Clinical applications of antidepressant drugs in childhood behavioral and emotional disorders. *Psychiatric Annals* 1985; 15:88–100.
145. Gittelman-Klein R, Klein D, Katz S, et al: Comparative effects of methylphenidate and thioridiazine in hyperkinetic children. *Arch Gen Psychiatry* 1976; 33:1217–1231.
146. Rapoport JL: The use of drugs, trends in research, in Rutter M (ed): *Developmental Neuropsychiatry*. New York, The Guilford Press, 1983.
147. Langer DH, Rapoport JL, Brown GL, et al: Behavioral effects of carbidopa/levidopa in hyperactive boys. *J Am Acad Child Psychiatry* 1982; 21:10–18.
148. Backman J, Firestone P: A review of psychopharmacological and behavioral approaches to the treatment of hyperactive children. *Am J Orthopsychiatry* 1979; 49:500–504.
149. Mash EJ, Dalby JT: Behavioral interventions for hyperactivity, in Trites RL (ed): *Hyperactivity in Children: Etiology, Measurement and Treatment Implications*. Baltimore, University Park Press, 1979.
150. Loney J, Weissenburger FE, Woolson RF, et al: Comparing psychological and pharmacological treatments for hyperactive boys and their classmates. *J Abnorm Child Psychol* 1979; 7:133–143.
151. Thurston LP: Comparison of the effects of parent training and of Ritalin in treating hyperactive children, in Gittelman M (ed): *Strategic Interventions for Hyperactive Children*. New York, M.E. Sharpe, Inc., 1981.
152. Douglas VI: Treatment and training approaches to hyperactivity: Establishing internal or external control, in Whalen C, Henker B (eds): *Hyperactive Children: The Social Ecology of Identification and Treatment*. New York, Academic Press, 1980.
153. Vygotsky R: *Thought and Language*. New York, Wiley, 1962.
154. Luria A: *The Role of Speech in the Regulation of Normal and Abnormal Behaviors*. New York, Liveright, 1961.

155. Spivack G, Shure MB: The cognition of social adjustment: Interpersonal cognitive problem-solving thinking, in Lahey BB, Kazdin AE (eds): *Advances in Clinical Child Psychology*, New York, Plenum, 1982, vol 5.
156. Douglas VI: Stop, look and listen: The problem of sustained attention and impulse control in hyperactive and normal children. *Can J Behav Science* 1972; 4:259–281.
157. Douglas VI, Parry P, Marton P, et al: Assessment of a cognitive training program for hyperactive children. *J Abnormal Child Psychol* 1976; 4:389–410.
158. Meichenbaum D: Application of cognitive-behavior modification procedures to hyperactive children, in Gittelman M (ed): *Strategic Interventions for Hyperactive Children*. New York, M.E. Sharpe, Inc., 1981.
159. Yellin AM, Kendall PC, Greenberg LM: Cognitive-behavioral therapy and methylphenidate with hyperactive children: Preliminary comparisons. *Research Communications in Psychology and Psychiatry and Behavior* 1981; 6:213–227.
160. Meichenbaum D, Goodman J: Training impulsive children to talk to themselves: A means of developing self-control. *J Abnorm Psychol* 1971; 77:115–126.
161. Kendall PC, Finch AJ: Developing non-impulsive behavior in children: Cognitive-behavioral strategies for self-control, in Kendall PC, Hollon SD (eds): *Cognitive-Behavioral Interventions: Theory, Research and Procedures*. New York, Academic Press, 1979.
162. Meichenbaum D, Asarnow J: Cognitive-behavioral modification and metacognitive development: Implications for the classroom, in Kendall PC, Hollon SD (eds): *Cognitive-Behavioral Interventions: Theory, Research and Procedures*. New York, Academic Press, 1979.
163. Kennedy R: Cognitive-behavioral approaches to the modification of aggressive behavior in children. *School Psychol Review* 1982; VII:47–55.
164. Urbain ES, Kendall PC: Review of social-cognitive problem-solving interventions with children. *Psychol Bull* 1980; 88:109–143.
165. Hinshaw SP, Henker B, Whalen CK: Self-control in hyperactive boys in anger inducing situations: Effects of cognitive-behavioral training and methylphenidate. *J Abnorm Child Psychol*, 1984; 12:55–77.
166. Feingold B: *Why Your Child Is Hyperactive*. New York, Random House, 1975.
167. Henker B, Whalen CK: The changing faces of hyperactivity: Retrospect and prospect, in Whalen CK, Henker B (eds): *Hyperactive Children*. New York, Academic Press, 1980.
168. Mattes JA: The Feingold diet: A current reappraisal. *J Learning Disabilities* 1983; 16:319–323.
169. Kavale KA, Forness SR: Hyperactivity and diet treatment: A meta-analysis of the Feingold hypothesis. *J Learning Disabilities* 1983; 16:324–330.
170. Varley CK: Diet and the behavior of children with attention deficit disorder. *J Am Acad Child Psychiatry* 1984; 23:182–185.
171. Rimland B: The Feingold diet: An assessment of the reviews by Mattes, by Kavale and Forness, and others. *J Learning Disabilities* 1983; 16:331–333.
172. David OJ, Hoffman SP, Sverd J, et al: Lead and hyperactivity: Behavioral response to chelation: A pilot study. *Am J Psychiatry* 1976; 133:1155–1158.

DEBORAH JACOBVITZ, L. ALAN SROUFE, MARK STEWART, & NANCY LEFFERT

Treatment of attentional and hyperactivity problems in children with sympathomimetic drugs: A comprehensive review

The practice of treating children with stimulant drugs (primarily methylphenidate) is widespread and apparently increasing. For example, a recent survey in Baltimore County revealed that by 1987 5.96% of all public elementary school students (approximately 10% of all males) were receiving stimulant medication (Safer and Krager, 1988). The rate of medication has doubled every 2 to 4 years since 1971. This study also showed the rate currently to be increasing disproportionately in females and in secondary school populations, two very recent trends. Proposals have been made to extend treatment deliberately into the adolescent period and beyond (Wender, 1987). In light of the continued use of stimulant medication with hundreds of thousands of children, it seems prudent to review the current status of research concerning the effects of stimulants on children. Data now exist on issues for which there was no information 10 or 15 years ago (Sroufe and Stewart, 1973), and numerous studies exist on issues where once there was only scant information. It is time for a comprehensive review.

Major questions that have persisted over time are the following:

1. Are the effects of stimulant medications with hyperactive children (now called children with attention deficit/hyperactivity disorder) (ADHD) atypical or "paradoxical"; that is, do stimulants affect these children uniquely? Until recently, there were no direct data on this question, though numerous studies with normal adults have suggested that the responses of hyperactive children were quite usual (Sroufe and Stewart, 1973).
2. Is there a relationship between specifiable neurological or biochemical abnormality and ADHD, and is drug response predictable from such markers? This literature has been plagued by inconsistency.
3. Do the demonstrable short-term effects of stimulant medications persist? Is enhanced attention still in evidence after several months of treatment? Are there long-term gains in school achievement and social behavior? Is there carryover of positive effects following termination of treatment? Are there long-term negative consequences of prolonged stimulant medication? There were virtually no data on these questions 15 years ago. This issue is critical.

A related question of current interest concerns differential diagnosis, especially the problem of distinguishing ADHD from learning disabilities and conduct disorders. This issue also will be addressed.

Before examining current data on these questions, the authors will begin by briefly reviewing the overwhelming evidence for the short-term impact of stimulants on attention and behavior. These dramatic, incontrovertible effects underlie the widespread use of stimulant medication. After all, there is pressing need to address the problems of children with attentional and activity problems.

SHORT-TERM EFFECTS

Over the past 25 years, there have been hundreds of controlled studies demonstrating the short-term efficacy of stimulant drugs. These studies have been reviewed frequently (Sroufe, 1975; Klein et al., 1980; Barkley, 1981; Ross and Ross, 1982; Solanto, 1984) and will be summarized only briefly.

Ratings by parents and professionals reveal improved behavior and performance following stimulant drug treatment. Task irrelevant activity, such as fidgetiness, finger tapping, and fine motor movement, declines, classroom disturbance lessens, and attention is en-

SOURCE: *Journal of the American Academy of Child and Adolescent Psychiatry*, 29, pp. 677–688, 1990.

hanced, all in comparison to placebo treated control groups.

Significant drug-placebo differences also have been reported on any array of prolonged, routinized laboratory tasks. Especially after many trials on repetitive reaction time tasks, medicated hyperactive children show shorter response latency and improved performance (Rapport et al., 1982). Errors of omission and errors of commission decline on vigilance tasks and performance improves on perceptual search tasks, including matching familiar figures and maze tracing. Stimulant drugs also facilitate performance on certain subscales of standard intelligence tests.

Researchers now are examining stimulant drug effects on children in settings other than laboratory situations. Researchers observing the effects of stimulants on classroom behavior find improvements on arithmetic and graphing tasks and enhanced attention (Whalen et al., 1978). There are also reductions in gross and minor motor movements, noncompliance, interferences, and overall hyperactivity (Abikoff and Gittelman, 1985a). Taken together, these short-term effects of stimulants for ADHD children are impressive.

Though stimulants improve the ability to sustain attention, there is little evidence that stimulants enhance retention, retrieval and relearning of material, or the control of anger. In numerous studies, hyperactive children, following stimulant treatment, failed to show improvement in achievement (Gittelman-Klein and Klein, 1976; Rie et al., 1976a, 1976b). Based on Cunningham and Barkley's (1978) review of 17 such studies using 55 independent measures of academic achievement, Barkley (1981) concluded that "these drugs have almost no effect on scholastic achievement" (p. 197).

There are various explanations for poor outcomes with achievement in the face of positive short-term outcomes on behavior. Douglas et al. (1986) suggest that methodological and conceptual weaknesses may have led to these conclusions. For example, most academic achievement tests do not contain enough items at appropriate levels of complexity to detect short-term changes, and few investigators have carefully matched forms of tests for repeated testing.

Alternatively, Sprague and Sleator (1977) offer an explanation based on differential dose response curves, with the dose of stimulants used to affect targeted behavior difficulties so high that they inhibit the child's ability to learn. This matter is unresolved. More recent studies (Douglas et al., 1986, 1988) suggest that even low doses (e.g., 0.15 to 0.3 mg/kg) lead to behavioral improvement. However, in contrast to behavioral changes that show improvements up to 0.6 mg/kg or even 1.0 mg/kg, there does appear to be a leveling off, if not a decline, in effectiveness on cognitive performance (arithmetic tasks, paired associate learning) at moderate dosages (e.g., 0.6 mg/kg). Dosages higher than 0.6 mg/kg may be ill-advised if the goal is improved cognitive task performance.

Over the past decade, stimulant drug effects on hyperactive children's relationships with mothers and teachers also have been examined. Drug treatment appears to increase child compliance and decrease maternal (Humphries et al., 1978; Tallmadge and Barkley, 1983; Barkley et al., 1985; Barkley, 1989) and teacher control (Whalen et al., 1980, 1981), though, generally, such differences appear only during structured tasks and not free play (Barkley, 1989). Although these studies used sequential analysis, it remains unclear whether the child's compliance elicits or is a consequence of less controlling behavior. Still, changes in adult behavior are important short-term outcomes.

ATYPICAL DRUG RESPONSE

A positive stimulant response by ADHD children has been used as evidence of central neurophysiological disturbance (Shaywitz et al., 1978). One assumption of this model is that reductions in task irrelevant activity in structured classroom settings and improved performance on repetitive tasks following medication distinguish those who suffer from ADHD from other children and adults (Wender, 1971.)

The accumulated literature clearly refutes the notion of an atypical stimulant response of ADHD children. First, substantial work with adult military personnel showed that stimulants enhanced concentration and performance, especially in repetitive, routinized situations (Weiss and Laties, 1962; Laties and Weiss, 1967). Second, those few studies of stimulant drug effects using a normal comparison group or clinically referred nonADHD children show that the response of these groups to stimulants is similar to that of ADHD children. For example, Rapoport et al. (1978) conducted a double-blind study administering 0.5 mg/kg body weight of amphetamines to ADHD children, normal children, and normal adults. Despite differences in age and clinical status, all groups responded to amphetamines with reduced activity level and enhanced vigilance and memory performance in a laboratory task situation. Peloquin and Klorman (1986), working with normal children and adults, found methylphenidate to enhance several aspects of psychomotor performance, such as reaction time and vigilance. Werry and Aman (1984) report enhanced reaction time and vigilance following administrations of methylphenidate to ADHD children as well as enuretic nonADHD controls.

In addition, stimulant effects on ADHD children themselves are not genuinely paradoxical. The children are not "slowed down." While researchers report reductions in activity during tasks performance or in structured classroom situations, these are in part an indirect consequence of enhanced attention and concentration, the effects stimulants have on all populations. Activity level may not be reduced in truly "free field" situations (e.g., on the playground), although the literature is inconsistent here (Ellis et al., 1974;

Solanto, 1984; Cunningham et al., 1985). Finally, the increases in heart rate and blood pressure routinely reported argue against a subduing effect.

ATTENTION DEFICIT HYPERACTIVITY DISORDER AND ORGANIC DYSFUNCTION

Although not logically necessitated, an organic basis for ADHD has often served as a rationale for prescribing stimulant drugs. Despite the plethora of research findings over the past 2 decades, the underlying deficits in hyperactivity remain poorly understood, leading to dozens of labels attached to these children (minimal brain dysfunction, hyperkinetic impulse disorder, etc.).

Brain Injury

ADHD was initially traced to brain injury resulting from traumatic events such as illness, injury, and prenatal and perinatal problems (Still, 1902; Ebaugh, 1923). Research, however, has shown that neurological abnormalities have been present in only a small proportion of ADHD children (Werry, 1968; Nichols and Chen, 1981); that pregnancy and delivery complications have contributed little to the prediction of hyperactivity in school children (Nichols and Chen, 1981; Taylor, 1986; Jacobvitz, 1988, unpublished dissertation); and that brain damaged children commonly have shown no overactivity (Rutter et al., 1970). The lack of evidence concerning brain dysfunction in hyperactivity could stem from failure to locate specific sites of the dysfunction; one candidate being the frontal lobe (Lou et al., 1984; Zametkin and Rapoport, 1987; Hamdan-Allen et al., submitted for publication).

ADHD, Arousal, and Biochemical and Neurological Dysfunction

Many researchers now postulate that ADHD children, rather than having any specific brain lesion, are underaroused or overaroused in autonomic and central nervous system functioning. The underarousal model (e.g., Zentall and Zentall, 1983) assumes that all organisms have a biologically determined optimal level of stimulation, and behavioral activity serves as a homeostatic regulator. Stimulant drugs have been prescribed for children with ADHD symptoms in order to increase their level of cortical arousal, thereby reducing their need to seek external stimulation. In the overarousal model, one version being a noradrenergic hypothesis, it is assumed that the effects of stimulants are paradoxical, perhaps through competition with norepinephrine at postsynaptic receptor sites (Kornetsky, 1970).

While there is abundant evidence that stimulants affect neurotransmitter functioning, there is little evidence for the underarousal theories of ADHD or overarousal theories that preceded them. Dozens of studies have examined psychophysiological indices of arousal in hyperactive children. Studies comparing heart rate, indices of skin conductance, cortical evoked potentials and electroencephalograms of ADHD children and normal controls have been inconsistent, usually showing no significant differences. (An alternative possibility to over- or underarousal per se is that ADHD children may suffer from difficulties modulating and regulating arousal to meet situational demands [Douglas and Peters, 1979]. This is a plausible idea. The physiological mechanism underlying such difficulties, however, awaits elaboration.)

More promising is research on brain neurophysiological mechanisms that may underlie ADHD. Research has focused on the hypothesis that stimulants affect catecholamines, their metabolism, or their action on receptor sites and that it may be possible to understand the exact nature of this disorder through an understanding of stimulant drug action (Zametkin and Rapoport, 1987).

A major area of research has centered on differences between children with ADHD and controls on peripheral measures of CNS neurotransmitter functioning from blood and urine assays. Differences obtained from such studies have been rather uniformly disappointing (Bhagauan et al., 1975; Mikkelson et al., 1981; Shekim et al., 1982; and others). However, such peripheral measure are indirect, imperfect indicators of brain functioning.

Another active area of research has been concerned with the effect of various drugs on neurotransmitter functioning and correlated behavior change in ADHD. Drugs that would specifically interfere with or enhance functioning of particular neurotransmitters have been examined as well as drugs which, like stimulants, affect a broad range of catecholamines (e.g., monoamine oxidase inhibitors). This very complex literature has been summarized by Zametkin and Rapoport (1987) in the following way: (1) specific agents, such as dopamine agonists (L-dopa) or antagonists (haloperidol, etc.) have not yielded impressive results in terms of behavior change; (2) more broadly acting drugs, such as methylphenidate and dextroamphetamine, do have demonstrable effects on catecholamine metabolism and behavior; (3) such changes have been shown in some studies to be correlated; that is, nonbehavioral responders do not show change in the catecholamine metabolite (e.g., 3-methoxy-4-hydroxyphenylethyleneglycol [MPHG]) under examination while responders do (Shekim et al., 1979; Yu-cun and Yu-feng, 1984), though not always (Brown et al., 1981).

Without proper controls, such research cannot demonstrate that any metabolite/behavioral correlations are unique to ADHD children. Nor can it demonstrate the biogenetic origins of ADHD; that is, whether any anomalous reaction of ADHD children is inherent or is the product of experience with arousal modulation problems over time. There is little information available on the prevalence of biochemical or other organic signs in the general child population and on the rates that such signs are associated with ADHD. Also, while organic deviations may produce ADHD symptoms, it is also possible that

ADHD symptoms produce biological abnormalities (Connors, 1977). Experiential factors have been found to produce change in PT (plasma testosterone) hormones in male rhesus monkeys. For example, when low-ranking males were given the opportunity to sexually dominate several females, their PT hormones rose sharply, and when they later returned to a cage with higher-ranking males, their PT levels decreased again (Rose et al., 1972). Similarly, levels of neurotransmitters linked with depression have been shown to increase in young monkeys following separation from their mothers (McKinney, 1977). The direction of causality between biochemical factors and behavior does not move in one direction only. Much more research, including longitudinal studies, will be needed to sort out cause–effect relationships.

Sill, the authors agree with Zametkin and Rapoport that research on neurotransmitters and recent work with brain imaging has a potential for helping to identify subgroups of ADHD children, perhaps ultimately identifying a subset or subsets of children for whom medication has unique advantages. This important goal remains elusive at present.

PREDICTORS OF DRUG RESPONSE

In response to stimulant medication, the symptoms of at least 25% of ADHD children either remain unchanged or become worse (Barkley, 1976; Safer and Krager, 1984). Dozens of studies have been conducted to isolate predictors of drug response among ADHD children (Sroufe, 1975; Solanto, 1984). Symptom severity, EEG abnormalities, soft signs, ratings of inattention, activity, and tests of memory all have failed to consistently distinguish responders and nonresponders. In fact, Rie et al. (1976b) found that hyperactive children with organic impairments actually responded more poorly to stimulants. The few studies demonstrating organic predictors have either not been replicated or show contradictory results. For example, responders, compared with nonresponders, have shown greater visual and auditory average evoked responses (Satterfield et al., 1972; Buchsbaum and Wender, 1973) but also smaller responses (Prichep et al., 1976). Skin conductance responses can be interpreted as showing underarousal (Satterfield et al., 1972) or overarousal (Zahn et al., 1975). Heart rates of responders have been reported to be slower (Porges et al., 1975) and faster (Barkley and Jackson, 1978). Variations in predrug catecholamine metabolites (e.g., MHPG) do not distinguish ADHD children from normal controls (Shekim et al., 1979; Yu-cun and Yu-Feng, 1984).

The difficulty in establishing predictors of drug response may be due to a number of factors. There are serious methodological difficulties, including wide variations in drug response measurements across studies, the confounding of pharmacological effects with who will take the drug, and the lack of reliable methods of determining the psychological and physiological effects of different doses for difference children. Nevertheless, it remains the case that there is no biochemical aberration or other marker that has been established as specific to ADHD children or which can guide the decision to medicate. This remains an important area for additional research.

LONG-TERM OUTCOME OF DRUG TREATMENT

Researchers and clinicians agree that ADHD is not a passing phase (Weiss and Hechtman, 1986). Rather, problems of these children undergo developmental transformation. Hyperactivity per se is not the critical feature beyond middle childhood. However, some ADHD symptoms, such as impulsiveness and inattentiveness, persist into adolescence and adulthood with associated academic failure (Lambert, 1988; Mannuzza et al., 1988), low self-esteem, and poor peer relations during adolescence (Hoy et al., 1978), although a substantial minority are functioning normally in adulthood, perhaps especially in the work arena (Weiss and Hechtman, 1986). In adolescence, delinquency and antisocial behavior are also reported (Feldman et al., 1979; Satterfield et al., 1982; Weiss, 1983), presumably a continuation of the conduct disorder that is so often associated with ADHD.

Critical questions regarding long-term effects of stimulant drugs can be divided into two areas: (1) do children habituate to the drug, losing beneficial effects; and (2) does medicating ADHD children predict overall long-range behavioral improvement?

Whether children develop a tolerance to stimulant drugs is still not resolved. Although side effects usually disappear after a few weeks, particularly if the dosage is monitored and adjusted, it is still logically possible that positive effects persist. For logistical reasons, however, studies following ADHD children who are taking stimulants, with some notable exceptions, have generally not lasted more than a few weeks or months, so the persistence of positive effects often is not fully investigated. The observation of deteriorating performance on removal from stimulants is not conclusive, because deterioration in performance would be expected if tolerance had developed (a disruptive effect) *or* if the drug were still being effective. To resolve this question, patients would need to be tested regularly (e.g., weekly) for several months.

Most critical is the overall long-term effectiveness of stimulants in treating ADHD children. Developmental psychologists agree that the crucial challenges adolescents face are successful adjustment to school, formation of close friendships, a relative absence of substance abuse, and other problems such as antisocial behavior. The long-term efficacy of stimulant drug treatment will first be evaluated with respect to these criteria.

Academic Performance

Researchers have reported immediate improvement in performance on arithmetic (Whalen et al., 1980; Rapport et al., 1982: Pelham et al., 1985); and spelling (Stephens et al., 1984). Such changes occur too quickly to reflect an actual increase in math and reading achievement and are best interpreted as improved ability to function in the test setting. Here, the authors examine data concerning actual change in achievement scores over time.

To date, there is no evidence that stimulants enhance academic performance. In the 5-year follow-up conducted by Weiss et al. (1975), there were no differences between treated and untreated hyperactive children in the number of grades failed. In addition, lower performance during adolescence on achievement tests such as the Wide-Range Achievement Test (WRAT) (Riddle and Rapoport, 1976), the spelling subtest on the Stanford Achievement Test (SAT), and the word knowledge subtest on the Metropolitan Achievement Test (MAT) (Hoy et al., 1978) reveal persistent problems in retaining and mastering new materials. Other studies also show that treated ADHD children do not significantly differ from untreated children on achievement tests such as the WRAT (Riddle and Rapoport, 1976; Blouin et al., 1978; Charles and Schain, 1981) and Peabody Individual Achievement Test (PIAT) (Charles and Schain, 1981). These results held up whether stimulant drug treatment lasted 2 years (Riddle and Rapoport, 1976) or 4 years (Charles and Schain, 1981) and even when positive and poor drug responders were compared (Blouin et al., 1978).

Only one study has examined the scholastic performance of ADHD children followed into young adulthood (16 to 24 years old). Hechtman et al. (1984) compared 20 hyperactive children receiving methylphenidate, 20 untreated hyperactive children, and 20 normal controls. Without regard to medication, hyperactive children attended fewer junior colleges and universities and in high school failed more grades and dropped out more frequently due to poor marks than did normal controls. (Such differences suggest that these measures have adequate reliability and validity.) Medicated hyperactive children, however, did not significantly differ from untreated hyperactive children on any of these variables. Though more studies of school performance are needed, at present there is no evidence that learning, as assessed by schoolwork and achievement tests, is enhanced by stimulant drug treatment. Rather than using global measures of academic performance, such as college enrollment, studies that address particular abilities such as writing or mathematical computation skills might reveal specific stimulant drug effects, but this is yet to be established in long-term outcome studies.

These negative results have been subject to a number of critiques (Douglas et al., 1986; Pelham, 1986). Pelham (1986), for example, raises questions about the "sensitivity of achievement tests, individual differences, drug dosage, compliance, and time-course effects" (p. 267). In addition, the presence of learning disabilities or gaps in knowledge before drug treatment may influence results. These are leads for additional research.

Peer Relations

Peer relationship problems of ADHD children have been well documented (King and Young, 1982; Johnston et al., 1985; Carlson et al., 1987). In comparison with normal children, ADHD children more often engage in controlling and dominating behaviors (Cunningham et al., 1985) and negative, aggressive interactions with peers (Pelham and Bender, 1982; Clark et al., 1988). They are more likely to be targets for others' aggression (Klein and Young, 1979) and receive lower sociometric nominations by their peers (Pelham and Bender, 1982), compared with controls. Recent work suggests that ADHD children communicate less effectively with peers, failing to modulate their social communication as task demands shifted (Landau and Milich, 1988) and engaging in fewer reciprocal verbal exchanges, compared with nonADHD dyads (Clark et al., 1988). Grenell et al. (1987) report that ADHD children's peers difficulties are apparent during actual peer interactions as well as on assessments of their social knowledge. Researchers have linked poor peer relations during middle childhood with an increased risk for later adjustment difficulties in general (Kohlberg et al., 1972) and specifically, with delinquency and academic problems in adolescence (Kupersmidt, 1983) and psychiatric problems in adulthood (Cowen et al., 1973). Difficulties with peers is clearly a critical concern.

Studies of the immediate effects of stimulant medication show few significant positive effects and a high incidence of negative effects. Pelham and Bender (1982) failed to find declines in negative nonverbal behavior in either direct observations or the sociometric rankings of ADHD children by their peers. This could be because methylphenidate leads to decreased social interactions and adversely affects mood (Schleifer et al., 1975), with medicated children rated as less happy and pleased with themselves and more dysphoric (Whalen et al., 1979). Such negative findings may be the result of high drug dosages sometimes used. Cunningham et al. (1985) compared the interactions of children at different dosage levels. At the lowest dose (0.15 mg/kg), but not at higher doses commonly used, they reported a significant decline in controlling and dominating behaviors of ADHD children and a reciprocal decrease in controlling responses by normal peers. Significant differences, however, were found only in a highly structured, simulated school setting. Consistent with previous work (Pelham and Bender, 1982), peer interactions of ADHD children following drug administration did not significantly change in free play and cooperative task settings where most peer interactions take place. The decline in controlling responses in structured classroom situations reported by Cunningham et al. may be related to the significant increase in the percent of time spent on-task at both dosage levels. Additionally, there was no change in popularity following medication at any dosage. Studies of longer duration are needed to determine if stimulant drug treatment helps break the chain of negative interactions, allowing ADHD children to develop better social skills and form lasting friendships. At present, no studies have examined the effects of drug treatment during the school years on children's formation of friendships during adolescence. There is critical need for additional research here.

Antisocial Behavior

Antisocial behavior and delinquency during adolescence are more likely among children previously diagnosed as ADHD. Hyperactive children were more likely to have been arrested for a serious offense (Satterfield et al., 1982), appeared in court more often (Mendelson et al., 1971), had more frequent difficulties with police, and had more frequent detentions in the principal's office (Hoy et al., 1978). Depending on diagnosis (minimal brain dysfunction versus ADHD) and seriousness of the offense (difficulties with police versus third time arrest), prevalence estimates of antisocial behavior range from 10% (Feldman et al., 1979) to 25% (Mendelson et al., 1971; Weiss, 1983) to 45% (Satterfield et al., 1982) during the early high school years. To some degree, the link between ADHD and later delinquent behavior may be due to the comorbidity of attention and aggressive behavioral/conduct disorder symptoms (August et al., 1983).

Neither Blouin et al. (1978) nor Weiss et al. (1975) found significant differences in delinquency during adolescence between hyperactive children treated and not treated with drugs. In a 10-year follow-up of 110 ADHD boys and 88 controls, Satterfield et al. (1982) found significantly more delinquency (placement in juvenile halls and probation camps) among hyperactive children compared with controls even though most of the ADHD children were treated with stimulant drugs for at least 25 months. (A later study where evidence is presented for the efficacy of medication plus psychological treatment is discussed below.) If delinquency during adolescence is due to aggression rather than ADHD, it is not surprising that stimulant drug effects targeted at reducing the core symptoms of ADHD do not diminish antisocial behavior. Many physicians currently argue against prescribing stimulant medication for conduct disorders (Cantwell, 1987; Garfinkel, 1987).

Overview of Long-Term Studies of Stimulant Treatment

Comprehensive studies of long-lasting effects of stimulants have been conducted on five different samples of ADHD children, each carried out by a different group of researchers (Weiss et al., 1975; Riddle and Rapoport, 1976; Blouin et al., 1978: Charles and Schain, 1981: Satterfield et al., 1982). These studies focused primarily on academic performance (Weiss et al., 1975; Riddle and Rapoport, 1976; Blouin et al., 1978; Charles and Schain, 1981) or antisocial behavior (Mendelson et al., 1971; Blouin et al., 1978; Satterfield et al., 1982), and, on the whole, show little support for the efficacy of drug treatment.

Hechtman, Weiss, and colleagues (e.g., Weiss and Hechtman, 1986) reported some positive effects on questionnaire measure of self-esteem in young adults. Results were not fully consistent (with some differences favoring the nonmedication group), were nested within many statistical tests, and were not supported by more objective measures. Nonetheless, the subjects' feelings are important, and this is a lead for additional research.

A variety of explanations are possible for the failure to find lasting improvement on academic tasks or a reduction in delinquent behavior among ADHD children following treatment with stimulant drugs. Increasing attention has been given to the overlap among children with symptoms of both ADHD and conduct disorder (Schachar et al., 1981; Taylor, 1986; Hinshaw, 1987; Rutter and Tuma, 1988). Since antisocial behavior during childhood predicts similar behavior during adolescence and adulthood (Robins, 1978), some researchers argue that antisocial behavior during adolescence may be more related to childhood aggression and conduct disorder than to ADHD symptoms. After separating children with antisocial behavior from those manifesting core ADHD symptoms (inattention, impulsivity, and overactivity) Loney et al. (1981) found that aggressiveness, not ADHD symptoms, predicted antisocial behavior. Gittelman et al. (1985) prospectively followed 107 males originally diagnosed as hyperactive (between 6 and 12 years old) into young adulthood. They found that the greatest risk factor for developing antisocial behavior was the maintenance of ADHD symptoms even after separating out ADHD children who were also diagnosed with conduct disorder during childhood. Overlapping symptoms of impulsivity and aggression (but not necessarily conduct disorder) in children diagnosed ADHD may account for the high incidence of antisocial behavior during adolescence. Additional research is needed in this area.

Another explanation for finding relatively few enduring drug effects is that none of the studies were experimental, with children randomly assigned to drug and no drug conditions. It is possible that children placed on medication had more severe problems than nonmedicated children. Also, in such studies, there are concerns about drug compliance. The disappointing long-term drug effects reported may stem from children's inconsistent drug intake or discontinuation of stimulant drugs entirely. While some researchers have checked whether children were taking stimulant drugs by contacting schools weekly (Satterfield et al., 1987), others did not examine such facts (Weiss et al., 1975; Blouin et al., 1978) or report how many children discontinued medication (Charles and Schain, 1981).

Charles and Schain (1981) explored the relationship between length of treatment on stimulants and ADHD children's performance on achievement tests at a 4-year follow-up. Children were separated into five groups on the basis of length of treatment—0 to 6 months to 2 years, 2 to 3 years, 3 to 4 years, and children still on medication. Although there were significant differences between some of the groups on their academic achievement test scores at the 4-year follow-up, ADHD children in all groups were functioning well below the norms for children their age. Additionally, children still on stimulants were not different from children who had discontinued medication.

Subject attrition in studies of long-term drug effects may also influence the finding reported. Subjects who dropped out of the study may be those who improved on the drug and discontinued drug usage leaving those who were functioning more poorly. In Riddle and Rapoport's (1976) 2-year follow-up, only 5% of the subjects dropped out, but in the other four outcome studies discussed above (Weiss et al., 1975; Blouin et al., 1978; Charles and Schain, 1981; Satterfield et al., 1982), attrition ranged from about 30% to 50%. Sometimes attrition stemmed primarily from difficulties in locating subjects rather than in subjects declining participation (Charles and Schain, 1981). In other cases, subjects were deliberately excluded to make comparison groups more homogeneous (Weiss et al., 1975) or to tighten standards for inclusion of subjects (Satterfield et al., 1982). Although most of the researchers found no significant differences on relevant measures such as IQ, socioeconomic status (SES), symptom severity, age, and parent education between subjects who dropped out of the study and those who remained (Weiss et al., 1975; Charles and Schain, 1981; Satterfield et al., 1982), one study did not examine differences between the two groups (Blouin et al., 1978).

Finally, failure to include relevant control groups limits interpretation of the research findings. In some cases, ADHD children were not initially matched on relevant variables such as IQ which could have influenced achievement test scores at the 2-year follow-up (Riddle and Rapoport, 1976); while other studies did not include an untreated ADHD group (Riddle and Rapoport, 1976), a nonclinical "normal" comparison group (Weiss et al., 1975; Blouin et al., 1978; Charles and Schain, 1981; Satterfield et al., 1987), or a nonADHD clinical control group (Weiss et al., 1975; Riddle and Rapoport, 1976; Charles and Schain, 1981; Satterfield et al., 1987).

Satterfield and his colleagues (1987) compared ADHD children who received drug treatment and brief counseling (the Drug Treatment Only [DTO] group) with ADHD children who underwent both drug treatment and intensive psychological treatment (the Multiple Method Treatment [MMT] group). The MMT group showed significantly less delinquency than the DTO group. This does suggest that medication should be used within a broader treatment approach. However, it cannot be taken as evidence for the effectiveness of medication. There was no psychological treatment alone group. Thus it is unclear whether finding reductions in delinquency over a 2- to 3-year period among ADHD boys in the MMT group, compared with the DTO group, was due to the combination of drugs and psychological intervention or to the psychological intervention alone.

To date, evidence of long-term benefits following stimulant drug treatment is inconclusive. The available data base remains limited, and additional studies exploring long-term stimulant effects are clearly needed.

Multimodal Treatment

Multimodal treatment programs have increased dramatically during the 1970s and 1980s. Using medication alone has been increasingly challenged. Specifically, concerns have been raised over the prolonged use of medication (Ross and Ross, 1982); lack of evidence for altering the eventual outcome for ADHD children; the heterogeneity of children diagnosed ADHD; the limited evidence for effects on important aspects of cognitive ability, such as learning, problem solving, and reasoning (Abikoff and Gittelman, 1985b); reluctance of parents to give children psychoactive drugs; and the dislike many ADHD children have of taking medications (Firestone, 1982). Given the limitations of solely treating ADHD children with psychoactive drugs, the relative benefits of alternative interventions alone and in combination with stimulant drugs will be examined.

Cognitive-behavioral training (CBT) has been one of the most frequently researched adjuncts or alternatives to medication (Abikoff and Gittelman, 1985b; Pelham and Murphy, 1986). CBT has been found effective primarily for brief durations, in circumscribed contexts, and with nonclinical samples of children experiencing difficulties with self-control (Kendall and Braswell, 1984). While some short-term benefits on ADHD children's capacity for self-control have been reported (Hinshaw et al., 1984b), lasting effects on ADHD children have been disappointing (Abikoff and Gittelman, 1985b; Brown et al., 1986). Even when using multiple materials, trainers, and settings and encouraging teachers and parents to continue the treatment at home and at school, CBT has shown limited generalization for ADHD children (Cohen et al., 1981; Brown et al., 1985; Abikoff, 1987).

Whether ADHD children benefit more from stimulants by themselves or in combination with CBT remains inconclusive. Some researchers report little additional benefit of combining treatments (Abikoff and Gittelman, 1985b; Brown et al., 1986). Others, such as Hinshaw and his colleagues, were able to increase ADHD children's capacity to cope with anger (Hinshaw et al., 1984a) and to accurately self-monitor their own behavior (Hinshaw et al., 1984b) using a combination of pharmacotherapy and cognitive-behavioral methods. Pelham and Murphy (1986) argue that available multimodal studies are filled with methodological limitations, such as, among others, failure to provide uniform treatment across conditions, small sample sizes, and inadequate outcome measures, that may obscure combination treatment effects. To date, few studies have investigated the long-term effects of combined treatments.

Other approaches are currently being developed, including educational training and psychotherapy with the child and family. Recent work by Satterfield and his colleagues lends evidence for the beneficial effects of psychotherapy for each ADHD child or each child and family as part of a comprehensive treatment plan (Satterfield et al., 1982). In light of the poor prognosis for children diagnosed ADHD and the limitations of current treatment programs, there is a pressing need for more effective treatment programs. More work which considers individual needs and then examines the effectiveness of various treatment combinations is required.

NEGATIVE CONSEQUENCES OF STIMULANT MEDICATION

Potential negative consequences of the widespread use of the stimulant medications are both indirect and direct. Perhaps one of the most noteworthy consequences of adopting stimulants as the treatment of choice for ADHD is the paucity of research on nonorganic contributors to this disorder. Likewise, relatively little research has been done on educational or psychological interventions, although this may be changing (see above). When organic dysfunction in the child is viewed as the problem, and medication as the solution, motivation to deal more comprehensively with these children may be compromised. This is an addition to possible physical side effects.

Most of the physical side effects of stimulant drugs commonly reported, including appetite loss, insomnia, weight loss, headaches, irritability, and sudden mood changes, are transient, disappearing after a short while, and reversible either with dosage reduction or drug withdrawal (see Klein et al., 1980, for a detailed review of side effects).

Growth suppression, the most widely researched side effect, was first described by Safer et al. in 1972. Decrements in height were estimated to be as much as 3 cm per year for children given dosages of methylphenidate exceeding 20 mg for a least 3 years (Safer and Allen, 1973; Mattes and Gittelman, 1979) and after only 1 and 2 years (Greenhill et al., 1981). Others report that height rebounds toward normal after the first year of treatment (Gross, 1976). The most extensive investigation of growth effects to date is that of Rachel Gittelman-Klein and colleagues. In one report (Gittelman-Klein et al., 1988), a growth rebound effect during summer vacations from medications was demonstrated. After one such summer, weight was higher for the group removed from medication; after 2 summers, height, but not weight, showed a rebound effect. (See also Safer et al., 1975, for other evidence of growth rebound following termination of stimulant treatment.) In a second paper, Gittelman-Klein and Mannuzza (1988) report that adult height of treated children did not differ from a nontreated, non-ADHD normal control group. While not an experimental study, groups were matched on key variables of SES and race, and age differences at outcome were controlled statistically. These data attest to the possibility that height rebounds following termination of stimulant treatment. However, the average duration of treatment for these subjects was 2.24 years, and almost all were under age 13 when treatment was terminated. Consequences of longer treatment, and treatment through the adolescent growth spurt, remain to be investigated.

Researchers have sought to understand the mechanism underlying the documented growth suppression during stimulant drug treatment. An important lead has been discovered here. Research reveals that methylphenidate stimulates daytime release of growth hormone, disrupting the usual nocturnal release (Greenhill et al., 1977; Jensen and Garfinkel, 1988). This finding is troublesome since disturbances in the normal cycle of release of growth hormone may not only influence height velocity but may also have an impact on other critical aspects of physical development such as sexual maturation. This would be of special concern if stimulant treatment is increased for adolescents. For some children, especially those treated over time, the growth hormone suppression disappears. This finding, of course, raises questions as to whether tolerance develops.

In recent years, much has been written concerning a possible link between stimulant treatment and either onset or exacerbation of tics, especially in children having or predisposed to having Tourette syndrome. Such a connection was implied by early case studies (Denckla et al., 1976; Golden, 1977). As recently as 1982, a report in the *Journal of the American Medical Association*, based on careful monitoring of 15 cases (Lowe et al., 1982), concluded that the presence of tics, or Tourette syndrome, or a family history of such problems contraindicates using stimulant medications. Others, however, have interpreted these data differently (Shapiro and Shapiro, 1981; Comings and Comings, 1987), arguing that the association between tics and stimulants, if any, is quite small, may be an effect of excessive dosage, and may even be artifactual. In a large scale study, Comings and Comings (1987) report that symptoms of ADHD often precede the onset of Tourette syndrome, usually by more than 2 years. Additionally, they report that this gap is unaffected by stimulant medication. Their conclusion is that the onset of Tourette symptoms occurs independently of stimulant treatment and they, in fact, argue that stimulants may be useful in combination with haloperidol. At present, this issue is not fully resolved. It should be noted that none of these studies has been experimental, with random assignment and proper controls. Moreover, contrary to their claim, the Comings and Comings study was not prospective, but, rather, relied on questionnaire reports concerning the onset of hyperactivity and Tourette symptoms. The authors would agree with Cohen [and colleagues (1984)] that "at this time, stimulants should be used cautiously with ADHD children who have a close relative with TS and should be terminated with the onset of tics in children who were previously tic free" (p. 13).

Also of concern regarding side effects of stimulant medication is the lack of information about possible health consequences in adult life. Given the recent advocacy of extending treatment into the adolescent years, children may now be on such medication for 8 to 10 years or more. Only a handful of children treated extensively with stimulants have reached middle age. It will be important to begin conducting such follow-up research. The foci of an investigation might be vascular, cardiac, or kidney function.

FUTURE DIRECTIONS FOR RESEARCH

Some researchers suggest that the lack of long-term effectiveness of these treatments is due to the heterogeneity of the disorder, in terms of definition and etiology. There are several ways to decrease the heterogeneity among children who are being investigated. One is to apply strict criteria; that is, to be faithful to the letter of the *DSM-III-R* when diagnosing children. Another is to insist that children's symptoms are "pervasive" versus "situational" (Taylor, 1988). Last, reliability and validity would be improved by using a battery of diagnostic instruments and administering these tests more than once, with at least a month between examinations.

When studying children with ADHD, reading disability and conduct disorder should be targets as well, since they are the most obvious correlates of ADHD (August et al., 1983). Conduct disorder has been associated with ADHD along a continuum, from no "acting out" to a full blown aggressive conduct disorder. In a large scale epidemiological study (August and Garfinkel, 1989), two types of children with attention deficits and hyperactivity were found, the first marked by behavior problems, and the second by reading disability. A third group had both the behavioral and cognitive problems. This analysis may provide clues as to which subtypes of ADHD will benefit the most from stimulant drugs or other treatments.

Longitudinal studies of children before they develop the disorder are needed to identify various etiological influences. At present, only one study has followed children from birth through age 8 and examined both early caregiving and biological variables (Jacobvitz and Sroufe, 1987; Jacobvitz 1988, unpublished dissertation). In this study, three assessments of the early child-caregiver relationship (parental intrusiveness at 6 months and overstimulation at 24 and 42 months) were examined. The 42 biological variables assessed included temperament measures (e.g., physical anomalies, prematurity, delivery complications, and indicators of early neurological dysfunction [e.g., newborn reflexes]). Two of the three caregiving measures, intrusiveness at 6 months and overstimulation at 42 months, and one of the 42 biological measures (a 7- and 10-day composite of motor immaturity during the newborn period) significantly distinguished 27 children, later showing ADHD symptoms, from 27 normal controls during kindergarten and the early school years (Jacobvitz and Sroufe, 1987; Jacobvitz, 1988, unpublished dissertation). This study suggests that experiential factors should not be overlooked in searching for the etiology of ADHD and that there may be multiple pathways to this disorder. Much more work is needed along these lines.

Jensen and Garfinkel (1988) and Taylor (1988), among others, emphasize the need to identify biological markers of ADHD and to confirm their validity through replication. Establishing prevalence rates of such markers and their unique presence in ADHD children is an important goal. Screening children whose difficulties stem from exogenous experiences could aid in distinguishing children with organic problems and help identify any subset of children who are indeed true responders to stimulant drugs.

CONCLUSIONS

The regulation of attention and activity are often problematic in childhood, and such anomalies can give rise to painful conflicts for children, families, and teachers. And while the manifest form of the misbehavior changes with age, children with such problems often suffer for years, if not for a lifetime. The motivations of professionals to deal swiftly and efficiently with such problems is therefore reasonable. This motivation and the often clear, dramatic, short-term impact of stimulant medication make it understandable how the widespread practice of stimulant medication came into being.

However, the paucity of data showing continued or lasting impact of stimulant medication for these children is disconcerting. A case for the long-term effectiveness of stimulant medication simply cannot be made at this time. This is especially troubling because some of the very aspects of functioning and development we would most hope to impact—school achievement, relationships with peers, and the behavior problems common to adolescence—have been the central focus in the outcome studies that have been done. ADHD children often continue to have problems in adolescence and having been treated with stimulant medication in childhood has had little demonstrable effect. Nor is there evidence that stimulant medication continues to benefit children after several months, though here the situation is mostly a lack of pertinent evidence rather than negative findings.

There are several possible explanations for the absence of demonstrable long-term benefits of stimulant drug medication. First, children with attentional behavioral problems likely are a very heterogeneous group. If only a subset of these children, especially if that subset is small, have a specific biochemical abnormality, drug treatment effects would be obscured. Second, drug treatment alone may represent inadequate treatment for most children, even those having an organic contribution to their problems. (Thus, studies using medication in combination with other treatments, such as that by Satterfield et al. [1987] are of great importance.) Finally, children, like adults, may commonly develop tolerance for stimulant medication so that drug effects in time disappear. Existing evidence does not allow firm conclusions concerning the relative importance of each of these factors.

At present, the decision to prescribe stimulant medication remains an individual clinical decision. Current research would not seem to justify sustained treatment with medication alone, widespread drug trials as a diagnostic procedure, or unrestrained use of stimulant medication. The Baltimore County study (Safer and Krager, 1988) revealed that 6% of public school children were being treated with stimulant medication. While rates certainly vary locally, this figure is striking. The estimated prevalence of ADHD is 3% (American Psychiatric Association, 1987), and only a yet to be defined subset of these children are appropriate targets of stimulant medication. The authors would urge greater caution and a much more restricted use of stimulant treatment pending more research on long-term effects, both concerning positive and negative consequences, and an increased ability to identify the subset of children having a specific biochemical abnormality.

REFERENCES

Abikoff, H. (1987), An evaluation of cognitive behavior therapy for hyperactive children. In: *Advances in Clinical Child Psychology*, Vol. 10, eds. B. B. Lahey & A. E. Kazdin. New York: Plenum, pp. 171–216.

——— Gittelman, R. (1985a), The normalizing effects of methylphenidate on the classroom behavior of ADHD children. *J. Abnorm. Child Psychol.*, 13: 33–44.

——— ——— (1985b), Hyperactive children treated with stimulants: is cognitive training a useful adjunct? *Arch. Gen. Psychiatry*, 42:953–961.

American Psychiatric Association, Committee on Nomenclature and Statistics. (1987), *Diagnostic and Statistical Manual of Mental Disorders, (3rd ed.—Revised)*. Washington, DC: American Psychiatric Association.

August, G. J. & Garfinkel, B. D. (1989), Behavioral and cognitive subtypes of ADHD. *J. Am. Acad. Child Adolesc. Psychiatry*, 28:739–748.

——— Stewart, M. A. & Holmes, C. S. (1983), A four-year follow-up of hyperactive boys with and without conduct disorder. *Br. J. Psychiatry*, 143: 192–198.

Barkley, R. A. (1976), Predicting the response of hyperkinetic children to stimulant drugs: a review. *J. Abnorm. Child Psychol.*, 4:327–348.

——— (1981), *Hyperactive Children: A Handbook for Diagnosis and Treatment*. New York: Guilford Press.

——— (1989), Hyperactive girls and boys: stimulant drug effects on mother–child interaction. *J. Child Psychol. Psychiatry*, 30:379–390.

——— Jackson, T. (1978), Hyperkinesis, autonomic nervous system activity and stimulant drug effects. *J. Child Psychol. Psychiatry*, 18:347–358.

——— Karlsson, J., Pollard, S. & Murphy, J. (1985), Developmental changes in the mother–child interactions of hyperactive boys: effects of two dose levels of Ritalin. *J. Child Psychol. Psychiatry*, 26:705–715.

Bhagauan, H. N., Coleman, M. & Coursina, D. B. (1975), The effect of pyridoxine hydrochloride on blood serotonin and pyridoxal phosphate contents in hyperactive children. *Pediatrics*, 55: 437–441.

Blouin, A. G., Bornstein, R. A. & Trites, R. L. (1978), Teenage alcohol use among hyperactive and nonhyperactive children: a five-year follow-up study. *J. Pediatr. Psychol.*, 3:188–194.

Brown, G. L., Ebert, M. H., Hunt, R. D. & Rapoport, J. L. (1981), Urinary 3-methoxy-4-hydroxyphenylglycol and homovanillic acid response to d-amphetamine in hyperactive children. *Biological Psychiatry*, 16:779–787.

Brown, R. T., Borden, K. A., Wynne, M. E., Schleser, R. & Clingermann, S. R. (1986), Methylphenidate and cognitive therapy with ADD children: a methodological reconsideration. *J. Abnorm. Child Psychol.*, 14:481–497.

——— Wynne, M. E. & Medenis, R. (1985), Methylphenidate and cognitive therapy: a comparison of treatment approaches with hyperactive boys. *J. Abnorm. Child Psychol.*, 13:69–87.

Buchsbaum, M. & Wender, P. (1973), Average evoked responses in normal and minimally brain dysfunctioned children treated with amphetamine: a preliminary report. *Arch. Gen. Psychiatry*, 29:764–770.

Cantwell, D. (1987, June). *Developmental and Longitudinal Aspects of Attention Deficit Disorders*. Workshop at the Conference on Attention Deficit Hyperactivity in Children and Adolescents: Assessment and Intervention, Minneapolis, Minnesota.

Carlson, C. L., Lahey, B. B., Frame, C. L., Walker, J. & Hynd, G. W. (1987), Sociometric status of clinic-referred children with attention deficit disorders with and without hyperactivity. *J. Abnorm. Child Psychol.*, 15:537–547.

Charles, L. & Schain, R. (1981), A four-year follow-up study of the effects of methylphenidate on the behavior and academic achievement of hyperactive children. *J. Abnorm. Child Psychol.*, 9:495–505.

Clark, M. L., Cheyne, J. A., Cunningham, C. E. & Siegel, L. S. (1988), Dyadic peer interaction and task orientation in attention-deficit-disordered children. *J. Abnorm. Child Psychol.*, 16:1–15.

Cohen, D., Leckman, J. & Shaywitz, B. (1985), The Tourette syndrome and other tics. In: *The Clinical Guide to Child Psychiatry*, eds. D. Shaffer, A. Ehrhardt & L. Greenhill. New York: Free Press, pp. 3–28.

Cohen N. J., Sullivan, J., Minde, K., Novak, C. & Helwig, C. (1981), Evaluations of the relative effectiveness of methylphenidate and cognitive behavior modification in the treatment of kindergarten-aged hyperactive children. *J. Abnorm. Child. Psychol.*, 9:43–54.

Comings, D. E. & Comings, B. G. (1987), A controlled study of Tourette syndrome: I. Attention-deficit disorder, learning disorders and school problems. *Am. J. Hum. Genet.*, 41:701–741.

Conners, C. K. (1977), Discussion of Rapoport's chapter. In: *Depression in Childhood*, eds. J. Schulterbrandt & A. Raskin. New York: Raven Press, pp. 101–104.

Cowen, E. L., Pederson, A., Babijian, H., Izzo, L. & Trost, M. A. (1973), Long-term follow-up of early detected vulnerable children. *J. Consult. Clin. Psychol.*, 41:438–446.

Cunningham, C. E., & Barkley, R. A. (1978), The role of academic failure in hyperactive behavior. *Journal of Learning Disabilities*, 11:15–21.

——— Siegel, L. S. & Offord, D. R. (1985), A developmental dose-response analysis of the effects of methylphenidate on the peer interactions of attention deficit disordered boys. *J. Child Psychol. Psychiat.*, 26:955–971.

Denckla, M. B., Bemporad, J. R. & Mackay, M. C. (1976), Tics following methylphenidate administration. *JAMA*, 235:1349–1351.

Douglas, V. I., & Peters, K. G. (1979), Toward a clearer definition of the attentional deficit of hyperactive children. In: *Attention and the Development of Cognitive Skills*, eds. G. A. Hale & M. Lewis. New York: Plenum Press, pp. 173–247.

——— Barr, R. G., O'Neill, M. E., & Britton, B. G. (1986), Short term effects of methylphenidate on the cognitive learning and academic performance of children with attention deficit disorder in the laboratory and the classroom. *J. Child Psychol. Psychiat.*, 27:191–211.

——— Amin, K., O'Neill, M. E. & Britton, B. G. (1988), Dosage effects and individual responsivity to methylphenidate in attention deficit disorder. *J. Child Psychol. Psychiat.*, 29:453–475.

Ebaugh, F. G. (1923), Neuropsychiatric sequelae of acute epidemic encephalitis in children. *Am. J. Dis. Child.*, 25: 89–97.

Ellis, M. J., Witt, P. A., Reynolds, R. & Sprague, R. L. (1974), Methylphenidate and the activity of hyperactives in the informal setting. *Child Dev.*, 45: 217–220.

Feldman, S., Denhoff, E. & Denhoff. (1979), The attention disorders and related syndromes: outcome in adolescence and young adult life. In: *Minimal Brain Dysfunction: A Developmental Approach:* eds. L. Starr & E. Denhoff. New York: Mason, pp. 133–148.

Firestone, P. (1982), Factors associated with children's adherence to stimulant medication. *Am. J. of Orthopsychiatry*, 52: 447–457.

——— Peters, S., Rivier, M. & Knights, R. M. (1978), Minor physical anomalies in hyperactive, retarded and normal children and their families. *J. Child Psychol. Psychiat.*, 19:155–160.

Garfinkel, B. (1987, June), *Treatment strategies for AD-HD.* Paper presented at the conference on Attention-Deficit Hyperactivity Disorders in Children and Adolescents, Minneapolis, Minnesota.

Gittelman-Klein, R. & Klein, D. F. (1976), Methylphenidate effects in learning disabilities: psychometric changes. *Arch. Gen. Psychiatry*, 33: 655–664.

——— Mannuzza, S. (1988), Hyperactive boys almost grown up: III. Methylphenidate effects on ultimate height. *Arch. Gen. Psychiatry*, 45:1131–1134.

Gittelman, R., Mannuzza, S., Shenker, R., & Bonagura, N. (1985), Hyperactive boys almost grown up: I. Psychiatric status. *Archives of General Psychiatry*, 42: 937–947.

——— Landa, B., Mattes, J. A. & Klein, D. F. (1988), Methylphenidate and growth in hyperactive children: a controlled withdrawal study. *Arch. Gen. Psychiatry*, 45:1127–1130.

Golden, G. S. (1977), The effect of central nervous system stimulants on Tourette syndrome. *Ann. Neurol.*, 2: 69–70.

Greenhill, L., Puig-Antich, K. & Sassin, J. (1977), Hormone and growth response in hyperkinetic children on stimulant medication. *Psychopharmacol Bull.*, 12: 33–34.

——— Puig-Antich, J., Chambers, W., Rubinstein, B., Halpern, F. & Sachar, E. J. (1981), Growth hormone, prolactin, and growth responses in hyperkinetic males treated with D-amphetamine. *J. Am. Acad. Child Psychiatry*, 20:84–103.

Grenell, M. M., Glass, C. R. & Katz, K. S. (1987), Hyperactive children and peer interaction: knowledge and performance of social skills. *J. Abnorm. Child Psychol.*, 15:1–13.

Gross, M. D. (1976), Dextroamphetamine, desipramine, growth, hyperkinetic syndrome, imipramine, methylphenidate. *Pediatrics*, 58:423–431.

Hechtman, L. ,Weiss, G., Perlman, T. & Amsel, R. (1984), Hyperactives as young adults: initial predictors of adult outcome. *J. Am. Acad. Child Adolesc Psychiatry*, 23:250–260.

Hinshaw, S. P. (1987), On the distinction between attentional deficits/hyperactivity and conduct problems/aggression in child psychopathology. *Psychol. Bull.*, 101:443–463.

——— Henker, B. & Whalen, C. K. (1984a), Cognitive-behavioral and pharmacological interventions for hyperactive boys: comparative and combined effects. *J. Consult. Clin. Psychol.*, 52:739–749.

——— ——— ——— (1984b), Self-control in hyperactive boys in anger-inducing situations: effect of cognitive-behavioral training and methylphenidate. *J. Abnorm. Child Psychol.*, 12:55–77.

Hoy, E., Weiss, G., Minde, K. & Cohen, N. (1978), The hyperactive child at adolescence: emotional, social, and cognitive functioning. *J. Abnorm. Child Psychol.*, 6:311–324.

Humphries, T., Kinsbourne, M. & Swanson, J. M. (1978), Stimulant effects on cooperation and social interaction between hyperactive children and their mothers. *J. Child Psychol. Psychiat.*, 19: 13–22.

Jacobvitz, D. (1988), *The early caregiver–child relationship and attention-deficit hyperactivity disorder in schoolchildren*. Ph.D. dissertation, University of Minnesota.

——— & Sroufe, L. A. (1987), The early caregiver–child relationship and Attention Deficit Disorder with Hyperactivity in kindergarten: a prospective study. *Child Dev.*, 58:1488–1495.

Jensen, J. B. & Garfinkel, B. D. (1988), Neuroendocrine aspects of attention deficit hyperactivity disorder. *Endocrinol. Metab. Clin. North Am.*, 17: 111–127.

Johnston, C. Pelham, W. E. & Murphy, H. A. (1985), Peer relationships in ADHD and normal children: a developmental analysis of peer and teacher ratings. *J. Abnorm. Child Psychol.*, 13:89–100.

Kendall, P. C. & Braswell, L. (1984), *Cognitive-Behavioral Therapy for Impulsive Children*. New York: Guilford Press.

King, L. A. & Young, R. D. (1982), Attentional deficits with and without hyperactivity: teacher and peer perceptions. *J. Abnorm. Child Pychol.*, 10: 483–495.

Klein, A. R. & Young, R. D. (1979), Hyperactive boys in their classroom assessment of teachers and peer perceptions, interactions, and classroom behavior. *J. Abnorm. Child Psychol.*, 7:425–442.

Klein, D. F., Gittelman, R., Quitkin, A. & Rifkin, A. (1980), Side effects of antipsychotic drugs and their treatment. In: *A Diagnosis and Treatment of Psychiatric Disorder: Adults and Children, (2nd ed.)*, eds. D. F. Klein, R. Gittelman, A. Quitkin & A. Rifkin. Baltimore: William & Wilkins, pp. 174–214.

Kohlberg, L., LaCrosse, J. & Ricks, D. (1972), The predictability of adult mental health from childhood behavior. In: *Manual of Child Psychopathology*, ed. B. B. Wolman. New York: McGraw-Hill, pp. 1217–1284.

Kornetsky, C. (1970), Psychoactive drugs in the immature organism. *Psychopharmacologia*, 17:105–136.

Kupersmidt, J. B. (1983, April), Predicting delinquency and academic problems from childhood peer status. *Strategies for Identifying Children at Social Risk: Longitudinal Correlates and Consequences*. Symposium presented at the biennial meeting of the Society for Research in Child Development, Detroit.

Lambert, N. M. (1988), Adolescent outcomes for hyperactive children: perspectives on general and specific patterns of childhood risk for adolescent educational, social and mental health problems. *Am. J. Psychol.*, 43:786–799.

Landau, S. & Milich, R. (1988), Social communication patterns of attention-deficit-disordered boys. *J. Abnorm. Child Psychol.*, 16:69–81.

Laties, V. G. & Weiss, B. (1967), Performance enhancement by the amphetamines: a new appraisal. In: *Neuropharmacology*, eds. H. Brill, J. O. Cole, P. Deniker, H. Hopkins & P. D. Bradley. Amsterdam: Excerpta Medica Foundation, pp. 800–808.

Loney, J., Kramer, J. & Milich, R. (1981), The hyperactive child grows up: predictors of symptoms, delinquency, and achievement at follow-up. In: *Psychosocial Aspects of Drug Treatment for Hyperactivity*, eds. K. Gadow & J. Loney. Boulder, CO: Westview Press, pp. 381–415.

Lou, H. C., Henricksen, & Bruhn, P. (1984), Focal cerebral hypoperfusion in children with dysphasia and/or attention deficit disorder. *Arch. Neurol.*, 41:825–829.

Lowe, T. L., Cohen, D. J., Detlor, J., Kaeonenitzer, M. W. & Shaywitz B. A. (1982), Stimulant medications precipitate Tourette's syndrome. JAMA, 247:1729–1731.

Mannuzza, S., Gittelman-Klein, R., Bonagura, N., Horowitz-Konig, P. & Shenker, R. (1988), Hyperactive boys almost grown up. *Arch. Gen. Psychiatry*, 45:13–18.

Mattes, J. & Gittelman, R. (1979), Drug linked to growth problem in children. *Psychiatric News*, 14:17.

McKinney, W. (1977), Animal behavioral/biological models relevant to depression and affective disorders in humans. In: *Depression in Childhood*, eds. J. Schulterbrandt & A. Raskin. New York: Raven Press, pp. 107–122.

Mendelson, J. H., Johnson, N. E. & Stewart, M. A. (1971), Hyperactive children as teenagers: a follow-up study. *J. Nerv. Ment. Dis.*, 153:273–279.

Mikkelson, E., Lake, C. R., Brown, G. L., Ziegler, M. G. & Ebert, M. H. (1981), The hyperactive child syndrome: peripheral sympathetic nervous system function and the effect of d-amphetamine. *Psychiatry Res.*, 4:157–169.

Nichols, P. L. & Chen, T. C. (1981), *Minimal Brain Dysfunction: A Prospective Study*. Hillsdale, NJ: Erlbaum.

Pelham, W. (1986), The effects of psychostimulant drugs on learning and academic achievement in children with attention-deficit disorders and learning disabilities. In: *Psychological and Educational Perspectives on Learning Disabilities*, eds. J. Torgesen & B. Wong. New York: Academic Press, pp. 259–295.

——— Bender, M. E. (1982), Peer relationships in hyperactive children: description and treatment. In: *Advances in Learning and Behavioral Disabilities, Vol. 1*, eds. K. Gadow & I. Bailer. Greenwich, CT: JAI Press, pp. 365–436.

——— Caddell, J., Booth, S. & Moore, S. (1985), Methylphenidate and children with attention deficit disorder: dose effects on classroom academic and social behavior. *Arch. Gen. Psychiatry*, 42: 948–952.

——— Murphy, H. A. (1986), Behavioral and pharmacological treatment of hyperactivity and attention deficit disorders. In: *Pharmacological and Behavioral Treatment: An Integrative Approach*, eds. M. Hersen & S. E. Breuning. New York: Wiley, pp. 108–147.

Peloquin, L. J. & Klorman, R. (1986), Effects of methylphenidate on normal children's mood, event-related potentials and performance in memory, scanning and vigilance. *J. Abnorm. Psychol.*, 95:88–98.

Porges, S. W, Walter, G. F., Korb, R. J. & Sprague, R. L. (1975), The influence of methylphenidate on heart rate and behavioral measures of attention in hyperactive children. *Child Dev.*, 46: 727–733.

Prichep, L., Sutton, S. & Hakerem, G. (1976), Evoked potentials in hyperkinetic and normal children under certainty and uncertainty. *Psychophysiology*, 13:419–428.

Rapoport, J. L., Buchsbaum, M., Zahn, T. P., Weingartner, H., Ludlow G. & Mikkelsen, E. (1978), Dextroamphetamine: cognitive and behavioral effects in normal prepubertal boys. *Science*, 199:560–562.

Rapport, M. D., Murphy, H. A. & Bailey, J. S. (1982), Ritalin vs. response cost in the control of hyperactive children: a within-subject comparison. *J. Appl. Behav. Anal.*, 15:205–216.

Riddle, K. D. & Rapoport, J. L. (1976), A 2-year follow-up of 72 hyperactive boys. *J. Nerv. Ment. Dis.*, 162:126–134.

Rie, H. E., Rie, E. D., Stewart, M. & Ambuel, J. P. (1976a), Effects of methylphenidate on underachieving children. *J. Consult. Clin. Psychol.*, 44:250–260.

——— ——— ——— ——— (1976b), Effects of Ritalin on underachieving children: a replication. *J. Orthopsychiatry*, 46:313–322.

Robins, L. N. (1978), Sturdy childhood predictors of adult outcomes: replications from longitudinal studies. *Psychol. Med.*, 8:611–622.

Rose, R. M., Gordon, T. P. Bernstein, I. S. (1972), Plasma testosterone in the male rhesus: influences of sexual and social stimuli. *Science*, 178:643–645.

Ross, D. & Ross, S. (1982), *Hyperactivity*. New York: Wiley.

Rutter, M., Graham, P. & Yule, W. (1970), A neuropsychiatric study in childhood. In: *Clinics in Developmental Medicine, Nos. 35–36*. London: Spastics International Medical Publications/Heinemann Medical Books.

——— Tuma, A. H. (1988), Diagnosis and classification: Some outstanding issues. In: *Assessment and Diagnosis in Child Psychopathology*, eds. M. Rutter, A. H. Tuma & I. S. Lann. New York: Guilford Press, pp. 3–17.

Safer D. J. & Allen, R. P. (1973), Factors influencing the suppressant effects of two stimulant drugs on the growth of hyperactive children. *Pediatrics*, 51: 660–667.

——— Krager, J. M. (1984), Trends in medication therapy for hyperactivity: national and international perspectives. *Adv. Learn. Behav. Dis.*, 3:125–149.

——— ——— (1988), A survey of medication treatment for hyperactive/inattentive students. *JAMA*, 260:2256–2258.

——— ——— Barr, E. (1972), Depression of growth in hyperactive children on stimulant drugs. *N. Engl. J. Med.*, 287:217–220.

——— ——— ———(1975), Growth rebound after termination of stimulant drugs. *J. Pediatr.*, 86:113–116.

Satterfield, J., Cantwell, D., Lesser, L. & Posodin, R. (1972), Physiological studies of the hyperkinetic child: I. *Am. J. Psychiatry*, 128:1418–1424.

——— Hoppe, C. M. & Schell, A. M. (1982), A prospective study of delinquency in 110 adolescent boys with attention deficit disorder and 88 normal adolescent boys. *Am. J. Psychiatry*, 139:797–798.

——— Satterfield, B. T. & Schell, A. M. (1987), Therapeutic interventions to prevent delinquency in hyperactive boys. *J. Am. Acad. Child Adolesc. Psychiatry*, 26:56-64.

Schachar, R., Rutter, M. & Smith, A. (1981), Situationally and pervasively hyperactive children. *J. Child Psychol. Psychiatry*, 22:375–392.

Schleifer, M., Weiss, G., Cohen, N., Elman, M., Crejic, H. & Kruger, E. (1975), Hyperactivity in preschoolers and the effect of methylphenidate. *Am. J. Orthopsychiatry*, 45:33–50.

Shapiro, A. K. & Shapiro, E. (1981), Do stimulants provoke, cause or exacerbate tics and Tourette syndrome? *Compr. Psychiatry*, 22:265–273.

Shaywitz, S. E., Cohen, D. J. & Shaywitz, S. E. (1978), The biochemical basis of minimal brain dysfunction. *Am. J. Dis. Child.*, 92:179–187.

Shekim, W. O., Dekirmenjian, H. & Chapel, J. L. (1979), Urinary MHPG excretion in minimal brain dysfunction and its modification by d-amphetamine. *Am. J. Psychiatry*, 136:667–671.

——— Davis, L. G., Bylund, D. B., Brunngraber, E., Fikes, L. & Lanham, J. (1982), Platelet MAO in children with attention deficit disorder and hyperactivity: a pilot study. *Am. J. Psychiatry*, 139:936–938.

Solanto, M. V. (1984), Neuropharmacological basis of stimulant drug action in attention deficit disorder with hyperactivity: a review and synthesis. *Psychol. Bull.*, 95:387–409.

Sprague, R. L. & Sleator, E. K. (1977), Methylphenidate in hyperkinetic children: differences in dose effects on learning and social behavior. *Science*, 198:1274–1276.

Sroufe, L. A. (1975), Drug treatment of children with behavior problems. In: *Review of Child Development Research, Vol. 4*, ed. F. Horowitz. Chicago: University of Chicago Press, pp. 347–407.

——— Stewart, M. A. (1973), Treating problem children with stimulant drugs. *N. Engl. J. Med.*, 289:407–413.

Stephens, R., Pelham, W. E. & Skinner, R. (1984), The state-dependent and main effects of pemoline and methylphenidate on paired-associate learning and spelling in hyperactive children. *J. Consult. Clin. Psychol.*, 52:104–113.

Still, G. F. (1902), The Coulstonian Lectures on some abnormal physical conditions in children. *Lancet*, 1:1008–1012, 1077–1082, 1163–1168.

Tallmadge, J. & Barkley, R. A. (1983), The interactions of hyperactive and normal boys with their fathers and mothers. *J. Abnorm. Child Psychol.*, 11:565–580.

Taylor, E. A. (1986), Childhood hyperactivity. *Br. J. Psychiatry*, 149:562–573.

——— (1988), Attention deficit and conduct disorder syndromes. In: *Assessment and Diagnosis in Child Psychopathology*, eds. M. Rutter, A. H. Tuma & I. S. Lann. New York: Guilford Press, pp. 377–407.

Weiss, G. (1983), Long term outcome of hyperkinetic syndrome: empirical findings, conceptual problems and practical implications. In: *Developmental Neuropsychiatry*, ed. M. Rutter. New York, Guilford Press, pp. 422–436.

——— Laties, V. G. (1962), Enhancement of human performance by caffeine and the amphetamines. *Pharmacol. Rev.*, 14:1–36.

——— Kruger, E., Danielson, V. & Elman, M. (1975), Effects of long-term treatment of hyperactive children with methylphenidate. *Can. Med. Assoc. J.*, 112:159–165.

——— Hechtman, L. T. (1986), *Hyperactive Children Grown Up*. New York, Guilford.

Wender, P. H. (1971), *Minimal Brain Dysfunction in Children*. New York, Wiley-Interscience.

——— (1987), *The Hyperactive Child, Adolescent, and Adult: Attention Deficit Disorder through the Lifespan*. New York: Oxford University Press.

Werry, J. S. (1968), Studies on the hyperactive child: IV. An empirical analysis of the minimal brain dysfunction syndrome. *Arch. Gen. Psychiatry*, 19:9–16.

——— Aman, M. (1984), Methylphenidate in hyperactive and enuretic children. *The Psychobiology of Childhood: Profile of Current Issues*, eds. B. Shopsin, & L. Greenhill. Jamaica, NY: Spectrum, pp. 183–195.

Whalen, C. K. & Henker, B. (1980), The social ecology of psychostimulant treatment: a model for conceptual and empirical analysis. In: *Hyperactive Children: The Social Ecology of Identification and Treatment*, eds. C. K. Whalen & B. Henker. New York: Academic Press, pp. 3–51.

——— ——— Alkus, S. R., Adams, D. & Stapp, J. (1978), Behavior observations of hyperactive children and methylphenidate (Ritalin) effects in systematically structured classroom environments: now you see them, now you don't. *J. Pediatr. Psychol.*, 3:177–184.

——— ——— Fink, D. & Dotemoto, S. (1979), A social ecology of hyperactive boys: medication effects in structured classroom environments. *J. Appl. Behav. Anal.*, 12:65–82.

——— ——— Dotemoto, S. (1980), Methylphenidate and hyperactivity: effects on teachers' behaviors. *Science*, 208:1280–1282.

——— ——— ——— (1981), Teacher response to the methylphenidate (Ritalin) versus placebo status of hyperactive boys in the classroom. *Child Dev.*, 52:1005–1014.

Yu-cun, S. & Yu-feng, W. (1984), Urinary 3-methoxy-4-hydroxyphenylglycol sulfate excretion in seventy-three school children minimal brain dysfunction syndrome. *Biol. Psychiatry*, 19:861–870.

Zahn, T. P., Abate, F., Little, B. & Wender, P. (1975), Minimal brain dysfunction, stimulant drugs, and autonomic nervous system activity. *Arch. Gen. Psychiatry*, 32:381–387.

Zametkin, A. J. & Rapoport, J. L. (1987), Neurobiology of attention deficit disorder with hyperactivity: where have we come in 50 years? *J. Am. Acad. Child Adolesc. Psychiatry*, 26:676–686.

Zentall, S. S. & Zentall, T. R. (1983), Optimal stimulation: a model of disordered activity and performance in normal and deviant children *Psychol. Bull.*, 94:446–471.

DISCUSSION

Despite their differences, the authors of these two articles agree on at least two major points: Stimulant medications exert dramatic short-term effects on the behavior and cognition of most ADHD children, and the long-term effects of stimulant medications on the interpersonal and academic functioning of ADHD children have not been compellingly demonstrated. The latter issue warrants further elaboration. One of the principal focal points for the debate concerning the use of stimulants with ADHD children is the apparent absence of long-term benefits. Dulcan contends that we should not necessarily expect a medication to exhibit long-term effects following its withdrawal. Indeed, many commonly used medications exhibit pronounced short-term effects but few or no long-term effects. Aspirin, for example, alleviates the immediate symptoms of headache, even though it does not diminish the long-term incidence of headaches. Nevertheless, a critic might respond (as Jacobvitz, Sroufe, Stewart, and Leffert might) that if stimulants do not produce long-term effects among ADHD children, the implication is that these medications are being used primarily for control rather than for treatment. In other words, a skeptic could justifiably argue that stimulants are administered more for the short-run convenience of parents and teachers, who are forced to contend with the frustrating and often exasperating behavior of ADHD children, than for the lasting benefit of ADHD children themselves.

The absence of reported long-term stimulant effects is difficult to interpret, however, in light of the research designs used to assess these effects. As Jacobvitz, Sroufe, Stewart, and Leffert note, these designs are without exception quasi-experimental, rather than experimental: ADHD subjects are not randomly assigned to treatment (experimental) and no-treatment (control) groups. (See Chapter 10 for a review of the difference between quasiexperimental and experimental designs.) Random assignment is a crucial component of experimental designs, and such designs are necessary if one is to draw definitive conclusions regarding cause-and-effect relationships. In studies examining the long-term effects of stimulants, however, ADHD children have not been randomly assigned to receive medication or not. Instead, the decisions regarding whether to administer stimulants or not were presumably made by physicians, perhaps in conjunction with parents and teachers, based on each child's clinical status and perceived need for medication.

This point introduces the potential problem of selection (Cook & Campbell, 1979), which, as you may recall from Chapter 10, occurs when differences between two groups in outcome are attributable to preexisting differences between these groups, rather than to the treatment or manipulation in question (in this case, stimulant medication). The problem of selection is especially worrisome in regard to stimulant medication of ADHD children, because it seems plausible, if not likely, that the ADHD children who receive medication are on average more severely disturbed than those who do not. (Imagine yourself a physician asked to treat two children with ADHD, one with severe symptoms and the other with relatively mild symptoms. For which child are you most likely to prescribe stimulants?) If this is the case, then the ADHD children who were administered stimulants in these studies may indeed have exhibited greater improvements compared with the ADHD children who were not administered stimulants—although these improvements might have been masked by the poorer initial adjustment of the ADHD children who received stimulants. Given the absence of random assignment of ADHD children to experimental conditions, however, we simply do not know.

In any case, the reported absence of long-term stimulant effects has led many clinicians and researchers to suggest that greater emphasis should be placed on "skills" rather than "pills" in the treatment of ADHD (O'Leary, 1980). Many critics are concerned that stimulants remedy the short-term difficulties of ADHD children without providing them with the long-term techniques needed to modulate and control their problematic behaviors. Consequently, over the past decade or so, increasing attention has been devoted to supplementing stimulant treatment with behavioral and cognitive-behavioral interventions. Behavioral interventions typically involve reinforcing ADHD children for appropriate behavior (for example, with tokens that can later be traded in for food or other "goodies") and punishing or extinguishing them for inappropriate behavior. Many cognitive-behavioral interventions are designed to help ADHD children to "stop, look, and listen." **Self-instructional training** (Meichenbaum & Asarnow, 1979), for example, attempts to teach ADHD children "self talk" (see also Chapter 13) that will assist them in inhibiting their tendencies toward cognitive and motoric impulsivity. For example, ADHD children may be taught to say the following sentences to themselves before attempting a task: "I must stop and think before I begin. What plans can I try? How would it work out if I did that?" (Douglas, Parry, Marton, & Garson, 1976, p. 408). The rationale underlying self-instructional training is that ADHD children have deficits in internalized language (Meichenbaum & Asarnow, 1979). Although the results of recent studies are somewhat mixed, the combination of stimulants with behavioral and cognitive-behavioral interventions appears in certain cases to be superior to stimulants alone (Hinshaw, 1991; Pelham, Vodde-Hamilton, Murphy, Greenstein, & Vallano, 1991), although self-instructional training by itself does not seem to be especially effective for ADHD (Hinshaw & Melnick, 1992). Because the long-term effects on ADHD of behavioral and cognitive-behavioral interventions have not been investigated, however, it is not yet known whether such interventions will provide ADHD children with the enduring "skills" that many clinicians and researchers have hoped for.

Another issue that merits additional discussion is the rationale for stimulant administration. As Jacobvitz, Sroufe, Stewart, and Leffert point out, the ostensible presence of organic deficits among ADHD children, such as neurological anomalies and abnormal electroencephalograms (which have been difficult to demonstrate consistently), has frequently been invoked to justify the use of stimulants with these children. Presumably, if a group of children exhibit physiological abnormalities, these abnormalities are best remedied by means of a somatic (that is, physiological) intervention. But does this logic hold up?

In actuality, as I mentioned in the introduction to Part III, the etiology and treatment of a condition bear no necessary logical relationship to each other. For instance, the presence of a biological etiology does not imply that biological interventions should constitute the treatment of choice; nor does it imply that environmental interventions cannot be successful. Thus, the question of whether ADHD children exhibit physiological abnormalities is irrelevant to whether stimulants are an appropriate treatment. In fact, as Rapaport et al. (1978) and others have shown, ADHD children and non-ADHD children respond to stimulants in essentially the same fashion: Both groups exhibit enhanced attention and diminished activity. Thus, the diagnosis of ADHD—or, for that matter, any biological abnormality that might ultimately turn out to be associated with this diagnosis—is not a specific indicator of a positive response to stimulants. If an argument is to be made for administering stimulants to ADHD children, it must ultimately be that ADHD children (because of their problems in attention and other domains) need stimulant medication more than other children do, not that ADHD children exhibit a unique response to this medication.

Finally, a comprehensive understanding of the effects of stimulants on ADHD may eventually have to accommodate the possibility (many would say likelihood), mentioned briefly in the introduction to this chapter, that ADHD is a heterogeneous category composed of children with etiologically diverse conditions (Prior & Sanson, 1986). In particular, there is some evidence that ADHD children with concomitant aggression may be substantially different from ADHD children without concomitant aggression: The more aggressive ADHD children are at higher risk for antisocial and criminal behaviors in adulthood; are more likely to have family histories of antisocial personality disorder, somatization disorder, and perhaps alcoholism; and appear to differ from ADHD children without aggression on certain biochemical indices (Lilienfeld & Waldman, 1990). The possibility that ADHD comprises two or more relatively distinct subtypes has generated understandable interest in identifying predictors of a good stimulant response. Despite the remarkable short-term effects of stimulants on most ADHD children, approximately 20% to 30% of these children show little or no clinical response. Moreover, even among those who do respond, marked individual differences in response exist (Pelham et al., 1991). Nevertheless, as Jacobvitz, Sroufe, Stewart, and Leffert point out, efforts to find consistent predictors of stimulant response have, to put it mildly, generally been disappointing. The identification of such predictors may have to await further clarification of the possible etiological heterogeneity of ADHD.

QUESTIONS TO STIMULATE DISCUSSION

1. A number of investigators have found that stimulant medications exert essentially the same effects on children without ADHD as on children with ADHD. Is there thus a justification for administering stimulants to non-ADHD children who are experiencing either temporary or long-term attentional difficulties? Explain your reasoning.
2. As Jacobvitz, Sroufe, Stewart, and Leffert note, researchers have generally failed to detect consistent differences between ADHD children who respond to stimulants and those who do not. Why might this be? How would you investigate the possibility that certain features of ADHD predict a successful response to stimulants? What types of variables would you select as potential predictors of stimulant response?
3. A number of researchers have reported that behavioral interventions can sometimes be an effective treatment for ADHD. If you were treating an ADHD child, would you administer a behavioral intervention before resorting to stimulants? Or would you administer stimulants before resorting to a behavioral intervention? Or would you use both treatments in conjunction? Explain what factors would influence your decision.
4. If you were a physician intending to prescribe stimulant medication for an ADHD child, what would you tell the parents about the pros and cons of this medication? What would you tell them about the likely long-term effects and the short-term side effects of stimulants?

SUGGESTIONS FOR FURTHER READING

Cowart, V. S. (1988). The Ritalin controversy: What's made this drug's opponents hyperactive? *Journal of the American Medical Association, 259*, 2521–2523.
Cowart reviews the recent furor concerning the prescription of stimulants for ADHD and presents commentary from well-known child psychiatrists (including Judith Rapaport and Dennis Cantwell) regarding this controversy.

Greenhill, L. L., & Osman, B. B. (Eds.) (1991). *Ritalin: Theory and patient management*. New York: Mary Ann Liebert, Inc.
This edited volume contains 26 chapters dealing with a variety of research and clinical issues relevant to the use of Ritalin among ADHD children. Among the topics covered are the use of stimulants in adults with ADHD, alternative medications for ADHD, the use of Ritalin to treat attentional problems in children with mental retardation and brain injury, the effects of Ritalin on classroom and laboratory performance, and research and theorizing on the biochemical mechanisms of stimulant drug action.

Kavale, K. (1982). The efficacy of stimulant drug treatment for hyperactivity: A meta-analysis. *Journal of Learning Disabilities, 15*, 280–289.
Kavale presents a comprehensive meta-analysis of the short-term effects of stimulant medication on activity level, attention and concentration, achievement, motor abilities, memory, and other variables. He concludes that convincing evidence exists for the short-term efficacy of using stimulants to treat ADHD.

McGuinness, D. (1989). Attention deficit disorder: The emperor's clothes, animal "pharm," and other fiction. In S. Fisher & R.P. Greenberg (Eds.), *The limits of biological treatments for psychological distress: Comparisons with psychotherapy and placebo* (pp. 151–187). Hillsdale, NJ: Erlbaum.
In a highly critical analysis, McGuinness reviews the literature on the assessment and diagnosis of ADHD and the efficacy of stimulants. She concludes that "the data consistently fail to support any benefits from stimulant medication" (p. 183). Although her chapter is well written and reasonably comprehensive, it is flawed by polemics and misstatements. Such assertions as "methodologically rigorous research . . . indicates that ADD and hyperactivity as 'syndromes' simply do not exist" (p. 155) are not only overstated but empirically false.

Paltin, D. M. (1993). *The parents' hyperactivity handbook: Helping the fidgety child*. New York: Insight Books.
In this highly readable guide, the author discusses a number of controversial issues concerning ADHD, including theories of its etiology, the use of food additives in treating ADHD, and disciplinary techniques with ADHD children. The chapter on ADHD and medication provides a balanced overview of the risks and benefits of stimulants.

Rapport, M. D. (1984). Hyperactivity and stimulant treatment: *Abusus non tollit usum. Behavior Therapist, 7*, 133–134.
Rapport argues that the side effects of stimulant drugs tend to be relatively mild and dose dependent, that studies purporting to show that stimulant treatment produces no long-term gains in academic performance are methodologically flawed, and that there is no persuasive evidence that the effects of stimulants diminish over time. He concludes that *abusus non tollit usum*: "The misuse of a treatment does not negate its potential value" (p. 134).

Ross, D., & Ross, S. (1982). *Hyperactivity: Current issues, research, and theory*. New York: Wiley.
The authors provide a comprehensive overview of the major issues pertaining to the diagnosis, assessment, etiology, and treatment of ADHD. Among the specialized issues covered are

the use of stimulants, the effectiveness of traditional treatments and behavior therapy, ADHD and its implications for the school setting, and preventive approaches.

Solanto, M. V. (1984). Neuropharmacological basis of stimulant drug action in attention deficit disorder with hyperactivity: A review and synthesis. *Psychological Bulletin, 95*, 387–409.
Solanto reviews the literature on the impact of stimulants upon a number of behavioral, cognitive, and psychophysiological variables among ADHD children and focuses on animal models of stimulant effects. She hypothesizes that the beneficial effects of stimulants on attention in humans are similar to the increased frequency of stereotypical behavior following stimulant administration in animals. This article is appropriate for readers with at least some background in physiological psychology.

Stewart, M. A. (1978). The pros and cons of treating problem children with stimulant drugs: A dialogue. In J. P. Brody & H. K. H. Brodie (Eds.), *Controversy in psychiatry* (pp. 269–276). Philadelphia: Saunders.
In this entertaining chapter, Stewart creates an imaginary dialogue between two psychiatrists to illustrate the potential benefits and risks of stimulant medication. You may also want to see the chapter in this book that was written by Cantwell, titled "CNS Activating Drugs in the Treatment of Hyperactive Children" (pp. 237–268), which provides a comprehensive, although somewhat dated, review of the clinical use and short- and long-term effects of stimulants with ADHD children.

Thurber, S., & Walker, C. E. (1983). Medication and hyperactivity: A meta-analysis. *The Journal of General Psychology, 108*, 79–86.
Like Kavale (1982), the authors of this article report the results of a meta-analysis of stimulant effectiveness. They conclude that attentional variables are substantially affected by stimulants, whereas performance on achievement and intelligence tests are only weakly affected.

Weiss, G. (1981). Controversial issues of the pharmacotherapy of the hyperactive child. *Canadian Journal of Psychiatry, 26*, 385–392.
Weiss discusses a number of controversial topics concerning the use of stimulants with ADHD children, including their side effects, differential effects on ADHD symptoms, overprescription, and potential for producing low self-esteem.

REFERENCES

American Psychiatric Association (1994). *Diagnostic and statistical manual of mental disorders* (4th ed.). Washington, DC: Author.

Box, S. (1978, Summer). Hyperactivity: The scandalous silence. *American Educator*, pp. 22–24.

Bradley, C. (1937). The behavior of children receiving benzedrine. *American Journal of Psychiatry, 94*, 577–585.

Cook, T. D., & Campbell, D. T. (1979). *Quasi-experimentation: Design and analysis for field settings*. Chicago: Rand McNally.

Cowart, V. S. (1988). The Ritalin controversy: What's made this drug's opponents hyperactive? *Journal of the American Medical Association, 259*, 2521–2523.

Douglas, V., Parry, P., Marton, P., & Garson, C. (1976). Assessment of a cognitive training program for hyperactive children. *Journal of Abnormal Child Psychology, 4*, 389–410.

Hinshaw, S. P. (1991). Stimulant medication and the treatment of aggression in children with attentional deficits. *Journal of Clinical Child Psychology, 20*, 301–312.

Hinshaw, S. P., & Melnick, S. (1992). Self management therapies and attention-deficit hyperactivity disorder. *Behavior Modification, 16*, 253–273.

Lilienfeld, S. O., & Waldman, I. D. (1990). The relation between childhood attention-deficit hyperactivity disorder and adult antisocial behavior reexamined: The problem of heterogeneity. *Clinical Psychology Review, 10*, 699–725.

Meichenbaum, D., & Asarnow, J. (1979). Cognitive-behavioral modification and metacognitive development: Implications for the classroom. In P. C. Kendall & S. D. Hollon (Eds.), *Cognitive-behavioral interventions: Theory, research, and procedures* (pp. 11–35). New York: Academic Press.

O'Leary, K. D. (1980). Pills or skills for hyperactive children. *Journal of Applied Behavior Analysis, 13*, 191–204.

Pelham, W. E., Vodde-Hamilton, M., Murphy, D. A., Greenstein, J. & Vallano, G. (1991). The effects of methylphenidate on ADHD adolescents in recreational, peer group, and classroom settings. *Journal of Clinical Child Psychology, 20*, 293–300.

Prior, M., & Sanson, A. (1986). Attention deficit disorder with hyperactivity: A critique. *Journal of Child Psychology and Psychiatry, 27*, 307–319.

Rapaport, J. L., Buchsbaum, M., Zahn, T. P., Weingartner, H., Ludlow, G., & Mikkelsen, E. (1978). Dextroamphetamine: Cognitive and behavioral effects in normal prepubertal boys. *Science, 199*, 560–562.

Rutter, M. (1982). Syndromes attributed to "minimal brain dysfunction" in childhood. *American Journal of Psychiatry, 139*, 21–33.

Rutter, M., & Garmezy, N. (1983). Developmental psychopathology. In P. H. Mussen (Ed.), *Handbook of child psychology* (4th Ed., pp. 775–911). New York: Wiley.

Sandberg, S. T., Wieselberg, M., & Schaffer, D. (1980). Hyperkinetic and conduct problem children in a primary school population: Some epidemiological considerations. *Journal of Child Psychology and Psychiatry, 21*, 293–311.

Satterfield, J. H. (1978). The hyperactive child syndrome: A precursor of adult psychopathy? In R. D. Hare & D. Schalling (Eds.), *Psychopathic behaviour: Approaches to research* (pp. 329–346). Chichester, England: Wiley.

Weiss, G., & Hechtman, L. T. (1986). *Hyperactive children grown up: Empirical findings and theoretical considerations*. New York: Guilford Press.

CHAPTER

16

Should electroconvulsive therapy be used to treat depression?

PRO Sackeim, H. A. (1989). The efficacy of electroconvulsive therapy in the treatment of major depressive disorder. In S. Fisher & R. P. Greenberg (Eds.), *The limits of biological treatments for psychological distress: Comparisons with therapy and placebo* (pp. 275–307). Hillsdale, NJ: Lawrence Erlbaum.

CON Breggin, P. R. (1991). "Shock treatment is not good for your brain." In P. R. Breggin, *Toxic psychiatry* (pp. 184–215). New York: St. Martin's Press.

OVERVIEW OF THE CONTROVERSY: Harold A. Sackeim reviews the literature on the efficacy and side effects of electroconvulsive therapy and concludes that it is an effective and relatively safe treatment for major depression. Peter R. Breggin discusses the evidence regarding the detrimental effects of electroconvulsive therapy on memory and brain functioning and its efficacy and clinical uses. He concludes that ECT is a physically dangerous and abusive treatment that should be discontinued.

CONTEXT OF THE PROBLEM

No psychiatric treatment has aroused as much heated controversy and acrimonious debate as has electroconvulsive therapy (ECT). The modern roots of ECT—which is sometimes referred to as electrotherapy, electric shock therapy, or more colloquially, "shock therapy"—can be traced to one of those bizarre instances of serendipidity that have periodically punctuated the history of medicine. In the 1920s, a number of researchers believed—entirely erroneously—that epilepsy and schizophrenia were antagonistic conditions (Kiloh, 1982). That is, epilepsy was mistakenly thought to somehow buffer individuals against the development of schizophrenia and vice versa.* So, the logic went, if schizophrenics could be made to experience epileptic-like symptoms, their condition should improve dramatically or perhaps even remit completely. This reasoning, based on a mistaken premise, provided the impetus for many of the early treatments for schizophrenia.

In the early 1930s, for example, Nyiro transfused schizophrenics with the blood of epileptics, only to meet with spectacular failure: no improvements were found. At about the same time, Manfred Sakel was taking the additional step of inducing epileptic-like seizures in schizophrenic patients. His now-defunct technique, insulin coma therapy, involved the production of a state of hypoglycemic coma by administering progressively increasing dosages of insulin over a 2- to 4-week period. A complete course of treatment often involved the induction of 100 or more comas (Gulevich, 1977). Each coma was typically followed by seizures, which Sakel originally

*Although it is not known precisely how this strange misconception originated, it may be a result of scientists misinterpreting the confluence of two rare events: Because both epilepsy and schizophrenia are infrequent, very few individuals have both conditions. Nevertheless, this extremely low rate of combined epilepsy and schizophrenia does not imply that these two conditions are less likely to co-occur than would be expected by chance.

believed to be an essential ingredient of the treatment. Although there is some suggestion that insulin coma therapy is effective in some cases of schizophrenia, the treatments are dangerous, arduous, and expensive (Gulevich, 1977). In 1933, the Hungarian psychiatrist Ladislas Meduna began to induce seizures in schizophrenics by means of camphor (a white medicinal substance extracted from the camphor tree) administered intramuscularly and, later, by means of Metrazol (a synthetic form of camphor) administered intravenously. Meduna's technique, although apparently effective for some schizophrenics (Brandon, 1981), never really caught on and is now little more than a historical footnote. Most patients apparently found the treatments to be terrifying (Gulevich, 1977).

It was not until 1938 that two Italian physicians, Ugo Cerletti and Lucio Bini, first administered electric shock to the brain of a psychiatric patient. According to eyewitness accounts, the initial demonstration of ECT was barbaric. The patient loudly exclaimed, "Not again! It will kill me!" following the delivery of the first shock, but Bini continued with the shocks anyway (Brandon, 1981). This episode eerily foreshadows many of the later misuses of ECT. ECT was introduced into the United States in 1940 (Kalinowsky, 1982) and achieved increasing popularity over the next several decades.

Ironically, however, ECT was eventually found to be more effective for depression than for schizophrenia, the condition for which it was initially developed (and upon which its theoretical rationale was originally premised). Today, ECT is almost always administered to profoundly depressed individuals, particularly those with so-called endogenous depression (see also Chapter 6). Among the characteristics of endogenous depression are profound slowing of movement, pervasive loss of pleasure, absence of reactivity to pleasant events, and weight loss. (This form of depression is often referred to as endogenous because some researchers believe it to be primarily of biological origin.) ECT is typically administered as a treatment of last resort to depressed patients who have failed to respond to other interventions, such as tricyclic antidepressants. ECT also appears to be effective in certain cases of schizophrenia, but its use for this disorder remains controversial (Simpson & May, 1985). Although the mechanism of action of ECT is not fully understood, it is known that ECT produces marked alterations in the activity of a variety of substances in the central nervous system, including endorphins (endogenous opiates) and neurotransmitters (chemical messengers) such as norepinephrine (Gulevich, 1977; Weiner, 1984).

In the first several decades of its use, ECT was a fairly hazardous—many would argue brutal—treatment. For example, a number of patients suffered bone fractures as a consequence of the violent convulsions accompanying the seizures. With the likely exception of certain Third World countries (Weiner, 1984), however, ECT is today a far safer and more humane procedure. The patient is first administered a barbiturate (such as Brevital) to induce anesthesia and a muscle relaxant (such as succinylcholine) to suppress convulsions. A 0.04 to 1 second current of between 70 and 150 volts is passed through the patient's head, either unilaterally (with the two shock electrodes placed on the same side of the head, usually the right hemisphere) or bilaterally (with the two shock electrodes placed on opposite sides of the head). This current triggers a seizure, physiologically indistinguishable from an epileptic seizure, which typically lasts between 45 and 60 seconds. Because the muscle relaxant interferes with breathing, the patient is often administered oxygen following the seizure. The patient awakens from anesthesia several minutes thereafter. ECT is typically administered two to three times a week for several weeks, for an average total of 6 to 12 treatments.

Although ECT has its vocal supporters in the psychiatric and psychological communities, many patients' rights advocates insist that it is a physically harmful treatment of dubious efficacy. For example, a number of critics have argued that ECT produces brain damage and severe long-term memory deficits (see Weiner, 1984, for a review). Moreover, some have called the efficacy of ECT into question, claiming that comparisons of ECT with a placebo control condition known as sham ECT do not provide compelling evidence for ECT's effectiveness. Still others have not questioned ECT's efficacy but have maintained that ECT "works" by erasing painful memories or perhaps even by satisfying depressed individuals' unconscious needs for punishment. Finally, those who have read Ken Kesey's *One Flew Over the Cuckoo's Nest* or seen the powerful film based on it know that ECT was occasionally used during the 1950s and 1960s as a weapon of control in mental institutions. Although such abuses were probably relatively rare, they may have contributed to a general mistrust of ECT on the part of the public. As discussed in the reading by Breggin in this chapter, these and other factors have led to mounting pressure in some states to ban ECT entirely. In 1982, for example, the citizens of Berkeley, California, voted to make the use of ECT a crime, although this referendum was overturned shortly thereafter (Sackeim, 1985). Do the data bear out the concerns of ECT's critics?

THE CONTROVERSY: Sackeim vs. Breggin

Sackeim

Harold Sackeim first reviews controlled comparisons of real ECT and sham ECT, a placebo control treatment. He concludes that real ECT is clearly more effective for depression than is sham ECT and that negative findings are attributable to methodological shortcomings. Sackeim then reviews comparisons of bilateral and unilateral ECT and concludes that they appear to be approximately equal in efficacy, with some studies suggesting a slight advantage for bilateral ECT. Bilateral ECT, however, produces a higher rate of short-term and perhaps long-term memory deficits than does unilateral ECT. Sackeim next discusses studies comparing ECT with antidepressant medications and argues that ECT is probably the most effective available treatment for depression. Finally, he reviews the literature on relapse following ECT and contends that continued antidepressant treatment following ECT can reduce the relapse rate. Sackeim also notes that administering ECT on an episodic basis following an initial positive response may be helpful, although he acknowledges that insufficient evidence on this issue exists. Sackeim concludes that the safety and efficacy of ECT "present a standard approached by few other interventions in medicine" (p. 302).

Breggin

Peter Breggin presents two case histories of individuals to support his assertion that ECT is capable of producing profound brain damage. He notes that elderly women are the most frequent recipients of ECT and that ECT is administered to approximately 100,000 individuals per year in the United States alone. Breggin reviews the evidence for the effects of ECT on brain functioning and memory, including the results of animal studies. He maintains that ECT almost invariably produces an acute organic brain syndrome or delirium, as well as severe long-term deficits in both cognitive and emotional functioning. To the extent that ECT "works," Breggin claims, it does so by causing brain damage: The patient is then able to deny the existence of personal difficulties. Breggin then presents a litany of misuses of ECT, including its use for "erasing" women's memories and for "reprogramming." Although a number of studies clearly demonstrate that ECT produces memory loss, Breggin contends, the American Psychiatric Association has consistently ignored and distorted the findings of such studies. In addition, he argues, there is little evidence that ECT is "effective" beyond 4 weeks or that it reduces suicide risk. Breggin maintains that two recent innovations, modified ECT and nondominant unilateral ECT, are no less dangerous than are earlier forms of ECT, their supporters' claims notwithstanding. Breggin concludes by applauding the efforts of individuals to ban ECT.

KEY CONCEPTS AND TERMS

anosognosia Condition, sometimes associated with right hemisphere brain damage, in which the patient denies or minimizes clear-cut physical or psychological impairments.

anterograde amnesia Loss of memory for newly learned material. Compare with retrograde amnesia.

bilateral ECT Electroconvulsive therapy delivered through both sides of the head. Compare with unilateral ECT.

delirium Condition characterized by marked confusion, grossly disorganized thinking, and severely diminished capacity to sustain attention to existing stimuli and shift attention to new stimuli.

frontal lobe syndrome Constellation of deficits resulting from damage to the brain's frontal lobes, including apathy, slowing, poor planning ability, diminished anxiety and impulse control, and deficient self-awareness.

retrograde amnesia Loss of memory for old material. Compare with anterograde amnesia.

sham ECT Placebo condition sometimes used for evaluating the efficacy of electroconvulsive therapy. In sham ECT, the patient is exposed to the same procedures as in genuine ECT (such as administration of a sedative and a muscle relaxant) except for the administration of electrical current.

unilateral ECT Electroconvulsive therapy delivered on one side of the head, typically the "nondominant" (usually the right) hemisphere. Compare with bilateral ECT.

PREVIEW QUESTIONS

1. According to Sackeim, what conclusions can be drawn from studies comparing real with sham ECT?
2. According to Sackeim, how do bilateral and unilateral ECT compare in their efficacy and side effects?
3. According to Sackeim, what do comparisons between ECT and antidepressant medications indicate?
4. What is known, according to Sackeim, concerning the prediction and prevention of relapse following ECT?
5. According to Breggin, which individuals are most likely to receive ECT? Approximately how many individuals receive ECT in the United States each year?
6. What evidence does Breggin cite for the existence of brain damage and memory loss following ECT?
7. What is Breggin's hypothesis regarding how ECT "works"? What is his reading of the literature on the effectiveness of ECT for depression and suicide?

HAROLD A. SACKEIM

The efficacy of electroconvulsive therapy in the treatment of major depressive disorder

Electroconvulsive therapy (ECT) was first used in 1938 in the treatment of psychiatric patients. Prior to the introduction of electricity as a means of eliciting seizures, pharmacological methods were used. In 1934, Laszlo Meduna first administered camphor in solution intramuscularly with the aim of provoking cerebral seizures. Meduna held the view, now since discarded, that there was an antagonism between epilepsy and schizophrenia, such that schizophrenia was underrepresented in patients with epilepsy and that epilepsy was rare in schizophrenic patients. He reasoned that there may be therapeutic benefit to artificially inducing epileptic-like seizures in schizophrenic patients. On the basis of clinical observation in a fairly substantial number of patients, Meduna (1935) reported that indeed the procedure was of benefit in relieving psychotic symptomatology.

Despite the introduction of malarial or fever therapy by Wagner-Jauregg in 1917 for treatment of general paresis, the era in which convulsive therapy was introduced was characterized by therapeutic nihilism. Within biological perspectives of psychopathology, the dominant belief was that the major psychiatric disturbances were untreatable and reflected primary genetic and/or neuropathological disturbance. Meduna's findings were treated in some camps with considerable skepticism. Indeed, his direct contradiction of the view that psychotic conditions were untreatable led to his losing his clinical and academic appointments. However, within a matter of a few years other somatic treatments were developed. Insulin coma therapy was first used in 1933 by Sakel, followed in 1935 by Moniz's introduction of psychosurgery. The reported success of these procedures in ameliorating psychopathological states (Sakel, 1938) ushered in an era of new therapeutic optimism, setting the stage for the development of the psychopharmacological approaches in the 1950s.

The introduction of psychopharmacological agents was strongly related to the virtual abandonment of insulin coma treatment and the marked reduction in use of psychosurgery. However, convulsive therapy has remained, and is now considered the form of somatic treatment with the longest continuous history of use in psychiatry. Soon after Meduna's report, it was recognized that other pharmacological agents could more reliably and safely induce seizures than camphor. In the 1930s and 1940s, pentylenetetrazol (Cardiozol, Metrazol) was frequently used. Cerletti and Bini were responsible for the substitution of an electrical stimulus for a chemical convulsant agent, and comparative trials evaluating efficacy and side effects of the two approaches continued until the 1960s (Small, 1974). In the 1950s, administration of a muscle relaxant and general anesthesia became commonplace, so that patients are unconscious during the procedure and protected from violent convulsive movements of the body. In the 1960s a series of studies began evaluating the relevant benefits and risks of administering the electrical stimulus either to one side of the head (unilateral ECT) or bilaterally, on both sides of the head. To date, there have been in excess of 40 such comparative trials, with research in this area continuing. In the 1970s and 1980s considerable attention was given to the nature of the electrical stimulus, with new devices introduced to minimize the electrical intensity required to elicit seizures, with the hope of thereby lessening side effects. With respect to mechanisms of action, there have been concerted attempts since the 1940s to identify the critical neurophysiological and neurochemical consequences of ECT.

Despite its long history of use and the continuing attention ECT has received from the research community, this form of treatment remains the most controversial in psychiatry. There are a variety of factors that have fueled this controversy (Sackeim, 1985), a number of which only indirectly bear on the issue of efficacy. However, in this [reading], the focus is on evaluating what is known about the therapeutic properties of ECT. Specific topics are reviewed,

This work was supported in part by grant MH35636 from the National Institute of Mental Health. I thank Richard P. Brown, M.D., Paolo Decina, M.D., D. P. Devanand, M.D., Sidney Malitz, M.D., and Joan Prudic, M.D. for critical discussions of various issues raised here and Victoria P. Maddatu for editorial assistance.

specifically in relation to the use of ECT in treatment of major depressive disorder. Attention is given to comparisons of ECT with experimental conditions involving only administration of anesthetic agents. . . . Comparisons of the differential therapeutic effects of different forms of ECT and comparisons of the therapeutic effects of ECT and antidepressant medications are examined. This discussion concludes with a review of the problem of relapse following clinical response to ECT.

REAL VERSUS SHAM ECT

It has long been argued that the elicitation of a generalized tonic-clonic seizure of the brain provides the necessary and sufficient conditions for the efficacy of ECT (d'Elia, Ottosson, & Strömgren, 1983; Ottosson, 1960). This view stipulates that the neurophysiological changes that ensue with seizures are fundamental to mechanisms of antidepressant response. This position rules out a number of psychological theories regarding efficacy.

Some psychological theories point out that ECT can be highly ritualized. Prior to starting a course of treatments, patients typically undergo a series of medical examinations to uncover conditions that may increase risk (e.g., space-occupying lesions). They fast from the evening before a treatment until its completion. With modern technique, at the treatment session they are attended to by staff that usually includes a psychiatrist, an anesthesiologist, nurses, and aides. Prior to induction of anesthesia and until the completion of the treatment they are monitored with EKG and often EEG. The treatment involves administration of a number of medications, principally a short-acting barbiturate anesthetic (e.g., methohexital), so that patients are unconscious for the few minutes that the procedure requires, and a muscle relaxant (e.g., succinylcholine), so that motor manifestations of the seizure are blunted. This intricate set of activities is repeated at either a two or a three treatments per week schedule.

Some psychological theories of efficacy have focused on the notion that this repetitive, intricate set of operations instills a magical quality to ECT, not only making the procedure the most "medical" or "surgical" of current psychiatric treatments, but also satisfying patient needs for attention and dependence. Related views emphasize that the expectations regarding positive clinical outcome are so high with ECT, with patients typically informed that the response rate in depressed patients is approximately 80% to 90%, that this combined with the intricate set of operations makes for a maximal placebo effect. Other theories have focused on the presumed need of depressed patients to experience real or symbolic punishment. Such views emphasize that patients may be fearful of the treatment and unconsciously identify the passage of current through the brain, the elicitation of a seizure, and other aspects of the procedure as punitive acts, thereby satisfying needs for self-directed or introjected anger. Still other theories emphasize the repeated experience of loss of consciousness, either as a result of seizure elicitation or anesthesia. The reconstitution that is established upon awakening with the gradual dissipation of confusion and disorientation is viewed as in some way restorative. Regardless of the focus, such theories reject the belief that the physiological changes that accompany seizure elicitation are intrinsic to the antidepressant properties of ECT (see Fink, 1979, and Miller, 1967, for reviews of psychological theories).

A method that has been used extensively to test the plausibility of such notions is the "real versus sham ECT" comparison. Such studies involve random assignment of patients to conditions in which they receive either a typical course of ECT ("real") or a course in which the same procedures are followed, including the repeated induction of anesthesia and application of electrodes, but no current is passed and consequently no seizure is elicited. When conducted properly such studies are double-blind, given that neither patients nor those engaged in clinical evaluation are aware of assignment to real or sham conditions. Superiority of real ECT, relative to sham conditions, would strongly suggest that either the passage of electricity or the elicitation of a seizure is critical to efficacy. Equivalence in therapeutic response would suggest that such factors are irrelevant to antidepressant effects, providing indirect support for some of the psychological theories just described.

A number of such comparative trials were conducted in the 1950s and early 1960s (Brill, Crumpton, Eiduson, Grayson, & Hellman, 1959; Fahy, Imiah, & Harrington, 1963; Harris & Robin, 1960; Sainz, 1959; Ulett, Smith, & Gleser, 1956). The findings from such studies have been reviewed elsewhere (Barton, 1977; Fink, 1979, 1980; Janicak et al., 1985; Scovern & Kilmann, 1980). In general, the results of these investigations indicated superior short-term clinical outcome with real versus sham ECT. However, these findings were inconsistent across studies and a number of methodological problems characterized much of the work. In particular, in some studies patient samples that were heterogeneous with respect to diagnosis included patients with chronic schizophrenic conditions, and did not involve random assignment or blind evaluation with objective instruments; in much of this work sample sizes were exceedingly small. In the 1970s and 1980s a spate of new studies emerged, all conducted in the United Kingdom.

The impetus for much of this new work was a report by Lambourn and Gill (1978) that found equivalent efficacy for real ECT compared to repeated anesthesia alone (see Table 1) and concern about the methodological inadequacies in the studies from the prior era. Given the clinical implications, several independent groups conducted new trials. The characteristics and findings of the

TABLE 1 Recent Comparative Studies of Real versus Sham ECT

		# of Pts.			
Study	*Methods*	*Started*	*Completed*	*Outcome*	*Comments*
Freeman et al. (1978)	Random Double-blind 2 sham vs. 2 real ECT followed by real ECT	 20 20	 14 18	Hamilton scores after 2 sham vs. 2 real ECT; more subsequent real ECT given the initial sham group	TCAs and BZD given during trial; handling of dropout may have enhanced real ECT efficacy
Lambourn & Gill (1978)	Random Double-blind 6 sham ECT vs. 6 real ECT	 16 16	 16 16	Nonsignificant outcome differences favoring real ECT	BZD given during trial; use of low dose, unilateral ECT may have weak efficacy; restriction to 6 treatments unlike clinical practice and too severe
West (1981)	Randomness and blindness uncertain 6 sham ECT vs. 6 real ECT	 12 13	 11 11	Marked advantage for real ECT; after 6 treatments 10 of 11 sham and no real patients switched to new treatment	TCA and BZD; limited methodology details available, with unresolved issues about sample selection and blindness; small sample size
Johnstone et al. (1980)	Random Double-blind 8 sham ECT 8 real ECT	 35 35	 31 31	Small advantage for real ECT; substantial clinical response to sham ECT; delusional patients responded better to real ECT: neurotic depressives had no difference	BZD; high percentage of ward admissions entered in the trial
Brandon et al. (1984)	Random Double-blind Up to 8 sham ECT Up to 8 real ECT	 42 53	 29 43	Marked advantage for real ECT, particularly in delusional/retarded patients	BZD; relatively high dropout rate
Gregory et al. (1985)	Random Double-blind Sham ECT vs. Real bilateral ECT vs. Real unilateral ECT No. treatments determined by clinical need	 23 23 23	 20 21 19	Marked advantage for both bilateral and unilateral ECT in improvement and number of treatments; bilateral required fewer treatments than unilateral ECT	BZD; unclear how dropout was handled

TCA = tricyclic antidepressant; BZD = benzodiazepine.

studies in depressed patients are summarized in Table 1. Across these trials, it is evident that short-term clinical outcome was superior with real compared to sham ECT. Give the cumulative experience over the last 30 years, the issue as to whether ECT is more efficacious in major depressive disorder than repeated anesthesia alone is now clearly determined. The medical risks of ECT with respect to morbidity and mortality largely center on the administration of anesthetic agents. It has been argued that new real versus sham ECT trials directed at addressing these same issues would be difficult to justify on either ethical or scientific grounds (Sackeim, 1986).

Several important factors should be considered in evaluating this work. First, the negative findings of Lambourn and Gill (1978) were puzzling. Even given the small sample size (16 real patients, 16 sham patients), it was unclear at the time why equal rates of clinical response were obtained in the two conditions. Lambourn and Gill used a form of ECT that has subsequently been identified as weak in therapeutic properties. They administered unilateral right (nondominant) ECT with an electrical stimulus characterized by low intensity and ultra-brief pulse width. Sackeim, Decina, Kanzler, Kerr, and Malitz (1987; Malitz, Sackeim, Decina, Kanzler, & Kerr, 1986) contrasted unilateral right and bilateral ECT, with extremely low stimulus intensity determined by adjusting stimulus dose for each patient to be just above seizure threshold. In this double-blind, random assignment trial, using conservative outcome criteria, 70% of patients were classified as responding to low dosage bilateral ECT. However, only 28% of patients responded to low dosage unilateral right ECT. This led to the suggestion . . . that at low stimulus intensity, unilateral ECT may lose a good deal of its efficacy. Concerned with this possibility, Gill and colleagues (Gregory, Shawcross, & Gill, 1985) completed another real versus sham ECT trial, this time comparing both bilateral and unilateral ECT to sham conditions, and using higher levels of stimulus intensity. The findings of this study indicated that both real ECT modalities were clearly superior in efficacy to the sham condition, although patients needed fewer treatments to achieve comparable therapeutic gains with bilateral than unilateral ECT.

The findings of Sackeim, Decina, Kanzler et al. (1987) are relevant in this context for another reason. The magnitude of the efficacy difference obtained between bilateral and unilateral ECT was dramatic. Yet patients in the unilateral right ECT condition not only experienced repeated anesthesia, but had generalized seizures of the same duration as the bilateral group. The acute cardiovascular changes that accompany seizure elicitation were equivalent in the two treatment conditions (Prudic et al., 1987). Nonetheless, the response rate obtained with low dose unilateral right ECT was the same as or less than that reported in the comparative studies for sham ECT conditions. Such findings indicate that it is highly unlikely that the psychological theories described above provide sufficient conditions for the efficacy of ECT. As discussed later, this particular set of findings also suggested that factors over and above seizure elicitation per se are critical in accounting for the efficacy of the treatment.

Across the recent series of real versus sham ECT trials, relative uniformity was observed in rates of response to real ECT conditions. The magnitude of differences between the conditions in rates of therapeutic response seemed more tied to variability in the "effectiveness" of the sham treatment. Why might this be and what might it suggest regarding the nature of response to ECT?

Sham ECT is usually intended to serve as a placebo condition. The intricate procedures involved in performing ECT would necessarily unblind patients to whether they were receiving active treatment, if the "placebo" condition was like that in pharmacological trials and involved administering a pill. Consequently, all aspects of traditional ECT were followed in these studies, except for the passage of current and seizure induction. The variability observed in rate of response of "sham" ECT suggests three alternatives: rater effects, sampling differences, and intrinsic antidepressant properties to anesthesia induction.

One might account for the intertrial differences in rates of response to repeated anesthesia by presuming that different clinical research centers differed in criteria for determining good outcome and/or in expectations for overall positive results. The relative lack of variability with respect to real ECT outcome rates makes this alternative less attractive. A more likely possibility pertains to differences among the trials in patient characteristics. Although undocumented, it is commonly believed that there are national differences in the extent to which ECT is used as a treatment of first choice or as a treatment of last resort. Even more likely are physician and clinical center differences along this dimension. The typical rate of placebo response in psychopharmacological trials in major depression is approximately 30% (e.g., Klein, Gittelman, Quitkin, & Rifkin, 1980). One might anticipate that those centers that administer ECT principally to medication-resistant patients would have a considerable lower rate of "placebo" response. The reason for this is that the medication-resistant patient has already experienced one, and often many, extended trials of biological treatment and should have already manifested a placebo response were it to occur. Unfortunately, information on the rates of medication-resistance in the recent series of real versus sham ECT trials is for the most part lacking, and has never been examined in relation to different rates of response to ECT versus anesthesia alone. It has been commented, however, that one of the trials (Johnstone et al., 1980) that overall showed a smaller advantage than typical for real ECT included a remarkably high rate of consecutive admissions with major depression in the study (Kendell, 1981).

The third alternative is that sham ECT or repeated administration of anesthesia should not be considered as an "active placebo," but as a weak antidepressant treatment. In psychopharmacological trials, an inactive placebo is inert and essentially has no effects on the individual. Active placebos share many of the side effects of the psychotropic medication with which they are compared, but lack efficacy with regard to the psychopathological condition being treated. For example, in studies of the effects of scopolamine, a central anticholinergic agent, it is often useful to administer methscopolamine as placebo. The latter is also an anticholinergic agent in the periphery, but does not cross the blood brain barrier. The avowed intention in using repeated anesthesia as a contrast condition is to provide an active placebo. No only are patients thereby blind to whether or not they experienced seizure induction, but many of the acute effects of traditional ECT are mimicked, including a period of disorientation following awakening and some somatic side effects. However, there are some reasons to believe that repeated anesthesia may have therapeutic properties. Although never subject to rigorous evaluation of efficacy, the administration of barbiturates and the use of chemically induced sleep therapy was an accepted mode of treatment for various forms of psychopathology prior to the introduction of ECT and other somatic treatments (Kalinowsky & Hippius, 1972). On theoretical grounds, the view has been raised that antidepressant effects may be obtained by acting on the same neurochemical systems that subserve the principal mode of action of the barbiturate anesthetics (Lloyd, Morselli, & Bartholini, 1987; Sackeim, 1986; Sackeim, Decina, Prohovnik, Malitz, & Resor, 1983). It is also noteworthy that the dosage of anesthetic agent used in the real versus sham ECT trials seemed roughly correlated with the obtained rate of therapeutic response. For example, Brandon et al. (1984), reporting one of the lowest response rates to sham ECT (20%), used 1.0 mg/kg of methohexital, whereas Johnstone et al. (1980) had a response rate of 40% and used 1.5 mg/kg of the same agent. Finally, in an earlier literature on treatment of depression, comparisons of ECT efficacy are available with medication placebo or no-treatment conditions (e.g., Greenblatt, Grooser, & Wechsler, 1964; Kiloh, Child, & Latner, 1960). It is noteworthy that for the most part these biologically inactive conditions yielded smaller response rates than those obtained with sham ECT and typically even larger differences with ECT.

In summary, at this point it is incontrovertible that ECT is an effective antidepressant agent and considerably more so than administration of repeated anesthesia. This focuses the issues of accounting for efficacy on other questions. These include the aspects of ECT that are critical to antidepressant response, [including] the areas of the brain stimulated (e.g., bilateral vs. unilateral ECT), the induction of seizures; the longevity of therapeutic response, that is, relapse rates; and the issue of the relative efficacy of ECT compared to other treatments of depression. . . .

BILATERAL VERSUS UNILATERAL ECT

No other set of issues in the field of ECT has received more research attention than the comparative efficacy and side effects of bilateral and unilateral ECT. Although unilateral ECT techniques had previously been employed, the first comparative trial of unilateral and bilateral techniques was reported by Lancaster, Steinert, and Frost (1958). This report ushered in a wave of clinical trials with its suggestion that unilateral ECT may have a considerable advantage with respect to a lower side effect profile, while being equal in efficacy to bilateral ECT.

Bilateral ECT involves placement of stimulus electrodes symmetrically, on both sides of the head. In virtually all studies in the modern era, the same electrode placement has been used for bilateral ECT, that is, frontotemporal. This placement results in a current density path in the brain which shows a marked anterior-posterior (caudality) gradient in the cortex. The anterior prefrontal pole is likely to receive the greatest current density, with a sharp drop-off in more posterior tissue (Rush & Driscoll, 1968; Sackeim & Mukherjee, 1986; Weaver et al., 1977). Relative to unilateral ECT, bilateral placement is likely to result in greater current density in deep, subcortical structures. A variety of electrode placements have been used for unilateral ECT (d'Elia & Raotma, 1975). The most common have been the Lancaster and d'Elia placements. All unilateral ECT placements involve positioning one of the electrodes in the same frontotemporal position as in bilateral ECT. The second electrode has varied in its placement over the ipsilateral hemisphere. The d'Elia placement involves positioning slightly down from the vertex, over parietal cortex. The Lancaster placement positions the electrode a few centimeters below the d'Elia placement, over temporoparietal areas. Regardless of exact placement, current density with unilateral ECT will be substantially greater in the hemisphere ipsilateral than contralateral to the electrodes. Although in gross motor and EEG manifestations seizures induced with unilateral ECT will appear to be generalized, fine-grained quantitative analyses of EEG can demonstrate asymmetries in the onset of seizures, the amplitude of the seizure discharge, and in postictal EEG slowing (e.g., d'Elia, 1970; Staton, Hass, & Brumback, 1981). Asymmetric transient neurological signs have also been observed following unilateral ECT (Kriss, Halliday, & Pratt, 1980). Within each hemisphere, unilateral ECT is likely to have a relatively even current density distribution over the anterior two thirds of the cortex. This difference in current density paths between the electrode placements is most likely due to the patterns of current shunting across the scalp. Therefore, bilateral and unilateral placements differ not only in lateralization but also in regionality of cur-

rent density distributions. Although not fully appreciated in the literature, this patterning suggests that differences between the modalities in behavioral consequences should not be assumed to be only a function of functional brain asymmetry.

Differences in the side effect profiles between bilateral and unilateral right ECT are well established. The extent and duration of disorientation are greater with bilateral ECT (Daniel & Crovitz, 1986; Sackeim et al., 1986). Although not documented, it is most likely that the probability of developing an organic brain syndrome (prolonged period of clouded consciousness) is significantly greater with bilateral ECT. Verbal anterograde and retrograde amnestic deficits are also greater with bilateral ECT immediately following a treatment and several days following the end of the treatment course. It is controversial whether bilateral ECT also results in greater disruption of nonverbal memory functions, and in particular those subserved to a greater extent by the right hemisphere. Evidence that this might be the case was reported by Squire and Slater (1978), although the "nonverbal" task used in this study, memory for geometric designs, could have been readily subject to verbal coding. Sackeim et al. (1986) suggested that the issue of whether bilateral and unilateral ECT differ in nonverbal amnestic deficits may be an oversimplification. They found that bilateral ECT produced greater retrograde amnesia for nonsense shape recognition, but was equivalent to unilateral right ECT in producing anterograde and retrograde deficits for face recognition. Given the differences between the modalities in current density paths and, as a likely result, in patterns of seizure discharge within the right hemisphere, it may be that findings of equivalent or differential right hemisphere deficits are task dependent.

Once patients recover from the acute postictal disorientation, the cognitive effects of ECT are highly selective with respect to memory functions. Other aspects of cognitive performance typically are unchanged or improved (e.g., Malloy, Small, Miller, & Milstein, 1982). In particular, tasks highly dependent on attention and concentration reveal deficient performance in depressed patients prior to ECT and often enhanced performance following the ECT course, with the extent of change related to measures of therapeutic response. On the other hand, retrieval of information learned shortly before or during the ECT course or retrieval of information newly learned but tested after a delay will be areas of clear impairment (Cronholm & Ottosson, 1961; Sackeim & Steif, 1988; Steif, Sackeim, Portnoy, Decina, & Malitz, 1986). Traditionally, beyond a week following the ECT course, differences between the modalities in cognitive effects have been difficult to document. This may be because the cognitive effects of ECT are most intense immediately following seizure induction and there is sharp recovery of functioning as time from ECT increases. Consequently, regardless of modality, there is remarkably little objective evidence of persistent cognitive deficits a few weeks beyond the end of the ECT course (e.g., Squire, 1986; Weiner, 1984). An exception is likely to be spottiness in memory for personal and impersonal events that occurred within the months preceding and the weeks following the ECT course. In this domain there well may be permanent loss, with the interpretation that ECT interferes with the consolidation of recent memories (Squire, 1986). Indeed, recently a greater long-term memory loss was documented for bilateral relative to unilateral ECT. Weiner, Rogers, Davidson, and Squire (1986) observed that compared both to non-ECT-depressed patient controls and to patients who had received unilateral ECT, bilateral ECT patients had a persistent deficit in memory for personal events, particularly those that occurred within the year preceding ECT. Therefore, given the established difference in short-term side effects and a possible difference in long-term cognitive profiles, the decision to use unilateral or bilateral ECT has important implications for risk/benefit considerations.

This summary concerned contrasts between bilateral and unilateral right ECT. Unilateral left ECT is a technique rarely used in treatment of major depression. With respect to orientation and verbal memory functions, early studies indicated that unilateral left ECT had a side effect profile similar to bilateral ECT (Daniel & Crovitz 1982; d'Elia, 1970; Halliday, Davison, Browne, & Kreeger, 1968; Lancaster et al., 1958). Particularly because these deficits are most bothersome to patients, unilateral left ECT was essentially abandoned. It should be noted also that of six comparative studies that examined efficacy of unilateral left and right ECT, three investigations had findings that suggested superior antidepressant response with electrode placement over the right hemisphere (see Malitz, Sackeim, & Decina, 1982, for a discussion). Such findings are supportive of the view that functional brain asymmetry contributes to manifestation of affective disorder (e.g., Sackeim et al., 1982), in addition to being critical in understanding the nature of ECT modality side effects profiles.

Despite a history of more than 35 comparative trials of the relative efficacy of unilateral and bilateral ECT, this area continues to be a source of controversy. Indeed, most academic reviews (with important exceptions; see Abrams, 1986a; Overall & Rhoades, 1986) have concluded that if differences in efficacy exist they are slight, statistical in nature, and of doubtful clinical consequence. The report of the Task Force of the American Psychiatric Association (Frankel et al., 1978) strongly recommended the use of unilateral right ECT, and some have questioned whether bilateral ECT is ever indicated (Strömgren, 1984). In contrast, surveys of clinical practice suggest that clinicians predominantly rely on bilateral ECT (e.g., Frankel et al., 1978; Pippard & Ellam, 1981).

The literature on the comparative efficacy of bilateral and unilateral ECT has been subject to a number of reviews and has been subject to meta-analysis (Abrams, 1986b; d'Elia & Raotma, 1975; Fink, 1979; Janicak et al., 1985; Overall & Rhoades, 1986; Pettinati, Mathisen, Rosenberg, & Lynch, 1986). Rather than recover this well-worn ground, a number of considerations are offered here to aid in interpreting this literature.

The large bulk of studies in this area failed to find significant efficacy differences between the modalities, although the majority reported trends favoring bilateral ECT. This has been interpreted variously as indicating a nonmeaningful efficacy difference (d'Elia & Raotma, 1975) or as signaling a difference of clinical consequence. Likewise, meta-analyses of the same studies have yielded rather different conclusions (Janicak et al., 1985; Overall & Rhoades, 1986), partly because of reliance of different statistical techniques for assessing interstudy findings. It should be noted here that the median sample size of studies comparing bilateral and unilateral ECT has been only 20 patients per treatment condition. Particularly in the major meta-analytic approaches, efficacy was determined by examining the categorical rate of response in each group. This means, of course, that the power in most comparative trials was remarkably low, lessening the confidence in null results. Further, dichotomous classification as responders or nonresponders is inherently insensitive to the issue as to whether the modalities differ in quality of response (i.e., the nature and extent of residual symptomatology in patients who have sustained clinical benefit).

A few studies have shown clear-cut efficacy differences, and with notable exception (e.g., Welch et al., 1982), these effects have favored bilateral ECT. Of more concern, some studies have obtained large differences favoring bilateral ECT (Abrams et al., 1983; Gregory et al., 1985; Sackeim, Decina, Kanzler, et al., 1987), and these studies are among those that used the strictest methodological conditions and are among the most recent. Indeed, given the recent history of findings, it is probably no longer viable to frame the question as to whether bilateral and unilateral ECT are equal in efficacy. Instead, the issue should be identification of the conditions under which unilateral ECT can be as effective as bilateral ECT.

There are a number of possibilities that may explain why more recent work has demonstrated more robust therapeutic advantages for bilateral ECT. Two factors that are raised here concern patient selection and technical factors in the administration of the treatment. Although there was at one time a host of studies that examined patient factors that predict response to ECT generally (e.g., Carney, Roth, & Garside, 1965; Mendels, 1967), there has been very limited work discerning whether unilateral and bilateral ECT differ in patient factors related to outcome. One exception is a study of Heshe, Roeder, and Theilgaard (1978), which found that bilateral ECT held a particular advantage for elderly patients. Although not well documented, it is likely that the nature of patient populations receiving ECT in academic and clinical settings has changed over the last two or more decades. Not only has there been diagnostic refinement regarding what constitutes major depressive disorder, but it is likely that ECT practice has increasingly centered on medication-resistant or medication-intolerant patients. Particularly in the United States, a major indication for ECT has become failure to respond to adequate trials with antidepressant medication or inability to sustain such trials due to side effect considerations (e.g., Frankel et al., 1978). As discussed later, there are no data documenting relative rates of response to ECT in medication-resistant patients and in those who have not failed adequate medication trials. Intuitively, one might expect that those who failed prior courses of antidepressant treatment would be less likely to respond to ECT than those who had not. Speculatively, it may also be the case that a larger representation of medication-resistant patients in research conducted at often tertiary academic centers magnifies efficacy differences between unilateral and bilateral ECT. A related possibility concerns patients with delusional or psychotic depression. There is a fair documentation that at high rates such patients fail to respond to monotherapy with antidepressants or antipsychotics (e.g., Spiker et al., 1985), and they respond at high rates to bilateral ECT (Avery & Lubrano, 1979; Crow & Johnstone, 1986). Some have contended that psychosis involves perturbation of left hemisphere processes (e.g., Flor-Henry, 1983), which could suggest a preferential response to bilateral ECT. In turn, if both the factors of medication-resistance and psychosis have become more represented in ECT samples, this may result in patient groups that are older, and with greater representation of highly recurrent affective disorder.

It has been suggested that a major methodological confound has characterized virtually all comparative trials of unilateral and bilateral ECT (Sackeim, Decina, Kanzler, et al., 1987). The typical paradigm has been to have ECT devices deliver the same electrical intensity to all patients, regardless of modality. Although this equates treatment conditions in terms of the raw amount of electricity being administered, it produces inequality in the amount that reaches the brain. With constant-current, brief pulse devices, seizure threshold is lower with right unilateral ECT (d'Elia placement) than with bilateral ECT (Sackeim, Decina, Portnoy, Neeley, & Malitz, 1987). Consequently, if the same electrical dose is administered to both conditions, it will exceed seizure threshold to a greater extent with unilateral than bilateral ECT. [There is evidence] that both the therapeutic and adverse effects of ECT are more related to the degree to which stimulus intensity exceeds seizure threshold than the absolute dose administered (Sackeim, Decina, Prohovnik, & Malitz, 1987). By this view, much of the previous comparative work was biased in favor of the efficacy of unilateral right ECT (underestimated therapeutic differences). This view also suggests that the side effect profile differences were also underestimated. In addition, it has been argued that for unilateral ECT to be efficacious, it, in particular, must be delivered with stimulus intensity that clearly exceeds threshold.

This perspective has been applied in analyses of extant findings regarding efficacy differences between bilateral and unilateral ECT (Abrams, 1986a; Pettinati et al., 1986). There are suggestions that trials that found advantages for bilateral ECT had greater representation of older patients, male patients, used shorter interelectrode distances for unilateral ECT, and/or permitted use of benzodiazepines during the ECT course for anxiolytic or hypnotic purposes. Each of these factors is associated with an increased seizure threshold. Therefore, given the hypothesized sensitivity of unilateral ECT to electrical dosage effects, such practices may have weakened the efficacy of this condition. The most recent studies are more likely to have used ECT devices that delivered more electrically efficient and less intense stimulation. This would have the same result.

If ongoing trials sustain this perspective, it is possible that the conditions under which unilateral and bilateral ECT are equally effective can be specified. Investigation in this area should also be revealing of mechanisms of therapeutic action of ECT. If stimulus intensity needs to be more grossly suprathreshold for unilateral ECT to be equivalent in efficacy, the question arises as to whether the greater efficacy is tied to the increased current density (or seizure discharge) in the ipsilateral or contralateral hemisphere. Do neurophysiological and neuropsychological studies reveal increased or decreased asymmetry when stimulus intensity is enhanced with unilateral ECT? At the practical level, this work will also require reassessment of whether there is a differential advantage with regard to cognitive side effects when each modality is delivered at the minimal intensity level that it requires to produce maximal clinical benefit.

ECT VERSUS ANTIDEPRESSANT MEDICATIONS

During the 1960s a series of trails were conducted that examined the relative efficacy of ECT compared to tricyclic antidepressants (TCAs) and monoamine oxidase inhibitors (MAOIs) (Bruce et al, 1960; Fahy et al., 1963; Greenblatt et al., 1964; Harris & Robin, 1960; Kiloh et al., 1960; Robin & Harris, 1962; Shepherd, 1965; Wilson, Vernon, Guin, & Sandifer, 1963). These trials were conducted soon after the introduction of the pharmacological agents, and the major American (Greenblatt et al., 1964) and British (Shepherd, 1965) studies in particular were geared to using ECT as a "gold standard" by which to measure the relative efficacy of the medications.

This literature has also been the subject of a number of recent reviews (e.g., Fink, 1980; Janicak et al., 1985; Rifkin, 1988). Broadly speaking there is consensus that across this work ECT was found to be as effective as or more effective than any other treatment for depression. On the basis of their meta-analysis, Janicak et al. (1985) summarized the literature as indicating that across studies that compared ECT to any other type of treatment, there was a 78% response rate to ECT, a 28% rate for sham ECT, a 37.6% rate for medication placebo conditions, a 64.3% rate for TCAs, and a 32% rate of response to MAOIs. Within the same set of studies, ECT had a 20% advantage in response rate over TCAs.

However, the situation is more complex. In most of this work and in the most critical studies, double-blind conditions did not pertain to the ECT groups. When patients receiving ECT and pharmacotherapy are being compared, it is impossible to disguise treatment conditions unless repeated anesthesia is administered to pharmacotherapy patients (e.g., Wilson et al., 1963). Such a procedure would not conform to clinical practice, it would enhance risks and conceivably it could interfere with medication effects. An alternative is to videotape clinical evaluations. References to or display of side effects that would indicate form of treatment (e.g., memory complaints or complaints of dry mouth, dizziness, etc.) can be edited out, with the tapes rated by clinicians blind to treatment and time period during the study (i.e., time-blind). Such procedures provide some control over rater bias, but not over differential patient expectancy and related placebo effects, and have been implemented recently in comparative studies of ECT and pharmacotherapy in the treatment of acute mania (Mukherjee, Sackeim, & Lee, 1988; Small et al., 1986).

As detailed by Rifkin (1988), the studies contrasting ECT and antidepressant medications also had limitations with respect to the nature of pharmacological treatment and statistical analyses. Since these studies were conducted, the standards for what are considered adequate trials of TCAs and MAOIs have been revised upwards. This has been based on findings that higher dosage and longer duration of treatment are associated with higher clinical response rate (e.g., Quitkin, Rabkin, Ross & McGrath, 1984). Therefore, by current standards one might question whether the superiority obtained for ECT was due to weak medication conditions. Further, in some trials that reported significant therapeutic advantages for ECT compared to specific comparative conditions, a significant between-group difference across all the conditions tested was not established prior to performing specific comparisons. This criticism loses some force when collapsing data across studies for purpose of meta-analysis.

Rifkin (1988) suggested that there is a pressing clinical need to determine more conclusively whether ECT is more effective than antidepressant medications. He argued that if, indeed, rates of ECT response exceed those with TCAs or MAOIs by approximately 20%, patients and clinicians should be informed of the greater likelihood of response with ECT. One can add to this that it is widely accepted that rates of medical morbidity and mortality are lower with ECT than with antidepressant medications, even though ECT is often used in patients with medical complications who cannot tolerate TCAs or MAOIs. However, this portrayal is also an oversimplification.

As described in the next section, current clinical practice dictates that following response to ECT, patients who have recovered from episodes of major depression receive antidepressant medications for a period of at least several months to prevent relapse of the same episode (e.g., Klein et al., 1980). Given that patients will in any case be exposed to antidepressant medications, it can be argued that unless there are other pressing indications for ECT, failure to respond to medications during the acute phase of illness typically should be established first. This would limit the extent of polytherapy and thereby decrease risk.

Another problem with how this literature has been framed concerns the fact that a large proportion of patients who receive ECT are therapeutically resistant to, or medically intolerant of, antidepressant medications. In evaluating the relative efficacy of these medications and ECT, it would be unfair to randomly assign a typical ECT sample to either ECT or medication conditions. Only a small proportion of medication-resistant patients would be expected to respond to the same class of drug if they already failed adequate trials during the same episode. Accordingly, one would expect a substantially higher response rate for ECT. On the other hand, one might concentrate work on patients untreated during that episode. Such research would be impractical or of limited meaning for three reasons. First, the nature of political climate surrounding ECT, at least in the United States, is such that one should expect high refusal rates in previously untreated patients for participation in a random assignment trial to medication or ECT. The outcome of such work may be compromised by a serious selection bias. Second, the availability of previously untreated patients, with depressions of sufficient severity to require ECT, is likely to be too low at academic centers to sustain this type of research. Third, such samples would not be representative of current ECT practice.

Assessment of the relative value of antidepressant and ECT treatment of depression is complicated by additional factors. Reviews of the comparative trials have centered on determining whether rate of clinical response differed for ECT or medications (e.g., Janicak et al., 1985; Rifkin, 1988). For the most part, this involved contrasts of the number of patients in the treatment conditions who were globally rated as improved. Traditionally, it has been claimed that not only is the rate of clinical response superior with ECT, but also the quality of clinical response. It is believed that patients considered improved or substantially improved will show less residual symptomatology, that is, more complete remission, if treated with ECT relative to medications. If true, this is a critical issue because residual symptomatology observed following maximal antidepressant response may be long persisting and possibly predictive of relapse. Unfortunately there are limited data regarding this issue. Hamilton (1982) reported an open, naturalistic study contrasting in his practice the distributions of the proportion of symptom score reductions with ECT and pharmacological treatment. Response to ECT was more bimodal than with antidepressant medication, with ECT characterized by a greater proportion of complete or near-complete remissions. From the point of view of prospective patients, the likely extent of residual symptoms may be as critical as the relative probability of sustaining improvement.

Finally, any evaluation of the relative merits of antidepressant medications and ECT must consider their respective side effect profiles. To some extent this is like comparing apples and oranges. The major concerns with the medications, particularly in the elderly, are systemic medical side effects, and in a small proportion, mortality. ECT has a marked advantage with regard to this domain. However, the frequency of such complications with medications is far lower than the universal acute cognitive side effects of ECT. Although research on the cognitive effects of TCAs and MAOIs is presently assuming more attention, it is unlikely that improvements in ECT technique in the near future will moderate acute cognitive side effects to a level that approaches the sustained effects of antidepressant medications. Further, within the domain of cognition there is likely to be specification by type of treatment, with differences between the medications and ECT in the areas affected. Indeed with ECT, the type and extent of cognitive side effects manifested are strongly related to when patients are assessed relative to their last treatment (e.g., Steif et al., 1986).

In summary, with a number of limitations, the comparative trials of ECT and TCAs or MAOIs are supportive of the view that ECT is the most effective antidepressant available. However, even assuming relative superiority in rates of clinical response, other factors must be considered in determining the priority of somatic treatments in relieving major depressive disorder. The issue as to whether quality of antidepressant response is also superior with ECT requires investigation. The increasing use of ECT in medication-resistant patients also poses issues of efficacy. It is established that medication-resistant patients respond to ECT at high rates (e.g., Avery & Lubrano, 1979). It has never been determined, however, whether their rate or quality of response is equivalent to that of patients who did not fail adequate medication trials in the same episode. It would be useful at the clinical level to determine whether established medication-resistance impinges on ECT response rates. Indeed, it would be highly unusual in therapeutics for patients who have failed adequate trials of accepted treatment for a condition to have equal probability of responding to another class of treatment as patients not determined to be treatment-resistant. If in fact this factor bears no relation to ECT outcome there would also be implications with respect to considerations of mechanisms of antidepressant action of ECT. A prominent approach in the study of such mechanisms has been the identification of the similarities between ECT and TCAs in neurophysiological effects (e.g., Sackeim, 1988). If previous failure to respond to adequate TCA trials is irrelevant with regard to efficacy of ECT, then it would seem less likely that ECT exerts its therapeutic properties via the same mechanisms as TCAs.

RELAPSE FOLLOWING RESPONSE TO ECT

This [reading] has focused on a variety of issues concerning the short-term efficacy of ECT. After 50 years of investigation, with comparisons to sham treatment . . . and placebo and active drug conditions, and within ECT, studies of a variety of technical factors, there is little room for doubt that ECT is a highly effective antidepressant treatment. From my viewpoint, the most pressing clinical question is not whether ECT works, but how best to prevent relapse.

Following response to antidepressant medication, relapse rates on the order of 50% are expected over the ensuing first several months if somatic treatment is discontinued at the point of critical response (Mindham, Howland, & Shepherd, 1973; Prien, Klett, & Caffey, 1973). This accords with notions that the underlying neurobiological abnormality persists until there is spontaneous remission. Relapse rates following a period of 6 months of sustained euthymia are expected to be considerably lower because by that point patients who have remained well are believed to be out of the index episode. Commonly, relapse after a sustained period of remission is considered a recurrence, that is, the expression of a new episode. This formulation results in the distinction among acute phase treatment, continuation phase treatment directed at preventing relapse, and maintenance or prophylactic phase treatment directed at preventing the occurrence of new episodes (e.g., Klein et al., 1980; Prien et al., 1984).

The available evidence indicates that continuing the same antidepressant medication to which patients responded during the acute phase will reduce relapse rate in the ensuing 6 months from approximately 50% to 20% (e.g., Mindham et al., 1973; Prien et al., 1973). The same type of pattern is believed to occur with ECT. If antidepressant treatment is not instituted following response, the evidence strongly indicates that relapse rates will be approximately 50% in the ensuing 4 to 6 months (e.g., Sackeim et al., 1990; Snaith, 1981). The standard view is that administration of TCAs or MAOIs following ECT reduces this rate to approximately 20%.

This view emanated from three comparative trials conducted in England during the 1960s (Imiah, Ryan, & Harrington, 1965; Kay, Fahy, & Garside, 1970; Seager & Bird, 1962). Table 2 presents the essential characteristics of these studies. These trials were conducted with two purposes in mind. The first was to determine whether concomitant treatment with antidepressant medications during the ECT course would result in need for fewer ECT treatments, that is, more rapid clinical response. This work and other studies indicated that proportion and speed of clinical response were not influenced by concomitant antidepressant treatment. The second goal was to determine whether continuing the antidepressant medications following response to ECT reduced rates of relapse.

TABLE 2 Prospective Studies of TCA Continuation Therapy Following Antidepressant Response to ECT

Study	*Methods*	*# of Pts.*	*Followup*	*Relapse*	
Seager & Bird (1962)	Random double-blind Imipramine Placebo	Entered 40 Completed followup 28	6 mo.	IMI 16% (2/12)	Placebo 68% (11/16)
Imlah et al. (1965)	Random not blind Imipramine Phenelzine No medication	Entered 150 Completed followup 111	6 mo.	IMI & PHZ 21% (15/70)	No meds 51 (21/41)
Kay et al. (1970)	Random double-blind Amitriptyline Diazepam	Entered 132 Completed followup 115	6 mo.	AMI 15% (8/52)	Diazepam 38% (24/63)

The bulk of patients in these trials received TCAs or MAOIs during the ECT course. In the majority of patients the continuation treatment phase did not involve being newly randomly assigned to medication or placebo (or no drug) conditions. Rather patients continued to receive the same pharmacological agent (or lack thereof) as during the ECT course. This raises the possibility that patients who benefited from the antidepressants as acute phase treatment also sustained benefit during the continuation phase. This problem is compounded by the fact that these trials were conducted soon after the introduction of the antidepressant medications, and at the time, ECT was often used as a treatment of first choice. Accordingly, one would expect that a fairly high proportion of depressed patients responded to the medications as acute phase treatment. As noted earlier, an increasing proportion of ECT practice centers on medication-resistant patients, and in many centers such patients comprise the great majority of those treated with ECT for depression. Nonetheless, the standard of practice in the field is to administer a TCA following clinical response to ECT, regardless of whether patients were found to be TCA-resistant during the acute phase of illness. Indeed, some have recommended that ECT be reserved for TCA-resistant patients and that all patients receive TCA continuation therapy following response to ECT (Klein et al., 1980).

Conceptually it is possible that patients benefit from use of medication as a continuation treatment that they failed to benefit from as an acute phase treatment. This circumstance rarely arises in psychopharmacological practice, because patients would ordinarily be continued on the same medication they responded to while in the acute phase. The rationale for such practice in the case of ECT centers on either the possibility that what needs to be accomplished from a neurobiological viewpoint differs during the acute and continuation phases or that prior ECT alters the neurobiological substrate such that the requisite pharmacological action can now be obtained (Sackeim, 1986).

To provide an initial examination of this issue, the Columbia group conducted a prospective, naturalistic study (Sackeim et al., 1990). Patients were monitored until relapse or for one year following clinical response to ECT. Several methods were used to evaluate relative medication resistance during the index depressive episode. Following ECT, somatic and psychotherapeutic treatment was uncontrolled and determined largely at the discretion of patients' referring clinicians. Across the sample, the relapse rate was high and clustered in the first 4 months following clinical response. If patients sustained remission beyond this point, relapse was rare. Regardless of method of evaluation, medication-resistance during the index episode was predictive of a substantially higher rate of relapse. In patients who were found to be medication-resistant prior to receiving ECT, adequacy of post-ECT pharmacotherapy had no relation to relapse rates. In particular, there was no evidence that patients who failed an adequate TCA trial prior to receiving ECT benefited from adequate TCA treatment following clinical response. On the other hand, adequate post-ECT pharmacotherapy was significantly associated with a lower relapse rate in patients who had not received an adequate medication trial prior to ECT. It is likely that a number of these patients would have responded to antidepressant medications had they received adequate trials prior to ECT.

These findings are suggestive that medication-resistance is predictive of a high relapse rate following ECT and that the standard pharmacological strategy of administering the same class of medication as continuation therapy that patients failed to respond to during the acute phase may be ineffective. Considerable caution is necessary in generalizing from these data. As in any naturalistic, uncontrolled study, it is conceivable that levels of treatment and patient characteristics are confounded. Although in this work such factors could not be identified, it is possible that treating clinicians instituted more vigorous continuation therapy in patients who were believed to be at higher risk of relapse. What is sorely needed in this area are prospective, random assignment, placebo-controlled evaluations of the utility of standard pharmacological continuation treatment in medication-resistant ECT-responsive patients. One such trial is ongoing.

It is noteworthy that ECT is the only somatic treatment of major depression that is typically discontinued following clinical response. Little data are available concerning the efficacy of continuing ECT on an intermittent basis following antidepressant response (e.g., Decina, Guthrie, Sackhein, Kahn, & Malitz, 1987; Stevenson & Geoghegan, 1951), although the case reports and clinical experience suggest that this approach can be highly effective in preventing relapse. The severity of cognitive side effects would be expected to be substantially moderated by such a procedure because their magnitude is linked to the temporal spacing of treatments (e.g., three times per week during the acute phase versus once every 2 or 3 weeks during the continuation treatment). The difficulties in this area are largely psychosocial. With euthymia, patients are frequently resistant to return periodically to hospitals to undergo anesthesia and seizure induction. An alternative is to evaluate the efficacy of different pharmacological treatment interventions to prevent relapse. This may involve use of standard classes of antidepressants for which medication-resistance was not established during the acute phase. Further, new classes of agents require attention. Particularly in light of developments in the study of the mechanisms of action of ECT, it would seem reasonable to attempt to sustain pharmacologically the same type of neurobiological effects as those produced by ECT in the first place. Ultimately such research offers the promise of replacing ECT with psychopharmacological interventions. This is a formidable task. With the clear exception in the area of cognitive side effects, the safety profile of ECT regarding medical morbidity and mortality and its remarkable short-term therapeutic efficacy present a standard approached by few other interventions in medicine.

REFERENCES

Abrams, R. (1986a). A hypothesis to explain divergent findings among studies comparing unilateral and bilateral ECT in depression. *Convulsive Therapy, 2*, 253–258.

Abrams, R. (1986b). Is unilateral electroconvulsive therapy really the treatment of choice in endogenous depression? *Annals of the New York Academy of Sciences, 462*, 50–55.

Abrams, R., Taylor, M., Faber, R., Tso, T., Williams, R., & Almy, G. (1983). Bilateral vs unilateral electroconvulsive therapy: Efficacy in melancholia. *American Journal of Psychiatry, 140*, 463–465.

Avery, D., & Lubrano, A. (1979). Depression treated with imipramine and ECT: The DeCarolis study reconsidered. *American Journal of Psychiatry, 136*, 559–562.

Barton, J. (1977). ECT in depression: The evidence of controlled studies. *Biological Psychiatry, 12*, 687–695.

Brandon, S., Cowley, P., McDonald, C., Neville, P., Palmer, R., & Wellstood-Eason, S. (1984). Electroconvulsive therapy: Results in depressive illness from the Leicestershire trial. *British Medical Journal, 228*, 22–25.

Brill, N. Q., Crumpton, E., Eiduson, S., Grayson, H. M., & Hellman, L. I. (1959). Predictive and concomitant variables related to improvement with actual and simulated ECT. *Archives of General Psychiatry, 1*, 263–272.

Bruce, E. M., Crone, N., Fitzpatrick, G., Frewin, S. J., Gillis, A., Lascelles, C. F., Levene, L. J., & Mersky, H. A. (1960). A comparative trial of ECT and Tofranil. *American Journal of Psychiatry, 117*, 76.

Carney, M. W. P., Roth, J., & Garside, R. F. (1965). The diagnosis of depressive syndromes and the prediction of E.C.T. response. *British Journal of Psychiatry, 111*, 659–674.

Carney, M. W. P., & Sheffield, B. F. (1974). The effects of pulse ECT in neurotic and endogenous depression. *British Journal of Psychiatry, 125*, 91–94.

Cronholm, B., & Ottosson, J.-O. (1961). Memory functions in endogenous depression before and after electroconvulsive therapy. *Archives of General Psychiatry, 5*, 193–199.

Cronholm, B., & Ottosson, J.-O. (1963). Ultrabrief stimulus technique in electroconvulsive therapy. II. Comparative studies of therapeutic effects and memory disturbances in treatment of endogenous depression with the Elther ES electroshock apparatus and Siemens Konvulsator III. *Journal of Nervous and Mental Disease, 137*, 268–276.

Crow, T. J., & Johnstone, E. C. (1986). Controlled trials of electroconvulsive therapy. *Annals of the New York Academy of Sciences, 462*, 12–29.

Daniel, W. F., & Crovitz, H. F. (1982). Recovery of orientation after electroconvulsive therapy. *Acta Psychiatrica Scandinavica, 66*, 421–428.

Daniel, W. F., & Crovitz, H. F. (1986). Disorientation during electroconvulsive therapy: Technical, theoretical, and neuropsychological issues. *Annals of the New York Academy of Sciences, 462*, 293–306.

Decina, P., Guthrie, E. B., Sackeim, H. A., Kahn, D., & Malitz, S. (1987). Continuation ECT in the management of relapses of major affective episodes. *Acta Psychiatrica Scandinavica, 75*, 559–562.

d'Elia, G. (1970). Unilateral electroconvulsive therapy. *Acta Psychiatrica Scandinavica (Supplement), 215*, 5–98.

d'Elia, G., Ottosson, J.-O., Strömgren, L. (1983). Present practice of electroconvulsive therapy in Scandinavia. *Archives of General Psychiatry, 40*, 577–581.

d'Elia, G., & Raotma, H. (1975). Is unilateral ECT less effective than bilateral ECT? *British Journal of Psychiatry, 126*, 83–89.

Devanand, D. P., & Sackeim, H. A. (1988). Seizure elicitation blocked by pretreatment with lidocaine. *Convulsive Therapy, 4*, 225–229.

Fahy, P., Imiah, N., & Harrington, J. A. (1963). A controlled comparison of electroconvulsive therapy, imipramine and thiopentone sleep in depression. *Journal of Neuropsychiatry, 4*, 310–314.

Fink, M. (1979). *Convulsive therapy: Theory and Practice*, New York: Raven Press.

Fink, M. (1980). Convulsive therapy and endogenous depression. *Pharmakopsychiatria, 13*, 49–54.

Fink, M., Kahn, R. L., & Green, M. A. (1958). Experimental studies of the electroshock process. *Diseases of the Nervous System, 19*, 113–118.

Flor-Henry, P. (1983). *Cerebral basis of psychopathology*. Boston: John Wright.

Frankel, F. H., Bidder, T. G., Fink, M. Mandel, M. R., Small, I. F., Wayne, G. J., Squire, L. R., Dutton, E. N., & Gurel, L. (1978). *Electroconvulsive therapy: Report of the task force of electroconvulsive therapy of the American Psychiatric Association*. Washington, DC: American Psychiatric Association.

Freeman, C. P., Basson, J. V., & Crighton, A. (1978) Double-blind controlled trial of electroconvulsive therapy (E.C.T.) and simulated E.C.T. in depressive illness. *Lancet, 1*, 738–740.

Gold, P. E., Macri, J., & McGaugh, J. L. (1973). Retrograde amnesia gradients: Effects of direct cortical stimulation. *Science, 179*, 1343–1345.

Greenblatt, M., Grooser, G. H., & Wechsler, H. A. (1964). Differential response of hospitalized depressed patients in somatic therapy. *American Journal of Psychiatry, 120*, 935–943.

Gregory, S., Shawcross, C. R., & Gill, D. (1985). The Nottingham ECT study: A double-blind comparison of bilateral, unilateral, and simulated ECT in depressive illness. *British Journal of Psychiatry, 146*, 520–524.

Halliday, A., Davison, K., Browne, M., & Kreeger, L. (1968). A comparison of the effects on depression and memory of bilateral ECT and unilateral ECT to the dominant and nondominant hemispheres. *British Journal of Psychiatry, 114*, 997–1012.

Hamilton, M. (1982). The effect of treatment on the melancholias (depressions). *British Journal of Psychiatry, 140,* 223–230.

Harris, J. A., & Robin, A. A. (1960). A controlled trial of phenelzine in depressive reactions. *Journal of Mental Science, 106,* 1432–1437.

Heshe, J., Roeder, F., & Theilgaard, A. (1978). Unilateral and bilateral ECT: A psychiatric and psychological study of therapeutic effect and side effects. *Acta Psychiatrica Scandinavica, (Supplement), 275,* 1–180.

Imiah, N. W., Ryan, E., & Harrington, J. A. (1965). The influence of antidepressant drugs on the response to electroconvulsive therapy and on subsequent relapse rates. *Neuropsychopharmacology, 4,* 438–442.

Janicak, P. G., Davis, J. M., Gibbons, R. D., Ericksen, S., Chang, S., & Gallagher, P. (1985). Efficacy of ECT: A meta-analysis. *American Journal of Psychiatry, 142,* 297–302.

Johnstone, E. C., Deakin, J. F. W., Lawler, P., Frith, C. D., Stevens, M., McPherson, K., & Crow, T. J. (1980). The Northwick Park electroconvulsive therapy trial. *Lancet, ii,* 1317–320.

Kalinowsky, L. B., & Hippius, H. (1972). *Pharmacological, convulsive and other treatments in psychiatry.* New York: Grune & Stratton.

Kay, D. W., Fahy, T., & Garside, R. F. (1970). A 7-month double-blind trial of amitriptyline and diazepam in ECT-treated depressed patients. *British Journal of Psychiatry, 117,* 667–671.

Kendall, B. S., Mills, W. B., & Thale, T. (1956). Comparison of two methods of electroshock in their effect on cognitive functions. *Journal of Consulting Psychology, 20,* 423–429.

Kendell, R. E. (1981). The present status of electroconvulsive therapy. *British Journal of Psychiatry, 139,* 265–283.

Kiloh, L. G., Child, J. P., & Latner, G. (1960). A controlled trial of iproniazid in the treatment of endogenous depression. *Journal of Mental Science, 106,* 1139–1144.

Klein, D., Gittelman, R., Quitkin, G., & Rifkin, A. (1980). *Diagnosis and drug treatment of psychiatric disorders: Adults and children.* Baltimore: Williams & Wilkins.

Kriss, A., Halliday, A. M., & Pratt, R. (1980). Neurological asymmetries immediately after unilateral ECT. *Journal of Neurology, Neurosurgery, and Psychiatry, 41,* 1135–1144.

Lambourn, J., & Gill, D. (1978). A controlled comparison of simulated and real ECT. *British Journal of Psychiatry, 133,* 514–519.

Lancaster, N., Steinert, R., & Frost, I. (1958). Unilateral electroconvulsive therapy. *Journal of Mental Science, 104,* 221–227.

Lloyd, K. G., Morselli, P. L., & Bartholini, G. (1987). GABA and affective disorders. *Medical Biology, 65,* 159–165.

Maletzky, B. M. (1978). Seizure duration and clinical effect in electroconvulsive therapy. *Comprehensive Psychiatry, 19,* 541–580.

Malitz, S., Sackeim, H. A., & Decina, P. (1982). ECT in the treatment of major affective disorders: Clinical and basic research issues. *Psychiatric Journal of the University of Ottawa, 7,* 126–134.

Malitz, S., Sackeim, H. A., Decina, P., Kanzler, M., & Kerr, B. (1986). The efficacy of ECT: Dose-response interactions with modality. *Annals of the New York Academy of Sciences, 462,* 58–64.

Malloy, F. W., Small, I. F., Miller, M. J., & Milstein, V. (1982). Changes in neuropsychological test performance after electroconvulsive therapy. *Biological Psychiatry, 17,* 61–67.

MECTA Corporation (1987). *Instruction manual: SR and JR models.* Portland, OR: MECTA Corporation.

Meduna, L. J. (1935). Versuche uber die biologische Beeinflussung des Abaufes der Schizophrenia: Camphor und Cardiozolkrampfe. *Zeitschrift Gesamte Neurologie Psychiatrie, 152,* 235–262.

Mendels, J. (1967). The prediction of response to electroconvulsive therapy. *American Journal of Psychiatry, 124,* 153–159.

Miller, E. (1967). Psychological theories of ECT: A review. *British Journal of Psychiatry, 113,* 301–311.

Mindham, R. H. S., Howland, C., & Shepherd, M. (1973). An evaluation of continuation therapy with tricyclic antidepressants in depressive illness. *Psychological Medicine, 3,* 5–17.

Mukherjee, S., Sackeim, H. A., & Lee, C. (1988). Unilateral ECT in the treatment of manic episodes. *Convulsive Therapy, 4,* 74–80.

Ottosson, J.-O. (1960). Experimental studies of the mode of action of electroconvulsive therapy. *Acta Psychiatrica Scandinavica, (Supplement), 145,* 1–141.

Ottosson, J.-O. (1985). Use and misuse of electroconvulsive treatment. *Biological Psychiatry, 20,* 933–946.

Overall, J. E. & Rhoades, H. M. (1986). A comment on the efficacy of unilateral versus bilateral ECT. *Convulsive Therapy, 2,* 245–251.

Pettinati, H. M., Mathisen, K. S., Rosenberg, J., & Lynch, J. F. (1986). Meta-analytical approach to reconciling discrepancies in efficacy between bilateral and unilateral electroconvulsive therapy. *Convulsive Therapy, 2,* 7–17.

Pippard, J., & Ellam, L. (1981). *Electroconvulsive treatment in Great Britain.* London: Gaskell.

Prien, R. F., Klett, C. J., & Caffey, E. M. J. (1973). Lithium carbonate and imipramine in prevention of affective episodes: A comparison in recurrent affective illness. *Archives of General Psychiatry, 29,* 420–425.

Prien, R., Kupfer, D., Mansky, P., Small, J., Tuason, V., Voss, C., & Johnson, W. (1984). Drug therapy in the prevention of recurrences in unipolar and bipolar affective disorders. *Archives of General Psychiatry, 41,* 1096–1104.

Prudic, J., Sackeim, H. A., Decina, P., Hopkins, N., Ross, F. R., & Malitz, S. (1987). Acute effects of ECT on cardiovascular functioning: Relations to patient and treatment variables. *Acta Psychiatrica Scandinavica, 75,* 344–351.

Quitkin, F. M., Rabkin, J. G., Ross, D., & McGrath, P. J. (1984). Duration of antidepressant drug treatment: What is an adequate trial? *Archives of General Psychiatry, 41,* 238–245.

Rifkin, A. (1988). ECT versus tricyclic antidepressants in depression: A review of the evidence. *Journal of Clinical Psychiatry, 49,* 3–7.

Robin, A. (in press). Current policy and rising trends. In B. Lerer (Ed.), *New Directions in Research in Affective Disorders.* New York: Elsevier.

Robin, A., & Harris, J. A. (1962). A controlled trial of imipramine and electroplexy. *Journal of Mental Science, 106*, 217–219.

Robin, A., & de Tissera, S. (1982). A double-blind controlled comparison of the therapeutic effects of low and high energy electroconvulsive therapies. *British Journal of Psychiatry, 141*, 357–366.

Rose, R. (1985). Consensus conference: Electroconvulsive therapy. *JAMA, 254*, 2103–2108.

Rush, S., & Driscoll, D. (1968). Current distribution in the brain from surface electrodes. *Anesthesia and Analgesia, 47*, 717–723.

Sackeim, H. A. (1985). The case for ECT. *Psychology Today, 19*, 36–40.

Sackeim, H. A. (1986). The efficacy of ECT. *Annals of the New York Academy of Sciences, 462*, 70–75.

Sackeim, H. A. (1988). Mechanisms of action of electroconvulsive therapy. In R. E. Hales & J. Frances (Eds.), *Annual Review of Psychiatry, Vol. 7*, (pp. 436–457). Washington, DC: American Psychiatric Press.

Sackeim, H. A. (in press). Stimulus intensity and ECT outcome. In B. Lerer (Ed.), *New directions in research in affective disorders*. New York: Elsevier.

Sackeim, H. A., Decina, P. Kanzler, M., Kerr, B., & Malitz, S. (1987). Effects of electrode placement on the efficacy of titrated, low-dose ECT. *American Journal of Psychiatry, 144*, 1449–1455.

Sackeim, H. A., Decina, P., Portnoy, S., Neeley, P., & Malitz, S. (1987). Studies of dosage, seizure threshold, and seizure duration in ECT. *Biological Psychiatry, 22*, 249–268.

Sackeim, H. A., Decina, P., Prohovnik, I., & Malitz, S. (1987). Seizure threshold in ECT: Effects of sex, age, electrode placement and number of treatments. *Archives of General Psychiatry, 44*, 355–360.

Sackeim, H. A., Decina, P., Prohovnik, I., Malitz, S., & Resor, S. (1983). Anticonvulsant and antidepressant properties of ECT: A proposed mechanism of action. *Biological Psychiatry, 18*, 1301–1310.

Sackeim, H. A., Greenberg, M. S., Weiman, A. L., Gur, R. C., Hungerbuhler, J. P., & Geschwind, N. (1982). Hemispheric asymmetry in the expression of positive and negative emotions: Neurologic evidence. *Archives of Neurology, 39*, 210–218.

Sackeim, H. A., & Mukherjee, S. (1986). Neurophysiological variability in the effects of the ECT stimulus. *Convulsive Therapy, 2*, 267–276.

Sackeim, H. A., Portnoy, S., Neeley, P., Steif, B., Decina, P., & Malitz, S. (1986). Cognitive consequences of low dosage ECT. *Annals of the New York Academy of Science, 462*, 398–410.

Sackeim, H. A., Prudic, J., Devanand, D. P., Decina, P., Kerr, B., & Malitz, S. (1990). The impact of medication resistance and continuation pharmacotherapy on relapse following responses to electroconvulsive therapy in major depression. *Journal of Clinical Psychopharmacology, 10*, 96–104.

Sackeim, H. A., & Steif, B. L. (1988). The neuropsychology of depression and mania. In A. Georgotas & R. Cancro (Eds.), *Depression and Mania* (pp. 265–289). New York: Elsevier.

Sainz, A. (1959). Clarification of the action of successful treatment in the depressions. *Diseases of the Nervous System (Supplement), 20*, 53–57.

Sakel, M. (1938). *Pharmacological treatment of schizophrenia*. New York: Nervous and Mental Disease Publishing.

Scovern, A. W., & Kilmann, P. R. (1980). Status of electroconvulsive therapy: Review of the outcome literature. *Psychological Bulletin, 87*, 260–303.

Seager, C. R., & Bird, R. L. (1962). Imipramine with electrical treatment in depression—a controlled trial. *Journal of Mental Science, 108*, 704–707.

Shepherd, M. (1965). Clinical trial of the treatment of depressive illness. *British Medical Journal, 1*, 881–886.

Small, I. F. (1974). Inhalant convulsive therapy. In M. Fink, S. Kety, J. McGaugh, & T. A. Williams (Eds.), *Psychobiology of convulsive therapy* (pp. 65–77). Washington DC: Winston & Sons.

Small, J. G., Milstein, V., Klapper, M. H., Kellams, J. J., Miller, M. J., & Small, I. F. (1986). Electroconvulsive therapy in the treatment of manic episodes. *Annals of the New York Academy of Sciences, 462*, 37–49.

Snaith, R. P. (1981). How much ECT does the depressed patient need? In R. L. Palmer (Ed.), *Electroconvulsive therapy: An appraisal* (pp. 61–64). New York: Oxford University Press.

Spiker, D. G., Weiss, J. C., Dealy, R. S., Griffin, S. J., Hanin, I., Neil, J. F., Perer, J. M., Rossi, A. J., & Soloff, P. H. (1985). The pharmacological treatment of delusional depression. *American Journal of Psychiatry, 142*, 430–436.

Squire, L. R. (1986). Memory functions as affected by electroconvulsive therapy. *Annals of the New York Academy of Sciences, 462*, 307–314.

Squire, L. R., & Slater, P. (1978). Bilateral and unilateral ECT: Effects on verbal and nonverbal memory. *American Journal of Psychology, 135*, 1316–1320.

Staton, R. D., Hass, P. J., & Brumback, R. A. (1981). Electroencephalographic recording during bitemporal and unilateral non-dominant hemisphere (Lancaster Position) electroconvulsive therapy. *Journal of Clinical Psychiatry, 42*, 264–269.

Steif, B. L., Sackeim, H. A., Portnoy, S., Decina, P., & Malitz, S. (1986). Effects of depression and ECT on anterograde memory. *Biological Psychiatry, 21*, 921–930.

Stevenson, G. H., & Geoghegan, J. J. (1951). Prophylactic electroshock: A five-year study. *American Journal of Psychiatry, 107*, 743–748.

Strömgren, L. (1984). Is bilateral ECT ever indicated? *Acta Psychiatrica Scandinavica, 69*, 484–490.

Ulett, G., Smith, K., & Gleser, G. (1956). Evaluation of convulsive and subconvulsive shock therapies utilizing a control group. *American Journal of Psychiatry, 112*, 795–802.

Valentine, M., Keddie, K., & Dunne, D. (1968). A comparison of techniques in electroconvulsive therapy. *British Journal of Psychiatry, 114*, 989–996.

Warren, E.W., & Groome, D. H. (1984). Memory test performance under three different waveforms of ECT for depression. *British Journal of Psychiatry, 144*, 370–375.

Weaver, L. A. J., Ives, J. O., Williams, R., & Nies, A. (1977). A comparison of standard alternating current and low-energy brief pulse electrotherapy. *Biological Psychiatry, 12*, 525–544.

Weaver, L. A. J., & Williams, R. W. (1986). Stimulus parameters and electroconvulsive therapy. *Annals of the New York Academy of Sciences, 462*, 174–185.

Weaver, L., Williams, R., & Rush, S. (1976). Current density in bilateral and unilateral ECT. *Biological Psychiatry, 11*, 303–312.

Weiner, R. D. (1980). ECT and seizure threshold: Effects of stimulus waveform and electrode placement. *Biological Psychiatry, 15*, 225–241.

Weiner, R. D., Rogers, H. J., Davidson, J. R. T., & Squire, L. R. (1986). Effects of stimulus parameters of cognitive side effects. *Annals of the New York Academy of Sciences, 462*, 315–325.

Welch, C. A., Weiner, R.D., Weir, D., Cahill, J. F., Rogers, H. J., Davidson, J., Miller, R. D., & Mandel, M. R. (1982). Efficacy of ECT in the treatment of depression: Waveform and electrode placement considerations. *Psychopharmacological Bulletin, 18*, 31–34.

West, E. D. (1981). Electric convulsive therapy in depression: A double-blind controlled trial. *British Medical Journal, 282*, 355–357.

Wilson, I. C., Vernon, J. T., Guin, T., & Sandifer, M. G. (1963). A controlled study of treatments of depression. *Journal of Neuropsychiatry, 4*, 331–337.

PETER R. BREGGIN

*"Shock treatment is not good for your brain"**

Well, what is the sense of ruining my head and erasing my memory, which is my capital, and putting me out of business. It was a brilliant cure but we lost the patient. It's a bum turn, Hotch, terrible.

—ERNEST HEMINGWAY, AFTER ECT AND SHORTLY BEFORE HE SHOT HIMSELF, QUOTED BY A. E. HOTCHNER IN *PAPA HEMINGWAY* (1967)

As a neurologist and electroencephalographer, I have seen many patients after ECT, and I have no doubt that ECT produces effects identical to those of a head injury. After multiple sessions of ECT, a patient has symptoms identical to those of a retired, punch-drunk boxer. . . . After a few sessions of ECT the symptoms are those of moderate cerebral contusion, and further enthusiastic use of ECT may result in the patient functioning at a subhuman level. Electroconvulsive therapy in effect may be defined as a controlled type of brain damage produced by electrical means.

—SIDNEY SAMANT, M.D., *CLINICAL PSYCHIATRY NEWS*, MARCH 1983

Electroshock in psychiatry involves the passage of an electrical current through the head and brain to produce unconsciousness and a convulsion.† When I mention to people that shock treatment is making a strong comeback, they often reply, "I thought that went out with *Cuckoo's Nest*,"‡ or "They did it to my grandmother and she was never the same. I can't believe they are still doing it." Many people mistakenly believe that shock has been outlawed.

In reality, 100,000 or more Americans are being shocked each year, and the number is rising rapidly. In California, where elderly women are the most frequent targets of shock, three San Francisco hospitals§ recently announced that they were starting to give the treatment—leading to a public outcry against it. A front-page headline in the November 28, 1990, *San Francisco Examiner* announced the controversy: CITY LOBBIED TO BAN SHOCK TREATMENT: EX-PATIENTS CALL PSYCHIATRIC TECHNIQUES "FRIGHTENING."

TWO SURVIVORS

Cynthia—an extremely intelligent young graphic designer who had taught courses in her field before completing her schooling—had been rendered permanently unable to teach or to work following a routine course of shock treatment (ECT). The ECT method used was state of the art, but her once-high IQ was now severely reduced and impaired.

Cynthia talked to me about what it was like to unexpectedly find herself with great gaps in her intelligence. Her entire identity

*This title is borrowed from neurologist John Friedberg's book *Shock Treatment Is Not Good for Your Brain* (San Francisco: Glide Publications, 1976).

†Electroshock treatment (EST), electroconvulsive therapy (ECT), electrotherapy, and convulsive therapy nowadays all refer to the application of electricity to the head to produce grand mal convulsions. In the past convulsions were produced by other methods as well, such as insulin overdose, stimulant drugs, and gases.

‡The reference is usually to the movie based on Ken Kesey's novel *One Flew Over the Cuckoo's Nest* (New York: Viking Press, 1962) in which the hero, McMurphy, is forced to undergo electroshock.

§The three are St. Mary's Hospital, Pacific Presbyterian Medical Center, and the Langley Porter Psychiatric Hospital at the University of California, San Francisco.

was changed. Her previous intellectual sources of pride, pleasure, and entertainment were gone. Her precocious professional achievements were now forever beyond her grasp. Even her former friendships, based largely on shared intellectual interests, were gone. Nor could she recall and savor many of her previous accomplishments or her educational experiences. Worse still, Cynthia had lost more than portions of her memory and IQ. The brain damage put gaping holes in her intellectual functions that no one with a normal brain would ever have to endure, even if he or she were of below average intelligence.

Although there can be significant brain damage from shock treatment without it being detectable with modern brain-imaging techniques, Cynthia's CT scan did show shrinkage of the cortex of her frontal and temporal lobes. Neuropsychological testing also showed generalized brain dysfunction. The psychologist was courageous enough to attribute the damage to the ECT.

Cynthia was painfully aware of the harm done to her, but more often than not, brain-damaged patients tend to deny the degree of their memory loss and mental dysfunction. This is true whether the damage has resulted from medical treatment, disease, or accidental trauma. Denial of impairment after brain injury is called anosognosia and is a very common finding.[1]

Manfred's attitude toward his ECT-induced mental dysfunction illustrates this principle. Manfred had become despairing a few years earlier following his wife's death, and a psychiatrist had given him shock treatment. Now Manfred had brain damage to add to his psychospiritual loss.

Manfred tried to ignore or to make light of his mental dysfunction. His family and friends, however, reported that ever since shock treatment, he had severe memory blanks for events during the year or two prior to the shock, almost complete memory loss for several months around the shock, and difficulty grasping or recalling new information and ideas.

I evaluated Manfred, and my clinical impression was generalized brain dysfunction with memory impairment, relatively shallow emotional responses, poor judgment, difficulty with intellectual functions, and problems focusing his attention. He had dementia—global mental deterioration—caused by shock treatment.

Manfred wasn't exaggerating his brain damage. During our lengthy interview and preliminary psychological testing, Manfred's mental dysfunction gradually became apparent. His daughter, who was with us most of the time, became increasingly upset over the confirmation of her worst fears; but Manfred made silly jokes about his difficulties and went off on tangents, talking about relatively trivial matters.

I recommended more thorough neuropsychological testing, which confirmed the diagnosis of brain damage. I also talked privately with several of Manfred's friends, and they described how he had become a "changed person," with shallow feelings, inappropriate conduct, and obvious intellectual and memory problems. In particular, they said he no longer had the same mental acuity, ability to plan ahead, judgment, and insight in social situations. Thus he had symptoms of a frontal lobe syndrome. . . . Since he had previously earned an advanced degree and had been known for his remarkable memory, intelligence, and wit, the change was striking.

One close friend, a health professional, said he hadn't told Manfred about the obvious damage after ECT for fear of upsetting him. After all, there was no hope of significant improvement now that it was three years after the shock.

Only one person who regularly saw Manfred reported no damage to his brain or mind: his psychiatrist, the one who had ordered the shock treatment. He didn't even notice or record any memory loss.* . . .

CELEBRATING SHOCK

Although it dates back to 1938 in Italy[2] and came to the United States soon after, electroshock treatment remains a revered symbol of authority in modern psychiatry. By promoting shock the new psychiatry reveals its ties to the old psychiatry and unabashedly defends this egregious assault on the patient. Thus when shock reached its fiftieth birthday in 1988, it literally was "celebrated" in an orchestrated fashion at meetings throughout the world, including the annual conventions of the American Psychiatric Association, the Society of Biological Psychiatry, the Royal College of Psychiatrists, and the International Psychiatric Congress. As if honoring a dead hero, shock's fiftieth birthday also was "celebrated" in an issue of the journal *Convulsive Therapy*, and "observances" were held at various hospitals that especially favor shock, such as the Friends Hospital in Philadelphia, the Oregon Health Sciences University, and Taylor Manor in Maryland. The festivities are lovingly described by Max Fink in "Fifty Years of ECT" in the May 1988 *Psychiatric Times*. . . .

WHO GETS SHOCKED

While preparing for the hearing in San Francisco I reviewed the data on the twenty-five hundred shock patients reported to the state each year in California. Since the data collection began over a decade ago, more than two-thirds have been women. Still more ominous, in recent times there has been an escalating percentage of elderly ECT patients. In 1977 only 28.7 percent of all patients were age sixty-five or older, but by 1983 it had leaped to 43.1 percent, and finally to 53.1 percent in 1988.[3] This means that *elderly women are among the most frequent victims of shock treatment in California*. The sexist and ageist implications of this national trend cannot be overlooked. . . .

The official report produced by the American Psychiatric Association, *The Practice of Electroconvulsive Therapy* (1990), strongly supports ECT for the elderly, citing a successful case involving a 102-year-old patient. Nonetheless, it acknowledges that the aged suffer "an increased likelihood of appreciable memory deficits and confusion during the course of treatment." The report also notes that it is harder to cause a convulsion in the elderly, *and therefore more electrical current must be used*. . . .

---

*I have found this time and again—everyone recognizes that the patient has been damaged, except the psychiatrist. Similarly, in a random selection of people, many are familiar with someone who has been "forever changed" by shock, except for psychiatrists, many of whom say they have never seen a bad outcome.

HOW MANY PATIENTS?

In my 1979 medical book *Electroshock: Its Brain-Disabling Effects*, I described the upswing of ECT and estimated that shock was being given to about 100,000 persons a year in the United States. This corresponded roughly with the APA estimate of over 88,000 per year in its 1978 *Task Force Report on Electroconvulsive Therapy* (see table 3 on p. 47), and now my estimate has been generally accepted. Even without an increase in the rate of shock treatment, a million or more people will be subjected to it in the coming decade.

The numbers of people shocked will escalate if the current promotional campaign continues to meet with so little scrutiny or opposition. Most unfortunately, these promotional efforts are being abetted by NAMI [National Alliance for the Mentally Ill], the parent group that so avidly supports biopsychiatry. The summer 1990 issue of *The Journal* of the California Alliance for the Mentally Ill (CAMI), the largest state branch of NAMI, devotes several articles to supporting shock. The featured testimonial is not from a patient but from an "Anonymous Father." Indeed, ECT testimonials are almost always from someone other than the patient.

THE IMPACT OF SHOCK TREATMENT

Electroshock or electroconvulsive therapy involves the passage of an electrical current through the brain of the patient to produce a grand mal or major epileptic seizure. Sometimes the two electrodes are placed over both temples (bilateral shock) and sometimes over one side of the head (unilateral).

The shock induces an electrical storm that obliterates the normal electrical patterns of the brain, driving the recording needle on the EEG up and down in violent, jagged swings. This period of extreme bursts of electrical energy often is followed by a briefer period of absolutely no electrical activity, called the isoelectric phase. The brain waves become temporarily flat, exactly as in brain death, and it may be that cell death takes place during this time.

A shock-induced seizure is typically far more severe than those suffered during spontaneous epilepsy. In earlier times, when the shock patient's body was not paralyzed by pharmacological agents, it would undergo muscle spasms sufficiently violent at times to crack vertebrae and break limb bones.

THE ACUTE ORGANIC BRAIN SYNDROME OR DELIRIUM

Typically the treatment is given three times a week for a total of at least six to ten sessions. After several sessions of shock, the patient awakens in a few (or sometimes many) minutes in a state of apathy and docility. There will be some memory loss and some confusion and often a headache, stiff neck, and nausea. As the course of shocks progresses, the patient's apathy, memory loss, and confusion increase. Judgment and general mental function become impaired. Sometimes the patient becomes temporarily giddy or artificially high. This generalized mental and emotional dysfunction is called an acute organic brain syndrome or delirium—the brain's typical response to severe stress or damage. Less frequently, extreme states of delirium develop in which the patient appears grossly psychotic, with hallucinations and delusions.

Even exponents of shock treatment usually admit in their professional publications that many or all shock patients develop an acute organic brain syndrome. In his 1988 book *Electroconvulsive Therapy*, shock advocate [Richard] Abrams says of all forms of shock treatment: "A patient recovering consciousness from ECT understandably exhibits multiform abnormalities of *all* aspects of thinking, feeling, and behaving, including disturbed memory, impaired comprehension, automatic movements, a dazed facial expression, and motor restlessness" (pp. 130–31).

In *Multiple-Monitored Electroconvulsive Therapy* (1981), Barry Maletzky points out that it "usually" takes two to four weeks for the EEG to return to normal after ECT; "However, some abnormalities may persist several months or longer and are considered to be poor prognostic signs" (p. 136). Some studies show that many patients never recover normal EEGs following shock treatment.[4]

THERE'S NO QUESTION ABOUT BRAIN DYSFUNCTION

Because shock treatment routinely causes an acute organic brain syndrome or delirium, the question is not whether shock can cause brain dysfunction. *Shock treatment always causes severe brain dysfunction*. The only legitimate question is, "How often is recovery complete?"

From what we know of head injury, we expect a high percentage of chronic impairments following other types of trauma much less severe than that incurred during ECT. In *Neurology: Problems in Primary Care* (1987), James Bernat and Frederick Vincent point out that "many patients following minor head trauma complain of difficulty with concentration, memory loss, dizziness, and headache" (p. 573). While some may be reacting psychologically, "as many as 50% of such patients studied with neuropsychiatric testing have demonstrated organic cognitive deficits."*

It is recognized in neurology that even mild head injury frequently results in lasting, debilitating problems, such as memory difficulties, deficiencies in fo-

*These patients have "minor head injury," typically without loss of consciousness, seizures, disorientation, or confusion. This is a much less traumatic state than that of post-ECT patients.

cusing and maintaining concentration, and loss of problem-solving skills. Frequently the person feels "changed" in a fundamental and catastrophic fashion. Often there is a frontal-lobe syndrome with loss of interest or emotional intensity, difficulties with abstract reasoning and planning, and so on. These responses to head injury are described vividly by Paul Chance in "Life After Head Injury," in the October 1986 *Psychology Today*.[5]

In their books, articles, and public statements, shock supporters, including the American Psychiatric Association, often ignore the vast literature on the damaging effects of even minor head injury. An exception (see ahead) is advocate Max Fink, who believes that shock treatment works by causing the typical aftermath of closed-head injury.

Evidence for Permanent Brain Damage

Brain damage from shock is amply demonstrated by animal research. Research conducted on dogs, cats, and monkeys in the 1940s and 1950s was so convincing that the search for further evidence came to a halt. Nonetheless, leading shock advocates, like Lothar Kalinowsky, claimed in their reviews that the animal research showed no damage. To the dismay of those of us who independently read the original investigations, most animal studies turned out to provide unequivocal proof of brain damage.[6] For example, in 1952 Hans Hartelius published a book-length report, "Cerebral Changes Following Electrically Induced Convulsions," as a supplement to *Acta Psychiatrica Neurologica Scandinavica* (vol. 77). He found scattered cell death and small hemorrhages in the brains of cats following relatively small doses of shock. Almost without exception, merely by examining their brains microscopically, he was able to predict which animals had been shocked.

Having first claimed that the early animal studies were negative, shock doctors instead now claim that these studies are too old or too flawed to count. If the studies showing brain damage were indeed outdated, it would be up to the shock doctors to stop using such a patently dangerous treatment while awaiting new studies with large animals, like dogs or monkeys. However, the older studies are not outdated, since they used less current than that applied to humans in modern ECT.

There is no reason to believe that modern shock is safer. The electrical stimulation must, in fact, be stronger nowadays, since the patients are sedated, and sedation makes it more difficult to convulse the patients. Cell death and widespread small, and sometimes large, hemorrhages are confirmed by human autopsy studies. Other evidence for persistent brain damage is found on EEG studies, neuropsychological testing, some brain-scan studies, and many clinical reports.[7]

The damage is caused by several factors that have been studied by direct examination of animal brains subjected to very small electrical stimulation: first, mechanical and heat trauma from the electric current; second, spasm and breakdown of blood vessel walls as the electricity travels down the vascular tree; and third, to a much lesser extent, the convulsions.[8]

Nowadays shock doctors are very sensitive to public and professional opinion, and therefore they maintain that the treatment is relatively harmless and that its method of action is unknown. But in the first couple of decades of use, many shock authorities boldly declared that the treatment works precisely by damaging the brain and that brain-cell death is the key to successful treatment.[9]

In April 1946 psychiatrist P. H. Wilcox complained in *Diseases of the Nervous System* that "there is a prevailing assumption that therapy of certain types of mental diseases must or can be accomplished only by destroying brain cells . . ." and that "this belief has become sufficiently current so that it is not unusual to hear prominent psychiatrists and neurologists express the opinion that improvement from any of the shock therapies in certain mental conditions must necessarily depend upon brain tissue destruction."

THE DAMAGE IS THE "CURE"

To the extent that it works at all, shock has its impact by disabling the brain.[10] It does so by causing an organic brain syndrome, with memory loss, confusion, and disorientation, and by producing lobotomy effects. For a few days or weeks the patient may be euphoric or high as a result of the brain damage, and this may be experienced as "feeling better." In the long run the patient becomes more apathetic and "makes fewer complaints."

Max Fink acknowledges that denial and euphoria are directly correlated to the degree of brain damage* as it is demonstrated by *abnormal* brain wave patterns and other signs of dysfunction; brain dysfunction is not, in Fink's own words, a "complication" or "side effect" but the "*sine qua non* of the mode of action." Clearly describing a patient with an organic brain syndrome following shock treatment, Fink declares that when a patient becomes "jovial and euphoric, denies his problems and sees his previous thoughts of suicide as 'silly,' a rating of 'much improved' is made." Fink declares that the basis of improvement is "similar to that of craniocerebral trauma" or head injury.[11] Finally, in the January/February 1978 issue of *Comprehensive Psychiatry*, Fink makes a statement that could have been attributed to those of us who oppose shock: "The principal complications of EST are death, brain damage, memory impairment, and spontaneous seizures. These complications are similar to those seen after head trauma, with which EST has been compared."[12]

---

*In some later papers and books the phrase *brain damage* is discarded and the euphemism *altered state of brain function* is used instead; but the import of what is said remains the same.

Fink's viewpoint is consistent with my own—that shock produces brain damage and dysfunction with denial and anosognosia.[13] This enables both the doctor and the patient to make believe that the patient has neither brain dysfunction nor personal problems.

That shock works by damaging the brain and by making patients more simpleminded, less self-aware, and docile is such an obnoxious idea to most people that the theory is never presented to the public or repeated in court, even by its main proponent, Max Fink. In public Fink states that shock's mode of action is unknown and that it may correct biochemical imbalances. When interviewed for a magazine article on shock treatment in 1989 Fink declared, "I can't prove there's no brain damage. I can't prove there are no other sentient beings in the universe, either. But scientists have been trying for thirty years to find both, and so far they haven't come up with a thing."[14]

ECT AND WOMEN

Survivors of ECT, their friends, and their families consistently report serious memory difficulties following ECT. And, as we shall see, some doctors actually use ECT purposely to erase memories.

In a startling report in a 1988 issue of *Research in the Sociology of Health Care* (7:283–300), Carol Warren studied ten women, including their family relationships, following shock treatment. Many of the patients thought that the erasure of memory was the actual intent or purpose of shock treatment. As one woman put it, "I can't remember a lot of things—but I'd rather not." Another woman, who felt rejected by her father, said, "I want to forget." Other patients resented losing their memory for what had happened in their lives to cause their problems. One woman felt the shock was given to her specifically to make her forget her resentment toward her husband for having committed her.

While the women were divided on the benefit of forgetting their problems, they "uniformly disliked the loss of everyday memory, as well as associated effects such as losing one's train of thought, incoherent speech or slowness of affect. What specifically was forgotten varied from matters of everyday routine to the existence of one or more of one's children. . . ."

The loss of everyday memory indicates ongoing memory dysfunction. Combined with "losing one's train of thought," "incoherence of thought," and "slowness of affect," we have convincing signs of dementia—chronic deterioration of the brain and mind. Such patients, when referred for neuropsychological testing, almost invariably will be diagnosed as suffering from dementia or a chronic organic brain syndrome. That the patients do not recognize the significance of their losses is again typical of serious brain damage and dysfunction. That Warren reports these symptoms without discussing their importance adds to their significance. Had she been on the lookout for signs of dementia, even more may have surfaced. The disclosure of several such cases in a small sample strengthens my concerns about ECT's severely damaging effects.

Forgetting the names or even the existence of other people was especially perplexing. One of the women never again felt that her child was her own. Warren comments on the irony that the same patient might be given shock to forget her memories and psychotherapy to recall them. Psychotherapy, of course, can do little to help recover memories lost through physical trauma and damage to the brain.

Some of Warren's most chilling observations concerned the viewpoint of husbands and other family members about the patient's memory loss. A husband said of the shock treatment, "They did a good job there," because his wife's long-term memory loss spanned the period of conflict with him when she was depressed. A patient who had been molested as a child by her mother's brother explained that her mother denied it and wanted her to have "the full treatment" to "make me forget all those things that happened."*

Three of the ten women lived in dread of ECT for years afterward; and therefore they refrained from expressing any angry feelings toward their husbands, for fear of being sent back to the hospital for involuntary shock treatment. One said, "Shock treatment is a helluva way to treat marital problems—the problems involved both of us." This confirms my impression that many shock survivors are too afraid to report their resentment of the treatment to anyone, and especially to the people they have reason to fear, such as their husbands—and their psychiatrists.

MAKING PEGGY INTO BELINDA

Not all shock doctors deny ECT's damaging effects on memory. H. C. Tien from Michigan has utilized it to erase memory and personality. In one case he reprogrammed a woman into a more docile mate, reminiscent of the Stepford wives, from the movie of the same name in which the men in a community murdered women and used their bodies to make "ideal wives." Nor was Tien's work done in obscurity. It was reported in detail in the November 1 and November 15, 1972, issues of *Frontiers in Psychiatry*, a Roche Laboratories (a pharmaceutical company) free handout sent to all psychiatrists in the country.

Tien, a self-styled "family psychiatrist," purposely used the older methods of shock to "maximize memory loss—

---

*ECT probably functions to suppress memories of and protests against physical and sexual abuse in many women. In *Women and Depression: Risk Factors and Treatment Issues* (1990) by the American Psychological Association National Task Force on Women and Depression, it is confirmed that a high percentage of depressed women suffer from past molestations. . . .

and for a very good reason," which was to eradicate the woman's identity or personality in order to reprogram it. Tien believes that the "memory loosening" and the "infantile" state produced by the electroshock make the patient amenable to drastic change. A relative helps reprogram the patient's personality according to a "blueprint" worked out prior to the shock.

Verbatim dialogues with Tien and a married couple dramatize how the wife believes, before her shock treatment, that she wants to leave her husband. She doesn't love him, he is never home, and he beats her in front of the children. Under threat that her husband would try to get custody of the children in a divorce, the wife, Peggy, agrees to undergo the treatment. After each ECT Peggy regresses to a childlike state and is "reprogrammed" by her bottle-feeding husband to believe that her past personality was bad and that her new one is "good." She assumes a new first name, Belinda, to signify the change.

Incidentally, Tien tells us, she became "paranoid" during the first treatment, accusing those around her of harming her; but then she submitted to a second series of shock. Afterward: "Belinda is more balanced, more mature and adaptable in social situations than Peggy was. Now, as Belinda, her marriage is reasonably stable."

Tien calls his method ELT, explaining that E is for electricity, L is for love, and T is for therapy.

Except for my own 1979 book, I am unaware of criticism of Tien and his technique from the psychiatric profession.

WITH A LITTLE HELP FROM THE CIA

Tien isn't the only psychiatrist to use shock to eradicate memories and even identities, usually those of women. In his book *The History of Shock Treatment* (1978) shock survivor Leonard Frank made probably the first public disclosure of the work of D. Ewen Cameron of Canada, who assaulted patients with massive drug doses, bizarre forms of conditioning, and what he called depatterning treatment. Cameron was professor of psychiatry at McGill University and the Allen Memorial Institute in Montreal. As president of the American Psychiatric Association (1953) and as the first president of the World Psychiatric Association, Cameron was one of the most revered and rewarded psychiatrists on the international scene.

Cameron subjected patients to twice-daily doses of six electroshocks, one after another, to maintain the individual in one prolonged stupor. Typically thirty to forty or more shocks were given in this blockbuster manner during his experiments on more than fifty patients in the late 1950s and early 1960s.

The result of this devastating treatment was a severe delirium; patients would lose their sense of identity and sometimes become delusional. Robbed of virtually all memory, the patients became completely focused on present sensations and feelings. With much or even all of their lifetime memory bank obliterated, six months would be taken to reprogram them with new memories of themselves and a more docile personality.

Around the time of Frank's disclosures about Cameron's treatments, Cameron's work suddenly became a major scandal. The outcry wasn't directed at the extreme treatments themselves, which were similar to numerous other regressive shock techniques, variations of which still are practiced in the United States (see below). What made Cameron suddenly newsworthy was the disclosure in newspaper reports and books that he had been secretly financed in part by CIA funds.

Eager to learn how to "brainwash" people and to wipe out their memories, the CIA found a willing ally in Cameron. Although Cameron was doing regressive shock on his own initiative as routine clinical practice, he accepted the CIA funds. His grisly, shameful methods, and their CIA funding, were documented in detail in John Marks's 1979 book *The Search for the "Manchurian Candidate."* In 1988, with Cameron deceased, some of his victims divided $750,000, individually receiving relatively small payments in a settlement from the CIA.[15]

I located one independent follow-up study of Cameron's shock treatments, by A. E. Schwartzman and P. Termansen in the April 1967 *Canadian Psychiatric Association Journal*, and directed Marks's researcher to it. It discloses severe chronic memory problems persisting many years after treatment. In their sample, 63 percent of patients still felt dependent on others for recalling aspects of their past. Sixty percent reported losses of memories spanning six months to ten years prior to the treatment. Except for the typical denial of symptoms that occurs with severe brain damage, undoubtedly many more would have reported serious lasting effects. In addition, 75 percent were found to suffer from "unsatisfactory or impoverished social adjustment."

Ironically, it is Cameron himself who waxed as eloquent as anyone in describing how important memory is. In the May 1963 *British Journal of Psychiatry* he wrote:

> Intelligence may be the pride—the towering distinction of man; emotion gives color and force to his actions; but memory is the bastion of his being. Without memory, there is no personal identity, there is no continuity to the days of his life. Memory provides the raw material for designs both small and great. Thus, governed and enriched by memory, all the enterprises of man go forward.

One of Cameron's patients, the wife of a Canadian politician, permanently lost all of her sense of self—memories and personality—for her entire life prior to the treatment.

Long before the scandal and lawsuits surrounding CIA sponsorship, Cameron wrote in graphic detail about his own work in major peer review journals, including the *Canadian Medical Association Journal* (January, 15, 1958) and

Comprehensive Psychiatry (February 1960 and April 1962). And, as we have seen, a follow-up was published in 1967 describing the fate of his victims. Cameron's extravagances were not the product of CIA financing or influence. Cameron already was carrying out his shock tortures before the CIA became interested. He would have carried on his work with or without the CIA, which never gave him more than $20,000 per year. Posthumously he would have remained one of the most renowned leaders in the history of psychiatry, except for the disclosure of his CIA connections. The irony is that the adverse publicity focused mostly on the CIA funding rather than on the most scandalous fact of all—that Cameron and his brutalities, although well known throughout the profession, were never criticized by mainstream psychiatry.

Nor was Cameron alone in inflicting sufficient amounts of shock to reduce patients to helpless, dilapidated, and demented human beings. In 1957 in the *Psychiatric Quarterly*, an official journal of the New York State Department of Mental Health, Glueck and his colleagues at Stoney Lodge, a private hospital in Ossining, New York, described giving shock until the patient became demented, unable to talk, lapsed into "utter apathy," and "behaves like a helpless infant, is incontinent of both bowel and bladder functions, requires spoon feeding and at times, tube feeding." It required a total of seventeen to sixty-four closely spaced treatments. Stoney Lodge continued these treatments at least until the 1970s, when I began to publicize them.

In *Multiple-Monitored Electroconvulsive Therapy* (1981) psychiatrist Barry Maletzky advocates and utilizes a contemporary version of intensive ECT called MMECT (multiple-monitored ECT). Patients are kept unconscious and almost continuously in a state of convulsion by several shocks in a row in each treatment session. As many as five seizures are induced in a period of up to fifty minutes of sustained convulsion. Several sessions are administered. According to the 1990 APA task force on ECT, a "substantial minority" of practitioners use the method.

The field of medicine is well acquainted with the effects of multiple, continuous seizures on the brain, whether these seizures are spontaneous, as in some forms of epilepsy, or caused by injury to the brain. A patient who suffers several convulsions in a row without regaining consciousness is defined as being in status epilepticus, which is recognized in neurology and medicine as a severe medical emergency requiring immediate intervention before it produces permanent brain damage.[16]

FURTHER EVIDENCE OF MEMORY LOSS AND MEMORY DYSFUNCTION

There is no way to get access to large numbers of shock patients for controlled studies except through the shock doctors themselves, and so meaningful scientific studies are few and far between. However, in the 1940s and 1950s I. L. Janis, a Yale psychologist, using controls, studied the effects of routine shock treatment on the recollection of personal memories. He found considerable losses at several weeks and then at a follow-up one year later.*

More recently, several shock doctors have found that a large percentage of ECT patients report significant memory blanks and continuing memory dysfunction years after shock treatment.[17] In a study by Larry Squire and Pamela Slater in the *British Journal of Psychiatry* in 1983 (pp. 1–8), patients questioned seven months after shock treatment reported memory loss spanning, on the average, a block of twenty-seven months surrounding the treatment. In another survey of routine shock patients in Scotland, by C. P. L. Freeman and R. E. Kendell in the *Annals of the New York Academy of Sciences* (vol. 462, 1986), patients returned to the hospital to be questioned face-to-face by the doctor who gave them the treatment. As Freeman and Kendell admit, patients might feel intimidated about criticizing shock under such conditions. Nonetheless, 74 percent mentioned "memory impairment" as a problem following shock treatment and "a striking 30 percent felt that their memory had been permanently affected."

In the same 1986 *Annals of the New York Academy of Sciences*, a team led by psychiatrist Richard Weiner of Duke University attempted to test for loss of personal subjective recollections of past experiences, because they are "most consistent with the nature of memory complaints by ECT patients themselves." Their memory inventory spanned several years prior to the shock and the testing. This was perhaps the first such study carried out in the several decades since those of Janis. Despite a strong bias toward shock treatment, the group found "objective personal memory losses." These lasted the duration of the study—six months—after bilateral ECT.

OLDER ECT PATIENTS

Because of the growing tendency to shock older people, it is important to understand their greater vulnerability to ECT-induced brain damage and dysfunction. Ongoing memory function is the subject of a study entitled "Cognitive Functioning in Depressed Geriatric Patients with a History of ECT," by Helen Pettinati and Kathryn Bonner, in the January 1984 *American Journal of Psychiatry*.[18] Among the older patients, performance was decreased on a test specifically aimed at disclosing "organic brain dysfunction" or "confusion." Short-term memory was impaired in both the older and the younger groups. As expected, age plus shock treatment produced the most deficits—a grave

*See I. L. Janis, "Psychological Effects of Electric Convulsive Treatments," *Journal of Nervous and Mental Diseases* (May 1950), and a more complete review of his publications in P. Breggin, *Electroshock: Its Brain-Disabling Effects* (1979).

warning to those who are promoting shock treatment as ideal for the elderly.

In "The Safety of ECT in Geriatric Psychiatry," by William Burke and his associates, in the June 1987 issue of the *Journal of the American Geriatrics Society*, it was found that ECT complications increase with age. Six of eight patients over seventy-five years of age had "some untoward event." The "common complications" included "confusion, falls, and cardiorespiratory problems."[19]

Gary Figiel and his colleagues, in "Brain Magnetic Resonance Imaging Findings in ECT-Induced Delirium," in the winter 1990 issue of the *Journal of Neuropsychiatry*, found that 11 percent of elderly patients developed an especially severe reaction characterized as delirium. They note concerns that elderly patients "may be at relatively high risk for developing encephalopathic side effects from the treatment."*

THE AMERICAN PSYCHIATRIC ASSOCIATION'S 1990 TASK FORCE

The APA's 1990 task force report, *The Practice of Electroconvulsive Therapy*, discusses and dismisses brain damage and memory loss from ECT—but without mentioning the relevant literature cited in the text and endnotes of this [reading], and in much greater detail in my 1979 textbook. For example, it does not refer to Hans Hartelius's definitive investigation of brain damage in cats or, for that matter, any of several other such animal studies by well-known American groups. Nor does it mention Janis's classic research on memory loss or Larry Squire and Pamela Slater's more recent research, although both are very well known in the field. Helen Pettinati and Kathryn Bonner's report on shock treatment of the elderly goes unmentioned. My publications, and those of John Friedberg and others, are not mentioned. Indeed, almost every article pertinent to memory dysfunction and brain damage is omitted from this latest APA report, including several that previously appeared in the two most widely used textbooks written by the advocates themselves.[20] Even the APA's own previous task force report on *Electroconvulsive Therapy* (1978) contains more information on memory loss. In psychiatry, "science" often goes backward!

The one negative study cited in the APA report is irresponsibly misrepresented. The task force declares that C. P. L. Freeman and R. E. Kendell found that "a small minority of patients, however, report persistent deficits" in memory. Freeman and Kendell, as already described, found that 74 percent of patients reported memory impairment and that a "striking 30%" said that their memory function was permanently impaired.

One must conclude that the APA report carefully paints an unblemished portrait of ECT in order to promote the treatment and to protect psychiatrists against malpractice suits. Thus the report was introduced at a press conference for the general media in late 1989 while still in the form of an unpublished manuscript.†

EVIDENCE FOR EFFICACY

A thorough review of the shock literature shows that there are no controlled studies indicating any "beneficial" effect beyond four weeks. Most show little or no improvement at all. The point was proven at the 1985 Consensus Conference on Electroconvulsive Therapy held by NIMH [National Institute of Mental Health] and NIH [National Institute of Health], at which psychologist and attorney Edward Opton, Jr., presented his review.‡ When none of the assembled shock doctors could provide any contradictory evidence, his conclusions were accepted in the Consensus Conference panel report, "Electroconvulsive Therapy," published in the October 18, 1985, *Journal of the American Medical Association*.

The four-week limit to treatment effectiveness is critical in two ways. First, it tends to confirm the brain-disabling hypothesis. Four weeks is the approximate period of time during which the patient's brain dysfunction, with associated euphoria or apathy, is most severe. Second, only four weeks of "relief' is very short considering the grave risks involved.

At the November 27, 1990, hearings in San Francisco, psychiatric survivor Wade Hudson reviewed the literature on electroshock, again focusing on controlled studies in which shock is compared to placebo in the form of simulated or "sham shock"—a mock shock procedure without the delivery of the electric current. The most recent relevant publication was by Timothy Crow and Eve Johnstone, "Controlled Trials of Electroconvulsive Therapy," in the 1986 New York Academy of Sciences proceedings, entitled *Electroconvulsive Therapy: Clinical and Basic Research Issues*. Crow and Johnstone confirm the power of placebo: simulated ECT resulted in "substantial improvements." They found only a slight and inconsistent tendency for ECT patients to perform better on a few test protocols for depression, and that was limited to the first month. They conclude, "Whether electrically induced convulsions exert therapeutic effects in certain types of depression . . . has yet to be clearly established."§After more than fifty years

*"Encephalopathic" refers to degenerative disease of the brain.

†By holding a press conference based on the unpublished version of the report, they gained national news coverage without fear of rebuttal from critics of the treatment, who had been refused access to the manuscript.

‡Opton's report was excluded from publication in the proceedings of the NIMH Consensus Conference. NIMH promotes all biopsychiatric treatments, including ECT.

§This is a most remarkable conclusion from the heart of the establishment, and it, too, was omitted from the APA task force report.

there is still no meaningful evidence that this dangerous treatment has any beneficial effect.[21]

SHOCK AS A "LIFESAVING" TREATMENT

As drastic as it is, does shock have some merit as a lifesaving treatment for suicidal people? Shock doctors frequently make that claim. But when confronted at the Consensus Conference they could cite only one paper in support of their thesis: David Avery and George Winokur's "Mortality in Depressed Patients Treated with Electroconvulsive Therapy and Antidepressants" in the September 1976 *Archives of General Psychiatry*. One of them even read the abstract of the paper to the audience in a manner too rushed to be comprehensible. This was not the first time I'd seen the specter of this paper raised, and so I pulled it from my files at lunchtime and distributed copies at the conference. What the paper actually says is the opposite of what the shock advocates claim: "In the present study, treatment was not shown to affect the suicide rate" (p. 1033).[22]

Despite the ease of studying suicide—one must merely follow up the patients and count the suicides—there is no published evidence whatsoever that electroshock helps. Instead, some clinicians, including neurologist John Friedberg and myself, are familiar with people who have killed themselves in despair over their brain damage from shock treatment, and we know many others who suffer lifelong despair. Happily, I also know a number of survivors who have recognized the damage but triumphed over it to lead full, rich lives—often as activists against psychiatric abuse.*

THE SAFETY OF THE "NEW" SHOCK TREATMENT

The most highly publicized alleged improvement is called modified ECT. It involves sedation, muscle paralysis, and artificial respiration. Despite the PR, this method is not new at all: I administered it more than twenty-five years ago in the early 1960s during my training at Harvard.[23] Furthermore, modified shock, of necessity, is *more* dangerous. First, the hazards of general anesthesia and muscle-paralyzing agents are added to those of the shock. Second, the intensity of current must be greater to overcome the anticonvulsant effect of the short-acting sedative that is injected immediately prior to the shock. In addition, patients in modern psychiatric hospitals frequently receive other medications, such as sedatives and minor tranquilizers, which further raise the seizure threshold. Furthermore, patients too often receive neuroleptics, antidepressants, and especially lithium, all of which can worsen the impact of shock.

Modified ECT wasn't introduced to reduce brain damage, since the shock doctors used to believe that the damage was therapeutic. The purpose of the modifications was to prevent fractures from muscle spasms. The claim that modified ECT reduces brain damage is a very recent public relations twist and has no validity whatsoever.

Another alleged improvement involves the use of differing types of electrical stimulation. But the relative safety of these innovations is controversial, and most of them have been around for decades. Besides, a great deal of shock is done at the same or higher energy levels used in the 1940s. The electrical current must in any case be sufficiently disruptive to produce a convulsion. Sometimes, if the patient is slow to "improve," an older machine will be brought in or the shock doctor will flip off the switch that protects the patient from especially high current intensities. While they won't admit it, many shock doctors act on the old axiom that the brain damage does the trick.

SACRIFICING THE RIGHT BRAIN

Another supposedly less harmful innovation is the placement of the two electrodes over the same side of the head—unilateral electroshock treatment. It is applied to the so-called nondominant or nonverbal side of the brain to focus the energy away from the verbal centers. In right-handed people the nonverbal side is usually, but not always, on the right. For a variety of technical reasons, this form of shock is potentially more dangerous than traditional bilateral shock.[24]

Why do shock advocates promote unilateral, nondominant shock? It's relatively easier for doctors to overlook harm done to the nonverbal side, because the patient can't speak about it. However, to people who use visual skills—such as homemakers, scientists, engineers, photographers, or artists—damage to the nondominant side may be more functionally devastating than damage to the more verbal side, even if the patient cannot communicate about it.[25]

The nonverbal side of the brain is involved in myriad subtle functions that are critical to a full, effective, happy life. . . . They include the creative faculties, such as imagination and the use of metaphor; visual and spatial capacities, as well as musical and motor abilities, such as coordination, dance, and athletics; the quality or vibrancy of

*Shock advocates frequently suggest that the eloquence of survivors like Leonard Frank is evidence that shock is not permanently damaging. I have known Leonard, and several other eloquent survivors, for almost twenty years, and I can vouch for the struggles they have undergone to recover as much as possible from the damage. These individuals are living proof of the capacity of the human being to triumph over brain damage and dysfunction. It seems cruel and self-serving for shock promoters to deny both their suffering and their heroic efforts to live life to the fullest despite their iatrogenic handicaps.

personality; initiative and autonomy; and insight.

It's ironic that modern psychology currently is placing so much emphasis on the importance of developing right brain function at the very moment that shock doctors are trying to tell us that we can more easily afford to sacrifice right brain function to repeated jolts of electricity. Notice also that the functions of the nondominant side mirror those of the frontal lobes—for example, initiative, autonomy, and insight—so that nondominant shock is potentially more lobotomylike than regular shock.

THE FDA, THE APA, AND ECT

Organized psychiatry realizes that shock cannot withstand scrutiny. In 1979 the FDA put shock machines into Class III, which means demonstrating "an unreasonable risk of illness or injury." Class III is the most restrictive category for medical devices and would have required manufacturers to provide premarketing data on safety and effectiveness.[26] This probably would have necessitated renewed animal testing.

Led by the American Psychiatric Association, psychiatry lobbied to have that decision reversed, and it succeeded. The FDA gave notice of its intention to reclassify shock machines into Class II, approving them as safe and efficacious and requiring no testing. It was a clear-cut illustration of psychiatry's lobbying strength at FDA.

A group of several hundred outraged shock survivors, organized by Marilyn Rice, began pressuring the FDA to maintain its earlier classification of the machines as dangerous and in need of testing. Most of the mail received by the FDA came from shock survivors testifying to the damage done to them.[27] The APA responded with its 1990 report claiming that the treatment is virtually harmless.

In September 1990 the FDA proposed a compromise that has satisfied neither side.[28] It would classify the machines as safe (Class II) for depression, but not for other disorders. The ruling permits shock machines to be used with impunity as long as the patient is diagnosed as very depressed. This will provide little protection to patients, since manipulating diagnoses to fit the treatment is commonplace in psychiatry. But it might open the way to more frequent malpractice suits against shock doctors when and if it can be shown that the patient failed to meet the proper diagnostic standard.

The FDA-ECT story illustrates how psychiatry places self-interest above both scientific inquiry and the well-being of its patients, as it stifled an examination of its treatment and rejected the outcry from the survivors. The story also confirms that the FDA has a greater commitment to placating psychiatry than to monitoring it. . . .

WHAT MANY PSYCHIATRISTS BELIEVE ABOUT SHOCK

Meanwhile, a large percentage of psychiatrists privately believe that the treatment is brain-damaging. How do we know? In a survey published in the earlier APA task force report on ECT (1978, p. 4), psychiatrists were asked, "Is it likely that ECT produces slight or subtle brain damage?" Forty-one percent voted yes and only 26 percent voted no. . . .

THE SURVIVORS FIGHT BACK

. . . [T]he main resistance to shock has come from those who have been damaged by it. Some have chained themselves to the gates or entrance doors of hospitals reputed to be shock mills. Leonard Frank also has debated shock doctors at their meetings and has written *The History of Shock Treatment* (1978) as well as the recently published comprehensive critique of ECT, "Electroshock: Death, Brain Damage, Memory Loss, and Brainwashing."[29] He was a founder of the national patients' rights movement and remains a heartening example to hundreds of survivors. Other survivors endure the stress of going on radio and television and of picketing the annual meetings of the American Psychiatric Association. Some have written about undergoing shock, like Janet Gotkin, with her husband Paul, in *Too Much Anger, Too Many Tears: A Personal Triumph Over Psychiatry* (1975). Marilyn Rice has become a watchdog of the FDA when it fails to perform its watchdog duties.

Most dramatically, one man—who was electroshocked at the age of six—managed for a few brief days to halt the use of shock in one of America's cities. Ted Chabasinski was a shy child genius growing up in a poor and dysfunctional family when a social worker removed him from his home and placed him in the psychiatric system. Soon he was subjected to shock treatment at the hands of one of the most famous child psychiatrists of all time, Loretta Bender.

Young Chabasinski was so confused and terrorized by the treatment that he inadvertently helped to maintain his long odyssey within the state mental hospital system. When the doctors asked the little boy "Do you hear voices?" he would dutifully reply yes, hoping to please his captors and to avoid further shock.

After being discharged from Rockland State in his teens it took Chabasinski several years to build a life for himself. In 1971, like so many other survivors, he joined the newly burgeoning ex-inmate movement in California and received enormous moral support from it. Eventually he went to law school and is now a practicing attorney and patients' rights advocate.

In 1982, before gaining his law degree, Chabasinski organized what eventually became the Berkeley ban, a citizens' movement aimed at stopping electroshock in Berkeley and specifically at Herrick Hospital, a general hospital with a psychiatric ward. An overwhelming victory was won at the polls as the people of Berkeley voted yes on a proposition to say no to shock. But within a few weeks the American Psychiatric Association had obtained a court order overturning the vote. Eventually the case was won by organized psychiatry, but for forty-one days in the winter of 1982 there was a "power outage" at Herrick.

As far as anyone knows, that was the only time anywhere in the world that shock treatment actually was banned. The following year Herrick Hospital shocked more people than ever before, and it is still going strong.

A few weeks ago, I had little positive with which to conclude this chapter. Shock treatment is on the rise, and elderly women are being targeted. The number of people subjected to shock is surpassing 100,000 per year in America, and it will keep on climbing unless the public takes an effective stand against it. But . . . there has been a series of encouraging events in California. As a result of reports that three more hospitals were starting to give shock in the San Francisco area, there were protests, public hearings, and surprisingly favorable media coverage of efforts to stymie the shock doctors. Led by Supervisor Angela Alioto, the Board of Supervisors of San Francisco (the city's governing body) has passed a resolution declaring its opposition to the "use and financing" of ECT. It also urged the state legislature to strengthen the requirements for informed consent, including my suggestion that potential patients be exposed to audio or video tapes by professionals who view ECT critically. On February 20, 1991, Mayor Art Agnos signed the resolution. While this resolution will not stop ECT in San Francisco, it is very encouraging to those of us who oppose the treatment, and hopefully will lead to further governmental actions around the country.

NOTES

1. See C. Miller Fisher, "Neurologic Fragments. II. Remarks on Anosognosia, Confabulation, Memory, and Other Topics; and an Appendix on Self-Observation," *Neurology* 39 (1989): 127–32. Fisher describes how brain-injured patients tend to deny their mental losses and to "confabulate" or make up stories to cover their deficits. The general tendency, called anosognosia or unawareness of neurologic deficit, is so common that Fisher declares, "Indeed, it may qualify as one of the general rules of cerebral dysfunction." Yet shock advocates persistently claim that ECT-damaged patients exaggerate their memory loss.
2. In the June 1960 *American Journal of Psychiatry* psychiatrist and shock advocate David Impastato describes the drama surrounding the first shock treatment in Italy. An involuntary patient had been subjected to one shock, which failed to make him convulse. "The Professor [Ugo Cerletti] suggested that another treatment with a higher voltage be given. The staff objected. They stated that if another treatment were given the patient would probably die and wanted further treatment postponed until the morrow. The Professor knew what that meant. [Presumably, that they would refuse to participate again.] He decided to go ahead right then and there, but before he could say so the patient suddenly sat up and pontifically proclaimed no longer in jargon, but in clear Italian, "Non una seconda! Mortifere!" (Not again, it will kill me.) This made the Professor think and swallow, but his courage was not lost. He gave the order to proceed at a higher voltage and a longer time; and the first electroconvulsion in man ensued. Thus was born EST out of one man and over the objection of his assistants."
3. Figures through 1983 are available in Carol Warren, "Electroconvulsive Therapy: 'New' Treatment of the 1980s," *Research in Law, Deviance and Social Control* 8 (1986): 41–55. More recent figures are from the State of California, Department of Mental Health, Statistics and Data Analysis Section, July 20, 1989.
4. See, for example, E. N. Zamora and R. Kaebling, "Memory and Electroconvulsive Therapy," *American Journal of Psychiatry* 122 (1965): 546–54. For a complete review, see Peter Breggin, *Electroshock: Its Brain-Disabling Effects*, pp. 63–70.
5. Also see Lewis Rowland, ed., *Merritt's Textbook of Neurology*, 8th ed. (Philadelphia: Lea and Fibiger, 1989). As with many other observations in this book, the comparison between ECT and closed-head injury did not fully dawn on me until emphasized by a survivor of the treatment.
6. I have reviewed the animal studies in detail in *Electroshock: Its Brain-Disabling Effects*. For short summaries, see Peter Breggin, "Neuropathology and Cognitive Dysfunction from ECT," *Psychopharmacology Bulletin* 22, no. 2 (1986): 476–79; Peter Breggin, "Disabling the Brain with Electroshock," in *Divergent Views in Psychiatry*, ed. M. Dongier and E. Wittkower (Hagerstown, Md.: Harper and Row, 1981); and John Friedberg, "Shock Treatment, Brain Damage, and Memory Loss: A Neurological Perspective," *American Journal of Psychiatry* 134 (1977): 1010–14.

   While psychiatrists tend to deny what shock is doing to their patients, psychologists have sometimes been more open about it. James McConnel, in *Understanding Human Behavior*, 4th ed. (New York: Holt, Rinehart and Winston, 1983), reviews my conclusions that ECT effects are "severe," "catastrophic," and "devastating" and concludes, "Most of the literature on ECT tends to support Breggin's view" (p. 565).
7. [See the advertisement "Informed ECT, at last" in *Psychiatric News*, September 7, 1990, p. 3.]
8. See Peter Breggin, *Electroshock: Its Brain-Disabling Effects*.
9. In Max Rinkel and Harold Himwich, eds., *Insulin Treatment in Psychiatry* (New York: Philosophical Library, 1959), shock advocate Hans Hoff states that the object of ECT is to kill brain cells: "cells that are sick, and new brain cells which are potentially sick have to be destroyed. Otherwise relapses will come. This means that one of the most important things is to see that really every cell which is affected is really destroyed" (p. 222). In

1941 Walter Freeman was given space in the prestigious journal *Diseases of the Nervous System* (vol. 2) to publish an editorial entitled "Brain-Damaging Therapeutics." Freeman postulates, "Among the explanations advanced to account for the success of the various shock methods of therapy in the psychoses, that of actual damage to the brain has not received adequate attention." He declares, "Maybe it will be shown that a mentally ill patient can think more clearly and more constructively with less brain in actual operation." Similarly, in a commentary at the end of an article by F. Ebaugh and others in the 1942 *Transactions of the American Neurological Association* (pp. 35–41), one of America's most influential psychiatrists, Abraham Myerson, speaks of how mental patients have "more intelligence than they can handle and that the reduction of intelligence is an important factor in the curative process." His remarks are made in a discussion of autopsy material gained from patients who died from electroshock treatment.

10. R. L. Kahn, M. Fink, and E. A. Weinstein, "Relation of Amobarbital to Clinical Improvement in Electroshock," *Archives of Neurology and Psychiatry* 76 (1956): 23–29. In a study of the amobarbital interview method, the authors again make clear that the test is useful as a "diagnostic test for the existence of structural brain disease." This is the test that is correlated with a positive clinical outcome following ECT. The meaning is clear: brain damage is considered an improvement. See R. L. Kahn, M. Fink, and E. Weinstein: "The 'Amytal Test' in Patients with Mental Illness," *Journal of the Hillside Hospital* 4 (1955): 3–13.
11. Fink's articles, which are cited in my 1979 book on shock, include those in the *Journal of the Hillside Hospital* 6 (1957): 197–206; *Archives of Neurology and Psychiatry* 80 (1958): 380–86; and *Diseases of the Nervous System* 19 (1958): 113–18. In his book *Convulsive Therapy: Theory and Practice* (New York: Raven, 1973), Fink again makes clear that the degree of improvement is correlated with brain dysfunction as reflected by psychological tests, brain wave studies, and other criteria (p. 127). He points out that "patients become more compliant and acquiescent with treatment" (p. 139) and also continues to connect improvement with denial, disorientation, brain trauma, cerebral dysfunction, and signs of an organic brain syndrome (p. 165). He also mentions anosognosia, the denial of physical damage after trauma to the brain, as a basis for the improvement. Nonetheless, in public Fink has contested my assertion that shock works by producing damage and dysfunction.
12. Max Fink, "Efficacy and Safety of Induced Seizures (EST) in Man," *Comprehensive Psychiatry* 19 (1978). This quote and several others originally were located by shock survivor Marilyn Rice.
13. For a discussion of anosognosia, see note 1. . . .
14. Russ Rymer, "Electroshock," *Hippocrates*, March/April 1989.
15. See David Remnick, "25 Years of Nightmares: Victims of CIA-Funded Mind Experiments Seek Damages from the Agency," *Washington Post*, July 28, 1985; Lee Hockstander, "Victims of 1950's Mind-Control Experiments Settle with CIA," *Washington Post*, October 5, 1988; Leonard Rubenstein, "The CIA and the Evil Doctor," *New York Times*, November 7, 1988; and a letter by Don Weitz, "Psychiatry Bears Guilt in Brainwashing Tests," *New York Times*, November 26, 1988.
16. See the classic article by A. V. Delgado-Escueta et al., "Management of Status Epilepticus," *New England Journal of Medicine* 306 (1982): 1337–40; or James Bernat and Frederick Vincent, eds., *Neurology: Problems in Primary Care* (Oradell, N.J.: Medical Economics, 1987), which states that status epilepticus is "a true medical emergency."
17. In the *British Journal of Psychiatry* (142 [1983]: 1–8), Larry Squire and Pamela Slater surveyed more than sixty patients long after they had received routine shock treatment. Seven months after ECT, patients reported a median memory loss spanning a period of two years prior to and three months after the shock—a total block of twenty-seven months. Three years after shock, they reported a smaller gross loss, from six months prior to two months after the ECT. The estimate at seven months is surely more accurate. Brain-injured patients, as described, tend to deny their losses (see note 1 . . .). While it's very unlikely that the brain would heal any further after seven months, over the years it would become easier for patients to deny the degree of their memory loss. Despite the tendency toward denial, more than half of the patients (55 percent) surveyed by Squire and Slater felt that they had not regained normal memory function over the years. In a personal discussion with me at the 1985 Consensus Conference on ECT, sponsored by NIMH in Bethesda, Maryland, Squire told me that one patient suffered significant memory losses over a span of ten years; but he said he did not consider it important to mention it in his report.

    In *Multiple-Monitored Electroconvulsive Therapy* (Boca Raton, Fla.: CRC Press, 1981), Barry Maletzky reports on a survey of forty-seven patients thirty-six months after his shock program. Thirty-six percent had ongoing or continuing cognitive problems, such as keeping sequences straight and remembering new things: "I have been following this soap opera for five years on TV but now I get confused about who is doing what to whom"; "I couldn't tell my neighbor how to get over to my uncle's house when she was driving me there the other day, but I have been going over there for years" (p. 180).
18. Two groups were studied, one with a mean age of 69.7 years and the other 41.7 years. There were control patients as well. None of them had had ECT for at least three months.
19. Nonetheless, the authors remain strong advocates of ECT.
20. Max Fink, *Convulsive Therapy: Theory and Practice* (New York: Raven,

1973); and Richard Abrams, *Electroconvulsive Therapy* (New York: Oxford University Press, 1988).

21. One controlled study using simulated ECT, by J. Lambourn and D. Gill, "A Controlled Comparison of Simulated and Real ECT" (*British Journal of Psychiatry* 133 [1978]: 514–19), found no difference and concludes, "This cast some doubt on current view of the effectiveness of electro-convulsive therapy in general." Even the often cited shock study, S. Brandon et al., "Electroconvulsive Therapy: Results in Depressive Illness from the Leicestershire Trial" (*British Medical Journal* 288 [1984]: 22–25), presents a bleak picture of ECT efficacy. While the authors emphasize an improvement on the Hamilton depression rating scale at four weeks, their data show absolutely no difference between shocked patients and sham patients at twelve or twenty-eight weeks. Their whole argument rests on the hope of a mere four weeks' relief from depression—the period of maximum brain dysfunction. But even in regard to the alleged improvement during the one-month period, the evidence is flimsy at best, relying on a few borderline test results. Wade Hudson summarizes:

    Whether due to the power of suggestion, the benefit of routine support from nursing staff, spontaneous healing, or a combination of the three, those who received simulated shock treatment improved dramatically, and on most measures, even 1–3 days right after treatment; [and] they improved as much as did those who had electricity passed through their brains.

22. It's unclear why shock advocates frequently misrepresent the Avery and Wonokur paper, but as I discuss in my 1979 book on shock (pp. 130–31), they may have gotten the wrong impression from Fink's citation of the paper in a paragraph misleadingly entitled "ECT and Suicide." On one occasion, a shock doctor tried to use the paper in a radio debate with me to prove the efficacy of shock in preventing suicide, but fortunately I was on the phone from my office and was able to locate the paper to quote it on the air. The Avery and Winokur paper is also misused in the APA task force report, *The Practice of Electroconvulsive Therapy* (1990), p. 53.
23. On many occasions I have referred to this as the shame of my life.
24. One-sided or unilateral shock can be more damaging than the usual bilateral shock, because the electrodes are placed closer together. The electrical current strikes the brain with more concentrated force, doing more intense focal damage. This is demonstrable in brain wave studies. It also is demonstrable in studies that show *increased* damage to the verbal centers when the electrodes are placed on the dominant side. Furthermore, attempts to shock the nondominant side will at times end up directing the full force of the shock inadvertently at the verbal centers. Many left-handers and some right-handers are dominant on the same, rather than the opposite, side of the brain.

    The dangerousness of unilateral shock is increased by the fact that it is harder to produce a convulsion with it. So sometimes the current controls on the shock machine are turned up higher to deliver a greater shock, or else more than one shock may be needed to produce a seizure. Often additional ECT treatments are given to achieve the desired level of post-ECT brain dysfunction.

    Denial and anosognosia are even more pronounced after damage to the nonverbal, or nondominant, side of the brain. Patients with strokes on that side of the brain will not recognize that they have very obvious ill effects, such as paralyzed limbs. Blakeslee remarks that the rest of the brain has trouble recognizing or communicating about any damage to the nonverbal side. Shock advocates are also well aware that nondominant shock makes their patients less aware of the damage done to them. In his 1988 book *Electroconvulsive Therapy*, Richard Abrams observes that anosognosia is especially "profound and striking" after nondominant shock. Yet shock doctors never admit that this causes patients to report falsely that they have less memory loss or mental dysfunction after nondominant ECT.
25. The relative impact of nondominant shock on nonverbal functions is reviewed in D. Fromm-Auch, "Comparison of Unilateral and Bilateral ECT: Evidence of Selective Memory Impairment," *British Journal of Psychiatry* 141 (1982): 608–13.
26. Margaret McDonald, "FDA Orders Tougher ECT Device Standards," *Psychiatric News*, December 7, 1979.
27. "Reclassification of ECT Devices Delayed," *Psychiatric News*, April 6, 1984.
28. See Rael Jean Isaac, "FDA's Shocking Treatment of a Valuable Device," *Wall Street Journal*, December 5, 1990; and Seth Farber, "US Food & Drug Administration Proposes Giving Electroshock the Rubber Stamp," *Dendron*, October 24, 1990. . . .
29. Leonard Frank, "Electroshock: Death, Brain Damage, Memory Loss, and Brainwashing," *Journal of Mind and Behavior* 11, nos. 3 and 4 (summer and autumn 1990).

DISCUSSION

The intrepid reader endeavoring to make sense of the ECT literature is immediately confronted with two radically different and seemingly irreconcilable perspectives. On the one hand, surveys of some patients who have undergone ECT indicate that this procedure is no more aversive than a trip to the dentist (Freeman & Kendell, 1980; Hughes, Barraclough, & Reeve, 1981). Moreover, a number of ECT practitioners and experts (for example, Fink, 1984) emphatically insist that the evidence that ECT produces long-term brain damage or memory loss is extremely weak, if not nonexistent. On the other hand, we readily encounter horror stories of patients who claim to have suffered permanent and severe cognitive and memory deficits as a consequence of ECT (Breggin, 1979; Friedberg, 1976). In addition, several highly visible psychiatrists, some of whom previously administered ECT themselves, interpret the literature as conclusively demonstrating that ECT produces long-term structural brain damage.

The authors of the two readings in this chapter squarely align themselves on opposing sides of this debate. Nevertheless, Sackeim and Breggin, for all of their differences, appear to agree on one important point: ECT alleviates the short-term symptoms of depression and perhaps other conditions. Sackeim, although not discussing in detail the possible mechanisms underlying ECT's effectiveness, suggests that the therapeutic efficacy of ECT is related to its induction of seizures and, in particular, to the extent to which the threshold for the induction of seizures is exceeded (see also Sackeim, 1984). In ways that are currently not well understood, these seizures presumably produce marked alterations in the levels of neurotransmitters (chemical messengers) and perhaps other brain chemicals, leading to a rapid and dramatic amelioration of depressive symptoms. Breggin embraces a radically different view of the reasons behind ECT's "effectiveness." ECT "works," Breggin maintains, by producing an organic brain syndrome characterized by anosognosia, a condition in which patients deny their psychological and physical difficulties. Because this anosognosia is transient, however, the effects of ECT on depressive symptoms tend to be similarly short-lived (that is, 1 month or less).

Thus, according to Breggin, the "effectiveness" of ECT is entirely superficial; this "effectiveness" can be likened to the effectiveness of "treating" a prolonged bad mood by ingesting an enormous dose of alcohol. As anyone who has attempted to drown their sorrows in alcohol surely knows, such a "treatment" typically allows the drinker to forget temporarily about his or her recent woes. As soon as the intoxicating effects of the alcohol wear off, however, the bad mood returns in full force. It is intriguing to note how Sackeim and Breggin differ in their conceptualization of the organic brain syndrome following ECT. For Sackeim, this syndrome is an unwanted but unavoidable short-term side effect. For Breggin, this syndrome is actually the key ingredient in ECT's "effectiveness."

To what extent do the data bear out Breggin's controversial contentions? In point of fact, certain elements of Breggin's arguments appear to be questionable or at least deserving of closer scrutiny. First, Breggin's reasoning concerning the mechanism of ECT's "effectiveness" would predict that the severity of the organic brain syndrome following ECT should be positively correlated with ECT's therapeutic success, because such "success" presumably derives from ECT's capacity to produce temporary cognitive dysfunction. In actuality, however, there is little evidence that the degree of cognitive impairment following ECT is correlated with its effectiveness (Weiner, 1984). Second, Breggin correctly notes that the introduction of muscular relaxants has necessitated the use of higher shock levels in ECT, because the muscle relaxants increase the threshold for electrically produced seizures. Breggin does not point out, however, that the administration of muscle relaxants has been found to buffer animals experiencing prolonged seizures from brain damage (Weiner, 1984).

A further complication involved in interpreting the long-term effects of ECT on memory functioning is the absence of control groups composed of individuals who did not receive ECT. Many or most of the claims of chronic memory loss produced by ECT derive from uncontrolled reports of patients who were administered ECT decades earlier. These reports, however, are potentially attributable to the tendency of individuals who are recuperating from memory loss to doubt that they have fully recovered (Squire, 1984). In other words, such patients might initially experience memory loss as a result of ECT and then recover more or less completely but mistakenly suspect that their memory is still faulty. In addition, patients who have received ECT might incorrectly attribute their commonplace, everyday memory lapses to the effects of treatment (Squire, 1984). All of us experience memory failures, some of them rather extreme ("Where did I leave my car keys?"), from time to time. The vast majority of us, who have not received ECT, attribute such failures to periodic lapses in concentration or to the inevitable effects of normal aging. But individuals who have received ECT may understandably be much more inclined to attribute such losses to the effects of treatment. A further difficulty in interpreting reports of chronic memory loss following ECT stems from the potential effect of depression on memory. Because depression is often characterized by profound disturbances in concentration and recall, patients' reports of long-term memory loss may be due to their prior depression rather than to ECT. Without a control group of previously depressed individuals who did not receive ECT, we have no way to know.

These interpretational problems aside, however, it would be premature to nonchalantly dismiss the possibility that ECT produces long-term memory loss or brain damage. Although intense disagreement regarding the long-term effects of ECT on memory and cognitive functioning persists, a scientific consensus has gradually emerged that prolonged administration of ECT (particularly bilateral ECT) may well, in some cases, result in a patchy loss of autobiographical memories lasting months or perhaps years (Coffey & Weiner, 1990; Weiner, 1984). Moreover, the possibility that ECT produces considerably more widespread and severe memory deficits in rare cases remains open (Weiner, 1984).

Thus, the decision regarding whether to administer ECT in an individual case must involve a careful evaluation of trade-offs. On the one hand, the possibility that ECT produces long-term cognitive deficits in certain individuals cannot be convincingly excluded. In addition, the chances of death associated with ECT administration, although statistically quite small—0.01% to 0.03% for each patient (Coffey & Weiner, 1990)—cannot be dismissed lightly. On the other hand, many medical treatments for life-threatening illnesses also have problematic side effects. For example, chemotherapy for cancer produces permanent hair loss in a small but not trivial number of cases (Price, 1984), and heart bypass surgery is associated with an increased risk of strokes.

Note my use of the term *life-threatening* in the previous paragraph; it was not accidental. Depression, like cancer and severe coronary heart disease, is associated with a markedly increased risk of death. The suicide rate of those with untreated depression has been estimated to be a staggering 15% (Avery & Winokur, 1976; Guze & Robins, 1970). More to the point, at least one study suggests that ECT may decrease the number of suicide attempts among depressed individuals (Avery & Winokur, 1978).* Thus, the clinician confronted with the difficult decision of whether to administer ECT to a given individual must, ideally in conjunction with the patient, judiciously balance the potential costs of the treatment against the potential costs—particularly suicide—of forgoing the treatment. Given the possible short- and long-term hazards associated with ECT, however, it seems likely that ECT will, at least in the foreseeable future, remain a treatment of last resort for depressed individuals.

*In his reading, Breggin cites an earlier study by Avery and Winokur (1976) that failed to find an effect of ECT on completed suicides among depressed individuals. (For reasons that are unclear, Breggin did not cite the later Avery and Winokur study.) Nevertheless, Avery and Winokur (1976) did find that ECT was associated with a lower death rate from causes other than suicide, such as heart attacks, compared with other treatments. Moreover, because the rate of completed suicides in Avery and Winokur's (1976) study was quite low, both among patients who did and did not receive ECT, their investigation does not provide an adequate test of ECT's effect on suicide rates.

QUESTIONS TO STIMULATE DISCUSSION

1. Clearly, considerable debate persists concerning ECT's precise mechanism of action. Is it ethically defensible to use a treatment even if the reasons for its effectiveness are largely or entirely unknown? Explain your reasoning.
2. How might you go about testing Breggin's hypothesis that ECT "works" by producing anosognosia? How would you assess anosognosia?
3. Both Sackeim and Breggin concur that the effects of ECT on depressive symptoms tend to be relatively short-lived. Some authors argue that this finding raises serious questions concerning the merits of ECT. In a commentary on ECT, for example, Pinel (1984) asserts that "it is difficult to justify [ECT's use] until ECT has been shown unambiguously to produce significant long-term therapeutic benefits" (p. 31). Do you agree with Pinel? What other medical treatments might be justifiable even though they do not produce long-term benefits?
4. Virtually every psychological and medical treatment has at least some undesirable side effects. Judging from what you have read, in what cases, if any, do you believe that the potential benefits of ECT outweigh its potential costs? Defend your answer.
5. What preconceptions did you hold regarding ECT prior to reading this chapter? From what sources were these preconceptions derived? How, if at all, have your views concerning ECT been changed by reading this chapter?

SUGGESTIONS FOR FURTHER READING

Abrams, R., & Essman, W. B. (Eds.). (1982). *Electroconvulsive therapy: Biological foundations and clinical applications*. New York: SP Medical & Scientific Books.

This edited volume contains chapters on such topics as the history of ECT, the techniques involved in ECT, neuropsychological consequences of ECT, changes in brain biochemistry following ECT, and ethical and legal issues concerning the use of ECT.

Breggin, P. (1979). *Electroshock: Its brain-disabling effects*. New York: Springer.

Breggin presents a detailed set of arguments to buttress his contention that ECT produces brain dysfunction. He reviews animal studies of ECT, human autopsy studies of ECT's effects, EEG and neurological studies of ECT, clinical and research studies of ECT's effects on acute and long-term brain damage, as well as hypotheses concerning ECT's mechanism of action. Breggin concludes with a discussion of informed consent and other ethical issues concerning the use of ECT.

Coffey, C. E., & Weiner, R. D. (1990). Electroconvulsive therapy: An update. *Hospital and Community Psychiatry, 41*, 515–521.

The authors briefly review the evolution and history of ECT and discuss recent developments in its application (for example, modifications in electrode placement and stimulus wave form). They recommend that psychiatrists and other relevant medical personnel receive formal academic and practical training in ECT administration.

Crowe, R. R. (1984). Electroconvulsive therapy: A current perspective. *New England Journal of Medicine, 311*, 163–166. (Reprinted in B. Slife & J. Rubinstein [1992], *Taking sides: Clashing views on controversial psychological issues* [7th ed.]. Guilford, CT: Dushkin Publishing Group.)
Crowe provides a brief and highly readable introduction to many of the central issues and controversies involving ECT. The major issues discussed include the evidence for ECT's efficacy, deaths resulting from ECT, side effects of ECT, recent modifications of ECT, and patient acceptance of ECT.

Fink, M. (1978). Is ECT a useful therapy in schizophrenia? In J. P. Brody & H. K. H. Brodie (Eds.), *Controversy in psychiatry* (pp. 183–193). Philadelphia: W. B. Saunders.
Fink reviews the evidence regarding the use of ECT to treat schizophrenia, including studies of its efficacy, safety, and mechanism of action. He concludes that although ECT's effectiveness in treating some cases of schizophrenia has been convincingly demonstrated, its potential side effects make it difficult to reach an informed judgment about its relative assets and liabilities.

Friedberg, J. (1976). *Shock treatment is not good for your brain*. San Francisco: Glide Publications.
In this highly readable but polemical book, Friedberg discusses his experiences as a psychiatrist battling the "ECT establishment" and briefly reviews the evidence regarding the efficacy and side effects of ECT. The remainder of the book is taken up primarily by interviews with psychiatric patients concerning their experiences with ECT.

Janicak, P. G., Davis, J. M., Gibbons, R. D., Eriksen, S., Chang, S., & Gallagher, P. (1985). Efficacy of ECT: A meta-analysis. *American Journal of Psychiatry, 142*, 297–302.
The authors report the results of a meta-analysis comparing the effectiveness of ECT with sham ECT, placebo, and antidepressants. They conclude that ECT is superior to all three in the treatment of depression. In addition, they conclude that unilateral and bilateral ECT are approximately equivalent in effectiveness.

Malitz, S., & Sackeim, H. A. (Eds.). (1986). Electroconvulsive therapy: Clinical and basic research issues. *Annals of the New York Academy of Sciences* (Vol. 462). New York: The New York Academy of Sciences.
This comprehensive edited volume contains chapters on diverse topics, including ECT's efficacy, biological and neuroendocrinological effects, neurophysiological and neuropsychological effects, and mechanism of action. The chapter by Crow and Johnstone provides a good overview of recent controlled trials of ECT. Sackeim concludes the section on ECT's efficacy with a reprise of the literature on ECT versus sham ECT, ECT's long-term effects, the use of ECT in disorders other than depression, and the comparative efficacy of unilateral and bilateral ECT.

Palmer, R. L. (1981). *Electroconvulsive therapy: An appraisal*. New York: Oxford University Press.
This edited volume covers a number of specialized topics relating to ECT, including the efficacy of ECT in treating schizophrenia, the use of ECT in elderly populations, and animal models of ECT. The chapter by Lambourn addresses the question of whether cognitive dysfunction is one of the key therapeutic components of ECT.

Weiner, R. D. (1984). Does electroconvulsive therapy cause brain damage? *Behavioral and Brain Sciences, 7*, 1–22.
Weiner presents a careful, comprehensive summary of data on the effects of ECT on brain anatomy and physiology from pathological, radiological, electrophysiological, biochemical, and neuropsychological perspectives. He concludes that, although the severity of brain damage resulting from ECT has probably been grossly overestimated by many of its opponents, the possibility of subtle effects on recent autobiographical memories or, more rarely, of global and persistent deficits, cannot be conclusively excluded on the basis of existing data. Weiner's article is appropriate for individuals with at least some background in physiological psychology and neurochemistry. Also see ensuing commentaries and the rejoinder to those commentaries by Weiner.

REFERENCES

Avery, D., & Winokur, G. (1976). Mortality in depressed patients treated with electroconvulsive therapy and antidepressants. *Archives of General Psychiatry, 33*, 1029–1037.

Avery, D., & Winokur, G. (1978). Suicide, attempted suicide, and relapse rates in depression: Occurrence after ECT and antidepressant therapy. *Archives of General Psychiatry, 35*, 749–753.

Brandon, S. (1981). The history of shock treatment. In R. L. Palmer (Ed.), *Electroconvulsive therapy: An appraisal* (pp. 3–10). New York: Oxford University Press.

Breggin, P. (1979). *Electroshock: Its brain-disabling effects*. New York: Springer.

Coffey, C. E., & Weiner, R. D. (1990). Electroconvulsive therapy: An update. *Hospital and Community Psychiatry, 41*, 515–521.

Fink, M. (1984). ECT—Verdict: Not guilty. *Behavioral and Brain Sciences, 7*, 26–27.

Freeman, C. P. L., & Kendell, R. E. (1980). Patients' experiences of and attitudes to ECT. *British Journal of Psychiatry, 137*, 8–16.

Friedberg, J. (1976). *Shock treatment is not good for your brain*. San Francisco: Glide Publications.

Gulevich, G. (1977). Convulsive and coma therapies and psychosurgery. In J. D. Barchas, P. A. Berger, R. D. Ciaranello, & G. R. Elliott (Eds.), *Psychopharmacology: From theory to practice* (pp. 514–525). New York: Oxford University Press.

Guze, S. B., & Robins, E. (1970). Suicide and primary affective disorders. *British Journal of Psychiatry, 117*, 437–438.

Hughes, J., Barraclough, B. M., & Reeve, W. (1981). Are patients shocked by ECT? *Journal of the Royal Society of Medicine, 74*, 283–285.

Kalinowsky, L. B. (1982). The history of electroconvulsive therapy. In R. Abrams & W. B. Essman (1982), *Electroconvulsive therapy: Biological foundations and clinical applications* (pp. 1–5). New York: SP Medical & Scientific Books.

Kiloh, L. G. (1982). Electroconvulsive therapy. In E. S. Paykel (Ed.), *Handbook of affective disorders* (pp. 262–275). New York: Guilford Press.

Pinel, J. P. J. (1984). After forty-five years ECT is still controversial. *Behavioral and Brain Sciences, 7,* 30–31.

Price, T. R. P. (1984). Modern ECT: Effective *and* safe. *Behavioral and Brain Sciences, 7,* 31–32.

Sackeim, H. (1984). Not all seizures are created equal: The importance of ECT dose-response variables. *Behavioral and Brain Sciences, 7,* 32–33.

Sackeim, H. (1985, June). The case for ECT. *Psychology Today, 19,* 36–40.

Simpson, G. M., & May, P. R. A. (1985). History and overview of schizophrenia. In H. I. Kaplan & B. J. Sadock (Eds.), *Comprehensive textbook of psychiatry* (4th ed., pp. 713–724). Baltimore: Williams & Wilkins.

Squire, L. R. (1984). Opinion and facts about ECT: Can science help? *Behavioral and Brain Sciences, 7,* 34–35.

Weiner, R. D. (1984). Does electroconvulsive therapy cause brain damage? *Behavioral and Brain Sciences, 7,* 1–22.

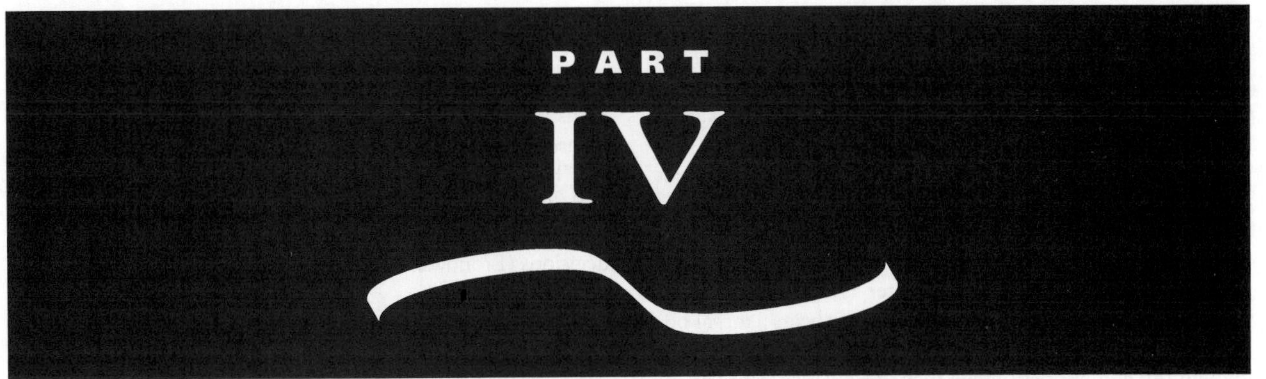

Legal and Ethical Issues

The science of medicine is like that of legislation in one respect:
that it is far more easy to point out what will do harm than what will do good.

—Charles Calel Colton, *Lacon* (1825)

INTRODUCTION

The "marriage" between law and psychology (alluded to by Alan Stone in Chapter 17) has generally been an uneasy, and at times openly embattled, one. To a large extent, the reasons for this less than blissful relationship can be traced to the contrasting assumptions held by individuals in these two disciplines regarding the causes of behavior and the proper relationship between society and the mentally ill. Although a variety of fundamental questions lie at the heart of the controversies involving law and psychology, two issues have stood out as especially resistant to a simple solution: whether human behavior is free or determined and to what extent society has a right or obligation to protect individuals from themselves.

Unlike most of the other questions addressed in this book, these two issues probably cannot be settled solely by recourse to data. Instead, the answers are rooted at least partly in deep-seated philosophical and ethical assumptions that lie outside the realm of science. The beginning student of abnormal psychology soon learns that not all questions in this discipline are purely empirical ones. Some can be answered only with reference to **zero-order beliefs**: fundamental assumptions (for example, the existence of reality) that cannot be justified on the basis of scientific findings and that form the logical foundation for other beliefs (Bem, 1970).

The **free will–determinism debate** provides one of the most dramatic lines of demarcation between law and psychology. Legal scholars tend to regard virtually all individuals as possessing free will. That is, with rare but significant exceptions, the legal system tends to treat individuals as autonomous agents who are responsible for their acts. In contrast, most psychological theorists and researchers—with the principal exception of those who subscribe to the humanistic/existential paradigm of personality—tend to regard behavior as determined by environmental factors, genetic factors, or both, even if these factors are not always identifiable in practice. In other words, the legal profession generally views behavior as chosen by the individual, whereas the psychological profession generally views behavior as caused by factors outside the individual's control.

The implications of the free will–determinism debate come into particularly sharp focus in the controversy regarding the insanity defense, which is discussed in Chapter 17. As Stone (1975) has pointed out, it is, paradoxically, the legal system's zero-order belief in the existence of free will that leads it to wholeheartedly embrace the insanity defense. If some individuals possess free will, then almost by definition others can be deprived of it; similarly, asserting that some individuals are "intelligent" implies that others are "unintelligent." If some acts can be freely chosen, others must not be. Thus, "the insanity defense is in every sense the exception that proves the rule" (Stone, 1975, p. 222).

The second issue at the interface of law and psychology that has proved to be surprisingly intractable has been the extent to which society should respect what former Supreme

Court Justice Louis Brandeis called "the right to be let alone" (Szasz, 1987). That is, should society adopt a paternalistic role toward individuals who are unable or unwilling to protect themselves, even if these individuals are not dangerous to others? This question assumes particular significance in the debate concerning the involuntary commitment of psychiatric patients, which is discussed in Chapter 19. Supporters of involuntary commitment contend that society bears a moral obligation to protect individuals from themselves; opponents of involuntary commitment argue that this practice deprives individuals of both their freedom and their responsibility.

Similar moral dilemmas have arisen in other domains. For example, psychiatrist Thomas Szasz (1986) questions the ethical propriety of coercively preventing individuals from attempting or completing suicide. For Szasz, although suicide is an act that psychologists and psychiatrists should generally discourage, it is ultimately a painful choice that must be left up to the individual. Szasz does not argue that psychologists and psychiatrists should not attempt to prevent suicide. He instead argues that they should refrain from implementing coercive interventions (such as involuntary hospitalization and imposition of physical restraints) in order to accomplish this goal. A somewhat related issue concerns the right of committed psychiatric patients to refuse treatment, particularly somatic interventions such as medication or ECT. Should patients who are confined to hospitals against their will because they are dangerous to themselves or others have the right to decline treatments intended to alleviate this dangerousness? U.S. courts have increasingly given an affirmative response to this question (see, for example, *United States* v. *Charters*, 1990), although they have also granted exceptions when patients appeared to be imminently dangerous to others (for example, *Dautremont* v. *Broadlawns Hospital*, 1987).

In grappling with this and other issues concerning the rights of the mentally ill, remember that many important questions in abnormal psychology have moral dimensions that transcend strictly scientific boundaries. Scientific research may be a value-free enterprise (and many would quarrel even with this assertion), but the application of this research to real-world problems almost inevitably entails difficult ethical decisions (Bronowski, 1965).

OVERVIEW OF PART IV

This fourth and final part comprises three chapters dealing with unresolved issues concerning the interface between law and ethics, on the one hand, and psychology, on the other. In Chapter 17, we examine the legal, moral, and psychological arguments for and against the insanity defense. In Chapter 18 we address a question with potentially important social policy implications: Are mentally ill individuals at heightened risk for dangerous behavior? Finally, in Chapter 19 we explore the controversy regarding the involuntary commitment of the mentally ill.

REFERENCES

Bem, D. J. (1970). *Beliefs, attitudes, and human affairs*. Pacific Grove, CA: Brooks/Cole.

Bronowski, J. (1965). *Science and human values*. New York: Harper & Row.

Dautremount v. *Broadlawns Hospital*, 827 F.2d 191, 8th Cir. (1987).

Stone, A. A. (1975). *Mental health and law: A system in transition*. Rockville, MD: National Institute of Mental Health.

Szasz, T. S. (1986). The case against suicide prevention. *American Psychologist*, *41*, 806–812.

Szasz, T. S. (1987). *Insanity: The idea and its consequences*. New York: Wiley.

United States v. *Charters*, 863 F.2d 302 (1990), cert. denied 494 U.S. 1016.

CHAPTER

17

Should the insanity defense be maintained?

PRO Stone, A. A. (1982). The insanity defense on trial. *Hospital and Community Psychiatry*, 33, 636–640.

CON Lykken, D. T. (1982). If a man be mad: A scientist testifies against the insanity defense. *The Sciences*, 22, 11–13.

OVERVIEW OF THE CONTROVERSY: Alan A. Stone reviews the major criticisms of the insanity defense—including its purported use by large numbers of criminals to avoid punishment, its reliance on dishonest testimony by psychiatrists, and its permissive message to criminals—and concludes that the insanity defense represents an important legal option that should not be abandoned. David T. Lykken argues that the insanity defense seriously tarnishes the reputation of both psychiatry and the law and that it represents a hopelessly misguided effort to "solve a legal problem with a psychiatric formula."

CONTEXT OF THE PROBLEM

At 2:25 P.M. on March 30, 1981, John W. Hinckley, Jr., pulled out a pistol and fired six shots at President Ronald Reagan and his aides outside the Washington Hilton Hotel in Washington, D.C. The first bullet hit Reagan's press secretary, James Brady, in the head, producing permanent brain damage; the sixth bullet ricocheted off the presidential limousine into Reagan's chest, only inches from his heart. Hinckley, as you may recall, was in love with actress Jodie Foster (whom he had never met but to whom he had sent numerous passionate letters, poems, and gifts) and entertained delusional fantasies of their becoming married and occupying the White House. He apparently believed that killing the president would so impress Ms. Foster that she would succumb to his amorous advances. Hinckley's unsuccessful assassination attempt, which was captured on camera and replayed hundreds of times on national television, sent shock waves through a country that was still recuperating from the assassination of a president less than two decades earlier.

The shock of Hinckley's assassination attempt seemed almost to pale in comparison with the national furor that erupted following Hinckley's acquittal 15 months later, in a Washington, D.C., courtroom, on the grounds of insanity. The public reaction to the Hinckley verdict was overwhelmingly negative: An ABC news poll indicated that more than three-fourths of all Americans objected to the decision. Prominent political columnists like George Will decried the use of the insanity defense, proclaiming that the conflicting psychiatric testimony regarding Hinckley's mental status only affirmed the unreliability of psychiatric diagnosis. (As you saw in Chapters 2 and 3, however, Will's contentions are contradicted by most existing evidence.) Calls to abolish or drastically reform the insanity defense came from many quarters, including lawyers, politicians, scientists, and mental health professionals.

How did the psychiatric and legal systems get themselves into such a quandary? The insanity plea—or, as it technically called, the "not guilty by reason of insanity" (NGRI) defense—has a long and rather checkered history. As early as the reign of Edward I of England in the late 1200s, a defense of insanity was used in the courtroom to lighten defendants' sentences (Davison & Neale, 1994). But it was not until over five centuries later that a formal rule was delineated for ascertaining sufficient grounds for acquittal by reason of insanity. The **irresistible impulse rule**, first formulated by an Ohio court in 1834, dictated that defendants could not be convicted if their criminal behaviors stemmed from an overpowering drive that they were deemed helpless to control. This rule, incidentally, was the defense with which Lorena Bobbitt, the woman who severed her husband's penis with a kitchen knife in response to years of apparent physical and sexual abuse, was acquitted in 1994. The problem with this rule, of course, has always been the potentially arbitrary nature of the word *irresistible.* How is a jury to decide whether an urge can be resisted?

More important, the concept of irresistible impulse highlights the fundamental difficulty that has bedeviled the insanity defense since its inception. If some impulses are irresistible, then others must necessarily be resistible. But the notion of a resistible impulse is premised on **free will**, the intuitively compelling belief that, with rare but significant exceptions, humans are capable of freely choosing their actions. Free will is a key assumption of the legal system, which holds individuals accountable for their criminal behaviors. But most scientific paradigms of human behavior, from Freudian psychoanalysis to Skinnerian radical behaviorism, are premised solidly on **determinism**, the belief that all psychological phenomena have potentially identifiable causes that can be explained in terms of scientific principles. Thus, the "irresistible impulse" defense, like other insanity rules, underscores the murky middle ground created by the shotgun wedding between law and psychiatry. The legal system asks if mentally deranged individuals should bear responsibility for their criminal acts; the psychiatric system responds that the judgment of responsibility is a moral and philosophical, rather than a scientific, decision. (Recall from Chapter 2 that sanity and insanity are legal, not psychiatric, concepts.)

Three other important insanity rules followed the "irresistible impulse" decision. The **M'Naughten rule** was formulated in 1843 in response to Daniel M'Naughten's murder of British Prime Minister Robert Peel's secretary, Edward Drummond. M'Naughten, who was apparently experiencing **command hallucinations** (that is, hallucinations directing an individual to perform a particular act) ordering him to murder the prime minister, shot Drummond after mistaking him for Peel. (In the days before television, well-known politicians were not always instantly recognizable.) The court ruled that M'Naughten's psychotic symptoms relieved him of criminal responsibility and acquitted him of murder. In response to the public outrage that ensued, the House of Lords appointed a panel of judges to delineate a set of guidelines for adjudicating a legal definition of insanity. Their guidelines, now known as the M'Naughten rule, asserted that defendants should be held insane, and thus not criminally responsible, if they were unaware either of the "nature or quality" of their criminal acts (in layperson's terms, if they did not know what they were doing) or that their criminal acts were morally wrong. The M'Naughten rule was thus relatively narrow in scope, because it emphasized the ability of defendants to distinguish right from wrong. Emotional factors, such as powerful urges, were not sufficient grounds for acquittal. This distinction probably explains why Jack Ruby, the man who assassinated Lee Harvey Oswald in front of millions of horrified viewers on national television, was unsuccessful in his attempt to plead insanity based on the M'Naughten defense. Ruby seemed to clearly comprehend the nature and quality, as well as the moral implications, of the crime he had committed.

The **Durham rule**, handed down in 1954, broadened the scope of the insanity defense considerably. Monte Durham was initially convicted in 1951 of breaking into a house but was acquitted on appeal after his lawyer argued that the M'Naughten rule was based on an outdated conception of behavior. The judge in the retrial ruled that individuals should not be held criminally responsible if their illegal behaviors were the product of a "mental disease or defect" (hence, the Durham rule is sometimes also called the product rule). The Durham rule thus greatly expanded the potential role of mental health professionals in insanity decisions, as expert witnesses were frequently required to render judgments regarding whether a defendant suffered from a diagnosable mental illness. The Durham rule, although initially adopted by a number of states, has since been abandoned in virtually all jurisdictions, largely because it resulted in an overreliance on expert testimony. New Hampshire is the only state currently using the Durham rule (Bootzin et al., 1993).

More recently, the **Brawner rule**, which combines elements of the irresistible impulse rule and the M'Naughten rule, was adopted by the American Law Institute (ALI). The Brawner rule asserts that defendants should be acquitted if they "lacked substantial capacity" either to understand the wrongfulness of their actions or to "conform [their] conduct to the requirements of the law" (American Law Institute, 1962, p. 66). The Brawner rule was adopted by a number of states and by the early 1980s was in place in all federal courts and approximately half of the country's lower courts. Nevertheless, the Hinckley verdict, which was based on the Brawner rule, raised serious questions concerning the wisdom of the ALI's guidelines. Largely in response to this verdict, the U.S. Congress enacted the Insanity Defense Reform Act of 1984, which heralded a return to a narrower M'Naughten-type insanity rule.

The article by Lykken in this chapter went to press as the Hinckley trial was still underway. Lykken prophesied (incorrectly) that "I find it hard to believe that this defense will succeed." But perhaps anticipating future developments, he rhetorically asked: "What if . . . the court is forced to find this man not guilty of a crime that millions of Americans witnessed on television? Could the American justice system survive such humiliation?" (p.12). Over a decade later, a number of legal and psychological experts still find themselves asking the same question.

THE CONTROVERSY: Stone vs. Lykken

Stone

Alan Stone notes that both the Durham rule and the concept of diminished capacity broadened the role of psychiatry in insanity decisions. Nevertheless, he points out that both of these insanity tests were overturned in the 1970s and 1980s. Indeed, an increasing number of lawyers and politicians have begun to call for the abolition of the insanity defense altogether. Stone then presents three major criticisms of the insanity defense and endeavors to rebut each:

- He disputes the claim that the insanity defense is overused. Statistics demonstrate, Stone contends, that the number of insanity acquittals in the United States is vanishingly small.
- He takes issue with the charge that the insanity defense is flawed because many psychiatrists are dishonest and will testify for either side in order to receive money or publicity. The American legal system, Stone maintains, is inherently adversarial, so that disagreements among expert witnesses are inevitable.
- He disagrees with the criticism that the insanity defense sends a permissive message to criminals. There is no evidence, Stone asserts, that criminals could be deterred by abolishing the insanity plea.

Stone also argues that the insanity defense was, until recently, "a profound hypocrisy," because criminals found not guilty by reason of insanity were often confined indefinitely in psychiatric institutions. Recent legal developments, however, have increased the likelihood that such criminals will be released after relatively brief stays. The insanity defense, Stone concludes, cannot be abolished, because the very foundation of the American legal system rests on the assumption of free will, as well as on the corollary assumption that free will is sometimes absent.

Lykken

David Lykken begins by briefly reviewing the history of the M'Naughten defense and notes that the interpretation of many of its concepts (such as "nature and quality of the act") have given rise to considerable confusion. Although trials involving insanity pleas are rare, he acknowledges, such trials seriously damage the reputation of both psychiatrists and lawyers. Lykken further contends that the Durham rule failed to remedy the deficiencies of the M'Naughten rule. Because psychologists and psychiatrists almost invariably adopt a deterministic view of human behavior, they will tend to find a mental "reason" for almost any criminal action. Lykken then delineates several differences between the premises of law and of psychiatry. For example, law aims to rehabilitate criminals, but rehabilitation has proven remarkably unsuccessful. Lykken maintains that the core assumptions of law and psychiatry are fundamentally incompatible. Law, which presumes free will, "wants to know who is responsible"; but psychiatry, which presumes determinism, cannot provide a meaningful answer to this question. Lykken concludes by proposing a modification to the traditional insanity defense. In Lykken's two-stage system, defendants would first be judged guilty or innocent based on whether they committed the act and meant to do so and would then be sentenced on the basis of their psychiatric status. In this way, Lykken contends, the question of guilt or innocence would be logically separated from the question of appropriate punishment.

KEY CONCEPTS AND TERMS

diminished capacity An extension of the traditional insanity defense to include instances in which the defendant's judgment was seriously impaired at the time of the criminal act.

mens rea Literally, "guilty mind"; the requirement that defendants be convicted of a criminal action only if they intended to commit this action at the time of the crime.

PREVIEW QUESTIONS

1. What is Stone's response to the familiar criticism that the insanity defense is overused by criminals?
2. How does Stone attempt to refute the charge that the insanity defense is flawed because some psychiatrists will testify for virtually any position in order to receive money or publicity?
3. What is Stone's answer to the charge that the insanity defense sends a permissive message to criminals?
4. According to Stone, what change over the past several decades has dramatically altered the impact of the insanity defense? What are the implications of this change for the use of the insanity defense?
5. According to Lykken, what has the insanity defense done to the reputation of psychiatrists and lawyers?
6. What is Lykken's criticism of the Durham rule?
7. According to Lykken, how do the assumptions of the legal system differ from those of psychiatry? Why do these differences make the insanity defense problematic?
8. What alternative does Lykken propose as a substitute for the traditional insanity defense?

ALAN A. STONE

The insanity defense on trial

It is sometimes said after a marriage ends in divorce, "Anyone who really knew them both could have told you it would never last." That is what is now being said about the marriage between law and psychiatry. "What could they have possibly seen in each other; they are so different. He, the law, is so formal, rigid, and traditional. She, psychiatry, is so flighty, expansive, and unconventional. His style is objective and judgmental; her style is subjective and understanding."

Yet 30 years ago there was in fact a great romance. Just 30 years ago progressive jurists were wooing psychiatry and urging the systematic reform of the criminal law in the light of the new scientific discoveries of modern psychoanalytic psychiatry.

During the decade of the 1950s, two major steps were taken to cement the relationship between law and psychiatry. In 1954, Judge David Bazelon authored the famous Durham decision, a new open-ended test of criminal responsibility (1). In subsequent decisions he not only gave more leeway for psychiatric testimony, but also scolded psychiatrists for not giving more to the relationship. What the law wanted, he said, was the complete psychodynamic explanation of how the defendant's disease or defect led to the alleged criminal act (2). The second, perhaps even more meaningful, step was taken on the other side of the continent in California. In 1959 the California Supreme Court decided that the law wanted to be guided by psychiatric wisdom not only on the plea of insanity but also on the concept of diminished capacity (3).

Diminished capacity allowed psychiatrists to go far beyond the boundary of legal insanity. They were now free to explore a more intimate relationship with law. Psychiatrists were to explain how mental disabilities less severe than those associated with "insanity" could nonetheless interfere with the capacity to premeditate or to choose to do evil. Diminished capacity could thus reduce first-degree murder to manslaughter. It could mitigate without absolving guilt in the eyes of the law.

As we move into the decade of the 1980s, both of these entanglements have been rejected. The D.C. court of appeals took less than 20 years to repudiate Durham (4), and this past year the California legislature abolished diminished capacity (5). And there is in the air a mood to go further, to abolish even the traditional insanity defense. One state has already done that. Many lawyers want to throw psychiatrists out of the temple of law. At the same time the sentiment is growing in the psychiatric establishment that it was led on, taken advantage of, and humiliated by this liaison with the law.

Americans have been hearing stories about this souring relationship. Many of them seem to believe that it has produced an increasing use of an expanded insanity defense and that law and order have been undermined as a result. President Richard Nixon created this impression ten years ago when he called for the abolition of the insanity defense as one of the central features of his administration's effort to reform the federal criminal law and get tough on crime in the streets (6). The debate over similar legislation being considered by this Congress focuses on the question of whether the traditional phrase "not guilty by reason of insanity" should be supplemented or supplanted by the phrase "guilty but insane" (7).

CRITICISMS OF THE DEFENSE

If the insanity defense, this child of law and psychiatry, is on trial, then like other defendants, it has a right to know what the charges are against it. The indictment, I think, includes the following particulars, abstracted from the *Congressional Record* of Tuesday, November 17, 1981, in a statement by the Honorable John Ashbrook of Ohio (8):

- The insanity defense has been successfully employed in large numbers by dangerous criminals, who thereby avoid punishment.
- Psychiatrists are particularly dishonest. They will say anything for money or to get their names in *Time* magazine. Representative Ashbrook spoke of psychiatric bogeymen who "have about as much understanding of the human mind as the butcher, the baker, and the candlestick maker." Therefore, the insanity defense does not work because the expert witnesses on whom the courts must rely say totally contra-

SOURCE: *Hospital and Community Psychiatry, 33*, pp. 636–640, 1982.

dictory things that cannot be trusted.
- The criminal justice system has been corrupted by psychiatry. Everywhere, as Lord Devlin said, "The concept of illness expands continually at the expense of the concept of moral responsibility" (9).

There have also been other charges against the insanity defense that often have been mutually contradictory. One distinguished psychiatrist called for its abolition because it is available only to the wealthy (10). Another abolitionist claimed it was applied only to the poor, to minorities, and to revolutionaries as a stigmatizing weapon of oppression (11). It should be apparent that almost no one favors this defendant, the insanity plea, and that opposition now comes from all sides of the political spectrum.

THE ISSUE IN PERSPECTIVE

The mystery, it seems to me, is how the insanity defense has survived at all since, not only now but all through history, there has been so much to be said against it. To answer the question first requires some perspective. This country has witnessed the assassination of John F. Kennedy, the murder of his assassin, the assassination of Robert F. Kennedy, the assassination of Martin Luther King, Jr., the two attempted assassinations of President Ford, the murder of John Lennon, the senseless killings by Son of Sam in New York, and the sadistic multiple murders by Gacy in Chicago. Is there anyone today who is completely confident that not one of these murderers was mentally ill? Yet every single one of these men and women was found guilty except Oswald, who was killed on national television. Ruby, Sirhan, Ray, Fromme, Moore, Chapman, Berkowitz, and Gacy—not one of them was found not guilty by reason of insanity in the courts of the United States.

It is important to remember, as these cases pointedly suggest, that in every plea of insanity a judge or jury will ultimately decide who is not guilty by reason of insanity—the decision is not left to psychiatrists. The record of history and the few scientific studies of the insanity defense clearly demonstrate that the value system of the judge and jury is far more important than either the testimony of the psychiatrist or the open-ended language of the test of criminal responsibility (12).

Unfortunately, we do not have good statistics on successful insanity defenses, but everyone who has attempted to compile and study the actual numbers has found that the frequency of insanity acquittals is surprisingly small. For example, in New York, a state plagued by crime, there were on average only eight successful insanity defenses a year between 1965 and 1971 (13). Many counties in the state of New York had no insanity acquittals at all during that period. Roughly one case in a thousand raises the insanity defense, and only 10 per cent of those are successful (14). These numbers make it clear how numerically insignificant the insanity defense really is.

Clearly then, the charge that the insanity defense is being exploited too much and excuses too many is false. This charge obscures the real problem; namely, the collapse of the criminal justice system. I shall give New York as an example again. When one arrest in a hundred ends in a prison sentence (15), when the vast majority of criminal cases are disposed of by plea bargaining (16), when first offenders convicted of armed robbery are routinely given suspended sentences (17), and when in several states across the country judges are forced to release convicted felons because the prisons are so overcrowded as to be found cruel and unusual punishment, then insanity acquittals are not the problem (17). Psychiatry and the insanity defense may be a pimple on the nose of Justice, but the patient is dying of congestive heart failure. It is a pipe dream to hope to reduce crime in the streets, rape, and murder by abolishing the insanity defense and throwing the psychiatrists out of the courtroom.

THE ADVERSARY SYSTEM

Let me consider the second charge—that psychiatrists are dishonest and will say anything for money or publicity. Cases that invoke the insanity defense are dramatic. In a certain sense, they are modern morality plays in which all of the courtroom participants assume that the defendant has done the deed and that what is at stake is whether the accused person is to be held legally responsible.

Every defendant in our legal system is entitled to an ardent advocate, even those who are arrested with the smoking pistol in their hand. Ours is the adversary system, and that means that if there is a possible insanity defense, the legal advocate has to get psychiatric testimony to make a case. The truth is that our adversary system demands that the lawyer try to find a psychiatric witness whose testimony will help the client.

That is inherent in our adversarial system of justice; it is not confined to psychiatric witnesses. When IBM is sued in an antitrust case, IBM's lawyers find an economist who will defend IBM's practices, using the very best economic arguments he or she can muster. The other side will hire an economist to attack, using the very best economic counterarguments. If a bridge collapses, one side will bring in engineers who will offer scientific evidence and claim negligence; the other side will bring in engineers to offer scientific evidence on the other side. The same can be said for medical testimony in malpractice cases and a host of other situations involving expert testimony. It is the lawyer's job to find a witness to support his or her argument. That is the very basis of our adversarial system.

Whatever the scientific status of psychiatry may be and whatever the ethical status of its practitioners may be, the public has to expect that psychiatrists, like all other expert witnesses, have been selected by lawyers who are advocates. Furthermore, in all important cases, the lawyer will have screened and then coached the psychiatrist on what to say and how to say it. To object to the contradictory testimony of psychiatrists is to object to the adversarial system of justice.

GETTING TOUGH ON CRIME

There is, however, another argument often made against the insanity defense. Doing away with the insanity defense, it is said, will send a message to the public and to the potential criminal that we arc getting tough on crime—we are no longer a permissive society that is going to coddle violent criminals.

My answer to this argument requires me first to consider what is meant by "a permissive society that is coddling violent criminals" and second to inquire how one goes about sending a message to criminals. No one who has been in prison or in jail or who has visited those institutions can possibly believe we coddle prisoners. Prisons like Attica may be better than they were but they are still terrifying, brutal institutions. Although there have been attempts at reform, our prisons are still overcrowded, and the idea of rehabilitation is no longer seriously believed by anyone. Prison is punishment and the only issue up for debate is whether the punishment of imprisonment is cruel and unusual.

Therefore, what is meant by coddling a criminal, if it has any meaning at all, must refer to what happens elsewhere in the criminal justice system outside confinement: bail, suspended sentences, probation, early parole, and the failure to confine known criminals or to confine them long enough. Surely this kind of coddling has little to do with psychiatry. These are the symptoms of a criminal justice system overwhelmed by the sheer weight of numbers.

Now what about the idea that abolishing the insanity defense will send a message to criminals? Could such a message have really influenced Ruby, Sirhan, Ray, Fromme, Moore, Chapman, Berkowitz, Gacy, or Hinckley? I am not someone who believes that the mentally ill cannot be deterred, but I am sure they cannot be deterred by abolishing the insanity defense.

Nor would such a message deter the criminal on the street who has made life unsafe in most of our major cities. The street criminal expects not to be caught. If he is caught, be expects not to serve time. If he does serve time, it will be because he has been caught more than once and not only will he not plead insanity, he will not even have a trial. His lawyer will plea bargain and make a deal. Psychiatrists and the insanity defense are not an important part of this realistic picture of the criminal justice system. Abolishing the insanity defense will send no real message to anyone.

FROM FICTION TO REALITY

But having rebutted these charges, I want to make a new and narrower charge of my own. I make it in the form of a question. "Are there some people, even a few, who, for example, kill and then invoke the plea of insanity and thereby avoid or spend less time confined?" We deal now with a very narrow question, and for the first time we hit on a charge against the insanity defense that is in my opinion quite justified.

However, until 20 years ago, the answer to even this narrow charge would have been "not true." Persons found not guilty by reason of insanity usually were confined for the rest of their lives in institutions for the criminally insane. Such institutions were even more awful than prisons. Unfortunately, the public was not aware of this reality. They believed that a successful plea of insanity meant that the defendant had escaped punishment. The fantasy of comfortable hospitals and the fiction of temporary insanity gave a completely incorrect impression.

Norval Morris, a distinguished professor of criminal law who did know the realities, wrote an article calling for the abolition of the insanity defense (18). He felt that the only humane value the insanity defense had served through history was to help societies avoid the use of capital punishment. Since at the time he wrote, capital punishment had been virtually abolished de facto if not de jure, it seemed to him that defendants found guilty of a capital offense would get a better deal in prison than if found not guilty by reason of insanity and condemned to live out their lives in these horrible institutions. But Professor Morris did not fully anticipate subsequent developments either in law or in psychiatry.

First, consider the law. In a series of decisions mainly predicated on constitutional grounds and civil liberties, the law has made it more difficult to confine and keep confined persons found not guilty by reason of insanity (19). These legal developments, which again arc not well understood by the public, are part of the great recent legal reforms of mental health law. Essentially what these particular legal reforms did was to reject the traditional practice of automatic indefinite confinement of persons found not guilty by reason of insanity. Such persons, it was decided, have rights; after trial they must be given a new hearing, and it must be determined that they are civilly committable, that is, they are still mentally ill and dangerous. If they are then committed, they are entitled to periodic review of their status so that they will not be needlessly confined. For example, in *People v. McQuillan* (19) the Supreme Court of Michigan found that the state's automatic commitment of insanity acquittals was a violation of due process and equal protection. Such people could be held for only 60 days. After that time they had exactly the same procedural rights as any civilly committed patient.

These developments took place at the same time that civil libertarians were making it much more difficult to civilly commit or to retain in commitment anyone whether a crime had been committed or not. Although temporary insanity as a defense had been mainly a fiction, these legal developments began to make it a reality. This was the work not of psychiatrists but of civil libertarians. They and federal judges agreed that psychiatrists had too much influence over the law in determining who should be confined in mental hospitals. The law decided that psychiatry was too subjective, and that it needed an objective standard. The objective standard announced by the court, and applicable to these cases, was imminent, likely, or probable danger to others (20).

Ironically, this objective standard is totally without empirical foundation. No one—not psychiatrists, not psychologists, not sociologists, not computers—can provide valid evidence about who does or does not meet this objective standard. This problem is particularly acute when a decision has to be made whether a person who was once dangerous is still dangerous. This is exactly the question that arises after a person is found not guilty by reason of insanity. No one can answer yes or no to this objective standard, which courts insist must be proven beyond a reasonable doubt. The law has lost touch with reality in its quest for objectivity.

These legal developments take on even greater import when we examine what happened in psychiatry during these same two decades. Until the second half of this century, long-term custodial confinement was an accepted practice of institutional psychiatry. Whether patients were dangerous or not, whether they came from the criminal courts or by ordinary civil commitment, the length of hospital stay could often be measured in years rather than in days. In 1958 the average length of hospitalization in the United States for schizophrenia was 13.1 years (21). As long as psychiatry endorsed or accepted the practice of long-term custodial confinement, mental institutions provided an extra measure of protection for the criminal justice system. Psychiatry, by calling this custodial confinement "treatment," gave legitimacy to the notion that the insanity defense was humane.

Later, when the community mental health approach began to dominate the therapeutic imagination, when effective drug treatments became available, and when psychiatrists finally opened their eyes to the evils of long-term institutionalization, a process began that, even without legal reform, might well have ended many of the abuses the civil libertarians decried. But these changes also radically altered the mental health system's ability to protect society. Institutions with revolving doors offer little security to the public. When therapeutic considerations alone determine the length of hospital stay, patients who formerly would have been hospitalized for years are now released after only a few days.

These psychiatric developments eventually reached even into the institutions for the criminally insane. Before a seriously mentally ill offender can be tried and plead insanity he must first, as a requirement of law, be restored to competency (22). Thus, if someone who is actually psychotic kills, he is confined, treated, restored to competency, and then goes to trial. From the psychiatrist's current perspective, almost everyone who has had sufficient treatment to be restored to competency has had as much inhospital treatment as is necessary for therapeutic reasons. Therefore, if his insanity plea is successful, there will be no therapeutic justification for his continued confinement.

Indeed, the more we improve conditions in institutions for the criminally insane, the more good psychiatrists we hire, the greater pressure there will be from the psychiatrists not to confine these patients. What this two-sided development means is that the laws created by the civil libertarians and the methods of treatment developed by psychiatrists now both push in the same direction, and the traditional way of dealing with persons found not guilty by reason of insanity has been drastically transformed.

CONFRONTING THE HYPOCRISY

For the last two hundred years, the insanity defense was a profound hypocrisy. The courts found defendants not guilty by reason of insanity and then relied on psychiatry to confine them for the rest of their lives. Thus there was no loss of protection to society. But beginning 20 years ago with the developments I have described, this hypocrisy was confronted. Perhaps for the first time in history, a successful plea of insanity has real bite.

Because the consequences of a successful plea of insanity have changed, it is now becoming increasingly attractive to criminal defendants, even defendants who have committed lesser crimes. For example, an average of eight insanity acquittals a year occurred in New York between 1965 and 1971. Then in 1972 there were 25 cases; in 1973, 37 cases; in 1974, 55 cases; in 1975, 61 cases (13). Furthermore, 31 persons charged with murder and given insanity acquittals had been discharged within a year. In addition, many insanity acquittals were given to defendants charged with less serious offenses, where there was no possibility of capital punishment or a lengthy sentence (13).

Compared with the debacle of the entire criminal justice system and the threat posed to the public by its failures, the insanity defense is trivial, notwithstanding these recent statistics. If, on the other hand, we compare the consequences of the insanity defense 20 years ago and the consequences today, a substantial change has taken place. The insanity defense, once a legal hypocrisy, has become a legal reality. It is this new legal reality that understandably has led to legislation that seeks to change the consequences of the insanity defense so as to restore the old hypocrisy.

What shall we do then—invent some new hypocrisy such as guilty but insane, or shall we once and for all abolish the insanity defense? In order to consider the question, one final, critical issue must be faced. Psychiatrists treat mental illness, often with great benefit to very sick patients, but that is not the same as curing them. Psychiatry certainly has not found a permanent cure for violence. We can treat people and return them to the community. They will function better, but we cannot guarantee that they are cured, and we certainly can make no promises that they will not be violent in the future.

For those who still support the insanity defense in 1982, it is not enough to say that it is morally wrong to punish an insane person. They must also be willing to submit to further risks at the hands of the insane rather than punish them or deprive them of due process and equal protection. Jesus Christ asked us to turn the other cheek. The American Civil Liberties Union proclaims that due process and equal protection are supreme legal values. But whether the American public will endorse this position is another matter.

BARRIERS TO ABOLITION

So, finally, why not abolish the insanity defense? Who is standing in the way? My answer is the law itself. I maintain that every moral philosopher in every culture has realized that morality requires that man has free will. Our legal system and the law are inspired by that moral intuition. At the same time, I maintain that every moral philosopher who has thought about human nature has also concluded that at *some* time in a man's life he feels he has no choice; he acts without choice.

The contradiction between this experience of being without choice and the moral intuition of free will is one of the inescapable contradictions of human existence. That contradiction is expressed and denied by the insanity defense. The insanity defense is the exception that "proves" the rule of law. I bowdlerized the maxim because today the insanity defense does more than test the law; it *demonstrates* that all other criminals had free will—the ability to choose between good and evil—but that they chose evil and therefore deserve to be punished.

It is not psychiatrists, it is not criminals, it is not the insane who need the insanity defense. The insanity defense is the exception that "proves" the rule of free will. It is required by the law itself, and it is this vision of law that has throughout history required resistance to abolition of the insanity defense. It is not for psychiatrists to choose between this vision of law and the new loss of protection to society. It is the law's own deeply social and cultural choice.

But if there is to be an insanity defense, there must be psychiatric testimony or some equivalent. Someone will be asked to help the court do the impossible, to distinguish the few who do not have free will from the multitude who do. So, in the end, I suggest that it is the law that cannot do without psychiatry. The marriage between law and psychiatry is therefore just like many other marriages in which one hears it said at times of crisis, "I don't know what to do. I can't live with her and I can't live without her."

REFERENCES

1. Durham v US, 214 F 2d 862 (DC Cir 1954)
2. Goldstein A: The Insanity Defense. New Haven, Yale University Press, 1967
3. People v Wells, 202 P 2d 53, 62–63 (Cal 1949) cert denied 337 US 919; People v Gorshen 336 P 2d 492, 503 (Cal 1959)
4. Brawner v US, 471 F 2d 969 (DC Cir 1972)
5. California Penal Code, See 28(b), 1981
6. Dershowitz A: Abolishing the insanity defense: the most significant feature of the administration's proposed criminal code: an essay. Criminal Law Bulletin 9:345, 1973
7. Ashbrook J: Statement on insanity defense. Congressional Record, Nov 17, 1981, p E5365
8. Gallo C in Ashbrook J: Statement on insanity defense. Congressional Record, Nov 17, 1981, p E5365
9. Devlin P: The Enforcement of Morals. London, Oxford University Press, 1959, p 17
10. Halleck SL: Psychiatry and the Dilemmas of Crime. New York, Harper & Row, 1962
11. Szasz T: Psychiatric Justice. New York, Macmillan, 1965
12. Simon R: The Jury and the Defense of Insanity. Boston, Little, Brown, 1967
13. Steadman HJ: Insanity acquittals in New York State, 1965–1978. American Journal of Psychiatry 137:321–326, 1980
14. Barclay RL: Criminal responsibility: an historical overview, p 11, unpublished paper cited in Criss ML, Racine DR: Impact of change in legal standard for those adjudicated not guilty by reason of insanity 1975–1979. Bulletin of the American Academy of Psychiatry and Law 8: 261, 1980
15. 99% of felony arrests in the city fail to bring terms of state prison. New York Times, January 4, 1981, p 1
16. Note: Plea bargaining and the transformation of criminal process. Harvard Law Review 90:564, 1977
17. Brooklyn office decides the treatment of cases that involve a felony charge. New York Times, Jan 4, 1981, p 78
18. Morris N: The dangerous criminal. Southern California Law Review 41: 514, 1968
19. Bolton v Harris, 395 F 2d 642 (DC Cir 1968); People v McQuillan, 392 Mich 511, 221 NW 2d 569 (1974)
20. Millard v Harris, 406 F 2d 964 (DC Cir 1968)
21. Bellak L (ed): Schizophrenia: A Review of the Syndrome. New York, Grune & Stratton, 1958, p 75
22. Pate v Robinson 383 US 375 (1966)

DAVID T. LYKKEN

If a man be mad: A scientist testifies against the insanity defense

Although not known for her wit, the young Queen Victoria indulged herself in one immortal quip: "We do not believe that anyone could be insane who wanted to murder a Conservative Prime Minister." She was referring to Daniel M'Naghten, a man tangled in paranoid delusions who, in 1843, thinking to strike back at the leader of the faction he believed to be persecuting him, determined to shoot Robert Peel, the Tory Prime Minister, but mistakenly murdered Peel's secretary instead. M'Naghten was reasonably intelligent and certainly not a raving lunatic, yet his delusions were obvious enough that the judge on the case, Chief Justice Tindal, directed the jury to find M'Naghten not guilty of murder by reason of insanity.

That a man might procure a weapon for the purpose of killing the prime minister, deliberately shoot to death a person whom he mistook for his intended victim, and yet escape the hangman, led to heated controversy. M'Naghten was not the first Englishman to succeed in an insanity plea, but the disconcerting method in his madness and the eminence of his target motivated the House of Lords to submit certain interrogatories to the judges of England. The judges replied with a simple-seeming formula that came to be known as the M'Naghten Rules for the adjudication of the insanity defense. Although the rules' legal standing was dubious, and certainly unique, and debate developed quickly as to what the phrases really meant in practice, the rules continue to define insanity in Britain and, also, in some thirty of the United States:

> . . . to establish a defense on the ground of insanity it must be clearly proved that, at the time of the committing of the act, the party accused was laboring under such a defect of reason, from disease of the mind, as not to know the nature and quality of the act he was doing; or, if he did know it, that he did not know he was doing wrong.

An able-bodied law clerk could not carry in one load all the exegeses of this simple text that have subsequently appeared: scholarly analyses of the intended or proper meaning of "defect of reason," "disease of the mind," "nature and quality," and especially, of course, those really difficult concepts, "know" and "wrong." A sane person knows the nature and quality of the act of homicide both intellectually (to terminate life) and emotionally (as dreadful and abhorrent). If the accused knows in the first sense but not in the second, is that person sane? Is an act wrong if it is against the law; or if it is held to be wrong in the common opinion; or if it is held wrong only because others do not know certain facts known to me; or if, although others consider it wrong, God has ordered me to do it?

A coherent and rational solution to this old problem is much to be desired, and for several reasons. Although they are infrequent, trials involving the insanity defense are protracted and expensive for all concerned. Psychiatry is displayed to bad advantage in the inevitable battle of expert witnesses. Most seriously, public respect for the law itself is injured whenever some obvious scoundrel attempts the insanity defense, even though these attempts very seldom succeed. In Minneapolis recently, a young hoodlum in a stolen car shot the police officer who stopped him for questioning, and then had the public defender register a plea of not guilty by reason of insanity on the grounds that he had been "high" on drugs that day and was therefore not responsible. That such a maneuver is possible might well lead the dead officer's colleagues to find justification for administering their own punishments in the future.

John W. Hinckley, Jr. tried to assassinate President Reagan and almost succeeded; one of his three victims lost a part of his brain that can never be replaced. The act was committed before television cameras and the perpetrator apprehended on the spot, gun in hand. Now, as this article goes to press, Hinckley's trial is in its third expensive week. He has pleaded insanity, and the prosecution is laboring to refute the claim that he was not responsible for his actions. Eminent psychiatrists have testified for both sides, confidently asserting plausible, yet contradictory, opinions. I find it hard to believe that this defense will succeed, but the mere fact that it can be attempted jeopardizes the vital consensus of confidence in the rule of

SOURCE: *The Sciences*, *22*, pp. 11–13, 1982. This article is reprinted by permission of *The Sciences* and is from the August/September 1982 issue. Individual subscriptions are $18.00 per year. Write to The Sciences, 2 East 63rd Street, New York, NY 10021 or call 1-800-THE-NYAS.

law. What if the prosecution blunders on some technicality and the court is forced to find this man not guilty of a crime that millions of citizens witnessed on television? Could the American justice system survive such humiliation?

Alienists have never been happy with the M'Naghten Rules nor with the concept of insanity itself, since it does not correspond to any psychiatric category. Persons who were plainly psychotic have failed the M'Naghten test as, indeed, M'Naghten, who was a paranoid psychotic, probably would have failed it himself had the rules been formulated earlier. A liberalization to include the idea of irresistible impulse has often been urged, sometimes successfully. American courts have tended to be more liberal (that is, more amenable to psychiatric opinion) than the British, beginning as early as 1869, with *New Hampshire* v. *Pike*, in which the appellate court ruled that the defendant should be acquitted if "the killing was the offspring or product of mental disease." Similarly, in a decision now known as the Durham Rule, Judge David Bazelon, in a District of Columbia case, concluded in 1954 that "an accused is not criminally responsible if his unlawful act was the product of mental disease or mental defect."

But many courts, reflecting as they must the general opinion, have resisted such liberalization. Counsel for Robert Pate, on trial in 1850 for the high misdemeanor of striking Queen Victoria with his walking stick, claimed irresistible impulse, but Baron Alderson, presiding, retorted, "A man might say that he picked a pocket from some uncontrollable impulse, and in that case the law would have an uncontrollable impulse to punish him for it."

The Durham Rule seems a perilously slippery slope, for there is probably no crime that, in the psychologist's perspective, would *not* appear to be the product of mental disease or defect. This is easily demonstrated by trying to imagine what category of offender a psychiatrist would reject as mentally healthy and thus outside his jurisdiction. The psychiatrist might say that he or she lacks the facilities necessary for treating this problem, or does not have a treatment, or that the defect that led to the criminal behavior has now spontaneously remitted. But the psychiatrist is committed to the deterministic view that all aberrant behavior is the product of aberrant psychological states or processes that, in principle, could be remedied.

The law's premises are more complicated than psychiatry's. First is the ancient doctrine of just deserts, which probably reflects the need for the King's justice to satisfy the public outrage lest citizens be too tempted to take justice back into their own hands. Second is the principle of deterrence. The miscreant and others who might be similarly tempted must be shown that such behavior will be punished. The deterrent effect equals the severity of the punishment multiplied by the presumed probability of getting caught. Since we are surprisingly inefficient at catching criminals, we try to compensate by punishing more harshly the ones we catch. The third premise of the criminal law is that society should be protected by the segregation of dangerous persons.

Finally, there is the principle of rehabilitation. Here, at least, the law stands shoulder to shoulder with psychiatry but its shoulders have slumped in discouragement in recent years. Rehabilitation does not seem to be working. For every inmate who completes a sentence with newly acquired job skills and a determination to go straight, there seems to be at least one other whose prison experience has so twisted or embittered him that he is now less likely to reform than if he had never been caught in the first place.

In earlier times, concern about the insanity defense centered on the issue of capital punishment. When Eliza Dart, in a fit of postpartum depression, drowned her infant child, hoping thereby to protect it from a sinful world, no reasonable person in Victorian England wanted Dart to hang on the same gibbet with a murderous highwayman. Yet even with the decreasing use of the death sentence, debate on this question remains vigorous, although the insanity defense is actually seldom offered and rarely sustained. Moreover, its success seems frequently to be an academic question from the viewpoint of the accused, since the only difference it makes to the accused is whether the grim institution in which he or she is incarcerated is called a prison or a hospital. A defendant who is plainly psychotic is unlikely now even to come to trial, but instead will be committed to a psychiatric hospital as unfit, by reason of mental illness, to assist in his or her own defense.

Our mistake, perhaps, has been to try to solve a legal problem with a psychiatric formula. The law wants to know who is responsible and who can be considered guilty of a crime. But psychiatry cannot make that distinction, cannot classify this act as determined and, therefore, guiltless, and that act as freely chosen and, therefore, blameworthy. If Dart intended that her child should die, then we must accept that she is guilty of the crime of murder. Defenders of the insanity plea resist this idea, confusing *guilty* ("having committed . . . a delinquency, crime, or sin") with *culpable* ("deserving of punishment"). No doubt it is burdensome to have it ordered that one was guilty of murder, even if one is never punished for it. But it is also burdensome to be mentally ill (or to be murdered, for that matter), and the law cannot undertake to protect us from all the unhappy consequences of our misfortunes. The question of what Dart did or meant to do (*mens rea*) can properly be decided by a jury in the usual way. It is conceivable that psychiatric testimony might be relevant at this stage, but only in exceptional circumstances.

In most cases, the question of mental illness ought to enter only later, after the facts of the case, of who did what to whom, have been decided. Once the defendant has been found guilty, the next step is to determine the proper disposition. Shall we sentence Dart to prison or shall we treat her depression and, when it has lifted, turn her loose? Shall we send Hinckley to the penitentiary for the statutory period, or shall we put him in a security hospital until the doctors are satisfied that he is no longer a menace to the community? These are decisions that a judge, advised by psychiatric experts, can probably arrive at more wisely than a jury can.

Florida has experimented with a bifurcated trial system in which the question of what happened is decided in stage one, while the question of insanity is threshed out by an adversarial process before the same jury in stage two. This would seem merely to prolong the agony without accomplishing any useful reform. Idaho's legislature recently voted to abolish the insanity defense altogether, while permitting the judge to consider evidence of mental illness in deciding on the length and type of sentence. Here one might question the lack of any formal mechanism to ensure that the defendant has been competently examined and that the judge will receive good psychiatric advice.

The defects of both systems might be circumvented by a modification of the two-stage process. If the defendant did the deed and meant to do it (as distinguished from an inadvertence or an accident), then he or she would be found guilty by a jury in stage one. Stage two would be designated as a hearing rather than a trial, and the jury would be replaced by a court-appointed panel of, say, two board-certified psychiatrists, a penologist or parole-board member, a police official (to help squelch police complaints of "coddling"), and one strong-minded lay person. Defense counsel would offer witnesses, including psychiatric experts, but the panel would be permitted to question them directly.

The object of this hearing would be, first, to determine whether the crime was a product of an identifiable mental disorder; if not, sentencing would proceed in the ordinary way. If the defendant is held to have been mentally ill when the crime was committed, the panel would make recommendations as to disposition, with dissenting opinions permitted. The judge would make the final decision, and the court's overriding concern would be the public safety. Should it be concluded that the crime was a result of some treatable disorder, a security hospital could be given the responsibility both to treat the illness and to determine when a cure had been effected and the patient could safely be released. Deranged but untreatable miscreants might be remitted to a hospital for custody rather than treatment, if it were felt that they would be a danger to themselves or others in a prison setting, or that they would continue to be a danger to society if released at the end of the normal prison term.

Let's test this proposal by imagining how it might deal with the trendy insanity defense based on the effects of premenstrual tension. According to a recent *New York Times* report, "Two women walked free from British criminal courts in November after having killed or threatened to kill. They were released after pleading that premenstrual tension had made them act out of character." Since there was no dispute as to the facts in either case, it can be presumed that both women would have pleaded guilty in my jurisdiction, thus avoiding the expenses of the stage-one trial.

Were I sitting on the panel at the stage-two hearing, I would listen sympathetically to expert testimony that, in some women, the hormonal tides preceding menstruation yield such a turmoil of emotion as might compel anyone to violence. I would suggest that the defendant be held in custody for several months of endocrinological study to determine if, in fact, her premenstrual changes were out of the ordinary range. If not, I would recommend the standard sentence for her offense. If the tests were positive, a regimen of monthly progesterone injections or other treatment could be implemented and tested for effectiveness by observing her behavior during, say, a year in a security hospital. On her release, I would recommend indefinite probation during which she would be required to present herself each month for prophylactic treatment. These measures would have no retributive intent but instead would be a reasonable response to the fact that, left to herself, the woman was periodically dangerous.

What about the law's agenda, those hard questions of fair punishment and adequate deterrence? The sense of fairness is most outraged when the client of a clever (and expensive) attorney is found to be "not guilty by reason of insanity." Even in Victorian times, alienists were pointing to defendants' long histories of immoral and violent behavior as evidence of mental disease, leading critics to suggest that previous depravity is a curious basis on which to beg forgiveness for a present offense. In the system recommended here, this sort of thing should never happen.

The question of deterrence concerns whether an onlooker might be led to suppose that he or she, too, could yield to some criminal impulse and yet avoid punishment. One wonders if this ever really happens, whether anyone reading about a successful insanity defense has cold-bloodedly proceeded with some outrage, planning to feign insanity as an escape route. Even if it seldom happens, as I would suppose, the fact that this seems a possibility to the ordinary citizen and imperils respect for the criminal justice system is sufficient cause for concern. Placing the final decision in the hands of the judge rather than the jury would seem to obviate this problem also. No clever lawyer will "get me off" on an insanity plea; if I commit a crime and am discovered, I will be found guilty. If I then suppose that, unassisted by legal technicalities, I can mislead the judge and his or her expert advisers, I am probably mad after all.

DISCUSSION

The differences between Stone and Lykken, like those between most proponents and opponents of the insanity plea, stem largely from a deeper and more fundamental disagreement regarding the free will–determinism issue and its implications for the interface betweeen law and psychiatry. Stone contends that the insanity defense is the exception that "proves the rule of free will." According to Stone, most or all of us intuitively believe that certain individuals should not be held accountable for their criminal actions. We do not perceive these actions as "freely" chosen because they appear to be instigated by forces (such as delusions and hallucinations) outside these individuals' control. Such reasoning implies, of course, that the behaviors of all other individuals, including criminal activities, are freely chosen (see also the Part IV introduction).

In contrast, Lykken does not take a stand on the free will–determinism issue but instead contends that the differing perspectives of the legal and psychiatric systems on this issue pose intractable difficulties for implementation of the insanity defense. Because the assumptions of psychiatry and psychology are almost invariably deterministic (see the introduction to this chapter), says Lykken, it is logically contradictory to ask psychiatric experts to distinguish individuals who are "responsible" for their actions from those who are not. Responsibility presumes the existence of free will, a concept alien to most of psychiatry and psychology.

Stone and Lykken also differ in their views concerning conflicting psychiatric testimony. Stone regards the differing opinions offered by expert witnesses at insanity trials as a necessary and unavoidable, albeit occasionally irritating, consequence of the adversarial U.S. system of justice. As he points out, the problem of contradictory testimony is not unique to psychiatry and can be observed at trials involving experts in other areas of medicine as well as in fields outside medicine, such as engineering. As long as the U.S. legal system insists that all criminal defendants have recourse to a legal advocate, the testimony of psychiatrists hired by the prosecution will frequently conflict with that of psychiatrists hired by the defense. Stone's arguments may not reassure critics who believe that the adversarial nature of the legal system is fundamentally incompatible with the ultimate goal of psychiatric diagnosis: the objective determination of an individual's mental status. As you saw in Chapter 2, psychiatric diagnosis cannot be meaningful without adequate levels of interrater reliability. Yet the adversarial nature of the legal system seems almost guaranteed to produce low levels of interrater reliability.

Lykken, in contrast, proposes to circumvent the difficulties posed by the adversarial system of justice with an impartial, court-appointed panel of experts—including psychiatrists—in a second-stage hearing. Because the question of the defendant's guilt or innocence would already be decided (without psychiatric testimony) in the initial trial, the need to call expert witnesses who are partial to either prosecution or defense would be obviated. Although Lykken's suggestion would not, of course, eliminate conflicting expert testimony, it would effectively ensure that whatever differences of opinion remain are a reflection of legitimate diagnostic disagreements rather than of preexisting biases engendered by the adversarial system of law. The principal barriers to Lykken's creative proposal appear to be logistical rather than logical: It would presumably require several psychiatric expert witnesses to be at each court's disposal.

Both Stone's and Lykken's articles were written prior to the Hinckley verdict (although, ironically, they both appeared in the same year as the verdict), which signaled a dramatic turning point in the history of the insanity defense. What changes in the status of the insanity defense have occurred in the aftermath of this controversial decision? Four developments seem especially likely to remain the focus of future debate. First, as noted in the introduction, the Insanity Defense Reform Law of 1984, which is now in effect in all federal courts, marked a turn away from the broader guidelines of the Brawner rule and toward the narrower M'Naughten guidelines. The M'Naughten rule is based almost exclusively on cognitive factors—in particular, individuals' capacity to understand right from wrong. In contrast, the Brawner rule is based on both cognitive factors and volitional factors (the latter defined as individuals' capacity to control their behavior). Largely in response to critics who charged that the assessment of volitional factors was considerably less reliable than was the assessment of cognitive factors, the Insanity Defense Reform Law abolished the volitional component of the insanity defense. Some observers believe, however, that this decision was motivated more by political considerations—a perceived need to respond to the public outcry over the Hinckley verdict by tightening the standards of the insanity defense—than by empirical data. In fact, research has shown that the assessment of the volitional component of the insanity defense is just as reliable as the assessment of the cognitive component (Rogers, 1987). Moreover, it is unlikely that the Hinckley verdict would have been different under the newer and more restrictive insanity defense standards. The principal basis for Hinckley's acquittal was his inability to comprehend the nature and quality of his actions rather than his capacity to control them (Rogers, 1987; Stone, 1984).

The second development is that the Insanity Defense Reform Law shifted the burden of proof from the prosecution to the defense. During the Hinckley trial, for example, the prosecution was required to demonstrate beyond a reasonable doubt that Hinckley was sane. Requiring the defense to demonstrate, with "clear and convincing evidence," that their defendant is insane is a subtle but not trivial attempt to raise the standards required for a successful insanity defense. It is still too early, however, to gauge the ultimate impact of this change on the prevalence of insanity acquittals.

The third development since the Hinckley trial is increasing interest in a new verdict, **guilty but mentally ill** (GBMI), which is an attempt to acknowledge the potential effects of mental illness on criminal behaviors while still holding individuals accountable for these behaviors. The proponents of this verdict argued that it would dramatically reduce the number of insanity acquittals. The GBMI verdict, unlike the not guilty by reason of insanity (NGRI) verdict, essentially eliminates the distinction between what Thomas Szasz (1963) has referred to as descriptive and ascriptive responsibility. **Descriptive responsibility** simply refers to whether the individual has committed the criminal act, whereas **ascriptive responsibility** refers to whether the individual who has committed the criminal act should be held morally accountable for it. The NGRI verdict distinguishes between these two forms of responsibility: Defendants judged insane are held to be descriptively, but not ascriptively, responsible for their illegal behaviors. In contrast, the GBMI verdict, like Lykken's two-stage proposal, holds defendants both descriptively and ascriptively responsible.

The GBMI verdict, which was introduced in 1975 in Michigan and passed in a number of states shortly after the Hinckley decision, permits defendants to be found guilty of criminal acts and sentenced to prison but to receive psychiatric treatment during their incarceration. In some cases, defendants convicted under this verdict are initially treated in psychiatric hospitals and complete the remainder of their sentence in prison (Simon & Aaronson, 1988). Thus, the GBMI verdict eliminates the insanity verdict while ostensibly preserving defendants' rights to have their psychiatric status considered in their punishment. Nevertheless, the GBMI verdict has been criticized on the grounds that it is a "counterfeit category created for the explicit purpose of misleading [jurors]" (Tanay, 1992, p. 573). Specifically, some authors maintain that this verdict differs only in name from the traditional guilty verdict and that it simply serves to funnel individuals who would otherwise be psychiatrically hospitalized into the correctional system. These criticisms appear to have at least some empirical foundation. Research has generally shown that individuals who receive GBMI verdicts frequently do not receive adequate psychiatric care while in prison (Keilitz & Fulton, 1984). Moreover, the GBMI verdict has apparently not led to a decrease in the number of NGRI acquittals (Simon & Aaronson, 1988) and has thus not accomplished one of its primary goals.

The fourth development since the Hinckley trial is that the Insanity Defense Reform Law prohibited expert witnesses from offering an opinion on the so-called **ultimate issue**—the question of the defendant's sanity or insanity. (This prohibition is known as the **ultimate issue rule.**) Recall that sanity and insanity are legal, not scientific, concepts that are premised on the notion of criminal "responsibility." Opponents of the ultimate issue rule maintain that it improperly limits expert witnesses from providing information regarding relevant issues about which they possess expertise, such as the defendant's capacity to understand right from wrong (Goldstein, 1989). Certain questions relevant to the defendant's sanity or insanity, opponents claim, are not entirely outside the scope of psychiatry or psychology. In contrast, proponents of the ultimate issue rule argue that permitting expert witnesses to testify on this issue blurs the crucial boundary between law and science. They contend that expert witnesses should be allowed to testify concerning the defendant's probable mental state at the time of the crime but should stop short of rendering judgment on an issue that is more appropriately left to juries. The American Psychiatric Association (1982), which favors the ultimate issue rule, framed this argument in the following way:

> When . . . "ultimate issue" questions are formulated by the law and put to the expert witness [the witness] is required to make a leap in logic. [The witness] no longer addresses himself [or herself] to medical concepts but instead must infer or intuit what is in fact unspeakable, namely, the probable relationship between medical concepts and legal or moral constructs such as free will. (p. 14)

Given the formidable conceptual and procedural complexities surrounding the NGRI defense, it is perhaps not surprising that three states—Montana, Idaho, and Utah—have abolished it entirely. Nevertheless, it is clear that the insanity defense will remain a longstanding, if not permament, fixture of the American legal system. How well the controversies associated with this defense can be resolved will depend largely on how well the conflicting presuppositions of the legal and psychiatric systems—particularly free will and determinism, respectively—can be reconciled.

QUESTIONS TO STIMULATE DISCUSSION

1. Judging from what you have read about the Hinckley verdict, do you believe that the jury made the appropriate decision given the insanity standard they were operating under (the Brawner rule)? Defend your answer.
2. Of the existing insanity standards discussed here (irresistible impulse, M'Naughten, Durham, Brawner), which do you find most reasonable? Why? What alternatives to the existing insanity rules might remedy the shortcomings of these rules? (Note: You can answer these questions even if you are opposed to the use of the insanity defense.)
3. The irresistible impulse standards and similar "volitional" insanity standards have generated substantial controversy. For which psychopathological conditions or states, if any, might such rules be justified?
4. Do you agree with Stone that the insanity defense does not send a permissive message to criminals? Explain your answer.

5. Do you believe that Lykken's two-stage proposal would effectively address most of the criticisms directed toward the NGRI defense? Or would it create problems of its own? Explain.
6. Do you agree with the ultimate issue rule? What do you view as the potential advantages and disadvantages (that is, dangers) of allowing expert witnesses to express opinions regarding the defendant's sanity or insanity?
7. If the insanity defense were abolished, how would the criminal justice system be affected? How would abolition of the insanity defense affect the mental health system?

SUGGESTIONS FOR FURTHER READING

Caplan, L. (1984). *The insanity defense and the trial of John W. Hinckley, Jr.* Boston: David R. Godine.
Caplan provides a detailed and fascinating account of the Hinckley trial and its aftermath. Chapter 2 contains a good discussion of criticisms and defenses of the insanity plea.

Halpern, A. L. (1984). Commentary: Further comments on the insanity defense in the aftermath of the Hinckley trial. *Psychiatric Quarterly, 56,* 62–69.
Halpern reviews the history of different perspectives on the insanity defense and contends that its abolition would benefit the public, criminal defendants, the law-abiding mentally ill, and the psychiatric and legal professions. He concludes that "the insanity defense is a tribute to our hypocrisy rather than to our morality" (p. 68).

Maeder, T. (1985). *Crime and madness: The origins and evolution of the insanity defense.* New York: Harper & Row.
Maeder reviews the history of the insanity defense through its origins in early English trials to its modern variants, including the guilty but mentally ill plea. He also discusses attacks on the insanity defense and recent efforts to abolish it.

National Commission on the Insanity Defense. (1983). *Myths and realities: A report of the National Commission on the Insanity Defense.* Arlington, VA: National Mental Health Association.
This brief and highly readable report begins with a history of the insanity defense and proceeds to debunk a number of popular misconceptions about it (for example, that the successful use of the insanity defense is frequent and that most insanity trials involve contradictory testimony by expert witnesses). The report concludes with 12 recommendations regarding the insanity defense.

Pasewark, R. A., & Pantle, M. L. (1979). Insanity plea: Legislator's view. *American Journal of Psychiatry, 136,* 222–223.
The authors found that state legislators in Wyoming grossly overestimated the frequency of insanity defenses in their state. Legislators estimated that, of a total of 21,012 felony convictions in Wyoming from 1970 to 1972, 4458 individuals pled not guilty by reason of insanity (NGRI) and 1794 of these pleas were successful. In fact, during this period only 102 individuals pled NGRI, and only 1 plea was successful.

Phillips, M. R., Wolf, A. S., & Coons, D. J. (1988). Psychiatry and the criminal justice system: Testing the myths. *American Journal of Psychiatry, 145,* 605–610.
The authors argue that a number of states have based their policies regarding the mentally ill on distorted perceptions of the crucial facts. Among their findings: In the state of Alaska, a successful insanity plea occurred in only 0.1% or less of all criminal cases. In addition, they report that, popular misconceptions notwithstanding, psychiatric expert witnesses agreed on key legal questions in 79% of cases.

Rogers, R. (1987). APA's position on the insanity defense: Empiricism versus emotionalism. *American Psychologist, 42,* 840–848.
Rogers reviews the empirical bases underlying insanity proposals by the American Psychological Association and American Bar Association in response to Hinckley's acquittal and finds them wanting. He outlines key empirical questions that need to be addressed before an informed decision on the insanity plea can be reached. He places particular emphasis on research concerning the cognitive and volitional prongs of the insanity defense.

Rowe, J. (1984, May). Why liberals should hate the insanity defense. *Washington Monthly, 16,* 39–46. (Reprinted in Slife, B., & Rubinstein, J. [1990]. *Taking sides: Clashing views on controversial psychological issues* [6th ed.]. Guilford, CT: Dushkin Publishing Group.)
Rowe contends that, because almost all individuals who commit crimes have psychological difficulties of one sort or another, the distinction between insanity and commonplace emotional problems is hopelessly fuzzy. Like Lykken, he argues that the question of defendants' guilt must be separated from that of their appropriate sentencing.

Sadoff, R. L. (1992). In defense of the insanity defense. *Psychiatric Annals, 22,* 556–560.
Sadoff reviews the history of, and the logic underlying, the insanity defense and defends it against a number of commonly made accusations, such as the problem of conflicting expert testimony. He concludes that the misuses of the insanity plea do not justify its abandonment and that this plea is needed to relieve severely mentally ill or mentally retarded individuals of criminal responsibility.

Simon, R. J., & Aaronson, D. E. (1988). *The insanity defense: A critical assessment of law and policy in the post-Hinckley era.* New York: Praeger.
This book contains detailed discussions of a number of issues relevant to the contemporary use of the insanity defense, including the use of expert witnesses, the guilty but mentally ill defense, and insanity defenses in other countries. The first two chapters provide a comprehensive history of various insanity tests, including the Insanity Defense Reform Act of 1984, which was passed by the U.S. Congress largely in response to Hinckley's acquittal.

Tanay, E. (1992). The verdict with two names. *Psychiatric Annals, 22,* 571–573.
The author takes aim at the recently devised guilty but mentally ill (GBMI) defense, arguing that it is not a genuine alter-

native to the NGRI defense. Instead, he maintains, the GBMI defense has resulted in a diversion of mentally ill criminals from psychiatric settings into the criminal justice system.

REFERENCES

American Law Institute. (1962). *Model penal code: Proposed official draft*. Philadelphia: Author.

American Psychiatric Association. (1982). *Statement on the insanity defense*. Washington, DC: Author.

Bootzin, R. R., Acorella, J. R., & Alloy, L. B. (1993) *Abnormal psychology: Current perspectives* (6th ed.). New York: McGraw Hill.

Davison, G. C., & Neale, J. M. (1994). *Abnormal psychology* (6th ed.). New York: Wiley.

Goldstein, R. L. (1989). The psychiatrist's guide to right and wrong: Part IV. The insanity defense and the ultimate issue rule. *Bulletin of the American Academy of Psychiatry and Law, 17*, 269–281.

Keilitz, I., & Fulton, J. (1984). *The insanity defense and its alternatives: A guide for policy makers*. Williamsburg, VA: National Center for State Courts, Institute on Mental Disability and the Law.

Rogers, R. (1987). APA's position on the insanity defense: Empiricism versus emotionalism. *American Psychologist, 42*, 840–848.

Simon, R. J., & Aaronson, D. E. (1988). *The insanity defense: A critical assessment of law and policy in the post-Hinckley era*. New York: Praeger.

Stone, A. A. (1984). *Law, psychiatry, and morality*. Washington, DC: American Psychiatric Press.

Szasz, T. S. (1963). *Law, liberty, and psychiatry*. New York: Macmillan.

Tanay, E. (1992). The verdict with two names. *Psychiatric Annals, 22*, 571–573.

CHAPTER

18

Is mental illness unrelated to violence?

PRO Teplin, L. A. (1985). The criminality of the mentally ill: A dangerous misconception. *American Journal of Psychiatry, 142*, 593–599.

CON Monahan, J. (1992). Mental disorder and violent behavior: Perceptions and evidence. *American Psychologist, 47*, 511–521.

OVERVIEW OF THE CONTROVERSY: Linda A. Teplin reports the findings from a study that she claims demonstrates an absence of an association between severe mental disorder and criminality and concludes that the widespread belief that the mentally ill are at heightened risk for violence is a pernicious myth. John Monahan reviews the literature on the relationship between mental illness and violence and argues that recent investigations lend strong support to the assertion that a variety of mental disorders are associated with a modest but consistent increase in the risk of violence.

CONTEXT OF THE PROBLEM

The violence of the mentally ill has commanded increasing public interest over the past several decades. The considerable publicity about such murderers as David Berkowitz ("Son of Sam"), Mark David Chapman (who killed John Lennon), and Jeffrey Dahmer, as well as such would-be murderers as John Hinckley, Jr. (see Chapter 17), have reinforced the widespread belief that violence is frequently accompanied by serious mental disorder. Popular films like *The Silence of the Lambs*, *Fatal Attraction*, and *In the Line of Fire*, which feature mentally disturbed (or, in the loose and imprecise vernacular often favored by the popular press, "deranged," "demented," or "psychopathic") individuals who engage in violence, have further contributed to this public perception. As Monahan points out in the article in this chapter, the notion that mental illness and violence are statistically associated has also been present from at least Greek and Roman times onward, as well as in both Western and non-Western cultures. But is this correlation real or illusory?

Before proceeding further, I should point out that simply because most individuals believe two characteristics are correlated in no way implies that that they are necessarily correlated in reality. We can be easily fooled by our preconceptions about the association between variables. In an ingenious series of studies that should be mandatory reading for all serious students of clinical psychology, Loren Chapman and Jean Chapman demonstrated that individuals readily form **illusory correlations** between attributes that are completely unrelated (Chapman & Chapman, 1967, 1969). Specifically, Chapman and Chapman asked subjects to estimate the extent to which certain signs on the Draw-a-Person (DAP) Test—a projective test in which respondents are asked to a draw a person in any way they wish—were associated with certain personality characteristics. Subjects were shown a series of fabricated DAP protocols containing certain features (such as large eyes or a big head), along with a description of the personality characteristics of the individual who purportedly produced each drawing (for example, paranoid or concerned about masculinity). The subjects were then asked to estimate the extent to which these features and personality characteristics co-occurred. Unbeknownst to the subjects, there was no statistical association whatsoever between the DAP features and the personality characteristics; these two variables had been paired randomly.

Nevertheless, subjects perceived certain DAP features to be strongly associated with certain personality traits. Interestingly, their errors seemed to correspond closely to individuals' implicit "theories" regarding which features go together with which personality traits. For example, subjects reported that individuals who produced DAP protocols with large eyes tended to be paranoid and that individuals who produced DAP protocols with large genitals tended to be concerned about their masculinity. Moreover, Chapman and Chapman found that these illusory correlations persisted in spite of strong and often overwhelming evidence to the contrary—in some cases, despite evidence that the features and personality traits were actually negatively correlated.

Chapman and Chapman's results suggest that individuals' preconceptions regarding the associations among characteristics can profoundly influence their estimates of the actual magnitude of these associations. The implications of their findings for the mental illness–violence debate cannot be overlooked: Individuals may perceive a correlation between mental illness and violence because this correlation conforms to their stereotypes of mentally ill individuals. Playing devil's advocate, however, one might argue that this interpretation begs the question. How do these stereotypes originate?

The question of whether the mentally ill are at increased risk for violence has a number of important social policy implications:

- As discussed in Chapter 17, the insanity defense is sometimes used to exculpate defendants from criminal responsibility for violent acts. The implicit assumption behind this practice is that certain psychological symptoms—particularly delusions, hallucinations, and other psychotic features—render individuals susceptible to criminal behavior.
- As Monahan notes in his article, mental health professionals and parole officials are frequently called on to predict whether patients and criminals are at risk for subsequent violence and to use these predictions to decide whether such individuals should be released into the community. The legal system has often assumed that mental health experts can accurately predict violence, largely because knowledge of individuals' psychiatric symptoms can presumably be used to make informed judgments about their risk for violence. As it turns out, however, experts' predictions regarding violence tend to be extremely poor (Monahan, 1981), largely because violence, although a societal problem of staggering proportions, is quite rare. Of course, one act of violence is too many, and the rate of violent crime in the United States is disturbingly high. The key point is that violent crimes, such as homicide, are statistically infrequent in the population at large. For reasons that I will not elaborate on here, rare events tend to be more difficult to predict than common events (Meehl & Rosen, 1955). Nevertheless, this fact has not prevented individuals from suing psychiatrists who have failed to correctly predict the violence of recently released mental patients (Appelbaum, 1988). Although some psychiatrists can probably be faulted for not erring sufficiently on the side of caution in their decisions to release potentially dangerous patients, in most cases the violent acts of psychiatric patients appear to be relatively "random" events—that is, occurrences that are exceptionally difficult to predict given our current (and rather primitive) state of knowledge.
- As you will learn in Chapter 19, one of the principal criteria in most states for the involuntary (civil) commitment of psychiatric patients is presumed dangerousness toward others. If the proneness of the severely mentally ill toward violence has been exaggerated, then many psychiatrists have probably been overly zealous in initiating commitment proceedings for psychiatric patients.
- The violence of the mentally ill has become an increasing focus of attention in many major American cities. You may be familiar with the case of Larry Hogue, the homeless man featured on CBS's television show *60 Minutes*, who for years physically and verbally harassed and threatened the citizens of West 96th Street in New York City until he was involuntarily committed. In another case, an 80-year-old New York City woman was bludgeoned to death in 1993 by a man who had been released from psychiatric hospitals twice in the 2 months preceding the murder (Lyall, 1993). In response to these and other highly publicized cases, New York City initiated a program in 1993 to send mental health workers into homeless shelters to identify mentally ill residents judged to be potentially dangerous and to initiate their commitment to state mental hospitals if necessary. This policy, although strongly supported by many New York City citizens and politicians, was vehemently attacked by both civil liberties organizations and advocates for the homeless and mentally ill (Lyall, 1993).

The debate on these controversial issues would be better informed by more accurate data on the mental illness–violence association.

THE CONTROVERSY: Teplin vs. Monahan

Teplin

Linda Teplin first reviews the literature on the relationship between mental illness and criminality. According to Teplin, recent studies suggest that previously reported differences in the rates of violence between the mentally ill and the nonmentally ill are attributable to sampling differences, such as demographic variables and previous criminality. Nevertheless, she notes, this conclusion must be tempered by the fact that most investigators have relied on official arrest records as indicators of crime and prior hospitalizations as indicators of mental disorder. Teplin then reports the design and results of a study conducted in a large U.S. city in which police-citizen encounters were meticulously observed over a 14-month period. In these encounters, citizens were rated as either severely mentally ill or not, using a standard set of criteria. Teplin reports that the severely mentally disordered were not significantly more likely to be involved in either violent or nonviolent crimes compared with the non-severely mentally disordered, although the former were somewhat more likely to be suspects. She concludes that the widely held stereotype of the mentally ill individual as dangerous is not warranted and that this stereotype is partly a consequence of misleading media portrayals of the mentally ill.

Monahan

John Monahan points out that beliefs regarding the relationship between mental illness and violence are important for two major reasons: These beliefs have significant implications for legal and mental health policies, and they influence our attitudes toward the mentally ill. Monahan then reviews historical, cross-cultural, and contemporary American perceptions of the mental illness–violence relationship and contends that the belief that the mentally ill are at increased risk for violence has been remarkably long-standing and pervasive. In stark contrast, however, most advocates for the mentally ill and many researchers have argued strenuously against the existence of this association. Monahan proceeds to discuss the evidence relevant to the mental illness–violence association from two sources: studies of the prevalence of violence among the mentally ill and studies of the prevalence of mental illness among the violent. He concludes that mental illness has consistently been associated with a modest increase in the rate of violence. In particular, Monahan maintains, the presence of psychotic features, such as delusions and hallucinations, is a consistent risk factor for violence. Monahan concludes by discussing four implications of the finding that mental illness and violence are associated. He cautions, however, that this finding does not justify increased restrictions on the rights of the mentally ill or imply that media portrayals of violence among the mentally ill are accurate.

KEY CONCEPTS AND TERMS

deinstitutionalization Massive program initiated in the 1960s to dramatically decrease the number of patients housed in mental hospitals. Deinstitutionalization has probably contributed to a substantial increase in the rate of homelessness.

Diagnostic Interview Schedule (DIS) Structured psychiatric interview that can be used by lay interviewers to establish DSM-III diagnoses of Axis I disorders.

external validity Extent to which the results of a study can be generalized to other situations.

PREVIEW QUESTIONS

1. According to Teplin, what do recent data on the criminality of former psychiatric patients indicate?
2. What methodological shortcomings identified by Teplin render the above conclusion tentative?
3. What is the design of Teplin's study, and what are her principal findings?
4. What does Teplin conclude regarding the commonly held belief that mentally ill individuals are prone to violent crime? What are her conjectures concerning the origins of this belief?
5. According to Monahan, why are beliefs concerning the violence of the mentally ill important?
6. According to Monahan, what is known regarding historical, cross-cultural, and modern American perceptions of the mental illness–violence association?
7. According to Monahan, what two major research approaches can be used to study the mental illness–violence association?
8. According to Monahan, what general conclusions can be drawn from the literature based on the two major research approaches? What factor seems to best predict the rates of violence among psychiatric patients?
9. According to Monahan, what are four major implications of the literature on the mental illness–violence association?

LINDA A. TEPLIN

The criminality of the mentally ill: A dangerous misconception

In recent years there has been a substantial increase in the number of mentally disordered persons residing in the community (1). This increase is a result of a number of complex factors including deinstitutionalization, more restrictive laws regarding commitment, and fiscal reductions in mental health programs (2). Unfortunately, the successful reentry of the mentally disordered person into the community may be hampered by the long-standing stereotype of the mentally ill individual as being dangerous (3–10).

A crucial issue is whether the stereotype of the mentally ill as dangerous and, therefore, more prone to commit crime is warranted. One way to verify this stereotype empirically is to observe police-citizen encounters (both police-initiated contact and citizen requests for service) and tabulate the relative frequency and types of crimes committed by persons exhibiting signs of serious mental disorder with that of non-mentally-disordered individuals. This report, based on quantified data from an observational study of 1,072 police-citizen encounters, presents the results of such an investigation and, in so doing, provides needed data on the relative criminality of the mentally ill.

PREVIOUS RESEARCH

With relatively few exceptions, the bulk of research in this area has attempted to verify the relative dangerousness of the psychiatric patient by comparing the arrest rates of former mental patients with those of the general population. Early investigations found arrest rates among former mental patients to be either lower than or equivalent to those in the general population (11–14). In contrast, most of the later investigations (15–21) found a higher arrest rate among formerly hospitalized persons than in the general population.

Steadman et al. (20, 21) offer an intriguing explanation for this apparent inconsistency over time. They found that the number of mental patients with prior arrests has increased substantially over the years and posited that the apparently higher arrest rate among former mental patients is a result of a marked change in the clientele of state hospitals (20). They pursued this line of investigation by comparing the rearrest rates of patients with and without criminal records (21). The results were striking: those patients without arrest records (approximately three-quarters of their sample) were arrested infrequently, i.e., at virtually the same rate as the general population. In contrast, patients who had multiple arrests before their psychiatric hospitalization were more likely to be rearrested after their hospital discharge. They concluded that it was not prior criminality per se that resulted in mental patients' being arrested more often than nonmental patients but the increased numbers of patients with criminal records entering psychiatric facilities. The lack of relationship between prior hospitalization and subsequent arrest was replicated in another investigation using an offender population (22). In that study, Steadman and Ribner found no relationship between the existence of a prior mental hospitalization and subsequent arrests made within 18 months after the offenders were released. To date, the only study finding higher arrest rates among former mental patients with no prior arrest record is an investigation conducted in California by Sosowsky (23). Although he reported arrest rates for former mental patients that were more than five times those of the general population, the study has been severely criticized for using inappropriate baseline data (24), thus rendering Sosowsky's conclusions somewhat suspect.

In sum, the latest research literature indicates that the apparently greater criminality of former mental patients found in recent studies can be attributed to a difference in the characteristics of the samples used in the earlier and the more current investigations (20). When samples are matched for demographic factors and prior criminal history, there is no consistent evidence that the true prevalence rate of criminal behavior among former mental patients exceeds the true prevalence rate of criminal behavior among the general population (24). However, while the logic of this argument is compelling, the

SOURCE: *American Journal of Psychiatry*, *142*(5), pp. 593–599, May 1985.

conclusion that the mentally ill are no more prone to crime is rendered problematic by several methodological limitations of the previous research.

Type of Data

With relatively few exceptions (25), previous investigators have largely relied on official arrest-rate statistics as a measure of criminal behavior. This procedure, whereby data can be efficiently collected on a large number of cases, was necessitated by the current state of knowledge in the area. Unfortunately, the value of such archival information is compromised by three basic problems.

First, although arrest rates are one important index of "true" criminal behavior (24), this operationalization has a serious limitation. By using arrest as the sole indicator of "crime," such studies eliminate those "truly" criminal incidents that result in the presence of the police but do not culminate in an arrest. Criminological research indicates that, even in situations in which criminal acts have occurred, informal dispositions predominate and arrest is a statistically rare event (26–28). As a consequence, studies based on arrest rates capture but a fraction of those "crimes" that occur and thus severely underrepresent the "true" prevalence of criminal behavior. What is needed is a data collection plan that captures a greater proportion of criminal events.

Second, the value of arrest-rate statistics is further compromised by the fact that arrests are by no means a random sample of all criminal events. The decision to arrest is the result of a complex discretionary process in which the commission of a crime is only one determining factor. Again, this is substantiated in the criminological literature. For example, arrest decisions have been found to be related to the prior arrest record of the suspect (29,30), the perceived helplessness of the citizen (31), and the mental status of the suspect (32). The fact that noncriminological variables may intrude into the decision to arrest may result in a severe sampling bias in studies using arrest-rate statistics. For example, the finding of Steadman et al. (20) that arrest rates vary for former mental patients with and without a previous arrest record may be less a function of the lesser criminality of mental patients than of the apparent inclination of the police to arrest prior offenders.

Finally, when one is using official statistics, the category of crime may have only a vague resemblance to the actual nature of the criminal event. For example, domestic disputes, which often involve assault or battery, rarely result in an arrest for either of these crimes. If an arrest occurs (in itself a rare event), the charge is most often "disorderly conduct," a lesser offense which has the function of temporarily removing the offender from the scene of conflict (28).

In sum, arrest rates cannot be equated with the commission or noncommission of a crime, nor can the type of charge be taken to reflect the actual nature of the criminal event. As a consequence, relying on arrest rate statistics as the sole indicator of "true" criminal behavior is likely to result in a biased sample of "crimes." The matter is further complicated by the fact that the direction of this bias is unknown. On the one hand, mentally disordered persons may be more likely to be arrested than the non-mentally-ill for similar offenses, particularly in situations where there is a paucity of alternative dispositions available to the officer (2). This would have the effect of making the mentally ill appear to be more criminal (i.e., have a higher arrest rate) than they "really" are. Alternatively, studies using arrest rates may underestimate the amount of crime committed by the mentally ill, particularly since those with a history of previous hospitalizations are often rehospitalized rather than arrested (5). Clearly, what is needed to assess the relative criminality of the mentally ill is a data base encompassing a more representative sample of criminal offenses than do arrest-rate statistics.

Type of Sample

Virtually all investigations have used prior hospitalization as the sole indicator of mental disorder. Moreover, with the exception of one study of prior offenders (22), all investigations have restricted their samples to persons who have been hospitalized in a state institution. There are two problems inherent in this sampling procedure.

First, if only persons from state hospitals are included, the sample, by definition, eliminates private patients. Monahan and Steadman (24) point out that this sampling strategy biases the results in the direction of finding greater criminality among former mental patients. They reason that rates of criminal behavior might be expected to be higher for former state hospital patients than for the entire group of formerly hospitalized individuals (i.e., those in both public and private hospitals). Persons treated in state hospitals tend to be of a lower social class than those treated as outpatients or in private facilities, and many studies find a correlation between criminal behavior and lower social class (24).

Second, this rather restrictive sampling strategy excludes those mentally ill persons who, due to a lack of sophistication or community resources or to pure happenstance, are not given inpatient treatment. Here the problem is one of external validity; it would be desirable to extend the findings of the previous research to samples other than an inpatient population. What is needed is to base the operationalization of mental disorder less on treatment (i.e., former mental patients) than on the broader indicators of mental illness.

In conclusion, what is needed to move beyond the previous research literature is a study designed so as to avoid the aforementioned problems inherent in using arrest-rate statistics and restrictive sampling criteria. A logical extension of the body of research in this area is to focus on the *initial* point in the criminal justice system—the police-citizen encounter. In this way, we may ascertain the actual frequency of criminal acts committed by mentally disordered persons, as well as compare the relative prevalence of crimes committed by persons exhibiting signs of mental disorder with baseline data (i.e., non-mentally-disordered individuals). In so doing, this report presents additional evidence needed to ascertain the relative criminality of mentally disordered persons.

METHOD

The data used in this report were part of a larger research effort that examined police handling of the mentally ill. The overall investigation included a large-scale observational study of everyday police activity in order to observe first-hand their involvement with mentally disordered persons. To this end, police officers in a large northern city with a Standard Metropolitan Area population of more than 1 million were observed in their everyday interactions with citizens for 2,200 hours over a 14-month period during 1980–1981; 283 randomly selected officers were included. This data base is also ideal for examining the presence of mental disorder vis-à-vis the relative frequency of criminal acts and of incidents that require the presence of the police.

Observers included myself and five clinical psychology graduate students (three men and two women). Observations were conducted during all hours of the day; evenings and weekends were oversampled in order to obtain a maximum of data within a minimum amount of time. Data were collected in two busy urban police precincts that included residents ranging from the lowest socioeconomic level to the very wealthy. These two precincts were judged to be typical of this city as well as of any large northern urban area. All types of police-citizen interactions were observed, irrespective of any mental health component. Such a procedure was necessary to obtain data on situations not related to mental health for use as baseline comparisons.

Although a standardized mode of assessment to test for the presence of mental disorder would have been preferable, the naturalistic setting of the research obviously precluded making in-depth streetcorner psychiatric examinations. In view of the limitations imposed by the naturalistic setting, the presence of mental disorder was ascertained by the fieldworker by use of a symptom checklist that listed the characteristics of severe mental disorder, e.g., confusion/disorientation; withdrawal/unresponsiveness; paranoid, inappropriate, or bizarre speech and/or behavior; and self-destructive behaviors. Thus, criminal behavior per se was not defined as being indicative of mental disorder, despite the fact that it is included in *DSM-III* as a symptom of sociopathy (*DSM-III* diagnosis 301.70). The focus was on identifying those persons suffering from the more severe forms of mental illness such as schizophrenia and major affective disorder. A person was defined as being mentally disordered if he or she possessed at least one of the above-mentioned traits and was also given a global rating indicating the presence of severe mental disorder by the fieldworker. Both the presence of traits and the global rating were necessary in order to avoid categorizing persons as being mentally ill when, in fact, they were merely exhibiting bizarre or unusual behavior. Thus, the environmental context and a number of extrapsychiatric cues were taken into account by the fieldworkers when making these judgments. An example will clarify the need for this procedure.

A street person who was found by police to be loudly shouting and running down the street naked on a cold night in January would be coded as "mentally disordered." However, similar behaviors exhibited on a warm June evening by a group of drunken college students would have been recognized as being simply bizarre, albeit within the range of "normality." The high reliability of this measure (greater than 95%) is probably due to the fact that all fieldworkers were students in a doctoral program in clinical psychology and had received extensive training in conventional psychiatric assessment techniques as part of their graduate training.

To ensure that this measure accurately discriminated between persons who did and did not exhibit signs of serious mental disorder, I conducted a separate validity study. Using a sample of 61 randomly selected jail detainees, I compared the results of the measure used in the present investigation with those generated by a standard diagnostic instrument, the NIMH [National Institute of Mental Health] Diagnostic Interview Schedule (DIS). The validity study involved diagnosing the 61 subjects as being "severely mentally disordered" or "not severely disordered" by both the DIS and our specially devised observational measure. The observational measure was recorded after a brief period of interaction (approximately 5–10 minutes), an amount of time which would approximate that which the observer would have with a person during a police-citizen encounter. Subsequently, the 61 jail detainees were interviewed using the DIS. There was 93.4% agreement between the observational measure and the DIS as to the presence or absence of severe mental disorder (psychosis). The results of two statistical tests indicate that the two measures are highly correlated; Fisher's exact test, $p < .001$; Kendall's $\tau - \beta = .739$. The strong relationship between our observational measure and the DIS confirms the validity of our instrument in detecting the presence of psychosis. Thus, the results of this validity study indicate that the categories generated by our observational instrument (severely disordered/nondisordered) are a fairly reliable substitute for conventional assessment techniques in assessing the presence or absence of current severe mental disorder.

For the purpose of minimizing evaluation apprehension on the part of the police officer, use of a tape recorder and extensive note taking were not permitted during the observations. The apparent lack of an obvious formal data collection procedure appeared to enhance cooperation between the police officer and the observer. After the first hour or so of observation, most officers tended to accept the fieldworker as a quasi-peer, often sharing their insights into street life and human nature with the observer.

To facilitate recollection of the data for subsequent transcription, fieldworkers were allowed to make a list of all the police-citizen encounters that took place during the observational period. A sample list might read: "1) 9:20 p.m., shoplifting at drug store, 2) 10:15 p.m., disturbance in schoolyard, Washington Elementary School," and so on. This list was later used by the fieldworker to facilitate data transcription. Data recording was conducted by later coding the objective characteristics of the encounter according to an instrument specifically developed for this purpose, the incident coding form. This instrument was designed to record the concrete behaviors and descriptive categories central to all aspects of the police-citizen encounter. In an extensive pilot test before the data collection began, interrater reliability values exceeded 97% for the coded information, including items concerning the presence of mental disorder. An incident coding form was completed for every encounter between a police officer and a citizen that involved at least three verbal exchanges. In order to maximize interobserver reliability, all fieldworkers were given 250 hours of training over a 3-month period, using both videotapes and field situations. In addition, reliability was subsequently monitored through periodic spot-checks.

Overall, 1,072 police-citizen encounters involving 2,122 citizens were observed and coded. Since the focus of the investigation was on the relative criminality of the mentally ill, data on 310 traffic citations (e.g., parking tickets, moving traffic violations) involving 433 citizens were omitted from the analyses. The size and breadth of our data base make it an appropriate vehicle for assessing the frequency with which apparently mentally disordered persons become involved in the kinds of situations that result in the presence of the police.

RESULTS

Overall, police encounters with mentally disordered persons were a relatively rare event; of the 2,122 persons involved with police, only 85 (4%) exhibited signs of serious mental disorder. A major question is whether persons suffering from mental disorder were predominantly suspects or victims of crimes. Table 1 shows that the presence of mental disorder was significantly related to the role of the citizen ($\chi^2 = 44.78$, $p < .001$). The table shows that mentally disordered persons were far less likely to be victims or complainants than non-mentally-ill individuals, but were twice as likely as non-mentally-disordered persons to be either subjects of concern or objects of assistance. In addition, they were somewhat more likely (35.3% versus 23.4% for non-mentally-disordered persons) to be suspects.

The next step in the analysis was to ascertain the extent to which mentally disordered suspects were involved in more serious crimes. To this end, the type of criminal incident was divided into six major categories: violent personal crime, interpersonal conflict, major property crime, minor property crime, public health, safety or decency offense, and public order offense. These six categories were derived from a complex coding scheme that included more than 120 subcategories of crime. Violent personal crime included homicide, rape, and serious assault. Less serious disturbances between persons were coded as interpersonal conflict. Major property crime differed from minor property crime in that the former involved the presence of a weapon (i.e., robbery) or was a felonious theft. Public health, safety, or decency offenses included all drug offenses as well as offenses against the normative order, e.g., prostitution or gambling. Public order offenses involved some type of minor disturbance, e.g., disorderly persons, public intoxication or vagrancy, and suspicious persons or situations. Incidents initially coded in multiple categories were later recoded according to the more serious incident.

Table 2 shows that the type of incident was not significantly related to the presence or absence of mental disorder for the 506 suspects ($\chi^2 = 4.58$, n.s.). These data indicate that mentally disordered persons did not differ significantly from non-mentally-ill individuals in the type of violation.

In sum, the data indicate that the mentally ill did not present an overwhelming burden for police in terms of frequency of encounters. More important, while they exhibited a slight trend to be suspects more frequently than did non-mentally-disordered persons, the

TABLE 1 Relationship between Severe Mental Disorder and Roles of Citizens Involved with Urban Police Officers[a]

	Severe Mental Disorder					
	Yes (N = 85)		*No (N = 2,037)*		*Total (N = 2,122)*	
Role of Citizen	*N*	*%*	*N*	*%*	*N*	*%*
Victim/complainant	13	15.3	653	32.1	666	31.4
Suspect	30	35.3	476	23.4	506	23.8
Witness/complainant	2	2.4	354	17.4	356	16.8
Subject of concern	25	29.4	293	14.4	318	15.0
Object of assistance	14	16.5	163	8.0	177	8.3
Other	1	1.2	98	4.8	99	4.7

[a]Significant difference: $\chi^2 = 44.78$, df = 5, $p < .001$.

TABLE 2 Relationship between Severe Mental Disorder and Type of Incident among Suspects Involved with Urban Police Officers[a]

	Severe Mental Disorder					
	Yes (N = 30)		*No (N = 476)*		*Total (N = 506)*	
Type of Incident	*N*	*%*	*N*	*%*	*N*	*%*
Violent personal crime	3	10.0	17	3.6	20	4.0
Interpersonal conflict	9	30.0	148	31.1	157	31.0
Major property crime	1	3.3	12	2.5	13	2.6
Minor property crime	1	3.3	49	10.3	50	9.9
Public health, safety, or decency offense	1	3.3	23	4.8	24	4.7
Public order offense	15	50.0	227	47.7	242	47.8

[a]Nonsignificant difference: $\chi^2 = 4.58$, df = 5, $p > .25$.

mentally ill did not commit serious crimes at a rate disproportionate to their numbers. From these data, it appears that the pattern of crime among the mentally ill is substantially similar to that of the general population, at least in this large northern city.

DISCUSSION

This study shows that contact by police with mentally disordered citizens was a relatively infrequent event; mentally disordered citizens made up less than 5% of the persons who were involved with the police. This figure is within the expected range indicated by recent epidemiological studies of the true prevalence of serious mental disorder in the United States. Estimates of the rate of psychoses in community populations range from 0% to 8.3%, and the median rate is 1.7% (33). Although the frequency of police involvement with the mentally ill was higher than the median prevalence rate of psychosis, this may be explained by the characteristics of the neighborhoods we studied. Specifically, the data collection site included two "deviant ghettos" (34), i.e., neighborhoods that contained a number of halfway houses and residential hotels housing former mental patients. In communities such as these, one would expect the number of contacts with police to be somewhat higher than the median rate found in the national epidemiological studies.

However, contact between a mentally disordered person and the police was not likely to have been a result of his or her having committed a crime. Mentally ill persons were involved as suspects only slightly more often than would be expected by their numbers. The modal involvement between police and the mentally ill was not one of a crazed suspect committing a heinous crime, but was more likely to involve a person engaging in behavior harmful to himself or herself. These findings thus confirm the use of police as a major community mental health resource (35–38). Clearly the police officer operates, at least to some extent, as a street-corner psychiatrist. Put in this context, there is ample reason to expect the mentally ill to have contact with the police inasmuch as the mentally ill represent one of the needier segments of the population.

Perhaps the most important finding of this study is that there were no appreciable differences between the mentally disordered suspects and the non-mentally-disordered suspects regarding the type of crimes that were perpetrated. This result is inconsistent with many of the previous investigations using arrest-rate data. One explanation for this discrepancy may be the unique methodology used in this study. Previous research has relied largely on archival data, e.g., studying the arrest records of former mental patients. As mentioned earlier, there is great potential slippage between the commission of an illegal act and that incident's being labeled a crime via arrest. Only a small proportion of criminal incidents actually become crimes (i.e., result in arrests). In our study, for example, only 29.2% of the 506 suspects were actually arrested (32). Moreover, illegal acts that result in arrest are neither a random nor a representative sample of crimes that occur. The decision to arrest is known to be influenced by a variety of sociopsychological and sociostructural exigencies (28). Labeling theorists suggest that initially bestowed definitions such as "prior offender" and "mental patient" become a type of master status that substantially affects the ways in which that person's subsequent behavior is defined, interpreted, and processed (39, 40). Since labels such as "prior criminal record" and "presence of obvious symptoms of severe mental disorder" are known to increase the probability of arrest (32), the apparently greater criminality of the mentally ill found in the arrest-rate studies may be an artifact of the propensity of the mentally ill to be arrested rather than a tendency toward criminality per se.

It is interesting to note that the results of this study largely substantiate the recent findings of Steadman and Felson (25) and provide indirect support for the position of Monahan and Steadman (24). In an exhaustive review of the pertinent research literature, Monahan and Steadman concluded that if a number of sociodemographic factors known to be related to crime are taken into account (e.g., race, age, and prior criminality), the relationship between mental disorder and criminality substantially diminishes. The present study, unlike previous investigations, encompassed all detected violations, regardless of the police officer's disposition of the incident. Thus, it is relatively uncontaminated by the effects of the variables Monahan and Steadman believed might have produced an artifactual relationship between mental disorder and criminality. The results of this study indicate that future investigators should attempt to design studies so as to avoid the biases inherent in archival data.

In conclusion, the stereotype of the mentally ill as dangerous is not substantiated by our data from police-citizen encounters. Thus, it is particularly unfortunate that the mentally ill continue to be portrayed by the news and entertainment media as crazed and violent people. Selective media reporting of instances in which mental illness and criminal behavior appear to be linked feeds the stereotype of the mentally ill as dangerous (10). Similarly, television and movie producers appear to be addicted to "mad slasher" plots in which grisly crimes are almost invariably committed by a newly released mental patient. One wonders if such metaevidence is responsible for the recent proliferation of the more combative tactics (e.g., nets, toxic substances) police now use to respond to calls involving mentally disordered persons (41).

The crucial issue is that with the advent of deinstitutionalization the mentally ill have no choice but to reside within the community. Unfortunately, reintegration into the community is made more difficult by the presumption that the mentally ill person is dangerous and prone to crime (42). Until such time as this stereotype is substantiated by empirical evidence, we must find ways to correct this misconception and, in so doing, provide a more receptive environment for the reentry of the mentally ill into the community setting.

REFERENCES

1. Additions and Resident Patients at End of Year in State and County Mental Hospitals by Age and Diagnosis, by State. Rockville, MD, NIMH Div. of Biometry and Epidemiology, 1981
2. Teplin LA: The criminalization of the mentally ill: speculation in search of data. Psychol Bull 94:54–67, 1983
3. Shah SA: Dangerousness and civil commitment of the mentally ill: some public policy considerations. Am J Psychiatry 132:501–505, 1975
4. Schag DS: Predicting dangerousness: an analysis of procedures in a mental health center and two police agencies (doctoral dissertation). University of California, Santa Cruz, Department of Psychology, 1977
5. Rabkin J: Criminal behavior of discharged mental patients: a critical appraisal of the research. Psychol Bull 86:1–27, 1979
6. Fracchia J, Canale D, Cambria E, et al: Public views of ex-mental patients: a note on perceived dangerousness and unpredictability. Psychiatr Reports 38:495–498, 1976
7. Olmstead DW, Durham K: Stability of mental health attitudes: a semantic differential study. J Health Soc Behav 17:35–44, 1976
8. Mechanic D: Mental Health and Social Policy. Englewood Cliffs, NJ, Prentice-Hall, 1969
9. Nunnally J: Popular Conceptions of Mental Health: Their Development and Change. New York, Holt, Rinehart & Winston, 1961
10. Steadman H, Cocozza J: Selective reporting and the public's misconceptions of the criminally insane. Public Opinion Quarterly 41:523–533, 1978
11. Ashley M: Outcome of 1,000 cases paroled from the Middletown State Homeopathic Hospital. State Hospital Quarterly 8: 64–70, 1922
12. Pollock H: Is the paroled patient a menace to the community? Psychiatr Q 12:236–244, 1938
13. Cohen L, Freeman H: How dangerous to the community are state hospital patients? Conn State Med J 9: 697–700, 1945
14. Brill H, Malzberg B: Statistical Report on the Arrest Record of Male Expatients, Age 16 and Over, Released From New York State Mental Hospitals During the Period 1946–48: Mental Hospital Services Supplemental Report 135. Washington, DC, American Psychiatric Association, 1962
15. Rappeport JR, Lassen G: Dangerousness-arrest rate comparisons of discharged patients and the general population. Am J Psychiatry 121: 776–783, 1965
16. Rappeport JR, Lassen G: The dangerousness of female patients: a comparison of the arrest rate of discharged psychiatric patients and the general population. Am J Psychiatry 123: 413–419, 1966
17. Giovannoni J, Gurel L: Socially disruptive behavior of ex-mental patients. Arch Gen Psychiatry 17:146–153, 1967
18. Zitrin A, Hardesty AS, Burdock EL: Crime and violence among mental patients. Am J Psychiatry 133:142–146, 1976
19. Durbin JR, Pasewark RA, Albers D: Criminality and mental illness: a study of arrest rates in a rural state. Am J Psychiatry 134:80–83, 1977
20. Steadman HJ, Cocozza JJ, Melick ME: Explaining the increased arrest rate among mental patients: the changing clientele of state hospitals. Am J Psychiatry 135:816–820, 1978
21. Steadman HJ, Vanderwyst D, Ribner SA: Comparing arrest rates of mental patients and criminal offenders. Am J Psychiatry 135:1218–1220, 1978
22. Steadman HJ, Ribner SA: Changing perceptions of the mental health needs of inmates in local jails. Am J Psychiatry 137:1115–1116, 1980
23. Sosowsky L: Explaining the increased arrest rate among mental patients: a cautionary note. Am J Psychiatry 137:1602–1605, 1980
24. Monahan J, Steadman H: Crime and mental disorder: an epidemiological approach, in Crime and Justice: An Annual Review of Research. Edited by Morris N, Tonry M. Chicago, University of Chicago Press, 1983
25. Steadman H, Felson R: Self-reports of violence: ex-mental patients, ex-offenders, and the general population. Criminology 22:321–342, 1984
26. Reiss A: The Police and the Public. New Haven, Conn, Yale University Press, 1971
27. Manning P: Police Work: The Social Organization of Policing. Cambridge, Mass, MIT Press, 1977
28. Black D: The Manners and Customs of the Police. New York, Academic Press, 1980
29. Thomas CW, Sieverdes CM: Juvenile

court intake: an analysis of discretionary decision-making. Criminology 12:413 432, 1975
30. Blankenship RL, Singh BK: Differential labeling of juveniles: a multivariate analysis. Criminology 13:420–423, 1976
31. Nimmer RT: Two Million Unnecessary Arrests: Removing a Social Service Concern From the Criminal Justice System. Chicago, American Bar Foundation, 1971
32. Teplin LA: Criminalizing mental disorder: the comparative arrest rate of the mentally ill. Am Psychol 39:794–803, 1984
33. Neugebauer R, Dohrenwend BP, Dohrenwend BS: Formulation of hypotheses about the true prevalence of functional psychiatric disorders among adults in the United States, in Mental Illness in the United States: Epidemiological Estimates. Edited by Dohrenwend BP, Dohrenwend BS, Gould MS, et al. New York, Praeger, 1980
34. Scull T: Decarceration Community and the Deviant—A Radical View. Englewood Cliffs, NJ, Prentice-Hall, 1977
35. Bittner E: Police discretion in emergency apprehension of mentally ill persons. Social Problems 14:278–292, 1967
36. Matthews A: Observations on police policy and procedures for emergency detention of the mentally ill. J Criminal Law, Criminology, and Police Science 61:283–295, 1970
37. Teplin LA, Filstead W, Hefter G, et al: Police involvement with the psychiatric emergency patient. Psychiatr Annals 10:202–207, 1980
38. Teplin LA: Mental Health and Criminal Justice. Newbury Park, Calif, Sage Publications, 1984
39. Rosenhan DL.: On being sane in insane places. Science 179:250–258, 1973
40. Becker H: Outsiders. New York, Free Press, 1963
41. Basler B: Police in city will use nets to subdue the deranged. New York Times, January 27, 1981, p 1
42. Steadman HJ: Critically reassessing the accuracy of public perceptions of the dangerousness of the mentally ill. J Health Soc Behav 22:310–316, 1981

JOHN MONAHAN

Mental disorder and violent behavior: Perceptions and evidence

Is there a relationship between mental disorder and violent behavior? Few questions in mental health law are as empirically complex or as politically controversial. On the one hand, the general public and their elected representatives appear firmly committed to the view that mental disorder and violence are connected. On the other hand, many social science researchers and the patient advocates who cite them seem equally convinced that no such connection exists. Although I have long been in the latter camp (e.g., Monahan, 1981), I now believe that there may be a relationship between mental disorder and violent behavior, one that cannot be fobbed off as chance or explained away by other factors that may cause them both. The relationship, if it exists, probably is not large, but may be important both for legal theory and for social policy. In this article, I lay before you the evidence and the inferences that have persuaded me to modify my views. I first consider the relationship between mental disorder and violence as it has been perceived by public and professional audiences, and then present an epidemiological framework within which the question can be empirically addressed.

MENTAL DISORDER AND VIOLENCE: PUBLIC AND PROFESSIONAL PERCEPTIONS

Beliefs that mental disorder is linked to violent behavior are important for two reasons. The first is that such beliefs drive the formal laws and policies by

Author's note: My work on this topic has been supported by the MacArthur Research Network on Mental Health and the Law. The views expressed here are my own.

I am grateful to the members of the Network and to Lawrence Fitch, S. Ken Hoge, Deidre Klassen, Bruce Link, Lee Robins, Joan Roth, Jeffrey Swanson, Linda Teplin, and Simon Wessely for their comments on the manuscript.

SOURCE: *American Psychologist*, 47(4), pp. 511–521, April 1992.

which society attempts to control the behavior of disordered people and to regulate the provision of mental health care. Coherent theories of mental health law can be constructed that are not premised on the assumption that the mentally disordered are more prone to violence than is the rest of the general population (e.g., "Developments in the Law," 1974). But there can be little doubt that this assumption has played an animating role in the prominence of *dangerous to others* as a criterion for civil commitment and the commitment of persons acquitted of crime by reason of insanity, in the creation of special statutes for the extended detention of mentally disordered prisoners, and in the imposition of tort liability on psychologists and psychiatrists who fail to anticipate the violence of their patients (Appelbaum, 1988; Grisso, 1991).

The second and perhaps more important reason why beliefs in the violence potential of the mentally disordered are important is that they not only drive formal law and policy toward the mentally disordered as a class, but they also determine our informal responses and modes of interacting with individuals who are perceived to be mentally ill. An ingenious study by Link, Cullen, Frank, and Wozniak (1987) vividly makes this point. These researchers investigated the extent to which a person's status as a former mental patient fostered social distance on the part of others, measured by questions tapping the willingness of the respondent to have as a co-worker or neighbor someone described in a vignette as having once been a patient in a mental hospital. Consistent with much prior research (e.g., Gove, 1980), Link et al. (1987) found no main effect of the former-patient label. But when they disaggregated their subjects—adults drawn from the open community—by means of a "perceived dangerousness scale" into those who believed that mental disorder was linked to violence and those who did not, strong labeling effects emerged. Remarkably, people who believed that there was no connection between mental disorder and violence exhibited what might be called an affirmative action effect: They responded as if they were *more* willing to have as a co-worker or neighbor someone who had been a mental patient than someone who had never been hospitalized. People who believed that the mentally disordered were prone to violence, however, strongly rejected and wished to distance themselves from the former patient.

Before considering the contemporary nature of public and professional perceptions of the relationship between mental disorder and violence, it may be useful to briefly set the topic in historical and cultural perspective.

Perceptions in Other Times and Other Places

From the very origins of Western civilization, most people's experience with the mentally disordered have led them to assume that there was a connection of some kind between mental disorder and violence (Monahan, 1992). References in Greek and Roman literature to the violence potential of the mentally disordered date from the fifth century before the Christian era began. As the historian George Rosen (1968) noted, in the ancient world "two forms of behavior were considered particularly characteristic of the mentally disordered, their habit of wandering about and their proneness to violence" (p. 98). Plato, for example, in "Alcibiades II," records a dialogue between Socrates and a friend. The friend claimed that many citizens of Athens were "mad." Socrates refuted this claim by arguing that the rate of mental disorder in Athens could not possibly be very high because the rate of violence in Athens was very low.

> How could we live in safety with so many crazy people? Should we not long ago have paid the penalty at their hands, and have been struck and beaten and endured every other form of ill usage which madmen are wont to inflict? (cited in Rosen, p. 100)

Likewise, Plautus, in a play written about 270 B.C., titled *Casina*, wrote of a maid who had taken up a sword and was threatening to murder a lover. One character describes the situation: "She's chasing everyone through the house there, and won't let a soul come near her; they're hiding under chests and couches afraid to breathe a word." To this, her lover asks, "What the deuce has gotten into her all of a sudden this way?" The answer he received seemed to suffice for an explanation: "She's gone crazy" (cited in Rosen, p. 99). Advice to those responsible for the care of the mentally disordered in Greece and Rome often made reference to their dangerousness and to the necessity of keeping them in restraints, lest their caretakers be injured.

It is important to emphasize that even in ancient times, the public perception was not that all or most or even many of the mentally disordered were violent, just that a disproportionate number were. The Roman philosopher Philo Judaeus, for example, divided the mentally disordered into two groups. The larger one was made up of disordered people "of the easy-going gentle style," and the other, smaller one, consisted of those "whose madness was . . . of the fierce and savage kind, which is dangerous both to the madmen themselves and those who approach them" (cited in Rosen, 1968, p. 89).

Such public attitudes persisted throughout the Middle Ages and the Renaissance. Care of the disordered was left to family and friends; "only those considered too dangerous to keep at home . . . were dealt with by communal authorities" (Rosen, 1968, p. 139). An early form of the *dangerousness standard* for civil commitment is illustrated by the 1493 German case of a disordered man who had committed a violent act and was ordered locked up in a tower of the city wall. When he no longer appeared violent, he was released from the tower to the custody of his family,

> upon condition that they would confine him themselves should he again become violent. In this event, his wife would confine him in her house or arrange to keep him elsewhere at her expense. If required, the council would lend her a jail. (Rosen, p. 143)

Little in terms of public attitudes changed as the Renaissance gave way to the modern era. In 1843, the London *Times* published the following ditty on its editorial page on the day after Daniel McNaughten was acquitted by reason of insanity of murdering the secretary to the prime minister:

> Ye people of England exult and be glad
> For ye're now at the mercy of the merciless mad!

In the United States, as in Europe, the perception of a link between mental disorder and violence is as old as recorded history. The first general hospital in the American colonies to include a ward for the mentally disordered—the cellar—was founded at the urging of no less than Benjamin Franklin. After arguing in vain that the Pennsylvania colony was morally obligated to provide for the disordered, he switched tacks and petitioned the Assembly in 1751 that

> the Number of Persons distempered in Mind and deprived of their rational Faculties has increased greatly in this province. Some of them going at large are a terror to their Neighbors, who are daily apprehensive of the Violences they may commit. (cited in Deutsch, 1949, p. 59)

This argument hit a responsive chord, and the Pennsylvania Hospital still stands in Philadelphia.

The belief that mental disorder is conducive to violence runs deep in Western culture, but is by no means peculiar to it. Westermeyer and Kroll (1978) studied all persons known as *baa*, or crazy, in 27 villages in Laos, a country that at the time of the research was without a single psychiatrist, psychologist, or mental hospital. They questioned family members, neighbors, and the people seen as *baa* themselves about the occurrence of violence and its relationship to mental disorder. They were told that 11 % of their subjects exhibited violent behavior before they began acting in a *baa* manner, whereas 54% were reported to have acted violently once they became *baa*. At approximately the same time, Jones and Horne (1973) studied almost 1,000 people in four isolated aboriginal missions in the Australian desert.

> Frequently, [they concluded,] an aggressive act by the patient causes him to present clinically, but with an explanation that was culturally appropriate—he would claim, for example, that his symptoms have been inflicted upon him by magical means and his aggression was his way of protecting himself. (p. 225)

Finally, Jane Murphy (1976), the noted anthropologist, reviewed in *Science* a great deal of research on responses to mental disorder among a variety of Northwestern Native American and several Central African ethnic groups. She reported great similarities among people in very different traditional societies, societies that had never had contact with one another:

> There seems to be little that is distinctively cultural in the attitudes and actions directed toward the mentally ill, except in such matters as that an abandoned anthill could not be used as an asylum in the arctic or a barred igloo in the tropics. . . . If the behavior indicates helplessness, help tends to be given, especially in food and clothes. If the behavior appears foolish or incongruous . . . , laughter is the response. If the behavior is noisy and agitated, the response may be to quiet, sometimes by herbs and sometimes by other means. If the behavior is violent or threatening, the response is to restrain or to subdue. (p. 1025)

Of course, the anthropological fact that a popular belief has persisted since antiquity and is found in all known societies does not mean that the belief is true. Unfounded prejudices may also be enduring and shared. But if the assumption that mental disorder sometimes predisposes toward violent behavior is a myth, it may still be worth noting that it is a myth that is both culturally universal and historically invariant.

Contemporary American Perceptions

In modern times and in modern societies, of course, we no longer have to rely on historians and anthropologists to tell us what we believe. We have survey researchers to quantify our opinions. One poll conducted by the Field Institute (1984) for the California Department of Mental Health asked 1,500 representative California adults whether they agreed with the statement, "A person who is diagnosed as schizophrenic is more likely to commit a violent crime than a normal person." Almost two thirds of the sample (61%) said that they definitely or probably agreed. In modern as in ancient times, however, the public by no means believes that mental disorder inevitably or even frequently leads to violence. In a survey of 1,000 adults from all parts of the United States, conducted by the DYG Corporation (1990) for the Robert Wood Johnson Foundation Program on Chronic Mental Illness, 24% of the respondents agreed with the statement, "People with chronic mental illness are, by far, more dangerous than the general population," whereas twice as many (48%) agreed with the proposition, "The mentally ill are far *less* of a danger than most people believe."

Although ancient attitudes about the relationship between mental disorder and violence were, of necessity, based on personal observation or word-of-mouth, contemporary opinions no doubt reflect the additional impact of the image of the mentally disordered relentlessly promoted by the media (Steadman & Cocozza, 1978). One content analysis performed for the National Institute of Mental Health (Gerbner, Gross, Morgan, & Signorielli, 1981) found that 17% of all prime-time American television programs could charitably be classified as dramas depicting a character as mentally ill. Of these mentally ill characters, 73% were portrayed as violent, compared with 40% of the "normal" characters (!), and 23% of the mentally ill characters were shown to be homicidal, compared with 10% of the normal characters. Nor are such caricatures limited to television. A content analysis of stories from the United Press International database (Shain & Phillips, 1991) found that in 86% of all print stories dealing with former mental patients, a violent crime—"usually murder or mass murder" (p. 64)—was the focus of the article.

Professional Perceptions

From reading the literature in this area, it would appear that there are only two identifiable groups in modern society who do *not* believe that mental disorder and violence are associated at greater than chance levels. The first group is composed of advocates for the mentally disordered, both of the traditional and ex-patient schools. The most recent pamphlet of the established National Mental Health Association (1987), for example, stated that "people with mental illnesses pose no more of a crime threat than do other members of the general population" (p. 2). Likewise, a recent volume produced by a leading ex-patient advocacy group for the California Department of Mental Health (Campbell & Schraiber, 1989) stated that "studies show that while, like all groups, some members are violent, mental health clients are no more violent than the general population" (p. 88). In making such statements, patient advocates are clearly and commendably motivated by the desire to dispel vivid homicidal maniac images pandered by the media and to counter the stigma and social distancing that are bred by public fear. Given the findings of Link et al. (1987), they surely are right to be concerned.

The second group in society that apparently believes that mental disorder is not associated with any increase in the risk of violence consists of many sociological and psychological researchers. Henry Steadman and I (Monahan & Steadman, 1983a), for example, reviewed over 200 studies on the association between crime and mental disorder for the National Institute of Justice. This was our summary:

> The conclusion to which our review is drawn is that the relation between . . . crime and mental disorder can be accounted for largely by demographic and historical characteristics that the two groups share. When appropriate statistical controls are applied for factors such as age, gender, race, social class, and previous institutionalization, whatever relations between crime and mental disorder are reported tend to disappear. (p. 152)

I now believe that this conclusion is at least premature and may well be wrong. I say this for two reasons. First, to statistically control for factors, such as social class and previous institutionalization, that are highly related to mental disorder is problematic. For example, if in some cases mental disorder causes people to decline in social class (perhaps because they became psychotic at work) and also to become violent, then to control for low social class is, to some unknown extent, to attenuate the relationship that will be found between mental disorder and violence. "The problem," as Bruce Dohrenwend (1990) has noted, "remains what it has always been: how to unlock the riddle that low SES can be either a cause or a consequence of psychopathology" (p. 45). If, in other cases, mental disorder causes people to be repetitively violent and therefore institutionalized, then to control for previous institutionalization also masks, to some unknown degree, the relationship that will be found between mental disorder and violence.

The second reason that I now think the no-relationship conclusion may be wrong is that new research—by no means perfect, yet by all accounts vastly superior to what had been in the literature even a few years ago—has become available. These new studies find a consistent, albeit modest, relationship between mental disorder and violent behavior. I will now turn to this literature, both old and new. As before (Monahan & Steadman, 1983a), I find an epidemiological framework conducive to clear thinking on this topic.

MENTAL DISORDER AND VIOLENCE: EVIDENCE FOR A RELATIONSHIP

There are two ways to determine whether a relationship exists between mental disorder and violent behavior and, if it does, to estimate the strength of that relationship. If being mentally disordered raises the likelihood that a person will commit a violent act—that is, if mental disorder is a risk factor for the occurrence of violent behavior—then the actual (or true) prevalence rate for violence should be higher among disordered than among nondisordered populations. And to the extent that mental disorder is a contributing cause to the occurrence of violence, the true prevalence rate of mental disorder should be higher among people who commit violent acts than among people who do not. These two complementary ways of estimating relationships with epidemiological methods follow.

1. True prevalence of violent behavior among persons with mental disorder
   a. Among identified mental patients
   b. Among random community samples
2. True prevalence of mental disorder among persons committing violent behavior
   a. Among identified criminal offenders
   b. Among random community samples

Within each generic category, two types of research exist. The first seeks to estimate the relationship between mental disorder and violence by studying people who are being treated either for mental disorder (in hospitals) or for violent behavior (in jails and prisons). The second seeks to estimate the relationship between mental disorder and violence by studying people unselected for treatment status in the open community. Both types of studies are valuable in themselves, but both have limitations taken in isolation, as will become clear.

Violence among the Disordered

Three types of studies provide data from hospitalized mental patients that can be used to estimate the relationship between mental disorder and violence. One type looks at the prevalence of violent acts committed by patients before they entered the hospital. A second type looks at the prevalence of violent incidents committed by mental patients during their hospital stay. A final type of study addresses the prevalence of violent behavior among mental patients after they have been released from the hospital. I restrict myself here to remarking on findings on violent behavior toward others and exclude violence toward self, verbal threats of violence, and property damage. By *mental disorder*, I refer, unless otherwise noted, to those major disorders of thought or affect that form a subset of Axis I of the *Diagnostic and Statistical Manual of Mental Disorders*, 3rd edition, revised (*DSM-III-R*; American Psychiatric Association 1987). Three excellent recent reviews (Mullen, 1992; Otto, 1992; Wessely & Taylor, 1991) make my task of summarizing these studies much easier.

Together, these three reviews report on 11 studies published over the past 15 years that provide data on the prevalence of violent behavior among persons who eventually became mental patients. The time period investigated was typically the two weeks prior to hospital admission. The findings across the various studies vary considerably: Between approximately 10% and 40% of the patient samples (with a median rate of 15%) committed a physically assaultive act against another shortly before they were hospitalized; 12 studies with data on the prevalence of violence by patients on mental hospital wards are found in these reviews. The periods studied varied from a few days to a year. The findings here also range from about 10% to 40% (with a median rate of 25%; see also Davis, 1991).

There is a very large literature, going back to the 1920s, on violent behavior by mental patients after they have been discharged from civil hospitals (Rabkin, 1979). The best recent studies are clearly those of Klassen and O'Connor (1988, 1990). They find that approximately 25%–30% of male subjects with at least one violent incident in their past—a very relevant, but highly selective sample of patients—are violent within a year of release from the hospital. The ongoing MacArthur Risk Assessment Study (Steadman et al., 1992) is finding that 27% of released male and female patients report at least one violent act within a mean of four months after discharge.

Each of these three types of research has important policy and practice implications. Studies of violence before hospitalization supply data on the workings of civil commitment laws and the interaction between the mental health and criminal justice systems (Monahan & Steadman, 1983b). Studies of violence during hospitalization have significance for the level of security required in mental health facilities and the need for staff training in managing aggressive incidents (Binder & McNiel, 1988; Roth, 1985). Studies of violence after hospitalization provide essential base-rate information for use in the risk assessments involved in release decision making and in after-care planning (Monahan, 1988).

For the purpose of determining whether there is a fundamental relationship between mental disorder and violent behavior, however, each of these three types of research is unavailing. Only rarely did the studies provide any comparative data on the prevalence of similarly defined violence among nonhospitalized groups. Steadman and Felson (1984) is one study that did. The authors interviewed former mental patients and a random sample of the general community in Albany County, New York. The percentage of ex-patients who reported at least one dispute involving hitting during the past year was 22.3, compared with 15.1% for the community sample. For disputes in which a weapon had been used, the figures were 8.1% for the ex-patients and 1.6% for the community sample. When demographic factors were controlled, however, these differences were not significant. Although the rates of violence by mental patients before, during, or after hospitalization reported in the other studies certainly appear much higher than would be expected by chance, the general lack of data from nonpatients makes comparison speculative. But even if such data were available, several sources of systematic bias would make their use for epidemiological purposes highly suspect. Because these studies dealt with persons who were subsequently, simultaneously, or previously institutionalized as mental patients, none of them can distinguish between the *participation* of the mentally disordered in violence—the topic of interest here—and the *selection* of that subset of the mentally disordered persons who are violent for treatment in the public-sector inpatient settings in which the research was carried out. (There is virtually no research on private hospitals or on outpatients.) Furthermore, studies of violence after hospitalization suffer from the additional selection bias that only those patients clinically predicted to be nonviolent were released. Nor can the studies of violence during and after hospitalization distinguish the effect of the treatment of potentially violent patients in the hospital from the existence of a prior relationship between mental disorder and violence.

For example, to use the prevalence of violence before hospitalization as an index of the fundamental relationship between mental disorder and violence would be to thoroughly confound rates of violence with the legal criteria for hospitalization. Given the rise of the dangerousness standard for civil commitment in the United States and throughout the world (Monahan & Shah, 1989), it would be amazing if many patients were not violent before they were hospitalized: Violent behavior is one of the reasons that these disordered people were selected out of the total disordered population for hospitalization. Likewise, the level of violent behavior exhibited on the ward during hospitalization is determined not only by the differential selection of violent people for hospitalization (or, within the hospital, the further selection of "violence-prone" patients for placement in the locked wards that were often the sites of the research), but by the skill of ward staff in defusing potentially violent incidents and by the efficacy of treatment in mitigating disorder (or by the effect of medication in sedating patients). As Werner, Rose, and Yesavage (1983) have stated,

> To the extent that hostile, excited, suspicious, and recent assaultive behavior is viewed by ward staffing as presaging imminent violence, it is the patient manifesting such behavior who is singled out for special treatment (e.g., additional medications, more psychotherapy); such selection may reduce the likelihood of engaging in violence. Thus, paradoxically, if the patient who "looks" imminently violent in this setting is given effective treatments that forestall violent behavior, he will not in fact engage in violence as predicted. (p. 824)

Because the prevalence of violence after hospitalization may be a function of (a) the type of patients selected for hospitalization, (b) the nature and duration of the treatment administered during hospitalization, and (c) the risk assessment cutoffs used in determining eligibility for discharge, these data, too, tell us little about whether a basic relationship between mental disorder and violence exists. Only by augmenting studies of the prevalence of violence among treated (i.e., hospitalized) samples of the mentally disordered with studies of the prevalence of violence among samples of disordered people unselected for treatment status in the community can population estimates free of selection and treatment biases be offered. Fortunately, a recent and seminal study by Swanson, Holzer, Ganju, and Jono (1990) provides this essential information. Swanson and his colleagues drew their data from the National Institute of Mental Health's Epidemiological Catchment Area (ECA) study (Robins & Regier, 1991). Representative weighted samples of adult household residents of Baltimore, Durham, and Los Angeles were pooled to form a data base of approximately 10,000 people. The Diagnostic Interview Schedule (DIS), a structured interview designed for use by trained lay persons, was used to establish mental disorder according to *Diagnostic and Statistical Manual of Mental Disorders*, third edition (*DSM-III*; American Psychiatric Association, 1980) criteria. Five items on the DIS[1]—four embedded among the criteria for antisocial personality disorder and one that formed part of the diagnosis of alcohol abuse/dependence—were used to indicate violent behavior. A respondent was counted as positive for violence if he or she endorsed at least one of these items and reported that the act occurred during the year preceding the interview. This index of violent behavior, as Swanson et al. noted, is a "blunt measure": It is based on self-report without corroboration, the questions overlap considerably, and it does not differentiate in terms of the frequency or the severity of violence. Yet there is little doubt that each of the target behaviors is indeed "violent," and I believe that the measure is a reasonable estimate of the prevalence of violent behavior.

Confidence in the Swanson et al. (1990) findings is increased by their conformity to the demographic correlates of violence known from the criminological literature. As Tables 1 and 2 indicate, violence in the ECA study was seven times as prevalent among the young as among the old, twice as prevalent among men as among women, and three times as prevalent among persons of the lowest social class as among persons of the highest social class.

But it is the clinical findings that are of direct interest here. Table 3 presents the prevalence of violent behavior during the past year by *DSM-III* diagnosis. For these data, exclusion criteria were not used: A subject who met the criteria for more than one disorder was counted as a case of each.

Three findings are immediately evident: (a) The prevalence of violence is more than five times higher among people who meet criteria for a *DSM-III* Axis I diagnosis than among people who are not diagnosable. (b) The prevalence of violence among persons who meet criteria for a diagnosis of schizophrenia, major depression, or mania/bipolar disorder are remarkably similar. (c) The prevalence of violence among persons who meet criteria for a diagnosis of alcoholism is 12 times that of persons who receive no diagnosis, and the prevalence of violence among persons who meet criteria for being diagnosed as abusing drugs is 16 times that of persons who receive no diagnosis. When both demographic and clinical factors were combined in a regression equation to predict the occurrence of violence, several significant predictors emerged. Violence was most likely to occur among young, lower class men, among those with a substance abuse diagnosis, and among those with a diagnosis of major

TABLE 1 Percentage Violent during Past Year in ECA Sample, by Age

Age Group	*% Violent*
18–29	7.3
30–44	3.6
45–64	1.2
65+	0.1

Note: ECA = Epidemiologic Catchment Area. From "Violence and Psychiatric Disorder in the Community: Evidence from the Epidemiologic Catchment Area Survey" by J. Swanson, C. Holzer, V. Ganju, and R. Jono, 1990, *Hospital and Community Psychiatry, 41,* p. 764. Copyright 1990 by the American Psychiatric Association. Adapted by permission.

TABLE 2 Percentage Violent during Past Year Among 18–29-Year-Olds in ECA Sample, by Gender and SES

SES	*Men*	*Women*
1 (lowest)	16.1	9.1
2	11.7	5.0
3	8.1	2.5
4 (highest)	6.1	3.3

Note: ECA = Epidemiologic Catchment Area; SES = socioeconomic status. From "Violence and Psychiatric Disorder in the Community: Evidence from the Epidemiologic Catchment Area Survey" by J. Swanson, C. Holzer, V. Ganju, and R. Jono, 1990, *Hospital and Community Psychiatry, 41,* p. 764. Copyright 1990 by the American Psychiatric Association. Adapted by permission.

TABLE 3 Percentage Violent during Past Year in ECA Sample, by Diagnosis

Diagnosis	*% Violent*
No disorder	2.1
Schizophrenia	12.7
Major depression	11.7
Mania or bi-polar	11.0
Alcohol abuse/dependence	24.6
Drug abuse/dependence	34.7

Note: ECA = Epidemiologic Catchment Area. From "Violence and Psychiatric Disorder in the Community: Evidence from the Epidemiologic Catchment Area Survey" by J. Swanson, C. Holzer, V. Ganju, and R. Jono, 1990, *Hospital and Community Psychiatry, 41*, p. 765. Copyright 1990 by the American Psychiatric Association. Adapted by permission.

mental disorder (see Swanson & Holzer. 1991).

One final and equally notable study not only confirms the ECA data but takes them a large step further. Link, Andrews, and Cullen (1992) analyzed data from a larger study conducted by Bruce Dohrenwend and his colleagues (Shrout et al., 1988), using the Psychiatric Epidemiology Research Interview (PERI) to measure symptoms and life events. Link et al. (in press) compared rates of arrest and of self-reported violence (including hitting, fighting, weapon use, and "hurting someone badly") in a sample of approximately 400 adults from the Washington Heights area of New York City who had never been in a mental hospital or sought help from a mental health professional with rates of arrest and self-reported violence in several samples of former mental patients from the same area. To eliminate alternative explanations of their data, the researchers controlled, in various analyses, for an extraordinary number of factors: age, gender, educational level, ethnicity (Black, White, and Hispanic), socioeconomic status, family composition (e.g., married with children), homicide rate of the census tract in which a subject lived, and the subject's "need for approval." This last variable was measured by the Crowne-Marlowe (1960) Social Desirability scale and was included to control for the possibility that patients might be more willing to report socially undesirable behavior (such as violence) than were nonpatients.

The study found that the patient groups were almost always more violent than the never-treated community sample, often two to three times as violent. As in the ECA study (Swanson et al., 1990), demographic factors clearly related to violence (e.g., men, the less educated, and those from high-crime neighborhoods were more likely to be violent). But even when all the demographic and personal factors, such as social desirability, were taken into account, significant differences between the patients and the never-treated community residents remained. The association between mental patient status and violent behavior, as the authors noted, was "remarkably robust" to attempts to explain it away as artifact.

Most important, Link et al. (1992) then controlled for "current symptomatology." They did this by using the False Beliefs and Perceptions scale of the PERI, which measures core psychotic symptoms via questions such as, "How often have you felt that thoughts were put into your head that were not your own?", "How often have you thought you were possessed by a spirit or devil?", and "How often have you felt that your mind was dominated by forces beyond your control?" Remarkably, *not a single difference in rates of recent violent behavior between patients and never-treated community residents remained significant when current psychotic symptoms were controlled*. The Psychotic Symptomatology scale, on the other hand, was significantly and strongly related to most indices of recent violent behavior, even when additional factors, such as alcohol and drug use, were taken into account. Thus, almost all of the difference in rates of violence between patients and nonpatients could be accounted for by the level of active psychotic symptoms that the patients were experiencing. In other words, when mental patients were actively experiencing psychotic symptoms like delusions and hallucinations, their risk of violence was significantly elevated, compared with that of nonpatients, and when patients were not actively experiencing psychotic symptoms, their risk of violence was not appreciably higher than demographically similar members of their home community who had never been treated. Finally, Link et al. (1992) also found that the Psychotic Symptomatology scale significantly predicted violent behavior among the never-treated community residents. Even among people who had never been formally treated for mental disorder, actively experiencing psychotic symptoms was associated with the commission of violent acts.

The data independently reported by Swanson et al. (1990) and Link et al. (1992) are remarkable and provide the crucial missing element that begins to fill out the epidemiological picture of mental disorder and violence. Together, these two studies suggest that the currently mentally disordered—those actively experiencing serious psychotic symptoms—are involved in violent behavior at rates several times those of nondisordered members of the general population, and that this difference persists even when a wide array of demographic and social factors are taken into consideration. Because the studies were conducted using representative samples of the open community, selection biases are not a plausible alternative explanation for their findings.

Disorder among the Violent

Recall that there is a second empirical tack that might be taken to determine whether a fundamental relationship between mental disorder and violence exists and to estimate what the magnitude of that relationship might be. If mental disorder is in fact a contributing cause to the occurrence of violence, then the prevalence of mental disorder should be higher among people who commit violent acts than among people who do not. As before, there are two ways to ascertain the existence of such a relationship: by studying treated cases—in this instance, people "treated" for violence by being institutionalized in local jails and state prisons—and determining their rates of mental disorder, and by studying untreated cases—people in the open community who are violent but not institutionalized for it—and determining their rates of mental disorder.

A large number of studies exist that estimate the prevalence of mental disorder among jail and prison inmates. Of course, not all jail and prison inmates have been convicted of a violent crime. Yet 66% of state prisoners have a current or past conviction for violence (Bureau of Justice Statistics, 1991), and there is no evidence that the rates of disorder of jail inmates charged with violent offenses differ from those of jail inmates charged with nonviolent offenses. So I believe that data on the prevalence of disorder among inmates in general also apply reasonably well to violent inmates in particular.

Teplin (1990) reviewed 18 studies of mental disorder among jail samples performed in the past 15 years. Most of the studies were conducted on inmates referred for a mental health evaluation, and thus present obviously inflated rates of disorder. Among those few studies that randomly sampled jail inmates, rates of mental disorder varied widely, from 5% to 16% psychotic. Roth (1980), in reviewing the literature on the prevalence of mental disorder among prison inmates, concluded that the rate of psychosis was "on the order of 5 percent or less of the total prison population" (p. 688), and the rate of any form of disorder was in the 15%–20% range. More recent studies have reported somewhat higher rates of serious mental disorder. Steadman, Fabisiak, Dvoskin, and Holohean (1987), in a level-of-care survey of more than 3,000 prisoners in New York State, concluded that 8% had "severe mental disabilities" and another 16% had "significant mental disabilities" (see also Taylor & Gunn, 1984).

TABLE 4 Current Prevalence of Mental Disorder (%) among California Prisoners, Chicago Jail Detainees, and ECA Sample

Diagnosis	*Prison*	*Jail*	*ECA*
Schizophrenia	3.1	2.7	0.9
Major depression	3.5	3.9	1.1
Mania or bi-polar	0.7	1.4	0.1
Any severe disorder	7.9	6.4	1.8

Note: ECA = Epidemiologic Catchment Area. The data in columns 2 and 3 are from "The Prevalence of Severe Mental Disorder Among Male Urban Jail Detainees" by L. Teplin, 1990, *American Journal of Public Health, 80,* p. 665. Copyright 1990 by the American Public Health Association. Adapted by permission. The data in column 1 are from *Current Description, Evaluation, and Recommendations for Treatment of Mentally Disordered Criminal Offenders,* 1989, Sacramento: California Department of Corrections.

Although the rates of mental disorder among jail and prison inmates appear very high, comparison data for similarly defined mental disorder among the general noninstitutionalized population were typically not available. As well, the methods of diagnosing mental disorder in the jail and prison studies often consisted of unstandardized clinical interviews or the use of proxy variables, such as prior mental hospitalization (see, e.g., Steadman, Monahan, Duffee, Hartstone, & Robbins, 1984).

Recently, however, four studies, one with jail inmates and three with prisoners, have become available that use the DIS as their diagnostic instrument. This not only allows for a standardized method of assessing disorder independent of previous hospitalization, it permits comparison across the studies and between these institutionalized populations and the random community samples of the ECA research.

In the first study, Teplin (1990) administered the DIS to a stratified random sample—one half misdemeanants and one half felons—of 728 men from the Cook County (Chicago) jail. In the most comparable of the prison studies, the California Department of Corrections (1989) commissioned a consortium of research organizations to administer the DIS to a stratified random sample of 362 male inmates in California prisons (see also Collins & Schlesinger, 1983; Hodgins & Cote, 1990; Neighbors et al., 1987). Comparative data from the ECA study for male respondents were provided by Teplin (1990). The findings for current disorder are summarized in Table 4.

It can be seen that the prevalence of schizophrenia is approximately 3 times higher in the jail and prison samples than in the general population samples, the prevalence of major depression 3–4 times higher, the prevalence of mania or bi-polar disorder 7–14 times higher, and overall, the prevalence of any severe disorder (i.e., any of the above diagnoses) 3–4 times higher. Although there were no controls for demographic factors in the prison study, Teplin (1990) controlled for race and age in the jail study, and the jail–general population differences persisted. Although these studies all relied on male inmates, even more dramatic data for female prisoners have been reported in one study (Daniel, Robins, Reid, & Wilfley, 1988).

These findings on the comparatively high prevalence of mental disorder among jail and prison inmates have enormous policy implications for mental health screening of admissions to these facilities and for the need for mental health treatment in correctional institutions (Steadman, McCarty, & Morrissey, 1989). But given the systematic bias inherent in the use of identified criminal offenders, they cannot fully address the issue of whether there is a fundamental relationship between mental disorder and violence. Mentally

TABLE 5 Current Prevalence of Mental Disorder (%) among Persons in ECA Sample Who Reported Violence or No Violence during Past Year

Violence	*Schizophrenia*	*Major Affective*	*Substance Abuse*	*Any Disorder*
Yes	3.9	9.4	41.6	55.5
No	1.0	3.0	4.9	19.6

Note: ECA = Epidemiologic Catchment Area. From "Violence and Psychiatric Disorder in the Community: Evidence from the Epidemiologic Catchment Area Survey" by J. Swanson, C. Holzer, V. Ganju, and R. Jono, 1990, *Hospital and Community Psychiatry, 41*, p. 765. Copyright 1990 by the American Psychiatric Association. Adapted by permission.

disordered offenders may be more or less likely to be arrested and imprisoned than are non-disordered offenders. On the one hand, Robertson (1988) found that offenders who were schizophrenic were much more likely than were non-disordered offenders to be arrested at the scene of the crime or to give themselves up to the police. Teplin (1985), in the only actual field study in this area, found the police more likely to arrest disordered than nondisordered suspects. On the other hand, Klassen and O'Connor (1988) found that released mental patients whose violence in the community evoked an official response were twice as likely to be rehospitalized—and thereby avoid going to jail—than they were to be arrested. An individual's status as a jail or prison inmate, in short, is not independent of the presence of mental disorder.

As before, complementary data on the prevalence of mental disorder among unselected samples of people in the open community who commit violent acts is necessary to fully address this issue. And as before, the analysis of the ECA data by Swanson et al. (1990) provides the required information, which is summarized in Table 5.

The prevalence of schizophrenia among respondents who endorsed at least one of the five questions indicating violent behavior in the past year was approximately four times higher than among respondents who did not report violence, the prevalence of affective disorder was three times higher, the prevalence of substance abuse (either alcohol or other drugs) was eight times higher, and overall, the prevalence of any measured DIS diagnosis—which here included anxiety disorders—was almost three times higher.

IMPLICATIONS FOR RESEARCH AND POLICY

The data that have recently become available, fairly read, suggest the one conclusion I did not want to reach: Whether the measure is the prevalence of violence among the disordered or the prevalence of disorder among the violent, whether the sample is people who are selected for treatment as inmates or patients in institutions or people randomly chosen from the open community, and no matter how many social and demographic factors are statistically taken into account, there appears to be a relationship between mental disorder and violent behavior. Mental disorder may be a robust and significant risk factor for the occurrence of violence, as an increasing number of clinical researchers in recent years have averred (Bloom, 1989; Krakowski, Volavka, & Brizer, 1986; Mullen, 1992; Wessely & Taylor, 1991).

Should further research solidify this conclusion, would it mean—to return to the points we began with—that laws that restrict the freedom of mentally disordered people for long periods of time or the pervasive social rejection of former mental patients are justified, or that the media is correct in its portrayal of people with mental disorder as threats to the social order? No, it would not and for two reasons.

First, as the Link et al. (1992) study makes clear, it is only people currently experiencing psychotic symptoms who may be at increased risk of violence. Being a former patient in a mental hospital—that is, having experienced psychotic symptoms *in the past*—bears no direct relationship to violence, and bears an indirect relationship to violence only in the attenuated sense that previous disorder may raise the risk of current disorder.

Second and more important, demonstrating the existence of a statistically significant relationship between mental disorder and violence is one thing; demonstrating the social and policy significance of the magnitude of that relationship is another. By all indications, the great majority of people who are currently disordered—approximately 90% from the ECA study—are not violent. None of the data give any support to the sensationalized caricature of the mentally disordered served up by the media, the shunning of former patients by employers and neighbors in the community, or regressive "lock 'em all up" laws proposed by politicians pandering to public fears. The policy implications of mental disorder as a risk factor for violent behavior can be understood only in relative terms. Compared with the magnitude of risk associated with the combination of male gender, young age, and lower socioeconomic status, for example, the risk of violence presented by mental disorder is modest. Compared with the magnitude of risk associated with alcoholism and other drug abuse, the risk associated with major mental disorders such as schizophrenia and affective disorder is modest indeed. Clearly, mental health status makes at best a trivial contribution to the overall level of violence in society. (But see "Developments in the Law", 1974, on the legal justification—"because [the mentally disordered] are . . . unable to make autonomous decisions" (p. 1233)—for preventively intervening in the lives of disordered people in situations in which we do not intervene with nondisordered people, even when the nondisordered people present a higher risk of violence.)

What, then, are the implications of the conclusion that mental disorder may be a significant, albeit modest, risk factor for the occurrence of violent behavior? I see four principal ones. First, the empirical question of the relationship between mental disorder and violent behavior has only begun to be addressed. That *major mental disorder* as a generic category relates to violence would be important to know, but it is by no means all that clinicians and policymakers need to know. They need to know the specific features of mental disorder that carry the increased risk. Do disordered perceptions (e.g., hallucinations), disordered assumptions (e.g., delusions), or disordered processes of reasoning or affect relate most closely to the occurrence of violent behavior? It is unclear whether mental disorder should be unpacked by diagnosis, by course, by symptom pattern, or by specific types of offender-victim interactions for the purpose of answering these crucial questions. Indeed, the victim's manner of reacting or overreacting to "fear-inducing" aspects of the disordered person's behavior may itself be a mediating factor in the occurrence of violence (Link et al., 1992). Violence itself may be only a by-product of a more generic tendency to "norm violation" that accompanies some forms of mental disorder. Epidemiological methods have yielded considerable insights in this general research area to date. "It is questionable, however, whether this group comparison approach can shed a great deal of light on more refined questions that may be posed at this point regarding the relationship between mental illness and criminality" (Mulvey, Blumstein, & Cohen, 1986, p. 60). The use of more longitudinal "career" methods at the individual level of analysis may have much to offer in this regard. Such studies could investigate, for example, how a person's likelihood of violence changes as his or her symptoms and life circumstances change.

Second, the data suggest that public education programs by advocates for the mentally disordered along the lines of "people with mental illness are no more violent than the rest of us" may be doomed to failure, as indeed research shows they have always failed (Cumming & Cumming, 1957). And they should fail: The claim, it turns out, may well be untrue. It will no doubt be difficult for mental health advocates to convey more accurate but more complex information about the relationship between mental disorder and violence in the sound bites and bumper stickers that have come to frame our public discourse. But the flat denial that any relationship exists between disorder and violence can no longer credibly be prefaced by "research shows" (Steadman, 1981). As Swanson et al. (1990), in commenting on their ECA data, stated, public fear of violence committed by the mentally disordered in the community is "largely unwarranted, though not totally groundless" (p. 769). I agree with Bloom (1989): "Few are interested in either heightening the stigmatization of the mentally ill or impeding the progress of the mentally ill in the community. Yet this progress is bound to be critically slowed without a realistic look at dangerousness" (p. 253).

Third, the antipathy toward dangerousness to others as one criterion for involuntary hospitalization frequently expressed by mental health professionals and professional organizations may be unwarranted. A concern with violence to others may not be a responsibility arbitrarily foisted on the mental health professions by an ignorant public that would better be left exclusively to the police. A somewhat heightened risk of violence may inhere in the disorders that it is the business of psychologists and psychiatrists to treat. It is not unreasonable of society to ask us to attend to this risk, within the limits of our ability to assess it (Grisso & Appelbaum, 1992; Monahan, 1993).

Finally, the data underscore the need for readily available mental health services in the community and in correctional institutions. If the experience of psychotic symptoms elevates the risk of violence and if psychotic symptoms can usually be controlled with treatment (Krakowski, Jaeger, & Volavka, 1988), then the provision of treatment to people in need of it can be justified as a small contribution to community safety, as well as a telling reflection on our common humanity.

NOTE

1. The items were, (a) Did you ever hit or throw things at your wife/husband/partner? [If so] Were you ever the one who threw things first, regardless of who started the argument? Did you hit or throw things first on more than one occasion? (b) Have you ever spanked or hit a child (yours or anyone else's) hard enough so that he or she had bruises or had to stay in bed or see a doctor? (c) Since age 18, have you been in more than one fight that came to swapping blows, other than fights with your husband/wife/partner? (d) Have you ever used a weapon like a stick, knife, or gun in a fight since you were 18? (e) Have you ever gotten into physical fights while drinking?

REFERENCES

American Psychiatric Association. (1980). *Diagnostic and statistical manual of mental disorders* (3rd ed.). Washington, DC: Author.

American Psychiatric Association. (1987). *Diagnostic and statistical manual of mental disorders* (3rd ed., rev.). Washington, DC: Author.

Appelbaum, P. (1988). The new preventive detention: Psychiatry's problematic responsibility for the control of violence. *American Journal of Psychiatry, 145*, 779–785.

Binder, R., & McNiel, D. (1988). Effects of diagnosis and context on dangerousness. *American Journal of Psychiatry, 145*, 728–732.

Bloom, J. (1989). The character of danger

in psychiatric practice: Are the mentally ill dangerous? *Bulletin of the American Academy of Psychiatry and the Law, 17,* 241–254.

Bureau of Justice Statistics. (1991). *Violent crime in the United States* (Report No. NCJ-127855). Washington, DC: Author.

California Department of Corrections, Office of Health Care Services. (1989). *Current description, evaluation, and recommendations for treatment of mentally disordered criminal offenders.* Sacramento: Author.

Campbell, J., & Schraiber, R. (1989). *In pursuit of wellness: The Well-being Project* (Vol. 6). Sacramento: California Department of Mental Health.

Collins, J., & Schlesinger, W. (1983, November). *The prevalence of psychiatric disorder among admissions to prison.* Paper presented at the meeting of the American Society of Criminology, Denver, CO.

Crowne, D., & Marlowe, D. (1960). A new scale of social desirability independent of psychopathology. *Journal of Consulting Psychology, 24,* 349–354.

Cumming, E., & Cumming, J. (1957). *Closed ranks: An experiment in mental health.* Cambridge, MA: Harvard University Press.

Daniel, A., Robins, A., Reid, J., & Wilfley, D. (1988). Lifetime and six-month prevalence of psychiatric disorders among sentenced female offenders. *Bulletin of the American Academy of Psychiatry and the Law, 16,* 333–342.

Davis, S. (1991). Violence by psychiatric inpatients: A review. *Hospital and Community Psychiatry, 42,* 585–590.

Deutsch, A. (1949). *The mentally ill in America: A history of their care and treatment from colonial times* (2nd ed.). New York: Columbia University Press.

Developments in the law: Civil commitment of the mentally ill. (1974). *Harvard Law Review, 87,* 1190–1406.

Dohrenwend, B. (1990). Socioeconomic status (SES) and psychiatric disorders: Are the issues still compelling? *Social Psychiatry and Psychiatric Epidemiology, 25,* 41–47.

DYG Corporation. (1990). *Public attitudes toward people with chronic mental illness.* Elmsford, NY: Author.

Field Institute. (1984). *In pursuit of wellness: A survey of California adults* (Vol. 4). Sacramento: California Department of Mental Health.

Gerbner, G., Gross, L., Morgan, M., & Signorielli, N. (1981). Health and medicine on television. *The New England Journal of Medicine, 305,* 901–904.

Gove, W. (1980). Labeling and mental illness: A critique. In W. Gove (Ed.), *The labeling of deviance: Evaluating a perspective* (2nd ed., pp. 264–270). Newbury Park, CA: Sage.

Grisso, T. (1991). Clinical assessments for legal decisionmaking: Research recommendations. In S. Shah & B. Sales (Eds.), *Law and mental health: Major developments and research needs* (pp. 49–80). Washington, DC: U.S. Department of Health and Human Services.

Grisso, T., & Appelbaum, P. (1992). Is it unethical to offer predictions of future violence? *Law and Human Behavior, 16,* 621–633.

Hodgins, S., & Cote, G. (1990, September). Prevalence of mental disorders among penitentiary inmates in Quebec. *Canada's Mental Health,* 1–4.

Jones, I., & Horne, D. (1973). Psychiatric disorders among aborigines of the Australian desert: Further data and discussion. *Social Science and Medicine, 1,* 219–228.

Klassen, D., & O'Connor, W. (1988). Crime, inpatient admissions, and violence among male mental patients. *International Journal of Law and Psychiatry, 11,* 305–312.

Klassen, D., & O'Connor, W. (1990). Assessing the risk of violence in released mental patients: A cross-validation study. *Psychological Assessment: A Journal of Consulting and Clinical Psychology, 1,* 75–81.

Krakowski, M., Jaeger, J., & Volavka, J. (1988). Violence and psychopathology: A longitudinal study. *Comprehensive Psychiatry, 29,* 174–181.

Krakowski, M., Volavka, J., & Brizer, D. (1986). Psychopathology and violence: A review of literature. *Comprehensive Psychiatry, 27,* 131–148.

Link, B., Andrews, H., & Cullen, F. (1992). The violent and illegal behavior of mental patients reconsidered. *American Sociological Review, 57,* 275–292.

Link, B., Cullen, F., Frank, J., & Wozniak, J. (1987). The social rejection of former mental patients: Understanding why labels matter. *American Journal of Sociology, 92,* 1461–1500.

Monahan, J. (1981). *The clinical prediction of violent behavior.* Washington, DC: U.S. Government Printing Office.

Monahan, J. (1988). Risk assessment of violence among the mentally disordered: Generating useful knowledge. *International Journal of Law and Psychiatry, 11,* 249–257.

Monahan, J. (1992). "A terror to their neighbors": Beliefs about mental disorder and violence in historical and cultural perspective. *Bulletin of the American Academy of Psychiatry and the Law, 20,* 191–195.

Monahan, J. (1993). Limiting therapist exposure to Tarasoff liability: Guidelines for risk containment. *American Psychologist,* 48, 242–250

Monahan, J., & Shah, S. (1989). Dangerousness and commitment of the mentally disordered in the United States. *Schizophrenia Bulletin, 15,* 541–553.

Monahan, J., & Steadman, H. (1983a). Crime and mental disorder: An epidemiological approach. In M. Tonry & N. Morris (Eds.), *Crime and justice: An annual review of research* (Vol. 4, pp. 145–189). Chicago: University of Chicago Press.

Monahan, J., & Steadman, H. (Eds.). (1983b). *Mentally disordered offenders: Perspectives from law & social science.* New York: Plenum Press.

Mullen, P. E. (1992). The clinical prediction of dangerousness. In D. Kavanaugh (Ed.), *Schizophrenia: An overview and practical handbook* (pp. 309–319). London: Chapman & Hall.

Mulvey, E., Blumstein, A., & Cohen, J. (1986). Reframing the research question of mental patient criminality. *International Journal of Law and Psychiatry, 9,* 57–65.

Murphy, J. (1976). Psychiatric labeling in crosscultural perspective. *Science, 191,* 1019–1028.

National Mental Health Association. (1987). *Stigma: A lack of awareness and understanding*. Alexandria, VA: Author.

Neighbors, H., Williams, D., Gunnings, T. Lipscomb, W., Broman, C., & Lepkowski, J. (1987). *The prevalence of mental disorder in Michigan prisons*. Lansing: Michigan Department of Corrections.

Otto, R. (1992). The prediction of dangerous behavior: A review and analysis of "second generation" research. *Forensic Reports, 5*, 103–133.

Rabkin, J. (1979). Criminal behavior of discharged mental patients: A critical appraisal of the research. *Psychological Bulletin, 86*, 1–27.

Robertson, G. (1988). Arrest patterns among mentally disordered offenders. *British Journal of Psychiatry, 153*, 313–316.

Robins, L., & Regier, D. (Eds.). (1991). *Psychiatric disorders in America: The Epidemiological Catchment Area study*. New York: Free Press.

Rosen, G. (1968). *Madness in society: Chapters in the historical sociology of mental illness*. Chicago: University of Chicago Press.

Roth, L. (1980). Correctional psychiatry. In W. Curran, A. McGarry, & C. Petty (Eds.), *Modern legal medicine, psychiatry and forensic science*. Philadelphia: Davis.

Roth, L. (Ed.). (1985). *Clinical treatment of the violent person*. Washington, DC: U.S. Government Printing Office.

Shain, R., & Phillips, J. (1991). The stigma of mental illness: Labeling and stereotyping in the news. In L. Wilkins & P. Patterson (Eds.), *Risky business: Communicating issues of science, risk, and public policy*(pp. 61–74). Westport, CT: Greenwood Press.

Shrout, P., Lyons, M., Dohrenwend, B., Skodol, A., Solomon, M., & Kass, F. (1988). Changing time frames on symptom inventories: Effects on the Psychiatric Epidemiology Research Interview. *Journal of Consulting and Clinical Psychology, 56*, 567–572.

Steadman, H. (1981). Critically reassessing the accuracy of public perceptions of the dangerousness of the mentally ill. *Journal of Health and Social Behavior, 22*, 310–316.

Steadman, H., & Cocozza, J. (1978). Selective reporting and the public's misconceptions of the criminally insane. *The Public Opinion Quarterly, 41*, 523–533.

Steadman, H., Fabisiak, S., Dvoskin, J., & Holohean, E. (1987). A survey of mental disability among state prison inmates. *Hospital and Community Psychiatry, 38*, 1086–1090.

Steadman, H., & Felson, R. (1984). Self-reports of violence: Ex-mental patients, ex-offenders, and the general population. *Criminology, 22*, 321–342.

Steadman, H., McCarty, D., & Morrissey, J. (1989). *The mentally ill in jail: Planning for essential services*. New York: Guilford Press.

Steadman, H., Monahan, J., Duffee, B., Hartstone, E., & Robbins, P. (1984). The impact of state mental hospital deinstitutionalization on United States prison populations, 1968–1978. *The Journal of Criminal Law and Criminology, 75*, 474–490.

Steadman, H., Monahan, J., Robbins, P., Appelbaum, P., Grisso, T., Klassen, D., Mulvey, E., & Roth, L. (1992). *From dangerousness to risk assessment: Implications for appropriate research strategies*. Unpublished manuscript.

Swanson, J., & Holzer, C. (1991). Violence and the ECA data. *Hospital and Community Psychiatry, 42*, 79–80.

Swanson, J., Holzer, C., Ganju, V., & Jono, R. (1990). Violence and psychiatric disorder in the community: Evidence from the Epidemiologic Catchment Area surveys. *Hospital and Community Psychiatry, 41*, 761–770.

Taylor, P., & Gunn, J. (1984). Violence and psychosis: I. Risk of violence among psychotic men. *British Medical Journal, 288*, 1945–1949.

Teplin, L. (1985). The criminality of the mentally ill: A dangerous misconception. *American Journal of Psychiatry, 142*, 593–599.

Teplin, L. (1990). The prevalence of severe mental disorder among male urban jail detainees: Comparison with the Epidemiologic Catchment Area program. *American Journal of Public Health, 80*, 663–669.

Werner, P., Rose, T., & Yesavage, J. (1983). Reliability, accuracy, and decision-making strategy in clinical predictions of imminent dangerousness. *Journal of Consulting and Clinical Psychology, 51*, 815–825.

Wessely, S., & Taylor, P. (1991). Madness and crime: Criminology versus psychiatry. *Criminal Behaviour and Mental Health, 1*, 193–228.

Westermeyer, J., & Kroll, J. (1978). Violence and mental illness in a peasant society: Characteristics of violent behaviours and "folk" use of restraints. *British Journal of Psychiatry, 133*, 529–541.

DISCUSSION

The contradictory conclusions drawn by Teplin and Monahan on the mental illness–violence relationship remind us of an obvious but all too easily overlooked lesson: The answer one gets to a research question depends on the question one asks. Careful scrutiny of Teplin's and Monahan's reasoning reveals that these two investigators are actually asking somewhat different questions about the association between psychopathology and violence.

In her review of the literature, Teplin concludes that the relationship between mental illness and criminality essentially disappears after one controls statistically for a variety of demographic factors, such as age and socioeconomic status, and for prior criminal history. This result indicates, argues Teplin, that mental illness per se is not associated with an increased risk of criminality or violence. Instead, certain factors that are themselves often associated with mental illness, such as poverty, are actually responsible for the heightened rate of criminality among the mentally ill. In contrast, Monahan argues that the practice of controlling statistically for the demographic and other variables that are associated with mental disorder is logically questionable. According to Monahan, controlling for such influences may mask the genuine relationship between psychopathology and violence.

The issue of statistical "control" is a deceptively complex one. Not uncommonly, one hears news reports like the following: "Investigators Smith and Jones found an association between alcohol intake and risk for heart attacks. But after Smith and Jones controlled for cigarette smoking, diet, and exercise, this association disappeared." What does this statement really mean? Essentially, when researchers control for extraneous variables, they are using statistical techniques to remove the effects of these variables from the correlation between two other variables. In essence, Smith and Jones are saying, "All other things being equal, there is no correlation between alcohol intake and heart attacks."

The extraneous variables that investigators often control for—in Smith and Jones's case, cigarette smoking, diet, and exercise—are sometimes referred to as **nuisance variables**, because they are a "nuisance" to investigators who are attempting to draw a causal inference from a correlation. You may be understandably confused by this last sentence. Introductory psychology courses teach us that "correlation is not causation," meaning that because two variables are statistically associated with one another does not imply that they are necessarily causally related. But why isn't correlation causation?

The primary reason that correlation is not causation can be traced to the so-called **third-variable problem**: Given a correlation between two variables, A and B, a third variable C (and a fourth variable D, and a fifth variable E, and so on) may be correlated with both A and B, and may therefore be producing the correlation between A and B. If so, A and B can be correlated without having a direct causal relationship to one another. Most psychologists have their own favorite example of the third-variable problem. Here's mine, for which I am indebted to Dr. Daryl Bem of Cornell University: There is a substantial negative correlation between the number of doctoral degrees awarded in a state and the number of mules in that state. How can we explain this preposterous correlation? Are the mules frightening away prospective Ph.D.s? Are prospective Ph.D.s capturing mules and transporting them to other states? Although both of these explanations are theoretically possible, they are rather implausible. Instead, it is most likely that a third variable, namely rural or urban location, is responsible for the negative correlation between doctoral degrees and mules. Rural states (like Wyoming) tend to have few universities (and thus award few doctoral degrees) and many mules, whereas urban states (like my home state of New York) have many universities but are not especially renowned for their abundance of mules.

Thus, correlation is not causation because third variables (that is, nuisance variables) can produce a correlation between two other variables. But by controlling for nuisance variables, the investigator can often attempt to draw a causal inference from a correlation by eliminating other plausible explanations of this correlation. To understand what I mean, let's return to the study of the association between alcohol intake and heart attacks. Presumably, Smith and Jones elected to control for cigarette smoking, diet, and exercise because they wished to rule out the possibility that these nuisance variables were spuriously producing the correlation between alcohol use and heart attacks. After all, we know that individuals who smoke heavily, eat unhealthy foods, and engage in little or no exercise are at elevated risk for heart attacks. By controlling for these variables, Smith and Jones attempted to exclude the hypothesis that it was these three nuisance variables, rather than alcohol intake per se, that were associated with heart attacks. Certainly, Smith and Jones were correct to control for these variables—right?

But wait: The issue is not quite this clear-cut. As Paul Meehl (1970, 1971) has pointed out, whenever we control for a nuisance variable, we are making an important assumption regarding the causal relationship between this variable (C) and our two principal variables of interest (A and B). Specifically, we are assuming that this nuisance variable C causes both A and B, just as in the Ph.D.-mule example. But this assumption may be erroneous. In the case of Smith and Jones's study, let's imagine that heavy drinking causes individuals to become apathetic and thus to care less about their health. In turn, this lack of concern about health may lead, in at least certain individuals, to cigarette smoking, poor diet, and a lack of exercise. According to this scenario, then, alcohol intake (at least to some extent) causes these three nuisance variables rather than the reverse. If so, controlling for these three variables will actually mask the true correlation between alcohol intake and heart attacks, because by controlling for these variables we are in effect also removing some of the variance that is psychologically related to alcohol use.

Now let us see if we can apply some of this esoteric statistical logic to the dispute between Teplin and Monahan. Recall that when researchers control for nuisance variables, they are attempting to draw a causal inference from a correlation. In effect, then, Teplin is asking is this question: Does mental illness cause criminality and violence? Essentially, she is arguing that the correlation between mental illness and violence is not due to mental illness itself but is due instead to variables (such as social class) that happen to be associated with mental illness. Teplin's assumptions, although potentially defensible, are also open to question. Let's imagine, for example, that mental disorders cause some individuals to become poorer, perhaps because mental illness interferes with the ability to gain and maintain employment. If so, controlling for social class would obscure the true relationship between mental illness and violence, because this procedure would eliminate some of the variance relevant to mental illness.

Monahan, in contrast, is asking a more straightforward question: Is mental illness correlated with criminality and violence? His review of the literature suggests that the answer is yes, particularly for disorders characterized by psychotic symptoms such as delusions and hallucinations. It is important to note, however, that the findings reviewed by Monahan do not allow us to conclude definitively that mental illness is causally related to violence, plausible as this possibility might seem in certain cases. The old dictum that correlation is not causation applies.

The conclusion that mental illness is associated with a somewhat increased rate of violence must be tempered by two crucial caveats. First, it is necessary to recognize that the question constituting this chapter's title, although a useful starting point for research purposes, is almost surely too simple. If you have learned anything by this point in the book, it is (I would hope) that mental disorders constitute an enormously heterogeneous collection of conditions differing greatly in their clinical manifestations and etiologies. It seems exceedingly unlikely that all these conditions would be associated with an increased risk of violence. Indeed, although this possibility has not been adequately researched, it may well be that certain mental illnesses, such as anxiety disorders and mood disorders (which are typically characterized by behavioral withdrawal and inhibition), are actually associated with a reduced risk of violence. For example, in their review of the literature, Krakowski, Volavka, and Brizer (1986) conclude that some types of severely mentally disordered individuals (for example, chronic schizophrenics) may be at decreased risk for violence, simply because they are so incapacitated that they are unable to initiate and complete a physical assault. Thus, the overall positive correlation between mental illness and violence obscures the possibility that certain psychopathological conditions are essentially unrelated, or perhaps even negatively related, to violence.

The second crucial caveat, as Monahan points out, is that, although certain types of psychopathology are apparently associated with a slightly increased risk of criminality and violence, the vast majority of mentally ill individuals—about 90%, according to recent estimates—are not dangerous. Teplin's warnings concerning the dangers of stereotyping the mentally ill are thus well taken. Mental health professionals bear a substantial responsibility to avoid perpetuating this stereotype, both in their predictions of violence among the mentally ill and their statements to the popular press and general public.

QUESTIONS TO STIMULATE DISCUSSION

1. As discussed in the introduction to this chapter, mental health professionals (even experts) have been found to be highly fallible in their predictions of dangerousness. What are the implications of Monahan's conclusions regarding the mental illness–violence association for the capacity of mental health professionals to forecast dangerousness? Can the findings he cites be used to improve this predictive capacity? If so, how?
2. If Monahan is correct in stating that certain mental illnesses are associated with an increased risk of violence, should prisoners' psychiatric diagnoses, symptoms, or both be taken into account in parole decisions? What would be the ethical implications of doing so?
3. Monahan contends that psychotic symptomatology is perhaps the best predictor of violence among psychiatric patients. Is the association between psychosis and violence causal in nature? How could causality be tested?
4. Teplin and Monahan concur that the large majority of mentally ill individuals are not dangerous. How, then, did the widespread stereotype of the mentally ill individual as dangerous originate? What research approaches might shed light on this question?

SUGGESTIONS FOR FURTHER READING

Krakowski, M., Volavka, J., & Brizer, D. (1986). Psychopathology and violence: A review of the literature. *Comprehensive Psychiatry, 27*, 131–148.
After reviewing the literature on the relationship between mental illness and violence, the authors conclude that diagnosis, natural history, and certain symptom constellations are related to the risk of violence among psychiatric patients. They also conclude that certain personality disorders are disproportionately represented among violent individuals.

Monahan, J. (1981). *The clinical prediction of violent behavior.* Washington, DC: U.S. Government Printing Office.
This superb monograph provides a detailed overview of the difficulties involved in the clinical prediction of violence, including the problems inherent in the prediction of low base-rate events. In addition, Monahan reviews the research literature on the prediction of violence and discusses the potential advantages and disadvantages of statistical approaches to violence prediction.

Monahan, J., & Shah, S. (1989). Dangerousness and commitment of the mentally disordered in the United States. *Schizophrenia Bulletin, 15*, 541–553.
The authors briefly review recent changes in U.S. mental health laws bearing on the dangerousness of psychiatric patients to self and others. In addition, they discuss the current status of research on dangerousness and its prediction.

Monahan, J., & Steadman, H. J. (1983). Crime and mental disorder: An epidemiological approach. In M. Tonry & N. Morris (Eds.), *Crime and justice: An annual review of research* (pp. 145–189). Chicago: University of Chicago Press.
The authors provide a comprehensive review of the epidemiological data on the relationship between mental illness and criminality. They conclude that the rates of true and treated mental disorder among criminals exceed those of the general population, as do the rates of true and treated crime among mentally ill individuals. Nevertheless, they find that when various demographic factors (such as age and social class) and life history factors (such as prior contacts with the criminal

justice system) are controlled for statistically, these differences essentially disappear.

Monahan, J., & Steadman, H. (Eds.). (1983). *Mentally disordered offenders: Perspectives from law and social science*. New York: Plenum Press.

This volume contains chapters dealing with a variety of topics relevant to mental illness and criminality, including competency to stand trial, the insanity defense, mental illness among sex offenders, and the transfer of prisoners to mental hospitals.

Rabkin, J. (1979). Criminal behavior of discharged mental patients: A critical appraisal of the research. *Psychological Bulletin, 86*, 1–27.

Rabkin discusses methodological issues in the study of dangerousness among the mentally ill and reviews the literature on the arrest and conviction rates of discharged psychiatric patients. She concludes that discharged patients have arrest rates that considerably exceed those of the general public and of other patients, although this difference is largely or entirely attributable to prior criminal history.

Teplin, L. A., Abram, K. M., & McClelland, G. M. (1994). Does psychiatric disorder predict violent crime among released jail detainees? A six-year longitudinal study. *American Psychologist, 49*, 335–342.

The authors report the results of a follow-up study of jail detainees with major psychiatric disorders, such as schizophrenia, depression, and substance abuse and dependence. They find that neither severe mental disorders nor substance use disorders were associated with rates of violent crime after six years, although there was a slight but statistically nonsignificant trend for delusions and hallucinations to be correlated with higher arrest rates for violence.

REFERENCES

Appelbaum, P. (1988). The new preventative detention: Psychiatry's problematic responsibility for the control of violence. *American Journal of Psychiatry, 145*, 779–785.

Chapman, L. J., & Chapman, J. P. (1967). Genesis of popular but erroneous psychodiagnostic observations. *Journal of Abnormal Psychology, 72*, 193–204.

Chapman, L. J., & Chapman, J. P. (1969). Illusory correlation as an obstacle to the use of valid psychodiagnostic signs. *Journal of Abnormal Psychology, 74*, 271–280.

Krakowski, M., Volavka, J., & Brizer, D. (1986). Psychopathology and violence: A review of the literature. *Comprehensive Psychiatry, 27*, 131–148.

Lyall, S. (1993, January 22). Danger of mentally ill homeless to be reevaluated in New York. *New York Times*, pp. A1, B2.

Meehl, P. E. (1970). Nuisance variables and the ex post facto design. In M. Radner & S. Winokur (Eds.), *Minnesota studies in the philosophy of science, IV* (pp. 373–402). Minneapolis: University of Minnesota Press.

Meehl, P. E. (1971). High school yearbooks: A reply to Schwarz. *Journal of Abnormal Psychology, 77*, 143–148.

Meehl, P. E., & Rosen, A. (1955). Antecedent probability and the efficiency of cutting scores. *Psychological Bulletin, 52*, 194–216.

Monahan, J. (1981). *The clinical prediction of violent behavior*. Washington, DC: U.S. Government Printing Office.

CHAPTER

19

Should psychiatric patients be hospitalized against their will?

PRO	Chodoff, P. (1976). The case for involuntary hospitalization of the mentally ill. *American Journal of Psychiatry*, *133*, 496–501.
CON	Szasz, T. S. (1978). Should psychiatric patients ever be hospitalized involuntarily? Under any circumstances—No. In J. P. Brady & H. K. H. Brodie (Eds.), *Controversy in psychiatry* (pp. 965–977). Philadelphia: W. B. Saunders.

OVERVIEW OF THE CONTROVERSY: Paul Chodoff reviews three perspectives on involuntary hospitalization—the "abolitionist" view, the "medical model" view, and the civil liberties view—and defends the practice of committing certain severely mentally ill individuals against their will. Thomas S. Szasz delineates the parallels between involuntary hospitalization and slavery and argues that civil commitment is a coercive practice that deprives patients of their freedom and dignity.

CONTEXT OF THE PROBLEM

The concept of liberty is so deeply ingrained in us as members of Western society that we have come almost to take it for granted. Most of us readily accept the premise that individuals should be free to engage in a remarkably wide range of behaviors, provided that these behaviors do not interfere with the rights of others. Notwithstanding differences of opinion regarding what constitute "the rights of others" (for example, does your right to use offensive language infringe on my right not to hear it?), we generally concur that individuals should enjoy considerable latitude in their actions unless these actions pose a threat to others. At the same time, however, most of us are strongly committed to the principle that society should do its utmost to assist those who are ill, infirm, or otherwise unable to help themselves. It is on the issue of the involuntary (that is, civil) commitment of psychiatric patients that these two fundamental precepts—liberty and altruism—come most squarely into conflict. For herein lies the crux of the dispute: Should society coercively restrict the rights of severely disturbed individuals who are unable or unwilling to care for themselves? Because approximately 55% of all admissions to public psychiatric hospitals are involuntary (Brakel, 1985), this question is of enormous societal significance.

As Szasz points out in the reading in this chapter, the involuntary confinement of the mentally ill has a lengthy history. From the time that mental hospitals were first built—in the 15th through 17th centuries in Spain, France, and the remainder of Europe—the practice of involuntary institutionalization of the severely psychiatrically ill has typically gone unquestioned. For many years in the United States, the primary criteria for civil commitment were that patients be severely mentally disturbed and in dire need of treatment (Appelbaum, 1993). But most civil libertarians have never felt entirely comfortable with these criteria. Why should the state, these critics ask, have the right to involuntarily commit individuals who are not dangerous to others? More recently, U.S. courts have generally reaffirmed the state's power to involuntarily commit some mentally ill individuals but have placed increasing restrictions on it.

In 1974, in the case of ***O'Connor v. Donaldson***, the U.S. Supreme Court ruled that nondangerous individuals who are capable of living independently cannot be confined in a psychiatric hospital against their will without treatment. In that same year, in the case of ***Lessard v. Schmidt***, the Supreme Court ruled that individuals have a right to be treated with the **least restrictive alternative** possible. In other words, individuals must be permitted to remain in the setting that places the fewest limitations on their freedom, provided that this setting meets their treatment needs. Finally, in 1979, in ***Addington v. Texas***, the Supreme Court ruled that to be involuntarily committed, patients must be judged to be both mentally ill and a "clear and convincing" danger to either themselves or others. Thus, the standards for civil commitment have subtly but progressively shifted away from what Chodoff, in the article in this chapter, terms medical criteria and toward criteria emphasizing dangerousness toward self and others.

Although involuntary commitment laws and procedures differ from state to state, most states require that one or more specific criteria be fulfilled in order to confine patients against their will for a prolonged period of time. In addition to being mentally ill, patients must be imminently dangerous toward others, imminently dangerous toward themselves, or incapable of caring for themselves. In general, the commitment process begins with a petition from a concerned individual, typically a police officer, mental health professional, friend, or relative. A judge then typically appoints several individuals (at least one of whom is often a psychiatrist) to conduct a detailed psychiatric evaluation. A formal hearing before the judge is usually held within several weeks of the initial petition. In most states, patients can be involuntarily committed for emergency purposes for brief periods (perhaps several days) if two physicians sign a certificate (a "hold order") stating that the individual is imminently dangerous to self or others.

The bizarre and celebrated case of Joyce Brown, who called herself Billy Boggs, highlights many of the complex ethical and legal issues involved in involuntary commitment. In 1987, Mayor Edward Koch of New York City initiated a program to canvass the city streets for severely mentally ill individuals and to hospitalize them against their will if necessary. The first patient they encountered as part of this program was Joyce Brown, a 40-year-old homeless black woman who defecated in her pants, spoke to herself, harassed and shouted profanities at black males, and burnt money given to her by strangers. She was not physically violent toward others, however. Several years earlier, Brown had become preoccupied with Bill Boggs, the host of a New York City television program, whom she visited on several occasions and named herself after. When Koch, on a tour with city officials, came upon Brown lying injured on the ground, he insisted that she be institutionalized against her will. She was then brought to Bellevue Hospital and given a diagnosis of paranoid schizophrenia.

Despite her unusual behaviors, Brown appeared surprisingly lucid and rational when asked to testify on her own behalf. In fact, in February 1988 she spoke articulately at a Harvard Law School forum on the civil liberties of the mentally ill. Brown soon became a focal point for the debate over the involuntary commitment of the mentally ill. Opponents of her commitment, including lawyers from the American Civil Liberties Union, maintained that she was a sane individual who was being unjustly deprived of her freedom. Supporters of her commitment, including Koch, contended that she was a grossly psychotic person who was incapable of rational decision making. The dispute attracted considerable public attention as Brown's advocates and Koch became embroiled in an increasingly vitriolic debate regarding the rights of the mentally ill versus the rights of the government to protect individuals from themselves.

Although the controversy largely subsided when Brown was released from Bellevue Hospital 84 days after her commitment, the questions raised by her involuntary hospitalization seem no closer to a satisfactory resolution today than they did in the late 1980s. Careful consideration of Brown's case reveals that two separable issues are at stake. First, where do the rights of individuals end and those of society begin? In other words, at what point, if any, does society have the right to curtail the rights of individuals simply because it finds their behavior offensive, threatening, or simply extremely annoying? Second, does society have the right to be paternalistic toward its own citizens? In other words, at what point, if any, does society possess the right to protect individuals from themselves, even if they do not pose a direct threat to others? Bear these two questions in mind when pondering the implications of the readings in this chapter.

THE CONTROVERSY: Chodoff vs. Szasz

Chodoff

Paul Chodoff begins by presenting several cases of psychiatrically disturbed individuals that illustrate the dilemma clinicians confront when deciding whether to institute involuntary commitment proceedings. He then reviews the three principal perspectives on involuntary hospitalization: the "abolitionist" view, the "medical model" view, and the civil liberties view. Many abolitionists reject the notion that mental illness exists; they contend that this label is a weapon of control on the part of the psychiatric profession. Moreover, abolitionists believe that involuntary commitment undermines both the freedoms and responsibilities of the mentally ill. In contrast, advocates of the "medical model" maintain that mental illness stems from an underlying "disease" and that many severely mentally ill individuals are incapable of making rational decisions concerning their own welfare. The criteria for involuntary hospitalization put forth by advocates of this view typically include mental illness, interference with functioning, and need for care and treatment. Finally, proponents of the civil liberties view accept the need for involuntary hospitalization but object to the use of medical criteria. Instead, civil liberties advocates focus on imminent dangerousness to others as the principal criterion for civil commitment. Chodoff criticizes this view on six grounds, including its neglect of nondangerous individuals who urgently require treatment and its blurring of the boundaries between criminal and civil commitment. Chodoff argues that proponents of the abolitionist and civil liberties views have adopted a narrow and short-sighted definition of freedom and suggests a return to medical criteria for civil commitment.

Szasz

Thomas Szasz notes that the involuntary commitment of psychiatric patients, which dates back to the Middle Ages, has consistently reflected a paternalistic attitude on the part of psychiatry. He reviews four sources of evidence against involuntary commitment: medical, moral, historical, and literary. Involuntary commitment, Szasz argues, is not genuinely intended to protect or benefit the mentally ill but is instead designed to segregate unpleasant and annoying individuals from the remainder of society. It is thus similar in its aims to criminal punishment, although Szasz points out that the mentally ill individual actually enjoys fewer legal rights and protections than does the accused criminal. Szasz then discusses the parallels between involuntary hospitalization and slavery. Just as slavery was justified by its advocates on the grounds that blacks were happier and safer when enslaved, involuntary hospitalization is justified by its advocates on the grounds that mental patients are happier and safer when institutionalized. Moreover, the relationship between master and slave can in many ways be likened to the relationship between psychiatrist and patient. Szasz concludes that involuntary commitment is a coercive and unethical practice that unjustly deprives psychiatric patients of their most fundamental civil liberties.

KEY CONCEPTS AND TERMS

"medical model" View that mental illnesses are a product of an underlying "disease."

moral treatment Form of treatment, pioneered by individuals such as Philippe Pinel in the late 1700s and early 1800s, that emphasizes humane and compassionate care of the psychiatrically ill.

parens patriae Literally, the "parent of the country"; the doctrine that the country or state should assume the role of legal guardian for individuals who are unable to care for or protect themselves.

PREVIEW QUESTIONS

1. According to Chodoff, what are the major tenets of the "abolitionists"?
2. According to Chodoff, what are the principal assumptions of proponents of the "medical model" view?
3. What are the major commitment criteria proposed by advocates of the "medical model" view? What are the principal objections to these criteria?
4. What is the key criterion for civil commitment proposed by civil liberties lawyers? What does Chodoff view as the major weaknesses of this criterion?
5. According to Szasz, what are the four major sources of evidence against involuntary commitment?
6. In what respects, according to Szasz, is involuntary commitment similar to slavery? How are the rationalizations of proponents of involuntary commitment similar to those previously made by proponents of slavery?
7. In what respects, according to Szasz, is the relationship between psychiatrist and patient similar to that between master and slave?
8. According to Szasz, what are the practical implications of recognizing the commonalities between slavery and involuntary hospitalization?

PAUL CHODOFF

The case for involuntary hospitalization of the mentally ill

I will begin this paper with a series of vignettes designed to illustrate graphically the question that is my focus: under what conditions, if any, does society have the right to apply coercion to an individual to hospitalize him against his will, by reason of mental illness?

Case 1. A woman in her mid 50s, with no previous overt behavioral difficulties, comes to believe that she is worthless and insignificant. She is completely preoccupied with her guilt and is increasingly unavailable for the ordinary demands of life. She eats very little because of her conviction that the food should go to others whose need is greater than hers, and her physical condition progressively deteriorates. Although she will talk to others about herself, she insists that she is not sick, only bad. She refuses medication, and when hospitalization is suggested she also refuses that on the grounds that she would be taking up space that otherwise could be occupied by those who merit treatment more than she.

Case 2. For the past 6 years the behavior of a 42-year-old woman has been disturbed for periods of 3 months or longer. After recovery from her most recent episode she has been at home, functioning at a borderline level. A month ago she again started to withdraw from her environment. She pays increasingly less attention to her bodily needs, talks very little, and does not respond to questions or attention from those about her. She lapses into a mute state and lies in her bed in a totally passive fashion. She does not respond to other people, does not eat, and does not void. When her arm is raised from the bed it remains for several minutes in the position in which it is left. Her medical history and a physical examination reveal no evidence of primary physical illness.

Case 3. A man with a history of alcoholism has been on a binge for several weeks. He remains at home doing little else than drinking. He eats very little. He becomes tremulous and misinterprets spots on the wall as animals about to attack him, and he complains of "creeping" sensations in his body, which he attributes to infestation by insects. He does not seek help voluntarily, insists there is nothing wrong with him, and despite his wife's entreaties he continues to drink.

Case 4. Passersby and station personnel observe that a young woman has been spending several days at Union Station in Washington, DC. Her behavior appears strange to others. She is finally befriended by a newspaper reporter who becomes aware that her perception of her situation is profoundly unrealistic and that she is, in fact, delusional. He persuades her to accompany him to St. Elizabeth's Hospital, where she is examined by a psychiatrist who recommends admission. She refuses hospitalization and the psychiatrist allows her to leave. She returns to Union Station. A few days later she is found dead, murdered, on one of the surrounding streets.

Case 5. A government attorney in his late 30s begins to display pressured speech and hyperactivity. He is too busy to sleep and eats very little. He talks rapidly, becomes irritable when interrupted, and makes phone calls all over the country in furtherance of his political ambitions, which are to begin a campaign for the Presidency of the United States. He makes many purchases, some very expensive, thus running through a great deal of money. He is rude and tactless to his friends, who are offended by his behavior, and his job is in jeopardy. In spite of his wife's pleas he insists that he does not have the time to seek or accept treatment, and he refuses hospitalization. This is not the first such disturbance for this individual; in fact, very similar episodes have been occurring at roughly 2-year intervals since he was 18 years old.

Case 6. Passersby in a campus area observe two young women standing together, staring at each other, for over an hour. Their behavior

SOURCE: *American Journal of Psychiatry, 133* (5), pp. 496–501, May 1976.

> attracts attention, and eventually the police take the pair to a nearby precinct station for questioning. They refuse to answer questions and sit mutely, staring into space. The police request some type of psychiatric examination but are informed by the city attorney's office that state law (Michigan) allows persons to be held for observation only if they appear obviously dangerous to themselves or others. In this case, since the women do not seem homicidal or suicidal, they do not qualify for observation and are released.
>
> Less than 30 hours later the two women are found on the floor of their campus apartment, screaming and writhing in pain with their clothes ablaze from a self-made pyre. One woman recovers; the other dies. There is no conclusive evidence that drugs were involved (1).

Most, if not all, people would agree that the behavior described in these vignettes deviates significantly from even elastic definitions of normality. However, it is clear that there would not be a similar consensus on how to react to this kind of behavior and that there is a considerable and increasing ferment about what attitude the organized elements of our society should take toward such individuals. Everyone has a stake in this important issue, but the debate about it takes place principally among psychiatrists, lawyers, the courts, and law enforcement agencies.

Points of view about the question of involuntary hospitalization fall into the following three principal groups: the "abolitionists," medical model psychiatrists, and civil liberties lawyers.

THE ABOLITIONISTS

Those holding this position would assert that in none of the cases I have described should involuntary hospitalization be a viable option because, quite simply, it should never be resorted to under any circumstances. As Szasz (2) has put it, "we should value liberty more highly than mental health no matter how defined" and "no one should be deprived of his freedom for the sake of his mental health." Ennis (3) has said that the goal "is nothing less than the abolition of involuntary hospitalization."

Prominent among the abolitionists are the "anti-psychiatrists," who, somewhat surprisingly, count in their ranks a number of well-known psychiatrists. For them mental illness simply does not exist in the field of psychiatry (4). They reject entirely the medical model of mental illness and insist that acceptance of it relies on a fiction accepted jointly by the state and by psychiatrists as a device for exerting social control over annoying or unconventional people. The anti-psychiatrists hold that these people ought to be afforded the dignity of being held responsible for their behavior and required to accept its consequences. In addition, some members of this group believe that the phenomena of "mental illness" often represent essentially a tortured protest against the insanities of an irrational society (5). They maintain that society should not be encouraged in its oppressive course by affixing a pejorative label to its victims.

Among the abolitionists are some civil liberties lawyers who both assert their passionate support of the magisterial importance of individual liberty and react with repugnance and impatience to what they see as the abuses of psychiatric practice in this field—the commitment of some individuals for flimsy and possibly self-serving reasons and their inhuman warehousing in penal institutions wrongly called "hospitals."

The abolitionists do not oppose psychiatric treatment when it is conducted with the agreement of those being treated. I have no doubt that they would try to gain the consent of the individuals described earlier to undergo treatment, including hospitalization. The psychiatrists in this group would be very likely to confine their treatment methods to psychotherapeutic efforts to influence the aberrant behavior. They would be unlikely to use drugs and would certainly eschew such somatic therapies as ECT [electroconvulsive therapy]. If efforts to enlist voluntary compliance with treatment failed, the abolitionists would not employ any means of coercion. Instead, they would step aside and allow social, legal, and community sanctions to take their course. If a human being should be jailed or a human life lost as a result of this attitude, they would accept it as a necessary evil to be tolerated in order to avoid the greater evil of unjustified loss of liberty for others (6).

THE MEDICAL MODEL PSYCHIATRISTS

I use this admittedly awkward and not entirely accurate label to designate the position of a substantial number of psychiatrists. They believe that mental illness is a meaningful concept and that under certain conditions its existence justifies the state's exercise, under the doctrine of parens patriae, of its right and obligation to arrange for the hospitalization of the sick individual even though coercion is involved and he is deprived of his liberty. I believe that these psychiatrists would recommend involuntary hospitalization for all six of the patients described earlier.

The Medical Model

There was a time, before they were considered to be ill, when individuals who displayed the kind of behavior I described earlier were put in "ships of fools" to wander the seas or were left to the mercies, sometimes tender but often savage, of uncomprehending communities that regarded them as either possessed or bad. During the Enlightenment and the early nineteenth century, however, these individuals gradually came to be regarded as sick people to be included under the humane and caring umbrella of the Judeo-Christian attitude toward illness. This attitude, which may have reached its height during the era of moral treatment in the early nineteenth century, has had unexpected and ambiguous consequences. It became overextended and partially perverted, and these excesses led to the reaction that is so strong a current in today's attitude toward mental illness.

However, reaction itself can go too far, and I believe that this is already happening. Witness the disastrous consequences of the precipitate dehospitalization that is occurring all over the country. To remove the protective mantle of illness from these disturbed people is to expose them, their families, and their communities to consequences that are certainly maladaptive and possibly irreparable. Are we really acting in accordance with their best interests when we allow them to "die with their rights on" (1) or when we condemn them to a "preservation of liberty which is actually so destructive as to constitute another form of imprisonment" (7)? Will they not suffer "if [a] liberty they cannot enjoy is made superior to a health that must sometimes be forced on them" (8)?

Many of those who reject the medical model out of hand as inapplicable to so-called "mental illness" have tended to oversimplify its meaning and have, in fact, equated it almost entirely with organic disease. It is necessary to recognize that it is a complex concept and that there is a lack of agreement about its meaning. Sophisticated definitions of the medical model do not require only the demonstration of unequivocal organic pathology. A broader formulation, put forward by sociologists and deriving largely from Talcott Parsons' description of the sick role (9), extends the domain of illness to encompass certain forms of social deviance as well as biological disorders. According to this definition, the medical model is characterized not only by organicity but also by being negatively valued by society, by "nonvoluntariness," thus exempting its exemplars from blame, and by the understanding that physicians are the technically competent experts to deal with its effects (10).

Except for the question of organic disease, the patients I described earlier conform well to this broader conception of the medical model. They are all suffering both emotionally and physically, they are incapable by an effort of will of stopping or changing their destructive behavior, and those around them consider them to be in an undesirable sick state and to require medical attention.

Categorizing the behavior of these patients as involuntary may be criticized as evidence of an intolerably paternalistic and antitherapeutic attitude that fosters the very failure to take responsibility for their lives and behavior that the therapist should uncover rather than encourage. However, it must also be acknowledged that these severely ill people are not capable at a conscious level of deciding what is best for themselves and that in order to help them examine their behavior and motivation, it is necessary that they be alive and available for treatment. Their verbal message that they will not accept treatment may at the same time be conveying other more covert messages—that they are desperate and want help even though they cannot ask for it (11).

Although organic pathology may not be the only determinant of the medical model, it is of course an important one and it should not be avoided in any discussion of mental illness. There would be no question that the previously described patient with delirium tremens is suffering from a toxic form of brain disease. There are a significant number of other patients who require involuntary hospitalization because of organic brain syndrome due to various causes. Among those who are not overtly organically ill, most of the candidates for involuntary hospitalization suffer from schizophrenia or one of the major affective disorders. A growing and increasingly impressive body of evidence points to the presence of an important genetic-biological factor in these conditions; thus, many of them qualify on these grounds as illnesses.

Despite the revisionist efforts of the anti-psychiatrists, mental illness *does* exist. It does not by any means include all of the people being treated by psychiatrists (or by nonpsychiatrist physicians), but it does encompass those few desperately sick people for whom involuntary commitment must be considered. In the words of a recent article, "The problem is that mental illness is not a myth. It is not some palpable falsehood propagated among the populace by power-mad psychiatrists, but a cruel and bitter reality that has been with the human race since antiquity" (12, p. 1483).

Criteria for Involuntary Hospitalization

Procedures for involuntary hospitalization should be instituted for individuals who require care and treatment because of diagnosable mental illness that produces symptoms, including marked impairment in judgment, that disrupt their intrapsychic and interpersonal functioning. All three of these criteria must be met before involuntary hospitalization can be instituted.

1. *Mental illness*. This concept has already been discussed, but it should be repeated that only a belief in the existence of illness justifies involuntary commitment. It is a fundamental assumption that makes aberrant behavior a medical matter and its care the concern of physicians.
2. *Disruption of functioning*. This involves combinations of serious and often obvious disturbances that are both intrapsychic (for example, the suffering of severe depression) and interpersonal (for example, withdrawal from others because of depression). It does not include minor peccadilloes or eccentricities. Furthermore, the behavior in question must represent symptoms of the mental illness from which the patient is suffering. Among these symptoms are actions that are imminently or potentially dangerous in a physical sense to self or others, as well as other manifestations of mental illness such as those in the cases I have described. This is not

to ignore dangerousness as a criterion for commitment but rather to put it in its proper place as one of a number of symptoms of the illness. A further manifestation of the illness, and indeed, the one that makes involuntary rather than voluntary hospitalization necessary, is impairment of the patient's judgment to such a degree that he is unable to consider his condition and make decisions about it in his own interests.

3. *Need for care and treatment.* The goal of physicians is to treat and cure their patients; however, sometimes they can only ameliorate the suffering of their patients and sometimes all they can offer is care. It is not possible to predict whether someone will respond to treatment; nevertheless, the need for treatment and the availability of facilities to carry it out constitute essential preconditions that must be met to justify requiring anyone to give up his freedom. If mental hospital patients have a right to treatment, then psychiatrists have a right to ask for treatability as a front-door as well as a back-door criterion for commitment (7). All of the six individuals I described earlier could have been treated with a reasonable expectation of returning to a more normal state of functioning.

I believe that the objections to this formulation can be summarized as follows.

1. The whole structure founders for those who maintain that mental illness is a fiction.
2. These criteria are also untenable to those who hold liberty to be such a supreme value that the presence of mental illness per se does not constitute justification for depriving an individual of his freedom; only when such illness is manifested by clearly dangerous behavior may commitment be considered. For reasons to be discussed later, I agree with those psychiatrists (13, 14) who do not believe that dangerousness should be elevated to primacy above other manifestations of mental illness as a sine qua non for involuntary hospitalization.
3. The medical model criteria are "soft" and subjective and depend on the fallible judgment of psychiatrists. This is a valid objection. There is no reliable blood test for schizophrenia and no method for injecting gray cells into psychiatrists. A relatively small number of cases will always fall within a gray area that will be difficult to judge. In those extreme cases in which the question of commitment arises, competent and ethical psychiatrists should be able to use these criteria without doing violence to individual liberties and with the expectation of good results. Furthermore, the possible "fuzziness" of some aspects of the medical model approach is certainly no greater than that of the supposedly "objective" criteria for dangerousness, and there is little reason to believe that lawyers and judges are any less fallible than psychiatrists.
4. Commitment procedures in the hands of psychiatrists are subject to intolerable abuses. Here, as Peszke said, "It is imperative that we differentiate between the principle of the process of civil commitment and the practice itself" (13, p. 825). Abuses can contaminate both the medical and the dangerousness approaches, and I believe that the abuses stemming from the abolitionist view of no commitment at all are even greater. Measures to abate abuses of the medical approach include judicial review and the abandonment of indeterminate commitment. In the course of commitment proceedings and thereafter, patients should have access to competent and compassionate legal counsel. However, this latter safeguard may itself be subject to abuse if the legal counsel acts solely in the adversary tradition and undertakes to carry out the patient's wishes even when they may be destructive.

Comment

The criteria and procedures outlined will apply most appropriately to initial episodes and recurrent attacks of mental illness. To put it simply, it is necessary to find a way to satisfy legal and humanitarian considerations and yet allow psychiatrists access to initially or acutely ill patients in order to do the best they can for them. However, there are some involuntary patients who have received adequate and active treatment but have not responded satisfactorily. An irreducible minimum of such cases, principally among those with brain disorders and process schizophrenia, will not improve sufficiently to be able to adapt to even a tolerant society.

The decision of what to do at this point is not an easy one, and it should certainly not be in the hands of psychiatrists alone. With some justification they can state that they have been given the thankless job of caring, often with inadequate facilities, for badly damaged people and that they are now being subjected to criticism for keeping these patients locked up. No one really knows what to do with these patients. It may be that when treatment has failed they exchange their sick role for what has been called the impaired role (15), which implies a permanent negative evaluation of them coupled with a somewhat less benign societal attitude. At this point, perhaps a case can be made for giving greater importance to the criteria for dangerousness and releasing such patients if they do not pose a threat to others. However, I do not believe that the release into the community of these severely malfunctioning individuals will serve their interests even though it may satisfy formal notions of right and wrong.

It should be emphasized that the number of individuals for whom involuntary commitment must be considered is small (although, under the influence of current pressures, it may be smaller than it should be). Even severe mental illness can often be handled by securing the cooperation of the patient, and certainly one of the favorable effects of the current ferment has been to encourage such efforts. However, the distinction between voluntary and involuntary hospitalization is sometimes more formal than meaningful. How "voluntary" are the actions of an individual who is being buffeted by the threats, entreaties, and tears of his family?

I believe, however, that we are at a point (at least in some jurisdictions) where, having rebounded from an era in which involuntary commitment was too easy and employed too often, we are now entering one in which it is becoming very difficult to commit anyone, even in urgent cases. Faced with the moral obloquy that has come to pervade the atmosphere in which the decision to involuntarily hospitalize is considered, some psychiatrists, especially younger ones, have become, as Stone (16) put it, "soft as grapes" when faced with the prospect of committing anyone under any circumstances.

THE CIVIL LIBERTIES LAWYERS

I use this admittedly inexact label to designate those members of the legal profession who do not in principle reject the necessity for involuntary hospitalization but who do reject or wish to diminish the importance of medical model criteria in the hands of psychiatrists. Accordingly, the civil liberties lawyers, in dealing with the problem of involuntary hospitalization, have enlisted themselves under the standard of dangerousness, which they hold to be more objective and capable of being dealt with in a sounder evidentiary manner than the medical model criteria. For them the question is not whether mental illness, even of disabling degree, is present, but only whether it has resulted in the probability of behavioral dangerous to others or to self. Thus they would scrutinize the cases previously described for evidence of such dangerousness and would make the decision about involuntary hospitalization accordingly. They would probably feel that commitment is not indicated in most of these cases, since they were selected as illustrative of severe mental illness in which outstanding evidence of physical dangerousness was not present.

The dangerousness standard is being used increasingly not only to supplement criteria for mental illness but, in fact, to replace them entirely. The recent Supreme Court decision in *O'Connor v. Donaldson* (17) is certainly a long step in this direction. In addition, "dangerousness" is increasingly being understood to refer to the probability that the individual will inflict harm on himself or others in a specific physical manner rather than in other ways. This tendency has perhaps been carried to its ultimate in the *Lessard v. Schmidt* case (18) in Wisconsin, which restricted suitability for commitment to the "extreme likelihood that if the person is not confined, he will do immediate harm to himself or others." (This decision was set aside by the U.S. Supreme Court in 1974.) In a recent Washington, DC., Superior Court case (19) the instructions to the jury stated that the government must prove that the defendant was likely to cause "substantial physical harm to himself or others in the reasonably foreseeable future."

For the following reasons, the dangerousness standard is an inappropriate and dangerous indicator to use in judging the conditions under which someone should be involuntarily hospitalized. Dangerousness is being taken out of its proper context as one among other symptoms of the presence of severe mental illness that should be the determining factor.

1. To concentrate on dangerousness (especially to others) as the sole criterion for involuntary hospitalization deprives many mentally ill persons of the protection and treatment that they urgently require. A psychiatrist under the constraints of the dangerousness rule, faced with an out-of-control manic individual whose frantic behavior the psychiatrist truly believes to be a disguised call for help, would have to say. "Sorry, I would like to help you but I can't because you haven't threatened anybody and you are not suicidal." Since psychiatrists are admittedly not very good at accurately predicting dangerousness to others, the evidentiary standards for commitment will be very stringent. This will result in mental hospitals becoming prisons for a small population of volatile, highly assaultive, and untreatable patients (14).
2. The attempt to differentiate rigidly (especially in regard to danger to self) between physical and other kinds of self-destructive behavior is artificial, unrealistic, and unworkable. It will tend to confront psychiatrists who want to help their patients with the same kind of dilemma they were faced with when justification for therapeutic abolition on psychiatric grounds depended on evidence of suicidal intent. The advocates of the dangerousness standard seem to be more comfortable with and pay more attention to the factor of dangerousness to others even though it is a much less frequent and much less significant consequence of mental illness than is danger to self.
3. The emphasis on dangerousness (again, especially to others) is a real obstacle to the right-to-treatment movement since it prevents the hospitalization and therefore the treatment of the population most amenable to various kinds of therapy.
4. Emphasis on the criterion of dangerousness to others moves involuntary commitment from a civil to a criminal procedure, thus, as Stone (14) put it, imposing the procedures of one terrible system on another. Involuntary commitment on these

grounds becomes a form of preventive detention and makes the psychiatrist a kind of glorified policeman.

5. Emphasis on dangerousness rather than mental disability and helplessness will hasten the process of deinstitutionalization. Recent reports (20, 21) have shown that these patients are not being rehabilitated and reintegrated into the community, but rather, that the burden of custodialism has been shifted from the hospital to the community.
6. As previously mentioned, emphasis on the dangerousness criterion may be a tactic of some of the abolitionists among the civil liberties lawyers (22) to end involuntary hospitalization by reducing it to an unworkable absurdity.

DISCUSSION

It is obvious that it is good to be at liberty and that it is good to be free from the consequences of disabling and dehumanizing illness. Sometimes these two values are incompatible, and in the heat of the passions that are often aroused by opposing views of right and wrong, the partisans of each view may tend to minimize the importance of the other. Both sides can present their horror stories—the psychiatrists, their dead victims of the failure of the involuntary hospitalization process, and the lawyers, their Donaldsons. There is a real danger that instead of acknowledging the difficulty of the problem, the two camps will become polarized, with a consequent rush toward extreme and untenable solutions rather than working toward reasonable ones.

The path taken by those whom I have labeled the abolitionists is an example of the barren results that ensue when an absolute solution is imposed on a complex problem. There are human beings who will suffer greatly if the abolitionists succeed in elevating an abstract principle into an unbreakable law with no exceptions. I find myself oppressed and repelled by their position, which seems to stem from an ideological rigidity which ignores that element of the contingent immanent in the structure of human existence. It is devoid of compassion.

The positions of those who espouse the medical model and the dangerousness approaches to commitment are, one hopes, not completely irreconcilable. To some extent these differences are a result of the vantage points from which lawyers and psychiatrists view mental illness and commitment. The lawyers see and are concerned with the failures and abuses of the process. Furthermore, as a result of their training, they tend to apply principles to classes of people rather than to take each instance as unique. The psychiatrists, on the other hand, are required to deal practically with the singular needs of individuals. They approach the problem from a clinical rather than a deductive stance. As physicians, they want to be in a position to take care of and to help suffering people whom they regard as sick patients. They sometimes become impatient with the rules that prevent them from doing this.

I believe we are now witnessing a pendular swing in which the rights of the mentally ill to be treated and protected are being set aside in the rush to give them their freedom at whatever cost. But is freedom defined only by the absence of external constraints? Internal physiological or psychological processes can contribute to a throttling of the spirit that is as painful as any applied from the outside. The "wild" manic individual without his lithium, the panicky hallucinator without his injection of fluphenazine hydrochloride and the understanding support of a concerned staff, the sodden alcoholic—are they free? Sometimes, as Woody Guthrie said, "Freedom means no place to go."

Today the civil liberties lawyers are in the ascendancy and the psychiatrists on the defensive to a degree that is harmful to individual needs and the public welfare. Redress and a more balanced position will not come from further extension of the dangerousness doctrine. I favor a return to the use of medical criteria by psychiatrists—psychiatrists, however, who have been chastened by the buffeting they have received and are quite willing to go along with even strict legal safeguards as long as they are constructive and not tyrannical.

REFERENCES

1. Treffert DA: The practical limits of patients' rights. Psychiatric Annals 5(4):91–96, 1971
2. Szasz T: Law, Liberty and Psychiatry. New York, Macmillan Co, 1963
3. Ennis B: Prisoners of Psychiatry. New York, Harcourt Brace Jovanovich, 1972
4. Szasz T: The Myth of Mental Illness. New York, Harper & Row, 1961
5. Laing R: The Politics of Experience. New York, Ballantine Books, 1967
6. Ennis B: Ennis on "Donaldson." Psychiatric News, Dec 3, 1975, pp 4, 19, 37
7. Peele R, Chodoff P, Taub N: Involuntary hospitalization and treatability. observations from the DC experience. Catholic University Law Review 23:744–753, 1974
8. Michels R: The Right to Refuse Psychotropic Drugs. Hastings Center Report. Hastings-on-Hudson, NY, Hastings Institute of Health and Human Values, 1973
9. Parsons T: The Social System. New York, Free Press, 1951
10. Veatch RM: The medical model: its nature and problems. Hastings Center Studies 1(3):59–76, 1973
11. Katz J: The right to treatment—an enchanting legal fiction? University of Chicago Law Review 36:755–783, 1969
12. Moore MS: Some myths about "mental illness." Arch Gen Psychiatry 32: 1483–1497, 1975
13. Peszke MA: Is dangerousness an issue for physicians in emergency commitment? Am J Psychiatry 132:825–828, 1975
14. Stone AA: Comment on Peszke MA:

is dangerousness an issue for physicians in emergency commitment? Ibid, 829–831

15. Siegler M, Osmond H: Models of Madness, Models of Medicine. New York, Macmillan Co, 1974
16. Stone A: Lecture for course on The Law, Litigation, and Mental Health Services. Adelphi, Md, Mental Health Study Center, September 1974
17. O'Connor v Donaldson, 43 USLW 4929 (1975)
18. Lessard v Schmidt, 349 F Supp 1078, 1092 (ED Wis 1972)
19. In re Johnnie Hargrove. Washington, DC, Superior Court Mental Health number 506-75, 1975
20. Rachlin S, Pam A, Milton J: Civil liberties versus involuntary hospitalization. Am J Psychiatry 132: 189–191, 1975
21. Kirk SA, Therrien ME: Community mental health myths and the fate of former hospitalized patients. Psychiatry 38:209–217, 1975
22. Dershowitz AA: Dangerousness as a criterion for confinement. Bulletin of the American Academy of Psychiatry and the Law 2:172–179, 1974

THOMAS S. SZASZ

Should psychiatric patients ever be hospitalized involuntarily? Under any circumstances—No

My answer to this question is an emphatic and unqualified "No." Before setting forth my reasons for this answer, I should like to clarify and comment on the key terms used in the question that makes up the title of this [reading].

Who is a psychiatric patient? Ostensibly, it is someone suffering from a mental disease. This presents an immediate obstacle for anyone who believes, as I do, that there are not mental diseases. It also presents an immediate opportunity for demystifying a persistent psychiatric problem. I maintain that being a psychiatric patient has, in fact, nothing to do with having a mental illness. Instead, it has to do with defining oneself, or being defined by someone else, as needing the professional services of a psychiatrist; and with assuming the patient role, or being cast into it, vis-à-vis a psychiatrist (or other mental health professional) (Szasz, 1961).

The issue of consent—that is, of the voluntariness or involuntariness of the patient's relationship to the psychiatrist—thus arises prior to mental hospitalization. It does so with an antecedent question that might be framed as follows: "Should or should not a particular person be regarded and treated as a psychiatric patient?" I contend that in a free society no one should be cast into the role of mental patient against his will (Szasz, 1963). If this premise is granted, the problem of involuntary mental hospitalization is, as it were, aborted: it is "solved" because it cannot come into being. If all psychiatric patients are voluntary, there can be no involuntary psychiatry—just as if all workers are voluntary there can be no involuntary servitude.

The second key term in the title is "hospitalized involuntarily." What is involuntary hospitalization? Ostensibly, it is placing a patient in a medical institution for the purpose of treating his illness. Actually, in the case of so-called psychiatric patients, the term is a euphemistic misnomer, and indeed doubly so: first, because the alleged patient is not sick; and second, because the so-called hospital is in fact a prison.

Much of my argument *against* coercive psychiatry, and much of the argument of those who are *for* it, thus turns on whether we regard the involuntary mental patient as an object or an agent; on whether we treat him as an irresponsible organism or as a responsible person; and on whether we accept involuntary mental hospitalization as a helpful medical-therapeutic intervention or reject it as a harmful judicial-penal sanction.

Portions of this essay have appeared previously in *Ideology and Insanity: Essays on the Psychiatric Dehumanization of Man*. Garden City, N.Y., Doubleday Co., Inc., 1970, pp. 113–139. Copyright 1970 by Thomas S. Szasz; reprinted by permission of Doubleday & Company.

SOURCE: *Controversy in Psychiatry*, by J. P. Brady and H. Keith H. Brodie (Eds.), pp. 968–977, 1978. Copyright © 1978 by W. B. Saunders Company. Reprinted by permission of the author.

HISTORY

Involuntary mental hospitalization—or compulsory admission to hospital, as it is called in England—has always been, and still is, the paradigmatic policy of psychiatry. Whenever and wherever psychiatry has been recognized and practiced as the medical specialty dealing with the treatment of insanity, madness, or mental disease, then and there persons have been incarcerated in insane asylums, madhouses, or mental hospitals.

The coercion and restraint of the mental patient by the psychiatrist—or, better, of the madman by the alienist, as these protagonists were first called—is thus coeval with the origin and development of psychiatry. As a discrete discipline, psychiatry began in the seventeenth century with the building of insane asylums, first in France, then throughout the civilized world. These institutions were, of course, prisons in which not only so-called madmen were confined but all of society's undesirables—abandoned children, prostitutes, incurably sick persons, the aged and indigent (Szasz, 1970, pp. 13–16).

How did people generally, and in particular those directly responsible for these confinements—the legislators and jurists, the physicians and the victims' relatives—justify such incarceration of persons not guilty of criminal offenses? The answer is: by means of the imagery and rhetoric of madness, insanity, psychosis, schizophrenia, mental illness—call it what you will—which transformed the inmate into a "patient," his prison into a "hospital," and his warden into a "doctor." Characteristically, the first official proposition of the Association of Medical Superintendents of American Institutions for the Insane, the organization which became, in 1921, the American Psychiatric Association, was: "Resolved, that it is the unanimous sense of this convention that the attempt to abandon entirely the use of all means of personal restraint is not sanctioned by the true interests of the "insane" (Ridenour, 1961, p. 76).

Ever since then, this paternalistic justification of psychiatric coercion has been a prominent theme in psychiatry, not only in America but throughout the world. Thus, in 1967—123 years after the drafting of its first resolution—the American Psychiatric Association reaffirmed its support of psychiatric coercion and restraint. In a "Position Statement on the Question of the Adequacy of Treatment," the Association declared that "restraints may be imposed [on the patient] from within by pharmacologic means or by locking the door of a ward. Either imposition may be a legitimate component of a treatment program" (APA, 1967).

Justifications for involuntary psychiatric interventions of all kinds, and especially for involuntary mental hospitalization, similar to those accepted in the United States have, of course, been advanced, and continue to be advanced, in other countries. In short, just as, for millennia, involuntary servitude had been accepted as a proper economic and social arrangement, so for centuries, involuntary psychiatry has been accepted as a proper medical and therapeutic arrangement.

It is this entire system of interlocking psychiatric ideas and institutions, justifications and practices which—beginning some twenty years ago, first in a series of articles, and then in a series of books—I have analyzed and attacked. In these publications I describe and document the precise legal status of the mental hospital patient—as an innocent person incarcerated in a psychiatric prison; articulate my objections to institutional psychiatry—as an extralegal system of penology and punishments; and demonstrate what seems to me, in a free society, our only morally proper option with respect to the problem of so-called psychiatric abuses—namely, the complete abolition of all involuntary psychiatric interventions (Szasz, 1961, 1963, 1970, 1977).

EVIDENCE AGAINST INVOLUNTARY HOSPITALIZATION

Let me now consider the evidence that supports my contention that involuntary mental hospitalization does not serve the purpose of helping or treating so-called mentally ill persons; and that, regardless of its avowed or actual purposes, involuntary psychiatry, like involuntary servitude, is incompatible with the moral principles and legal procedures of a free society.

> *The medical evidence*. Mental illness is a metaphor. If by "disease" we mean a disorder of the physicochemical machinery of the human body, then it is clear that what we call functional mental diseases are not diseases at all. Persons said to be suffering from such disorders are socially deviant or inept, or in conflict with individuals, groups, or institutions. Since they do not suffer from disease, it is impossible to "treat" them for any sickness.

Although the term "mentally ill" is usually applied to persons who do not suffer from bodily disease, it is sometimes applied also to persons who do—for example, to individuals intoxicated with alcohol or other drugs, or to elderly people suffering from degenerative disease of the brain. When such persons are hospitalized involuntarily, the primary purpose is to exercise social control over their behavior; treatment of the disease is, at best, a secondary consideration. Frequently, therapy is nonexistent, and custodial care is dubbed "treatment."

In short, the commitment of persons suffering from "functional psychoses" serves moral and social, rather than medical and therapeutic, purposes. Hence, even if, as a result of future research, certain conditions now believed to be "functional" mental illnesses were to be shown to be "organic," my argument against involuntary mental hospitalization would remain unaffected.

> *The moral evidence.* In free societies, the relationship between physician and patient is predicated on the legal assumption that the individual "owns" his body and his personality. The physician can examine and treat a patient only with his consent; the latter is free to reject treatment—for example, an operation for cancer. As John Stuart Mill put it, ". . . each person is the proper guardian of his own health, whether bodily, or mental and spiritual" (Mill 1859). Commitment is incompatible with this moral principle.
>
> *The historical evidence.* Commitment practices flourished long before there were any mental or psychiatric "treatments" of "mental diseases." Indeed, madness or mental illness was not always a necessary condition for commitment. For example, in the seventeenth century, "children of artisans and other poor inhabitants of Paris up to the age of 25, . . . girls who were debauched or in evident danger of being debauched," and other "miserables" of the community, such as epileptics, people with venereal disease, and poor people with chronic diseases of all sorts, were all considered fit subjects for confinement in the Hôpital Général (Rosen, 1963). In 1860, when Mrs. Packard was incarcerated for disagreeing with her minister-husband, the commitment laws of the State of Illinois explicitly proclaimed that "married women . . . may be entered or detained in the hospital at the request of the husband of the woman or guardian . . . without the evidence of insanity required in other cases" (Szasz, 1970, p. 307).
>
> *The literary evidence.* Involuntary mental hospitalization plays a significant part in numerous short stories and novels from many countries. In none that I have encountered is commitment portrayed as helpful to the hospitalized person; instead, it is always depicted as an arrangement serving interests antagonistic to those of the so-called patient.

In short, I am suggesting that commitment constitutes a social arrangement whereby one part of society secures certain advantages for itself at the expense of another part. To do so, the oppressors must possess an ideology to justify their aims and actions; and they must be able to enlist the police power of the state to impose their will on the oppressed members. What makes such an arrangement morally legitimate or illegitimate? If the use of state power to punish lawbreakers is legitimate, why is its use to commit the insane not also legitimate?

In the first place, the difference between committing the "insane" and imprisoning the "criminal" is essentially the same as the difference between the rule of man and the rule of law: whereas the "insane" are subjected to the coercive controls of the state because persons more powerful than they have labeled them as "psychotic," "criminals" are subjected to such controls because they have violated legal rules applicable equally to all.

The second difference between these two proceedings lies in their professed aims. The principal purpose of imprisoning criminals is to protect the liberties of the law-abiding members of society. Since the individual subject to commitment is not considered a threat to liberty in the same way as the accused criminal is—if he were, he would be prosecuted—his removal from society cannot be justified on the same grounds. Justification for commitment must thus rest on its therapeutic promise and potential: it will help restore the "patients" to "mental health." But if this can be accomplished only at the cost of robbing the individual of liberty, involuntary mental hospitalization becomes only a verbal camouflage for what is, in effect, punishment. Such "therapeutic" punishment differs, however, from traditional judicial punishment, in that the accused criminal enjoys a rich panoply of constitutional protections against false accusation and illegal prosecution, whereas the accused mental patient is deprived of these protections.

To lend further support to my argument against involuntary mental hospitalization, I shall now briefly review the similarities between chattel slavery and involuntary psychiatry.

INVOLUNTARY PSYCHIATRY AND SLAVERY

Suppose that a person wished to study slavery. How would he go about doing so? First, he might study slaves. He would then find that such persons are generally brutish, poor, and uneducated, and he might accordingly conclude that slavery is their "natural" or appropriate social state. Such, indeed, have been the methods and conclusions of innumerable men throughout the ages. Even the great Aristotle held that slaves were "naturally" inferior and were hence justly subdued. "From the hour of their birth," he asserted, "some are marked for subjection, others for rule" (Davis, 1966, p. 70). This view is similar to the modern concept of "schizophrenia" as a genetically caused disease.

Another student, "biased" by contempt for the institution of slavery, might proceed differently. He would maintain that there can be no slave without a master holding him in bondage. Accordingly, he would consider slavery a type of human relationship and, more generally, a social institution, supported by custom, law, religion, and force. From this point of view, the study of masters is at least as relevant to the study of slavery as is the study of slaves.

The latter point of view is generally accepted today with regard to involuntary servitude, but not with regard to involuntary psychiatry. "Mental illness" of the type found in psychiatric hospitals has been investigated for centuries, and continues to be investigated today, in much the same ways as slaves had been studied in the antebellum South and before. Then, the "existence" of slaves was taken for granted; their biological and social characteristics were accordingly noted and catalogued. Today, the "existence" of "mental patients" is taken for granted; their biological and social characteristics are accordingly noted and catalogued. The fundamental parallel between master and slave on the one hand, and the institutional psychiatrist and involuntarily hospitalized patient on the other, thus lies in this: in each instance, the former member of the pair *defines* the social role of the latter, and *casts* him in that role by force (Szasz, 1977).

Wherever there is slavery, there must be criteria for who may and who may not be enslaved. In ancient times, any people could be enslaved. Bondage was the usual consequence of military defeat. After the advent of Christianity, although the people of Europe continued to make war upon each other, they ceased enslaving prisoners who were Christians. According to Dwight Dumond, ". . . the theory that a Christian could not be enslaved soon gained such wide endorsement as to be considered a point of international law" (Dumond, 1961, p. 4). By the time of the colonization of America, the people of the Western world considered only black persons appropriate subjects for slave trade.

The criteria for distinguishing between those who may be incarcerated in mental hospitals and those who may not be has had a similar history and evolution. At first—300 years ago—virtually anyone could be; later—in the nineteenth century—only madmen and madwomen could be; now only "mental patients" who are "dangerous to themselves or others" can be. It is significant that in each case narrowing the criteria for enslavement in the one, for commitment in the other—has greatly strengthened the moral legitimacy of a fundamentally immoral practice.

A basic assumption of American slavery was that the black was racially inferior to the white. Similarly, the basic assumption of institutional psychiatry is that the mentally ill person is psychiatrically inferior to the mentally healthy. Like the black slave, the mental patient is like a child: he does not know what is in his best interest and therefore needs others to control and protect him. Psychiatrists often care deeply for their involuntary patients, whom they consider—in contrast with the merely "neurotic" persons—"psychotic," which is to say, "very sick." Hence, such patients must be cared for as the "irresponsible children" they are considered to be.

This perspective of paternalism has played an exceedingly important part in justifying both slavery and involuntary hospitalization. Aristotle defined slavery as "an essentially domestic relationship"; in so doing, writes Davis, he "endowed it with the sanction of paternal authority, and helped to establish a precedent that would govern discussions of political philosophers as late as the eighteenth century" (Davis, 1966, p. 69). The relationship between psychiatrists and mental patients has been, and continues to be, viewed in the same way. "If a man brings his daughter to me from California," declares Braceland, "because she is in manifest danger of falling into vice or in some way disgracing herself, he doesn't expect me to let her loose in my hometown for that same thing to happen" (Braceland, 1961, p. 71). Almost any article or book dealing with the "care" of involuntary mental patients may be cited to illustrate the contention that physicians fall back on paternalism to justify their coercive control over the uncooperative patient. "Certain cases," writes Solomon in an article on suicide, ". . . must be considered irresponsible, not only with respect to violent impulses, but also in all medical matters." In this class, which he labels, "The Irresponsible," he places "Children," "The Mentally Retarded," "The Psychotic," and "The Severely or Terminally Ill." Solomon's conclusion is that "Repugnant though it may be, he [the physician] may have to act against the patient's wishes in order to protect the patient's life and that of others" (Solomon, 1967). The fact that, as in the case of slavery, the physician needs the police power of the state to maintain his relationship with his involuntary patient does not seem to affect this self-serving image of institutional psychiatry.

Paternalism is the crucial explanation for the stubborn contradiction and conflict about whether the practices employed by slaveholders and institutional psychiatrists are "therapeutic" or "noxious." Masters and mad-doctors profess their benevolence; their slaves and captives protest against their malevolence. In *Ward 7*, Valeriy Tarsis presents the following dialogue between his protagonist-patient and the mental hospital physician: "This is the position. I don't regard you as a doctor. You call this a hospital. I call it a prison. . . . So now, let's get everything straight. I am your prisoner, you are my jailer, and there isn't going to be any nonsense about my health . . . or treatment" (Tarsis, 1965, p. 62).

This is the monotonous dialogue between oppressors and oppressed. The ruler looks in the mirror and sees a liberator; the ruled looks at the ruler and sees a tyrant. If the physician has the power to incarcerate the patient and uses it, their relationship will inevitably fit into this mold. If one cannot ask the subject whether he likes being enslaved or committed, whipped or electroshocked—because he is not a fit judge of his own "best interests"—then one is left with the contending opinions of the practitioners and their critics. The practitioners insist that their coercive measures are beneficial; the critics, that they are harmful.

The defenders of slavery thus claimed that the black "is happier . . . as a slave, than he could be as a free man; this is the result of the peculiarities of his character" (Elkins, 1963, p. 190); that "it was actually an act of liberation to remove Negroes from their harsh world of sin and dark superstition"; and that "Negroes were better off in a Christian land, even as slaves, than living like beasts in Africa" (Davis, 1966, pp. 186, 190).

Similarly, the defenders of involuntary mental hospitalization claim that the mental patient is healthier—the twentieth-century synonym for the nineteenth century term "happier"—as a psychiatric prisoner than he would be as a free citizen; that "[t]he basic purpose of commitment is to make sure that sick human beings get the care that is appropriate to their needs . . ." (Ewalt, 1961, p. 75); and the "[i]t is a feature of some illnesses that people do not have insight into the fact that they are sick. In short, sometimes it is necessary to protect them [the mentally ill] for a while from themselves . . ." (Braceland, 1961, p. 64). It requires no great feat of imagination to see how comforting—indeed, how absolutely necessary—these views were to the advocates of involuntary servitude, and are now to the advocates of involuntary psychiatry.

THE MASTER-SUBJECT RELATIONSHIP

There are essential similarities in all relationships between masters and subjects—whether they be between plantation owners and black slaves, or institutional psychiatrists and committed mental patients.

To maintain a relationship of personal or class superiority, it is necessary, as a rule, that the oppressor keep the oppressed uninformed, especially about matters pertinent to their relationship. In America the history of the systematic efforts by the whites to keep the black ignorant is well known. A dramatic example is the law passed in 1824 by the Virginia Assembly that provided a $50 fine and two month's imprisonment for teaching *free* blacks to read and write (Dumond, 1961, p. 11).

A similar effort educationally to degrade and psychologically to impoverish their charges characterizes the acts of the managers of madhouses. In most prisons in the United States, it is possible for a convict to obtain a high-school diploma, to learn a trade, to become an amateur lawyer, or to write a book. None of these things is possible in a mental hospital. The principal requirement for an inmate of such an institution is to accept the psychiatric ideology of his "illness" and the things he must do to "recover" from it. The committed patient must thus accept the view that he is "sick" and that his captors are "well"; that his own view of himself is false and that of his captors true; and that to effect any change in his social situation he must relinquish his "sick" views and adopt the "healthy" views of those who have power over him. By accepting himself as "sick," and his institutional environment and the various manipulations imposed on him by the staff as "treatment," the mental patient is compelled to authenticate the psychiatrist's role as that of a benevolent physician curing mental illness. The mental patient who maintains the forbidden image of reality that the institutional psychiatrist is a jailer is considered paranoid. Moreover, since most patients—as do oppressed people generally—sooner or later accept the ideas imposed on them by their superiors, hospital psychiatrists are constantly immersed in an environment where their identity as "doctors" is affirmed. The moral superiority of white men over black was similarly authenticated and affirmed through the association between slaveowners and slaves.

In both situations, the oppressor first subjugates his adversary and then cites his oppressed status as proof of his inferiority. Once this process is set in motion, it develops its own momentum and psychological logic.

Looking at the relationship, the oppressor will see his superiority and hence his well-deserved dominance, and the oppressed will see his inferiority and hence his well-deserved submission. In race relations in the United States, we continue to reap the bitter results of his philosophy, while in psychiatry we are even now sowing the seeds of this poisonous fruit whose eventual harvest may be equally bitter and long.

Oppression and degradation are unpleasant to behold and are, therefore, frequently disguised or concealed. One method for doing so is to segregate—in special areas, as in camps or "hospitals"—the degraded human beings. Another is to conceal the social realities behind the fictional facade of our "language games." While psychiatric language games may seem fanciful, the psychiatric idiom is actually only a dialect of the common language of oppressors. Slaveholders called the slaves "livestock," mothers "breeders," their children "increase," and gave the term "drivers" to the men set over them at work (Dumond, 1961, p. 251). The defenders of psychiatric imprisonment call their institutions "hospitals," the inmates "patients," and the keepers "doctors"; they refer to the sentence as "treatment," and to the deprivation of liberty as "protection of the patient's best interests."

In both cases, the semantic deceptions are supplemented by appeals to tradition, to morality, and to social necessity. The proslavery forces in America argued that the abolitionists were wrong because "they were seeking to overthrow an ancient institution, one which was recognized by the Scriptures, recognized by the Constitution, and imbedded in the structure of southern society" (Dumond, 1961, p. 233). Thus, an editorial in the Washington Telegraph in 1837 asserted, "As a man, a Christian, and a citizen, we believe that slavery is right; that the condition of the slave, as it now exists in slaveholding states, is the best existing organization of civil society"; while another proslavery author, writing in 1862, defended the institution on mainly religious grounds: "Slavery, authorized by God, permitted by Jesus Christ, sanctioned by the apostles, maintained by good men of all ages, is still existing in a portion of our beloved country" (Elkins, 1963, p. 36). One has only to scan present-day psychiatric journals, popular magazines, or daily newspapers to find involuntary mental hospitalization similarly extolled and defended.

The contemporary reader may find it difficult to believe how unquestioningly slavery was accepted as a natural beneficial social arrangement. Even as great a liberal thinker as John Locke did not advocate its abolition. Moreover, protests against the slave trade would have provoked the hostility of powerful religious and economic interests. Opposition to it, as Davis observes, would therefore have required "considerable independence of mind, since the Portuguese slave posts were closely connected with missionary establishments and criticism of the African slave trade might challenge the very ideal of spreading the faith" (Davis, 1966, p. 187).

Indeed, the would-be critic or opponent of slavery would have found himself at odds with all the tradition and wisdom of Western civilization. ". . . [O]ne could not lightly challenge," writes Davis, "an institution approved not only by the Fathers and canons of the church, but by the most illustrious writers of antiquity. . . . [T]he revival of classical learning, which may have helped to liberate the mind of Europe from bondage to ignorance and superstition, only reinforced the traditional justification for human slavery. . . . [H]ow could an institution supported by so many authorities and sanctioned by the general custom of nations be intrinsically unjust or repugnant to natural reason?" (Davis, 1966, pp. 107, 115).

[T]here are thus two contradictory views on commitment. According to the one, involuntary mental hospitalization is an indispensable method of medical healing and a humane type of social control; according to the other, it is a contemptible abuse of the medical relationship and a type of imprisonment without trial. We adopt the former view and consider commitment "proper" if we use it on victims of our own choosing whom we despise; we adopt the latter view and consider commitment "improper" if our enemies use it on victims of their choosing whom we esteem.

PRACTICAL IMPLICATIONS

The change in perspective—from seeing slavery occasioned by the "inferiority" of the black and commitment by the "insanity" of the patient, to seeing each occasioned by the interplay of, and especially the power relations between, the participants—has far-reaching practical implications. In the case of slavery, it meant not only that the slaves had an obligation to revolt and emancipate themselves, but also that the masters had an even greater obligation to renounce their roles as slaveholders. Naturally, a slaveholder with such ideas felt compelled to set his slaves free, at whatever cost to himself. This is precisely what some slaveowners did. Their action had profound consequences in a social system based on slavery.

For the individual slaveholder who set his slaves free, the act led invariably to his expulsion from the community—through economic pressure or personal harassment or both. Such persons usually emigrated to the North. For the nation as a whole, these acts and the abolitionist sentiments behind them, symbolized a fundamental moral rift between those who regarded blacks as objects or slaves, and those who regarded them as persons or citizens. The former could persist in regarding the slave as existing in nature, whereas the latter could not deny his own moral responsibility for creating man in the image, not of God, but of the slave-animal.

The implications of this perspective for involuntary psychiatry are equally clear. A psychiatrist who accepts as his "patient" a person who does not wish to be his patient, defines him as a "mentally ill" person, then incarcerates him in an institution, bars his escape from the institution and from the role of mental patient, and proceeds to "treat" him against his will—such a psychiatrist, I maintain, creates "mental illness" and "mental patients." He does so in exactly the same way as the white man who sailed for Africa, captured the black, brought him to America in shackles, and then sold him as if he were an animal, created slavery and slaves.

The parallel between involuntary servitude and involuntary psychiatry may be carried one step further: denunciation of slavery and the renouncing of slaveholding by some slaveowners led to certain social problems, such as black unemployment, the importation of cheap European labor, and a gradual splitting of the country into pro- and antislavery factions. Similarly, criticisms of involuntary mental hospitalization and the renouncing by some psychiatrists of relationships with involuntary mental patients have led to professional problems in the past, and are likely to do so again in the future. Psychiatrists restricting their work to psychoanalysis and psychotherapy have been accused of not being "real doctors"—as if depriving a person of his liberty required medical skills; of "shirking their responsibilities" to their colleagues and to society by accepting only the "easier cases" and refusing to treat the "seriously mentally ill" patient—as if avoiding treating persons who do not want to be treated were itself a kind of unprofessional conduct; and of undermining the profession of psychiatry—as if practicing self-control and eschewing violence were newly discovered forms of immorality.

For millennia, people did not question the social necessity, and hence the moral legitimacy, of involuntary servitude. Today, they do not generally question the social necessity, and hence the moral legitimacy, of involuntary psychiatry. There is now a massive consensus, not only in the United States but throughout the "civilized" world, that, when "properly used," involuntary mental hospitalization is socially necessary for the nonpatients outside of mental hospitals and is personally beneficial for the patients inside them. Hence it is only possible to debate *who* should be hospitalized, or *how*, or for *how long*—but not *whether anyone should* be. I submit, however, that just as it is improper to enslave anyone—whether he is black or white, Moslem or Christian—so it is improper to hospitalize anyone without his consent—whether he is depressed or paranoid, hysterical or schizophrenic.

Our unwillingness to look at this problem searchingly may be compared to the unwillingness of the South to look at slavery. ". . . [A] democratic people," writes Elkins, "no longer 'reasons' with itself when it is all of the same mind. Men will then only warn and exhort each other, that their solidarity may be yet more perfect. The South's intellectuals, after the 1830s, did really little more than this. And when the enemy's reality disappears, when his concreteness recedes, then intellect itself, with nothing more to resist it and give it reasonance, merges with the mass and stultifies, and shadows become monsters" (Elkins, 1963, p. 222).

Our growing preoccupation with the menace of mental illness may be a manifestation of just such a process—in which "concreteness recedes . . . and shadows become monsters." A democratic nation, as we have been warned by Tocqueville, is especially vulnerable to the hazards of a surfeit of agreement: "The authority of a king is physical, and controls the actions of men without subduing their will. But the majority possesses a power that is physical and moral at the same time, which acts upon the will as much as upon the actions, and represses not only all contests, but all controversy" (Tocqueville, 1835–40, Vol. I, p. 273).

The idea that a person accused of crime is innocent until proven guilty is not shared by people everywhere but is, as I need hardly belabor, characteristically English in its historical origin and singularly Anglo-American in its consistent social application. And so is its corollary, namely that an individual has an inalienable right to personal liberty unless he has been duly convicted in court of an offense punishable by imprisonment. Because this magnificent edifice of dignity and liberty has been undermined, and continues to be undermined, by psychiatry, I consider the abolition of involuntary psychiatric interventions to be an especially important link in the chain I have tried to forge for restraining this mortal enemy of individualism and self-determination. I hope that my work will help people to discriminate between two types of physicians: those who heal, not so much because they are saints, but because *that is their job;* and those who harm, not so much because they are sinners, but because *that is their job.* And if some doctors harm—torture rather than treat, murder the soul rather than minister to the body—that is, in part, because society, through the state, asks them, and pays them, to do so.

We saw it happen in Nazi Germany, and we hanged many of the doctors. We [saw] it happen in the Soviet Union, and we [denounced] the doctors with righteous indignation. But when will we recognize—and publicly identify—the medical criminals among us? Or is the very possibility of perceiving many of our leading psychiatrists and psychiatric institutions in this way precluded by the fact that they represent the officially "correct" views and practices? By the fact that they have the ears of our lawyers and legislators, journalists and judges? And by the fact that they control the vast funds, collected by the state through taxing the citizens, which finance an enterprise whose basic moral legitimacy I have called into question?

NOTE

1. In contemporary practice there is a gray area composed of persons who do not formally or verbally consent to being psychiatric patients but who also make no protest against being so treated. For the sake of clarity, I shall here either not consider the particular circumstances of such persons, or shall consider their cases as falling in the category of voluntary psychiatric patients. My argument is thus addressed to the involuntary hospitalization of individuals who object, verbally or behaviorally, to psychiatric confinement, and who are demonstrably restrained by legal and medical authorities.

REFERENCES

American Psychiatric Association (APA): Position statement on the question of the adequacy of treatment. Am. J. Psychiatry, *123:* 1458–1460, 1967, p. 1459.

Braceland, F. J.: *In* Constitutional Rights of the Mentally Ill. Washington, D.C., U.S. Government Printing Office, 1961, pp. 63–74.

Davis, D. B.: The Problems of Slavery in Western Culture. Ithaca, N.Y., Cornell University Press, 1966.

Dumond, D. L.: Antislavery: The Crusade for Freedom. Ann Arbor, University of Michigan Press, 1961.

Elkins, S. M.: Slavery: A Problem in American Institutional and Intellectual Life. New York, University Library, 1963.

Ewalt, J. *In* Constitutional Rights of the Mentally Ill. Washington, D.C., U.S. Government Printing Office, 1961, pp. 74–89.

Mill, J. S.: On Liberty [1859]. Chicago, Henry Regnery Company, 1955, p. 18.

Ridenour, N.: Mental Health in the United States: A Fifty-Year History. Cambridge, Mass., Harvard University Press, 1961, p. 76.

Rosen, G.: Social attitudes to irrationality and madness in 17th and 18th century Europe. J. Hist Med. Allied Sci. *18:* 220–240, 1963.

Solomon, P.: The burden of responsibility in suicide. J.A.M.A., *199:*321–324, 1967.

Szasz, T. S.: The Myth of Mental Illness: Foundations of a Theory of Personal Conduct. New York, Hoeber-Harper, 1961; rev. ed., New York, Harper & Row, 1974.

Szasz, T. S.: Law, Liberty, and Psychiatry: An Inquiry into the Social Uses of Mental Health Practices, New York, Macmillan, Inc., 1963.

Szasz, T. S.: The Manufacture of Madness: A Comparative Study of the Inquisition and the Mental Health Movement. New York, Harper & Row, 1970.

Szasz, T. S.: Psychiatry Slavery: The Dilemma of Involuntary Psychiatry as Exemplified by the Case of Kenneth Donaldson. New York, The Free Press, 1977.

Tarsis, V.: Ward 7: An Autobiographical Novel. London, Collins, and Harvill, 1965.

Tocqueville, A. de.: Democracy in America [1835–40]. New York, Vintage, 1945.

DISCUSSION

In some respects, we have returned full circle to the fundamental questions with which this book began. Recall that I opened the book with the controversy regarding the validity and utility of the concept of mental illness. In that first chapter, Szasz argued that "mental illness" is nothing more than a summary label for unwanted behavior and that this label implies a misleading analogy to medical illness. Ausubel, in contrast, maintained that mental illness is a genuine entity that fulfills the same criteria for disease (that is, marked deviation from a desirable range of functioning) as does medical illness. Eighteen chapters later, we see how differing presuppositions regarding the nature of mental illness can lead to radically divergent views concerning important social issues—in this case, the question of whether the mentally ill should be institutionalized against their will.

Chodoff, who embraces what he terms a "medical model" of mental illness (while acknowledging that the current boundaries of "mental illness" are not clear-cut), contends that the principal criteria for involuntary commitment should be medical: mental illness, severe personal or interpersonal impairment, and dire need for care and treatment. Thus, Chodoff believes that the primary rationale for involuntary commitment is treatment of a disease—mental illness. In contrast, Szasz, who denies the reality of "mental illness," argues that involuntary commitment is used primarily or exclusively for the purpose of coercive social control. For Szasz, the imaginary concept of "mental illness" serves as a face-saving rationale to justify our segregation of "undesirable" individuals from the remainder of society. The "mental illness" concept allows us to believe that we are behaving altruistically while sparing us the discomfort of interacting with individuals whose behavior we find aversive.

The debate between Chodoff and Szasz does not imply that the controversy regarding involuntary commitment can be reduced to a dispute between those who do and do not believe in the existence of mental illness. For example, one can believe that mental illness is a real entity but oppose the use of state power to impose coercive interventions on the grounds that such procedures violate psychiatric patients' civil liberties. At the same time, however, the dispute between Chodoff and Szasz dramatically underscores the way that fundamental differences in assumptions about mental illness can produce fundamental differences in social policy.

The controversy regarding coercive psychiatric procedures is not limited to the question of involuntary commitment. As noted in the introduction to Part IV, a related issue that has arisen in recent years is whether institutionalized psychiatric patients should be permitted to refuse treatments, particularly somatic interventions such as psychotropic medications and electroconclusive therapy (see White & White, 1981, for a review). In general, U.S. courts have ruled that committed patients can refuse medication, except when these patients pose an imminent physical danger to themselves or others (Davison & Neale, 1994). Nevertheless, some have argued that granting involuntary patients the right to refuse treatment only reinforces the widespread perception of psychiatric hospitals as prisonlike warehouses of detention (Appelbaum, 1993). Legalizing the right to refuse treatment, critics claim, would render many or most cases of involuntary hospitalization essentially meaningless: Patients committed against their will for the principal purpose of treating their mental disorders could refuse to accept such treatments in the first place.

Thus, the debate between the proponents and opponents of coercive psychiatric procedures appears stalemated. Is there any way out of this seemingly insoluble impasse? Yes, at least according to Szasz. In a daring and controversial article, Szasz (1982) proposes a potential resolution to the debate between what he terms the "psychiatric protectionists"—those like Chodoff who favor the use of coercive procedures (such as involuntary hospitalization and treatment) to protect psychiatric patients from themselves—and the "psychiatric voluntarists"—those like himself who oppose coercive procedures but support psychiatric patients' rights to voluntarily obtain hospitalization and treatment. Specifically, Szasz suggests that individuals be granted the option of executing a **psychiatric will** while they are still of sound mind. (The psychiatric will is modeled after the "living will," which permits individuals to prohibit the administration of artificial life-sustaining procedures in the event of an incurable disease or injury, such as massive and irreversible brain damage.) The psychiatric will would explicitly allow individuals to forbid others from imposing coercive psychiatric procedures in the event that they are subsequently judged to be psychotic or irrational. Individuals who had elected not to complete such a will would, however, be subject to coercive psychiatric procedures.*

The psychiatric will has the potential to provide a middle ground for psychiatric protectionists and psychiatric voluntarists. Society would retain the right to impose coercive procedures on those who implicitly acknowledged (by failing to execute a psychiatric will) that they did not object to such procedures, whereas society would renounce the right to impose such procedures on those who have explicitly registered objections to their use.

Szasz's bold proposal is not without its critics. Some have suggested, for example, that the psychiatric will is meaningful only when the principal criteria for commitment are medical. When the primary criterion for commitment is dangerousness toward others, the rationale for such a will becomes less compelling, because the state will presumably disregard the individual's wishes in order to safeguard its citizens (Ennis, 1982). Still others have pointed to logistical difficulties associated with the psychiatric will. For example, how is the sanity of the individual executing the will to be ascertained? Presumably, such a determination would require the participation of both psychiatrists and lawyers, which could ultimately result in decreased, rather than increased, individual autonomy and control over the decision-making process (Schmidt, 1983). Moreover, because psychiatric wills would almost certainly be completed less often by individuals who are uneducated, uninformed, or poor, the formalization of such a will could, paradoxically, result in proportionately higher rates of involuntary commitment among those who possess the least power in society (Schmidt, 1983). Thus, the psychiatric will, although offering the hope of a resolution to the controversy regarding the use of coercive psychiatric interventions, may prove considerably more difficult to implement in practice than in principle.

QUESTIONS TO STIMULATE DISCUSSION

1. What do you view as the potential advantages and disadvantages of "medical criteria" for involuntary commitment, such as those proposed by Chodoff? Do you agree with Chodoff that the abolitionists and civil libertarians have defined freedom in an overly restrictive fashion?
2. Chodoff cites six reasons why the "dangerousness standard" for involuntary commitment is inappropriate. Now place yourself in the shoes of a proponent of the dangerousness standard. What reasons can you offer in its favor?
3. Do you concur with Szasz that involuntary commitment is directly analogous to slavery? Can you think of any circumstances in which this analogy does not appear to hold?
4. Szasz believes that individuals who violate the law should always be imprisoned, regardless of their "mental" status. Conversely, he believes that individuals who do not violate the law should never be confined against their will, regardless of their mental status. But how might Szasz deal with people who appear imminently dangerous (for example, who are threatening to murder someone and have apparently taken steps to do so) but have not yet broken the law? Do they pose logical difficulties for his anticoercion position?
5. If you had the option of completing a psychiatric will, would you do so? Do you believe that you possess sufficient information regarding the effects of mental illness and the nature of psychiatric interventions to execute such a will? Do you think that at least some training in abnormal psychology is needed to properly execute a psychiatric will?
6. In a highly controversial 1986 article, "The Case against Suicide Prevention," Szasz takes a firm stand against the use of coercive procedures, including involuntary hospitalization, to prevent individuals from attempting or completing suicide. (He does, however, endorse the right of mental health professionals to prevent suicide if a suicidal individual willingly asks them to do so.) Where do you stand on this issue and why? Is it possible to agree with Szasz on the issue of involuntary commitment and yet disagree with him on the issue of suicide prevention? How might Szasz deal with individuals who normally are nonsuicidal but who suddenly become suicidal following an acute overdose of drugs, such as LSD?

SUGGESTIONS FOR FURTHER READING

Appelbaum, P. S. (1993). Civil commitment. In J. O. Cavenar, Jr., R. Michels, & H. K. H. Brodie (Eds.), *Psychiatry* (Vol. 3, pp. 1–18). Philadelphia & New York: Lippincott & Basic Books.
In this comprehensive chapter, Appelbaum reviews the history and current status of civil commitment, criticisms of commitment law, and systematic research on civil commitment. He discusses many of the difficulties clinicians confront when dealing with a commitment system centered around patient dangerousness.

Bloom, B. L., & Asher, S. J. (Eds.) (1982). *Psychiatric patient rights and patient advocacy: Issues and evidence*. New York: Human Sciences Press.
This edited volume covers a variety of topics relevant to the ethical and legal rights of psychiatric patients, including the right to receive and refuse treatment, patient confidentiality and privacy, and the insanity plea. The chapter by Spensley and Werme provides a balanced review of the empirical literature bearing on involuntary commitment.

*Szasz (1982) also discussed the possibility of a "stronger" version of the psychiatric will, in which individuals would be subject to involuntary interventions only if they had explicitly requested their imposition in advance.

Kopolow, L. E. (1976). A review of major implications of the O'Connor v. Donaldson decision. *American Journal of Psychiatry, 133*, 379–383.

Kopolow reviews the background leading to the historic *O'Connor v. Donaldson* decision, the details of the case, and its implications for the relationship between dangerousness and civil commitment. He concludes that this case may herald a trend for psychiatrists to be held increasingly liable for their decisions to involuntarily commit patients.

LaFond, J. Q., & Durham, M. L. (1992). *Back to the asylum: The future of mental health law and policy in the United States*. New York: Oxford University Press.

LaFond and Durham examine the changes in laws and societal attitudes concerning the mentally ill over the past three decades. Chapters 4 and 5 contrast involuntary commitment practices in the "liberal era," which emphasized patient rights, with those of the more modern "neoconservative era," which emphasize society's obligation to protect patients from themselves.

Lindsey, K. P., & Paul, G. L. (1989). Involuntary commitments to public mental institutions: Issues involving the overrepresentation of blacks and assessment of relevant functioning. *Psychological Bulletin, 106*, 171–183.

The authors review literature indicating that African-Americans are involuntarily institutionalized at disproportionately high rates. They discuss potential explanations for this phenomenon and conclude with recommendations for research addressing this issue.

Szasz, T. S. (1977). *Psychiatric slavery*. New York: Free Press.

Szasz reviews the *Donaldson v. O'Connor* decision in detail and discusses its implications for the practice of involuntary commitment. He argues that the U.S. Supreme Court's decision, far from representing a triumph for psychiatric patients' rights, was actually an implicit affirmation of involuntary commitment. In Chapter 9, Szasz reviews the parallels between involuntary hospitalization and slavery.

Szasz, T. S. (1982). The psychiatric will: A new mechanism for protecting persons against "psychosis" and psychiatry. *American Psychologist, 37*, 762–770.

In this provocative article, Szasz proposes a new procedure that he believes will satisfy the objections of both those favoring involuntary commitment and those opposed to it. Specifically, he suggests that individuals who do not wish to be confined involuntarily sign a "psychiatric will" (analogous to a "living will") while they are still of sound mind. Such a will would prohibit their involuntary commitment in the event that they subsequently develop "mental illness."

Wexler, D. B. (1981). *Mental health law: Major issues*. New York: Plenum Press.

In the first part of this book, the author outlines the theoretical underpinnings of civil commitment and criminal commitment and discusses their relationship. The second half of the book focuses on legal issues pertaining to psychological and somatic therapies, including the use of psychosurgery and token economies and the obligation of therapists to warn third parties of potential harm.

REFERENCES

Appelbaum, P. S. (1993). Civil commitment. In J. O. Cavenar, Jr., R. Michels, & H. K. H. Brodie (Eds.), *Psychiatry* (Vol. 3, pp. 1–18). Philadelphia & New York: Lippincott & Basic Books.

Brakel, S. J. (1985). Involuntary institutionalization. In S. J. Brakel, J. Parry, & B. A. Weiner (Eds.), *The mentally disabled and the law* (3rd ed.). Chicago: American Bar Association.

Davison, G. C., & Neale, J. M. (1994). *Abnormal psychology* (6th. ed.). New York: Wiley.

Ennis, B. J. (1982). The psychiatric will: Odysseus at the mast. *American Psychologist, 37*, 854.

Schmidt, J. P. (1983). The psychiatric will: Is the cure worse than the illness? *American Psychologist, 38*, 342–343.

Szasz, T. S. (1982). The psychiatric will: A new mechanism for protecting persons against "psychosis" and psychiatry. *American Psychologist, 37*, 762–770.

Szasz, T. S. (1986). The case against suicide prevention. *American Psychologist, 41*, 806–812.

White, M. D., & White, C. A. (1981). Involuntarily committed patients' constitutional rights to refuse treatment: A challenge to psychology. *American Psychologist, 36*, 953–962.

APPENDIX

Additional controversies in abnormal psychology

This appendix lists a number of additional controversial issues in abnormal psychology, with two suggested readings for each one that adopt opposing or substantially different views. Although this list is not meant to be exhaustive, it is intended to provide readers and instructors with a broad range of topics for further reading and discussion.

CLASSIFICATION AND DIAGNOSIS

1. *Has DSM-III solved the problem of diagnostic unreliability?*

PRO: Spitzer, R. L., Forman, J., & Nee, J. (1979). DSM-III field trials: I. Initial interrater diagnostic reliability. *American Journal of Psychiatry, 136*, 815–817.

CON: Kutchins, H., & Kirk, S. A. (1986). The reliability of DSM-III: A critical review. *Social Work Research and Abstracts, 22*, 3–12.

2. *Is DSM-IV premature?*

PRO: Zimmerman, M. (1988). Why are we rushing to publish DSM-IV? *Archives of General Psychiatry, 45*, 1135–1138.

CON: Frances, A., Widiger, T. A., & Pincus, H. A. (1989). The development of DSM-IV. *Archives of General Psychiatry, 46*, 373–375.

3. *Should the diagnostic threshold for psychiatric conditions be adjusted depending upon their prevalence?*

PRO: Finn, S. (1982). Base rates, utilities, and DSM-III: Shortcomings of fixed-rule systems of psychodiagnosis. *Journal of Abnormal Psychology, 91*, 194–302.

CON: Widiger, T. A. (1983). Utilities and fixed diagnostic rules: Comments on Finn. *Journal of Abnormal Psychology, 92*, 493–498.

4. *Should homosexuality be included in the diagnostic nomenclature?*

PRO: Bieber, I. (1973). Homosexuality—An adaptive consequence of disorder in psychosexual development. *American Journal of Psychiatry, 130*, 1209–1211.

CON: Spitzer, R. L. (1973). A proposal about homosexuality and the APA nomeclature: Homosexuality as an irregular form of sexual behavior and sexual orientation disturbance as a psychiatric disorder. *American Journal of Psychiatry, 130*, 1214–1216.

5. *Should premenstrual syndrome be included in the diagnostic nomenclature?*

PRO: Spitzer, R. L., Severino, S. K., Williams, J. B. W., & Parry, B. L. (1989). Late luteal phase disorder and DSM-IV. *American Journal of Psychiatry, 146*, 892–897.

CON: Gallant, S. J., & Hamilton, J. A. (1988). On a premenstrual diagnosis: What's in a name? *Professional Psychology: Research and Practice*, *19*, 271–278.

PSYCHOPATHOLOGY: ITS CHARACTERISTICS AND CAUSES

6. Is an excess number of schizophrenics born during the winter?

PRO: Bradbury, T. N., & Miller, G. A. (1985). Season of birth in schizophrenia: A review of evidence, methodology, and etiology. *Psychological Bulletin*, *98*, 569–594.

CON: Lewis, M. S., & Griffin, P. A. (1981). An explanation for the season of birth effect in schizophrenia and certain other diseases. *Psychological Bulletin*, *89*, 589–596.

7. Are individuals evolutionarily "prepared" to develop phobic reactions toward certain stimuli?

PRO: Seligman, M. E. P. (1971). Phobias and preparedness. *Behavior Therapy*, *2*, 307–320.

CON: McNally, R. J. (1987). Preparedness and phobias: A review. *Psychological Bulletin*, *101*, 283–303.

8. Do cognitive factors cause depression?

PRO: Haaga, D. A., Dyck, M. J., & Ernst, D. (1991). Empirical status of cognitive theory of depression. *Psychological Bulletin*, *110*, 215–236.

CON: Coyne, J. C., & Gotlib, I. H. (1983). The role of cognition in depression: A critical appraisal. *Psychological Bulletin*, *94*, 472–505.

9. Are depressed individuals "sadder but wiser"? (Or, Is "depressive realism" real?)

PRO: Layne, C. (1983). Painful truths about depressives' cognitions. *Journal of Clinical Psychology*, *39*, 848–853.

CON: Ackerman, R., & DeRubeis, R. J. (1991). Is depressive realism real? *Clinical Psychology Review*, *11*, 565–584.

10. Does a single gene underlie bipolar disorder?

PRO: Egeland, J. A., et al. (1987). Bipolar affective disorders linked to DNA markers on chromosome 11. *Nature*, *325*, 783–787.

CON: Kelsoe, J. R., et al. (1989). Reevaluation of the linkage relationship between chromosome 11p loci and the gene for bipolar affective disorder in the Old Order Amish. *Nature*, *342*, 238–243.

11. Can suicide be rational?

PRO: Barrington, M. R. (1980). Apologia for suicide. In M. P. Batten & D. Mayo (Eds.), *Suicide: The philosophical issues* (pp. 90–103). New York: St. Martin's Press.

CON: Hendin, H. (1982). The right to suicide. In H. Hendin, *Suicide in America* (pp. 209–228). New York: W. W. Norton.

Note: Both readings are reprinted in Slife, B., & Rubinstein, J. (1990). *Taking sides: Clashing views on controversial psychological issues* (6th ed.). Guilford, CT: Dushkin Publishing Group.

12. Does alcoholism have a substantial genetic component?

PRO: Goodwin, D. W. (1985). Alcoholism and genetics: The sins of the fathers. *Archives of General Psychiatry*, *42*, 171–174.

CON: Searles, J. (1988). The role of genetics in the pathogenesis of alcoholism. *Journal of Abnormal Psychology*, *97*, 153–167.

13. Should personality disorders be conceptualized dimensionally rather than categorically?

PRO: Widiger, T. A. (1993). The DSM-III-R categorical personality disorder diagnoses: A critique and an alternative. *Psychological Inquiry*, *4*, 75–90.

CON: Gunderson, J. G., Links, P. S., & Reich, J. H. (1991). Competing models of personality disorders. *Journal of Personality Disorders*, *5*, 60–68.

14. Is self-defeating personality disorder a valid diagnostic entity?

PRO: Simons, R. C. (1987). Self-defeating and sadistic personality disorders: Needed additions to the diagnostic nomenclature. *Journal of Personality Disorders*, *1*, 161–167.

CON: Skodol, A. E., Oldham, J. M., Gallaher, P. E., & Bezirganian, S. (1994). Validity of self-defeating personality disorder. *American Journal of Psychiatry*, *151*, 560–567.

15. Does criminality have a substantial genetic component?

PRO: Mednick, S. A., Gabrielli, W. F., & Hutchings, B. (1984). Genetic influence in criminal convictions: Evidence from an adoption cohort. *Science*, *224*, 891–894.

CON: Walters, G. D. (1992). A meta-analysis of the gene-crime relationship. *Criminology, 30*, 595–613.

16. *Are males with the XYY genotype at heightened risk for violence?*

PRO: Jarvik, L. F., Klodin, V., & Matsuyama, S. S. (1973). Human aggression and the extra Y chromosome: Fact or fantasy? *American Psychologist, 28*, 674–682.

CON: Witkin, H. A., Mednick, S. A., Schulsinger, F., Bakkestrom, E., Christiansen, K. O., Goodenough, D. R., Hirschhorn, K., Lundsteen, C., Owen, D. R., Philip, J., Rubin, D. B., & Stocking, M. (1976). Criminality in XYY and XXY men. *Science, 193*, 547–555.

17. *Is there convincing evidence that victims of child abuse are at increased risk for later criminality?*

PRO: Widom, C. S. (1989). The cycle of violence. *Science, 244*, 160–166.

CON: DiLalla, L. F., & Gottesman, I. I. (1991). Biological and genetic contributors to violence—Widom's untold tale. *Psychological Bulletin, 109*, 125–129.

Note: See also Widom, C. S. (1991). A tail on an untold tale: Response to "Biological and genetic contributors to violence—Widom's untold tale." *Psychological Bulletin, 109*, 130–132.

18. *Is bulimia a manifestation of depression?*

PRO: Lee, N. F., Rush, A., & Mitchell, J. E. (1985). Bulimia and depression. *Journal of Affective Disorders, 9*, 231–238.

CON: Hinz, L. D., & Williamson, D. A. (1987). Bulimia and depression: A review of the affective variant hypothesis. *Psychological Bulletin, 102*, 150–158.

19. *Does the Type A behavior pattern predispose to coronary artery disease?*

PRO: Thoresen, C. E., & Powell, L. H. (1992). Type A behavior pattern: New perspectives on theory, assessment, and intervention. *Journal of Consulting and Clinical Psychology, 60*, 595–604.

CON: Ragland, D. R., & Brand, R. J. (1988). Type A behavior and mortality from coronary heart disease. *New England Journal of Medicine, 318*, 65–69.

20. *Is attention-deficit/hyperactivity disorder produced by "minimal brain dysfunction"?*

PRO: Bloomingdale, L. M., & Bloomingdale, E. C. (1980). Minimal brain dysfunction: A new screening test and theoretical considerations. *Psychiatric Journal of the University of Ottawa, 5*, 295–306.

CON: Rutter, M. (1982). Syndromes attributed to "minimal brain dysfunction" in childhood. *American Journal of Psychiatry, 139*, 21–33.

21. *Does sugar contribute to hyperactivity?*

PRO: Prinz, R. J., Roberts, W. A., & Hantmann, E. (1980). Dietary correlates of hyperactive behavior in children. *Journal of Consulting and Clinical Psychology, 48*, 760–769.

CON: Wolraich, M. L., Lindgren, S. D., Stumbo, P. J., Stegink, L. D., Appelbaum, M. I., & Kiritsy, M. C. (1994). Effects of diets high in sucrose or aspartame on the behavior and cognitive performance of children. *New England Journal of Medicine, 330*, 301–307.

22. *Do food additives contribute to hyperactivity?*

PRO: Feingold, B. F. (1976). Hyperkinesis and learning disabilities linked to the ingestion of artificial food colors and flavors. *Journal of Learning Disabilities, 9*, 551–559.

CON: Kavale, K. A., & Forness, S. R. (1983). Hyperactivity and diet treatment: A meta-analysis of the Feingold hypothesis. *Journal of Learning Disabilities, 16*, 324–330.

PSYCHOLOGICAL AND SOMATIC TREATMENTS

23. *Should psychotherapy incorporate religious values?*

PRO: Bergin, A. E. (1980). Psychotherapy and religious values. *Journal of Consulting and Clinical Psychology, 48*, 95–105.

CON: Ellis, A. (1980). Psychotherapy and atheistic values: A response to A. E. Bergin's "Psychotherapy and religious values." *Journal of Consulting and Clinical Psychology, 48*, 635–639.

Note: Both articles are reprinted in Slife, B., & Rubinstein, J. (1992). *Taking sides: Clashing views on controversial psychological issues* (7th ed.). Guilford, CT: Dushkin Publishing Group.

24. *Can psychoanalysis and behavior therapy be integrated?*

PRO: Wachtel, P. L. (1984). On theory, practice, and the nature of integration. In H. Arkowitz & S. B. Messer (Eds.), *Psychoanalytic and behavior therapy: Is integration possible?* (pp. 31–52). New York: Plenum Press.

CON: Messer, S. B., & Winokur, M. (1980). Some limits to the integration of psychoanalytic and behavioral therapy. *American Psychologist, 35*, 818–827.

Note: Those who are interested in this issue may first want to read (particularly Chapters 1–5) Wachtel, P. L. (1977). *Psychoanalysis and behavior therapy: Toward an integration*. New York: Basic Books.

25. *Does "facilitated communication" enhance the ability of autistic children to communicate?*

PRO: Biklen, D., & Schubert, A. (1991). New words: The communication of students with autism. *Remedial and Special Education, 12*, 46–57.

CON: Mulick, J. A., Jacobson, J. W., & Kobe, F. H. (1993). Anguished silence and helping hands: Autism and facilitated communication. *Skeptical Inquirer, 17*, 270–280.

26. *Does fluoxetine (Prozac) produce an increased risk for suicide?*

PRO: Teicher, M. H., Glod, C., & Cole, J. O. (1990). Emergence of intense suicidal preoccupation during fluoxetine treatment. *American Journal of Psychiatry, 147*, 207–210.

CON: Fava, M., & Rosenbaum, J. F. (1991). Suicidality and fluoxetine: Is there a relationship? *Journal of Clinical Psychiatry, 52*, 108–111.

LEGAL AND ETHICAL ISSUES

27. *Is the expert testimony of psychologists trusthworthy?*

PRO: Matarazzo, J. D. (1990). Psychological assessment versus psychological testing: Validation from Binet to the school, clinic, and courtroom. *American Psychologist, 45*, 999–1017.

CON: Faust, D., & Ziskin, J. (1988). The expert witness in psychology and psychiatry. *Science, 241*, 31–35.

28. *Should anatomically correct dolls be used in expert testimony on sexual abuse?*

PRO: Yates, A. (1988). Anatomically correct dolls: Should they be used as the basis for expert testimony? *Journal of the American Academy of Child and Adolescent Psychiatry, 27*, 254–255.

CON: Terry, L. (1988). Anatomically correct dolls: Should they be used as the basis for expert testimony? *Journal of the American Academy of Child and Adolescent Psychiatry, 27*, 255–257.

29. *Should punishment be used to treat certain childhood behavior problems?*

PRO: Axelrod, S. (1990). Myths that (mis)guide our profession. In A. C. Repp & N. N. Singh (Eds.), *Perspectives on the use of nonaversive and aversive interventions for persons with developmental disabilities* (pp. 59–72). Sycamore, IL: Sycamore Publishing.

CON: Durand, V. M. (1987). "Look homeward angel": A call to return to our (functional) roots. *The Behavior Analyst, 10*, 299–302.

30. *Should psychologists and psychiatrists avoid using coercive means to prevent suicide?*

PRO: Szasz, T. (1986). The case against suicide prevention. *American Psychologist, 41*, 806–812.

CON: (1987). C. B. Holmes, "Comment on Szasz's view of suicide prevention"; D. B. Mather, "The case against preventing suicide prevention: Comments on Szasz"; and G. Clum, "Abandon the suicidal: A reply to Szasz" in *American Psychologist, 42*, 882–885.

31. *Should psychologists refuse to assist individuals who wish to change their sexual orientation?*

PRO: Davison, G. C. (1976). Homosexuality: The ethical challenge. *Journal of Consulting and Clinical Psychology, 44*, 157–162.

CON: Bieber, I. (1976). A discussion of "Homosexuality: The ethical challenge." *Journal of Consulting and Clinical Psychology, 44*, 163–166.

32. *Should psychologists be allowed to prescribe psychotropic medications?*

PRO: DeLeon, P. H., Fox, R. E., Graham, S. R. (1991). Prescription privileges: Psychology's next frontier. *American Psychologist*, 46, 384–393.

CON: DeNelsky, G. Y. (1991). Prescription privileges for psychologists: The case against. *Professional Psychology: Research and Practice*, 22, 188–193.

MISCELLANEOUS

33. *Should clinicians combine assessment data statistically rather than clinically?*

PRO: Dawes, R. M., Faust, D., & Meehl, P. E. (1989). Clinical versus actuarial judgment. *Science*, 243, 1668–1674.

CON: Holt, R. R. (1958). Clinical and statistical prediction: A reformulation and some new data. *Journal of Abnormal and Social Psychology*, 56, 1–12.

34. *Has the prevalence of "recovered memories" of child abuse been overestimated?*

PRO: Loftus, E. F. (1993). The reality of repressed memories. *American Psychologist*, 48, 518–537.

CON: Olio, K. A. (1994). Truth in memory. *American Psychologist*, 49, 442–443.

NAME INDEX

SUBJECT INDEX

Page numbers in **boldface** indicate definitions of terms and concepts.

TO THE OWNER OF THIS BOOK:

We hope that you have found *Seeing Both Sides* useful. So that this book can be improved in a future edition, would you take the time to complete this sheet and return it? Thank you.

School and address: ______________________________

Department: ______________________________

Instructor's name: ______________________________

1. What I like most about this book is: ______________________________

____

____

2. What I like least about this book is: ______________________________

____

____

3. My general reaction to this book is: ______________________________

____

4. The name of the course in which I used this book is: ______________________________

____

5. Were all of the chapters of the book assigned for you to read? ______________

If not, which ones weren't? ______________________________

6. In the space below, or on a separate sheet of paper, please write specific suggestions for improving this book and anything else you'd care to share about your experience in using the book.

____

____

____

____

____

____

Optional:

Your name: ______________________ Date: ______________________

May Brooks/Cole quote you, either in promotion for *Seeing Both Sides* or in future publishing ventures?

Yes: ________ No: ________

Sincerely,

Scott O. Lilienfeld

FOLD HERE

NO POSTAGE NECESSARY IF MAILED IN THE UNITED STATES

BUSINESS REPLY MAIL

FIRST CLASS PERMIT NO. 358 PACIFIC GROVE, CA

POSTAGE WILL BE PAID BY ADDRESSEE

ATT: *Scott O. Lilienfeld*

Brooks/Cole Publishing Company
511 Forest Lodge Road
Pacific Grove, California 93950-9968

FOLD HERE